PAULINE PARALLELS

PAULINE PARALLELS

Designed and Edited by

Fred O. Francis and J. Paul Sampley

BIP 89

Fortress Press

Philadelphia, Pennsylvania

and

Scholars Press

Missoula, Montana

PAULINE PARALLELS
Sources for Biblical Study 9

Copyright © 1975

by

SOCIETY OF BIBLICAL LITERATURE

The Bible text in this publication is from the Revised Standard Version of the Bible, copyrighted 1946, 1952, © 1971, 1973 by the Division of Christian Education of the National Council of the Churches of Christ in the U.S.A., and is used by permission.

The text of the ten Pauline Letters is taken from the *RSV Common Bible* by permission of the publisher, Collins.

Library of Congress Catalog Card Number 74-26346

ISBN 0-8006-1206-X

Printed in the U.S.A.   1-1206

4026175

to
NILS A. DAHL

for whom
we do not cease to give thanks

TABLE OF CONTENTS

ACKNOWLEDGEMENTS

In a publication where two presses collaborate, the number of co-operating persons increases greatly. The staffs of Fortress and Scholars Presses, under the leadership of the respective editors, Norman A. Hjelm and Robert W. Funk, receive our thanks for their consistent co-operation and good will.

Norman A. Hjelm, who first made a commitment to the project more than two years ago, deserves considerable credit for his willingness to undertake and see through a publication whose format is a bit unusual.

To Robert Funk we owe a special debt of gratitude. He gave support to the venture and personally directed the preparation of the manuscript for printing. He made possible the book's appearance at this time.

We express our thanks to the Society of Biblical Literature for its support of this endeavor.

We are grateful to William Collins Sons & Company, Limited, for permission photographically to reproduce the text of the Common Bible.

We thank our wives.

INTRODUCTION

Pauline Parallels is offered as a working tool for students of the apostle Paul. The aim of the volume is to facilitate comparative study of various passages in the Pauline corpus that might illuminate one another by juxtaposition. Such a book is possible and useful because in his various letters Paul touches upon similar themes and images and employs common letter structures and rhetorical devices. *Pauline Parallels* provides a direct, handy means of viewing thematically and structurally similar passages alongside one another.

Past Efforts

Past efforts at a handbook of Paul's letters often have been thematic tables that listed where Paul dealt with various subjects such as the kingdom of God or justification. The earliest extant effort of this kind seems to have been by an anonymous fourth century author.[1] Similar treatments continue into the modern era but sometimes suffer from importation of non-pauline categories or lack of comprehensiveness, and too frequently such treatments allow the dissipation of the discreteness of the letter occasions. A reductionist and simplistic understanding of Paul often results from such an approach.

The nearest modern analogy to what is here offered in the *Pauline Parallels* is the work of Goodspeed and Mitton on Ephesians[2] but their efforts are marred by the severe fragmentation of the text into small phrases in an effort to demonstrate a use-hypothesis, namely that Ephesians is a pastiche or mosaic of the other Pauline letters and is composed by a Paulinist. *Pauline Parallels* seeks to avoid fragmentation and fosters no such methodology or hypothesis.

The reader familiar with various Gospel parallels will see certain similarities in the layout of this volume. Comparable sense-units are arranged across the top of each numbered paragraph; secondary materials and information may be found below. Unlike the Gospels, however, the letters of Paul manifest little or no literary interdependence. Further, each of the letters is particularly wed to concrete historical circumstances and most nearly approximates one side of a written conversation.

Table of Parallels

The following description of the volume's layout as well as the format of the individual paragraphs should facilitate the use of the *Pauline Parallels*. The detailed *table of parallels* divides each letter into thought-units or sense-units and lists the primary parallels for each passage. This table is the key to the entire volume. It shows what passages are associated with each other and is a direct means for readers to find their way by the paragraph number (or page number) to a given passage in its primary context. Familiarity with the table of parallels will enhance the usefulness of this working tool.

The text of the *Pauline Parallels* is composed of a sequential presentation of each of the ten chief letters attributed to Paul:

Romans, 1 and 2 Corinthians, Galatians, Ephesians, Philippians, Colossians, 1 and 2 Thessalonians and Philemon. The letters stand in their canonical order, each in its own entirety: that is, Romans is followed through to its end, then 1 Corinthians is treated in like fashion, then 2 Corinthians and so forth throughout the ten letters. In this way each letter is retained in its own integrity and is pursued, one sense- or thought-unit after another, to the conclusion of that document. Such a procedure, of course, contributes to repetition as the volume unfolds but preserves the integrity of the letters as they now stand.

Authorship

Pauline Parallels makes no prejudgment concerning the authorship of 2 Thessalonians, Ephesians, and Colossians. Persons who dispute the authorship of these three letters will have occasion to test their judgment as the passages are placed beside other Pauline letters. Persons who consider these three as genuine Pauline letters will find no impediment to their examination alongside the remaining Pauline letters.

From this layout of the volume it should be apparent that if one wishes to study a particular passage, for example from 1 Thessalonians, he or she ought to turn first to the section of the *Pauline Parallels* where 1 Thessalonians is being followed in sequence, sense-unit after sense-unit. Only in that way can the passage in question be considered in its fullest context and the reader see the materials especially chosen for association with the particular thought-unit.

Layout of Paragraphs

The *layout of each paragraph* of the volume is separated into two parts, each reading completely across the folio. The *upper section of each paragraph* is divided into ten columns, always following from left to right the canonical order of the Pauline letters. On any given folio, the letter under consideration will be highlighted by bold vertical lines on either side of the column where it appears. All other passages printed on that folio are suggested to illuminate the principal passage. Across the upper portion of the paragraph, therefore, the reader will discover what we judge to be primary parallels, always printed in full sense-units. Our desire to avoid over-fragmentation is reflected in this decision to print whole thought-units at every point in the upper section.

Upper Section of Paragraph

Criteria for Primary Parallels

The criteria employed in the juxtaposition of primary passages alongside a particular Pauline text are fundamentally the following: 1) similarity of language; 2) similarity of images; or 3) similarity of letter structure or form. In keeping with our view of this volume as a working tool, we encourage readers to use blank spaces in the text to include further passages they deem helpful.

Lower Section of Paragraph

The *lower section of each paragraph* is devoted to secondary parallels and even to contrasts at times. All of the entries on this section of the page are keyed to the major passage in question at the top. In these notes there has been no effort to reproduce total sense-units as is the practice in the primary parallels. Insofar as space allows we have printed these verses and part-verses rather than simply give reference numbers.

Lower Left

Lower Right

On the *lower left* are located pertinent passages from Acts and the pastoral epistles (1 and 2 Timothy and Titus) along with a few references to other New Testament documents. On the *lower right*, Old Testament quotations and strong allusions are listed along with textual variants and their manuscript witnesses for those instances of some consequence (see ''The Text'' below).

Lower Middle

Across the *lower middle* of each paragraph are verses that have been chosen from the ten Pauline letters for the additional light they cast on the primary passage in question.

Where a parallel passage is pertinent to two sequential paragraphs under examination we have not hesitated to reprint it in the hope that the student will find leafing backwards and forward through the book to be a minimal problem. Each paragraph therefore has its own completeness in terms of the parallels suggested for consideration to a given passage.

Index

For convenience of cross-references an *index* is included at the end of the volume. There the reader may find not only the paragraphs where a particular passage of interest appears, but also a full index of references to Acts and the pastoral epistles in the notes.

Letter Structure

Formal Similarities

The Pauline letters have major structural sections such as the following: salutation, thanksgiving/blessing, body, appeal, greetings, grace. These are parallelled even when thematically disparate. We have also taken note of certain other formal similarities within the letters for example, virtue and vice lists.

On occasion we have arranged more than one passage in the primary column. We did so when it appeared that such juxtaposition might offer telling comparison.

Though we have consistently tried to avoid imposing any particular methodology on the study of Paul by our construction of this volume, we are concerned that we do not contribute to a simplistic, conflationary or synthesizing methodology whereby fragments of Paul are recast in the thought patterns of the interpreter. It is our hope that a clearer notion of thought-units within a given letter and a stronger sense of context for a given passage might heighten the understanding of the diversity of occasions and communities that are represented in these different letters. Much as synoptic Gospel studies have moved from a coalescing of the various parallels into one synthetic account towards an increased sensitivity to the idiosyncracies of a given Gospel, we hope that the study of Paul may become more sophisticated by highlighting the diversity and complexity of Paul's letters.

J. Paul Sampley
Indiana University
Bloomington, Indiana

Fred O. Francis
Chapman College
Orange, California

[1] John Wordsworth and Henry J. White, and others, *Novum Testamentum Domini Nostri Iesu Christi Latine Secundum Editionem Sancti Hieronymi* (Oxford, 1889-1954), II, 12-16.

[2] Edgar J. Goodspeed, *The Meaning of Ephesians* (Chicago, 1933), and C. Leslie Mitton, *The Epistle to the Ephesians: Its Authorship, Origin and Purpose* (Oxford, 1951).

THE TEXT

None of the Pauline epistles is preserved in the original. Instead, what has come down to us across the centuries are hundreds and hundreds of manuscripts — copies hand-written in Greek or papyri and vellum, quotations and commentaries by the Fathers of the early church, lectionary texts for use in liturgy, and Latin, Syriac, Coptic, and other early versions.

In copying and re-copying the epistles over a period of several centuries, scribes made all the typical mistakes of eye and ear inherent in the production of hand-written documents. They also harmonized one portion of the text with another, and occasionally made theological or other modifications.

It is the task of textual criticism to determine from this mass of manuscripts (MSS) what Paul originally wrote or at least the earliest form of the text available. The *Common Bible* (Revised Standard Version) text in this volume is based upon modern critical editions of the Greek New Testament which pull together the documentary evidence by means of such textual study.[1]

Ernest Cadman Colwell, a leading American text critic, characterized the comprehensive question of New Testament textual criticism as, "What is the best New Testament?"[2] He constructs the outline of the last four hundred fifty years of study of the text in the following way:

1500-1633, the best New Testament is Greek: the development of the Received Text from the first printed editions to the second edition of Elzevir brothers.[3]

1633-1831, the best New Testament is the first one printed: the reign of the Received Text.

1831-1880, the best New Testament is the oldest one: the impact of manuscript discovery and the new editions.

1880-1925, the best New Testament is the one with the best family tree: the development of the geneological method for MSS and classification of local text types.

1925-1950, the best New Testament must be chosen verse by verse: the exercise of eclectic judgment.

1950-——, the best New Testament is still to be: efforts toward a new, comprehensive collection of data pointing toward preparation of a new text.

This scheme should not mislead one into thinking that efforts toward the grouping of families of MSS and judgments on particular passages by means of a variety of criteria are now in the past. Not at all, but those of Colwell's mind believe an accurate New Testament awaits a new presentation of data and the new methods that possibly would follow. Other scholars proceed on the assumption that future textual criticism will build directly upon the last century of scholarship.[4]

The notes in the *Parallels* contain a selection of textual variants, some of the more important cases when MSS differ on the wording of passages in the epistles.[5] Such notes approximately reflect the present state of the discipline: an interest in the oldest MSS, use of MSS to represent certain text types, eclectic weighing of individual cases.

The main types of text represented in the notes in this volume are the Alexandrian (a short, but not highly polished text; circulated by the second century in Egypt and in the Eastern Church), the Western (a long text marked by striking "omissions" and "insertions;" circulated by the second century in the western Mediterranian with influence elsewhere), and the Koine (a stylistically and linguistically smooth text that harmonizes parallel passages; circulated by the fourth century in the Byzantine Empire). Other types of text have been identified, such as the Caesarean and other families among medieval MSS. Readings from MSS of the Alexandrian type are generally given greatest weight, though editors at times favor readings of other textual families.

The Greek Manuscript Evidence

Papyri Cited number	date	name	general text type[6]	location
p[46]	about 200	Chester Beatty	Alexandrian	Dublin/Ann Arbor
p[61]	about 700	p.Colt 5	Alexandrian	New York
p[65]	III		Alexandrian	Florence

Others cited sign	date	name	general text type	location
S	IV	Sinaiticus	Alexandrian	London
A	V	Alexandrinus	Alexandrian	London
B	IV	Vaticanus	Alexandrian	Rome
C	V	Ephraemi Rescriptus	Alexandrian	Paris
D	VI	Claromontanus	Western	Paris
F	IX	Augiensis	Western	Cambridge
G	IX	Boernerianus	Western	Dresden
L	IX	Angelicus	Koine	Rome
P	IX	Porphyrianus	Alexandrian	Leningrad
Koine	the reading of a majority of Koine MSS (third to sixteenth centuries)			
Lect	the reading of a majority of lectionaries (ninth to fifteenth centuries)			

Ancient Versions Cited

it	Itala or Old Latin (second to forth century)	Western
vg	Vulgate (fourth century)	Western
vg(clem)	Clementine edition (3rd ed., 1598; continued publication into this century) cited when differs from vg(w-w)	
vg(w-w)	Wordsworth and White edition (3 vols., 1889-1954) cited when differs from vg(clem)	

syr	Syriac (fifth to seventh century versions cited) mixed		
syr(pes)	The Peshitta	V	
syr(pal)	Palestinian	V	
syr(har)	Harclean	616	
cop	Coptic (third to fifth century)	Alexandrian	
cop(sa)	Sahidic	III	
cop(bo)	Bohairic	III or V	

Church Fathers Cited

name	location	date of death (often approximate)
Ambrose	Milan	397
Ambrosiaster	?	IV
Chrysostom	Constantinople	407
Clement	Alexandria	215
Ephraem	Edessa	373
Hippolytus	Rome	235
Irenaeus	Lyons	202
Marcion	Rome	II
Origen	Alexandria/Caesarea	254
Pelagius	Rome	412
Tertullian	Carthage	220

The following symbols are used in connection with the citation of certain Greek MSS:

*	the reading of the original hand of a MS
c	corrector of a MS
c,2,3	multiple correctors of a MS
a,b,c	multiple correctors of MSS S and D

---

[1] The two most important editions for the RSV text are Eberhard Nestle and Erwin Nestle, *Novum Testamentum Graece* (17th ed., Stuttgart, 1941), and other editions, and behind that, B.F. Westcott and F.J.A. Hort, *The New Testament in the Original Greek* (Cambridge, 1881), 2 Vols. (2nd ed. of vol. 2, 1896).

[2] E.C. Colwell, *What Is the Best New Testament?* (Chicago, 1947).

[3] The received text, or Textus Receptus, was the common text of the Byzantine world. Medieval MSS of this text type were the ones readily available during the renewed interest in antiquity in the Renaissance. It has a number of other names: Koine (common)—the name used in the notes to the *Parallels*, Byzantine, Ecclesiastical, Traditional, *etc.*

[4] Cf. for example, Bruce M. Metzger, *The Text of the New Testament: Its Transmission, Corruption, and Restoration* (New York, 1964).

[5] The Nestle text (n. 3 above) and K. Aland, M. Black, B. M. Metzger, A. Wikgren, edd., *The Greek New Testament* (London, 1966), were most useful to the editors in the preparation of the textual notes.

[6] The classification of text types in this table applies only to the Pauline Corpus in a MS.

TABLE OF PARALLELS

§		Rom	1 Cor	2 Cor	Gal	Eph	Phil	Col	1 Thes	2 Thes	Phm	Page
1	**Paul to God's beloved in Rome**	1:1-7	1:1-3 §71	1:1-2 §146	1:1-5 §193	1:1-2 §218	1:1-2 §237	1:1-2 §256	1:1 §275	1:1-2 §294	1-3 §305	34
2	**I thank my God**	1:8-15	1:4-9 §72				1:3-11 §238	1:3-14 §257	1:2-10 §276	1:3-12 §295	4-7 §306	34
3	**Gospel as power of God**	1:16-17		10:1-6 §176			1:12-18 §239					36
4	**God's wrath revealed**	1:18-23	3:18-23 §82 1:18-25 §74	11:16-21a §182		5:15-20 §231				2:1-12 §296		36
5	**God gave them up**	1:24-28	5:1-5 §87 5:9-13 §89 6:9-11 §91 6:12-20 §92						4:1-8 §284	2:1-12 §296		38
6	**All manner of wickedness**	1:29-32	5:9-13 §89 6:9-11 §91	12:19-21 §188	5:16-26 §213	4:25-5:14 §228-230		3:5-11 §266				38
7	**Man's judgment and God's judgment**	2:1-5			2:11-14 §198							40
8	**To every man according to his work**	2:6-11	1:10-17 §73	5:6-10 §162						2:1-15 §296-297		40
9	**Doers of the law will be justified**	2:12-16	4:1-5 §83 8:7-13 §104 9:19-23 §107 10:23-11:1 §111									42
10	**Boasting in the law**	2:17-24		11:21b-29 §183	1:13-14 §195 2:11-14 §198 6:11-17 §216		3:2-11 §247					42

§		Rom	1 Cor	2 Cor	Gal	Eph	Phil	Col	1 Thes	2 Thes	Phm	Page
33	Those who love God, who are called	8:28-30	1:4-9 §72			1:3-23 §219		1:15-20 §258	5:1-11 §287	2:13-15 §297		66
34	God is for us	8:31-39	4:1-5 §83	4:7-12 §159 6:1-10 §165		3:14-19 §223			3:1-5 §281			66
35	Advantage of Israel	9:1-5		3:7-18 §156-157 11:21b-29 §183	3:19-20 §204	2:11-22 §221	3:17-21 §249					68
36	Children of God	9:6-13			4:21-31 §210	1:3-23 §219						68
37	Not man's will but God's mercy	9:14-18				2:1-10 §220						70
38	Freedom of God	9:19-29				1:3-23 §219		1:24-2:3 §260	5:1-11 §287			70
39	Righteousness through faith	9:30-33	1:18-25 §74		2:15-21 §199 5:1-12 §211		3:2-11 §247					72
40	Israel ignorant of the righteousness that comes from God	10:1-4			1:13-14 §195 3:19-25 §204-205		3:2-11 §247					72
41	Everyone who calls upon the name of the Lord will be saved	10:5-13	12:1-3 §116 12:13 §118 15:1-19 §131-132		3:10-14 §202 3:26-29 §206		2:1-11 §242	3:5-11 §266	1:2-10 §276			74
42	Faith comes from what is heard	10:14-17			3:1-5 §200		4:8-9 §252	1:21-23 §259	2:13-16 §279			74
43	Have they not heard?	10:18-21						1:3-14 §257	1:2-10 §276			76
44	God has not rejected his people	11:1-6		11:21b-29 §183	2:15-21 §199	2:1-10 §220	3:2-11 §247					76

§		Rom	1 Cor	2 Cor	Gal	Eph	Phil	Col	1 Thes	2 Thes	Phm	Page
45	Some of Israel hardened	11:7-10								2:1-12 §296		78
46	Israel's stumbling means riches for Gentiles	11:11-12				2:11-22 §221						78
47	Their acceptance: life from the dead	11:13-16	5:6-8 §88	5:14-21 §164	2:1-14 §197-198	3:1-13 §222		1:21-2:3 §259-260				80
48	Olive tree	11:17-24	1:26-31 §75 4:6-7 §84			2:1-10 §220 2:11-22 §221						80
49	Gifts and call of God irrevocable	11:25-32				4:17-24 §227	3:17-21 §249	1:24-2:3 §260				82
50	Riches, wisdom and knowledge of God	11:33-36	2:6-16 §77 8:4-6 §103			3:1-19 §222-223		1:15-20 §258				82
51	Present your body as a living sacrifice	12:1-2	1:10-17 §73	10:1-6 §176		4:1-10 §225	4:10-20 §253 2:14-18 §244		4:1-8 §284	2:1-12 §296	8-14 §307	84
52	Gifts differ according to grace	12:3-8	10:14-22 §110 12:4-31 §117-120			2:1-10 §220 4:11-16 §226						84
53	Overcome evil with good	12:9-21	13:4-7 §122	13:11-13 §191		4:25-32 §228	2:1-11 §242 4:4-7 §251	3:12-17 §267	4:9-12 §285 5:12-22 §288			86
54	Governing authorities instituted by God	13:1-7	4:1-5 §83 6:1-8 §90 8:7-13 §104									86
55	Love is the fulfilling of the law	13:8-10	13:1-3 §121		5:13-15 §212				4:9-12 §285		15-20 §308	88
56	Night is far gone; salvation nearer	13:11-14	5:9-13 §89 6:9-11 §91	12:19-21 §188	5:16-26 §213	4:17-24 §227 5:3-20 §230-231 6:10-17 §233		3:5-11 §266	5:1-11 §287			88

§		Rom	1 Cor	2 Cor	Gal	Eph	Phil	Col	1 Thes	2 Thes	Phm	Page
57	**Man who is weak in faith**	14:1-4	8:1-3 §102 10:23-11:1 §111 11:17-22 §113									90
58	**Whether we live or die, we are the Lord's**	14:5-12	4:1-5 §83 7:17-24 §97		4:8-11 §208	5:15-20 §231	1:19-26 §240	2:16-19 §263 3:12-17 §267	5:1-11 §287			90
59	**Whatever does not proceed from faith is sin**	14:13-23	4:1-5 §83 8:7-13 §104 10:23-11:1 §111									92
60	**Strong ought to bear with failings of the weak**	15:1-6	1:10-17 §73 10:23-11:1 §111 14:1-5 §124	13:5-13 §190-191	6:1-6 §214		2:1-11 §242	3:12-17 §267				92
61	**Christ confirms the promises**	15:7-13			3:6-9 §201 3:10-14 §202						15-20 §308	94
62	**Paul, minister of Christ Jesus to Gentiles**	15:14-21	2:1-5 §76 3:10-15 §80	10:13-18 §178 12:11-13 §186		3:1-13 §222	1:3-11 §238	1:3-14 §257	1:2-10 §276			94
63	**Going to Jerusalem with aid for the saints**	15:22-29	16:1-4 §138 16:5-9 §139	1:15-22 §149 1:23-2:4 §150 8:1-9:15 §171-175 12:14-13:4 §187-189	2:1-10 §197				2:17-20 §280		21-22 §309	96
64	**Strive together with me in your prayers**	15:30-33				6:18-20 §234		4:2-4 §269	5:25 §290	3:1-5 §299 3:16 §302		96
65	**I commend Phoebe**	16:1-2	16:10-12 §140 16:15-18 §142	3:1-3 §154 8:16-24 §173			2:19-24 §245 2:25-3:1 §246				8-20 §307-308	98

§		Rom	1 Cor	2 Cor	Gal	Eph	Phil	Col	1 Thes	2 Thes	Phm	Page
66	**Greetings**	**16:3-16** **16:21-23 §69**	16:19-20 §143	13:11-13 §191			4:21-22 §254	4:10-15 §272	5:26 §291		23-24 §310	98
67	**Note those who create dissensions**	**16:17-20a**	5:1-5 §87 5:9-13 §89	6:14-7:1 §167 11:12-15 §181			3:17-21 §249		2:1-8 §277			100
68	**Grace**	**16:20b**	16:23-24 §145	13:14 §192	6:18 §217	6:23-24 §236	4:23 §255	4:18b §274	5:28 §293	3:18 §304	25 §311	100
69	**Timothy and others greet you**	**16:21-23** **16:3-16 §66**	16:19-20 §143	13:11-13 §191			4:21-22 §254	4:10-15 §272	5:26 §291		23-24 §310	102
70	**To him be glory**	**16:25-27**				3:20-21 §224		1:24-2:3 §260				102
71	**Paul to the church at Corinth**	1:1-7 §1	**1:1-3**	1:1-2 §146	1:1-5 §193	1:1-2 §218	1:1-2 §237	1:1-2 §256	1:1 §275	1:1-2 §294	1-3 §305	104
72	**I give thanks to God**	1:8-15 §2	**1:4-9**				1:3-11 §238	1:3-14 §257	1:2-10 §276 3:11-13 §283	1:3-12 §295	4-7 §306	104
73	**Quarreling among you**	12:1-2 §51	**1:10-17**	10:1-6 §176		4:1-10 §225	4:1-3 §250		4:1-8 §284	2:1-12 §296	8-14 §307	106
74	**Word of the cross**	1:16-17 §3 1:18-23 §4 9:30-33 §39 11:33-36 §50	**1:18-25**	12:1-10 §185					2:13-16 §279			106
75	**Consider your call**	3:27-31 §15	**1:26-31** **3:18-23 §82** **4:6-13** **§84-85**									108
76	**Jesus Christ and him crucified**	15:14-21 §62	**2:1-5**	10:7-12 §177 12:11-13 §186	4:12-20 §209				1:2-10 §276			108

§		Rom	1 Cor	2 Cor	Gal	Eph	Phil	Col	1 Thes	2 Thes	Phm	Page
77	Secret and hidden wisdom of God	8:26-27 §32 11:33-36 §50	2:6-16 1:4-9 §72		6:1-6 §214	4:11-16 §226		1:24-2:3 §260				110
78	Behaving like ordinary men		3:1-4	5:14-21 §164		2:1-10 §220						110
79	Apollos and Paul, fellow workers for God	1:1-7 §1	3:5-9			2:11-22 §221						112
80	No other foundation	2:1-11 §7-8	3:10-15		2:1-10 §197	3:1-13 §222			1:3-12 §295			112
81	God's temple		3:16-17	6:14-7:1 §81		2:11-22 §221						114
82	Wisdom of this world is folly with God	8:31-39 §34	3:18-23			3:14-19 §223						114
83	It is the Lord who judges	2:12-16 §9 8:26-27 §32 13:1-7 §54 14:13-23 §59	4:1-5			3:1-13 §222		1:24-2:3 §260 2:16-19 §263				116
84	Why do you boast?	3:21-26 §14 11:17-24 §48 12:3-8 §52	4:6-7			2:1-10 §220						116
85	Already you are filled		4:8-13	1:3-11 §147 4:7-12 §159 6:1-10 §165 11:21b-29 §183					2:9-12 §278	3:6-13 §300		118
86	I became your father	1:8-15 §2 15:22-29 §63	4:14-21	1:15-2:4 §149-150 10:1-6 §176 12:14-13:10 §187-190			1:19-30 §240-241 2:19-24 §245		2:1-12 §277-278 2:17-3:5 §280-281	3:6-13 §300	21-22 §309	120
87	Immorality among you	16:17-20a §67	5:1-5	6:14-7:1 §167						3:14-15 §301		122

§		Rom	1 Cor	2 Cor	Gal	Eph	Phil	Col	1 Thes	2 Thes	Phm	Page
88	**Christ our paschal lamb**		**5:6-8**			5:1-2 §229						122
89	**Drive out the wicked from among you**	1:29-32 §6 13:11-14 §56 16:17-20 §67	**5:9-13**	6:14-7:1 §167 12:19-21 §188	5:16-26 §213	4:17-32 §227 5:3-14 §230		3:5-11 §266		3:14-15 §301		124
90	**Brother goes to law against brother**	13:1-7 §54	**6:1-8**					4:5-6 §270			15-20 §308	124
91	**Unrighteous will not inherit the Kingdom**	1:29-32 §6 13:11-14 §56	**6:9-11**	12:19-21 §188	5:16-26 §213	4:17-32 §227 5:3-14 §230		3:5-11 §266		2:13-15 §297		126
92	**Glorify God in your body**	6:1-23 §23-25	**6:12-20**			2:11-22 §221						126
93	**Each has his own special gift**		**7:1-7**						4:1-8 §284			128
94	**To the unmarried and widows**		**7:8-9**									128
95	**To the married**	7:1-6 §26	**7:10-11**									130
96	**Unbelieving partner**	7:1-6 §26	**7:12-16**	6:14-7:1 §167								130
97	**Let everyone lead the life in which God has called him**	2:25-29 §11 6:15-23 §25	**7:17-24**		5:1-12 §211 6:11-17 §216						8-20 §307-308	132
98	**Concerning the unmarried**	13:11-14 §56	**7:25-31**						5:1-11 §287	2:1-12 §296		132
99	**Free from anxieties about worldly affairs**		**7:32-35**			5:21-6:9 §232	4:4-7 §251	3:18-4:1 §268 2:4-7 §261	4:1-8 §284			134
100	**He who refrains from marriage does better**		**7:36-38**									134

§		Rom	1 Cor	2 Cor	Gal	Eph	Phil	Col	1 Thes	2 Thes	Phm	Page
101	Wife bound to her husband as long as he lives	7:1-6 §26	**7:39-40**									136
102	Love builds up, knowledge puffs up	14:1-4 §57	**8:1-3**									136
103	No God but one	11:33-36 §50 14:5-12 §58	**8:4-6**			4:1-10 §225		1:15-20 §258				138
104	Food will not commend us to God	2:12-16 §9 14:13-23 §59	**8:7-13**									138
105	Am I not an apostle?		**9:1-14**	3:1-3 §154 11:7-11 §180 12:14-18 §187	1:15-24 §196 6:1-6 §214		4:10-20 §253		2:9-12 §278	3:6-13 §300		140
106	Gospel free of charge		**9:15-18**	11:7-11 §180 11:12-15 §106		3:1-13 §222			2:1-8 §277			140
107	All things to all men	15:1-6 §60 2:12-16 §9	**9:19-23**		5:13-15 §212 2:1-10 §197							142
108	Run that you may attain the prize		**9:24-27**				3:12-16 §248					142
109	Baptized into Moses	6:11-14 §24	**10:1-13**		5:16-26 §213			3:5-11 §266		2:1-12 §296		144
110	Cup of the Lord; cup of demons		**10:14-22**	6:14-7:1 §167								144
111	Do all to the glory of God	2:12-16 §9 14:5-12 §58 15:1-6 §60	**10:23-11:1**	6:14-7:1 §167	2:11-14 §198	5:15-20 §231		3:12-17 §267	2:13-16 §279	3:6-13 §300		146
112	If a woman will not veil herself		**11:2-16**			5:21-6:9 §232	4:8-9 §252			3:14-15 §301		146
113	It is not the Lord's supper	14:1-4 §57	**11:17-22**									148

§		Rom	1 Cor	2 Cor	Gal	Eph	Phil	Col	1 Thes	2 Thes	Phm	Page
114	Proclaim the Lord's death until he comes		**11:23-26**									148
115	One who eats and drinks without discerning the body	14:13-23 §59	**11:27-34**	13:5-10 §190								150
116	Now concerning spiritual gifts		**12:1-3**		4:8-11 §208	2:11-22 §221			1:2-10 §276			150
117	Manifestation of the Spirit for the common good	12:3-8 §52	**12:4-11** *12:27-31 §120*			4:1-10 §225 4:11-16 §226						152
118	By one Spirit we were baptized into one body		**12:12-13**		3:26-29 §206	2:11-22 §221		3:5-11 §266				152
119	Body consists of many members	11:17-24 §48	**12:14-26**	1:3-7 §147 4:7-15 §159-160								154
120	Individually members of the body of Christ	12:3-8 §52	**12:27-31** *12:4-11 §117*			4:11-16 §226						154
121	If I have not love	16:25-27 §70	**13:1-3**			3:1-13 §222		1:24-2:3 §260				156
122	Love is patient and kind	12:9-21 §53 13:8-10 §55	**13:4-7**		5:13-15 §212		2:1-11 §242		4:9-12 §285		8-20 §307-308	156
123	Greatest of these is love		**13:8-13**	1:12-14 §148		4:11-16 §226 3:14-19 §223					4-7 §306	158
124	He who prophesies edifies the church	15:1-6 §60	**14:1-5**									158
125	How will anyone know what is said?	1:8-15 §2 10:14-17 §42	**14:6-12**	1:12-14 §148								160

§		Rom	1 Cor	2 Cor	Gal	Eph	Phil	Col	1 Thes	2 Thes	Phm	Page
126	I would rather speak five words with my mind	8:26-27 §32	**14:13-19**			5:15-20 §231		3:12-17 §267				160
127	Tongues a sign for unbelievers, prophecy for believers		**14:20-25**			4:11-16 §226		4:5-6 §270				162
128	Let all things be done for edification	12:3-8 §52	**14:26-33a**			5:15-20 §231		3:12-17 §267	5:12-22 §288	3:16 §302		162
129	Women should keep silence in the churches		**14:33b-36** 11:2-16 §112									164
130	All things should be done in order		**14:37-40**						3:14-15 §301	8:14 §307		164
131	I delivered to you what I also received	5:6-11 §21 6:1-10 §23	**15:1-11**	5:14-21 §164	1:15-24 §196 2:1-10 §197	2:1-10 §220 3:1-13 §222	1:12-18 §239 3:17-21 §249	2:8-15 §262				166
132	If Christ has not been raised	5:1-5 §20 6:1-10 §23	**15:12-19**	5:14-21 §164		2:1-10 §220	3:17-21 §249	2:8-15 §262	4:13-18 §286			168
133	In Adam all die; in Christ shall all be made alive	5:12-21 §22	**15:20-28**	10:1-6 §176		1:3-23 §219	3:17-21 §249	1:15-20 §258	4:13-18 §286	2:1-12 §296		170
134	If the dead are not raised		**15:29-34**	4:7-12 §159 6:1-10 §165 11:21b-29 §183			1:19-26 §240	1:24-2:3 §260	3:1-5 §281			170
135	With what kind of body are the dead raised?	8:18-25 §31	**15:35-41**	4:16-5:5 §161				3:17-21 §249				172
136	How are the dead raised?	5:12-21 §22	**15:42-50**		6:7-10 §215			3:17-21 §249	1:15-20 §258 3:5-11 §266			172
137	We shall all be changed	7:7-13 §27	**15:51-58**	4:16-5:5 §161		4:17-24 §227		3:5-11 §266	4:13-18 §286			174

§		Rom	1 Cor	2 Cor	Gal	Eph	Phil	Col	1 Thes	2 Thes	Phm	Page
138	Concerning contribution for the saints	15:14-21 §62	**16:1-4**	8:1-9:15 §171-175	2:1-10 §197							174
139	I hope to spend some time with you	15:22-29 §63	**16:5-9**	1:15-22 §149 1:23-2:4 §150 12:11-13:4 §186-189					2:17-20 §280		21-22 §309	176
140	When Timothy comes; as for Apollos	16:1-2 §65	**16:10-12**	3:1-3 §154 8:16-24 §173			2:19-24 §245 2:25-3:1 §246				8:20 §307-308	176
141	Stand firm	13:8-14 §55-56	**16:13-14**		5:13-15 §212	6:10-17 §233		4:2-4 §269	5:1-11 §287	2:13-17 §297		178
142	Give recognition to such men	16:1-2 §65	**16:15-18**	3:1-3 §154 8:16-24 §173			2:19-24 §245 2:25-3:1 §246		5:12-22 §288		8-20 §307-308	178
143	Greetings	16:3-16 §66 16:21-23 §69	**16:19-20**	13:11-13 §191			4:21-22 §254	4:10-15 §272	5:26 §291		23-24 §310	180
144	Our Lord, come		**16:21-22**		6:11-17 §216			4:16-18a §273	5:27 §292	3:17 §303		180
145	Grace	16:20b §68	**16:23-24**	13:14 §192	6:18 §217	6:23-24 §236	4:23 §255	4:18b §274	5:28 §293	3:18 §304	25 §311	182
146	Paul to the church at Corinth	1:1-7 §1	1:1-3 §71	**1:1-2**	1:1-5 §193	1:1-2 §218	1:1-2 §237	1:1-2 §256	1:1 §275	1:1-2 §294	1-3 §305	184
147	Blessed be God	5:1-5 §20		**1:3-11**		1:3-23 §219			3:1-10 §281-282	1:3-12 §295 2:16-17 §298		186
148	We have behaved with holiness and sincerity	5:1-5 §20	4:1-5 §83 9:15-18 §106	**1:12-14**					2:9-12 §278			186
149	Do I make my plans like a worldly man?	5:1-5 §20 15:22-29 §63	16:5-9 §139	**1:15-22**	3:21-25 §205	1:3-23 §219			2:17-20 §280		21-22 §309	188

§		Rom	1 Cor	2 Cor	Gal	Eph	Phil	Col	1 Thes	2 Thes	Phm	Page
150	I wrote you out of much affliction and anguish		4:14-21 §86 16:13-14 §141	1:23-2:4			1:27-30 §241		3:6-10 §282			188
151	Forgive and comfort him	16:17-20a §67	5:1-5 §87	2:5-11	6:1-6 §214							190
152	A door was opened for me			2:12-13				4:2-4 §269	2:17-3:5 §280-281			190
153	We are the aroma of Christ to God		9:15-18 §106	2:14-17			1:12-18 §239 4:10-20 §253		2:1-8 §277			192
154	You are a letter from Christ	7:1-6 §26 16:1-2 §65	16:10-12 §140 16:15-18 §142	3:1-3			2:19-24 §245 2:25-3:1 §246				8-20 §307-308	192
155	Ministers of a new covenant	7:1-6 §26	4:6-7 §84	3:4-6			3:2-11 §247 3:12-16 §248					194
156	Dispensation of death; dispensation of Spirit	3:21-26 §14 5:6-11 §21 7:1-6 §26 9:1-5 §35 15:7-13 §61		3:7-11			3:2-11 §247					194
157	When a man turns to the Lord the veil is removed	7:1-6 §26 11:25-32 §49		3:12-18	4:21-31 §210							196
158	We do not lose heart	1:1-7 §1	2:1-5 §76	4:1-6		3:1-13 §222		1:24-2:3 §260	2:1-8 §277			196
159	Treasure in earthen vessels	5:1-5 §20 8:31-39 §34	4:8-13 §85	4:7-12			1:12-18 §239 1:19-26 §240					198
160	We believe and so we speak	6:1-10 §23	15:12-19 §132	4:13-15			3:17-21 §249	3:1-4 §265	4:13-18 §286			198
161	Momentary affliction is preparing eternal weight of glory	8:18-25 §31	15:51-58 §137	4:16-5:5		3:14-19 §223		3:5-11 §266				200

§		Rom	1 Cor	2 Cor	Gal	Eph	Phil	Col	1 Thes	2 Thes	Phm	Page
162	We walk by faith, not by sight	2:6-16 §8		**5:6-10**			1:19-26 §240					200
163	What we are is known to God		4:1-5 §83	**5:11-13**								202
164	Ministry of reconciliation	5:6-11 §21 6:1-10 §23 11:13-16 §47	15:1-11 §131	**5:14-21**	2:15-21 §199			1:15-20 §258				202
165	Now is the day of salvation	5:1-5 §20 8:31-39 §34	4:8-13 §85	**6:1-10**	5:16-26 §213	4:1-10 §225	4:8-20 §252-253	3:12-17 §267	2:1-8 §277			204
166	Widen your hearts		4:14-21 §86 3:1-4 §78	**6:11-13**								204
167	Do not be mismated with unbelievers	16:17-20a §67	3:16-17 §81 5:1-5 §87 5:9-13 §89 6:12-20 §92 7:12-16 §96	**6:14-7:1**		5:3-14 §230			2:1-8 §277			206
168	You are in our hearts			**7:2-4**			4:10-20 §253		2:1-8 §277	1:3-12 §295	4-7 §306	206
169	Godly grief	5:1-5 §20		**7:5-13a**					2:17-3:5 §280-281	2:16-17 §298		208
170	Boasting before Titus has proved true			**7:13b-16**			2:12-13 §243		3:1-5 §299			208
171	Macedonia's wealth of liberality	15:22-29 §63	16:1-4 §138	**8:1-7**	2:1-10 §197 5:16-26 §213	4:1-10 §225	4:8-9 §252	3:12-17 §267	1:2-10 §276			210
172	Complete what you began a year ago	15:22-29 §63	16:1-4 §138	**8:8-15**	2:1-10 §197 6:1-6 §214		2:1-11 §242					210
173	We aim at what is honorable	15:22-29 §63 16:1-2 §65	16:1-4 §138 16:10-12 §140 16:15-18 §142	**8:16-24**	2:1-10 §197		2:19-24 §245 2:25-3:1 §246				8-20 §307-308	212

		Rom	1 Cor	2 Cor	Gal	Eph	Phil	Col	1 Thes	2 Thes	Phm	Page
174	Not an exaction but a willing gift	15:22-29 §63	16:1-4 §138	9:1-5	2:1-10 §197				1:2-10 §276			212
175	He who sows bountifully will reap bountifully	15:22-29 §63	9:1-14 §105 16:1-4 §138	9:6-15	2:1-10 §197	3:20-21 §224						214
176	We destroy every obstacle to the knowledge of God	1:16-17 §3 12:1-2 §51 13:11-14 §56	4:14-21 §86	10:1-6		6:10-17 §233			2:1-8 §277 5:1-11 §287			214
177	We, too, are Christ's		2:1-5 §76 3:18-23 §82	10:7-12								216
178	Let him who boasts, boast of the Lord	3:27-31 §15 15:14-21 §62	3:10-15 §80 4:1-5 §83	10:13-18								216
179	I betrothed you to Christ		2:1-5 §76	11:1-6	1:6-12 §194	5:21-6:9 §232						218
180	I did not burden anyone		9:15-18 §106	11:7-11			4:10-20 §253		2:9-12 §278			218
181	False apostles, deceitful workmen	16:17-20a §67	9:15-18 §106	11:12-15	1:6-12 §194					2:1-12 §296		220
182	You gladly bear with fools	1:18-23 §4 3:27-31 §15	1:26-31 §75	11:16-21a								220
183	Greater labors, more imprisonments	2:17-24 §10 3:27-31 §15 9:1-5 §35 11:1-6 §44	4:8-13 §85	11:21b-29			3:2-11 §247	1:24-2:3 §260	2:1-8 §277 3:1-5 §281			222
184	I boast of things that show my weakness		1:26-31 §75	11:30-33								222
185	Caught up to the third heaven	5:1-5 §20 8:26-27 §32		12:1-10	4:12-20 §209		4:10-20 §253	2:16-19 §263				224

§		Rom	1 Cor	2 Cor	Gal	Eph	Phil	Col	1 Thes	2 Thes	Phm	Page
186	Signs of a true apostle were performed among you	15:14-21 §62	2:1-5 §76	**12:11-13**			4:10-20 §253		1:2-10 §276 2:9-12 §278	2:1-12 §296		224
187	I seek not what is yours but you		4:14-21 §86	**12:14-18**					2:1-8 §277			226
188	Not what I wish; not what you wish	1:29-32 §6 13:11-14 §56	5:9-13 §89 6:9-11 §91	**12:19-21**	5:16-26 §213	4:17-32 §227-228 5:3-14 §230		3:5-11 §266				226
189	I warn those who sinned	1:16-17 §3	1:18-25 §74 4:14-21 §86 5:1-5 §87	**13:1-4**								228
190	We pray for your improvement	15:1-6 §60	4:14-21 §86	**13:5-10**								228
191	Live in peace	12:9-21 §53 16:3-16 §66	16:19-20 §143	**13:11-13**			4:21-22 §254	4:10-15 §272	5:26 §291	3:16 §302	23-24 §310	230
192	Grace	16:20b §68	16:23-24 §145	**13:14**	6:18 §217	6:23-24 §236	4:23 §255	4:18b §274	5:28 §293	3:18 §304	25 §311	230
193	Paul to the churches of Galatia	1:1-7 §1	1:1-3 §71	1:1-2 §146	**1:1-5**	1:1-2 §218	1:1-2 §237	1:1-2 §256	1:1 §275	1:1-2 §294	1-3 §305	232
194	Not that there is another gospel	16:17-20a §67	11:23-26 §114 15:1-11 §131	11:1-6 §179 11:12-21a §181-182 5:11-13 §163	**1:6-12**				2:1-8 §277 2:13-16 §279			232
195	Former life in Judaism	2:17-24 §10 10:1-4 §40 11:1-6 §44		11:21b-29 §183	**1:13-14**		3:2-11 §247					234
196	I did not confer with flesh and blood		1:10-17 §73 9:1-14 §105 15:1-11 §131		**1:15-24**	3:1-13 §222	3:2-11 §247 3:12-16 §248	1:24-2:3 §260				234

§		Rom	1 Cor	2 Cor	Gal	Eph	Phil	Col	1 Thes	2 Thes	Phm	Page
197	We should go to the Gentiles	11:13-16 §47 15:22-29 §63	3:10-15 §80 9:19-23 §107 15:1-11 §131 16:1-4 §138	8:1-7 §171 9:1-5 §174	2:1-10	3:1-13 §222		1:24-2:3 §260				236
198	I opposed Cephas to his face	2:1-5 §7 2:17-24 §10 11:13-16 §47	10:23-11:1 §111		2:11-14							236
199	Justification through faith, not works of the law	3:9-20 §13 6:1-14 §23-24 8:9-17 §30 9:30-33 §39 11:1-6 §44		5:14-21 §164	2:15-21	2:1-10 §220	3:2-11 §247					238
200	Works of the law or hearing with faith	8:9-17 §30 10:14-17 §42 16:17-20a §67			3:1-5			2:8-15 §262	1:2-10 §276			238
201	Men of faith are sons of Abraham	4:1-8 §16 15:7-13 §61			3:6-9							240
202	Redeemed from curse of the law	2:25-29 §11 3:9-20 §13 1:16-17 §3 10:5-13 §41			3:10-14							240
203	Law does not annul a previously ratified covenant	4:13-15 §18		3:4-6 §155	3:15-18							242
204	Why the law?	5:12-21 §22 9:1-5 §35 10:1-4 §40			3:19-20							242
205	Law was our custodian until Christ came	3:9-20 §13 6:11-14 §24 7:7-13 §27 11:25-32 §49		1:15-22 §149	3:21-25							244

22

§		Rom	1 Cor	2 Cor	Gal	Eph	Phil	Col	1 Thes	2 Thes	Phm	Page
206	Neither Jew nor Greek	10:5-13 §41	12:12-13 §118		3:26-29	2:11-22 §221		3:5-11 §266				244
207	No longer a slave, but a son	5:1-5 §20 8:9-17 §30			4:1-7							246
208	How can you turn back?	14:5-12 §58	8:4-6 §103 12:1-3 §116		4:8-11			2:16-23 §263-264	1:2-10 §276			246
209	I am perplexed about you		2:1-5 §76 4:14-21 §86	7:5-13a §169 12:1-10 §185	4:12-20				1:2-10 §276			248
210	Not children of the slave but of the free woman	9:6-13 §36		3:12-18 §157	4:21-31							248
211	Faith working through love	2:6-11 §8 2:25-29 §11 6:15-23 §25 9:30-33 §39	5:6-8 §88 7:17-24 §97		5:1-12							250
212	Called to freedom	6:15-23 §25 13:8-10 §55	9:19-23 §107		5:13-15							250
213	Walk by the Spirit	1:29-32 §6 7:14-25 §28 8:1-8 §29 13:11-14 §56	6:9-11 §91 10:1-13 §109 5:9-13 §89	6:1-10 §165 8:1-7 §171 12:19-21 §188	5:16-26	4:1-10 §225 4:17-32 §227 5:3-14 §230	4:8-9 §252	3:5-17 §266-267				252
214	Bear one another's burdens	15:1-6 §60	2:6-16 §77 9:1-14 §105	2:5-11 §151 8:8-15 §172 13:5-10 §190	6:1-6					3:14-15 §301		254
215	Whatever a man sows, that he will also reap	6:15-23 §25	15:42-50 §136		6:7-10					3:6-13 §300		256
216	A new creation	2:17-24 §10 2:25-29 §11	16:21-22 §144 7:17-24 §97		6:11-17			4:16-18a §273	5:27 §292	3:17 §303		256

§		Rom	1 Cor	2 Cor	Gal	Eph	Phil	Col	1 Thes	2 Thes	Phm	Page
217	**Grace**	16:20b §68	16:23-24 §145	13:14 §192	**6:18**	6:23-24 §236	4:23 §255	4:18b §274	5:28 §293	3:18 §304	25 §311	258
218	**Paul to the saints**	1:1-7 §1	1:1-3 §71	1:1-2 §146	1:1-5 §193	**1:1-2**	1:1-2 §237	1:1-2 §256	1:1 §275	1:1-2 §294	1-3 §305	260
219	**Blessed be God**	3:21-26 §14 8:28-30 §33 9:19-29 §38 9:6-13 §36	15:20-28 §133	1:3-11 §147 1:15-22 §149		**1:3-23**	2:1-11 §242	1:15-20 §258 1:24-2:3 §260			4-7 §306	262
220	**You he made alive**	3:21-26 §14 3:27-31 §15 6:1-10 §23 9:14-18 §37 11:1-6 §44 11:17-24 §48 12:3-8 §52	3:1-4 §78 4:6-7 §84		2:15-21 §199	**2:1-10**		2:8-15 §262 3:1-11 §265-266				264
221	**You have been brought near**	5:6-11 §21 9:1-5 §35 11:11-12 §46 11:17-24 §48 15:7-13 §61	3:5-9 §79 3:16-17 §81 6:12-20 §92 12:1-3 §116 12:12-13 §118	5:14-21 §164		**2:11-22**		1:21-23 §259 1:15-20 §258				266
222	**Of this gospel I was made a minister**	1:1-7 §1 11:13-16 §47 11:33-36 §50 15:14-21 §62	3:10-15 §80 4:1-5 §83 9:15-18 §106		1:15-24 §196 2:1-10 §197 4:1-7 §207	**3:1-13**		1:24-2:3 §260				268
223	**I bow my knees before the Father**	8:31-39 §34	3:18-23 §82	4:16-5:5 §161		**3:14-19**		2:4-7 §261				270
224	**To God be glory**	16:25-27 §70		9:6-15 §175		**3:20-21**						270
225	**Lead a life worthy of the calling**	12:1-8 §52-52	1:10-17 §73 8:4-6 §103 12:4-13 §117-118	10:1-6 §176 6:1-10 §165	5:16-26 §213 3:26-29 §206	**4:1-10**	4:10-20 §253 4:8-9 §252 1:27-30 §241	3:12-17 §267 1:15-20 §258	4:1-8 §284	2:1-12 §296	8:14 §307	272

§		Rom	1 Cor	2 Cor	Gal	Eph	Phil	Col	1 Thes	2 Thes	Phm	Page
226	Unity of the faith and of the knowledge of God's Son	12:3-8 §52	2:6-16 §77 3:1-4 §78 12:4-11 §117 12:14-26 §119 12:27-31 §120			**4:11-16**	3:12-16 §248	2:16-19 §263				274
227	No longer live as the Gentiles	1:29-32 §6 13:11-14 §56 1:18-28 §4-5 11:25-32 §49	6:9-11 §91	12:19-21 §188	5:16-26 §213	**4:17-24**		3:5-11 §266				276
228	Putting away falsehood	1:29-32 §6 13:11-14 §56 12:9-21 §53	6:9-11 §91 5:9-13 §89	6:1-10 §165 12:19-21 §188	5:16-26 §213	**4:25-32**	4:8-9 §252	3:5-11 §266 3:12-17 §267	5:12-22 §288	3:6-13 §300		278
229	Be imitators of God		5:6-8 §88	2:14-17 §153		**5:1-2**						280
230	Immorality must not even be named among you	1:29-32 §6 13:11-14 §56 2:1-5 §7	5:9-13 §89 6:9-11 §91 7:32-35 §99	12:19-21 §188 6:14-7:1 §167	5:16-26 §213	**5:3-14**		3:5-11 §266 2:4-7 §261	5:1-11 §287			280
231	Be filled with the Spirit	1:18-23 §4 14:5-12 §58	10:23-11:1 §111 14:13-19 §126 14:26-33a §128			**5:15-20**		3:12-17 §267				282
232	Be subject to one another		7:32-35 §99 11:2-16 §112 14:33b-36 §129	11:1-6 §179		**5:21-6:9**		3:18-4:1 §268				282
233	Put on the whole armor of God	13:11-14 §56	16:13-14 §141	10:1-6 §176		**6:10-17**			5:1-11 §287			284
234	Pray at all times in the Spirit	8:26-27 §32 15:30-33 §64				**6:18-20**		4:2-3 §269 1:24-2:3 §260	5:25 §290	3:1-5 §299		284
235	I have sent Tychicus to you		4:14-21 §86 16:10-12 §140			**6:21-22**	2:25-3:1 §246	4:7-9 §271				286

§		Rom	1 Cor	2 Cor	Gal	Eph	Phil	Col	1 Thes	2 Thes	Phm	Page
236	Peace and grace	16:20b §68	16:23-24 §145	13:14 §192	6:18 §217	6:23-24	4:23 §255	4:18b §274	5:28 §293	3:18 §304	25 §311	286
237	Paul and Timothy, to the saints at Philippi	1:1-7 §1	1:1-3 §71	1:1-2 §146	1:1-5 §193	1:1-2 §218	1:1-2	1:1-2 §256	1:1 §275	1:1-2 §294	1-3 §305	288
238	I thank my God	1:8-15 §2 15:14-21 §62	1:4-9 §72				1:3-11	1:3-14 §257	1:2-10 §276 3:6-13 §282-283	1:3-12 §295	4-7 §306	288
239	My imprisonment is for Christ	1:16-17 §3 2:6-11 §8	15:1-11 §131				1:12-18					290
240	Christ will be honored in my body	14:5-12 §58	4:14-21 §86	4:7-12 §159 5:6-10 §162			1:19-26				21-22 §309	290
241	Striving for the faith of the gospel			1:23-2:4 §150		4:1-10 §225	1:27-30	2:4-7 §261	3:6-10 §282	1:3-12 §295	21-22 §309	292
242	Obedient unto death	2:6-11 §8 8:1-8 §29 8:9-17 §30 10:5-13 §41 12:9-21 §53 15:1-6 §60	13:4-7 §122	8:8-15 §172		4:1-10 §225 1:3-23 §219	2:1-11					292
243	God is at work in you			7:13b-16 §170			2:12-13				21-22 §309	294
244	Do all things without grumbling	12:1-2 §51		1:12-14 §148			2:14-18		5:1-11 §287			294
245	Timothy's worth you know	16:1-2 §65	16:10-12 §140 16:15-18 §142 4:14-21 §86	3:1-3 §154 8:16-24 §173			2:19-24				8-14 §307	296
246	Receive Epaphroditus in the Lord	16:1-2 §65	16:10-12 §140 16:15-18 §142	3:1-3 §154 8:16-24 §173			2:25-3:1				8-14 §307	296

§		Rom	1 Cor	2 Cor	Gal	Eph	Phil	Col	1 Thes	2 Thes	Phm	Page
258	**In him all things were created**	5:6-11 §21 8:28-30 §33 11:13-16 §47 11:33-36 §50	8:4-6 §103 15:20-28 §133 15:42-50 §136	5:14-21 §164		1:3-23 §219 4:1-10 §225 2:11-22 §221		**1:15-20**				312
259	**You he has now reconciled**	11:13-16 §47 12:1-2 §51	15:51-58 §137	4:13-15 §160		2:11-22 §221		**1:21-23**				314
260	**I became a minister**	9:19-29 §38 16:25-27 §70	1:4-9 §72 2:6-16 §77 4:1-5 §83	11:21b-29 §183	1:15-24 §196	1:3-23 §219 3:1-13 §222		**1:24-2:3**				316
261	**Firmness of your faith in Christ**		7:32-35 §99			5:3-14 §230	1:27-30 §241	**2:4-7**	2:1-8 §277	2:13-15 §297		318
262	**See that no one makes prey of you**	6:1-10 §23	15:1-11 §131		3:1-5 §200 3:21-29 §205-206 4:8-11 §208	2:1-10 §220		**2:8-15**				318
263	**Let no one pass judgment on you**	14:5-12 §58	4:1-5 §83	12:1-10 §185	4:8-11 §208	4:11-16 §226		**2:16-19**				320
264	**If with Christ you died**	6:11-14 §24						**2:20-23**				320
265	**If you have been raised with Christ**	6:11-14 §24 8:1-8 §29		4:13-15 §160		2:1-10 §220		**3:1-4**				322
266	**Put to death what is earthly**	1:29-32 §6 2:1-5 §7 6:11-14 §24 8:9-17 §30 13:1-14 §54-56	5:9-13 §89 6:9-11 §91 10:1-13 §109 12:12-13 §118 15:42-50 §136	4:16-5:5 §161 12:19-21 §188	3:26-29 §206 5:16-26 §213	4:17-24 §227 5:3-14 §230		**3:5-11**				324
267	**Put on love**	12:9-21 §53 15:1-6 §60	10:23-11:1 §111 14:26-33a §128	6:1-10 §165	5:16-26 §213	4:1-10 §225 5:15-20 §231	4:8-9 §252	**3:12-17**				324
268	**Subject in the Lord**		7:32-35 §99			5:21-6:9 §232		**3:18-4:1**				326

§		Rom	1 Cor	2 Cor	Gal	Eph	Phil	Col	1 Thes	2 Thes	Phm	Page
269	Continue steadfastly in prayer	15:30-33 §64	16:13-14 §141	2:12-13 §152		6:18-20 §234		**4:2-4**	5:25 §290	3:1-5 §299	21-22 §309	328
270	Conduct yourself wisely towards outsiders		6:1-8 §90 14:13-19 §126					**4:5-6**	4:9-12 §285			328
271	Tychicus and Onesimus will tell you of everything here					6:21-22 §235	2:25-3:1 §246	**4:7-9**			8-14 §307	330
272	Greetings	16:3-16 §66 16:21-23 §69	16:19-20 §143	13:11-13 §191			4:21-22 §254	**4:10-15**	5:26 §291		23-24 §310	330
273	Exchange letters; Archippus' ministry		16:21-22 §144		6:11-17 §216			**4:16-18a**	5:27 §292	3:17 §303		332
274	Grace	16:20b §68	16:23-24 §145	13:14 §192	6:18 §217	6:23-24 §236	4:23 §255	**4:18b**	5:28 §293	3:18 §304	25 §311	332
275	Paul, Silvanus and Timothy to the Thessalonians	1:1-7 §1	1:1-3 §71	1:1-2 §146	1:1-5 §193	1:1-2 §218	1:1-2 §237	1:1-2 §256	**1:1**	1:1-2 §294	1-3 §305	334
276	We give thanks to God	1:8-15 §2 10:5-13 §41 15:14-21 §62	1:4-9 §72 2:1-5 §76 10:14-22 §110	8:1-7 §171 9:1-5 §174	3:1-5 §200 4:12-20 §209 4:8-11 §208		1:3-11 §238 3:17-21 §249	1:3-14 §257	**1:2-10**	1:3-12 §295 2:13-15 §297	4-7 §306	336
277	Our visit to you was not in vain	16:17-20a §67	4:14-21 §86 9:15-18 §106	4:1-6 §158 6:1-10 §165 7:2-4 §168 10:1-6 §176 12:14-18 §187				2:4-7 §261	**2:1-8**			338
278	You remember our labor and toil		4:8-13 §85 4:14-21 §86 9:1-14 §105	1:12-14 §148			4:10-20 §253		**2:9-12**	3:6-13 §300		338
279	You became imitators of the churches in Judea	10:14-17 §42 16:17-20a §67	1:18-25 §74		1:6-12 §194				**2:13-16**			340

§		Rom	1 Cor	2 Cor	Gal	Eph	Phil	Col	1 Thes	2 Thes	Phm	Page
280	You are our glory and joy	15:22-29 §63	4:14-21 §86 16:5-9 §139	1:15-22 §149 2:12-13 §152 7:5-13a §169			4:1-3 §250		**2:17-20**			340
281	I sent Timothy that I might know your faith	8:31-39 §34	4:8-13 §85	1:3-11 §147 7:5-13a §169 11:21b-29 §183			4:10-20 §253		**3:1-5**			342
282	We live, if you stand fast in the Lord			1:3-11 §147					**3:6-10**			342
283	May the Lord establish your hearts in holiness		1:4-9 §72						**3:11-13**	2:16-17 §298		344
284	We beseech you in the Lord	12:1-2 §51	1:10-17 §73 7:1-7 §93 7:32-35 §99 7:39-40 §101 14:37-40 §130 *5:1-8 §87-88*	10:1-6 §176		4:1-10 §225			**4:1-8**	2:1-12 §296	8-14 §307	344
285	Concerning love of the brethren	12:9-21 §53 13:8-10 §55	13:4-7 §122		5:13-15 §212			4:5-6 §270	**4:9-12**	3:6-13 §300		346
286	Those who have fallen asleep and we who are alive		15:12-28 §132-133 15:51-58 §137	4:13-15 §160 4:16-5:5 §161			3:17-21 §249		**4:13-18**	2:1-12 §296		346
287	Like a thief in the night	8:28-30 §33 9:19-29 §38 13:11-14 §56 14:5-12 §58	7:25-31 §98 16:13-14 §141	10:1-6 §176		6:10-17 §233 5:3-14 §230	2:14-18 §244		**5:1-11**	2:1-12 §296		348
288	Hold fast what is good	12:9-21 §53	16:15-18 §142			4:25-32 §228			**5:12-22**	3:6-13 §300		350
289	May God sanctify you		1:4-9 §72						**5:23-24**	3:16 §302		350

§		Rom	1 Cor	2 Cor	Gal	Eph	Phil	Col	1 Thes	2 Thes	Phm	Page
290	Pray for us	15:30-33 §64				6:18-20 §234		4:2-4 §269	5:25	3:1-5 §299	21-22 §309	352
291	Greet all the brethren	16:3-16 §66 16:21-23 §69	16:19-20 §143	13:11-13 §191			4:21-22 §254	4:10-15 §272	5:26		23-24 §310	354
292	Read this letter to the brethren		16:21-22 §144		6:11-17 §216			4:16-18a §273	5:27	3:17 §303		354
293	Grace	16:20b §68	16:23-24 §145	13:14 §192	6:18 §217	6:23-24 §236	4:23 §255	4:18b §274	5:28	3:18 §304	25 §311	356
294	Paul, Silvanus and Timothy to the Thessalonians	1:1-7 §1	1:1-3 §71	1:1-2 §146	1:1-5 §193	1:1-2 §218	1:1-2 §237	1:1-2 §256	1:1 §275	1:1-2	1-3 §305	358
295	We are bound to give thanks	1:8-15 §2	1:4-9 §72 3:10-15 §80	1:3-11 §147 7:2-4 §168			1:3-11 §238 1:27-30 §241 3:17-21 §249	1:3-14 §257	1:2-10 §276	1:3-12	4-7 §306	360
296	Concerning the coming of our Lord	1:18-23 §4 1:24-28 §5 2:6-11 §8 11:7-10 §45	7:25-31 §98 10:1-13 §109 15:20-28 §133	12:11-13 §186 11:12-15 §181			3:17-21 §249		4:13-18 §286 5:1-11 §287	2:1-12		362
297	God chose you from the beginning	2:6-11 §8 8:28-30 §33	16:13-14 §141				4:8-9 §252	2:4-7 §261		2:13-15		364
298	May our Lord comfort your hearts			1:3-11 §147					3:11-13 §283	2:16-17		364
299	Pray that we be delivered from wicked men	15:30-33 §64		7:13b-16 §170		6:18-20 §234		4:2-4 §269	5:25 §290	3:1-5	21-22 §309	366
300	If any one will not work		9:1-14 §105			4:25-32 §228			2:9-12 §278 4:9-12 §285 5:12-22 §288	3:6-13		366
301	If any one refuses to obey what we say		5:9-13 §89 14:37-40 §130 16:21-22 §144							3:14-15		368

§		Rom	1 Cor	2 Cor	Gal	Eph	Phil	Col	1 Thes	2 Thes	Phm	Page
302	May the Lord give you peace	15:30-33 §64							5:23-24 §289	3:16		368
303	It is the way I write		16:21-22 §144		6:11-17 §216			4:16-18a §273	5:27 §292	3:17		370
304	Grace	16:20b §68	16:23-24 §145	13:14 §192	6:18 §217	6:23-24 §236	4:23 §255	4:18b §274	5:28 §293	3:18	25 §311	370
305	Paul and Timothy to Philemon	1:1-7 §1	1:1-3 §71	1:1-2 §146	1:1-5 §193	1:1-2 §218	1:1-2 §237	1:1-2 §256	1:1 §275	1:1-2 §294	1-3	372
306	I thank my God	1:8-15 §2	1:4-9 §72	7:2-4 §168			1:3-11 §238	1:3-14 §257	1:2-10 §276	1:3-12 §295	4-7	372
307	I appeal to you for Onesimus	12:1-2 §51 16:1-2 §65	1:10-17 §73 7:17-24 §97 16:10-12 §140 16:15-18 §142	3:1-3 §154 8:16-24 §173 10:1-6 §176		4:1-10 §225	2:19-24 §245 2:25-3:1 §246	4:7-9 §271	4:1-8 §284		8-14	374
308	Receive him as you would receive me	13:8-10 §55 15:7-13 §61 16:1-2 §65	7:17-24 §97 16:10-12 §140	3:1-3 §154 8:16-24 §173							15-20	374
309	Confident of your obedience		4:14-21 §86 16:5-9 §139	1:15-22 §149			1:19-26 §240 1:27-30 §241 2:19-24 §245 2:12-13 §243		5:25 §290		21-22	376
310	Greetings	16:3-16 §66 16:21-23 §69	16:19-20 §143	13:11-13 §191			4:21-22 §254	4:10-15 §272	5:26 §291		23-24	376
311	Grace	16:20b §68	16:23-24 §145	13:14 §192	6:18 §217	6:23-24 §236	4:23 §255	4:18b §274	5:28 §293	3:18 §304	25	378

1

Rom 1:1-7

1 Paul, a servant of Jesus Christ, called to be an apostle, set apart for the gospel of God 2 which he promised beforehand through his prophets in the holy scriptures, 3 the gospel concerning his Son, who was descended from David according to the flesh 4 and designated Son of God in power according to the Spirit of holiness by his resurrection from the dead, Jesus Christ our Lord, 5 through whom we have received grace and apostleship to bring about the obedience of faith for the sake of his name among all the nations, 6 including yourselves who are called to belong to Jesus Christ;

7 To all God's beloved in Rome, who are called to be saints:

Grace to you and peace from God our Father and the Lord Jesus Christ.

1 Cor 1:1-3 (§71)

1 Paul, called by the will of God to be an apostle of Christ Jesus, and our brother Sos'thenes,

2 To the church of God which is at Corinth, to those sanctified in Christ Jesus, called to be saints together with all those who in every place call on the name of our Lord Jesus Christ, both their Lord and ours:

3 Grace to you and peace from God our Father and the Lord Jesus Christ.

2 Cor 1:1-2 (§146)

1 Paul, an apostle of Christ Jesus by the will of God, and Timothy our brother.

To the church of God which is at Corinth, with all the saints who are in the whole of Acha'ia:

2 Grace to you and peace from God our Father and the Lord Jesus Christ.

Gal 1:1-5 (§193)

1 Paul an apostle—not from men nor through man, but through Jesus Christ and God the Father, who raised him from the dead—2 and all the brethren who are with me,

To the churches of Galatia:

3 Grace to you and peace from God the Father and our Lord Jesus Christ, 4 who gave himself for our sins to deliver us from the present evil age, according to the will of our God and Father; 5 to whom be the glory for ever and ever. Amen.

Eph 1:1-2 (§218)

1 Paul, an apostle of Christ Jesus by the will of God,

To the saints who are also faithful in Christ Jesus:

2 Grace to you and peace from God our Father and the Lord Jesus Christ.

▶ **1:1-7 Acts 9:15** 15 But the Lord said to him, "Go, for he is a chosen instrument of mine to carry my name before the Gentiles and kings and the sons of Israel;

▶ **1:1-7 Acts 26:16-18** 16 But rise and stand upon your feet; for I have appeared to you for this purpose, to appoint you to serve and bear witness to the things in which you have seen me and to those in which I will appear to you, 17 delivering you from the people and from the Gentiles —to whom I send you 18 to open their eyes, that they may turn from darkness to light and from the power of Satan to God, that they may receive forgiveness of sins and a place among those who are sanctified by faith in me.'

▶ **1:1 2 Cor 4:5** 5 For what we preach is not ourselves, but Jesus Christ as Lord, with ourselves as your servants for Jesus' sake.

▶ **1:2 Eph 3:9** 9 and to make all men see what is the plan of the mystery hidden for ages in God who created all things;

▶ **1:3-4 1 Cor 15:3-5** 3 For I delivered to you as of first importance what I also received, that Christ died for our sins in accordance with the scriptures, 4 that he was buried, that he was raised on the third day in accordance with the scriptures, 5 and that he appeared to Cephas, then to the twelve.

2. I thank my God

2

Rom 1:8-15

8 First, I thank my God through Jesus Christ for all of you, because your faith is proclaimed in all the world. 9 For God is my witness, whom I serve with my spirit in the gospel of his Son, that without ceasing I mention you always in my prayers, 10 asking that somehow by God's will I may now at last succeed in coming to you. 11 For I long to see you, that I may impart to you some spiritual gift to strengthen you, 12 that is, that we may be mutually encouraged by each other's faith, both yours and mine. 13 I want you to know, brethren, that I have often intended to come to you (but thus far have been prevented), in order that I may reap some harvest among you as well as among the rest of the Gentiles. 14 I am under obligation both to Greeks and to barbarians, both to the wise and to the foolish: 15 so I am eager to preach the gospel to you also who are in Rome.

1 Cor 1:4-9 (§72)

4 I give thanks to God always for you because of the grace of God which was given you in Christ Jesus, 5 that in every way you were enriched in him with all speech and all knowledge— 6 even as the testimony to Christ was confirmed among you— 7 so that you are not lacking in any spiritual gift, as you wait for the revealing of our Lord Jesus Christ; 8 who will sustain you to the end, guiltless in the day of our Lord Jesus Christ. 9 God is faithful, by whom you were called into the fellowship of his Son, Jesus Christ our Lord.

▶ **1:8 2 Tim 1:3** 3 I thank God whom I serve with a clear conscience, as did my fathers, when I remember you constantly in my prayers.

▶ **1:10 Acts 18:2** 2 And he found a Jew named Aquila, a native of Pontus, lately come from Italy with his wife Priscilla, because Claudius had commanded all the Jews to leave Rome. And he went to see them;

▶ **1:11 Acts 19:21** 21 Now after these events Paul resolved in the Spirit to pass through Macedo'nia and Acha'ia and go to Jerusalem, saying, "After I have been there, I must also see Rome."

▶ **1:10 15:23-24, 32** 23 But now, since I no longer have any room for work in these regions, and since I have longed for many years to come to you, 24 I hope to see you in passing as I go to Spain, and to be sped on my journey there by you, once I have enjoyed your company for a little. 32 so that by God's will I may come to you with joy and be refreshed in your company.

▶ **1:13 15:22** 22 This is the reason why I have so often been hindered from coming to you.

1

Phil 1:1-2 (§237)

1 Paul and Timothy, servants of Christ Jesus,

To all the saints in Christ Jesus who are at Philippi, with the bishops and deacons:

2 Grace to you and peace from God our Father and the Lord Jesus Christ.

Col 1:1-2 (§256)

1 Paul, an apostle of Christ Jesus by the will of God, and Timothy our brother,

2 To the saints and faithful brethren in Christ at Colos´sae:

Grace to you and peace from God our Father.

1 Thes 1:1 (§275)

1 Paul, Silva´nus, and Timothy,

To the church of the Thessalo´-nians in God the Father and the Lord Jesus Christ:

Grace to you and peace.

2 Thes 1:1-2 (§294)

1 Paul, Silva´nus, and Timothy,

To the church of the Thessalo´-nians in God our Father and the Lord Jesus Christ:

2 Grace to you and peace from God the Father and the Lord Jesus Christ.

Phm 1-3 (§305)

1 Paul, a prisoner for Christ Jesus, and Timothy our brother,

To Phile´mon our beloved fellow worker 2 and Ap´phia our sister and Archip´pus our fellow soldier, and the church in your house:

3 Grace to you and peace from God our Father and the Lord Jesus Christ.

▶ 1:5 1 Cor 9:1-2,

Am I not free? Am I not an apostle? Have I not seen Jesus our Lord? Are not you my workmanship in the Lord? 2 If to others I am not an apostle, at least I am to you; for you are the seal of my apostleship in the Lord.

15:9-10 9 For I am the least of the apostles, unfit to be called an apostle, because I persecuted the church of God. 10 But by the grace of God I am what I am, and his grace toward me was not in vain. On the contrary, I worked harder than any of them, though it was not I, but the grace of God which is with me.

Gal 1:15-16a 15 But when he who had set me apart before I was born, and had called me through his grace, 16 was pleased to reveal his Son to me, in order that I might preach him among the Gentiles,

▶ 1:7 (Rome) omit in Rome: G Origen

2. I thank my God

2

Phil 1:3-11 (§238)

3 I thank my God in all my remembrance of you, 4 always in every prayer of mine for you all making my prayer with joy, 5 thankful for your partnership in the gospel from the first day until now. 6 And I am sure that he who began a good work in you will bring it to completion at the day of Jesus Christ. 7 It is right for me to feel thus about you all, because I hold you in my heart, for you are all partakers with me of grace, both in my imprisonment and in the defense and confirmation of the gospel. 8 For God is my witness, how I yearn for you all with the affection of Christ Jesus. 9 And it is my prayer that your love may abound more and more, with knowledge and all discernment, 10 so that you may approve what is excellent, and may be pure and blameless for the day of Christ, 11 filled with the fruits of righteousness which come through Jesus Christ, to the glory and praise of God.

Col 1:3-14 (§257)

3 We always thank God, the Father of our Lord Jesus Christ, when we pray for you, 4 because we have heard of your faith in Christ Jesus and of the love which you have for all the saints, 5 because of the hope laid up for you in heaven. Of this you have heard before in the word of the truth, the gospel 6 which has come to you, as indeed in the whole world it is bearing fruit and growing—so among yourselves, from the day you heard and understood the grace of God in truth, 7 as you learned it from Ep´aphras our beloved fellow servant. He is a faithful minister of Christ on our behalf 8 and has made known to us your love in the Spirit.

9 And so, from the day we heard of it, we have not ceased to pray for you, asking that you may be filled with the knowledge of his will in all spiritual wisdom and understanding, 10 to lead a life worthy of the Lord, fully pleasing to him, bearing fruit in every good work and increasing in the knowledge of God. 11 May you be strengthened with all power, according to his glorious might,

1 Thes 1:2-10 (§276)

2 We give thanks to God always for you all, constantly mentioning you in our prayers, 3 remembering before our God and Father your work of faith and labor of love and steadfastness of hope in our Lord Jesus Christ. 4 For we know, brethren beloved by God, that he has chosen you; 5 for our gospel came to you not only in word, but also in power and in the Holy Spirit and with full conviction. You know what kind of men we proved to be among you for your sake. 6 And you became imitators of us and of the Lord, for you received the word in much affliction, with joy inspired by the Holy Spirit; 7 so that you became an example to all the believers in Macedo´nia and in Acha´ia. 8 For not only has the word of the Lord

for all endurance and patience with joy, 12 giving thanks to the Father, who has qualified us to share in the inheritance of the saints in light. 13 He has delivered us from the dominion of darkness and transferred us to the kingdom of his beloved Son, 14 in whom we have redemption, the forgiveness of sins.

2 Thes 1:3-12 (§295)

3 We are bound to give thanks to God always for you, brethren, as is fitting, because your faith is growing abundantly, and the love of every one of you for one another is increasing. 4 Therefore we ourselves boast of you in the churches of God for your steadfastness and faith in all your persecutions and in the afflictions which you are enduring.

5 This is evidence of the righteous judgment of God, that you may be made worthy of the kingdom of God, for which you are suffering—6 since indeed God deems it just to repay with affliction those who afflict you, 7 and to grant rest with us to you who are af-

sounded forth from you in Macedo´nia and Acha´ia, but your faith in God has gone forth everywhere, so that we need not say anything. 9 For they themselves report concerning us what a welcome we had among you, and how you turned to God from idols, to serve a living and true God, 10 and to wait for his Son from heaven, whom he raised from the dead, Jesus who delivers us from the wrath to come.

Phm 4-7 (§306)

4 I thank my God always when I remember you in my prayers, 5 because I hear of your love and of the faith which you have toward the Lord Jesus and all the saints, 6 and I pray that the sharing of your faith may promote the knowledge of all the good that is ours in Christ. 7 For I have derived much joy and comfort from your love, my brother, because the hearts of the saints have been refreshed through you.

flicted, when the Lord Jesus is revealed from heaven with his mighty angels in flaming fire, 8 inflicting vengeance upon those who do not know God and upon those who do not obey the gospel of our Lord Jesus. 9 They shall suffer the punishment of eternal destruction and exclusion from the presence of the Lord and from the glory of his might, 10 when he comes on that day to be glorified in his saints, and to be marveled at in all who have believed, because our testimony to you was believed. 11 To this end we always pray for you, that our God may make you worthy of his call, and may fulfil every good resolve and work of faith by his power, 12 so that the name of our Lord Jesus may be glorified in you, and you in him, according to the grace of our God and the Lord Jesus Christ.

▶ 1:14 1 Cor 9:16 16 For if I preach the gospel, that gives me no ground for boasting. For necessity is laid upon me. Woe to me if I do not preach the gospel!

▶ 1:8-15 2 Cor 1:3-6 3 Blessed be the God and Father of our Lord Jesus Christ, the Father of mercies and God of all comfort, 4 who comforts us in all our affliction, so that we may be able to comfort those who are in any affliction, with the comfort with which we ourselves are comforted by God. 5 For as we share abundantly in Christ's sufferings, so through Christ we share abundantly in comfort too. 6 If we are afflicted, it is for your comfort and salvation; and if we are comforted, it is for your comfort, which you experience when you patiently endure the same sufferings that we suffer.

▶ 1:15 (Rome) omit in Rome: G Origen

3

Rom 1:16-17

16 For I am not ashamed of the gospel: it is the power of God for salvation to every one who has faith, to the Jew first and also to the Greek. 17 For in it the righteousness of God is revealed through faith for faith; as it is written, "He who through faith is righteous shall live."

2 Cor 10:1-6 (§176)

10 I, Paul, myself entreat you, by the meekness and gentleness of Christ—I who am humble when face to face with you, but bold to you when I am away!— 2 I beg of you that when I am present I may not have to show boldness with such confidence as I count on showing against some who suspect us of acting in worldly fashion. 3 For though we live in the world we are not carrying on a worldly war, 4 for the weapons of our warfare are not worldly but have divine power to destroy strongholds. 5 We destroy arguments and every proud obstacle to the knowledge of God, and take every thought captive to obey Christ, 6 being ready to punish every disobedience, when your obedience is complete.

▶ 1:16 2 Tim 1:8,
8 Do not be ashamed then of testifying to our Lord, nor of me his prisoner, but share in suffering for the gospel in the power of God,

12,
I do. But I am not ashamed, for I know whom I have believed, and I am sure that he is able to guard until that Day what has been entrusted to me.

12 and therefore I suffer as

16
16 May the Lord grant mercy to the household of Onesiph'orus, for he often refreshed me; he was not ashamed of my chains,

▶ 1:16 Phil 1:20
it is my eager expectation and hope that I shall not be at all ashamed, but that with full courage now as always Christ will be honored in my body, whether by life or by death.

20 as

▶ 1:16-17 3:21-26
21 But now the righteousness of God has been manifested apart from law, although the law and the prophets bear witness to it, 22 the righteousness of God through faith in Jesus Christ for all who believe. For there is no distinction; 23 since all have sinned and fall short of the glory of God, 24 they are justified by his grace as a gift, through the redemption which is in Christ Jesus, 25 whom God put forward as an expiation by his blood, to be received by faith. This was to show God's righteousness, because in his divine forbearance he had passed over former sins; 26 it was to prove at the present time that he himself is righteous and that he justifies him who has faith in Jesus.

4. God's wrath revealed

4

Rom 1:18-23

18 For the wrath of God is revealed from heaven against all ungodliness and wickedness of men who by their wickedness suppress the truth. 19 For what can be known about God is plain to them, because God has shown it to them. 20 Ever since the creation of the world his invisible nature, namely, his eternal power and deity, has been clearly perceived in the things that have been made. So they are without excuse; 21 for although they knew God they did not honor him as God or give thanks to him, but they became futile in their thinking and their senseless minds were darkened. 22 Claiming to be wise, they became fools, 23 and exchanged the glory of the immortal God for images resembling mortal man or birds or animals or reptiles.

1 Cor 3:18-23 (§82)

18 Let no one deceive himself. If any one among you thinks that he is wise in this age, let him become a fool that he may become wise. 19 For the wisdom of this world is folly with God. For it is written, "He catches the wise in their craftiness," 20 and again, "The Lord knows that the thoughts of the wise are futile." 21 So let no one boast of men. For all things are yours, 22 whether Paul or Apol'los or Cephas or the world or life or death or the present or the future, all are yours; 23 and you are Christ's; and Christ is God's.

1 Cor 1:18-25 (§74)

18 For the word of the cross is folly to those who are perishing, but to us who are being saved it is the power of God. 19 For it is written,
   "I will destroy the wisdom of the wise,
   and the cleverness of the clever I will thwart."
20 Where is the wise man? Where is the scribe? Where is the debater of this age? Has not God made foolish the wisdom of the world? 21 For since, in the wisdom

2 Cor 11:16-21a (§182)

16 I repeat, let no one think me foolish; but even if you do, accept me as a fool, so that I too may boast a little. 17 (What I am saying I say not with the Lord's authority but as a fool, in this boastful confidence; 18 since many boast of worldly things, I too will boast.) 19 For you gladly bear with fools, being wise yourselves! 20 For you bear it if a man makes slaves of you, or preys upon you, or takes advantage of you, or puts on airs, or strikes you in the face. 21 To my shame, I must say, we were too weak for that!

of God, the world did not know God through wisdom, it pleased God through the folly of what we preach to save those who believe. 22 For Jews demand signs and Greeks seek wisdom, 23 but we preach Christ crucified, a stumbling block to Jews and folly to Gentiles, 24 but to those who are called, both Jews and Greeks, Christ the power of God and the wisdom of God. 25 For the foolishness of God is wiser than men, and the weakness of God is stronger than men.

Eph 5:15-20 (§231)

15 Look carefully then how you walk, not as unwise men but as wise, 16 making the most of the time, because the days are evil. 17 Therefore do not be foolish, but understand what the will of the Lord is. 18 And do not get drunk with wine, for that is debauchery; but be filled with the Spirit, 19 addressing one another in psalms and hymns and spiritual songs, singing and making melody to the Lord with all your heart, 20 always and for everything giving thanks in the name of our Lord Jesus Christ to God the Father.

▶ 1:18 Acts 3:26,
26 God, having raised up his servant, sent him to you first, to bless you in turning every one of you from your wickedness."

18:6
they opposed and reviled him, he shook out his garments and said to them, "Your blood be upon your heads! I am innocent. From now on I will go to the Gentiles."

6 And when

▶ 1:20 1 Tim 1:17
17 To the King of ages, immortal, invisible, the only God, be honor and glory for ever and ever. Amen.

▶ 1:23 Acts 17:29
29 Being then God's offspring, we ought not to think that the Deity is like gold, or silver, or stone, a representation by the art and imagination of man.

▶ 1:18-23 1 Cor 4:10
10 We are fools for Christ's sake, but you are wise in Christ. We are weak, but you are strong. You are held in honor, but we in disrepute.

2 Thes 1:7-8
7 and to grant rest with us to you who are afflicted, when the Lord Jesus is revealed from heaven with his mighty angels in flaming fire, 8 inflicting vengeance upon those who do not know God and upon those who do not obey the gospel of our Lord Jesus.

3

Phil 1:12-18 (§239)

12 I want you to know, brethren, that what has happened to me has really served to advance the gospel, 13 so that it has become known throughout the whole praetorian guard and to all the rest that my imprisonment is for Christ; 14 and most of the brethren have been made confident in the Lord because of my imprisonment, and are much more bold to speak the word of God without fear.

15 Some indeed preach Christ from envy and rivalry, but others from good will. 16 The latter do it out of love, knowing that I am put here for the defense of the gospel; 17 the former proclaim Christ out of partisanship, not sincerely but thinking to afflict me in my imprisonment. 18 What then? Only that in every way, whether in pretense or in truth, Christ is proclaimed; and in that I rejoice.

▶1:17 Hab 2:4
4 Behold, he whose soul is not upright in him shall fail, but the righteous shall live by his faith.

▶1:16 2:9-10 9 There will be tribulation and distress for every human being who does evil, the Jew first and also the Greek, 10 but glory and honor and peace for every one who does good, the Jew first and also the Greek.

3:9
9 What then? Are we Jews any better off? No, not at all; for I have already charged that all men, both Jews and Greeks, are under the power of sin,

4. God's wrath revealed

4

2 Thes 2:1-12 (§296)

2 Now concerning the coming of our Lord Jesus Christ and our assembling to meet him, we beg you, brethren, 2 not to be quickly shaken in mind or excited, either by spirit or by word, or by letter purporting to be from us, to the effect that the day of the Lord has come. 3 Let no one deceive you in any way; for that day will not come, unless the rebellion comes first, and the man of lawlessness*a* is revealed, the son of perdition, 4 who opposes and exalts himself against every so-called god or object of worship, so that he takes his seat in the temple of God, proclaiming himself to be God. 5 Do you not remember that when I was still with you I told you this? 6And you know what is restraining him now so that he may be revealed in his time. 7 For the mystery of lawlessness is already at work; only he who now restrains it will do so until he is out of the way. 8And then the lawless one will be revealed, and the Lord Jesus will slay him with the breath of his mouth and destroy him by his appearing and his coming. 9 The coming of the lawless one by the activity of Satan will be with all power and with pretended signs and wonders, 10 and with all wicked deception for those who are to perish, because they refused to love the truth and so be saved. 11 Therefore God sends upon them a strong delusion, to make them believe what is false, 12 so that all may be condemned who did not believe the truth but had pleasure in unrighteousness.

▶1:18 (God) omit God: Marcion

5

Rom 1:24-28

24 Therefore God gave them up in the lusts of their hearts to impurity, to the dishonoring of their bodies among themselves, 25 because they exchanged the truth about God for a lie and worshiped and served the creature rather than the Creator, who is blessed for ever! Amen.

26 For this reason God gave them up to dishonorable passions. Their women exchanged natural relations for unnatural, 27 and the men likewise gave up natural relations with women and were consumed with passion for one another, men committing shameless acts with men and receiving in their own persons the due penalty for their error.

28 And since they did not see fit to acknowledge God, God gave them up to a base mind and to improper conduct.

▶ 1:24 12:1-2

I appeal to you therefore, brethren, by the mercies of God, to present your bodies as a living sacrifice, holy and acceptable to God, which is your spiritual worship. 2 Do not be conformed to this world but be transformed by the renewal of your mind, that you may prove what is the will of God, what is good and acceptable and perfect.

1 Cor 5:1-5 (§87)

5 It is actually reported that there is immorality among you, and of a kind that is not found even among pagans; for a man is living with his father's wife. 2 And you are arrogant! Ought you not rather to mourn? Let him who has done this be removed from among you.

3 For though absent in body I am present in spirit, and as if present, I have already pronounced judgment 4 in the name of the Lord Jesus on the man who has done such a thing. When you are assembled, and my spirit is present, with the power of our Lord Jesus, 5 you are to deliver this man to Satan for the destruction of the flesh, that his spirit may be saved in the day of the Lord Jesus.

1 Cor 5:9-13 (§89)

9 I wrote to you in my letter not to associate with immoral men; 10 not at all meaning the immoral of this world, or the greedy and robbers, or idolaters, since then you would need to go out of the world. 11 But rather I wrote not to associate with any one who bears the name of brother if he is guilty of immorality or greed, or is an idolater, reviler, drunkard, or robber—not even to eat with such a one. 12 For what have I to do with judging outsiders? Is it not those inside the church whom you are to judge? 13 God judges those outside. "Drive out the wicked person from among you."

1 Cor 6:9-11 (§91)

9 Do you not know that the unrighteous will not inherit the kingdom of God? Do not be deceived; neither the immoral, nor idolaters, nor adulterers, nor sexual perverts, 10 nor thieves, nor the greedy, nor drunkards, nor revilers, nor robbers will inherit the kingdom of God. 11 And such were some of you. But you were washed, you were sanctified, you were justified in the name of the Lord Jesus Christ and in the Spirit of our God.

1 Cor 6:12-20 (§92)

12 "All things are lawful for me," but not all things are helpful. "All things are lawful for me," but I will not be enslaved by anything. 13 "Food is meant for the stomach and the stomach for food"—and God will destroy both one and the other. The body is not meant for immorality, but for the Lord, and the Lord for the body. 14 And God raised the Lord and will also raise us up by his power. 15 Do you not know that your bodies are members of Christ? Shall I therefore take the members of Christ and make them members of a prostitute? Never! 16 Do you not know that he who joins himself to a prostitute becomes one body with her? For, as it is written, "The two shall become one flesh." 17 But he who is united to the Lord becomes one spirit with him. 18 Shun immorality. Every other sin which a man commits is outside the body; but the immoral man sins against his own body. 19 Do you not know that your body is a temple of the Holy Spirit within you, which you have from God? You are not your own; 20 you were bought with a price. So glorify God in your body.

1 Thes 4:3-7 ... 3 For this is the will of God, your sanctification: that you abstain from unchastity; 4 that each one of you know how to take a wife for himself in holiness and honor, 5 not in the passion of lust like heathen who do not know God; 6 that no man transgress, and wrong his brother in this matter, because the Lord is an avenger in all these things, as we solemnly forewarned you. 7 For God has not called us for uncleanness, but in holiness.

▶ 1:24-28 8:20-23 ... 20 for the creation was subjected to futility, not of its own will but by the will of him who subjected it in hope; 21 because the creation itself will be set free from its bondage to decay and obtain the glorious liberty of the children of God. 22 We know that the whole creation has been groaning in travail together until now; 23 and not only the creation, but we ourselves, who have the first fruits of the Spirit, groan inwardly as we wait for adoption as sons, the redemption of our bodies.

6. All manner of wickedness

6

Rom 1:29-32

29 They were filled with all manner of wickedness, evil, covetousness, malice. Full of envy, murder, strife, deceit, malignity, they are gossips, 30 slanderers, haters of God, insolent, haughty, boastful, inventors of evil, disobedient to parents, 31 foolish, faithless, heartless, ruthless. 32 Though they know God's decree that those who do such things deserve to die, they not only do them but approve those who practice them.

1 Cor 5:9-13 (§89)

9 I wrote to you in my letter not to associate with immoral men; 10 not at all meaning the immoral of this world, or the greedy and robbers, or idolaters, since then you would need to go out of the world. 11 But rather I wrote to you not to associate with any one who bears the name of brother if he is guilty of immorality or greed, or is an idolater, reviler, drunkard, or robber—not even to eat with such a one. 12 For what have I to do with judging outsiders? Is it not those inside the church whom you are to judge? 13 God judges those outside. "Drive out the wicked person from among you."

1 Cor 6:9-11 (§91)

9 Do you not know that the unrighteous will not inherit the kingdom of God? Do not be deceived; neither the immoral, nor idolaters, nor adulterers, nor sexual perverts, 10 nor thieves, nor the greedy, nor drunkards, nor revilers, nor robbers will inherit the kingdom of God. 11 And such were some of you. But you were washed, you were sanctified, you were justified in the name of the Lord Jesus Christ and in the Spirit of our God.

2 Cor 12:19-21 (§188)

19 Have you been thinking all along that we have been defending ourselves before you? It is in the sight of God that we have been speaking in Christ, and all for your upbuilding, beloved. 20 For I fear that perhaps I may come and find you not what I wish, and that you may find me not what you wish; that perhaps there may be quarreling, jealousy, anger, selfishness, slander, gossip, conceit, and disorder. 21 I fear that when I come again my God may humble me before you, and I may have to mourn over many of those who sinned before and have not repented of the impurity, immorality, and licentiousness which they have practiced.

Gal 5:16-26 (§213)

16 But I say, walk by the Spirit, and do not gratify the desires of the flesh. 17 For the desires of the flesh are against the Spirit, and the desires of the Spirit are against the flesh; for these are opposed to each other, to prevent you from doing what you would. 18 But if you are led by the Spirit you are not under the law. 19 Now the works of the flesh are plain: fornication, impurity, licentiousness, 20 idolatry, sorcery, enmity, strife, jealousy, anger, selfishness, dissension, party spirit, 21 envy, drunkenness, carousing, and the like. I warn you, as I warned you before, that those who do such things shall not inherit the kingdom of God. 22 But the fruit of the Spirit is love, joy, peace, patience, kindness, goodness, faithfulness, 23 gentleness, self-control; against such there is no law. 24 And those who belong to Christ Jesus have crucified the flesh with its passions and desires.

25 If we live by the Spirit, let us also walk by the Spirit. 26 Let us have no self-conceit, no provoking of one another, no envy of one another.

Eph 4:25-5:14 (§228-230)

25 Therefore, putting away falsehood, let every one speak the truth with his neighbor, for we are members one of another. 26 Be angry but do not sin; do not let the sun go down on your anger, 27 and give no opportunity to the devil. 28 Let the thief no longer steal, but rather let him labor, doing honest work with his hands, so that he may be able to give to those in need. 29 Let no evil talk come out of your mouths, but only such as is good for edifying, as fits the occasion, that it may impart grace to those who hear. 30 And do not grieve the Holy Spirit of God, in whom you were sealed for the day of redemption. 31 Let all bitterness and wrath and anger and clamor and slander be put away from you, with all malice, 32 and be kind to one another, tenderhearted, forgiving one another, as God in Christ forgave you.

5 Therefore be imitators of God, as beloved children. 2 And walk in love, as Christ loved us and gave himself up for us, a fragrant offering and sacrifice to God.

Lord Jesus Christ and in the Spirit of our God.

▶ 1:29-32 1 Tim 1:9, ... 9 understanding this, that the law is not laid down for the just but for the lawless and disobedient, for the ungodly and sinners, for the unholy and profane, for murderers of fathers and murderers of mothers, for manslayers,

6:4-5 ... 4 he is puffed up with conceit, he knows nothing; he has a morbid craving for controversy and for disputes about words, which produce envy, dissension, slander, base suspicions, 5 and wrangling among men who are depraved in mind and bereft of the truth, imagining that godliness is a means of gain.

Tit 3:3 ... 3 For we ourselves were once foolish, disobedient, led astray, slaves to various passions and pleasures, passing our days in malice and envy, hated by men and hating one another;

2 Tim 3:2-4 ... 2 For men will be lovers of self, lovers of money, proud, arrogant, abusive, disobedient to their parents, ungrateful, unholy, 3 inhuman, implacable, slanderers, profligates, fierce, haters of good, 4 treacherous, reckless, swollen with conceit, lovers of pleasure rather than lovers of God,

1 Pet 4:3 ... 3 Let the time that is past suffice for doing what the Gentiles like to do, living in licentiousness, passions, drunkenness, revels, carousing, and lawless idolatry.

1 Thes 4:1-8 (§284)

4 Finally, brethren, we beseech and exhort you in the Lord Jesus, that as you learned from us how you ought to live and to please God, just as you are doing, you do so more and more. 2 For you know what instructions we gave you through the Lord Jesus. 3 For this is the will of God, your sanctification: that you abstain from unchastity; 4 that each one of you know how to take a wife for himself in holiness and honor 5 not in the passion of lust like heathen who do not know God; 6 that no man transgress, and wrong his brother in this matter, because the Lord is an avenger in all these things, as we solemnly forewarned you. 7 For God has not called us for uncleanness, but in holiness. 8 Therefore whoever disregards this, disregards not man but God, who gives his Holy Spirit to you.

2 Thes 2:1-12 (§296)

2 Now concerning the coming of our Lord Jesus Christ and our assembling to meet him, we beg you, brethren, 2 not to be quickly shaken in mind or excited, either by spirit or by word, or by letter purporting to be from us, to the effect that the day of the Lord has come. 3 Let no one deceive you in any way; for that day will not come, unless the rebellion comes first, and the man of lawlessness is revealed, the son of perdition, 4 who opposes and exalts himself against every so-called god or object of worship, so that he takes his seat in the temple of God, proclaiming himself to be God. 5 Do you not remember that when I was still with you I told you this? 6 And you know what is restraining him now so that he may be revealed in his time. 7 For the mystery of lawlessness is already at work; only he who now restrains it will do so until he is out of the way. 8 And then the lawless one will be revealed, and the Lord Jesus will slay him with the breath of his mouth and destroy him by his appearing and his coming. 9 The coming of the lawless one by the activity of Satan will be with all power and with pretended signs and wonders, 10 and with all wicked deception for those who are to perish, because they refused to love the truth and so be saved. 11 Therefore God sends upon them a strong delusion, to make them believe what is false, 12 so that all may be condemned who did not believe the truth but had pleasure in unrighteousness.

6. All manner of wickedness

Eph (cont)

3 But fornication and all impurity or covetousness must not even be named among you, as is fitting among saints. 4 Let there be no filthiness, nor silly talk, nor levity, which are not fitting; but instead let there be thanksgiving. 5 Be sure of this, that no fornicator or impure man, or one who is covetous (that is, an idolater), has any inheritance in the kingdom of Christ and of God. 6 Let no one deceive you with empty words, for it is because of these things that the wrath of God comes upon the sons of disobedience. 7 Therefore do not associate with them, 8 for once you were darkness, but now you are light in the Lord; walk as children of light 9 (for the fruit of light is found in all that is good and right and true), 10 and try to learn what is pleasing to the Lord. 11 Take no part in the unfruitful works of darkness, but instead expose them. 12 For it is a shame even to speak of the things that they do in secret; 13 but when anything is exposed by the light it becomes visible, for anything that becomes visible is light. 14 Therefore it is said,

"Awake, O sleeper, and arise from the dead,
and Christ shall give you light."

Col 3:5-11 (§266)

5 Put to death therefore what is earthly in you: fornication, impurity, passion, evil desire, and covetousness, which is idolatry. 6 On account of these the wrath of God is coming. 7 In these you once walked, when you lived in them. 8 But now put them all away: anger, wrath, malice, slander, and foul talk from your mouth. 9 Do not lie to one another, seeing that you have put off the old nature with its practices 10 and have put on the new nature, which is being renewed in knowledge after the image of its creator. 11 Here there cannot be Greek and Jew, circumcised and uncircumcised, barbarian, Scyth'ian, slave, free man, but Christ is all, and in all.

7

Rom 2:1-5

2 Therefore you have no excuse, O man, whoever you are, when you judge another; for in passing judgment upon him you condemn yourself, because you, the judge, are doing the very same things. 2 We know that the judgment of God rightly falls upon those who do such things. 3 Do you suppose, O man, that when you judge those who do such things and yet do them yourself, you will escape the judgment of God? 4 Or do you presume upon the riches of his kindness and forbearance and patience? Do you not know that God's kindness is meant to lead you to repentance? 5 But by your hard and impenitent heart you are storing up wrath for yourself on the day of wrath when God's righteous judgment will be revealed.

Gal 2:11-14 (§198)

11 But when Cephas came to Antioch I opposed him to his face, because he stood condemned. 12 For before certain men came from James, he ate with the Gentiles; but when they came he drew back and separated himself, fearing the circumcision party. 13 And with him the rest of the Jews acted insincerely, so that even Barnabas was carried away by their insincerity. 14 But when I saw that they were not straightforward about the truth of the gospel, I said to Cephas before them all, "If you, though a Jew, live like a Gentile and not like a Jew, how can you compel the Gentiles to live like Jews?"

▶2:4 1 Tim 1:16
16 but I received mercy for this reason, that in me, as the foremost, Jesus Christ might display his perfect patience for an example to those who were to believe in him for eternal life.

Tit 3:4-5a
4 but when the goodness and loving kindness of God our Savior appeared, 5 he saved us, not because of deeds done by us in righteousness, but in virtue of his own mercy,

2 Tim 2:24-25a
24 And the Lord's servant must not be quarrelsome but kindly to every one, an apt teacher, forbearing, 25 correcting his opponents with gentleness.

▶2:1-5 14:3-4a,
3 Let not him who eats despise him who abstains, and let not him who abstains pass judgment on him who eats; for God has welcomed him. 4 Who are you to pass judgment on the servant of another? It is before his own master that he stands or falls.

10
10 Why do you pass judgment on your brother? Or you, why do you despise your brother? For we shall all stand before the judgment seat of God;

▶2:5 Eph 5:6
6 On account of these the wrath of God is coming.

8

Rom 2:6-11

6 For he will render to every man according to his works: 7 to those who by patience in well-doing seek for glory and honor and immortality, he will give eternal life; 8 but for those who are factious and do not obey the truth, but obey wickedness, there will be wrath and fury. 9 There will be tribulation and distress for every human being who does evil, the Jew first and also the Greek, 10 but glory and honor and peace for every one who does good, the Jew first and also the Greek. 11 For God shows no partiality.

1 Cor 1:10-17 (§73)

10 I appeal to you, brethren, by the name of our Lord Jesus Christ, that all of you agree and that there be no dissensions among you, but that you be united in the same mind and the same judgment. 11 For it has been reported to me by Chlo'e's people that there is quarreling among you, my brethren. 12 What I mean is that each one of you says, "I belong to Paul," or "I belong to Apol'los," or "I belong to Cephas," or "I belong to Christ." 13 Is Christ divided? Was Paul crucified for you? Or were you baptized in the name of Paul? 14 I am thankful that I baptized none of you except Crispus and Ga'ius; 15 lest any one should say that you were baptized in my name. 16 (I did baptize also the household of Steph'anas. Beyond that, I do not know whether I baptized any one else.) 17 For Christ did not send me to baptize but to preach the gospel, and not with eloquent wisdom, lest the cross of Christ be emptied of its power.

2 Cor 5:6-10 (§162)

6 So we are always of good courage; we know that while we are at home in the body we are away from the Lord, 7 for we walk by faith, not by sight. 8 We are of good courage, and we would rather be away from the body and at home with the Lord. 9 So whether we are at home or away, we make it our aim to please him. 10 For we must all appear before the judgment seat of Christ, so that each one may receive good or evil, according to what he has done in the body.

▶2:7 2 Tim 1:10
10 and now has manifested through the appearing of our Savior Christ Jesus, who abolished death and brought life and immortality to light through the gospel.

▶2:9 Acts 10:34
34 And Peter opened his mouth and said: "Truly I perceive that God shows no partiality,

▶2:8 Gal 1:6-9
6 I am astonished that you are so quickly deserting him who called you in the grace of Christ and turning to a different gospel—7 not that there is another gospel, but there are some who trouble you and want to pervert the gospel of Christ. 8 But even if we, or an angel from heaven, should preach to you a gospel contrary to that which we preached to you, let him be accursed. 9 As we have said before, so now I say again, If any one is preaching to you a gospel contrary to that which you received, let him be accursed.

▶2:9-10 1:16,
16 For I am not ashamed of the gospel: it is the power of God for salvation to every one who has faith, to the Jew first and also to the Greek.

3:9
9 What then? Are we Jews any better off? No, not at all; for I have already charged that all men, both Jews and Greeks, are under the power of sin,

7

Col 3:6
[6] Let no one deceive you with empty words, for it is because of these things that the wrath of God comes upon the sons of disobedience.

1 Thes 1:9-10 [9] For they themselves report concerning us what a welcome we had among you, and how you turned to God from idols, to serve a living and true God, [10] and to wait for his Son from heaven, whom he raised from the dead, Jesus who delivers us from the wrath to come.

8. To every man according to his work

2 Thes 2:1-15 (§296-297)

2 Now concerning the coming of our Lord Jesus Christ and our assembling to meet him, we beg you, brethren, [2] not to be quickly shaken in mind or excited, either by spirit or by word, or by letter purporting to be from us, to the effect that the day of the Lord has come. [3] Let no one deceive you in any way; for that day will not come, unless the rebellion comes first, and the man of lawlessness is revealed, the son of perdition, [4] who opposes and exalts himself against every so-called god or object of worship, so that he takes his seat in the temple of God, proclaiming himself to be God. [5] Do you not remember that when I was still with you I told you this? [6] And you know what is restraining him now so that he may be revealed in his time. [7] For the mystery of lawlessness is already at work; only he who now restrains it will do so until he is out of the way. [8] And then the lawless one will be revealed, and the Lord Jesus will slay him with the breath of his mouth and destroy him by his appearing and his coming. [9] The coming of the lawless one by the activity of Satan will be with all power and with pretended signs and wonders, [10] and with all wicked deception for those who are to perish, because they refused to love the truth and so be saved. [11] Therefore God sends upon them a strong delusion, to make them believe what is false, [12] so that all may be condemned who did not believe the truth but had pleasure in unrighteousness.

[13] But we are bound to give thanks to God always for you, brethren beloved by the Lord, because God chose you from the beginning to be saved, through sanctification by the Spirit[c] and belief in the truth. [14] To this he called you through our gospel, so that you may obtain the glory of our Lord Jesus Christ. [15] So then, brethren, stand firm and hold to the traditions which you were taught by us, either by word of mouth or by letter.

8

3:22 [22] the righteousness of God through faith in Jesus Christ for all who believe. For there is no distinction;

9

Rom 2:12-16

12 All who have sinned without the law will also perish without the law, and all who have sinned under the law will be judged by the law. 13 For it is not the hearers of the law who are righteous before God, but the doers of the law who will be justified. 14 When Gentiles who have not the law do by nature what the law requires, they are a law to themselves, even though they do not have the law. 15 They show that what the law requires is written on their hearts, while their conscience also bears witness and their conflicting thoughts accuse or perhaps excuse them 16 on that day when, according to my gospel, God judges the secrets of men by Christ Jesus.

▶ 2:13ff Acts 10:35
35 but in every nation any one who fears him and does what is right is acceptable to him.

1 Cor 4:1-5 (§83)

4 This is how one should regard us, as servants of Christ and stewards of the mysteries of God. 2 Moreover it is required of stewards that they be found trustworthy. 3 But with me it is a very small thing that I should be judged by you or by any human court. I do not even judge myself. 4 I am not aware of anything against myself, but I am not thereby acquitted. It is the Lord who judges me. 5 Therefore do not pronounce judgment before the time, before the Lord comes, who will bring to light the things now hidden in darkness and will disclose the purposes of the heart. Then every man will receive his commendation from God.

1 Cor 8:7-13 (§104)

7 However, not all possess this knowledge. But some, through being hitherto accustomed to idols, eat food as really offered to an idol; and their conscience, being weak, is defiled. 8 Food will not commend us to God. We are no worse off if we do not eat, and no better off if we do. 9 Only take care lest this liberty of yours somehow be-

Heb 8:10b,
I will put my laws into their minds,
and write them on their hearts,
and I will be their God,
and they shall be my people.

come a stumbling block to the weak. 10 For if any one sees you, a man of knowledge, at table in an idol's temple, might he not be encouraged, if his conscience is weak, to eat food offered to idols? 11And so by your knowledge this weak man is destroyed, the brother for whom Christ died. 12 Thus, sinning against your brethren and wounding their conscience when it is weak, you sin against Christ. 13 Therefore, if food is a cause of my brother's falling, I will never eat meat, lest I cause my brother to fall.

1 Cor 9:19-23 (§107)

19 For though I am free from all men, I have made myself a slave to all, that I might win the more. 20 To the Jews I became as a Jew, in order to win Jews; to those under the law I became as one under the law—though not being myself under the law—that I might win those under the law. 21 To those outside the law I became as one outside the law—not being without law toward God but under the law of Christ

10:16
16 "This is the covenant that I will make with them
after those days, says the Lord:
I will put my laws on their hearts,
and write them on their minds,"

—that I might win those outside the law. 22 To the weak I became weak, that I might win the weak. I have become all things to all men, that I might by all means save some. 23 I do it all for the sake of the gospel, that I may share in its blessings.

1 Cor 10:23-11:1 (§111)

23 "All things are lawful," but not all things are helpful. "All things are lawful," but not all things build up. 24 Let no one seek his own good, but the good of his neighbor. 25 Eat whatever is sold in the meat market without raising any question on the ground of conscience. 26 For "the earth is the Lord's, and everything in it." 27 If one of the unbelievers invites you to dinner and you are disposed to go, eat whatever is set before you without raising any question on the ground of conscience. 28 (But if some one says to you, "This has been offered in sacrifice," then out of consideration for the man who informed you, and for conscience' sake— 29 I mean his conscience, not yours—do not

▶ 2:16 Acts 10:42,
42And he commanded us to preach to the people, and to testify that he is the one ordained by God to be judge of the living and the dead.

eat it.) For why should my liberty be determined by another man's scruples? 30 If I partake with thankfulness, why am I denounced because of that for which I give thanks?

31 So, whether you eat or drink, or whatever you do, do all to the glory of God. 32 Give no offense to Jews or to Greeks or to the church of God, 33 just as I try to please all men in everything I do, not seeking my own advantage, but that of many, that they may be

11

saved. 1 Be imitators of me, as I am of Christ.

17:31
31 because he has fixed a day on which he will judge the world in righteousness by a man whom he has appointed, and of this he has given assurance to all men by raising him from the dead."

▶ 2:12-16 13:5,
5 Therefore one must be subject, not only to avoid God's wrath but also for the sake of conscience.

10. Boasting in the law

10

Rom 2:17-24

17 But if you call yourself a Jew and rely upon the law and boast of your relation to God 18 and know his will and approve what is excellent, because you are instructed in the law, 19 and if you are sure that you are a guide to the blind, a light to those who are in darkness, 20 a corrector of the foolish, a teacher of children, having in the law the embodiment of knowledge and truth— 21 you then who teach others, will you not teach yourself? While you preach against stealing, do you steal? 22 You who say that one must not commit adultery, do you commit adultery? You who abhor idols, do you rob temples? 23 You who boast in the law, do you dishonor God by breaking the law? 24 For, as it is written, "The name of God is blasphemed among the Gentiles because of you."

▶ 2:20 2 Tim 1:13
13 Follow the pattern of the sound words which you have heard from me, in the faith and love which are in Christ Jesus;

2 Cor 11:21b-29 (§183)

But whatever any one dares to boast of—I am speaking as a fool—I also dare to boast of that. 22Are they Hebrews? So am I. Are they Israelites? So am I. Are they descendants of Abraham? So am I. 23Are they servants of Christ? I am a better one—I am talking like a madman—with far greater labors, far more imprisonments, with countless beatings, and often near death. 24 Five times I have received at the hands of the Jews the forty lashes less one. 25 Three times I have been beaten with rods; once I was stoned. Three times I have been shipwrecked; a night and a day I have been adrift at sea; 26 on frequent journeys, in danger from rivers, danger from robbers, danger from my own people, danger from Gentiles, danger in the city, danger in the wilderness, danger at sea, danger from false brethren; 27 in toil and hardship, through many a sleepless night, in hunger and thirst, often without food, in cold and exposure. 28And, apart from other things, there is the daily pressure upon me of my anxiety for all the churches. 29 Who is weak, and I am not weak? Who is made to fall, and I am not indignant?

Gal 1:13-14 (§195)

13 For you have heard of my former life in Judaism, how I persecuted the church of God violently and tried to destroy it; 14 and I advanced in Judaism beyond many of my own age among my people, so extremely zealous was I for the traditions of my fathers.

Gal 2:11-14 (§198)

11 But when Cephas came to Antioch I opposed him to his face, because he stood condemned. 12 For before certain men came from James, he ate with the Gentiles; but when they came he drew back and separated himself, fearing the circumcision party. 13And with him the rest of the Jews acted insincerely, so that even Barnabas was carried away by their insincerity. 14 But when I saw that they were not straightforward about the truth of the gospel, I said to Cephas before them all, "If you, though a Jew, live like a Gentile and not like a Jew, how can you compel the Gentiles to live like Jews?"

Gal 6:11-17 (§216)

11 See with what large letters I am writing to you with my own hand. 12 It

is those who want to make a good showing in the flesh that would compel you to be circumcised, and only in order that they may not be persecuted for the cross of Christ. 13 For even those who receive circumcision do not themselves keep the law, but they desire to have you circumcised that they may glory in your flesh. 14 But far be it from me to glory except in the cross of our Lord Jesus Christ, by which the world has been crucified to me, and I to the world. 15 For neither circumcision counts for anything, nor uncircumcision, but a new creation. 16 Peace and mercy be upon all who walk by this rule, upon the Israel of God.

17 Henceforth let no man trouble me; for I bear on my body the marks of Jesus.

8-10

8 Owe no one anything, except to love one another; for he who loves his neighbor has fulfilled the law. 9 The commandments, "You shall not commit adultery, You shall not kill, You shall not steal, You shall not covet," and any other commandment, are summed up in this sentence, "You shall love your neighbor as yourself." 10 Love does no wrong to a neighbor; therefore love is the fulfilling of the law.

2 Cor 3:3

3 and you show that you are a letter from Christ delivered by us, written not with ink but with the Spirit of the living God, not on tablets of stone but on tablets of human hearts.

Gal 5:13-14

13 For you were called to freedom, brethren; only do not use your freedom as an opportunity for the flesh, but through love be servants of one another. 14 For the whole law is fulfilled in one word, "You shall love your neighbor as yourself."

10. Boasting in the law

Phil 3:2-11 (§247)

2 Look out for the dogs, look out for the evil-workers, look out for those who mutilate the flesh. 3 For we are the true circumcision, who worship God in spirit, and glory in Christ Jesus, and put no confidence in the flesh. 4 Though I myself have reason for confidence in the flesh also. If any other man thinks he has reason for confidence in the flesh, I have more: 5 circumcised on the eighth day, of the people of Israel, of the tribe of Benjamin, a Hebrew born of Hebrews; as to the law a Pharisee, 6 as to zeal a persecutor of the church, as to righteousness under the law blameless. 7 But whatever gain I had, I counted as loss for the sake of Christ. 8 Indeed I count everything as loss because of the surpassing worth of knowing Christ Jesus my Lord. For his sake I have suffered the loss of all things, and count them as refuse, in order that I may gain Christ 9 and be found in him, not having a righteousness of my own, based on law, but that which is through faith in Christ, the righteousness from God that depends on faith; 10 that I may know him and the power of his resurrection, and may share his sufferings, becoming like him in his death, 11 that if possible I may attain the resurrection from the dead.

▶ 2:24 Is 52:5

5 Now therefore what have I here, says the LORD, seeing that my people are taken away for nothing? Their rulers wail, says the LORD, and continually all the day my name is despised.

11. True circumcision

11

Rom 2:25-29

25 Circumcision indeed is of value if you obey the law; but if you break the law, your circumcision becomes uncircumcision. 26 So, if a man who is uncircumcised keeps the precepts of the law, will not his uncircumcision be regarded as circumcision? 27 Then those who are physically uncircumcised but keep the law will condemn you who have the written code and circumcision but break the law. 28 For he is not a real Jew who is one outwardly, nor is true circumcision something external and physical. 29 He is a Jew who is one inwardly, and real circumcision is a matter of the heart, spiritual and not literal. His praise is not from men but from God.

1 Cor 7:17-24 (§97)

17 Only, let every one lead the life which the Lord has assigned to him, and in which God has called him. This is my rule in all the churches. 18 Was any one at the time of his call already circumcised? Let him not seek to remove the marks of circumcision. Was any one at the time of his call uncircumcised? Let him not seek circumcision. 19 For neither circumcision counts for anything nor uncircumcision, but keeping the commandments of God. 20 Every one should remain in the state in which he was called. 21 Were you a slave when called? Never mind. But if you can gain your freedom, avail yourself of the opportunity. 22 For he who was called in the Lord as a slave is a freedman of the Lord. Likewise he who was free when called is a slave of Christ. 23 You were bought with a price; do not become slaves of men. 24 So, brethren, in whatever state each was called, there let him remain with God.

Gal 3:10-14 (§202)

10 For all who rely on works of the law are under a curse; for it is written, "Cursed be every one who does not abide by all things written in the book of the law, and do them." 11 Now it is evident that no man is justified before God by the law; for "He who through faith is righteous shall live"; 12 but the law does not rest on faith, for "He who does them shall live by them." 13 Christ redeemed us from the curse of the law, having become a curse for us—for it is written, "Cursed be every one who hangs on a tree"—14 that in Christ Jesus the blessing of Abraham might come upon the Gentiles, that we might receive the promise of the Spirit through faith.

Gal 5:1-12 (§211)

5 For freedom Christ has set us free; stand fast therefore, and do not submit again to a yoke of slavery.

2 Now I, Paul, say to you that if you receive circumcision, Christ will be of no advantage to you. 3 I testify again to every man who receives circumcision that he is bound to keep the whole law.

4 You are severed from Christ, you who would be justified by the law; you have fallen away from grace. 5 For through the Spirit, by faith, we wait for the hope of righteousness. 6 For in Christ Jesus neither circumcision nor uncircumcision is of any avail, but faith working through love. 7 You were running well; who hindered you from obeying the truth? 8 This persuasion is not from him who calls you. 9 A little leaven leavens the whole lump. 10 I have confidence in the Lord that you will take no other view than mine; and he who is troubling you will bear his judgment, whoever he is. 11 But if I, brethren, still preach circumcision, why am I still persecuted? In that case the stumbling block of the cross has been removed. 12 I wish those who unsettle you would mutilate themselves!

Gal 6:11-17 (§216)

11 See with what large letters I am writing to you with my own hand. 12 It is those who want to make a good showing in the flesh that would compel you to be circumcised, and only in order

▶ 2:26 Acts 10:35

35 but in every nation any one who fears him and does what is right is acceptable to him.

▶ 2:29 Acts 7:51

51 "You stiff-necked people, uncircumcised in heart and ears, you always resist the Holy Spirit. As your fathers did, so do you.

▶ 2:25ff 9:6-8

6 But it is not as though the word of God had failed. For not all who are descended from Israel belong to Israel, 7 and not all are children of Abraham because they are his descendants; but "Through Isaac shall your descendants be named." 8 This means that it is not the children of the flesh who are the children of God, but the children of the promise are reckoned as descendants.

Col 3:11

11 Here there cannot be Greek and Jew, circumcised and uncircumcised, barbarian, Scyth'ian, slave, free man, but Christ is all, and in all.

*cf. Gal 4:21-31

▶ 2:29 1 Cor 4:5b

Then every man will receive his commendation from God.

12. Advantage of the Jew and the faithfulness of God

12

Rom 3:1-8

3 Then what advantage has the Jew? Or what is the value of circumcision? 2 Much in every way. To begin with, the Jews are entrusted with the oracles of God. 3 What if some were unfaithful? Does their faithlessness nullify the faithfulness of God? 4 By no means! Let God be true though every man be false, as it is written,

"That thou mayest be justified in thy words,
and prevail when thou art judged."

5 But if our wickedness serves to show the justice of God, what shall we say? That God is unjust to inflict wrath on us? (I speak in a human way.) 6 By no means! For then how could God judge the world? 7 But if through my falsehood God's truthfulness abounds to his glory, why am I still being condemned as a sinner? 8 And why not do evil that good may come?—as some people slanderously charge us with saying. Their condemnation is just.

Rom 9:1-5 (§35)

9 I am speaking the truth in Christ, I am not lying; my conscience bears me witness in the Holy Spirit, 2 that I have great sorrow and unceasing anguish in my heart. 3 For I could wish that I myself were accursed and cut off from Christ for the sake of my brethren, my kinsmen by race. 4 They are Israelites, and to them belong the sonship, the glory, the covenants, the giving of the law, the worship, and the promises; 5 to them belong the patriarchs, and of their race, according to the flesh, is the Christ. God who is over all be blessed for ever. Amen.

▶ 3:3 2 Tim 2:13

13 if we are faithless, he remains faithful—
for he cannot deny himself.

▶ 3:1 11:28-29

28 As regards the gospel they are enemies of God, for your sake; but as regards election they are beloved for the sake of their forefathers. 29 For the gifts and the call of God are irrevocable.

▶ 3:1-8 cf. 3:9ff

▶ 3:8 cf. 6:1ff

Phil 3:2-11 (§247)

2 Look out for the dogs, look out for the evil-workers, look out for those who mutilate the flesh. 3 For we are the true circumcision, who worship God in spirit,ᵉ and glory in Christ Jesus, and put no confidence in the flesh. 4 Though I myself have reason for confidence in the flesh also. If any other man thinks he has reason for confidence in the flesh, I have more: 5 circumcised on the

Gal (cont)

that they may not be persecuted for the cross of Christ. 13 For even those who receive circumcision do not themselves keep the law, but they desire to have you circumcised that they may glory in your flesh. 14 But far be it from me to glory except in the cross of our Lord Jesus Christ, by which the world has been crucified to me, and I to the world. 15 For neither circumcision counts for anything, nor uncircumcision, but a new creation. 16 Peace and mercy be upon all who walk by this rule, upon the Israel of God.

17 Henceforth let no man trouble me; for I bear on my body the marks of Jesus.

eighth day, of the people of Israel, of the tribe of Benjamin, a Hebrew born of Hebrews; as to the law a Pharisee, 6 as to zeal a persecutor of the church, as to righteousness under the law blameless. 7 But whatever gain I had, I counted as loss for the sake of Christ. 8 Indeed I count everything as loss because of the surpassing worth of knowing Christ Jesus my Lord. For his sake I have suffered the loss of all things, and count them as refuse, in order that I may gain Christ 9 and be found in him, not having a righteousness of my own, based on law, but that which is through faith in Christ, the righteousness from God that depends on faith; 10 that I may know him and the power of his resurrection, and may share his sufferings, becoming like him in his death, 11 that if possible I may attain the resurrection from the dead.

11

12. Advantage of the Jew and the faithfulness of God

12

▶ 3:4 Ps 51:4
4 Against thee, thee only, have I sinned,
and done that which is evil in thy sight,
so that thou art justified in thy sentence
and blameless in thy judgment.

45

13. Advantage of the Jew and the power of sin

13

Rom 3:9-20

9 What then? Are we Jews any better off? No, not at all; for I have already charged that all men, both Jews and Greeks, are under the power of sin, 10 as it is written:
"None is righteous, no, not one;
11 no one understands, no one seeks for God.
12 All have turned aside, together they have gone wrong;
no one does good, not even one."
13 "Their throat is an open grave, they use their tongues to deceive."
"The venom of asps is under their lips."
14 "Their mouth is full of curses and bitterness."
15 "Their feet are swift to shed blood, 16 in their paths are ruin and misery, 17 and the way of peace they do not know."
18 "There is no fear of God before their eyes."
19 Now we know that whatever the law says it speaks to those who are under the law, so that every mouth may be stopped, and the whole world may be held accountable to God. 20 For no human being will be justified in his sight by works of the law, since through the law comes knowledge of sin.

▶ 3:20 Acts 13:39
39 and by him every one that believes is freed from everything from which you could not be freed by the law of Moses.

▶ 3:9 7:7
7 What then shall we say? That the law is sin? By no means! Yet, if it had not been for the law, I should not have known sin. I should not have known what it is to covet if the law had not said, "You shall not covet."

11:32
32 For God has consigned all men to disobedience, that he may have mercy upon all.

*cf. 2:11

Gal 2:15-21 (§199)
15 We ourselves, who are Jews by birth and not Gentile sinners, 16 yet who know that a man is not justified by works of the law but through faith in Jesus Christ, even we have believed in Christ Jesus, in order to be justified by faith in Christ, and not by works of the law, because by works of the law shall no one be justified. 17 But if, in our endeavor to be justified in Christ, we ourselves were found to be sinners, is Christ then an agent of sin? Certainly not! 18 But if I build up again those things which I tore down, then I prove myself a transgressor. 19 For I through the law died to the law, that I might live to God. 20 I have been crucified with Christ; it is no longer I who live, but Christ who lives in me; and the life I now live in the flesh I live by faith in the Son of God, who loved me and gave himself for me. 21 I do not nullify the grace of God; for if justification[e] were through the law, then Christ died to no purpose.

Gal 3:10-14 (§202)
10 For all who rely on works of the law are under a curse; for it is written,

▶ 3:10-12 Ps 14:1-2
The fool says in his heart,
"There is no God."
They are corrupt, they do abominable deeds,
there is none that does good.

2 The LORD looks down from heaven
upon the children of men,
to see if there are any that act wisely,
that seek after God.

"Cursed be every one who does not abide by all things written in the book of the law, and do them." 11 Now it is evident that no man is justified before God by the law; for "He who through faith is righteous shall live"; 12 but the law does not rest on faith, for "He who does them shall live by them." 13 Christ redeemed us from the curse of the law, having become a curse for us—for it is written, "Cursed be every one who hangs on a tree"—14 that in Christ Jesus the blessing of Abraham might come upon the Gentiles, that we might receive the promise of the Spirit through faith.

Gal 3:21-25 (§205)
21 Is the law then against the promises of God? Certainly not; for if a law had been given which could make alive, then righteousness would indeed be by the law. 22 But the scripture consigned all things to sin, that what was promised to faith in Jesus Christ might be given to those who believe.
23 Now before faith came, we were

Ps 53:1-2
The fool says in his heart,
"There is no God."
They are corrupt, doing abominable iniquity;
there is none that does good.

2 God looks down from heaven
upon the sons of men
to see if there are any that are wise,
that seek after God.

14. Righteousness of God for all who believe

14

Rom 3:21-26

21 But now the righteousness of God has been manifested apart from law, although the law and the prophets bear witness to it, 22 the righteousness of God through faith in Jesus Christ for all who believe. For there is no distinction; 23 since all have sinned and fall short of the glory of God, 24 they are justified by his grace as a gift, through the redemption which is in Christ Jesus, 25 whom God put forward as an expiation by his blood, to be received by faith. This was to show God's righteousness, because in his divine forbearance he had passed over former sins; 26 it was to prove at the present time that he himself is righteous and that he justifies him who has faith in Jesus.

▶ 3:24 Tit 3:7
7 so that we might be justified by his grace and become heirs in hope of eternal life.

1 Cor 4:6-7 (§84)
6 I have applied all this to myself and Apol'los for your benefit, brethren, that you may learn by us not to go beyond what is written, that none of you may be puffed up in favor of one against another. 7 For who sees anything different in you? What have you that you did not receive? If then you received it, why do you boast as if it were not a gift?

▶ 3:25 Acts 14:16,
16 In past generations he allowed all the nations to walk in their own ways;

17:30
30 The times of ignorance God overlooked, but now he commands all men everywhere to repent,

▶ 3:21 1:17
17 For in it the righteousness of God is revealed through faith for faith; as it is written, "He who through faith is righteous shall live."

▶ 3:24 1 Cor 15:10
10 But by the grace of God I am what I am, and his grace toward me was not in vain. On the contrary, I worked harder than any of them, though it was not I, but the grace of God which is with me.

Eph 2:1-10 (§220)
2 And you he made alive, when you were dead through the trespasses and sins 2 in which you once walked, following the course of this world, following the prince of the power of the air, the spirit that is now at work in the sons of disobedience; 3 among these we all once lived in the passions of our flesh, following the desires of body and mind, and so we were by nature children of wrath, like the rest of mankind. 4 But God, who is rich in mercy, out of the great love with which he loved us, 5 even when we were dead through our trespasses, made us alive together with Christ (by grace you have been saved), 6 and raised us up with him, and made us sit with him in the heavenly places in Christ Jesus, 7 that in the coming ages he might show the immeasurable riches of his grace in kindness toward us in Christ Jesus. 8 For by grace you have been saved through faith; and this is not your own doing, it is the gift of God—9 not because of works, lest any man should boast. 10 For we are his workmanship, created in Christ Jesus for good works, which God prepared beforehand, that we should walk in them.

▶ 3:22-23 1:16
16 For I am not ashamed of the gospel: it is the power of God for salvation to every one who has faith, to the Jew first and also to the Greek.

13

Gal (cont)

confined under the law, kept under restraint until faith should be revealed. 24 So that the law was our custodian until Christ came, that we might be justified by faith. 25 But now that faith has come, we are no longer under a custodian;

▶ 3:13 Ps 5:9,   140:3
9 For there is no truth in their mouth;
   their heart is destruction,
their throat is an open sepulchre,
   they flatter with their tongue.

3 They make their tongue sharp as a
   serpent's,
and under their lips is the poison
   of vipers.

▶ 3:14 Ps 10:7
7 His mouth is filled with cursing and
   deceit and oppression;
under his tongue are mischief and
   iniquity.

▶ 3:15-17 Is 59:7-8
7 Their feet run to evil,
   and they make haste to shed innocent blood;
their thoughts are thoughts of iniquity,

desolation and destruction are in
   their highways.
8 The way of peace they know not,
   and there is no justice in their
   paths;
they have made their roads crooked,
   no one who goes in them knows
   peace.

▶ 3:18 Ps 36:1
   Transgression speaks to the
wicked
deep in his heart;
there is no fear of God
   before his eyes.

14. Righteousness of God for all who believe

14

Phil 3:2-11 (§247)

2 Look out for the dogs, look out for the evil-workers, look out for those who mutilate the flesh. 3 For we are the true circumcision, who worship God in spirit, and glory in Christ Jesus, and put no confidence in the flesh. 4 Though I myself have reason for confidence in the flesh also. If any other man thinks he has reason for confidence in the flesh, I have more: 5 circumcised on the eighth day, of the people of Israel, of the tribe of Benjamin, a Hebrew born of Hebrews; as to the law a Pharisee, 6 as to zeal a persecutor of the church, as to righteousness under the law blameless. 7 But whatever gain I had, I counted as loss for the sake of Christ. 8 Indeed I count everything as loss because of the surpassing worth of knowing Christ Jesus my Lord. For his sake I have suffered the loss of all things, and count them as refuse, in order that I may gain Christ 9 and be found in him, not having a righteousness of my own, based on law, but that which is through faith in Christ, the righteousness from God that depends on faith; 10 that I may know him and the power of his resurrection,

and may share his sufferings, becoming like him in his death, 11 that if possible I may attain the resurrection from the dead.

2:9-11   9 There will be tribulation and distress for every human being
who does evil, the Jew first and also the
Greek, 10 but glory and honor and
peace for every one who does good, the
Jew first and also the Greek. 11 For
God shows no partiality.

3:9
   9 What then? Are we Jews any better
off? No, not at all; for I have already
charged that all men, both Jews and
Greeks, are under the power of sin,

15

Rom 3:27-31

27 Then what becomes of our boasting? It is excluded. On what principle? On the principle of works? No, but on the principle of faith. 28 For we hold that a man is justified by faith apart from works of law. 29 Or is God the God of Jews only? Is he not the God of Gentiles also? Yes, of Gentiles also, 30 since God is one; and he will justify the circumcised on the ground of their faith and the uncircumcised through their faith. 31 Do we then overthrow the law by this faith? By no means! On the contrary, we uphold the law.

1 Cor 1:26-31 (§75)

26 For consider your call, brethren; not many of you were wise according to worldly standards, not many were powerful, not many were of noble birth; 27 but God chose what is foolish in the world to shame the wise, God chose what is weak in the world to shame the strong, 28 God chose what is low and despised in the world, even things that are not, to bring to nothing things that are, 29 so that no human being might boast in the presence of God. 30 He is the source of your life in Christ Jesus, whom God made our wisdom, our righteousness and sanctification and redemption; 31 therefore, as it is written, "Let him who boasts, boast of the Lord."

2 Cor 10:13-18 (§178)

13 But we will not boast beyond limit, but will keep to the limits God has apportioned us, to reach even to you. 14 For we are not overextending ourselves, as though we did not reach you; we were the first to come all the way to you with the gospel of Christ. 15 We do not boast beyond limit, in other men's labors; but our hope is that as your faith increases, our field among you may be greatly enlarged, 16 so that we may preach the gospel in lands beyond you, without boasting of work already done in another's field. 17 "Let him who boasts, boast of the Lord." 18 For it is not the man who commends himself that is accepted, but the man whom the Lord commends.

2 Cor 11:16-21a (§182)

16 I repeat, let no one think me foolish; but even if you do, accept me as a fool, so that I too may boast a little. 17 (What I am saying I say not with the Lord's authority but as a fool, in this boastful confidence; 18 since many boast of worldly things, I too will boast.) 19 For you gladly bear with fools, being wise yourselves! 20 For you bear it if a man makes slaves of you, or preys upon you, or takes advantage of you, or puts on airs, or strikes you in the face. 21 To my shame, I must say, we were too weak for that!

2 Cor 11:21b-12:10 (§183)

But whatever any one dares to boast of—I am speaking as a fool—I also dare to boast of that. 22 Are they Hebrews? So am I. Are they Israelites? So am I. Are they descendants of Abraham? So am I. 23 Are they servants of Christ? I am

a better one—I am talking like a madman—with far greater labors, far more imprisonments, with countless beatings, and often near death. 24 Five times I have received at the hands of the Jews the forty lashes less one. 25 Three times I have been beaten with rods; once I was stoned. Three times I have been shipwrecked; a night and a day I have been adrift at sea; 26 on frequent journeys, in danger from rivers, danger from robbers, danger from my own people, danger from Gentiles, danger in the city, danger in the wilderness, danger at sea, danger from false brethren; 27 in toil and hardship, through many a sleepless night, in hunger and thirst, often without food, in cold and exposure. 28 And, apart from other things, there is the daily pressure upon me of my anxiety for all the churches. 29 Who is weak, and I am not weak? Who is made to fall, and I am not indignant?

30 If I must boast, I will boast of the things that show my weakness. 31 The God and Father of the Lord Jesus, he who is blessed for ever, knows that I do not lie. 32 At Damascus, the governor under King Ar′etas guarded the city of Damascus in order to seize me, 33 but I was let down in a basket through a window in the wall, and escaped his hands.

12

I must boast; there is nothing to be gained by it, but I will go on to visions and revelations of the Lord. 2 I know a man in Christ who fourteen years ago was caught up to the third heaven—whether in the body or out of the body I do not know, God knows. 3 And I know that this man was caught

Eph 2:1-10 (§220)

2

And you he made alive, when you were dead through the trespasses and sins 2 in which you once walked, following the course of this world, following the prince of the power of the air, the spirit that is now at work in the sons of disobedience. 3 Among these we all once lived in the passions of our flesh, following the desires of body and mind, and so we were by nature children of wrath, like the rest of mankind. 4 But God, who is rich in mercy, out of the great love with which he loved us, 5 even when we were dead through our trespasses, made us alive together with Christ (by grace you have been saved), 6 and raised us up with him, and made us sit with him in the heavenly places in Christ Jesus, 7 that in the coming ages he might show the immeasurable riches of his grace in kindness toward us in Christ Jesus. 8 For by grace you have been saved through faith; and this is not your own doing, it is the gift of God— 9 not because of works, lest any man should boast. 10 For we are his workmanship, created in Christ Jesus for good works, which God prepared beforehand, that we should walk in them.

up into Paradise—whether in the body or out of the body I do not know, God knows—4 and he heard things that cannot be told, which man may not utter. 5 On behalf of this man I will boast, but on my own behalf I will not boast, except of my weaknesses. 6 Though if I wish to boast, I shall not be a fool, for I shall be speaking the truth. But I refrain from it, so that no one may think more of me than he sees in me or hears

---

▶ 3:28 Acts 13:39
39 and by him every one that believes is freed from everything from which you could not be freed by the law of Moses.

▶ 3:29 Acts 10:34
34 And Peter opened his mouth and said: "Truly I perceive that God shows no partiality,

▶ 3:27 2:17
17 But if you call yourself a Jew and rely upon the law and boast of your relation to God

2:23
23 You who boast in the law, do you dishonor God by breaking the law?

5:2-3
2 Through him we have obtained access to this grace in which we stand, and we rejoice in our hope of sharing the glory of God. 3 More than that, we rejoice in our sufferings, knowing that suffering produces endurance,

15:17
Jesus, then, I have reason to be proud of my work for God.

1Cor 3:21
21 So let no one boast of men. For all things are yours,

17 In Christ

4:7
7 For who sees anything different in you? What have you that you did not receive? If then you received it, why do you boast as if it were not a gift?

5:6
6 Your boasting is not good. Do you not know that a little leaven leavens the whole lump?

▶ 3:28 *cf. 3:21-26
*cf. 9:30-32

▶ 3:31 *cf. 6:14-8:25, esp. 7:7

16

Rom 4:1-8

4

What then shall we say about Abraham, our forefather according to the flesh? 2 For if Abraham was justified by works, he has something to boast about, but not before God. 3 For what does the scripture say? "Abraham believed God, and it was reckoned to him as righteousness." 4 Now to one who works, his wages are not reckoned as a gift but as his due. 5 And to one who does not work but trusts him who justifies the ungodly, his faith is reckoned as

righteousness. 6 So also David pronounces a blessing upon the man to whom God reckons righteousness apart from works:
7 "Blessed are those whose iniquities are forgiven, and whose sins are covered;
8 blessed is the man against whom the Lord will not reckon his sin."

Gal 3:15-20 (§203-204)

15 To give a human example, brethren: no one annuls even a man's will, or adds to it, once it has been ratified. 16 Now the promises were made to Abraham and to his offspring. It does not say, "And to offsprings," referring to many; but, referring to one, "And to your offspring," which is Christ. 17 This is what I mean: the law, which came four hundred and thirty years afterward, does not annul a covenant previously ratified by God, so as to make the promise void. 18 For if the inheritance is by the law, it is no longer

by promise; but God gave it to Abraham by a promise.

19 Why then the law? It was added because of transgressions, till the offspring should come to whom the promise had been made; and it was ordained by angels through an intermediary. 20 Now an intermediary implies more than one; but God is one.

▶ 4:1-8 Jas 2:21-26 21 Was not Abraham our father justified by works, when he offered his son Isaac upon the altar? 22 You see that faith was active along with his works, and faith was completed by works, 23 and the scripture was fulfilled which says, "Abraham believed God, and it was reckoned to him as righteousness"; and he was called the friend of God. 24 You see

that a man is justified by works and not by faith alone. 25 And in the same way was not also Rahab the harlot justified by works when she received the messengers and sent them out another way? 26 For as the body apart from the spirit is dead, so faith apart from works is dead.

▶ 4:3 Gen 15:6
6 And he believed the LORD; and he reckoned it to him as righteousness.

▶ 4:7 Ps 32:1-2
Blessed is he whose transgression is forgiven, whose sin is covered.
2 Blessed is the man to whom the LORD imputes no iniquity, and in whose spirit there is no deceit.

15

Phil 3:2-11 (§247)

2 Look out for the dogs, look out for the evil-workers, look out for those who mutilate the flesh. 3 For we are the true circumcision, who worship God in spirit,*e* and glory in Christ Jesus, and put no confidence in the flesh. 4 Though I myself have reason for confidence in the flesh also. If any other man thinks he has reason for confidence in the flesh, I have more: 5 circumcised on the eighth day, of the people of Israel, of the tribe of Benjamin, a Hebrew born of Hebrews; as to the law a Pharisee, 6 as to zeal a persecutor of the church, as to righteousness under the law blameless. 7 But whatever gain I had, I counted as loss for the sake of Christ. 8 Indeed I count everything as loss because of the surpassing worth of knowing Christ Jesus my Lord. For his sake I have suffered the loss of all things, and count them as refuse, in order that I may gain Christ 9 and be found in him, not having a righteousness of my own, based on law, but that which is through faith in Christ, the righteousness from God that depends on faith; 10 that I may know him and the power of his resurrection,

and may share his sufferings, becoming like him in his death, 11 that if possible I may attain the resurrection from the dead.

2 Cor (cont)

from me. 7And to keep me from being too elated by the abundance of revelations, a thorn was given me in the flesh, a messenger of Satan, to harass me, to keep me from being too elated. 8 Three times I besought the Lord about this, that it should leave me; 9 but he said to me, "My grace is sufficient for you, for my power is made perfect in weakness." I will all the more gladly boast of my weaknesses, that the power of Christ

may rest upon me. 10 For the sake of Christ, then, I am content with weaknesses, insults, hardships, persecutions, and calamities; for when I am weak, then I am strong.

9:15b-16a   For I would rather die than have any one deprive me of my ground for boasting. 16 For if I preach the gospel, that gives me no ground for boasting.

2 Cor 1:12-14

12 For our boast is this, the testimony of our conscience that we have behaved in the world, and still more

toward you, with holiness and godly sincerity, not by earthly wisdom but by the grace of God. 13 For we write you nothing but what you can read and understand; I hope you will understand fully, 14 as you have understood in part, that you can be proud of us as we can be of you, on the day of the Lord Jesus.

5:12   12 We are not commending ourselves to you again but giving you cause to be proud of us, so that you may be able to answer those who pride themselves on a man's position and not on his heart.

13,13 But we will not boast beyond limit, but will keep to the limits God has apportioned us, to reach even to you.

10:8,   8 For even if I boast a little too much of our authority, which the Lord gave for building you up and not for destroying you, I shall not be put to shame.

18   18 For it is not the man who commends himself that is accepted, but the man whom the Lord commends.

Gal 6:13   13 For even those who receive circumcision do not themselves keep the law, but they desire to have you circumcised that they may glory in your flesh.

1 Thes 2:19   19 For what is our hope or joy or crown of boasting before our Lord Jesus at his coming? Is it not you?

16. Abraham righteous by faith, not by works

16

▶4:1 (about) *read* was gained by: SACDG Koine Lect it vg syr(pal) cop(sa, bo); *text:* B Origen Ephraem

17

Rom 4:9-12

9 Is this blessing pronounced only upon the circumcised, or also upon the uncircumcised? We say that faith was reckoned to Abraham as righteousness. 10 How then was it reckoned to him? Was it before or after he had been circumcised? It was not after, but before he was circumcised. 11 He received circumcision as a sign or seal of the righteousness which he had by faith while he was still uncircumcised. The purpose was to make him the father of all who believe without being circumcised and who thus have righteousness reckoned to them, 12 and likewise the father of the circumcised who are not merely circumcised but also follow the example of the faith which our father Abraham had before he was circumcised.

18. Abraham righteous by faith, not by law.

18

Rom 4:13-15

13 The promise to Abraham and his descendants, that they should inherit the world, did not come through the law but through the righteousness of faith. 14 If it is the adherents of the law who are to be the heirs, faith is null and the promise is void. 15 For the law brings wrath, but where there is no law there is no transgression.

Gal 3:15-20 (§203-204)

15 To give a human example, brethren: no one annuls even a man's will, or adds to it, once it has been ratified. 16 Now the promises were made to Abraham and to his offspring. It does not say, "And to offsprings," referring to many; but, referring to one, "And to your offspring," which is Christ. 17 This is what I mean: the law, which came four hundred and thirty years afterward, does not annul a covenant previously ratified by God, so as to make the promise void. 18 For if the inheritance is by the law, it is no longer by promise; but God gave it to Abraham by a promise.

19 Why then the law? It was added because of transgressions, till the offspring should come to whom the promise had been made; and it was ordained by angels through an intermediary. 20 Now an intermediary implies more than one; but God is one.

▶ 4:14 2:12-13
12 All who have sinned without the law will also perish without the law, and all who have sinned under the law will be judged by the law. 13 For it is not the hearers of the law who are righteous before God, but the doers of the law who will be justified.

▶ 4:15 7:7b   Yet, if it had not been for the law, I should not have known sin. I should not have known what it is to covet if the law had not said, "You shall not covet."

17

▶ 4:11 Gen 17:10   [10] This is my covenant, which you shall keep, between me and you and your descendants after you: Every male among you shall be circumcised.

18. Abraham righteous by faith, not by law.

18

▶ 4:13 Gen 17:4-6
[4] "Behold, my covenant is with you, and you shall be the father of a multitude of nations. [5] No longer shall your name be Abram, but your name shall be Abraham; for I have made you the father of a multitude of nations. [6] I will make you exceedingly fruitful; and I will make nations of you, and kings shall come forth from you.

19

Rom 4:16-25

16 That is why it depends on faith, in order that the promise may rest on grace and be guaranteed to all his descendants—not only to the adherents of the law but also to those who share the faith of Abraham, for he is the father of us all, 17 as it is written, "I have made you the father of many nations"—in the presence of the God in whom he believed, who gives life to the dead and calls into existence the things that do not exist. 18 In hope he believed against hope, that he should become the father of many nations; as he had been told, "So shall your descendants be." 19 He did not weaken in faith when he considered his own body, which was as good as dead because he was about a hundred years old, or when he considered the barrenness of Sarah's womb. 20 No distrust made him waver concerning the promise of God, but he grew strong in his faith as he gave glory to God, 21 fully convinced that God was able to do what he had promised. 22 That is why his faith was "reckoned to him as righteousness." 23 But the words, "it was reckoned to him," were written not for his sake alone, 24 but for ours also. It will be reckoned to us who believe in him that raised from the dead Jesus our Lord, 25 who was put to death for our trespasses and raised for our justification.

▶ 4:23-24 2 Tim 3:16-17 16All scripture is inspired by God and profitable for teaching, for reproof, for correction, and for training in righteousness, 17 that the man of God may be complete, equipped for every good work.

▶ 4:24 Acts 2:24 24 But God raised him up, having loosed the pangs of death, because it was not possible for him to be held by it.

▶ 4:16-25 Gal 4:21-31
21 Tell me, you who desire to be under law, do you not hear the law? 22 For it is written that Abraham had two sons, one by a slave and one by a free woman. 23 But the son of the slave was born according to the flesh, the son of the free woman through promise. 24 Now this is an allegory: these women are two covenants. One is from Mount Sinai, bearing children for slavery; she is Hagar. 25 Now Hagar is Mount Sinai in Arabia; she corresponds to the present Jerusalem, for she is in slavery with her children. 26 But the Jerusalem above is free, and she is our mother. 27 For it is written,
"Rejoice, O barren one who does not bear;
break forth and shout, you who are not in travail;
for the children of the desolate one are many more
than the children of her that is married."
28 Now we, brethren, like Isaac, are children of promise. 29 But as at that time he who was born according to the flesh persecuted him who was born according to the Spirit, so it is now. 30 But what does the scripture say? "Cast out the slave and her son; for the son of the slave shall not inherit with the son of the free woman." 31 So, brethren, we are not children of the slave but of the free woman.

20. Since we are justified by faith

20

Rom 5:1-5

5 Therefore, since we are justified by faith, we have peace with God through our Lord Jesus Christ. 2 Through him we have obtained access to this grace in which we stand, and we rejoice in our hope of sharing the glory of God. 3 More than that, we rejoice in our sufferings, knowing that suffering produces endurance, 4 and endurance produces character, and character produces hope, 5 and hope does not disappoint us, because God's love has been poured into our hearts through the Holy Spirit which has been given to us.

2 Cor 1:3-11 (§147)

3 Blessed be the God and Father of our Lord Jesus Christ, the Father of mercies and God of all comfort, 4 who comforts us in all our affliction, so that we may be able to comfort those who are in any affliction, with the comfort with which we ourselves are comforted by God. 5 For as we share abundantly in Christ's sufferings, so through Christ we share abundantly in comfort too. 6 If we are afflicted, it is for your comfort and salvation; and if we are comforted, it is for your comfort, which you experience when you patiently endure the same sufferings that we suffer. 7 Our hope for you is unshaken; for we know that as you share in our sufferings, you will also share in our comfort.
8 For we do not want you to be ignorant, brethren, of the affliction we experienced in Asia; for we were so utterly, unbearably crushed that we despaired of life itself. 9 Why, we felt that we had received the sentence of death; but that was to make us rely not on ourselves but on God who raises the dead; 10 he delivered us from so deadly a peril, and he will deliver us; on him we have set our hope that he will deliver us again. 11 You also must help us by prayer, so that many will give thanks on our behalf for the blessing granted us in answer to many prayers.

2 Cor 4:7-12 (§159)

7 But we have this treasure in earthen vessels, to show that the transcendent power belongs to God and not to us. 8 We are afflicted in every way, but not crushed; perplexed, but not driven to despair; 9 persecuted, but not forsaken; struck down, but not destroyed; 10 always carrying in the body the death of Jesus, so that the life of Jesus may also be manifested in our bodies. 11 For while we live we are always being given up to death for Jesus' sake, so that the life of Jesus may be manifested in our mortal flesh. 12 So death is at work in us, but life in you.

2 Cor 6:1-10 (§165)

6 Working together with him, then, we entreat you not to accept the grace of God in vain. 2 For he says,
"At the acceptable time I have listened to you,
and helped you on the day of salvation."
Behold, now is the acceptable time; behold, now is the day of salvation.
3 We put no obstacle in any one's way, so that no fault may be found with our ministry, 4 but as servants of God we commend ourselves in every way: through great endurance, in afflictions, hardships, calamities, 5 beatings, imprisonments, tumults, labors, watching, hunger; 6 by purity, knowledge, forbearance, kindness, the Holy Spirit, genuine love, 7 truthful speech, and the power of God; with the weapons of righteousness for the right hand and for the left; 8 in honor and dishonor, in ill repute and good repute. We are treated as impostors, and yet are true; 9 as unknown, and yet well known; as dying, and behold we live; as punished, and yet not killed; 10 as sorrowful, yet always rejoicing; as poor, yet making many rich; as having nothing, and yet possessing everything.

▶ 5:5 Acts 2:17-18,
17 'And in the last days it shall be, God declares,
that I will pour out my Spirit upon all flesh,
and your sons and your daughters shall prophesy,
and your young men shall see visions,
and your old men shall dream dreams;

18 yea, and on my menservants and my maidservants in those days
I will pour out my Spirit; and they shall prophesy.

33 33 Being therefore exalted at the right hand of God, and having received from the Father the promise of the Holy Spirit, he has poured out this which you see and hear.

Acts 10:45
45And the believers from among the circumcised who came with Peter were amazed, because the gift of the Holy Spirit had been poured out even on the Gentiles.

Tit 3:6 6 which he poured out upon us richly through Jesus Christ our Savior,

▶ 5:1 *cf. 3:17 15:33

▶ 5:1-5 *cf. 8:1-27

▶ 5:2 Col 1:27 27 To them God chose to make known how great among the Gentiles are the riches of the glory of this mystery, which is Christ in you, the hope of glory.

▶ 5:3 Gal 5:22 22 he has put his seal upon us and given us his Spirit in our hearts as a guarantee.

19

▶ 4:17 Gen 17:5   5 No longer shall your name be Abram, but your name shall be Abraham; for I have made you the father of a multitude of nations.

▶ 4:18 Gen 15:5   5And he brought him outside and said, "Look toward heaven, and number the stars, if you are able to number them." Then he said to him, "So shall your descendants be."

▶4:19 Gen 17:17,   17 Then Abraham fell on his face and laughed, and said to himself, "Shall a child be born to a man who is a hundred years old? Shall Sarah, who is ninety years old, bear a child?"

18:11   11 Now Abraham and Sarah were old, advanced in age; it had ceased to be with Sarah after the manner of women.

▶ 4:22 Gen 15:6   6And he believed the LORD; and he reckoned it to him as righteousness.

20. Since we are justified by faith

20

2 Cor 12:1-10 (§185)

12 I must boast; there is nothing to be gained by it, but I will go on to visions and revelations of the Lord. 2 I know a man in Christ who fourteen years ago was caught up to the third heaven—whether in the body or out of the body I do not know, God knows. 3And I know that this man was caught up into Paradise—whether in the body or out of the body I do not know, God knows—4 and he heard things that cannot be told, which man may not utter. 5 On behalf of this man I will boast, but on my own behalf I will not boast, except of my weaknesses. 6 Though if I wish to boast, I shall not be a fool, for I shall be speaking the truth. But I refrain from it, so that no one may think more of me than he sees in me or hears from me. 7And to keep me from being too elated by the abundance of revelations, a thorn was given me in the flesh, a messenger of Satan, to harass me, to keep me from being too elated. 8 Three times I besought the Lord about this, that it should leave me; 9 but he said to me, "My grace is sufficient for you, for my power is made perfect in weakness." I will all the more gladly boast of my weaknesses, that the power of Christ may rest upon me. 10 For the sake of Christ, then, I am content with weaknesses, insults, hardships, persecutions, and calamities; for when I am weak, then I am strong.

▶ 5:3-4 *cf. 2 Cor 11:21b-29

▶ 5:5 12:11-12   11 Never flag in zeal, be aglow with the Spirit, serve the Lord. 12 Rejoice in your hope, be patient in tribulation, be constant in prayer.

2 Cor 1:22   22 But the fruit of the Spirit is love, joy, peace, patience, kindness, goodness, faithfulness,

Gal 4:6   6And because you are sons, God has sent the Spirit of his Son into our hearts, crying, "Abba! Father!"

▶ 5:1 (we) read let us: S*AB*CD it (most) vg syr (pes pal) cop(bo) Marcion Tertullian; text: SaB3G(Greek) Koine Lect it(few) syr(har) cop(sa) Ephraem

▶ 5:2 (access) add by faith: S*C Koine Lect it(most) vg syr cop(bo) Chrysostom; text: BDG it(some) cop(sa) Ephraem

21

Rom 5:6-11

6 While we were still weak, at the right time Christ died for the ungodly. 7 Why, one will hardly die for a righteous man—though perhaps for a good man one will dare even to die. 8 But God shows his love for us in that while we were yet sinners Christ died for us. 9 Since, therefore, we are now justified by his blood, much more shall we be saved by him from the wrath of God. 10 For if while we were enemies we were reconciled to God by the death of his Son, much more, now that we are reconciled, shall we be saved by his life. 11 Not only so, but we also rejoice in God through our Lord Jesus Christ, through whom we have now received our reconciliation.

▶ 5:10 2 Tim 2:17-18a
17 and their talk will eat its way like gangrene. Among them are Hymenae'us and Phile'tus, 18 who have swerved from the truth by holding that the resurrection is past already.

1 Cor 15:1-11 (§131)

15 Now I would remind you, brethren, in what terms I preached to you the gospel, which you received, in which you stand, 2 by which you are saved, if you hold it fast —unless you believed in vain.

3 For I delivered to you as of first importance what I also received, that Christ died for our sins in accordance with the scriptures, 4 that he was buried, that he was raised on the third day in accordance with the scriptures, 5 and that he appeared to Cephas, then to the twelve. 6 Then he appeared to more than five hundred brethren at one time, most of whom are still alive, though some have fallen asleep. 7 Then he appeared to James, then to all the apostles. 8 Last of all, as to one untimely born, he appeared also to me. 9 For I am the least of the apostles, unfit to be called an apostle, because I persecuted the church of God. 10 But by the grace of God I am what I am, and his grace toward me was not in vain. On the contrary, I worked harder than any of them, though it was not I, but the grace

▶ 5:9 1:18
18 For the wrath of God is revealed from heaven against all ungodliness and wickedness of men who by their wickedness suppress the truth.

2 Cor 5:14-21 (§164)

14 For the love of Christ controls us, because we are convinced that one has died for all; therefore all have died. 15 And he died for all, that those who live might live no longer for themselves but for him who for their sake died and was raised.

16 From now on, therefore, we regard no one from a human point of view; even though we once regarded Christ from a human point of view, we regard him thus no longer. 17 Therefore, if any one is in Christ, he is a new creation; the old has passed away, behold, the new has come. 18 All this is from God, who through Christ reconciled us to himself and gave us the ministry of reconciliation; 19 that is, in Christ God was reconciling the world to himself, not counting their trespasses against them, and entrusting to us the message of reconciliation. 20 So we are ambassadors for Christ, God making his appeal through us. We beseech you

▶ 5:10 11:28
28 As regards the gospel they are enemies of God, for your sake; but as regards election they are beloved for the sake of their forefathers.

Eph 2:11-22 (§221)

11 Therefore remember that at one time you Gentiles in the flesh, called the uncircumcision by what is called the circumcision, which is made in the flesh by hands—12 remember that you were at that time separated from Christ, alienated from the commonwealth of Israel, and strangers to the covenants of promise, having no hope and without God in the world. 13 But now in Christ Jesus you who once were far off have been brought near in the blood of Christ. 14 For he is our peace, who has made us both one, and has broken down the dividing wall of hostility, 15 by abolishing in his flesh the law of commandments and ordinances, that he might create in himself one new man in place of the two, so making peace, 16 and might reconcile us both to God in one body through the cross, thereby bringing the hostility to an end. 17 And he came and preached peace to you who were far off and peace to those who were near; 18 for through him we both have access in one Spirit to the Father. 19 So then you are no longer strangers and sojourners, but you are fellow citizens

on behalf of Christ, be reconciled to God. 21 For our sake he made him to be sin who knew no sin, so that in him we might become the righteousness of God.

of God which is with me. 11 Whether then it was I or they, so we preach and so you believed.

22

Rom 5:12-21

12 Therefore as sin came into the world through one man and death through sin, and so death spread to all men because all men sinned—13 sin indeed was in the world before the law was given, but sin is not counted where there is no law. 14 Yet death reigned from Adam to Moses, even over those whose sins were not like the transgression of Adam, who was a type of the one who was to come.

15 But the free gift is not like the trespass. For if many died through one man's trespass, much more have the grace of God and the free gift in the grace of that one man Jesus Christ abounded for many. 16 And the free gift is not like the effect of that one man's sin. For the judgment following one trespass brought condemnation, but the free gift following many trespasses brings justification. 17 If, because of one man's trespass, death reigned through that one man, much more will those who receive the abundance of grace and the free gift of righteousness reign in life through the one man Jesus Christ. 18 Then as one man's trespass led to

▶ 5:15 Acts 15:11
11 But we believe that we shall be saved through the grace of the Lord Jesus, just as they will."

1 Cor 15:20-28 (§133)

20 But in fact Christ has been raised from the dead, the first fruits of those who have fallen asleep. 21 For as by a man came death, by a man has come also the resurrection of the dead. 22 For as in Adam all die, so also in Christ shall all be made alive. 23 But each in his own order: Christ the first fruits, then at his coming those who belong to Christ. 24 Then comes the end, when he delivers the kingdom to God the Father after destroying every rule and every authority and power. 25 For he must reign until he has put all his enemies under his feet. 26 The last enemy to be

condemnation for all men, so one man's act of righteousness leads to acquittal and life for all men. 19 For as by one man's disobedience many were made sinners, so by one man's obedience many will be made righteous. 20 Law came in, to increase the trespass; but where sin increased, grace abounded all the more, 21 so that, as sin reigned in death, grace also might reign through righteousness to eternal life through Jesus Christ our Lord.

1 Tim 2:5
5 For there is one God, and there is one mediator between God and men, the man Christ Jesus,

destroyed is death. 27 "For God has put all things in subjection under his feet." But when it says, "All things are put in subjection under him," it is plain that he is excepted who put all things under him. 28 When all things are subjected to him, then the Son himself will also be subjected to him who put all things under him, that God may be everything to every one.

1 Cor 15:42-50 (§136)

42 So is it with the resurrection of the dead. What is sown is perishable, what is raised is imperishable. 43 It is sown in dishonor, it is raised in glory. It is sown in weakness, it is raised in power. 44 It is sown a physical body, it is raised a spiritual body. If there is a physical body, there is also a spiritual body. 45 Thus it is written, "The first man Adam became a living being"; the last Adam became a life-giving spirit. 46 But it is not the spiritual which is first but the physical, and then the spiritual. 47 The first man was from the earth, a man of dust; the second man is from heaven. 48 As was the man of dust, so are those who are of the dust; and as is the

man of heaven, so are those who are of heaven. 49 Just as we have borne the image of the man of dust, we shall also bear the image of the man of heaven. 50 I tell you this, brethren: flesh and blood cannot inherit the kingdom of God, nor does the perishable inherit the imperishable.

Gal 3:19-20 (§204)

19 Why then the law? It was added because of transgressions, till the offspring should come to whom the promise had been made; and it was ordained by angels through an intermediary. 20 Now an intermediary implies more than one; but God is one.

Eph 4:1-10 (§225)

4 I therefore, a prisoner for the Lord, beg you to lead a life worthy of the calling to which you have been called, 2 with all lowliness and meekness, with patience, forbearing one another in love, 3 eager to maintain the unity of the Spirit in the bond of peace. 4 There is one body and one Spirit, just as you were called to the one hope that belongs to your call, 5 one Lord, one faith, one baptism, 6 one God and Father of us all, who is above all and through all and in all. 7 But grace was given to each of us according to the measure of Christ's gift. 8 Therefore it is said,
"When he ascended on high he led a
    host of captives,
and he gave gifts to men."
9 (In saying, "He ascended," what does it mean but that he had also descended into the lower parts of the earth? 10 He who descended is he who also ascended far above all the heavens, that he might fill all things.)

▶ 5:20 1 Tim 1:14
14 and the grace of our Lord overflowed for me with the faith and love that are in Christ Jesus.

▶ 5:12-21 *cf. 6:20-23   *cf. 1 Cor 15:45-59   ▶ 5:20 *cf. 7:7-12

Col 1:15-23 (§258-259)

15 He is the image of the invisible God, the first-born of all creation; 16 for in him all things were created, in heaven and on earth, visible and invisible, whether thrones or dominions or principalities or authorities—all things were created through him and for him. 17 He is before all things, and in him all things hold together. 18 He is the head of the body, the church; he is the beginning, the first-born from the dead, that in everything he might be pre-eminent. 19 For in him all the fulness of God was pleased to dwell, 20 and through him to reconcile to himself all things, whether on earth or in heaven, making peace by the blood of his cross. 21 And you, who once were estranged and hostile in mind, doing evil deeds, 22 he has now reconciled in his body of flesh by his death, in order to present you holy and blameless and irreproachable before him, 23 provided that you continue in the faith, stable and steadfast, not shifting from the hope of the gospel which you heard, which has been preached to every creature under heaven, and of which I, Paul, became a minister.

Eph (cont)

with the saints and members of the household of God, 20 built upon the foundation of the apostles and prophets, Christ Jesus himself being the cornerstone, 21 in whom the whole structure is joined together and grows into a holy temple in the Lord; 22 in whom you also are built into it for a dwelling place of God in the Spirit.

22. Through Adam death; through Christ life

22

Phil 2:1-11 (§242)

2 So if there is any encouragement in Christ, any incentive of love, any participation in the Spirit, any affection and sympathy, 2 complete my joy by being of the same mind, having the same love, being in full accord and of one mind. 3 Do nothing from selfishness or conceit, but in humility count others better than yourselves. 4 Let each of you look not only to his own interests, but also to the interests of others. 5 Have this mind among yourselves, which is yours in Christ Jesus, 6 who, though he was in the form of God, did not count equality with God a thing to be grasped, 7 but emptied himself, taking the form of a servant, being born in the likeness of men. 8 And being found in human form he humbled himself and became obedient unto death, even death on a cross. 9 Therefore God has highly exalted him and bestowed on him the name which is above every name, 10 that at the name of Jesus every knee should bow, in heaven and on earth and under the earth, 11 and every tongue confess that Jesus Christ is Lord, to the glory of God the Father.

23. Dead to sin

Rom 6:1-10

23 **6** What shall we say then? Are we to continue in sin that grace may abound? 2 By no means! How can we who died to sin still live in it? 3 Do you not know that all of us who have been baptized into Christ Jesus were baptized into his death? 4 We were buried therefore with him by baptism into death, so that as Christ was raised from the dead by the glory of the Father, we too might walk in newness of life.

5 For if we have been united with him in a death like his, we shall certainly be united with him in a resurrection like his. 6 We know that our old self was crucified with him so that the sinful body might be destroyed, and we might no longer be enslaved to sin. 7 For he who has died is freed from sin. 8 But if we have died with Christ, we believe that we shall also live with him. 9 For we know that Christ being raised from the dead will never die again; death no longer has dominion over him. 10 The death he died he died to sin, once for all, but the life he lives he lives to God.

▶ 6:3 Acts 2:38, 38And Peter said to them, "Repent, and be baptized every one of you in the name of Jesus Christ for the forgiveness of your sins; and you shall receive the gift of the Holy Spirit.

8:16 16for it had not yet fallen on any of them, but they had only been baptized in the name of the Lord Jesus.

Acts 19:5 5 On hearing this, they were baptized in the name of the Lord Jesus.

2 Cor 4:13-15 (§160)

13 Since we have the same spirit of faith as he had who wrote, "I believed, and so I spoke," we too believe, and so we speak, 14 knowing that he who raised the Lord Jesus will raise us also with Jesus and bring us with you into his presence. 15 For it is all for your sake, so that as grace extends to more and more people it may increase thanksgiving, to the glory of God.

▶ 6:8 2 Tim 2:11 11The saying is sure: If we have died with him, we shall also live with him;

▶ 6:9 Acts 2:24 24 But God raised him up, having loosed the pangs of death, because it was not possible for him to be held by it.

Eph 2:1-10 (§220)

2 And you he made alive, when you were dead through the trespasses and sins 2 in which you once walked, following the course of this world, following the prince of the power of the air, the spirit that is now at work in the sons of disobedience. 3Among these we all once lived in the passions of our flesh, following the desires of body and mind, and so we were by nature children of wrath, like the rest of mankind. 4 But God, who is rich in mercy, out of the great love with which he loved us, 5 even when we were dead through our trespasses, made us alive together with Christ (by grace you have been saved), 6 and raised us up with him, and made us sit with him in the heavenly places in Christ Jesus, 7 that in the coming ages he might show the immeasurable riches of his grace in kindness toward us in Christ Jesus. 8 For by grace you have been saved through faith; and this is not your own doing, it is the gift of God— 9 not because of works, lest any man should boast. 10 For we are his workmanship, created in Christ Jesus for

▶ 6:1ff 3:5-8 5 But if our wickedness serves to show the justice of God, what shall we say? That God is unjust to inflict wrath on us? (I speak in a human way.) 6 By no means! For then how could God judge the world? 7 But if through my falsehood God's truthfulness abounds to his glory, why am I still being condemned as a sinner? 8And why not do evil that good may come?—as some people slanderously charge us with saying. Their condemnation is just.

24. Alive to God

Gal 3:21-25 (§205)

21 Is the law then against the promises of God? Certainly not; for if a law had been given which could make alive, then righteousness would indeed be by the law. 22 But the scripture consigned all things to sin, that what was promised to faith in Jesus Christ might be given to those who believe. 23 Now before faith came, we were confined under the law, kept under restraint until faith should be revealed. 24 So that the law was our custodian until Christ came, that we might be justified by faith. 25 But now that faith has come, we are no longer under a custodian;

Rom 6:11-14

24 11 So you also must consider yourselves dead to sin and alive to God in Christ Jesus.

12 Let not sin therefore reign in your mortal bodies, to make you obey their passions. 13 Do not yield your members to sin as instruments of wickedness, but yield yourselves to God as men who have been brought from death to life, and your members to God as instruments of righteousness. 14 For sin will have no dominion over you, since you are not under law but under grace.

▶ 6:12-14 12:1-2 I appeal to you therefore, brethren, by the mercies of God, to present your bodies as a living sacrifice, holy and acceptable to God, which is your spiritual worship. 2 Do not be conformed to this world but be transformed by the renewal of your mind, that you may prove what is the will of God, what is good and acceptable and perfect.

▶ 6:14 1 Cor 9:21 21 To those outside the law I became as one outside the law—not being without law toward God but under the law of Christ —that I might win those outside the law.

Gal 4:21 21 Tell me, you who desire to be under law, do you not hear the law?

Col 2:8-15 (§262)

8 See to it that no one makes a prey of you by philosophy and empty deceit, according to human tradition, according to the elemental spirits of the universe, and not according to Christ. 9 For in him the whole fulness of deity dwells bodily, 10 and you have come to fulness of life in him, who is the head of all rule and authority. 11 In him also you were circumcised with a circumcision made without hands, by putting off the body of flesh in the circumcision of Christ; 12 and you were buried with him in baptism, in which you were also raised with him through faith in the working of God, who raised him from the dead. 13 And you, who were dead in trespasses and the uncircumcision of your flesh, God made alive together with him, having forgiven us all our trespasses, 14 having canceled the bond which stood against us with its legal demands; this he set aside, nailing it to the cross. 15 He disarmed the principalities and powers and made a public example of them, triumphing over them in him.

Eph (cont)
good works, which God prepared beforehand, that we should walk in them.

▶ 6:3 Gal 3:26-29 26 for in Christ Jesus you are all sons of God, through faith. 27 For as many of you as were baptized into Christ have put on Christ. 28 There is neither Jew nor Greek, there is neither slave nor free, there is neither male nor female; for you are all one in Christ Jesus. 29 And if you are Christ's, then you are Abraham's offspring, heirs according to promise.

▶ 6:5 2 Cor 5:14-15
14 For the love of Christ controls us, because we are convinced that one has died for all; therefore all have died. 15 And he died for all, that those who live might live no longer for themselves but for him who for their sake died and was raised.

Phil 3:10-11   10 that I may know him and the power of his resurrection, and may share his sufferings, becoming like him in his death, 11 that if possible I may attain the resurrection from the dead.

24. Alive to God

24

Col 2:20-3:11 (§264)

20 If with Christ you died to the elemental spirits of the universe, why do you live as if you still belonged to the world? Why do you submit to regulations, 21 "Do not handle, Do not taste, Do not touch" 22 (referring to things which all perish as they are used), according to human precepts and doctrines? 23 These have indeed an appearance of wisdom in promoting rigor of devotion and self-abasement and severity to the body, but they are of no value in checking the indulgence of the flesh.

3 If then you have been raised with Christ, seek the things that are above, where Christ is, seated at the right hand of God. 2 Set your minds on things that are above, not on things that are on earth. 3 For you have died, and your life is hid with Christ in God. 4 When Christ who is our life appears, then you also will appear with him in glory.

5 Put to death therefore what is earthly in you: fornication, impurity, passion, evil desire, and covetousness, which is idolatry. 6 On account of these the wrath of God is coming. 7 In these you once walked, when you lived in them. 8 But now put them all away: anger, wrath, malice, slander, and foul talk from your mouth. 9 Do not lie to one another, seeing that you have put off the old nature with its practices 10 and have put on the new nature, which is being renewed in knowledge after the image of its creator. 11 Here there cannot be Greek and Jew, circumcised and uncircumcised, barbarian, Scyth'ian, slave, free man, but Christ is all, and in all.

▶ 6:12 (passions) read it: p46DG it(some) Irenaeus(Latin) Tertullian; text: SABC* it(most) vg cop Origen Ambrosiaster

25. Freed from sin; enslaved to righteousness

§25

Rom 6:15-23

15 What then? Are we to sin because we are not under law but under grace? By no means! 16 Do you not know that if you yield yourselves to any one as obedient slaves, you are slaves of the one whom you obey, either of sin, which leads to death, or of obedience, which leads to righteousness? 17 But thanks be to God, that you who were once slaves of sin have become obedient from the heart to the standard of teaching to which you were committed, 18 and, having been set free from sin, have become slaves of righteousness. 19 I am speaking in human terms, because of your natural limitations. For just as you once yielded your members to impurity and to greater and greater iniquity, so now yield your members to righteousness for sanctification.

20 When you were slaves of sin, you were free in regard to righteousness. 21 But then what return did you get from the things of which you are now ashamed? The end of those things is death. 22 But now that you have been set free from sin and have become slaves of God, the return you get is sanctifica-

1 Cor 7:17-24 (§97)

17 Only, let every one lead the life which the Lord has assigned to him, and in which God has called him. This is my rule in all the churches. 18 Was any one at the time of his call already circumcised? Let him not seek to remove the marks of circumcision. Was any one at the time of his call uncircumcised? Let him not seek circumcision. 19 For neither circumcision counts for anything nor uncircumcision, but keeping the commandments of God. 20 Every one should remain in the state in which he was called. 21 Were you a slave when called? Never mind. But if you can gain your freedom, avail yourself of the opportunity. 22 For he who was called in the Lord as a slave is a freedman of the Lord. Likewise he who was free when called is a slave of Christ. 23 You were bought with a price; do not become slaves of men. 24 So, brethren, in whatever state each was called, there let him remain with God.

tion and its end, eternal life. 23 For the wages of sin is death, but the free gift of God is eternal life in Christ Jesus our Lord.

▶ 6:23 Jas 1:15   15 Then desire when it has conceived gives birth to sin; and sin when it is full-grown brings forth death.

Gal 5:1-12 (§211)

5 For freedom Christ has set us free; stand fast therefore, and do not submit again to a yoke of slavery.

2 Now I, Paul, say to you that if you receive circumcision, Christ will be of no advantage to you. 3 I testify again to every man who receives circumcision that he is bound to keep the whole law. 4 You are severed from Christ, you who would be justified by the law; you have fallen away from grace. 5 For through the Spirit, by faith, we wait for the hope of righteousness. 6 For in Christ Jesus neither circumcision nor uncircumcision is of any avail, but faith working through love. 7 You were running well; who hindered you from obeying the truth? 8 This persuasion is not from him who calls you. 9 A little leaven leavens the whole lump. 10 I have confidence in the Lord that you will take no other view than mine; and he who is troubling you will bear his judgment, whoever he is. 11 But if I, brethren, still preach circumcision, why am I still persecuted? In that case the stumbling block of the cross has been removed. 12 I wish those who unsettle you would mutilate themselves!

Gal 5:13-15 (§212)

13 For you were called to freedom, brethren; only do not use your freedom as an opportunity for the flesh, but through love be servants of one another. 14 For the whole law is fulfilled in one word, "You shall love your neighbor as yourself." 15 But if you bite and devour one another take heed that you are not consumed by one another.

Gal 6:7-10 (§215)

7 Do not be deceived; God is not mocked, for whatever a man sows, that he will also reap. 8 For he who sows to his own flesh will from the flesh reap corruption; but he who sows to the Spirit will from the Spirit reap eternal life. 9 And let us not grow weary in well-doing, for in due season we shall reap, if we do not lose heart. 10 So then, as we have opportunity, let us do good to all men, and especially to those who are of the household of faith.

26. Old written code; new life of Spirit

§26

Rom 7:1-6

7 Do you not know, brethren—for I am speaking to those who know the law—that the law is binding on a person only during his life? 2 Thus a married woman is bound by law to her husband as long as he lives; but if her husband dies she is discharged from the law concerning the husband. 3 Accordingly, she will be called an adulteress if she lives with another man while her husband is alive. But if her husband dies she is free from that law, and if she marries another man she is not an adulteress.

4 Likewise, my brethren, you have died to the law through the body of Christ, so that you may belong to another, to him who has been raised from the dead in order that we may bear fruit for God. 5 While we were living in the flesh, our sinful passions, aroused by the law, were at work in our members to bear fruit for death. 6 But now we are discharged from the law, dead to that which held us captive, so that we serve not under the old written code but in the new life of the Spirit.

▶ 7:4 Eph 2:15   15 by abolishing in his flesh the law of commandments and ordinances, that he might create in himself one new man in place of the two, so making peace,

1 Cor 7:8-9 (§94)

8 To the unmarried and the widows I say that it is well for them to remain single as I do. 9 But if they cannot exercise self-control, they should marry. For it is better to marry than to be aflame with passion.

1 Cor 7:10-11 (§95)

10 To the married I give charge, not I but the Lord, that the wife should not separate from her husband 11 (but if she does, let her remain single or else be reconciled to her husband)—and that the husband should not divorce his wife.

1 Cor 7:39-40 (§101)

39 A wife is bound to her husband as long as he lives. If the husband dies, she is free to be married to whom she wishes, only in the Lord. 40 But in my judgment she is happier if she remains as she is. And I think that I have the Spirit of God.

▶ 7:5 5:20   20 Law came in, to increase the trespass; but where sin increased, grace abounded all the more,

2 Cor 3:1-18 (§154-157)

3 Are we beginning to commend ourselves again? Or do we need, as some do, letters of recommendation to you, or from you? 2 You yourselves are our letter of recommendation, written on your hearts, to be known and read by all men; 3 and you show that you are a letter from Christ delivered by us, written not with ink but with the Spirit of the living God, not on tablets of stone but on tablets of human hearts.

4 Such is the confidence that we have through Christ toward God. 5 Not that we are competent of ourselves to claim anything as coming from us; our competence is from God, 6 who has made us competent to be ministers of a new covenant, not in a written code but in the Spirit; for the written code kills, but the Spirit gives life.

7 Now if the dispensation of death, carved in letters on stone, came with such splendor that the Israelites could not look at Moses' face because of its brightness, fading as this was, 8 will not the dispensation of the Spirit be attended with greater splendor? 9 For if there was splendor in the dispensation

Gal 2:15-21 (§199)

15 We ourselves, who are Jews by birth and not Gentile sinners, 16 yet who know that a man is not justified by works of the law but through faith in Jesus Christ, even we have believed in Christ Jesus, in order to be justified by faith in Christ, and not by works of the law, because by works of the law shall no one be justified. 17 But if, in our endeavor to be justified in Christ, we ourselves were found to be sinners, is Christ then an agent of sin? Certainly not! 18 But if I build up again those things which I tore down, then I prove myself a transgressor. 19 For I through the law died to the law, that I might live to God. 20 I have been crucified with Christ; it is no longer I who live, but Christ who lives in me; and the life I now live in the flesh I live by faith in the Son of God, who loved me and gave himself for me. 21 I do not nullify the grace of God; for if justification were through the law, then Christ died to no purpose.

of condemnation, the dispensation of righteousness must far exceed it in splendor. 10 Indeed, in this case, what once had splendor has come to have no splendor at all, because of the splendor that surpasses it. 11 For if what faded away came with splendor, what is permanent must have much more splendor.

12 Since we have such a hope, we are very bold, 13 not like Moses, who put a

Gal 3:21-25 (§205)

21 Is the law then against the promises of God? Certainly not; for if a law had been given which could make alive, then righteousness would indeed be by the law. 22 But the scripture consigned all things to sin, that what was promised to faith in Jesus Christ might be given to those who believe.

23 Now before faith came, we were confined under the law, kept under restraint until faith should be revealed. 24 So that the law was our custodian until Christ came, that we might be justified by faith. 25 But now that faith has come, we are no longer under a custodian;

veil over his face so that the Israelites might not see the end of the fading splendor. 14 But their minds were hardened; for to this day, when they read the old covenant, that same veil remains unlifted, because only through Christ is it taken away. 15 Yes, to this day whenever Moses is read a veil lies over their minds; 16 but when a man turns to the Lord the veil is removed. 17 Now the Lord is the Spirit, and where the Spirit of the Lord is, there is freedom. 18 And we all, with unveiled face, beholding the glory of the Lord, are being changed into his likeness from one degree of glory to another; for this comes from the Lord who is the Spirit.

25

26. Old written code; new life of Spirit

26

▶7:6 (dead) *read* of death which: DG it vg(clem); *text*: SABC Koine Lect vg(w-w) syr cop Tertullian

Rom 7:7-13

27

7 What then shall we say? That the law is sin? By no means! Yet, if it had not been for the law, I should not have known sin. I should not have known what it is to covet if the law had not said, "You shall not covet." 8 But sin, finding opportunity in the commandment, wrought in me all kinds of covetousness. Apart from the law sin lies dead. 9 I was once alive apart from the law, but when the commandment came, sin revived and I died; 10 the very commandment which promised life proved to be death to me. 11 For sin, finding opportunity in the commandment, deceived me and by it killed me. 12 So the law is holy, and the commandment is holy and just and good.

13 Did that which is good, then, bring death to me? By no means! It was sin, working death in me through what is good, in order that sin might be shown to be sin, and through the commandment might become sinful beyond measure.

1 Cor 15:51-58 (§137)

51 Lo! I tell you a mystery. We shall not all sleep, but we shall all be changed, 52 in a moment, in the twinkling of an eye, at the last trumpet. For the trumpet will sound, and the dead will be raised imperishable, and we shall be changed. 53 For this perishable nature must put on the imperishable, and this mortal nature must put on immortality. 54 When the perishable puts on the imperishable, and the mortal puts on immortality, then shall come to pass the saying that is written:
"Death is swallowed up in victory." 55 "O death, where is thy victory? O death, where is thy sting?" 56 The sting of death is sin, and the power of sin is the law. 57 But thanks be to God, who gives us the victory through our Lord Jesus Christ.

58 Therefore, my beloved brethren, be steadfast, immovable, always abounding in the work of the Lord, knowing that in the Lord your labor is not in vain.

Gal 3:21-25 (§205)

21 Is the law then against the promises of God? Certainly not; for if a law had been given which could make alive, then righteousness would indeed be by the law. 22 But the scripture consigned all things to sin, that what was promised to faith in Jesus Christ might be given to those who believe.

23 Now before faith came, we were confined under the law, kept under restraint until faith should be revealed. 24 So that the law was our custodian until Christ came, that we might be justified by faith. 25 But now that faith has come, we are no longer under a custodian;

▶ 7:12 1 Tim 1:8
8 Now we know that the law is good, if any one uses it lawfully,

▶ 7:7 5:20
20 Law came in, to increase the trespass; but where sin increased, grace abounded all the more,

Gal 3:19-20
19 Why then the law? It was added because of transgressions, till the offspring should come to whom the promise had been made; and it was ordained by angels through an intermediary. 20 Now an intermediary implies more than one; but God is one.

▶ 7:10 Gal 3:12
12 but the law does not rest on faith, for "He who does them shall live by them."

▶ 7:12 3:31
31 Do we then overthrow the law by this faith? By no means! On the contrary, we uphold the law.

12:2
2 Do not be conformed to this world but be transformed by the renewal of your mind, that you may prove what is the will of God, what is good and acceptable and perfect.

28. Wretched man that I am

Rom 7:14-25

28

14 We know that the law is spiritual; but I am carnal, sold under sin. 15 I do not understand my own actions. For I do not do what I want, but I do the very thing I hate. 16 Now if I do what I do not want, I agree that the law is good. 17 So then it is no longer I that do it, but sin which dwells within me. 18 For I know that nothing good dwells within me, that is, in my flesh. I can will what is right, but I cannot do it. 19 For I do not do the good I want, but the evil I do not want is what I do. 20 Now if I do what I do not want, it is no longer I that do it, but sin which dwells within me.

21 So I find it to be a law that when I want to do right, evil lies close at hand. 22 For I delight in the law of God, in my inmost self, 23 but I see in my members another law at war with the law of my mind and making me captive to the law of sin which dwells in my members. 24 Wretched man that I am! Who will deliver me from this body of death? 25 Thanks be to God through Jesus Christ our Lord! So then, I of myself serve the law of God with my mind, but with my flesh I serve the law of sin.

1 Cor 3:1-4 (§78)

3 But I, brethren, could not address you as spiritual men, but as men of the flesh, as babes in Christ. 2 I fed you with milk, not solid food; for you were not ready for it; and even yet you are not ready, 3 for you are still of the flesh. For while there is jealousy and strife among you, are you not of the flesh, and behaving like ordinary men? 4 For when one says, "I belong to Paul," and another, "I belong to Apol′los," are you not merely men?

Gal 5:16-26 (§213)

16 But I say, walk by the Spirit, and do not gratify the desires of the flesh. 17 For the desires of the flesh are against the Spirit, and the desires of the Spirit are against the flesh; for these are opposed to each other, to prevent you from doing what you would. 18 But if you are led by the Spirit you are not under the law. 19 Now the works of the flesh are plain: fornication, impurity, licentiousness, 20 idolatry, sorcery, enmity, strife, jealousy, anger, selfishness, dissension, party spirit, 21 envy, drunkenness, carousing, and the like. I warn you, as I warned you before, that those who do such things shall not inherit the kingdom of God. 22 But the fruit of the Spirit is love, joy, peace, patience, kindness, goodness, faithfulness, 23 gentleness, self-control; against such there is no law. 24 And those who belong to Christ Jesus have crucified the flesh with its passions and desires.

25 If we live by the Spirit, let us also walk by the Spirit. 26 Let us have no self-conceit, no provoking of one another, no envy of one another.

▶ 7:25 1 Cor 9:21
21 To those outside the law I became as one outside the law—not being without law toward God but under the law of Christ—that I might win those outside the law.

Gal 6:2
2 Bear one another's burdens, and so fulfil the law of Christ.

27

▶ 7:7 Ex 20:17

17 "You shall not covet your neighbor's house; you shall not covet your neighbor's wife, or his manservant, or his maidservant, or his ox, or his ass, or anything that is your neighbor's."

Deut 5:21

21 " 'Neither shall you covet your neighbor's wife; and you shall not desire your neighbor's house, his field, or his manservant, or his maidservant, his ox, or his ass, or anything that is your neighbor's.'

28. Wretched man that I am

28

29

Rom 8:1-8

8 There is therefore now no condemnation for those who are in Christ Jesus. 2 For the law of the Spirit of life in Christ Jesus has set me free from the law of sin and death. 3 For God has done what the law, weakened by the flesh, could not do: sending his own Son in the likeness of sinful flesh and for sin, he condemned sin in the flesh, 4 in order that the just requirement of the law might be fulfilled in us, who walk not according to the flesh but according to the Spirit. 5 For those who live according to the flesh set their minds on the things of the flesh, but those who live according to the Spirit set their minds on the things of the Spirit. 6 To set the mind on the flesh is death, but to set the mind on the Spirit is life and peace. 7 For the mind that is set on the flesh is hostile to God; it does not submit to God's law, indeed it cannot; 8 and those who are in the flesh cannot please God.

1 Cor 3:1-4 (§78)

3 But I, brethren, could not address you as spiritual men, but as men of the flesh, as babes in Christ. 2 I fed you with milk, not solid food; for you were not ready for it; and even yet you are not ready, 3 for you are still of the flesh. For while there is jealousy and strife among you, are you not of the flesh, and behaving like ordinary men? 4 For when one says, "I belong to Paul," and another, "I belong to Apol′los," are you not merely men?

Gal 5:16-26 (§213)

16 But I say, walk by the Spirit, and do not gratify the desires of the flesh. 17 For the desires of the flesh are against the Spirit, and the desires of the Spirit are against the flesh; for these are opposed to each other, to prevent you from doing what you would. 18 But if you are led by the Spirit you are not under the law. 19 Now the works of the flesh are plain: fornication, impurity, licentiousness, 20 idolatry, sorcery, enmity, strife, jealousy, anger, selfishness, dissension, party spirit, 21 envy, drunkenness, carousing, and the like. I warn you, as I warned you before, that those who do such things shall not inherit the kingdom of God. 22 But the fruit of the Spirit is love, joy, peace, patience, kindness, goodness, faithfulness, 23 gentleness, self-control; against such there is no law. 24 And those who belong to Christ Jesus have crucified the flesh with its passions and desires.

25 If we live by the Spirit, let us also walk by the Spirit. 26 Let us have no self-conceit, no provoking of one another, no envy of one another.

▶ 8:3 Acts 13:39
39 and by him every one that believes is freed from everything from which you could not be freed by the law of Moses.

▶ 8:2 1 Cor 15:45
45 Thus it is written, "The first man Adam became a living being"; the last Adam became a life-giving spirit.

▶ 8:3 Col 1:22
22 he has now reconciled in his body of flesh by his death, in order to present you holy and blameless and irreproachable before him,

2 Cor 5:16
16 From now on, therefore, we regard no one from a human point of view; even though we once regarded Christ from a human point of view, we regard him thus no longer.

▶ 8:4 13:8,
8 Owe no one anything, except to love one another; for he who loves his neighbor has fulfilled the law.

10
10 Love does no wrong to a neighbor; therefore love is the fulfilling of the law.

30. Sons of God in the Spirit

30

Rom 8:9-17

9 But you are not in the flesh, you are in the Spirit, if in fact the Spirit of God dwells in you. Any one who does not have the Spirit of Christ does not belong to him. 10 But if Christ is in you, although your bodies are dead because of sin, your spirits are alive because of righteousness. 11 If the Spirit of him who raised Jesus from the dead dwells in you, he who raised Christ Jesus from the dead will give life to your mortal bodies also through his Spirit which dwells in you.

12 So then, brethren, we are debtors, not to the flesh, to live according to the flesh—13 for if you live according to the flesh you will die, but if by the Spirit you put to death the deeds of the body you will live. 14 For all who are led by the Spirit of God are sons of God. 15 For you did not receive the spirit of slavery to fall back into fear, but you have received the spirit of sonship. When we cry, "Abba! Father!" 16 it is the Spirit himself bearing witness with our spirit that we are children of God, 17 and if children, then heirs, heirs of God and fellow heirs with Christ, provided we suffer with him in order that we may also be glorified with him.

1 Cor 3:16-17 (§81)

16 Do you not know that you are God's temple and that God's Spirit dwells in you? 17 If any one destroys God's temple, God will destroy him. For God's temple is holy, and that temple you are.

1 Cor 6:12-20 (§92)

12 "All things are lawful for me," but not all things are helpful. "All things are lawful for me," but I will not be enslaved by anything. 13 "Food is meant for the stomach and the stomach for food"—and God will destroy both one and the other. The body is not meant for immorality, but for the Lord, and the Lord for the body. 14 And God raised the Lord and will also raise us up by his power. 15 Do you not know that your bodies are members of Christ? Shall I therefore take the members of Christ and make them members of a prostitute? Never! 16 Do you not know that he who joins himself to a prostitute becomes one body with her? For, as it is written, "The two shall become one flesh." 17 But he who is united to the Lord becomes one spirit with him. 18 Shun immorality. Every other sin which a man commits is outside the body; but the immoral man sins against his own body. 19 Do you not know that your body is a temple of the Holy Spirit within you, which you have from God? You are not your own; 20 you were bought with a price. So glorify God in your body.

Gal 2:15-21 (§199) 15 We ourselves, who are Jews by birth and not Gentile sinners, 16 yet who know that a man is not justified by works of the law but through faith in Jesus Christ, even we have believed in Christ Jesus, in order to be justified by faith in Christ, and not by works of the law, because by works of the law shall no one be justified. 17 But if, in our endeavor to be justified in Christ, we ourselves were found to be sinners, is Christ then an agent of sin? Certainly not! 18 But if I build up again those things which I tore down, then I prove myself a transgressor. 19 For I through the law died to the law, that I might live to God. 20 I have been crucified with Christ; it is no longer I who live, but Christ who lives in me; and the life I now live in the flesh I live by faith in the Son of God, who loved me and gave himself for me. 21 I do not nullify the grace of God; for if justification were through the law, then Christ died to no purpose.

Gal 4:1-7 (§207)

4 I mean that the heir, as long as he is a child, is no better than a slave, though he is the owner of all the estate; 2 but he is under guardians and trustees until the date set by the father. 3 So with us; when we were children, we were slaves to the elemental spirits of the universe. 4 But when the time had fully come, God sent forth his Son, born of woman, born under the law, 5 to redeem those who were under the law, so that we might receive adoption as sons. 6 And because you are sons, God has sent the Spirit of his Son into our hearts, crying, "Abba! Father!" 7 So through God you are no longer a slave but a son, and if a son then an heir.

▶ 8:9 2 Tim 1:14
14 guard the truth that has been entrusted to you by the Holy Spirit who dwells within us.

▶ 8:15 2 Tim 1:7
7 for God did not give us a spirit of timidity but a spirit of power and love and self-control.

▶ 8:16 Acts 5:32
32 And we are witnesses to these things, and so is the Holy Spirit whom God has given to those who obey him."

▶ 8:17 Acts 20:32
32 And now I commend you to God and to the word of his grace, which is able to build you up and to give you the inheritance nong all those who are sanctified.

2 Tim 2:12
12 if we endure, we shall also reign with him;
if we deny him, he also will deny us;

Tit 3:7
7 so that we might be justified by his grace and become heirs in hope of eternal life.

29

Phil 2:1-11 (§242)

2 So if there is any encouragement in Christ, any incentive of love, any participation in the Spirit, any affection and sympathy, 2 complete my joy by being of the same mind, having the same love, being in full accord and of one mind. 3 Do nothing from selfishness or conceit, but in humility count others better than yourselves. 4 Let each of you look not only to his own interests, but also to the interests of others. 5 Have this mind among yourselves, which is yours in Christ Jesus, 6 who, though he was in the form of God, did not count equality with God a thing to be grasped, 7 but emptied himself, taking the form of a servant, being born in the likeness of men. 8 And being found in human form he humbled himself and became obedient unto death, even death on a cross. 9 Therefore God has highly exalted him and bestowed on him the name which is above every name, 10 that at the name of Jesus every knee should bow, in heaven and on earth and under the earth, 11 and every tongue confess that Jesus Christ is Lord, to the glory of God the Father.

▶8:5 Gal 6:8 8 For he who sows to his own flesh will from the flesh reap corruption; but he who sows to the Spirit will from the Spirit reap eternal life.

Gal 5:14 4 For the whole law is fulfilled in one word, "You shall love your neighbor as yourself."

Col 3:1-4 (§265)

3 If then you have been raised with Christ, seek the things that are above, where Christ is, seated at the right hand of God. 2 Set your minds on things that are above, not on things that are on earth. 3 For you have died, and your life is hid with Christ in God. 4 When Christ who is our life appears, then you also will appear with him in glory.

▶ 8:1 (Jesus) add and do not walk according to the flesh: AD[b] it(most) vg Ephraem; add and do not walk according to the flesh but according to the Spirit: S[c]D[c] Koine Lect it (few) Theodoret; text: S*BC[2]D*G it (few) cop Marcion

▶8:2 (me) read you: SBG it(some) syr(pes) Tertullian Ephraem; read us: syr (pal) cop(bo) Marcion Origen; text: AD Koine Lect it(most) vg syr(har) cop(sa) Clement

30. Sons of God in the Spirit

30

Phil 2:1-11 (§242)

2 So if there is any encouragement in Christ, any incentive of love, any participation in the Spirit, any affection and sympathy, 2 complete my joy by being of the same mind, having the same love, being in full accord and of one mind. 3 Do nothing from selfishness or conceit, but in humility count others better than yourselves. 4 Let each of you look not only to his own interests, but also to the interests of others. 5 Have this mind among yourselves, which is yours in Christ Jesus, 6 who, though he was in the form of God, did not count equality with God a thing to be grasped, 7 but emptied himself, taking the form of a servant, being born in the likeness of men. 8 And being found in human form he humbled himself and became obedient unto death, even death on a cross. 9 Therefore God has highly exalted him and bestowed on him the name which is above every name, 10 that at the name of Jesus every knee should bow, in heaven and on earth and under the earth, 11 and every tongue confess that Jesus Christ is Lord, to the glory of God the Father.

▶ 8:10 2 Cor 13:5 5 Examine yourselves, to see whether you are holding to your faith. Test yourselves. Do you not realize that Jesus Christ is in you?—unless indeed you fail to meet the test!

Col 3:5-11 (§266)

5 Put to death therefore what is earthly in you: fornication, impurity, passion, evil desire, and covetousness, which is idolatry. 6 On account of these the wrath of God is coming. 7 In these you once walked, when you lived in them. 8 But now put them all away: anger, wrath, malice, slander, and foul talk from your mouth. 9 Do not lie to one another, seeing that you have put off the old nature with its practices 10 and have put on the new nature, which is being renewed in knowledge after the image of its creator. 11 Here there cannot be Greek and Jew, circumcised and uncircumcised, barbarian, Scyth'ian, slave, free man, but Christ is all, and in all.

Gal 4:19 19 My little children, with whom I am again in travail until Christ be formed in you!

▶8:13 Gal 5:24 24 And those who belong to Christ Jesus have crucified the flesh with its passions and desires.

▶8:16 2 Cor 1:22 22 he has put his seal upon us and given us his Spirit in our hearts as a guarantee.

▶8:17 Eph 3:6 6 that is, how the Gentiles are fellow heirs, members of the same body, and partakers of the promise in Christ Jesus through the gospel.

2 Cor 1:5f 5 For as we share abundantly in Christ's sufferings, so through Christ we share abundantly in comfort too.

31. Present sufferings and future glory

31

Rom 8:18-25

18 I consider that the sufferings of this present time are not worth comparing with the glory that is to be revealed to us. ¹⁹ For the creation waits with eager longing for the revealing of the sons of God; ²⁰ for the creation was subjected to futility, not of its own will but by the will of him who subjected it in hope; ²¹ because the creation itself will be set free from its bondage to decay and obtain the glorious liberty of the children of God. ²² We know that the whole creation has been groaning in travail together until now; ²³ and not only the creation, but we ourselves, who have the first fruits of the Spirit, groan inwardly as we wait for adoption as sons, the redemption of our bodies. ²⁴ For in this hope we were saved. Now hope that is seen is not hope. For who hopes for what he sees? ²⁵ But if we hope for what we do not see, we wait for it with patience.

2 Cor 4:16-5:5 (§161)

16 So we do not lose heart. Though our outer nature is wasting away, our inner nature is being renewed every day. ¹⁷ For this slight momentary affliction is preparing for us an eternal weight of glory beyond all comparison, ¹⁸ because we look not to the things that are seen but to the things that are unseen; for the things that are seen are transient, but the things that are unseen are eternal.

5 For we know that if the earthly tent we live in is destroyed, we have a building from God, a house not made with hands, eternal in the heavens. ² Here indeed we groan, and long to put on our heavenly dwelling, ³ so that by putting it on we may not be found naked. ⁴ For while we are still in this tent, we sigh with anxiety; not that we would be unclothed, but that we would be further clothed, so that what is mortal may be swallowed up by life. ⁵ He who has prepared us for this very thing is God, who has given us the Spirit as a guarantee.

Gal 4:1-7 (§207)

4 I mean that the heir, as long as he is a child, is no better than a slave, though he is the owner of all the estate; ² but he is under guardians and trustees until the date set by the father. ³ So with us; when we were children, we were slaves to the elemental spirits of the universe. ⁴ But when the time had fully come, God sent forth his Son, born of woman, born under the law, ⁵ to redeem those who were under the law, so that we might receive adoption as sons. ⁶And because you are sons, God has sent the Spirit of his Son into our hearts, crying, "Abba! Father!" ⁷ So through God you are no longer a slave but a son, and if a son then an heir.

▶ 8:18 Tit 2:13
¹³ awaiting our blessed hope, the appearing of the glory of our great God and Savior Jesus Christ,

▶ 8:21 Acts 3:21
²¹ whom heaven must receive until the time for establishing all that God spoke by the mouth of his holy prophets from of old.

▶ 8:24 Tit 3:7
⁷ so that we might be justified by his grace and become heirs in hope of eternal life.

Heb 11:1
Now faith is the assurance of things hoped for, the conviction of things not seen.

▶ 8:18 Col 3:4
⁴ When Christ who is our life appears, then you also will appear with him in glory.

▶ 8:22 *cf. Col 1:15-20

▶ 8:23 2 Cor 1:22
²² he has put his seal upon us and given us his Spirit in our hearts as a guarantee.

32. Spirit intercedes for us

32

Rom 8:26-27

26 Likewise the Spirit helps us in our weakness; for we do not know how to pray as we ought, but the Spirit himself intercedes for us with sighs too deep for words. ²⁷And he who searches the hearts of men knows what is the mind of the Spirit, because the Spirit intercedes for the saints according to the will of God.

1 Cor 2:6-16 (§77)

6 Yet among the mature we do impart wisdom, although it is not a wisdom of this age or of the rulers of this age, who are doomed to pass away. ⁷ But we impart a secret and hidden wisdom of God, which God decreed before the ages for our glorification. ⁸ None of the rulers of this age understood this; for if they had, they would not have crucified the Lord of glory. ⁹ But, as it is written,
"What no eye has seen, nor ear heard,
nor the heart of man conceived,
what God has prepared for those who love him,"
¹⁰ God has revealed to us through the Spirit. For the Spirit searches everything, even the depths of God. ¹¹ For what person knows a man's thoughts except the spirit of the man which is in him? So also no one comprehends the thoughts of God except the Spirit of God. ¹² Now we have received not the spirit of the world, but the Spirit which is from God, that we might understand the gifts bestowed on us by God. ¹³And we impart this in words not taught by human wisdom but taught by the Spirit,

interpreting spiritual truths to those who possess the Spirit.
14 The unspiritual man does not receive the gifts of the Spirit of God, for they are folly to him, and he is not able to understand them because they are spiritually discerned. ¹⁵ The spiritual man judges all things, but is himself to be judged by no one. ¹⁶ "For who has known the mind of the Lord so as to instruct him?" But we have the mind of Christ.

1 Cor 4:1-5 (§83)

4 This is how one should regard us, as servants of Christ and stewards of the mysteries of God. ² Moreover it is required of stewards that they be found trustworthy. ³ But with me it is a very small thing that I should be judged by you or by any human court. I do not even judge myself. ⁴ I am not aware of anything against myself, but I am not thereby acquitted. It is the Lord who judges me. ⁵ Therefore do not pronounce judgment before the time, before the Lord comes, who will bring to light the things now hidden in darkness and will disclose the purposes of the heart. Then every man will receive his commendation from God.

▶ 8:27 Acts 1:24
²⁴And they prayed and said, "Lord, who knowest the hearts of all men, show which one of these two thou hast chosen

▶ 8:26 8:15b-16
When we cry, "Abba! Father!" ¹⁶ it is the Spirit himself bearing witness with our spirit that we are children of God,

Gal 4:6
⁶And because you are sons, God has sent the Spirit of his Son into our hearts, crying, "Abba! Father!"

Gal 5:5

⁵ For through the Spirit, by faith, we wait for the hope of righteousness.

5:22-23

²² But the fruit of the Spirit is love, joy, peace, patience, kindness, goodness, faithfulness, ²³ gentleness, self-control; against such there is no law.

▶8:24 2 Cor 5:7

⁷ for we walk by faith, not by sight.

▶8:23 (sons) *omit* adoption as sons: p⁴⁶ DG it(some) Ambrosiaster Ephraem; *text:* SABC Koine Lect it vg syr cop Origen(Latin)

32. Spirit intercedes for us

32

33

Rom 8:28-30

28 We know that in everything God works for good with those who love him, who are called according to his purpose. 29 For those whom he foreknew he also predestined to be conformed to the image of his Son, in order that he might be the first-born among many brethren. 30And those whom he predestined he also called; and those whom he called he also justified; and those whom he justified he also glorified.

1 Cor 1:4-9 (§72)

4 I give thanks to God always for you because of the grace of God which was given you in Christ Jesus, 5 that in every way you were enriched in him with all speech and all knowledge— 6 even as the testimony to Christ was confirmed among you—7 so that you are not lacking in any spiritual gift, as you wait for the revealing of our Lord Jesus Christ; 8 who will sustain you to the end, guiltless in the day of our Lord Jesus Christ. 9 God is faithful, by whom you were called into the fellowship of his Son, Jesus Christ our Lord.

Eph 1:3-23 (§219)

3 Blessed be the God and Father of our Lord Jesus Christ, who has blessed us in Christ with every spiritual blessing in the heavenly places, 4 even as he chose us in him before the foundation of the world, that we should be holy and blameless before him. 5 He destined us in love to be his sons through Jesus Christ, according to the purpose of his will, 6 to the praise of his glorious grace which he freely bestowed on us in the Beloved. 7 In him we have redemption through his blood, the forgiveness of our trespasses, according to the riches of his grace 8 which he lavished upon us. 9 For he has made known to us in all wisdom and insight the mystery of his will, according to his purpose which he set forth in Christ 10 as a plan for the fulness of time, to unite all things in him, things in heaven and things on earth.

11 In him, according to the purpose of him who accomplishes all things according to the counsel of his will, 12 we who first hoped in Christ have been destined and appointed to live for the

▶ 8:29 2 Tim 1:9
9 who saved us and called us with a holy calling, not in virtue of our works but in virtue of his own purpose and the grace which he gave us in Christ Jesus ages ago,

▶ 8:28-30 *cf. 9:19-29 11:25

▶ 8:29 11:2
2 God has not rejected his people whom he foreknew. Do you not know what the scripture says of Eli′jah, how he pleads with God against Israel?

34. God is for us

34

Rom 8:31-39

31 What then shall we say to this? If God is for us, who is against us? 32 He who did not spare his own Son but gave him up for us all, will he not also give us all things with him? 33 Who shall bring any charge against God's elect? It is God who justifies; 34 who is to condemn? Is it Christ Jesus, who died, yes, who was raised from the dead, who is at the right hand of God, who indeed intercedes for us? 35 Who shall separate us from the love of Christ? Shall tribulation, or distress, or persecution, or famine, or nakedness, or peril, or sword? 36As it is written,
"For thy sake we are being killed all the day long;
we are regarded as sheep to be slaughtered."
37 No, in all these things we are more than conquerors through him who loved us. 38 For I am sure that neither death, nor life, nor angels, nor principalities, nor things present, nor things to come, nor powers, 39 nor height, nor depth, nor anything else in all creation, will be able to separate us

1 Cor 4:1-5 (§83)

4 This is how one should regard us, as servants of Christ and stewards of the mysteries of God. 2 Moreover it is required of stewards that they be found trustworthy. 3 But with me it is a very small thing that I should be judged by you or by any human court. I do not even judge myself. 4 I am not aware of anything against myself, but I am not thereby acquitted. It is the Lord who judges me. 5 Therefore do not pronounce judgment before the time, before the Lord comes, who will bring to light the things now hidden in darkness and will disclose the purposes of the heart. Then every man will receive his commendation from God.

2 Cor 4:7-12 (§159)

7 But we have this treasure in earthen vessels, to show that the transcendent power belongs to God and not to us. 8 We are afflicted in every way, but not crushed; perplexed, but not driven to despair; 9 persecuted, but not forsaken; struck down, but not destroyed; 10 always carrying in the body the death of Jesus, so that the life of Jesus may also be manifested in our bodies. 11 For while we live we are always being given up to death for Jesus' sake, so that the life of Jesus may be manifested in our mortal flesh. 12 So death is at work in us, but life in you.

2 Cor 6:1-10 §165

6 Working together with him, then, we entreat you not to accept the grace of God in vain. 2 For he says,
"At the acceptable time I have listened to you,
and helped you on the day of salvation."
Behold, now is the acceptable time; behold, now is the day of salvation. 3 We put no obstacle in any one's way, so that no fault may be found with our ministry, 4 but as servants of God we

commend ourselves in every way: through great endurance, in afflictions, hardships, calamities, 5 beatings, imprisonments, tumults, labors, watching, hunger; 6 by purity, knowledge, forbearance, kindness, the Holy Spirit, genuine love, 7 truthful speech, and the power of God; with the weapons of righteousness for the right hand and for the left; 8 in honor and dishonor, in ill repute and good repute. We are treated as impostors, and yet are true; 9 as unknown, and yet well known; as dying, and behold we live; as punished, and yet not killed; 10 as sorrowful, yet always rejoicing; as poor, yet making many rich; as having nothing, and yet possessing everything.

Eph 3:14-19 (§223)

14 For this reason I bow my knees before the Father, 15 from whom every family in heaven and on earth is named, 16 that according to the riches of his glory he may grant you to be strengthened with might through his Spirit in the inner man, 17 and that Christ may dwell in your hearts through faith; that you, being rooted and grounded in love, 18 may have power to comprehend with all the saints what is the breadth and length and height and depth, 19 and to know the love of Christ which surpasses knowledge, that you may be filled with all the fulness of God.

from the love of God in Christ Jesus our Lord.

▶ 8:34 Acts 2:24
24 But God raised him up, having loosed the pangs of death, because it was not possible for him to be held by it.

▶8:36 Acts 20:24
24 But I do not account my life of any value nor as precious to myself, if only I may accomplish my course and the ministry which I received from the Lord Jesus, to testify to the gospel of the grace of God.

▶ 8:32 4:25
25 who was put to death for our trespasses and raised for our justification.

▶ 8:36 1 Cor 4:9,
9 For I think that God has exhibited us apostles as last of all, like men sentenced to death; because we have become a spectacle to the world, to angels and to men.

15:30
30 Why am I in peril every hour?

▶8:38-39 1 Cor 3:21-23,
21 So let no one boast of men. For all things are yours, 22 whether Paul or Apol′los or Cephas or the world or life or death or the present or the future, all are yours; 23 and you are Christ's; and Christ is God's.

33

Eph (cont)

praise of his glory. 13 In him you also, who have heard the word of truth, the gospel of your salvation, and have believed in him, were sealed with the promised Holy Spirit, 14 which is the guarantee of our inheritance until we acquire possession of it, to the praise of his glory.

15 For this reason, because I have heard of your faith in the Lord Jesus and your love toward all the saints, 16 I do not cease to give thanks for you, remembering you in my prayers, 17 that the God of our Lord Jesus Christ, the Father of glory, may give you a spirit of wisdom and of revelation in the knowledge of him, 18 having the eyes of your hearts enlightened, that you may know what is the hope to which he has called you, what are the riches of his glorious inheritance in the saints, 19 and what is the immeasurable greatness of his power in us who believe, according to the working of his great might 20 which he accomplished in Christ when he raised him from the dead and made him sit at

Col 1:15-20 (§258)

15 He is the image of the invisible God, the first-born of all creation; 16 for in him all things were created, in heaven and on earth, visible and invisible, whether thrones or dominions or principalities or authorities—all things were created through him and for him. 17 He is before all things, and in him all things hold together. 18 He is the head of the body, the church; he is the beginning, the first-born from the dead, that in everything he might be pre-eminent. 19 For in him all the fulness of God was pleased to dwell, 20 and through him to reconcile to himself all things, whether on earth or in heaven, making peace by the blood of his cross.

his right hand in the heavenly places, 21 far above all rule and authority and power and dominion, and above every name that is named, not only in this age but also in that which is to come; 22 and he has put all things under his feet and has made him the head over all things for the church, 23 which is his body, the fulness of him who fills all in all.

1 Thes 5:1-11 (§287)

5 But as to the times and the seasons, brethren, you have no need to have anything written to you. 2 For you yourselves know well that the day of the Lord will come like a thief in the night. 3 When people say, "There is peace and security," then sudden destruction will come upon them as travail comes upon a woman with child, and there will be no escape. 4 But you are not in darkness, brethren, for that day to surprise you like a thief. 5 For you are all sons of light and sons of the day; we are not of the night or of darkness. 6 So then, let us not sleep, as others do, but let us keep awake and be sober. 7 For those who sleep sleep at night, and those who get drunk are drunk at night. 8 But, since we belong to the day, let us be sober, and put on the breastplate of faith and love, and for a helmet the hope of salvation. 9 For God has not destined us for wrath, but to obtain salvation through our Lord Jesus Christ, 10 who died for us so that whether we wake or sleep we might live with him. 11 Therefore encourage one another and build one another up, just as you are doing.

2 Thes 2:13-15 (§297)

13 But we are bound to give thanks to God always for you, brethren beloved by the Lord, because God chose you from the beginning to be saved, through sanctification by the Spirit and belief in the truth. 14 To this he called you through our gospel, so that you may obtain the glory of our Lord Jesus Christ. 15 So then, brethren, stand firm and hold to the traditions which you were taught by us, either by word of mouth or by letter.

▶ 8:28 (in every thing God) *omit* God: SCD G Koine Lect it vg syr cop(bo) Clement Origen(most); *text*: p⁴⁶AB cop(sa) Origen(some)

34. God is for us

34

1 Thes 3:1-5 (§281)

3 Therefore when we could bear it no longer, we were willing to be left behind at Athens alone, 2 and we sent Timothy, our brother and God's servant in the gospel of Christ, to establish you in your faith and to exhort you, 3 that no one be moved by these afflictions. You yourselves know that this is to be our lot. 4 For when we were with you, we told you beforehand that we were to suffer affliction; just as it has come to pass, and as you know. 5 For this reason, when I could bear it no longer, I sent that I might know your faith, for fear that somehow the tempter had tempted you and that our labor would be in vain.

15:24

24 Then comes the end, when he delivers the kingdom to God the Father after destroying every rule and every authority and power.

▶ 8:36 Ps 44:22

22 Nay, for thy sake we are slain all the
  day long,
  and accounted as sheep for the
  slaughter.

▶ 8:35 (Christ) *read* God: S cop(sa) Origen(some); *read* God in Christ Jesus: B Origen(some); *text*: ACDG Koine Lect it vg syr cop(bo) Tertullian Origen(some)

35

Rom 9:1-5

9 I am speaking the truth in Christ, I am not lying; my conscience bears me witness in the Holy Spirit, 2 that I have great sorrow and unceasing anguish in my heart. 3 For I could wish that I myself were accursed and cut off from Christ for the sake of my brethren, my kinsmen by race. 4 They are Israelites, and to them belong the sonship, the glory, the covenants, the giving of the law, the worship, and the promises; 5 to them belong the patriarchs, and of their race, according to the flesh, is the Christ. God who is over all be blessed for ever. Amen.

▶ 9:1 1 Tim 2:7
7 For this I was appointed a preacher and apostle (I am telling the truth, I am not lying), a teacher of the Gentiles in faith and truth.

▶ 9:4 Acts 2:39,
39 For the promise is to you and to your children and to all that are far off, every one whom the Lord our God calls to him."

3:25 25 You are the sons of the prophets and of the covenant which God gave to your fathers, saying to Abraham, 'And in your posterity shall all the families of the earth be blessed.'

2 Cor 3:7-18 (§156-157)

7 Now if the dispensation of death, carved in letters on stone, came with such splendor that the Israelites could not look at Moses' face because of its brightness, fading as this was, 8 will not the dispensation of the Spirit be attended with greater splendor? 9 For if there was splendor in the dispensation of condemnation, the dispensation of righteousness must far exceed it in splendor. 10 Indeed, in this case, what once had splendor has come to have no splendor at all, because of the splendor that surpasses it. 11 For if what faded away came with splendor, what is permanent must have much more splendor.

12 Since we have such a hope, we are very bold, 13 not like Moses, who put a veil over his face so that the Israelites might not see the end of the fading splendor. 14 But their minds were hardened; for to this day, when they read the old covenant, that same veil remains unlifted, because only through Christ is it taken away. 15 Yes, to this day whenever Moses is read a veil lies over their minds; 16 but when a man turns to the Lord the veil is removed. 17 Now the Lord is the Spirit, and where the Spirit of the Lord is, there is freedom. 18 And we all, with unveiled face, beholding the glory of the Lord, are being changed into his likeness from one degree of glory to another; for this comes from the Lord who is the Spirit.

2 Cor 11:21b-29 (§183)

But whatever any one dares to boast of—I am speaking as a fool—I also dare to boast of that. 22 Are they Hebrews? So am I. Are they Israelites? So am I. Are they descendants of Abraham? So am I. 23 Are they servants of Christ? I am a better one—I am talking like a madman—with far greater labors, far more imprisonments, with countless beatings, and often near death. 24 Five times I have received at the hands of the Jews

Acts 13:32 32 And we bring you the good news that what God promised to the fathers,

Gal 3:19-20 §204)

19 Why then the law? It was added because of transgressions, till the offspring should come to whom the promise had been made; and it was ordained by angels through an intermediary. 20 Now an intermediary implies more than one; but God is one.

▶ 9:1 Gal 1:20
20 (In what I am writing to you, before God, I do not lie!)

Eph 2:11-22 (§221)

11 Therefore remember that at one time you Gentiles in the flesh, called the uncircumcision by what is called the circumcision, which is made in the flesh by hands—12 remember that you were at that time separated from Christ, alienated from the commonwealth of Israel, and strangers to the covenants of promise, having no hope and without God in the world. 13 But now in Christ Jesus you who once were far off have been brought near in the blood of Christ. 14 For he is our peace, who has made us both one, and has broken down the dividing wall of hostility, 15 by abolishing in his flesh the law of commandments and ordinances, that he might create in himself one new man in

the forty lashes less one. 25 Three times I have been beaten with rods; once I was stoned. Three times I have been shipwrecked; a night and a day I have been adrift at sea; 26 on frequent journeys, in danger from rivers, danger from robbers, danger from my own people, danger from Gentiles, danger in the city, danger in the wilderness,

2 Cor 11:31 31 The God and Father of the Lord Jesus, he who is blessed for ever, knows that I do not lie.

36. Children of God

36

Rom 9:6-13

6 But it is not as though the word of God had failed. For not all who are descended from Israel belong to Israel, 7 and not all are children of Abraham because they are his descendants; but "Through Isaac shall your descendants be named." 8 This means that it is not the children of the flesh who are the children of God, but the children of the promise are reckoned as descendants. 9 For this is what the promise said, "About this time I will return and Sarah shall have a son." 10 And not only so, but also when Rebecca had conceived children by one man, our forefather Isaac, 11 though they were not yet born and had done nothing either good or bad, in order that God's purpose of election might continue, not because of works but because of his call, 12 she was told, "The elder will serve the younger." 13 As it is written, "Jacob I loved, but Esau I hated."

▶ 9:6 2:28-29 28 For he is not a real Jew who is one outwardly, nor is true circumcision something external and physical. 29 He is a Jew who is one inwardly, and real circumcision is a matter of the heart, spiritual and not literal. His praise is not from men but from God.

Gal 6:16 16 Peace and mercy be upon all who walk by this rule, upon the Israel of God.

Gal 4:21-31 (§210)

21 Tell me, you who desire to be under law, do you not hear the law? 22 For it is written that Abraham had two sons, one by a slave and one by a free woman. 23 But the son of the slave was born according to the flesh, the son of the free woman through promise. 24 Now this is an allegory: these women are two covenants. One is from Mount Sinai, bearing children for slavery; she is Hagar. 25 Now Hagar is Mount Sinai in Arabia; she corresponds to the present Jerusalem, for she is in slavery with her children. 26 But the Jerusalem above is free, and she is our mother. 27 For it is written,

"Rejoice, O barren one who does not bear;
break forth and shout, you who are not in travail;
for the children of the desolate one are many more
than the children of her that is married."

28 Now we, brethren, like Isaac, are children of promise. 29 But as at that time he who was born according to the flesh persecuted him who was born according to the Spirit, so it is now. 30 But what does the scripture say? "Cast out the slave and her son; for the son of the slave shall not inherit with the son of the free woman." 31 So, brethren, we are not children of the slave but of the free woman.

▶ 9:7 4:11b-12 The purpose was to make him the father of all who believe without being circumcised and who thus have righteousness reckoned to them, 12 and likewise the father of the circumcised who are not merely circumcised but also follow the example of the faith which our father Abraham had before he was circumcised.

Eph 1:3-23 (§219)

3 Blessed be the God and Father of our Lord Jesus Christ, who has blessed us in Christ with every spiritual blessing in the heavenly places, 4 even as he chose us in him before the foundation of the world, that we should be holy and blameless before him. 5 He destined us in love to be his sons through Jesus Christ, according to the purpose of his will, 6 to the praise of his glorious grace which he freely bestowed on us in the Beloved. 7 In him we have redemption through his blood, the forgiveness of our trespasses, according to the riches of his grace 8 which he lavished upon us. 9 For he has made known to us in all wisdom and insight the mystery of his will, according to his purpose which he set forth in Christ 10 as a plan for the fulness of time, to unite all things in

cording to the Spirit, so it is now. 30 But what does the scripture say? "Cast out the slave and her son; for the son of the slave shall not inherit with the son of the free woman." 31 So, brethren, we are not children of the slave but of the free woman.

▶ 9:11 8:28-30
28 We know that in everything God works for good with those who love him, who are called according to his purpose. 29 For those whom he foreknew he also predestined to be conformed to the image of his Son, in order that he might be the first-born among many brethren. 30 And those whom he predestined he also called; and those whom he called he also justified; and those whom he justified he also glorified.

35

Phil 3:17-21 (§249)

17 Brethren, join in imitating me, and mark those who so live as you have an example in us. 18 For many, of whom I have often told you and now tell you even with tears, live as enemies of the cross of Christ. 19 Their end is destruction, their god is the belly, and they glory in their shame, with minds set on earthly things. 20 But our commonwealth is in heaven, and from it we await a Savior, the Lord Jesus Christ, 21 who will change our lowly body to be like his glorious body, by the power which enables him even to subject all things to himself.

Eph (cont)

place of the two, so making peace, 16 and might reconcile us both to God in one body through the cross, thereby bring-

ing the hostility to an end. 17And he came and preached peace to you who were far off and peace to those who were near; 18 for through him we both have access in one Spirit to the Father. 19 So then you are no longer strangers and sojourners, but you are fellow citizens with the saints and members of the household of God, 20 built upon the foundation of the apostles and prophets, Christ Jesus himself being the cornerstone, 21 in whom the whole structure is joined together and grows into a holy temple in the Lord; 22 in whom you also are built into it for a dwelling place of God in the Spirit.

2 Cor (cont)

danger at sea, danger from false brethren; 27 in toil and hardship, through many a sleepless night, in hunger and thirst, often without food, in cold and exposure. 28And, apart from other things, there is the daily pressure

upon me of my anxiety for all the churches. 29 Who is weak, and I am not weak? Who is made to fall, and I am not indignant?

▶ 9:2 11:13-14

13 Now I am speaking to you Gentiles. Inasmuch then as I am an apostle to the Gentiles, I magnify my ministry 14 in order to make my fellow Jews jealous, and thus save some of them.

2 Cor 1:23-24

23 But I call God to witness against me—it was to spare you that I refrained from coming to Corinth. 24 Not that we lord it over your faith; we work with you for your joy, for you stand

▶ 9:3 Gal 1:8 8 But even if we, or an angel from heaven, should preach to you a gospel contrary to that which we preached to you, let him be accursed.

Phil 1:21-24 21 For to me to live is Christ, and to die is gain. 22 If it is to be life in the flesh, that means fruitful labor for me. Yet which I shall choose I cannot tell. 23 I am hard pressed between the two. My desire is to depart and be with Christ, for that is far better. 24 But to remain in the flesh is more necessary on your account.

▶ 9:4 3:1-2

Then what advantage has the Jew? Or what is the value of circumcision? 2 Much in every way. To begin with, the Jews are entrusted with the oracles of God.

11:1 I ask, then, has God rejected his people? By no means! I myself am an Israelite, a descendant of Abraham, a member of the tribe of Benjamin.

15:8 8 For I tell you that Christ became a servant to the circumcised to show God's truthfulness, in order to confirm the promises given to the patriarchs,

▶ 9:5 1:3 3 the gospel concerning his Son, who was descended from David according to the flesh

36. Children of God

36

Eph (cont)

him, things in heaven and things on earth.

11 In him, according to the purpose of him who accomplishes all things according to the counsel of his will, 12 we who first hoped in Christ have been destined and appointed to live for the praise of his glory. 13 In him you also, who have heard the word of truth, the gospel of your salvation, and have believed in him, were sealed with the promised Holy Spirit, 14 which is the guarantee of our inheritance until we acquire possession of it, to the praise of his glory.

15 For this reason, because I have heard of your faith in the Lord Jesus and your love toward all the saints, 16 I do not cease to give thanks for you, remembering you in my prayers, 17 that the God of our Lord Jesus Christ, the Father of glory, may give you a spirit of wisdom and of revelation in the knowledge of him, 18 having the eyes of your hearts enlightened, that you may know what is the hope to which he has called

you, what are the riches of his glorious inheritance in the saints, 19 and what is the immeasurable greatness of his power in us who believe, according to the working of his great might 20 which he accomplished in Christ when he raised him from the dead and made him sit at his right hand in the heavenly places, 21 far above all rule and authority and power and dominion, and above every name that is named, not only in this age but also in that which is to come; 22 and he has put all things under his feet and has made him the head over all things for the church, 23 which is his body, the fulness of him who fills all in all.

▶ 9:7 Gen 21:12

12 But God said to Abraham, "Be not displeased because of the lad and because of your slave woman; whatever Sarah says to you, do as she tells you, for through Isaac shall your descendants be named.

▶ 9:9 Gen 18:10

10 The LORD said, "I will surely return to you in the spring, and Sarah your wife shall have a son." And Sarah was listening at the tent door behind him.

▶ 9:10 Gen 25:21 21And Isaac prayed to the LORD for his wife, because she was barren; and the LORD granted his prayer, and Rebekah his wife conceived.

▶ 9:12 Gen 25:23

23And the LORD said to her, "Two nations are in your womb, and two peoples, born of you, shall be divided; the one shall be stronger than the other, the elder shall serve the younger."

▶ 9:13 Mal 1:2-3

2 "I have loved you," says the LORD. But you say, "How hast thou loved us?" "Is not Esau Jacob's brother?" says the LORD. "Yet I have loved Jacob 3 but I have hated Esau; I have laid waste his hill country and left his heritage to jackals of the desert."

37. Not man's will but God's mercy

37

Rom 9:14-18

14 What shall we say then? Is there injustice on God's part? By no means! 15 For he says to Moses, "I will have mercy on whom I have mercy, and I will have compassion on whom I have compassion." 16 So it depends not upon man's will or exertion, but upon God's mercy. 17 For the scripture says to Pharaoh, "I have raised you up for the very purpose of showing my power in you, so that my name may be proclaimed in all the earth." 18 So then he has mercy upon whomever he wills, and he hardens the heart of whomever he wills.

▶ 9:16 Tit 3:5
5 he saved us, not because of deeds done by us in righteousness, but in virtue of his own mercy, by the washing of regeneration and renewal in the Holy Spirit,

▶9:14-18 11:32 32 For God has consigned all men to disobedience, that he may have mercy upon all.

*cf. 8:28-30

Eph 2:1-10 (§220)

2 And you he made alive, when you were dead through the trespasses and sins 2 in which you once walked, following the course of this world, following the prince of the power of the air, the spirit that is now at work in the sons of disobedience. 3 Among these we all once lived in the passions of our flesh, following the desires of body and mind, and so we were by nature children of wrath, like the rest of mankind. 4 But God, who is rich in mercy, out of the great love with which he loved us, 5 even when we were dead through our trespasses, made us alive together with Christ (by grace you have been saved), 6 and raised us up with him, and made us sit with him in the heavenly places in Christ Jesus, 7 that in the coming ages he might show the immeasurable riches of his grace in kindness toward us in Christ Jesus. 8 For by grace you have been saved through faith; and this is not your own doing, it is the gift of God— 9 not because of works, lest any man should boast. 10 For we are his workmanship, created in Christ Jesus for

38. Freedom of God

38

Rom 9:19-29

19 You will say to me then, "Why does he still find fault? For who can resist his will?" 20 But who are you, a man, to answer back to God? Will what is molded say to its molder, "Why have you made me thus?" 21 Has the potter no right over the clay, to make out of the same lump one vessel for beauty and another for menial use? 22 What if God, desiring to show his wrath and to make known his power, has endured with much patience the vessels of wrath made for destruction, 23 in order to make known the riches of his glory for the vessels of mercy, which he has prepared beforehand for glory, 24 even us whom he has called, not from the Jews only but also from the Gentiles? 25 As indeed he says in Hose'a,
"Those who were not my people
I will call 'my people,'
and her who was not beloved
I will call 'my beloved.'"
26 "And in the very place where it was said to them, 'You are not my people,'
they will be called 'sons of the living God.'"

27 And Isaiah cries out concerning Israel: "Though the number of the sons of Israel be as the sand of the sea, only a remnant of them will be saved; 28 for the Lord will execute his sentence upon the earth with rigor and dispatch." 29 And as Isaiah predicted,
"If the Lord of hosts had not left us children,
we would have fared like Sodom and been made like Gomor'rah."

▶9:21 2 Tim 2:20
20 In a great house there are not only vessels of gold and silver but also of wood and earthenware, and some for noble use, some for ignoble.

▶ 9:19 *cf. 3:1-8
▶9:19-29 *cf. 8:28-30

▶ 9:22-23 2:4-5
4 Or do you presume upon the riches of his kindness and forbearance and patience? Do you not know that God's kindness is meant to lead you to repentance? 5 But by your hard and impenitent heart you are storing up wrath for yourself on the day of wrath when God's righteous judgment will be revealed.

▶9:23 Phil 4:19
19 And my God will supply every need of yours according to his riches in glory in Christ Jesus.

Eph 3:16
16 that according to the riches of his glory he may grant you to be strengthened with might through his Spirit in the inner man,

▶9:20 Is 29:16,
16 You turn things upside down!
Shall the potter be regarded as the clay;
that the thing made should say of its maker,
"He did not make me";
or the thing formed say of him who formed it,
"He has no understanding"?

45:9
9 "Woe to him who strives with his Maker,
an earthen vessel with the potter!
Does the clay say to him who fashions it, 'What are you making?'
or 'Your work has no handles'?

Eph 1:3-23 (§219)

3 Blessed be the God and Father of our Lord Jesus Christ, who has blessed us in Christ with every spiritual blessing in the heavenly places, 4 even as he chose us in him before the foundation of the world, that we should be holy and blameless before him. 5 He destined us in love to be his sons through Jesus Christ, according to the purpose of his will, 6 to the praise of his glorious grace which he freely bestowed on us in the Beloved. 7 In him we have redemption through his blood, the forgiveness of our trespasses, according to the riches of his grace 8 which he lavished upon us. 9 For he has made known to us in all wisdom and insight the mystery of his will, according to his purpose which he set forth in Christ 10 as a plan for the fulness of time, to unite all things in him, things in heaven and things on earth.

11 In him, according to the purpose of him who accomplishes all things according to the counsel of his will, 12 we who first hoped in Christ have been destined and appointed to live for the

Eph (cont)

good works, which God prepared beforehand, that we should walk in them.

▶ 9:15 Ex 33:19

¹⁹And he said, "I will make all my goodness pass before you, and will proclaim before you my name 'The LORD'; and I will be gracious to whom I will be gracious, and will show mercy on whom I will show mercy.

▶ 9:17 Ex 9:16

¹⁶ but for this purpose have I let you live, to show you my power, so that my name may be declared throughout all the earth.

38. Freedom of God

Eph (cont)

praise of his glory. ¹³ In him you also, who have heard the word of truth, the gospel of your salvation, and have believed in him, were sealed with the promised Holy Spirit, ¹⁴ which is the guarantee of our inheritance until we acquire possession of it, to the praise of his glory.

15 For this reason, because I have heard of your faith in the Lord Jesus and your love[c] toward all the saints, ¹⁶ I do not cease to give thanks for you, remembering you in my prayers, ¹⁷ that the God of our Lord Jesus Christ, the Father of glory, may give you a spirit of wisdom and of revelation in the knowledge of him, ¹⁸ having the eyes of your hearts enlightened, that you may know what is the hope to which he has called you, what are the riches of his glorious inheritance in the saints, ¹⁹ and what is the immeasurable greatness of his power in us who believe, according to the working of his great might ²⁰ which he accomplished in Christ when he raised him from the dead and made him sit at his right hand in the heavenly places,

Col 1:24-2:3 (§260)

24 Now I rejoice in my sufferings for your sake, and in my flesh I complete what is lacking in Christ's afflictions for the sake of his body, that is, the church, ²⁵ of which I became a minister according to the divine office which was given to me for you, to make the word of God fully known, ²⁶ the mystery hidden for ages and generations but now made manifest to his saints. ²⁷ To them God chose to make known how great among the Gentiles are the riches of the glory of this mystery, which is Christ in you, the hope of glory. ²⁸ Him we proclaim, warning every man and teaching every man in all wisdom, that we may present every man mature in Christ. ²⁹ For this I toil, striving with all the energy which he mightily inspires within me.

21 far above all rule and authority and power and dominion, and above every name that is named, not only in this age but also in that which is to come; ²² and he has put all things under his feet and has made him the head over all things for the church, ²³ which is his body, the fulness of him who fills all in all.

1 Thes 5:1-11 (§287)

5 But as to the times and the seasons, brethren, you have no need to have anything written to you. ² For you yourselves know well that the day of the Lord will come like a thief in the night. ³ When people say, "There is peace and security," then sudden destruction will come upon them as travail comes upon a woman with child, and there will be no escape. ⁴ But you are not in darkness, brethren, for that day to surprise you like a thief. ⁵ For you are all sons of light and sons of the day; we are not of the night or of darkness. ⁶ So then, let us not sleep, as others do, but let us keep awake and be sober. ⁷ For those who sleep sleep at night, and those who get

2 For I want you to know how greatly I strive for you, and for those at La-odice′a, and for all who have not seen my face, ² that their hearts may be encouraged as they are knit together in love, to have all the riches of assured understanding and the knowledge of God's mystery, of Christ, ³ in whom are hid all the treasures of wisdom and knowledge.

drunk are drunk at night. ⁸ But, since we belong to the day, let us be sober, and put on the breastplate of faith and love, and for a helmet the hope of salvation. ⁹ For God has not destined us for wrath, but to obtain salvation through our Lord Jesus Christ, ¹⁰ who died for us so that whether we wake or sleep we might live with him. ¹¹ Therefore encourage one another and build one another up, just as you are doing.

▶ 9:25 Hos 2:23

23 and I will sow him for myself in the land.
And I will have pity on Not pitied,
and I will say to Not my people,
'You are my people';
and he shall say, 'Thou art my God.' "

▶ 9:26 Hos 1:10

10 Yet the number of the people of Israel shall be like the sand of the sea, which can be neither measured nor numbered; and in the place where it was said to them, "You are not my people," it shall be said to them, "Sons of the living God."

▶ 9:27 Is 10:22-23

22 For though your people Israel be as the sand of the sea, only a remnant of them will return. Destruction is decreed, overflowing with righteousness. 23 For the Lord, the LORD of hosts, will make a full end, as decreed, in the midst of all the earth.

Gen 22:17,

17 I will indeed bless you, and I will multiply your descendants as the stars of heaven and as the sand which is on the seashore. And your descendants shall possess the gate of their enemies,

Hos 1:10

10 Yet the number of the people of Israel shall be like the sand of the sea, which can be neither measured nor numbered; and in the place where it was said to them, "You are not my people," it shall be said to them, "Sons of the living God."

▶ 9:29 Is 1:9

9 If the LORD of hosts
had not left us a few survivors,
we should have been like Sodom,
and become like Gomor′rah.

39. Righteousness through faith

Rom 9:30-33

30 What shall we say, then? That Gentiles who did not pursue righteousness have attained it, that is, righteousness through faith; 31 but that Israel who pursued the righteousness which is based on law did not succeed in fulfilling that law. 32 Why? Because they did not pursue it through faith, but as if it were based on works. They have stumbled over the stumbling stone, 33 as it is written,

"Behold, I am laying in Zion a stone
that will make men stumble,
a rock that will make them fall;
and he who believes in him will not
be put to shame."

1 Cor 1:18-25 (§74)

18 For the word of the cross is folly to those who are perishing, but to us who are being saved it is the power of God. 19 For it is written,
"I will destroy the wisdom of the wise,
and the cleverness of the clever I will thwart."
20 Where is the wise man? Where is the scribe? Where is the debater of this age? Has not God made foolish the wisdom of the world? 21 For since, in the wisdom of God, the world did not know God through wisdom, it pleased God through the folly of what we preach to save those who believe. 22 For Jews demand signs and Greeks seek wisdom, 23 but we preach Christ crucified, a stumbling block to Jews and folly to Gentiles, 24 but to those who are called, both Jews and Greeks, Christ the power of God and the wisdom of God. 25 For the foolishness of God is wiser than men, and the weakness of God is stronger than men.

Gal 2:15-21 (§199) 15 We ourselves, who are Jews by birth and not Gentile sinners, 16 yet who know that a man is not justified by works of the law but through faith in Jesus Christ, even we have believed in Christ Jesus, in order to be justified by faith in Christ, and not by works of the law, because by works of the law shall no one be justified. 17 But if, in our endeavor to be justified in Christ, we ourselves were found to be sinners, is Christ then an agent of sin? Certainly not! 18 But if I build up again those things which I tore down, then I prove myself a transgressor. 19 For I through the law died to the law, that I might live to God. 20 I have been crucified with Christ; it is no longer I who live, but Christ who lives in me; and the life I now live in the flesh I live by faith in the Son of God, who loved me and gave himself for me. 21 I do not nullify the grace of God; for if justification[e] were through the law, then Christ died to no purpose.

Gal 5:1-12 (§211)

5 For freedom Christ has set us free; stand fast therefore, and do not submit again to a yoke of slavery.

2 Now I, Paul, say to you that if you receive circumcision, Christ will be of no advantage to you. 3 I testify again to every man who receives circumcision that he is bound to keep the whole law. 4 You are severed from Christ, you who would be justified by the law; you have fallen away from grace. 5 For through the Spirit, by faith, we wait for the hope of righteousness. 6 For in Christ Jesus neither circumcision nor uncircumcision is of any avail, but faith working through love. 7 You were running well; who hindered you from obeying the truth? 8 This persuasion is not from him who calls you. 9 A little leaven leavens the whole lump. 10 I have confidence in the Lord that you will take no other view than mine; and he who is troubling you will bear his judgment, whoever he is. 11 But if I, brethren, still preach circumcision, why am I still persecuted? In that case the stumbling block of the cross has been removed. 12 I wish those who unsettle you would mutilate themselves!

▶ 9:30-31 1 Tim 6:11
11 But as for you, man of God, shun all this; aim at righteousness, godliness, faith, love, steadfastness, gentleness.

2 Tim 2:22
22 So shun youthful passions and aim at righteousness, faith, love, and peace, along with those who call upon the Lord from a pure heart.

▶ 9:30-33 *cf. 2:12-16 3:31 7:7

▶ 9:32-33 1 Cor 8:13
13 Therefore, if food is a cause of my brother's falling, I will never eat meat, lest I cause my brother to fall.

Rom 14:13
13 Then let us no more pass judgment on one another, but rather decide never to put a stumbling block or hindrance in the way of a brother.

40. Israel ignorant of the righteousness that comes from God

Rom 10:1-4

10 Brethren, my heart's desire and prayer to God for them is that they may be saved. 2 I bear them witness that they have a zeal for God, but it is not enlightened. 3 For, being ignorant of the righteousness that comes from God, and seeking to establish their own, they did not submit to God's righteousness. 4 For Christ is the end of the law, that every one who has faith may be justified.

Gal 1:13-14 (§195) 13 For you have heard of my former life in Judaism, how I persecuted the church of God violently and tried to destroy it; 14 and I advanced in Judaism beyond many of my own age among my people, so extremely zealous was I for the traditions of my fathers.

Gal 3:19-25 (§204-205)
19 Why then the law? It was added because of transgressions, till the offspring should come to whom the promise had been made; and it was ordained by angels through an intermediary. 20 Now an intermediary implies more than one; but God is one.

21 Is the law then against the promises of God? Certainly not; for if a law had been given which could make alive, then righteousness would indeed be by the law. 22 But the scripture consigned all things to sin, that what was promised to faith in Jesus Christ might be given to those who believe.

23 Now before faith came, we were confined under the law, kept under restraint until faith should be revealed. 24 So that the law was our custodian until Christ came, that we might be justified by faith. 25 But now that faith has come, we are no longer under a custodian;

▶ 10:2 Acts 22:13
13 came to me, and standing by me said to me, 'Brother Saul, receive your sight.' And in that very hour I received my sight and saw him.

▶ 10:1-4 6:14
14 For sin will have no dominion over you, since you are not under law but under grace.

7:4-6
4 Likewise, my brethren, you have died to the law through the body of Christ, so that you may belong to another, to him who has been raised from the dead in order that we may bear fruit for God. 5 While we were living in the flesh, our sinful passions, aroused by the law, were at work in our members to bear fruit for death. 6 But now we are discharged from the law, dead to that which held us captive, so that we serve not under the old written code but in the new life of the Spirit.

7:25
25 Thanks be to God through Jesus Christ our Lord! So then, I of myself serve the law of God with my mind, but with my flesh I serve the law of sin.

3 For *cf. 9:1-5 1 Cor 9:19-23

8:3-4
God has done what the law, weakened by the flesh, could not do: sending his own Son in the likeness of sinful flesh and for sin, he condemned sin in the flesh, 4 in order that the just requirement of the law might be fulfilled in us, who walk not according to the flesh but according to the Spirit.

Phil 3:2-11 (§247)

39

2 Look out for the dogs, look out for the evil-workers, look out for those who mutilate the flesh. 3 For we are the true circumcision, who worship God in spirit, and glory in Christ Jesus, and put no confidence in the flesh. 4 Though I myself have reason for confidence in the flesh also. If any other man thinks he has reason for confidence in the flesh, I have more: 5 circumcised on the eighth day, of the people of Israel, of the tribe of Benjamin, a Hebrew born of Hebrews; as to the law a Pharisee, 6 as to zeal a persecutor of the church, as to righteousness under the law blameless. 7 But whatever gain I had, I counted as loss for the sake of Christ. 8 Indeed I count everything as loss because of the surpassing worth of knowing Christ Jesus my Lord. For his sake I have suffered the loss of all things, and count them as refuse, in order that I may gain Christ 9 and be found in him, not having a righteousness of my own, based on law, but that which is through faith in Christ, the righteousness from God that depends on faith; 10 that I may know him and the power of his resurrection,

and may share his sufferings, becoming like him in his death, 11 that if possible I may attain the resurrection from the dead.

▶ 9:33 Is 28:16
16 therefore thus says the Lord GOD,
"Behold, I am laying in Zion for a
foundation
a stone, a tested stone,
a precious cornerstone, of a sure
foundation:
'He who believes will not be in
haste.'

Phil 3:2-11 (§247)

40

2 Look out for the dogs, look out for the evil-workers, look out for those who mutilate the flesh. 3 For we are the true circumcision, who worship God in spirit, and glory in Christ Jesus, and put no confidence in the flesh. 4 Though I myself have reason for confidence in the flesh also. If any other man thinks he has reason for confidence in the flesh, I have more: 5 circumcised on the eighth day, of the people of Israel, of the tribe of Benjamin, a Hebrew born of Hebrews; as to the law a Pharisee, 6 as to zeal a persecutor of the church, as to righteousness under the law blameless. 7 But whatever gain I had, I counted as loss for the sake of Christ. 8 Indeed I count everything as loss because of the surpassing worth of knowing Christ Jesus my Lord. For his sake I have suffered the loss of all things, and count them as refuse, in order that I may gain Christ 9 and be found in him, not having a righteousness of my own, based on law, but that which is through faith in Christ, the righteousness from God that depends on faith; 10 that I may know him and the power of his resurrection,

and may share his sufferings, becoming like him in his death, 11 that if possible I may attain the resurrection from the dead.

▶ 10:4 3:31
31 Do we then overthrow the law by this faith? By no means! On the contrary, we uphold the law.

40. Israel ignorant of the righteousness that comes from God

41

Rom 10:5-13

5 Moses writes that the man who practices the righteousness which is based on the law shall live by it. 6 But the righteousness based on faith says, Do not say in your heart, "Who will ascend into heaven?" (that is, to bring Christ down) 7 or "Who will descend into the abyss?" (that is, to bring Christ up from the dead). 8 But what does it say? The word is near you, on your lips and in your heart (that is, the word of faith which we preach); 9 because, if you confess with your lips that Jesus is Lord and believe in your heart that God raised him from the dead, you will be saved. 10 For man believes with his heart and so is justified, and he confesses with his lips and so is saved. 11 The scripture says, "No one who believes in him will be put to shame." 12 For there is no distinction between Jew and Greek; the same Lord is Lord of all and bestows his riches upon all who call upon him. 13 For, "every one who calls upon the name of the Lord will be saved."

1 Cor 12:1-3 (§116)

12 Now concerning spiritual gifts, brethren, I do not want you to be uninformed. 2 You know that when you were heathen, you were led astray to dumb idols, however you may have been moved. 3 Therefore I want you to understand that no one speaking by the Spirit of God ever says "Jesus be cursed!" and no one can say "Jesus is Lord" except by the Holy Spirit.

1 Cor 12:12-13 (§118)

12 For just as the body is one and has many members, and all the members of the body, though many, are one body, so it is with Christ. 13 For by one Spirit we were all baptized into one body—Jews or Greeks, slaves or free—and all were made to drink of one Spirit.

1 Cor 15:1-19 (§131-132)

15 Now I would remind you, brethren, in what terms I preached to you the gospel, which you received, in which you stand, 2 by which you are saved, if you hold it fast —unless you believed in vain.

3 For I delivered to you as of first importance what I also received, that Christ died for our sins in accordance with the scriptures, 4 that he was buried, that he was raised on the third day in accordance with the scriptures, 5 and that he appeared to Cephas, then to the twelve. 6 Then he appeared to more than five hundred brethren at one time, most of whom are still alive, though some have fallen asleep. 7 Then he appeared to James, then to all the apostles. 8 Last of all, as to one untimely born, he appeared also to me. 9 For I am the least of the apostles, unfit to be called an apostle, because I persecuted the church of God. 10 But by the grace of God I am what I am, and his grace toward me was not in vain. On the contrary, I worked harder than any of them, though it was not I, but the grace of God which is with me. 11 Whether then it was I or they, so we preach and so you believed.

12 Now if Christ is preached as raised from the dead, how can some of you say that there is no resurrection of the dead? 13 But if there is no resurrection of the dead, then Christ has not been

Gal 3:10-14 (§202)

10 For all who rely on works of the law are under a curse; for it is written, "Cursed be every one who does not abide by all things written in the book of the law, and do them." 11 Now it is evident that no man is justified before God by the law; for "He who through faith is righteous shall live"; 12 but the law does not rest on faith, for "He who does them shall live by them." 13 Christ redeemed us from the curse of the law, raised; 14 if Christ has not been raised, then our preaching is in vain and your faith is in vain. 15 We are even found to be misrepresenting God, because we testified of God that he raised Christ, whom he did not raise if it is true that the dead are not raised. 16 For if the dead are not raised, then Christ has not been raised. 17 If Christ has not been raised, your faith is futile and you are still in your sins. 18 Then those also who have fallen asleep in Christ have perished. 19 If for this life only we have hoped in Christ, we are of all men most to be pitied.

having become a curse for us—for it is written, "Cursed be every one who hangs on a tree"—14 that in Christ Jesus the blessing of Abraham might come upon the Gentiles, that we might receive the promise of the Spirit through faith.

Gal 3:26-29 (§206)

26 for in Christ Jesus you are all sons of God, through faith. 27 For as many of you as were baptized into Christ have put on Christ. 28 There is neither Jew nor Greek, there is neither slave nor free, there is neither male nor female; for you are all one in Christ Jesus. 29 And if you are Christ's, then you are Abraham's offspring, heirs according to promise.

▶ 10:9 Acts 2:24, 24 But God raised him up, having loosed the pangs of death, because it was not possible for him to be held by it.

▶ 10:9 16:31

31 And they said, "Believe in the Lord Jesus, and you will be saved, you and your household."

▶ 10:12 Acts 10:36 36 You know the word which he sent to Israel, preaching good news of peace by Jesus Christ (he is Lord of all),

▶ 10:13 Acts 2:21

21 And it shall be that whoever calls on the name of the Lord shall be saved.'

▶ 10:5 Gal 5:3 3 I testify again to every man who receives circumcision that he is bound to keep the whole law.

▶ 10:6-7 Eph 4:8-10 8 To me, though I am the very least of all the saints, this grace was given, to preach to the Gentiles the unsearchable riches of Christ, 9 and to make all men see what is the plan of the mystery hidden for ages in God who created all things; 10 that through the church the manifold wisdom of God might now be made known to the principalities and powers in the heavenly places.

▶ 10:9 2 Cor 5:14-15 14 knowing that he who raised the Lord Jesus will raise us also with Jesus and bring us with you into his presence. 15 For it is all for your sake, so that as grace extends to more and more

▶ 10:12 2:11 11 For God shows no partiality.

3:22 22 the righteousness of God through faith in Jesus Christ for all who believe. For there is no distinction;

people may increase thanksgiving, to the glory of God.

42. Faith comes from what is heard

42

Rom 10:14-17

14 But how are men to call upon him in whom they have not believed? And how are they to believe in him of whom they have never heard? And how are they to hear without a preacher? 15 And how can men preach unless they are sent? As it is written, "How beautiful are the feet of those who preach good news!" 16 But they have not all obeyed the gospel; for Isaiah says, "Lord, who has believed what he has heard from us?" 17 So faith comes from what is heard, and what is heard comes by the preaching of Christ.

Gal 3:1-5 (§200)

3 O foolish Galatians! Who has bewitched you, before whose eyes Jesus Christ was publicly portrayed as crucified? 2 Let me ask you only this: Did you receive the Spirit by works of the law, or by hearing with faith? 3 Are you so foolish? Having begun with the Spirit, are you now ending with the flesh? 4 Did you experience so many things in vain?—if it really is in vain. 5 Does he who supplies the Spirit to you and works miracles among you do so by works of the law, or by hearing with faith?

▶ 10:14 Acts 8:31 31 And he said, "How can I, unless some one guides me?" And he invited Philip to come up and sit with him.

Tit 1:3 3 and at the proper time manifested in his word through the preaching with which I have been entrusted by command of God our Savior;

▶ 10:17 Eph 2:17 17 that the God of our Lord Jesus Christ, the Father of glory, may give you a spirit of wisdom and of revelation in the knowledge of him,

▶ 10:15 Gal 4:12-15 12 Brethren, I beseech you, become as I am, for I also have become as you are. You did me no wrong; 13 you know it was because of a bodily ailment that I preached the gospel to you at first; 14 and though my condition was a trial to you, you did not scorn or despise me, but received me as an angel of God, as Christ Jesus. 15 What has become of the satisfaction you felt? For I bear you witness that, if possible, you would have plucked out your eyes and given them to me.

41.

Phil 2:1-11 (§242)

2 So if there is any encouragement in Christ, any incentive of love, any participation in the Spirit, any affection and sympathy, 2 complete my joy by being of the same mind, having the same love, being in full accord and of one mind. 3 Do nothing from selfishness or conceit, but in humility count others better than yourselves. 4 Let each of you look not only to his own interests, but also to the interests of others. 5 Have this mind among yourselves, which is yours in Christ Jesus, 6 who, though he was in the form of God, did not count equality with God a thing to be grasped, 7 but emptied himself, taking the form of a servant, being born in the likeness of men. 8 And being found in human form he humbled himself and became obedient unto death, even death on a cross. 9 Therefore God has highly exalted him and bestowed on him the name which is above every name, 10 that at the name of Jesus every knee should bow, in heaven and on earth and under the earth, 11 and every tongue confess that Jesus Christ is Lord, to the glory of God the Father.

▶ 10:5 Lev 18:5
5 You shall therefore keep my statutes and my ordinances, by doing which a man shall live: I am the LORD.

Col 3:5-11 (§266)

5 Put to death therefore what is earthly in you: fornication, impurity, passion, evil desire, and covetousness, which is idolatry. 6 On account of these the wrath of God is coming. 7 In these you once walked, when you lived in them. 8 But now put them all away: anger, wrath, malice, slander, and foul talk from your mouth. 9 Do not lie to one another, seeing that you have put off the old nature with its practices 10 and have put on the new nature, which is being renewed in knowledge after the image of its creator. 11 Here there cannot be Greek and Jew, circumcised and uncircumcised, barbarian, Scyth′ian, slave, free man, but Christ is all, and in all.

▶ 10:6 Deut 30:12-13
12 It is not in heaven, that you should say, 'Who will go up for us to heaven, and bring it to us, that we may hear it and do it?' 13 Neither is it beyond the sea, that you should say, 'Who will go over the sea for us, and bring it to us, that we may hear it and do it?'

1 Thes 1:2-10 (§276)

2 We give thanks to God always for you all, constantly mentioning you in our prayers, 3 remembering before our God and Father your work of faith and labor of love and steadfastness of hope in our Lord Jesus Christ. 4 For we know, brethren beloved by God, that he has chosen you; 5 for our gospel came to you not only in word, but also in power and in the Holy Spirit and with full conviction. You know what kind of men we proved to be among you for your sake. 6 And you became imitators of us and of the Lord, for you received the word in much affliction, with joy inspired by the Holy Spirit; 7 so that you became an example to all the believers in Macedo′nia and in Acha′ia. 8 For not only has the word of the Lord sounded forth from you in Macedo′nia and Acha′ia, but your faith in God has gone forth everywhere, so that we need not say anything. 9 For they themselves report concerning us what a welcome we had among you, and how you turned to God from idols, to serve a living and true God, 10 and to wait for his Son from heaven, whom he raised from the dead, Jesus who delivers us from the wrath to come.

▶ 10:8 Deut 30:14
14 But the word is very near you; it is in your mouth and in your heart, so that you can do it.

▶ 10:11 Is 28:16
16 therefore thus says the Lord GOD,
"Behold, I am laying in Zion for a foundation
a stone, a tested stone,
a precious cornerstone, of a sure foundation:
'He who believes will not be in haste.'

▶ 10:13 Joel 2:32
32 And it shall come to pass that all who call upon the name of the LORD shall be delivered; for in Mount Zion and in Jerusalem there shall be those who escape, as the LORD has said, and among the survivors shall be those whom the LORD calls.

42. Faith comes from what is heard

42.

Phil 4:8-9 (§252)

8 Finally, brethren, whatever is true, whatever is honorable, whatever is just, whatever is pure, whatever is lovely, whatever is gracious, if there is any excellence, if there is anything worthy of praise, think about these things. 9 What you have learned and received and heard and seen in me, do; and the God of peace will be with you.

▶ 10:15 Is 52:7
7 How beautiful upon the mountains are the feet of him who brings good tidings,
who publishes peace, who brings good tidings of good,
who publishes salvation,
who says to Zion, "Your God reigns."

Col 1:21-23 (§259)

21 And you, who once were estranged and hostile in mind, doing evil deeds, 22 he has now reconciled in his body of flesh by his death, in order to present you holy and blameless and irreproachable before him, 23 provided that you continue in the faith, stable and steadfast, not shifting from the hope of the gospel which you heard, which has been preached to every creature under heaven, and of which I, Paul, became a minister.

1 Thes 2:13-16 (§279)

13 And we also thank God constantly for this, that when you received the word of God which you heard from us, you accepted it not as the word of men but as what it really is, the word of God, which is at work in you believers. 14 For you, brethren, became imitators of the churches of God in Christ Jesus which are in Judea; for you suffered the same things from your own countrymen as they did from the Jews, 15 who killed both the Lord Jesus and the prophets, and drove us out, and displease God and oppose all men 16 by hindering us from speaking to the Gentiles that they may be saved—so as always to fill up the measure of their sins. But God's wrath has come upon them at last!

▶ 10:16 Is 53:1
Who has believed what we have heard?
And to whom has the arm of the LORD been revealed?

43

Rom 10:18-21

18 But I ask, have they not heard? Indeed they have; for

"Their voice has gone out to all the earth,
and their words to the ends of the world."

19 Again I ask, did Israel not understand? First Moses says,

"I will make you jealous of those who are not a nation;
with a foolish nation I will make you angry."

20 Then Isaiah is so bold as to say,

"I have been found by those who did not seek me;
I have shown myself to those who did not ask for me."

21 But of Israel he says, "All day long I have held out my hands to a disobedient and contrary people."

▶ 10:19 11:11

11 So I ask, have they stumbled so as to fall? By no means! But through their trespass salvation has come to the Gentiles, so as to make Israel jealous.

▶ 10:20 *cf. 9:30-33

2:14   14 When Gentiles who have not the law do by nature what the law requires, they are a law to themselves, even though they do not have the law.

44. God has not rejected his people

44

Rom 11:1-6

11 I ask, then, has God rejected his people? By no means! I myself am an Israelite, a descendant of Abraham, a member of the tribe of Benjamin. 2 God has not rejected his people whom he foreknew. Do you not know what the scripture says of Eli'jah, how he pleads with God against Israel? 3 "Lord, they have killed thy prophets, they have demolished thy altars, and I alone am left, and they seek my life." 4 But what is God's reply to him? "I have kept for myself seven thousand men who have not bowed the knee to Ba'al." 5 So too at the present time there is a remnant, chosen by grace. 6 But if it is by grace, it is no longer on the basis of works; otherwise grace would no longer be grace.

2 Cor 11:21b-29 (§183)

But whatever any one dares to boast of—I am speaking as a fool—I also dare to boast of that. 22 Are they Hebrews? So am I. Are they Israelites? So am I. Are they descendants of Abraham? So am I. 23 Are they servants of Christ? I am a better one—I am talking like a madman—with far greater labors, far more imprisonments, with countless beatings, and often near death. 24 Five times I have received at the hands of the Jews the forty lashes less one. 25 Three times I have been beaten with rods; once I was stoned. Three times I have been shipwrecked; a night and a day I have been adrift at sea; 26 on frequent journeys, in danger from rivers, danger from robbers, danger from my own people, danger from Gentiles, danger in the city, danger in the wilderness, danger at sea, danger from false brethren; 27 in toil and hardship, through many a sleepless night, in hunger and thirst, often without food, in cold and exposure. 28 And, apart from other things, there is the daily pressure upon me of my anxiety for all the churches. 29 Who is weak, and I am not

Gal 2:15-21 (§199) 15 We ourselves, who are Jews by birth and not Gentile sinners, 16 yet who know that a man is not justified by works of the law but through faith in Jesus Christ, even we have believed in Christ Jesus, in order to be justified by faith in Christ, and not by works of the law, because by works of the law shall no one be justified. 17 But if, in our endeavor to be justified in Christ, we ourselves were found to be sinners, is Christ then an agent of sin? Certainly not! 18 But if I build up again those things which I tore down, then I prove myself a transgressor. 19 For I through the law died to the law, that I might live to God. 20 I have been crucified with Christ; it is no longer I who live, but Christ who lives in me; and the life I now live in the flesh I live by faith in the Son of God, who loved me and gave himself for me. 21 I do not nullify the grace of God; for if justification were through the law, then Christ died to no purpose.

Eph 2:1-10 (§220)

2 And you he made alive, when you were dead through the trespasses and sins 2 in which you once walked, following the course of this world, following the prince of the power of the air, the spirit that is now at work in the sons of disobedience. 3 Among these we all once lived in the passions of our flesh, following the desires of body and mind, and so we were by nature children of wrath, like the rest of mankind. 4 But God, who is rich in mercy, out of the great love with which he loved us, 5 even when we were dead through our trespasses, made us alive together with Christ (by grace you have been saved), 6 and raised us up with him, and made us sit with him in the heavenly places in Christ Jesus, 7 that in the coming ages he might show the immeasurable riches of his grace in kindness toward us in Christ Jesus. 8 For by grace you have been saved through faith; and this is not your own doing, it is the gift of God— 9 not because of works, lest any man should boast. 10 For we are his workmanship, created in Christ Jesus for good works, which God prepared beforehand, that we should walk in them.

weak? Who is made to fall, and I am not indignant?

▶ 11:1-2 8:29-30

29 For those whom he foreknew he also predestined to be conformed to the image of his Son, in order that he might be the first-born among many brethren. 30 And those whom he predestined he also called; and those whom he called he also justified; and those whom he justified he also glorified.

9:11

11 though they were not yet born and had done nothing either good or bad, in order that God's purpose of election might continue, not because of works but because of his call,

*cf. Gal 1:15

*cf. Rom 9:19-29

▶ 11:2 11:28-29

28 As regards the gospel they are enemies of God, for your sake; but as regards election they are beloved for the sake of their forefathers. 29 For the gifts and the call of God are irrevocable.

▶ 11:3 1 Thes 2:15   15 who killed both the Lord Jesus and the prophets, and drove us out, and displease God and oppose all men

43

Col 1:3-14 (§257)

3 We always thank God, the Father of our Lord Jesus Christ, when we pray for you, 4 because we have heard of your faith in Christ Jesus and of the love which you have for all the saints, 5 because of the hope laid up for you in heaven. Of this you have heard before in the word of the truth, the gospel 6 which has come to you, as indeed in the whole world it is bearing fruit and growing—so among yourselves, from the day you heard and understood the grace of God in truth, 7 as you learned it from Ep'aphras our beloved fellow servant. He is a faithful minister of Christ on our behalf 8 and has made known to us your love in the Spirit.

9 And so, from the day we heard of it, we have not ceased to pray for you, asking that you may be filled with the knowledge of his will in all spiritual wisdom and understanding, 10 to lead a life worthy of the Lord, fully pleasing to him, bearing fruit in every good work and increasing in the knowledge of God. 11 May you be strengthened with all power, according to his glorious might,

1 Thes 1:2-10 (§276)

2 We give thanks to God always for you all, constantly mentioning you in our prayers, 3 remembering before our God and Father your work of faith and labor of love and steadfastness of hope in our Lord Jesus Christ. 4 For we know, brethren beloved by God, that he has chosen you; 5 for our gospel came to you not only in word, but also in power and in the Holy Spirit and with full conviction. You know what kind of men we proved to be among you for your sake. 6 And you became imitators of us and of the Lord, for you received the word in much affliction, with joy inspired by the Holy Spirit; 7 so that you became an example to all the believers in Macedo'nia and in Acha'ia.

for all endurance and patience with joy, 12 giving thanks to the Father, who has qualified us to share in the inheritance of the saints in light. 13 He has delivered us from the dominion of darkness and transferred us to the kingdom of his beloved Son, 14 in whom we have redemption, the forgiveness of sins.

8 For not only has the word of the Lord sounded forth from you in Macedo'nia and Acha'ia, but your faith in God has gone forth everywhere, so that we need not say anything. 9 For they themselves report concerning us what a welcome we had among you, and how you turned to God from idols, to serve a living and true God, 10 and to wait for his Son from heaven, whom he raised from the dead, Jesus who delivers us from the wrath to come.

▶ 10:18 Ps 19:4

1 yet their voice goes out through all the earth,
  and their words to the end of the world.

In them he has set a tent for the sun,

▶ 10:19 Deut 32:21

21 They have stirred me to jealousy with what is no god;
  they have provoked me with their idols.
So I will stir them to jealousy with those who are no people;
I will provoke them with a foolish nation.

▶ 10:20 Is 65:1

I was ready to be sought by those who did not ask for me;
I was ready to be found by those who did not seek me.
I said, "Here am I, here am I," to a nation that did not call on my name.

▶ 10:21 Is 65:2

2 I spread out my hands all the day to a rebellious people,
  who walk in a way that is not good,
  following their own devices;

44. God has not rejected his people

44

Phil 3:2-11 (§247)

2 Look out for the dogs, look out for the evil-workers, look out for those who mutilate the flesh. 3 For we are the true circumcision, who worship God in spirit, and glory in Christ Jesus, and put no confidence in the flesh. 4 Though I myself have reason for confidence in the flesh also. If any other man thinks he has reason for confidence in the flesh, I have more: 5 circumcised on the eighth day, of the people of Israel, of the tribe of Benjamin, a Hebrew born of Hebrews; as to the law a Pharisee, 6 as to zeal a persecutor of the church, as to righteousness under the law blameless. 7 But whatever gain I had, I counted as loss for the sake of Christ. 8 Indeed I count everything as loss because of the surpassing worth of knowing Christ Jesus my Lord. For his sake I have suffered the loss of all things, and count them as refuse, in order that I may gain Christ 9 and be found in him, not having a righteousness of my own, based on law, but that which is through faith in Christ, the righteousness from God that

depends on faith; 10 that I may know him and the power of his resurrection, and may share his sufferings, becoming like him in his death, 11 that if possible I may attain the resurrection from the dead.

▶ 11:3 1 Kng 19:10

10 He said, "I have been very jealous for the LORD, the God of hosts; for the people of Israel have forsaken thy covenant, thrown down thy altars, and slain thy prophets with the sword; and I, even I only, am left; and they seek my life, to take it away."

▶ 11:4 1 Kng 19:18

18 Yet I will leave seven thousand in Israel, all the knees that have not bowed to Ba'al, and every mouth that has not kissed him."

▶ 11:1 (people) read inheritance: p46 G it (few) Ambrosiaster Ambrose

§45

45

Rom 11:7-10

7 What then? Israel failed to obtain what it sought. The elect obtained it, but the rest were hardened, 8 as it is written,

"God gave them a spirit of stupor,
    eyes that should not see and ears that
        should not hear,
down to this very day."
9 And David says,
    "Let their table become a snare and a
        trap,
    a pitfall and a retribution for them;
10 let their eyes be darkened so that they
        cannot see,
    and bend their backs for ever."

▶ 11:7-10 9:30-32a

30 What shall we say, then? That Gentiles who did not pursue righteousness have attained it, that is, righteousness through faith; 31 but that Israel who pursued the righteousness which is based on law did not succeed in fulfilling that law. 32 Why? Because they did not pursue it through faith, but as if it were based on works.

9:17-18

17 For the scripture says to Pharaoh, "I have raised you up for the very purpose of showing my power in you, so that my name may be proclaimed in all the earth." 18 So then he has mercy upon whomever he wills, and he hardens the heart of whomever he wills.

8:29-30 29 For those whom he foreknew he also predestined to be conformed to the image of his Son, in order that he might be the first-born among many brethren. 30And those whom he predestined he also called; and those whom he called he also justified; and those whom he justified he also glorified.

46

Rom 11:11-12

11 So I ask, have they stumbled so as to fall? By no means! But through their trespass salvation has come to the Gentiles, so as to make Israel jealous. 12 Now if their trespass means riches for the world, and if their failure means riches for the Gentiles, how much more will their full inclusion mean!

46. Israel's stumbling means riches for Gentiles

Eph 2:11-22 (§221)

11 Therefore remember that at one time you Gentiles in the flesh, called the uncircumcision by what is called the circumcision, which is made in the flesh by hands—12 remember that you were at that time separated from Christ, alienated from the commonwealth of Israel, and strangers to the covenants of promise, having no hope and without God in the world. 13 But now in Christ Jesus you who once were far off have been brought near in the blood of Christ. 14 For he is our peace, who has made us both one, and has broken down the dividing wall of hostility, 15 by abolishing in his flesh the law of commandments and ordinances, that he might create in himself one new man in place of the two, so making peace, 16 and might reconcile us both to God in one body through the cross, thereby bringing the hostility to an end. 17And he came and preached peace to you who were far off and peace to those who were near; 18 for through him we both have access in one Spirit to the Father. 19 So then you are no longer strangers and sojourners, but you are fellow citizens

▶ 11:11 Acts 13:46,   46And Paul and Barnabas spoke out boldly, saying, "It was necessary that the word of God should be spoken first to you. Since you thrust it from you, and judge yourselves unworthy of eternal life, behold, we turn to the Gentiles.

28:28

28 Let it be known to you then that this salvation of God has been sent to the Gentiles; they will listen."

▶11:11-12 *cf. 11:1

45

2 Thes 2:1-12 (§296)

2 Now concerning the coming of our Lord Jesus Christ and our assembling to meet him, we beg you, brethren, [2] not to be quickly shaken in mind or excited, either by spirit or by word, or by letter purporting to be from us, to the effect that the day of the Lord has come. [3] Let no one deceive you in any way; for that day will not come, unless the rebellion comes first, and the man of lawlessness is revealed, the son of perdition, [4] who opposes and exalts himself against every so-called god or object of worship, so that he takes his seat in the temple of God, proclaiming himself to be God. [5] Do you not remember that when I was still with you I told you this? [6]And you know what is restraining him now so that he may be revealed in his time. [7] For the mystery of lawlessness is already at work; only he who now restrains it will do so until he is out of the way. [8]And then the lawless one will be revealed, and the Lord Jesus will slay him with the breath of his mouth and destroy him by his appearing and his coming. [9] The coming of the lawless one by the activity of Satan will be with all power and with pretended signs and wonders, [10] and with all wicked deception for those who are to perish, because they refused to love the truth and so be saved. [11] Therefore God sends upon them a strong delusion, to make them believe what is false, [12] so that all may be condemned who did not believe the truth but had pleasure in unrighteousness.

▶11:8 Is 29:10

[10] For the LORD has poured out upon
       you
    a spirit of deep sleep,
and has closed your eyes, the proph-
    ets,
    and covered your heads, the seers.

Deut 29:4   [4] but to
this day the LORD has not given you a
mind to understand, or eyes to see, or
ears to hear.

▶11:9 Ps 69:22-23

[22] Let their own table before them be-
       come a snare;
    let their sacrificial feasts be a trap.
[23] Let their eyes be darkened, so that
       they cannot see;
    and make their loins tremble con-
       tinually.

46. Israel's stumbling means riches for Gentiles

46

Eph (cont)

with the saints and members of the household of God, [20] built upon the foundation of the apostles and prophets, Christ Jesus himself being the corner-stone, [21] in whom the whole structure is joined together and grows into a holy temple in the Lord; [22] in whom you also are built into it for a dwelling place of God in the Spirit.

47

Rom 11:13-16

13 Now I am speaking to you Gentiles. Inasmuch then as I am an apostle to the Gentiles, I magnify my ministry [14] in order to make my fellow Jews jealous, and thus save some of them. [15] For if their rejection means the reconciliation of the world, what will their acceptance mean but life from the dead? [16] If the dough offered as first fruits is holy, so is the whole lump; and if the root is holy, so are the branches.

1 Cor 5:6-8 (§88)

6 Your boasting is not good. Do you not know that a little leaven leavens the whole lump? [7] Cleanse out the old leaven that you may be a new lump, as you really are unleavened. For Christ, our paschal lamb, has been sacrificed. [8] Let us, therefore, celebrate the festival, not with the old leaven, the leaven of malice and evil, but with the unleavened bread of sincerity and truth.

2 Cor 5:14-21 (§164)

[14] For the love of Christ controls us, because we are convinced that one has died for all; therefore all have died. [15] And he died for all, that those who live might live no longer for themselves but for him who for their sake died and was raised.

16 From now on, therefore, we regard no one from a human point of view; even though we once regarded Christ from a human point of view, we regard him thus no longer. [17] Therefore, if any one is in Christ, he is a new creation; the old has passed away, behold, the new has come. [18] All this is from God, who through Christ reconciled us to himself and gave us the ministry of reconciliation; [19] that is, in Christ God was reconciling the world to himself, not counting their trespasses against them, and entrusting to us the message of reconciliation. [20] So we are ambassadors for Christ, God making his appeal through us. We beseech you on behalf of Christ, be reconciled to God. [21] For our sake he made him to be sin who knew no sin, so that in him we might become the righteousness of God.

Gal 2:1-14 (§197-198)

2 Then after fourteen years I went up again to Jerusalem with Barnabas, taking Titus along with me. [2] I went up by revelation; and I laid before them (but privately before those who were of repute) the gospel which I preach among the Gentiles, lest somehow I should be running or had run in vain. [3] But even Titus, who was with me, was not compelled to be circumcised, though he was a Greek. [4] But because of false brethren secretly brought in, who slipped in to spy out our freedom which we have in Christ Jesus, that they might bring us into bondage— [5] to them we did not yield submission even for a moment, that the truth of the gospel might be preserved for you. [6] And from those who were reputed to be something (what they were makes no difference to me; God shows no partiality)—those, I say, who were of repute added nothing to me; [7] but on the contrary, when they saw that I had been entrusted with the gospel to the uncircumcised, just as Peter had been entrusted with the gospel to the cir-

Eph 3:1-13 (§222)

3 For this reason I, Paul, a prisoner for Christ Jesus on behalf of you Gentiles— [2] assuming that you have heard of the stewardship of God's grace that was given to me for you, [3] how the mystery was made known to me by revelation, as I have written briefly. [4] When you read this you can perceive my insight into the mystery of Christ, [5] which was not made known to the sons of men in other generations as it has now been revealed to his holy apostles and prophets by the Spirit; [6] that is, how the Gentiles are fellow heirs, members of the same body, and partakers of the promise in Christ Jesus through the gospel.

cumcised [8] (for he who worked through Peter for the mission to the circumcised worked through me also for the Gentiles), [9] and when they perceived the grace that was given to me, James and Cephas and John, who were reputed to be pillars, gave to me and Barnabas the right hand of fellowship, that we should go to the Gentiles and they to the cir-

▶ 11:13 Acts 9:15 [15] But the Lord said to him, "Go, for he is a chosen instrument of mine to carry my name before the Gentiles and kings and the sons of Israel;

▶ 11:14 1 Tim 2:4 [4] who desires all men to be saved and to come to the knowledge of the truth.

Rom 15:15-16 [15] But on some points I have written to you very boldly by way of reminder, because of the grace given me by God [16] to be a minister of Christ Jesus to the Gentiles in the priestly service of the gospel of God, so that the offering of the Gentiles may be acceptable, sanctified by the Holy Spirit.

▶ 11:13 1:5 [5] through whom we have received grace and apostleship to bring about the obedience of faith for the sake of his name among all the nations,

Eph 4:11-12 [11] And his gifts were that some should be apostles, some prophets, some evangelists, some pastors and teachers, [12] to equip the saints for the work of ministry, for building up the body of Christ,

▶ 11:15 *cf. 5:6-11

48. Olive tree

48

Rom 11:17-24

17 But if some of the branches were broken off, and you, a wild olive shoot, were grafted in their place to share the richness of the olive tree, [18] do not boast over the branches. If you do boast, remember it is not you that support the root, but the root that supports you. [19] You will say, "Branches were broken off so that I might be grafted in." [20] That is true. They were broken off because of their unbelief, but you stand fast only through faith. So do not become proud, but stand in awe. [21] For if God did not spare the natural branches, neither will he spare you. [22] Note then the kindness and the severity of God: severity toward those who have fallen, but God's kindness to you, provided you continue in his kindness; otherwise you too will be cut off. [23] And even the others, if they do not persist in their unbelief, will be grafted in, for God has the power to graft them in again. [24] For if you have been cut from what is by nature a wild olive tree, and grafted, contrary to nature, into a cultivated olive tree, how much more will these natural branches be grafted back into their own olive tree.

1 Cor 1:26-31 (§75)

26 For consider your call, brethren; not many of you were wise according to worldly standards, not many were powerful, not many were of noble birth; [27] but God chose what is foolish in the world to shame the wise, God chose what is weak in the world to shame the strong, [28] God chose what is low and despised in the world, even things that are not, to bring to nothing things that are, [29] so that no human being might boast in the presence of God. [30] He is the source of your life in Christ Jesus, whom God made our wisdom, our righteousness and sanctification and redemption; [31] therefore, as it is written, "Let him who boasts, boast of the Lord."

1 Cor 4:6-7 (§84)

6 I have applied all this to myself and Apol'los for your benefit, brethren, that you may learn by us not to go beyond what is written, that none of you may be puffed up in favor of one against another. [7] For who sees anything different in you? What have you that you did not receive? If then you received it, why do you boast as if it were not a gift?

Eph 2:1-10 (§220)

2 And you he made alive, when you were dead through the trespasses and sins [2] in which you once walked, following the course of this world, following the prince of the power of the air, the spirit that is now at work in the sons of disobedience. [3] Among these we all once lived in the passions of our flesh, following the desires of body and mind, and so we were by nature children of wrath, like the rest of mankind. [4] But God, who is rich in mercy, out of the great love with which he loved us, [5] even when we were dead through our trespasses, made us alive together with Christ (by grace you have been saved), [6] and raised us up with him, and made us sit with him in the heavenly places in Christ Jesus, [7] that in the coming ages he might show the immeasurable riches of his grace in kindness toward us in Christ Jesus. [8] For by grace you have been saved through faith; and this is not your own doing, it is the gift of God— [9] not because of works, lest any man should boast. [10] For we are his workmanship, created in Christ Jesus for good works, which God prepared beforehand, that we should walk in them.

▶ 11:18 1 Tim 6:17 [17] As for the rich in this world, charge them not to be haughty, nor to set their hopes on uncertain riches but on God who richly furnishes us with everything to enjoy.

▶ 11:20 Gal 5:1 For freedom Christ has set us free; stand fast therefore, and do not submit again to a yoke of slavery.

▶ 11:22 2:4 [4] Or do you presume upon the riches of his kindness and forbearance and patience? Do you not know that God's kindness is meant to lead you to repentance?

47

Eph (cont)

7 Of this gospel I was made a minister according to the gift of God's grace which was given me by the working of his power. 8 To me, though I am the very least of all the saints, this grace was given, to preach to the Gentiles the unsearchable riches of Christ, 9 and to make all men see what is the plan of the mystery hidden for ages in God who created all things; 10 that through the church the manifold wisdom of God might now be made known to the principalities and powers in the heavenly places. 11 This was according to the eternal purpose which he has realized in Christ Jesus our Lord, 12 in whom we have boldness and confidence of access through our faith in him. 13 So I ask you not to lose heart over what I am suffering for you, which is your glory.

Gal (cont)

cumcised; 10 only they would have us remember the poor, which very thing I was eager to do.

11 But when Cephas came to Antioch I opposed him to his face, because he stood condemned. 12 For before certain

Col 1:21-2:3 (§259-260)

21 And you, who once were estranged and hostile in mind, doing evil deeds, 22 he has now reconciled in his body of flesh by his death, in order to present you holy and blameless and irreproachable before him, 23 provided that you continue in the faith, stable and steadfast, not shifting from the hope of the gospel which you heard, which has been preached to every creature under heaven, and of which I, Paul, became a minister.

24 Now I rejoice in my sufferings for your sake, and in my flesh I complete

men came from James, he ate with the Gentiles; but when they came he drew back and separated himself, fearing the circumcision party. 13 And with him the rest of the Jews acted insincerely, so that even Barnabas was carried away by their insincerity. 14 But when I saw that they were not straightforward about the truth of the gospel, I said to Cephas before them all, "If you, though a Jew, live like a Gentile and not like a Jew, how can you compel the Gentiles to live like Jews?"

what is lacking in Christ's afflictions for the sake of his body, that is, the church, 25 of which I became a minister according to the divine office which was given to me for you, to make the word of God fully known, 26 the mystery hidden for ages and generations but now made manifest to his saints. 27 To them God chose to make known how great among the Gentiles are the riches of the glory of this mystery, which is Christ in you, the hope of glory. 28 Him we proclaim, warning every man and teaching every man in all wisdom, that we may present every man mature in Christ. 29 For this I toil, striving with all the energy which he mightily inspires within me.

2 For I want you to know how greatly I strive for you, and for those at La-odice′a, and for all who have not seen my face, 2 that their hearts may be encouraged as they are knit together in love, to have all the riches of assured understanding and the knowledge of God's mystery, of Christ, 3 in whom are hid all the treasures of wisdom and knowledge.

▶11:16 (and if) *omit* if: p⁴⁶G it(few) Chrysostom

48. Olive tree

48

Eph (cont)

Eph 2:11-22 (§221)

11 Therefore remember that at one time you Gentiles in the flesh, called the uncircumcision by what is called the circumcision, which is made in the flesh by hands—12 remember that you were at that time separated from Christ, alienated from the commonwealth of Israel, and strangers to the covenants of promise, having no hope and without God in the world. 13 But now in Christ Jesus you who once were far off have been brought near in the blood of Christ. 14 For he is our peace, who has made us both one, and has broken down the dividing wall of hostility, 15 by abolishing in his flesh the law of commandments and ordinances, that he might create in himself one new man in place of the two, so making peace, 16 and might reconcile us both to God in one body through the cross, thereby bringing the hostility to an end. 17 And he came and preached peace to you who were far off and peace to those who were near; 18 for through him we both have access in one Spirit to the Father. 19 So

then you are no longer strangers and sojourners, but you are fellow citizens with the saints and members of the household of God, 20 built upon the foundation of the apostles and prophets, Christ Jesus himself being the cornerstone, 21 in whom the whole structure is joined together and grows into a holy temple in the Lord; 22 in whom you also are built into it for a dwelling place of God in the Spirit.

▶11:17 (richness) *read* rich root: S*BC; *read* root and richness: SᶜADᵇᶜ Koine Lect it(some) vg syr(pes har) Origen(Latin); *text:* p⁴⁶ D*G it(some) cop(bo) Irenaeus (Latin)

49. Gifts and call of God irrevocable

Rom 11:25-32

49 25 Lest you be wise in your own conceits, I want you to understand this mystery, brethren: a hardening has come upon part of Israel, until the full number of the Gentiles come in, 26 and so all Israel will be saved; as it is written,
"The Deliverer will come from Zion, he will banish ungodliness from Jacob";
27 "and this will be my covenant with them
when I take away their sins."
28 As regards the gospel they are enemies of God, for your sake; but as regards election they are beloved for the sake of their forefathers. 29 For the gifts and the call of God are irrevocable. 30 Just as you were once disobedient to God but now have received mercy because of their disobedience, 31 so they have now been disobedient in order that by the mercy shown to you they also may receive mercy. 32 For God has consigned all men to disobedience, that he may have mercy upon all.

▶11:27 2 Tim 1:9 9 who saved us and called us with a holy calling, not in virtue of our works but in virtue of his own purpose and the grace which he gave us in Christ Jesus ages ago,

▶11:32 1 Tim 2:4 4 who desires all men to be saved and to come to the knowledge of the truth.

▶11:25 1 Cor 2:7-9 7 But we impart a secret and hidden wisdom of God, which God decreed before the ages for our glorification. 8 None of the rulers of this age understood this; for if they had, they would not have crucified the Lord of glory. 9 But, as it is written, "What no eye has seen, nor ear heard, nor the heart of man conceived,

what God has prepared for those who love him,"

2 Thes 1:11 11 To this end we always pray for you, that our God may make you worthy of his call, and may fulfil every good resolve and work of faith by his power,

Eph 4:17-24 (§227)

17 Now this I affirm and testify in the Lord, that you must no longer live as the Gentiles do, in the futility of their minds; 18 they are darkened in their understanding, alienated from the life of God because of the ignorance that is in them, due to their hardness of heart; 19 they have become callous and have given themselves up to licentiousness, greedy to practice every kind of uncleanness. 20 You did not so learn Christ!— 21 assuming that you have heard about him and were taught in him, as the truth is in Jesus. 22 Put off your old nature which belongs to your former manner of life and is corrupt through deceitful lusts, 23 and be renewed in the spirit of your minds, 24 and put on the new nature, created after the likeness of God in true righteousness and holiness.

50. Riches, wisdom and knowledge of God

Rom 11:33-36

50 33 O the depth of the riches and wisdom and knowledge of God! How unsearchable are his judgments and how inscrutable his ways!
34 "For who has known the mind of the Lord,
or who has been his counselor?"
35 "Or who has given a gift to him that he might be repaid?"
36 For from him and through him and to him are all things. To him be glory for ever. Amen.

▶11:33-36 Col 2:1-3 For I want you to know how greatly I strive for you, and for those at La-odice a, and for all who have not seen my face, 2 that their hearts may be encouraged as they are knit together in love, to have all the riches of assured understanding and the knowledge of

1 Cor 2:6-16 (§77)

6 Yet among the mature we do impart wisdom, although it is not a wisdom of this age or of the rulers of this age, who are doomed to pass away. 7 But we impart a secret and hidden wisdom of God, which God decreed before the ages for our glorification. 8 None of the rulers of this age understood this; for if they had, they would not have crucified the Lord of glory. 9 But, as it is written, "What no eye has seen, nor ear heard, nor the heart of man conceived, what God has prepared for those who love him," 10 God has revealed to us through the Spirit. For the Spirit searches everything, even the depths of God. 11 For what person knows a man's thoughts except the spirit of the man which is in him? So also no one comprehends the thoughts of God except the Spirit of God. 12 Now we have received not the spirit of the world, but the Spirit which is from God, that we might understand the gifts bestowed on us by God. 13 And we impart this in words not taught by human wisdom but taught by the Spirit,

God's mystery, of Christ, 3 in whom are hid all the treasures of wisdom and knowledge.

interpreting spiritual truths to those who possess the Spirit.
14 The unspiritual man does not receive the gifts of the Spirit of God, for they are folly to him, and he is not able to understand them because they are spiritually discerned. 15 The spiritual man judges all things, but is himself to be judged by no one. 16 "For who has known the mind of the Lord so as to instruct him?" But we have the mind of Christ.

1 Cor 8:4-6 (§103)

4 Hence, as to the eating of food offered to idols, we know that "an idol has no real existence," and that "there is no God but one." 5 For although there may be so-called gods in heaven or on earth—as indeed there are many "gods" and many "lords"—6 yet for us there is one God, the Father, from whom are all things and for whom we exist, and one Lord, Jesus Christ, through whom are all things and through whom we exist.

1 Cor 1:21 21 For since, in the wisdom of God, the world did not know God through wisdom, it pleased God through the folly of what we preach to save those who believe.

Eph 3:1-19 (§222-223)

3 For this reason I, Paul, a prisoner for Christ Jesus on behalf of you Gentiles— 2 assuming that you have heard of the stewardship of God's grace that was given to me for you, 3 how the mystery was made known to me by revelation, as I have written briefly. 4 When you read this you can perceive my insight into the mystery of Christ, 5 which was not made known to the sons of men in other generations as it has now been revealed to his holy apostles and prophets by the Spirit; 6 that is, how the Gentiles are fellow heirs, members of the same body, and partakers of the promise in Christ Jesus through the gospel.
7 Of this gospel I was made a minister according to the gift of God's grace which was given me by the working of his power. 8 To me, though I am the very least of all the saints, this grace was given, to preach to the Gentiles the unsearchable riches of Christ, 9 and to make all men see what is the plan of the mystery hidden for ages in God who created all things; 10 that through the church the manifold wisdom of God

49

Phil 3:17-21 (§249)

17 Brethren, join in imitating me, and mark those who so live as you have an example in us. 18 For many, of whom I have often told you and now tell you even with tears, live as enemies of the cross of Christ. 19 Their end is destruction, their god is the belly, and they glory in their shame, with minds set on earthly things. 20 But our commonwealth is in heaven, and from it we await a Savior, the Lord Jesus Christ, 21 who will change our lowly body to be like his glorious body, by the power which enables him even to subject all things to himself.

▶11:28 5:6-10
6 While we were still weak, at the right time Christ died for the ungodly. 7 Why, one will hardly die for a righteous man—though perhaps for a good man one will dare even to die. 8 But God shows his love for us in that while we were yet sinners Christ died for us. 9 Since, therefore, we are now justified by his blood, much more shall we be saved by him from the wrath of God. 10 For if while we were enemies we were reconciled to God by the death of his Son, much more, now that we are reconciled, shall we be saved by his life.

Col 1:24-2:3 (§260)

24 Now I rejoice in my sufferings for your sake, and in my flesh I complete what is lacking in Christ's afflictions for the sake of his body, that is, the church, 25 of which I became a minister according to the divine office which was given to me for you, to make the word of God fully known, 26 the mystery hidden for ages and generations but now made manifest to his saints. 27 To them God chose to make known how great among the Gentiles are the riches of the glory of this mystery, which is Christ in you, the hope of glory. 28 Him we proclaim, warning every man and teaching every man in all wisdom, that we may present every man mature in Christ. 29 For this I toil, striving with all the energy which he mightily inspires within me.

2 For I want you to know how greatly I strive for you, and for those at La-odice′a, and for all who have not seen my face, 2 that their hearts may be encouraged as they are knit together in love, to have all the riches of assured understanding and the knowledge of God's mystery, of Christ, 3 in whom are hid all the treasures of wisdom and knowledge.

▶11:32 Phil 2:9-11
9 Therefore God has highly exalted him and bestowed on him the name which is above every name, 10 that at the name of Jesus every knee should bow, in heaven and on earth and under the earth, 11 and every tongue confess that Jesus Christ is Lord, to the glory of God the Father.

▶11:26 Is 59:20f
20 "And he will come to Zion as Redeemer,
to those in Jacob who turn from transgression, says the LORD.

▶11:27 Jer 31:33
33 But this is the covenant which I will make with the house of Israel after those days, says the LORD: I will put my law within them, and I will write it upon their hearts; and I will be their God, and they shall be my people.

▶11:31 (may) *add* now:
SBD(Greek) cop(bo)

50. Riches, wisdom and knowledge of God

50

Col 1:15-20 (§258)

15 He is the image of the invisible God, the first-born of all creation; 16 for in him all things were created, in heaven and on earth, visible and invisible, whether thrones or dominions or principalities or authorities—all things were created through him and for him. 17 He is before all things, and in him all things hold together. 18 He is the head of the body, the church; he is the beginning, the first-born from the dead, that in everything he might be pre-eminent. 19 For in him all the fulness of God was pleased to dwell, 20 and through him to reconcile to himself all things, whether on earth or in heaven, making peace by the blood of his cross.

Eph (cont)
might now be made known to the principalities and powers in the heavenly places. 11 This was according to the eternal purpose which he has realized in Christ Jesus our Lord, 12 in whom we have boldness and confidence of access through our faith in him. 13 So I ask you not to lose heart over what I am suffering for you, which is your glory.

14 For this reason I bow my knees before the Father, 15 from whom every family in heaven and on earth is named, 16 that according to the riches of his glory he may grant you to be strengthened with might through his Spirit in the inner man, 17 and that Christ may dwell in your hearts through faith; that you, being rooted and grounded in love, 18 may have power to comprehend with all the saints what is the breadth and length and height and depth, 19 and to know the love of Christ which surpasses knowledge, that you may be filled with all the fulness of God.

▶11:34 Is 40:13-14
13 Who has directed the Spirit of the LORD,
or as his counselor has instructed him?
14 Whom did he consult for his enlightenment,
and who taught him the path of justice,
and taught him knowledge,
and showed him the way of understanding?

▶11:35 Job 35:7,
7 If you are righteous, what do you give to him;
or what does he receive from your hand?

41:11
11 Who has given to me, that I should repay him?
Whatever is under the whole heaven is mine.

51.

Rom 12:1-2

12 I appeal to you therefore, brethren, by the mercies of God, to present your bodies as a living sacrifice, holy and acceptable to God, which is your spiritual worship. 2 Do not be conformed to this world but be transformed by the renewal of your mind, that you may prove what is the will of God, what is good and acceptable and perfect.

1 Cor 1:10-17 (§73)

10 I appeal to you, brethren, by the name of our Lord Jesus Christ, that all of you agree and that there be no dissensions among you, but that you be united in the same mind and the same judgment. 11 For it has been reported to me by Chlo'e's people that there is quarreling among you, my brethren. 12 What I mean is that each one of you says, "I belong to Paul," or "I belong to Apol'los," or "I belong to Cephas," or "I belong to Christ." 13 Is Christ divided? Was Paul crucified for you? Or were you baptized in the name of Paul? 14 I am thankful[b] that I baptized none of you except Crispus and Ga'ius; 15 lest any one should say that you were baptized in my name. 16 (I did baptize also the household of Steph'anas. Beyond that, I do not know whether I baptized any one else.) 17 For Christ did not send me to baptize but to preach the gospel, and not with eloquent wisdom, lest the cross of Christ be emptied of its power.

2 Cor 10:1-6 (§176)

10 I, Paul, myself entreat you, by the meekness and gentleness of Christ—I who am humble when face to face with you, but bold to you when I am away!— 2 I beg of you that when I am present I may not have to show boldness with such confidence as I count on showing against some who suspect us of acting in worldly fashion. 3 For though we live in the world we are not carrying on a worldly war, 4 for the weapons of our warfare are not worldly but have divine power to destroy strongholds. 5 We destroy arguments and every proud obstacle to the knowledge of God, and take every thought captive to obey Christ, 6 being ready to punish every disobedience, when your obedience is complete.

Eph 4:1-10 (§225)

4 I therefore, a prisoner for the Lord, beg you to lead a life worthy of the calling to which you have been called, 2 with all lowliness and meekness, with patience, forbearing one another in love, 3 eager to maintain the unity of the Spirit in the bond of peace. 4 There is one body and one Spirit, just as you were called to the one hope that belongs to your call, 5 one Lord, one faith, one baptism, 6 one God and Father of us all, who is above all and through all and in all. 7 But grace was given to each of us according to the measure of Christ's gift. 8 Therefore it is said,

"When he ascended on high he led a host of captives,
and he gave gifts to men."

9 (In saying, "He ascended," what does it mean but that he had also descended into the lower parts of the earth? 10 He who descended is he who also ascended far above all the heavens, that he might fill all things.)

▶12:2 Tit 3:5
5 he saved us, not because of deeds done by us in righteousness, but in virtue of his own mercy, by the washing of regeneration and renewal in the Holy Spirit,

▶12:1 11:32
32 For God has consigned all men to disobedience, that he may have mercy upon all.

2 Cor 1:3
3 Blessed be the God and Father of our Lord Jesus Christ, the Father of mercies and God of all comfort,

1 Thes 5:12
12 But we beseech you, brethren, to respect those who labor among you and are over you in the Lord and admonish you,

▶12:2 7:12
12 So the law is holy, and the commandment is holy and just and good.

52. Gifts differ according to grace

52.

Rom 12:3-8

3 For by the grace given to me I bid every one among you not to think of himself more highly than he ought to think, but to think with sober judgment, each according to the measure of faith which God has assigned him. 4 For as in one body we have many members, and all the members do not have the same function, 5 so we, though many, are one body in Christ, and individually members one of another. 6 Having gifts that differ according to the grace given to us, let us use them: if prophecy, in proportion to our faith; 7 if service, in our serving; he who teaches, in his teaching; 8 he who exhorts, in his exhortation; he who contributes, in liberality; he who gives aid, with zeal; he who does acts of mercy, with cheerfulness.

1 Cor 10:14-22 (§110)

14 Therefore, my beloved, shun the worship of idols. 15 I speak as to sensible men; judge for yourselves what I say. 16 The cup of blessing which we bless, is it not a participation in the blood of Christ? The bread which we break, is it not a participation in the body of Christ? 17 Because there is one bread, we who are many are one body, for we all partake of the one bread. 18 Consider the people of Israel; are not those who eat the sacrifices partners in the altar? 19 What do I imply then? That food offered to idols is anything, or that an idol is anything? 20 No, I imply that what pagans sacrifice they offer to demons and not to God. I do not want you to be partners with demons. 21 You cannot drink the cup of the Lord and the cup of demons. You cannot partake of the table of the Lord and the table of demons. 22 Shall we provoke the Lord to jealousy? Are we stronger than he?

1 Cor 12:4-31 (§117-120)

4 Now there are varieties of gifts, but the same Spirit; 5 and there are varieties of service, but the same Lord; 6 and there are varieties of working, but it is the same God who inspires them all in every one. 7 To each is given the manifestation of the Spirit for the common good. 8 To one is given through the Spirit the utterance of wisdom, and to another the utterance of knowledge according to the same Spirit, 9 to another faith by the same Spirit, to another gifts of healing by the one Spirit, 10 to another the working of miracles, to another prophecy, to another the ability to distinguish between spirits, to another various kinds of tongues, to another the interpretation of tongues. 11 All these are inspired by one and the same Spirit, who apportions to each one individually as he wills.

12 For just as the body is one and has many members, and all the members of the body, though many, are one body, so it is with Christ. 13 For by one Spirit we were all baptized into one body—Jews or Greeks, slaves or free—and all were made to drink of one Spirit.

14 For the body does not consist of one member but of many. 15 If the foot should say, "Because I am not a hand, I do not belong to the body," that would not make it any less a part of the body. 16 And if the ear should say, "Because I am not an eye, I do not belong to the body," that would not make it any less a part of the body. 17 If the whole body were an eye, where would be the hearing? If the whole body were an ear, where would be the sense of smell? 18 But as it is, God arranged the organs in the body, each one of them, as he chose. 19 If all were a single organ, where would the body be? 20 As it is, there are many parts, yet one body. 21 The eye cannot say to the hand, "I have no need of you," nor again the head to the feet, "I have no need of you." 22 On the contrary, the parts of the body which seem to be weaker are indispensable, 23 and those parts of the body which we think less honorable we invest with the greater honor, and our unpresentable parts are treated with greater modesty, 24 which our more presentable parts do not require. But God has so composed the body, giving the greater honor to the inferior part, 25 that there may be no discord in the body, but that the members may have the same care for one another. 26 If one member suffers, all suffer together; if one member is honored, all rejoice together.

27 Now you are the body of Christ and individually members of it. 28 And God has appointed in the church first apostles, second prophets, third teachers, then workers of miracles, then healers, helpers, administrators, speakers in various kinds of tongues. 29 Are all apostles? Are all prophets? Are all teachers? Do all work miracles? 30 Do all possess gifts of healing? Do all speak with tongues? Do all interpret? 31 But earnestly desire the higher gifts.

And I will show you a still more excellent way.

Eph 2:1-10 (§220)

2 And you he made alive, when you were dead through the trespasses and sins 2 in which you once walked, following the course of this world, following the prince of the power of the air, the spirit that is now at work in the sons of disobedience. 3 Among these we all once lived in the passions of our

▶12:6 1 Tim 4:14
14 Do not neglect the gift you have, which was given you by prophetic utterance when the council of elders laid their hands upon you.

▶12:8 Acts 13:15
15 After the reading of the law and the prophets, the rulers of the synagogue sent to them, saying, "Brethren, if you have any word of exhortation for the people, say it."

1 Tim 5:17
17 Let the elders who rule well be considered worthy of double honor, especially those who labor in preaching and teaching;

▶12:4 Eph 4:25
25 Therefore, putting away falsehood, let every one speak the truth with his neighbor, for we are members one of another.

▶12:5 Eph 1:23,
23 which is his body, the fulness of him who fills all in all.

5:30
30 because we are members of his body.

51. Present your body as a living sacrifice

Phil 4:10-20 (§253)

10 I rejoice in the Lord greatly that now at length you have revived your concern for me; you were indeed concerned for me, but you had no opportunity. 11 Not that I complain of want; for I have learned, in whatever state I am, to be content. 12 I know how to be abased, and I know how to abound; in any and all circumstances I have learned the secret of facing plenty and hunger, abundance and want. 13 I can do all things in him who strengthens me.

14 Yet it was kind of you to share my trouble. 15And you Philippians yourselves know that in the beginning of the gospel, when I left Macedo'nia, no church entered into partnership with me in giving and receiving except you only; 16 for even in Thessaloni'ca you sent me help once and again. 17 Not that I seek the gift; but I seek the fruit which increases to your credit. 18 I have received full payment, and more; I am filled, having received from Epaphrodi'tus the gifts you sent, a fragrant offering, a sacrifice acceptable and pleasing to God. 19And my God will supply every need of yours according to his riches in glory in Christ Jesus. 20 To our God and Father be glory for ever and ever. Amen.

Phil 2:14-18 (§244)

14 Do all things without grumbling or questioning, 15 that you may be blameless and innocent, children of God without blemish in the midst of a crooked and perverse generation, among whom you shine as lights in the world, 16 holding fast the word of life, so that in the day of Christ I may be proud that I did not run in vain or labor in vain. 17 Even if I am to be poured as a libation upon the sacrificial offering of your faith, I am glad and rejoice with you all. 18 Likewise you also should be glad and rejoice with me.

1 Thes 4:1-8 (§284)

4 Finally, brethren, we beseech and exhort you in the Lord Jesus, that as you learned from us how you ought to live and to please God, just as you are doing, you do so more and more. 2 For you know what instructions we gave you through the Lord Jesus. 3 For this is the will of God, your sanctification: that you abstain from unchastity; 4 that each one of you know how to take a wife for himself in holiness and honor 5not in the passion of lust like heathen who do not know God; 6that no man transgress, and wrong his brother in this matter, because the Lord is an avenger in all these things, as we solemnly forewarned you. 7 For God has not called us for uncleanness, but in holiness. 8 Therefore whoever disregards this, disregards not man but God, who gives his Holy Spirit to you.

2 Thes 2:1-12 (§296)

2 Now concerning the coming of our Lord Jesus Christ and our assembling to meet him, we beg you, brethren, 2 not to be quickly shaken in mind or excited, either by spirit or by word, or by letter purporting to be from us, to the effect that the day of the Lord has come. 3 Let no one deceive you in any way; for that day will not come, unless the rebellion comes first, and the man of lawlessness is revealed, the son of perdition, 4 who opposes and exalts himself against every so-called god or object of worship, so that he takes his seat in the temple of God, proclaiming himself to be God. 5 Do you not remember that when I was still with you I told you this? 6And you know what is restraining him now so that he may be revealed in his time. 7 For the mystery of lawlessness is already at work; only he who now restrains it will do so until he is out of the way. 8And then the lawless one will be revealed, and the Lord Jesus will slay him with the breath of his mouth and destroy him by his appearing and his coming. 9 The coming of the lawless one by the activity of Satan will be with all power and with pretended signs and wonders, 10 and

Phm 8-14 (§307)

8 Accordingly, though I am bold enough in Christ to command you to do what is required, 9 yet for love's sake I prefer to appeal to you—I, Paul, an ambassador and now a prisoner also for Christ Jesus—10 I appeal to you for my child, Ones'imus, whose father I have become in my imprisonment. 11 (Formerly he was useless to you, but now he is indeed useful to you and to me.) 12 I am sending him back to you, sending my very heart. 13 I would have been glad to keep him with me, in order that he might serve me on your behalf during my imprisonment for the gospel; 14 but I preferred to do nothing without your consent in order that your goodness might not be by compulsion but of your own free will.

with all wicked deception for those who are to perish, because they refused to love the truth and so be saved. 11 Therefore God sends upon them a strong delusion, to make them believe what is false, 12 so that all may be condemned who did not believe the truth but had pleasure in unrighteousness.

51

52. Gifts differ according to grace

52

Eph (cont)

flesh, following the desires of body and mind, and so we were by nature children of wrath, like the rest of mankind. 4 But God, who is rich in mercy, out of the great love with which he loved us, 5 even when we were dead through our trespasses, made us alive together with Christ (by grace you have been saved), 6 and raised us up with him, and made us sit with him in the heavenly places in Christ Jesus, 7 that in the coming ages he might show the immeasurable riches of his grace in kindness toward us in Christ Jesus. 8 For by grace you have been saved through faith; and this is not your own doing, it is the gift of God— 9 not because of works, lest any man should boast. 10 For we are his workmanship, created in Christ Jesus for good works, which God prepared beforehand, that we should walk in them.

Eph 4:11-16 (§226)

11And his gifts were that some should be apostles, some prophets, some evangelists, some pastors and teachers, 12to equip the saints for the work of ministry, for building up the body of Christ, 13 until we all attain to the unity of the faith and of the knowledge of the Son of God, to mature manhood, to the measure of the stature of the fulness of Christ; 14 so that we may no longer be children, tossed to and fro and carried about with every wind of doctrine, by the cunning of men, by their craftiness in deceitful wiles. 15 Rather, speaking the truth in love, we are to grow up in every way into him who is the head, into Christ, **16 from whom the whole body, joined and knit together by every joint with which it is supplied, when each part is working properly, makes bodily growth and upbuilds itself in love.**

Col 1:18, 18 He is the head of the body, the church; he is the beginning, the first-born from the dead, that in everything he might be pre-eminent.

2:19, 19 and not holding fast to the Head, from whom the whole body, nourished and knit together through its joints and ligaments, grows with a growth that is from God.

3:15 15And let the peace of Christ rule in your hearts, to which indeed you were called in the one body. And be thankful.

53

Rom 12:9-21

9 Let love be genuine; hate what is evil, hold fast to what is good; 10 love one another with brotherly affection; outdo one another in showing honor. 11 Never flag in zeal, be aglow with the Spirit, serve the Lord. 12 Rejoice in your hope, be patient in tribulation, be constant in prayer. 13 Contribute to the needs of the saints, practice hospitality.

14 Bless those who persecute you; bless and do not curse them. 15 Rejoice with those who rejoice, weep with those who weep. 16 Live in harmony with one another; do not be haughty, but associate with the lowly; never be conceited. 17 Repay no one evil for evil, but take thought for what is noble in the sight of all. 18 If possible, so far as it depends upon you, live peaceably with all. 19 Beloved, never avenge yourselves, but leave it¹ to the wrath of God; for it is written, "Vengeance is mine, I will repay, says the Lord." 20 No, "if your enemy is hungry, feed him; if he is thirsty, give him drink; for by so doing you will heap burning coals upon his head." 21 Do not be overcome by evil, but overcome evil with good.

▶12:9 1 Tim 1:5   ⁵ whereas the aim of our charge is love that issues from a pure heart and a good conscience and sincere faith.

1 Cor 13:4-7 (§122)

4 Love is patient and kind; love is not jealous or boastful; ⁵ it is not arrogant or rude. Love does not insist on its own way; it is not irritable or resentful; ⁶ it does not rejoice at wrong, but rejoices in the right. ⁷ Love bears all things, believes all things, hopes all things, endures all things.

▶12:12 Acts 1:14   ¹⁴All these with one accord devoted themselves to prayer, together with the women and Mary the mother of Jesus, and with his brothers.

2 Cor 13:11-13 (§191)

11 Finally, brethren, farewell. Mend your ways, heed my appeal, agree with one another, live in peace, and the God of love and peace will be with you. 12 Greet one another with a holy kiss. ¹³All the saints greet you.

1 Tim 2:1

First of all, then, I urge that supplications, prayers, intercessions, and thanksgivings be made for all men,

Eph 4:25-32 (§228)

25 Therefore, putting away falsehood, let every one speak the truth with his neighbor, for we are members one of another. 26 Be angry but do not sin; do not let the sun go down on your anger, 27 and give no opportunity to the devil. 28 Let the thief no longer steal, but rather let him labor, doing honest work with his hands, so that he may be able to give to those in need. 29 Let no evil talk come out of your mouths, but only such as is good for edifying, as fits the occasion, that it may impart grace to those who hear. 30And do not grieve the Holy Spirit of God, in whom you were sealed for the day of redemption. 31 Let all bitterness and wrath and anger and clamor and slander be put away from you, with all malice, 32 and be kind to one another, tenderhearted, forgiving one another, as God in Christ forgave you.

54. Governing authorities instituted by God

54

Rom 13:1-7

13 Let every person be subject to the governing authorities. For there is no authority except from God, and those that exist have been instituted by God. 2 Therefore he who resists the authorities resists what God has appointed, and those who resist will incur judgment. 3 For rulers are not a terror to good conduct, but to bad. Would you have no fear of him who is in authority? Then do what is good, and you will receive his approval, 4 for he is God's servant for your good. But if you do wrong, be afraid, for he does not bear the sword in vain; he is the servant of God to execute his wrath on the wrongdoer. 5 Therefore one must be subject, not only to avoid God's wrath but also for the sake of conscience. 6 For the same reason you also pay taxes, for the authorities are ministers of God, attending to this very thing. 7 Pay all of them their dues, taxes to whom taxes are due, revenue to whom revenue is due, respect to whom respect is due, honor to whom honor is due.

▶13:1 Tit 3:1   Remind them to be submissive to rulers and authorities, to be obedient, to be ready for any honest work,

1 Cor 4:1-5 (§83)

4 This is how one should regard us, as servants of Christ and stewards of the mysteries of God. 2 Moreover it is required of stewards that they be found trustworthy. 3 But with me it is a very small thing that I should be judged by you or by any human court. I do not even judge myself. 4 I am not aware of anything against myself, but I am not thereby acquitted. It is the Lord who judges me. 5 Therefore do not pronounce judgment before the time, before the Lord comes, who will bring to light the things now hidden in darkness and will disclose the purposes of the heart. Then every man will receive his commendation from God.

1 Cor 6:1-8 (§90)

6 When one of you has a grievance against a brother, does he dare go to law before the unrighteous instead of the saints? 2 Do you not know that the saints will judge the world? And if the world is to be judged by you, are you incompetent to try trivial cases? 3 Do you not know that we are to judge angels? How much more, matters pertaining to this life! 4 If then you have

▶13:1-7 1 Pet 2:13-17   13 Be subject for the Lord's sake to every human institution, whether it be to the emperor as supreme, 14 or to governors as sent by him to punish those who do wrong and to praise those who do right. 15 For it is God's will that by doing right you should put to silence

such cases, why do you lay them before those who are least esteemed by the church? ⁵ I say this to your shame. Can it be that there is no man among you wise enough to decide between members of the brotherhood, ⁶ but brother goes to law against brother, and that before unbelievers?

7 To have lawsuits at all with one another is defeat for you. Why not rather suffer wrong? Why not rather be defrauded? ⁸ But you yourselves wrong and defraud, and that even your own brethren.

1 Cor 8:7-13 (§104)

7 However, not all possess this knowledge. But some, through being hitherto accustomed to idols, eat food as really offered to an idol; and their conscience, being weak, is defiled. ⁸ Food will not commend us to God. We are no worse off if we do not eat, and no better off if we do. 9 Only take care lest this liberty of yours somehow become a stumbling block to the weak. 10 For if any one sees you, a man of

the ignorance of foolish men. 16 Live as free men, yet without using your freedom as a pretext for evil; but live as servants of God. 17 Honor all men. Love the brotherhood. Fear God. Honor the emperor.

*cf. Tit 2:1-10   *cf. 1 Tim 6:1

knowledge, at table in an idol's temple, might he not be encouraged, if his conscience is weak, to eat food offered to idols? ¹¹And so by your knowledge this weak man is destroyed, the brother for whom Christ died. 12 Thus, sinning against your brethren and wounding their conscience when it is weak, you sin against Christ. 13 Therefore, if food is a cause of my brother's falling, I will never eat meat, lest I cause my brother to fall.

▶13:1-7 Eph 5:21   21 Be subject to one another out of reverence for Christ.

Col 3:18

18 Wives, be subject to your husbands, as is fitting in the Lord.

Phil 2:1-11 (§242)

2 So if there is any encouragement in Christ, any incentive of love, any participation in the Spirit, any affection and sympathy, 2 complete my joy by being of the same mind, having the same love, being in full accord and of one mind. 3 Do nothing from selfishness or conceit, but in humility count others better than yourselves. 4 Let each of you look not only to his own interests, but also to the interests of others. 5 Have this mind among yourselves, which is yours in Christ Jesus, 6 who, though he was in the form of God, did not count equality with God a thing to be grasped, 7 but emptied himself, taking the form of a servant, being born in the likeness of men. 8 And being found in human form he humbled himself and became obedient unto death, even death on a cross. 9 Therefore God has highly exalted him and bestowed on him the name which is above every name, 10 that at the name of Jesus every knee should bow, in heaven and on earth and under the earth, 11 and every tongue confess that Jesus Christ is Lord, to the glory of God the Father.

▶ 12:19 Lev 19:18
18 You shall not take vengeance or bear any grudge against the sons of your own people, but you shall love your neighbor as yourself: I am the LORD.

Col 3:12-17 (§267)

12 Put on then, as God's chosen ones, holy and beloved, compassion, kindness, lowliness, meekness, and patience, 13 forbearing one another and, if one has a complaint against another, forgiving each other; as the Lord has forgiven you, so you also must forgive. 14 And above all these put on love, which binds everything together in perfect harmony. 15 And let the peace of Christ rule in your hearts, to which indeed you were called in the one body. And be thankful. 16 Let the word of Christ dwell in you richly, teach and admonish one another in all wisdom, and sing psalms and hymns and spiritual songs with thankfulness in your hearts to God. 17 And whatever you do, in word or deed, do everything in the name of the Lord Jesus, giving thanks to God the Father through him.

Phil 4:4-7 (§251)

4 Therefore, my brethren, whom I love and long for, my joy and crown, stand firm thus in the Lord, my beloved.

Deut 32:35
35 Vengeance is mine, and recompense,
for the time when their foot shall slip;
for the day of their calamity is at hand,
and their doom comes swiftly.

1 Thes 4:9-12 (§285)

9 But concerning love of the brethren you have no need to have any one write to you, for you yourselves have been taught by God to love one another; 10 and indeed you do love all the brethren throughout Macedo'nia. But we exhort you, brethren, to do so more and more, 11 to aspire to live quietly, to mind your own affairs, and to work with your hands, as we charged you; 12 so that you may command the respect of outsiders, and be dependent on nobody.

1 Thes 5:12-22 (§288)

12 But we beseech you, brethren, to respect those who labor among you and are over you in the Lord and admonish you, 13 and to esteem them very highly in love because of their work. Be at peace among yourselves. 14 And we exhort you, brethren. admonish the idlers,

2 I entreat Eu-o'dia and I entreat Syn'tyche to agree in the Lord. 3 And I ask you also, true yokefellow, help these women, for they have labored side by side with me in the gospel together with Clement and the rest of my

▶ 12:20 Prov 25:21-22
21 If your enemy is hungry, give him bread to eat;
and if he is thirsty, give him water to drink;
22 for you will heap coals of fire on his head,
and the LORD will reward you.

encourage the fainthearted, help the weak, be patient with them all. 15 See that none of you repays evil for evil, but always seek to do good to one another and to all. 16 Rejoice always, 17 pray constantly, 18 give thanks in all circumstances; for this is the will of God in Christ Jesus for you. 19 Do not quench the Spirit, 20 do not despise prophesying, 21 but test everything; hold fast what is good, 22 abstain from every form of evil.

fellow workers, whose names are in the book of life.

4 Rejoice in the Lord always; again I will say, Rejoice. 5 Let all men know your forbearance. The Lord is at hand. 6 Have no anxiety about anything, but in everything by prayer and supplication with thanksgiving let your requests be made known to God. 7 And the peace of God, which passes all understanding, will keep your hearts and your minds in Christ Jesus.

54. Governing authorities instituted by God

▶ 13:5 *cf. 2:12-16, 1 Cor 10:25-29

§55-56

55. Love is the fulfilling of the law

Rom 13:8-10

55 8 Owe no one anything, except to love one another; for he who loves his neighbor has fulfilled the law. 9 The commandments, "You shall not commit adultery, You shall not kill, You shall not steal, You shall not covet," and any other commandment, are summed up in this sentence, "You shall love your neighbor as yourself." 10 Love does no wrong to a neighbor; therefore love is the fulfilling of the law.

1 Cor 13:1-3 (§121)

13 If I speak in the tongues of men and of angels, but have not love, I am a noisy gong or a clanging cymbal. 2And if I have prophetic powers, and understand all mysteries and all knowledge, and if I have all faith, so as to remove mountains, but have not love, I am nothing. 3 If I give away all I have, and if I deliver my body to be burned, but have not love, I gain nothing.

Gal 5:13-15 (§212)

13 For you were called to freedom, brethren; only do not use your freedom as an opportunity for the flesh, but through love be servants of one another. 14 For the whole law is fulfilled in one word, "You shall love your neighbor as yourself." 15 But if you bite and devour one another take heed that you are not consumed by one another.

▶ 13:10 1 Tim 1:5 5 whereas the aim of our charge is love that issues from a pure heart and a good conscience and sincere faith.

▶ 13:8 Gal 6:2 2 Bear one another's burdens, and so fulfil the law of Christ.

Eph 5:2 2And walk in love, as Christ loved us and gave himself up for us, a fragrant offering and sacrifice to God.

▶ 13:10 Col 3:14 14And above all these put on love, which binds everything together in perfect harmony.

56. Night is far gone; salvation nearer

Rom 13:11-14

56 11 Besides this you know what hour it is, how it is full time now for you to wake from sleep. For salvation is nearer to us now than when we first believed; 12 the night is far gone, the day is at hand. Let us then cast off the works of darkness and put on the armor of light; 13 let us conduct ourselves becomingly as in the day, not in reveling and drunkenness, not in debauchery and licentiousness, not in quarreling and jealousy. 14 But put on the Lord Jesus Christ, and make no provision for the flesh, to gratify its desires.

1 Cor 5:9-13 (§89)

9 I wrote to you in my letter not to associate with immoral men; 10 not at all meaning the immoral of this world, or the greedy and robbers, or idolaters, since then you would need to go out of the world. 11 But rather I wrote to you not to associate with any one who bears the name of brother if he is guilty of immorality or greed, or is an idolater, reviler, drunkard, or robber—not even to eat with such a one. 12 For what have I to do with judging outsiders? Is it not those inside the church whom you are to judge? 13 God judges those outside. "Drive out the wicked person from among you."

1 Cor 6:9-11 (§91)

9 Do you not know that the unrighteous will not inherit the kingdom of God? Do not be deceived; neither the immoral, nor idolaters, nor adulterers, nor sexual perverts, 10nor thieves, nor the greedy, nor drunkards, nor revilers, nor robbers will inherit the kingdom of God. 11And such were some of you. But you were washed, you were sanctified, you were justified in the name of the Lord Jesus Christ and in the Spirit of our God.

2 Cor 12:19-21 (§188)

19 Have you been thinking all along that we have been defending ourselves before you? It is in the sight of God that we have been speaking in Christ, and all for your upbuilding, beloved. 20 For I fear that perhaps I may come and find you not what I wish, and that you may find me not what you wish; that perhaps there may be quarreling, jealousy, anger, selfishness, slander, gossip, conceit, and disorder. 21 I fear that when I come again my God may humble me before you, and I may have to mourn over many of those who sinned before and have not repented of the impurity, immorality, and licentiousness which they have practiced.

Gal 5:16-26 (§213)

16 But I say, walk by the Spirit, and do not gratify the desires of the flesh. 17 For the desires of the flesh are against the Spirit, and the desires of the Spirit are against the flesh; for these are opposed to each other, to prevent you from doing what you would. 18 But if you are led by the Spirit you are not under the law. 19 Now the works of the flesh are plain: fornication, impurity, licentiousness, 20 idolatry, sorcery, enmity, strife, jealousy, anger, selfishness, dissension, party spirit, 21 envy, drunkenness, carousing, and the like. I warn you, as I warned you before, that those who do such things shall not inherit the kingdom of God. 22 But the fruit of the Spirit is love, joy, peace, patience, kindness, goodness, faithfulness, 23 gentleness, self-control; against such there is no law. 24And those who belong to Christ Jesus have crucified the flesh with its passions and desires. 25 If we live by the Spirit, let us also walk by the Spirit. 26 Let us have no self-conceit, no provoking of one another, no envy of one another.

Eph 4:17-24 (§227)

17 Now this I affirm and testify in the Lord, that you must no longer live as the Gentiles do, in the futility of their minds; 18 they are darkened in their understanding, alienated from the life of God because of the ignorance that is in them, due to their hardness of heart; 19 they have become callous and have given themselves up to licentiousness, greedy to practice every kind of uncleanness. 20 You did not so learn Christ!— 21 assuming that you have heard about him and were taught in him, as the truth is in Jesus. 22 Put off your old nature which belongs to your former manner of life and is corrupt through deceitful lusts, 23 and be renewed in the spirit of your minds, 24 and put on the new nature, created after the likeness of God in true righteousness and holiness.

Eph 5:3-20 (§230-231)

3 But fornication and all impurity or covetousness must not even be named among you, as is fitting among saints. 4 Let there be no filthiness, nor silly talk, nor levity, which are not fitting; but instead let there be thanksgiving.

▶ 13:13 1:29-32 29 They were filled with all manner of wickedness, evil, covetousness, malice. Full of envy, murder, strife, deceit, malignity, they are gossips, 30 slanderers, haters of God, insolent, haughty, boastful, inventors of evil, disobedient to parents, 31 foolish, faithless, heartless, ruthless. 32 Though they know God's decree that those who do such things deserve to die, they not only do them but approve those who practice them.

55

1 Thes 4:9-12 (§285)

9 But concerning love of the brethren you have no need to have any one write to you, for you yourselves have been taught by God to love one another; 10 and indeed you do love all the brethren throughout Macedo′nia. But we exhort you, brethren, to do so more and more, 11 to aspire to live quietly, to mind your own affairs, and to work with your hands, as we charged you; 12 so that you may command the respect of outsiders, and be dependent on nobody.

Phm 15-20(§308)

15 Perhaps this is why he was parted from you for a while, that you might have him back for ever, 16 no longer as a slave but more than a slave, as a beloved brother, especially to me but how much more to you, both in the flesh and in the Lord. 17 So if you consider me your partner, receive him as you would receive me. 18 If he has wronged you at all, or owes you anything, charge that to my account. 19 I, Paul, write this with my own hand, I will repay it—to say nothing of your owing me even your own self. 20 Yes, brother, I want some benefit from you in the Lord. Refresh my heart in Christ.

▶ 13:9 Ex 20:13-14

13 "You shall not kill.
14 "You shall not commit adultery.

Deut 5:17-18

17 " 'You shall not kill.
18 " 'Neither shall you commit adultery.

Lev 19:18

18 You shall not take vengeance or bear any grudge against the sons of your own people, but you shall love your neighbor as yourself: I am the LORD.

56. Night is far gone; salvation nearer

56

Eph (cont)

5 Be sure of this, that no fornicator or impure man, or one who is covetous (that is, an idolater), has any inheritance in the kingdom of Christ and of God. 6 Let no one deceive you with empty words, for it is because of these things that the wrath of God comes upon the sons of disobedience. 7 Therefore do not associate with them, 8 for once you were darkness, but now you are light in the Lord; walk as children of light 9 (for the fruit of light is found in all that is good and right and true), 10 and try to learn what is pleasing to the Lord. 11 Take no part in the unfruitful works of darkness, but instead expose them. 12 For it is a shame even to speak of the things that they do in secret; 13 but when anything is exposed by the light it becomes visible, for anything that becomes visible is light. 14 Therefore it is said,
"Awake, O sleeper, and arise from the dead,
and Christ shall give you light."
15 Look carefully then how you walk,

Col 3:5-11 (§266)

5 Put to death therefore what is earthly in you: fornication, impurity, passion, evil desire, and covetousness, which is idolatry. 6 On account of these the wrath of God is coming. 7 In these you once walked, when you lived in them. 8 But now put them all away: anger, wrath, malice, slander, and foul talk from your mouth. 9 Do not lie to one another, seeing that you have put off the old nature with its practices 10 and have put on the new nature, which is being renewed in knowledge after the image of its creator. 11 Here there cannot be Greek and Jew, circumcised and uncircumcised, barbarian, Scyth′ian, slave, free man, but Christ is all, and in all.

not as unwise men but as wise, 16 making the most of the time, because the days are evil. 17 Therefore do not be foolish, but understand what the will of the Lord is. 18 And do not get drunk with wine, for that is debauchery; but be filled with the Spirit, 19 addressing one another in psalms and hymns and spiritual songs, singing and making

1 Thes 5:1-11 (§287)

5 But as to the times and the seasons, brethren, you have no need to have anything written to you. 2 For you your-

melody to the Lord with all your heart, 20 always and for everything giving thanks in the name of our Lord Jesus Christ to God the Father.

Eph 6:10-17 (§233)

10 Finally, be strong in the Lord and in the strength of his might. 11 Put on the whole armor of God, that you may be able to stand against the wiles of the devil. 12 For we are not contending against flesh and blood, but against the principalities, against the powers, against the world rulers of this present darkness, against the spiritual hosts of wickedness in the heavenly places. 13 Therefore take the whole armor of God, that you may be able to withstand in the evil day, and having done all, to stand. 14 Stand therefore, having girded your loins with truth, and having put on the breastplate of righteousness, 15 and having shod your feet with the equipment of the gospel of peace; 16 besides all these, taking the shield of faith, with which you can quench all the flaming darts of the evil one. 17 And take the helmet of salvation, and the sword of the Spirit, which is the word of God.

selves know well that the day of the Lord will come like a thief in the night. 3 When people say, "There is peace and security," then sudden destruction will come upon them as travail comes upon a woman with child, and there will be no escape. 4 But you are not in darkness, brethren, for that day to surprise you like a thief. 5 For you are all sons of light and sons of the day; we are not of the night or of darkness. 6 So then, let us not sleep, as others do, but let us keep awake and be sober. 7 For those who sleep sleep at night, and those who get drunk are drunk at night. 8 But, since we belong to the day, let us be sober, and put on the breastplate of faith and love, and for a helmet the hope of salvation. 9 For God has not destined us for wrath, but to obtain salvation through our Lord Jesus Christ, 10 who died for us so that whether we wake or sleep we might live with him. 11 Therefore encourage one another and build one another up, just as you are doing.

57. Man who is weak in faith

57

Rom 14:1-4

14 As for the man who is weak in faith, welcome him, but not for disputes over opinions. 2 One believes he may eat anything, while the weak man eats only vegetables. 3 Let not him who eats despise him who abstains, and let not him who abstains pass judgment on him who eats; for God has welcomed him. 4 Who are you to pass judgment on the servant of another? It is before his own master that he stands or falls. And he will be upheld, for the Master is able to make him stand.

▶ 14:1 1 Cor 9:22
22 To the weak I became weak, that I might win the weak. I have become all things to all men, that I might by all means save some.

1 Cor 8:1-3 (§102)

8 Now concerning food offered to idols: we know that "all of us possess knowledge." "Knowledge" puffs up, but love builds up. 2 If any one imagines that he knows something, he does not yet know as he ought to know. 3 But if one loves God, one is known by him.

1 Cor 10:23-11:1 (§111)

23 "All things are lawful," but not all things are helpful. "All things are lawful," but not all things build up. 24 Let no one seek his own good, but the good of his neighbor. 25 Eat whatever is sold in the meat market without raising any question on the ground of conscience. 26 For "the earth is the Lord's, and everything in it." 27 If one of the unbelievers invites you to dinner and you are disposed to go, eat whatever is set before you without raising any question on the ground of conscience. 28 (But if some one says to you, "This has been offered in sacrifice," then out of consideration for the man who informed you, and for conscience' sake— 29 I mean his conscience, not yours—do not

▶ 14:4 *cf. 2:1-3

eat it.) For why should my liberty be determined by another man's scruples? 30 If I partake with thankfulness, why am I denounced because of that for which I give thanks?

31 So, whether you eat or drink, or whatever you do, do all to the glory of God. 32 Give no offense to Jews or to Greeks or to the church of God, 33 just as I try to please all men in everything I do, not seeking my own advantage, but that of many, that they may be **11** saved. 1 Be imitators of me, as I am of Christ.

1 Cor 11:17-22 (§113)

17 But in the following instructions I do not commend you, because when you come together it is not for the better but for the worse. 18 For, in the first place, when you assemble as a church, I hear that there are divisions among you; and I partly believe it, 19 for there must be factions among you in order that those who are genuine among you may be recognized. 20 When you meet together, it is not the Lord's supper that you eat. 21 For in eating, each one goes ahead with his own meal, and one is

hungry and another is drunk. 22 What! Do you not have houses to eat and drink in? Or do you despise the church of God and humiliate those who have nothing? What shall I say to you? Shall I commend you in this? No, I will not.

---

58. Whether we live or die, we are the Lord's

58

Rom 14:5-12

5 One man esteems one day as better than another, while another man esteems all days alike. Let every one be fully convinced in his own mind. 6 He who observes the day, observes it in honor of the Lord. He also who eats, eats in honor of the Lord, since he gives thanks to God; while he who abstains, abstains in honor of the Lord and gives thanks to God. 7 None of us lives to himself, and none of us dies to himself. 8 If we live, we live to the Lord, and if we die, we die to the Lord; so then, whether we live or whether we die, we are the Lord's. 9 For to this end Christ died and lived again, that he might be Lord both of the dead and of the living. 10 Why do you pass judgment on your brother? Or you, why do you despise your brother? For we shall all stand before the judgment seat of God; 11 for it is written,

"As I live, says the Lord, every knee
    shall bow to me,
and every tongue shall give praise to
    God."
12 So each of us shall give account of himself to God.

▶ 14:10 Acts 17:31
31 because he has fixed a day on which he will judge the world in righteousness by a man whom he has appointed, and of this he has given assurance to all men by raising him from the dead."

1 Cor 4:1-5 (§83)

4 This is how one should regard us, as servants of Christ and stewards of the mysteries of God. 2 Moreover it is required of stewards that they be found trustworthy. 3 But with me it is a very small thing that I should be judged by you or by any human court. I do not even judge myself. 4 I am not aware of anything against myself, but I am not thereby acquitted. It is the Lord who judges me. 5 Therefore do not pronounce judgment before the time, before the Lord comes, who will bring to light the things now hidden in darkness and will disclose the purposes of the heart. Then every man will receive his commendation from God.

1 Cor 7:17-24 (§97)

17 Only, let every one lead the life which the Lord has assigned to him, and in which God has called him. This is my rule in all the churches. 18 Was any one at the time of his call already circumcised? Let him not seek to remove the marks of circumcision. Was any one at the time of his call uncircumcised? Let him not seek circumcision. 19 For neither circumcision counts for any-

▶ 14:9 2 Cor 4:11-12
11 For while we live we are always being given up to death for Jesus' sake, so that the life of Jesus may be manifested in our mortal flesh. 12 So death is at work in us, but life in you.

thing nor uncircumcision, but keeping the commandments of God. 20 Every one should remain in the state in which he was called. 21 Were you a slave when called? Never mind. But if you can gain your freedom, avail yourself of the opportunity. 22 For he who was called in the Lord as a slave is a freedman of the Lord. Likewise he who was free when called is a slave of Christ. 23 You were bought with a price; do not become slaves of men. 24 So, brethren, in whatever state each was called, there let him remain with God.

*cf. 8:38-39   ▶ 14:10 *cf. 2:1-5 2 Cor 5:10

▶ 14:10 *cf 1 Cor 5:3, 12-13

Gal 4:8-11 (§208)

8 Formerly, when you did not know God, you were in bondage to beings that by nature are no gods; 9 but now that you have come to know God, or rather to be known by God, how can you turn back again to the weak and beggarly elemental spirits, whose slaves you want to be once more? 10 You observe days, and months, and seasons, and years! 11 I am afraid I have labored over you in vain.

▶ 14:11 Phil 2:9-11
9 Therefore God has highly exalted him and bestowed on him the name which is above every name, 10 that at the name of Jesus every knee should bow, in heaven and on earth and under the earth, 11 and every tongue confess

Eph 5:15-20 (§231)

15 Look carefully then how you walk, not as unwise men but as wise, 16 making the most of the time, because the days are evil. 17 Therefore do not be foolish, but understand what the will of the Lord is. 18 And do not get drunk with wine, for that is debauchery; but be filled with the Spirit, 19 addressing one another in psalms and hymns and spiritual songs, singing and making melody to the Lord with all your heart, 20 always and for everything giving thanks in the name of our Lord Jesus Christ to God the Father.

that Jesus Christ is Lord, to the glory of God the Father.

58. Whether we live or die, we are the Lord's

Phil 1:19-26 (§240)

19 Yes, and I shall rejoice. For I know that through your prayers and the help of the Spirit of Jesus Christ this will turn out for my deliverance, 20 as it is my eager expectation and hope that I shall not be at all ashamed, but that with full courage now as always Christ will be honored in my body, whether by life or by death. 21 For to me to live is Christ, and to die is gain. 22 If it is to be life in the flesh, that means fruitful labor for me. Yet which I shall choose I cannot tell. 23 I am hard pressed between the two. My desire is to depart and be with Christ, for that is far better. 24 But to remain in the flesh is more necessary on your account. 25 Convinced of this, I know that I shall remain and continue with you all, for your progress and joy in the faith, 26 so that in me you may have ample cause to glory in Christ Jesus, because of my coming to you again.

Col 2:16-19 (§263)

16 Therefore let no one pass judgment on you in questions of food and drink or with regard to a festival or a new moon or a sabbath. 17 These are only a shadow of what is to come; but the substance belongs to Christ. 18 Let no one disqualify you, insisting on self-abasement and worship of angels, taking his stand on visions, puffed up without reason by his sensuous mind, 19 and not holding fast to the Head, from whom the whole body, nourished and knit together through its joints and ligaments, grows with a growth that is from God.

Col 3:12-17 (§267)

12 Put on then, as God's chosen ones, holy and beloved, compassion, kindness, lowliness, meekness, and patience, 13 forbearing one another and, if one has a complaint against another, forgiving each other; as the Lord has forgiven you, so you also must forgive. 14And above all these put on love, which binds everything together in perfect harmony. 15And let the peace of Christ rule in your hearts, to which indeed you were called in the one body. And be thankful. 16 Let the word of Christ dwell in you richly, teach and admonish one another in all wisdom, and sing psalms and hymns and spiritual songs with thankfulness in your hearts to God. 17And whatever you do, in word or deed, do everything in the name of the Lord Jesus, giving thanks to God the Father through him.

1 Thes 5:1-11 (§287)

5 But as to the times and the seasons, brethren, you have no need to have anything written to you. 2 For you yourselves know well that the day of the Lord will come like a thief in the night. 3 When people say, "There is peace and security," then sudden destruction will come upon them as travail comes upon a woman with child, and there will be no escape. 4 But you are not in darkness, brethren, for that day to surprise you like a thief. 5 For you are all sons of light and sons of the day; we are not of the night or of darkness. 6 So then, let us not sleep, as others do, but let us keep awake and be sober. 7 For those who sleep sleep at night, and those who get drunk are drunk at night. 8 But, since we belong to the day, let us be sober, and put on the breastplate of faith and love, and for a helmet the hope of salvation. 9 For God has not destined us for wrath, but to obtain salvation through our Lord Jesus Christ, 10 who died for us so that whether we wake or sleep we might live with him. 11 Therefore encourage one another and build one another up, just as you are doing.

▶ 14:11 Is 45:23

23 By myself I have sworn,
   from my mouth has gone forth in
      righteousness
   a word that shall not return:
'To me every knee shall bow,
   every tongue shall swear.'

59

Rom 14:13-23

13 Then let us no more pass judgment on one another, but rather decide never to put a stumbling block or hindrance in the way of a brother. 14 I know and am persuaded in the Lord Jesus that nothing is unclean in itself; but it is unclean for any one who thinks it unclean. 15 If your brother is being injured by what you eat, you are no longer walking in love. Do not let what you eat cause the ruin of one for whom Christ died. 16 So do not let your good be spoken of as evil. 17 For the kingdom of God is not food and drink but righteousness and peace and joy in the Holy Spirit; 18 he who thus serves Christ is acceptable to God and approved by men. 19 Let us then pursue what makes for peace and for mutual upbuilding. 20 Do not, for the sake of food, destroy the work of God. Everything is indeed clean, but it is wrong for any one to make others fall by what he eats; 21 it is right not to eat meat or drink wine or do anything that makes your brother stumble. *c* 22 The faith that you have, keep between yourself and God; happy is he who has no

1 Cor 4:1-5 (§83)

4 This is how one should regard us, as servants of Christ and stewards of the mysteries of God. 2 Moreover it is required of stewards that they be found trustworthy. 3 But with me it is a very small thing that I should be judged by you or by any human court. I do not even judge myself. 4 I am not aware of anything against myself, but I am not thereby acquitted. It is the Lord who judges me. 5 Therefore do not pronounce judgment before the time, before the Lord comes, who will bring to light the things now hidden in darkness and will disclose the purposes of the heart. Then every man will receive his commendation from God.

1 Cor 8:7-13 (§104)

7 However, not all possess this knowledge. But some, through being hitherto accustomed to idols, eat food as really offered to an idol; and their

reason to judge himself for what he approves. 23 But he who has doubts is condemned, if he eats, because he does not act from faith; for whatever does not proceed from faith is sin.

conscience, being weak, is defiled. 8 Food will not commend us to God. We are no worse off if we do not eat, and no better off if we do. 9 Only take care lest this liberty of yours somehow become a stumbling block to the weak. 10 For if any one sees you, a man of knowledge, at table in an idol's temple, might he not be encouraged, if his conscience is weak, to eat food offered to idols? 11 And so by your knowledge this weak man is destroyed, the brother for whom Christ died. 12 Thus, sinning against your brethren and wounding their conscience when it is weak, you sin against Christ. 13 Therefore, if food is a cause of my brother's falling, I will never eat meat, lest I cause my brother to fall.

1 Cor 10:23-11:1 (§111)

23 "All things are lawful," but not all things are helpful. "All things are lawful," but not all things build up. 24 Let no one seek his own good, but the good of his neighbor. 25 Eat whatever is sold in the meat market without raising any question on the ground of conscience.

26 For "the earth is the Lord's, and everything in it." 27 If one of the unbelievers invites you to dinner and you are disposed to go, eat whatever is set before you without raising any question on the ground of conscience. 28 (But if some one says to you, "This has been offered in sacrifice," then out of consideration for the man who informed you, and for conscience' sake— 29 I mean his conscience, not yours—do not eat it.) For why should my liberty be determined by another man's scruples? 30 If I partake with thankfulness, why am I denounced because of that for which I give thanks?

31 So, whether you eat or drink, or whatever you do, do all to the glory of God. 32 Give no offense to Jews or to Greeks or to the church of God, 33 just as I try to please all men in everything I do, not seeking my own advantage, but that of many, that they may be

11

saved. 1 Be imitators of me, as I am of Christ.

▶ 14:14 Acts 10:15, 15 And the voice came to him again a second time, "What God has cleansed, you must not call common."

28 and he said to them, "You yourselves know how unlawful it is for a Jew to associate with or to visit any one of another nation; but God has shown me that I should not call any man common or unclean.

▶ 14:16 Tit 2:5 5 to be sensible, chaste, domestic, kind, and submissive to their husbands, that the word of God may not be discredited.

▶ 14:19 2 Tim 2:22 22 So shun youthful passions and aim at righteousness, faith, love, and peace, along with those who call upon the Lord from a pure heart.

▶ 14:22-23 2:15-56 15 They show that what the law requires is written on their hearts, while their conscience also bears witness and their conflicting thoughts accuse or perhaps excuse them 16 on that day when, according to my gospel, God judges the secrets of men by Christ Jesus.

60. Strong ought to bear with failings of the weak

60

Rom 15:1-6

15 We who are strong ought to bear with the failings of the weak, and not to please ourselves; 2 let each of us please his neighbor for his good, to edify him. 3 For Christ did not please himself; but, as it is written, "The reproaches of those who reproached thee fell on me." 4 For whatever was written in former days was written for our instruction, that by steadfastness and by the encouragement of the scriptures we might have hope. 5 May the God of steadfastness and encouragement grant you to live in such harmony with one another, in accord with Christ Jesus, 6 that together you may with one voice glorify the God and Father of our Lord Jesus Christ.

1 Cor 1:10-17 (§73)

10 I appeal to you, brethren, by the name of our Lord Jesus Christ, that all of you agree and that there be no dissensions among you, but that you be united in the same mind and the same judgment. 11 For it has been reported to me by Chloe's people that there is quarreling among you, my brethren. 12 What I mean is that each one of you says, "I belong to Paul," or "I belong to Apollos," or "I belong to Cephas," or "I belong to Christ." 13 Is Christ divided? Was Paul crucified for you? Or were you baptized in the name of Paul? 14 I am thankful that I baptized none of you except Crispus and Gaius; 15 lest any one should say that you were baptized in my name. 16 (I did baptize also the household of Stephanas. Beyond that, I do not know whether I baptized any one else.) 17 For Christ did not send me to baptize but to preach the gospel, and not with eloquent wisdom, lest the cross of Christ be emptied of its power.

1 Cor 10:23-11:1 (§111)

23 "All things are lawful," but not all things are helpful. "All things are lawful," but not all things build up. 24 Let

2 Cor 13:5-13 (§190-191)

5 Examine yourselves, to see whether you are holding to your faith. Test yourselves. Do you not realize that Jesus Christ is in you?—unless indeed you fail to meet the test! 6 I hope you will find out that we have not failed. 7 But we pray God that you may not do wrong—not that we may appear to have met the test, but that you may do what is right, though we may seem to have failed. 8 For we cannot do anything against the truth, but only for the truth. 9 For we are glad when we are weak and you are strong. What we pray for is your improvement. 10 I write this while I am away from you, in order that when I come I may not have to be severe in my use of the authority which the Lord has given me for building up and not for tearing down.

11 Finally, brethren, farewell. Mend your ways, heed my appeal, agree with one another, live in peace, and the God of love and peace will be with you. 12 Greet one another with a holy kiss. 13 All the saints greet you.

no one seek his own good, but the good

Gal 6:1-6 (§214)

6 Brethren, if a man is overtaken in any trespass, you who are spiritual should restore him in a spirit of gentleness. Look to yourself, lest you too be tempted. 2 Bear one another's burdens, and so fulfil the law of Christ. 3 For if any one thinks he is something, when he is nothing, he deceives himself. 4 But let each one test his own work, and then his reason to boast will be in himself alone and not in his neighbor. 5 For each man will have to bear his own load.

6 Let him who is taught the word share all good things with him who teaches.

of his neighbor. 25 Eat whatever is sold in the meat market without raising any question on the ground of conscience. 26 For "the earth is the Lord's, and everything in it." 27 If one of the unbelievers invites you to dinner and you are disposed to go, eat whatever is set before you without raising any question on the ground of conscience. 28 (But if some one says to you, "This has been offered in sacrifice," then out of consideration for the man who informed

you, and for conscience' sake— 29 I mean his conscience, not yours—do not eat it.) For why should my liberty be determined by another man's scruples? 30 If I partake with thankfulness, why am I denounced because of that for which I give thanks?

31 So, whether you eat or drink, or whatever you do, do all to the glory of God. 32 Give no offense to Jews or to Greeks or to the church of God, 33 just as I try to please all men in everything I do, not seeking my own advantage, but that of many, that they may be

11

saved. 1 Be imitators of me, as I am of Christ.

1 Cor 14:1-5 (§124)

14

Make love your aim, and earnestly desire the spiritual gifts, especially that you may prophesy. 2 For one who speaks in a tongue speaks not to men but to God; for no one understands him, but he utters mysteries in the Spirit. 3 On the other hand, he who prophesies speaks to men for their upbuilding and encouragement and con-

▶ 15:4 2 Tim 3:16-17 16 All scripture is inspired by God and profitable for teaching, for reproof, for correction, and for training in righteousness, 17 that the man of God may be complete, equipped for every good work.

▶ 15:1 1 Cor 1:27 27 but God chose what is foolish in the world to shame the wise, God chose what is weak in the world to shame the strong.

▶ 15:2 1 Thes 5:11 11 Therefore encourage one another and build one another up, just as you are doing.

▶ 15:4 1 Cor 9:10, 10 Does he not speak entirely for our sake? It was written for our sake, because the plowman should plow in hope and the thresher thresh in hope of a share in the crop.

10:6, 6 Now these things are warnings for us, not to desire evil as they did.

10:11 11 Now these things happened to them as a warning, but they were written down for our instruction, upon whom the end of the ages has come.

*cf. 14:1-4

▶14:19 (let us) *read* we: SABG (Greek); *text:* CD Koine Lect it vg syr cop Origen (Latin)

▶14:21 (stumble) *read* be upset: S*; *add* or be weakened: syr (pal); *read* be upset or sin or be weakened: P; *add* sin or be weakened: S°BDG Koine Lect it(most) vg syr(har)

cop(sa) Ambrosiaster; *text:* Sª AC syr(pes) cop(bo) Marcion Origen

▶14:23 (sin) *add 16:25-27 here only:* L Koine Lect it(few) syr(har) Chrysoston; *add 16:25-27 both here and at 16:25:* AP; *text:* S BCD it(some) vg syr cop Clement Origen(Latin)

60. Strong ought to bear with failings of the weak

Phil 2:1-11 (§242)

2 So if there is any encouragement in Christ, any incentive of love, any participation in the Spirit, any affection and sympathy, 2 complete my joy by being of the same mind, having the same love, being in full accord and of one mind. 3 Do nothing from selfishness or conceit, but in humility count others better than yourselves. 4 Let each of you look not only to his own interests, but also to the interests of others. 5 Have this mind among yourselves, which is yours in Christ Jesus, 6 who, though he was in the form of God, did not count equality with God a thing to be grasped, 7 but emptied himself, taking the form of a servant, being born in the likeness of men. 8And being found in human form he humbled himself and became

Col 3:12-17 (§267)

12 Put on then, as God's chosen ones, holy and beloved, compassion, kindness, lowliness, meekness, and patience, 13 forbearing one another and, if one has a complaint against another, forgiving each other; as the Lord has forgiven you, so you also must forgive. 14And above all these put on love, which binds everything together in perfect harmony. 15And let the peace of Christ rule in your hearts, to which indeed you were called in the one body. And be thankful. 16 Let the word of Christ dwell in you richly, teach and admonish one another in all wisdom, and sing psalms and hymns and spiritual songs

obedient unto death, even death on a cross. 9 Therefore God has highly exalted him and bestowed on him the name which is above every name, 10 that at the name of Jesus every knee should bow, in heaven and on earth and under the earth, 11 and every tongue confess that Jesus Christ is Lord, to the glory of God the Father.

with thankfulness in your hearts to God. 17And whatever you do, in word or deed, do everything in the name of the Lord Jesus, giving thanks to God the Father through him.

1 Cor (cont)

solation. 4 He who speaks in a tongue edifies himself, but he who prophesies edifies the church. 5 Now I want you all to speak in tongues, but even more to prophesy. He who prophesies is greater than he who speaks in tongues, unless some one interprets, so that the church may be edified.

▶ 15:3 Ps 69:9

9 For zeal for thy house has consumed
    me,
  and the insults of those who insult
    thee have fallen on me.

61

Rom 15:7-13

7 Welcome one another, therefore, as Christ has welcomed you, for the glory of God. 8 For I tell you that Christ became a servant to the circumcised to show God's truthfulness, in order to confirm the promises given to the patriarchs, 9 and in order that the Gentiles might glorify God for his mercy. As it is written,

"Therefore I will praise thee among the Gentiles,
and sing to thy name";

10 and again it is said,

"Rejoice, O Gentiles, with his people";

11 and again,

"Praise the Lord, all Gentiles,
and let all the peoples praise him";

12 and further Isaiah says,

"The root of Jesse shall come,
he who rises to rule the Gentiles;
in him shall the Gentiles hope."

13 May the God of hope fill you with all joy and peace in believing, so that by the power of the Holy Spirit you may abound in hope.

▶ 15:8 Acts 3:26
26 God, having raised up his servant, sent him to you first, to bless you in turning every one of you from your wickedness."

▶ 15:7 *cf. 14:1-3

▶ 15:13 1 Thes 2:19-20
19 For what is our hope or joy or crown of boasting before our Lord Jesus at his coming? Is it not you? 20 For you are our glory and joy.

9:4-5 4 They are Israelites, and to them belong the sonship, the glory, the covenants, the giving of the law, the worship, and the promises; 5 to them belong the patriarchs, and of their race, according to the flesh, is the Christ. God who is over all be blessed for ever. Amen.

Gal 3:6-9 (§201)

6 Thus Abraham "believed God, and it was reckoned to him as righteousness." 7 So you see that it is men of faith who are the sons of Abraham. 8 And the scripture, foreseeing that God would justify the Gentiles by faith, preached the gospel beforehand to Abraham, saying, "In you shall all the nations be blessed." 9 So then, those who are men of faith are blessed with Abraham who had faith.

Gal 3:10-14 (§202)

10 For all who rely on works of the law are under a curse; for it is written, "Cursed be every one who does not abide by all things written in the book of the law, and do them." 11 Now it is evident that no man is justified before God by the law; for "He who through faith is righteous shall live";ᶠ 12 but the law does not rest on faith, for "He who does them shall live by them." 13 Christ redeemed us from the curse of the law, having become a curse for us—for it is written, "Cursed be every one who hangs on a tree"—14 that in Christ Jesus the blessing of Abraham might come upon the Gentiles, that we might receive the promise of the Spirit through faith.

2 Cor 1:20 20 For all the promises of God find their Yes in him. That is why we utter the Amen through him, to the glory of God.

▶ 15:13 Eph 2:12 12 remember that you were at that time separated from Christ, alienated from the commonwealth of Israel, and strangers to the covenants of promise, having no hope and without God in the world.

1 Thes 1:5 5 for our gospel came to you not only in word, but also in power and in the Holy Spirit and with full conviction. You know what kind of men we proved to be among you for your sake.

62. Paul, minister of Christ Jesus to Gentiles

62

Rom 15:14-21

14 I myself am satisfied about you, my brethren, that you yourselves are full of goodness, filled with all knowledge, and able to instruct one another. 15 But on some points I have written to you very boldly by way of reminder, because of the grace given me by God 16 to be a minister of Christ Jesus to the Gentiles in the priestly service of the gospel of God, so that the offering of the Gentiles may be acceptable, sanctified by the Holy Spirit. 17 In Christ Jesus, then, I have reason to be proud of my work for God. 18 For I will not venture to speak of anything except what Christ has wrought through me to win obedience from the Gentiles, by word and deed, 19 by the power of signs and wonders, by the power of the Holy Spirit, so that from Jerusalem and as far round as Illyr′icum I have fully preached the gospel of Christ, 20 thus making it my ambition to preach the gospel, not where Christ has already been named, lest I build on another man's foundation, 21 but as it is written,

"They shall see who have never been told of him,

1 Cor 2:1-5 (§76)

2 When I came to you, brethren, I did not come proclaiming to you the testimonyᶜ of God in lofty words or wisdom. 2 For I decided to know nothing among you except Jesus Christ and him crucified. 3 And I was with you in weakness and in much fear and trembling; 4 and my speech and my message were not in plausible words of wisdom, but in demonstration of the Spirit and of power, 5 that your faith might not rest in the wisdom of men but in the power of God.

1 Cor 3:10-15 (§80)

10 According to the grace of God given to me, like a skilled master builder I laid a foundation, and another man is building upon it. Let each man take care how he builds upon it. 11 For no other foundation can any one lay than that which is laid, which is Jesus Christ. 12 Now if any one builds on the foundation with gold, silver, precious stones, wood, hay, straw—13 each man's work will become manifest; for the Day will disclose it, because it will

and they shall understand who have never heard of him."

2 Cor 10:13-18 (§178)

13 But we will not boast beyond limit, but will keep to the limits God has apportioned us, to reach even to you. 14 For we are not overextending ourselves, as though we did not reach you; we were the first to come all the way to you with the gospel of Christ. 15 We do not boast beyond limit, in other men's labors; but our hope is that as your faith increases, our field among you may be greatly enlarged, 16 so that we may preach the gospel in lands beyond you, without boasting of work already done in another's field. 17 "Let him who boasts, boast of the Lord." 18 For it is not the man who commends himself that is accepted, but the man whom the Lord commends.

2 Cor 12:11-13 (§186)

11 I have been a fool! You forced me

be revealed with fire, and the fire will test what sort of work each one has done. 14 If the work which any man has built on the foundation survives, he will receive a reward. 15 If any man's work is burned up, he will suffer loss, though he himself will be saved, but only as through fire.

to it, for I ought to have been commended by you. For I was not at all inferior to these superlative apostles, even though I am nothing. 12 The signs of a true apostle were performed among you in all patience, with signs and wonders and mighty works. 13 For in what were you less favored than the rest of the churches, except that I myself did not burden you? Forgive me this wrong!

Eph 3:1-13 (§222)

3 For this reason I, Paul, a prisoner for Christ Jesus on behalf of you Gentiles— 2 assuming that you have heard of the stewardship of God's grace that was given to me for you, 3 how the mystery was made known to me by revelation, as I have written briefly. 4 When you read this you can perceive my insight into the mystery of Christ, 5 which was not made known to the sons of men in other generations as it has now been revealed to his holy apostles and prophets by the Spirit; 6 that is, how the Gentiles are fellow heirs, members of the same body, and partakers of the promise in Christ Jesus through the gospel.

7 Of this gospel I was made a minister according to the gift of God's grace which was given me by the working of his power. 8 To me, though I am the very least of all the saints, this grace was given, to preach to the Gentiles the unsearchable riches of Christ, 9 and to make all men see what is the plan of the mystery hidden for ages in God who created all things; 10 that through the church the manifold wisdom of God

▶ 15:16 Acts 9:15 15 But the Lord said to him, "Go, for he is a chosen instrument of mine to carry my name before the Gentiles and kings and the sons of Israel;

▶ 15:18 Acts 21:19 19 After greeting them, he related one by one the things that God had done among the Gentiles through his ministry.

▶ 15:18-19 Acts 15:12 12 And all the assembly kept silence; and they listened to Barnabas and Paul as they related what signs and wonders God had done through them among the Gentiles. ▶ 15:19 Acts 19:11, 11 And God did extraordinary miracles by the hands of Paul,

22:17-21 17 "When I had returned to Jerusalem and was praying in the temple, I fell into a trance 18 and saw him saying to me, 'Make haste and get quickly out of Jerusalem, because they will not accept your testimony about me.' 19 And I said, 'Lord, they themselves know that in every synagogue I imprisoned and beat those who believed in thee. 20 And when the blood of Stephen thy witness was shed, I also was standing by and approving, and keeping the garments of those who killed him.' 21 And he said to me, 'Depart; for I will send you far away to the Gentiles.'"

▶ 15:14-21 1 Cor 11:2 2 I commend you because you remember me in everything and maintain the traditions even as I have delivered them to you.

61

Phm 15-20 (§308)

15 Perhaps this is why he was parted from you for a while, that you might have him back for ever, 16 no longer as a slave but more than a slave, as a beloved brother, especially to me but how much more to you, both in the flesh and in the Lord. 17 So if you consider me your partner, receive him as you would receive me. 18 If he has wronged you at all, or owes you anything, charge that to my account. 19 I, Paul, write this with my own hand, I will repay it—to say nothing of your owing me even your own self. 20 Yes, brother, I want some benefit from you in the Lord. Refresh my heart in Christ.

▶ 15:9 Ps 18:49
49 For this I will extol thee, O Lord,
among the nations,
and sing praises to thy name.

▶ 15:10 Deut 32:43
43 "Praise his people, O you nations;
for he avenges the blood of his servants,
and takes vengeance on his adversaries,
and makes expiation for the land of his people."

▶ 15:11 Ps 117:1
Praise the Lord, all nations!
Extol him, all peoples!

▶ 15:12 Is 11:10
10 In that day the root of Jesse shall stand as an ensign to the peoples; him shall the nations seek, and his dwellings shall be glorious.

62. Paul, minister of Christ Jesus to Gentiles

62

Phil 1:3-11 (§238)

3 I thank my God in all my remembrance of you, 4 always in every prayer of mine for you all making my prayer with joy, 5 thankful for your partnership in the gospel from the first day until now. 6 And I am sure that he who began a good work in you will bring it to completion at the day of Jesus Christ. 7 It is right for me to feel thus about you all, because I hold you in my heart, for you are all partakers with me of grace, both in my imprisonment and in the defense and confirmation of the gospel. 8 For God is my witness, how I yearn for you all with the affection of Christ Jesus. 9 And it is my prayer that your love may abound more and more, with

Eph (cont)

might now be made known to the principalities and powers in the heavenly places. 11 This was according to the eternal purpose which he has realized in Christ Jesus our Lord, 12 in whom we have boldness and confidence of access through our faith in him. 13 So I ask you not to lose heart over what I am suffering for you, which is your glory.

Col 1:3-14 (§257)

3 We always thank God, the Father of our Lord Jesus Christ, when we pray for you, 4 because we have heard of your faith in Christ Jesus and of the love which you have for all the saints, 5 because of the hope laid up for you in heaven. Of this you have heard before in the word of the truth, the gospel 6 which has come to you, as indeed in the whole world it is bearing fruit and growing—so among yourselves, from the day you heard and understood the grace of God in truth, 7 as you learned it from Ep'aphras our beloved fellow

knowledge and all discernment, 10 so that you may approve what is excellent, and may be pure and blameless for the day of Christ, 11 filled with the fruits of righteousness which come through Jesus Christ, to the glory and praise of God.

1 Thes 1:2-10 (§276)

2 We give thanks to God always for you all, constantly mentioning you in our prayers, 3 remembering before our God and Father your work of faith and

servant. He is a faithful minister of Christ on our behalf 8 and has made known to us your love in the Spirit.

9 And so, from the day we heard of it, we have not ceased to pray for you, asking that you may be filled with the knowledge of his will in all spiritual wisdom and understanding, 10 to lead a life worthy of the Lord, fully pleasing to him, bearing fruit in every good work and increasing in the knowledge of God. 11 May you be strengthened with all power, according to his glorious might, for all endurance and patience with joy, 12 giving thanks to the Father, who has qualified us to share in the inheritance of the saints in light. 13 He has delivered us from the dominion of darkness and transferred us to the kingdom of his beloved Son, 14 in whom we have redemption, the forgiveness of sins.

labor of love and steadfastness of hope in our Lord Jesus Christ. 4 For we know, brethren beloved by God, that he has chosen you; 5 for our gospel came to you not only in word, but also in power and in the Holy Spirit and with full conviction. You know what kind of men we proved to be among you for your sake. 6 And you became imitators of us and of the Lord, for you received the word in much affliction, with joy inspired by the Holy Spirit; 7 so that you became an example to all the believers in Macedo'nia and in Acha'ia. 8 For not only has the word of the Lord sounded forth from you in Macedo'nia and Acha'ia, but your faith in God has gone forth everywhere, so that we need not say anything. 9 For they themselves report concerning us what a welcome we had among you, and how you turned to God from idols, to serve a living and true God, 10 and to wait for his Son from heaven, whom he raised from the dead, Jesus who delivers us from the wrath to come.

▶ 15:16 Phil 4:18
18 I have received full payment, and more; I am filled, having received from Epaphrodi'tus the gifts you sent, a fragrant offering, a sacrifice acceptable and pleasing to God.

2 Cor 2:14-17
14 But thanks be to God, who in Christ always leads us in triumph, and through us spreads the fragrance of the knowledge of him everywhere. 15 For we are the aroma of Christ to God among those who are being saved and among those who are perishing, 16 to one a fragrance from death to death, to the other a fragrance from life to life. Who is sufficient for these things? 17 For we are not, like so many, peddlers of God's word; but as men of sincerity, as commissioned by God, in the sight of God we speak in Christ.

Eph 5:2
2 And walk in love, as Christ loved us and gave himself up for us, a fragrant offering and sacrifice to God.

▶ 15:19 2 Thes 2:9
9 The coming of the lawless one by the activity of Satan will be with all power and with pretended signs and wonders,

2 Cor 10:16
16 so that we may preach the gospel in lands beyond you, without boasting of work already done in another's field.

▶ 15:21 Is 52:15
15 so shall he startle many nations;
kings shall shut their mouths because of him;
for that which has not been told them they shall see,
and that which they have not heard they shall understand.

63

Rom 15:22-29

22 This is the reason why I have so often been hindered from coming to you. 23 But now, since I no longer have any room for work in these regions, and since I have longed for many years to come to you, 24 I hope to see you in passing as I go to Spain, and to be sped on my journey there by you, once I have enjoyed your company for a little. 25 At present, however, I am going to Jerusalem with aid for the saints. 26 For Macedo'nia and Acha'ia have been pleased to make some contribution for the poor among the saints at Jerusalem; 27 they were pleased to do it, and indeed they are in debt to them, for if the Gentiles have come to share in their spiritual blessings, they ought also to be of service to them in material blessings. 28 When therefore I have completed this, and have delivered to them what has been raised, I shall go on by way of you to Spain; 29 and I know that when I come to you I shall come in the fulness of the blessing of Christ.

1 Cor 16:1-4 (§138)

16 Now concerning the contribution for the saints: as I directed the churches of Galatia, so you also are to do. 2 On the first day of every week, each of you is to put something aside and store it up, as he may prosper, so that contributions need not be made when I come. 3 And when I arrive, I will send those whom you accredit by letter to carry your gift to Jerusalem. 4 If it seems advisable that I should go also, they will accompany me.

1 Cor 16:5-9 (§139)

5 I will visit you after passing through Macedo'nia, for I intend to pass through Macedo'nia, 6 and perhaps I will stay with you or even spend the winter, so that you may speed me on my journey, wherever I go. 7 For I do not want to see you now just in passing; I hope to spend some time with you, if the Lord permits. 8 But I will stay in Ephesus until Pentecost, 9 for a wide door for effective work has opened to me, and there are many adversaries.

2 Cor 1:15-22 (§149)

15 Because I was sure of this, I wanted to come to you first, so that you might have a double pleasure; 16 I wanted to visit you on my way to Macedo'nia, and to come back to you from Macedo'nia and have you send me on my way to Judea. 17 Was I vacillating when I wanted to do this? Do I make my plans like a worldly man, ready to say Yes and No at once? 18 As surely as God is faithful, our word to you has not been Yes and No. 19 For the Son of God, Jesus Christ, whom we preached among you, Silva'nus and Timothy and I, was not Yes and No; but in him it is always Yes. 20 For all the promises of God find their Yes in him. That is why we utter the Amen through him, to the glory of God. 21 But it is God who establishes us with you in Christ, and has commissioned us; 22 he has put his seal upon us and given us his Spirit in our hearts as a guarantee.

2 Cor 1:23-2:4 (§150)

23 But I call God to witness against me—it was to spare you that I refrained from coming to Corinth. 24 Not that we lord it over your faith; we work with you for your joy, for you stand 2 firm in your faith. 1 For I made up my mind not to make you another painful visit. 2 For if I cause you pain, who is there to make me glad but the one whom I have pained? 3 And I wrote as I did, so that when I came I might not suffer pain from those who should have made me rejoice, for I felt sure of all of you, that my joy would be the joy of you all. 4 For I wrote you out of much affliction and anguish of heart and with many tears, not to cause you pain but to let you know the abundant love that I have for you.

2 Cor 8:1-9:15 (§171-175)

8 We want you to know, brethren, about the grace of God which has

Gal 2:1-10 (§197)

2 Then after fourteen years I went up again to Jerusalem with Barnabas, taking Titus along with me. 2 I went up by revelation; and I laid before them (but privately before those who were of repute) the gospel which I preach among the Gentiles, lest somehow I should be running or had run in vain. 3 But even Titus, who was with me, was not compelled to be circumcised, though he was a Greek. 4 But because of false brethren secretly brought in, who slipped in to spy out our freedom which we have in Christ Jesus, that they might bring us into bondage— 5 to them we did not yield submission even for a moment, that the truth of the gospel might be preserved for you. 6 And from those who were reputed to be something (what they were makes no difference to me; God shows no partiality)—those, I say, who were of repute added nothing to me; 7 but on the contrary, when they saw that I had been entrusted with the gospel to the uncircumcised, just as Peter had been entrusted with the gospel to the circumcised 8 (for he who worked through Peter for the mission to the circumcised worked through me also for the Gentiles), 9 and when they perceived the grace that was given to me, James and Cephas and John, who were reputed to be pillars, gave to me and Barnabas the right hand of fellowship, that we should go to the Gentiles and they to the circumcised; 10 only they would have us remember the poor, which very thing I was eager to do.

been shown in the churches of Macedo'nia, 2 for in a severe test of affliction, their abundance of joy and their extreme poverty have overflowed in a wealth of liberality on their part. 3 For they gave according to their means, as I can testify, and beyond their means, of their own free will, 4 begging us earnestly for the favor of taking part in the relief of the saints— 5 and this, not as we expected, but first they gave themselves to the Lord and to us by the will of God. 6 Accordingly we have urged Titus that as he had already made a beginning, he should also complete among you this gracious work. 7 Now as you excel in everything—in faith, in utterance, in knowledge, in all earnestness, and in your love for us—see that you excel in this gracious work also.

8 I say this not as a command, but to prove by the earnestness of others that your love also is genuine. 9 For you know the grace of our Lord Jesus Christ, that though he was rich, yet for your sake he became poor, so that by his poverty you might become rich. 10 And in this matter I give my advice:

it is best for you now to complete what a year ago you began not only to do but to desire, 11 so that your readiness in desiring it may be matched by your completing it out of what you have. 12 For if the readiness is there, it is acceptable according to what a man has, not according to what he has not. 13 I do not mean that others should be eased and you burdened, 14 but that as a matter of equality your abundance at the present time should supply their want, so that their abundance may supply your want, that there may be equality. 15 As it is written, "He who gathered much had nothing over, and he who gathered little had no lack."

16 But thanks be to God who puts the same earnest care for you into the heart of Titus. 17 For he not only accepted our appeal, but being himself very earnest he is going to you of his own accord. 18 With him we are sending the brother who is famous among all the churches for his preaching of the gospel; 19 and

▶ 15:23 Acts 19:21
21 Now after these events Paul resolved in the Spirit to pass through Macedo'nia and Acha'ia and go to Jerusalem, saying, "After I have been there, I must also see Rome."

▶ 15:25 Acts 15:31   31 And when they read it, they rejoiced at the exhortation.

▶ 15:29 Acts 19:21
21 Now after these events Paul resolved in the Spirit to pass through Macedo'nia and Acha'ia and go to Jerusalem, saying, "After I have been there, I must also see Rome."

64. Strive together with me in your prayers

64

Rom 15:30-33

30 I appeal to you, brethren, by our Lord Jesus Christ and by the love of the Spirit, to strive together with me in your prayers to God on my behalf, 31 that I may be delivered from the unbelievers in Judea, and that my service for Jerusalem may be acceptable to the saints, 32 so that by God's will I may come to you with joy and be refreshed in your company. 33 The God of peace be with you all. Amen.

Eph 6:18-20 (§234)

18 Pray at all times in the Spirit, with all prayer and supplication. To that end keep alert with all perseverance, making supplication for all the saints, 19 and also for me, that utterance may be given me in opening my mouth boldly to proclaim the mystery of the gospel, 20 for which I am an ambassador in chains; that I may declare it boldly, as I ought to speak.

▶ 15:31 Acts 9:13
13 But Anani'as answered, "Lord, I have heard from many about this man, how much evil he has done to thy saints at Jerusalem;

2 Tim 3:11
11 my persecutions, my sufferings, what befell me at Antioch, at Ico'nium, and at Lystra, what persecutions I endured; yet from them all the Lord rescued me.

▶ 15:32 Acts 18:21,   21 but on taking leave of them he said, "I will return to you if God wills," and he set sail from Ephesus.

19:22   22 And having sent into Macedo'nia two of his helpers, Timothy and Eras'tus, he himself stayed in Asia for a while.

▶ 15:30 2 Cor 1:11
11 You also must help us by prayer, so that many will give thanks on our behalf for the blessing granted us in answer to many prayers.

Phil 4:6
6 Have no anxiety about anything, but in everything by prayer and supplication with thanksgiving let your requests be made known to God.

2 Cor (cont)

not only that, but he has been appointed by the churches to travel with us in this gracious work which we are carrying on, for the glory of the Lord and to show our good will. 20 We intend that no one should blame us about this liberal gift which we are administering, 21 for we aim at what is honorable not only in the Lord's sight but also in the sight of men. 22 And with them we are sending our brother whom we have often tested and found earnest in many matters, but who is now more earnest than ever because of his great confidence in you. 23 As for Titus, he is my partner and fellow worker in your service; and as for our brethren, they are messengers of the churches, the glory of Christ. 24 So give proof, before the churches, of your love and of our boasting about you to these men.

9 Now it is superfluous for me to write to you about the offering for the saints, 2 for I know your readiness, of which I boast about you to the people of Macedo′nia, saying that Acha′ia has been ready since last year; and your zeal has stirred up most of them. 3 But I am sending the brethren so that our boasting about you may not prove vain in this case, so that you may be ready, as I said you would be; 4 lest if some Macedo′nians come with me and find that you are not ready, we be humiliated—to say nothing of you—for being so confident. 5 So I thought it necessary to urge the brethren to go on to you before me, and arrange in advance for this gift you have promised, so that it may be ready not as an exaction but as a willing gift.

6 The point is this: he who sows sparingly will also reap sparingly, and he who sows bountifully will also reap bountifully. 7 Each one must do as he has made up his mind, not reluctantly or under compulsion, for God loves a cheerful giver. 8 And God is able to provide you with every blessing in abundance, so that you may always have enough of everything and may provide in abundance for every good work. 9 As it is written,

"He scatters abroad, he gives to the poor;
his righteousness endures for ever."

10 He who supplies seed to the sower and bread for food will supply and multiply your resources and increase the harvest of your righteousness. 11 You will be enriched in every way for great generosity, which through us will produce thanksgiving to God; 12 for the rendering of this service not only supplies the wants of the saints but also overflows in many thanksgivings to God. 13 Under the test of this service, you will glorify God by your obedience in acknowledging the gospel of Christ, and by the generosity of your contribution for them and for all others; 14 while they long for you and pray for you, because of the surpassing grace of God in you. 15 Thanks be to God for his inexpressible gift!

2 Cor 12:14-13:4 (§187-189)

14 Here for the third time I am ready to come to you. And I will not be a burden, for I seek not what is yours but you; for children ought not to lay up for their parents, but parents for their children. 15 I will most gladly spend and be spent for your souls. If I love you the more, am I to be loved the less? 16 But granting that I myself did not burden you, I was crafty, you say, and got the better of you by guile. 17 Did I take advantage of you through any of those whom I sent to you? 18 I urged Titus to go, and sent the brother with him. Did Titus take advantage of you? Did we not act in the same spirit? Did we not take the same steps?

1 Thes 2:17-20 (§280)

17 But since we were bereft of you, brethren, for a short time, in person not in heart, we endeavored the more eagerly and with great desire to see you face to face; 18 because we wanted to come to you—I, Paul, again and again—but Satan hindered us. 19 For what is our hope or joy or crown of boasting before our Lord Jesus at his coming? Is it not you? 20 For you are our glory and joy.

19 Have you been thinking all along that we have been defending ourselves before you? It is in the sight of God that we have been speaking in Christ, and all for your upbuilding, beloved. 20 For I fear that perhaps I may come and find you not what I wish, and that you may find me not what you wish; that perhaps there may be quarreling, jealousy, anger, selfishness, slander, gossip, conceit, and disorder. 21 I fear that when I come again my God may humble me before you, and I may have to mourn over many of those who sinned before and have not repented of the impurity, immorality, and licentiousness which they have practiced.

13 This is the third time I am coming to you. Any charge must be sustained by the evidence of two or three witnesses. 2 I warned those who sinned before and all the others, and I warn them now while absent, as I did when present on my second visit, that if I come again I will not spare them—3 since you desire proof that Christ is speaking in me. He is not weak in dealing with you, but is powerful in you. 4 For he was crucified in weakness, but lives by the power of God. For we are weak in him, but in dealing with you we shall live with him by the power of God.

Phm 21-22 (§309)

21 Confident of your obedience, I write to you, knowing that you will do even more than I say. 22 At the same time, prepare a guest room for me, for I am hoping through your prayers to be granted to you.

63

▶ 15:22 1:13 13 I want you to know, brethren, that I have often intended to come to you (but thus far have been prevented), in order that I may reap some harvest among you as well as among the rest of the Gentiles.

▶ 15:23 1 Thes 3:6 6 But now that Timothy has come to us from you, and has brought us the good news of your faith and love and reported that you always remember us kindly and long to see us, as we long to see you—

▶ 15:27 1 Cor 9:11 11 If we have sown spiritual good among you, is it too much if we reap your material benefits?

▶ 15:29 (blessing) add of the gospel: Sc Koine Lect vg(clem) syr(pes har) Chrysostom

64. Strive together with me in your prayers

Col 4:2-4 (§269)

2 Continue steadfastly in prayer, being watchful in it with thanksgiving; 3 and pray for us also, that God may open to us a door for the word, to declare the mystery of Christ, on account of which I am in prison, 4 that I may make it clear, as I ought to speak.

1 Thes 5:25 (§290)

25 Brethren, pray for us.

2 Thes 3:1-5 (§299)

3 Finally, brethren, pray for us, that the word of the Lord may speed on and triumph, as it did among you, 2 and that we may be delivered from wicked and evil men; for not all have faith. 3 But the Lord is faithful; he will strengthen you and guard you from evil. 4 And we have confidence in the Lord about you, that you are doing and will do the things which we command. 5 May the Lord direct your hearts to the love of God and to the steadfastness of Christ.

‡ 2 Thes 3:16 (§302)

16 Now may the Lord of peace himself give you peace at all times in all ways. The Lord be with you all.

64

▶ 15:31 Gal 2:10 10 only they would have us remember the poor, which very thing I was eager to do.

▶ 15:33 (Amen) omit Amen: AG it(few); omit Amen and add 16:25-27 here only: p46

65

Rom 16:1-2

16 I commend to you our sister Phoebe, a deaconess of the church at Cen′chre-ae, 2 that you may receive her in the Lord as befits the saints, and help her in whatever she may require from you, for she has been a helper of many and of myself as well.

1 Cor 16:10-12 (§140)

10 When Timothy comes, see that you put him at ease among you, for he is doing the work of the Lord, as I am. 11 So let no one despise him. Speed him on his way in peace, that he may return to me; for I am expecting him with the brethren.

12 As for our brother Apol′los, I strongly urged him to visit you with the other brethren, but it was not at all his will to come now. He will come when he has opportunity.

1 Cor 16:15-18 (§142)

15 Now, brethren, you know that the household of Steph′anas were the first converts in Acha′ia, and they have devoted themselves to the service of the saints; 16 I urge you to be subject to such men and to every fellow worker and laborer. 17 I rejoice at the coming of Steph′anas and Fortuna′tus and Acha′-icus, because they have made up for your absence; 18 for they refreshed my spirit as well as yours. Give recognition to such men.

2 Cor 3:1-3 (§154)

3 Are we beginning to commend ourselves again? Or do we need, as some do, letters of recommendation to you, or from you? 2 You yourselves are our letter of recommendation, written on your hearts, to be known and read by all men; 3 and you show that you are a letter from Christ delivered by us, written not with ink but with the Spirit of the living God, not on tablets of stone but on tablets of human hearts.

2 Cor 8:16-24 (§173)

16 But thanks be to God who puts the same earnest care for you into the heart of Titus. 17 For he not only accepted our appeal, but being himself very earnest he is going to you of his own accord. 18 With him we are sending the brother who is famous among all the churches for his preaching of the gospel; 19 and not only that, but he has been appointed by the churches to travel with us in this gracious work which we are carrying on, for the glory of the Lord and to show our good will. 20 We intend that no one should blame us about this liberal gift which we are administering, 21 for we

aim at what is honorable not only in the Lord's sight but also in the sight of men. 22And with them we are sending our brother whom we have often tested and found earnest in many matters, but who is now more earnest than ever because of his great confidence in you. 23As for Titus, he is my partner and fellow worker in your service; and as for our brethren, they are messengers of the churches, the glory of Christ. 24 So give proof, before the churches, of your love and of our boasting about you to these men.

▶16:1 Acts 18:18
18 After this Paul stayed many days longer, and then took leave of the brethren and sailed for Syria, and with him Priscilla and Aquila. At Cen′chre-ae he cut his hair, for he had a vow.

▶16:1-2 *cf. Phil 4:2-3

66. Greetings

66

Rom 16:3-16

3 Greet Prisca and Aquila, my fellow workers in Christ Jesus, 4 who risked their necks for my life, to whom not only I but also all the churches of the Gentiles give thanks; 5 greet also the church in their house. Greet my beloved Epae′netus, who was the first convert in Asia for Christ. 6 Greet Mary, who has worked hard among you. 7 Greet Androni′cus and Ju′nias, my kinsmen and my fellow prisoners; they are men of note among the apostles, and they were in Christ before me. 8 Greet Amplia′tus, my beloved in the Lord. 9 Greet Urba′nus, our fellow worker in Christ, and my beloved Stachys. 10 Greet Apel′les, who is approved in Christ. Greet those who belong to the family of Aristobu′lus. 11 Greet my kinsman Hero′dion. Greet those in the Lord who belong to the family of Narcis′sus. 12 Greet those workers in the Lord, Tryphae′na and Trypho′sa. Greet the beloved Persis, who has worked hard in the Lord. 13 Greet Rufus, eminent in the Lord, also his mother and mine. 14 Greet Asyn′critus, Phlegon, Hermes, Pat′robas, Hermas,

1 Cor 16:19-20 (§143)

19 The churches of Asia send greetings. Aquila and Prisca, together with the church in their house, send you hearty greetings in the Lord. 20All the brethren send greetings. Greet one another with a holy kiss.

and the brethren who are with them. 15 Greet Philol′ogus, Julia, Nereus and his sister, and Olym′pas, and all the saints who are with them. 16 Greet one another with a holy kiss. All the churches of Christ greet you.

Rom 16:21-23 (§69)

21 Timothy, my fellow worker, greets you; so do Lucius and Jason and Sosip′ater, my kinsmen.

22 I Tertius, the writer of this letter, greet you in the Lord.

23 Ga′ius, who is host to me and to the whole church, greets you. Eras′tus, the city treasurer, and our brother Quartus, greet you.

2 Cor 13:11-13 (§191)

11 Finally, brethren, farewell. Mend your ways, heed my appeal, agree with one another, live in peace, and the God of love and peace will be with you. 12 Greet one another with a holy kiss. 13All the saints greet you.

▶ 16:3 Acts 18:2
2And he found a Jew named Aquila, a native of Pontus, lately come from Italy with his wife Priscilla, because Claudius had commanded all the Jews to leave Rome. And he went to see them;

▶16:4 Acts 15:26
26men who have risked their lives for the sake of our Lord Jesus Christ.

▶16:3 Acts 18:18
18 After this Paul stayed many days longer, and then took leave of the brethren and sailed for Syria, and with him Priscilla and Aquila. At Cen′chre-ae he cut his hair, for he had a vow.

Phil 2:19-24 (§245)

19 I hope in the Lord Jesus to send Timothy to you soon, so that I may be cheered by news of you. 20 I have no one like him, who will be genuinely anxious for your welfare. 21 They all look after their own interests, not those of Jesus Christ. 22 But Timothy's worth you know, how as a son with a father he has served with me in the gospel. 23 I hope therefore to send him just as soon as I see how it will go with me; 24 and I trust in the Lord that shortly I myself shall come also.

Phil 2:25-3:1 (§246)

25 I have thought it necessary to send to you Epaphrodi'tus my brother and fellow worker and fellow soldier, and your messenger and minister to my need, 26 for he has been longing for you all, and has been distressed because you heard that he was ill. 27 Indeed he was ill, near to death. But God had mercy on him, and not only on him but on me also, lest I should have sorrow upon sorrow. 28 I am the more eager to send him, therefore, that you may rejoice at seeing him again, and that I may be less anxious. 29 So receive him in the Lord with all joy; and honor such men, 30 for he nearly died for the work of Christ, risking his life to complete your service to me.

3 Finally, my brethren, rejoice in the Lord. To write the same things to you is not irksome to me, and is safe for you.

Phm 8-20 (§307-308)

8 Accordingly, though I am bold enough in Christ to command you to do what is required, 9 yet for love's sake I prefer to appeal to you—I, Paul, an ambassador and now a prisoner also for Christ Jesus—10 I appeal to you for my child, Ones'imus, whose father I have become in my imprisonment. 11 (Formerly he was useless to you, but now he is indeed useful to you and to me.) 12 I am sending him back to you, sending my very heart. 13 I would have been glad to keep him with me, in order that he might serve me on your behalf during my imprisonment for the gospel; 14 but I preferred to do nothing without your consent in order that your goodness might not be by compulsion but of your own free will. 15 Perhaps this is why he was parted from you for a while, that you might have him back for ever, 16 no longer as a slave but more than a slave, as a beloved brother, especially to me but how much more to you, both in the flesh and in the Lord. 17 So if you consider me your partner, receive him as you would receive me. 18 If he has wronged you at all, or owes you anything, charge that to my account. 19 I, Paul, write this with my own hand, I will repay it—to say nothing of your owing me even your own self. 20 Yes, brother, I want some benefit from you in the Lord. Refresh my heart in Christ.

66. Greetings

Phil 4:21-22 (§254)

21 Greet every saint in Christ Jesus. The brethren who are with me greet you. 22 All the saints greet you, especially those of Caesar's household.

Col 4:10-15 (§272)

10 Aristar'chus my fellow prisoner greets you, and Mark the cousin of Barnabas (concerning whom you have received instructions—if he comes to you, receive him), 11 and Jesus who is called Justus. These are the only men of the circumcision among my fellow workers for the kingdom of God, and they have been a comfort to me. 12 Ep'aphras, who is one of yourselves, a servant of Christ Jesus, greets you, always remembering you earnestly in his prayers, that you may stand mature and fully assured in all the will of God. 13 For I bear him witness that he has worked hard for you and for those in La-odice'a and in Hi-erap'olis. 14 Luke the beloved physician and Demas greet you. 15 Give my greetings to the brethren at La-odice'a, and to Nympha and the church in her house.

1 Thes 5:26 (§291)

26 Greet all the brethren with a holy kiss.

Phm 23-24 (§310)

23 Ep'aphras, my fellow prisoner in Christ Jesus, sends greetings to you, 24 and so do Mark, Aristar'chus, Demas, and Luke, my fellow workers.

65

66

67

Rom 16:17-20a

17 I appeal to you, brethren, to take note of those who create dissensions and difficulties, in opposition to the doctrine which you have been taught; avoid them. 18 For such persons do not serve our Lord Christ, but their own appetites, and by fair and flattering words they deceive the hearts of the simple-minded. 19 For while your obedience is known to all, so that I rejoice over you, I would have you wise as to what is good and guileless as to what is evil; 20 then the God of peace will soon crush Satan under your feet.

1 Cor 5:1-5 (§87)

5 It is actually reported that there is immorality among you, and of a kind that is not found even among pagans; for a man is living with his father's wife. 2 And you are arrogant! Ought you not rather to mourn? Let him who has done this be removed from among you.

3 For though absent in body I am present in spirit, and as if present, I have already pronounced judgment 4 in the name of the Lord Jesus on the man who has done such a thing. When you are assembled, and my spirit is present, with the power of our Lord Jesus, 5 you are to deliver this man to Satan for the destruction of the flesh, that his spirit may be saved in the day of the Lord Jesus.

1 Cor 5:9-13 (§89)

9 I wrote to you in my letter not to associate with immoral men; 10 not at all meaning the immoral of this world, or the greedy and robbers, or idolaters, since then you would need to go out of the world. 11 But rather I wrote to you not to associate with any one who bears

2 Cor 6:14-7:1 (§167)

14 Do not be mismated with unbelievers. For what partnership have righteousness and iniquity? Or what fellowship has light with darkness? 15 What accord has Christ with Be'lial? Or what has a believer in common with an unbeliever? 16 What agreement has the temple of God with idols? For we are the temple of the living God; as God said,

"I will live in them and move among them,
and I will be their God,
and they shall be my people.
17 Therefore come out from them,
and be separate from them, says the Lord,
and touch nothing unclean;

then I will welcome you,
18 and I will be a father to you,
and you shall be my sons and daughters,
says the Lord Almighty."

7 Since we have these promises, beloved, let us cleanse ourselves from every defilement of body and spirit, and make holiness perfect in the fear of God.

2 Cor 11:12-15 (§181)

12 And what I do I will continue to do, in order to undermine the claim of those who would like to claim that in their boasted mission they work on the same terms as we do. 13 For such men are false apostles, deceitful workmen, disguising themselves as apostles of Christ. 14 And no wonder, for even Satan disguises himself as an angel of light. 15 So it is not strange if his servants also disguise themselves as servants of righteousness. Their end will correspond to their deeds.

the name of brother if he is guilty of immorality or greed, or is an idolater, reviler, drunkard, or robber—not even to eat with such a one. 12 For what have I to do with judging outsiders? Is it not those inside the church whom you are to judge? 13 God judges those outside. "Drive out the wicked person from among you."

▶ 16:17 Acts 19:9
" but when some were stubborn and disbelieved, speaking evil of the Way before the congregation, he withdrew from them, taking the disciples with him, and argued daily in the hall of Tyrannus.

Tit 3:10 10 As for a man who is factious, after admonishing him once or twice, have nothing more to do with him,

Acts 20:1-2
After the uproar ceased, Paul sent for the disciples and having exhorted them took leave of them and departed for Macedo'nia. 2 When he had gone through these parts and had given them much encouragement, he came to Greece.

1 Tim 1:3,
3 As I urged you when I was going to Macedo'nia, remain at Ephesus that you may charge certain persons not to teach any different doctrine,

6:3-5
one teaches otherwise and does not agree with the sound words of our Lord Jesus Christ and the teaching which accords with godliness, 4 he is puffed up with conceit, he knows nothing; he has a morbid craving for controversy and for disputes about words, which produce envy, dissension, slander, base

3 If any

suspicions, 5 and wrangling among men who are depraved in mind and bereft of the truth, imagining that godliness is a means of gain.

68. Grace

68

Rom 16:20b
The grace of our Lord Jesus Christ be with you.

1 Cor 16:23-24 (§145)
23 The grace of the Lord Jesus be with you. 24 My love be with you all in Christ Jesus. Amen.

2 Cor 13:14 (§192)
14 The grace of the Lord Jesus Christ and the love of God and the fellowship of the Holy Spirit be with you all.

Gal 6:18 (§217)
18 The grace of our Lord Jesus Christ be with your spirit, brethren. Amen.

Eph 6:23-24 (§236)
23 Peace be to the brethren, and love with faith, from God the Father and the Lord Jesus Christ. 24 Grace be with all who love our Lord Jesus Christ with love undying.

Phil 3:17-21 (§249)

17 Brethren, join in imitating me, and mark those who so live as you have an example in us. 18 For many, of whom I have often told you and now tell you even with tears, live as enemies of the cross of Christ. 19 Their end is destruction, their god is the belly, and they glory in their shame, with minds set on earthly things. 20 But our commonwealth is in heaven, and from it we await a Savior, the Lord Jesus Christ, 21 who will change our lowly body to be like his glorious body, by the power which enables him even to subject all things to himself.

1 Thes 2:1-8 (§277)

2 For you yourselves know, brethren, that our visit to you was not in vain; 2 but though we had already suffered and been shamefully treated at Philippi, as you know, we had courage in our God to declare to you the gospel of God in the face of great opposition. 3 For our appeal does not spring from error or uncleanness, nor is it made with guile; 4 but just as we have been approved by God to be entrusted with the gospel, so we speak, not to please men, but to please God who tests our hearts. 5 For we never used either words of flattery, as you know, or a cloak for greed, as God is witness; 6 nor did we seek glory from men, whether from you or from others, though we might have made demands as apostles of Christ. 7 But we were gentle among you, like a nurse taking care of her children. 8 So, being affectionately desirous of you, we were ready to share with you not only the gospel of God but also our own selves, because you had become very dear to us.

▶ 16:18 Gal 1:10

10 Am I now seeking the favor of men, or of God? Or am I trying to please men? If I were still pleasing men, I should not be a servant of Christ.

▶ 16:19 Col 2:4

4 I say this in order that no one may delude you with beguiling speech.

1 Cor 14:20

20 Brethren, do not be children in your thinking; be babes in evil, but in thinking be mature.

▶ 16:20 1 Cor 15:24-28

24 Then comes the end, when he delivers the kingdom to God the Father after destroying every rule and every authority and power. 25 For he must reign until he has put all his enemies under his feet. 26 The last enemy to be destroyed is death. 27 "For God has put all things in subjection under his feet." But when it says, "All things are put in subjection under him," it is plain that he is excepted who put all things under him. 28 When all things are subjected to him, then the Son himself will also be subjected to him who put all things under him, that God may be everything to every one.

1 Thes 1:9-10 9 For they themselves report concerning us what a welcome we had among you, and how you turned to God from idols, to serve a living and true God, 10 and to wait for his Son from heaven, whom he raised from the dead, Jesus who delivers us from the wrath to come.

68. Grace

Phil 4:23 (§255)

23 The grace of the Lord Jesus Christ be with your spirit.

Col 4:18b (§274)

Remember my fetters. Grace be with you.

1 Thes 5:28 (§293)

28 The grace of our Lord Jesus Christ be with you.

2 Thes 3:18 (§304,

18 The grace of our Lord Jesus Christ be with you all.

Phm 25 (§311)

25 The grace of the Lord Jesus Christ be with your spirit.

▶ 16:20b (you) omit Christ: p⁴⁶SB; omit 16:20b entirely: DG it(some)

69

Rom 16:21-23

21 Timothy, my fellow worker, greets you; so do Lucius and Jason and Sosip′ater, my kinsmen.
22 I Tertius, the writer of this letter, greet you in the Lord.
23 Ga′ius, who is host to me and to the whole church, greets you. Eras′tus, the city treasurer, and our brother Quartus, greet you.

Rom 16:3-16 (§66)

3 Greet Prisca and Aquila, my fellow workers in Christ Jesus, 4 who risked their necks for my life, to whom not only I but also all the churches of the Gentiles give thanks; 5 greet also the church in their house. Greet my beloved Epae′netus, who was the first convert in Asia for Christ. 6 Greet Mary, who has worked hard among you. 7 Greet Androni′cus and Ju′nias, my kinsmen and my fellow prisoners; they are men of note among the apostles, and they were in Christ before me. 8 Greet Amplia′tus, my beloved in the Lord. 9 Greet Urba′nus, our fellow worker in Christ, and my beloved Stachys. 10 Greet Apel′les, who is approved in

1 Cor 16:19-20 (§143)

19 The churches of Asia send greetings. Aquila and Prisca, together with the church in their house, send you hearty greetings in the Lord. 20All the brethren send greetings. Greet one another with a holy kiss.

Christ. Greet those who belong to the family of Aristobu′lus. 11 Greet my kinsman Hero′dion. Greet those in the Lord who belong to the family of Narcis′sus. 12 Greet those workers in the Lord, Tryphae′na and Trypho′sa. Greet the beloved Persis, who has worked hard in the Lord. 13 Greet Rufus, eminent in the Lord, also his mother and mine. 14 Greet Asyn′critus, Phlegon, Hermes, Pat′robas, Hermas, and the brethren who are with them. 15 Greet Philol′ogus, Julia, Nereus and his sister, and Olym′pas, and all the saints who are with them. 16 Greet one another with a holy kiss. All the churches of Christ greet you.

2 Cor 13:11-13 (§191)

11 Finally, brethren, farewell. Mend your ways, heed my appeal, agree with one another, live in peace, and the God of love and peace will be with you. 12 Greet one another with a holy kiss. 13All the saints greet you.

▶16:21 Acts 13:1,
Now in the church at Antioch there were prophets and teachers, Barnabas, Simeon who was called Niger, Lucius of Cyre′ne, Man′a-en a member of the court of Herod the tetrarch, and Saul.

16:1
And he came also to Derbe and to Lystra. A disciple was there, named Timothy, the son of a Jewish woman who was a believer; but his father was a Greek.

▶16:23 Acts 19:29, 29 So the city was filled with the confusion; and they rushed together into the theater, dragging with them Ga′ius and Aristar′chus, Macedo′nians who were Paul's companions in travel.

20:4 4 Sop′ate. of Beroe′a, the son of Pyrrhus, accompanied him; and of the Thessalo′nians, Aristar′chus and Secun′dus; and Ga′ius of Derbe, and Timothy; and the Asians, Tych′icus and Troph′imus.

70. To him be glory

70

Rom 16:25-27

25 Now to him who is able to strengthen you according to my gospel and the preaching of Jesus Christ, according to the revelation of the mystery which was kept secret for long ages 26 but is now disclosed and through the prophetic writings is made known to all nations, according to the command of the eternal God, to bring about the obedience of faith—27 to the only wise God be glory for evermore through Jesus Christ! Amen.

Eph 3:20-21 (§224)

20 Now to him who by the power at work within us is able to do far more abundantly than all that we ask or think, 21 to him be glory in the church and in Christ Jesus to all generations, for ever and ever. Amen.

Phil 4:21-22 (§254)

21 Greet every saint in Christ Jesus. The brethren who are with me greet you. 22 All the saints greet you, especially those of Caesar's household.

Col 4:10-15 (§272)

10 Aristar'chus my fellow prisoner greets you, and Mark the cousin of Barnabas (concerning whom you have received instructions—if he comes to you, receive him), 11 and Jesus who is called Justus. These are the only men of the circumcision among my fellow workers for the kingdom of God, and they have been a comfort to me. 12 Ep'aphras, who is one of yourselves, a servant of Christ Jesus, greets you, always remembering you earnestly in his prayers, that you may stand mature and fully assured in all the will of God. 13 For I bear him witness that he has worked hard for you and for those in La-odice'a and in Hi-erap'olis. 14 Luke the beloved physician and Demas greet you. 15 Give my greetings to the brethren at La-odice'a, and to Nympha and the church in her house.

1 Thes 5:26 (§291)

26 Greet all the brethren with a holy kiss.

Phm 23-24 (§310)

23 Ep'aphras, my fellow prisoner in Christ Jesus, sends greetings to you, 24 and so do Mark, Aristar'chus, Demas, and Luke, my fellow workers.

69

▶ 16:23 (you) *add verse 24 here* (The grace of our Lord Jesus Christ be with you all. Amen): Koine Lect it (some) vg(clem) syr(har) Theodoret

70. To him be glory

Col 1:24-2:3 (§260)

24 Now I rejoice in my sufferings for your sake, and in my flesh I complete what is lacking in Christ's afflictions for the sake of his body, that is, the church, 25 of which I became a minister according to the divine office which was given to me for you, to make the word of God fully known, 26 the mystery hidden for ages and generations but now made manifest to his saints. 27 To them God chose to make known how great among the Gentiles are the riches of the glory of this mystery, which is Christ in you, the hope of glory. 28 Him we proclaim, warning every man and teaching every man in all wisdom, that we may present every man mature in Christ. 29 For this I toil, striving with all the energy which he mightily inspires within me.

2 For I want you to know how greatly I strive for you, and for those at La-odice'a, and for all who have not seen my face, 2 that their hearts may be encouraged as they are knit together in love, to have all the riches of assured understanding and the knowledge of God's mystery, of Christ, 3 in whom are hid all the treasures of wisdom and knowledge.

70

▶ 16:27 (Amen) *read 16:25-27 here and following 14:23:* AP; *omit 16:25-27 here and add following 15:33 only:* p⁴⁶; *omit 16:25-27:* F(Greek)G few others; *text:* p⁶¹ SBCD   it(some) vg syr(pes) cop Clement Origen(Latin)

71. Paul to the church at Corinth

Rom 1:1-7 (§1)	1 Cor 1:1-3	2 Cor 1:1-2 (§146)	Gal 1:1-5 (§193)	Eph 1:1-2 (§218)
71 **1** Paul, a servant of Jesus Christ, called to be an apostle, set apart for the gospel of God ² which he promised beforehand through his prophets in the holy scriptures, ³ the gospel concerning his Son, who was descended from David according to the flesh ⁴ and designated Son of God in power according to the Spirit of holiness by his resurrection from the dead, Jesus Christ our Lord, ⁵ through whom we have received grace and apostleship to bring about the obedience of faith for the sake of his name among all the nations, ⁶ including yourselves who are called to belong to Jesus Christ; 7 To all God's beloved in Rome, who are called to be saints: Grace to you and peace from God our Father and the Lord Jesus Christ.	**1** Paul, called by the will of God to be an apostle of Christ Jesus, and our brother Sos′thenes, 2 To the church of God which is at Corinth, to those sanctified in Christ Jesus, called to be saints together with all those who in every place call on the name of our Lord Jesus Christ, both their Lord and ours: 3 Grace to you and peace from God our Father and the Lord Jesus Christ.	**1** Paul, an apostle of Christ Jesus by the will of God, and Timothy our brother. To the church of God which is at Corinth, with all the saints who are in the whole of Acha′ia: 2 Grace to you and peace from God our Father and the Lord Jesus Christ.	**1** Paul an apostle—not from men nor through man, but through Jesus Christ and God the Father, who raised him from the dead— ² and all the brethren who are with me, To the churches of Galatia: 3 Grace to you and peace from God the Father and our Lord Jesus Christ, ⁴ who gave himself for our sins to deliver us from the present evil age, according to the will of our God and Father; ⁵ to whom be the glory for ever and ever. Amen.	**1** Paul, an apostle of Christ Jesus by the will of God, To the saints who are also faithful in Christ Jesus: 2 Grace to you and peace from God our Father and the Lord Jesus Christ.

▶1:1 Acts 18:17
¹⁷And they all seized Sos′thenes, the ruler of the synagogue, and beat him in front of the tribunal. But Gallio paid no attention to this.

▶1:2 Acts 2:21,
²¹ And it shall be that whoever calls on the name of the Lord shall be saved.'

9:21,
²¹And all who heard him were amazed, and said, "Is not this the man who made havoc in Jerusalem of those who called on this name? And he has come here for this purpose, to bring them bound before the chief priests."

14 ¹⁴ and here he has authority from the chief priests to bind all who call upon thy name."

Acts 18:1
After this he left Athens and went to Corinth.

72. I give thanks to God

Rom 1:8-15 (§2)	1 Cor 1:4-9
72 8 First, I thank my God through Jesus Christ for all of you, because your faith is proclaimed in all the world. ⁹ For God is my witness, whom I serve with my spirit in the gospel of his Son, that without ceasing I mention you always in my prayers, ¹⁰ asking that somehow by God's will I may now at last succeed in coming to you. ¹¹ For I long to see you, that I may impart to you some spiritual gift to strengthen you, ¹² that is, that we may be mutually encouraged by each other's faith, both yours and mine. ¹³ I want you to know, brethren, that I have often intended to come to you (but thus far have been prevented), in order that I may reap some harvest among you as well as among the rest of the Gentiles. ¹⁴ I am under obligation both to Greeks and to barbarians, both to the wise and to the foolish: ¹⁵ so I am eager to preach the gospel to you also who are in Rome.	4 I give thanks to God always for you because of the grace of God which was given you in Christ Jesus, ⁵ that in every way you were enriched in him with all speech and all knowledge— ⁶ even as the testimony to Christ was confirmed among you— ⁷ so that you are not lacking in any spiritual gift, as you wait for the revealing of our Lord Jesus Christ; ⁸ who will sustain you to the end, guiltless in the day of our Lord Jesus Christ. ⁹ God is faithful, by whom you were called into the fellowship of his Son, Jesus Christ our Lord.

▶1:6 1 Tim 2:6 ⁶ who gave himself as a ransom for all, the testimony to which was borne at the proper time.

2 Tim 1:8,
8 Do not be ashamed then of testifying to our Lord, nor of me his prisoner, but share in suffering for the gospel in the power of God,

12 ¹² and therefore I suffer as I do. But I am not ashamed, for I know whom I have believed, and I am sure that he is able to guard until that Day what has been entrusted to me.

▶1:6 Acts 18:5
5 When Silas and Timothy arrived from Macedo′nia, Paul was occupied with preaching, testifying to the Jews that the Christ was Jesus.

▶1:9 2 Tim 2:13
¹³ if we are faithless, he remains faithful— for he cannot deny himself.

cf.* 12:1-11

▶1:5 Rom 15:14
14 I myself am satisfied about you, my brethren, that you yourselves are full of goodness, filled with all knowledge, and able to instruct one another.

▶ 1:7 Rom 12:6a
⁶ Having gifts that differ according to the grace given to us, let us use them:

71

Phil 1:1-2 (§237)

1 Paul and Timothy, servants of Christ Jesus,

To all the saints in Christ Jesus who are at Philippi, with the bishops and deacons:

2 Grace to you and peace from God our Father and the Lord Jesus Christ.

Col 1:1-2 (§256)

1 Paul, an apostle of Christ Jesus by the will of God, and Timothy our brother,

2 To the saints and faithful brethren in Christ at Colos′sae:

Grace to you and peace from God our Father.

1 Thes 1:1 (§275)

1 Paul, Silva′nus, and Timothy,

To the church of the Thessalo′-nians in God the Father and the Lord Jesus Christ:

Grace to you and peace.

2 Thes 1:1-2 (§294)

1 Paul, Silva′nus, and Timothy,

To the church of the Thessalo′-nians in God our Father and the Lord Jesus Christ:

2 Grace to you and peace from God the Father and the Lord Jesus Christ.

Phm 1-3 (§305)

1 Paul, a prisoner for Christ Jesus, and Timothy our brother,

To Phile′mon our beloved fellow worker 2 and Ap′phia our sister and Archip′pus our fellow soldier, and the church in your house:

3 Grace to you and peace from God our Father and the Lord Jesus Christ.

---

2 Tim 2:22

22 So shun youthful passions and aim at righteousness, faith, love, and peace, along with those who call upon the Lord from a pure heart.

▶1:2 1:30-31

30 He is the source of your life in Christ Jesus, whom God made our wisdom, our righteousness and sanctification and redemption; 31 therefore, as it is written, "Let him who boasts, boast of the Lord."

6:11

11And such were some of you. But you were washed, you were sanctified, you were justified in the name of the Lord Jesus Christ and in the Spirit of our God.

7:14

14 For the unbelieving husband is consecrated through his wife, and the unbelieving wife is consecrated through her husband. Otherwise, your children would be unclean, but as it is they are holy.

72. I give thanks to God

72

Phil 1:3-11 (§238)

3 I thank my God in all my remembrance of you, 4 always in every prayer of mine for you all making my prayer with joy, 5 thankful for your partnership in the gospel from the first day until now. 6And I am sure that he who began a good work in you will bring it to completion at the day of Jesus Christ. 7 It is right for me to feel thus about you all, because I hold you in my heart, for you are all partakers with me of grace, both in my imprisonment and in the defense and confirmation of the gospel. 8 For God is my witness, how I yearn for you all with the affection of Christ Jesus. 9And it is my prayer that your love may abound more and more, with knowledge and all discernment, 10 so that you may approve what is excellent, and may be pure and blameless for the day of Christ, 11 filled with the fruits of righteousness which come through Jesus Christ, to the glory and praise of God.

Col 1:3-14 (§257)

3 We always thank God, the Father of our Lord Jesus Christ, when we pray for you, 4 because we have heard of your faith in Christ Jesus and of the love which you have for all the saints, 5 because of the hope laid up for you in heaven. Of this you have heard before in the word of the truth, the gospel 6 which has come to you, as indeed in the whole world it is bearing fruit and growing—so among yourselves, from the day you heard and understood the grace of God in truth, 7 as you learned it from Ep′aphras our beloved fellow servant. He is a faithful minister of Christ on our behalf 8 and has made known to us your love in the Spirit.

9 And so, from the day we heard of it, we have not ceased to pray for you, asking that you may be filled with the knowledge of his will in all spiritual wisdom and understanding, 10 to lead a life worthy of the Lord, fully pleasing to him, bearing fruit in every good work and increasing in the knowledge of God, 11May you be strengthened with all power, according to his glorious might, for all endurance and patience with joy, 12 giving thanks to the Father, who has qualified us to share in the inheritance of the saints in light. 13 He has delivered us from the dominion of darkness and transferred us to the kingdom of his beloved Son, 14 in whom we have redemption, the forgiveness of sins.

1 Thes 1:2-10 (§276)

2 We give thanks to God always for you all, constantly mentioning you in our prayers, 3 remembering before our God and Father your work of faith and labor of love and steadfastness of hope in our Lord Jesus Christ. 4 For we know, brethren beloved by God, that he has chosen you; 5 for our gospel came to you not only in word, but also in power and in the Holy Spirit and with full conviction. You know what kind of men we proved to be among you for your sake. 6And you became imitators of us and of the Lord, for you received the word in much affliction, with joy inspired by the Holy Spirit; 7 so that you became an example to all the believers in Macedo′nia and in Acha′ia. 8 For not only has the word of the Lord sounded forth from you in Macedo′nia and Acha′ia, but your faith in God has gone forth everywhere, so that we need not say anything. 9 For they themselves report concerning us what a welcome we had among you, and how you turned to God from idols, to serve a living and true God, 10 and to wait for his Son from heaven, whom he raised from the dead, Jesus who delivers us from the wrath to come.

2 Thes 1:3-12 (§295)

3 We are bound to give thanks to God always for you, brethren, as is fitting, because your faith is growing abundantly, and the love of every one of you for one another is increasing. 4 Therefore we ourselves boast of you in the churches of God for your steadfastness and faith in all your persecutions and in the afflictions which you are enduring.

5 This is evidence of the righteous judgment of God, that you may be made worthy of the kingdom of God, for which you are suffering—6 since indeed God deems it just to repay with affliction those who afflict you, 7 and to grant rest with us to you who are afflicted, when the Lord Jesus is revealed from heaven with his mighty angels in

1 Thes 3:11-13 (§283)

11 Now may our God and Father himself, and our Lord Jesus, direct our way to you; 12 and may the Lord make you increase and abound in love to one another and to all men, as we do to you, 13 so that he may establish your hearts unblamable in holiness before our God and Father, at the coming of our Lord Jesus with all his saints.

Phm 4-7 (§306)

4, I thank my God always when I remember you in my prayers, 5 because I hear of your love and of the faith which you have toward the Lord Jesus and all the saints, 6 and I pray that the sharing of your faith may promote the knowledge of all the good that is ours in Christ. 7 For I have derived much joy and comfort from your love, my brother, because the hearts of the saints have been refreshed through you.

flaming fire, 8 inflicting vengeance upon those who do not know God and upon those who do not obey the gospel of our Lord Jesus. 9 They shall suffer the punishment of eternal destruction and exclusion from the presence of the Lord and from the glory of his might, 10 when he comes on that day to be glorified in his saints, and to be marveled at in all who have believed, because our testimony to you was believed. 11 To this end we always pray for you, that our God may make you worthy of his call, and may fulfil every good resolve and work of faith by his power, 12 so that the name of our Lord Jesus may be glorified in you, and you in him, according to the grace of our God and the Lord Jesus Christ.

Phil 3:20

20 But our commonwealth is in heaven, and from it we await a Savior, the Lord Jesus Christ,

2 Thes 1:7

7 and to grant rest with us to you who are afflicted, when the Lord Jesus is revealed from heaven with his mighty angels in flaming fire,

▶1:9 10:13b

God is faithful, and he will not let you be tempted beyond your strength, but with the temptation will also provide the way of escape, that you may be able to endure it.

Rom 3:3

God is 3 What if some were unfaithful? Does their faithlessness nullify the faithfulness of God?

2 Cor 1:18

18As surely as God is faithful, our word to you has not been Yes and No.

1 Thes 5:24

24 He who calls you is faithful, and he will do it.

2 Thes 3:3

3 But the Lord is faithful; he will strengthen you and guard you from evil.

▶1:4 (God) read my God: SᵃACDG it vg syr cop Origen; text: S*B Ephraem

▶1:8 (Christ) omit Christ: p⁴⁶B

73

Rom 12:1-2 (§51)

12 I appeal to you therefore, brethren, by the mercies of God, to present your bodies as a living sacrifice, holy and acceptable to God, which is your spiritual worship. 2 Do not be conformed to this world but be transformed by the renewal of your mind, that you may prove what is the will of God, what is good and acceptable and perfect.

1 Cor 1:10-17

10 I appeal to you, brethren, by the name of our Lord Jesus Christ, that all of you agree and that there be no dissensions among you, but that you be united in the same mind and the same judgment. 11 For it has been reported to me by Chloe's people that there is quarreling among you, my brethren. 12 What I mean is that each one of you says, "I belong to Paul," or "I belong to Apol'los," or "I belong to Cephas," or "I belong to Christ." 13 Is Christ divided? Was Paul crucified for you? Or were you baptized in the name of Paul? 14 I am thankful that I baptized none of you except Crispus and Ga'ius; 15 lest any one should say that you were baptized in my name. 16 (I did baptize also the household of Steph'anas. Beyond that, I do not know whether I baptized any one else.) 17 For Christ did not send me to baptize but to preach the gospel, and not with eloquent wisdom, lest the cross of Christ be emptied of its power.

2 Cor 10:1-6 (§176)

10 I, Paul, myself entreat you, by the meekness and gentleness of Christ—I who am humble when face to face with you, but bold to you when I am away!— 2 I beg of you that when I am present I may not have to show boldness with such confidence as I count on showing against some who suspect us of acting in worldly fashion. 3 For though we live in the world we are not carrying on a worldly war, 4 for the weapons of our warfare are not worldly but have divine power to destroy strongholds. 5 We destroy arguments and every proud obstacle to the knowledge of God, and take every thought captive to obey Christ, 6 being ready to punish every disobedience, when your obedience is complete.

Eph 4:1-10 (§225)

4 I mean that the heir, as long as he is a child, is no better than a slave, though he is the owner of all the estate; 2 but he is under guardians and trustees until the date set by the father. 3 So with us; when we were children, we were slaves to the elemental spirits of the universe. 4 But when the time had fully come, God sent forth his Son, born of woman, born under the law, 5 to redeem those who were under the law, so that we might receive adoption as sons. 6 And because you are sons, God has sent the Spirit of his Son into our hearts, crying, "Abba! Father!" 7 So through God you are no longer a slave but a son, and if a son then an heir.

8 Formerly, when you did not know God, you were in bondage to beings that by nature are no gods; 9 but now that you have come to know God, or rather to be known by God, how can you turn back again to the weak and beggarly elemental spirits, whose slaves you want to be once more? 10 You observe days, and months, and seasons, and years!

▶1:12 Acts 18:24-19:1
24 Now a Jew named Apol'los, a native of Alexandria, came to Ephesus. He was an eloquent man, well versed in the scriptures. 25 He had been instructed in the way of the Lord; and being fervent in spirit, he spoke and taught accurately the things concerning Jesus, though he knew only the baptism of John. 26 He began to speak boldly in the synagogue; but when Priscilla and Aquila heard him, they took him and expounded to him the way of God more accurately. 27 And when he wished to cross to Acha'ia, the brethren encouraged him, and wrote to the disciples to receive him. When he arrived, he greatly helped those who through grace had believed, 28 for he powerfully confuted the Jews in public, showing by the scriptures that the Christ was Jesus.
19 While Apol'los was at Corinth, Paul passed through the upper country and came to Ephesus. There he found some disciples.

▶1:13 Acts 2:38 38 And Peter said to them, "Repent, and be baptized every one of you in the name of Jesus Christ for the forgiveness of your sins; and you shall receive the gift of the Holy Spirit.

▶1:14 Acts 18:8, 8 Crispus, the ruler of the synagogue, believed in the Lord, together with all his household; and many of the Corinthians hearing Paul believed and were baptized.

19:29 was filled with the confusion; and they rushed together into the theater, dragging with them Ga'ius and Aristar'chus, Macedo'nians who were Paul's companions in travel.

29 So the city

▶1:10 Rom 15:5-6
5 May the God of steadfastness and encouragement grant you to live in such harmony with one another, in accord with Christ Jesus, 6 that together you may with one voice glorify the God and Father of our Lord Jesus Christ.

74. Word of the cross.

74

Rom 1:16-17 (§3)

16 For I am not ashamed of the gospel: it is the power of God for salvation to every one who has faith, to the Jew first and also to the Greek. 17 For in it the righteousness of God is revealed through faith for faith; as it is written, "He who through faith is righteous shall live."

Rom 1:18-23 (§4)

18 For the wrath of God is revealed from heaven against all ungodliness and wickedness of men who by their wickedness suppress the truth. 19 For what can be known about God is plain to them, because God has shown it to them. 20 Ever since the creation of the world his invisible nature, namely, his eternal power and deity, has been clearly perceived in the things that have been made. So they are without excuse; 21 for although they knew God they did not honor him as God or give thanks to him, but they became futile in their thinking and their senseless minds were darkened. 22 Claiming to be wise, they became fools, 23 and exchanged the glory of the immortal God for images resembling mortal man or birds or animals or reptiles.

1 Cor 1:18-25

18 For the word of the cross is folly to those who are perishing, but to us who are being saved it is the power of God. 19 For it is written,
"I will destroy the wisdom of the wise,
and the cleverness of the clever I will thwart."
20 Where is the wise man? Where is the scribe? Where is the debater of this age? Has not God made foolish the wisdom of the world? 21 For since, in the wisdom of God, the world did not know God through wisdom, it pleased God through the folly of what we preach to save those who believe. 22 For Jews demand signs and Greeks seek wisdom, 23 but we preach Christ crucified, a stumbling block to Jews and folly to Gentiles, 24 but to those who are called, both Jews and Greeks, Christ the power of God and the wisdom of God. 25 For the foolishness of God is wiser than men, and the weakness of God is stronger than men.

2 Cor 12:1-10 (§185)

12 I must boast; there is nothing to be gained by it, but I will go on to visions and revelations of the Lord. 2 I know a man in Christ who fourteen years ago was caught up to the third heaven—whether in the body or out of the body I do not know, God knows. 3 And I know that this man was caught up into Paradise—whether in the body or out of the body I do not know, God knows—4 and he heard things that cannot be told, which man may not utter. 5 On behalf of this man I will boast, but on my own behalf I will not boast, except of my weaknesses. 6 Though if I wish to boast, I shall not be a fool, for I shall be speaking the truth. But I refrain from it, so that no one may think more of me than he sees in me or hears from me. 7 And to keep me from being too elated by the abundance of revelations, a thorn was given me in the flesh, a messenger of Satan, to harass me, to keep me from being too elated. 8 Three times I besought the Lord about this, that it should leave me; 9 but he said to me, "My grace is sufficient for you, for my power is made perfect in weakness." I will all the more gladly boast of my weaknesses, that the power of Christ may rest upon me. 10 For the sake of Christ, then, I am content with weaknesses, insults, hardships, persecutions, and calamities; for when I am weak, then I am strong.

Rom 9:30-33 (§39)

30 What shall we say, then? That Gentiles who did not pursue righteousness have attained it, that is, righteousness through faith; 31 but that Israel who pursued the righteousness which is based on law did not succeed in fulfilling that law. 32 Why? Because they did not pursue it through faith, but as if it were based on works. They have stumbled over the stumbling stone, 33 as it is written,
"Behold, I am laying in Zion a stone that will make men stumble,
a rock that will make them fall;
and he who believes in him will not be put to shame."

Rom 11:33-36 (§50)

33 O the depth of the riches and wisdom and knowledge of God! How unsearchable are his judgments and how inscrutable his ways!
34 "For who has known the mind of the Lord,
or who has been his counselor?"
35 "Or who has given a gift to him that he might be repaid?"
36 For from him and through him and to him are all things. To him be glory for ever. Amen.

▶1:21 1 Tim 4:16 16 Take heed to yourself and to your teaching; hold to that, for by so doing you will save both yourself and your hearers.

▶1:18 2 Cor 2:15, 15 For we are the aroma of Christ to God among those who are being saved and among those who are perishing,

4:3 3 And even if our gospel is veiled, it is veiled only to those who are perishing.

▶1:23 Gal 5:11 11 But if I, brethren, still preach circumcision, why am I still persecuted? In that case the stumbling block of the cross has been removed.

▶1:25 2 Cor 13:3b-4 He is not weak in dealing with you, but is powerful in you. 4 For he was crucified in weakness, but lives by the power of God. For we are weak in him, but in dealing with you we shall live with him by the power of God.

▶1:18 *cf 2 Tim 1:8

▶1:20 *cf Acts 6:10

73

Phil 4:1-3 (§250)

4 Therefore, my brethren, whom I love and long for, my joy and crown, stand firm thus in the Lord, my beloved.

2 I entreat Eu-o′dia and I entreat Syn′tyche to agree in the Lord. 3 And I ask you also, true yokefellow, help these women, for they have labored side by side with me in the gospel together with Clement and the rest of my fellow workers, whose names are in the book of life.

1 Thes 4:1-8 (§284)

4 Finally, brethren, we beseech and exhort you in the Lord Jesus, that as you learned from us how you ought to live and to please God, just as you are doing, you do so more and more. 2 For you know what instructions we gave you through the Lord Jesus. 3 For this is the will of God, your sanctification: that you abstain from unchastity; 4 that each one of you know how to take a wife for himself in holiness and honor 5 not in the passion of lust like heathen who do not know God; 6 that no man transgress, and wrong his brother in this matter, because the Lord is an avenger in all these things, as we solemnly forewarned you. 7 For God has not called us for uncleanness, but in holiness. 8 Therefore whoever disregards this, disregards not man but God, who gives his Holy Spirit to you.

2 Thes 2:1-12 (§296)

2 Now concerning the coming of our Lord Jesus Christ and our assembling to meet him, we beg you, brethren, 2 not to be quickly shaken in mind or excited, either by spirit or by word, or by letter purporting to be from us, to the effect that the day of the Lord has come. 3 Let no one deceive you in any way; for that day will not come, unless the rebellion comes first, and the man of lawlessness is revealed, the son of perdition, 4 who opposes and exalts himself against every so-called god or object of worship, so that he takes his seat in the temple of God, proclaiming himself to be God. 5 Do you not remember that when I was still with you I told you this? 6 And you know what is restraining him now so that he may be revealed in his time. 7 For the mystery of lawlessness is already at work; only he who now restrains it will do so until he is out of the way. 8 And then the lawless one will be revealed, and the Lord Jesus will slay him with the breath of his mouth and destroy him by his appearing and his coming. 9 The coming of the lawless one by the activity of Satan will be with all power and with pretended signs and wonders, 10 and

Phm 8-14 (§307)

8 Accordingly, though I am bold enough in Christ to command you to do what is required, 9 yet for love's sake I prefer to appeal to you—I, Paul, an ambassador and now a prisoner also for Christ Jesus—10 I appeal to you for my child, Ones′imus, whose father I have become in my imprisonment. 11 (Formerly he was useless to you, but now he is indeed useful to you and to me.) 12 I am sending him back to you, sending my very heart. 13 I would have been glad to keep him with me, in order that he might serve me on your behalf during my imprisonment for the gospel; 14 but I preferred to do nothing without your consent in order that your goodness might not be by compulsion but of your own free will.

with all wicked deception for those who are to perish, because they refused to love the truth and so be saved. 11 Therefore God sends upon them a strong delusion, to make them believe what is false, 12 so that all may be condemned who did not believe the truth but had pleasure in unrighteousness.

Phil 2:1-2
So if there is any encouragement in Christ, any incentive of love, any participation in the Spirit, any affection and sympathy, 2 complete my joy by being of the same mind, having the same love, being in full accord and of one mind.

▶ 1:11 7:1a
Now concerning the matters about which you wrote

16:17
17 I rejoice at the coming of Steph′anas and Fortuna′tus and Acha′icus, because they have made up for your absence;

11:18-19 18 For, in the first place, when you assemble as a church, I hear that there are divisions among you; and I partly believe it, 19 for there must be factions among you in order that those who are genuine among you may be recognized.

▶ 1:12 *cf. 3:4-9, 2 Cor 10:7

▶ 1:16 16:15-16 15 Now, brethren, you know that the household of Steph′anas were the first converts in Acha′ia, and they have devoted themselves to the service of the saints; 16 I urge you to be subject to such men and to every fellow worker and laborer.

▶ 1:17 *cf. 2:4-5 Gal 1:15f

▶ 1:14 (thankful) *read* I thank God: SᶜCDG Koine Lect it(some) vg syr(har) Tertullian Origen(Latin); *text:* S*B Clement Origen

74. Word of the cross.

74

1 Thes 2:13-16 (§279)

13 And we also thank God constantly for this, that when you received the word of God which you heard from us, you accepted it not as the word of men but as what it really is, the word of God, which is at work in you believers. 14 For you, brethren, became imitators of the churches of God in Christ Jesus which are in Judea; for you suffered the same things from your own countrymen as they did from the Jews, 15 who killed both the Lord Jesus and the prophets, and drove us out, and displease God and oppose all men 16 by hindering us from speaking to the Gentiles that they may be saved—so as always to fill up the measure of their sins. But God's wrath has come upon them at last!

▶ 1:19 Is 29:14
14 therefore, behold, I will again do marvelous things with this people,
wonderful and marvelous;
and the wisdom of their wise men shall perish,
and the discernment of their discerning men shall be hid."

75. Consider your call

75

Rom 3:27-31 (§15)

27 Then what becomes of our boasting? It is excluded. On what principle? On the principle of works? No, but on the principle of faith. 28 For we hold that a man is justified by faith apart from works of law. 29 Or is God the God of Jews only? Is he not the God of Gentiles also? Yes, of Gentiles also, 30 since God is one; and he will justify the circumcised on the ground of their faith and the uncircumcised through their faith. 31 Do we then overthrow the law by this faith? By no means! On the contrary, we uphold the law.

1 Cor 1:26-31

26 For consider your call, brethren; not many of you were wise according to worldly standards, not many were powerful, not many were of noble birth; 27 but God chose what is foolish in the world to shame the wise, God chose what is weak in the world to shame the strong, 28 God chose what is low and despised in the world, even things that are not, to bring to nothing things that are, 29 so that no human being might boast in the presence of God. 30 He is the source of your life in Christ Jesus, whom God made our wisdom, our righteousness and sanctification and redemption; 31 therefore, as it is written, "Let him who boasts, boast of the Lord."

1 Cor 3:18-23 (§82)

18 Let no one deceive himself. If any one among you thinks that he is wise in this age, let him become a fool that he may become wise. 19 For the wisdom of this world is folly with God. For it is written, "He catches the wise in their craftiness," 20 and again, "The Lord knows that the thoughts of the wise are futile." 21 So let no one boast of men.

For all things are yours, 22 whether Paul or Apol'los or Cephas or the world or life or death or the present or the future, all are yours; 23 and you are Christ's; and Christ is God's.

1 Cor 4:6-13 (§84-85)

6 I have applied all this to myself and Apol'los for your benefit, brethren, that you may learn by us not to go beyond what is written, that none of you may be puffed up in favor of one against another. 7 For who sees anything different in you? What have you that you did not receive? If then you received it, why do you boast as if it were not a gift?

8 Already you are filled! Already you have become rich! Without us you have become kings! And would that you did reign, so that we might share the rule with you! 9 For I think that God has exhibited us apostles as last of all, like men sentenced to death; because we have become a spectacle to the world, to angels and to men. 10 We are fools for Christ's sake, but you are wise in Christ. We are weak, but you are strong. You are held in honor, but we in disrepute. 11 To the present hour we hunger and thirst, we are ill-clad and buffeted and homeless, 12 and we labor, working with our own hands. When reviled, we bless; when persecuted, we endure; 13 when slandered, we try to conciliate; we have become, and are now, as the refuse of the world, the offscouring of all things.

▶ 1:26 Jas 2:5   5 Listen, my beloved brethren. Has not God chosen those who are poor in the world to be rich in faith and heirs of the kingdom which he has promised to those who love him?

▶ 1:26 6:9-11   9 Do you not know that the unrighteous will not inherit the kingdom of God? Do not be deceived; neither the immoral, nor idolaters, nor adulterers, nor sexual perverts, 10 nor thieves, nor the greedy, nor drunkards, nor revilers, nor robbers will inherit the kingdom of God. 11 And such were some of you. But you were washed, you were sanctified, you were justified in the name of the Lord Jesus Christ and in the Spirit of our God.

▶ 1:28 Rom 4:17   17 as it is written, "I have made you the father of many nations"—in the presence of the God in whom he believed, who gives life to the dead and calls into existence the things that do not exist.

▶ 1:29 Eph 2:8-9   8 For by grace you have been saved through faith; and this is not your own doing, it is the gift of God— 9 not because of works, lest any man should boast.

76. Jesus Christ and him crucified

76

Rom 15:14-21 (§62)

14 I myself am satisfied about you, my brethren, that you yourselves are full of goodness, filled with all knowledge, and able to instruct one another. 15 But on some points I have written to you very boldly by way of reminder, because of the grace given me by God 16 to be a minister of Christ Jesus to the Gentiles in the priestly service of the gospel of God, so that the offering of the Gentiles may be acceptable, sanctified by the Holy Spirit. 17 In Christ Jesus, then, I have reason to be proud of my work for God. 18 For I will not venture to speak of anything except what Christ has wrought through me to win obedience from the Gentiles, by word and deed, 19 by the power of signs and wonders, by the power of the Holy Spirit, so that from Jerusalem and as far round as Illyr icum I have fully preached the gospel of Christ, 20 thus making it my ambition to preach the gospel, not where Christ has already been named, lest I build on another man's foundation, 21 but as it is written,
"They shall see who have never been told of him,
and they shall understand who have never heard of him."

1 Cor 2:1-5

2 When I came to you, brethren, I did not come proclaiming to you the testimony of God in lofty words or wisdom. 2 For I decided to know nothing among you except Jesus Christ and him crucified. 3 And I was with you in weakness and in much fear and trembling; 4 and my speech and my message were not in plausible words of wisdom, but in demonstration of the Spirit and of power, 5 that your faith might not rest in the wisdom of men but in the power of God.

2 Cor 10:7-12 (§177)

7 Look at what is before your eyes. If any one is confident that he is Christ's, let him remind himself that as he is Christ's, so are we. 8 For even if I boast a little too much of our authority, which the Lord gave for building you up and not for destroying you, I shall not be put to shame. 9 I would not seem to be frightening you with letters. 10 For they say, "His letters are weighty and strong, but his bodily presence is weak, and his speech of no account." 11 Let such people understand that what we say by letter when absent, we do when present. 12 Not that we venture to class or compare ourselves with some of those who commend themselves. But when they measure themselves by one another, and compare themselves with one another, they are without understanding.

2 Cor 12:11-13 (§186)

11 I have been a fool! You forced me to it, for I ought to have been commended by you. For I was not at all inferior to these superlative apostles, even though I am nothing. 12 The signs of a true apostle were performed among you in all patience, with signs and wonders and mighty works. 13 For in what were you less favored than the rest of the churches, except that I myself did not burden you? Forgive me this wrong!

Gal 4:12-20 (§209)

12 Brethren, I beseech you, become as I am, for I also have become as you are. You did me no wrong; 13 you know it was because of a bodily ailment that I preached the gospel to you at first; 14 and though my condition was a trial to you, you did not scorn or despise me, but received me as an angel of God, as Christ Jesus. 15 What has become of the satisfaction you felt? For I bear you witness that, if possible, you would have plucked out your eyes and given them to me. 16 Have I then become your enemy by telling you the truth?h 17 They make much of you, but for no good purpose; they want to shut you out, that you may make much of them. 18 For a good purpose it is always good to be made much of, and not only when I am present with you. 19 My little children, with whom I am again in travail until Christ be formed in you! 20 I could wish to be present with you now and to change my tone, for I am perplexed about you.

▶ 2:3 Acts 18:1   After this he left Athens and went to Corinth.

▶ 2:1 2 Cor 11:6   6 Even if I am unskilled in speaking, I am not in knowledge; in every way we have made this plain to you in all things.

▶ 2:2 Gal 6:14   14 But far be it from me to glory except in the cross of our Lord Jesus Christ, by which the world has been crucified to me, and I to the world.

▶ 2:4 4:20   20 For the kingdom of God does not consist in talk but in power. 21 What do you wish? Shall I come to you with a rod, or with love in a spirit of gentleness?

▶1:31 Jer 9:24
24 but let him who glories glory in this, that he understands and knows me, that I am the LORD who practice steadfast love, justice, and righteousness in the earth; for in these things I delight, says the LORD."

76. Jesus Christ and him crucified

76

1 Thes 1:2-10 (§276)

2 We give thanks to God always for you all, constantly mentioning you in our prayers, 3 remembering before our God and Father your work of faith and labor of love and steadfastness of hope in our Lord Jesus Christ. 4 For we know, brethren beloved by God, that he has chosen you; 5 for our gospel came to you not only in word, but also in power and in the Holy Spirit and with full conviction. You know what kind of men we proved to be among you for your sake. 6And you became imitators of us and of the Lord, for you received the word in much affliction, with joy inspired by the Holy Spirit; 7 so that you became an example to all the believers in Macedo′nia and in Acha′ia. 8 For not only has the word of the Lord sounded forth from you in Macedo′nia and Acha′ia, but your faith in God has gone forth everywhere, so that we need not say anything. 9 For they themselves report concerning us what a welcome we had among you, and how you turned to God from idols, to serve a living and true God, 10 and to wait for his Son from heaven, whom he raised from the dead, Jesus who delivers us from the wrath to come.

▶2:1 (testimony) *read* mystery: p46S*AC it (few) syr(pes) cop(bo) Hippolytus

77. Secret and hidden wisdom of God

77

Rom 8:26-27 (§32)

26 Likewise the Spirit helps us in our weakness; for we do not know how to pray as we ought, but the Spirit himself intercedes for us with sighs too deep for words. 27And he who searches the hearts of men knows what is the mind of the Spirit, because the Spirit intercedes for the saints according to the will of God.

Rom 11:33-36 (§50)

33 O the depth of the riches and wisdom and knowledge of God! How unsearchable are his judgments and how inscrutable his ways!
34 "For who has known the mind of the Lord,
or who has been his counselor?"
35 "Or who has given a gift to him
that he might be repaid?"
36 For from him and through him and to him are all things. To him be glory for ever. Amen.

1 Cor 2:6-16

6 Yet among the mature we do impart wisdom, although it is not a wisdom of this age or of the rulers of this age, who are doomed to pass away. 7 But we impart a secret and hidden wisdom of God, which God decreed before the ages for our glorification. 8 None of the rulers of this age understood this; for if they had, they would not have crucified the Lord of glory. 9 But, as it is written,
"What no eye has seen, nor ear heard,
nor the heart of man conceived,
what God has prepared for those who love him,"
10 God has revealed to us through the Spirit. For the Spirit searches everything, even the depths of God. 11 For what person knows a man's thoughts except the spirit of the man which is in him? So also no one comprehends the thoughts of God except the Spirit of God. 12 Now we have received not the spirit of the world, but the Spirit which is from God, that we might understand the gifts bestowed on us by God. 13And we impart this in words not taught by human wisdom but taught by the Spirit, interpreting spiritual truths to those who possess the Spirit.

14 The unspiritual man does not receive the gifts of the Spirit of God, for they are folly to him, and he is not able to understand them because they are spiritually discerned. 15 The spiritual man judges all things, but is himself to be judged by no one. 16 "For who has known the mind of the Lord so as to instruct him?" But we have the mind of Christ.

1 Cor 1:4-9 (§72)

4 I give thanks to God always for you because of the grace of God which was given you in Christ Jesus, 5 that in every way you were enriched in him with all speech and all knowledge— 6 even as the testimony to Christ was confirmed among you—7 so that you are not lacking in any spiritual gift, as you wait for the revealing of our Lord Jesus Christ; 8 who will sustain you to the end, guiltless in the day of our Lord Jesus Christ. 9 God is faithful, by whom you were called into the fellowship of his Son, Jesus Christ our Lord.

Gal 6:1-6 (§214)

6 Brethren, if a man is overtaken in any trespass, you who are spiritual should restore him in a spirit of gentleness. Look to yourself, lest you too be tempted. 2 Bear one another's burdens, and so fulfil the law of Christ. 3 For if any one thinks he is something, when he is nothing, he deceives himself. 4 But let each one test his own work, and then his reason to boast will be in himself alone and not in his neighbor. 5 For each man will have to bear his own load.

6 Let him who is taught the word share all good things with him who teaches.

Eph 4:11-16 (§226)

11And his gifts were that some should be apostles, some prophets, some evangelists, some pastors and teachers, 12 to equip the saints for the work of ministry, for building up the body of Christ, 13 until we all attain to the unity of the faith and of the knowledge of the Son of God, to mature manhood, to the measure of the stature of the fulness of Christ; 14 so that we may no longer be children, tossed to and fro and carried about with every wind of doctrine, by the cunning of men, by their craftiness in deceitful wiles. 15 Rather, speaking the truth in love, we are to grow up in every way into him who is the head, into Christ, 16 from whom the whole body, joined and knit together by every joint with which it is supplied, when each part is working properly, makes bodily growth and upbuilds itself in love.

▶2:8 Acts 7:2,
2And Stephen said:
"Brethren and fathers, hear me. The God of glory appeared to our father Abraham, when he was in Mesopota´mia, before he lived in Haran,

13:27 27 For those who live in Jerusalem and their rulers, because they did not recognize him nor understand the utterances of the prophets which are read every sabbath, fulfilled these by condemning him.

▶2:6ff *cf. 1:26-29   ▶2:7 *cf. Rom 16:25 Eph 3:4-5   ▶2:12 *cf. 1:7   *cf. 12:1-11

---

78. Behaving like ordinary men

78

1 Cor 3:1-4

3 But I, brethren, could not address you as spiritual men, but as men of the flesh, as babes in Christ. 2 I fed you with milk, not solid food; for you were not ready for it; and even yet you are not ready, 3 for you are still of the flesh. For while there is jealousy and strife among you, are you not of the flesh, and behaving like ordinary men? 4 For when one says, "I belong to Paul," and another, "I belong to Apol´los," are you not merely men?

2 Cor 5:14-21 (§164)

14 For the love of Christ controls us, because we are convinced that one has died for all; therefore all have died. 15And he died for all, that those who live might live no longer for themselves but for him who for their sake died and was raised.

16 From now on, therefore, we regard no one from a human point of view; even though we once regarded Christ from a human point of view, we regard him thus no longer. 17 Therefore, if any one is in Christ, he is a new creation; the old has passed away, behold, the new has come. 18All this is from God, who through Christ reconciled us to himself and gave us the ministry of reconciliation; 19 that is, in Christ God was reconciling the world to himself, not counting their trespasses against them, and entrusting to us the message of reconciliation. 20 So we are ambassadors for Christ, God making his appeal through us. We beseech you on behalf of Christ, be reconciled to God. 21 For our sake he made him to be sin who knew no sin, so that in him we might become the righteousness of God.

Eph 2:1-10 (§220)

2 And you he made alive, when you were dead through the trespasses and sins 2 in which you once walked, following the course of this world, following the prince of the power of the air, the spirit that is now at work in the sons of disobedience. 3Among these we all once lived in the passions of our flesh, following the desires of body and mind, and so we were by nature children of wrath, like the rest of mankind. 4 But God, who is rich in mercy, out of the great love with which he loved us, 5 even when we were dead through our trespasses, made us alive together with Christ (by grace you have been saved), 6 and raised us up with him, and made us sit with him in the heavenly places in Christ Jesus, 7 that in the coming ages he might show the immeasurable riches of his grace in kindness toward us in Christ Jesus. 8 For by grace you have been saved through faith; and this is not your own doing, it is the gift of God— 9 not because of works, lest any man should boast. 10 For we are his workmanship, created in Christ Jesus for

▶3:1-2 Heb 5:13f   13 for every one who lives on milk is unskilled in the word of righteousness, for he is a child.
1 Pet 2:2
2 Like newborn babes, long for the pure spiritual milk, that by it you may grow up to salvation;

▶3:1 Rom 7:14   14 We know that the law is spiritual; but I am carnal, sold under sin.
▶3:1-2 4:14   14 I do not write this to make you ashamed, but to admonish you as my beloved children.

14:20   20 Brethren, do not be children in your thinking; be babes in evil, but in thinking be mature.
2 Cor 6:13   13 In return—I speak as to children—widen your hearts also.

Gal 4:19   19 My little children, with whom I am again in travail until Christ be formed in you!
*cf. Gal 4:21-31
Phil 2:22   22 But Timothy's worth you know, how as a son with a father he has served with me in the gospel.

Eph 5:1   Therefore be imitators of God, as beloved children.
▶3:1-4 Rom 8:3-13   3 For God has done what the law, weakened by the flesh, could not do: sending his own Son in the likeness of sinful flesh and for sin, he condemned sin in the flesh, 4 in order that the just require-

ment of the law might be fulfilled in us, who walk not according to the flesh but according to the Spirit. 5 For those who live according to the flesh set their minds on the things of the flesh, but those who live according to the Spirit set their minds on the things of the Spirit. 6 To set the mind on the flesh is death, but to set the mind on the Spirit is life and peace. 7 For the mind that is

set on the flesh is hostile to God; it does not submit to God's law, indeed it cannot; 8 and those who are in the flesh cannot please God.

9 But you are not in the flesh, you are in the Spirit, if in fact the Spirit of God dwells in you. Any one who does not have the Spirit of Christ does not belong to him. 10 But if Christ is in you, although your bodies are dead because of

77

Col 1:24-2:3 (§260)

24 Now I rejoice in my sufferings for your sake, and in my flesh I complete what is lacking in Christ's afflictions for the sake of his body, that is, the church, 25 of which I became a minister according to the divine office which was given to me for you, to make the word of God fully known, 26 the mystery hidden for ages and generations but now made manifest to his saints. 27 To them God chose to make known how great among the Gentiles are the riches of the glory of this mystery, which is Christ in you, the hope of glory. 28 Him we proclaim, warning every man and teaching every man in all wisdom, that we may present every man mature in Christ. 29 For this I toil, striving with all the energy which he mightily inspires within me.

2 For I want you to know how greatly I strive for you, and for those at La-odice′a, and for all who have not seen my face, 2 that their hearts may be encouraged as they are knit together in love, to have all the riches of assured understanding and the knowledge of God's mystery, of Christ, 3 in whom are hid all the treasures of wisdom and knowledge.

▶ 2:9 Is 64:4
4 From of old no one has heard
   or perceived by the ear,
no eye has seen a God besides thee,
   who works for those who wait for
     him.

▶2:16 Is 40:13
13 Who has directed the Spirit of the
   LORD,
   or as his counselor has instructed
   him?

78. Behaving like ordinary men

78

Eph(cont)
good works, which God prepared beforehand, that we should walk in them.

...in, your spirits are alive because of ...ghteousness. 11 If the Spirit of him ...ho raised Jesus from the dead dwells ... you, he who raised Christ Jesus from ...e dead will give life to your mortal ...odies also through his Spirit which ...wells in you.
12 So then, brethren, we are debtors, ...ot to the flesh, to live according to the

flesh—13 for if you live according to the flesh you will die, but if by the Spirit you put to death the deeds of the body you will live.

▶ 3:3 Gal 5:20-21
20 idolatry, sorcery, enmity, strife, jealousy, anger, selfishness, dissension, party spirit, 21 envy, drunkenness, carousing, and the like. I warn you, as I warned you before, that those who do such things shall not inherit the kingdom of God.

Col 3:9-10   9 Do not lie to one another, seeing that you have put off the old nature with its practices 10 and have put on the new nature, which is being renewed in knowledge after the image of its creator.

▶ 3:4 1:12   12 What I mean is that each one of you says, "I belong to Paul," or "I belong to Apol′los," or "I belong to Cephas," or "I belong to Christ."

3:22   22 whether Paul or Apol′los or Cephas or the world or life or death or the present or the future, all are yours;

4:6 6 I have applied all this to myself and Apol′los for your benefit, brethren, that you may learn by us not to go beyond what is written, that none of you may be puffed up in favor of one against another.

79

Rom 1:1-7 (§1)

1 Paul, a servant of Jesus Christ, called to be an apostle, set apart for the gospel of God ² which he promised beforehand through his prophets in the holy scriptures, ³ the gospel concerning his Son, who was descended from David according to the flesh ⁴ and designated Son of God in power according to the Spirit of holiness by his resurrection from the dead, Jesus Christ our Lord, ⁵ through whom we have received grace and apostleship to bring about the obedience of faith for the sake of his name among all the nations, ⁶ including yourselves who are called to belong to Jesus Christ;

7 To all God's beloved in Rome, who are called to be saints:

Grace to you and peace from God our Father and the Lord Jesus Christ.

1 Cor 3:5-9

5 What then is Apol′los? What is Paul? Servants through whom you believed, as the Lord assigned to each. ⁶ I planted, Apol′los watered, but God gave the growth. ⁷ So neither he who plants nor he who waters is anything, but only God who gives the growth. ⁸ He who plants and he who waters are equal, and each shall receive his wages according to his labor. ⁹ For we are God's fellow workers; you are God's field, God's building.

Eph 2:11-22 (§221)

11 Therefore remember that at one time you Gentiles in the flesh, called the uncircumcision by what is called the circumcision, which is made in the flesh by hands—¹² remember that you were at that time separated from Christ, alienated from the commonwealth of Israel, and strangers to the covenants of promise, having no hope and without God in the world. ¹³ But now in Christ Jesus you who once were far off have been brought near in the blood of Christ. ¹⁴ For he is our peace, who has made us both one, and has broken down the dividing wall of hostility, ¹⁵ by abolishing in his flesh the law of commandments and ordinances, that he might create in himself one new man in place of the two, so making peace, ¹⁶ and might reconcile us both to God in one body through the cross, thereby bringing the hostility to an end. ¹⁷And he came and preached peace to you who were far off and peace to those who were near; ¹⁸ for through him we both have access in one Spirit to the Father. ¹⁹ So then you are no longer strangers and sojourners, but you are fellow citizens

▶ 3:6 Acts 18:4-11, ⁴And he argued in the synagogue every sabbath, and persuaded Jews and Greeks.
5 When Silas and Timothy arrived from Macedo′nia, Paul was occupied with preaching, testifying to the Jews that the Christ was Jesus. ⁶And when they opposed and reviled him, he shook out his garments and said to them, "Your blood be upon your heads! I am innocent. From now on I will go to the Gentiles." ⁷And he left there and went to the house of a man named Titius Justus, a worshiper of God; his house was next door to the synagogue. ⁸ Crispus, the ruler of the synagogue, believed in the Lord, together with all his household; and many of the Corinthians hearing Paul believed and were baptized. ⁹And the Lord said to Paul one night in a vision, "Do not be afraid, but speak and do not be silent; ¹⁰ for I am with you, and no man shall attack you to harm you; for I have many people in this city." ¹¹And he stayed a year and six months, teaching the word of God among them.

24
24 Now a Jew named Apol′los, a native of Alexandria, came to Ephesus. He was an eloquent man, well versed in the scriptures.

▶ 3:5 *cf Acts 16:17

▶ 3:5-9 *cf. 9:1-18 Gal 6:7-9

▶ 3:7 Rom 9:16
¹⁶ So it depends not upon man's will or exertion, but upon God's mercy.

80

Rom 2:1-11 (§7-8)

2 Therefore you have no excuse, O man, whoever you are, when you judge another; for in passing judgment upon him you condemn yourself, because you, the judge, are doing the very same things. ² We know that the judgment of God rightly falls upon those who do such things. ³ Do you suppose, O man, that when you judge those who do such things and yet do them yourself, you will escape the judgment of God? ⁴ Or do you presume upon the riches of his kindness and forbearance and patience? Do you not know that God's kindness is meant to lead you to repentance? ⁵ But by your hard and impenitent heart you are storing up wrath for yourself on the day of wrath when God's righteous judgment will be revealed. ⁶ For he will render to every man according to his works: ⁷ to those who by patience in well-doing seek for glory and honor and immortality, he will give eternal life; ⁸ but for those who are factious and do not obey the truth, but obey wickedness, there will be wrath and fury. ⁹ There will be tribulation and distress for every human being

1 Cor 3:10-15

10 According to the grace of God given to me, like a skilled master builder I laid a foundation, and another man is building upon it. Let each man take care how he builds upon it. ¹¹ For no other foundation can any one lay than that which is laid, which is Jesus Christ. ¹² Now if any one builds on the foundation with gold, silver, precious stones, wood, hay, straw—¹³ each man's work will become manifest; for the Day will disclose it, because it will be revealed with fire, and the fire will test what sort of work each one has done. ¹⁴ If the work which any man has built on the foundation survives, he will receive a reward. ¹⁵ If any man's work is burned up, he will suffer loss, though he himself will be saved, but only as through fire.

80. No other foundation

Gal 2:1-10 (§197)

2 Then after fourteen years I went up again to Jerusalem with Barnabas, taking Titus along with me. ² I went up by revelation; and I laid before them (but privately before those who were of repute) the gospel which I preach among the Gentiles, lest somehow I should be running or had run in vain. ³ But even Titus, who was with me, was not compelled to be circumcised, though he was a Greek. ⁴ But because of false brethren secretly brought in, who slipped in to spy out our freedom which we have in Christ Jesus, that they might bring us into bondage— ⁵ to them we did not yield submission even for a moment, that the truth of the gospel might be preserved for you. ⁶And from those who were reputed to be something (what they were makes no difference to me; God shows no partiality)—those, I say, who were of repute added nothing to me; ⁷ but on the contrary, when they saw that I had been entrusted with the gospel to the uncircumcised, just as Peter had been entrusted with the gospel to the circumcised ⁸ (for he who worked through

Eph 3:1-13 (§222)

3 For this reason I, Paul, a prisoner for Christ Jesus on behalf of you Gentiles— ² assuming that you have heard of the stewardship of God's grace that was given to me for you, ³ how the mystery was made known to me by revelation, as I have written briefly. ⁴ When you read this you can perceive my insight into the mystery of Christ, ⁵ which was not made known to the sons of men in other generations as it has now been revealed to his holy apostles and prophets by the Spirit; ⁶ that is, how the Gentiles are fellow heirs, members of the same body, and partakers of the promise in Christ Jesus through the

Peter for the mission to the circumcised worked through me also for the Gentiles), ⁹ and when they perceived the grace that was given to me, James and Cephas and John, who were reputed to be pillars, gave to me and Barnabas the right hand of fellowship, that we should go to the Gentiles and they to the circumcised; ¹⁰ only they would have us remember the poor, which very thing I was eager to do.

who does evil, the Jew first and also the Greek, ¹⁰ but glory and honor and peace for every one who does good, the Jew first and also the Greek. ¹¹ For God shows no partiality.

▶3:10-14 2 Tim 2:19-20
¹⁹ But God's firm foundation stands, bearing this seal: "The Lord knows those who are his," and, "Let every one who names the name of the Lord depart from iniquity."
20 In a great house there are not only vessels of gold and silver but also of wood and earthenware, and some for noble use, some for ignoble.

▶ 3:10-14 Rom 15:20 20 thus making it my ambition to preach the gospel, not where Christ has already been named, lest I build on another man's foundation,

Eph 2:20 20 built upon the foundation of the apostles and prophets, Christ Jesus himself being the cornerstone,

▶ 3:13 Rom 2:16 16 on that day when, according to my gospel, God judges the secrets of men by Christ Jesus.

▶ 3:15 5:3-5
3 For though absent in body I am present in spirit, and as if present, I have already pronounced judgment ⁴ in the name of the Lord Jesus on the man who has done such a thing. When you are assembled, and my spirit is present, with the power of our Lord Jesus, ⁵ you are to deliver this man to Satan for the destruction of the flesh, that his spirit may be saved in the day of the Lord Jesus.

79

Eph(cont)
with the saints and members of the household of God, 20 built upon the foundation of the apostles and prophets, Christ Jesus himself being the corner-stone, 21 in whom the whole structure is joined together and grows into a holy temple in the Lord; 22 in whom you also are built into it for a dwelling place of God in the Spirit.

▶ 3:9 16:10
10 When Timothy comes, see that you put him at ease among you, for he is doing the work of the Lord, as I am.

Phil 2:25
25 I have thought it necessary to send to you Epaphrodi′tus my brother and fellow worker and fellow soldier, and your messenger and minister to my need,

Col 4:11 11 and Jesus who is called Justus. These are the only men of the circumcision among my fellow workers for the kingdom of God, and they have been a comfort to me.

80. No other foundation

80

2 Thes 1:3-12 (§295)

3 We are bound to give thanks to God always for you, brethren, as is fitting, because your faith is growing abundantly, and the love of every one of you for one another is increasing. 4 Therefore we ourselves boast of you in the churches of God for your stead-fastness and faith in all your persecu-tions and in the afflictions which you are enduring.
5 This is evidence of the righteous judgment of God, that you may be made worthy of the kingdom of God, for which you are suffering—6 since indeed God deems it just to repay with affliction those who afflict you, 7 and to grant rest with us to you who are af-flicted, when the Lord Jesus is revealed from heaven with his mighty angels in flaming fire, 8 inflicting vengeance upon those who do not know God and upon those who do not obey the gospel of our Lord Jesus. 9 They shall suffer the punishment of eternal destruction and exclusion from the presence of the Lord and from the glory of his might, 10 when he comes on that day to be glorified in his saints, and to be marveled at in all who have believed, because our testi-mony to you was believed. 11 To this end we always pray for you, that our God may make you worthy of his call, and may fulfil every good resolve and work of faith by his power, 12 so that the name of our Lord Jesus may be glorified in you, and you in him, ac-cording to the grace of our God and the Lord Jesus Christ.

Eph(cont)
gospel.
7 Of this gospel I was made a minister according to the gift of God's grace which was given me by the working of his power. 8 To me, though I am the very least of all the saints, this grace was given, to preach to the Gentiles the un-searchable riches of Christ, 9 and to make all men see what is the plan of the mystery hidden for ages in God who created all things; 10 that through the church the manifold wisdom of God might now be made known to the principalities and powers in the heav-enly places. 11 This was according to the eternal purpose which he has realized in Christ Jesus our Lord, 12 in whom we have boldness and confidence of access through our faith in him. 13 So I ask you not to lose heart over what I am suffering for you, which is your glory.

▶3:10 (God) *omit* of God: p⁴⁶ it(few) Clement

81

1 Cor 3:16-17

16 Do you not know that you are God's temple and that God's Spirit dwells in you? 17 If any one destroys God's temple, God will destroy him. For God's temple is holy, and that temple you are.

2 Cor 6:14-7:1 (§81)

14 Do not be mismated with unbelievers. For what partnership have righteousness and iniquity? Or what fellowship has light with darkness? 15 What accord has Christ with Be'lial? Or what has a believer in common with an unbeliever? 16 What agreement has the temple of God with idols? For we are the temple of the living God; as God said,
"I will live in them and move among them,
and I will be their God,
and they shall be my people.
17 Therefore come out from them,
and be separate from them, says the Lord,
and touch nothing unclean;
then I will welcome you,
18 and I will be a father to you,
and you shall be my sons and daughters,
says the Lord Almighty."
7 Since we have these promises, beloved, let us cleanse ourselves from every defilement of body and spirit, and make holiness perfect in the fear of God.

Eph 2:11-22 (§221)

11 Therefore remember that at one time you Gentiles in the flesh, called the uncircumcision by what is called the circumcision, which is made in the flesh by hands—12 remember that you were at that time separated from Christ, alienated from the commonwealth of Israel, and strangers to the covenants of promise, having no hope and without God in the world. 13 But now in Christ Jesus you who once were far off have been brought near in the blood of Christ. 14 For he is our peace, who has made us both one, and has broken down the dividing wall of hostility, 15 by abolishing in his flesh the law of commandments and ordinances, that he might create in himself one new man in place of the two, so making peace, 16 and might reconcile us both to God in one body through the cross, thereby bringing the hostility to an end. 17And he came and preached peace to you who were far off and peace to those who were near; 18 for through him we both have access in one Spirit to the Father. 19 So then you are no longer strangers and sojourners, but you are fellow citizens

▶ 3:16-17 6:12-20
12 "All things are lawful for me," but not all things are helpful. "All things are lawful for me," but I will not be enslaved by anything. 13 "Food is meant for the stomach and the stomach for food"—and God will destroy both one and the other. The body is not meant for immorality, but for the Lord, and the Lord for the body. 14And God raised the Lord and will also raise us up by his power. 15 Do you not know that your bodies are members of Christ? Shall I therefore take the members of Christ and make them members of a prostitute? Never! 16 Do you not know that he who joins himself to a prostitute becomes one body with her? For, as it is written, "The two shall become one flesh." 17But he who is united to the Lord becomes one spirit with him.

18 Shun immorality. Every other sin which a man commits is outside the body; but the immoral man sins against his own body. 19 Do you not know that your body is a temple of the Holy Spirit within you, which you have from God? You are not your own; 20 you were bought with a price. So glorify God in your body.

▶ 3:16-17 *cf Rom 8:9-11

82. Wisdom of this world is folly with God

82

Rom 8:31-39 (§34)

31 What then shall we say to this? If God is for us, who is against us? 32 He who did not spare his own Son but gave him up for us all, will he not also give us all things with him? 33 Who shall bring any charge against God's elect? It is God who justifies; 34 who is to condemn? Is it Christ Jesus, who died, yes, who was raised from the dead, who is at the right hand of God, who indeed intercedes for us? 35 Who shall separate us from the love of Christ? Shall tribulation, or distress, or persecution, or famine, or nakedness, or peril, or sword? 36As it is written,
"For thy sake we are being killed all the day long;
we are regarded as sheep to be slaughtered."
37 No, in all these things we are more than conquerors through him who loved us. 38 For I am sure that neither death, nor life, nor angels, nor principalities, nor things present, nor things to come, nor powers, 39 nor height, nor depth, nor anything else in all creation, will be able to separate us from the love of God in Christ Jesus our Lord.

1 Cor 3:18-23

18 Let no one deceive himself. If any one among you thinks that he is wise in this age, let him become a fool that he may become wise. 19 For the wisdom of this world is folly with God. For it is written, "He catches the wise in their craftiness," 20 and again, "The Lord knows that the thoughts of the wise are futile." 21 So let no one boast of men. For all things are yours, 22 whether Paul or Apol'los or Cephas or the world or life or death or the present or the future, all are yours; 23 and you are Christ's; and Christ is God's.

Eph 3:14-19 (§223)

14 For this reason I bow my knees before the Father, 15 from whom every family in heaven and on earth is named, 16 that according to the riches of his glory he may grant you to be strengthened with might through his Spirit in the inner man, 17 and that Christ may dwell in your hearts through faith; that you, being rooted and grounded in love, 18 may have power to comprehend with all the saints what is the breadth and length and height and depth, 19 and to know the love of Christ which surpasses knowledge, that you may be filled with all the fulness of God.

▶ 3:18 Gal 6:7
7 Do not be deceived; God is not mocked, for whatever a man sows, that he will also reap.

▶ 3:18-23 *cf. 1:18-2:9

▶ 3:22 *cf 1:12-13, 3:4-6, 4:6

▶ 3:23 11:3 3 But I want you to understand that the head of every man is Christ, the head of a woman is her husband, and the head of Christ is God.

▶ 3:21 *cf Rom 3:27

81

Eph (cont)

with the saints and members of the household of God, [20] built upon the foundation of the apostles and prophets, Christ Jesus himself being the cornerstone, [21] in whom the whole structure is joined together and grows into a holy temple in the Lord; [22] in whom you also are built into it for a dwelling place of God in the Spirit.

82. Wisdom of this world is folly with God

82

▶3:19 Job 5:13

[13] He takes the wise in their own craftiness; and the schemes of the wily are brought to a quick end.

▶ 3:20 Ps 94:11

[11] the LORD, knows the thoughts of man, that they are but a breath.

83

Rom 2:12-16 (§9)

12 All who have sinned without the law will also perish without the law, and all who have sinned under the law will be judged by the law. 13 For it is not the hearers of the law who are righteous before God, but the doers of the law who will be justified. 14 When Gentiles who have not the law do by nature what the law requires, they are a law to themselves, even though they do not have the law. 15 They show that what the law requires is written on their hearts, while their conscience also bears witness and their conflicting thoughts accuse or perhaps excuse them 16 on that day when, according to my gospel, God judges the secrets of men by Christ Jesus.

Rom 8:26-27 (§32)

26 Likewise the Spirit helps us in our weakness; for we do not know how to pray as we ought, but the Spirit himself intercedes for us with sighs too deep for words. 27 And he who searches the hearts of men knows what is the mind of the Spirit, because the Spirit intercedes for the saints according to the will of God.

▶ 4:1 1 Tim 1:7   7 desiring to be teachers of the law, without understanding either what they are saying or the things about which they make assertions.

1 Cor 4:1-5

4 This is how one should regard us, as servants of Christ and stewards of the mysteries of God. 2 Moreover it is required of stewards that they be found trustworthy. 3 But with me it is a very small thing that I should be judged by you or by any human court. I do not even judge myself. 4 I am not aware of anything against myself, but I am not thereby acquitted. It is the Lord who judges me. 5 Therefore do not pronounce judgment before the time, before the Lord comes, who will bring to light the things now hidden in darkness and will disclose the purposes of the heart. Then every man will receive his commendation from God.

Rom 13:1-7 (§54)

13 Let every person be subject to the governing authorities. For there is no authority except from God, and those that exist have been instituted by God. 2 Therefore he who resists the authorities resists what God has appointed, and those who resist will incur judgment. 3 For rulers are not a terror to good conduct, but to bad.

▶ 4:4 Acts 23:1   And Paul, looking intently at the council, said, "Brethren, I have lived before God in all good conscience up to this day."

Would you have no fear of him who is in authority? Then do what is good, and you will receive his approval, 4 for he is God's servant for your good. But if you do wrong, be afraid, for he does not bear the sword in vain; he is the servant of God to execute his wrath on the wrongdoer. 5 Therefore one must be subject, not only to avoid God's wrath but also for the sake of conscience. 6 For the same reason you also pay taxes, for the authorities are ministers of God, attending to this very thing. 7 Pay all of them their dues, taxes to whom taxes are due, revenue to whom revenue is due, respect to whom respect is due, honor to whom honor is due.

Rom 14:13-23 (§59)

13 Then let us no more pass judgment on one another, but rather decide never to put a stumbling block or hindrance in the way of a brother. 14 I know and am persuaded in the Lord Jesus that nothing is unclean in itself; but it is unclean for any one who thinks it unclean. 15 If your brother is being injured by what you eat, you are no

▶ 4:1 2:1   When I came to you, brethren, I did not come proclaiming to you the testimony of God in lofty words or wisdom.

longer walking in love. Do not let what you eat cause the ruin of one for whom Christ died. 16 So do not let your good be spoken of as evil. 17 For the kingdom of God is not food and drink but righteousness and peace and joy in the Holy Spirit; 18 he who thus serves Christ is acceptable to God and approved by men. 19 Let us then pursue what makes for peace and for mutual upbuilding. 20 Do not, for the sake of food, destroy the work of God. Everything is indeed clean, but it is wrong for any one to make others fall by what he eats; 21 it is right not to eat meat or drink wine or do anything that makes your brother stumble. *v* 22 The faith that you have, keep between yourself and God; happy is he who has no reason to judge himself for what he approves. 23 But he who has doubts is condemned, if he eats, because he does not act from faith; for whatever does not proceed from faith is sin.

14:2   2 For one who speaks in a tongue speaks not to men but to God; for no one understands him, but he utters mysteries in the Spirit.

Rom 11:25,   25 Lest you be wise in your own conceits, I want you to understand this mystery, brethren: a hardening has come upon part of Israel, until the full number of the Gentiles come in,

Eph 3:1-13 (§222)

3 For this reason I, Paul, a prisoner for Christ Jesus on behalf of you Gentiles— 2 assuming that you have heard of the stewardship of God's grace that was given to me for you, 3 how the mystery was made known to me by revelation, as I have written briefly. 4 When you read this you can perceive my insight into the mystery of Christ, 5 which was not made known to the sons of men in other generations as it has now been revealed to his holy apostles and prophets by the Spirit; 6 that is, how the Gentiles are fellow heirs, members of the same body, and partakers of the promise in Christ Jesus through the gospel. 7 Of this gospel I was made a minister according to the gift of God's grace which was given me by the working of his power. 8 To me, though I am the very least of all the saints, this grace was given, to preach to the Gentiles the unsearchable riches of Christ, 9 and to make all men see what is the plan of the mystery hidden for ages in God who created all things; 10 that through the church the manifold wisdom of God

16:25   25 Now to him who is able to strengthen you according to my gospel and the preaching of Jesus Christ, according to the revelation of the mystery which was kept secret for long ages

84. Why do you boast?

84

Rom 3:21-26 (§14)

21 But now the righteousness of God has been manifested apart from law, although the law and the prophets bear witness to it, 22 the righteousness of God through faith in Jesus Christ for all who believe. For there is no distinction; 23 since all have sinned and fall short of the glory of God, 24 they are justified by his grace as a gift, through the redemption which is in Christ Jesus, 25 whom God put forward as an expiation by his blood, to be received by faith. This was to show God's righteousness, because in his divine forbearance he had passed over former sins; 26 it was to prove at the present time that he himself is righteous and that he justifies him who has faith in Jesus.

Rom 11:17-24 (§48)

17 But if some of the branches were broken off, and you, a wild olive shoot, were grafted in their place to share the richness of the olive tree, 18 do not boast over the branches. If you do boast, remember it is not you that support the root, but the root that supports you. 19 You will say, "Branches were

▶ 4:6 1:12-13   12 What I mean is that each one of you says, "I belong to Paul," or "I belong to Apol'los," or "I belong to Cephas," or "I belong to Christ." 13 Is Christ divided? Was Paul crucified for you? Or were you baptized in the name of Paul?

1 Cor 4:6-7

6 I have applied all this to myself and Apol'los for your benefit, brethren, that you may learn by us not to go beyond what is written, that none of you may be puffed up in favor of one against another. 7 For who sees anything different in you? What have you that you did not receive? If then you received it, why do you boast as if it were not a gift?

broken off so that I might be grafted in." 20 That is true. They were broken off because of their unbelief, but you stand fast only through faith. So do not become proud, but stand in awe. 21 For if God did not spare the natural branches, neither will he spare you. 22 Note then the kindness and the severity of God: severity toward those who have fallen, but God's kindness to you, provided you continue in his kindness; otherwise you too will be cut off. 23 And even the others, if they do not persist in their unbelief, will be grafted in, for God has the power to graft them in again. 24 For if you have been cut from what is by nature a wild olive tree,

3:4-6   4 For when one says, "I belong to Paul," and another, "I belong to Apol'los," are you not merely men? 5 What then is Apol'los? What is Paul? Servants through whom you believed, as the Lord assigned to each. 6 I planted, Apol'los watered, but God gave the growth.

and grafted, contrary to nature, into a cultivated olive tree, how much more will these natural branches be grafted back into their own olive tree.

Rom 12:3-8 (§52)

3 For by the grace given to me I bid every one among you not to think of himself more highly than he ought to think, but to think with sober judgment, each according to the measure of faith which God has assigned him. 4 For as in one body we have many members, and all the members do not have the same function, 5 so we, though many, are one body in Christ, and individually members one of another. 6 Having gifts that differ according to the grace given to us, let us use them: if prophecy, in proportion to our faith; 7 if service, in our serving; he who teaches, in his teaching; 8 he who exhorts, in his exhortation; he who contributes, in liberality; he who gives aid, with zeal; he who does acts of mercy, with cheerfulness.

3:21-23   21 So let no one boast of men. For all things are yours, 22 whether Paul or Apol'los or Cephas or the world or life or death or the present or the future, all are yours; 23 and you are Christ's; and Christ is God's.

Col 2:18   18 Let no one disqualify you, insisting on self-abasement and worship of angels, taking his stand on visions, puffed up without reason by his sensuous mind,

Eph 2:1-10 (§220)

2 And you he made alive, when you were dead through the trespasses and sins 2 in which you once walked, following the course of this world, following the prince of the power of the air, the spirit that is now at work in the sons of disobedience. 3 Among these we all once lived in the passions of our flesh, following the desires of body and mind, and so we were by nature children of wrath, like the rest of mankind. 4 But God, who is rich in mercy, out of the great love with which he loved us, 5 even when we were dead through our trespasses, made us alive together with Christ (by grace you have been saved), 6 and raised us up with him, and made us sit with him in the heavenly places in Christ Jesus, 7 that in the coming ages he might show the immeasurable riches of his grace in kindness toward us in Christ Jesus. 8 For by grace you have been saved through faith; and this is not your own doing, it is the gift of God— 9 not because of works, lest any man should boast. 10 For we are his workmanship, created in Christ Jesus for

Col 1:24-2:3 (§260)

24 Now I rejoice in my sufferings for your sake, and in my flesh I complete what is lacking in Christ's afflictions for the sake of his body, that is, the church, 25 of which I became a minister according to the divine office which was given to me for you, to make the word of God fully known, 26 the mystery hidden for ages and generations[c] but now made manifest to his saints. 27 To them God chose to make known how great among the Gentiles are the riches of the glory of this mystery, which is Christ in you, the hope of glory. 28 Him we proclaim, warning every man and teaching every man in all wisdom, that we may present every man mature in Christ. 29 For this I toil, striving with all the energy which he mightily inspires within me.

2 For I want you to know how greatly I strive for you, and for those at La-odice'a, and for all who have not seen my face, 2 that their hearts may be encouraged as they are knit together in love, to have all the riches of assured understanding and the knowledge of God's mystery, of Christ, 3 in whom

are hid all the treasures of wisdom and knowledge.

Col 2:16-19 (§263)

16 Therefore let no one pass judgment on you in questions of food and drink or with regard to a festival or a new moon or a sabbath. 17 These are only a shadow of what is to come; but the substance belongs to Christ. 18 Let no one disqualify you, insisting on self-abasement and worship of angels, taking his stand on visions, puffed up without reason by his sensuous mind, 19 and not holding fast to the Head, from whom the whole body, nourished and knit together through its joints and ligaments, grows with a growth that is from God.

Eph (cont)

might now be made known to the principalities and powers in the heavenly places. 11 This was according to the eternal purpose which he has realized in Christ Jesus our Lord, 12 in whom we have boldness and confidence of access through our faith in him. 13 So I ask you not to lose heart over what I am suffering for you, which is your glory.

Eph 6:19

19 and also for me, that utterance may be given me in opening my mouth boldly to proclaim the mystery of the gospel,

Col 4:3

3 and pray for us also, that God may open to us a door for the word, to declare the mystery of Christ, on account of which I am in prison,

2 Thes 2:7

7 For the mystery of lawlessness is already at work; only he who now restrains it will do so until he is out of the way.

▶ 4:1-5 8:7-10

7 However, not all possess this knowledge. But some, through being hitherto accustomed to idols, eat food as really offered to an idol; and their conscience, being weak, is defiled. 8 Food will not commend us to God. We are no worse off if we do not eat, and no better off if we do. 9 Only take care lest this liberty of yours somehow become a stumbling block to the weak. 10 For if any one sees you, a man of knowledge, at table in an idol's temple, might he not be encouraged, if his conscience is weak, to eat food offered to idols?

10:25-29

25 Eat whatever is sold in the meat market without raising any question on the ground of conscience. 26 For "the earth is the Lord's, and everything in it." 27 If one of the unbelievers invites you to dinner and you are disposed to go, eat whatever is set before you without raising any question on the ground of conscience. 28 (But if some one says to you, "This has been offered in sacrifice," then out of consideration for the man who informed you, and for conscience' sake— 29 I mean his conscience, not yours—do not eat it.) For why should my liberty be determined by another man's scruples?

84. Why do you boast?

84

Eph (cont)

good works, which God prepared beforehand, that we should walk in them.

85

1 Cor 4:8-13

8 Already you are filled! Already you have become rich! Without us you have become kings! And would that you did reign, so that we might share the rule with you! 9 For I think that God has exhibited us apostles as last of all, like men sentenced to death; because we have become a spectacle to the world, to angels and to men. 10 We are fools for Christ's sake, but you are wise in Christ. We are weak, but you are strong. You are held in honor, but we in disrepute. 11 To the present hour we hunger and thirst, we are ill-clad and buffeted and homeless, 12 and we labor, working with our own hands. When reviled, we bless; when persecuted, we endure; 13 when slandered, we try to conciliate; we have become, and are now, as the refuse of the world, the offscouring of all things.

2 Cor 1:3-11 (§147)

3 Blessed be the God and Father of our Lord Jesus Christ, the Father of mercies and God of all comfort, 4 who comforts us in all our affliction, so that we may be able to comfort those who are in any affliction, with the comfort with which we ourselves are comforted by God. 5 For as we share abundantly in Christ's sufferings, so through Christ we share abundantly in comfort too. 6 If we are afflicted, it is for your comfort and salvation; and if we are comforted, it is for your comfort, which you experience when you patiently endure the same sufferings that we suffer. 7 Our hope for you is unshaken; for we know that as you share in our sufferings, you will also share in our comfort.

8 For we do not want you to be ignorant, brethren, of the affliction we experienced in Asia; for we were so utterly, unbearably crushed that we despaired of life itself. 9 Why, we felt that we had received the sentence of death; but that was to make us rely not on ourselves but on God who raises the dead; 10 he delivered us from so deadly a peril, and he will deliver us; on him we have set our hope that he will deliver us again. 11 You also must help us by prayer, so that many will give thanks on our behalf for the blessing granted us in answer to many prayers.

2 Cor 4:7-12 (§159)

7 But we have this treasure in earthen vessels, to show that the transcendent power belongs to God and not to us. 8 We are afflicted in every way, but not crushed; perplexed, but not driven to despair; 9 persecuted, but not forsaken; struck down, but not destroyed; 10 always carrying in the body the death of Jesus, so that the life of Jesus may also be manifested in our bodies. 11 For while we live we are always being given up to death for Jesus' sake, so that the life of Jesus may be manifested in our mortal flesh. 12 So death is at work in us, but life in you.

2 Cor 6:1-10 (§165)

6 Working together with him, then, we entreat you not to accept the grace of God in vain. 2 For he says,

"At the acceptable time I have listened to you,
and helped you on the day of salva-tion."

Behold, now is the acceptable time; behold, now is the day of salvation. 3 We put no obstacle in any one's way, so that no fault may be found with our ministry, 4 but as servants of God we commend ourselves in every way: through great endurance, in afflictions, hardships, calamities, 5 beatings, imprisonments, tumults, labors, watching, hunger; 6 by purity, knowledge, forbearance, kindness, the Holy Spirit, genuine love, 7 truthful speech, and the power of God; with the weapons of righteousness for the right hand and for the left; 8 in honor and dishonor, in ill repute and good repute. We are treated as impostors, and yet are true; 9 as unknown, and yet well known; as dying, and behold we live; as punished, and yet not killed; 10 as sorrowful, yet always rejoicing; as poor, yet making many rich; as having nothing, and yet possessing everything.

2 Cor 11:21b-29 (§183)

But whatever any one dares to boast of—I am speaking as a fool—I also dare to boast of that. 22 Are they Hebrews? So am I. Are they Israelites? So am I.

▶ 4:9 Acts 5:40
40 So they took his advice, and when they had called in the apostles, they beat them and charged them not to speak in the name of Jesus, and let them go.

▶ 4:10 Acts 17:18,
18 Some also of the Epicurean and Stoic philosophers met him. And some said, "What would this babbler say?" Others said, "He seems to be a preacher of foreign divinities"—because he preached Jesus and the resurrection

26:24
24 And as he thus made his defense, Festus said with a loud voice, "Paul, you are mad; your great learning is turning you mad."

▶ 4:12 Acts 18:3 3 and because he was of the same trade he stayed with them, and they worked, for by trade they were tentmakers.

▶ 4:9 15:7-11 7 Then he appeared to James, then to all the apostles. 8 Last of all, as to one untimely born, he appeared also to me. 9 For I am the least of the apostles, unfit to be called an apostle, because I persecuted the church of God. 10 But by the grace of God I am what I am, and his grace toward me was not in vain. On the contrary, I worked harder than any of them, though it was not I, but the grace of God which is with me. 11 Whether then it was I or they, so we preach and so you believed.

2 Cor 11:12-15,
12 And what I do I will continue to do, in order to undermine the claim of those who would like to claim that in their boasted mission they work on the same terms as we do. 13 For such men are false apostles, deceitful workmen, disguising themselves as apostles of Christ. 14 And no wonder, for even Satan disguises himself as an angel of light. 15 So it is not strange if his servants also disguise themselves as servants of righteousness. Their end will correspond to their deeds.

2 Cor (cont)

Are they descendants of Abraham? So am I. 23Are they servants of Christ? I am a better one—I am talking like a madman—with far greater labors, far more imprisonments, with countless beatings, and often near death. 24 Five times I have received at the hands of the Jews the forty lashes less one. 25 Three times I have been beaten with rods; once I was stoned. Three times I have been shipwrecked; a night and a day I have been adrift at sea; 26 on frequent journeys, in danger from rivers, danger from robbers, danger from my own people, danger from Gentiles, danger in the city, danger in the wilderness, danger at sea, danger from false brethren; 27 in toil and hardship, through many a sleepless night, in hunger and thirst, often without food, in cold and exposure. 28And, apart from other things, there is the daily pressure upon me of my anxiety for all the churches. 29 Who is weak, and I am not weak? Who is made to fall, and I am not indignant?

12:11-13

11 I have been a fool! You forced me to it, for I ought to have been commended by you. For I was not at all inferior to these superlative apostles, even though I am nothing. 12 The signs of a true apostle were performed among you in all patience, with signs and wonders and mighty works. 13 For in what were you less favored than the rest of the churches, except that I myself did not burden you? Forgive me this wrong!

1 Thes 3:1-5

Therefore when we could bear it no longer, we were willing to be left behind at Athens alone, 2 and we sent Timothy, our brother and God's servant in the gospel of Christ, to establish you in your faith and to exhort you, 3 that no one be moved by these afflictions. You yourselves know that this is to be our lot. 4 For when we were with you, we told you beforehand that we were to suffer affliction; just as it has come to pass, and as you know. 5 For this reason, when I could bear it no longer, I sent that I might know your faith, for fear that somehow the tempter had tempted you and that our labor would be in vain.

1 Thes 2:9-12 (§278)

9 For you remember our labor and toil, brethren; we worked night and day, that we might not burden any of you, while we preached to you the gospel of God. 10 You are witnesses, and God also, how holy and righteous and blameless was our behavior to you believers; 11 for you know how, like a father with his children, we exhorted each one of you and encouraged you and charged you 12 to lead a life worthy of God, who calls you into his own kingdom and glory.

Gal 1:17 17 nor did I go up to Jerusalem to those who were apostles before me, but I went away into Arabia; and again I returned to Damascus.

2 Thes 3:6-13 (§300)

6 Now we command you, brethren, in the name of our Lord Jesus Christ, that you keep away from any brother who is living in idleness and not in accord with the tradition that you received from us. 7 For you yourselves know how you ought to imitate us; we were not idle when we were with you, 8 we did not eat any one's bread without paying, but with toil and labor we worked night and day, that we might not burden any of you. 9 It was not because we have not that right, but to give you in our conduct an example to imitate. 10 For even when we were with you, we gave you this command: If any one will not work, let him not eat. 11 For we hear that some of you are living in idleness, mere busybodies, not doing any work. 12 Now such persons we command and exhort in the Lord Jesus Christ to do their work in quietness and to earn their own living. 13 Brethren, do not be weary in well-doing.

▶ 4:12 9:6 6 yet for us there is one God, the Father, from whom are all things and for whom we exist, and one Lord, Jesus Christ, through whom are all things and through whom we exist.

86

Rom 1:8-15 (§2)

8 First, I thank my God through Jesus Christ for all of you, because your faith is proclaimed in all the world. 9 For God is my witness, whom I serve with my spirit in the gospel of his Son, that without ceasing I mention you always in my prayers, 10 asking that somehow by God's will I may now at last succeed in coming to you. 11 For I long to see you, that I may impart to you some spiritual gift to strengthen you, 12 that is, that we may be mutually encouraged by each other's faith, both yours and mine. 13 I want you to know, brethren, that I have often intended to come to you (but thus far have been prevented), in order that I may reap some harvest among you as well as among the rest of the Gentiles. 14 I am under obligation both to Greeks and to barbarians, both to the wise and to the foolish; 15 so I am eager to preach the gospel to you also who are in Rome.

Rom 15:22-29 (§63)

22 This is the reason why I have so often been hindered from coming to you. 23 But now, since I no longer have any room for work in these regions, and since I have longed for many years to come to you, 24 I hope to see you in passing as I go to Spain, and to be sped on my journey there by you, once I have enjoyed your company for a little. 25 At present, however, I am going to Jerusalem with aid for the saints. 26 For Macedo'nia and Acha'ia have been pleased to make some contribution for the poor among the saints at Jerusalem; 27 they were pleased to do it, and indeed they are in debt to them, for if the Gentiles have come to share in their spiritual blessings, they ought also to be of service to them in material blessings. 28 When therefore I have completed this, and have delivered to them what has been raised, I shall go on by way of you to Spain; 29 and I know that when I come to you I shall come in the fulness of the blessing of Christ.

1 Cor 4:14-21

14 I do not write this to make you ashamed, but to admonish you as my beloved children. 15 For though you have countless guides in Christ, you do not have many fathers. For I became your father in Christ Jesus through the gospel. 16 I urge you, then, be imitators of me. 17 Therefore I sent to you Timothy, my beloved and faithful child in the Lord, to remind you of my ways in Christ, as I teach them everywhere in every church. 18 Some are arrogant, as though I were not coming to you. 19 But I will come to you soon, if the Lord wills, and I will find out not the talk of these arrogant people but their power. 20 For the kingdom of God does not consist in talk but in power. 21 What do you wish? Shall I come to you with a rod, or with love in a spirit of gentleness?

2 Cor 1:15-2:4 (§ 147-150)

15 Because I was sure of this, I wanted to come to you first, so that you might have a double pleasure; 16 I wanted to visit you on my way to Macedo'nia, and to come back to you from Macedo'nia and have you send me on my way to Judea. 17 Was I vacillating when I wanted to do this? Do I make my plans like a worldly man, ready to say Yes and No at once? 18 As surely as God is faithful, our word to you has not been Yes and No. 19 For the Son of God, Jesus Christ, whom we preached among you, Silva'nus and Timothy and I, was not Yes and No; but in him it is always Yes. 20 For all the promises of God find their Yes in him. That is why we utter the Amen through him, to the glory of God. 21 But it is God who establishes us with you in Christ; and has commissioned us; 22 he has put his seal upon us and given us his Spirit in our hearts as a guarantee. 23 But I call God to witness against me—it was to spare you that I refrained from coming to Corinth. 24 Not that we lord it over your faith; we work with you for your joy, for you stand 2 firm in your faith. 1 For I made up my mind not to make you another painful visit. 2 For if I cause you pain, who is there to make me glad but the one whom I have pained? 3 And I wrote as I did, so that when I came I might not suffer pain from those who should have made me rejoice, for I felt sure of all of you, that my joy would be the joy of you all. 4 For I wrote you out of much affliction and anguish of heart and with many tears, not to cause you pain but to let you know the abundant love that I have for you.

2 Cor 10:1-6 (§176)

10 I, Paul, myself entreat you, by the meekness and gentleness of Christ—I who am humble when face to face with you, but bold to you when I am away!— 2 I beg of you that when I am present I may not have to show boldness with such confidence as I count on showing against some who

suspect us of acting in worldly fashion. 3 For though we live in the world we are not carrying on a worldly war, 4 for the weapons of our warfare are not worldly but have divine power to destroy strongholds. 5 We destroy arguments and every proud obstacle to the knowledge of God, and take every thought captive to obey Christ, 6 being ready to punish every disobedience, when your obedience is complete.

2 Cor 12:14-13:10 (§187-190)

14 Here for the third time I am ready to come to you. And I will not be a burden, for I seek not what is yours but you; for children ought not to lay up for their parents, but parents for their children. 15 I will most gladly spend and be spent for your souls. If I love you the more, am I to be loved the less? 16 But granting that I myself did not burden you, I was crafty, you say, and got the better of you by guile. 17 Did I take advantage of you through any of those whom I sent to you? 18 I urged Titus to go, and sent the brother with him. Did Titus take advantage of you? Did we not act in the same spirit? Did we not take the same steps?

19 Have you been thinking all along that we have been defending ourselves before you? It is in the sight of God that we have been speaking in Christ, and all for your upbuilding, beloved. 20 For I fear that perhaps I may come and find you not what I wish, and that you may find me not what you wish; that perhaps there may be quarreling, jealousy, anger, selfishness, slander, gossip, conceit, and disorder. 21 I fear that when I come again my God may humble me before you, and I may have to mourn over many of those who sinned before and have not repented of the impurity, immorality, and licentiousness which they have practiced.

13 This is the third time I am coming to you. Any charge must be sustained by the evidence of two or three witnesses. 2 I warned those who sinned before and all the others, and I warn them now while absent, as I did

when present on my second visit, that if I come again I will not spare them— 3 since you desire proof that Christ is speaking in me. He is not weak in dealing with you, but is powerful in you. 4 For he was crucified in weakness, but lives by the power of God. For we are weak in him, but in dealing with you we shall live with him by the power of God.

5 Examine yourselves, to see whether you are holding to your faith. Test yourselves. Do you not realize that Jesus Christ is in you?—unless indeed you fail to meet the test! 6 I hope you will find out that we have not failed. 7 But we pray God that you may not do wrong—not that we may appear to have met the test, but that you may do what is right, though we may seem to have failed. 8 For we cannot do anything against the truth, but only for the truth. 9 For we are glad when we are weak and you are strong. What we pray for is your improvement. 10 I write this while I am away from you, in order that when I come I may not have to be severe in my use of the authority which the Lord has given me for building up and not for tearing down.

▶4:17 Acts 16:1
    And he came also to Derbe and to Lystra. A disciple was there, named Timothy, the son of a Jewish woman who was a believer; but his father was a Greek.

▶4:14 14:20
    20 Brethren, do not be children in your thinking; be babes in evil, but in thinking be mature.

2 Cor 6:13   13 In return—I speak as to children—widen your hearts also.

Gal 4:19   19 My little children, with whom I am again in travail until Christ be formed in you!

Eph 5:1
    Therefore be imitators of God, as beloved children.

Phm 10   10 I appeal to you for my child, Ones'imus, whose father I have become in my imprisonment.

▶4:16 11:1
    1 Be imitators of me, as I am of Christ.

Gal 4:12
    12 Brethren, I beseech you, become as I am, for I also have become as you are. You did me no wrong;

Phil 3:17
    17 Brethren, join in imitating me, and mark those who so live as you have an example in us.

1 Thes 1:6,
    6 And you became imitators of us and of the Lord, for you received the word in much affliction, with joy inspired by the Holy Spirit;

2:14a
    14 For you, brethren, became imitators of the churches of God in Christ Jesus which are in Judea;

Phil 1:19-30 (§240-241)

19 Yes, and I shall rejoice. For I know that through your prayers and the help of the Spirit of Jesus Christ this will turn out for my deliverance, 20 as it is my eager expectation and hope that I shall not be at all ashamed, but that with full courage now as always Christ will be honored in my body, whether by life or by death. 21 For to me to live is Christ, and to die is gain. 22 If it is to be life in the flesh, that means fruitful labor for me. Yet which I shall choose I cannot tell. 23 I am hard pressed between the two. My desire is to depart and be with Christ, for that is far better. 24 But to remain in the flesh is more necessary on your account. 25 Convinced of this, I know that I shall remain and continue with you all, for your progress and joy in the faith, 26 so that in me you may have ample cause to glory in Christ Jesus, because of my coming to you again.

27 Only let your manner of life be worthy of the gospel of Christ, so that whether I come and see you or am absent, I may hear of you that you stand firm in one spirit, with one mind striving side by side for the faith of the gospel, 28 and not frightened in anything by your opponents. This is a clear omen to them of their destruction, but of your salvation, and that from God. 29 For it has been granted to you that for the sake of Christ you should not only believe in him but also suffer for his sake, 30 engaged in the same conflict which you saw and now hear to be mine.

Phil 2:19-24 (§245)

19 I hope in the Lord Jesus to send Timothy to you soon, so that I may be cheered by news of you. 20 I have no one like him, who will be genuinely anxious for your welfare. 21 They all look after their own interests, not those of Jesus Christ. 22 But Timothy's worth you know, how as a son with a father he has served with me in the gospel. 23 I hope therefore to send him just as soon as I see how it will go with me; 24 and I

trust in the Lord that shortly I myself shall come also.

1 Thes 2:1-12 (§277-278)

2 For you yourselves know, brethren, that our visit to you was not in vain; 2 but though we had already suffered and been shamefully treated at Philippi, as you know, we had courage in our God to declare to you the gospel of God in the face of great opposition. 3 For our appeal does not spring from error or uncleanness, nor is it made with guile; 4 but just as we have been approved by God to be entrusted with the gospel, so we speak, not to please men, but to please God who tests our hearts. 5 For we never used either words of flattery, as you know, or a cloak for greed, as God is witness; 6 nor did we seek glory from men, whether from you or from others, though we might have made demands as apostles of Christ. 7 But we were gentle among you, like a nurse taking care of her children. 8 So, being affectionately desirous of you, we were ready to share with you not only the gospel of God but also our own selves, because you had become very dear to us.

9 For you remember our labor and toil, brethren; we worked night and day, that we might not burden any of you, while we preached to you the gospel of God. 10 You are witnesses, and God also, how holy and righteous and blameless was our behavior to you believers; 11 for you know how, like a father with his children, we exhorted each one of you and encouraged you and charged you 12 to lead a life worthy of God, who calls you into his own kingdom and glory.

1 Thes 2:17-3:5 (§280-281)

17 But since we were bereft of you, brethren, for a short time, in person not in heart, we endeavored the more eagerly and with great desire to see you face to face; 18 because we wanted to come to you—I, Paul, again and again—but Satan hindered us. 19 For what is our hope or joy or crown of boasting before our Lord Jesus at his coming? Is it not you? 20 For you are our glory and joy.

2 Thes 3:6-13 (§300)

6 Now we command you, brethren, in the name of our Lord Jesus Christ, that you keep away from any brother who is living in idleness and not in accord with the tradition that you received from us. 7 For you yourselves know how you ought to imitate us; we were not idle when we were with you, 8 we did not eat any one's bread without paying, but with toil and labor we worked night and day, that we might not burden any of you. 9 It was not because we have not that right, but to give you in our conduct an example to imitate. 10 For even when we were with you, we gave you this command: If any one will not work, let him not eat. 11 For we hear that some of you are living in idleness, mere busybodies, not doing any work. 12 Now such persons we command and exhort in the Lord Jesus Christ to do their work in quietness and to earn their own living. 13 Brethren, do not be weary in well-doing.

3 Therefore when we could bear it no longer, we were willing to be left behind at Athens alone, 2 and we sent Timothy, our brother and God's servant in the gospel of Christ, to establish you in your faith and to exhort you, 3 that no one be moved by these afflictions. You yourselves know that this is to be our lot. 4 For when we were with you, we told you beforehand that we were to suffer affliction; just as it has come to pass, and as you know. 5 For this reason, when I could bear it no longer, I sent that I might know your faith, for fear that somehow the tempter had tempted you and that our labor would be in vain.

Phm 21-22 (§309)

21 Confident of your obedience, I write to you, knowing that you will do even more than I say. 22 At the same time, prepare a guest room for me, for I am hoping through your prayers to be granted to you.

▶ 4:19 16:5-9

5 I will visit you after passing through Macedonia, for I intend to pass through Macedonia, 6 and perhaps I will stay with you or even spend the winter, so that you may speed me on my journey, wherever I go. 7 For I do not want to see you now just in passing; I hope to spend some time with you, if the Lord permits. 8 But I will stay in Ephesus until Pentecost, 9 for a wide door for effective work has opened to me, and there are many adversaries.

▶ 4:20 Rom 14:17

17 For the kingdom of God is not food and drink but righteousness and peace and joy in the Holy Spirit;

▶ 4:21 Gal 6:1

Brethren, if a man is overtaken in any trespass, you who are spiritual should restore him in a spirit of gentleness. Look to yourself, lest you too be tempted.

87. Immorality among you

87

Rom 16:17-20a (§67)

17 I appeal to you, brethren, to take note of those who create dissensions and difficulties, in opposition to the doctrine which you have been taught; avoid them. 18 For such persons do not serve our Lord Christ, but their own appetites, and by fair and flattering words they deceive the hearts of the simple-minded. 19 For while your obedience is known to all, so that I rejoice over you, I would have you wise as to what is good and guileless as to what is evil; 20 then the God of peace will soon crush Satan under your feet.

1 Cor 5:1-5

5 It is actually reported that there is immorality among you, and of a kind that is not found even among pagans; for a man is living with his father's wife. 2And you are arrogant! Ought you not rather to mourn? Let him who has done this be removed from among you.

3 For though absent in body I am present in spirit, and as if present, I have already pronounced judgment 4 in the name of the Lord Jesus on the man who has done such a thing. When you are assembled, and my spirit is present, with the power of our Lord Jesus, 5 you are to deliver this man to Satan for the destruction of the flesh, that his spirit may be saved in the day of the Lord Jesus.

2 Cor 6:14-7:1 (§167)

14 Do not be mismated with unbelievers. For what partnership have righteousness and iniquity? Or what fellowship has light with darkness? 15 What accord has Christ with Be′lial? Or what has a believer in common with an unbeliever? 16 What agreement has the temple of God with idols? For we are the temple of the living God; as God said,

"I will live in them and move among them,
and I will be their God,
and they shall be my people.
17 Therefore come out from them,
and be separate from them, says the Lord,
and touch nothing unclean;
then I will welcome you,
18 and I will be a father to you,
and you shall be my sons and daughters,
says the Lord Almighty."

7 Since we have these promises, beloved, let us cleanse ourselves from every defilement of body and spirit, and make holiness perfect in the fear of God.

▶5:5 1 Tim 1:20   20 among them Hymenae′us and Alexander, whom I have delivered to Satan that they may learn not to blaspheme.

▶5:1-5 *cf. 5:9-13 2 Cor 13:10

▶5:3 Col 2:5
5 For though I am absent in body, yet I am with you in spirit, rejoicing to see your good order and the firmness of your faith in Christ.

▶5:3-5 2 Cor 13:2-3
2 I warned those who sinned before and all the others, and I warn them now while absent, as I did when present on my second visit, that if I come again I will not spare them—

3 since you desire proof that Christ is speaking in me. He is not weak in dealing with you, but is powerful in you.

88. Christ our paschal lamb

88

1 Cor 5:6-8

6 Your boasting is not good. Do you not know that a little leaven leavens the whole lump? 7 Cleanse out the old leaven that you may be a new lump, as you really are unleavened. For Christ, our paschal lamb, has been sacrificed. 8 Let us, therefore, celebrate the festival, not with the old leaven, the leaven of malice and evil, but with the unleavened bread of sincerity and truth.

Eph 5:1-2 (§229)

5 Therefore be imitators of God, as beloved children. 2And walk in love, as Christ loved us and gave himself up for us, a fragrant offering and sacrifice to God.

▶5:7 *cf. Rom 15:16 Gal 5:8

▶5:8 Gal 4:10-11   10 You observe days, and months, and seasons, and years! 11 I am afraid I have labored over you in vain.

Col 2:16
16 Therefore let no one pass judgment on you in questions of food and drink or with regard to a festival or a new moon or a sabbath.

Rom 14:5-9
5 One man esteems one day as better than another, while another man esteems all days alike. Let every one be fully convinced in his own mind. 6 He who observes the day, observes it in honor of the Lord. He also who eats, eats in honor of the Lord, since he gives thanks to God; while he who abstains, abstains in honor of the Lord and gives thanks to God. 7 None of us lives to himself, and none of us dies to himself. 8 If we live, we live to the Lord, and if we die, we die to the Lord; so then, whether we live or whether we die, we are the Lord's. 9 For to this end Christ died and lived again, that he might be Lord both of the dead and of the living

87

2 Thes 3:14-15 (§301)

14 If any one refuses to obey what we say in this letter, note that man, and have nothing to do with him, that he may be ashamed. 15 Do not look on him as an enemy, but warn him as a brother.

▶ 5:2 *cf 2Cor 2:5-11

▶5:5 (Jesus) *omit* Jesus: p⁴⁶B Marcion Tertullian; *add* Christ: ADG it vg(clem) syr(pes) cop; *text:* S Koine Lect vg(w-w) syr(har) Origen(Latin)

88. **Christ our paschal lamb**

88

89

Rom 1:29-32 (§6)

29 They were filled with all manner of wickedness, evil, covetousness, malice. Full of envy, murder, strife, deceit, malignity, they are gossips, 30 slanderers, haters of God, insolent, haughty, boastful, inventors of evil, disobedient to parents, 31 foolish, faithless, heartless, ruthless. 32 Though they know God's decree that those who do such things deserve to die, they not only do them but approve those who practice them.

Rom 13:11-14 (§56)

11 Besides this you know what hour it is, how it is full time now for you to wake from sleep. For salvation is nearer to us now than when we first believed; 12 the night is far gone, the day is at hand. Let us then cast off the works of darkness and put on the armor of light; 13 let us conduct ourselves becomingly as in the day, not in reveling and drunkenness, not in debauchery and licentiousness, not in quarreling and jealousy. 14 But put on the Lord Jesus Christ, and make no provision for the flesh, to gratify its desires.

▶ 5:11 Acts 19:9
9 but when some were stubborn and disbelieved, speaking evil of the Way before the congregation, he withdrew from them, taking the disciples with him, and argued daily in the hall of Tyran nus.

1 Cor 5:9-13

9 I wrote to you in my letter not to associate with immoral men; 10 not at all meaning the immoral of this world, or the greedy and robbers, or idolaters, since then you would need to go out of the world. 11 But rather I wrote to you not to associate with any one who bears the name of brother if he is guilty of immorality or greed, or is an idolater, reviler, drunkard, or robber—not even to eat with such a one. 12 For what have I to do with judging outsiders? Is it not those inside the church whom you are to judge? 13 God judges those outside. "Drive out the wicked person from among you."

Rom 16:17-20 (§67)

17 I appeal to you, brethren, to take note of those who create dissensions and difficulties, in opposition to the doctrine which you have been taught; avoid them. 18 For such persons do not serve our Lord Christ, but their own appetites, and by fair and flattering words they deceive the hearts of the simple-minded. 19 For while your obedience is known to all, so that I re-

▶ 5:9-11 *cf. Rom 1:28 *cf. 10:14-32

▶ 5:9-13 Phil 3:18-19 18 For many, of whom I have often told you and now tell you even with tears, live as enemies of the cross of Christ. 19 Their end is destruction, their god is the belly, and they glory in their shame, with minds set on earthly things.

*cf. 11:27-32

2 Cor 6:14-7:1 (§167)

14 Do not be mismated with unbelievers. For what partnership have righteousness and iniquity? Or what fellowship has light with darkness? 15 What accord has Christ with Be'lial? Or what has a believer in common with an unbeliever? 16 What agreement has the temple of God with idols? For we are the temple of the living God; as God said,
"I will live in them and move among them,
and I will be their God,
and they shall be my people.
17 Therefore come out from them,
and be separate from them, says the Lord,
and touch nothing unclean;
then I will welcome you,
18 and I will be a father to you,
and you shall be my sons and

joice over you, I would have you wise as to what is good and guileless as to what is evil; 20 then the God of peace will soon crush Satan under your feet. The grace of our Lord Jesus Christ be with you.

▶ 5:11 10:7
not be idolaters as some of them were; as it is written, "The people sat down to eat and drink and rose up to dance."

Gal 5:16-26 (§213)

16 But I say, walk by the Spirit, and do not gratify the desires of the flesh. 17 For the desires of the flesh are against the Spirit, and the desires of the Spirit are against the flesh; for these are opposed to each other, to prevent you from doing what you would. 18 But if you are led by the Spirit you are not under the law. 19 Now the works of the flesh are plain: fornication, impurity, licentiousness, 20 idolatry, sorcery, enmity, strife, jealousy, anger, selfishness, dissension, party spirit, 21 envy, drunkenness, carousing, and the like. I warn you, as I warned you before, that those who do such things shall not inherit the

daughters,
says the Lord Almighty."

7 Since we have these promises, beloved, let us cleanse ourselves from every defilement of body and spirit, and make holiness perfect in the fear of God.

2 Cor 12:19-21 (§188)

19 Have you been thinking all along that we have been defending ourselves before you? It is in the sight of God that

7 Do

6:9-10
9 Do you not know that the unrighteous will not inherit the kingdom of God? Do not be deceived; neither the immoral, nor idolaters, nor adulterers, nor sexual perverts, 10 nor thieves, nor

Eph 4:17-32 (§227)

17 Now this I affirm and testify in the Lord, that you must no longer live as the Gentiles do, in the futility of their minds; 18 they are darkened in their understanding, alienated from the life of God because of the ignorance that is in them, due to their hardness of heart; 19 they have become callous and have given themselves up to licentiousness,

kingdom of God. 22 But the fruit of the Spirit is love, joy, peace, patience, kindness, goodness, faithfulness, 23 gentleness, self-control; against such there is no law. 24 And those who belong to Christ Jesus have crucified the flesh with its passions and desires.

25 If we live by the Spirit, let us also walk by the Spirit. 26 Let us have no self-conceit, no provoking of one another, no envy of one another.

we have been speaking in Christ, and all for your upbuilding, beloved. 20 For I fear that perhaps I may come and find you not what I wish, and that you may find me not what you wish; that perhaps there may be quarreling, jealousy, anger, selfishness, slander, gossip, conceit,

the greedy, nor drunkards, nor revilers, nor robbers will inherit the kingdom of God.

90. Brother goes to law against brother

90

Rom 13:1-7 (§54)

13 Let every person be subject to the governing authorities. For there is no authority except from God, and those that exist have been instituted by God. 2 Therefore he who resists the authorities resists what God has appointed, and those who resist will incur judgment. 3 For rulers are not a terror to good conduct, but to bad. Would you have no fear of him who is in authority? Then do what is good, and you will receive his approval, 4 for he is God's servant for your good. But if you do wrong, be afraid, for he does not bear the sword in vain; he is the servant of God to execute his wrath on the wrongdoer. 5 Therefore one must be subject, not only to avoid God's wrath but also for the sake of conscience. 6 For the same reason you also pay taxes, for the authorities are ministers of God, attending to this very thing. 7 Pay all of them their dues, taxes to whom taxes are due, revenue to whom revenue is due, respect to whom respect is due, honor to whom honor is due.

1 Cor 6:1-8

6 When one of you has a grievance against a brother, does he dare go to law before the unrighteous instead of the saints? 2 Do you not know that the saints will judge the world? And if the world is to be judged by you, are you incompetent to try trivial cases? 3 Do you not know that we are to judge angels? How much more, matters pertaining to this life! 4 If then you have such cases, why do you lay them before those who are least esteemed by the church? 5 I say this to your shame. Can it be that there is no man among you wise enough to decide between members of the brotherhood, 6 but brother goes to law against brother, and that before unbelievers?

7 To have lawsuits at all with one another is defeat for you. Why not rather suffer wrong? Why not rather be defrauded? 8 But you yourselves wrong and defraud, and that even your own brethren.

▶ 6:6 1 Tim 5:8· 8 If any one does not provide for his relatives, and especially for his own family, he has disowned the faith and is worse than an unbeliever.

▶ 6:1-2 *cf 1Tim 5:19-21

▶ 6:3 11:10
10 That is why a woman ought to have a veil on her head, because of the angels.

▶ 6:7 Gal 6:10 10 So then, as we have opportunity, let us do good to all men, and especially to those who are of the household of faith.

1 Thes 5:15 15 See that none of you repays evil for evil, but always seek to do good to one another and to all.

▶ 6:4-5 *cf 2 Cor 13:1, 1Thes 4:9-12

Eph (cont)

greedy to practice every kind of uncleanness. 20 You did not so learn Christ!— 21 assuming that you have heard about him and were taught in him, as the truth is in Jesus. 22 Put off your old nature which belongs to your former manner of life and is corrupt through deceitful lusts, 23 and be renewed in the spirit of your minds, 24 and put on the new nature, created after the likeness of God in true righteousness and holiness.

25 Therefore, putting away falsehood, let every one speak the truth with his neighbor, for we are members one of another. 26 Be angry but do not sin; do not let the sun go down on your anger, 27 and give no opportunity to the devil. 28 Let the thief no longer steal, but rather let him labor, doing honest work

2 Cor (cont)

and disorder. 21 I fear that when I come again my God may humble me before you, and I may have to mourn over many of those who sinned before and have not repented of the impurity, immorality, and licentiousness which they have practiced.

2 Thes 3:6

6 Now we command you, brethren, in the name of our Lord Jesus Christ, that you keep away from any brother who is living in idleness and not in accord with the tradition that you received from us.

Col 3:5-11 (§266)

5 Put to death therefore what is earthly in you: fornication, impurity, passion, evil desire, and covetousness, which is idolatry. 6 On account of these the wrath of God is coming. 7 In these you once walked, when you lived in them. 8 But now put them all away: anger, wrath, malice, slander, and foul talk from your mouth. 9 Do not lie to one another, seeing that you have put off the old nature with its practices 10 and have put on the new nature, which is being renewed in knowledge after the image of its creator. 11 Here there cannot be Greek and Jew, circumcised and uncircumcised, barbarian, Scyth'ian, slave, free man, but Christ is all, and in all.

Col 4:5-6 (§270)

5 Conduct yourselves wisely toward outsiders, making the most of the time. 6 Let your speech always be gracious, seasoned with salt, so that you may know how you ought to answer every one.

Eph 5:3-14 (§230)

3 But fornication and all impurity or covetousness must not even be named among you, as is fitting among saints. 4 Let there be no filthiness, nor silly talk, nor levity, which are not fitting; but instead let there be thanksgiving. 5 Be sure of this, that no fornicator or impure man, or one who is covetous (that is, an idolater), has any inheritance in the kingdom of Christ and of God. 6 Let no one deceive you with empty words, for it is because of these things that the wrath of God comes upon the sons of disobedience. 7 Therefore do not associate with them, 8 for once you were darkness, but now you are light in the Lord; walk as children of light 9 (for the fruit of light is found in all that is good and right and true), 10 and try to learn what is pleasing to the Lord. 11 Take no part in the unfruitful works of darkness, but instead expose them. 12 For it is a shame even to speak of the things that they do in secret; 13 but when anything is exposed by the light it becomes visible, for anything that becomes visible is light. 14 Therefore it is said,
"Awake, O sleeper, and arise from the dead,
and Christ shall give you light."

2 Thes 3:14-15 (§301)

14 If any one refuses to obey what we say in this letter, note that man, and have nothing to do with him, that he may be ashamed. 15 Do not look on him as an enemy, but warn him as a brother.

(with his hands, so that he may be able to give to those in need. 29 Let no evil talk come out of your mouths, but only such as is good for edifying, as fits the occasion, that it may impart grace to those who hear. 30 And do not grieve the Holy Spirit of God, in whom you were sealed for the day of redemption. 31 Let all bitterness and wrath and anger and clamor and slander be put away from you, with all malice, 32 and be kind to one another, tenderhearted, forgiving one another, as God in Christ forgave you.)

89

90. Brother goes to law against brother

Phm 15-20 (§308)

15 Perhaps this is why he was parted from you for a while, that you might have him back for ever, 16 no longer as a slave but more than a slave, as a beloved brother, especially to me but how much more to you, both in the flesh and in the Lord. 17 So if you consider me your partner, receive him as you would receive me. 18 If he has wronged you at all, or owes you anything, charge that to my account. 19 I, Paul, write this with my own hand, I will repay it—to say nothing of your owing me even your own self. 20 Yes, brother, I want some benefit from you in the Lord. Refresh my heart in Christ.

90

91

Rom 1:29-32 (§6)

29 They were filled with all manner of wickedness, evil, covetousness, malice. Full of envy, murder, strife, deceit, malignity, they are gossips, 30 slanderers, haters of God, insolent, haughty, boastful, inventors of evil, disobedient to parents, 31 foolish, faithless, heartless, ruthless. 32 Though they know God's decree that those who do such things deserve to die, they not only do them but approve those who practice them.

Rom 13:11-14 (§56)

11 Besides this you know what hour it is, how it is full time now for you to wake from sleep. For salvation is nearer to us now than when we first believed; 12 the night is far gone, the day is at hand. Let us then cast off the works of darkness and put on the armor of light; 13 let us conduct ourselves becomingly as in the day, not in reveling and drunkenness, not in debauchery and licentiousness, not in quarreling and jealousy. 14 But put on the Lord Jesus Christ, and make no provision for the flesh, to gratify its desires.

1 Cor 6:9-11 —

9 Do you not know that the unrighteous will not inherit the kingdom of God? Do not be deceived; neither the immoral, nor idolaters, nor adulterers, nor sexual perverts, 10 nor thieves, nor the greedy, nor drunkards, nor revilers, nor robbers will inherit the kingdom of God. 11 And such were some of you. But you were washed, you were sanctified, you were justified in the name of the Lord Jesus Christ and in the Spirit of our God.

2 Cor 12:19-21 (§188)

19 Have you been thinking all along that we have been defending ourselves before you? It is in the sight of God that we have been speaking in Christ, and all for your upbuilding, beloved. 20 For I fear that perhaps I may come and find you not what I wish, and that you may find me not what you wish; that perhaps there may be quarreling, jealousy, anger, selfishness, slander, gossip, conceit, and disorder. 21 I fear that when I come again my God may humble me before you, and I may have to mourn over many of those who sinned before and have not repented of the impurity, immorality, and licentiousness which they have practiced.

Gal 5:16-26 (§213)

16 But I say, walk by the Spirit, and do not gratify the desires of the flesh. 17 For the desires of the flesh are against the Spirit, and the desires of the Spirit are against the flesh; for these are opposed to each other, to prevent you from doing what you would. 18 But if you are led by the Spirit you are not under the law. 19 Now the works of the flesh are plain: fornication, impurity, licentiousness, 20 idolatry, sorcery, enmity, strife, jealousy, anger, selfishness, dissension, party spirit, 21 envy, drunkenness, carousing, and the like. I warn you, as I warned you before, that those who do such things shall not inherit the kingdom of God. 22 But the fruit of the Spirit is love, joy, peace, patience, kindness, goodness, faithfulness, 23 gentleness, self-control; against such there is no law. 24 And those who belong to Christ Jesus have crucified the flesh with its passions and desires.

25 If we live by the Spirit, let us also walk by the Spirit. 26 Let us have no self-conceit, no provoking of one another, no envy of one another.

Eph 4:17-32 (§227)

17 Now this I affirm and testify in the Lord, that you must no longer live as the Gentiles do, in the futility of their minds; 18 they are darkened in their understanding, alienated from the life of God because of the ignorance that is in them, due to their hardness of heart; 19 they have become callous and have given themselves up to licentiousness, greedy to practice every kind of uncleanness. 20 You did not so learn Christ!— 21 assuming that you have heard about him and were taught in him, as the truth is in Jesus. 22 Put off your old nature which belongs to your former manner of life and is corrupt through deceitful lusts, 23 and be renewed in the spirit of your minds, 24 and put on the new nature, created after the likeness of God in true righteousness and holiness.

25 Therefore, putting away falsehood, let every one speak the truth with his neighbor, for we are members one of another. 26 Be angry but do not sin; do not let the sun go down on your anger, 27 and give no opportunity to the devil. 28 Let the thief no longer steal, but

▶ 6:9 1 Tim 1:10
10 For even when we were with you, we gave you this command: If any one will not work, let him not eat.

▶ 6:11 Acts 22:16
16 And now why do you wait? Rise and be baptized, and wash away your sins, calling on his name.'

▶ 6:9-10 5:10-11
10 not at all meaning the immoral of this world, or the greedy and robbers, or idolaters, since then you would need to go out of the world. 11 But rather I wrote to you not to associate with any one who bears the name of brother if he is guilty of immorality or greed, or is an idolater, reviler, drunkard, or robber—not even to eat with such a one.

▶ 6:11 1:30
30 Why am I in peril every hour?

Rom 3:21-26
21 But now the righteousness of God has been manifested apart from law, although the law and the prophets bear witness to it, 22 the righteousness of God through faith in Jesus Christ for

all who believe. For there is no distinction; 23 since all have sinned and fall short of the glory of God, 24 they are justified by his grace as a gift, through the redemption which is in Christ Jesus, 25 whom God put forward as an expiation by his blood, to be received by faith. This was to show God's righteousness, because in his divine

92. Glorify God in your body

92

Rom 6:1-23 (§23-25)

6 What shall we say then? Are we to continue in sin that grace may abound? 2 By no means! How can we who died to sin still live in it? 3 Do you not know that all of us who have been baptized into Christ Jesus were baptized into his death? 4 We were buried therefore with him by baptism into death, so that as Christ was raised from the dead by the glory of the Father, we too might walk in newness of life.

5 For if we have been united with him in a death like his, we shall certainly be united with him in a resurrection like his. 6 We know that our old self was crucified with him so that the sinful body might be destroyed, and we might no longer be enslaved to sin. 7 For he who has died is freed from sin. 8 But if we have died with Christ, we believe that we shall also live with him. 9 For we know that Christ being raised from the dead will never die again; death no longer has dominion over him. 10 The death he died he died to sin, once for all, but the life he lives he lives to God. 11 So you also must consider yourselves dead to sin and

1 Cor 6:12-20

12 "All things are lawful for me," but not all things are helpful. "All things are lawful for me," but I will not be enslaved by anything. 13 "Food is meant for the stomach and the stomach for food"—and God will destroy both one and the other. The body is not meant for immorality, but for the Lord, and the Lord for the body. 14 And God raised the Lord and will also raise us up by his power. 15 Do you not know that your bodies are members of Christ? Shall I therefore take the members of Christ and make them members of a prostitute? Never! 16 Do you not know that he who joins himself to a prostitute becomes one body with her? For, as it is written, "The two shall become one flesh." 17 But he who is united to the Lord becomes one spirit with him. 18 Shun immorality. Every other sin which a man commits is outside the body; but the immoral man sins against

his own body. 19 Do you not know that your body is a temple of the Holy Spirit within you, which you have from God? You are not your own; 20 you were bought with a price. So glorify God in your body.

yield yourselves to God as men who have been brought from death to life, and your members to God as instruments of righteousness. 14 For sin will have no dominion over you, since you are not under law but under grace.

15 What then? Are we to sin because we are not under law but under grace? By no means! 16 Do you not know that if you yield yourselves to any one as obedient slaves, you are slaves of the one whom you obey, either of sin, which leads to death, or of obedience, which leads to righteousness? 17 But thanks be to God, that you who were once slaves of sin have become obedient from the heart to the standard of teaching to which you were committed, 18 and, having been set free from sin, have become slaves of righteousness. 19 I am speaking in human terms, because

of your natural limitations. For just as you once yielded your members to impurity and to greater and greater iniquity, so now yield your members to righteousness for sanctification.

20 When you were slaves of sin, you were free in regard to righteousness. 21 But then what return did you get from the things of which you are now ashamed? The end of those things is death. 22 But now that you have been set free from sin and have become slaves of God, the return you get is sanctification and its end, eternal life. 23 For the wages of sin is death, but the free gift of God is eternal life in Christ Jesus our Lord.

Eph 2:11-22 (§221)

11 Therefore remember that at one time you Gentiles in the flesh, called the uncircumcision by what is called the circumcision, which is made in the flesh by hands—12 remember that you were at that time separated from Christ, alienated from the commonwealth of Israel, and strangers to the covenants of promise, having no hope and without God in the world. 13 But now in Christ Jesus you who once were far off have been brought near in the blood of Christ. 14 For he is our peace, who has made us both one, and has broken down the dividing wall of hostility, 15 by abolishing in his flesh the law of commandments and ordinances, that he might create in himself one new man in place of the two, so making peace, 16 and might reconcile us both to God in one body through the cross, thereby bringing the hostility to an end. 17 And he came and preached peace to you who were far off and peace to those who were near; 18 for through him we both have access in one Spirit to the Father. 19 So then you are no longer strangers and sojourners, but you are fellow citizens

▶ 6:14 Acts 2:24
24 But God raised him up, having loosed the pangs of death, because it was not possible for him to be held by it.

▶ 6:20 Acts 20:28
28 Take heed to yourselves and to all the flock, in which the Holy Spirit has made you overseers, to care for the church of God which he obtained with the blood of his own Son.

▶ 6:12 *cf. 10:23
▶ 6:13, 18 Rom 14:17
17 For the kingdom of God is not food and drink but righteousness and peace and joy in the Holy Spirit;

1 Thes 4:3
3 For this is the will of God, your sanctification: that you abstain from unchastity;
1 Cor 8:8
8 Food will not commend us to God. We are no worse off if we do not eat, and no better off if we do.

▶ 6:14 15:20
20 But in fact Christ has been raised from the dead, the first fruits of those who have fallen asleep.

2 Cor 4:14
14 knowing that he who raised the Lord Jesus will raise us also with Jesus and bring us with you into his presence.

91

Eph (cont)

rather let him labor, doing honest work with his hands, so that he may be able to give to those in need. 29 Let no evil talk come out of your mouths, but only such as is good for edifying, as fits the occasion, that it may impart grace to those who hear. 30And do not grieve the Holy Spirit of God, in whom you were sealed for the day of redemption. 31 Let all bitterness and wrath and anger and clamor and slander be put away from you, with all malice, 32 and be kind to one another, tenderhearted, forgiving one another, as God in Christ forgave you.

Eph 5:3-14 (§230)

3 But fornication and all impurity or covetousness must not even be named among you, as is fitting among saints. 4 Let there be no filthiness, nor silly talk, nor levity, which are not fitting; but instead let there be thanksgiving. 5 Be sure of this, that no fornicator or impure man, or one who is covetous (that is, an idolater), has any inheritance in the kingdom of Christ and of God. 6 Let no one deceive you with empty

forbearance he had passed over former sins; 26 it was to prove at the present time that he himself is righteous and that he justifies him who has faith in Jesus.

Col 3:5-11 (§266)

5 Put to death therefore what is earthly in you: fornication, impurity, passion, evil desire, and covetousness, which is idolatry. 6 On account of these the wrath of God is coming. 7 In these you once walked, when you lived in them. 8 But now put them all away: anger, wrath, malice, slander, and foul talk from your mouth. 9 Do not lie to one another, seeing that you have put off the old nature with its practices 10 and have put on the new nature, which is being renewed in knowledge after the image of its creator. 11 Here there cannot be Greek and Jew, circumcised and uncircumcised, barbarian, Scyth′ian, slave, free man, but Christ is all, and in all.

words, for it is because of these things that the wrath of God comes upon the sons of disobedience. 7 Therefore do not associate with them, 8 for once you were darkness, but now you are light in the Lord; walk as children of light 9 (for the fruit of light is found in all that is good and right and true), 10 and try to learn what is pleasing to the

Lord. 11 Take no part in the unfruitful works of darkness, but instead expose them. 12 For it is a shame even to speak of the things that they do in secret; 13 but when anything is exposed by the light it becomes visible, for anything that becomes visible is light. 14 Therefore it is said,
"Awake, O sleeper, and arise from the dead,
and Christ shall give you light."

2 Thes 2:13-15 (§297)

13 But we are bound to give thanks to God always for you, brethren beloved by the Lord, because God chose you from the beginning to be saved, through sanctification by the Spirit and belief in the truth. 14 To this he called you through our gospel, so that you may obtain the glory of our Lord Jesus Christ. 15 So then, brethren, stand firm and hold to the traditions which you were taught by us, either by word of mouth or by letter.

92. Glorify God in your body

92

Eph (cont)

with the saints and members of the household of God, 20 built upon the foundation of the apostles and prophets, Christ Jesus himself being the cornerstone, 21 in whom the whole structure is joined together and grows into a holy temple in the Lord; 22 in whom you also are built into it for a dwelling place of God in the Spirit.

Phil 3:10-11 10 that I may know him and the power of his resurrection, and may share his sufferings, becoming like him in his death, 11 that if possible I may attain the resurrection from the dead.

Col 2:12 12 and you were buried with him in baptism, in which you were also raised with him through faith in the working of God, who raised him from the dead.

▶ **6:17 Rom 8:9** 9 But you are not in the flesh, you are in the Spirit, if in fact the Spirit of God dwells in you. Any one who does not have the Spirit of Christ does not belong to him.

Gal 2:20 20 I have been crucified with Christ; it is no longer I who live, but Christ who lives in me; and the life I now live in the flesh I live by faith in the Son of God, who loved me and gave himself for me.

▶ **6:18-19 Phil 1:20** 20 as it is my eager expectation and hope that I shall not be at all ashamed, but that with full courage now as always Christ will be honored in my body, whether by life or by death.

▶ **6:19 3:16** 16 Do you not know that you are God's temple and that God's Spirit dwells in you?

▶ **6:20 7:23** 23 You were bought with a price; do not become slaves of men.

93

1 Cor 7:1-7

7 Now concerning the matters about which you wrote. It is well for a man not to touch a woman. 2 But because of the temptation to immorality, each man should have his own wife and each woman her own husband. 3 The husband should give to his wife her conjugal rights, and likewise the wife to her husband. 4 For the wife does not rule over her own body, but the husband does; likewise the husband does not rule over his own body, but the wife does. 5 Do not refuse one another except perhaps by agreement for a season, that you may devote yourselves to prayer; but then come together again, lest Satan tempt you through lack of self-control. 6 I say this by way of concession, not of command. 7 I wish that all were as I myself am. But each has his own special gift from God, one of one kind and one of.another.

▶ 7:1 7:25
25 Now concerning the unmarried, I have no command of the Lord, but I give my opinion as one who by the Lord's mercy is trustworthy.

8:1 Now concerning food offered to idols: we know that "all of us possess knowledge." "Knowledge" puffs up, but love builds up.

12:1 Now concerning spiritual gifts, brethren, I do not want you to be uninformed.

16:1 Now concerning the contribution for the saints: as I directed the churches of Galatia, so you also are to do.

1 Thes 4:9
9 But concerning love of the brethren you have no need to have any one write to you, for you yourselves have been taught by God to love one another;
1 Thes 4:13.
13 But we would not have you ignorant, brethren, concerning those who are asleep, that you may not grieve as others do who have no hope.

Rom 5:1
But as to the times and the seasons, brethren, you have no need to have anything written to you.
▶ 7:4 Eph 5:28-29
28 Even so husbands should love their wives as their own bodies. He who loves his wife loves himself. 29 For no man ever hates his own flesh, but nourishes and cherishes it, as Christ does the church,

▶ 7:5 2 Cor 2:11, 11 to keep Satan from gaining the advantage over us; for we are not ignorant of his designs.

11:14 14And no wonder, for even Satan disguises himself as an angel of light.

▶ 7:6 7:25,
25 Now concerning the unmarried, I have no command of the Lord, but I give my opinion as one who by the Lord's mercy is trustworthy.

94. To the unmarried and widows

94

1 Cor 7:8-9

8 To the unmarried and the widows I say that it is well for them to remain single as I do. 9 But if they cannot exercise self-control, they should marry. For it is better to marry than to be aflame with passion.

▶ 7:8-9 1 Tim 5:14
14 So I would have younger widows marry, bear children, rule their households, and give the enemy no occasion to revile us.

▶ 7:9 9:25
25 Every athlete exercises self-control in all things. They do it to receive a perishable wreath, but we an imperishable.

Gal 5:16-23
16 But I say, walk by the Spirit, and do not gratify the desires of the flesh. 17 For the desires of the flesh are against the Spirit, and the desires of the Spirit are against the flesh; for these are opposed to each other, to prevent you from doing what you would. 18 But if you are led by the Spirit you are not under the law. 19 Now the works of the flesh are plain: fornication, impurity, licentiousness, 20 idolatry, sorcery, enmity, strife, jealousy, anger, selfishness, dissension, party spirit, 21 envy, drunkenness, carousing, and the like. I warn you, as I warned you before, that those who do such things shall not inherit the kingdom of God. 22 But the fruit of the Spirit is love, joy, peace, patience, kindness, goodness, faithfulness, 23 gentleness, self-control; against such there is no law.

1 Thes 4:1-8 (§284)

4 Finally, brethren, we beseech and exhort you in the Lord Jesus, that as you learned from us how you ought to live and to please God, just as you are doing, you do so more and more. [2] For you know what instructions we gave you through the Lord Jesus. [3] For this is the will of God, your sanctification: that you abstain from unchastity; [4] that each one of you know how to take a wife for himself[x] in holiness and honor [5] not in the passion of lust like heathen who do not know God; [6] that no man transgress, and wrong his brother in this matter,[c] because the Lord is an avenger in all these things, as we solemnly forewarned you. [7] For God has not called us for uncleanness, but in holiness. [8] Therefore whoever disregards this, disregards not man but God, who gives his Holy Spirit to you.

---

35 [35] I say this for your own benefit, not to lay any restraint upon you, but to promote good order and to secure your undivided devotion to the Lord.

14:37
[37] If any one thinks that he is a prophet, or spiritual, he should acknowledge that what I am writing to you is a command of the Lord.

2 Cor 8:8,
[8] I say this not as a command, but to prove by the earnestness of others that your love also is genuine.

11:17
[17] (What I am saying I say not with the Lord's authority but as a fool, in this boastful confidence;

Phm 8-9
[8] Accordingly, though I am bold enough in Christ to command you to do what is required, [9] yet for love's sake I prefer to appeal to you—I, Paul, an ambassador and now a prisoner also for Christ Jesus—

▶ 7:7 *cf. 12:1-11 Rom 12:3-8

▶7:5 (prayer) *add* fasting: S[c] Koine Lect syr Ephraem

94. To the unmarried and widows

94

95

Rom 7:1-6 (§26)

7 Do you not know, brethren—for I am speaking to those who know the law—that the law is binding on a person only during his life? 2 Thus a married woman is bound by law to her husband as long as he lives; but if her husband dies she is discharged from the law concerning the husband. 3Accordingly, she will be called an adulteress if she lives with another man while her husband is alive. But if her husband dies she is free from that law, and if she marries another man she is not an adulteress.

4 Likewise, my brethren, you have died to the law through the body of Christ, so that you may belong to another, to him who has been raised from the dead in order that we may bear fruit for God. 5 While we were living in the flesh, our sinful passions, aroused by the law, were at work in our members to bear fruit for death. 6 But now we are discharged from the law, dead to that which held us captive, so that we serve not under the old written code but in the new life of the Spirit.

1 Cor 7:10-11

10 To the married I give charge, not I but the Lord, that the wife should not separate from her husband 11 (but if she does, let her remain single or else be reconciled to her husband)—and that the husband should not divorce his wife.

▶7:10-11 Mk 10:2-12
2 And Pharisees came up and in order to test him asked, "Is it lawful for a man to divorce his wife?" 3 He answered them, "What did Moses command you?" 4 They said, "Moses allowed a man to write a certificate of divorce, and to put her away." 5 But Jesus said to them, "For your hardness of heart he wrote you this commandment. 6 But from the beginning of creation, 'God made them male and female.' 7 'For this reason a man shall leave his father and mother and be joined to his wife, 8and the two shall become one flesh.' So they are no longer two but one flesh. 9What therefore God has joined together, let not man put asunder."

10 And in the house the disciples asked him again about this matter. 11And he said to them, "Whoever divorces his wife and marries another, commits adultery against her; 12 and if she divorces her husband and marries another, she commits adultery."

▶7:10 *cf. 7:12, 25

96. Unbelieving partner

96

Rom 7:1-6 (§26)

7 Do you not know, brethren—for I am speaking to those who know the law—that the law is binding on a person only during his life? 2 Thus a married woman is bound by law to her husband as long as he lives; but if her husband dies she is discharged from the law concerning the husband. 3Accordingly, she will be called an adulteress if she lives with another man while her husband is alive. But if her husband dies she is free from that law, and if she marries another man she is not an adulteress.

4 Likewise, my brethren, you have died to the law through the body of Christ, so that you may belong to another, to him who has been raised from the dead in order that we may bear fruit for God. 5 While we were living in the flesh, our sinful passions, aroused by the law, were at work in our members to bear fruit for death. 6 But now we are discharged from the law, dead to that which held us captive, so that we serve not under the old written code but in the new life of the Spirit.

1 Cor 7:12-16

12 To the rest I say, not the Lord, that if any brother has a wife who is an unbeliever, and she consents to live with him, he should not divorce her. 13 If any woman has a husband who is an unbeliever, and he consents to live with her, she should not divorce him. 14 For the unbelieving husband is consecrated through his wife, and the unbelieving wife is consecrated through her husband. Otherwise, your children would be unclean, but as it is they are holy. 15 But if the unbelieving partner desires to separate, let it be so; in such a case the brother or sister is not bound. For God has called us to peace. 16 Wife, how do you know whether you will save your husband? Husband, how do you know whether you will save your wife?

2 Cor 6:14-7:1 (§167)

14 Do not be mismated with unbelievers. For what partnership have righteousness and iniquity? Or what fellowship has light with darkness? 15 What accord has Christ with Be'lial? Or what has a believer in common with an unbeliever? 16 What agreement has the temple of God with idols? For we are the temple of the living God; as God said,
"I will live in them and move among them,
and I will be their God,
and they shall be my people.
17 Therefore come out from them,
and be separate from them, says the Lord,
and touch nothing unclean;
then I will welcome you,
18 and I will be a father to you,
and you shall be my sons and daughters,
says the Lord Almighty."

7 Since we have these promises, beloved, let us cleanse ourselves from every defilement of body and spirit, and make holiness perfect in the fear of God.

▶7:16 *cf. 1 Pet 3:1-2   ▶7:12 *cf. 7:10 2 Cor 11:17   ▶7:14 Rom 11:16   1 Thes 4:4   ▶7:15 Rom 14:19   19Let us then pursue what makes for peace and for mutual upbuilding.   *cf. 7:39f   ▶7:16 *cf. Eph 5:21-33

▶ 7:12-16 *cf Mk 10:10-12
16 If the dough offered as first fruits is holy, so is the whole lump; and if the root is holy, so are the branches.
4 that each one of you know how to take a wife for himself in holiness and honor

95

96. Unbelieving partner

96

▶ 7:15 (us) *read* you:S*AC cop(bo) Pelagius

97

Rom 2:25-29 (§11)

25 Circumcision indeed is of value if you obey the law; but if you break the law, your circumcision becomes uncircumcision. 26 So, if a man who is uncircumcised keeps the precepts of the law, will not his uncircumcision be regarded as circumcision? 27 Then those who are physically uncircumcised but keep the law will condemn you who have the written code and circumcision but break the law. 28 For he is not a real Jew who is one outwardly, nor is true circumcision something external and physical. 29 He is a Jew who is one inwardly, and real circumcision is a matter of the heart, spiritual and not literal. His praise is not from men but from God.

Rom 6:15-23 (§25)

15 What then? Are we to sin because we are not under law but under grace? By no means! 16 Do you not know that if you yield yourselves to any one as obedient slaves, you are slaves of the one whom you obey, either of sin, which leads to death, or of obedience, which leads to righteousness? 17 But thanks be to God, that you who were

1 Cor 7:17-24

17 Only, let every one lead the life which the Lord has assigned to him, and in which God has called him. This is my rule in all the churches. 18 Was any one at the time of his call already circumcised? Let him not seek to remove the marks of circumcision. Was any one at the time of his call uncircumcised? Let him not seek circumcision. 19 For neither circumcision counts for anything nor uncircumcision, but keeping the commandments of God. 20 Every one should remain in the state in which he was called. 21 Were you a slave when called? Never mind. But if you can gain your freedom, avail yourself of the opportunity. 22 For he who was called in the Lord as a slave is a freedman of the Lord. Likewise he who was free when called is a slave of Christ. 23 You were bought with a price; do not become slaves of men. 24 So, brethren, in whatever state each was called, there let him remain with God.

once slaves of sin have become obedient from the heart to the standard of teaching to which you were committed,

18 and, having been set free from sin, have become slaves of righteousness. 19 I am speaking in human terms, because of your natural limitations. For just as you once yielded your members to impurity and to greater and greater iniquity, so now yield your members to righteousness for sanctification.

20 When you were slaves of sin, you were free in regard to righteousness. 21 But then what return did you get from the things of which you are now ashamed? The end of those things is death. 22 But now that you have been set free from sin and have become slaves of God, the return you get is sanctification and its end, eternal life. 23 For the wages of sin is death, but the free gift of God is eternal life in Christ Jesus our Lord.

Gal 5:1-12 (§211)

5 For freedom Christ has set us free; stand fast therefore, and do not submit again to a yoke of slavery.

2 Now I, Paul, say to you that if you receive circumcision, Christ will be of no advantage to you. 3 I testify again to every man who receives circumcision that he is bound to keep the whole law. 4 You are severed from Christ, you who would be justified by the law; you have fallen away from grace. 5 For through the Spirit, by faith, we wait for the hope of righteousness. 6 For in Christ Jesus neither circumcision nor uncircumcision is of any avail, but faith working through love. 7 You were running well; who hindered you from obeying the truth? 8 This persuasion is not from him who calls you. 9 A little leaven leavens the whole lump. 10 I have confidence in the Lord that you will take no other view than mine; and he who is troubling you will bear his judgment, whoever he is. 11 But if I, brethren, still preach circumcision, why am I still persecuted? In that case the stumbling block of the cross has been removed. 12 I wish those who unsettle you would mutilate themselves!

Gal 6:11-17 (§216)

11 See with what large letters I am writing to you with my own hand. 12 It is those who want to make a good showing in the flesh that would compel you to be circumcised, and only in order that they may not be persecuted for the cross of Christ. 13 For even those who receive circumcision do not themselves keep the law, but they desire to have you circumcised that they may glory in your flesh. 14 But far be it from me to glory except in the cross of our Lord Jesus Christ, by which the world has been crucified to me, and I to the world. 15 For neither circumcision counts for anything, nor uncircumcision, but a new creation. 16 Peace and mercy be upon all who walk by this rule, upon the Israel of God.

17 Henceforth let no man trouble me; for I bear on my body the marks of Jesus.

▶ 7:18 Acts 15:1-2
But some men came down from Judea and were teaching the brethren, "Unless you are circumcised according to the custom of Moses, you cannot be saved." 2 And when Paul and Barnabas had no small dissension and debate with them, Paul and Barnabas and some of the others were appointed to go up to Jerusalem to the apostles and the elders about this question.

▶ 7:17 4:17
17 Therefore I sent to you Timothy, my beloved and faithful child in the Lord, to remind you of my ways in Christ, as I teach them everywhere in every church.

11:16
16 If any one is disposed to be contentious, we recognize no other practice, nor do the churches of God.

Rom 12:3
3 For by the grace given to me I bid every one among you not to think of himself more highly than he ought to think, but to think with sober judgment, each according to the measure of faith which God has assigned him.

2 Cor 8:18
18 With him we are sending the brother who is famous among all the churches for his preaching of the gospel;

2 Cor 11:28   28 And, apart from other things, there is the daily pressure upon me of my anxiety for all the churches.
▶ 7:23 6:20   20 you were bought with a price. So glorify God in your body.

98. Concerning the unmarried

98

Rom 13:11-14 (§56)

11 Besides this you know what hour it is, how it is full time now for you to wake from sleep. For salvation is nearer to us now than when we first believed; 12 the night is far gone, the day is at hand. Let us then cast off the works of darkness and put on the armor of light; 13 let us conduct ourselves becomingly as in the day, not in reveling and drunkenness, not in debauchery and licentiousness, not in quarreling and jealousy. 14 But put on the Lord Jesus Christ, and make no provision for the flesh, to gratify its desires.

1 Cor 7:25-31

25 Now concerning the unmarried, I have no command of the Lord, but I give my opinion as one who by the Lord's mercy is trustworthy. 26 I think that in view of the present distress it is well for a person to remain as he is. 27 Are you bound to a wife? Do not seek to be free. Are you free from a wife? Do not seek marriage. 28 But if you marry, you do not sin, and if a girl marries she does not sin. Yet those who marry will have worldly troubles, and I would spare you that. 29 I mean, brethren, the appointed time has grown very short; from now on, let those who have wives live as though they had none, 30 and those who mourn as though they were not mourning, and those who rejoice as though they were not rejoicing, and those who buy as though they had no goods, 31 and those who deal with the world as though they had no dealings with it. For the form of this world is passing away.

▶ 7:25 1 Tim 1:12
12 I thank him who has given me strength for this, Christ Jesus our Lord, because he judged me faithful by appointing me to his service,

▶ 7:25 *cf. 7:10, 12 4:2 2 Cor 4:1   ▶ 7:26 10:11
11 Now these things happened to them as a warning, but they were written down for our instruction, upon whom the end of the ages has come.

▶ 7:31 *cf. Rom 8:18-25

97

Phm 8-20 (§307-308)

8 Accordingly, though I am bold enough in Christ to command you to do what is required, 9 yet for love's sake I prefer to appeal to you—I, Paul, an ambassador and now a prisoner also for Christ Jesus—10 I appeal to you for my child, Ones'imus, whose father I have become in my imprisonment. 11 (Formerly he was useless to you, but now he is indeed useful to you and to me.) 12 I am sending him back to you, sending my very heart. 13 I would have been glad to keep him with me, in order that he might serve me on your behalf during my imprisonment for the gospel; 14 but I preferred to do nothing without your consent in order that your goodness might not be by compulsion but of your own free will.

15 Perhaps this is why he was parted from you for a while, that you might have him back for ever, 16 no longer as a slave but more than a slave, as a beloved brother, especially to me but how much more to you, both in the flesh and in the Lord. 17 So if you consider me your partner, receive him as you would receive me. 18 If he has wronged you at all, or owes you anything, charge that to my account. 19 I, Paul, write this with my own hand, I will repay it—to say nothing of your owing me even your own self. 20 Yes, brother, I want some benefit from you in the Lord. Refresh my heart in Christ.

98. Concerning the unmarried

98

1 Thes 5:1-11 (§287)

5 But as to the times and the seasons, brethren, you have no need to have anything written to you. 2 For you yourselves know well that the day of the Lord will come like a thief in the night. 3 When people say, "There is peace and security," then sudden destruction will come upon them as travail comes upon a woman with child, and there will be no escape. 4 But you are not in darkness, brethren, for that day to surprise you like a thief. 5 For you are all sons of light and sons of the day; we are not of the night or of darkness. 6 So then, let us not sleep, as others do, but let us keep awake and be sober. 7 For those who sleep sleep at night, and those who get drunk are drunk at night. 8 But, since we belong to the day, let us be sober, and put on the breastplate of faith and love, and for a helmet the hope of salvation. 9 For God has not destined us for wrath, but to obtain salvation through our Lord Jesus Christ, 10 who died for us so that whether we wake or sleep we might live with him. 11 Therefore encourage one another and build one another up, just as you are doing.

2 Thes 2:1-12 (§296)

2 Now concerning the coming of our Lord Jesus Christ and our assembling to meet him, we beg you, brethren, 2 not to be quickly shaken in mind or excited, either by spirit or by word, or by letter purporting to be from us, to the effect that the day of the Lord has come. 3 Let no one deceive you in any way; for that day will not come, unless the rebellion comes first, and the man of lawlessness is revealed, the son of perdition, 4 who opposes and exalts himself against every so-called god or object of worship, so that he takes his seat in the temple of God, proclaiming himself to be God. 5 Do you not remember that when I was still with you I told you this? 6 And you know what is restraining him now so that he may be revealed in his time. 7 For the mystery of lawlessness is already at work; only he who now restrains it will do so until he is out of the way. 8 And then the lawless one will be revealed, and the Lord Jesus will slay him with the breath of his mouth and destroy him by his appearing and his coming. 9 The coming of the lawless one by the activity of Satan will be with all power and with pretended signs and wonders, 10 and with all wicked deception for those who are to perish, because they refused to love the truth and so be saved. 11 Therefore God sends upon them a strong delusion, to make them believe what is false, 12 so that all may be condemned who did not believe the truth but had pleasure in unrighteousness.

99

1 Cor 7:32-35

32 I want you to be free from anxieties. The unmarried man is anxious about the affairs of the Lord, how to please the Lord; 33 but the married man is anxious about worldly affairs, how to please his wife, 34 and his interests are divided. And the unmarried woman or girl is anxious about the affairs of the Lord, how to be holy in body and spirit; but the married woman is anxious about worldly affairs, how to please her husband. 35 I say this for your own benefit, not to lay any restraint upon you, but to promote good order and to secure your undivided devotion to the Lord.

Eph 5:21-6:9 (§232)

21 Be subject to one another out of reverence for Christ. 22 Wives, be subject to your husbands, as to the Lord. 23 For the husband is the head of the wife as Christ is the head of the church, his body, and is himself its Savior. 24 As the church is subject to Christ, so let wives also be subject in everything to their husbands. 25 Husbands, love your wives, as Christ loved the church and gave himself up for her, 26 that he might sanctify her, having cleansed her by the washing of water with the word, 27 that he might present the church to himself in splendor, without spot or wrinkle or any such thing, that she might be holy and without blemish. 28 Even so husbands should love their wives as their own bodies. He who loves his wife loves himself. 29 For no man ever hates his own flesh, but nourishes and cherishes it, as Christ does the church, 30 because we are members of his body. 31 "For this reason a man shall leave his father and mother and be joined to his wife, and the two shall become one flesh." 32 This mystery is a profound one, and I am saying that it

▶ 7:32 1 Tim 5:5
5 She who is a real widow, and is left all alone, has set her hope on God and continues in supplications and prayers night and day;

▶ 7:32 Rom 8:8
8 and those who are in the flesh cannot please God.

▶ 7:32-34 7:14
14 For the unbelieving husband is consecrated through his wife, and the unbelieving wife is consecrated through her husband. Otherwise, your children would be unclean, but as it is they are holy.

12:25
25 that there may be no discord in the body, but that the members may have the same care for one another.

▶ 7:35 7:6
6 I say this by way of concession, not of command.

100

1 Cor 7:36-38

36 If any one thinks that he is not behaving properly toward his betrothed, if his passions are strong, and it has to be, let him do as he wishes: let them marry—it is no sin. 37 But whoever is firmly established in his heart, being under no necessity but having his desire under control, and has determined this in his heart, to keep her as his betrothed, he will do well. 38 So that he who marries his betrothed does well; and he who refrains from marriage will do better.

▶ 7:36-38 *cf. 7:8-9, 25-31

▶ 7:37 Phm 14
14 but I preferred to do nothing without your consent in order that your goodness might not be by compulsion but of your own free will.

Phil 4:4-7 (§251)

4 Rejoice in the Lord always; again I will say, Rejoice. 5 Let all men know your forbearance. The Lord is at hand. 6 Have no anxiety about anything, but in everything by prayer and supplication with thanksgiving let your requests be made known to God. 7 And the peace of God, which passes all understanding, will keep your hearts and your minds in Christ Jesus.

Eph (cont)

refers to Christ and the church; 33 however, let each one of you love his wife as himself, and let the wife see that she respects her husband.

6 Children, obey your parents in the Lord, for this is right. 2 "Honor your father and mother" (this is the first commandment with a promise), 3 "that it may be well with you and that you may live long on the earth." 4 Fathers, do not provoke your children to anger, but bring them up in the discipline and instruction of the Lord.

5 Slaves, be obedient to those who are your earthly masters, with fear and trembling, in singleness of heart, as to Christ; 6 not in the way of eyeservice,

Col 3:18-4:1 (§268)

18 Wives, be subject to your husbands, as is fitting in the Lord. 19 Husbands, love your wives, and do not be harsh with them. 20 Children, obey your parents in everything, for this pleases the Lord. 21 Fathers, do not provoke your children, lest they become discouraged. 22 Slaves, obey in everything those who are your earthly masters, not with eyeservice, as men-pleasers, but in singleness of heart, fearing the Lord. 23 Whatever your task, work heartily, as serving the Lord and not men, 24 knowing that from the Lord you will receive the inheritance as your reward;

as men-pleasers, but as servants of Christ, doing the will of God from the heart, 7 rendering service with a good will as to the Lord and not to men, 8 knowing that whatever good any one does, he will receive the same again from the Lord, whether he is a slave or free. 9 Masters, do the same to them, and forbear threatening, knowing that he who is both their Master and yours is in heaven, and that there is no partiality with him.

1 Thes 4:1-8 (§284)

4 Finally, brethren, we beseech and exhort you in the Lord Jesus, that as you learned from us how you ought to live and to please God, just as you are doing, you do so more and more. 2 For you know what instructions we gave you through the Lord Jesus. 3 For this is the will of God, your sanctifica-

you are serving the Lord Christ. 25 For the wrongdoer will be paid back for the wrong he has done, and there is no partiality.

4 Masters, treat your slaves justly and fairly, knowing that you also have a Master in heaven.

Col 2:4-7 (§261)

4 I say this in order that no one may delude you with beguiling speech. 5 For though I am absent in body, yet I am with you in spirit, rejoicing to see your good order and the firmness of your faith in Christ.

6 As therefore you received Christ Jesus the Lord, so live in him, 7 rooted and built up in him and established in the faith, just as you were taught, abounding in thanksgiving.

tion: that you abstain from unchastity; 4 that each one of you know how to take a wife for himself in holiness and honor 5 not in the passion of lust like heathen who do not know God; 6 that no man transgress, and wrong his brother in this matter, because the Lord is an avenger in all these things, as we solemnly forewarned you. 7 For God has not called us for uncleanness, but in holiness. 8 Therefore whoever disregards this, disregards not man but God, who gives his Holy Spirit to you.

100. He who refrains from marriage does better

101

Rom 7:1-6 (§26)

7 Do you not know, brethren—for I am speaking to those who know the law—that the law is binding on a person only during his life? ² Thus a married woman is bound by law to her husband as long as he lives; but if her husband dies she is discharged from the law concerning the husband. ³Accordingly, she will be called an adulteress if she lives with another man while her husband is alive. But if her husband dies she is free from that law, and if she marries another man she is not an adulteress.

4 Likewise, my brethren, you have died to the law through the body of Christ, so that you may belong to another, to him who has been raised from the dead in order that we may bear fruit for God. ⁵ While we were living in the flesh, our sinful passions, aroused by the law, were at work in our members to bear fruit for death. ⁶ But now we are discharged from the law, dead to that which held us captive, so that we serve not under the old written code but in the new life of the Spirit.

1 Cor 7:39-40

39 A wife is bound to her husband as long as he lives. If the husband dies, she is free to be married to whom she wishes, only in the Lord. ⁴⁰ But in my judgment she is happier if she remains as she is. And I think that I have the Spirit of God.

▶ 7:39 7:12-13
12 To the rest I say, not the Lord, that if any brother has a wife who is an unbeliever, and she consents to live with him, he should not divorce her. ¹³ If any woman has a husband who is an unbeliever, and he consents to live with her, she should not divorce him.

▶ 7:40 2 Cor 10:7
7 Look at what is before your eyes. If any one is confident that he is Christ's, let him remind himself that as he is Christ's, so are we.

1 Cor 7:8,
8 To the unmarried and the widows I say that it is well for them to remain single as I do.

25
25 Now concerning the unmarried, I have no command of the Lord, but I give my opinion as one who by the Lord's mercy is trustworthy.

102. Love builds up, knowledge puffs up

102

Rom 14:1-4 (§57)

14 As for the man who is weak in faith, welcome him, but not for disputes over opinions. ² One believes he may eat anything, while the weak man eats only vegetables. ³ Let not him who eats despise him who abstains, and let not him who abstains pass judgment on him who eats; for God has welcomed him. ⁴ Who are you to pass judgment on the servant of another? It is before his own master that he stands or falls. And he will be upheld, for the Master is able to make him stand.

1 Cor 8:1-3

8 Now concerning food offered to idols: we know that "all of us possess knowledge." "Knowledge" puffs up, but love builds up. ² If any one imagines that he knows something, he does not yet know as he ought to know. ³ But if one loves God, one is known by him.

▶ 8:1 Acts 15:20 20 but should write to them to abstain from the pollutions of idols and from unchastity and from what is strangled and from blood.

29 ²⁹ that you abstain from what has been sacrificed to idols and from blood and from what is strangled and from unchastity. If you keep yourselves from these, you will do well. Farewell."

▶ 8:2 1 Tim 6:4-5 4 he is puffed up with conceit, he knows nothing; he has a morbid craving for controversy and for disputes about words, which produce envy, dissension, slander, base suspicions, ⁵ and wrangling among men who are depraved in mind and bereft of the truth, imagining that godliness is a means of gain.

▶ 8:1 Rom 15:14 14 I myself am satisfied about you, my brethren, that you yourselves are full of goodness, filled with all knowledge, and able to instruct one another.

▶ 8:2 Gal 6:3 ³ For if any one thinks he is something, when he is nothing, he deceives himself.

▶ 8:3 Gal 4:9 ⁹ but now that you have come to know God, or rather to be known by God, how can you turn back again to the weak and beggarly elemental spirits, whose slaves you want to be once more?

101

102. Love builds up, knowledge puffs up

102

▶8:2 (something) *omit* something: p⁴⁶ ▶8:3 (God) *omit* God: p⁴⁶S* Clement; (him)
Tertullian Origen   *omit* by him: p⁴⁶S* Clement

103

Rom 11:33-36 (§50)

33 O the depth of the riches and wisdom and knowledge of God! How unsearchable are his judgments and how inscrutable his ways! 34 "For who has known the mind of the Lord, or who has been his counselor?" 35 "Or who has given a gift to him that he might be repaid?" 36 For from him and through him and to him are all things. To him be glory for ever. Amen.

Rom 14:5-12 (§58)

5 One man esteems one day as better than another, while another man esteems all days alike. Let every one be fully convinced in his own mind. 6 He who observes the day, observes it in honor of the Lord. He also who eats, eats in honor of the Lord, since he gives thanks to God; while he who abstains, abstains in honor of the Lord and gives thanks to God. 7 None of us lives to himself, and none of us dies to himself. 8 If we live, we live to the Lord, and if we die, we die to the Lord; so then, whether we live or whether we die, we are the Lord's. 9 For to this end Christ

▶ 8:4 Acts 14:15

15 "Men, why are you doing this? We also are men, of like nature with you, and bring you good news, that you should turn from these vain things to a living God who made the heaven and the earth and the sea and all that is in them.

1 Cor 8:4-6

4 Hence, as to the eating of food offered to idols, we know that "an idol has no real existence," and that "there is no God but one." 5 For although there may be so-called gods in heaven or on earth—as indeed there are many "gods" and many "lords"—6 yet for us there is one God, the Father, from whom are all things and for whom we exist, and one Lord, Jesus Christ, through whom are all things and through whom we exist.

died and lived again, that he might be Lord both of the dead and of the living.

10 Why do you pass judgment on your brother? Or you, why do you despise your brother? For we shall all stand before the judgment seat of God; 11 for it is written,
"As I live, says the Lord, every knee shall bow to me,
and every tongue shall give praise*u* to God."
12 So each of us shall give account of himself to God.

▶ 8:6 1 Tim 2:5

5 For there is one God, and there is one mediator between God and men, the man Christ Jesus,

▶ 8:4 *cf. 10:19-20

▶ 8:6 Rom 14:9-12

9 For to this end Christ died and lived again, that he might be Lord both of the dead and of the living.
10 Why do you pass judgment on your brother? Or you, why do you despise your brother? For we shall all stand before the judgment seat of God; 11 for it is written,
"As I live, says the Lord, every knee shall bow to me,
and every tongue shall give praise to God."
12 So each of us shall give account of himself to God.

Eph 4:1-10 (§225)

4 I therefore, a prisoner for the Lord, beg you to lead a life worthy of the calling to which you have been called, 2 with all lowliness and meekness, with patience, forbearing one another in love, 3 eager to maintain the unity of the Spirit in the bond of peace. 4 There is one body and one Spirit, just as you were called to the one hope that belongs to your call, 5 one Lord, one faith, one baptism, 6 one God and Father of us all, who is above all and through all and in all. 7 But grace was given to each of us according to the measure of Christ's gift. 8 Therefore it is said,
"When he ascended on high he led a host of captives,
and he gave gifts to men."
9 (In saying, "He ascended," what does it mean but that he had also descended into the lower parts of the earth? 10 He who descended is he who also ascended far above all the heavens, that he might fill all things.)

104. Food will not commend us to God

104

Rom 2:12-16 (§9)

12 All who have sinned without the law will also perish without the law, and all who have sinned under the law will be judged by the law. 13 For it is not the hearers of the law who are righteous before God, but the doers of the law who will be justified. 14 When Gentiles who have not the law do by nature what the law requires, they are a law to themselves, even though they do not have the law. 15 They show that what the law requires is written on their hearts, while their conscience also bears witness and their conflicting thoughts accuse or perhaps excuse them 16 on that day when, according to my gospel, God judges the secrets of men by Christ Jesus.

Rom 14:13-23 (§59)

13 Then let us no more pass judgment on one another, but rather decide never to put a stumbling block or hindrance in the way of a brother. 14 I know and am persuaded in the Lord Jesus that nothing is unclean in itself; but it is unclean for any one who thinks it unclean. 15 If your brother is being injured by what you eat, you are no

▶ 8:10 Acts 15:20

20 but should write to them to abstain from the pollutions of idols and from unchastity and from what is strangled and from blood.

1 Cor 8:7-13

7 However, not all possess this knowledge. But some, through being hitherto accustomed to idols, eat food as really offered to an idol; and their conscience, being weak, is defiled. 8 Food will not commend us to God. We are no worse off if we do not eat, and no better off if we do. 9 Only take care lest this liberty of yours somehow become a stumbling block to the weak. 10 For if any one sees you, a man of knowledge, at table in an idol's temple, might he not be encouraged, if his conscience is weak, to eat food offered to idols? 11 And so by your knowledge this weak man is destroyed, the brother for whom Christ died. 12 Thus, sinning against your brethren and wounding their conscience when it is weak, you sin against Christ. 13 Therefore, if food is a cause of my brother's falling, I will never eat meat, lest I cause my brother to fall.

longer walking in love. Do not let what you eat cause the ruin of one for whom Christ died. 16 So do not let your good be spoken of as evil. 17 For the kingdom of God is not food and drink but

▶ 8:7 10:19-20

19 What do I imply then? That food offered to idols is anything, or that an idol is anything? 20 No, I imply that what pagans sacrifice they offer to demons and not to God. I do not want you to be partners with demons.

▶ 8:7-13 *cf. 10:23-11:1 4:1-5

righteousness and peace and joy in the Holy Spirit; 18 he who thus serves Christ is acceptable to God and approved by men. 19 Let us then pursue what makes for peace and for mutual upbuilding. 20 Do not, for the sake of food, destroy the work of God. Everything is indeed clean, but it is wrong for any one to make others fall by what he eats; 21 it is right not to eat meat or drink wine or do anything that makes your brother stumble. 22 The faith that you have, keep between yourself and God; happy is he who has no reason to judge himself for what he approves. 23 But he who has doubts is condemned, if he eats, because he does not act from faith; for whatever does not proceed from faith is sin.

▶ 8:8 Rom 14:17

17 For the kingdom of God is not food and drink but righteousness and peace and joy in the Holy Spirit;

▶ 8:11-13 9:22

22 To the weak I became weak, that I might win the weak. I have become all things to all men, that I might by all means save some.

103

Col 1:15-20 (§258)

15 He is the image of the invisible God, the first-born of all creation; 16 for in him all things were created, in heaven and on earth, visible and invisible, whether thrones or dominions or principalities or authorities—all things were created through him and for him. 17 He is before all things, and in him all things hold together. 18 He is the head of the body, the church; he is the beginning, the first-born from the dead, that in everything he might be pre-eminent. 19 For in him all the fulness of God was pleased to dwell, 20 and through him to reconcile to himself all things, whether on earth or in heaven, making peace by the blood of his cross.

▶8:4 *cf 1Thes 1:9
▶8:5 *cf 2 Thes 2:4

104. Food will not commend us to God

104

105

1 Cor 9:1-14

9 Am I not free? Am I not an apostle? Have I not seen Jesus our Lord? Are not you my workmanship in the Lord? [2] If to others I am not an apostle, at least I am to you; for you are the seal of my apostleship in the Lord.

3 This is my defense to those who would examine me. [4] Do we not have the right to our food and drink? [5] Do we not have the right to be accompanied by a wife, as the other apostles and the brothers of the Lord and Cephas? [6] Or is it only Barnabas and I who have no right to refrain from working for a living? [7] Who serves as a soldier at his own expense? Who plants a vineyard without eating any of its fruit? Who tends a flock without getting some of the milk?

8 Do I say this on human authority? Does not the law say the same? [9] For it is written in the law of Moses, "You shall not muzzle an ox when it is treading out the grain." Is it for oxen that God is concerned? [10] Does he not speak entirely for our sake? It was written for our sake, because the plowman should plow in hope and the thresher thresh in

2 Cor 3:1-3 (§154)

3 Are we beginning to commend ourselves again? Or do we need, as some do, letters of recommendation to you, or from you? [2] You yourselves are our letter of recommendation, written on your hearts, to be known and read by all men; [3] and you show that you are a letter from Christ delivered by us, written not with ink but with the Spirit of the living God, not on tablets of stone but on tablets of human hearts.

hope of a share in the crop. [11] If we have sown spiritual good among you, is it too much if we reap your material benefits? [12] If others share this rightful claim upon you, do not we still more?

Nevertheless, we have not made use of this right, but we endure anything rather than put an obstacle in the way of the gospel of Christ. [13] Do you not know that those who are employed in the temple service get their food from the temple, and those who serve at the altar share in the sacrificial offerings? [14] In the same way, the Lord commanded that those who proclaim the gospel should get their living by the gospel.

Gal 1:15-24 (§196)   15 But when he who had set me apart before I was born, and had called me through his grace, [16] was pleased to reveal his Son to me, in

2 Cor 11:7-11 (§180)

7 Did I commit a sin in abasing myself so that you might be exalted, because I preached God's gospel without cost to you? [8] I robbed other churches by accepting support from them in order to serve you. [9]And when I was with you and was in want, I did not burden any one, for my needs were supplied by the brethren who came from Macedo'nia. So I refrained and will refrain from burdening you in any way. [10]As the truth of Christ is in me, this boast of mine shall not be silenced in the regions of Acha'ia. [11]And why? Because I do not love you? God knows I do!

2 Cor 12:14-18 (§187)

14 Here for the third time I am ready to come to you. And I will not be a burden, for I seek not what is yours but you; for children ought not to lay up for their parents, but parents for their children. [15] I will most gladly spend and be spent for your souls. If I love you the

order that I might preach him among the Gentiles, I did not confer with flesh and blood, [17] nor did I go up to Jerusalem to those who were apostles before me, but I went away into Arabia; and again I returned to Damascus.

18 Then after three years I went up to Jerusalem to visit Cephas, and remained with him fifteen days. [19] But I saw none of the other apostles except James the Lord's brother. [20] (In what I am writing to you, before God, I do not lie!) [21] Then I went into the regions of Syria and Cili'cia. [22]And I was still not known by sight to the churches of Christ in Judea; [23] they only heard it said, "He who once persecuted us is now preaching the faith he once tried to

more, am I to be loved the less? [16] But granting that I myself did not burden you, I was crafty, you say, and got the better of you by guile. [17] Did I take advantage of you through any of those whom I sent to you? [18] I urged Titus to go, and sent the brother with him. Did Titus take advantage of you? Did we not act in the same spirit? Did we not take the same steps?

▶ 9:1 Acts 9:3.
[3] Now as he journeyed he approached Damascus, and suddenly a light from heaven flashed about him.

17
[17] So Anani'as departed and entered the house. And laying his hands on him he said, "Brother Saul, the Lord Jesus who appeared to you on the road by which you came, has sent me that you may regain your sight and be filled with the Holy Spirit."

18:9 [9]And the Lord said to Paul one night in a vision, "Do not be afraid, but speak and do not be silent;

22:14, [14]And he said, 'The God of our fathers appointed you to know his will, to see the Just One and to hear a voice from his mouth;

18 [18] and saw him saying to me, 'Make haste and get quickly out of Jerusalem, because they will not accept your testimony about me.'

23:11
11 The following night the Lord stood by him and said, "Take courage, for as you have testified about me at Jerusalem, so you must bear witness also at Rome."

1 Tim 2:7
7 For this I was appointed a preacher and apostle (I am telling the truth, I am not lying), a teacher of the Gentiles in faith and truth.

2 Tim 1:11   11 For this gospel I was appointed a preacher and apostle and teacher,

106. Gospel free of charge

106

1 Cor 9:15-18

15 But I have made no use of any of these rights, nor am I writing this to secure any such provision. For I would rather die than have any one deprive me of my ground for boasting. [16] For if I preach the gospel, that gives me no ground for boasting. For necessity is laid upon me. Woe to me if I do not preach the gospel! [17] For if I do this of my own will, I have a reward; but if not of my own will, I am entrusted with a commission. [18] What then is my reward? Just this: that in my preaching I may make the gospel free of charge, not making full use of my right in the gospel.

2 Cor 11:7-11 (§180)

7 Did I commit a sin in abasing myself so that you might be exalted, because I preached God's gospel without cost to you? [8] I robbed other churches by accepting support from them in order to serve you. [9]And when I was with you and was in want, I did not burden any one, for my needs were supplied by the brethren who came from Macedo'nia. So I refrained and will refrain from burdening you in any way. [10]As the truth of Christ is in me, this boast of mine shall not be silenced in the regions of Acha'ia. [11]And why? Because I do not love you? God knows I do!

2 Cor 11:12-15 (§106)

12 And what I do I will continue to do, in order to undermine the claim of those who would like to claim that in their boasted mission they work on the same terms as we do. [13] For such men are false apostles, deceitful workmen, disguising themselves as apostles of Christ. [14]And no wonder, for even Satan disguises himself as an angel of light. [15] So it is not strange if his servants also disguise themselves as servants

Eph 3:1-13 (§222)

3 For this reason I, Paul, a prisoner for Christ Jesus on behalf of you Gentiles— [2] assuming that you have heard of the stewardship of God's grace that was given to me for you, [3] how the mystery was made known to me by revelation, as I have written briefly. [4] When you read this you can perceive my insight into the mystery of Christ, [5] which was not made known to the sons of men in other generations as it has now been revealed to his holy apostles and prophets by the Spirit; [6] that is, how the Gentiles are fellow heirs, members of the same body, and partakers of the promise in Christ Jesus through the gospel.

7 Of this gospel I was made a minister according to the gift of God's grace which was given me by the working of his power. [8] To me, though I am the very least of all the saints, this grace was given, to preach to the Gentiles the unsearchable riches of Christ, [9] and to make all men see what is the plan of the mystery hidden for ages in God who created all things; [10] that through the church the manifold wisdom of God

of righteousness. Their end will correspond to their deeds.

▶ 9:18 Acts 18:3 [3] and because he was of the same trade he stayed with them, and they worked, for by trade they were tentmakers.

▶ 9:15 2 Cor 1:12,
12 For our boast is this, the testimony of our conscience that we have behaved in the world, and still more toward you, with holiness and godly sincerity, not by earthly wisdom but by the grace of God.

11:10
[10]As the truth of Christ is in me, this boast of mine shall not be silenced in the regions of Acha'ia.

Phil 4:11,
11 Not that I complain of want; for I have learned, in whatever state I am, to be content.

17
that I seek the gift; but I seek the fruit which increases to your credit.

▶ 9:16 2 Cor 4:5 [5] For what we preach is not ourselves, but Jesus Christ as Lord, with ourselves as your servants for Jesus' sake.

105

106

Phil 4:10-20 (§253)

10 I rejoice in the Lord greatly that now at length you have revived your concern for me; you were indeed concerned for me, but you had no opportunity. 11 Not that I complain of want; for I have learned, in whatever state I am, to be content. 12 I know how to be abased, and I know how to abound; in any and all circumstances I have

Gal (cont)

destroy." 24And they glorified God because of me.

Gal 6:1-6 (§214)

6 Brethren, if a man is overtaken in any trespass, you who are spiritual should restore him in a spirit of gentleness. Look to yourself, lest you too be tempted. 2 Bear one another's burdens, and so fulfil the law of Christ. 3 For if any one thinks he is something, when he is nothing, he deceives himself. 4 But let each one test his own work, and then his reason to boast will be in himself alone and not in his neighbor. 5 For each man will have to bear his own load.

6 Let him who is taught the word share all good things with him who teaches.

learned the secret of facing plenty and hunger, abundance and want. 13 I can do all things in him who strengthens me.

14 Yet it was kind of you to share my trouble. 15And you Philippians yourselves know that in the beginning of the gospel, when I left Macedo'nia, no church entered into partnership with me in giving and receiving except you only; 16 for even in Thessaloni'ca you sent me help once and again. 17 Not that I seek the gift; but I seek the fruit which increases to your credit. 18 I have received full payment, and more; I am filled, having received from Epaphrodi'tus the gifts you sent, a fragrant offering, a sacrifice acceptable and pleasing to God. 19And my God will supply every need of yours according to his riches in glory in Christ Jesus. 20 To our God and Father be glory for ever and ever. Amen.

1 Thes 2:9-12 (§278)

9 For you remember our labor and toil, brethren; we worked night and day, that we might not burden any of you, while we preached to you the gospel of God. 10 You are witnesses, and God also, how holy and righteous and blameless was our behavior to you believers; 11 for you know how, like a father with his children, we exhorted each one of you and encouraged you and charged you 12 to lead a life worthy of God, who calls you into his own kingdom and glory.

2 Thes 3:6-13 (§300)

6 Now we command you, brethren, in the name of our Lord Jesus Christ, that you keep away from any brother who is living in idleness and not in accord with the tradition that you received from us. 7 For you yourselves know how you ought to imitate us; we were not idle when we were with you, 8 we did not eat any one's bread without paying, but with toil and labor we worked night and day, that we might not burden any of you. 9 It was not because we have not that right, but to give you in our conduct an example to imitate. 10 For even when we were with you, we gave you this command: If any one will not work, let him not eat. 11 For we hear that some of you are living in idleness, mere busybodies, not doing any work. 12 Now such persons we command and exhort in the Lord Jesus Christ to do their work in quietness and to earn their own living. 13 Brethren, do not be weary in well-doing.

▶ 9:7, 10 2 Tim 2:4-6
4No soldier on service gets entangled in civilian pursuits, since his aim is to satisfy the one who enlisted him. 5An athlete is not crowned unless he competes according to the rules.

▶ 9:9, 14 1 Tim 5:18
18 for the scripture says, "You shall not muzzle an ox when it is treading out the grain," and, "The laborer deserves his wages."

▶ 9:1 *cf. 3:5-15

▶ 9:1-2 *cf. 15:3-8

▶ 9:11 Rom 15:27
27 they were pleased to do it, and indeed they are in debt to them, for if the Gentiles have come to share in their spiritual blessings, they ought also to be of service to them in material blessings.

Gal 6:7-10
7 Do not be deceived; God is not mocked, for whatever a man sows, that he will also reap. 8 For he who sows to his own flesh will from the flesh reap corruption; but he who sows to the Spirit will from the Spirit reap eternal life. 9And let us not grow weary in well-doing, for in due season we shall reap, if

we do not lose heart. 10 So then, as we have opportunity, let us do good to all men, and especially to those who are of the household of faith.

▶ 9:9 Deut 25:4
4 "You shall not muzzle an ox when it treads out the grain.

▶ 9:12 2 Cor 11:20-21
20 For you bear it if a man makes slaves of you, or preys upon you, or takes advantage of you, or puts on airs, or strikes you in the face. 21 To my shame, I must say, we were too weak for that!
But whatever any one dares to boast of—I am speaking as a fool—I also dare to boast of that.

106. Gospel free of charge

1 Thes 2:1-8 (§277)

2 For you yourselves know, brethren, that our visit to you was not in vain; 2 but though we had already suffered and been shamefully treated at Philippi, as you know, we had courage in our God to declare to you the gospel of God in the face of great opposition. 3 For our appeal does not spring from error or uncleanness, nor is it made with guile; 4 but just as we have been approved by God to be entrusted with the gospel, so we speak, not to please men, but to please God who tests our hearts. 5 For we never used either words of flattery, as you know, or a cloak for greed, as God is witness; 6 nor did we seek glory from men, whether from you or from others, though we might have made demands as apostles of Christ. 7 But we were gentle among you, like a nurse taking care of her children. 8 So, being affectionately desirous of you, we were ready to share with you not only the gospel of God but also our own selves, because you had become very dear to us.

Eph (cont)

might now be made known to the principalities and powers in the heavenly places. 11 This was according to the eternal purpose which he has realized in Christ Jesus our Lord, 12 in whom we have boldness and confidence of access through our faith in him. 13 So I ask you not to lose heart over what I am suffering for you, which is your glory.

107

Rom 15:1-6 (§100)

15 We who are strong ought to bear with the failings of the weak, and not to please ourselves; 2 let each of us please his neighbor for his good, to edify him. 3 For Christ did not please himself; but, as it is written, "The reproaches of those who reproached thee fell on me." 4 For whatever was written in former days was written for our instruction, that by steadfastness and by the encouragement of the scriptures we might have hope. 5 May the God of steadfastness and encouragement grant you to live in such harmony with one another, in accord with Christ Jesus, 6 that together you may with one voice glorify the God and Father of our Lord Jesus Christ.

Rom 2:12-16 (§9)

12 All who have sinned without the law will also perish without the law, and all who have sinned under the law will be judged by the law. 13 For it is not the hearers of the law who are righteous before God, but the doers of the law who will be justified. 14 When Gentiles who have not the law do by nature what the law requires, they are a law to them-

1 Cor 9:19-23

19 For though I am free from all men, I have made myself a slave to all, that I might win the more. 20 To the Jews I became as a Jew, in order to win Jews; to those under the law I became as one under the law—though not being myself under the law—that I might win those under the law. 21 To those outside the law I became as one outside the law—not being without law toward God but under the law of Christ —that I might win those outside the law. 22 To the weak I became weak, that I might win the weak. I have become all things to all men, that I might by all means save some. 23 I do it all for the sake of the gospel, that I may share in its blessings.

selves, even though they do not have the law. 15 They show that what the law requires is written on their hearts, while their conscience also bears witness and their conflicting thoughts accuse or perhaps excuse them 16 on that day when, according to my gospel, God judges the secrets of men by Christ Jesus.

▶ 9:20 Acts 16:3, 21:23-26
3 Paul wanted Timothy to accompany him; and he took him and circumcised him because of the Jews that were in those places, for they all knew that his father was a Greek.

23 Do therefore what we tell you. We have four men who are under a vow; 24 take these men and purify yourself along with them and pay their expenses, so that they may shave their heads. Thus all will know that there is nothing in what they have been told about you but that you yourself live in observance of the law. 25 But as for the Gentiles who have believed, we have sent a letter with our judgment that they should abstain from what has been sacrificed to idols and from blood and from what is strangled and from unchastity." 26 Then Paul took the men, and the next day he purified himself with them and went into the temple, to give notice when the days of purification would be fulfilled and the offering presented for every one of them.

1 Cor 9:24-27

24 Do you not know that in a race all the runners compete, but only one receives the prize? So run that you may obtain it. 25 Every athlete exercises self-control in all things. They do it to receive a perishable wreath, but we an imperishable. 26 Well, I do not run aimlessly, I do not box as one beating the air; 27 but I pommel my body and subdue it, lest after preaching to others I myself should be disqualified.

▶ 9:19 *cf. 9:1

▶ 9:19-21 *cf. Rom 11:13

Gal 5:13-15 (§212)

13 For you were called to freedom, brethren; only do not use your freedom as an opportunity for the flesh, but through love be servants of one another. 14 For the whole law is fulfilled in one word, "You shall love your neighbor as yourself." 15 But if you bite and devour one another take heed that you are not consumed by one another.

Gal 2:1-10 (§197)

2 Then after fourteen years I went up again to Jerusalem with Barnabas, taking Titus along with me. 2 I went up by revelation; and I laid before them (but privately before those who were of repute) the gospel which I preach among the Gentiles, lest somehow I should be running or had run in vain. 3 But even Titus, who was with me, was not compelled to be circumcised, though he was a Greek. 4 But because of false brethren secretly brought in, who slipped in to spy out our freedom which we have in Christ Jesus, that they might bring us into bondage— 5 to them we did not yield submission even for a moment, that the truth of the gospel might be preserved

for you. 6 And from those who were reputed to be something (what they were makes no difference to me; God shows no partiality)—those, I say, who were of repute added nothing to me; 7 but on the contrary, when they saw that I had been entrusted with the gospel to the uncircumcised, just as Peter had been entrusted with the gospel to the circumcised 8 (for he who worked through Peter for the mission to the circumcised worked through me also for the Gentiles), 9 and when they perceived the grace that was given to me, James and Cephas and John, who were reputed to be pillars, gave to me and Barnabas the right hand of fellowship, that we should go to the Gentiles and they to the circumcised; 10 only they would have us remember the poor, which very thing I was eager to do.

▶ 9:20 Gal 2:11-14,
11 But when Cephas came to Antioch I opposed him to his face, because he stood condemned. 12 For before certain men came from James, he ate with the Gentiles; but when they came he drew back and separated himself, fearing the circumcision party. 13 And with him the rest of the Jews acted insincerely, so that even Barnabas was carried away by their insincerity. 14 But when I saw that they were not straightforward about the truth of the gospel, I said to Cephas before them all, "If you, though a Jew, live like a Gentile and not like a Jew, how can you compel the Gentiles to live like Jews?"

108. Run that you may attain the prize

108

▶ 9:24-27 2 Tim 4:7-8
7 I have fought the good fight, I have finished the race, I have kept the faith. 8 Henceforth there is laid up for me the crown of righteousness, which the Lord, the righteous judge, will award to me on that Day, and not only to me but also to all who have loved his appearing.

▶ 9:25 2 Tim 2:5 5 An athlete is not crowned unless he competes according to the rules.

Jas 1:12
12 Blessed is the man who endures trial, for when he has stood the test he will receive the crown of life which God has promised to those who love him.

2 Pet 1:6
6 and knowledge with self-control, and self-control with steadfastness, and steadfastness with godliness,

▶ 9:24 Gal 2:2
2 I
went up by revelation; and I laid before them (but privately before those who were of repute) the gospel which I preach among the Gentiles, lest somehow I should be running or had run in vain.

▶ 9:25 7:5,
5 Do not refuse one another except perhaps by agreement for a season, that you may devote yourselves to prayer; but then come together again, lest Satan tempt you through lack of self-control.

5:11
¹¹But if I, brethren, still preach circumcision, why am I still persecuted? In
that case the stumbling block of the cross
has been removed.

▶9:21 7:19
¹⁹ For
neither circumcision counts for anything nor uncircumcision, but keeping
the commandments of God.

*cf. Gal 6:2

*cf. Eph 3:1-13

Eph 2:12
¹² remember that you
were at that time separated from Christ,
alienated from the commonwealth of
Israel, and strangers to the covenants of
promise, having no hope and without
God in the world.

▶9:22 8:11-13
¹¹And so by your knowledge this
weak man is destroyed, the brother for
whom Christ died. ¹² Thus, sinning
against your brethren and wounding
their conscience when it is weak, you
sin against Christ. ¹³ Therefore, if food
is a cause of my brother's falling, I will
never eat meat, lest I cause my brother
to fall.

Rom 14:1
As for the man who is weak in
faith, welcome him, but not for
disputes over opinions.

2 Cor 11:29
²⁹ Who is weak, and I am not
weak? Who is made to fall, and I am not
indignant?

▶9:23 Phil 1:5
⁵ thankful for your partnership
in the gospel from the first day until
now.

108. Run that you may attain the prize

108

Phil 3:12-16 (§248)

12 Not that I have already obtained
this or am already perfect; but I press
on to make it my own, because Christ
Jesus has made me his own. ¹³ Brethren,
I do not consider that I have made it my
own; but one thing I do, forgetting what
lies behind and straining forward to
what lies ahead, ¹⁴ I press on toward the
goal for the prize of the upward call of
God in Christ Jesus. ¹⁵ Let those of us
who are mature be thus minded; and if
in anything you are otherwise minded,
God will reveal that also to you. ¹⁶ Only
let us hold true to what we have attained.

9.
⁹ But if they cannot exer-
cise self-control, they should marry.
For it is better to marry than to be
aflame with passion.

37
³⁷ But whoever is
firmly established in his heart, being
under no necessity but having his desire
under control, and has determined this
in his heart, to keep her as his betrothed, he will do well.

▶9:27 Col 2:18
¹⁸ Let
no one disqualify you, insisting on
self-abasement and worship of angels,
taking his stand on visions, puffed up
without reason by his sensuous mind,

109

Rom 6:11-14 (§24)

11 So you also must consider yourselves dead to sin and alive to God in Christ Jesus.

12 Let not sin therefore reign in your mortal bodies, to make you obey their passions. 13 Do not yield your members to sin as instruments of wickedness, but yield yourselves to God as men who have been brought from death to life, and your members to God as instruments of righteousness. 14 For sin will have no dominion over you, since you are not under law but under grace.

1 Cor 10:1-13

10 I want you to know, brethren, that our fathers were all under the cloud, and all passed through the sea, 2 and all were baptized into Moses in the cloud and in the sea, 3 and all ate the same supernatural food 4 and all drank the same supernatural drink. For they drank from the supernatural Rock which followed them, and the Rock was Christ. 5 Nevertheless with most of them God was not pleased; for they were overthrown in the wilderness.

6 Now these things are warnings for us, not to desire evil as they did. 7 Do not be idolaters as some of them were; as it is written, "The people sat down to eat and drink and rose up to dance." 8 We must not indulge in immorality as some of them did, and twenty-three thousand fell in a single day. 9 We must not put the Lord to the test, as some of them did and were destroyed by serpents; 10 nor grumble, as some of them did and were destroyed by the Destroyer. 11 Now these things happened to them as a warning, but they were written down for our instruction, upon whom the end of the ages has come. 12 Therefore let any one who thinks that he stands take heed lest he fall. 13 No temptation has overtaken you that is not common to man. God is faithful, and he will not let you be tempted beyond your strength, but with the temptation will also provide the way of escape, that you may be able to endure it.

Gal 5:16-26 (§213)

16 But I say, walk by the Spirit, and do not gratify the desires of the flesh. 17 For the desires of the flesh are against the Spirit, and the desires of the Spirit are against the flesh; for these are opposed to each other, to prevent you from doing what you would. 18 But if you are led by the Spirit you are not under the law. 19 Now the works of the flesh are plain: fornication, impurity, licentiousness, 20 idolatry, sorcery, enmity, strife, jealousy, anger, selfishness, dissension, party spirit, 21 envy, drunkenness, carousing, and the like. I warn you, as I warned you before, that those who do such things shall not inherit the kingdom of God. 22 But the fruit of the Spirit is love, joy, peace, patience, kindness, goodness, faithfulness, 23 gentleness, self-control; against such there is no law. 24 And those who belong to Christ Jesus have crucified the flesh with its passions and desires.

25 If we live by the Spirit, let us also walk by the Spirit. 26 Let us have no self-conceit, no provoking of one another, no envy of one another.

▶10:2 Acts 21:20
20 And when they heard it, they glorified God. And they said to him, "You see, brother, how many thousands there are among the Jews of those who have believed; they are all zealous for the law,

▶10:11 2 Tim 3:16 16 All scripture is inspired by God and profitable for teaching, for reproof, for correction, and for training in righteousness,

▶10:13 2 Tim 2:13
13 if we are faithless, he remains faithful—
for he cannot deny himself.

▶10:2 Gal 3:27 27 For as many of you as were baptized into Christ have put on Christ.

▶10:10 Phil 2:14
14 Do all things without grumbling or questioning,

▶10:11 9:10 10 Does he not speak entirely for our sake? It was written for our sake, because the plowman should plow in hope and the thresher thresh in hope of a share in the crop.

Rom 4:23-24 23 But the words, "it was reckoned to him," were written not for his sake alone, 24 but for ours also. It will be reckoned to us who believe in him that raised from the dead Jesus our Lord,

15:4 4 For whatever was written in former days was written for our instruction, that by steadfastness and by the encouragement of the scriptures we might have hope.

*cf. Rom 15:24

▶10:12 Rom 11:20
20 That is true. They were broken off because of their unbelief, but you stand fast only through faith. So do not become proud, but stand in awe.

▶10:13 1:9 9 God is faithful, by whom you were called into the fellowship of his Son, Jesus Christ our Lord.

2 Cor 1:18 18 As surely as God is faithful, our word to you has not been Yes and No.

1 Thes 5:24 24 He who calls you is faithful, and he will do it.

2 Thes 3:3, 3 But the Lord is faithful; he will strengthen you and guard you from evil.

2:13
13 But we are bound to give thanks to God always for you, brethren beloved by the Lord, because God chose you from the beginning to be saved, through sanctification by the Spirit and belief in the truth.

▶10:3 Ex 16:4,
4 Then the LORD said to Moses, "Behold, I will rain bread from heaven for you; and the people shall go out and gather a day's portion every day, that I may prove them, whether they will walk in my law or not.

25 25 Moses said, "Eat it today, for today is a sabbath to the LORD; today you will not find it in the field.

▶10:4 Ex 17:6
6 Behold, I will stand before you there on the rock at Horeb; and you shall strike the rock, and water shall come out of it, that the people may drink." And Moses did so, in the sight of the elders of Israel.

Num 20:11 11 And Moses lifted up his hand and struck the rock with his rod twice; and water came forth abundantly, and the congregation drank, and their cattle.

▶10:5 Num 14:29-30
29 your dead bodies shall fall in this wilderness; and of all your number, numbered from twenty years old and upward, who have murmured against me, 30 not one shall come into the land where I swore that I would make you dwell, except Caleb the son of Jephun'neh and Joshua the son of Nun.

▶10:6 Num 11:4,
4 Now the rabble that was among them had a strong craving; and the people of Israel also wept again, and said, "O that we had meat to eat!

34 34 Therefore the name of that place was called Kib'roth-hatta'avah, because there they buried the people who had the craving.

110. Cup of the Lord; cup of demons

1 Cor 10:14-22

14 Therefore, my beloved, shun the worship of idols. 15 I speak as to sensible men; judge for yourselves what I say. 16 The cup of blessing which we bless, is it not a participation in the blood of Christ? The bread which we break, is it not a participation in the body of Christ? 17 Because there is one bread, we who are many are one body, for we all partake of the one bread. 18 Consider the people of Israel; are not those who eat the sacrifices partners in the altar? 19 What do I imply then? That food offered to idols is anything, or that an idol is anything? 20 No, I imply that what pagans sacrifice they offer to demons and not to God. I do not want you to be partners with demons. 21 You cannot drink the cup of the Lord and the cup of demons. You cannot partake of the table of the Lord and the table of demons. 22 Shall we provoke the Lord to jealousy? Are we stronger than he?

2 Cor 6:14-7:1 (§167)

14 Do not be mismated with unbelievers. For what partnership have righteousness and iniquity? Or what fellowship has light with darkness? 15 What accord has Christ with Be'lial? Or what has a believer in common with an unbeliever? 16 What agreement has the temple of God with idols? For we are the temple of the living God; as God said,

"I will live in them and move among them,
and I will be their God,
and they shall be my people.
17 Therefore come out from them,
and be separate from them, says the Lord,
and touch nothing unclean;
then I will welcome you,
18 and I will be a father to you,
and you shall be my sons and daughters,
says the Lord Almighty."

7 Since we have these promises, beloved, let us cleanse ourselves from every defilement of body and spirit, and make holiness perfect in the fear of God.

▶10:16 Acts 2:42
42 And they devoted themselves to the apostles' teaching and fellowship, to the breaking of bread and the prayers.

▶10:14-22 11:23-26
23 For I received from the Lord what I also delivered to you, that the Lord Jesus on the night when he was betrayed took bread, 24 and when he had given thanks, he broke it, and said, "This is my body which is for you. Do this in remembrance of me." 25 In the same way also the cup, after supper, saying, "This cup is the new covenant in my blood. Do this, as often as you drink it, in remembrance of me." 26 For as often as you eat this bread and drink the cup, you proclaim the Lord's death until he comes.

▶10:15 4:10 10 We are fools for Christ's sake, but you are wise in Christ. We are weak, but you are strong. You are held in honor, but we in disrepute.

2 Cor 11:19 19 For you gladly bear with fools, being wise yourselves!

▶10:17 12:12-13
12 For just as the body is one and has many members, and all the members of the body, though many, are one body, so it is with Christ. 13 For by one Spirit we were all baptized into one body—Jews or Greeks, slaves or free—and all were made to drink of one Spirit.

*cf. Rom 12:5

▶10:19-21 *cf. 8:4-6

Col 3:5-11 (§266)

5 Put to death therefore what is earthly in you: fornication, impurity, passion, evil desire, and covetousness, which is idolatry. 6 On account of these the wrath of God is coming. 7 In these you once walked, when you lived in them. 8 But now put them all away: anger, wrath, malice, slander, and foul talk from your mouth. 9 Do not lie to one another, seeing that you have put off the old nature with its practices 10 and have put on the new nature, which is being renewed in knowledge after the image of its creator. 11 Here there cannot be Greek and Jew, circumcised and uncircumcised, barbarian, Scyth'ian, slave, free man, but Christ is all, and in all.

2 Thes 2:1-12 (§296)

2 Now concerning the coming of our Lord Jesus Christ and our assembling to meet him, we beg you, brethren, 2 not to be quickly shaken in mind or excited, either by spirit or by word, or by letter purporting to be from us, to the effect that the day of the Lord has come. 3 Let no one deceive you in any way; for that day will not come, unless the rebellion comes first, and the man of lawlessness is revealed, the son of perdition, 4 who opposes and exalts himself against every so-called god or object of worship, so that he takes his seat in the temple of God, proclaiming himself to be God. 5 Do you not remember that when I was still with you I told you this? 6And you know what is restraining him now so that he may be revealed in his time. 7 For the mystery of lawlessness is already at work; only he who now restrains it will do so until he is out of the way. 8And then the lawless one will be revealed, and the Lord Jesus will slay him with the breath of his mouth and destroy him by his appearing and his coming. 9 The coming of the lawless one by the activity of Satan will be with all power and with pretended signs and wonders, 10 and with all wicked deception for those who are to perish, because they refused to love the truth and so be saved. 11 Therefore God sends upon them a strong delusion, to make them believe what is false, 12 so that all may be condemned who did not believe the truth but had pleasure in unrighteousness.

§109-110 **109**

▶ 10:7 Ex 32:4, 4And he received the gold at their hand, and fashioned it with a graving tool, and made a molten calf; and they said, "These are your gods, O Israel, who brought you up out of the land of Egypt!"

6 6And they rose up early on the morrow, and offered burnt offerings and brought peace offerings; and the people sat down to eat and drink, and rose up to play.

▶ 10:8 Num 25:1-18
While Israel dwelt in Shittim the people began to play the harlot with the daughters of Moab. 2 These invited the people to the sacrifices of their gods, and the people ate, and bowed down to their gods. 3 So Israel yoked himself to Ba'al of Pe'or. And the anger of the LORD was kindled against Israel; 4 and the LORD said to Moses, "Take all the chiefs of the people, and hang them in the sun before the LORD, that the fierce anger of the LORD may turn away from Israel." 5And Moses said to the judges of Israel, "Every one of you slay his men who have yoked themselves to Ba'al of Pe'or."

6 And behold, one of the people of Israel came and brought a Mid'ianite woman to his family, in the sight of Moses and in the sight of the whole congregation of the people of Israel, while they were weeping at the door of the tent of meeting. 7 When Phin'ehas the son of Elea'zar, son of Aaron the priest, saw it, he rose and left the congregation, and took a spear in his hand 8 and went after the man of Israel into the inner room, and pierced both of them, the man of Israel and the woman, through her body. Thus the plague was stayed from the people of Israel. 9 Nevertheless those that died by the plague were twenty-four thousand.

10 And the LORD said to Moses, 11 "Phin'ehas the son of Elea'zar, son of Aaron the priest, has turned back my wrath from the people of Israel, in that he was jealous with my jealousy among them, so that I did not consume the people of Israel in my jealousy. 12 Therefore say, 'Behold, I give to him my covenant of peace; 13 and it shall be to him, and to his descendants after him, the covenant of a perpetual priesthood, because he was jealous for his God, and made atonement for the people of Israel.' "

14 The name of the slain man of Israel, who was slain with the Mid'ianite woman, was Zimri the son of Salu, head of a fathers' house belonging to the Simeonites. 15And the name of the Mid'ianite woman who was slain was Cozbi the daughter of Zur, who was the head of the people of a fathers' house in Mid'ian.

16 And the LORD said to Moses, 17 "Harass the Mid'ianites, and smite them; 18 for they have harassed you with their wiles, with which they beguiled you in the matter of Pe'or, and in the matter of Cozbi, the daughter of the prince of Mid'ian, their sister, who was slain on the day of the plague on account of Pe'or."

▶ 10:9 Num 21:5-6 5And the people spoke against God and against Moses, "Why have you brought us up out of Egypt to die in the wilderness? For there is no food and no water, and we loathe this worthless food." 6 Then the LORD sent fiery serpents among the people, and they bit the people, so that many people of Israel died.

▶ 10:10 Num 16:41, 41 But on the morrow all the congregation of the people of Israel murmured against Moses and against Aaron, saying, "You have killed the people of the LORD."

49
49 Now those who died by the plague were fourteen thousand seven hundred, besides those who died in the affair of Korah.

▶ 10:9 (Lord) read Christ: p⁴⁶DG Koine Lect it vg syr cop Marcion Irenaeus(Latin)

110. Cup of the Lord; cup of demons

110

▶ 10:18 Lev 7:6
6 Every male among the priests may eat of it; it shall be eaten in a holy place; it is most holy.

111

Rom 2:12-16 (§9)

12 All who have sinned without the law will also perish without the law, and all who have sinned under the law will be judged by the law. 13 For it is not the hearers of the law who are righteous before God, but the doers of the law who will be justified. 14 When Gentiles who have not the law do by nature what the law requires, they are a law to themselves, even though they do not have the law. 15 They show that what the law requires is written on their hearts, while their conscience also bears witness and their conflicting thoughts accuse or perhaps excuse them 16 on that day when, according to my gospel, God judges the secrets of men by Christ Jesus.

Rom 14:5-12 (§58)

5 One man esteems one day as better than another, while another man esteems all days alike. Let every one be fully convinced in his own mind. 6 He who observes the day, observes it in honor of the Lord. He also who eats, eats in honor of the Lord, since he gives thanks to God; while he who abstains, abstains in honor of the Lord and gives thanks to God. 7 None of us lives to himself, and none of us dies to himself. 8 If we live, we live to the Lord, and if we die, we die to the Lord; so then whether we live or whether we die, we are the Lord's. 9 For to this end Christ died and lived again, that he might be Lord both of the dead and of the living.

1 Cor 10:23-11:1

23 "All things are lawful," but not all things are helpful. "All things are lawful," but not all things build up. 24 Let no one seek his own good, but the good of his neighbor. 25 Eat whatever is sold in the meat market without raising any question on the ground of conscience. 26 For "the earth is the Lord's, and everything in it." 27 If one of the unbelievers invites you to dinner and you are disposed to go, eat whatever is set before you without raising any question on the ground of conscience. 28 (But if some one says to you, "This has been offered in sacrifice," then out of consideration for the man who informed you, and for conscience' sake— 29 I mean his conscience, not yours—do not eat it.) For why should my liberty be determined by another man's scruples? 30 If I partake with thankfulness, why am I denounced because of that for which I give thanks?

31 So, whether you eat or drink, or

10 Why do you pass judgment on your brother? Or you, why do you despise your brother? For we shall all stand before the judgment seat of God; 11 for it is written,
"As I live, says the Lord, every knee shall bow to me,
and every tongue shall give praise to God."
12 So each of us shall give account of himself to God.

2 Cor 6:14-7:1 (§167)

14 Do not be mismated with unbelievers. For what partnership have righteousness and iniquity? Or what fellowship has light with darkness? 15 What accord has Christ with Be'lial? Or what has a believer in common with an unbeliever? 16 What agreement has the temple of God with idols? For we are the temple of the living God; as God said,
"I will live in them and move among them,
and I will be their God,
and they shall be my people.
17 Therefore come out from them, and be separate from them, says the Lord,
and touch nothing unclean;

whatever you do, do all to the glory of God. 32 Give no offense to Jews or to Greeks or to the church of God, 33 just as I try to please all men in everything I do, not seeking my own advantage, but that of many, that they may be saved. **11** 1 Be imitators of me, as I am of Christ.

Rom 15:1-6 (§60)

15 We who are strong ought to bear with the failings of the weak, and not to please ourselves; 2 let each of us please his neighbor for his good, to edify him. 3 For Christ did not please himself; but, as it is written, "The reproaches of those who reproached thee fell on me." 4 For what-

Gal 2:11-14 (§198)

11 But when Cephas came to Antioch I opposed him to his face, because he stood condemned. 12 For before certain men came from James, he ate with the Gentiles; but when they came he drew back and separated himself, fearing the circumcision party. 13 And with him the rest of the Jews acted insincerely, so that even Barnabas was carried away by their insincerity. 14 But when I saw that they were not straightforward about the truth of the gospel, I said to Cephas before them all, "If you, though a Jew, live like a Gentile and not like a Jew, how can you compel the Gentiles to live like Jews?"

then I will welcome you,
18 and I will be a father to you,
and you shall be my sons and daughters,
says the Lord Almighty."
7 Since we have these promises, beloved, let us cleanse ourselves from every defilement of body and spirit, and make holiness perfect in the fear of God.

ever was written in former days was written for our instruction, that by steadfastness and by the encouragement of the scriptures we might have hope. 5 May the God of steadfastness and encouragement grant you to live in such harmony with one another, in accord with Christ Jesus, 6 that together you may with one voice glorify the God and Father of our Lord Jesus Christ.

Eph 5:15-20 (§231)

15 Look carefully then how you walk, not as unwise men but as wise, 16 making the most of the time, because the days are evil. 17 Therefore do not be foolish, but understand what the will of the Lord is. 18 And do not get drunk with wine, for that is debauchery; but be filled with the Spirit, 19 addressing one another in psalms and hymns and spiritual songs, singing and making melody to the Lord with all your heart, 20 always and for everything giving thanks in the name of our Lord Jesus Christ to God the Father.

▶ 10:26 1 Tim 4:4   4 For everything created by God is good, and nothing is to be rejected if it is received with thanksgiving;

▶ 10:32 Acts 24:16   16 So I always take pains to have a clear conscience toward God and toward men.

▶ 10:23 *cf. 6:12

▶ 10:24 Gal 6:2   2 Bear one another's burdens, and so fulfil the law of Christ.

▶ 10:25 *cf. 8:7-13, 4:3-4, Rom 14:17-23

▶ 10:27 5:9-13   9 I wrote to you in my letter not to associate with immoral men; 10 not at all meaning the immoral of this world, or the greedy and robbers, or idolaters, since then you would need to go out of the world. 11 But rather I wrote to you not to associate with any one who bears the name of brother if he is guilty of immorality or greed, or is an idolater, reviler, drunkard, or robber—not even to eat with such a one. 12 For what have I to do with judging outsiders? Is it not those inside the church whom you are to judge? 13 God judges those outside. "Drive out the wicked person from among you."

▶ 10:30 Gal 5:11   11 But if I, brethren, still preach circumcision, why am I still persecuted? In that case the stumbling block of the cross has been removed.

▶ 10:32 9:19-23   19 For though I am free from all men, I have made myself a slave to all, that I might win the more. 20 To the Jews I became as a Jew, in order to win Jews; to those under the law I became as one under the law—though not being myself under the law—that might win those under the law. 21 T those outside the law I became as on outside the law—not being without la toward God but under the law of Chri —that I might win those outside th law. 22 To the weak I became weak, th I might win the weak. I have become a things to all men, that I might by a means save some. 23 I do it all for th

112. If a woman will not veil herself

112

Eph 5:21-6:9 (§232)

21 Be subject to one another out of reverence for Christ. 22 Wives, be subject to your husbands, as to the Lord. 23 For the husband is the head of the wife as Christ is the head of the church, his body, and is himself its Savior. 24 As the church is subject to Christ, so let wives also be subject in everything to their husbands. 25 Husbands, love your wives, as Christ loved the church and gave himself up for her, 26 that he might sanctify her, having cleansed her by the washing of water with the word, 27 that he might present the church to himself in splendor, without spot or wrinkle or any such thing, that she might be holy and without blemish. 28 Even so husbands should love their wives as their own bodies. He who loves his wife loves himself. 29 For no man

1 Cor 11:2-16

2 I commend you because you remember me in everything and maintain the traditions even as I have delivered them to you. 3 But I want you to understand that the head of every man is Christ, the head of a woman is her husband, and the head of Christ is God. 4 Any man who prays or prophesies with his head covered dishonors his head, 5 but any woman who prays or prophesies with her head unveiled dishonors her head—it is the same as if her head were shaven. 6 For if a woman will not veil herself, then she should cut off her hair; but if it is disgraceful for a woman to be shorn or shaven, let her wear a veil. 7 For a man ought not to cover his head, since he is the image and glory of God; but woman is the glory of man. 8 (For man was not made from woman, but woman from man. 9 Neither was man created for woman, but woman for man.) 10 That is why a woman ought to have a veil on her head, because of the angels. 11 (Nevertheless, in the Lord woman is not independent of man nor man of woman; 12 for as woman was made from man, so man is now born of woman. And all things are from God.) 13 Judge for yourselves; is it proper for a woman to pray to God with her head uncovered? 14 Does not nature itself teach you that for a man to wear long hair is degrading to him, 15 but if a woman has long hair, it is her pride? For her hair is given to her for a covering. 16 If any one is disposed to be contentious, we recognize no other practice, nor do the churches of God.

▶ 11:5 Acts 21:9   9 And he had four unmarried daughters, who prophesied.

▶ 11:8 1 Tim 2:13   13 For Adam was formed first, then Eve;

▶ 11:2 15:1-3   Now I would remind you, brethren, in what terms I preached to you the gospel, which you received, in which you stand, 2 by which you are saved, if you hold it fast—unless you believed in vain. 3 For I delivered to you as of first importance what I also received, that Christ died for our sins in accordance with the scriptures,

11:23   23 For I received from the Lord what I also delivered to you, that the Lord Jesus on the night when he was betrayed took bread,

Rom 6:17   17 But thanks be to God, that you who were once slaves of sin have become obedient from the heart to the standard of teaching to which you were committed.

1 Thes 2:13-14a   13 And we also thank God constantly for this, that when you received the word of God which you heard from us, you accepted it not as the word of men but as what it really is, the word of God, which is at work in you believers. 14 For you, brethren, became imitators of the churches of God in Christ Jesus which are in Judea;

▶ 11:3 3:23   23 and you are Christ's; and Christ is God's.

14:33b-36   As in all the churches of the saints, 34 the women should keep silence in the churches. For they are not permitted to speak, but should be subordinate, as even the law says. 35 If there is anything they desire to know, let them ask their husbands at home. For it is shameful for a woman to speak in church. 36 What! Did the word of God originate with you, or are you the only ones it has reached?

Col 3:12-17 (§267)

12 Put on then, as God's chosen ones, holy and beloved, compassion, kindness, lowliness, meekness, and patience, 13 forbearing one another and, if one has a complaint against another, forgiving each other; as the Lord has forgiven you, so you also must forgive. 14 And above all these put on love, which binds everything together in perfect harmony. 15 And let the peace of Christ rule in your hearts, to which indeed you were called in the one body. And be thankful. 16 Let the word of Christ dwell in you richly, teach and admonish one another in all wisdom, and sing psalms and hymns and spiritual songs with thankfulness in your hearts to God. 17 And whatever you do, in word or deed, do everything in the name of the Lord Jesus, giving thanks to God the Father through him.

1 Thes 2:13-16 (§279)

13 And we also thank God constantly for this, that when you received the word of God which you heard from us, you accepted it not as the word of men but as what it really is, the word of God, which is at work in you believers. 14 For you, brethren, became imitators of the churches of God in Christ Jesus which are in Judea; for you suffered the same things from your own countrymen as they did from the Jews, 15 who killed both the Lord Jesus and the prophets, and drove us out, and displease God and oppose all men 16 by hindering us from speaking to the Gentiles that they may be saved—so as always to fill up the measure of their sins. But God's wrath has come upon them at last!

2 Thes 3:6-13 (§300)

6 He must not be a recent convert, or he may be puffed up with conceit and fall into the condemnation of the devil; 7 moreover he must be well thought of by outsiders, or he may fall into reproach and the snare of the devil.

8 Deacons likewise must be serious, not double-tongued, not addicted to much wine, not greedy for gain; 9 they must hold the mystery of the faith with a clear conscience. 10 And let them also be tested first; then if they prove themselves blameless let them serve as deacons. 11 The women likewise must be serious, no slanderers, but temperate, faithful in all things. 12 Let deacons be the husband of one wife, and let them manage their children and their households well; 13 for those who serve well as deacons gain a good standing for themselves and also great confidence in the faith which is in Christ Jesus.

111

sake of the gospel, that I may share in its blessings.
Rom 11:13-14
13 Now I am speaking to you Gentiles. Inasmuch then as I am an apostle to the Gentiles, I magnify my ministry 14 in order to make my fellow Jews jealous, and thus save some of them.

▶ 10:33 Phil 2:4   4 Let each of you look not only to his own interests, but also to the interests of others.

▶ 11:1 4:16   16 I urge you, then, be imitators of me.

Gal 4:12   12 Brethren, I beseech you, become as I am, for I also have become as you are. You did me no wrong;

1 Thes 1:6   6 And you became imitators of us and of the Lord, for you received the word in much affliction, with joy inspired by the Holy Spirit;

▶ 10:26 Ps 24:1   The earth is the Lord's and the fulness thereof, the world and those who dwell therein;

112. If a woman will not veil herself

2 Thes 3:14-15 (§301)

14 If any one refuses to obey what we say in this letter, note that man, and have nothing to do with him, that he may be ashamed. 15 Do not look on him as an enemy, but warn him as a brother.

112

Phil 4:8-9 (§252)
8 Finally, brethren, whatever is true, whatever is honorable, whatever is just, whatever is pure, whatever is lovely, whatever is gracious, if there is any excellence, if there is anything worthy of praise, think about these things. 9 What you have learned and received and heard and seen in me, do; and the God of peace will be with you.

Eph (cont)
ever hates his own flesh, but nourishes and cherishes it, as Christ does the church, 30 because we are members of his body. 31 "For this reason a man shall leave his father and mother and be joined to his wife, and the two shall become one flesh." 32 This mystery is a profound one, and I am saying that it refers to Christ and the church; 33 how-

ever, let each one of you love his wife as himself, and let the wife see that she respects her husband.

6 Children, obey your parents in the Lord, for this is right. 2 "Honor your father and mother" (this is the first commandment with a promise), 3 "that it may be well with you and that you may live long on the earth." 4 Fathers, do not provoke your children to anger, but bring them up in the discipline and instruction of the Lord.

5 Slaves, be obedient to those who are your earthly masters, with fear and trembling, in singleness of heart, as to Christ; 6 not in the way of eyeservice, as men-pleasers, but as servants of Christ, doing the will of God from the heart, 7 rendering service with a good will as to the Lord and not to men,

8 knowing that whatever good any one does, he will receive the same again from the Lord, whether he is a slave or free. 9 Masters, do the same to them, and forbear threatening, knowing that he who is both their Master and yours is in heaven, and that there is no partiality with him.

ph 1:22,   22 and
e has put all things under his feet and as made him the head over all things r the church,

Col 2:19
19 and not holding fast to the Head, from whom the whole body, nourished and knit together through its joints and ligaments, grows with a growth that is from God.

:15   15 Rather, speaking the truth in ove, we are to grow up in every way nto him who is the head, into Christ,

▶ 11:10 6:3   3 Do you not know that we are to judge angels? How much more, matters pertaining to this life!

▶ 11:11 7:4   4 For the wife does not rule over her own body, but the husband does; likewise the husband does not rule over his own body, but the wife does.

▶ 11:14 Rom 1:26   26 For this reason God gave them up to dishonorable passions. Their women exchanged natural relations for unnatural,

*cf. Rom 2:14

▶ 11:16 7:17   17 Only, let every one lead the life which the Lord has assigned to him, and in which God has called him. This is my rule in all the churches.

14:38   38 If any one does not recognize this, he is not recognized.

113

Rom 14:1-4 (§57)

14 As for the man who is weak in faith, welcome him, but not for disputes over opinions. 2 One believes he may eat anything, while the weak man eats only vegetables. 3 Let not him who eats despise him who abstains, and let not him who abstains pass judgment on him who eats; for God has welcomed him. 4 Who are you to pass judgment on the servant of another? It is before his own master that he stands or falls. And he will be upheld, for the Master is able to make him stand.

1 Cor 11:17-22

17 But in the following instructions I do not commend you, because when you come together it is not for the better but for the worse. 18 For, in the first place, when you assemble as a church, I hear that there are divisions among you; and I partly believe it, 19 for there must be factions among you in order that those who are genuine among you may be recognized. 20 When you meet together, it is not the Lord's supper that you eat. 21 For in eating, each one goes ahead with his own meal, and one is hungry and another is drunk. 22 What! Do you not have houses to eat and drink in? Or do you despise the church of God and humiliate those who have nothing? What shall I say to you? Shall I commend you in this? No, I will not.

▶ 11:17 11:2
2 I commend you because you remember me in everything and maintain the traditions even as I have delivered them to you.

▶ 11:17, 22 2 Cor 12:11
11 I have been a fool! You forced me to it, for I ought to have been commended by you. For I was not at all inferior to these superlative apostles, even though I am nothing.

▶ 11:18 1:10-12
10 I appeal to you, brethren, by the name of our Lord Jesus Christ, that all of you agree and that there be no dissensions among you, but that you be united in the same mind and the same judgment. 11 For it has been reported to me by Chlo′e's people that there is quarreling among you, my brethren. 12 What I mean is that each one of you says, "I belong to Paul," or "I belong to Apol′los," or "I belong to Cephas," or "I belong to Christ."

*cf. Phil 2:1-11

114

1 Cor 11:23-26

23 For I received from the Lord what I also delivered to you, that the Lord Jesus on the night when he was betrayed took bread, 24 and when he had given thanks, he broke it, and said, "This is my body which is for you. Do this in remembrance of me." 25 In the same way also the cup, after supper, saying, "This cup is the new covenant in my blood. Do this, as often as you drink it, in remembrance of me." 26 For as often as you eat this bread and drink the cup, you proclaim the Lord's death until he comes.

▶ 11:23-26 10:16
16 The cup of blessing which we bless, is it not a participation in the blood of Christ? The bread which we break, is it not a participation in the body of Christ?

▶ 11:26 1:23
preach Christ crucified, a stumbling block to Jews and folly to Gentiles, 2:1-5
When I came to you, brethren, I did not come proclaiming to you the testimony of God in lofty words or wisdom. 2 For I decided to know nothing among you except Jesus Christ and

23 but we
him crucified. 3And I was with you in weakness and in much fear and trembling; 4 and my speech and my message were not in plausible words of wisdom, but in demonstration of the Spirit and of power, 5 that your faith might not rest in the wisdom of men but in the power of God.

Rom 13:11-12
11 Besides this you know what hour it is, how it is full time now for you to wake from sleep. For salvation is nearer to us now than when we first believed; 12 the night is far gone, the day is at hand. Let us then cast off the works of darkness and put on the armor of light;

Gal 6:14 14 But far be it from me to glory except in the cross of our Lord Jesus Christ, by which the world has been crucified to me, and I to the world.

1 Thes 4:15,
15 For this we declare to you by the word of the Lord, that we who are alive, who are left until the coming of the Lord, shall not precede those who have fallen asleep.

▶ 11:22 *cf. 11:33-34

5:2   ²And you are arrogant!
Ought you not rather to mourn? Let
him who has done this be removed from
among you.

2 Thes 2:1-3
    Now concerning the coming of our
Lord Jesus Christ and our assembling to meet him, we beg you, brethren, ² not to be quickly shaken in mind
or excited, either by spirit or by word,
or by letter purporting to be from us, to
the effect that the day of the Lord has
come. ³ Let no one deceive you in any
way; for that day will not come, unless
the rebellion comes first, and the man
of lawlessness is revealed, the son of
perdition,

▶ 11:24 (for) *read* broken for: S^c C^3 D^{bc} G
Koine Lect it(few) syr Ambrosiaster; *read*
given for: it(most) vg cop

115

Rom 14:13-23 (§59)

13 Then let us no more pass judgment on one another, but rather decide never to put a stumbling block or hindrance in the way of a brother. 14 I know and am persuaded in the Lord Jesus that nothing is unclean in itself; but it is unclean for any one who thinks it unclean. 15 If your brother is being injured by what you eat, you are no longer walking in love. Do not let what you eat cause the ruin of one for whom Christ died. 16 So do not let your good be spoken of as evil. 17 For the kingdom of God is not food and drink but righteousness and peace and joy in the Holy Spirit; 18 he who thus serves Christ is acceptable to God and approved by men. 19 Let us then pursue what makes for peace and for mutual upbuilding. 20 Do not, for the sake of food, destroy the work of God. Everything is indeed clean, but it is wrong for any one to make others fall by what he eats; 21 it is right not to eat meat or drink wine or do anything that makes your brother stumble. 22 The faith that you have, keep between yourself and God; happy is he who has no

▶ 11:32 1 Pet 4:17   17 For the time has come for judgment to begin with the household of God; and if it begins with us, what will be the end of those who do not obey the gospel of God?

1 Cor 11:27-34

27 Whoever, therefore, eats the bread or drinks the cup of the Lord in an unworthy manner will be guilty of profaning the body and blood of the Lord. 28 Let a man examine himself, and so eat of the bread and drink of the cup. 29 For any one who eats and drinks without discerning the body eats and drinks judgment upon himself. 30 That is why many of you are weak and ill, and some have died. 31 But if we judged ourselves truly, we should not be judged. 32 But when we are judged by the Lord, we are chastened so that we may not be condemned along with the world.

33 So then, my brethren, when you come together to eat, wait for one another— 34 if any one is hungry, let him eat at home—lest you come together to be condemned. About the other things I will give directions when I come.

reason to judge himself for what he approves. 23 But he who has doubts is condemned, if he eats, because he does not act from faith; for whatever does not proceed from faith is sin.

▶ 11:28 Gal 6:4   4 But let each one test his own work, and then his reason to boast will be in himself alone and not in his neighbor.

2 Cor 13:5-10 (§190)

5 Examine yourselves, to see whether you are holding to your faith. Test yourselves. Do you not realize that Jesus Christ is in you?—unless indeed you fail to meet the test! 6 I hope you will find out that we have not failed. 7 But we pray God that you may not do wrong—not that we may appear to have met the test, but that you may do what is right, though we may seem to have failed. 8 For we cannot do anything against the truth, but only for the truth. 9 For we are glad when we are weak and you are strong. What we pray for is your improvement. 10 I write this while I am away from you, in order that when I come I may not have to be severe in my use of the authority which the Lord has given me for building up and not for tearing down.

116. Now concerning spiritual gifts

116

1 Cor 12:1-3

12 Now concerning spiritual gifts, brethren, I do not want you to be uninformed. 2 You know that when you were heathen, you were led astray to dumb idols, however you may have been moved. 3 Therefore I want you to understand that no one speaking by the Spirit of God ever says "Jesus be cursed!" and no one can say "Jesus is Lord" except by the Holy Spirit.

▶ 12:1 Acts 17:29   29 Being then God's offspring, we ought not to think that the Deity is like gold, or silver, or stone, a representation by the art and imagination of man.

▶ 12:1 1:7   7 so that you are not lacking in any spiritual gift, as you wait for the revealing of our Lord Jesus Christ;

2:12 12 Now we have received not the spirit of the world, but the Spirit which is from God, that we might understand the gifts bestowed on us by God.

Gal 4:8-11 (§208)

8 Formerly, when you did not know God, you were in bondage to beings that by nature are no gods; 9 but now that you have come to know God, or rather to be known by God, how can you turn back again to the weak and beggarly elemental spirits, whose slaves you want to be once more? 10 You observe days, and months, and seasons, and years! 11 I am afraid I have labored over you in vain.

▶ 12:2 1 Thes 1:9   9 For they themselves report concerning us what a welcome we had among you, and how you turned to God from idols, to serve a living and true God,

Eph 2:11-22 (§221)

11 Therefore remember that at one time you Gentiles in the flesh, called the uncircumcision by what is called the circumcision, which is made in the flesh by hands—12 remember that you were at that time separated from Christ, alienated from the commonwealth of Israel, and strangers to the covenants of promise, having no hope and without God in the world. 13 But now in Christ Jesus you who once were far off have been brought near in the blood of Christ. 14 For he is our peace, who has made us both one, and has broken down the dividing wall of hostility, 15 by abolishing in his flesh the law of commandments and ordinances, that he might create in himself one new man in place of the two, so making peace, 16 and might reconcile us both to God in one body through the cross, thereby bringing the hostility to an end. 17 And he came and preached peace to you who were far off and peace to those who were near; 18 for through him we both have access in one Spirit to the Father. 19 So then you are no longer strangers and sojourners, but you are fellow citizens

▶ 12:3 Rom 10:9   9 because, if you confess with your lips that Jesus is Lord and believe in your heart that God raised him from the dead, you will be saved.

Phil 2:11 11 and every tongue confess that Jesus Christ is Lord, to the glory of God the Father.

115

116. Now concerning spiritual gifts

1 Thes 1:2-10(§276)

[2] but though we had already suffered and been shamefully treated at Philippi, as you know, we had courage in our God to declare to you the gospel of God in the face of great opposition. [3] For our appeal does not spring from error or uncleanness, nor is it made with guile; [4] but just as we have been approved by God to be entrusted with the gospel, so we speak, not to please men, but to please God who tests our hearts. [5] For we never used either words of flattery, as you know, or a cloak for greed, as God is witness; [6] nor did we seek glory from men, whether from you or from others, though we might have made demands as apostles of Christ. [7] But we were gentle[a] among you, like a nurse taking care of her children. [8] So, being affectionately desirous of you, we were ready to share with you not only the gospel of God but also our own selves, because you had become very dear to us. [9] For you remember our labor and toil, brethren; we worked night and day, that we might not burden any of you, while we preached to you the gospel of God. [10] You are witnesses, and God also, how holy and righteous and blameless was our behavior to you believers;

116

Eph (cont)

with the saints and members of the household of God, [20] built upon the foundation of the apostles and prophets, Christ Jesus himself being the cornerstone, [21] in whom the whole structure is joined together and grows into a holy temple in the Lord; [22] in whom you also are built into it for a dwelling place of God in the Spirit.

117

Rom 12:3-8 (§52)

3 For by the grace given to me I bid every one among you not to think of himself more highly than he ought to think, but to think with sober judgment, each according to the measure of faith which God has assigned him. 4 For as in one body we have many members, and all the members do not have the same function, 5 so we, though many, are one body in Christ, and individually members one of another. 6 Having gifts that differ according to the grace given to us, let us use them: if prophecy, in proportion to our faith; 7 if service, in our serving; he who teaches, in his teaching; 8 he who exhorts, in his exhortation; he who contributes, in liberality; he who gives aid, with zeal; he who does acts of mercy, with cheerfulness.

1 Cor 12:4-11

4 Now there are varieties of gifts, but the same Spirit; 5 and there are varieties of service, but the same Lord; 6 and there are varieties of working, but it is the same God who inspires them all in every one. 7 To each is given the manifestation of the Spirit for the common good. 8 To one is given through the Spirit the utterance of wisdom, and to another the utterance of knowledge according to the same Spirit, 9 to another faith by the same Spirit, to another gifts of healing by the one Spirit, 10 to another the working of miracles, to another prophecy, to another the ability to distinguish between spirits, to another various kinds of tongues, to another the interpretation of tongues. 11All these are inspired by one and the same Spirit, who apportions to each one individually as he wills.

*cf 1 Cor 12:27-31(§120)

Eph 4:1-10 (§225)

4 I therefore, a prisoner for the Lord, beg you to lead a life worthy of the calling to which you have been called, 2 with all lowliness and meekness, with patience, forbearing one another in love, 3 eager to maintain the unity of the Spirit in the bond of peace. 4 There is one body and one Spirit, just as you were called to the one hope that belongs to your call, 5 one Lord, one faith, one baptism, 6 one God and Father of us all, who is above all and through all and in all. 7 But grace was given to each of us according to the measure of Christ's gift. 8 Therefore it is said,
"When he ascended on high he led a host of captives,
and he gave gifts to men."
9 (In saying, "He ascended," what does it mean but that he had also descended into the lower parts of the earth? 10 He who descended is he who also ascended far above all the heavens, that he might fill all things.)

Eph 4:11-16 (§226)

11And his gifts were that some should be apostles, some proph-

▶12:4 Gal 5:22 22 But the fruit of the Spirit is love, joy, peace, patience, kindness, goodness, faithfulness,
▶12:6 Eph 1:23 23 which is his body, the fulness of him who fills all in all.

▶12:7 6:12 12 "All things are lawful for me," but not all things are helpful. "All things are lawful for me," but I will not be enslaved by anything.

14:26-33a 26 What then, brethren? When you come together, each one has a hymn, a lesson, a revelation, a tongue, or an interpretation. Let all things be done for edification. 27 If any speak in a tongue, let there be only two or at most three, and each in turn; and let one interpret. 28 But if there is no one to interpret, let each of them keep silence in church and speak to himself and to God. 29 Let two or three prophets speak, and let the others weigh what is said. 30 If a revelation is made to another sitting by, let the first be silent. 31 For you can all prophesy one by one, so that all may learn and all be encouraged; 32 and the spirits of prophets are subject to prophets. 33 For God is not a God of confusion but of peace.

10:23 23 "All things are lawful," but not all things are helpful. "All things are lawful," but not all things build up.

▶12:10 1 Thes 5:19-21 19 Do not quench the Spirit, 20 do not despise prophesying, 21 but test everything; hold fast what is good,

118. By one Spirit we were baptized into one body

118

1 Cor 12:12-13

12 For just as the body is one and has many members, and all the members of the body, though many, are one body, so it is with Christ. 13 For by one Spirit we were all baptized into one body—Jews or Greeks, slaves or free—and all were made to drink of one Spirit.

Gal 3:26-29 (§206)

26 for in Christ Jesus you are all sons of God, through faith. 27 For as many of you as were baptized into Christ have put on Christ. 28 There is neither Jew nor Greek, there is neither slave nor free, there is neither male nor female; for you are all one in Christ Jesus. 29And if you are Christ's, then you are Abraham's offspring, heirs according to promise.

Eph 2:11-22 (§221)

11 Therefore remember that at one time you Gentiles in the flesh, called the uncircumcision by what is called the circumcision, which is made in the flesh by hands—12 remember that you were at that time separated from Christ, alienated from the commonwealth of Israel, and strangers to the covenants of promise, having no hope and without God in the world. 13 But now in Christ Jesus you who once were far off have been brought near in the blood of Christ. 14 For he is our peace, who has made us both one, and has broken down the dividing wall of hostility, 15 by abolishing in his flesh the law of commandments and ordinances, that he might create in himself one new man in place of the two, so making peace, 16 and might reconcile us both to God in one body through the cross, thereby bringing the hostility to an end. 17And he came and preached peace to you who were far off and peace to those who were near; 18 for through him we both have access in one Spirit to the Father. 19 So then you are no longer strangers and sojourners, but you are fellow citizens

▶ 12:12-13 *cf. Rom 12:4-5   ▶ 12:13 *cf Acts 19:5-6

117

Eph (cont)

ets, some evangelists, some pastors and teachers, [12] to equip the saints for the work of ministry, for building up the body of Christ, [13] until we all attain to the unity of the faith and of the knowledge of the Son of God, to mature manhood, to the measure of the stature of the fulness of Christ; [14] so that we may no longer be children, tossed to and fro and carried about with every wind of doctrine, by the cunning of men, by their craftiness in deceitful wiles. [15] Rather, speaking the truth in love, we are to grow up in every way into him who is the head, into Christ, [16] from whom the whole body, joined and knit together by every joint with which it is supplied, when each part is working properly, makes bodily growth and upbuilds itself in love.

118. By one Spirit we were baptized into one body

118

Col 3:5-11 (§266)

5 Put to death therefore what is earthly in you: fornication, impurity, passion, evil desire, and covetousness, which is idolatry. [6] On account of these the wrath of God is coming. [7] In these you once walked, when you lived in them. [8] But now put them all away: anger, wrath, malice, slander, and foul talk from your mouth. [9] Do not lie to one another, seeing that you have put off the old nature with its practices [10] and have put on the new nature, which is being renewed in knowledge after the image of its creator. [11] Here there cannot be Greek and Jew, circumcised and uncircumcised, barbarian, Scyth´ian, slave, free man, but Christ is all, and in all.

Eph (cont)

with the saints and members of the household of God, [20] built upon the foundation of the apostles and prophets, Christ Jesus himself being the cornerstone, [21] in whom the whole structure is joined together and grows into a holy temple in the Lord; [22] in whom you also are built into it for a dwelling place of God in the Spirit.

119

Rom 11:17-24 (§48)

17 But if some of the branches were broken off, and you, a wild olive shoot, were grafted in their place to share the richness of the olive tree, 18 do not boast over the branches. If you do boast, remember it is not you that support the root, but the root that supports you. 19 You will say, "Branches were broken off so that I might be grafted in." 20 That is true. They were broken off because of their unbelief, but you stand fast only through faith. So do not become proud, but stand in awe. 21 For if God did not spare the natural branches, neither will he spare you. 22 Note then the kindness and the severity of God: severity toward those who have fallen, but God's kindness to you, provided you continue in his kindness; otherwise you too will be cut off. 23 And even the others, if they do not persist in their unbelief, will be grafted in, for God has the power to graft them in again. 24 For if you have been cut from what is by nature a wild olive tree, and grafted, contrary to nature, into a cultivated olive tree, how much more will these natural branches be grafted back into their own olive tree.

▶12:18 15:38
38 But God gives it a body as he has chosen, and to each kind of seed its own body.

1 Cor 12:14-26

14 For the body does not consist of one member but of many. 15 If the foot should say, "Because I am not a hand, I do not belong to the body," that would not make it any less a part of the body. 16 And if the ear should say, "Because I am not an eye, I do not belong to the body," that would not make it any less a part of the body. 17 If the whole body were an eye, where would be the hearing? If the whole body were an ear, where would be the sense of smell? 18 But as it is, God arranged the organs in the body, each one of them, as he chose. 19 If all were a single organ, where would the body be? 20 As it is, there are many parts, yet one body. 21 The eye cannot say to the hand, "I have no need of you," nor again the head to the feet, "I have no need of you." 22 On the contrary, the parts of the body which seem to be weaker are indispensable, 23 and those parts of the body which we think less honorable we invest with the greater honor, and our unpresentable parts are treated with greater modesty, 24 which our more presentable parts do not require. But

▶12:24 1:26-31
26 For consider your call, brethren; not many of you were wise according to worldly standards, not many were powerful, not many were of noble birth; 27 but God chose what is foolish in the world to shame the wise, God chose what is weak in the world to shame the strong, 28 God chose what is low and despised in the world, even things that are not, to bring to nothing things that are, 29 so that no human being might boast in the presence of God. 30 He is the source of your life in Christ Jesus, whom God made our wisdom, our righteousness and sanctification and redemption; 31 therefore, as it is written, "Let him who boasts, boast of the Lord."

2 Cor 1:3-7 (§147)

3 Blessed be the God and Father of our Lord Jesus Christ, the Father of mercies and God of all comfort, 4 who comforts us in all our affliction, so that we may be able to comfort those who are in any affliction, with the comfort with which we ourselves are comforted by God. 5 For as we share abundantly in Christ's sufferings, so through Christ we share abundantly in comfort too. 6 If we are afflicted, it is for your comfort and salvation; and if we are comforted, it is for your comfort, which you experience when you patiently endure the same sufferings that we suffer. 7 Our hope for you is unshaken; for we know that as you share in our sufferings, you will also share in our comfort.

God has so composed the body, giving the greater honor to the inferior part, 25 that there may be no discord in the body, but that the members may have the same care for one another. 26 If one member suffers, all suffer together; if one member is honored, all rejoice together.

▶12:26 2 Cor 11:28-29
28 Let a man examine himself, and so eat of the bread and drink of the cup. 29 For any one who eats and drinks without discerning the body eats and drinks judgment upon himself.

2 Cor 4:7-15 (§159-160)

7 so you should rather turn to forgive and comfort him, or he may be overwhelmed by excessive sorrow. 8 So I beg you to reaffirm your love for him. 9 For this is why I wrote, that I might test you and know whether you are obedient in everything. 10 Any one whom you forgive, I also forgive. What I have forgiven, if I have forgiven anything, has been for your sake in the presence of Christ, 11 to keep Satan from gaining the advantage over us; for we are not ignorant of his designs.

12 When I came to Tro'as to preach the gospel of Christ, a door was opened for me in the Lord; 13 but my mind could not rest because I did not find my brother Titus there. So I took leave of them and went on to Macedo'nia.

14 But thanks be to God, who in Christ always leads us in triumph, and through us spreads the fragrance of the knowledge of him everywhere. 15 For we are the aroma of Christ to God among those who are being saved and among those who are perishing,

120. Individually members of the body of Christ

120

Rom 12:3-8 (§52)

3 For by the grace given to me I bid every one among you not to think of himself more highly than he ought to think, but to think with sober judgment, each according to the measure of faith which God has assigned him. 4 For as in one body we have many members, and all the members do not have the same function, 5 so we, though many, are one body in Christ, and individually members one of another. 6 Having gifts that differ according to the grace given to us, let us use them: if prophecy, in proportion to our faith; 7 if service, in our serving; he who teaches, in his teaching; 8 he who exhorts, in his exhortation; he who contributes, in liberality; he who gives aid, with zeal; he who does acts of mercy, with cheerfulness.

▶12:27 10:16-17
16 The cup of blessing which we bless, is it not a participation in the blood of Christ? The bread which we break, is it not a participation in the body of Christ? 17 Because there is one bread, we who are many are one body, for we all partake of the one bread.

1 Cor 12:27-31

27 Now you are the body of Christ and individually members of it. 28 And God has appointed in the church first apostles, second prophets, third teachers, then workers of miracles, then healers, helpers, administrators, speakers in various kinds of tongues. 29 Are all apostles? Are all prophets? Are all teachers? Do all work miracles? 30 Do all possess gifts of healing? Do all speak with tongues? Do all interpret? 31 But earnestly desire the higher gifts.

And I will show you a still more excellent way.

*cf 1 Cor 12:4-11 (§117)

11:27
27 Whoever, therefore, eats the bread or drinks the cup of the Lord in an unworthy manner will be guilty of profaning the body and blood of the Lord.

▶12:28-30 *cf Acts 13:1, 6:3-4, 19:11-12, 1Tim 5:17

Rom 7:4
4 Likewise, my brethren, you have died to the law through the body of Christ, so that you may belong to another, to him who has been raised from the dead in order that we may bear fruit for God.

Eph 4:11-16 (§226)

11 And his gifts were that some should be apostles, some prophets, some evangelists, some pastors and teachers, 12 to equip the saints for the work of ministry, for building up the body of Christ, 13 until we all attain to the unity of the faith and of the knowledge of the Son of God, to mature manhood, to the measure of the stature of the fulness of Christ; 14 so that we may no longer be children, tossed to and fro and carried about with every wind of doctrine, by the cunning of men, by their craftiness in deceitful wiles. 15 Rather, speaking the truth in love, we are to grow up in every way into him who is the head, into Christ, 16 from whom the whole body, joined and knit together by every joint with which it is supplied, when each part is working properly, makes bodily growth and upbuilds itself in love.

Eph 1:22-23,
22 and he has put all things under his feet and has made him the head over all things for the church, 23 which is his body, the fulness of him who fills all in all.

4:12
12 to equip the saints for the work of ministry, for building up the body of Christ,

Col 1:22,
22 he has now reconciled in his body of flesh by his death, in order to present you holy and blameless and irreproachable before him,

2:17
17 These are only a shadow of what is to come; but the substance belongs to Christ.

119

120. **Individually members of the body of Christ**

120

121

Rom 16:25-27 (§70)

25 Now to him who is able to strengthen you according to my gospel and the preaching of Jesus Christ, according to the revelation of the mystery which was kept secret for long ages 26 but is now disclosed and through the prophetic writings is made known to all nations, according to the command of the eternal God, to bring about the obedience of faith—27 to the only wise God be glory for evermore through Jesus Christ! Amen.

1 Cor 13:1-3

13 If I speak in the tongues of men and of angels, but have not love, I am a noisy gong or a clanging cymbal. 2And if I have prophetic powers, and understand all mysteries and all knowledge, and if I have all faith, so as to remove mountains, but have not love, I am nothing. 3 If I give away all I have, and if I deliver my body to be burned, but have not love, I gain nothing.

Eph 3:1-13 (§222)

3 For this reason I, Paul, a prisoner for Christ Jesus on behalf of you Gentiles— 2 assuming that you have heard of the stewardship of God's grace that was given to me for you, 3 how the mystery was made known to me by revelation, as I have written briefly. 4 When you read this you can perceive my insight into the mystery of Christ, 5 which was not made known to the sons of men in other generations as it has now been revealed to his holy apostles and prophets by the Spirit; 6 that is, how the Gentiles are fellow heirs, members of the same body, and partakers of the promise in Christ Jesus through the gospel.

7 Of this gospel I was made a minister according to the gift of God's grace which was given me by the working of his power. 8 To me, though I am the very least of all the saints, this grace was given, to preach to the Gentiles the unsearchable riches of Christ, 9 and to make all men see what is the plan of the mystery hidden for ages in God who created all things; 10 that through the church the manifold wisdom of God

▶13:2 8:1
Now concerning food offered to idols: we know that "all of us possess knowledge." "Knowledge" puffs up, but love builds up.

Gal 5:6   6 For in Christ Jesus neither circumcision nor uncircumcision is of any avail, but faith working through love.

Eph 3:19   19 and to know the love of Christ which surpasses knowledge, that you may be filled with all the fulness of God.

▶13:3 15:30-32
30 Why am I in peril every hour? 31 I protest, brethren, by my pride in you which I have in Christ Jesus our Lord, I die every day! 32 What do I gain if, humanly speaking, I fought with beasts at Ephesus? If the dead are not raised, "Let us eat and drink, for tomorrow we die."

122. **Love is patient and kind**

122

Rom 12:9-21 (§53)

9 Let love be genuine; hate what is evil, hold fast to what is good; 10 love one another with brotherly affection; outdo one another in showing honor. 11 Never flag in zeal, be aglow with the Spirit, serve the Lord. 12 Rejoice in your hope, be patient in tribulation, be constant in prayer. 13 Contribute to the needs of the saints, practice hospitality.

14 Bless those who persecute you; bless and do not curse them. 15 Rejoice with those who rejoice, weep with those who weep. 16 Live in harmony with one another; do not be haughty, but associate with the lowly; never be conceited. 17 Repay no one evil for evil, but take thought for what is noble in the sight of all. 18 If possible, so far as it depends upon you, live peaceably with all. 19 Beloved, never avenge yourselves, but leave it to the wrath of God; for it is written, "Vengeance is mine, I will repay, says the Lord." 20 No, "if your enemy is hungry, feed him; if he is thirsty, give him drink; for by so doing you will heap burning coals upon his head." 21 Do not be overcome by evil, but overcome evil with good.

1 Cor 13:4-7

4 Love is patient and kind; love is not jealous or boastful; 5 it is not arrogant or rude. Love does not insist on its own way; it is not irritable or resentful; 6 it does not rejoice at wrong, but rejoices in the right. 7 Love bears all things, believes all things, hopes all things, endures all things.

Rom 13:8-10 (§55)

8 Owe no one anything, except to love one another; for he who loves his neighbor has fulfilled the law. 9 The commandments, "You shall not commit adultery, You shall not kill, You shall not steal, You shall not covet," and any other commandment, are summed up in this sentence, "You shall love your neighbor as yourself." 10 Love does no wrong to a neighbor; therefore love is the fulfilling of the law.

Gal 5:13-15 (§212)

13 For you were called to freedom, brethren; only do not use your freedom as an opportunity for the flesh, but through love be servants of one another. 14 For the whole law is fulfilled in one word, "You shall love your neighbor as yourself." 15 But if you bite and devour one another take heed that you are not consumed by one another.

▶13:5 Acts 15:39   39And there arose a sharp contention, so that they separated from each other; Barnabas took Mark with him and sailed away to Cyprus,

▶13:4-7 Col 3:14   14And above all these put on love, which binds everything together in perfect harmony.

▶13:4-6 *cf Tit 3:2

▶13:4-5 *cf Eph 4:2

121

Col 1:24-2:3 (§260)

24 Now I rejoice in my sufferings for your sake, and in my flesh I complete what is lacking in Christ's afflictions for the sake of his body, that is, the church, 25 of which I became a minister according to the divine office which was given to me for you, to make the word of God fully known, 26 the mystery hidden for ages and generations but now made manifest to his saints. 27 To them God chose to make known how great among the Gentiles are the riches of the glory of this mystery, which is Christ in you, the hope of glory. 28 Him we proclaim, warning every man and teaching every man in all wisdom, that we may present every man mature in Christ. 29 For this I toil, striving with all the energy which he mightily inspires within me.

2 For I want you to know how greatly I strive for you, and for those at La-odice′a, and for all who have not seen my face, 2 that their hearts may be encouraged as they are knit together in love, to have all the riches of assured understanding and the knowledge of God's mystery, of Christ, 3 in whom are hid all the treasures of wisdom and knowledge.

Eph (cont)

might now be made known to the principalities and powers in the heavenly places. 11 This was according to the eternal purpose which he has realized in Christ Jesus our Lord, 12 in whom we have boldness and confidence of access through our faith in him. 13 So I ask you not to lose heart over what I am suffering for you, which is your glory.

▶13:3 (burned) *read* body that I may glory: p⁴⁶SAB cop Clement Origen; *text:* CDG Koine it vg syr Tertullian Origen

122. Love is patient and kind

122

Phil 2:1-11 (§242)

2 So if there is any encouragement in Christ, any incentive of love, any participation in the Spirit, any affection and sympathy, 2 complete my joy by being of the same mind, having the same love, being in full accord and of one mind. 3 Do nothing from selfishness or conceit, but in humility count others better than yourselves. 4 Let each of you look not only to his own interests, but also to the interests of others. 5 Have this mind among yourselves, which is yours in Christ Jesus, 6 who, though he was in the form of God, did not count equality with God a thing to be grasped, 7 but emptied himself, taking the form of a servant, being born in the likeness of men. 8And being found in human form he humbled himself and became obedient unto death, even death on a cross. 9 Therefore God has highly exalted him and bestowed on him the name which is above every name, 10 that at the name of Jesus every knee should bow, in heaven and on earth and under the earth, 11 and every tongue confess that Jesus Christ is Lord, to the glory of God the Father.

1 Thes 4:9-12 (§285)

9 But concerning love of the brethren you have no need to have any one write to you, for you yourselves have been taught by God to love one another; 10 and indeed you do love all the brethren throughout Macedo′nia. But we exhort you, brethren, to do so more and more, 11 to aspire to live quietly, to mind your own affairs, and to work with your hands, as we charged you; 12 so that you may command the respect of outsiders, and be dependent on nobody.

Phm 8-20(§307-308)

8 Accordingly, though I am bold enough in Christ to command you to do what is required, 9 yet for love's sake I prefer to appeal to you—I, Paul, an ambassador and now a prisoner also for Christ Jesus—10 I appeal to you for my child, Ones′imus, whose father I have become in my imprisonment. 11 (Formerly he was useless to you, but now he is indeed useful to you and to me.) 12 I am sending him back to you, sending my very heart. 13 I would have been glad to keep him with me, in order that he might serve me on your behalf during my imprisonment for the gospel; 14 but I preferred to do nothing without your consent in order that your goodness might not be by compulsion but of your own free will. 15 Perhaps this is why he was parted from you for a while, that you might have him back for ever, 16 no longer as a slave but more than a slave, as a beloved brother, especially to me but how much more to you, both in the flesh and in the Lord. 17 So if you consider me your partner, receive him as you would receive me. 18 If he has wronged you at all, or owes you anything, charge that to my account. 19 I, Paul, write this with my own hand, I will repay it—to say nothing of your owing me even your own self. 20 Yes, brother, I want some benefit from you in the Lord. Refresh my heart in Christ.

123

1 Cor 13:8-13

8 Love never ends; as for prophecies, they will pass away; as for tongues, they will cease; as for knowledge, it will pass away. 9 For our knowledge is imperfect and our prophecy is imperfect; 10 but when the perfect comes, the imperfect will pass away. 11 When I was a child, I spoke like a child, I thought like a child, I reasoned like a child; when I became a man, I gave up childish ways. 12 For now we see in a mirror dimly, but then face to face. Now I know in part; then I shall understand fully, even as I have been fully understood. 13 So faith, hope, love abide, these three; but the greatest of these is love.

2 Cor 1:12-14(§148)

12 For our boast is this, the testimony of our conscience that we have behaved in the world, and still more toward you, with holiness and godly sincerity, not by earthly wisdom but by the grace of God. 13 For we write you nothing but what you can read and understand; I hope you will understand fully, 14 as you have understood in part, that you can be proud of us as we can be of you, on the day of the Lord Jesus.

Eph 4:11-16(§226)

11 And his gifts were that some should be apostles, some prophets, some evangelists, some pastors and teachers, 12 to equip the saints for the work of ministry, for building up the body of Christ, 13 until we all attain to the unity of the faith and of the knowledge of the Son of God, to mature manhood, to the measure of the stature of the fulness of Christ; 14 so that we may no longer be children, tossed to and fro and carried about with every wind of doctrine, by the cunning of men, by their craftiness in deceitful wiles. 15 Rather, speaking the truth in love, we are to grow up in every way into him who is the head, into Christ, 16 from whom the whole body, joined and knit together by every joint with which it is supplied, when each part is working properly, makes bodily growth and upbuilds itself in love.

*cf Eph 3:14-19(§223)

▶ 13:12 *cf Jas 1:23

▶ 13:8 *cf 1Tim 4:14

▶ 13:11 *cf 2 Tim 2:22

▶ 13:8 1 Thes 5:20
20 do not despise prophesying,

*cf Phil 1:9, Col 2:2

▶ 13:9-10 8:1-3
Now concerning food offered to idols: we know that "all of us possess knowledge." "Knowledge" puffs up, but love builds up. 2 If any one imagines that he knows something, he does not yet know as he ought to know. 3 But if one loves God, one is known by him.

▶ 13:11 3:1-4
But I, brethren, could not address you as spiritual men, but as men of the flesh, as babes in Christ. 2 I fed you with milk, not solid food; for you were not ready for it; and even yet you are not ready, 3 for you are still of the flesh. For while there is jealousy and strife among you, are you not of the flesh, and behaving like ordinary men? 4 For when one says, "I belong to Paul," and another, "I belong to Apol'los," are you not merely men?

14:20
20 Brethren, do not be children in your thinking; be babes in evil, but in thinking be mature.

124. He who prophesies edifies the church

124

Rom 15:1-6 (§60)

15 We who are strong ought to bear with the failings of the weak, and not to please ourselves; 2 let each of us please his neighbor for his good, to edify him. 3 For Christ did not please himself; but, as it is written, "The reproaches of those who reproached thee fell on me." 4 For whatever was written in former days was written for our instruction, that by steadfastness and by the encouragement of the scriptures we might have hope. 5 May the God of steadfastness and encouragement grant you to live in such harmony with one another, in accord with Christ Jesus, 6 that together you may with one voice glorify the God and Father of our Lord Jesus Christ.

1 Cor 14:1-5

14 Make love your aim, and earnestly desire the spiritual gifts, especially that you may prophesy. 2 For one who speaks in a tongue speaks not to men but to God; for no one understands him, but he utters mysteries in the Spirit. 3 On the other hand, he who prophesies speaks to men for their upbuilding and encouragement and consolation. 4 He who speaks in a tongue edifies himself, but he who prophesies edifies the church. 5 Now I want you all to speak in tongues, but even more to prophesy. He who prophesies is greater than he who speaks in tongues, unless some one interprets, so that the church may be edified.

▶ 14:1 8:1
Now concerning food offered to idols: we know that "all of us possess knowledge." "Knowledge" puffs up, but love builds up.

▶ 14:1-5 *cf Acts 2:4-8, 17

▶ 14:2-3 *cf Eph 3:4-5

▶ 14:4 *cf 6:12

Phm 4-7(§306)

123

4 I thank my God always when I remember you in my prayers, 5 because I hear of your love and of the faith which you have toward the Lord Jesus and all the saints, 6 and I pray that the sharing of your faith may promote the knowledge of all the good that is ours in Christ. 7 For I have derived much joy and comfort from your love, my brother, because the hearts of the saints have been refreshed through you.

▶ 13:12 2 Cor 5:7
7 for we walk by faith, not by sight.

▶ 13:13 Gal 5:5-6   5 For through the Spirit, by faith, we wait for the hope of righteousness. 6 For in Christ Jesus neither circumcision nor uncircumcision is of any avail, but faith working through love.

Col 1:3-5
3 We always thank God, the Father of our Lord Jesus Christ, when we pray for you, 4 because we have heard of your faith in Christ Jesus and of the love which you have for all the saints, 5 because of the hope laid up for you in heaven. Of this you have heard before in the word of the truth, the gospel

1 Thes 1:3
3 remembering before our God and Father your work of faith and labor of love and steadfastness of hope in our Lord Jesus Christ.

1 Thes 5:8   8 But, since we belong to the day, let us be sober, and put on the breastplate of faith and love, and for a helmet the hope of salvation.

124. He who prophesies edifies the church

124

125

Rom 1:8-15 (§2)

8 First, I thank my God through Jesus Christ for all of you, because your faith is proclaimed in all the world. 9 For God is my witness, whom I serve with my spirit in the gospel of his Son, that without ceasing I mention you always in my prayers, 10 asking that somehow by God's will I may now at last succeed in coming to you. 11 For I long to see you, that I may impart to you some spiritual gift to strengthen you, 12 that is, that we may be mutually encouraged by each other's faith, both yours and mine. 13 I want you to know, brethren, that I have often intended to come to you (but thus far have been prevented), in order that I may reap some harvest among you as well as among the rest of the Gentiles. 14 I am under obligation both to Greeks and to barbarians, both to the wise and to the foolish: 15 so I am eager to preach the gospel to you also who are in Rome.

Rom 10:14-17 (§42)

14 But how are men to call upon him in whom they have not believed? And how are they to believe in him of whom

1 Cor 14:6-12

6 Now, brethren, if I come to you speaking in tongues, how shall I benefit you unless I bring you some revelation or knowledge or prophecy or teaching? 7 If even lifeless instruments, such as the flute or the harp, do not give distinct notes, how will any one know what is played? 8 And if the bugle gives an indistinct sound, who will get ready for battle? 9 So with yourselves; if you in a tongue utter speech that is not intelligible, how will any one know what is said? For you will be speaking into the air. 10 There are doubtless many different languages in the world, and none is without meaning; 11 but if I do not

they have never heard? And how are they to hear without a preacher? 15 And how can men preach unless they are sent? As it is written, "How beautiful are the feet of those who preach good news!" 16 But they have not all obeyed the gospel; for Isaiah says, "Lord, who has believed what he has heard from us?" 17 So faith comes from what is heard, and what is heard comes by the preaching of Christ.

2 Cor 1:12-14(§148)

12 For our boast is this, the testimony of our conscience that we have behaved in the world, and still more toward you, with holiness and godly sincerity, not by earthly wisdom but by the grace of God. 13 For we write you nothing but what you can read and understand; I hope you will understand fully, 14 as you have understood in part,

know the meaning of the language, I shall be a foreigner to the speaker and the speaker a foreigner to me. 12 So with yourselves; since you are eager for manifestations of the Spirit, strive to excel in building up the church.

that you can be proud of us as we can be of you, on the day of the Lord Jesus.

▶14:10 Acts 2:5-6
5 Now there were dwelling in Jerusalem Jews, devout men from every nation under heaven. 6 And at this sound the multitude came together, and they were bewildered, because each one heard them speaking in his own language.

▶14:9 9:26 26 Well, I do not run aimlessly, I do not box as one beating the air;

▶14:12 Eph 4:12
12 to equip the saints for the work of ministry, for building up the body of Christ,

▶ *cf 2 Cor 13:10, 1 Thes 5:11

126. I would rather speak five words with my mind

126

Rom 8:26-27(§32)

26 Likewise the Spirit helps us in our weakness; for we do not know how to pray as we ought, but the Spirit himself intercedes for us with sighs too deep for words. 27 And he who searches the hearts of men knows what is the mind of the Spirit, because the Spirit intercedes for the saints according to the will of God.

1 Cor 14:13-19

13 Therefore, he who speaks in a tongue should pray for the power to interpret. 14 For if I pray in a tongue, my spirit prays but my mind is unfruitful. 15 What am I to do? I will pray with the spirit and I will pray with the mind also; I will sing with the spirit and I will sing with the mind also. 16 Otherwise, if you bless with the spirit, how can any one in the position of an outsider say the "Amen" to your thanksgiving when he does not know what you are saying? 17 For you may give thanks well enough, but the other man is not edified. 18 I thank God that I speak in tongues more than you all; 19 nevertheless, in church I would rather speak five words with my mind, in order to instruct others, than ten thousand words in a tongue.

Eph 5:15-20 (§231)

15 Look carefully then how you walk, not as unwise men but as wise, 16 making the most of the time, because the days are evil. 17 Therefore do not be foolish, but understand what the will of the Lord is. 18 And do not get drunk with wine, for that is debauchery; but be filled with the Spirit, 19 addressing one another in psalms and hymns and spiritual songs, singing and making melody to the Lord with all your heart, 20 always and for everything giving thanks in the name of our Lord Jesus Christ to God the Father.

▶14:16 2 Cor 1:20
20 For all the promises of God find their Yes in him. That is why we utter the Amen through him, to the glory of God.

▶ 14:19 Rom 7:23-25
23 but I see in my members another law at war with the law of my mind and making me captive to the law of sin which dwells in my members. 24 Wretched man that I am! Who will deliver me from this body of death? 25 Thanks be to God through Jesus Christ our Lord! So then, I of myself

serve the law of God with my mind, but with my flesh I serve the law of sin.

▶ 14:15 *cf Acts 22:17

125

Col 3:12-17 (§267)

12 Put on then, as God's chosen ones, holy and beloved, compassion, kindness, lowliness, meekness, and patience, [13] forbearing one another and, if one has a complaint against another, forgiving each other; as the Lord has forgiven you, so you also must forgive. [14]And above all these put on love, which binds everything together in perfect harmony. [15]And let the peace of Christ rule in your hearts, to which indeed you were called in the one body. And be thankful. [16] Let the word of Christ dwell in you richly, teach and admonish one another in all wisdom, and sing psalms and hymns and spiritual songs with thankfulness in your hearts to God. [17]And whatever you do, in word or deed, do everything in the name of the Lord Jesus, giving thanks to God the Father through him.

126. I would rather speak five words with my mind

126

127

1 Cor 14:20-25

20 Brethren, do not be children in your thinking; be babes in evil, but in thinking be mature. 21 In the law it is written, "By men of strange tongues and by the lips of foreigners will I speak to this people, and even then they will not listen to me, says the Lord." 22 Thus, tongues are a sign not for believers but for unbelievers, while prophecy is not for unbelievers but for believers. 23 If, therefore, the whole church assembles and all speak in tongues, and outsiders or unbelievers enter, will they not say that you are mad? 24 But if all prophesy, and an unbeliever or outsider enters, he is convicted by all, he is called to account by all, 25 the secrets of his heart are disclosed; and so, falling on his face, he will worship God and declare that God is really among you.

Eph 4:11-16 (§226)

11 And his gifts were that some should be apostles, some prophets, some evangelists, some pastors and teachers, 12 to equip the saints for the work of ministry, for building up the body of Christ, 13 until we all attain to the unity of the faith and of the knowledge of the Son of God, to mature manhood, to the measure of the stature of the fulness of Christ; 14 so that we may no longer be children, tossed to and fro and carried about with every wind of doctrine, by the cunning of men, by their craftiness in deceitful wiles. 15 Rather, speaking the truth in love, we are to grow up in every way into him who is the head, into Christ, 16 from whom the whole body, joined and knit together by every joint with which it is supplied, when each part is working properly, makes bodily growth and upbuilds itself in love.

▶ 14:23 Acts 2:13   13 But others mocking said, "They are filled with new wine."

▶ 14:20 13:11   11 When I was a child, I spoke like a child, I thought like a child, I reasoned like a child; when I became a man, I gave up childish ways.

Rom 16:19   19 For while your obedience is known to all, so that I rejoice over you, I would have you wise as to what is good and guileless as to what is evil;

Phil 3:15   15 Let those of us who are mature be thus minded; and if in anything you are otherwise minded, God will reveal that also to you.

▶ 14:23-24 *cf 1 Thes 4:12

▶ 14:25 Eph 5:13   13 but when anything is exposed by the light it becomes visible, for anything that becomes visible is light.

▶ 14:21 Is 28:11-12   11 Nay, but by men of strange lips and with an alien tongue the LORD will speak to this people, 12 to whom he has said, "This is rest; give rest to the weary; and this is repose"; yet they would not hear.

128. Let all things be done for edification

128

Rom 12:3-8 (§52)

3 For by the grace given to me I bid every one among you not to think of himself more highly than he ought to think, but to think with sober judgment, each according to the measure of faith which God has assigned him. 4 For as in one body we have many members, and all the members do not have the same function, 5 so we, though many, are one body in Christ, and individually members one of another. 6 Having gifts that differ according to the grace given to us, let us use them: if prophecy, in proportion to our faith; 7 if service, in our serving; he who teaches, in his teaching; 8 he who exhorts, in his exhortation; he who contributes, in liberality; he who gives aid, with zeal; he who does acts of mercy, with cheerfulness.

1 Cor 14:26-33a

26 What then, brethren? When you come together, each one has a hymn, a lesson, a revelation, a tongue, or an interpretation. Let all things be done for edification. 27 If any speak in a tongue, let there be only two or at most three, and each in turn; and let one interpret. 28 But if there is no one to interpret, let each of them keep silence in church and speak to himself and to God. 29 Let two or three prophets speak, and let the others weigh what is said. 30 If a revelation is made to another sitting by, let the first be silent. 31 For you can all prophesy one by one, so that all may learn and all be encouraged; 32 and the spirits of prophets are subject to prophets. 33 For God is not a God of confusion but of peace.

Eph 5:15-20 (§231)

15 Look carefully then how you walk, not as unwise men but as wise, 16 making the most of the time, because the days are evil. 17 Therefore do not be foolish, but understand what the will of the Lord is. 18 And do not get drunk with wine, for that is debauchery; but be filled with the Spirit, 19 addressing one another in psalms and hymns and spiritual songs, singing and making melody to the Lord with all your heart, 20 always and for everything giving thanks in the name of our Lord Jesus Christ to God the Father.

▶ 14:29 Acts 17:11   11 Now these Jews were more noble than those in Thessaloni′ca, for they received the word with all eagerness, examining the scriptures daily to see if these things were so.

▶ 14:26 Rom 14:19,   19 Let us then pursue what makes for peace and for mutual upbuilding.

15:2   2 let each of us please his neighbor for his good, to edify him.

Gal 2:18   18 But if I build up again those things which I tore down, then I prove myself a transgressor.

1 Thes 5:11   11 Therefore encourage one another and build one another up, just as you are doing.

▶ 14:33 7:15,   15 But if the unbelieving partner desires to separate, let it be so; in such a case the brother or sister is not bound. For God has called us to peace.

Col 4:5-6 (§270)

5 Conduct yourselves wisely toward outsiders, making the most of the time. 6 Let your speech always be gracious, seasoned with salt, so that you may know how you ought to answer every one.

128. Let all things be done for edification

Col 3:12-17 (§267)

12 Put on then, as God's chosen ones, holy and beloved, compassion, kindness, lowliness, meekness, and patience, 13 forbearing one another and, if one has a complaint against another, forgiving each other; as the Lord has forgiven you, so you also must forgive. 14And above all these put on love, which binds everything together in perfect harmony. 15And let the peace of Christ rule in your hearts, to which indeed you were called in the one body. And be thankful. 16 Let the word of Christ dwell in you richly, teach and admonish one another in all wisdom, and sing psalms and hymns and spiritual songs with thankfulness in your hearts to God. 17And whatever you do, in word or deed, do everything in the name of the Lord Jesus, giving thanks to God the Father through him.

1 Thes 5:12-22(§288)

12 But we beseech you, brethren, to respect those who labor among you and are over you in the Lord and admonish you, 13 and to esteem them very highly in love because of their work. Be at peace among yourselves. 14And we exhort you, brethren, admonish the idlers, encourage the fainthearted, help the weak, be patient with them all. 15 See that none of you repays evil for evil, but always seek to do good to one another and to all. 16 Rejoice always, 17 pray constantly, 18 give thanks in all circumstances; for this is the will of God in Christ Jesus for you. 19 Do not quench the Spirit, 20 do not despise prophesying, 21 but test everything; hold fast what is good, 22 abstain from every form of evil.

2 Thes 3:16(§302)

16 Now may the Lord of peace himself give you peace at all times in all ways. The Lord be with you all.

---

35   35 I say this for your own benefit, not to lay any restraint upon you, but to promote good order and to secure your undivided devotion to the Lord.

Rom 15:33
    33 The God of peace be with you all. Amen.

*cf 1 Thes 5:23

129

1 Cor 14:33b-36

As in all the churches of the saints, [34] the women should keep silence in the churches. For they are not permitted to speak, but should be subordinate, as even the law says. [35] If there is anything they desire to know, let them ask their husbands at home. For it is shameful for a woman to speak in church. [36] What! Did the word of God originate with you, or are you the only ones it has reached?

1 Cor 11:2-16 (§112)

[2] I commend you because you remember me in everything and maintain the traditions even as I have delivered them to you. [3] But I want you to understand that the head of every man is Christ, the head of a woman is her husband, and the head of Christ is God. [4] Any man who prays or prophesies with his head covered dishonors his head, [5] but any woman who prays or prophesies with her head unveiled dishonors her head—it is the same as if her head were shaven. [6] For if a woman will not veil herself, then she should cut off her hair; but if it is disgraceful for a woman to be shorn or shaven, let her wear a veil. [7] For a man ought not to cover his head, since he is the image and glory of God; but woman is the glory of man. [8] (For man was not made from woman, but woman from man. [9] Neither was man created for woman, but woman for man.) [10] That is why a woman ought to have a veil[r] on her head, because of the angels. [11] (Nevertheless, in the Lord woman is not independent of man nor man of woman; [12] for as woman was made from man, so man is now born of woman. And all things are from God.) [13] Judge for yourselves; is it proper for a woman to pray to God with her head uncovered? [14] Does not nature itself teach you that for a man to wear long hair is degrading to him, [15] but if a woman has long hair, it is her pride? For her hair is given to her for a covering. [16] If any one is disposed to be contentious, we recognize no other practice, nor do the churches of God.

▶ 14:34 1 Tim 2:11-12
[11] Let a woman learn in silence with all submissiveness. [12] I permit no woman to teach or to have authority over men; she is to keep silent.

Tit 2:5 [5] to be sensible, chaste, domestic, kind, and submissive to their husbands, that the word of God may not be discredited.

14:35 Eph 5:22-23 [22] Wives, be subject to your husbands, as to the Lord. [23] For the husband is the head of the wife as Christ is the head of the church, his body, and is himself its Savior.

Col 3:18 [18] Wives, be subject to your husbands, as is fitting in the Lord.

▶ 14:36 7:17 [17] Only, let every one lead the life which the Lord has assigned to him, and in which God has called him. This is my rule in all the churches.

130. **All things should be done in order**

130

1 Cor 14:37-40

[37] If any one thinks that he is a prophet, or spiritual, he should acknowledge that what I am writing to you is a command of the Lord. [38] If any one does not recognize this, he is not recognized. [39] So, my brethren, earnestly desire to prophesy, and do not forbid speaking in tongues; [40] but all things should be done decently and in order.

▶ 14:37 3:1-4
But I, brethren, could not address you as spiritual men, but as men of the flesh, as babes in Christ. [2] I fed you with milk, not solid food; for you were not ready for it; and even yet you are not ready, [3] for you are still of the flesh. For while there is jealousy and strife among you, are you not of the flesh, and behaving like ordinary men? [4] For when one says, "I belong to Paul," and another, "I belong to Apol'los," are you not merely men?

7:6, [6] I say this by way of concession, not of command.

10, [10] To the married I give charge, not I but the Lord, that the wife should not separate from her husband

12, [12] To the rest I say, not the Lord, that if any brother has a wife who is an unbeliever, and she consents to live with him, he should not divorce her.

25 [25] Now concerning the unmarried, I have no command of the Lord, but I give my opinion as one who by the Lord's mercy is trustworthy.

2Cor 8:8, [8] I say this not as a command, but to prove by the earnestness of others that your love also is genuine.

129

▶ 14:34-35 (church) *omit 14:34-35 here and add following 14:40:* DG it(some) Ambrosiaster

130. All things should be done in order

2 Thes 3:14-15 (§301)

14 If any one refuses to obey what we say in this letter, note that man, and have nothing to do with him, that he may be ashamed. 15 Do not look on him as an enemy, but warn him as a brother.

Phm 8-14 (§307)

8 Accordingly, though I am bold enough in Christ to command you to do what is required, 9 yet for love's sake I prefer to appeal to you—I, Paul, an ambassador and now a prisoner also for Christ Jesus—10 I appeal to you for my child, Ones'imus, whose father I have become in my imprisonment. 11 (Formerly he was useless to you, but now he is indeed useful to you and to me.) 12 I am sending him back to you, sending my very heart. 13 I would have been glad to keep him with me, in order that he might serve me on your behalf during my imprisonment for the gospel; 14 but I preferred to do nothing without your consent in order that your goodness might not be by compulsion but of your own free will.

130

10
10And in this matter I give my advice: it is best for you now to complete what a year ago you began not only to do but to desire,

▶ 14:40 7:35
35 I say this for your own benefit, not to lay any restraint upon you, but to promote good order and to secure your undivided devotion to the Lord.

▶ 14:40 (order) *add 14:34-35 here only:* DG it(some) Ambrosiaster

131

Rom 5:6-11 (§21)

6 While we were still weak, at the right time Christ died for the ungodly. 7 Why, one will hardly die for a righteous man—though perhaps for a good man one will dare even to die. 8 But God shows his love for us in that while we were yet sinners Christ died for us. 9 Since, therefore, we are now justified by his blood, much more shall we be saved by him from the wrath of God. 10 For if while we were enemies we were reconciled to God by the death of his Son, much more, now that we are reconciled, shall we be saved by his life. 11 Not only so, but we also rejoice in God through our Lord Jesus Christ, through whom we have now received our reconciliation.

Rom 6:1-10 (§23)

6 What shall we say then? Are we to continue in sin that grace may abound? 2 By no means! How can we who died to sin still live in it? 3 Do you not know that all of us who have been baptized into Christ Jesus were baptized into his death? 4 We were buried therefore with him by baptism into death, so that as Christ was raised from the dead by the glory of the Father, we too might walk in newness of life.

5 For if we have been united with him in a death like his, we shall certainly be united with him in a resurrection like his. 6 We know that our old self was crucified with him so that the sinful body might be destroyed, and we might no longer be enslaved to sin. 7 For he who has died is freed from sin. 8 But if we have died with Christ, we believe that we shall also live with him. 9 For we know that Christ being raised from the dead will never die again; death no longer has dominion over him. 10 The death he died he died to sin, once for all, but the life he lives he lives to God.

1 Cor 15:1-11

15 Now I would remind you, brethren, in what terms I preached to you the gospel, which you received, in which you stand, 2 by which you are saved, if you hold it fast—unless you believed in vain.

3 For I delivered to you as of first importance what I also received, that Christ died for our sins in accordance with the scriptures, 4 that he was buried, that he was raised on the third day in accordance with the scriptures, 5 and that he appeared to Cephas, then to the twelve. 6 Then he appeared to more than five hundred brethren at one time, most of whom are still alive, though some have fallen asleep. 7 Then he appeared to James, then to all the apostles. 8 Last of all, as to one untimely born, he appeared also to me. 9 For I am the least of the apostles, unfit to be called an apostle, because I persecuted the church of God. 10 But by the grace of God I am what I am, and his grace toward me was not in vain. On the contrary, I worked harder than any of them, though it was not I, but the grace of God which is with me. 11 Whether then it was I or they, so we preach and so you believed.

2 Cor 5:14-21 (§164)

14 For the love of Christ controls us, because we are convinced that one has died for all; therefore all have died. 15 And he died for all, that those who live might live no longer for themselves but for him who for their sake died and was raised.

16 From now on, therefore, we regard no one from a human point of view; even though we once regarded Christ from a human point of view, we regard him thus no longer. 17 Therefore, if any one is in Christ, he is a new creation; the old has passed away, behold, the new has come. 18 All this is from God, who through Christ reconciled us to himself and gave us the ministry of reconciliation; 19 that is, in Christ God was reconciling the world to himself, not counting their trespasses against them, and entrusting to us the message of reconciliation. 20 So we are ambassadors for Christ, God making his appeal through us. We beseech you on behalf of Christ, be reconciled to God. 21 For our sake he made him to be sin who knew no sin, so that in him we might become the righteousness of God.

Gal 1:15-24 (§196)

15 But when he who had set me apart before I was born, and had called me through his grace, 16 was pleased to reveal his Son to me, in order that I might preach him among the Gentiles, I did not confer with flesh and blood, 17 nor did I go up to Jerusalem to those who were apostles before me, but I went away into Arabia; and again I returned to Damascus.

18 Then after three years I went up to Jerusalem to visit Cephas, and remained with him fifteen days. 19 But I saw none of the other apostles except James the Lord's brother. 20 (In what I am writing to you, before God, I do not lie!) 21 Then I went into the regions of Syria and Cili'cia. 22 And I was still not known by sight to the churches of Christ in Judea; 23 they only heard it said, "He who once persecuted us is now preaching the faith he once tried to destroy." 24 And they glorified God because of me.

Gal 2:1-10 (§197)

2 Then after fourteen years I went up again to Jerusalem with Barnabas, taking Titus along with me. 2 I went up by revelation; and I laid before them (but privately before those who were of repute) the gospel which I preach among the Gentiles, lest somehow I should be running or had run in vain. 3 But even Titus, who was with me, was not compelled to be circumcised, though he was a Greek. 4 But because of false brethren secretly brought in, who slipped in to spy out our freedom which we have in Christ Jesus, that they might bring us into bondage— 5 to them we did not yield submission even for a moment, that the truth of the gospel might be preserved for you. 6 And from those who were reputed to be something (what they were makes no difference to me; God shows no partiality)—those, I say, who were of repute added nothing to me; 7 but on the contrary, when they saw that I had been entrusted with the gospel to the uncircumcised, just as Peter had been entrusted with the gospel to the circumcised 8 (for he who worked through Peter for the mission to the circumcised worked through me also for the Gentiles), 9 and when they perceived the grace that was given to me, James and Cephas and John, who were reputed to be pillars, gave to me and Barnabas the right hand of fellowship, that we should go to the Gentiles and they to the cir-

Eph 2:1-10 (§220)

2 And you he made alive, when you were dead through the trespasses and sins 2 in which you once walked, following the course of this world, following the prince of the power of the air, the spirit that is now at work in the sons of disobedience. 3 Among these we all once lived in the passions of our flesh, following the desires of body and mind, and so we were by nature children of wrath, like the rest of mankind. 4 But God, who is rich in mercy, out of the great love with which he loved us, 5 even when we were dead through our trespasses, made us alive together with Christ (by grace you have been saved), 6 and raised us up with him, and made us sit with him in the heavenly places in Christ Jesus, 7 that in the coming ages he might show the immeasurable riches of his grace in kindness toward us in Christ Jesus. 8 For by grace you have been saved through faith; and this is not your own doing, it is the gift of God— 9 not because of works, lest any man should boast. 10 For we are his workmanship, created in Christ Jesus for good works, which God prepared beforehand, that we should walk in them.

Eph 3:1-13 (§222)

3 For this reason I, Paul, a prisoner for Christ Jesus on behalf of you Gentiles— 2 assuming that you have heard of the stewardship of God's grace that was given to me for you, 3 how the mystery was made known to me by revelation, as I have written briefly. 4 When you read this you can perceive my insight into the mystery of Christ, 5 which was not made known to the sons of men in other generations as it has now been revealed to his holy apostles and prophets by the Spirit; 6 that is, how the Gentiles are fellow heirs, members of the same body, and partakers of the promise in Christ Jesus through the gospel.

7 Of this gospel I was made a minister according to the gift of God's grace which was given me by the working of his power. 8 To me, though I am the very least of all the saints, this grace was given, to preach to the Gentiles the unsearchable riches of Christ, 9 and to make all men see what is the plan of the mystery hidden for ages in God who

cumcised; 10 only they would have us remember the poor, which very thing I was eager to do.

▶ 15:3 Acts 8:32-33, 32 Now the passage of the scripture which he was reading was this: "As a sheep led to the slaughter or a lamb before its shearer is dumb, so he opens not his mouth. 33 In his humiliation justice was denied him. Who can describe his generation? For his life is taken up from the earth."

17:2-3 2 And Paul went in, as was his custom, and for three weeks he argued with them from the scriptures, 3 explaining and proving that it was necessary for the Christ to suffer and to rise from the dead, and saying, "This Jesus, whom I proclaim to you, is the Christ."

▶ 15:3-4 Acts 26:22-23 22 To this day I have had the help that comes from God, and so I stand here testifying both to small and great, saying nothing but what the prophets and Moses said would come to pass: 23 that the Christ must suffer, and that, by being the first to rise from the dead, he would proclaim light both to the people and to the Gentiles."

▶ 15:7 Acts 1:3-4 3 To them he presented himself alive after his passion by many proofs, appearing to them during forty days, and speaking of the kingdom of God. 4 And while staying with them he charged them not to depart from Jerusalem, but to wait for the promise of the Father, which, he said, "you heard from me,

▶ 15:4 Acts 2:24, 24 But God raised him up, having loosed the pangs of death, because it was not possible for him to be held by it.

31 31 he foresaw and spoke of the resurrection of the Christ, that he was not abandoned to Hades, nor did his flesh see corruption.

▶ 15:8-9 Acts 9:3-4 3 Now as he journeyed he approached Damascus, and suddenly a light from heaven flashed about him. 4 And he fell to the ground and heard a voice saying to him, "Saul, Saul, why do you persecute me?"

22:6-7 6 "As I made my journey and drew near to Damascus, about noon a great light from heaven suddenly shone about me. 7 And I fell to the ground and heard a voice saying to me, 'Saul, Saul, why do you persecute me?'

Acts 26:12-18 12 "Thus I journeyed to Damascus with the authority and commission of the chief priests. 13 At midday, O king, I saw on the way a light from heaven,

*cf Acts 9:1-30, 22:3-21

brighter than the sun, shining round me and those who journeyed with me. 14 And when we had all fallen to the ground, I heard a voice saying to me in the Hebrew language, 'Saul, Saul, why do you persecute me? It hurts you to kick against the goads.' 15 And I said, 'Who are you, Lord?' And the Lord said, 'I am Jesus whom you are persecuting. 16 But rise and stand upon your feet; for I have appeared to you for this purpose, to appoint you to serve and bear witness to the things in which you have seen me and to those in which I will appear to you, 17 delivering you from the people and from the Gentiles

Phil 1:12-18 (§239)

12 I want you to know, brethren, that what has happened to me has really served to advance the gospel, 13 so that it has become known throughout the whole praetorian guard and to all the rest that my imprisonment is for Christ; 14 and most of the brethren have been made confident in the Lord because of my imprisonment, and are much more bold to speak the word of God without fear.

15 Some indeed preach Christ from envy and rivalry, but others from good will. 16 The latter do it out of love, knowing that I am put here for the defense of the gospel; 17 the former proclaim Christ out of partisanship, not sincerely but thinking to afflict me in my imprisonment. 18 What then? Only that in every way, whether in pretense or in truth, Christ is proclaimed; and in that I rejoice.

Phil 3:17-21 (§249)

17 Brethren, join in imitating me, and mark those who so live as you have an example in us. 18 For many, of whom I have often told you and now tell you even with tears, live as enemies of the cross of Christ. 19 Their end is destruction, their god is the belly, and they glory in their shame, with minds set on earthly things. 20 But our commonwealth is in heaven, and from it we await a Savior, the Lord Jesus Christ, 21 who will change our lowly body to be like his glorious body, by the power which enables him even to subject all things to himself.

Col 2:8-15 (§262)

8 See to it that no one makes a prey of you by philosophy and empty deceit, according to human tradition, according to the elemental spirits of the universe, and not according to Christ. 9 For in him the whole fulness of deity dwells bodily, 10 and you have come to fulness of life in him, who is the head of all rule and authority. 11 In him also you were circumcised with a circumcision made without hands, by putting off the body of flesh in the circumcision of Christ; 12 and you were buried with him in baptism, in which you were also raised with him through faith in the working of God, who raised him from the dead. 13 And you, who were dead in trespasses and the uncircumcision of your flesh, God made alive together with him, having forgiven us all our trespasses, 14 having canceled the bond which stood against us with its legal demands; this he set aside, nailing it to the cross. 15 He disarmed the principalities and powers and made a public example of them, triumphing over them in him.

Eph (cont)

created all things; 10 that through the church the manifold wisdom of God might now be made known to the principalities and powers in the heavenly places. 11 This was according to the eternal purpose which he has realized in Christ Jesus our Lord, 12 in whom we have boldness and confidence of access through our faith in him. 13 So I ask you not to lose heart over what I am suffering for you, which is your glory.

—to whom I send you 18 to open their eyes, that they may turn from darkness to light and from the power of Satan to God, that they may receive forgiveness of sins and a place among those who are sanctified by faith in me.'

1 Tim 1:15

15 The saying is sure and worthy of full acceptance, that Christ Jesus came into the world to save sinners. And I am the foremost of sinners;

▶ 15:10 1 Tim 4:10

10 For to this end we toil and strive, because we have our hope set on the living God, who is the Savior of all men, especially of those who believe.

▶15:1-3 11:23

23 For I received from the Lord what I also delivered to you, that the Lord Jesus on the night when he was betrayed took bread,

▶ 15:3-4 1 Thes 1:9-10,

9 For they themselves report concerning us what a welcome we had among you, and how you turned to God from idols, to serve a living and true God, 10 and to wait for his Son from heaven, whom he raised from the dead, Jesus who delivers us from the wrath to come.

4:14

14 For since we believe that Jesus died and rose again, even so, through Jesus, God will bring with him those who have fallen asleep.

▶15:9 2 Cor 11:5

5 I think that I am not in the least inferior to these superlative apostles.

▶ 15:10 2 Cor 6:1,

Working together with him, then, we entreat you not to accept the grace of God in vain.

11:21b-23

But whatever any one dares to boast of—I am speaking as a fool—I also dare to boast of that. 22 Are they Hebrews? So am I. Are they Israelites? So am I. Are they descendants of Abraham? So am I. 23 Are they servants of Christ? I am a better one—I am talking like a madman—with far greater labors, far more imprisonments, with countless beatings, and often near death.

132

5 Therefore, since we are justified by faith, we have peace with God through our Lord Jesus Christ. [2] Through him we have obtained access to this grace in which we stand, and we rejoice in our hope of sharing the glory of God. [3] More than that, we rejoice in our sufferings, knowing that suffering produces endurance, [4] and endurance produces character, and character produces hope, [5] and hope does not disappoint us, because God's love has been poured into our hearts through the Holy Spirit which has been given to us.

6 What shall we say then? Are we to continue in sin that grace may abound? [2] By no means! How can we who died to sin still live in it? [3] Do you not know that all of us who have been baptized into Christ Jesus were baptized into his death? [4] We were buried therefore with him by baptism into death, so that as Christ was raised from the dead by the glory of the Father, we too might walk in newness of life.
[5] For if we have been united with him in a death like his, we shall certainly be united with him in a resurrection like his. [6] We know that our old self was crucified with him so that the sinful body might be destroyed, and we might no longer be enslaved to sin. [7] For he who has died is freed from sin. [8] But if we have died with Christ, we believe that we shall also live with him. [9] For we know that Christ being raised from the dead will never die again; death no longer has dominion over him. [10] The death he died he died to sin, once for all, but the life he lives he lives to God.

[12] Now if Christ is preached as raised from the dead, how can some of you say that there is no resurrection of the dead? [13] But if there is no resurrection of the dead, then Christ has not been raised; [14] if Christ has not been raised, then our preaching is in vain and your faith is in vain. [15] We are even found to be misrepresenting God, because we testified of God that he raised Christ, whom he did not raise if it is true that the dead are not raised. [16] For if the dead are not raised, then Christ has not been raised. [17] If Christ has not been raised, your faith is futile and you are still in your sins. [18] Then those also who have fallen asleep in Christ have perished. [19] If for this life only we have hoped in Christ, we are of all men most to be pitied.

[14] For the love of Christ controls us, because we are convinced that one has died for all; therefore all have died. [15] And he died for all, that those who live might live no longer for themselves but for him who for their sake died and was raised.
[16] From now on, therefore, we regard no one from a human point of view; even though we once regarded Christ from a human point of view, we regard him thus no longer. [17] Therefore, if any one is in Christ, he is a new creation; the old has passed away, behold, the new has come. [18] All this is from God, who through Christ reconciled us to himself and gave us the ministry of reconciliation; [19] that is, in Christ God was reconciling the world to himself, not counting their trespasses against them, and entrusting to us the message of reconciliation. [20] So we are ambassadors for Christ, God making his appeal through us. We beseech you on behalf of Christ, be reconciled to God. [21] For our sake he made him to be sin who knew no sin, so that in him we might become the righteousness of God.

2 And you he made alive, when you were dead through the trespasses and sins [2] in which you once walked, following the course of this world, following the prince of the power of the air, the spirit that is now at work in the sons of disobedience. [3] Among these we all once lived in the passions of our flesh, following the desires of body and mind, and so we were by nature children of wrath, like the rest of mankind. [4] But God, who is rich in mercy, out of the great love with which he loved us, [5] even when we were dead through our trespasses, made us alive together with Christ (by grace you have been saved), [6] and raised us up with him, and made us sit with him in the heavenly places in Christ Jesus, [7] that in the coming ages he might show the immeasurable riches of his grace in kindness toward us in Christ Jesus. [8] For by grace you have been saved through faith; and this is not your own doing, it is the gift of God— [9] not because of works, lest any man should boast. [10] For we are his workmanship, created in Christ Jesus for good works, which God prepared beforehand, that we should walk in them.

▶15:12 Acts 4:2,
[2] annoyed because they were teaching the people and proclaiming in Jesus the resurrection from the dead.

17:32,
[32] Now when they heard of the resurrection of the dead, some mocked; but others said, "We will hear you again about this."

23:8
[8] For the Sad'ducees say that there is no resurrection, nor angel, nor spirit; but the Pharisees acknowledge them all.

2 Tim 2:17-18
[17] and their talk will eat its way like gangrene. Among them are Hymenae'us and Phile'tus, [18] who have swerved from the truth by holding that the resurrection is past already. They are upsetting the faith of some.

▶15:15 Acts 2:24
[24] But God raised him up, having loosed the pangs of death, because it was not possible for him to be held by it.

▶15:19 Rom 8:24,
[24] For in this hope we were saved. Now hope that is seen is not hope. For who hopes for what he sees?

Phil 3:17-21 (§249)

17 Brethren, join in imitating me, and mark those who so live as you have an example in us. 18 For many, of whom I have often told you and now tell you even with tears, live as enemies of the cross of Christ. 19 Their end is destruction, their god is the belly, and they glory in their shame, with minds set on earthly things. 20 But our commonwealth is in heaven, and from it we await a Savior, the Lord Jesus Christ, 21 who will change our lowly body to be like his glorious body, by the power which enables him even to subject all things to himself.

Col 2:8-15 (§262)

8 See to it that no one makes a prey of you by philosophy and empty deceit, according to human tradition, according to the elemental spirits of the universe, and not according to Christ. 9 For in him the whole fulness of deity dwells bodily, 10 and you have come to fulness of life in him, who is the head of all rule and authority. 11 In him also you were circumcised with a circumcision made without hands, by putting off the body of flesh in the circumcision of Christ; 12 and you were buried with him in baptism, in which you were also raised with him through faith in the working of God, who raised him from the dead. 13 And you, who were dead in trespasses and the uncircumcision of your flesh, God made alive together with him, having forgiven us all our trespasses, 14 having canceled the bond which stood against us with its legal demands; this he set aside, nailing it to the cross. 15 He disarmed the principalities and powers and made a public example of them, triumphing over them in him.

1 Thes 4:13-18 (§286)

13 But we would not have you ignorant, brethren, concerning those who are asleep, that you may not grieve as others do who have no hope. 14 For since we believe that Jesus died and rose again, even so, through Jesus, God will bring with him those who have fallen asleep. 15 For this we declare to you by the word of the Lord, that we who are alive, who are left until the coming of the Lord, shall not precede those who have fallen asleep. 16 For the Lord himself will descend from heaven with a cry of command, with the archangel's call, and with the sound of the trumpet of God. And the dead in Christ will rise first; 17 then we who are alive, who are left, shall be caught up together with them in the clouds to meet the Lord in the air; and so we shall always be with the Lord. 18 Therefore comfort one another with these words.

15:13

13 May the God of hope fill you with all joy and peace in believing, so that by the power of the Holy Spirit you may abound in hope.

Eph 2:12 12 remember that you were at that time separated from Christ, alienated from the commonwealth of Israel, and strangers to the covenants of promise, having no hope and without God in the world.

133

Rom 5:12-21 (§22)

12 Therefore as sin came into the world through one man and death through sin, and so death spread to all men because all men sinned—13 sin indeed was in the world before the law was given, but sin is not counted where there is no law. 14 Yet death reigned from Adam to Moses, even over those whose sins were not like the transgression of Adam, who was a type of the one who was to come.

15 But the free gift is not like the trespass. For if many died through one man's trespass, much more have the grace of God and the free gift in the grace of that one man Jesus Christ abounded for many. 16And the free gift is not like the effect of that one man's sin. For the judgment following one trespass brought condemnation, but the free gift following many trespasses brings justification. 17 If, because of one man's trespass, death reigned through that one man, much more will those who receive the abundance of grace and the free gift of righteousness reign in life through the one man Jesus Christ. 18 Then as one man's trespass led to

▶15:20 Acts 2:24, 24 But God raised him up, having loosed the pangs of death, because it was not possible for him to be held by it.

1 Cor 15:20-28

20 But in fact Christ has been raised from the dead, the first fruits of those who have fallen asleep. 21 For as by a man came death, by a man has come also the resurrection of the dead. 22 For as in Adam all die, so also in Christ shall all be made alive. 23 But each in his own order: Christ the first fruits, then at his coming those who belong to Christ. 24 Then comes the end, when he delivers the kingdom to God the Father after destroying every rule and every authority and power. 25 For he must reign until he has put all his enemies under his feet. 26 The last enemy to be

condemnation for all men, so one man's act of righteousness leads to acquittal and life for all men. 19 For as by one man's disobedience many were made sinners, so by one man's obedience many will be made righteous. 20 Law came in, to increase the trespass; but where sin increased, grace abounded all the more, 21 so that, as sin reigned in death, grace also might reign through righteousness to eternal life through Jesus Christ our Lord.

26:22-23 22 To this day I have had the help that comes from God, and so I stand here testifying both to small and great, saying nothing but what the prophets and Moses said would come to pass: 23 that the Christ must suffer, and that, by being the first to rise from the dead, he would proclaim light both to the people and to the Gentiles."

2 Cor 10:1-6 (§176)

10 I, Paul, myself entreat you, by the meekness and gentleness of Christ—I who am humble when face to face with you, but bold to you when I am away!— 2 I beg of you that when I am present I may not have to show boldness with such confidence as I count on showing against some who suspect us of acting in worldly fashion. 3 For though we live in the world we are

not carrying on a worldly war, 4 for the weapons of our warfare are not worldly but have divine power to destroy strongholds. 5 We destroy arguments and every proud obstacle to the knowledge of God, and take every thought captive to obey Christ, 6 being ready to punish every disobedience, when your obedience is complete.

destroyed is death. 27 "For God has put all things in subjection under his feet." But when it says, "All things are put in subjection under him," it is plain that he is excepted who put all things under him. 28 When all things are subjected to him, then the Son himself will also be subjected to him who put all things under him, that God may be everything to every one.

▶15:28 3:21-23 21 So let no one boast of men. For all things are yours, 22 whether Paul or Apol'los or Cephas or the world or life or death or the present or the future, all are yours; 23 and you are Christ's; and Christ is God's.

▶15:27 Ps 8:6 6 Thou hast given him dominion over the works of thy hands; thou hast put all things under his feet,

Eph 1:3-23 (§219)

3 Blessed be the God and Father of our Lord Jesus Christ, who has blessed us in Christ with every spiritual blessing in the heavenly places, 4 even as he chose us in him before the foundation of the world, that we should be holy and blameless before him. 5 He destined us in love to be his sons through Jesus Christ, according to the purpose of his will, 6 to the praise of his glorious grace which he freely bestowed on us in the Beloved. 7 In him we have redemption through his blood, the forgiveness of our trespasses, according to the riches of his grace 8 which he lavished upon us. 9 For he has made known to us in all wisdom and insight the mystery of his will, according to his purpose which he set forth in Christ 10 as a plan for the fulness of time, to unite all things in him, things in heaven and things on earth.

11 In him, according to the purpose of him who accomplishes all things according to the counsel of his will, 12 we who first hoped in Christ have been destined and appointed to live for the

134. If the dead are not raised

134

1 Cor 15:29-34

29 Otherwise, what do people mean by being baptized on behalf of the dead? If the dead are not raised at all, why are people baptized on their behalf? 30 Why am I in peril every hour? 31 I protest, brethren, by my pride in you which I have in Christ Jesus our Lord, I die every day! 32 What do I gain if, humanly speaking, I fought with beasts at Ephesus? If the dead are not raised, "Let us eat and drink, for tomorrow we die." 33 Do not be deceived: "Bad company ruins good morals." 34 Come to your right mind, and sin no more. For some have no knowledge of God. I say this to your shame.

▶15:30 Gal 5:11 11But if I, brethren, still preach circumcision, why am I still persecuted? In that case the stumbling block of the cross has been removed.

▶15:34 Gal 4:9 9 but now that you have come to know God, or rather to be known by God, how can you turn back again to the weak and beggarly elemental spirits, whose slaves you want to be once more?

2 Cor 4:7-12 (§159)

7 But we have this treasure in earthen vessels, to show that the transcendent power belongs to God and not to us. 8 We are afflicted in every way, but not crushed; perplexed, but not driven to despair; 9 persecuted, but not forsaken; struck down, but not destroyed; 10 always carrying in the body the death of Jesus, so that the life of Jesus may also be manifested in our bodies. 11 For while we live we are always being given up to death for Jesus' sake, so that the life of Jesus may be manifested in our mortal flesh. 12 So death is at work in us, but life in you.

2 Cor 6:1-10 (§165)

6 Working together with him, then, we entreat you not to accept the grace of God in vain. 2 For he says,
"At the acceptable time I have listened to you,
and helped you on the day of salvation."
Behold, now is the acceptable time; behold, now is the day of salvation. 3 We put no obstacle in any one's way, so that no fault may be found with our ministry, 4 but as servants of God we

▶15:32 Is 22:13 13 and behold, joy and gladness, slaying oxen and killing sheep, eating flesh and drinking wine. "Let us eat and drink, for tomorrow we die."

commend ourselves in every way: through great endurance, in afflictions, hardships, calamities, 5 beatings, imprisonments, tumults, labors, watching, hunger; 6 by purity, knowledge, forbearance, kindness, the Holy Spirit, genuine love, 7 truthful speech, and the power of God; with the weapons of righteousness for the right hand and for the left; 8 in honor and dishonor, in ill repute and good repute. We are treated as impostors, and yet are true; 9 as unknown, and yet well known; as dying, and behold we live; as punished, and yet not killed; 10 as sorrowful, yet always rejoicing; as poor, yet making many rich; as having nothing, and yet possessing everything.

2 Cor 11:21b-29 (§183)

But whatever any one dares to boast of—I am speaking as a fool—I also dare to boast of that. 22Are they Hebrews? So am I. Are they Israelites? So am I. Are they descendants of Abraham? So am I. 23Are they servants of Christ? I am a better one—I am talking like a madman—with far greater labors, far more imprisonments, with countless beatings, and often near death. 24 Five times I

have received at the hands of the Jews the forty lashes less one. 25 Three times I have been beaten with rods; once I was stoned. Three times I have been shipwrecked; a night and a day I have been adrift at sea; 26 on frequent journeys, in danger from rivers, danger from robbers, danger from my own people, danger from Gentiles, danger in the city, danger in the wilderness, danger at sea, danger from false brethren; 27 in toil and hardship, through many a sleepless night, in hunger and thirst, often without food, in cold and exposure. 28And, apart from other things, there is the daily pressure upon me of my anxiety for all the churches. 29 Who is weak, and I am not weak? Who is made to fall, and I am not indignant?

Phil 3:17-21 (§249)

17 Brethren, join in imitating me, and mark those who so live as you have an example in us. 18 For many, of whom I have often told you and now tell you even with tears, live as enemies of the cross of Christ. 19 Their end is destruction, their god is the belly, and they glory in their shame, with minds set on earthly things. 20 But our commonwealth is in heaven, and from it we await a Savior, the Lord Jesus Christ, 21 who will change our lowly body to be like his glorious body, by the power which enables him even to subject all things to himself.

Eph (cont)

praise of his glory. 13 In him you also, who have heard the word of truth, the gospel of your salvation, and have believed in him, were sealed with the promised Holy Spirit, 14 which is the guarantee of our inheritance until we acquire possession of it, to the praise of his glory.

15 For this reason, because I have heard of your faith in the Lord Jesus and your love toward all the saints, 16 I do not cease to give thanks for you, remembering you in my prayers, 17 that the God of our Lord Jesus Christ, the Father of glory, may give you a spirit of wisdom and of revelation in the knowledge of him, 18 having the eyes of your

Col 1:15-20 (§258)

15 He is the image of the invisible God, the first-born of all creation; 16 for in him all things were created, in heaven and on earth, visible and invisible, whether thrones or dominions or principalities or authorities—all things were created through him and for him. 17 He is before all things, and in him all things hold together. 18 He is the head of the body, the church; he is the beginning, the first-born from the dead, that in everything he might be pre-eminent. 19 For in him all the fulness of God was pleased to dwell, 20 and through him to reconcile to himself all things, whether on earth or in heaven, making peace by the blood of his cross.

hearts enlightened, that you may know what is the hope to which he has called you, what are the riches of his glorious inheritance in the saints, 19 and what is the immeasurable greatness of his power in us who believe, according to the working of his great might 20 which he accomplished in Christ when he raised him from the dead and made him sit at his right hand in the heavenly places, 21 far above all rule and authority and power and dominion, and above every name that is named, not only in this age but also in that which is to come; 22 and he has put all things under his feet and has made him the head over all things for the church, 23 which is his body, the fulness of him who fills all in all.

1 Thes 4:13-18 (§286)

13 But we would not have you ignorant, brethren, concerning those who are asleep, that you may not grieve as others do who have no hope. 14 For since we believe that Jesus died and rose again, even so, through Jesus, God will bring with him those who have fallen asleep. 15 For this we declare to you by the word of the Lord, that we who are alive, who are left until the coming of the Lord, shall not precede those who have fallen asleep. 16 For the Lord himself will descend from heaven with a cry of command, with the archangel's call, and with the sound of the trumpet of God. And the dead in Christ will rise first; 17 then we who are alive, who are left, shall be caught up together with them in the clouds to meet the Lord in the air; and so we shall always be with the Lord. 18 Therefore comfort one another with these words.

2 Thes 2:1-12 (§296)

2 Now concerning the coming of our Lord Jesus Christ and our assembling to meet him, we beg you, brethren, 2 not to be quickly shaken in mind or excited, either by spirit or by word, or by letter purporting to be from us, to the effect that the day of the Lord has come. 3 Let no one deceive you in any way; for that day will not come, unless the rebellion comes first, and the man of lawlessness is revealed, the son of perdition, 4 who opposes and exalts himself against every so-called god or object of worship, so that he takes his seat in the temple of God, proclaiming himself to be God. 5 Do you not remember that when I was still with you I told you this? 6 And you know what is restraining him now so that he may be revealed in his time. 7 For the mystery of lawlessness is already at work; only he who now restrains it will do so until he is out of the way. 8 And then the lawless one will be revealed, and the Lord Jesus will slay him with the breath of his mouth and destroy him by his appearing and his coming. 9 The coming of the lawless one by the activity of

Satan will be with all power and with pretended signs and wonders, 10 and with all wicked deception for those who are to perish, because they refused to love the truth and so be saved. 11 Therefore God sends upon them a strong delusion, to make them believe what is false, 12 so that all may be condemned who did not believe the truth but had pleasure in unrighteousness.

133

Phil 1:19-26 (§240)

19 Yes, and I shall rejoice. For I know that through your prayers and the help of the Spirit of Jesus Christ this will turn out for my deliverance, 20 as it is my eager expectation and hope that I shall not be at all ashamed, but that with full courage now as always Christ will be honored in my body, whether by life or by death. 21 For to me to live is Christ, and to die is gain. 22 If it is to be life in the flesh, that means fruitful labor for me. Yet which I shall choose I cannot tell. 23 I am hard pressed between the two. My desire is to depart and be with Christ, for that is far better. 24 But to remain in the flesh is more necessary on your account. 25 Convinced of this, I know that I shall remain and continue with you all, for your progress and joy in the faith, 26 so that in me you may have ample cause to glory in Christ Jesus, because of my coming to you again.

Col 1:24-2:3 (§260)

24 Now I rejoice in my sufferings for your sake, and in my flesh I complete what is lacking in Christ's afflictions for the sake of his body, that is, the church, 25 of which I became a minister according to the divine office which was given to me for you, to make the word of God fully known, 26 the mystery hidden for ages and generations but now made manifest to his saints. 27 To them God chose to make known how great among the Gentiles are the riches of the glory of this mystery, which is Christ in you, the hope of glory. 28 Him we proclaim, warning every man and teaching every man in all wisdom, that we may present every man mature in Christ. 29 For this I toil, striving with all the energy which he mightily inspires within me.

2 For I want you to know how greatly I strive for you, and for those at La-odice′a, and for all who have not seen my face, 2 that their hearts may be encouraged as they are knit together in love, to have all the riches of assured understanding and the knowledge of God's mystery, of Christ, 3 in whom are hid all the treasures of wisdom and knowledge.

134. If the dead are not raised

1 Thes 3:1-5 (§281)

3 Therefore when we could bear it no longer, we were willing to be left behind at Athens alone, 2 and we sent Timothy, our brother and God's servant in the gospel of Christ, to establish you in your faith and to exhort you, 3 that no one be moved by these afflictions. You yourselves know that this is to be our lot. 4 For when we were with you, we told you beforehand that we were to suffer affliction; just as it has come to pass, and as you know. 5 For this reason, when I could bear it no longer, I sent that I might know your faith, for fear that somehow the tempter had tempted you and that our labor would be in vain.

134

▶ 15:33 Meander, *Thais.*

135

Rom 8:18-25 (§31)

18 I consider that the sufferings of this present time are not worth comparing with the glory that is to be revealed to us. 19 For the creation waits with eager longing for the revealing of the sons of God; 20 for the creation was subjected to futility, not of its own will but by the will of him who subjected it in hope; 21 because the creation itself will be set free from its bondage to decay and obtain the glorious liberty of the children of God. 22 We know that the whole creation has been groaning in travail together until now; 23 and not only the creation, but we ourselves, who have the first fruits of the Spirit, groan inwardly as we wait for adoption as sons, the redemption of our bodies. 24 For in this hope we were saved. Now hope that is seen is not hope. For who hopes for what he sees? 25 But if we hope for what we do not see, we wait for it with patience.

▶15:35 Acts 26:8
8 Why is it thought incredible by any of you that God raises the dead?

1 Cor 15:35-41

35 But some one will ask, "How are the dead raised? With what kind of body do they come?" 36 You foolish man! What you sow does not come to life unless it dies. 37 And what you sow is not the body which is to be, but a bare kernel, perhaps of wheat or of some other grain. 38 But God gives it a body as he has chosen, and to each kind of seed its own body. 39 For not all flesh is alike, but there is one kind for men, another for animals, another for birds, and another for fish. 40 There are celestial bodies and there are terrestrial bodies; but the glory of the celestial is one, and the glory of the terrestrial is another. 41 There is one glory of the sun, and another glory of the moon, and another glory of the stars; for star differs from star in glory.

▶15:35-41 Rom 8:9-11
9 But you are not in the flesh, you are in the Spirit, if in fact the Spirit of God dwells in you. Any one who does not have the Spirit of Christ does not belong to him. 10 But if Christ is in you, although your bodies are dead because of sin, your spirits are alive because of righteousness. 11 If the Spirit of him who raised Jesus from the dead dwells in you, he who raised Christ Jesus from the dead will give life to your mortal bodies also through his Spirit which dwells in you.

2 Cor 4:16-5:5 (§161)

16 So we do not lose heart. Though our outer nature is wasting away, our inner nature is being renewed every day. 17 For this slight momentary affliction is preparing for us an eternal weight of glory beyond all comparison, 18 because we look not to the things that are seen but to the things that are unseen; for the things that are seen are transient, but the things that are unseen are eternal.

5 For we know that if the earthly tent we live in is destroyed, we have a building from God, a house not made with hands, eternal in the heavens. 2 Here indeed we groan, and long to put on our heavenly dwelling, 3 so that by putting it on we may not be found naked. 4 For while we are still in this tent, we sigh with anxiety; not that we would be unclothed, but that we would be further clothed, so that what is mortal may be swallowed up by life. 5 He who has prepared us for this very thing is God, who has given us the Spirit as a guarantee.

136. How are the dead raised?

136

Rom 5:12-21 (§22)

12 Therefore as sin came into the world through one man and death through sin, and so death spread to all men because all men sinned—13 sin indeed was in the world before the law was given, but sin is not counted where there is no law. 14 Yet death reigned from Adam to Moses, even over those whose sins were not like the transgression of Adam, who was a type of the one who was to come.

15 But the free gift is not like the trespass. For if many died through one man's trespass, much more have the grace of God and the free gift in the grace of that one man Jesus Christ abounded for many. 16 And the free gift is not like the effect of that one man's sin. For the judgment following one trespass brought condemnation, but the free gift following many trespasses brings justification. 17 If, because of one man's trespass, death reigned through that one man, much more will those who receive the abundance of grace and the free gift of righteousness reign in life through the one man Jesus Christ. 18 Then as one man's trespass led to

▶15:45 *cf. Rom 8:11

1 Cor 15:42-50

42 So is it with the resurrection of the dead. What is sown is perishable, what is raised is imperishable. 43 It is sown in dishonor, it is raised in glory. It is sown in weakness, it is raised in power. 44 It is sown a physical body, it is raised a spiritual body. If there is a physical body, there is also a spiritual body. 45 Thus it is written, "The first man Adam became a living being"; the last Adam became a life-giving spirit. 46 But it is not the spiritual which is first but the physical, and then the spiritual. 47 The first man was from the earth, a man of dust; the second man is from heaven. 48 As was the man of dust, so are those who are of the dust; and as is the man of heaven, so are those who are of heaven. 49 Just as we have borne the image of the man of dust, we shall also bear the image of the man of heaven. 50 I tell you this, brethren: flesh and blood cannot inherit the kingdom of God, nor does the perishable inherit the imperishable.

condemnation for all men, so one man's act of righteousness leads to acquittal and life for all men. 19 For as by one man's disobedience many were made sinners, so by one man's obedience many will be made righteous. 20 Law came in, to increase the trespass; but where sin increased, grace abounded all the more, 21 so that, as sin reigned in death, grace also might reign through righteousness to eternal life through Jesus Christ our Lord.

▶15:45 Gen 2:7
7 then the LORD God formed man of dust from the ground, and breathed into his nostrils the breath of life; and man became a living being.

Gal 6:7-10 (§215)

7 Do not be deceived; God is not mocked, for whatever a man sows, that he will also reap. 8 For he who sows to his own flesh will from the flesh reap corruption; but he who sows to the Spirit will from the Spirit reap eternal life. 9 And let us not grow weary in well-doing, for in due season we shall reap, if we do not lose heart. 10 So then, as we have opportunity, let us do good to all men, and especially to those who are of the household of faith.

135

Phil 3:17-21 (§249)

17 Brethren, join in imitating me, and mark those who so live as you have an example in us. 18 For many, of whom I have often told you and now tell you even with tears, live as enemies of the cross of Christ. 19 Their end is destruction, their god is the belly, and they glory in their shame, with minds set on earthly things. 20 But our commonwealth is in heaven, and from it we await a Savior, the Lord Jesus Christ, 21 who will change our lowly body to be like his glorious body, by the power which enables him even to subject all things to himself.

136. How are the dead raised?

136

Phil 3:17-21 (§249)

17 Brethren, join in imitating me, and mark those who so live as you have an example in us. 18 For many, of whom I have often told you and now tell you even with tears, live as enemies of the cross of Christ. 19 Their end is destruction, their god is the belly, and they glory in their shame, with minds set on earthly things. 20 But our commonwealth is in heaven, and from it we await a Savior, the Lord Jesus Christ, 21 who will change our lowly body to be like his glorious body, by the power which enables him even to subject all things to himself.

Col 1:15-20 (§258)

15 He is the image of the invisible God, the first-born of all creation; 16 for in him all things were created, in heaven and on earth, visible and invisible, whether thrones or dominions or principalities or authorities—all things were created through him and for him. 17 He is before all things, and in him all things hold together. 18 He is the head of the body, the church; he is the beginning, the first-born from the dead, that in everything he might be pre-eminent. 19 For in him all the fulness of God was pleased to dwell, 20 and through him to reconcile to himself all things, whether on earth or in heaven, making peace by the blood of his cross.

Col 3:5-11 (§266)

5 Put to death therefore what is earthly in you: fornication, impurity, passion, evil desire, and covetousness, which is idolatry. 6 On account of these the wrath of God is coming. 7 In these you once walked, when you lived in them. 8 But now put them all away: anger, wrath, malice, slander, and foul talk from your mouth. 9 Do not lie to one another, seeing that you have put off the old nature with its practices 10 and have put on the new nature, which is being renewed in knowledge after the image of its creator. 11 Here there cannot be Greek and Jew, circumcised and uncircumcised, barbarian, Scyth'ian, slave, free man, but Christ is all, and in all.

▶15:49 (shall) *read* let us: p46SACDG Koine it vg cop(bo) Marcion Clement; *text*: B Lect cop(sa) Irenaeus Origen

137

Rom 7:7-13 (§27)

7 What then shall we say? That the law is sin? By no means! Yet, if it had not been for the law, I should not have known sin. I should not have known what it is to covet if the law had not said, "You shall not covet." 8 But sin, finding opportunity in the commandment, wrought in me all kinds of covetousness. Apart from the law sin lies dead. 9 I was once alive apart from the law, but when the commandment came, sin revived and I died; 10 the very commandment which promised life proved to be death to me. 11 For sin, finding opportunity in the commandment, deceived me and by it killed me. 12 So the law is holy, and the commandment is holy and just and good.

13 Did that which is good, then, bring death to me? By no means! It was sin, working death in me through what is good, in order that sin might be shown to be sin, and through the commandment might become sinful beyond measure.

▶15:56 Rom 7:25
25 Thanks be to God through Jesus Christ our Lord! So then, I of myself serve the law of God with my mind, but with my flesh I serve the law of sin.

1 Cor 15:51-58

51 Lo! I tell you a mystery. We shall not all sleep, but we shall all be changed, 52 in a moment, in the twinkling of an eye, at the last trumpet. For the trumpet will sound, and the dead will be raised imperishable, and we shall be changed. 53 For this perishable nature must put on the imperishable, and this mortal nature must put on immortality. 54 When the perishable puts on the imperishable, and the mortal puts on immortality, then shall come to pass the saying that is written:
"Death is swallowed up in victory."
55 "O death, where is thy victory?
O death, where is thy sting?"
56 The sting of death is sin, and the power of sin is the law. 57 But thanks be to God, who gives us the victory through our Lord Jesus Christ.

58 Therefore, my beloved brethren, be steadfast, immovable, always abounding in the work of the Lord, knowing that in the Lord your labor is not in vain.

▶15:58 Gal 2:2   2 I
went up by revelation; and I laid before them (but privately before those who were of repute) the gospel which I preach among the Gentiles, lest somehow I should be running or had run in vain.

Phil 2:16
16 holding fast the word of life, so that in the day of Christ I may be proud that I did not run in vain or labor in vain.

2 Cor 4:16-5:5 (§161)

16 So we do not lose heart. Though our outer nature is wasting away, our inner nature is being renewed every day. 17 For this slight momentary affliction is preparing for us an eternal weight of glory beyond all comparison, 18 because we look not to the things that are seen but to the things that are unseen; for the things that are seen are transient, but the things that are unseen are eternal.

5 For we know that if the earthly tent we live in is destroyed, we have a building from God, a house not made with hands, eternal in the heavens. 2 Here indeed we groan, and long to put on our heavenly dwelling, 3 so that by putting it on we may not be found naked. 4 For while we are still in this tent, we sigh with anxiety; not that we would be unclothed, but that we would be further clothed, so that what is mortal may be swallowed up by life. 5 He who has prepared us for this very thing is God, who has given us the Spirit as a guarantee.

Col 2:4-7 4 I say this in order that no one may delude you with beguiling speech. 5 For though I am absent in body, yet I am with you in spirit, rejoicing to see your good order and the firmness of your faith in Christ.
6 As therefore you received Christ Jesus the Lord, so live in him, 7 rooted and built up in him and established in the faith, just as you were taught, abounding in thanksgiving.

Eph 4:17-24 (§227)

17 Now this I affirm and testify in the Lord, that you must no longer live as the Gentiles do, in the futility of their minds; 18 they are darkened in their understanding, alienated from the life of God because of the ignorance that is in them, due to their hardness of heart; 19 they have become callous and have given themselves up to licentiousness, greedy to practice every kind of uncleanness. 20 You did not so learn Christ!— 21 assuming that you have heard about him and were taught in him, as the truth is in Jesus. 22 Put off your old nature which belongs to your former manner of life and is corrupt through deceitful lusts, 23 and be renewed in the spirit of your minds, 24 and put on the new nature, created after the likeness of God in true righteousness and holiness.

1 Thes 3:5   5 For
this reason, when I could bear it no longer, I sent that I might know your faith, for fear that somehow the tempter had tempted you and that our labor would be in vain.

138. Concerning contribution for the saints

138

Rom 15:14-21 (§62)

14 I myself am satisfied about you, my brethren, that you yourselves are full of goodness, filled with all knowledge, and able to instruct one another. 15 But on some points I have written to you very boldly by way of reminder, because of the grace given me by God 16 to be a minister of Christ Jesus to the Gentiles in the priestly service of the gospel of God, so that the offering of the Gentiles may be acceptable, sanctified by the Holy Spirit. 17 In Christ Jesus, then, I have reason to be proud of my work for God. 18 For I will not venture to speak of anything except what Christ has wrought through me to win obedience from the Gentiles, by word and deed, 19 by the power of signs and wonders, by the power of the Holy Spirit, so that from Jerusalem and as far round as Illyr'icum I have fully preached the gospel of Christ, 20 thus making it my ambition to preach the gospel, not where Christ has already been named, lest I build on another man's foundation, 21 but as it is written,
"They shall see who have never been told of him,
and they shall understand who have never heard of him."

▶16:1 Acts 11:29,
29And the disciples determined, every one according to his ability, to send relief to the brethren who lived in Judea;

1 Cor 16:1-4

16 Now concerning the contribution for the saints: as I directed the churches of Galatia, so you also are to do. 2 On the first day of every week, each of you is to put something aside and store it up, as he may prosper, so that contributions need not be made when I come. 3And when I arrive, I will send those whom you accredit by letter to carry your gift to Jerusalem. 4 If it seems advisable that I should go also, they will accompany me.

24:17   17 Now after
some years I came to bring to my nation alms and offerings.

2 Cor 8:1-9:15 (§171-175)

8 We want you to know, brethren, about the grace of God which has been shown in the churches of Macedo'nia, 2 for in a severe test of affliction, their abundance of joy and their extreme poverty have overflowed in a wealth of liberality on their part. 3 For they gave according to their means, as I can testify, and beyond their means, of their own free will, 4 begging us earnestly for the favor of taking part in the relief of the saints— 5 and this, not as we expected, but first they gave themselves to the Lord and to us by the will of God. 6Accordingly we have urged Titus that as he had already made a beginning, he should also complete among you this gracious work. 7 Now as you excel in everything—in faith, in utterance, in knowledge, in all earnestness, and in your love for us—see that you excel in this gracious work also.

8 I say this not as a command, but to prove by the earnestness of others that your love also is genuine. 9 For you know the grace of our Lord Jesus Christ, that though he was rich, yet for your sake he became poor, so that by his poverty you might become rich.

▶16:2 Acts 20:7
7 On the first day of the week, when we were gathered together to break bread, Paul talked with them, intending to depart on the morrow; and he prolonged his speech until midnight.

Gal 2:1-10 (§197)

2 Then after fourteen years I went up again to Jerusalem with Barnabas, taking Titus along with me. 2 I went up by revelation; and I laid before them (but privately before those who were of repute) the gospel which I preach among the Gentiles, lest somehow I should be running or had run in vain. 3 But even Titus, who was with me, was not compelled to be circumcised, though he was a Greek. 4 But because of false brethren secretly brought in, who slipped in to spy out our freedom which we have in Christ Jesus, that they might bring us into bondage— 5 to them we did not yield submission even for a moment, that the truth of the gospel might be preserved for you. 6And from those who were reputed to be something (what they were

10And in this matter I give my advice: it is best for you now to complete what a year ago you began not only to do but to desire, 11 so that your readiness in desiring it may be matched by your completing it out of what you have. 12 For if the readiness is there, it is acceptable according to what a man has, not according to what he has not. 13 I do not mean that others should be eased and you burdened, 14 but that as a matter of equality your abundance at

makes no difference to me; God shows no partiality)—those, I say, who were of repute added nothing to me; 7 but on the contrary, when they saw that I had been entrusted with the gospel to the uncircumcised, just as Peter had been entrusted with the gospel to the circumcised 8 (for he who worked through Peter for the mission to the circumcised worked through me also for the Gentiles), 9 and when they perceived the grace that was given to me, James and Cephas and John, who were reputed to be pillars, gave to me and Barnabas the right hand of fellowship, that we should go to the Gentiles and they to the circumcised; 10 only they would have us remember the poor, which very thing I was eager to do.

the present time should supply their want, so that their abundance may supply your want, that there may be equality. 15As it is written, "He who gathered much had nothing over, and he who gathered little had no lack."

16 But thanks be to God who puts the same earnest care for you into the heart of Titus. 17 For he not only accepted our appeal, but being himself very earnest he is going to you of his own accord. 18 With him we are sending the brother who is famous among all the churches

137

Col 3:5-11 (§266)

5 Put to death therefore what is earthly in you: fornication, impurity, passion, evil desire, and covetousness, which is idolatry. 6 On account of these the wrath of God is coming. 7 In these you once walked, when you lived in them. 8 But now put them all away: anger, wrath, malice, slander, and foul talk from your mouth. 9 Do not lie to one another, seeing that you have put off the old nature with its practices 10 and have put on the new nature, which is being renewed in knowledge after the image of its creator. 11 Here there cannot be Greek and Jew, circumcised and uncircumcised, barbarian, Scyth'ian, slave, free man, but Christ is all, and in all.

1 Thes 4:13-18 (§286)

13 But we would not have you ignorant, brethren, concerning those who are asleep, that you may not grieve as others do who have no hope. 14 For since we believe that Jesus died and rose again, even so, through Jesus, God will bring with him those who have fallen asleep. 15 For this we declare to you by the word of the Lord, that we who are alive, who are left until the coming of the Lord, shall not precede those who have fallen asleep. 16 For the Lord himself will descend from heaven with a cry of command, with the archangel's call, and with the sound of the trumpet of God. And the dead in Christ will rise first; 17 then we who are alive, who are left, shall be caught up together with them in the clouds to meet the Lord in the air; and so we shall always be with the Lord. 18 Therefore comfort one another with these words.

▶ 15:54 Is 25:8   8 He will swallow up death for ever, and the Lord God will wipe away tears from all faces, and the reproach of his people he will take away from all the earth; for the Lord has spoken.

▶ 15:55 Hos 13:14
14 Shall I ransom them from the power of Sheol?
Shall I redeem them from Death?
O Death, where are your plagues?
O Sheol, where is your destruction?
Compassion is hid from my eyes.

▶ 15:51 (changed) *read* we shall not all sleep but we shall not all be changed: p⁴⁶ Aᶜ Origen; *read* we shall sleep but we shall not all be changed: SCG (Greek) Origen; *read* we

shall rise but we shall not all be changed: D* it (most) vg Marcion Terullian; *text:* BDᶜ Koine lect syr cop Tertullian Origen

138. Concerning contribution for the saints

138

2 Cor (cont)

for his preaching of the gospel; 19 and not only that, but he has been appointed by the churches to travel with us in this gracious work which we are carrying on, for the glory of the Lord and to show our good will. 20 We intend that no one should blame us about this liberal gift which we are administering, 21 for we aim at what is honorable not only in the Lord's sight but also in the sight of men. 22 And with them we are sending our brother whom we have often tested and found earnest in many matters, but who is now more earnest than ever because of his great confidence in you. 23 As for Titus, he is my partner and fellow worker in your service; and as for our brethren, they are messengers of the churches, the glory of Christ. 24 So give proof, before the churches, of your love and of our boasting about you to these men.

9 Now it is superfluous for me to write to you about the offering for the saints, 2 for I know your readiness, of which I boast about you to the people of Macedo'nia, saying that Acha'ia has been ready since last year; and your zeal

has stirred up most of them. 3 But I am sending the brethren so that our boasting about you may not prove vain in this case, so that you may be ready, as I said you would be; 4 lest if some Macedo'nians come with me and find that you are not ready, we be humiliated—to say nothing of you—for being so confident. 5 So I thought it necessary to urge the brethren to go on to you before me, and arrange in advance for this gift you have promised, so that it may be ready not as an exaction but as a willing gift.

6 The point is this: he who sows sparingly will also reap sparingly, and he who sows bountifully will also reap bountifully. 7 Each one must do as he has made up his mind, not reluctantly or under compulsion, for God loves a cheerful giver. 8 And God is able to provide you with every blessing in abundance, so that you may always have enough of everything and may provide in abundance for every good work. 9 As it is written,

"He scatters abroad, he gives to the poor;
his righteousness endures for ever."
10 He who supplies seed to the sower

and bread for food will supply and multiply your resources and increase the harvest of your righteousness. 11 You will be enriched in every way for great generosity, which through us will produce thanksgiving to God; 12 for the rendering of this service not only supplies the wants of the saints but also overflows in many thanksgivings to God. 13 Under the test of this service, you will glorify God by your obedience in acknowledging the gospel of Christ, and by the generosity of your contribution for them and for all others; 14 while they long for you and pray for you, because of the surpassing grace of God in you. 15 Thanks be to God for his inexpressible gift!

139

Rom 15:22-29 (§63)

22 This is the reason why I have so often been hindered from coming to you. 23 But now, since I no longer have any room for work in these regions, and since I have longed for many years to come to you, 24 I hope to see you in passing as I go to Spain, and to be sped on my journey there by you, once I have enjoyed your company for a little. 25 At present, however, I am going to Jerusalem with aid for the saints. 26 For Macedo'nia and Acha'ia have been pleased to make some contribution for the poor among the saints at Jerusalem; 27 they were pleased to do it, and indeed they are in debt to them, for if the Gentiles have come to share in their spiritual blessings, they ought also to be of service to them in material blessings. 28 When therefore I have completed this, and have delivered to them what has been raised, I shall go on by way of you to Spain; 29 and I know that when I come to you I shall come in the fulness of the blessing of Christ.

1 Cor 16:5-9

5 I will visit you after passing through Macedo'nia, for I intend to pass through Macedo'nia, 6 and perhaps I will stay with you or even spend the winter, so that you may speed me on my journey, wherever I go. 7 For I do not want to see you now just in passing; I hope to spend some time with you, if the Lord permits. 8 But I will stay in Ephesus until Pentecost, 9 for a wide door for effective work has opened to me, and there are many adversaries.

2 Cor 1:15-22 (§149)

15 Because I was sure of this, I wanted to come to you first, so that you might have a double pleasure; 16 I wanted to visit you on my way to Macedo'nia, and to come back to you from Macedo'nia and have you send me on my way to Judea. 17 Was I vacillating when I wanted to do this? Do I make my plans like a worldly man, ready to say Yes and No at once? 18 As surely as God is faithful, our word to you has not been Yes and No. 19 For the Son of God, Jesus Christ, whom we preached among you, Silva'nus and Timothy and I, was not Yes and No; but in him it is always Yes. 20 For all the promises of God find their Yes in him. That is why we utter the Amen through him, to the glory of God. 21 But it is God who establishes us with you in Christ, and has commissioned us; 22 he has put his seal upon us and given us his Spirit in our hearts as a guarantee.

2 Cor 1:23-2:4 (§150)

23 But I call God to witness against me—it was to spare you that I refrained from coming to Corinth. 24 Not that we lord it over your faith; we work with you for your joy, for you stand

2 firm in your faith. 1 For I made up my mind not to make you another painful visit. 2 For if I cause you pain, who is there to make me glad but the one whom I have pained? 3 And I wrote as I did, so that when I came I might not suffer pain from those who should have made me rejoice, for I felt sure of all of you, that my joy would be the joy of you all. 4 For I wrote you out of much affliction and anguish of heart and with many tears, not to cause you pain but to let you know the abundant love that I have for you.

2 Cor 12:11-13:4 (§186-189)

11 I have been a fool! You forced me to it, for I ought to have been commended by you. For I was not at all inferior to these superlative apostles, even though I am nothing. 12 The signs of a true apostle were performed among you in all patience, with signs and wonders and mighty works. 13 For in what were you less favored than the rest of the churches, except that I myself did not burden you? Forgive me this wrong!

14 Here for the third time I am ready to come to you. And I will not be a burden, for I seek not what is yours but you; for children ought not to lay up for their parents, but parents for their children. 15 I will most gladly spend and be spent for your souls. If I love you the more, am I to be loved the less? 16 But granting that I myself did not burden you, I was crafty, you say, and got the better of you by guile. 17 Did I take advantage of you through any of those whom I sent to you? 18 I urged Titus to go, and sent the brother with him. Did Titus take advantage of you? Did we not act in the same spirit? Did we not take the same steps?

19 Have you been thinking all along that we have been defending ourselves before you? It is in the sight of God that we have been speaking in Christ, and all for your upbuilding, beloved. 20 For I fear that perhaps I may come and find you not what I wish, and that you may find me not what you wish; that perhaps there may be quarreling, jealousy, anger, selfishness, slander, gossip, conceit, and disorder. 21 I fear that when I come again my God may humble me before you, and I may have to mourn over many of those who sinned before and

▶16:5 Acts 19:21
21 Now after these events Paul resolved in the Spirit to pass through Macedo'nia and Acha'ia and go to Jerusalem, saying, "After I have been there, I must also see Rome."

▶16:7 Acts 18:21
21 but on taking leave of them he said, "I will return to you if God wills," and he set sail from Ephesus.

▶16:8 Acts 18:19
19 And they came to Ephesus, and he left them there; but he himself went into the synagogue and argued with the Jews.

*cf 20:16

▶16:9 Acts 14:27,
27 And when they arrived, they gathered the church together and declared all that God had done with them, and how he had opened a door of faith to the Gentiles.

19:9 9 but when some were stubborn and disbelieved, speaking evil of the Way before the congregation, he withdrew from them, taking the disciples with him, and argued daily in the hall of Tyran'nus.

▶16:5-9 1 Cor 4:18
18 Some are arrogant, as though I were not coming to you.

140. When Timothy comes; as for Apollos

140

Rom 16:1-2 (§65)

16 I commend to you our sister Phoebe, a deaconess of the church at Cen'chre-ae, 2 that you may receive her in the Lord as befits the saints, and help her in whatever she may require from you, for she has been a helper of many and of myself as well.

1 Cor 16:10-12

10 When Timothy comes, see that you put him at ease among you, for he is doing the work of the Lord, as I am. 11 So let no one despise him. Speed him on his way in peace, that he may return to me; for I am expecting him with the brethren.

12 As for our brother Apol'los, I strongly urged him to visit you with the other brethren, but it was not at all his will to come now. He will come when he has opportunity.

2 Cor 3:1-3 (§154)

3 Are we beginning to commend ourselves again? Or do we need, as some do, letters of recommendation to you, or from you? 2 You yourselves are our letter of recommendation, written on your hearts, to be known and read by all men; 3 and you show that you are a letter from Christ delivered by us, written not with ink but with the Spirit of the living God, not on tablets of stone but on tablets of human hearts.

2 Cor 8:16-24 (§173)

16 But thanks be to God who puts the same earnest care for you into the heart of Titus. 17 For he not only accepted our appeal, but being himself very earnest he is going to you of his own accord. 18 With him we are sending the brother who is famous among all the churches for his preaching of the gospel; 19 and not only that, but he has been appointed by the churches to travel with us in this gracious work which we are carrying on, for the glory of the Lord and to show our good will. 20 We intend that no one should blame us about this liberal gift which we are administering, 21 for we aim at what is honorable not only in the Lord's sight but also in the sight of men. 22 And with them we are sending our brother whom we have often tested and found earnest in many matters, but who is now more earnest than ever because of his great confidence in you. 23 As for Titus, he is my partner and fellow worker in your service; and as for our brethren, they are messengers of the churches, the glory of Christ. 24 So give proof, before the churches, of your love and of our boasting about you to these men.

▶16:10 Acts 16:1
And he came also to Derbe and to Lystra. A disciple was there, named Timothy, the son of a Jewish woman who was a believer; but his father was a Greek.

▶16:11 1 Tim 4:12
12 Let no one despise your youth, but set the believers an example in speech and conduct, in love, in faith, in purity.

▶16:12 Acts 18:24
24 Now a Jew named Apol'los, a native of Alexandria, came to Ephesus. He was an eloquent man, well versed in the scriptures.

▶16:10 4:17
17 Therefore I sent to you Timothy, my beloved and faithful child in the Lord, to remind you of my ways in Christ, as I teach them everywhere in every church.

2 Cor 1:19
19 For the Son of God, Jesus Christ, whom we preached among you, Silva'nus and Timothy and I, was not Yes and No; but in him it is always Yes.

1 Thes 3:2,
2 and we sent Timothy, our brother and God's servant in the gospel of Christ, to establish you in your faith and to exhort you,

139

1 Thes 2:17-20 (§280)

17 But since we were bereft of you, brethren, for a short time, in person not in heart, we endeavored the more eagerly and with great desire to see you face to face; 18 because we wanted to come to you—I, Paul, again and again—but Satan hindered us. 19 For what is our hope or joy or crown of boasting before our Lord Jesus at his coming? Is it not you? 20 For you are our glory and joy.

Phm 21-22 (§309)

21 Confident of your obedience, I write to you, knowing that you will do even more than I say. 22At the same time, prepare a guest room for me, for I am hoping through your prayers to be granted to you.

2 Cor (cont)

have not repented of the impurity, immorality, and licentiousness which they have practiced.

13 This is the third time I am coming to you. Any charge must be sustained by the evidence of two or three witnesses. 2 I warned those who sinned before and all the others, and I warn them now while absent, as I did when present on my second visit, that if I come again I will not spare them— 3 since you desire proof that Christ is speaking in me. He is not weak in dealing with you, but is powerful in you. 4 For he was crucified in weakness, but lives by the power of God. For we are weak in him, but in dealing with you we shall live with him by the power of God.

10:1-6,

I, Paul, myself entreat you, by the meekness and gentleness of Christ—I who am humble when face to face with you, but bold to you when I am away!— 2 I beg of you that when I am present I may not have to show boldness with such confidence as I count on showing against some who

suspect us of acting in worldly fashion. 3 For though we live in the world we are not carrying on a worldly war, 4 for the weapons of our warfare are not worldly but have divine power to destroy strongholds. 5 We destroy arguments and every proud obstacle to the knowledge of God, and take every thought captive to obey Christ, 6 being ready to

punish every disobedience, when your obedience is complete.

13:10   10 I write this while I am away from you, in order that when I come I may not have to be severe in my use of the authority which the Lord has given me for building up and not for tearing down.

Phil 1:27   27 Only let your manner of life be worthy of the gospel of Christ, so that whether I come and see you or am absent, I may hear of you that you stand

firm in one spirit, with one mind striving side by side for the faith of the gospel,

140. When Timothy comes; as for Apollos

Phm 8-20 (§307-308)

8 Accordingly, though I am bold enough in Christ to command you to do what is required, 9 yet for love's sake I prefer to appeal to you—I, Paul, an ambassador and now a prisoner also for Christ Jesus—10 I appeal to you for my child, Ones'imus, whose father I have become in my imprisonment. 11 (Formerly he was useless to you, but now he is indeed useful to you and to me.) 12 I am sending him back to you, sending my very heart. 13 I would have been glad to keep him with me, in order that he might serve me on your behalf during my imprisonment for the gospel; 14 but I preferred to do nothing without your consent in order that your goodness might not be by compulsion but of your own free will.

15 Perhaps this is why he was parted from you for a while, that you might have him back for ever, 16 no longer as a slave but more than a slave, as a beloved brother, especially to me but how much more to you, both in the flesh and in the Lord. 17 So if you consider me your partner, receive him as you would receive me. 18 If he has wronged you at all, or owes you anything, charge that to my account. 19 I, Paul, write this with my own hand, I will repay it—to say nothing of your owing me even your own self. 20 Yes, brother, I want some benefit from you in the Lord. Refresh my heart in Christ.

140

Phil 2:19-24 (§245)

19 I hope in the Lord Jesus to send Timothy to you soon, so that I may be cheered by news of you. 20 I have no one like him, who will be genuinely anxious for your welfare. 21 They all look after their own interests, not those of Jesus Christ. 22 But Timothy's worth you know, how as a son with a father he has served with me in the gospel. 23 I hope therefore to send him just as soon as I see how it will go with me; 24 and I trust in the Lord that shortly I myself shall come also.

Phil 2:25-3:1 (§246)

25 I have thought it necessary to send to you Epaphrodi'tus my brother and fellow worker and fellow soldier, and your messenger and minister to my need, 26 for he has been longing for you all, and has been distressed because you heard that he was ill. 27 Indeed he was ill, near to death. But God had mercy on him, and not only on him but on me also, lest I should have sorrow upon sorrow. 28 I am the more eager to send him, therefore, that you may rejoice at seeing him again, and that I may be less anxious. 29 So receive him in the Lord

with all joy; and honor such men, 30 for he nearly died for the work of Christ, risking his life to complete your service to me.

3 Finally, my brethren, rejoice in the Lord. To write the same things to you is not irksome to me, and is safe for you.

6

6 But now that Timothy has come to us from you, and has brought us the good news of your faith and love and reported that you always remember us kindly and long to see us, as we long to see you—

▶16:12 1:12   12 What I mean is that each one of you says, "I belong to Paul," or "I belong to Apol'los," or "I belong to Cephas," or "I belong to Christ."

3:4-6
4 For when one says, "I belong to Paul," and another, "I belong to Apol'los," are you not merely men? 5 What then is Apol'los? What is Paul? Servants through whom you believed, as the Lord assigned to each. 6 I planted, Apol'los watered, but God gave the growth.

3:22-23   22 whether Paul or Apol'los or Cephas or the world or life or death or the present or the future, all are yours; 23 and you are Christ's; and Christ is God's.

4:6
6 I have applied all this to myself and Apol'los for your benefit, brethren, that you may learn by us not to go beyond what is written, that none of you may be puffed up in favor of one against another.

141

Rom 13:8-14 (§55-56)

8 Owe no one anything, except to love one another; for he who loves his neighbor has fulfilled the law. 9 The commandments, "You shall not commit adultery, You shall not kill, You shall not steal, You shall not covet," and any other commandment, are summed up in this sentence, "You shall love your neighbor as yourself." 10 Love does no wrong to a neighbor; therefore love is the fulfilling of the law.

11 Besides this you know what hour it is, how it is full time now for you to wake from sleep. For salvation is nearer to us now than when we first believed; 12 the night is far gone, the day is at hand. Let us then cast off the works of darkness and put on the armor of light; 13 let us conduct ourselves becomingly as in the day, not in reveling and drunkenness, not in debauchery and licentiousness, not in quarreling and jealousy. 14 But put on the Lord Jesus Christ, and make no provision for the flesh, to gratify its desires.

1 Cor 16:13-14

13 Be watchful, stand firm in your faith, be courageous, be strong. 14 Let all that you do be done in love.

Gal 5:13-15 (§212)

13 For you were called to freedom, brethren; only do not use your freedom as an opportunity for the flesh, but through love be servants of one another. 14 For the whole law is fulfilled in one word, "You shall love your neighbor as yourself." 15 But if you bite and devour one another take heed that you are not consumed by one another.

Eph 6:10-17 (§233)

10 Finally, be strong in the Lord and in the strength of his might. 11 Put on the whole armor of God, that you may be able to stand against the wiles of the devil. 12 For we are not contending against flesh and blood, but against the principalities, against the powers, against the world rulers of this present darkness, against the spiritual hosts of wickedness in the heavenly places. 13 Therefore take the whole armor of God, that you may be able to withstand in the evil day, and having done all, to stand. 14 Stand therefore, having girded your loins with truth, and having put on the breastplate of righteousness, 15 and having shod your feet with the equipment of the gospel of peace; 16 besides all these, taking the shield of faith, with which you can quench all the flaming darts of the evil one. 17 And take the helmet of salvation, and the sword of the Spirit, which is the word of God.

▶16:13 15:58
58 Therefore, my beloved brethren, be steadfast, immovable, always abounding in the work of the Lord, knowing that in the Lord your labor is not in vain.

Gal 5:1
For freedom Christ has set us free; stand fast therefore, and do not submit again to a yoke of slavery.

Phil 1:27
27 Only let your manner of life be worthy of the gospel of Christ, so that whether I come and see you or am absent, I may hear of you that you stand firm in one spirit, with one mind striving side by side for the faith of the gospel,

Col 1:23
23 provided that you continue in the faith, stable and steadfast, not shifting from the hope of the gospel which you heard, which has been preached to every creature under heaven, and of which I, Paul, became a minister.

1 Thes 3:6-10
6 But now that Timothy has come to us from you, and has brought us the good news of your faith and love and reported that you always remember us kindly and long to see us, as we long to see you—7 for this reason, brethren,

in all our distress and affliction we have been comforted about you through your faith; 8 for now we live, if you stand fast in the Lord. 9 For what thanksgiving can we render to God for you, for all the joy which we feel for your sake before our God, 10 praying earnestly night and day that we may see you face to face and supply what is lacking in your faith?

142. Give recognition to such men

142

Rom 16:1-2 (§65)

16 I commend to you our sister Phoebe, a deaconess of the church at Cen′chre-ae, 2 that you may receive her in the Lord as befits the saints, and help her in whatever she may require from you, for she has been a helper of many and of myself as well.

1 Cor 16:15-18

15 Now, brethren, you know that the household of Steph′anas were the first converts in Acha′ia, and they have devoted themselves to the service of the saints; 16 I urge you to be subject to such men and to every fellow worker and laborer. 17 I rejoice at the coming of Steph′anas and Fortuna′tus and Acha′icus, because they have made up for your absence; 18 for they refreshed my spirit as well as yours. Give recognition to such men.

2 Cor 3:1-3 (§154)

3 Are we beginning to commend ourselves again? Or do we need, as some do, letters of recommendation to you, or from you? 2 You yourselves are our letter of recommendation, written on your hearts, to be known and read by all men; 3 and you show that you are a letter from Christ delivered by us, written not with ink but with the Spirit of the living God, not on tablets of stone but on tablets of human hearts.

2 Cor 8:16-24 (§173)
16 But thanks be to God who puts the same earnest care for you into the heart of Titus. 17 For he not only accepted our appeal, but being himself very earnest he is going to you of his own accord. 18 With him we are sending the brother who is famous among all the churches for his preaching of the gospel; 19 and not only that, but he has been appointed by the churches to travel with us in this gracious work which we are carrying on, for the glory of the Lord and to show our good will. 20 We intend that no one should blame us about this liberal gift which we are administering, 21 for we aim at what is honorable not only in the

Lord's sight but also in the sight of men. 22 And with them we are sending our brother whom we have often tested and found earnest in many matters, but who is now more earnest than ever because of his great confidence in you. 23 As for Titus, he is my partner and fellow worker in your service; and as for our brethren, they are messengers of the churches, the glory of Christ. 24 So give proof, before the churches, of your love and of our boasting about you to these men.

▶16:15-18 16:10-12
10 When Timothy comes, see that you put him at ease among you, for he is doing the work of the Lord, as I am. 11 So let no one despise him. Speed him on his way in peace, that he may return to me; for I am expecting him with the brethren.
12 As for our brother Apol′los, I

strongly urged him to visit you with the other brethren, but it was not at all his will to come now. He will come when he has opportunity.

▶16:15 *cf. Rom 16:5

*cf Acts 17:18

▶16:17 1 Thes 2:17-3:2
17 But since we were bereft of you, brethren, for a short time, in person not in heart, we endeavored the more eagerly and with great desire to see your face to face; 18 because we wanted to come to you—I, Paul, again and again—but Satan hindered us. 19 For what is our hope or joy or crown of boasting

before our Lord Jesus at his coming? Is it not you? 20 For you are our glory and joy.
3 Therefore when we could bear it no longer, we were willing to be left behind at Athens alone, 2 and we sent Timothy, our brother and God's servant in the gospel of Christ, to establish you in your faith and to exhort you,

▶16:18 Gal 6:6
6 Let him who is taught the word share all good things with him who teaches.

Phm 7 7 For I have derived much joy and comfort from your love, my brother, because the hearts of the saints have been refreshed through you.

141

Col 4:2-4 (§269)

2 Continue steadfastly in prayer, being watchful in it with thanksgiving; 3 and pray for us also, that God may open to us a door for the word, to declare the mystery of Christ, on account of which I am in prison, 4 that I may make it clear, as I ought to speak.

1 Thes 5:1-11 (§287)

5 But as to the times and the seasons, brethren, you have no need to have anything written to you. 2 For you yourselves know well that the day of the Lord will come like a thief in the night. 3 When people say, "There is peace and security," then sudden destruction will come upon them as travail comes upon a woman with child, and there will be no escape. 4 But you are not in darkness, brethren, for that day to surprise you like a thief. 5 For you are all sons of light and sons of the day; we are not of the night or of darkness. 6 So then, let us not sleep, as others do, but let us keep awake and be sober. 7 For those who sleep sleep at night, and those who get drunk are drunk at night. 8 But, since we belong to the day, let us be sober, and put on the breastplate of faith and love, and for a helmet the hope of salvation. 9 For God has not destined us for wrath, but to obtain salvation through our Lord Jesus Christ, 10 who died for us so that whether we wake or sleep we might live with him. 11 Therefore encourage one another and build one another up, just as you are doing.

2 Thes 2:13-17 (§297)

13 But we are bound to give thanks to God always for you, brethren beloved by the Lord, because God chose you from the beginning to be saved, through sanctification by the Spirit and belief in the truth. 14 To this he called you through our gospel, so that you may obtain the glory of our Lord Jesus Christ. 15 So then, brethren, stand firm and hold to the traditions which you were taught by us, either by word of mouth or by letter.

16 Now may our Lord Jesus Christ himself, and God our Father, who loved us and gave us eternal comfort and good hope through grace, 17 comfort your hearts and establish them in every good work and word.

142. Give recognition to such men

142

Phil 2:19-24 (§245)

19 I hope in the Lord Jesus to send Timothy to you soon, so that I may be cheered by news of you. 20 I have no one like him, who will be genuinely anxious for your welfare. 21 They all look after their own interests, not those of Jesus Christ. 22 But Timothy's worth you know, how as a son with a father he has served with me in the gospel. 23 I hope therefore to send him just as soon as I see how it will go with me; 24 and I trust in the Lord that shortly I myself shall come also.

Phil 2:25-3:1 (§246)

25 I have thought it necessary to send to you Epaphrodi′tus my brother and fellow worker and fellow soldier, and your messenger and minister to my need, 26 for he has been longing for you all, and has been distressed because you heard that he was ill. 27 Indeed he was ill, near to death. But God had mercy on him, and not only on him but on me also, lest I should have sorrow upon sorrow. 28 I am the more eager to send him, therefore, that you may rejoice at seeing him again, and that I may be less anxious. 29 So receive him in the Lord

with all joy; and honor such men, 30 for he nearly died for the work of Christ, risking his life to complete your service to me.

3 Finally, my brethren, rejoice in the Lord. To write the same things to you is not irksome to me, and is safe for you.

1 Thes 5:12-22 (§288)

12 But we beseech you, brethren, to respect those who labor among you and are over you in the Lord and admonish you, 13 and to esteem them very highly in love because of their work. Be at peace among yourselves. 14 And we exhort you, brethren, admonish the idlers, encourage the fainthearted, help the weak, be patient with them all. 15 See that none of you repays evil for evil, but always seek to do good to one another and to all. 16 Rejoice always, 17 pray constantly, 18 give thanks in all circumstances; for this is the will of God in Christ Jesus for you. 19 Do not quench the Spirit, 20 do not despise prophesying, 21 but test everything; hold fast what is good, 22 abstain from every form of evil.

Phm 8-20 (§307-308)

8 Accordingly, though I am bold enough in Christ to command you to do what is required, 9 yet for love's sake I prefer to appeal to you—I, Paul, an ambassador and now a prisoner also for Christ Jesus—10 I appeal to you for my child, Ones′imus, whose father I have become in my imprisonment. 11 (Formerly he was useless to you, but now he is indeed useful to you and to me.) 12 I am sending him back to you, sending my very heart. 13 I would have been glad to keep him with me, in order that he might serve me on your behalf during my imprisonment for the gospel; 14 but I preferred to do nothing without your consent in order that your goodness might not be by compulsion but of your own free will.

15 Perhaps this is why he was parted from you for a while, that you might have him back for ever, 16 no longer as a slave but more than a slave, as a beloved brother, especially to me but how much more to you, both in the flesh and in the Lord. 17 So if you consider me your partner, receive him as you would receive me. 18 If he has wronged you at all, or owes you anything, charge that to my account. 19 I, Paul, write this with my own hand, I will repay it—to say nothing of your owing me even your own self. 20 Yes, brother, I want some benefit from you in the Lord. Refresh my heart in Christ.

143

Rom 16:3-16 (§66)

3 Greet Prisca and Aquila, my fellow workers in Christ Jesus, 4 who risked their necks for my life, to whom not only I but also all the churches of the Gentiles give thanks; 5 greet also the church in their house. Greet my beloved Epae′netus, who was the first convert in Asia for Christ. 6 Greet Mary, who has worked hard among you. 7 Greet Androni′cus and Ju′nias, my kinsmen and my fellow prisoners; they are men of note among the apostles, and they were in Christ before me. 8 Greet Amplia′tus, my beloved in the Lord. 9 Greet Urba′nus, our fellow worker in Christ, and my beloved Stachys. 10 Greet Apel′les, who is approved in Christ. Greet those who belong to the family of Aristobu′lus. 11 Greet my kinsman Hero′dion. Greet those in the Lord who belong to the family of Narcis′sus. 12 Greet those workers in the Lord, Tryphae′na and Trypho′sa. Greet the beloved Persis, who has worked hard in the Lord. 13 Greet Rufus, eminent in the Lord, also his mother and mine. 14 Greet Asyn′critus, Phlegon, Hermes, Pat′robas, Hermas,

▶ 16:19 Acts 18:2   2And he found a Jew named Aquila, a native of Pontus, lately come from Italy with his wife Priscilla, because Claudius had commanded all the Jews to leave Rome. And he went to see them;

1 Cor 16:19-20

19 The churches of Asia send greetings. Aquila and Prisca, together with the church in their house, send you hearty greetings in the Lord. 20All the brethren send greetings. Greet one another with a holy kiss.

and the brethren who are with them. 15 Greet Philol′ogus, Julia, Nereus and his sister, and Olym′pas, and all the saints who are with them. 16 Greet one another with a holy kiss. All the churches of Christ greet you.

Rom 16:21-23 (§69)

21 Timothy, my fellow worker, greets you; so do Lucius and Jason and Sosip′ater, my kinsmen. 22 I Tertius, the writer of this letter, greet you in the Lord. 23 Ga′ius, who is host to me and to the whole church, greets you. Eras′tus, the city treasurer, and our brother Quartus, greet you.

*cf 2 Tim 4:19-21, Tit 3:15a-b

2 Cor 13:11-13 (§191)

11 Finally, brethren, farewell. Mend your ways, heed my appeal, agree with one another, live in peace, and the God of love and peace will be with you. 12 Greet one another with a holy kiss. 13All the saints greet you.

144

144. Our Lord, come

1 Cor 16:21-22

21 I, Paul, write this greeting with my own hand. 22 If any one has no love for the Lord, let him be accursed. Our Lord, come!

Gal 6:11-17 (§216)

11 See with what large letters I am writing to you with my own hand. 12 It is those who want to make a good showing in the flesh that would compel you to be circumcised, and only in order that they may not be persecuted for the cross of Christ. 13 For even those who receive circumcision do not themselves keep the law, but they desire to have you circumcised that they may glory in your flesh. 14 But far be it from me to glory except in the cross of our Lord Jesus Christ, by which the world has been crucified to me, and I to the world. 15 For neither circumcision counts for anything, nor uncircumcision, but a new creation. 16 Peace and mercy be upon all who walk by this rule, upon the Israel of God.

17 Henceforth let no man trouble me; for I bear on my body the marks of Jesus.

▶ 16:22 12:1-3   Now concerning spiritual gifts, brethren, I do not want you to be uninformed. 2 You know that when you were heathen, you were led astray to dumb idols, however you may have been moved. 3 Therefore I want you to understand that no one speaking by the Spirit of God ever says "Jesus be cursed!" and no one can say "Jesus is Lord" except by the Holy Spirit.

Phil 4:21-22 (§254)

21 Greet every saint in Christ Jesus. The brethren who are with me greet you. 22All the saints greet you, especially those of Caesar's household.

Col 4:10-15 (§272)

10 Aristar′chus my fellow prisoner greets you, and Mark the cousin of Barnabas (concerning whom you have received instructions—if he comes to you, receive him), 11 and Jesus who is called Justus. These are the only men of the circumcision among my fellow workers for the kingdom of God, and they have been a comfort to me. 12 Ep′aphras, who is one of yourselves, a servant of Christ Jesus, greets you, always remembering you earnestly in his prayers, that you may stand mature and fully assured in all the will of God. 13 For I bear him witness that he has worked hard for you and for those in La-odice′a and in Hi-erap′olis. 14 Luke the beloved physician and Demas greet you. 15 Give my greetings to the brethren at La-odice′a, and to Nympha and the church in her house.

1 Thes 5:26 (§291)

26 Greet all the brethren with a holy kiss.

Phm 23-24 (§310)

23 Ep′aphras, my fellow prisoner in Christ Jesus, sends greetings to you, 24 and so do Mark, Aristar′chus, Demas, and Luke, my fellow workers.

143

144. Our Lord, come

Col 4:16-18a (§273)

16And when this letter has been read among you, have it read also in the church of the La-odice′ans; and see that you read also the letter from La-odice′a. 17And say to Archip′pus, "See that you fulfil the ministry which you have received in the Lord."

18 I, Paul, write this greeting with my own hand.

1 Thes 5:27 (§292)

27 I adjure you by the Lord that this letter be read to all the brethren.

2 Thes 3:17 (§303)

17 I, Paul, write this greeting with my own hand. This is the mark in every letter of mine; it is the way I write.

144

145. Grace

145

Rom 16:20b (§68)

The grace of our Lord Jesus Christ be with you.

1 Cor 16:23-24
23 The grace of the Lord Jesus be with you. 24 My love be with you all in Christ Jesus. Amen.

2 Cor 13:14 (§192)

14 The grace of the Lord Jesus Christ and the love of God and the fellowship of the Holy Spirit be with you all.

Gal 6:18 (§236)

18 The grace of our Lord Jesus Christ be with your spirit, brethren. Amen.

Eph 6:23-24 (§236)

23 Peace be to the brethren, and love with faith, from God the Father and the Lord Jesus Christ. 24 Grace be with all who love our Lord Jesus Christ with love undying.

▶ 16:23 *cf 1 Tim 6:21b, 2 Tim 4:22, Tit 3:15c

Phil 4:23 (§255)	Col 4:18b (§274)	1 Thes 5:28 (§293)	2 Thes 3:18 (§304)	Phm 25 (§311)
23 The grace of the Lord Jesus Christ be with your spirit.	Remember my fetters. Grace be with you.	28 The grace of our Lord Jesus Christ be with you.	18 The grace of our Lord Jesus Christ be with you all.	25 The grace of the Lord Jesus Christ be with your spirit.

145

146

Rom 1:1-7 (§1)	1 Cor 1:1-3 (§71)	2 Cor 1:1-2	Gal 1:1-5 (§193)	Eph 1:1-2 (§218)
1 Paul, a servant of Jesus Christ, called to be an apostle, set apart for the gospel of God ² which he promised beforehand through his prophets in the holy scriptures, ³ the gospel concerning his Son, who was descended from David according to the flesh ⁴ and designated Son of God in power according to the Spirit of holiness by his resurrection from the dead, Jesus Christ our Lord, ⁵ through whom we have received grace and apostleship to bring about the obedience of faith for the sake of his name among all the nations, ⁶ including yourselves who are called to belong to Jesus Christ; 7 To all God's beloved in Rome, who are called to be saints: Grace to you and peace from God our Father and the Lord Jesus Christ.	**1** Paul, called by the will of God to be an apostle of Christ Jesus, and our brother Sos'thenes, 2 To the church of God which is at Corinth, to those sanctified in Christ Jesus, called to be saints together with all those who in every place call on the name of our Lord Jesus Christ, both their Lord and ours: 3 Grace to you and peace from God our Father and the Lord Jesus Christ.	**1** Paul, an apostle of Christ Jesus by the will of God, and Timothy our brother. To the church of God which is at Corinth, with all the saints who are in the whole of Acha'ia: 2 Grace to you and peace from God our Father and the Lord Jesus Christ.	**1** Paul an apostle—not from men nor through man, but through Jesus Christ and God the Father, who raised him from the dead—² and all the brethren who are with me, To the churches of Galatia: 3 Grace to you and peace from God the Father and our Lord Jesus Christ, ⁴ who gave himself for our sins to deliver us from the present evil age, according to the will of our God and Father; ⁵ to whom be the glory for ever and ever. Amen.	**1** Paul, an apostle of Christ Jesus by the will of God, To the saints who are also faithful in Christ Jesus: 2 Grace to you and peace from God our Father and the Lord Jesus Christ.

▶ 1:1 Acts 16:1,
And he came also to Derbe and to Lystra. A disciple was there, named Timothy, the son of a Jewish woman who was a believer; but his father was a Greek.

18:1
After this he left Athens and went to Corinth.

1 Tim 1:1
Paul, a servant of God and an apostle of Jesus Christ, to further the faith of God's elect and their knowledge of the truth which accords with godliness,

2 Tim 1:1
Paul, an apostle of Christ Jesus by command of God our Savior and of Christ Jesus our hope,

Tit 1:1
Paul, an apostle of Christ Jesus by the will of God according to the promise of the life which is in Christ Jesus,

Phil 1:1-2 (§237)	Col 1:1-2 (§256)	1 Thes 1:1 (§275)	2 Thes 1:1-2 (§294)	Phm 1-3 (§305)

1 Paul and Timothy, servants of Christ Jesus,

To all the saints in Christ Jesus who are at Philippi, with the bishops and deacons:

2 Grace to you and peace from God our Father and the Lord Jesus Christ.

1 Paul, an apostle of Christ Jesus by the will of God, and Timothy our brother,

2 To the saints and faithful brethren in Christ at Colos'sae:

Grace to you and peace from God our Father.

1 Paul, Silva'nus, and Timothy,

To the church of the Thessalo'-nians in God the Father and the Lord Jesus Christ:

Grace to you and peace.

1 Paul, Silva'nus, and Timothy,

To the church of the Thessalo'-nians in God our Father and the Lord Jesus Christ:

2 Grace to you and peace from God the Father and the Lord Jesus Christ.

1 Paul, a prisoner for Christ Jesus, and Timothy our brother,

To Phile'mon our beloved fellow worker 2 and Ap'phia our sister and Archip'pus our fellow soldier, and the church in your house:

3 Grace to you and peace from God our Father and the Lord Jesus Christ.

146

147. Blessed be God

147

Rom 5:1-5 (§20)

5 Therefore, since we are justified by faith, we have peace with God through our Lord Jesus Christ. [2] Through him we have obtained access to this grace in which we stand, and we rejoice in our hope of sharing the glory of God. [3] More than that, we rejoice in our sufferings, knowing that suffering produces endurance, [4] and endurance produces character, and character produces hope, [5] and hope does not disappoint us, because God's love has been poured into our hearts through the Holy Spirit which has been given to us.

2 Cor 1:3-11

3 Blessed be the God and Father of our Lord Jesus Christ, the Father of mercies and God of all comfort, [4] who comforts us in all our affliction, so that we may be able to comfort those who are in any affliction, with the comfort with which we ourselves are comforted by God. [5] For as we share abundantly in Christ's sufferings, so through Christ we share abundantly in comfort too. [6] If we are afflicted, it is for your comfort and salvation; and if we are comforted, it is for your comfort, which you experience when you patiently endure the same sufferings that we suffer. [7] Our hope for you is unshaken; for we know that as you share in our sufferings, you will also share in our comfort.

8 For we do not want you to be ignorant, brethren, of the affliction we experienced in Asia; for we were so utterly, unbearably crushed that we despaired of life itself. [9] Why, we felt that we had received the sentence of death; but that was to make us rely not on ourselves but on God who raises the dead; [10] he delivered us from so deadly a peril, and he will deliver us; on him we have set our hope that he will deliver us again. [11] You also must help us by prayer, so that many will give thanks on our behalf for the blessing granted us in answer to many prayers.

Eph 1:3-23 (§219)

3 Blessed be the God and Father of our Lord Jesus Christ, who has blessed us in Christ with every spiritual blessing in the heavenly places, [4] even as he chose us in him before the foundation of the world, that we should be holy and blameless before him. [5] He destined us in love to be his sons through Jesus Christ, according to the purpose of his will, [6] to the praise of his glorious grace which he freely bestowed on us in the Beloved. [7] In him we have redemption through his blood, the forgiveness of our trespasses, according to the riches of his grace [8] which he lavished upon us. [9] For he has made known to us in all wisdom and insight the mystery of his will, according to his purpose which he set forth in Christ [10] as a plan for the fulness of time, to unite all things in him, things in heaven and things on earth.

11 In him, according to the purpose of him who accomplishes all things according to the counsel of his will, [12] we who first hoped in Christ have been destined and appointed to live for the praise of his glory. [13] In him you also,

▶ 1:3 1 Pet 1:3

3 Blessed be the God and Father of our Lord Jesus Christ! By his great mercy we have been born anew to a living hope through the resurrection of Jesus Christ from the dead,

▶ 1:6-7 2 Tim 2:10

[10] and now has manifested through the appearing of our Savior Christ Jesus, who abolished death and brought life and immortality to light through the gospel.

▶ 1:8 Acts 16:6,

6 And they went through the region of Phryg'ia and Galatia, having been forbidden by the Holy Spirit to speak the word in Asia.

19:23-41

23 About that time there arose no little stir concerning the Way. [24] For a man named Deme'trius, a silversmith, who made silver shrines of Ar'temis, brought no little business to the craftsmen. [25] These he gathered together, with the workmen of like occupation, and said, "Men, you know that from this business we have our wealth. [26] And you see and hear that not only at Ephesus but almost throughout all Asia this Paul has persuaded and turned away a considerable company of people, saying that gods made with hands are not gods. [27] And there is danger not only that this trade of ours may come into disrepute but also that the temple of the great goddess Ar'temis may count for nothing, and that she may even be deposed from her magnificence, she whom all Asia and the world worship."

28 When they heard this they were enraged, and cried out, "Great is Ar'temis of the Ephesians!" [29] So the city was filled with the confusion; and they rushed together into the theater, dragging with them Ga'ius and Aristar'chus, Macedo'nians who were Paul's companions in travel. [30] Paul wished to go in among the crowd, but the disciples would not let him; [31] some of the A'si-archs also, who were friends of his, sent to him and begged him not to venture into the theater. [32] Now some cried one thing, some another; for the assembly was in confusion, and most of them did not know why they had come together. [33] Some of the crowd prompted Alexander, whom the Jews had put forward. And Alexander motioned with his hand, wishing to make a defense to the people. [34] But when they recognized that he was a Jew, for about two hours they all with one voice cried out, "Great is Ar'temis of the Ephesians!" [35] And when the town clerk had quieted the crowd, he said, "Men of Ephesus, what man is there who does not know that the city of the Ephesians is temple keeper of the great Ar'temis, and of the sacred stone that fell from the sky? [36] Seeing then that these things cannot be contradicted, you ought to be quiet and do nothing rash. [37] For you have brought these men here who are neither sacrilegious nor blasphemers of our goddess. [38] If therefore Deme'trius and the craftsmen with him have a complaint against any one, the courts are open, and there are proconsuls; let them bring charges against one another. [39] But if you seek anything further, it shall be settled in the regular assembly. [40] For we are in danger of being charged with rioting today, there being no cause that we can give to justify this commotion." [41] And when he had said this, he dismissed the assembly.

▶ 1:10 2 Tim 4:18

[18] The Lord will rescue me from every evil and save me for his heavenly kingdom. To him be the glory for ever and ever. Amen.

1 Tim 4:10

[10] For to this end we toil and strive, because we have our hope set on the living God, who is the Savior of all men, especially of those who believe.

▶ 1:3-7 1 Cor 4:13

[13] when slandered, we try to conciliate; we have become, and are now, as the refuse of the world, the offscouring of all things.

2 Cor 2:7-8,

[7] so you should rather turn to forgive and comfort him, or he may be overwhelmed by excessive sorrow. [8] So I beg you to reaffirm your love for him.

7:6,

[6] But God, who comforts the downcast, comforted us by the coming of Titus,

13

[13] Therefore we are comforted.

Eph 6:22

[22] I have sent him to you for this very purpose, that you may know how we are, and that he may encourage your hearts.

1 Thes 4:18

[18] Therefore comfort one another with these words.

Rom 15:1-6

We who are strong ought to bear with the failings of the weak, and not to please ourselves; [2] let each of us please his neighbor for his good, to edify him. [3] For Christ did not please himself; but, as it is written, "The reproaches of those who reproached thee fell on me." [4] For whatever was written in former days was written for our instruction, that by steadfastness and by the encouragement of the scriptures we might have hope. [5] May the God of steadfastness and encouragement grant you to live in such harmony with one another, in accord with Christ Jesus, [6] that together you may with one voice glorify the God and Father of our Lord Jesus Christ.

148. We have behaved with holiness and sincerity

148

Rom 5:1-5 (§20)

5 Therefore, since we are justified by faith, we have peace with God through our Lord Jesus Christ. [2] Through him we have obtained access to this grace in which we stand, and we rejoice in our hope of sharing the glory of God. [3] More than that, we rejoice in our sufferings, knowing that suffering produces endurance, [4] and endurance produces character, and character produces hope, [5] and hope does not disappoint us, because God's love has been poured into our hearts through the Holy Spirit which has been given to us.

1 Cor 4:1-5 (§83)

4 This is how one should regard us, as servants of Christ and stewards of the mysteries of God. [2] Moreover it is required of stewards that they be found trustworthy. [3] But with me it is a very small thing that I should be judged by you or by any human court. I do not even judge myself. [4] I am not aware of anything against myself, but I am not thereby acquitted. It is the Lord who judges me. [5] Therefore do not pronounce judgment before the time, before the Lord comes, who will bring to light the things now hidden in darkness and will disclose the purposes of the

2 Cor 1:12-14

12 For our boast is this, the testimony of our conscience that we have behaved in the world, and still more toward you, with holiness and godly sincerity, not by earthly wisdom but by the grace of God. [13] For we write you nothing but what you can read and understand; I hope you will understand fully, [14] as you have understood in part, that you can be proud of us as we can be of you, on the day of the Lord Jesus.

1 Cor 9:15-18 (§106)

15 But I have made no use of any of these rights, nor am I writing this to secure any such provision. For I would rather die than have any one deprive me of my ground for boasting. [16] For if I preach the gospel, that gives me no ground for boasting. For necessity is laid upon me. Woe to me if I do not preach the gospel! [17] For if I do this of my own will, I have a reward; but if not of my own will, I am entrusted with a commission. [18] What then is my reward? Just this: that in my preaching I may make the gospel free of charge, not making full use of my right in the gospel.

▶ 1:12 Acts 23:1

And Paul, looking intently at the council, said, "Brethren, I have lived before God in all good conscience up to this day."

▶ 1:12 Rom 14:22-23

[22] The faith that you have, keep between yourself and God; happy is he who has no reason to judge himself for what he approves. [23] But he who has doubts is condemned, if he eats, because he does not act from faith; for whatever does not proceed from faith is sin.

heart. Then every man will receive his commendation from God.

2 Cor 10:13-18

13 But we will not boast beyond limit, but will keep to the limits God has apportioned us, to reach even to you. [14] For we are not overextending ourselves, as though we did not reach you; we were the first to come all the way to you with the gospel of Christ. [15] We do not boast beyond limit, in other men's labors; but our hope is that as your faith increases, our field among you may be greatly enlarged, [16] so that we may preach the gospel in lands beyond you, without boasting of work already done in another's field. [17] "Let him who boasts, boast of the Lord." [18] For it is not the man who commends himself that is accepted, but the man whom the Lord commends.

2 Cor 11:12-15

12 And what I do I will continue to do, in order to undermine the claim of those who would like to claim that in their boasted mission they work on the same terms as we do. [13] For such men are false apostles, deceitful workmen, disguising themselves as apostles of Christ. [14] And no wonder, for even Satan disguises himself as an angel of light. [15] So it is not strange if his servants also disguise themselves as servants of righteousness. Their end will correspond to their deeds.

Eph (cont)

who have heard the word of truth, the gospel of your salvation, and have believed in him, were sealed with the promised Holy Spirit, 14 which is the guarantee of our inheritance until we acquire possession of it, to the praise of his glory.

15 For this reason, because I have heard of your faith in the Lord Jesus and your love toward all the saints, 16 I do not cease to give thanks for you, remembering you in my prayers, 17 that the God of our Lord Jesus Christ, the Father of glory, may give you a spirit of wisdom and of revelation in the knowledge of him, 18 having the eyes of your hearts enlightened, that you may know what is the hope to which he has called you, what are the riches of his glorious inheritance in the saints, 19 and what is the immeasurable greatness of his power in us who believe, according to the working of his great might 20 which he accomplished in Christ when he raised him from the dead and made him sit at his right hand in the heavenly places, 21 far above all rule and authority and power and dominion, and above every

name that is named, not only in this age but also in that which is to come; 22 and he has put all things under his feet and has made him the head over all things for the church, 23 which is his body, the fulness of him who fills all in all.

1 Thes 3:1-10 (§281-282)

3 Therefore when we could bear it no longer, we were willing to be left behind at Athens alone, 2 and we sent Timothy, our brother and God's servant in the gospel of Christ, to establish you in your faith and to exhort you, 3 that no one be moved by these afflictions. You yourselves know that this is to be our lot. 4 For when we were with you, we told you beforehand that we were to suffer affliction; just as it has come to pass, and as you know. 5 For this reason, when I could bear it no longer, I sent that I might know your faith, for fear that somehow the tempter had tempted you and that our labor would be in vain.

6 But now that Timothy has come to us from you, and has brought us the good news of your faith and love and reported that you always remember us kindly and long to see us, as we long to see you—7 for this reason, brethren, in all our distress and affliction we have been comforted about you through your faith; 8 for now we live, if you stand fast in the Lord. 9 For what thanksgiving can we render to God for you, for

2 Thes 1:3-12 (§295)

3 We are bound to give thanks to God always for you, brethren, as is fitting, because your faith is growing abundantly, and the love of every one of you for one another is increasing. 4 Therefore we ourselves boast of you in the churches of God for your steadfastness and faith in all your persecutions and in the afflictions which you are enduring.

5 This is evidence of the righteous judgment of God, that you may be made worthy of the kingdom of God, for which you are suffering—6 since indeed God deems it just to repay with affliction those who afflict you, 7 and to grant rest with us to you who are afflicted, when the Lord Jesus is revealed from heaven with his mighty angels in flaming fire, 8 inflicting vengeance upon those who do not know God and upon those who do not obey the gospel of our

Lord Jesus. 9 They shall suffer the punishment of eternal destruction and exclusion from the presence of the Lord and from the glory of his might, 10 when he comes on that day to be glorified in his saints, and to be marveled at in all who have believed, because our testimony to you was believed. 11 To this end we always pray for you, that our God may make you worthy of his call, and may fulfil every good resolve and work of faith by his power, 12 so that the name of our Lord Jesus may be glorified in you, and you in him, according to the grace of our God and the Lord Jesus Christ.

2 Thes 2:16-17 (§298)

16 Now may our Lord Jesus Christ himself, and God our Father, who loved us and gave us eternal comfort and good hope through grace, 17 comfort your hearts and establish them in every good work and word.

§147-148 147

▶ 1:3-11 4:7-12

7 But we have this treasure in earthen vessels, to show that the transcendent power belongs to God and not to us. 8 We are afflicted in every way, but not crushed; perplexed, but not driven to despair; 9 persecuted, but not forsaken; struck down, but not destroyed; 10 always carrying in the body the death of Jesus, so that the life of Jesus may also be manifested in our bodies. 11 For while we live we are always being given up to death for Jesus' sake, so that the life of Jesus may be manifested in our mortal flesh. 12 So death is at work in us, but life in you.

6:1-10

Working together with him, then, we entreat you not to accept the grace of God in vain. 2 For he says,
"At the acceptable time I have listened to you,
and helped you on the day of salvation."
Behold, now is the acceptable time; behold, now is the day of salvation.

3 We put no obstacle in any one's way, so that no fault may be found with our ministry, 4 but as servants of God we commend ourselves in every way: through great endurance, in afflictions, hardships, calamities, 5 beatings, imprisonments, tumults, labors, watching, hunger; 6 by purity, knowledge, forbearance, kindness, the Holy Spirit, genuine love, 7 truthful speech, and the power of God; with the weapons of righteousness for the right hand and for the left; 8 in honor and dishonor, in ill repute and good repute. We are treated as impostors, and yet are true; 9 as unknown, and yet well known; as dying, and behold we live; as punished, and yet not killed; 10 as sorrowful, yet always rejoicing; as poor, yet making many rich; as having nothing, and yet possessing everything.

▶ 1:7 Phil 3:10 10 that I may know him and the power of his resurrection, and may share his sufferings, becoming like him in his death,

Col 1:24

24 Now I rejoice in my sufferings for your sake, and in my flesh I complete what is lacking in Christ's afflictions for the sake of his body, that is, the church,

Eph 3:13 13 So I ask you not to lose heart over what I am suffering for you, which is your glory.

▶ 1:8 1 Cor 15:32 32 What do I gain if, humanly speaking, I fought with beasts at Ephesus? If the dead are not raised, "Let us eat and drink, for tomorrow we die."

▶ 1:9 Rom 4:17 17 as it is written, "I have made you the father of many nations"—in the presence of the God in whom he believed, who gives life to the dead and calls into existence the things that do not exist.

▶ 1:11 Phil 1:19 19 Yes, and I shall rejoice. For I know that through your prayers and the help of the Spirit of Jesus Christ this will turn out for my deliverance,

all the joy which we feel for your sake before our God, 10 praying earnestly night and day that we may see you face to face and supply what is lacking in your faith?

148. We have behaved with holiness and sincerity

§147-148 148

1 Thes 2:9-12 (§278)

9 For you remember our labor and toil, brethren; we worked night and day, that we might not burden any of you, while we preached to you the gospel of God. 10 You are witnesses, and God also, how holy and righteous and blameless was our behavior to you believers; 11 for you know how, like a father with his children, we exhorted each one of you and encouraged you and charged you 12 to lead a life worthy of God, who calls you into his own kingdom and glory.

Gal 6:13-14

13 For you were called to freedom, brethren; only do not use your freedom as an opportunity for the flesh, but through love be servants of one another. 14 For the whole law is fulfilled in one word, "You shall love your neighbor as yourself."

2 Cor 2:17 17 For we are not, like so many, peddlers of God's word; but as men of sincerity, as commissioned by God, in the sight of God we speak in Christ.

▶ 1:14 Phil 1:6, 6 And I am sure that he who began a good work in you will bring it to completion at the day of Jesus Christ.

10 10 so that you may approve what is excellent, and may be pure and blameless for the day of Christ,

1 Cor 1:8 8 who will sustain you to the end, guiltless in the day of our Lord Jesus Christ.

2 Cor 5:5 5 He who has prepared us for this very thing is God, who has given us the Spirit as a guarantee.

1 Thes 5:2 2 For you yourselves know well that the day of the Lord will come like a thief in the night.

2 Thes 2:2 2 not to be quickly shaken in mind or excited, either by spirit or by word, or by letter purporting to be from us, to the effect that the day of the Lord has come.

149

Rom 5:1-5 (§20)

5 Therefore, since we are justified by faith, we have peace with God through our Lord Jesus Christ. 2 Through him we have obtained access to this grace in which we stand, and we rejoice in our hope of sharing the glory of God. 3 More than that, we rejoice in our sufferings, knowing that suffering produces endurance, 4 and endurance produces character, and character produces hope, 5 and hope does not disappoint us, because God's love has been poured into our hearts through the Holy Spirit which has been given to us.

Rom 15:22-29 (§63)

22 This is the reason why I have so often been hindered from coming to you. 23 But now, since I no longer have any room for work in these regions, and since I have longed for many years to come to you, 24 I hope to see you in passing as I go to Spain, and to be sped on my journey there by you, once I have enjoyed your company for a little. 25 At present, however, I am going to Jerusalem with aid for the saints. 26 For Macedo'nia and Acha'ia have been

1 Cor 16:5-9 (§139)

5 I will visit you after passing through Macedo'nia, for I intend to pass through Macedo'nia, 6 and perhaps I will stay with you or even spend the winter, so that you may speed me on my journey, wherever I go. 7 For I do not want to see you now just in passing; I hope to spend some time with you, if the Lord permits. 8 But I will stay in Ephesus until Pentecost, 9 for a wide door for effective work has opened to me, and there are many adversaries.

pleased to make some contribution for the poor among the saints at Jerusalem; 27 they were pleased to do it, and indeed they are in debt to them, for if the Gentiles have come to share in their spiritual blessings, they ought also to be of service to them in material blessings. 28 When therefore I have completed this, and have delivered to them what has been raised, I shall go on by way of you to Spain; 29 and I know that when I come to you I shall come in the fulness of the blessing of Christ.

2 Cor 1:15-22

15 Because I was sure of this, I wanted to come to you first, so that you might have a double pleasure; 16 I wanted to visit you on my way to Macedo'nia, and to come back to you from Macedo'nia and have you send me on my way to Judea. 17 Was I vacillating when I wanted to do this? Do I make my plans like a worldly man, ready to say Yes and No at once? 18 As surely as God is faithful, our word to you has not been Yes and No. 19 For the Son of God, Jesus Christ, whom we preached among you, Silva'nus and Timothy and I, was not Yes and No; but in him it is always Yes. 20 For all the promises of God find their Yes in him. That is why we utter the Amen through him, to the glory of God. 21 But it is God who establishes us with you in Christ, and has commissioned us; 22 he has put his seal upon us and given us his Spirit in our hearts as a guarantee.

Gal 3:21-25 (§205)

21 Is the law then against the promises of God? Certainly not; for if a law had been given which could make alive, then righteousness would indeed be by the law. 22 But the scripture consigned all things to sin, that what was promised to faith in Jesus Christ might be given to those who believe.

23 Now before faith came, we were confined under the law, kept under restraint until faith should be revealed. 24 So that the law was our custodian until Christ came, that we might be justified by faith. 25 But now that faith has come, we are no longer under a custodian;

Eph 1:3-23 (§219)

3 Blessed be the God and Father of our Lord Jesus Christ, who has blessed us in Christ with every spiritual blessing in the heavenly places, 4 even as he chose us in him before the foundation of the world, that we should be holy and blameless before him. 5 He destined us in love to be his sons through Jesus Christ, according to the purpose of his will, 6 to the praise of his glorious grace which he freely bestowed on us in the Beloved. 7 In him we have redemption through his blood, the forgiveness of our trespasses, according to the riches of his grace 8 which he lavished upon us. 9 For he has made known to us in all wisdom and insight the mystery of his will, according to his purpose which he set forth in Christ 10 as a plan for the fulness of time, to unite all things in him, things in heaven and things on earth.

11 In him, according to the purpose of him who accomplishes all things according to the counsel of his will, 12 we who first hoped in Christ have been destined and appointed to live for the

▶ 1:16 Acts 19:21
21 Now after these events Paul resolved in the Spirit to pass through Macedo'nia and Acha'ia and go to Jerusalem, saying, "After I have been there, I must also see Rome."

▶ 1:19 Acts 15:22
22 Then it seemed good to the apostles and the elders, with the whole church, to choose men from among them and send them to Antioch with Paul and Barnabas. They sent Judas called Barsabbas, and Silas, leading men among the brethren,

▶ 1:15-22 1:23-2:4
23 But I call God to witness against me—it was to spare you that I refrained from coming to Corinth. 24 Not that we lord it over your faith; we work with you for your joy, for you stand 2 firm in your faith. 1 For I made up my mind not to make you another painful visit. 2 For if I cause you pain, who is there to make me glad but the one whom I have pained? 3 And I wrote as I did, so that when I came I might not suffer pain from those who should have made me rejoice, for I felt sure of all of you, that my joy would be the joy of you all. 4 For I wrote you out of much affliction and anguish of heart and with many tears, not to cause you pain but to let you know the abundant love that I have for you.

12:14-13:1
14 Here for the third time I am ready to come to you. And I will not be a burden, for I seek not what is yours but you; for children ought not to lay up for their parents, but parents for their children. 15 I will most gladly spend and be spent for your souls. If I love you the more, am I to be loved the less? 16 But granting that I myself did not burden you, I was crafty, you say, and got the better of you by guile. 17 Did I take advantage of you through any of those whom I sent to you? 18 I urged Titus to

150. I wrote you out of much affliction and anguish

150

1 Cor 4:14-21 (§86)

14 I do not write this to make you ashamed, but to admonish you as my beloved children. 15 For though you have countless guides in Christ, you do not have many fathers. For I became your father in Christ Jesus through the gospel. 16 I urge you, then, be imitators of me. 17 Therefore I sent to you Timothy, my beloved and faithful child in the Lord, to remind you of my ways in Christ, as I teach them everywhere in every church. 18 Some are arrogant, as though I were not coming to you. 19 But I will come to you soon, if the Lord wills, and I will find out not the talk of these arrogant people but their power. 20 For the kingdom of God does not consist in talk but in power. 21 What do you wish? Shall I come to you with a rod, or with love in a spirit of gentleness?

1 Cor 16:13-14 (§141)

13 Be watchful, stand firm in your faith, be courageous, be strong. 14 Let all that you do be done in love.

2 Cor 1:23-2:4

23 But I call God to witness against me—it was to spare you that I refrained from coming to Corinth. 24 Not that we lord it over your faith; we work with you for your joy, for you stand 2 firm in your faith. 1 For I made up my mind not to make you another painful visit. 2 For if I cause you pain, who is there to make me glad but the one whom I have pained? 3 And I wrote as I did, so that when I came I might not suffer pain from those who should have made me rejoice, for I felt sure of all of you, that my joy would be the joy of you all. 4 For I wrote you out of much affliction and anguish of heart and with many tears, not to cause you pain but to let you know the abundant love that I have for you.

▶ 2:4 Acts 20:31
31 Therefore be alert, remembering that for three years I did not cease night or day to admonish every one with tears.

▶ 1:23-2:4 12:14
14 Here for the third time I am ready to come to you. And I will not be a burden, for I seek not what is yours but you; for children ought not to lay up for their parents, but parents for their children.

13:1
This is the third time I am coming to you. Any charge must be sustained by the evidence of two or three witnesses.

▶ 1:23-24 1 Cor 15:1-2
Now I would remind you, brethren, in what terms I preached to you the gospel, which you received, in which you stand, 2 by which you are saved, if you hold it fast—unless you believed in vain.

▶ 1:23 Gal 1:20
20 (In what I am writing to you, before God, I do not lie!)

2 Cor 11:31
31 The God and Father of the Lord Jesus, he who is blessed for ever, knows that I do not lie.

Eph (cont)

praise of his glory. 13 In him you also, who have heard the word of truth, the gospel of your salvation, and have believed in him, were sealed with the promised Holy Spirit, 14 which is the guarantee of our inheritance until we acquire possession of it, to the praise of his glory.

15 For this reason, because I have heard of your faith in the Lord Jesus and your love[c] toward all the saints, 16 I do not cease to give thanks for you, remembering you in my prayers, 17 that the God of our Lord Jesus Christ, the Father of glory, may give you a spirit of wisdom and of revelation in the knowledge of him, 18 having the eyes of your hearts enlightened, that you may know what is the hope to which he has called you, what are the riches of his glorious inheritance in the saints, 19 and what is the immeasurable greatness of his power in us who believe, according to the working of his great might 20 which he accomplished in Christ when he raised him from the dead and made him sit at his right hand in the heavenly places, 21 far above all rule and authority and

power and dominion, and above every name that is named, not only in this age but also in that which is to come; 22 and he has put all things under his feet and has made him the head over all things for the church, 23 which is his body, the fulness of him who fills all in all.

1 Thes 2:17-20 (§280)

17 But since we were bereft of you, brethren, for a short time, in person not in heart, we endeavored the more eagerly and with great desire to see you face to face; 18 because we wanted to come to you—I, Paul, again and again— but Satan hindered us. 19 For what is our hope or joy or crown of boasting before our Lord Jesus at his coming? Is it not you? 20 For you are our glory and joy.

▶ 1:20 Rom 15:8

8 For I tell you that Christ became a servant to the circumcised to show God's truthfulness, in order to confirm the promises given to the patriarchs,

1 Cor 14:16

16 Otherwise, if you bless with the spirit, how can any one in the position of an outsider say the "Amen" to your thanksgiving when he does not know what you are saying?

Gal 3:17-18

17 This is what I mean: the law, which came four hundred and thirty years afterward, does not annul a covenant previously ratified by God, so as to make the promise void. 18 For if the inheritance is by the law, it is no longer by promise; but God gave it to Abraham by a promise.

▶ 1:22 Rom 8:16,

16 it is the Spirit himself bearing witness with our spirit that we are children of God,

Phm 21-22 (§309)

21 Confident of your obedience, I write to you, knowing that you will do even more than I say. 22 At the same time, prepare a guest room for me, for I am hoping through your prayers to be granted to you.

149

23   23 and not only the creation, but we ourselves, who have the first fruits of the Spirit, groan inwardly as we wait for adoption as sons, the redemption of our bodies.

2 Cor 5:5

5 He who has prepared us for this very thing is God, who has given us the Spirit as a guarantee.

▶ 1:15 (pleasure) *read* favor: S* ACDG Koine

Lect it vg syr cop(sa); *text:* ScBP cop(bo)

Theodoret

go, and sent the brother with him. Did Titus take advantage of you? Did we not act in the same spirit? Did we not take the same steps?

19 Have you been thinking all along that we have been defending ourselves before you? It is in the sight of God that we have been speaking in Christ, and all for your upbuilding, beloved. 20 For

I fear that perhaps I may come and find you not what I wish, and that you may find me not what you wish; that perhaps there may be quarreling, jealousy, anger, selfishness, slander, gossip, conceit, and disorder. 21 I fear that when I come again my God may humble me before you, and I may have to mourn over many of those who sinned before and

have not repented of the impurity, immorality, and licentiousness which they have practiced.

13   This is the third time I am coming to you. Any charge must be sustained by the evidence of two or three witnesses.

150. I wrote you out of much affliction and anguish

Phil 1:27-30 (§241)

27 Only let your manner of life be worthy of the gospel of Christ, so that whether I come and see you or am absent, I may hear of you that you stand firm in one spirit, with one mind striving side by side for the faith of the gospel, 28 and not frightened in anything by your opponents. This is a clear omen to them of their destruction, but of your salvation, and that from God. 29 For it has been granted to you that for the sake of Christ you should not only believe in him but also suffer for his sake, 30 engaged in the same conflict which you saw and now hear to be mine.

1 Thes 3:6-10 (§282)

6 But now that Timothy has come to us from you, and has brought us the good news of your faith and love and reported that you always remember us kindly and long to see us, as we long to see you—7 for this reason, brethren, in all our distress and affliction we have been comforted about you through your faith; 8 for now we live, if you stand fast in the Lord. 9 For what thanksgiving can we render to God for you, for all the joy which we feel for your sake before our God, 10 praying earnestly night and day that we may see you face to face and supply what is lacking in your faith?

150

▶ 1:24 Gal 5:1

For freedom Christ has set us free; stand fast therefore, and do not submit again to a yoke of slavery.

Phil 4:1

Therefore, my brethren, whom I love and long for, my joy and crown, stand firm thus in the Lord, my beloved.

▶ 2:3 7:16

16 I rejoice, because I have perfect confidence in you.

151

Rom 16:17-20a (§67)

17 I appeal to you, brethren, to take note of those who create dissensions and difficulties, in opposition to the doctrine which you have been taught; avoid them. 18 For such persons do not serve our Lord Christ, but their own appetites, and by fair and flattering words they deceive the hearts of the simple-minded. 19 For while your obedience is known to all, so that I rejoice over you, I would have you wise as to what is good and guileless as to what is evil; 20 then the God of peace will soon crush Satan under your feet.

1 Cor 5:1-5 (§87)

5 It is actually reported that there is immorality among you, and of a kind that is not found even among pagans; for a man is living with his father's wife. 2And you are arrogant! Ought you not rather to mourn? Let him who has done this be removed from among you.

3 For though absent in body I am present in spirit, and as if present, I have already pronounced judgment 4 in the name of the Lord Jesus on the man who has done such a thing. When you are assembled, and my spirit is present, with the power of our Lord Jesus, 5 you are to deliver this man to Satan for the destruction of the flesh, that his spirit may be saved in the day of the Lord Jesus.

2 Cor 2:5-11

5 But if any one has caused pain, he has caused it not to me, but in some measure—not to put it too severely—to you all. 6 For such a one this punishment by the majority is enough; 7 so you should rather turn to forgive and comfort him, or he may be overwhelmed by excessive sorrow. 8 So I beg you to reaffirm your love for him. 9 For this is why I wrote, that I might test you and know whether you are obedient in everything. 10Any one whom you forgive, I also forgive. What I have forgiven, if I have forgiven anything, has been for your sake in the presence of Christ, 11 to keep Satan from gaining the advantage over us; for we are not ignorant of his designs.

Gal 6:1-6 (§214)

6 Brethren, if a man is overtaken in any trespass, you who are spiritual should restore him in a spirit of gentleness. Look to yourself, lest you too be tempted. 2 Bear one another's burdens, and so fulfil the law of Christ. 3 For if any one thinks he is something, when he is nothing, he deceives himself. 4 But let each one test his own work, and then his reason to boast will be in himself alone and not in his neighbor. 5 For each man will have to bear his own load.

6 Let him who is taught the word share all good things with him who teaches.

▶ 2:5-11 6:14-7:1
14 Do not be mismated with unbelievers. For what partnership have righteousness and iniquity? Or what fellowship has light with darkness? 15 What accord has Christ with Be'lial? Or what has a believer in common with an unbeliever? 16 What agreement has the temple of God with idols? For we are the temple of the living God; as

God said,
"I will live in them and move among them,
and I will be their God,
and they shall be my people.
17 Therefore come out from them,
and be separate from them, says the Lord,
and touch nothing unclean;
then I will welcome you,
18 and I will be a father to you,

and you shall be my sons and daughters,
says the Lord Almighty."
7 Since we have these promises, beloved, let us cleanse ourselves from every defilement of body and spirit, and make holiness perfect in the fear of God.

▶ 2:7-8 Col 3:13-14
13 forbearing one another and, if one has a complaint against another, forgiving each other; as the Lord has forgiven you, so you also must forgive. 14And above all these put on love, which binds everything together in perfect harmony.

Eph 4:32   32 and be kind to one another, tenderhearted, forgiving one another, as God in Christ forgave you.

▶ 2:10-11 4:3-6
3And even if our gospel is veiled, it is veiled only to those who are perishing. 4 In their case the god of this world has blinded the minds of the unbelievers, to keep them from seeing the light of the gospel of the glory of Christ,

152. A door was opened for me

152

2 Cor 2:12-13

12 When I came to Tro'as to preach the gospel of Christ, a door was opened for me in the Lord; 13 but my mind could not rest because I did not find my brother Titus there. So I took leave of them and went on to Macedo'nia.

▶ 2:12 Acts 14:27,
27And when they arrived, they gathered the church together and declared all that God had done with them, and how he had opened a door of faith to the Gentiles.

16:8   8 so, passing by My'sia, they went down to Tro'as.

▶ 2:13 Tit 1:4
4 To Titus, my true child in a common faith:
Grace and peace from God the Father and Christ Jesus our Savior,

▶ 2:13 Gal 2:1-3
Then after fourteen years I went up again to Jerusalem with Barnabas, taking Titus along with me. 2 I went up by revelation; and I laid before them (but privately before those who were of repute) the gospel which I preach among the Gentiles, lest somehow I should be running or had run in

vain. 3 But even Titus, who was with me, was not compelled to be circumcised, though he was a Greek.

151

who is the likeness of God. 5 For what we preach is not ourselves, but Jesus Christ as Lord, with ourselves as your servants for Jesus' sake. 6 For it is the God who said, "Let light shine out of darkness," who has shone in our hearts to give the light of the knowledge of the glory of God in the face of Christ.

152. A door was opened for me

152

Col 4:2-4 (§269)

2 Continue steadfastly in prayer, being watchful in it with thanksgiving; 3 and pray for us also, that God may open to us a door for the word, to declare the mystery of Christ, on account of which I am in prison, 4 that I may make it clear, as I ought to speak.

1 Thes 2:17-3:5 (§280-281)

17 But since we were bereft of you, brethren, for a short time, in person not in heart, we endeavored the more eagerly and with great desire to see you face to face; 18 because we wanted to come to you—I, Paul, again and again—but Satan hindered us. 19 For what is our hope or joy or crown of boasting before our Lord Jesus at his coming? Is it not you? 20 For you are our glory and joy.

3 Therefore when we could bear it no longer, we were willing to be left behind at Athens alone, 2 and we sent Timothy, our brother and God's servant in the gospel of Christ, to establish you in your faith and to exhort you, 3 that no one be moved by these afflictions. You yourselves know that this is to be our lot. 4 For when we were with you, we told you beforehand that we were to suffer affliction; just as it has come to pass, and as you know. 5 For this reason, when I could bear it no longer, I sent that I might know your faith, for fear that somehow the tempter had tempted you and that our labor would be in vain.

153

1 Cor 9:15-18 (§106)

15 But I have made no use of any of these rights, nor am I writing this to secure any such provision. For I would rather die than have any one deprive me of my ground for boasting. 16 For if I preach the gospel, that gives me no ground for boasting. For necessity is laid upon me. Woe to me if I do not preach the gospel! 17 For if I do this of my own will, I have a reward; but if not of my own will, I am entrusted with a commission. 18 What then is my reward? Just this: that in my preaching I may make the gospel free of charge, not making full use of my right in the gospel.

2 Cor 2:14-17

14 But thanks be to God, who in Christ always leads us in triumph, and through us spreads the fragrance of the knowledge of him everywhere. 15 For we are the aroma of Christ to God among those who are being saved and among those who are perishing, 16 to one a fragrance from death to death, to the other a fragrance from life to life. Who is sufficient for these things? 17 For we are not, like so many, peddlers of God's word; but as men of sincerity, as commissioned by God, in the sight of God we speak in Christ.

▶ 2:14 Col 2:15
15 He disarmed the principalities and powers and made a public example of them, triumphing over them in him.

1 Cor 15:57   57 But thanks be to God, who gives us the victory through our Lord Jesus Christ.

▶ 2:15-16 Eph 5:2 2 And walk in love, as Christ loved us and gave himself up for us, a fragrant offering and sacrifice to God.

▶ 2:15 1 Cor 1:18
18 For the word of the cross is folly to those who are perishing, but to us who are being saved it is the power of God.

▶ 2:16 3:5   5 Not that we are competent of ourselves to claim anything as coming from us; our competence is from God,

▶ 2:17 12:19
19 Have you been thinking all along that we have been defending ourselves before you? It is in the sight of God that we have been speaking in Christ, and all for your upbuilding, beloved.

154. You are a letter from Christ

154

Rom 7:1-6 (§26)

7 Do you not know, brethren—for I am speaking to those who know the law—that the law is binding on a person only during his life? 2 Thus a married woman is bound by law to her husband as long as he lives; but if her husband dies she is discharged from the law concerning the husband. 3 Accordingly, she will be called an adulteress if she lives with another man while her husband is alive. But if her husband dies she is free from that law, and if she marries another man she is not an adulteress.
4 Likewise, my brethren, you have died to the law through the body of Christ, so that you may belong to another, to him who has been raised from the dead in order that we may bear fruit for God. 5 While we were living in the flesh, our sinful passions, aroused by the law, were at work in our members to bear fruit for death. 6 But now we are discharged from the law, dead to that which held us captive, so that we serve not under the old written code but in the new life of the Spirit.

1 Cor 16:10-12 (§140)

10 When Timothy comes, see that you put him at ease among you, for he is doing the work of the Lord, as I am. 11 So let no one despise him. Speed him on his way in peace, that he may return to me; for I am expecting him with the brethren.
12 As for our brother Apol'los, I strongly urged him to visit you with the other brethren, but it was not at all his will to come now. He will come when he has opportunity.

1 Cor 16:15-18 (§142)

15 Now, brethren, you know that the household of Steph'anas were the first converts in Acha'ia, and they have devoted themselves to the service of the saints; 16 I urge you to be subject to

Rom 16:1-2 (§65)

16 I commend to you our sister Phoebe, a deaconess of the church at Cen'chre-ae, 2 that you may receive her in the Lord as befits the saints, and help her in whatever she may require from you, for she has been a helper of many and of myself as well.

2 Cor 3:1-3

3 Are we beginning to commend ourselves again? Or do we need, as some do, letters of recommendation to you, or from you? 2 You yourselves are our letter of recommendation, written on your hearts, to be known and read by all men; 3 and you show that you are a letter from Christ delivered by us, written not with ink but with the Spirit of the living God, not on tablets of stone but on tablets of human hearts.

such men and to every fellow worker and laborer. 17 I rejoice at the coming of Steph'anas and Fortuna'tus and Acha'-icus, because they have made up for your absence; 18 for they refreshed my spirit as well as yours. Give recognition to such men.

▶ 3:1 Acts 18:27
27 And when he wished to cross to Acha'ia, the brethren encouraged him, and wrote to the disciples to receive him. When he arrived, he greatly helped those who through grace had believed,

▶ 3:1-3 2 Cor 8:16-24
16 But thanks be to God who puts the same earnest care for you into the heart of Titus. 17 For he not only accepted our appeal, but being himself very earnest he is going to you of his own accord. 18 With him we are sending the brother who is famous among all the churches for his preaching of the gospel; 19 and not only that, but he has been appointed by the churches to travel with us in this gracious work which we are carrying on, for the glory of the Lord and to show our good will. 20 We intend that no one should blame us about this liberal gift which we are administering, 21 for we aim at what is honorable not only in the Lord's sight but also in the sight of men.

22 And with them we are sending our brother whom we have often tested and found earnest in many matters, but who is now more earnest than ever because of his great confidence in you. 23 As for Titus, he is my partner and fellow worker in your service; and as for our brethren, they are messengers of the churches, the glory of Christ. 24 So give proof, before the churches, of your love and of our boasting about you to these men.

▶ 3:3 Rom 2:25-29
25 Circumcision indeed is of value if you obey the law; but if you break the law, your circumcision becomes uncircumcision. 26 So, if a man who is uncircumcised keeps the precepts of the law, will not his uncircumcision be regarded as circumcision? 27 Then those who are physically uncircumcised but keep the law will condemn you who have the written code and circumcision but break the law. 28 For he is not a real Jew who is one outwardly, nor is true circumcision something external and physical. 29 He is a Jew who is one in-

153

Phil 1:12-18 (§239)

12 I want you to know, brethren, that what has happened to me has really served to advance the gospel, 13 so that it has become known throughout the whole praetorian guard and to all the rest that my imprisonment is for Christ; 14 and most of the brethren have been made confident in the Lord because of my imprisonment, and are much more bold to speak the word of God without fear.

15 Some indeed preach Christ from envy and rivalry, but others from good will. 16 The latter do it out of love, knowing that I am put here for the defense of the gospel; 17 the former proclaim Christ out of partisanship, not sincerely but thinking to afflict me in my imprisonment. 18 What then? Only that in every way, whether in pretense or in truth, Christ is proclaimed; and in that I rejoice.

Phil 4:10-20 (§253)

10 I rejoice in the Lord greatly that now at length you have revived your concern for me; you were indeed concerned for me, but you had no opportunity. 11 Not that I complain of want;

for I have learned, in whatever state I am, to be content. 12 I know how to be abased, and I know how to abound; in any and all circumstances I have learned the secret of facing plenty and hunger, abundance and want. 13 I can do all things in him who strengthens me.

14 Yet it was kind of you to share my trouble. 15 And you Philippians yourselves know that in the beginning of the gospel, when I left Macedo'nia, no church entered into partnership with me in giving and receiving except you only; 16 for even in Thessaloni'ca you sent me help once and again. 17 Not that I seek the gift; but I seek the fruit which increases to your credit. 18 I have received full payment, and more; I am filled, having received from Epaphrodi'tus the gifts you sent, a fragrant offering, a sacrifice acceptable and pleasing to God. 19 And my God will supply every need of yours according to his riches in glory in Christ Jesus. 20 To our God and Father be glory for ever and ever. Amen.

1 Thes 2:1-8 (§277)

2 For you yourselves know, brethren, that our visit to you was not in vain; 2 but though we had already suffered and been shamefully treated at Philippi, as you know, we had courage in our God to declare to you the gospel of God in the face of great opposition. 3 For our appeal does not spring from error or uncleanness, nor is it made with guile; 4 but just as we have been approved by God to be entrusted with the gospel, so we speak, not to please men, but to please God who tests our hearts. 5 For we never used either words of flattery, as you know, or a cloak for greed, as God is witness; 6 nor did we seek glory from men, whether from you or from others, though we might have made demands as apostles of Christ. 7 But we were gentle among you, like a nurse taking care of her children. 8 So, being affectionately desirous of you, we were ready to share with you not only the gospel of God but also our own selves, because you had become very dear to us.

154. You are a letter from Christ

154

Phil 2:19-24 (§245)

19 I hope in the Lord Jesus to send Timothy to you soon, so that I may be cheered by news of you. 20 I have no one like him, who will be genuinely anxious for your welfare. 21 They all look after their own interests, not those of Jesus Christ. 22 But Timothy's worth you know, how as a son with a father he has served with me in the gospel. 23 I hope therefore to send him just as soon as I see how it will go with me; 24 and I trust in the Lord that shortly I myself shall come also.

Phil 2:25-3:1 (§246)

25 I have thought it necessary to send to you Epaphrodi'tus my brother and fellow worker and fellow soldier, and your messenger and minister to my need, 26 for he has been longing for you all, and has been distressed because you heard that he was ill. 27 Indeed he was ill, near to death. But God had mercy on him, and not only on him but on me also, lest I should have sorrow upon sorrow. 28 I am the more eager to send him, therefore, that you may rejoice at seeing him again, and that I may be less anxious. 29 So receive him in the Lord

wardly, and real circumcision is a matter of the heart, spiritual and not literal. His praise is not from men but from God.

with all joy; and honor such men, 30 for he nearly died for the work of Christ, risking his life to complete your service to me.

3 Finally, my brethren, rejoice in the Lord. To write the same things to you is not irksome to me, and is safe for you.

▶ 3:2 (your) *read* our: p46 ABCDG Koine Lect it vg syr cop; *text:* S

Phm 8-20 (§307-308)

8 Accordingly, though I am bold enough in Christ to command you to do what is required, 9 yet for love's sake I prefer to appeal to you—I, Paul, an ambassador and now a prisoner also for Christ Jesus—10 I appeal to you for my child, Ones'imus, whose father I have become in my imprisonment. 11 (Formerly he was useless to you, but now he is indeed useful to you and to me.) 12 I am sending him back to you, sending my very heart. 13 I would have been glad to keep him with me, in order that he might serve me on your behalf during my imprisonment for the gospel; 14 but I preferred to do nothing without your consent in order that your goodness might not be by compulsion but of your own free will.

15 Perhaps this is why he was parted from you for a while, that you might have him back for ever, 16 no longer as a slave but more than a slave, as a beloved brother, especially to me but how much more to you, both in the flesh and in the Lord. 17 So if you consider me your partner, receive him as you would receive me. 18 If he has wronged you at all, or owes you anything, charge that to my account. 19 I, Paul, write this with my own hand, I will repay it—to say nothing of your owing me even your own self. 20 Yes, brother, I want some benefit from you in the Lord. Refresh my heart in Christ.

155

Rom 7:1-6 (§26)

7 Do you not know, brethren—for I am speaking to those who know the law—that the law is binding on a person only during his life? 2 Thus a married woman is bound by law to her husband as long as he lives; but if her husband dies she is discharged from the law concerning the husband. 3 Accordingly, she will be called an adulteress if she lives with another man while her husband is alive. But if her husband dies she is free from that law, and if she marries another man she is not an adulteress.

4 Likewise, my brethren, you have died to the law through the body of Christ, so that you may belong to another, to him who has been raised from the dead in order that we may bear fruit for God. 5 While we were living in the flesh, our sinful passions, aroused by the law, were at work in our members to bear fruit for death. 6 But now we are discharged from the law, dead to that which held us captive, so that we serve not under the old written code but in the new life of the Spirit.

▶ 3:4 Eph 3:12
12 to equip the saints for the work of ministry, for building up the body of Christ,

1 Cor 4:6-7 (§84)

6 I have applied all this to myself and Apol′los for your benefit, brethren, that you may learn by us not to go beyond what is written, that none of you may be puffed up in favor of one against another. 7 For who sees anything different in you? What have you that you did not receive? If then you received it, why do you boast as if it were not a gift?

▶ 3:5 1 Cor 15:10
10 But by the grace of God I am what I am, and his grace toward me was not in vain. On the contrary, I worked harder than any of them, though it was not I, but the grace of God which is with me.

2 Cor 3:4-6

4 Such is the confidence that we have through Christ toward God. 5 Not that we are competent of ourselves to claim anything as coming from us; our competence is from God, 6 who has made us competent to be ministers of a new covenant, not in a written code but in the Spirit; for the written code kills, but the Spirit gives life.

▶ 3:6 Rom 7:6,
6 But now we are discharged from the law, dead to that which held us captive, so that we serve not under the old written code but in the new life of the Spirit.

2:29
29 He is a Jew who is one inwardly, and real circumcision is a matter of the heart, spiritual and not literal. His praise is not from men but from God.

1 Cor 11:25
25 In the same way also the cup, after supper, saying, "This cup is the new covenant in my blood. Do this, as often as you drink it, in remembrance of me."

Gal 3:15
15 To give a human example, brethren: no one annuls even a man's will, or adds to it, once it has been ratified.

156. Dispensation of death; dispensation of Spirit

156

Rom 3:21-26 (§14)

21 But now the righteousness of God has been manifested apart from law, although the law and the prophets bear witness to it, 22 the righteousness of God through faith in Jesus Christ for all who believe. For there is no distinction; 23 since all have sinned and fall short of the glory of God, 24 they are justified by his grace as a gift, through the redemption which is in Christ Jesus, 25 whom God put forward as an expiation by his blood, to be received by faith. This was to show God's righteousness, because in his divine forbearance he had passed over former sins; 26 it was to prove at the present time that he himself is righteous and that he justifies him who has faith in Jesus.

Rom 5:6-11 (§21)

6 While we were still weak, at the right time Christ died for the ungodly. 7 Why, one will hardly die for a righteous man—though perhaps for a good man one will dare even to die. 8 But God shows his love for us in that while we were yet sinners Christ died for us. 9 Since, therefore, we are now justified

▶ 3:7-11 Rom 1:18-23,
18 For the wrath of God is revealed from heaven against all ungodliness and wickedness of men who by their wickedness suppress the truth. 19 For what can be known about God is plain to them, because God has shown it to them. 20 Ever since the creation of the world his invisible nature, namely, his eternal

power and deity, has been clearly perceived in the things that have been made. So they are without excuse; 21 for although they knew God they did not honor him as God or give thanks to him, but they became futile in their thinking and their senseless minds were darkened. 22 Claiming to be wise, they became fools, 23 and exchanged the

by his blood, much more shall we be saved by him from the wrath of God. 10 For if while we were enemies we were reconciled to God by the death of his Son, much more, now that we are reconciled, shall we be saved by his life. 11 Not only so, but we also rejoice in God through our Lord Jesus Christ, through whom we have now received our reconciliation.

Rom 7:1-6 (§26)

7 Do you not know, brethren—for I am speaking to those who know the law—that the law is binding on a person only during his life? 2 Thus a married woman is bound by law to her husband as long as he lives; but if her husband dies she is discharged from the law concerning the husband. 3 Accordingly, she will be called an adulteress if she lives with another man while her husband is alive. But if her husband dies she is free from that law, and if she marries another man she is not an adulteress.

4 Likewise, my brethren, you have died to the law through the body of Christ, so that you may belong to another, to him who has been raised from

glory of the immortal God for images resembling mortal man or birds or animals or reptiles.

2 Cor 3:7-11

7 Now if the dispensation of death, carved in letters on stone, came with such splendor that the Israelites could not look at Moses' face because of its brightness, fading as this was, 8 will not the dispensation of the Spirit be attended with greater splendor? 9 For if there was splendor in the dispensation of condemnation, the dispensation of righteousness must far exceed it in splendor. 10 Indeed, in this case, what once had splendor has come to have no splendor at all, because of the splendor that surpasses it. 11 For if what faded away came with splendor, what is permanent must have much more splendor.

the dead in order that we may bear fruit for God. 5 While we were living in the flesh, our sinful passions, aroused by the law, were at work in our members to bear fruit for death. 6 But now we are discharged from the law, dead to that which held us captive, so that we serve not under the old written code but in the new life of the Spirit.

9:22-23
22 What if God, desiring to show his wrath and to make known his power, has endured with much patience the vessels of wrath made for destruction, 23 in order to make known the riches of his glory for the vessels of mercy, which he has prepared beforehand for glory, 24 even us

Rom 9:1-5 (§35)

9 I am speaking the truth in Christ, I am not lying; my conscience bears me witness in the Holy Spirit, 2 that I have great sorrow and unceasing anguish in my heart. 3 For I could wish that I myself were accursed and cut off from Christ for the sake of my brethren, my kinsmen by race. 4 They are Israelites, and to them belong the sonship, the glory, the covenants, the giving of the law, the worship, and the promises; 5 to them belong the patriarchs, and of their race, according to the flesh, is the Christ. God who is over all be blessed for ever. Amen.

Rom 15:7-13 (§61)

7 Welcome one another, therefore, as Christ has welcomed you, for the glory of God. 8 For I tell you that Christ became a servant to the circumcised to show God's truthfulness, in order to confirm the promises given to the patriarchs, 9 and in order that the Gentiles might glorify God for his mercy. As it is written,

"Therefore I will praise thee among the Gentiles,
and sing to thy name";

1 Cor 15:40-43
40 There are celestial bodies and there are terrestrial bodies; but the glory of the celestial is one, and the glory of the terrestrial is another. 41 There is one glory of the sun, and another glory of the moon, and another glory of the stars; for star differs from star in glory.
42 So is it with the resurrection of the

10 and again it is said,
"Rejoice, O Gentiles, with his people";
11 and again,
"Praise the Lord, all Gentiles,
and let all the peoples praise him";
12 and further Isaiah says,
"The root of Jesse shall come,

he who rises to rule the Gentiles;
in him shall the Gentiles hope."
13 May the God of hope fill you with all joy and peace in believing, so that by the power of the Holy Spirit you may abound in hope.

dead. What is sown is perishable, what is raised is imperishable. 43 It is sown in dishonor, it is raised in glory. It is sown in weakness, it is raised in power.

155

Phil 3:2-11 (§247)

2 Look out for the dogs, look out for the evil-workers, look out for those who mutilate the flesh. 3 For we are the true circumcision, who worship God in spirit, and glory in Christ Jesus, and put no confidence in the flesh. 4 Though I myself have reason for confidence in the flesh also. If any other man thinks he has reason for confidence in the flesh, I have more: 5 circumcised on the eighth day, of the people of Israel, of the tribe of Benjamin, a Hebrew born of Hebrews; as to the law a Pharisee, 6 as to zeal a persecutor of the church, as to righteousness under the law blameless. 7 But whatever gain I had, I counted as loss for the sake of Christ. 8 Indeed I count everything as loss because of the surpassing worth of knowing Christ Jesus my Lord. For his sake I have suffered the loss of all things, and count them as refuse, in order that I may gain Christ 9 and be found in him, not having a righteousness of my own, based on law, but that which is through faith in Christ, the righteousness from God that depends on faith; 10 that I may know him and the power of his resurrection,

and may share his sufferings, becoming like him in his death, 11 that if possible I may attain the resurrection from the dead.

Phil 3:12-16 (§248)

12 Not that I have already obtained this or am already perfect; but I press on to make it my own, because Christ Jesus has made me his own. 13 Brethren, I do not consider that I have made it my own; but one thing I do, forgetting what lies behind and straining forward to what lies ahead, 14 I press on toward the goal for the prize of the upward call of God in Christ Jesus. 15 Let those of us who are mature be thus minded; and if in anything you are otherwise minded, God will reveal that also to you. 16 Only let us hold true to what we have attained.

156. Dispensation of death; dispensation of Spirit

156

Phil 3:2-11 (§247)

2 Look out for the dogs, look out for the evil-workers, look out for those who mutilate the flesh. 3 For we are the true circumcision, who worship God in spirit, and glory in Christ Jesus, and put no confidence in the flesh. 4 Though I myself have reason for confidence in the flesh also. If any other man thinks he has reason for confidence in the flesh, I have more: 5 circumcised on the eighth day, of the people of Israel, of the tribe of Benjamin, a Hebrew born of Hebrews; as to the law a Pharisee, 6 as to zeal a persecutor of the church, as to righteousness under the law blameless. 7 But whatever gain I had, I counted as loss for the sake of Christ. 8 Indeed I count everything as loss because of the surpassing worth of knowing Christ Jesus my Lord. For his sake I have suffered the loss of all things, and count them as refuse, in order that I may gain Christ 9 and be found in him, not having a righteousness of my own, based on law, but that which is through faith in Christ, the righteousness from God that depends on faith; 10 that I may know him and the power of his resurrection,

and may share his sufferings, becoming like him in his death, 11 that if possible I may attain the resurrection from the dead.

▶ 3:7-8 Rom 5:20-21 20 Law came in, to increase the trespass; but where sin increased, grace abounded all the more, 21 so that, as sin reigned in death, grace also might reign through righteousness to eternal life through Jesus Christ our Lord.

▶ 3:7 Rom 4:15 15 For the law brings wrath, but where there is no law there is no transgression.

▶ 3:7 Ex 34:29-35 29 When Moses came down from Mount Sinai, with the two tables of the testimony in his hand as he came down from the mountain, Moses did not know that the skin of his face shone because he had been talking with God. 30 And when Aaron and all the people of Israel saw Moses, behold, the skin of his face shone, and they were afraid to come near him. 31 But Moses called to them; and Aaron and all the leaders of the congregation returned to him, and Moses talked with them. 32 And afterward all the people of Israel came near, and he gave them in commandment all that the LORD had spoken with him in Mount Sinai. 33 And when Moses had finished speaking with them, he put a veil on his face; 34 but whenever Moses went in before the LORD to speak with him, he took the veil off, until he came out; and when he came out, and told the people of Israel what he was commanded, 35 the people of Israel saw the face of Moses, that the skin of Moses' face shone; and Moses would put the veil upon his face again, until he went in to speak with him.

157

Rom 7:1-6 (§26)

7 Do you not know, brethren—for I am speaking to those who know the law—that the law is binding on a person only during his life? 2 Thus a married woman is bound by law to her husband as long as he lives; but if her husband dies she is discharged from the law concerning the husband. 3 Accordingly, she will be called an adulteress if she lives with another man while her husband is alive. But if her husband dies she is free from that law, and if she marries another man she is not an adulteress.

4 Likewise, my brethren, you have died to the law through the body of Christ, so that you may belong to another, to him who has been raised from the dead in order that we may bear fruit for God. 5 While we were living in the flesh, our sinful passions, aroused by the law, were at work in our members to bear fruit for death. 6 But now we are discharged from the law, dead to that which held us captive, so that we serve not under the old written code but in the new life of the Spirit.

▶ 3:12 Acts 4:13
13 Now when they saw the boldness of Peter and John, and perceived that they were uneducated, common men, they wondered; and they recognized that they had been with Jesus.

Rom 11:25-32 (§49)

25 Lest you be wise in your own conceits, I want you to understand this mystery, brethren: a hardening has come upon part of Israel, until the full number of the Gentiles come in, 26 and so all Israel will be saved; as it is written,

"The Deliverer will come from Zion,
    he will banish ungodliness from
    Jacob";
27 "and this will be my covenant with
    them
    when I take away their sins."
28 As regards the gospel they are enemies of God, for your sake; but as regards election they are beloved for the sake of their forefathers. 29 For the gifts and the call of God are irrevocable. 30 Just as you were once disobedient to God but now have received mercy because of their disobedience, 31 so they have now been disobedient in order that by the mercy shown to you they also may receive mercy. 32 For God has consigned all men to disobedience, that he may have mercy upon all.

▶ 3:15 Acts 15:21   21 For
from early generations Moses has had in every city those who preach him, for he is read every sabbath in the synagogues."

2 Cor 3:12-18

12 Since we have such a hope, we are very bold, 13 not like Moses, who put a veil over his face so that the Israelites might not see the end of the fading splendor. 14 But their minds were hardened; for to this day, when they read the old covenant, that same veil remains unlifted, because only through Christ is it taken away. 15 Yes, to this day whenever Moses is read a veil lies over their minds; 16 but when a man turns to the Lord the veil is removed. 17 Now the Lord is the Spirit, and where the Spirit of the Lord is, there is freedom. 18 And we all, with unveiled face, beholding the glory of the Lord, are being changed into his likeness from one degree of glory to another; for this comes from the Lord who is the Spirit.

▶ 3:17 Gal 5:1
For freedom Christ has set us free; stand fast therefore, and do not submit again to a yoke of slavery.

Gal 4:21-31 (§210)

21 Tell me, you who desire to be under law, do you not hear the law? 22 For it is written that Abraham had two sons, one by a slave and one by a free woman. 23 But the son of the slave was born according to the flesh, the son of the free woman through promise. 24 Now this is an allegory: these women are two covenants. One is from Mount Sinai, bearing children for slavery; she is Hagar. 25 Now Hagar is Mount Sinai in Arabia; she corresponds to the present Jerusalem, for she is in slavery with her children. 26 But the Jerusalem above is free, and she is our mother. 27 For it is written,

"Rejoice, O barren one who does not
    bear;
break forth and shout, you who are
    not in travail;
for the children of the desolate one
    are many more
    than the children of her that is
    married."
28 Now we, brethren, like Isaac, are children of promise. 29 But as at that time he who was born according to the flesh persecuted him who was born according to the Spirit, so it is now. 30 But what does the scripture say? "Cast out the slave and her son; for the son of the slave shall not inherit with the son of the free woman." 31 So, brethren, we are not children of the slave but of the free woman.

▶ 3:18 1 Cor 6:17
17 But he who is united to the Lord becomes one spirit with him.

158. We do not lose heart

158

Rom 1:1-7 (§1)

1 Paul, a servant of Jesus Christ, called to be an apostle, set apart for the gospel of God 2 which he promised beforehand through his prophets in the holy scriptures, 3 the gospel concerning his Son, who was descended from David according to the flesh 4 and designated Son of God in power according to the Spirit of holiness by his resurrection from the dead, Jesus Christ our Lord, 5 through whom we have received grace and apostleship to bring about the obedience of faith for the sake of his name among all the nations, 6 including yourselves who are called to belong to Jesus Christ;

7 To all God's beloved in Rome, who are called to be saints:

Grace to you and peace from God our Father and the Lord Jesus Christ.

▶ 4:3 1 Cor 1:18
18 For the word of the cross is folly to those who are perishing, but to us who are being saved it is the power of God.

1 Cor 2:1-5 (§76)

2 When I came to you, brethren, I did not come proclaiming to you the testimony of God in lofty words or wisdom. 2 For I decided to know nothing among you except Jesus Christ and him crucified. 3 And I was with you in weakness and in much fear and trembling; 4 and my speech and my message were not in plausible words of wisdom, but in demonstration of the Spirit and of power, 5 that your faith might not rest in the wisdom of men but in the power of God.

▶ 4:4 1 Cor 7:25
25 Now concerning the unmarried, I have no command of the Lord, but I give my opinion as one who by the Lord's mercy is trustworthy.

2 Cor 4:1-6

4 Therefore, having this ministry by the mercy of God, we do not lose heart. 2 We have renounced disgraceful, underhanded ways; we refuse to practice cunning or to tamper with God's word, but by the open statement of the truth we would commend ourselves to every man's conscience in the sight of God. 3 And even if our gospel is veiled, it is veiled only to those who are perishing. 4 In their case the god of this world has blinded the minds of the unbelievers, to keep them from seeing the light of the gospel of the glory of Christ, who is the likeness of God. 5 For what we preach is not ourselves, but Jesus Christ as Lord, with ourselves as your servants for Jesus' sake. 6 For it is the God who said, "Let light shine out of darkness," who has shone in our hearts to give the light of the knowledge of the glory of God in the face of Christ.

Rom 11:7-10
7 What then? Israel failed to obtain what it sought. The elect obtained it, but the rest were hardened, 8 as it is written,
"God gave them a spirit of stupor,
    eyes that should not see and ears that
    should not hear,
    down to this very day."

9 And David says,
"Let their table become a snare and a
    trap,
a pitfall and a retribution for them;
10 let their eyes be darkened so that they
    cannot see,

2 Thes 2:11-12   11 Therefore God sends upon them a strong delusion, to make them believe what is false, 12 so that all may be condemned who did not believe the truth but had pleasure in unrighteousness.

Eph 3:1-13 (§222)

3 For this reason I, Paul, a prisoner for Christ Jesus on behalf of you Gentiles— 2 assuming that you have heard of the stewardship of God's grace that was given to me for you, 3 how the mystery was made known to me by revelation, as I have written briefly. 4 When you read this you can perceive my insight into the mystery of Christ, 5 which was not made known to the sons of men in other generations as it has now been revealed to his holy apostles and prophets by the Spirit; 6 that is, how the Gentiles are fellow heirs, members of the same body, and partakers of the promise in Christ Jesus through the gospel.

7 Of this gospel I was made a minister according to the gift of God's grace which was given me by the working of his power. 8 To me, though I am the very least of all the saints, this grace was given, to preach to the Gentiles the unsearchable riches of Christ, 9 and to make all men see what is the plan of the mystery hidden for ages in God who created all things; 10 that through the church the manifold wisdom of God

Eph 2:1-2
And you he made alive, when you were dead through the trespasses and sins 2 in which you once walked, following the course of this world, following the prince of the power of the air, the spirit that is now at work in the sons of disobedience.

158. We do not lose heart

Col 1:24-2:3 (§260)

24 Now I rejoice in my sufferings for your sake, and in my flesh I complete what is lacking in Christ's afflictions for the sake of his body, that is, the church, 25 of which I became a minister according to the divine office which was given to me for you, to make the word of God fully known, 26 the mystery hidden for ages and generations but now made manifest to his saints. 27 To them God chose to make known how great among the Gentiles are the riches of the glory of this mystery, which is Christ in you, the hope of glory. 28 Him we proclaim, warning every man and teaching every man in all wisdom, that we may present every man mature in Christ. 29 For this I toil, striving with all the energy which he mightily inspires within me.

2 For I want you to know how greatly I strive for you, and for those at La-odice′a, and for all who have not seen my face, 2 that their hearts may be encouraged as they are knit together in love, to have all the riches of assured understanding and the knowledge of God's mystery, of Christ, 3 in whom are hid all the treasures of wisdom and knowledge.

1 Thes 2:1-8 (§277)

2 For you yourselves know, brethren, that our visit to you was not in vain; 2 but though we had already suffered and been shamefully treated at Philippi, as you know, we had courage in our God to declare to you the gospel of God in the face of great opposition. 3 For our appeal does not spring from error or uncleanness, nor is it made with guile; 4 but just as we have been approved by God to be entrusted with the gospel, so we speak, not to please men, but to please God who tests our hearts. 5 For we never used either words of flattery, as you know, or a cloak for greed, as God is witness; 6 nor did we seek glory from men, whether from you or from others, though we might have made demands as apostles of Christ. 7 But we were gentle among you, like a nurse taking care of her children. 8 So, being affectionately desirous of you, we were ready to share with you not only the gospel of God but also our own selves, because you had become very dear to us.

Eph (cont)

might now be made known to the principalities and powers in the heavenly places. 11 This was according to the eternal purpose which he has realized in Christ Jesus our Lord, 12 in whom we have boldness and confidence of access through our faith in him. 13 So I ask you not to lose heart over what I am suffering for you, which is your glory.

159

Rom 5:1-5 (§20)

5 Therefore, since we are justified by faith, we have peace with God through our Lord Jesus Christ. 2 Through him we have obtained access to this grace in which we stand, and we rejoice in our hope of sharing the glory of God. 3 More than that, we rejoice in our sufferings, knowing that suffering produces endurance, 4 and endurance produces character, and character produces hope, 5 and hope does not disappoint us, because God's love has been poured into our hearts through the Holy Spirit which has been given to us.

Rom 8:31-39 (§34)

31 What then shall we say to this? If God is for us, who is against us? 32 He who did not spare his own Son but gave him up for us all, will he not also give us all things with him? 33 Who shall bring any charge against God's elect? It is God who justifies; 34 who is to condemn? Is it Christ Jesus, who died, yes, who was raised from the dead, who is at the right hand of God, who indeed intercedes for us? 35 Who shall separate us from the love of Christ? Shall

1 Cor 4:8-13 (§85)

8 Already you are filled! Already you have become rich! Without us you have become kings! And would that you did reign, so that we might share the rule with you! 9 For I think that God has exhibited us apostles as last of all, like men sentenced to death; because we have become a spectacle to the world, to angels and to men. 10 We are fools for Christ's sake, but you are wise in Christ. We are weak, but you are strong. You are held in honor, but we in disrepute. 11 To the present hour we hunger and thirst, we are ill-clad and buffeted and homeless, 12 and we labor, working with our own hands. When reviled, we bless; when persecuted, we endure; 13 when slandered, we try to conciliate; we have become, and are now, as the refuse of the world, the offscouring of all things.

tribulation, or distress, or persecution, or famine, or nakedness, or peril, or sword? 36As it is written,
"For thy sake we are being killed all the day long;
we are regarded as sheep to be

2 Cor 4:7-12

7 But we have this treasure in earthen vessels, to show that the transcendent power belongs to God and not to us. 8 We are afflicted in every way, but not crushed; perplexed, but not driven to despair; 9 persecuted, but not forsaken; struck down, but not destroyed; 10 always carrying in the body the death of Jesus, so that the life of Jesus may also be manifested in our bodies. 11 For while we live we are always being given up to death for Jesus' sake, so that the life of Jesus may be manifested in our mortal flesh. 12 So death is at work in us, but life in you.

slaughtered."

37 No, in all these things we are more than conquerors through him who loved us. 38 For I am sure that neither death, nor life, nor angels, nor principalities, nor things present, nor things to come, nor powers, 39 nor height, nor depth, nor anything else in all creation, will be able to separate us from the love of God in Christ Jesus our Lord.

▶4:7 2 Tim 2:20
20 In a great house there are not only vessels of gold and silver but also of wood and earthenware, and some for noble use, some for ignoble.

▶4:7-12 11:24-29   24 Five times I have received at the hands of the Jews the forty lashes less one. 25 Three times I have been beaten with rods; once I was stoned. Three times I have been shipwrecked; a night and a day I have been adrift at sea; 26 on frequent journeys, in danger from rivers, danger from robbers, danger from my own

people, danger from Gentiles, danger in the city, danger in the wilderness, danger at sea, danger from false brethren; 27 in toil and hardship, through many a sleepless night, in hunger and thirst, often without food, in cold and exposure. 28And, apart from other things, there is the daily pressure upon me of my anxiety for all the

churches. 29 Who is weak, and I am not weak? Who is made to fall, and I am not indignant?

6:4-10 4 but as servants of God we commend ourselves in every way: through great endurance, in afflictions, hardships, calamities, 5 beatings, imprisonments, tumults, labors, watching, hunger; 6 by purity, knowledge, forbearance, kindness, the Holy Spirit,

genuine love, 7 truthful speech, and the power of God; with the weapons of righteousness for the right hand and for the left; 8 in honor and dishonor, in ill repute and good repute. We are treated as impostors, and yet are true; 9 as unknown, and yet well known; as dying,

160. We believe and so we speak

160

Rom 6:1-10 (§23)

6 What shall we say then? Are we to continue in sin that grace may abound? 2 By no means! How can we who died to sin still live in it? 3 Do you not know that all of us who have been baptized into Christ Jesus were baptized into his death? 4 We were buried therefore with him by baptism into death, so that as Christ was raised from the dead by the glory of the Father, we too might walk in newness of life.

5 For if we have been united with him in a death like his, we shall certainly be united with him in a resurrection like his. 6 We know that our old self was crucified with him so that the sinful body might be destroyed, and we might no longer be enslaved to sin. 7 For he who has died is freed from sin. 8 But if we have died with Christ, we believe that we shall also live with him. 9 For we know that Christ being raised from the dead will never die again; death no longer has dominion over him. 10 The death he died he died to sin, once for all, but the life he lives he lives to God.

1 Cor 15:12-19 (§132)

12 Now if Christ is preached as raised from the dead, how can some of you say that there is no resurrection of the dead? 13 But if there is no resurrection of the dead, then Christ has not been raised; 14 if Christ has not been raised, then our preaching is in vain and your faith is in vain. 15 We are even found to be misrepresenting God, because we testified of God that he raised Christ, whom he did not raise if it is true that the dead are not raised. 16 For if the dead are not raised, then Christ has not been raised. 17 If Christ has not been raised, your faith is futile and you are still in your sins. 18 Then those also who have fallen asleep in Christ have perished. 19 If for this life only we have hoped in Christ, we are of all men most to be pitied.

2 Cor 4:13-15

13 Since we have the same spirit of faith as he had who wrote, "I believed, and so I spoke," we too believe, and so we speak, 14 knowing that he who raised the Lord Jesus will raise us also with Jesus and bring us with you into his presence. 15 For it is all for your sake, so that as grace extends to more and more people it may increase thanksgiving, to the glory of God.

▶4:14 Acts 2:24   24 But God raised him up, having loosed the pangs of death, because it was not possible for him to be held by it.

▶4:13-15 Rom 8:11
11 If the Spirit of him who raised Jesus from the dead dwells in you, he who raised Christ Jesus from the dead will give life to your mortal bodies also through his Spirit which dwells in you.

1 Thes 1:9-10 9 For they themselves report concerning us what a welcome we had among you, and how you turned to God from idols, to serve a living and true God, 10 and to wait for his Son from heaven, whom he raised from the dead, Jesus who delivers us from the wrath to come.

▶4:13 Ps 116:10
10 I kept my faith, even when I said, "I am greatly afflicted";

159

Phil 1:12-18 (§239)

12 I want you to know, brethren, that what has happened to me has really served to advance the gospel, 13 so that it has become known throughout the whole praetorian guard and to all the rest that my imprisonment is for Christ; 14 and most of the brethren have been made confident in the Lord because of my imprisonment, and are much more bold to speak the word of God without fear.

15 Some indeed preach Christ from envy and rivalry, but others from good will. 16 The latter do it out of love, knowing that I am put here for the defense of the gospel; 17 the former proclaim Christ out of partisanship, not sincerely but thinking to afflict me in my imprisonment. 18 What then? Only that in every way, whether in pretense or in truth, Christ is proclaimed; and in that I rejoice.

Phil 1:19-26 (§240)

19 Yes, and I shall rejoice. For I know that through your prayers and the help of the Spirit of Jesus Christ this will turn out for my deliverance, 20 as it is my eager expectation and hope that I shall not be at all ashamed, but that with full courage now as always Christ will be honored in my body, whether by life or by death. 21 For to me to live is Christ, and to die is gain. 22 If it is to be life in the flesh, that means fruitful labor for me. Yet which I shall choose I cannot tell. 23 I am hard pressed between the two. My desire is to depart and be with Christ, for that is far better. 24 But to remain in the flesh is more necessary on your account. 25 Convinced of this, I know that I shall remain and continue with you all, for your progress and joy in the faith, 26 so that in me you may have ample cause to glory in Christ Jesus, because of my coming to you again.

and behold we live; as punished, and yet not killed; 10 as sorrowful, yet always rejoicing; as poor, yet making many rich; as having nothing, and yet possessing everything.

Phil 3:10-11   10 that I may know him and the power of his resurrection, and may share his sufferings, becoming like him in his death, 11 that if possible I may attain the resurrection from the dead.

▶ 4:8 2 Cor 1:8-10
8 For we do not want you to be ignorant, brethren, of the affliction we experienced in Asia; for we were so utterly, unbearably crushed that we despaired of life itself. 9 Why, we felt that we had received the sentence of death; but that was to make us rely not on ourselves but on God who raises the dead; 10 he delivered us from so deadly a peril, and he will deliver us; on him we have set our hope that he will deliver us again.

▶4:10 1 Cor 15:31
31 I protest, brethren, by my pride in you which I have in Christ Jesus our Lord, I die every day!

160. We believe and so we speak

160

Phil 3:17-21 (§249)

17 Brethren, join in imitating me, and mark those who so live as you have an example in us. 18 For many, of whom I have often told you and now tell you even with tears, live as enemies of the cross of Christ. 19 Their end is destruction, their god is the belly, and they glory in their shame, with minds set on earthly things. 20 But our commonwealth is in heaven, and from it we await a Savior, the Lord Jesus Christ, 21 who will change our lowly body to be like his glorious body, by the power which enables him even to subject all things to himself.

Col 3:1-4 (§265)

3 If then you have been raised with Christ, seek the things that are above, where Christ is, seated at the right hand of God. 2 Set your minds on things that are above, not on things that are on earth. 3 For you have died, and your life is hid with Christ in God. 4 When Christ who is our life appears, then you also will appear with him in glory.

1 Thes 4:13-18 (§286)

13 But we would not have you ignorant, brethren, concerning those who are asleep, that you may not grieve as others do who have no hope. 14 For since we believe that Jesus died and rose again, even so, through Jesus, God will bring with him those who have fallen asleep. 15 For this we declare to you by the word of the Lord, that we who are alive, who are left until the coming of the Lord, shall not precede those who have fallen asleep. 16 For the Lord himself will descend from heaven with a cry of command, with the archangel's call, and with the sound of the trumpet of God. And the dead in Christ will rise first; 17 then we who are alive, who are left, shall be caught up together with them in the clouds to meet the Lord in the air; and so we shall always be with the Lord. 18 Therefore comfort one another with these words.

161

Rom 8:18-25 (§31)

18 I consider that the sufferings of this present time are not worth comparing with the glory that is to be revealed to us. 19 For the creation waits with eager longing for the revealing of the sons of God; 20 for the creation was subjected to futility, not of its own will but by the will of him who subjected it in hope; 21 because the creation itself will be set free from its bondage to decay and obtain the glorious liberty of the children of God. 22 We know that the whole creation has been groaning in travail together until now; 23 and not only the creation, but we ourselves, who have the first fruits of the Spirit, groan inwardly as we wait for adoption as sons, the redemption of our bodies. 24 For in this hope we were saved. Now hope that is seen is not hope. For who hopes for what he sees? 25 But if we hope for what we do not see, we wait for it with patience.

1 Cor 15:51-58 (§137)

51 Lo! I tell you a mystery. We shall not all sleep, but we shall all be changed, 52 in a moment, in the twinkling of an eye, at the last trumpet. For the trumpet will sound, and the dead will be raised imperishable, and we shall be changed. 53 For this perishable nature must put on the imperishable, and this mortal nature must put on immortality. 54 When the perishable puts on the imperishable, and the mortal puts on immortality, then shall come to pass the saying that is written:
"Death is swallowed up in victory."
55 "O death, where is thy victory?
O death, where is thy sting?"
56 The sting of death is sin, and the power of sin is the law. 57 But thanks be to God, who gives us the victory through our Lord Jesus Christ.
58 Therefore, my beloved brethren, be steadfast, immovable, always abounding in the work of the Lord, knowing that in the Lord your labor is not in vain.

2 Cor 4:16-5:5

16 So we do not lose heart. Though our outer nature is wasting away, our inner nature is being renewed every day. 17 For this slight momentary affliction is preparing for us an eternal weight of glory beyond all comparison, 18 because we look not to the things that are seen but to the things that are unseen; for the things that are seen are transient, but the things that are unseen are eternal.

5 For we know that if the earthly tent we live in is destroyed, we have a building from God, a house not made with hands, eternal in the heavens. 2 Here indeed we groan, and long to put on our heavenly dwelling, 3 so that by putting it on we may not be found naked. 4 For while we are still in this tent, we sigh with anxiety; not that we would be unclothed, but that we would be further clothed, so that what is mortal may be swallowed up by life. 5 He who has prepared us for this very thing is God, who has given us the Spirit as a guarantee.

Eph 3:14-19 (§223)

14 For this reason I bow my knees before the Father, 15 from whom every family in heaven and on earth is named, 16 that according to the riches of his glory he may grant you to be strengthened with might through his Spirit in the inner man, 17 and that Christ may dwell in your hearts through faith; that you, being rooted and grounded in love, 18 may have power to comprehend with all the saints what is the breadth and length and height and depth, 19 and to know the love of Christ which surpasses knowledge, that you may be filled with all the fulness of God.

▶ 5:1 Acts 7:48
48 Yet the Most High does not dwell in houses made with hands; as the prophet says,

▶ 4:18 Col 1:15-16
15 He is the image of the invisible God, the first-born of all creation; 16 for in him all things were created, in heaven and on earth, visible and invisible, whether thrones or dominions or principalities or authorities—all things were created through him and for him.

▶ 5:2 Phil 1:23-24
23 I am hard pressed between the two. My desire is to depart and be with Christ, for that is far better. 24 But to remain in the flesh is more necessary on your account.

▶ 5:5 1:22
22 he has put his seal upon us and given us his Spirit in our hearts as a guarantee.

Rom 8:23
23 and not only the creation, but we ourselves, who have the first fruits of the Spirit, groan inwardly as we wait for adoption as sons, the redemption of our bodies.

162. We walk by faith, not by sight

162

Rom 2:6-16 (§8)

6 For he will render to every man according to his works: 7 to those who by patience in well-doing seek for glory and honor and immortality, he will give eternal life; 8 but for those who are factious and do not obey the truth, but obey wickedness, there will be wrath and fury. 9 There will be tribulation and distress for every human being who does evil, the Jew first and also the Greek, 10 but glory and honor and peace for every one who does good, the Jew first and also the Greek. 11 For God shows no partiality.
12 All who have sinned without the law will also perish without the law, and all who have sinned under the law will be judged by the law. 13 For it is not the hearers of the law who are righteous before God, but the doers of the law who will be justified. 14 When Gentiles who have not the law do by nature what the law requires, they are a law to themselves, even though they do not have the law. 15 They show that what the law requires is written on their hearts, while their conscience also bears witness and their conflicting thoughts accuse or

perhaps excuse them 16 on that day when, according to my gospel, God judges the secrets of men by Christ Jesus.

2 Cor 5:6-10

6 So we are always of good courage; we know that while we are at home in the body we are away from the Lord, 7 for we walk by faith, not by sight. 8 We are of good courage, and we would rather be away from the body and at home with the Lord. 9 So whether we are at home or away, we make it our aim to please him. 10 For we must all appear before the judgment seat of Christ, so that each one may receive good or evil, according to what he has done in the body.

▶ 5:10 Acts 10:42
42 And he commanded us to preach to the people, and to testify that he is the one ordained by God to be judge of the living and the dead.

▶ 5:6-10 Rom 14:10-12
10 Why do you pass judgment on your brother? Or you, why do you despise your brother? For we shall all stand before the judgment seat of God; 11 for it is written,
"As I live, says the Lord, every knee shall bow to me,
and every tongue shall give praise to

God."
12 So each of us shall give account of himself to God.

▶ 5:7 Rom 8:24-25
24 For in this hope we were saved. Now hope that is seen is not hope. For who hopes for what he sees? 25 But if we hope for what we do not see, we wait for it with patience.

1 Cor 13:12
12 For now we see in a mirror dimly, but then face to face. Now I know in part; then I shall understand fully, even as I have been fully understood.

▶ 5:10 Eph 6:8
8 knowing that whatever good any one does, he will receive the same again from the Lord, whether he is a slave or free.

— header —

Col 3:5-11 (§266)

5 Put to death therefore what is earthly in you: fornication, impurity, passion, evil desire, and covetousness, which is idolatry. 6 On account of these the wrath of God is coming. 7 In these you once walked, when you lived in them. 8 But now put them all away: anger, wrath, malice, slander, and foul talk from your mouth. 9 Do not lie to one another, seeing that you have put off the old nature with its practices 10 and have put on the new nature, which is being renewed in knowledge after the image of its creator. 11 Here there cannot be Greek and Jew, circumcised and uncircumcised, barbarian, Scyth'ian, slave, free man, but Christ is all, and in all.

161

162. We walk by faith, not by sight

162

Phil 1:19-26 (§240)

19 Yes, and I shall rejoice. For I know that through your prayers and the help of the Spirit of Jesus Christ this will turn out for my deliverance, 20 as it is my eager expectation and hope that I shall not be at all ashamed, but that with full courage now as always Christ will be honored in my body, whether by life or by death. 21 For to me to live is Christ, and to die is gain. 22 If it is to be life in the flesh, that means fruitful labor for me. Yet which I shall choose I cannot tell. 23 I am hard pressed between the two. My desire is to depart and be with Christ, for that is far better. 24 But to remain in the flesh is more necessary on your account. 25 Convinced of this, I know that I shall remain and continue with you all, for your progress and joy in the faith, 26 so that in me you may have ample cause to glory in Christ Jesus, because of my coming to you again.

1 Cor 3:8

8 He who plants and he who waters are equal, and each shall receive his wages according to his labor.

163

1 Cor 4:1-5 (§83)

4 This is how one should regard us, as servants of Christ and stewards of the mysteries of God. 2 Moreover it is required of stewards that they be found trustworthy. 3 But with me it is a very small thing that I should be judged by you or by any human court. I do not even judge myself. 4 I am not aware of anything against myself, but I am not thereby acquitted. It is the Lord who judges me. 5 Therefore do not pronounce judgment before the time, before the Lord comes, who will bring to light the things now hidden in darkness and will disclose the purposes of the heart. Then every man will receive his commendation from God.

2 Cor 5:11-13

11 Therefore, knowing the fear of the Lord, we persuade men; but what we are is known to God, and I hope it is known also to your conscience. 12 We are not commending ourselves to you again but giving you cause to be proud of us, so that you may be able to answer those who pride themselves on a man's position and not on his heart. 13 For if we are beside ourselves, it is for God; if we are in our right mind, it is for you.

▶ 5:12 10:12,
12 Not that we venture to class or compare ourselves with some of those who commend themselves. But when they measure themselves by one another, and compare themselves with one another, they are without understanding.

3:1
Are we beginning to commend ourselves again? Or do we need, as some do, letters of recommendation to you, or from you?

▶ 5:13 1 Cor 14:1-5
Make love your aim, and earnestly desire the spiritual gifts, especially that you may prophesy. 2 For one who speaks in a tongue speaks not to men but to God; for no one understands him, but he utters mysteries in the Spirit. 3 On the other hand, he who prophesies speaks to men for their upbuilding and encouragement and consolation. 4 He who speaks in a tongue edifies himself, but he who prophesies edifies the church. 5 Now I want you all to speak in tongues, but even more to prophesy. He who prophesies is greater than he who speaks in tongues, unless some one interprets, so that the church may be edified.

1 Cor 14:18
18 I thank God that I speak in tongues more than you all;

2 Cor 12:11-13
11All these are inspired by one and the same Spirit, who apportions to each one individually as he wills.
12 For just as the body is one and has many members, and all the members of the body, though many, are one body, so it is with Christ. 13 For by one Spirit we were all baptized into one body—Jews or Greeks, slaves or free—and all were made to drink of one Spirit.

164. Ministry of reconciliation

164

Rom 5:6-11 (§21)

6 While we were still weak, at the right time Christ died for the ungodly. 7 Why, one will hardly die for a righteous man—though perhaps for a good man one will dare even to die. 8 But God shows his love for us in that while we were yet sinners Christ died for us. 9 Since, therefore, we are now justified by his blood, much more shall we be saved by him from the wrath of God. 10 For if while we were enemies we were reconciled to God by the death of his Son, much more, now that we are reconciled, shall we be saved by his life. 11 Not only so, but we also rejoice in God through our Lord Jesus Christ, through whom we have now received our reconciliation.

Rom 6:1-10 (§23)

6 What shall we say then? Are we to continue in sin that grace may abound? 2 By no means! How can we who died to sin still live in it? 3 Do you not know that all of us who have been baptized into Christ Jesus were baptized into his death? 4 We were buried therefore with him by baptism into death, so that as Christ was raised from the dead by the glory of the Father, we too might walk in newness of life.

5 For if we have been united with him in a death like his, we shall certainly be united with him in a resurrection like his. 6 We know that our old self was crucified with him so that the sinful body might be destroyed, and we

1 Cor 15:1-11 (§131)

15 Now I would remind you, brethren, in what terms I preached to you the gospel, which you received, in which you stand, 2 by which you are saved, if you hold it fast —unless you believed in vain.

3 For I delivered to you as of first importance what I also received, that Christ died for our sins in accordance with the scriptures, 4 that he was buried, that he was raised on the third day in accordance with the scriptures, 5 and that he appeared to Cephas, then to the twelve. 6 Then he appeared to more than five hundred brethren at one time, most of whom are still alive, though some have fallen asleep. 7 Then he appeared to James, then to all the apostles. 8 Last of all, as to one untimely born, he appeared also to me. 9 For I am the least of the apostles; unfit to be called an apostle, because I persecuted the church of God. 10 But by the grace of God I am what I am, and his grace toward me was not in vain. On the contrary, I worked harder than any of them, though it was not I, but the grace of God which is with me. 11 Whether then it was I or they, so we preach and so you believed.

2 Cor 5:14-21

14 For the love of Christ controls us, because we are convinced that one has died for all; therefore all have died. 15And he died for all, that those who live might live no longer for themselves but for him who for their sake died and was raised.

16 From now on, therefore, we regard no one from a human point of view; even though we once regarded Christ from a human point of view, we regard him thus no longer. 17 Therefore, if any one is in Christ, he is a new creation; the old has passed away, behold, the new has come. 18All this is from God, who through Christ reconciled us to himself and gave us the ministry of reconciliation; 19that is, in Christ God was reconciling the world to himself, not counting their trespasses against them, and entrusting to us the message of reconciliation. 20 So we are ambassadors for Christ, God making his appeal through us. We beseech you on behalf of Christ, be reconciled to God. 21 For our sake he made him to be sin who knew no sin, so that in him we might become the righteousness of God.

Rom 11:13-16 (§47)
13 Now I am speaking to you Gentiles. Inasmuch then as I am an apostle to the Gentiles, I magnify my ministry 14 in order to make my fellow Jews jealous, and thus save some of them. 15 For if their rejection means the reconciliation of the world, what will

Gal 2:15-21 (§199) 15 We ourselves, who are Jews by birth and not Gentile sinners, 16 yet who know that a man is not justified by works of the law but through faith in Jesus Christ, even we have believed in Christ Jesus, in order to be justified by faith in Christ, and not by works of the law, because by works of the law shall no one be justified. 17 But if, in our endeavor to be justified in Christ, we ourselves were found to be sinners, is Christ then an agent of sin? Certainly not! 18 But if I build up again those things which I tore down, then I prove myself a transgressor. 19 For I through the law died to the law, that I might live to God. 20 I have been crucified with Christ; it is no longer I who live, but Christ who lives in me; and the life I now live in the flesh I live

by faith in the Son of God, who loved me and gave himself for me. 21 I do not nullify the grace of God; for if justification were through the law, then Christ died to no purpose.

on behalf of Christ, be reconciled to God. 21 For our sake he made him to be sin who knew no sin, so that in him we might become the righteousness of God.

their acceptance mean but life from the dead? 16 If the dough offered as first fruits is holy, so is the whole lump; and if the root is holy, so are the branches.

again; death no longer has dominion over him. 10 The death he died he died to sin, once for all, but the life he lives he lives to God.

sinful body might be destroyed, and we

▶ 5:18 Acts 20:24
24 But I do not account my life of any value nor as precious to myself, if only I may accomplish my course and the ministry which I received from the Lord Jesus, to testify to the gospel of the grace of God.

▶ 5:21 Acts 3:14
14 But you denied the Holy and Righteous One, and asked for a murderer to be granted to you,

▶5:14-15 Rom 6:11,
11 So you also must consider yourselves dead to sin and alive to God in Christ Jesus.

7:4
4 Likewise, my brethren, you have died to the law through the body of Christ, so that you may belong to another, to him who has been raised from the dead in order that we may bear fruit for God.

▶ 5:16 1 Cor 3:1-4
But I, brethren, could not address you as spiritual men, but as men of the flesh, as babes in Christ. 2 I fed you with milk, not solid food; for you were not ready for it; and even yet you are not ready, 3 for you are still of the flesh. For while there is jealousy and strife among you, are you not of the

flesh, and behaving like ordinary men? 4 For when one says, "I belong to Paul," and another, "I belong to Apol'los," are you not merely men?

▶ 5:17 Gal 6:15
15 For neither circumcision counts for anything, nor uncircumcision, but a new creation.

Eph 4:24
24 and put on the new nature, created after the likeness of God in true righteousness and holiness.

164. Ministry of reconciliation

164

Col 1:15-20 (§258)

15 He is the image of the invisible God, the first-born of all creation; 16 for in him all things were created, in heaven and on earth, visible and invisible, whether thrones or dominions or principalities or authorities—all things were created through him and for him. 17 He is before all things, and in him all things hold together. 18 He is the head of the body, the church; he is the beginning, the first-born from the dead, that in everything he might be pre-eminent. 19 For in him all the fulness of God was pleased to dwell, 20 and through him to reconcile to himself all things, whether on earth or in heaven, making peace by the blood of his cross.

▶ 5:20 Eph 6:20

20 for which I am an ambassador in chains; that I may declare it boldly, as I ought to speak.

▶ 5:21 1 Cor 1:30-31

30 He is the source of your life in Christ Jesus, whom God made our wisdom, our righteousness and sanctification and redemption; 31 therefore, as it is written, "Let him who boasts, boast of the Lord."

Gal 3:10-13

10 For all who rely on works of the law are under a curse; for it is written, "Cursed be every one who does not abide by all things written in the book of the law, and do them." 11 Now it is evident that no man is justified before God by the law; for "He who through faith is righteous shall live"; 12 but the law does not rest on faith, for "He who does them shall live by them." 13 Christ redeemed us from the curse of the law, having become a curse for us—for it is written, "Cursed be every one who hangs on a tree"—

165

Rom 5:1-5 (§20)

5 Therefore, since we are justified by faith, we have peace with God through our Lord Jesus Christ. 2 Through him we have obtained access to this grace in which we stand, and we rejoice in our hope of sharing the glory of God. 3 More than that, we rejoice in our sufferings, knowing that suffering produces endurance, 4 and endurance produces character, and character produces hope, 5 and hope does not disappoint us, because God's love has been poured into our hearts through the Holy Spirit which has been given to us.

Rom 8:31-39 (§34)

31 What then shall we say to this? If God is for us, who is against us? 32 He who did not spare his own Son but gave him up for us all, will he not also give us all things with him? 33 Who shall bring any charge against God's elect? It is God who justifies; 34 who is to condemn? Is it Christ Jesus, who died, yes, who was raised from the dead, who is at the right hand of God, who indeed intercedes for us? 35 Who shall separate us from the love of Christ? Shall tribulation, or distress, or persecution, or famine, or nakedness, or peril, or sword? 36 As it is written,

"For thy sake we are being killed all
    the day long;
we are regarded as sheep to be
    slaughtered."

37 No, in all these things we are more than conquerors through him who loved us. 38 For I am sure that neither

1 Cor 4:8-13 (§85)

8 Already you are filled! Already you have become rich! Without us you have become kings! And would that you did reign, so that we might share the rule with you! 9 For I think that God has exhibited us apostles as last of all, like men sentenced to death; because we have become a spectacle to the world, to angels and to men. 10 We are fools for Christ's sake, but you are wise in Christ. We are weak, but you are strong. You are held in honor, but we in disrepute. 11 To the present hour we hunger and thirst, we are ill-clad and buffeted and homeless, 12 and we labor, working with our own hands. When reviled, we bless; when persecuted, we endure; 13 when slandered, we try to conciliate; we have become, and are now, as the refuse of the world, the offscouring of all things.

death, nor life, nor angels, nor principalities, nor things present, nor things to come, nor powers, 39 nor height, nor depth, nor anything else in all creation, will be able to separate us from the love of God in Christ Jesus our Lord.

2 Cor 6:1-10

6 Working together with him, then, we entreat you not to accept the grace of God in vain. 2 For he says,
"At the acceptable time I have listened to you,
and helped you on the day of salvation."
Behold, now is the acceptable time; behold, now is the day of salvation. 3 We put no obstacle in any one's way, so that no fault may be found with our ministry, 4 but as servants of God we commend ourselves in every way: through great endurance, in afflictions, hardships, calamities, 5 beatings, imprisonments, tumults, labors, watching, hunger; 6 by purity, knowledge, forbearance, kindness, the Holy Spirit, genuine love, 7 truthful speech, and the power of God; with the weapons of righteousness for the right hand and for the left; 8 in honor and dishonor, in ill repute and good repute. We are treated as impostors, and yet are true; 9 as unknown, and yet well known; as dying, and behold we live; as punished, and yet not killed; 10 as sorrowful, yet always rejoicing; as poor, yet making many rich; as having nothing, and yet possessing everything.

Gal 5:16-26 (§213)

16 But I say, walk by the Spirit, and do not gratify the desires of the flesh. 17 For the desires of the flesh are against the Spirit, and the desires of the Spirit are against the flesh; for these are opposed to each other, to prevent you from doing what you would. 18 But if you are led by the Spirit you are not under the law. 19 Now the works of the flesh are plain: fornication, impurity, licentiousness, 20 idolatry, sorcery, enmity, strife, jealousy, anger, selfishness, dissension, party spirit, 21 envy, drunkenness, carousing, and the like. I warn you, as I warned you before, that those who do such things shall not inherit the kingdom of God. 22 But the fruit of the Spirit is love, joy, peace, patience, kindness, goodness, faithfulness, 23 gentleness, self-control; against such there is no law. 24 And those who belong to Christ Jesus have crucified the flesh with its passions and desires.

25 If we live by the Spirit, let us also walk by the Spirit. 26 Let us have no self-conceit, no provoking of one another, no envy of one another.

Eph 4:1-10 (§225)

4 I therefore, a prisoner for the Lord, beg you to lead a life worthy of the calling to which you have been called, 2 with all lowliness and meekness, with patience, forbearing one another in love, 3 eager to maintain the unity of the Spirit in the bond of peace. 4 There is one body and one Spirit, just as you were called to the one hope that belongs to your call, 5 one Lord, one faith, one baptism, 6 one God and Father of us all, who is above all and through all and in all. 7 But grace was given to each of us according to the measure of Christ's gift. 8 Therefore it is said,
"When he ascended on high he led a
    host of captives,
and he gave gifts to men."
9 (In saying, "He ascended," what does it mean but that he had also descended into the lower parts of the earth? 10 He who descended is he who also ascended far above all the heavens, that he might fill all things.)

▶ 6:4 Acts 9:16,
16 So it depends not upon man's will or exertion, but upon God's mercy.
2 Tim 2:24-25
24 And the Lord's servant must not be quarrelsome but kindly to every one, an apt teacher, forbearing, 25 correcting his opponents with gentleness. God may perhaps grant that they will repent and come to know the truth,

▶ 6:5 Acts 16:23   23 And wher they had inflicted many blows upon them, they threw them into prison, charging the jailer to keep them safely.
▶ 6:10 Acts 3:6
6 But Peter said, "I have no silver and gold, but I give you what I have; in the name of Jesus Christ of Nazareth, walk."

▶ 6:6-10 11:24-29   24 Five times I have received at the hands of the Jews the forty lashes less one. 25 Three times I have been beaten with rods; once I was stoned. Three times I have been shipwrecked; a night and a day I have been adrift at sea; 26 on frequent journeys, in danger from rivers, danger from robbers, danger from my own people, danger from Gentiles, danger in the city, danger in the wilderness, danger at sea, danger from false brethren; 27 in toil and hardship,

through many a sleepless night, in hunger and thirst, often without food, in cold and exposure. 28 And, apart from other things, there is the daily pressure upon me of my anxiety for all the churches. 29 Who is weak, and I am not weak? Who is made to fall, and I am not indignant?

4:7-12
7 But we have this treasure in earthen vessels, to show that the transcendent power belongs to God and not to us. 8 We are afflicted in every way, but not crushed; perplexed, but not driven to despair; 9 persecuted, but not forsaken; struck down, but not destroyed; 10 always carrying in the body

the death of Jesus, so that the life of Jesus may also be manifested in our bodies. 11 For while we live we are always being given up to death for Jesus' sake, so that the life of Jesus may be manifested in our mortal flesh. 12 So death is at work in us, but life in you.

166. Widen your hearts

166

1 Cor 4:14-21 (§86)

14 I do not write this to make you ashamed, but to admonish you as my beloved children. 15 For though you have countless guides in Christ, you do not have many fathers. For I became your father in Christ Jesus through the gospel. 16 I urge you, then, be imitators of me. 17 Therefore I sent to you Timothy, my beloved and faithful child in the Lord, to remind you of my ways in Christ, as I teach them everywhere in every church. 18 Some are arrogant, as though I were not coming to you. 19 But I will come to you soon, if the Lord wills, and I will find out not the talk of these arrogant people but their power. 20 For the kingdom of God does

2 Cor 6:11-13

11 Our mouth is open to you, Corinthians; our heart is wide. 12 You are not restricted by us, but you are restricted in your own affections. 13 In return—I speak as to children—widen your hearts also.

not consist in talk but in power. 21 What do you wish? Shall I come to you with a rod, or with love in a spirit of gentleness?

1 Cor 3:1-4 (§78)

3 But I, brethren, could not address you as spiritual men, but as men of the flesh, as babes in Christ. 2 I fed you with milk, not solid food; for you were not ready for it; and even yet you are

not ready, 3 for you are still of the flesh. For while there is jealousy and strife among you, are you not of the flesh, and behaving like ordinary men? 4 For when one says, "I belong to Paul," and another, "I belong to Apol'los," are you not merely men?

▶ 6:13 Heb 5:13-14   13 for every one who lives on milk is unskilled in the word of righteousness, for he is a child. 14 But solid food is for the mature, for those who have their faculties trained by practice to distinguish good from evil.

1 Pet 2:2
2 Like newborn babes, long for the pure spiritual milk, that by it you may grow up to salvation;

▶ 6:13 1 Cor 14:20
20 Brethren, do not be children in your thinking; be babes in evil, but in thinking be mature.

Gal 4:19
19 My little children, with whom I am again in travail until Christ be formed in you!

Phil 2:22
22 But Timothy's worth you know, how as a son with a father he has served with me in the gospel.

Eph 5:1
Therefore be imitators of God, as beloved children.

Phil 4:8-20 (§252-253)

8 Finally, brethren, whatever is true, whatever is honorable, whatever is just, whatever is pure, whatever is lovely, whatever is gracious, if there is any excellence, if there is anything worthy of praise, think about these things. 9 What you have learned and received and heard and seen in me, do; and the God of peace will be with you.

10 I rejoice in the Lord greatly that now at length you have revived your concern for me; you were indeed concerned for me, but you had no opportunity. 11 Not that I complain of want; for I have learned, in whatever state I am, to be content. 12 I know how to be abased, and I know how to abound; in any and all circumstances I have learned the secret of facing plenty and hunger, abundance and want. 13 I can do all things in him who strengthens me.

14 Yet it was kind of you to share my trouble. 15 And you Philippians yourselves know that in the beginning of the gospel, when I left Macedo'nia, no church entered into partnership with me in giving and receiving except you only; 16 for even in Thessaloni'ca you sent me help once and again. 17 Not that I seek the gift; but I seek the fruit which increases to your credit. 18 I have received full payment, and more; I am filled, having received from Epaphrodi'tus the gifts you sent, a fragrant offering, a sacrifice acceptable and pleasing

Col 3:12-17 (§267)

12 Put on then, as God's chosen ones, holy and beloved, compassion, kindness, lowliness, meekness, and patience, 13 forbearing one another and, if one has a complaint against another, forgiving each other; as the Lord has forgiven you, so you also must forgive. 14 And above all these put on love, which binds everything together in perfect harmony. 15 And let the peace of Christ rule in your hearts, to which indeed you were called in the one body. And be thankful. 16 Let the word of Christ dwell in you richly, teach and admonish one another in all wisdom, and sing psalms and hymns and spiritual songs with thankfulness in your hearts to God. 17 And whatever you do, in word or deed, do everything in the name of the Lord Jesus, giving thanks to God the Father through him.

1 Thes 2:1-8 (§277)

2 For you yourselves know, brethren, that our visit to you was not in vain; 2 but though we had already suffered and been shamefully treated at Philippi, as you know, we had courage in our God to declare to you the gospel of God in the face of great opposition. 3 For our appeal does not spring from error or uncleanness, nor is it made with guile; 4 but just as we have been approved by God to be entrusted with the gospel, so we speak, not to please men, but to please God who tests our hearts. 5 For we never used either words of flattery, as you know, or a cloak for greed, as God is witness; 6 nor did we seek glory from men, whether from you or from others, though we might have made demands as apostles of Christ. 7 But we were gentle among you, like a nurse taking care of her children. 8 So, being affectionately desirous of you, we were ready to share with you not only the gospel of God but also our own selves, because you had become very dear to us.

to God. 19 And my God will supply every need of yours according to his riches in glory in Christ Jesus. 20 To our God and Father be glory for ever and ever. Amen.

1:8-11

8 For we do not want you to be ignorant, brethren, of the affliction we experienced in Asia; for we were so utterly, unbearably crushed that we despaired of life itself. 9 Why, we felt that we had received the sentence of death; but that was to make us rely not on ourselves but on God who raises the dead; 10 he delivered us from so deadly a peril, and he will deliver us; on him we have set our hope that he will deliver us again. 11 You also must help us by prayer, so that many will give thanks on our behalf for the blessing granted us in answer to many prayers.

8:7

32 and be kind to one another, tenderhearted, forgiving one another, as God in Christ forgave you.

▶ 6:6 Eph 4:32

7 Now as you excel in everything—in faith, in utterance, in knowledge, in all earnestness, and in your love for us—see that you excel in this gracious work also.

▶ 6:2 Is 49:8

8 Thus says the LORD:
"In a time of favor I have answered you,
  in a day of salvation I have helped you;
I have kept you and given you
  as a covenant to the people,
to establish the land,
  to apportion the desolate heritages;

166. Widen your hearts

167

Rom 16:17-20a (§67)

17 I appeal to you, brethren, to take note of those who create dissensions and difficulties, in opposition to the doctrine which you have been taught; avoid them. 18 For such persons do not serve our Lord Christ, but their own appetites, and by fair and flattering words they deceive the hearts of the simple-minded. 19 For while your obedience is known to all, so that I rejoice over you, I would have you wise as to what is good and guileless as to what is evil; 20 then the God of peace will soon crush Satan under your feet.

1 Cor 3:16-17 (§81)

16 Do you not know that you are God's temple and that God's Spirit dwells in you? 17 If any one destroys God's temple, God will destroy him. For God's temple is holy, and that temple you are.

1 Cor 5:1-5 (§87)

5 It is actually reported that there is immorality among you, and of a kind that is not found even among pagans; for a man is living with his father's wife. 2 And you are arrogant! Ought you not rather to mourn? Let him who has done this be removed from among you.

3 For though absent in body I am present in spirit, and as if present, I have already pronounced judgment 4 in the name of the Lord Jesus on the man who has done such a thing. When you are assembled, and my spirit is present, with the power of our Lord Jesus, 5 you are to deliver this man to Satan for the destruction of the flesh, that his spirit may be saved in the day of the Lord Jesus.

2 Cor 6:14-7:1

14 Do not be mismated with unbelievers. For what partnership have righteousness and iniquity? Or what fellowship has light with darkness? 15 What accord has Christ with Be'lial? Or what has a believer in common with an unbeliever? 16 What agreement has the temple of God with idols? For we are the temple of the living God; as God said,
"I will live in them and move among them,
and I will be their God,
and they shall be my people.
17 Therefore come out from them,
and be separate from them, says the Lord,
and touch nothing unclean;
18 and I will be a father to you,
and you shall be my sons and daughters,
says the Lord Almighty."

7 Since we have these promises, beloved, let us cleanse ourselves from every defilement of body and spirit, and make holiness perfect in the fear of God.

1 Cor 7:12-16 (§96)

12 "All things are lawful for me," but not all things are helpful. "All things are lawful for me," but I will not be enslaved by anything. 13 "Food is meant for the stomach and the stomach for food"—and God will destroy both one and the other. The body is not meant for immorality, but for the Lord, and the Lord for the body. 14 And God raised the Lord and will also raise us up by his power. 15 Do you not know that your bodies are members of Christ? Shall I therefore take the members of Christ and make them members of a prostitute? Never! 16 Do you not know that he who joins himself to a prostitute becomes one body with her? For, as it is written, "The two shall become one flesh." 17 But he who is united to the Lord becomes one spirit with him. 18 Shun immorality. Every other sin which a man commits is outside the body; but the immoral man sins against his own body. 19 Do you not know that your body is a temple of the Holy Spirit within you, which you have from God?

Eph 5:3-14 (§230)

3 But fornication and all impurity or covetousness must not even be named among you, as is fitting among saints. 4 Let there be no filthiness, nor silly talk, nor levity, which are not fitting; but instead let there be thanksgiving. 5 Be sure of this, that no fornicator or impure man, or one who is covetous (that is, an idolater), has any inheritance in the kingdom of Christ and of God. 6 Let no one deceive you with empty words, for it is because of these things that the wrath of God comes upon the sons of disobedience. 7 Therefore do

You are not your own; 20 you were bought with a price. So glorify God in your body.

1 Cor 5:9-13 (§89)

9 I wrote to you in my letter not to associate with immoral men; 10 not at all meaning the immoral of this world, or the greedy and robbers, or idolaters, since then you would need to go out of the world. 11 But rather I wrote to you not to associate with any one who bears the name of brother if he is guilty of immorality or greed, or is an idolater,

---

▶ 6:17 Acts 19:9
9 but when some were stubborn and disbelieved, speaking evil of the Way before the congregation, he withdrew from them, taking the disciples with him, and argued daily in the hall of Tyran'nus.

▶ 6:14 4:6
6 For it is the God who said, "Let light shine out of darkness," who has shone in our hearts to give the light of the knowledge of the glory of God in the face of Christ.

▶ 6:15 11:12-15
12 for as woman was made from man, so man is now born of woman. And all things are from God.) 13 Judge for yourselves; is it proper for a woman to pray to God with her head uncovered? 14 Does not nature itself teach you that for a man to wear long hair is degrading to him, 15 but if a woman has long hair, it is her pride? For her hair is given to her for a covering.

▶ 6:16 1 Cor 10:19-22
19 What do I imply then? That food offered to idols is anything, or that an idol is anything? 20 No, I imply that what pagans sacrifice they offer to demons and not to God. I do not want you to be partners with demons. 21 You cannot drink the cup of the Lord and the cup of demons. You cannot partake of the table of the Lord and the table of demons. 22 Shall we provoke the Lord to jealousy? Are we stronger than he?

168. You are in our hearts

168

2 Cor 7:2-4

2 Open your hearts to us; we have wronged no one, we have corrupted no one, we have taken advantage of no one. 3 I do not say this to condemn you, for I said before that you are in our hearts, to die together and to live together. 4 I have great confidence in you; I have great pride in you; I am filled with comfort. With all our affliction, I am overjoyed.

▶ 7:2 Acts 20:33
33 I coveted no one's silver or gold or apparel.

▶ 7:2 6:11-13
11 Our mouth is open to you, Corinthians; our heart is wide. 12 You are not restricted by us, but you are restricted in your own affections. 13 In return—I speak as to children—widen your hearts also.

▶ 7:4 1:3-7
3 Blessed be the God and Father of our Lord Jesus Christ, the Father of mercies and God of all comfort, 4 who comforts us in all our affliction, so that we may be able to comfort those who are in any affliction, with the comfort with which we ourselves are comforted by God. 5 For as we share abundantly in Christ's sufferings, so through Christ we share abundantly in comfort too. 6 If we are afflicted, it is for your comfort and salvation; and if we are comforted, it is for your comfort, which you experience when you patiently endure the same sufferings that we suffer. 7 Our hope for you is unshaken; for we know that as you share in our sufferings, you will also share in our comfort.

1 Cor 4:14
14 I do not write this to make you ashamed, but to admonish you as my beloved children.

§167

Eph (cont)

not associate with them, 8 for once you were darkness, but now you are light in the Lord; walk as children of light 9 (for the fruit of light is found in all that is good and right and true), 10 and try to learn what is pleasing to the Lord. 11 Take no part in the unfruitful works of darkness, but instead expose them. 12 For it is a shame even to speak of the things that they do in secret; 13 but when anything is exposed by the light it becomes visible, for anything that becomes visible is light. 14 Therefore it is said,

"Awake, O sleeper, and arise from the dead,
and Christ shall give you light."

1 Cor (cont)

reviler, drunkard, or robber—not even to eat with such a one. 12 For what have I to do with judging outsiders? Is it not those inside the church whom you are to judge? 13 God judges those outside. "Drive out the wicked person from among you."

1 Cor 6:12-20 (§92)

12 To the rest I say, not the Lord, that if any brother has a wife who is an

unbeliever, and she consents to live with him, he should not divorce her. 13 If any woman has a husband who is an unbeliever, and he consents to live with her, she should not divorce him. 14 For the unbelieving husband is consecrated through his wife, and the unbelieving wife is consecrated through her husband. Otherwise, your children would be unclean, but as it is they are holy. 15 But if the unbelieving partner desires to separate, let it be so; in such a case the brother or sister is not bound. For God has called us to peace. 16 Wife, how do you know whether you will save your husband? Husband, how do you know whether you will save your wife?

1 Thes 2:1-8 (§277)

2 For you yourselves know, brethren, that our visit to you was not in vain; 2 but though we had already suffered and been shamefully treated at Philippi, as you know, we had courage in our God to declare to you the gospel of God in the face of great opposition. 3 For our appeal does not spring from error or uncleanness, nor is it made with guile; 4 but just as we have been approved by God to be entrusted with the gospel, so we speak, not to please men, but to please God who tests our hearts. 5 For we never used either words of flattery, as you know, or a cloak for greed, as God is witness; 6 nor did we seek glory from men, whether from you or from others, though we might have made demands as apostles of Christ. 7 But we were gentle among you, like a nurse taking care of her children. 8 So, being affectionately desirous of you, we were ready to share with you not only the gospel of God but also our own selves, because you had become very dear to us.

▶6:16 Ex 25:8,

8And let them make me a sanctuary, that I may dwell in their midst.

29:45 45And I will dwell among the people of Israel, and will be their God.

Lev 26:12

12And I will walk among you, and will be your God, and you shall be my people.

Ezek 37:27

27 My dwelling place shall be with them; and I will be their God, and they shall be my people.

Jer 31:1

"At that time, says the LORD, I will be the God of all the families of Israel, and they shall be my people."

▶6:17 Is 52:11
11 Depart, depart, go out thence,
    touch no unclean thing;
go out from the midst of her, purify
    yourselves,
you who bear the vessels of the
    LORD.

▶6:18 Hos 1:10
10 Yet the number of the people of Israel shall be like the sand of the sea, which can be neither measured nor numbered; and in the place where it was said to them, "You are not my people," it shall be said to them, "Sons of the living God."

Is 43:6
6 I will say to the north, Give up,
    and to the south, Do not withhold;
bring my sons from afar
    and my daughters from the end of
    the earth,

168. You are in our hearts

§168

Phil 4:10-20 (§253)

10 I rejoice in the Lord greatly that now at length you have revived your concern for me; you were indeed concerned for me, but you had no opportunity. 11 Not that I complain of want; for I have learned, in whatever state I am, to be content. 12 I know how to be abased, and I know how to abound; in any and all circumstances I have learned the secret of facing plenty and hunger, abundance and want. 13 I can do all things in him who strengthens me.

14 Yet it was kind of you to share my trouble. 15And you Philippians yourselves know that in the beginning of the gospel, when I left Macedo′nia, no church entered into partnership with me in giving and receiving except you only; 16 for even in Thessaloni′ca you sent me help once and again. 17 Not that I seek the gift; but I seek the fruit which increases to your credit. 18 I have received full payment, and more; I am filled, having received from Epaphrodi′tus the gifts you sent, a fragrant offering, a sacrifice acceptable and pleasing to God. 19And my God will supply

every need of yours according to his riches in glory in Christ Jesus. 20 To our God and Father be glory for ever and ever. Amen.

1 Thes 2:1-8 (§277)

2 For you yourselves know, brethren, that our visit to you was not in vain; 2 but though we had already suffered and been shamefully treated at Philippi, as you know, we had courage in our God to declare to you the gospel of God in the face of great opposition. 3 For our appeal does not spring from error or uncleanness, nor is it made with guile; 4 but just as we have been approved by God to be entrusted with the gospel, so we speak, not to please men, but to please God who tests our hearts. 5 For we never used either words of flattery, as you know, or a cloak for greed, as God is witness; 6 nor did we seek glory from men, whether from you or from others, though we might have made demands as apostles of Christ. 7 But we were gentle among you, like a nurse taking care of her children. 8 So, being affectionately desirous of you, we were ready to share with you not only the gospel of God but also our own selves, because you had become very dear to us.

2 Thes 1:3-12 (§295)

3 We are bound to give thanks to God always for you, brethren, as is fitting, because your faith is growing abundantly, and the love of every one of you for one another is increasing. 4 Therefore we ourselves boast of you in the churches of God for your steadfastness and faith in all your persecutions and in the afflictions which you are enduring.

5 This is evidence of the righteous judgment of God, that you may be made worthy of the kingdom of God, for which you are suffering—6 since indeed God deems it just to repay with affliction those who afflict you, 7 and to grant rest with us to you who are afflicted, when the Lord Jesus is revealed from heaven with his mighty angels in flaming fire, 8 inflicting vengeance upon those who do not know God and upon those who do not obey the gospel of our Lord Jesus. 9 They shall suffer the punishment of eternal destruction and exclusion from the presence of the Lord and from the glory of his might, 10 when he comes on that day to be glorified in his saints, and to be marveled at in all

Phm 4-7 (§306)

4 I thank my God always when I remember you in my prayers, 5 because I hear of your love and of the faith which you have toward the Lord Jesus and all the saints, 6 and I pray that the sharing of your faith may promote the knowledge of all the good that is ours in Christ. 7 For I have derived much joy and comfort from your love, my brother, because the hearts of the saints have been refreshed through you.

who have believed, because our testimony to you was believed. 11 To this end we always pray for you, that our God may make you worthy of his call, and may fulfil every good resolve and work of faith by his power, 12 so that the name of our Lord Jesus may be glorified in you, and you in him, according to the grace of our God and the Lord Jesus Christ.

169

Rom 5:1-5 (§20)

5 Therefore, since we are justified by faith, we have peace with God through our Lord Jesus Christ. 2 Through him we have obtained access to this grace in which we stand, and we rejoice in our hope of sharing the glory of God. 3 More than that, we rejoice in our sufferings, knowing that suffering produces endurance, 4 and endurance produces character, and character produces hope, 5 and hope does not disappoint us, because God's love has been poured into our hearts through the Holy Spirit which has been given to us.

2 Cor 7:5-13a

5 For even when we came into Macedo'nia, our bodies had no rest but we were afflicted at every turn—fighting without and fear within. 6 But God, who comforts the downcast, comforted us by the coming of Titus, 7 and not only by his coming but also by the comfort with which he was comforted in you, as he told us of your longing, your mourning, your zeal for me, so that I rejoiced still more. 8 For even if I made you sorry with my letter, I do not regret it (though I did regret it), for I see that that letter grieved you, though only for a while. 9 As it is, I rejoice, not because you were grieved, but because you were grieved into repenting; for you felt a godly grief, so that you suffered no loss through us. 10 For godly grief produces a repentance that leads to salvation and brings no regret, but worldly grief produces death. 11 For see what earnestness this godly grief has produced in you, what eagerness to clear yourselves, what indignation, what alarm, what longing, what zeal, what punishment! At every point you have proved yourselves guiltless in the matter. 12 So although I wrote to you, it was not on account of the one who did the wrong, nor on account of the one who suffered the wrong, but in order that your zeal for us might be revealed to you in the sight of God. 13 Therefore we are comforted.

▶ 7:5 Acts 20:1-6

After the uproar ceased, Paul sent for the disciples and having exhorted them took leave of them and departed for Macedo'nia. 2 When he had gone through these parts and had given them much encouragement, he came to Greece. 3 There he spent three months, and when a plot was made against him by the Jews as he was about to set sail for Syria, he determined to return through Macedo'nia. 4 Sop'ater of Beroe'a, the son of Pyrrhus, accompanied him; and of the Thessalo'nians, Aristar'chus and Secun'dus; and Ga'ius of Derbe, and Timothy; and the Asians, Tych'icus and Troph'imus. 5 These went on and were waiting for us at Tro'as, 6 but we sailed away from Philippi after the days of Unleavened Bread, and in five days we came to them at Tro'as, where we stayed for seven days.

▶ 7:10 Acts 11:18

18 When they heard this they were silenced. And they glorified God, saying, "Then to the Gentiles also God has granted repentance unto life."

▶ 7:5-13 1:3-7

3 Blessed be the God and Father of our Lord Jesus Christ, the Father of mercies and God of all comfort, 4 who comforts us in all our affliction, so that we may be able to comfort those who are in any affliction, with the comfort with which we ourselves are comforted by God. 5 For as we share abundantly in Christ's sufferings, so through Christ we share abundantly in comfort too. 6 If we are afflicted, it is for your comfort and salvation; and if we are comforted, it is for your comfort, which you experience when you patiently endure the same sufferings that we suffer. 7 Our hope for you is unshaken; for we know that as you share in our sufferings, you will also share in our comfort.

170. Boasting before Titus has proved true

170

2 Cor 7:13b-16

And besides our own comfort we rejoiced still more at the joy of Titus, because his mind has been set at rest by you all. 14 For if I have expressed to him some pride in you, I was not put to shame; but just as everything we said to you was true, so our boasting before Titus has proved true. 15 And his heart goes out all the more to you, as he remembers the obedience of you all, and the fear and trembling with which you received him. 16 I rejoice, because I have perfect confidence in you.

▶ 7:14 1 Cor 15:31

31 I protest, brethren, by my pride in you which I have in Christ Jesus our Lord, I die every day!

2 Cor 7:4,

4 I have great confidence in you; I have great pride in you; I am filled with comfort. With all our affliction, I am overjoyed.

8:24,
24 So give proof, before the churches, of your love and of our boasting about you to these men.

9:2-3,
2 for I know your readiness, of which I boast about you to the people of Macedo'nia, saying that Acha'ia has been ready since last year; and your zeal has stirred up most of them. 3 But I am sending the brethren so that our boasting about you may not prove vain in this case, so that you may be ready, as I said you would be;

Phil 2:16
16 holding fast the word of life, so that in the day of Christ I may be proud that I did not run in vain or labor in vain.

▶ 7:16 Gal 5:10
10 I have confidence in the Lord that you will take no other view than mine; and he who is troubling you will bear his judgment, whoever he is.

1 Thes 2:17-3:5 (§280-281)

17 But since we were bereft of you, brethren, for a short time, in person not in heart, we endeavored the more eagerly and with great desire to see you face to face; 18 because we wanted to come to you—I, Paul, again and again—but Satan hindered us. 19 For what is our hope or joy or crown of boasting before our Lord Jesus at his coming? Is it not you? 20 For you are our glory and joy.

3 Therefore when we could bear it no longer, we were willing to be left behind at Athens alone, 2 and we sent Timothy, our brother and God's servant in the gospel of Christ, to establish you in your faith and to exhort you, 3 that no one be moved by these afflictions. You yourselves know that this is to be our lot. 4 For when we were with you, we told you beforehand that we were to suffer affliction; just as it has come to pass, and as you know. 5 For this reason, when I could bear it no longer, I sent that I might know your faith, for fear that somehow the tempter had tempted you and that our labor would be in vain.

2 Thes 2:16-17 (§298)

16 Now may our Lord Jesus Christ himself, and God our Father, who loved us and gave us eternal comfort and good hope through grace, 17 comfort your hearts and establish them in every good work and word.

▶7:11 13:1-4

This is the third time I am coming to you. Any charge must be sustained by the evidence of two or three witnesses. 2 I warned those who sinned before and all the others, and I warn them now while absent, as I did when present on my second visit, that if I come again I will not spare them—

Phil 2:12-13 (§243)

12 Therefore, my beloved, as you have always obeyed, so now, not only as in my presence but much more in my absence, work out your own salvation with fear and trembling; 13 for God is at work in you, both to will and to work for his good pleasure.

3 since you desire proof that Christ is speaking in me. He is not weak in dealing with you, but is powerful in you. 4 For he was crucified in weakness, but lives by the power of God. For we are weak in him, but in dealing with you we shall live with him by the power of God.

▶7:12 2:5-11

5 But if any one has caused pain, he has caused it not to me, but in some measure—not to put it too severely—to you all. 6 For such a one this punishment by the majority is enough; 7 so you should rather turn to forgive and comfort him, or he may be overwhelmed by excessive sorrow. 8 So I

beg you to reaffirm your love for him. 9 For this is why I wrote, that I might test you and know whether you are obedient in everything. 10 Any one whom you forgive, I also forgive. What I have forgiven, if I have forgiven anything, has been for your sake in the presence of Christ, 11 to keep Satan from gaining the advantage over us; for we are not ignorant of his designs.

1 Cor 5:1-5

It is actually reported that there is immorality among you, and of a kind that is not found even among pagans; for a man is living with his father's wife. 2 And you are arrogant! Ought you not rather to mourn? Let him who has done this be removed from among you.

3 For though absent in body I am present in spirit, and as if present, I have already pronounced judgment 4 in the name of the Lord Jesus on the man who has done such a thing. When you are assembled, and my spirit is present, with the power of our Lord Jesus, 5 you are to deliver this man to Satan for the destruction of the flesh, that his spirit may be saved in the day of the Lord Jesus.

170. Boasting before Titus has proved true

2 Thes 3:1-5 (§299)

3 Finally, brethren, pray for us, that the word of the Lord may speed on and triumph, as it did among you, 2 and that we may be delivered from wicked and evil men; for not all have faith. 3 But the Lord is faithful; he will strengthen you and guard you from evil. 4 And we have confidence in the Lord about you, that you are doing and will do the things which we command. 5 May the Lord direct your hearts to the love of God and to the steadfastness of Christ.

171

Rom 15:22-29 (§63)

22 This is the reason why I have so often been hindered from coming to you. 23 But now, since I no longer have any room for work in these regions, and since I have longed for many years to come to you, 24 I hope to see you in passing as I go to Spain, and to be sped on my journey there by you, once I have enjoyed your company for a little. 25 At present, however, I am going to Jerusalem with aid for the saints. 26 For Macedo'nia and Acha'ia have been pleased to make some contribution for the poor among the saints at Jerusalem; 27 they were pleased to do it, and indeed they are in debt to them, for if the Gentiles have come to share in their spiritual blessings, they ought also to be of service to them in material blessings. 28 When therefore I have completed this, and have delivered to them what has been raised, I shall go on by way of you to Spain; 29 and I know that when I come to you I shall come in the fulness of the blessing of Christ.

▶ 8:4 Acts 11:29 29 And the disciples determined, every one according to his ability, to send relief to the brethren who lived in Judea;

1 Cor 16:1-4 (§138)

16 Now concerning the contribution for the saints: as I directed the churches of Galatia, so you also are to do. 2 On the first day of every week, each of you is to put something aside and store it up, as he may prosper, so that contributions need not be made when I come. 3 And when I arrive, I will send those whom you accredit by letter to carry your gift to Jerusalem. 4 If it seems advisable that I should go also, they will accompany me.

▶ 8:2 Rom 12:8 8 he who exhorts, in his exhortation; he who contributes, in liberality; he who gives aid, with zeal; he who does acts of mercy, with cheerfulness.

2 Cor 8:1-7

8 We want you to know, brethren, about the grace of God which has been shown in the churches of Macedo'nia, 2 for in a severe test of affliction, their abundance of joy and their extreme poverty have overflowed in a wealth of liberality on their part. 3 For they gave according to their means, as I can testify, and beyond their means, of their own free will, 4 begging us earnestly for the favor of taking part in the relief of the saints— 5 and this, not as we expected, but first they gave themselves to the Lord and to us by the will of God. 6 Accordingly we have urged Titus that as he had already made a beginning, he should also complete among you this gracious work. 7 Now as you excel in everything—in faith, in utterance, in knowledge, in all earnestness, and in your love for us—see that you excel in this gracious work also.

▶ 8:7 1 Cor 1:5 5 that in every way you were enriched in him with all speech and all knowledge—

Gal 2:1-10 (§197)

2 Then after fourteen years I went up again to Jerusalem with Barnabas, taking Titus along with me. 2 I went up by revelation; and I laid before them (but privately before those who were of repute) the gospel which I preach among the Gentiles, lest somehow I should be running or had run in vain. 3 But even Titus, who was with me, was not compelled to be circumcised, though he was a Greek. 4 But because of false brethren secretly brought in, who slipped in to spy out our freedom which we have in Christ Jesus, that they might bring us into bondage— 5 to them we did not yield submission even for a moment, that the truth of the gospel might be preserved for you. 6 And from those who were reputed to be something (what they were makes no difference to me; God shows no partiality)—those, I say, who were of repute added nothing to me; 7 but on the contrary, when they saw that I had been entrusted with the gospel to the uncircumcised, just as Peter had been entrusted with the gospel to the circumcised 8 (for he who worked through

2 Cor 6:6-8a 6 by purity, knowledge, forbearance, kindness, the Holy Spirit, genuine love, 7 truthful speech, and the power of God; with the weapons of righteousness for the right hand and for the left; 8 in honor and dishonor, in ill repute and good repute.

Eph 4:1-10 (§225)

4 I therefore, a prisoner for the Lord, beg you to lead a life worthy of the calling to which you have been called, 2 with all lowliness and meekness, with patience, forbearing one another in love, 3 eager to maintain the unity of the Spirit in the bond of peace. 4 There is one body and one Spirit, just as you were called to the one hope that belongs to your call, 5 one Lord, one faith, one baptism, 6 one God and Father of us all, who is above all and through all and in all. 7 But grace was given to each of us according to the measure of Christ's gift. 8 Therefore it is said,

"When he ascended on high he led a host of captives, and he gave gifts to men."

9 (In saying, "He ascended," what does it mean but that he had also descended into the lower parts of the earth? 10 He who descended is he who also ascended far above all the heavens, that he might fill all things.)

Peter for the mission to the circumcised worked through me also for the Gentiles), 9 and when they perceived the

Eph 4:32 32 and be kind to one another, tenderhearted, forgiving one another, as God in Christ forgave you.

172. Complete what you began a year ago

172

Rom 15:22-29 (§63)

22 This is the reason why I have so often been hindered from coming to you. 23 But now, since I no longer have any room for work in these regions, and since I have longed for many years to come to you, 24 I hope to see you in passing as I go to Spain, and to be sped on my journey there by you, once I have enjoyed your company for a little. 25 At present, however, I am going to Jerusalem with aid for the saints. 26 For Macedo'nia and Acha'ia have been pleased to make some contribution for the poor among the saints at Jerusalem; 27 they were pleased to do it, and indeed they are in debt to them, for if the Gentiles have come to share in their spiritual blessings, they ought also to be of service to them in material blessings. 28 When therefore I have completed this, and have delivered to them what has been raised, I shall go on by way of you to Spain; 29 and I know that when I come to you I shall come in the fulness of the blessing of Christ.

▶ 8:14 Acts 4:34 34 There was not a needy person among them, for as many as were possessors of lands or houses sold them, and brought the proceeds of what was sold

1 Cor 16:1-4 (§138)

16 Now concerning the contribution for the saints: as I directed the churches of Galatia, so you also are to do. 2 On the first day of every week, each of you is to put something aside and store it up, as he may prosper, so that contributions need not be made when I come. 3 And when I arrive, I will send those whom you accredit by letter to carry your gift to Jerusalem. 4 If it seems advisable that I should go also, they will accompany me.

▶ 8:8 1 Cor 7:6, 6 I say this by way of concession, not of command.

2 Cor 8:8-15

8 I say this not as a command, but to prove by the earnestness of others that your love also is genuine. 9 For you know the grace of our Lord Jesus Christ, that though he was rich, yet for your sake he became poor, so that by his poverty you might become rich. 10 And in this matter I give my advice: it is best for you now to complete what a year ago you began not only to do but to desire, 11 so that your readiness in desiring it may be matched by your completing it out of what you have. 12 For if the readiness is there, it is acceptable according to what a man has, not according to what he has not. 13 I do not mean that others should be eased and you burdened, 14 but that as a matter of equality your abundance at the present time should supply their want, so that their abundance may supply your want, that there may be equality. 15 As it is written, "He who gathered much had nothing over, and he who gathered little had no lack."

7:10, 10 To the married I give charge, not I but the Lord, that the wife should not separate from her husband

Gal 2:1-10 (§197)

2 Then after fourteen years I went up again to Jerusalem with Barnabas, taking Titus along with me. 2 I went up by revelation; and I laid before them (but privately before those who were of repute) the gospel which I preach among the Gentiles, lest somehow I should be running or had run in vain. 3 But even Titus, who was with me, was not compelled to be circumcised, though he was a Greek. 4 But because of false brethren secretly brought in, who slipped in to spy out our freedom which we have in Christ Jesus, that they might bring us into bondage— 5 to them we did not yield submission even for a moment, that the truth of the gospel might be preserved for you. 6 And from those who were reputed to be something (what they were makes no difference to me; God shows no partiality)—those, I say, who were of repute added nothing to me; 7 but on the contrary, when they saw that I had been entrusted with the gospel to the uncircumcised, just as Peter had been entrusted with the gospel to the circumcised 8 (for he who worked through

7:12, 12 To the rest I say, not the Lord, that if any brother has a wife who is an unbeliever, and she consents to live with him, he should not divorce her.

Peter for the mission to the circumcised worked through me also for the Gentiles), 9 and when they perceived the grace that was given to me, James and Cephas and John, who were reputed to be pillars, gave to me and Barnabas the right hand of fellowship, that we should go to the Gentiles and they to the circumcised; 10 only they would have us remember the poor, which very thing I was eager to do.

Gal 6:1-6 (§214)

6 Brethren, if a man is overtaken in any trespass, you who are spiritual should restore him in a spirit of gentleness. Look to yourself, lest you too be tempted. 2 Bear one another's burdens, and so fulfil the law of Christ. 3 For if any one thinks he is something, when he is nothing, he deceives himself. 4 But let each one test his own work, and then his reason to boast will be in himself alone and not in his neighbor. 5 For each man will have to bear his own load.

6 Let him who is taught the word share all good things with him who teaches.

7:25, 25 Now concerning the unmarried, I have no command of the Lord, but I give my opinion as one who by the Lord's mercy is trustworthy.

7:35 35 I say this for your own benefit, not to lay any restraint upon you, but to promote good order and to secure your undivided devotion to the Lord.

Phil 4:8-9 (§252)

8 Finally, brethren, whatever is true, whatever is honorable, whatever is just, whatever is pure, whatever is lovely, whatever is gracious, if there is any excellence, if there is anything worthy of praise, think about these things. 9 What you have learned and received and heard and seen in me, do; and the God of peace will be with you.

Gal (cont)

grace that was given to me, James and Cephas and John, who were reputed to be pillars, gave to me and Barnabas the right hand of fellowship, that we should go to the Gentiles and they to the circumcised; 10 only they would have us remember the poor, which very thing I was eager to do.

Gal 5:16-26 (§213)

16 But I say, walk by the Spirit, and do not gratify the desires of the flesh. 17 For the desires of the flesh are against the Spirit, and the desires of the Spirit are against the flesh; for these are opposed to each other, to prevent you from doing what you would. 18 But if you are led by the Spirit you are not

Col 3:12-17 (§267)

12 Put on then, as God's chosen ones, holy and beloved, compassion, kindness, lowliness, meekness, and patience, 13 forbearing one another and, if one has a complaint against another, forgiving each other; as the Lord has forgiven you, so you also must forgive. 14 And above all these put on love, which binds everything together in perfect harmony. 15 And let the peace of Christ rule in your hearts, to which indeed you were called in the one body. And be thankful. 16 Let the word of Christ dwell in you richly, teach and admonish one another in all wisdom, and sing psalms and hymns and spiritual songs with thankfulness in your hearts to God. 17 And whatever you do, in word or deed, do everything in the name of the Lord Jesus, giving thanks to God the Father through him.

under the law. 19 Now the works of the flesh are plain: fornication, impurity, licentiousness, 20 idolatry, sorcery, enmity, strife, jealousy, anger, selfishness, dissension, party spirit, 21 envy, drunkenness, carousing, and the like. I warn

1 Thes 1:2-10 (§276)

2 We give thanks to God always for you all, constantly mentioning you in our prayers, 3 remembering before our God and Father your work of faith and labor of love and steadfastness of hope in our Lord Jesus Christ. 4 For we know, brethren beloved by God, that he has chosen you; 5 for our gospel came to you not only in word, but also in power and in the Holy Spirit and with full conviction. You know what kind of men we proved to be among you for your sake. 6 And you became imitators

you, as I warned you before, that those who do such things shall not inherit the kingdom of God. 22 But the fruit of the Spirit is love, joy, peace, patience, kindness, goodness, faithfulness, 23 gentleness, self-control; against such there is no law. 24 And those who belong to Christ Jesus have crucified the flesh with its passions and desires.

25 If we live by the Spirit, let us also walk by the Spirit. 26 Let us have no self-conceit, no provoking of one another, no envy of one another.

of us and of the Lord, for you received the word in much affliction, with joy inspired by the Holy Spirit; 7 so that you became an example to all the believers in Macedo'nia and in Acha'ia. 8 For not only has the word of the Lord sounded forth from you in Macedo'nia and Acha'ia, but your faith in God has gone forth everywhere, so that we need not say anything. 9 For they themselves report concerning us what a welcome we had among you, and how you turned to God from idols, to serve a living and true God, 10 and to wait for his Son from heaven, whom he raised from the dead, Jesus who delivers us from the wrath to come.

171

▶ 8:7 (us) *read* our love for you: p⁴⁶ B syr(pes) cop Origen(Latin); *text:* SCDG Koine Lect it vg syr(har) Ambrosiaster

172. Complete what you began a year ago

Phil 2:1-11 (§242)

2 So if there is any encouragement in Christ, any incentive of love, any participation in the Spirit, any affection and sympathy, 2 complete my joy by being of the same mind, having the same love, being in full accord and of one mind. 3 Do nothing from selfishness or conceit, but in humility count others better than yourselves. 4 Let each of you look not only to his own interests, but also to the interests of others. 5 Have this mind among yourselves, which is yours in Christ Jesus, 6 who, though he was in the form of God, did not count equality with God a thing to be grasped, 7 but emptied himself, taking the form of a servant, being born in the likeness of men. 8 And being found in human form he humbled himself and became obedient unto death, even death on a cross. 9 Therefore God has highly exalted him and bestowed on him the name which is above every name, 10 that at the name of Jesus every knee should bow, in heaven and on earth and under the earth, 11 and every tongue confess that Jesus Christ is Lord, to the glory of God the Father.

172

Rom 12:9

9 Let love be genuine; hate what is evil, hold fast to what is good;

Phm 8-9

8 Accordingly, though I am bold enough in Christ to command you to do what is required, 9 yet for love's sake I prefer to appeal to you—I, Paul, an ambassador and now a prisoner also for Christ Jesus—

▶ 8:15 Ex 16:18 18 But when they measured it with an omer, he that gathered much had nothing over, and he that gathered little had no lack; each gathered according to what he could eat.

173

Rom 15:22-29 (§63)

22 This is the reason why I have so often been hindered from coming to you. 23 But now, since I no longer have any room for work in these regions, and since I have longed for many years to come to you, 24 I hope to see you in passing as I go to Spain, and to be sped on my journey there by you, once I have enjoyed your company for a little. 25 At present, however, I am going to Jerusalem with aid for the saints. 26 For Macedo'nia and Acha'ia have been pleased to make some contribution for the poor among the saints at Jerusalem; 27 they were pleased to do it, and indeed they are in debt to them, for if the Gentiles have come to share in their spiritual blessings, they ought also to be of service to them in material blessings. 28 When therefore I have completed this, and have delivered to them what has been raised, I shall go on by way of you to Spain; 29 and I know that when I come to you I shall come in the fulness of the blessing of Christ.

Rom 16:1-2 (§65)

16 I commend to you our sister Phoebe, a deaconess of the church

▶ 8:16-24 3:1-3
Are we beginning to commend ourselves again? Or do we need, as some do, letters of recommendation to you, or from you? 2 You yourselves are our letter of recommendation, written on your hearts, to be known and read by all men; 3 and you show that you are a letter from Christ delivered by us,

1 Cor 16:1-4 (§138)

16 Now concerning the contribution for the saints: as I directed the churches of Galatia, so you also are to do. 2 On the first day of every week, each of you is to put something aside and store it up, as he may prosper, so that contributions need not be made when I come. 3 And when I arrive, I will send those whom you accredit by letter to carry your gift to Jerusalem. 4 If it seems advisable that I should go also, they will accompany me.

1 Cor 16:10-12 (§140)

10 When Timothy comes, see that you put him at ease among you, for he is doing the work of the Lord, as I am. 11 So let no one despise him. Speed him on his way in peace, that he may return to me; for I am expecting him with the brethren.

12 As for our brother Apol'los, I strongly urged him to visit you with the

at Cen'chre-ae, 2 that you may receive her in the Lord as befits the saints, and help her in whatever she may require from you, for she has been a helper of many and of myself as well.

written not with ink but with the Spirit of the living God, not on tablets of stone but on tablets of human hearts.

▶ 8:24 7:4.
4 I have great confidence in you; I have great pride in you; I am filled with comfort. With all our affliction, I am overjoyed.

2 Cor 8:16-24

16 But thanks be to God who puts the same earnest care for you into the heart of Titus. 17 For he not only accepted our appeal, but being himself very earnest he is going to you of his own accord. 18 With him we are sending the brother who is famous among all the churches for his preaching of the gospel; 19 and not only that, but he has been appointed by the churches to travel with us in this gracious work which we are carrying on,

other brethren, but it was not at all his will[b] to come now. He will come when he has opportunity.

1 Cor 16:15-18 (§142)

15 Now, brethren, you know that the household of Steph'anas were the first converts in Acha'ia, and they have devoted themselves to the service of the saints; 16 I urge you to be subject to such men and to every fellow worker and laborer. 17 I rejoice at the coming of Steph'anas and Fortuna'tus and Acha'icus, because they have made up for your absence; 18 for they refreshed my spirit as well as yours. Give recognition to such men.

14 14 For if I have expressed to him some pride in you, I was not put to shame; but just as everything we said to you was true, so our boasting before Titus has proved true.

9:2-3 2 for I know your readiness, of which I boast about you to the people of Macedo'nia, saying that Acha'ia has been ready since last year; and your zeal has stirred up most of them. 3 But I am sending the brethren so that our boast-

Gal 2:1-10 (§197)

2 Then after fourteen years I went up again to Jerusalem with Barnabas, taking Titus along with me. 2 I went up by revelation; and I laid before them (but privately before those who were of repute) the gospel which I preach among the Gentiles, lest somehow I should be running or had run in vain. 3 But even Titus, who was with

for the glory of the Lord and to show our good will. 20 We intend that no one should blame us about this liberal gift which we are administering, 21 for we aim at what is honorable not only in the Lord's sight but also in the sight of men. 22 And with them we are sending our brother whom we have often tested and found earnest in many matters, but who is now more earnest than ever because of his great confidence in you. 23 As for Titus, he is my partner and fellow worker in your service; and as for our brethren, they are messengers of the churches, the glory of Christ. 24 So give proof, before the churches, of your love and of our boasting about you to these men.

ing about you may not prove vain in this case, so that you may be ready, as I said you would be;

me, was not compelled to be circumcised, though he was a Greek. 4 But because of false brethren secretly brought in, who slipped in to spy out our freedom which we have in Christ Jesus, that they might bring us into bondage— 5 to them we did not yield submission even for a moment, that the truth of the gospel might be preserved for you. 6 And from those who were reputed to be something (what they were makes no difference to me; God shows no partiality)—those, I say, who were of repute added nothing to me; 7 but on the contrary, when they saw that I had been entrusted with the gospel to the uncircumcised, just as Peter had been entrusted with the gospel to the circumcised 8 (for he who worked through Peter for the mission to the circumcised worked through me also for the Gentiles), 9 and when they perceived the grace that was given to me, James and Cephas and John, who were reputed to be pillars, gave to me and Barnabas the right hand of fellowship, that we should go to the Gentiles and they to the circumcised; 10 only they would have us remember the poor, which very thing I was eager to do.

1 Cor 15:31

31 I protest, brethren, by my pride in you which I have in Christ Jesus our Lord, I die every day!

174. Not an exaction but a willing gift

174

Rom 15:22-29 (§63)

22 This is the reason why I have so often been hindered from coming to you. 23 But now, since I no longer have any room for work in these regions, and since I have longed for many years to come to you, 24 I hope to see you in passing as I go to Spain, and to be sped on my journey there by you, once I have enjoyed your company for a little. 25 At present, however, I am going to Jerusalem with aid for the saints. 26 For Macedo'nia and Acha'ia have been pleased to make some contribution for the poor among the saints at Jerusalem; 27 they were pleased to do it, and indeed they are in debt to them, for if the Gentiles have come to share in their spiritual blessings, they ought also to be of service to them in material blessings. 28 When therefore I have completed this, and have delivered to them what has been raised, I shall go on by way of you to Spain; 29 and I know that when I come to you I shall come in the fulness of the blessing of Christ.

▶ 9:2-3 7:4.
4 I have great confidence in you; I have great pride in you; I am filled with comfort. With all our affliction, I am overjoyed.

1 Cor 16:1-4 (§138)

16 Now concerning the contribution for the saints: as I directed the churches of Galatia, so you also are to do. 2 On the first day of every week, each of you is to put something aside and store it up, as he may prosper, so that contributions need not be made when I come. 3 And when I arrive, I will send those whom you accredit by letter to carry your gift to Jerusalem. 4 If it seems advisable that I should go also, they will accompany me.

14 14 For if I have expressed to him some pride in you, I was not put to shame; but just as everything we said to you was true, so our boasting before Titus has proved true.

2 Cor 9:1-5

9 Now it is superfluous for me to write to you about the offering for the saints, 2 for I know your readiness, of which I boast about you to the people of Macedo'nia, saying that Acha'ia has been ready since last year; and your zeal has stirred up most of them. 3 But I am sending the brethren so that our boasting about you may not prove vain in this case, so that you may be ready, as I said you would be; 4 lest if some Macedo'nians come with me and find that you are not ready, we be humiliated—to say nothing of you—for being so confident. 5 So I thought it necessary to urge the brethren to go on to you before me, and arrange in advance for this gift you have promised, so that it may be ready not as an exaction but as a willing gift.

8:24 24 So give proof, before the churches, of your love and of our boasting about you to these men.

Gal 2:1-10 (§197)

2 Then after fourteen years I went up again to Jerusalem with Barnabas, taking Titus along with me. 2 I went up by revelation; and I laid before them (but privately before those who were of repute) the gospel which I preach among the Gentiles, lest somehow I should be running or had run in vain. 3 But even Titus, who was with me, was not compelled to be circumcised, though he was a Greek. 4 But because of false brethren secretly brought in, who slipped in to spy out our freedom which we have in Christ Jesus, that they might bring us into bondage— 5 to them we did not yield submission even for a moment, that the truth of the gospel might be preserved for you. 6 And from those who were reputed to be something (what they were makes no difference to me; God shows no partiality)—those, I say, who were of repute added nothing to me; 7 but on the contrary, when they saw that I had been entrusted with the gospel to the uncircumcised, just as Peter had been entrusted with the gospel to the circumcised 8 (for he who worked through

Peter for the mission to the circumcised worked through me also for the Gentiles), 9 and when they perceived the grace that was given to me, James and Cephas and John, who were reputed to be pillars, gave to me and Barnabas the right hand of fellowship, that we should go to the Gentiles and they to the circumcised; 10 only they would have us remember the poor, which very thing I was eager to do.

1 Cor 15:31

31 I protest, brethren, by my pride in you which I have in Christ Jesus our Lord, I die every day!

Phil 2:16

16 holding fast the word of life, so that in the day of Christ I may be proud that I did not run in vain or labor in vain.

▶ 9:4 12:21 21 I fear that when I come again my God may humble me before you, and I may have to mourn over many of those who sinned before and have not repented of the impurity, immorality, and licentiousness which they have practiced.

Phil 2:19-24 (§245)

19 I hope in the Lord Jesus to send Timothy to you soon, so that I may be cheered by news of you. 20 I have no one like him, who will be genuinely anxious for your welfare. 21 They all look after their own interests, not those of Jesus Christ. 22 But Timothy's worth you know, how as a son with a father he has served with me in the gospel. 23 I hope therefore to send him just as soon as I see how it will go with me; 24 and I trust in the Lord that shortly I myself shall come also.

Phil 2:25-3:1 (§246)

25 I have thought it necessary to send to you Epaphrodi′tus my brother and fellow worker and fellow soldier, and your messenger and minister to my need, 26 for he has been longing for you all, and has been distressed because you heard that he was ill. 27 Indeed he was ill, near to death. But God had mercy on him, and not only on him but on me also, lest I should have sorrow upon sorrow. 28 I am the more eager to send him, therefore, that you may rejoice at seeing him again, and that I may be less anxious. 29 So receive him in the Lord

with all joy; and honor such men, 30 for he nearly died for the work of Christ, risking his life to complete your service to me.

3 Finally, my brethren, rejoice in the Lord. To write the same things to you is not irksome to me, and is safe for you.

Phm 8-20 (§307-308)

8 Accordingly, though I am bold enough in Christ to command you to do what is required, 9 yet for love's sake I prefer to appeal to you—I, Paul, an ambassador and now a prisoner also for Christ Jesus—10 I appeal to you for my child, Ones′imus, whose father I have become in my imprisonment. 11 (Formerly he was useless to you, but now he is indeed useful to you and to me.) 12 I am sending him back to you, sending my very heart. 13 I would have been glad to keep him with me, in order that he might serve me on your behalf during my imprisonment for the gospel; 14 but I preferred to do nothing without your consent in order that your goodness might not be by compulsion but of your own free will.

15 Perhaps this is why he was parted from you for a while, that you might have him back for ever, 16 no longer as a slave but more than a slave, as a beloved brother, especially to me but how much more to you, both in the flesh and in the Lord. 17 So if you consider me your partner, receive him as you would receive me. 18 If he has wronged you at all, or owes you anything, charge that to my account. 19 I, Paul, write this with my own hand, I will repay it—to say nothing of your owing me even your own self. 20 Yes, brother, I want some benefit from you in the Lord. Refresh my heart in Christ.

173

174. Not an exaction but a willing gift

1 Thes 1:2-10 (§276)

2 but though we had already suffered and been shamefully treated at Philippi, as you know, we had courage in our God to declare to you the gospel of God in the face of great opposition. 3 For our appeal does not spring from error or uncleanness, nor is it made with guile; 4 but just as we have been approved by God to be entrusted with the gospel, so we speak, not to please men, but to please God who tests our hearts. 5 For we never used either words of flattery, as you know, or a cloak for greed, as God is witness; 6 nor did we seek glory from men, whether from you or from others, though we might have made demands as apostles of Christ. 7 But we were gentle among you, like a nurse taking care of her children. 8 So, being affectionately desirous of you, we were ready to share with you not only the gospel of God but also our own selves, because you had become very dear to us. 9 For you remember our labor and toil, brethren; we worked night and day, that we might not burden any of you, while we preached to you the gospel of God. 10 You are witnesses, and

God also, how holy and righteous and blameless was our behavior to you believers;

174

175

Rom 15:22-29 (§63)

22 This is the reason why I have so often been hindered from coming to you. 23 But now, since I no longer have any room for work in these regions, and since I have longed for many years to come to you, 24 I hope to see you in passing as I go to Spain, and to be sped on my journey there by you, once I have enjoyed your company for a little. 25 At present, however, I am going to Jerusalem with aid for the saints. 26 For Macedo′nia and Acha′ia have been pleased to make some contribution for the poor among the saints at Jerusalem; 27 they were pleased to do it, and indeed they are in debt to them, for if the Gentiles have come to share in their spiritual blessings, they ought also to be of service to them in material blessings. 28 When therefore I have completed this, and have delivered to them what has been raised, I shall go on by way of you to Spain; 29 and I know that when I come to you I shall come in the fulness of the blessing of Christ.

1 Cor 9:1-14 (§105)

9 Am I not free? Am I not an apostle? Have I not seen Jesus our Lord? Are not you my workmanship in the Lord? 2 If to others I am not an apostle, at least I am to you; for you are the seal of my apostleship in the Lord.

3 This is my defense to those who would examine me. 4 Do we not have the right to our food and drink? 5 Do we not have the right to be accompanied by a wife, as the other apostles and the brothers of the Lord and Cephas? 6 Or is it only Barnabas and I who have no right to refrain from working for a living? 7 Who serves as a soldier at his own expense? Who plants a vineyard without eating any of its fruit? Who tends a flock without getting some of the milk?

8 Do I say this on human authority? Does not the law say the same? 9 For it is written in the law of Moses, "You shall not muzzle an ox when it is treading out the grain." Is it for oxen that God is concerned? 10 Does he not speak entirely for our sake? It was written for our sake, because the plowman should plow in hope and the thresher thresh in

2 Cor 9:6-15

6 The point is this: he who sows sparingly will also reap sparingly, and he who sows bountifully will also reap bountifully. 7 Each one must do as he has made up his mind, not reluctantly or under compulsion, for God loves a cheerful giver. 8 And God is able to provide you with every blessing in abundance, so that you may always have enough of everything and may provide in abundance for every good work. 9 As it is written,

hope of a share in the crop. 11 If we have sown spiritual good among you, is it too much if we reap your material benefits? 12 If others share this rightful claim upon you, do not we still more?

Nevertheless, we have not made use of this right, but we endure anything rather than put an obstacle in the way of the gospel of Christ. 13 Do you not know that those who are employed in the temple service get their food from the temple, and those who serve at the altar share in the sacrificial offerings? 14 In the same way, the Lord commanded that those who proclaim the gospel should get their living by the gospel.

"He scatters abroad, he gives to the poor;
his righteousness endures for ever."

10 He who supplies seed to the sower and bread for food will supply and multiply your resources and increase the harvest of your righteousness. 11 You will be enriched in every way for great generosity, which through us will produce thanksgiving to God; 12 for the

1 Cor 16:1-4 (§138)

16 Now concerning the contribution for the saints: as I directed the churches of Galatia, so you also are to do. 2 On the first day of every week, each of you is to put something aside and store it up, as he may prosper, so that contributions need not be made

Gal 2:1-10 (§197)

2 Then after fourteen years I went up again to Jerusalem with Barnabas, taking Titus along with me. 2 I went up by revelation; and I laid before them (but privately before those who were of repute) the gospel which I preach among the Gentiles, lest somehow I should be running or had run in vain. 3 But even Titus, who was with

me, was not compelled to be circumcised, though he was a Greek. 4 But because of false brethren secretly brought in, who slipped in to spy out

Eph 3:20-21 (§224)

20 Now to him who by the power at work within us is able to do far more abundantly than all that we ask or think, 21 to him be glory in the church and in Christ Jesus to all generations, for ever and ever. Amen.

rendering of this service not only supplies the wants of the saints but also overflows in many thanksgivings to God. 13 Under the test of this service, you will glorify God by your obedience in acknowledging the gospel of Christ, and by the generosity of your contribution for them and for all others; 14 while they long for you and pray for you, because of the surpassing grace of God in you. 15 Thanks be to God for his inexpressible gift!

when I come. 3 And when I arrive, I will send those whom you accredit by letter to carry your gift to Jerusalem. 4 If it seems advisable that I should go also, they will accompany me.

▶9:7 Phm 14
14 but I preferred to do nothing without your consent in order that your goodness might not be by compulsion but of your own free will.

▶9:12 4:15
15 For it is all for your sake, so that as grace extends to more and more people it may increase thanksgiving, to the glory of God.

Eph 5:20
20 always and for everything giving thanks in the name of our Lord Jesus Christ to God the Father.

Col 3:15b-17
ful. 16 Let the word of Christ dwell in you richly, teach and admonish one another in all wisdom, and sing psalms and hymns and spiritual songs with thankfulness in your hearts to

And be thankful.
God. 17 And whatever you do, in word or deed, do everything in the name of the Lord Jesus, giving thanks to God the Father through him.

▶9:9 Ps 112:9
9 He has distributed freely, he has given to the poor;
his righteousness endures for ever;
his horn is exalted in honor.

176. We destroy every obstacle to the knowledge of God

176

Rom 1:16-17 (§3)

16 For I am not ashamed of the gospel: it is the power of God for salvation to every one who has faith, to the Jew first and also to the Greek. 17 For in it the righteousness of God is revealed through faith for faith; as it is written, "He who through faith is righteous shall live."

Rom 12:1-2 (§51)

12 I appeal to you therefore, brethren, by the mercies of God, to present your bodies as a living sacrifice, holy and acceptable to God, which is your spiritual worship. 2 Do not be conformed to this world but be transformed by the renewal of your mind, that you may prove what is the will of God, what is good and acceptable and perfect.

Rom 13:11-14 (§56)

11 Besides this you know what hour it is, how it is full time now for you to wake from sleep. For salvation is nearer to us now than when we first believed; 12 the night is far gone, the day is at hand. Let us then cast off the works of darkness and put on the armor of light; 13 let us conduct ourselves becomingly

1 Cor 4:14-21 (§86)

14 I do not write this to make you ashamed, but to admonish you as my beloved children. 15 For though you have countless guides in Christ, you do not have many fathers. For I became your father in Christ Jesus through the gospel. 16 I urge you, then, be imitators of me. 17 Therefore I sent to you Timothy, my beloved and faithful child in the Lord, to remind you of my ways in Christ, as I teach them everywhere in every church. 18 Some are arrogant, as though I were not coming to you. 19 But I will come to you soon, if the Lord wills, and I will find out not the talk of these arrogant people but their power. 20 For the kingdom of God does not consist in talk but in power. 21 What do you wish? Shall I come to you with a rod, or with love in a spirit of gentleness?

as in the day, not in reveling and drunkenness, not in debauchery and licentiousness, not in quarreling and jealousy. 14 But put on the Lord Jesus Christ, and make no provision for the flesh, to gratify its desires.

2 Cor 10:1-6

10 I, Paul, myself entreat you, by the meekness and gentleness of Christ—I who am humble when face to face with you, but bold to you when I am away!— 2 I beg of you that when I am present I may not have to show boldness with such confidence as I count on showing against some who suspect us of acting in worldly fashion. 3 For though we live in the world we are not carrying on a worldly war, 4 for the weapons of our warfare are not worldly but have divine power to destroy strongholds. 5 We destroy arguments and every proud obstacle to the knowledge of God, and take every thought captive to obey Christ, 6 being ready to punish every disobedience, when your obedience is complete.

Eph 6:10-17 (§233)

10 Finally, be strong in the Lord and in the strength of his might. 11 Put on the whole armor of God, that you may be able to stand against the wiles of the devil. 12 For we are not contending against flesh and blood, but against the principalities, against the powers, against the world rulers of this present darkness, against the spiritual hosts of wickedness in the heavenly places. 13 Therefore take the whole armor of God, that you may be able to withstand in the evil day, and having done all, to stand. 14 Stand therefore, having girded your loins with truth, and having put on the breastplate of righteousness, 15 and having shod your feet with the equipment of the gospel of peace; 16 besides all these, taking the shield of faith, with which you can quench all the flaming darts of the evil one. 17 And take the helmet of salvation, and the sword of the Spirit, which is the word of God.

▶10:4 1 Tim 1:18
18 This charge I commit to you, Timothy, my son, in accordance with the prophetic utterances which pointed to you, that inspired by them you may wage the good warfare,

▶10:1-6 13:10
10 I write this while I am away from you, in order that when I come I may not have to be severe in my use of the authority which the Lord has given me for building up and not for tearing down.

▶10:1 1 Cor 2:3
3 And I was with you in weakness and in much fear and trembling;

2 Cor 10:10
10 For they say, "His letters are weighty and strong, but his bodily presence is weak, and his speech of no account."

▶10:2 Rom 16:17-20
17 I appeal to you, brethren, to take note of those who create dissensions and difficulties, in opposition to the doctrine which you have been taught; avoid them. 18 For such persons do not serve our Lord Christ, but their own appetites, and by fair and flattering words they deceive the hearts of the

simple-minded. 19 For while your obedience is known to all, so that I rejoice over you, I would have you wise as to what is good and guileless as to what is evil; 20 then the God of peace will soon crush Satan under your feet. The grace of our Lord Jesus Christ be with you.

175

Gal (cont)
our freedom which we have in Christ Jesus, that they might bring us into bondage— 5 to them we did not yield submission even for a moment, that the truth of the gospel might be preserved for you. 6And from those who were reputed to be something (what they were makes no difference to me; God shows no partiality)—those, I say, who were of repute added nothing to me; 7 but on the contrary, when they saw that I had been entrusted with the gospel to the uncircumcised, just as Peter had been entrusted with the gospel to the circumcised 8 (for he who worked through Peter for the mission to the circumcised worked through me also for the Gentiles), 9 and when they perceived the grace that was given to me, James and Cephas and John, who were reputed to be pillars, gave to me and Barnabas the right hand of fellowship, that we should go to the Gentiles and they to the circumcised; 10 only they would have us remember the poor, which very thing I was eager to do.

176. We destroy every obstacle to the knowledge of God

176

1 Thes 2:1-8 (§277)

2 For you yourselves know, brethren, that our visit to you was not in vain; 2 but though we had already suffered and been shamefully treated at Philippi, as you know, we had courage in our God to declare to you the gospel of God in the face of great opposition. 3 For our appeal does not spring from error or uncleanness, nor is it made with guile; 4 but just as we have been approved by God to be entrusted with the gospel, so we speak, not to please men, but to please God who tests our hearts. 5 For we never used either words of flattery, as you know, or a cloak for greed, as God is witness; 6 nor did we seek glory from men, whether from you or from others, though we might have made demands as apostles of Christ. 7 But we were gentle among you, like a nurse taking care of her children. 8 So, being affectionately desirous of you, we were ready to share with you not only the gospel of God but also our own selves, because you had become very dear to us.

1 Thes 5:1-11 (§287)

5 But as to the times and the seasons, brethren, you have no need to have anything written to you. 2 For you yourselves know well that the day of the Lord will come like a thief in the night. 3 When people say, "There is peace and security," then sudden destruction will come upon them as travail comes upon a woman with child, and there will be no escape. 4 But you are not in darkness, brethren, for that day to surprise you like a thief. 5 For you are all sons of light and sons of the day; we are not of the night or of darkness. 6 So then,let us not sleep, as others do, but let us keep awake and be sober. 7 For those who sleep sleep at night, and those who get drunk are drunk at night. 8 But, since we belong to the day, let us be sober, and put on the breastplate of faith and love, and for a helmet the hope of salvation. 9 For God has not destined us for wrath, but to obtain salvation through our Lord Jesus Christ, 10 who died for us so that whether we wake or sleep we might live with him. 11 Therefore encourage one another and build one another up, just as you are doing.

▶10:3 6:7 7 truthful speech, and the power of God; with the weapons of righteousness for the right hand and for the left;

177

1 Cor 2:1-5 (§76)

2 When I came to you, brethren, I did not come proclaiming to you the testimony of God in lofty words or wisdom. 2 For I decided to know nothing among you except Jesus Christ and him crucified. 3 And I was with you in weakness and in much fear and trembling; 4 and my speech and my message were not in plausible words of wisdom, but in demonstration of the Spirit and of power, 5 that your faith might not rest in the wisdom of men but in the power of God.

1 Cor 3:18-23 (§82)

18 Let no one deceive himself. If any one among you thinks that he is wise in this age, let him become a fool that he may become wise. 19 For the wisdom of this world is folly with God. For it is

2 Cor 10:7-12

7 Look at what is before your eyes. If any one is confident that he is Christ's, let him remind himself that as he is Christ's, so are we. 8 For even if I boast a little too much of our authority, which the Lord gave for building you up and not for destroying you, I shall not be put to shame. 9 I would not seem to be frightening you with letters. 10 For they

written, "He catches the wise in their craftiness," 20 and again, "The Lord knows that the thoughts of the wise are futile." 21 So let no one boast of men. For all things are yours, 22 whether Paul or Apol'los or Cephas or the world or life or death or the present or the future, all are yours; 23 and you are Christ's; and Christ is God's.

say, "His letters are weighty and strong, but his bodily presence is weak, and his speech of no account." 11 Let such people understand that what we say by letter when absent, we do when present. 12 Not that we venture to class or compare ourselves with some of those who commend themselves. But when they measure themselves by one another, and compare themselves with one another, they are without understanding.

▶10:7 11:21b-23
But whatever any one dares to boast of—I am speaking as a fool—I also dare to boast of that. 22 Are they Hebrews? So am I. Are they Israelites? So am I. Are they descendants of Abraham? So am I. 23 Are they servants of Christ? I am a better one—I am talking like a madman—with far greater labors, far more imprisonments, with countless beatings, and often near death.

▶10:8 13:10
10 I write this while I am away from you, in order that when I come I may not have to be severe in my use of the authority which the Lord has given me for building up and not for tearing down.

Rom 1:16-17
16 For I am not ashamed of the gospel; it is the power of God for salvation to every one who has faith, to the Jew first and also to the Greek. 17 For in it the righteousness of God is revealed through faith for faith; as it is written, "He who through faith is righteous shall live."

1 Cor 5:4
4 in the name of the Lord Jesus on the man who has done such a thing. When you are assembled, and my spirit is present, with the power of our Lord Jesus,

Gal 2:18   18 But if I build up again those things which I tore down, then I prove myself a transgressor.

▶10:10 12:7
7 And to keep me from being too elated by the abundance of revelations, a thorn was given me in the flesh, a messenger of Satan, to harass me, to keep me from being too elated.

Gal 4:12-20
12 Brethren, I beseech you, become as I am, for I also have become as you are. You did me no wrong; 13 you know it was because of a bodily ailment that I preached the gospel to you at first; 14 and though my condition was a trial to you, you did not scorn or despise me, but received me as an angel of God,

as Christ Jesus. 15 What has become of the satisfaction you felt? For I bear you witness that, if possible, you would have plucked out your eyes and given them to me. 16 Have I then become your enemy by telling you the truth? 17 They make much of you, but for no good purpose; they want to shut you out, that you may make much of them. 18 For a good purpose it is always good to be made much of, and not only when I am present with you. 19 My little children, with whom I am again in travail until Christ be formed in you! 20 I could wish to be present with you now and to change my tone, for I am perplexed about you.

1 Cor 2:3   3 And I was with you in weakness and in much fear and trembling;

2 Cor 10:1,
I, Paul, myself entreat you, by the meekness and gentleness of Christ—I who am humble when face to face with you, but bold to you when I am away!—

11:6
6 Even if I am unskilled in speaking, I am not in knowledge; in every way we have made this plain to you in all things.

▶10:11 1:17-18   17 Was I vacillating when I wanted to do this? Do I make my plans like a worldly man, ready to say Yes and No at once? 18 As surely as God is faithful, our word to you has not been Yes and No.

▶10:10-12 12:11-12
11 I have been a fool! You forced me to it, for I ought to have been commended by you. For I was not at all inferior to these superlative apostles, even though I am nothing. 12 The signs of a true apostle were performed among you in all patience, with signs and wonders and mighty works.

178. Let him who boasts, boast of the Lord

178

Rom 3:27-31 (§15)
27 Then what becomes of our boasting? It is excluded. On what principle? On the principle of works? No, but on the principle of faith. 28 For we hold that a man is justified by faith apart from works of law. 29 Or is God the God of Jews only? Is he not the God of Gentiles also? Yes, of Gentiles also, 30 since God is one; and he will justify the circumcised on the ground of their faith and the uncircumcised through their faith. 31 Do we then overthrow the law by this faith? By no means! On the contrary, we uphold the law.

Rom 15:14-21 (§62)
14 I myself am satisfied about you, my brethren, that you yourselves are full of goodness, filled with all knowledge, and able to instruct one another. 15 But on some points I have written to you very boldly by way of reminder, because of the grace given me by God 16 to be a minister of Christ Jesus to the Gentiles in the priestly service of the gospel of God, so that the offering of the Gentiles may be acceptable, sanctified by the Holy Spirit. 17 In Christ Jesus, then, I have reason to be proud

1 Cor 4:1-5 (§83)

4 This is how one should regard us, as servants of Christ and stewards of the mysteries of God. 2 Moreover it is required of stewards that they be found trustworthy. 3 But with me it is a very small thing that I should be judged by you or by any human court. I do not even judge myself. 4 I am not aware of anything against myself, but I am not thereby acquitted. It is the Lord who judges me. 5 Therefore do not pronounce judgment before the time, before the Lord comes, who will bring to light the things now hidden in darkness and will disclose the purposes of the heart. Then every man will receive his commendation from God.

of my work for God. 18 For I will not venture to speak of anything except what Christ has wrought through me to win obedience from the Gentiles, by word and deed, 19 by the power of signs and wonders, by the power of the Holy Spirit, so that from Jerusalem and as far round as Illyr'icum I have fully preached the gospel of Christ, 20 thus making it my ambition to preach the gospel, not where Christ has already

2 Cor 10:13-18

13 But we will not boast beyond limit, but will keep to the limits God has apportioned us, to reach even to you. 14 For we are not overextending ourselves, as though we did not reach you; we were the first to come all the way to you with the gospel of Christ. 15 We do not boast beyond limit, in other men's labors; but our hope is that as your faith increases, our field among you may be greatly enlarged, 16 so that we may preach the gospel in lands beyond you, without boasting of work already done in another's field. 17 "Let him who boasts, boast of the Lord." 18 For it is not the man who commends himself that is accepted, but the man whom the Lord commends.

been named, lest I build on another man's foundation, 21 but as it is written,
"They shall see who have never been told of him,
and they shall understand who have never heard of him."

1 Cor 3:10-15 (§80)
10 According to the grace of God given to me, like a skilled master builder I laid a foundation, and another

man is building upon it. Let each man take care how he builds upon it. 11 For no other foundation can any one lay than that which is laid, which is Jesus Christ. 12 Now if any one builds on the foundation with gold, silver, precious stones, wood, hay, straw— 13 each man's work will become manifest; for the Day will disclose it, because it will be revealed with fire, and the fire will test what sort of work each one has done. 14 If the work which any man has built on the foundation survives, he will receive a reward. 15 If any man's work is burned up, he will suffer loss, though he himself will be saved, but only as through fire.

▶10:16 Acts 19:21
21 Now after these events Paul resolved in the Spirit to pass through Macedo'nia and Acha'ia and go to Jerusalem, saying, "After I have been there, I must also see Rome."

▶10:13 Rom 12:3
3 For by the grace given to me I bid every one among you not to think of himself more highly than he ought to think, but to think with sober judgment, each according to the measure of faith which God has assigned him.

▶10:17 Jer 9:24 (*cf. 1 Cor 1:31)
24 but let him who glories glory in this, that he understands and knows me, that I am the LORD who practice steadfast love, justice, and righteousness in the earth; for in these things I delight, says the LORD."

177

178. Let him who boasts, boast of the Lord

178

179. I betrothed you to Christ

179

1 Cor 2:1-5 (§76)

2 When I came to you, brethren, I did not come proclaiming to you the testimony of God in lofty words or wisdom. 2 For I decided to know nothing among you except Jesus Christ and him crucified. 3And I was with you in weakness and in much fear and trembling; 4 and my speech and my message were not in plausible words of wisdom, but in demonstration of the Spirit and of power, 5 that your faith might not rest in the wisdom of men but in the power of God.

2 Cor 11:1-6

11 I wish you would bear with me in a little foolishness. Do bear with me! 2 I feel a divine jealousy for you, for I betrothed you to Christ to present you as a pure bride to her one husband. 3 But I am afraid that as the serpent deceived Eve by his cunning, your thoughts will be led astray from a sincere and pure devotion to Christ. 4 For if some one comes and preaches another Jesus than the one we preached, or if you receive a different spirit from the one you received, or if you accept a different gospel from the one you accepted, you submit to it readily enough. 5 I think that I am not in the least inferior to these superlative apostles. 6 Even if I am unskilled in speaking, I am not in knowledge; in every way we have made this plain to you in all things.

Gal 1:6-12 (§194)

6 I am astonished that you are so quickly deserting him who called you in the grace of Christ and turning to a different gospel—7 not that there is another gospel, but there are some who trouble you and want to pervert the gospel of Christ. 8 But even if we, or an angel from heaven, should preach to you a gospel contrary to that which we preached to you, let him be accursed. 9As we have said before, so now I say again, If any one is preaching to you a gospel contrary to that which you received, let him be accursed.

10 Am I now seeking the favor of men, or of God? Or am I trying to please men? If I were still pleasing men, I should not be a servant of Christ.

11 For I would have you know, brethren, that the gospel which was preached by me is not man's gospel. 12 For I did not receive it from man, nor was I taught it, but it came through a revelation of Jesus Christ.

Eph 5:21-6:9 (§232)

21 Be subject to one another out of reverence for Christ. 22 Wives, be subject to your husbands, as to the Lord. 23 For the husband is the head of the wife as Christ is the head of the church, his body, and is himself its Savior. 24As the church is subject to Christ, so let wives also be subject in everything to their husbands. 25 Husbands, love your wives, as Christ loved the church and gave himself up for her, 26 that he might sanctify her, having cleansed her by the washing of water with the word, 27 that he might present the church to himself in splendor, without spot or wrinkle or any such thing, that she might be holy and without blemish. 28 Even so husbands should love their wives as their own bodies. He who loves his wife loves himself. 29 For no man ever hates his own flesh, but nourishes and cherishes it, as Christ does the church, 30 because we are members of his body. 31 "For this reason a man shall leave his father and mother and be joined to his wife, and the two shall become one flesh." 32This mystery is a profound one, and I am saying that it

▶11:3 1 Tim 2:14   14 and Adam was not deceived, but the woman was deceived and became a transgressor.

▶11:5 12:11   11 I have been a fool! You forced me to it, for I ought to have been commended by you. For I was not at all inferior to these superlative apostles, even though I am nothing.

▶11:6 10:10   10 For they say, "His letters are weighty and strong, but his bodily presence is weak, and his speech of no account."

180. I did not burden anyone

180

1 Cor 9:15-18 (§106)

15 But I have made no use of any of these rights, nor am I writing this to secure any such provision. For I would rather die than have any one deprive me of my ground for boasting. 16 For if I preach the gospel, that gives me no ground for boasting. For necessity is laid upon me. Woe to me if I do not preach the gospel! 17 For if I do this of my own will, I have a reward; but if not of my own will, I am entrusted with a commission. 18 What then is my reward? Just this: that in my preaching I may make the gospel free of charge, not making full use of my right in the gospel.

2 Cor 11:7-11

7 Did I commit a sin in abasing myself so that you might be exalted, because I preached God's gospel without cost to you? 8 I robbed other churches by accepting support from them in order to serve you. 9And when I was with you and was in want, I did not burden any one, for my needs were supplied by the brethren who came from Macedo′nia. So I refrained and will refrain from burdening you in any way. 10As the truth of Christ is in me, this boast of mine shall not be silenced in the regions of Acha′ia. 11And why? Because I do not love you? God knows I do!

▶11:7 Acts 18:3   3 and because he was of the same trade he stayed with them, and they worked, for by trade they were tentmakers.

▶11:9 Acts 18:5   5 When Silas and Timothy arrived from Macedo′nia, Paul was occupied with preaching, testifying to the Jews that the Christ was Jesus.

▶11:10 Acts 18:12   12 But when Gallio was proconsul of Acha′ia, the Jews made a united attack upon Paul and brought him before the tribunal,

▶11:7-9 2 Thes 3:7-9   7 For you yourselves know how you ought to imitate us; we were not idle when we were with you, 8 we did not eat any one's bread without paying, but with toil and labor we worked night and day, that we might not burden any of you. 9 It was not because we have not that right, but to give you in our conduct an example to imitate.

179

Eph (cont)

refers to Christ and the church; 33 however, let each one of you love his wife as himself, and let the wife see that she respects her husband.

6 Children, obey your parents in the Lord, for this is right. 2 "Honor your father and mother" (this is the first commandment with a promise), 3 "that it may be well with you and that you may live long on the earth." 4 Fathers, do not provoke your children to anger, but bring them up in the discipline and instruction of the Lord.

5 Slaves, be obedient to those who are your earthly masters, with fear and trembling, in singleness of heart, as to Christ; 6 not in the way of eyeservice, as men-pleasers, but as servants *f* of Christ, doing the will of God from the heart, 7 rendering service with a good will as to the Lord and not to men, 8 knowing that whatever good any one does, he will receive the same again from the Lord, whether he is a slave or free. 9 Masters, do the same to them, and forbear threatening, knowing that he who is both their Master and yours is in heaven, and that there is no partiality with him.

180. I did not burden anyone

180

Phil 4:10-20 (§253)

10 I rejoice in the Lord greatly that now at length you have revived your concern for me; you were indeed concerned for me, but you had no opportunity. 11 Not that I complain of want; for I have learned, in whatever state I am, to be content. 12 I know how to be abased, and I know how to abound; in any and all circumstances I have learned the secret of facing plenty and hunger, abundance and want. 13 I can do all things in him who strengthens me.

14 Yet it was kind of you to share my trouble. 15And you Philippians yourselves know that in the beginning of the gospel, when I left Macedo'nia, no church entered into partnership with me in giving and receiving except you only; 16 for even in Thessaloni'ca you sent me help*f* once and again. 17 Not that I seek the gift; but I seek the fruit which increases to your credit. 18 I have received full payment, and more; I am filled, having received from Epaphrodi'tus the gifts you sent, a fragrant offering, a sacrifice acceptable and pleasing to God. 19And my God will supply every need of yours according to his riches in glory in Christ Jesus. 20 To our God and Father be glory for ever and ever. Amen.

1 Thes 2:9-12 (§278)

9 For you remember our labor and toil, brethren; we worked night and day, that we might not burden any of you, while we preached to you the gospel of God. 10 You are witnesses, and God also, how holy and righteous and blameless was our behavior to you believers; 11 for you know how, like a father with his children, we exhorted each one of you and encouraged you and charged you 12 to lead a life worthy of God, who calls you into his own kingdom and glory.

181

Rom 16:17-20a (§67)

17 I appeal to you, brethren, to take note of those who create dissensions and difficulties, in opposition to the doctrine which you have been taught; avoid them. 18 For such persons do not serve our Lord Christ, but their own appetites, and by fair and flattering words they deceive the hearts of the simple-minded. 19 For while your obedience is known to all, so that I rejoice over you, I would have you wise as to what is good and guileless as to what is evil; 20 then the God of peace will soon crush Satan under your feet.

1 Cor 9:15-18 (§106)

15 But I have made no use of any of these rights, nor am I writing this to secure any such provision. For I would rather die than have any one deprive me of my ground for boasting. 16 For if I preach the gospel, that gives me no ground for boasting. For necessity is laid upon me. Woe to me if I do not preach the gospel! 17 For if I do this of my own will, I have a reward; but if not of my own will, I am entrusted with a commission. 18 What then is my reward? Just this: that in my preaching I may make the gospel free of charge, not making full use of my right in the gospel.

2 Cor 11:12-15

12 And what I do I will continue to do, in order to undermine the claim of those who would like to claim that in their boasted mission they work on the same terms as we do. 13 For such men are false apostles, deceitful workmen, disguising themselves as apostles of Christ. 14And no wonder, for even Satan disguises himself as an angel of light. 15 So it is not strange if his servants also disguise themselves as servants of righteousness. Their end will correspond to their deeds.

Gal 1:6-12 (§194)

6 I am astonished that you are so quickly deserting him who called you in the grace of Christ and turning to a different gospel—7 not that there is another gospel, but there are some who trouble you and want to pervert the gospel of Christ. 8 But even if we, or an angel from heaven, should preach to you a gospel contrary to that which we preached to you, let him be accursed. 9As we have said before, so now I say again, If any one is preaching to you a gospel contrary to that which you received, let him be accursed.

10 Am I now seeking the favor of men, or of God? Or am I trying to please men? If I were still pleasing men, I should not be a servant of Christ.

11 For I would have you know, brethren, that the gospel which was preached by me is not man's gospel. 12 For I did not receive it from man, nor was I taught it, but it came through a revelation of Jesus Christ.

▶11:13 Acts 20:30, 30and from among your own selves will arise men speaking perverse things, to draw away the disciples after them.

▶ 11:15 2 Tim 4:14 14Alexander the coppersmith did me great harm; the Lord will requite him for his deeds.

▶11:13 Phil 3:2 2 Look out for the dogs, look out for the evil-workers, look out for those who mutilate the flesh.

▶11:15 1 Thes 2:16 16 by hindering us from speaking to the Gentiles that they may be saved—so as always to fill up the measure of their sins. But God's wrath has come upon them at last!

182. You gladly bear with fools

182

Rom 1:18-23 (§4)

18 For the wrath of God is revealed from heaven against all ungodliness and wickedness of men who by their wickedness suppress the truth. 19 For what can be known about God is plain to them, because God has shown it to them. 20 Ever since the creation of the world his invisible nature, namely, his eternal power and deity, has been clearly perceived in the things that have been made. So they are without excuse; 21 for although they knew God they did not honor him as God or give thanks to him, but they became futile in their thinking and their senseless minds were darkened. 22 Claiming to be wise, they became fools, 23 and exchanged the glory of the immortal God for images resembling mortal man or birds or animals or reptiles.

Rom 3:27-31 (§15)

27 Then what becomes of our boasting? It is excluded. On what principle? On the principle of works? No, but on the principle of faith. 28 For we hold that a man is justified by faith apart from works of law. 29 Or is God the God of Jews only? Is he not the God of

1 Cor 1:26-31 (§75)

26 For consider your call, brethren; not many of you were wise according to worldly standards, not many were powerful, not many were of noble birth; 27 but God chose what is foolish in the world to shame the wise, God chose what is weak in the world to shame the strong, 28 God chose what is low and despised in the world, even things that are not, to bring to nothing things that are, 29 so that no human being might boast in the presence of God. 30 He is the source of your life in Christ Jesus, whom God made our wisdom, our righteousness and sanctification and redemption; 31 therefore, as it is written, "Let him who boasts, boast of the Lord."

Gentiles also? Yes, of Gentiles also, 30 since God is one; and he will justify the circumcised on the ground of their faith and the uncircumcised through their faith. 31 Do we then overthrow the law by this faith? By no means! On the contrary, we uphold the law.

2 Cor 11:16-21a

16 I repeat, let no one think me foolish; but even if you do, accept me as a fool, so that I too may boast a little. 17 (What I am saying I say not with the Lord's authority but as a fool, in this boastful confidence; 18 since many boast of worldly things, I too will boast.) 19 For you gladly bear with fools, being wise yourselves! 20 For you bear it if a man makes slaves of you, or preys upon you, or takes advantage of you, or puts on airs, or strikes you in the face. 21 To my shame, I must say, we were too weak for that!

▶11:17 1 Cor 7:6, 6 I say this by way of concession, not of command.
7:10, 10 To the married I give charge, not I but the Lord, that the wife should not separate from her husband

7:12, 12 To the rest I say, not the Lord, that if any brother has a wife who is an unbeliever, and she consents to live with him, he should not divorce her.
7:25, 25 Now concerning the unmarried, I have no command of the Lord, but I give my opinion as one who by the Lord's mercy is trustworthy.

7:35 35 I say this for your own benefit, not to lay any restraint upon you, but to promote good order and to secure your undivided devotion to the Lord.

Phm 8-9 8 Accordingly, though I am bold enough in Christ to command you to do what is required, 9 yet for love's sake I prefer to appeal to you—I, Paul, an ambassador and now a prisoner also for Christ Jesus—

▶11:18 10:13-18 13 But we will not boast beyond limit, but will keep to the limits God has apportioned us, to reach even to you. 14 For we are not overextending ourselves, as though we did not reach you; we were the first to come all the way to you with the gospel of Christ. 15 We do not boast beyond limit, in other men's

181. False apostles, deceitful workmen

§181-182

181

2 Thes 2:1-12 (§296)

2 Now concerning the coming of our Lord Jesus Christ and our assembling to meet him, we beg you, brethren, ² not to be quickly shaken in mind or excited, either by spirit or by word, or by letter purporting to be from us, to the effect that the day of the Lord has come. ³ Let no one deceive you in any way; for that day will not come, unless the rebellion comes first, and the man of lawlessness is revealed, the son of perdition, ⁴ who opposes and exalts himself against every so-called god or object of worship, so that he takes his seat in the temple of God, proclaiming himself to be God. ⁵ Do you not remember that when I was still with you I told you this? ⁶And you know what is restraining him now so that he may be revealed in his time. ⁷ For the mystery of lawlessness is already at work; only he who now restrains it will do so until he is out of the way. ⁸And then the lawless one will be revealed, and the Lord Jesus will slay him with the breath of his mouth and destroy him by his appearing and his coming. ⁹ The coming of the lawless one by the activity of Satan will be with all power and with pretended signs and wonders, ¹⁰ and with all wicked deception for those who are to perish, because they refused to love the truth and so be saved. ¹¹ Therefore God sends upon them a strong delusion, to make them believe what is false, ¹² so that all may be condemned who did not believe the truth but had pleasure in unrighteousness.

182. You gladly bear with fools

182

labors; but our hope is that as your faith increases, our field among you may be greatly enlarged, ¹⁶ so that we may preach the gospel in lands beyond you, without boasting of work already done in another's field. ¹⁷ "Let him who boasts, boast of the Lord." ¹⁸ For it is not the man who commends himself that is accepted, but the man whom the Lord commends.

11:21b-23a
But whatever any one dares to boast of—I am speaking as a fool—I also dare to boast of that. ²²Are they Hebrews? So am I. Are they Israelites? So am I. Are they descendants of Abraham? So am I. ²³Are they servants of Christ? I am a better one—I am talking like a madman—

Eph 2:8-9 ⁸ For by grace you have been saved through faith; and this is not your own doing, it is the gift of God— ⁹ not because of works, lest any man should boast.

*cf 11:30, 12:1, 5-6, 9

*cf Phil 3:4

183

Rom 2:17-24 (§10)

17 But if you call yourself a Jew and rely upon the law and boast of your relation to God 18 and know his will and approve what is excellent, because you are instructed in the law, 19 and if you are sure that you are a guide to the blind, a light to those who are in darkness, 20 a corrector of the foolish, a teacher of children, having in the law the embodiment of knowledge and truth— 21 you then who teach others, will you not teach yourself? While you preach against stealing, do you steal? 22 You who say that one must not commit adultery, do you commit adultery? You who abhor idols, do you rob temples? 23 You who boast in the law, do you dishonor God by breaking the law? 24 For, as it is written, "The name of God is blasphemed among the Gentiles because of you."

Rom 3:27-31 (§15)

27 Then what becomes of our boasting? It is excluded. On what principle? On the principle of works? No, but on the principle of faith. 28 For we hold that a man is justified by faith apart from works of law. 29 Or is God the

1 Cor 4:8-13 (§85)

8 Already you are filled! Already you have become rich! Without us you have become kings! And would that you did reign, so that we might share the rule with you! 9 For I think that God has exhibited us apostles as last of all, like men sentenced to death; because we have become a spectacle to the world, to angels and to men. 10 We are fools for Christ's sake, but you are wise in Christ. We are weak, but you are strong. You are held in honor, but we in disrepute. 11 To the present hour we hunger and thirst, we are ill-clad and buffeted and homeless, 12 and we labor, working with our own hands. When reviled, we bless; when persecuted, we endure; 13 when slandered, we try to conciliate; we have become, and are now, as the refuse of the world, the offscouring of all things.

God of Jews only? Is he not the God of Gentiles also? Yes, of Gentiles also, 30 since God is one; and he will justify the circumcised on the ground of their faith and the uncircumcised through their faith. 31 Do we then overthrow the law by this faith? By no means! On the

2 Cor 11:21b-29

But whatever any one dares to boast of—I am speaking as a fool—I also dare to boast of that. 22 Are they Hebrews? So am I. Are they Israelites? So am I. Are they descendants of Abraham? So am I. 23 Are they servants of Christ? I am a better one—I am talking like a madman—with far greater labors, far more imprisonments, with countless beatings, and often near death. 24 Five times I have received at the hands of the Jews the forty lashes less one. 25 Three times I have been beaten with rods; once I was stoned. Three times I have been

contrary, we uphold the law.

Rom 9:1-5 (§35)

9

I am speaking the truth in Christ, I am not lying; my conscience bears me witness in the Holy Spirit, 2 that I have great sorrow and unceasing anguish in my heart. 3 For I could wish that I myself were accursed and cut off from Christ for the sake of my brethren, my kinsmen by race. 4 They are Israelites, and to them belong the sonship, the glory, the covenants, the giving of the law, the worship, and the prom-

shipwrecked; a night and a day I have been adrift at sea; 26 on frequent journeys, in danger from rivers, danger from robbers, danger from my own people, danger from Gentiles, danger in the city, danger in the wilderness, danger at sea, danger from false brethren; 27 in toil and hardship, through many a sleepless night, in hunger and thirst, often without food, in cold and exposure. 28 And, apart from other things, there is the daily pressure upon me of my anxiety for all the churches. 29 Who is weak, and I am not weak? Who is made to fall, and I am not indignant?

ises; 5 to them belong the patriarchs, and of their race, according to the flesh, is the Christ. God who is over all be blessed for ever. Amen.

Rom 11:1-6 (§44)

11

I ask, then, has God rejected his people? By no means! I myself am an Israelite, a descendant of Abraham, a member of the tribe of Benjamin. 2 God has not rejected his people whom he foreknew. Do you not know what the scripture says of Eli'jah, how he pleads with God against Israel?

3 "Lord, they have killed thy prophets, they have demolished thy altars, and I alone am left, and they seek my life." 4 But what is God's reply to him? "I have kept for myself seven thousand men who have not bowed the knee to Ba'al." 5 So too at the present time there is a remnant, chosen by grace. 6 But if it is by grace, it is no longer on the basis of works; otherwise grace would no longer be grace.

▶11:23 Acts 9:16,

16 for I will show him how much he must suffer for the sake of my name."

16:23

23 And when they had inflicted many blows upon them, they threw them into prison, charging the jailer to keep them safely.

▶ 11:25-26 Acts 14:19

19 But Jews came there from Antioch and Ico'nium; and having persuaded the people, they stoned Paul and dragged him out of the city, supposing that he was dead.

▶11:25 Acts 16:22

22 The crowd joined in attacking them; and the magistrates tore the garments off them and gave orders to beat them with rods.

▶11:26 Acts 9:23,

23 When many days had passed, the Jews plotted to kill him,

13:45,

45 But when the Jews saw the multitudes, they were filled with jealousy, and contradicted what was spoken by Paul, and reviled him.

50,

50 But the Jews incited the devout women of high standing and the leading men of the city, and stirred up persecution against Paul and Barnabas, and drove them out of their district.

17:5,

5 But the Jews were jealous, and taking some wicked fellows of the rabble, they gathered a crowd, set the city in an uproar, and attacked the house of Jason, seeking to bring them out to the people.

13

13 But when the Jews of Thessaloni'ca learned that the word of God was proclaimed by Paul at Beroe'a also, they came there too, stirring up and inciting the crowds.

Acts 18:12,

12 But when Gallio was proconsul of Acha'ia, the Jews made a united attack upon Paul and brought him before the tribunal,

21:31,

31 And as they were trying to kill him, word came to the tribune of the cohort that all Jerusalem was in confusion.

27:42

42 The soldiers' plan was to kill the prisoners, lest any should swim away and escape;

▶11:28 Acts 20:18-21

18 And when they came to him, he said to them: "You yourselves know how I lived among you all the time from the first day that I set foot in Asia, 19 serving the Lord with all humility and with tears and with trials which befell me through the plots of the Jews; 20 how I did not shrink from declaring to you anything

that was profitable, and teaching you in public and from house to house, 21 testifying both to Jews and to Greeks of repentance to God and of faith in our Lord Jesus Christ.

184. I boast of things that show my weakness

184

1 Cor 1:26-31 (§75)

26 For consider your call, brethren; not many of you were wise according to worldly standards, not many were powerful, not many were of noble birth; 27 but God chose what is foolish in the world to shame the wise, God chose what is weak in the world to shame the strong, 28 God chose what is low and despised in the world, even things that are not, to bring to nothing things that are, 29 so that no human being might boast in the presence of God. 30 He is the source of your life in Christ Jesus, whom God made our wisdom, our righteousness and sanctification and redemption; 31 therefore, as it is written, "Let him who boasts, boast of the Lord."

2 Cor 11:30-33

30 If I must boast, I will boast of the things that show my weakness. 31 The God and Father of the Lord Jesus, he who is blessed for ever, knows that I do not lie. 32 At Damascus, the governor under King Ar'etas guarded the city of Damascus in order to seize me, 33 but I was let down in a basket through a window in the wall, and escaped his hands.

▶11:30-33 Acts 9:24-25

24 but their plot became known to Saul. They were watching the gates day and night, to kill him; 25 but his disciples took him by night and let him down over the wall, lowering him in a basket.

▶11:31 Gal 1:20

20 (In what I am writing to you, before God, I do not lie!)

2 Cor 1:23

23 But I call God to witness against me—it was to spare you that I refrained from coming to Corinth.

Phil 3:2-11 (§247)

2 Look out for the dogs, look out for the evil-workers, look out for those who mutilate the flesh. 3 For we are the true circumcision, who worship God in spirit,e and glory in Christ Jesus, and put no confidence in the flesh. 4 Though I myself have reason for confidence in the flesh also. If any other man thinks he has reason for confidence in the flesh, I have more: 5 circumcised on the eighth day, of the people of Israel, of the tribe of Benjamin, a Hebrew born of Hebrews; as to the law a Pharisee, 6 as to zeal a persecutor of the church, as to righteousness under the law blameless. 7 But whatever gain I had, I counted as loss for the sake of Christ. 8 Indeed I count everything as loss because of the surpassing worth of knowing Christ Jesus my Lord. For his sake I have suffered the loss of all things, and count them as refuse, in order that I may gain Christ 9 and be found in him, not having a righteousness of my own, based on law, but that which is through faith in Christ, the righteousness from God that depends on faith; 10 that I may know

Col 1:24-2:3 (§260)

24 Now I rejoice in my sufferings for your sake, and in my flesh I complete what is lacking in Christ's afflictions for the sake of his body, that is, the church, 25 of which I became a minister according to the divine office which was given to me for you, to make the word of God fully known, 26 the mystery hidden for ages and generationse but now made manifest to his saints. 27 To them God chose to make known how great among the Gentiles are the riches of the glory of this mystery, which is Christ in you, the hope of glory. 28 Him we proclaim, warning every man and teaching every man in all wisdom, that we may present every man mature in Christ. 29 For this I toil, striving with all the energy which he mightily inspires within me.

2 For I want you to know how greatly I strive for you, and for those at La-odice′a, and for all who have

him and the power of his resurrection, and may share his sufferings, becoming like him in his death, 11 that if possible I may attain the resurrection from the dead.

1 Thes 2:1-8 (§277)

2 For you yourselves know, brethren, that our visit to you was not in vain; 2 but though we had already suffered and been shamefully treated at Philippi, as you know, we had courage in our God to declare to you the gospel of God in the face of great opposition. 3 For our appeal does not spring from error or uncleanness, nor is it made with guile; 4 but just as we have been approved by God to be entrusted with the gospel, so we speak, not to please men, but to please God who tests our hearts. 5 For we never used either words of flattery, as you know, or a cloak for greed, as God is witness; 6 nor did we seek glory from men, whether from you or from others, though we might have made demands as apostles of Christ. 7 But we were gentle among you, like

not seen my face, 2 that their hearts may be encouraged as they are knit together in love, to have all the riches of assured understanding and the knowledge of God's mystery, of Christ, 3 in whom are hid all the treasures of wisdom and knowledge.

a nurse taking care of her children. 8 So, being affectionately desirous of you, we were ready to share with you not only the gospel of God but also our own selves, because you had become very dear to us.

1 Thes 3:1-5 (§281)

3 Therefore when we could bear it no longer, we were willing to be left behind at Athens alone, 2 and we sent Timothy, our brother and God's servant in the gospel of Christ, to establish you in your faith and to exhort you, 3 that no one be moved by these afflictions. You yourselves know that this is to be our lot. 4 For when we were with you, we told you beforehand that we were to suffer affliction; just as it has come to pass, and as you know. 5 For this reason, when I could bear it no longer, I sent that I might know your faith, for fear that somehow the tempter had tempted you and that our labor would be in vain.

183

▶11:21b-29 4:7-12

7 But we have this treasure in earthen vessels, to show that the transcendent power belongs to God and not to us. 8 We are afflicted in every way, but not crushed; perplexed, but not driven to despair; 9 persecuted, but not forsaken; struck down, but not destroyed; 10 always carrying in the body the death of Jesus, so that the life of Jesus may also be manifested in our bodies. 11 For while we live we are always being given up to death for Jesus' sake, so that the life of Jesus may be manifested in our mortal flesh. 12 So death is at work in us, but life in you.

6:4-10 4 but as servants of God we commend ourselves in every way: through great endurance, in afflictions, hardships, calamities, 5 beatings, imprisonments, tumults, labors, watching, hunger; 6 by purity, knowledge, forbearance, kindness, the Holy Spirit, genuine love, 7 truthful speech, and the power of God; with the weapons of righteousness for the right hand and for the left; 8 in honor and dishonor, in ill repute and good repute. We are treated as impostors, and yet are true; 9 as unknown, and yet well known; as dying, and behold we live; as punished, and yet not killed; 10 as sorrowful, yet always rejoicing; as poor, yet making many rich; as having nothing, and yet possessing everything.

1:3-11

3 Blessed be the God and Father of our Lord Jesus Christ, the Father of mercies and God of all comfort, 4 who comforts us in all our affliction, so that we may be able to comfort those who are in any affliction, with the comfort with which we ourselves are comforted by God. 5 For as we share abundantly in Christ's sufferings, so through Christ we share abundantly in comfort too." 6 If we are afflicted, it is for your comfort and salvation; and if we are comforted, it is for your comfort, which you experience when you patiently endure the same sufferings that we suffer. 7 Our hope for you is unshaken; for we know that as you share in our sufferings, you will also share in our comfort.

8 For we do not want you to be ignorant, brethren, of the affliction we experienced in Asia; for we were so utterly, unbearably crushed that we despaired of life itself. 9 Why, we felt that we had received the sentence of

death; but that was to make us rely not on ourselves but on God who raises the dead; 10 he delivered us from so deadly a peril, and he will deliver us; on him we have set our hope that he will deliver us again. 11 You also must help us by prayer, so that many will give thanks on our behalf for the blessing granted us in answer to many prayers.

184. I boast of things that show my weakness

184

185

Rom 5:1-5 (§20)

5 Therefore, since we are justified by faith, we have peace with God through our Lord Jesus Christ. 2 Through him we have obtained access· to this grace in which we stand, and we rejoice in our hope of sharing the glory of God. 3 More than that, we rejoice in our sufferings, knowing that suffering produces endurance, 4 and endurance produces character, and character produces hope, 5 and hope does not disappoint us, because God's love has been poured into our hearts through the Holy Spirit which has been given to us.

Rom 8:26-27 (§32)

26 Likewise the Spirit helps us in our weakness; for we do not know how to pray as we ought, but the Spirit himself intercedes for us with sighs too deep for words. 27And he who searches the hearts of men knows what is the mind of the Spirit, because the Spirit intercedes for the saints according to the will of God.

2 Cor 12:1-10

12 I must boast; there is nothing to be gained by it, but I will go on to visions and revelations of the Lord. 2 I know a man in Christ who fourteen years ago was caught up to the third heaven—whether in the body or out of the body I do not know, God knows. 3And I know that this man was caught up into Paradise—whether in the body or out of the body I do not know, God knows—4 and he heard things that cannot be told, which man may not utter. 5 On behalf of this man I will boast, but on my own behalf I will not boast, except of my weaknesses. 6 Though if I wish to boast, I shall not be a fool, for I shall be speaking the truth. But I refrain from it, so that no one may think more of me than' he sees in me or hears from me. 7And to keep me from being too elated by the abundance of revelations, a thorn was given me in the flesh, a messenger of Satan, to harass me, to keep me from being too elated. 8 Three times I besought the Lord about this, that it should leave me; 9 but he said to me, "My grace is sufficient for you, for my power is made perfect in weakness." I will all the more gladly boast of my weaknesses, that the power of Christ may rest upon me. 10 For the sake of Christ, then, I am content with weaknesses, insults, hardships, persecutions, and calamities; for when I am weak, then I am strong.

Gal 4:12-20 (§209)

12 Brethren, I beseech you, become as I am, for I also have become as you are. You did me no wrong; 13 you know it was because of a bodily ailment that I preached the gospel to you at first; 14 and though my condition was a trial to you, you did not scorn or despise me, but received me as an angel of God, as Christ Jesus. 15 What has become of the satisfaction you felt? For I bear you witness that, if possible, you would have plucked out your eyes and given them to me. 16 Have I then become your enemy by telling you the truth? 17 They make much of you, but for no good purpose; they want to shut you out, that you may make much of them. 18 For a good purpose it is always good to be made much of, and not only when I am present with you. 19 My little children, with whom I am again in travail until Christ be formed in you! 20 I could wish to be present with you now and to change my tone, for I am perplexed about you.

▶12:2 Acts 8:39
39And when they came up out of the water, the Spirit of the Lord caught up Philip; and the eunuch saw him no more, and went on his way rejoicing.

▶12:1 Gal 2:2   2 I went up by revelation; and I laid before them (but privately before those who were of repute) the gospel which I preach among the Gentiles, lest somehow I should be running or had run in vain.

1 Cor 15:8
8 Last of all, as to one untimely born, he appeared also to me.

9:1 Am I not free? Am I not an apostle? Have I not seen Jesus our Lord? Are not you my workmanship in the Lord?

2 Cor 5:16
16 From now on, therefore, we regard no one from a human point of view; even though we once regarded Christ from a human point of view, we regard him thus no longer.

▶12:5 11:30
30 If I must boast, I will boast of the things that show my weakness.

186. Signs of a true apostle were performed among you

186

Rom 15:14-21 (§62)

14 I myself am satisfied about you, my brethren, that you yourselves are full of goodness, filled with all knowledge, and able to instruct one another. 15 But on some points I have written to you very boldly by way of reminder, because of the grace given me by God 16 to be a minister of Christ Jesus to the Gentiles in the priestly service of the gospel of God, so that the offering of the Gentiles may be acceptable, sanctified by the Holy Spirit. 17 In Christ Jesus, then, I have reason to be proud of my work for God. 18 For I will not venture to speak of anything except what Christ has wrought through me to win obedience from the Gentiles, by word and deed, 19 by the power of signs and wonders, by the power of the Holy Spirit, so that from Jerusalem and as far round as Illyr'icum I have fully preached the gospel of Christ, 20 thus making it my ambition to preach the gospel, not where Christ has already been named, lest I build on another man's foundation, 21 but as it is written,
"They shall see who have never been told of him,
and they shall understand who have never heard of him."

1 Cor 2:1-5 (§76)

2 When I came to you, brethren, I did not come proclaiming to you the testimony of God in lofty words or wisdom. 2 For I decided to know nothing among you except Jesus Christ and him crucified. 3And I was with you in weakness and in much fear and trembling; 4 and my speech and my message were not in plausible words of wisdom, but in demonstration of the Spirit and of power, 5 that your faith might not rest in the wisdom of men but in the power of God.

2 Cor 12:11-13

11 I have been a fool! You forced me to it, for I ought to have been commended by you. For I was not at all inferior to these superlative apostles, even though I am nothing. 12 The signs of a true apostle were performed among you in all patience, with signs and wonders and mighty works. 13 For in what were you less favored than the rest of the churches, except that I myself did not burden you? Forgive me this wrong!

▶12:12 Acts 5:12
12 Now many signs and wonders were done among the people by the hands of the apostles. And they were all together in Solomon's Portico.

▶12:11-12 10:10-12   10 For they say, "His letters are weighty and strong, but his bodily presence is weak, and his speech of no account." 11 Let such people understand that what we say by letter when absent, we do when present. 12 Not that we venture to class or compare ourselves with some of those who commend themselves. But when they measure themselves by one another, and compare themselves with one another, they are without understanding.

▶12:11 11:5
5 I think that I am not in the least inferior to these superlative apostles.

2 Cor 5:12   12 We are not commending ourselves to you again but giving you cause to be proud of us, so that you may be able to answer those who pride themselves on a man's position and not on his heart.

185

Phil 4:10-20 (§253)

10 I rejoice in the Lord greatly that now at length you have revived your concern for me; you were indeed concerned for me, but you had no opportunity. 11 Not that I complain of want; for I have learned, in whatever state I am, to be content. 12 I know how to be abased, and I know how to abound; in any and all circumstances I have learned the secret of facing plenty and hunger, abundance and want. 13 I can do all things in him who strengthens me.

14 Yet it was kind of you to share my trouble. 15And you Philippians yourselves know that in the beginning of the gospel, when I left Macedo′nia, no church entered into partnership with me in giving and receiving except you only; 16 for even in Thessaloni′ca you sent me help once and again. 17 Not that I seek the gift; but I seek the fruit which increases to your credit. 18 I have received full payment, and more; I am filled, having received from Epaphrodi′tus the gifts you sent, a fragrant offering, a sacrifice acceptable and pleasing to God. 19And my God will supply

►12:9 Deut 3:26
26 But the LORD was angry with me on your account, and would not hearken to me; and the LORD said to me, 'Let it suffice you; speak no more to me of this matter.

Col 2:16-19 (§263)

16 Therefore let no one pass judgment on you in questions of food and drink or with regard to a festival or a new moon or a sabbath. 17 These are only a shadow of what is to come; but the substance belongs to Christ. 18 Let no one disqualify you, insisting on self-abasement and worship of angels, taking his stand on visions, puffed up without reason by his sensuous mind, 19 and not holding fast to the Head, from whom the whole body, nourished and knit together through its joints and ligaments, grows with a growth that is from God.

every need of yours according to his riches in glory in Christ Jesus. 20 To our God and Father be glory for ever and ever. Amen.

186. Signs of a true apostle were performed among you

186

Phil 4:10-20 (§253)

10 I rejoice in the Lord greatly that now at length you have revived your concern for me; you were indeed concerned for me, but you had no opportunity. 11 Not that I complain of want; for I have learned, in whatever state I am, to be content. 12 I know how to be abased, and I know how to abound; in any and all circumstances I have learned the secret of facing plenty and hunger, abundance and want. 13 I can do all things in him who strengthens me.

14 Yet it was kind of you to share my trouble. 15And you Philippians yourselves know that in the beginning of the gospel, when I left Macedo′nia, no church entered into partnership with me in giving and receiving except you only; 16 for even in Thessaloni′ca you sent me help once and again. 17 Not that I seek the gift; but I seek the fruit which increases to your credit. 18 I have received full payment, and more; I am filled, having received from Epaphrodi′tus the gifts you sent, a fragrant offering, a sacrifice acceptable and pleasing to God. 19And my God will supply

every need of yours according to his riches in glory in Christ Jesus. 20 To our God and Father be glory for ever and ever. Amen.

1 Thes 1:2-10(§276)

2 We give thanks to God always for you all, constantly mentioning you in our prayers, 3 remembering before our God and Father your work of faith and labor of love and steadfastness of hope in our Lord Jesus Christ. 4 For we know, brethren beloved by God, that he has chosen you; 5 for our gospel came to you not only in word, but also in power and in the Holy Spirit and with full conviction. You know what kind of men we proved to be among you for your sake. 6And you became imitators of us and of the Lord, for you received the word in much affliction, with joy inspired by the Holy Spirit; 7 so that you became an example to all the believers in Macedo′nia and in Acha′ia. 8 For not only has the word of the Lord sounded forth from you in Macedo′nia and Acha′ia, but your faith in God has gone forth everywhere, so that we need not say anything. 9 For they themselves report concerning us what a welcome we had among you, and how you turned to God from idols, to serve a living and true God, 10 and to wait for his Son from heaven, whom he raised from the dead, Jesus who delivers us from the wrath to come.

*cf 1 Thes 2:9-12(§278)

,2 Thes 2:1-12 (§296)

2 Now concerning the coming of our Lord Jesus Christ and our assembling to meet him, we beg you, brethren, 2 not to be quickly shaken in mind or excited, either by spirit or by word, or by letter purporting to be from us, to the effect that the day of the Lord has come. 3 Let no one deceive you in any way; for that day will not come, unless the rebellion comes first, and the man of lawlessness is revealed, the son of perdition, 4 who opposes and exalts himself against every so-called god or object of worship, so that he takes his seat in the temple of God, proclaiming himself to be God. 5 Do you not remember that when I was still with you I told you this? 6And you know what is restraining him now so that he may be revealed in his time. 7 For the mystery of lawlessness is already at work; only he who now restrains it will do so until he is out of the way. 8And then the lawless one will be revealed, and the Lord Jesus will slay him with the breath of his mouth and destroy him by his appearing and his coming. 9 The coming of the lawless one by the activity of

Satan will be with all power and with pretended signs and wonders, 10 and with all wicked deception for those who are to perish, because they refused to love the truth and so be saved. 11 Therefore God sends upon them a strong delusion, to make them believe what is false, 12 so that all may be condemned who did not believe the truth but had pleasure in unrighteousness.

187

1 Cor 4:14-21 (§86)

14 I do not write this to make you ashamed, but to admonish you as my beloved children. 15 For though you have countless guides in Christ, you do not have many fathers. For I became your father in Christ Jesus through the gospel. 16 I urge you, then, be imitators of me. 17 Therefore I sent to you Timothy, my beloved and faithful child in the Lord, to remind you of my ways in Christ, as I teach them everywhere in every church. 18 Some are arrogant, as though I were not coming to you. 19 But I will come to you soon, if the Lord wills, and I will find out not the talk of these arrogant people but their power. 20 For the kingdom of God does not consist in talk but in power. 21 What do you wish? Shall I come to you with a rod, or with love in a spirit of gentleness?

2 Cor 12:14-18

14 Here for the third time I am ready to come to you. And I will not be a burden, for I seek not what is yours but you; for children ought not to lay up for their parents, but parents for their children. 15 I will most gladly spend and be spent for your souls. If I love you the more, am I to be loved the less? 16 But granting that I myself did not burden you, I was crafty, you say, and got the better of you by guile. 17 Did I take advantage of you through any of those whom I sent to you? 18 I urged Titus to go, and sent the brother with him. Did Titus take advantage of you? Did we not act in the same spirit? Did we not take the same steps?

▶12:15 2 Tim 2:10
10 Therefore I endure everything for the sake of the elect, that they also may obtain salvation in Christ Jesus with its eternal glory.

▶2:14-18 Rom 16:17-20
17 I appeal to you, brethren, to take note of those who create dissensions and difficulties, in opposition to the doctrine which you have been taught; avoid them. 18 For such persons do not serve our Lord Christ, but their own appetites, and by fair and flattering words they deceive the hearts of the simple-minded. 19 For while your obedience is known to all, so that I rejoice over you, I would have you wise as to what is good and guileless as to what is evil; 20 then the God of peace will soon crush Satan under your feet. The grace of our Lord Jesus Christ be with you.

▶12:14 1:15-18,
15 Because I was sure of this, I wanted to come to you first, so that you might have a double pleasure, 16 I wanted to visit you on my way to Macedo'nia, and to come back to you from Macedo'nia and have you send me on my way to Judea. 17 Was I vacillating when I wanted to do this? Do I make my plans like a worldly man, ready to say Yes and No at once? 18 As surely as God is faithful, our word to you has not been Yes and No.

2:1,
For I made up my mind not to make you another painful visit.

188. Not what I wish; not what you wish

188

Rom 1:29-32 (§6)

29 They were filled with all manner of wickedness, evil, covetousness, malice. Full of envy, murder, strife, deceit, malignity, they are gossips, 30 slanderers, haters of God, insolent, haughty, boastful, inventors of evil, disobedient to parents, 31 foolish, faithless, heartless, ruthless. 32 Though they know God's decree that those who do such things deserve to die, they not only do them but approve those who practice them.

Rom 13:11-14 (§56)

11 Besides this you know what hour it is, how it is full time now for you to wake from sleep. For salvation is nearer to us now than when we first believed; 12 the night is far gone, the day is at hand. Let us then cast off the works of darkness and put on the armor of light; 13 let us conduct ourselves becomingly as in the day, not in reveling and drunkenness, not in debauchery and licentiousness, not in quarreling and jealousy. 14 But put on the Lord Jesus Christ, and make no provision for the flesh, to gratify its desires.

1 Cor 5:9-13 (§88)

9 I wrote to you in my letter not to associate with immoral men; 10 not at all meaning the immoral of this world, or the greedy and robbers, or idolaters, since then you would need to go out of the world. 11 But rather I wrote to you not to associate with any one who bears the name of brother if he is guilty of immorality or greed, or is an idolater, reviler, drunkard, or robber—not even to eat with such a one. 12 For what have I to do with judging outsiders? Is it not those inside the church whom you are to judge? 13 God judges those outside. "Drive out the wicked person from among you."

1 Cor 6:9-11 (§91)

9 Do you not know that the unrighteous will not inherit the kingdom of God? Do not be deceived; neither the immoral, nor idolaters, nor adulterers, nor sexual perverts, 10 nor thieves, nor the greedy, nor drunkards, nor revilers, nor robbers will inherit the kingdom of God. 11 And such were some of you. But you were washed, you were sanctified, you were justified in the name of the Lord Jesus Christ and in the Spirit of our God.

2 Cor 12:19-21

19 Have you been thinking all along that we have been defending ourselves before you? It is in the sight of God that we have been speaking in Christ, and all for your upbuilding, beloved. 20 For I fear that perhaps I may come and find you not what I wish, and that you may find me not what you wish; that perhaps there may be quarreling, jealousy, anger, selfishness, slander, gossip, conceit, and disorder. 21 I fear that when I come again my God may humble me before you, and I may have to mourn over many of those who sinned before and have not repented of the impurity, immorality, and licentiousness which they have practiced.

Gal 5:16-26 (§213)

16 But I say, walk by the Spirit, and do not gratify the desires of the flesh. 17 For the desires of the flesh are against the Spirit, and the desires of the Spirit are against the flesh; for these are opposed to each other, to prevent you from doing what you would. 18 But if you are led by the Spirit you are not under the law. 19 Now the works of the flesh are plain: fornication, impurity, licentiousness, 20 idolatry, sorcery, enmity, strife, jealousy, anger, selfishness, dissension, party spirit, 21 envy,k drunkenness, carousing, and the like. I warn you, as I warned you before, that those who do such things shall not inherit the kingdom of God. 22 But the fruit of the Spirit is love, joy, peace, patience, kindness, goodness, faithfulness, 23 gentleness, self-control; against such there is no law. 24 And those who belong to Christ Jesus have crucified the flesh with its passions and desires.

25 If we live by the Spirit, let us also walk by the Spirit. 26 Let us have no self-conceit, no provoking of one another, no envy of one another.

Eph 4:17-32(§227-228)

17 Now this I affirm and testify in the Lord, that you must no longer live as the Gentiles do, in the futility of their minds; 18 they are darkened in their understanding, alienated from the life of God because of the ignorance that is in them, due to their hardness of heart; 19 they have become callous and have given themselves up to licentiousness, greedy to practice every kind of uncleanness. 20 You did not so learn Christ!— 21 assuming that you have heard about him and were taught in him, as the truth is in Jesus. 22 Put off your old nature which belongs to your former manner of life and is corrupt through deceitful lusts, 23 and be renewed in the spirit of your minds, 24 and put on the new nature, created after the likeness of God in true righteousness and holiness.

25 Therefore, putting away falsehood, let every one speak the truth with his neighbor, for we are members one of another. 26 Be angry but do not sin; do not let the sun go down on your anger, 27 and give no opportunity to the devil. 28 Let the thief no longer steal, but

▶12:19 3:1,
Are we beginning to commend ourselves again? Or do we need, as some do, letters of recommendation to you, or from you?

2:17,
17 For we are not, like so many, peddlers of God's word; but as men of sincerity, as commissioned by God, in the sight of God we speak in Christ.

10:18
18 For it is not the man who commends himself that is accepted, but the man whom the Lord commends.

▶12:20 10:11
11 Let such people understand that what we say by letter when absent, we do when present.

▶12:21 9:4
4 lest if some Macedo'nians come with me and find that you are not ready, we be humiliated—to say nothing of you—for being so confident.

1 Thes 2:1-8 (§277)

2 For you yourselves know, brethren, that our visit to you was not in vain; 2 but though we had already suffered and been shamefully treated at Philippi, as you know, we had courage in our God to declare to you the gospel of God in the face of great opposition. 3 For our appeal does not spring from error or uncleanness, nor is it made with guile; 4 but just as we have been approved by God to be entrusted with the gospel, so we speak, not to please men, but to please God who tests our hearts. 5 For we never used either words of flattery, as you know, or a cloak for greed, as God is witness; 6 nor did we seek glory from men, whether from you or from others, though we might have made demands as apostles of Christ. 7 But we were gentle among you, like a nurse taking care of her children. 8 So, being affectionately desirous of you, we were ready to share with you not only the gospel of God but also our own selves, because you had become very dear to us.

13:1 This is the third time I am coming to you. Any charge must be sustained by the evidence of two or three witnesses.

▶ 12:15 Phil 2:17
17 Even if I am to be poured as a libation upon the sacrificial offering of your faith, I am glad and rejoice with you all.

▶ 12:18 8:6,
6Accordingly we have urged Titus that as he had already made a beginning, he should also complete among you this gracious work.

16-19
16 But thanks be to God who puts the same earnest care for you into the heart of Titus. 17 For he not only accepted our appeal, but being himself very earnest he is going to you of his own accord.

18 With him we are sending the brother who is famous among all the churches for his preaching of the gospel; 19 and not only that, but he has been appointed by the churches to travel with us in this gracious work which we are carrying on, for the glory of the Lord and to show our good will.

188. Not what I wish; not what you wish

Eph (cont)
rather let him labor, doing honest work with his hands, so that he may be able to give to those in need. 29 Let no evil talk come out of your mouths, but only such as is good for edifying, as fits the occasion, that it may impart grace to those who hear. 30And do not grieve the Holy Spirit of God, in whom you were sealed for the day of redemption. 31 Let all bitterness and wrath and anger and clamor and slander be put away from you, with all malice, 32 and be kind to one another, tenderhearted, forgiving one another, as God in Christ forgave you.

Eph 5:3-14 (§230)
3 But fornication and all impurity or covetousness must not even be named among you, as is fitting among saints. 4 Let there be no filthiness, nor silly talk, nor levity, which are not fitting; but instead let there be thanksgiving. 5 Be sure of this, that no fornicator or impure man, or one who is covetous (that is, an idolater), has any inheritance in the kingdom of Christ and of God. 6 Let no one deceive you with empty words, for it is because of these things

Col 3:5-11 (§266)
5 Put to death therefore what is earthly in you: fornication, impurity, passion; evil desire, and covetousness, which is idolatry. 6 On account of these the wrath of God is coming. 7 In these you once walked, when you lived in them. 8 But now put them all away: anger, wrath, malice, slander, and foul talk from your mouth. 9 Do not lie to one another, seeing that you have put off the old nature with its practices 10 and have put on the new nature, which is being renewed in knowledge

that the wrath of God comes upon the sons of disobedience. 7 Therefore do not associate with them, 8 for once you were darkness, but now you are light in the Lord; walk as children of light 9 (for the fruit of light is found in all that is good and right and true), 10 and try to learn what is pleasing to the Lord. 11 Take no part in the unfruitful works of darkness, but instead expose them. 12 For it is a shame even to speak of the things that they do in secret; 13 but when anything is exposed by the light it becomes visible, for anything that becomes visible is light. 14 There-

after the image of its creator. 11 Here there cannot be Greek and Jew, circumcised and uncircumcised, barbarian, Scyth'ian, slave, free man, but Christ is all, and in all.

fore it is said,
"Awake, O sleeper, and arise from the dead,
and Christ shall give you light."

189

Rom 1:16-17 (§3)

16 For I am not ashamed of the gospel: it is the power of God for salvation to every one who has faith, to the Jew first and also to the Greek. 17 For in it the righteousness of God is revealed through faith for faith; as it is written, "He who through faith is righteous shall live."

▶13:1 12:14
14 Here for the third time I am ready to come to you. And I will not be a burden, for I seek not what is yours but you; for children ought not to lay up for their parents, but parents for their children.

1 Cor 1:18-25 (§74)

18 For the word of the cross is folly to those who are perishing, but to us who are being saved it is the power of God. 19 For it is written,
"I will destroy the wisdom of the wise,
and the cleverness of the clever I will thwart."
20 Where is the wise man? Where is the scribe? Where is the debater of this age? Has not God made foolish the wisdom of the world? 21 For since, in the wisdom of God, the world did not know God through wisdom, it pleased God through the folly of what we preach to save those who believe. 22 For Jews demand signs and Greeks seek wisdom, 23 but we preach Christ crucified, a stumbling block to Jews and folly to Gentiles, 24 but to those who are called, both Jews and Greeks, Christ the power of God and the wisdom of God. 25 For the foolishness of God is wiser than men, and the weakness of God is stronger than men.

1 Cor 4:14-21 (§86)
14 I do not write this to make you ashamed, but to admonish you as my

*cf. 2 Cor 7:5-13

▶13:4 1 Cor 2:1-5
When I came to you, brethren, I did not come proclaiming to you the testimony of God in lofty words or wisdom. 2 For I decided to know nothing among you except Jesus Christ and him crucified. 3 And I was with you in weakness and in much fear and trembling; 4 and my speech and my

2 Cor 13:1-4

13 This is the third time I am coming to you. Any charge must be sustained by the evidence of two or three witnesses. 2 I warned those who sinned before and all the others, and I warn them now while absent, as I did when present on my second visit, that if I come again I will not spare them— 3 since you desire proof that Christ is speaking in me. He is not weak in dealing with you, but is powerful in you. 4 For he was crucified in weakness, but lives by the power of God. For we are weak in him, but in dealing with you we shall live with him by the power of God.

beloved children. 15 For though you have countless guides in Christ, you do not have many fathers. For I became your father in Christ Jesus through the gospel. 16 I urge you, then, be imitators of me. 17 Therefore I sent to you Timothy, my beloved and faithful child in the Lord, to remind you of my ways in Christ, as I teach them everywhere in every church. 18 Some are arrogant, as though I were not coming to you. 19 But I will come to you soon, if the

message were not in plausible words of wisdom, but in demonstration of the Spirit and of power, 5 that your faith might not rest in the wisdom of men but in the power of God.

Lord wills, and I will find out not the talk of these arrogant people but their power. 20 For the kingdom of God does not consist in talk but in power. 21 What do you wish? Shall I come to you with a rod, or with love in a spirit of gentleness?

1 Cor 5:1-5 (§87)

5 It is actually reported that there is immorality among you, and of a kind that is not found even among pagans; for a man is living with his father's wife. 2 And you are arrogant! Ought you not rather to mourn? Let him who has done this be removed from among you.

3 For though absent in body I am present in spirit, and as if present, I have already pronounced judgment 4 in the name of the Lord Jesus on the man who has done such a thing. When you are assembled, and my spirit is present, with the power of our Lord Jesus, 5 you are to deliver this man to Satan for the destruction of the flesh, that his spirit may be saved in the day of the Lord Jesus.

Phil 2:7
7 but emptied himself, taking the form of a servant, being born in the likeness of men.

190. We pray for your improvement

190

Rom 15:1-6 (§60)

15 We who are strong ought to bear with the failings of the weak, and not to please ourselves; 2 let each of us please his neighbor for his good, to edify him. 3 For Christ did not please himself; but, as it is written, "The reproaches of those who reproached thee fell on me." 4 For whatever was written in former days was written for our instruction, that by steadfastness and by the encouragement of the scriptures we might have hope. 5 May the God of steadfastness and encouragement grant you to live in such harmony with one another, in accord with Christ Jesus, 6 that together you may with one voice glorify the God and Father of our Lord Jesus Christ.

▶13:10 Tit 1:13
13 This testimony is true. Therefore rebuke them sharply, that they may be sound in the faith,

1 Cor 4:14-21 (§86)

14 I do not write this to make you ashamed, but to admonish you as my beloved children. 15 For though you have countless guides in Christ, you do not have many fathers. For I became your father in Christ Jesus through the gospel. 16 I urge you, then, be imitators of me. 17 Therefore I sent to you Timothy, my beloved and faithful child in the Lord, to remind you of my ways in Christ, as I teach them everywhere in every church. 18 Some are arrogant, as though I were not coming to you. 19 But I will come to you soon, if the Lord wills, and I will find out not the talk of these arrogant people but their power. 20 For the kingdom of God does not consist in talk but in power. 21 What do you wish? Shall I come to you with a rod, or with love in a spirit of gentleness?

▶13:5-6 2:9,
9 For this is why I wrote, that I might test you and know whether you are obedient in everything.

7:11
see what earnestness this godly grief has produced in you, what eagerness to clear yourselves, what indignation, what alarm, what longing, what zeal, what punishment! At every point you have proved yourselves guiltless in the matter.

2 Cor 13:5-10

5 Examine yourselves, to see whether you are holding to your faith. Test yourselves. Do you not realize that Jesus Christ is in you?—unless indeed you fail to meet the test! 6 I hope you will find out that we have not failed. 7 But we pray God that you may not do wrong— not that we may appear to have met the test, but that you may do what is right, though we may seem to have failed. 8 For we cannot do anything against the truth, but only for the truth. 9 For we are glad when we are weak and you are strong. What we pray for is your improvement. 10 I write this while I am away from you, in order that when I come I may not have to be severe in my use of the authority which the Lord has given me for building up and not for tearing down.

11 For
▶13:5 1 Cor 11:28
28 Let a man examine himself, and so eat of the bread and drink of the cup.

Gal 6:4
4 But let each one test his own work, and then his reason to boast will be in himself alone and not in his neighbor.

▶13:10 10:1-6,
I, Paul, myself entreat you, by the meekness and gentleness of Christ—I who am humble when face to face with you, but bold to you when I am away!— 2 I beg of you that when I am present I may not have to show boldness with such confidence as I count on showing against some who

190. We pray for your improvement

suspect us of acting in worldly fashion. ³ For though we live in the world we are not carrying on a worldly war, ⁴ for the weapons of our warfare are not worldly but have divine power to destroy strongholds. ⁵ We destroy arguments and every proud obstacle to the knowledge of God, and take every thought captive to obey Christ, ⁶ being ready to

punish every disobedience, when your obedience is complete.

8   ⁸ For even if I boast a little too much of our authority, which the Lord gave for building you up and not for destroying you, I shall not be put to shame.

Gal 2:18   ¹⁸ But if I build up again those things which I tore down, then I prove myself a transgressor.

191. Live in peace

191

Rom 12:9-21 (§53)

9 Let love be genuine; hate what is evil, hold fast to what is good; 10 love one another with brotherly affection; outdo one another in showing honor. 11 Never flag in zeal, be aglow with the Spirit, serve the Lord. 12 Rejoice in your hope, be patient in tribulation, be constant in prayer. 13 Contribute to the needs of the saints, practice hospitality.

14 Bless those who persecute you; bless and do not curse them. 15 Rejoice with those who rejoice, weep with those who weep. 16 Live in harmony with one another; do not be haughty, but associate with the lowly; never be conceited. 17 Repay no one evil for evil, but take thought for what is noble in the sight of all. 18 If possible, so far as it depends upon you, live peaceably with all. 19 Beloved, never avenge yourselves, but leave it to the wrath of God; for it is written, "Vengeance is mine, I will repay, says the Lord." 20 No, "if your enemy is hungry, feed him; if he is thirsty, give him drink; for by so doing you will heap burning coals upon his head." 21 Do not be overcome by evil, but overcome evil with good.

1 Cor 16:19-20 (§143)

19 The churches of Asia send greetings. Aquila and Prisca, together with the church in their house, send you hearty greetings in the Lord. 20 All the brethren send greetings. Greet one another with a holy kiss.

Rom 16:3-16 (§66)

3 Greet Prisca and Aquila, my fellow workers in Christ Jesus, 4 who risked their necks for my life, to whom not only I but also all the churches of the Gentiles give thanks; 5 greet also the church in their house. Greet my beloved Epae′netus, who was the first convert in Asia for Christ. 6 Greet Mary, who has worked hard among you. 7 Greet Androni′cus and Ju′nias, my kinsmen and my fellow prisoners; they are men of note among the apostles, and they were in Christ before me. 8 Greet Amplia′tus, my beloved in the Lord. 9 Greet Urba′nus, our fellow worker in Christ, and my beloved Stachys. 10 Greet Apel′les, who is approved in Christ. Greet those who belong to the family of Aristobu′lus. 11 Greet my kinsman Hero′dion. Greet those in the

2 Cor 13:11-13

11 Finally, brethren, farewell. Mend your ways, heed my appeal, agree with one another, live in peace, and the God of love and peace will be with you. 12 Greet one another with a holy kiss. 13 All the saints greet you.

Lord who belong to the family of Narcis′sus. 12 Greet those workers in the Lord, Tryphae′na and Trypho′sa. Greet the beloved Persis, who has worked hard in the Lord. 13 Greet Rufus, eminent in the Lord, also his mother and mine. 14 Greet Asyn′critus, Phlegon, Hermes, Pat′robas, Hermas, and the brethren who are with them. 15 Greet Philol′ogus, Julia, Nereus and his sister, and Olym′pas, and all the saints who are with them. 16 Greet one another with a holy kiss. All the churches of Christ greet you.

*cf Rom 16:21-33(§69)

▶ 13:11-13 *cf 2 Tim 4:19-21, Tit 3:15a

192. Grace

192

Rom 16:20b (§68)

The grace of our Lord Jesus Christ be with you.

1 Cor 16:23-24 (§145)

23 The grace of the Lord Jesus be with you. 24 My love be with you all in Christ Jesus. Amen.

2 Cor 13:14

14 The grace of the Lord Jesus Christ and the love of God and the fellowship of the Holy Spirit be with you all.

Gal 6:18 (§217)

18 The grace of our Lord Jesus Christ be with your spirit, brethren. Amen.

Eph 6:23-24 (§236)

23 Peace be to the brethren, and love with faith, from God the Father and the Lord Jesus Christ. 24 Grace be with all who love our Lord Jesus Christ with love undying.

▶ 13:14 *cf 1 Tim 6:21b, 2Tim 4:22, Tit 3:15b

Phil 4:21-22 (§254)

21 Greet every saint in Christ Jesus. The brethren who are with me greet you. 22 All the saints greet you, **especially those of Caesar's household.**

Col 4:10-15 (§272)

10 Aristar'chus my fellow prisoner greets you, and Mark the cousin of Barnabas (concerning whom you have received instructions—if he comes to you, receive him), 11 and Jesus who is called Justus. These are the only men of the circumcision among my fellow workers for the kingdom of God, and they have been a comfort to me. 12 Ep'aphras, who is one of yourselves, a servant of Christ Jesus, greets you, always remembering you earnestly in his prayers, that you may stand mature and fully assured in all the will of God. 13 For I bear him witness that he has worked hard for you and for those in La-odice'a and in Hi-erap'olis. 14 Luke the beloved physician and Demas greet you. 15 Give my greetings to the brethren at La-odice'a, and to Nympha and the church in her house.

1 Thes 5:23-24(§289)

23 May the God of peace himself sanctify you wholly; and may your spirit and soul and body be kept sound and blameless at the coming of our Lord Jesus Christ. 24 He who calls you is faithful, and he will do it.

1 Thes 5:26 (§291)

26 Greet all the brethren with a holy kiss.

2 Thes 3:16(§302)

16 Now may our Lord Jesus Christ himself, and God our Father, who loved us and gave us eternal comfort and good hope through grace, 17 comfort your hearts and establish them in every good work and word.

Phm 23-24 (§310)

23 Ep'aphras, my fellow prisoner in Christ Jesus, sends greetings to you, 24 and so do Mark, Aristar'chus, Demas, and Luke, my fellow workers.

191

192. Grace

Phil 4:23 (§255)

23 **The grace of the Lord Jesus Christ be with your spirit.**

Col 4:18b (§274)

Grace be with you.

1 Thes 5:28 (§293)

28 The grace of our Lord Jesus Christ be with you.

2 Thes 3:18 (§304)

18 The grace of our Lord Jesus Christ be with you all.

Phm 25 (§311)

25 The grace of the Lord Jesus Christ be with your spirit.

192

193

Rom 1:1-7 (§1)

1 Paul, a servant of Jesus Christ, called to be an apostle, set apart for the gospel of God 2 which he promised beforehand through his prophets in the holy scriptures, 3 the gospel concerning his Son, who was descended from David according to the flesh 4 and designated Son of God in power according to the Spirit of holiness by his resurrection from the dead, Jesus Christ our Lord, 5 through whom we have received grace and apostleship to bring about the obedience of faith for the sake of his name among all the nations, 6 including yourselves who are called to belong to Jesus Christ;

7 To all God's beloved in Rome, who are called to be saints:

Grace to you and peace from God our Father and the Lord Jesus Christ.

1 Cor 1:1-3 (§71)

1 Paul, called by the will of God to be an apostle of Christ Jesus, and our brother Sos´thenes,

2 To the church of God which is at Corinth, to those sanctified in Christ Jesus, called to be saints together with all those who in every place call on the name of our Lord Jesus Christ, both their Lord and ours:

3 Grace to you and peace from God our Father and the Lord Jesus Christ.

2 Cor 1:1-2 (§146)

1 Paul, an apostle of Christ Jesus by the will of God, and Timothy our brother.

To the church of God which is at Corinth, with all the saints who are in the whole of Acha´ia:

2 Grace to you and peace from God our Father and the Lord Jesus Christ.

Gal 1:1-5

1 Paul an apostle—not from men nor through man, but through Jesus Christ and God the Father, who raised him from the dead— 2 and all the brethren who are with me,

To the churches of Galatia:

3 Grace to you and peace from God the Father and our Lord Jesus Christ, 4 who gave himself for our sins to deliver us from the present evil age, according to the will of our God and Father; 5 to whom be the glory for ever and ever. Amen.

Eph 1:1-2 (§218)

1 Paul, an apostle of Christ Jesus by the will of God,
To the saints who are also faithful in Christ Jesus:

2 Grace to you and peace from God our Father and the Lord Jesus Christ.

▶ 1:1 Acts 2:24, 24 But God raised him up, having loosed the pangs of death, because it was not possible for him to be held by it.

9:15, 15 But the Lord said to him, "Go, for he is a chosen instrument of mine to carry my name before the Gentiles and kings and the sons of Israel;

20:24 24 But I do not account my life of any value nor as precious to myself, if only I may accomplish my course and the ministry which I received from the Lord Jesus, to testify to the gospel of the grace of God.

▶ 1:2 Acts 16:6 6 And they went through the region of Phryg´ia and Galatia, having been forbidden by the Holy Spirit to speak the word in Asia.

▶ 1:4 Acts 2:40, 40And he testified with many other words and exhorted them, saying, "Save yourselves from this crooked generation."

1 Tim 2:6 6 who gave himself as a ransom for all, the testimony to which was borne at the proper time.

194. Not that there is another gospel

194

Rom 16:17-20a (§67)

17 I appeal to you, brethren, to take note of those who create dissensions and difficulties, in opposition to the doctrine which you have been taught; avoid them. 18 For such persons do not serve our Lord Christ, but their own appetites, and by fair and flattering words they deceive the hearts of the simple-minded. 19 For while your obedience is known to all, so that I rejoice over you, I would have you wise as to what is good and guileless as to what is evil; 20 then the God of peace will soon crush Satan under your feet.

1 Cor 11:23-26 (§114)

23 For I received from the Lord what I also delivered to you, that the Lord Jesus on the night when he was betrayed took bread, 24 and when he had given thanks, he broke it, and said, "This is my body which is for you. Do this in remembrance of me." 25 In the same way also the cup, after supper, saying, "This cup is the new covenant in my blood. Do this, as often as you drink it, in remembrance of me." 26 For as often as you eat this bread and drink the cup, you proclaim the Lord's death until he comes.

1 Cor 15:1-11 (§131)

15 Now I would remind you, brethren, in what terms I preached to you the gospel, which you received, in which you stand, 2 by which you are saved, if you hold it fast—unless you believed in vain.

3 For I delivered to you as of first importance what I also received, that Christ died for our sins in accordance with the scriptures, 4 that he was buried, that he was raised on the third day in accordance with the scriptures, 5 and that he appeared to Cephas, then to the twelve. 6 Then he appeared to more than five hundred brethren at one time, most of whom are still alive, though some have fallen asleep. 7 Then he appeared to James, then to all the apostles. 8 Last of all, as to one untimely born, he appeared also to me. 9 For I am the least of the apostles, unfit to be called an apostle, because I persecuted the church of God. 10 But by the grace of God I am what I am, and his grace toward me was not in vain. On the contrary, I worked harder than any of them, though it was not I, but the grace

2 Cor 11:1-6 (§179)

11 I wish you would bear with me in a little foolishness. Do bear with me! 2 I feel a divine jealousy for you, for I betrothed you to Christ to present you as a pure bride to her one husband. 3 But I am afraid that as the serpent deceived Eve by his cunning, your thoughts will be led astray from a sincere and pure devotion to Christ. 4 For if some one comes and preaches another Jesus than the one we preached, or if you receive a different spirit from the one you received, or if you accept a different gospel from the one you accepted, you submit to it readily enough.

5 I think that I am not in the least inferior to these superlative apostles. 6 Even if I am unskilled in speaking, I am not in knowledge; in every way we have made this plain to you in all things.

2 Cor 11:12-21a (§181-182)

12 And what I do I will continue to do, in order to undermine the claim of those who would like to claim that in their boasted mission they work on the same terms as we do. 13 For such men are false apostles, deceitful workmen, disguising themselves as apostles of God which is with me. 11 Whether then it was I or they, so we preach and so you believed.

Gal 1:6-12

6 I am astonished that you are so quickly deserting him who called you in the grace of Christ and turning to a different gospel— 7 not that there is another gospel, but there are some who trouble you and want to pervert the gospel of Christ. 8 But even if we, or an angel from heaven, should preach to you a gospel contrary to that which we preached to you, let him be accursed. 9As we have said before, so now I say again, If any one is preaching to you a gospel contrary to that which you received, let him be accursed.

10 Am I now seeking the favor of men, or of God? Or am I trying to please men? If I were still pleasing men, I should not be a servant of Christ.

11 For I would have you know, brethren, that the gospel which was preached by me is not man's gospel. 12 For I did not receive it from man, nor was I taught it, but it came through a revelation of Jesus Christ.

Christ. 14And no wonder, for even Satan disguises himself as an angel of light. 15 So it is not strange if his servants also disguise themselves as servants of righteousness. Their end will correspond to their deeds.

16 I repeat, let no one think me foolish; but even if you do, accept me as a fool, so that I too may boast a little. 17 (What I am saying I say not with the Lord's authority but as a fool, in this boastful confidence; 18 since many boast of worldly things, I too will boast.) 19 For you gladly bear with fools, being wise yourselves! 20 For you bear it if a

---

▶ 1:6 3:1-5, O foolish Galatians! Who has bewitched you, before whose eyes Jesus Christ was publicly portrayed as crucified? 2 Let me ask you only this: Did you receive the Spirit by works of the law, or by hearing with faith? 3Are you so foolish? Having begun with the Spirit, are you now ending with the flesh? 4 Did you experience so many things in vain?—if it really is in vain. 5 Does he who supplies the Spirit to you and works miracles among you do so by works of the law, or by hearing with faith?

6:7, 7 Do not be deceived; God is not mocked, for whatever a man sows, that he will also reap.

5:12, 12 I wish those who unsettle you would mutilate themselves!

6:17 17 They make much of you, but for no good purpose; they want to shut you out, that you may make much of them.

▶ 1:7 4:17 17 Henceforth let no man trouble me; for I bear on my body the marks of Jesus.

2 Cor 12:11 11 I have been a fool! You forced me to it, for I ought to have been commended by you. For I was not at all inferior to these superlative apostles, even though I am nothing.

▶ 1:8 4:14 14 and though my condition was a trial to you, you did not scorn or despise me, but received me as an angel of God, as Christ Jesu:

Phil 1:1-2 (§237)

1 Paul and Timothy, servants of Christ Jesus,

To all the saints in Christ Jesus who are at Philippi, with the bishops and deacons:

2 Grace to you and peace from God our Father and the Lord Jesus Christ.

Col 1:1-2 (§256)

1 Paul, an apostle of Christ Jesus by the will of God, and Timothy our brother,

2 To the saints and faithful brethren in Christ at Colos'sae:

Grace to you and peace from God our Father.

1 Thes 1:1 (§275)

1 Paul, Silva'nus, and Timothy,

To the church of the Thessalo'nians in God the Father and the Lord Jesus Christ:

Grace to you and peace.

2 Thes 1:1-2 (§294)

1 Paul, Silva'nus, and Timothy,

To the church of the Thessalo'nians in God our Father and the Lord Jesus Christ:

2 Grace to you and peace from God the Father and the Lord Jesus Christ.

Phm 1-3 (§305)

1 Paul, a prisoner for Christ Jesus, and Timothy our brother,

To Phile'mon our beloved fellow worker 2 and Ap'phia our sister and Archip'pus our fellow soldier, and the church in your house:

3 Grace to you and peace from God our Father and the Lord Jesus Christ.

193

194. Not that there is another gospel

194

1 Thes 2:1-8 (§277)

2 For you yourselves know, brethren, that our visit to you was not in vain; 2 but though we had already suffered and been shamefully treated at Philippi, as you know, we had courage in our God to declare to you the gospel of God in the face of great opposition. 3 For our appeal does not spring from error or uncleanness, nor is it made with guile; 4 but just as we have been approved by God to be entrusted with the gospel, so we speak, not to please men, but to please God who tests our hearts. 5 For we never used either words of flattery, as you know, or a cloak for greed, as God is witness; 6 nor did we seek glory from men, whether from you or from others, though we might have made demands as apostles of Christ. 7 But we were gentle among you, like a nurse taking care of her children. 8 So, being affectionately desirous of you, we were ready to share with you not only the gospel of God but also our own selves, because you had become very dear to us.

1 Thes 2:13-16 (§279)

13 And we also thank God constantly for this, that when you received the word of God which you heard from us, you accepted it not as the word of men but as what it really is, the word of God, which is at work in you believers. 14 For you, brethren, became imitators of the churches of God in Christ Jesus which are in Judea; for you suffered the same things from your own countrymen as they did from the Jews, 15 who killed both the Lord Jesus and the prophets, and drove us out, and displease God and oppose all men 16 by hindering us from speaking to the Gentiles that they may be saved—so as always to fill up the measure of their sins. But God's wrath has come upon them at last!

2 Cor (cont)

man makes slaves of you, or preys upon you, or takes advantage of you, or puts on airs, or strikes you in the face. 21 To my shame, I must say, we were too weak for that!

2 Cor 5:11-13 (§163)

11 Therefore, knowing the fear of the Lord, we persuade men; but what we are is known to God, and I hope it is known also to your conscience. 12 We are not commending ourselves to you again but giving you cause to be proud of us, so that you may be able to answer those who pride themselves on a man's position and not on his heart. 13 For if we are beside ourselves, it is for God; if we are in our right mind, it is for you.

▶ 1:9 5:4
4 You are severed from Christ, you who would be justified by the law; you have fallen away from grace.

Rom 9:3
3 For I could wish that I myself were accursed and cut off from Christ for the sake of my brethren, my kinsmen by race.

1 Cor 16:22, 22 If any one has no love for the Lord, let him be accursed. Our Lord, come!

12:3 3 Therefore I want you to understand that no one speaking by the Spirit of God ever says "Jesus be cursed!" and no one can say "Jesus is Lord" except by the Holy Spirit.

▶ 1:12 1 Cor 15:8
8 Last of all, as to one untimely born, he appeared also to me.

2 Cor 12:1
I must boast; there is nothing to be gained by it, but I will go on to visions and revelations of the Lord.

1 Cor 9:1
Am I not free? Am I not an apostle? Have I not seen Jesus our Lord? Are not you my workmanship in the Lord?

195. Former life in Judaism

195

Rom 2:17-24 (§10)

17 But if you call yourself a Jew and rely upon the law and boast of your relation to God 18 and know his will and approve what is excellent, because you are instructed in the law, 19 and if you are sure that you are a guide to the blind, a light to those who are in darkness, 20 a corrector of the foolish, a teacher of children, having in the law the embodiment of knowledge and truth— 21 you then who teach others, will you not teach yourself? While you preach against stealing, do you steal? 22 You who say that one must not commit adultery, do you commit adultery? You who abhor idols, do you rob temples? 23 You who boast in the law, do you dishonor God by breaking the law? 24 For, as it is written, "The name of God is blasphemed among the Gentiles because of you."

Rom 10:1-4 (§40)

10 Brethren, my heart's desire and prayer to God for them is that they may be saved. 2 I bear them witness that they have a zeal for God, but it is not enlightened. 3 For, being ignorant of the righteousness that comes from God, and seeking to establish their own, they did not submit to God's righteousness. 4 For Christ is the end of the law, that every one who has faith may be justified.

Rom 11:1-6 (§44)

11 I ask, then, has God rejected his people? By no means! I myself am an Israelite, a descendant of Abraham, a member of the tribe of Benjamin. 2 God has not rejected his people whom he foreknew. Do you not know what the scripture says of Eli′jah, how he pleads with God against Israel? 3 "Lord, they have killed thy prophets, they have demolished thy altars, and I alone am left, and they seek my life." 4 But what is God's reply to him? "I have kept for myself seven thousand men who have not bowed the knee to Ba′al." 5 So too at the present time there is a remnant, chosen by grace. 6 But if it is by grace, it is no longer on the basis of works; otherwise grace would no longer be grace.

2 Cor 11:21b-29 (§183)

But whatever any one dares to boast of—I am speaking as a fool—I also dare to boast of that. 22 Are they Hebrews? So am I. Are they Israelites? So am I. Are they descendants of Abraham? So am I. 23 Are they servants of Christ? I am a better one—I am talking like a madman—with far greater labors, far more imprisonments, with countless beatings, and often near death. 24 Five times I have received at the hands of the Jews the forty lashes less one. 25 Three times I have been beaten with rods; once I was stoned. Three times I have been shipwrecked; a night and a day I have been adrift at sea; 26 on frequent journeys, in danger from rivers, danger from robbers, danger from my own people, danger from Gentiles, danger in the city, danger in the wilderness, danger at sea, danger from false brethren; 27 in toil and hardship, through many a sleepless night, in hunger and thirst, often without food, in cold and exposure. 28 And, apart from other things, there is the daily pressure upon me of my anxiety for all the churches. 29 Who is weak, and I am not weak? Who is made to fall, and I am not indignant?

Gal 1:13-14

13 For you have heard of my former life in Judaism, how I persecuted the church of God violently and tried to destroy it; 14 and I advanced in Judaism beyond many of my own age among my people, so extremely zealous was I for the traditions of my fathers.

▶1:13 Acts 9:21,
21 And all who heard him were amazed, and said, "Is not this the man who made havoc in Jerusalem of those who called on this name? And he has come here for this purpose, to bring them bound before the chief priests."

26:4-5
4 "My manner of life from my youth, spent from the beginning among my own nation and at Jerusalem, is known by all the Jews. 5 They have known for a long time, if they are willing to testify, that according to the strictest party of our religion I have lived as a Pharisee.

▶1:14 Acts 8:3,
3 But Saul was ravaging the church, and entering house after house, he dragged off men and women and committed them to prison.

22:3
3 "I am a Jew, born at Tarsus in Cili′cia, but brought up in this city at the feet of Gama′liel, educated according to the strict manner of the law of our fathers, being zealous for God as you all are this day.

▶1:13 Gal 1:23 23 they only heard it said, "He who once persecuted us is now preaching the faith he once tried to destroy."

1 Cor 15:9 9 For I am the least of the apostles, unfit to be called an apostle, because I persecuted the church of God.

196. I did not confer with flesh and blood

196

1 Cor 1:10-17 (§73)

10 I appeal to you, brethren, by the name of our Lord Jesus Christ, that all of you agree and that there be no dissensions among you, but that you be united in the same mind and the same judgment. 11 For it has been reported to me by Chlo′e's people that there is quarreling among you, my brethren. 12 What I mean is that each one of you says, "I belong to Paul," or "I belong to Apol′los," or "I belong to Cephas," or "I belong to Christ." 13 Is Christ divided? Was Paul crucified for you? Or were you baptized in the name of Paul? 14 I am thankful that I baptized none of you except Crispus and Ga′ius; 15 lest any one should say that you were baptized in my name. 16 (I did baptize also the household of Steph′anas. Beyond that, I do not know whether I baptized any one else.) 17 For Christ did not send me to baptize but to preach the gospel, and not with eloquent wisdom, lest the cross of Christ be emptied of its power.

1 Cor 9:1-14 (§105)

9 Am I not free? Am I not an apostle? Have I not seen Jesus our Lord? Are not you my workmanship in the Lord? 2 If to others I am not an apostle, at least I am to you; for you are the seal of my apostleship in the Lord.

3 This is my defense to those who would examine me. 4 Do we not have the right to our food and drink? 5 Do we not have the right to be accompanied by a wife, as the other apostles and the brothers of the Lord and Cephas? 6 Or is it only Barnabas and I who have no right to refrain from working for a living? 7 Who serves as a soldier at his own expense? Who plants a vineyard without eating any of its fruit? Who tends a flock without getting some of the milk?

8 Do I say this on human authority? Does not the law say the same? 9 For it is written in the law of Moses, "You shall not muzzle an ox when it is treading out the grain." Is it for oxen that God is concerned? 10 Does he not speak entirely for our sake? It was written for our sake, because the plowman should plow in hope and the thresher thresh in hope of a share in the crop. 11 If we have sown spiritual good among you, is it too much if we reap your material benefits? 12 If others share this rightful claim upon you, do not we still more?

Nevertheless, we have not made use of this right, but we endure anything rather than put an obstacle in the way of the gospel of Christ. 13 Do you not know that those who are employed in the temple service get their food from the temple, and those who serve at the altar share in the sacrificial offerings? 14 In the same way, the Lord commanded that those who proclaim the gospel should get their living by the gospel.

Gal 1:15-24

15 But when he who had set me apart before I was born, and had called me through his grace, 16 was pleased to reveal his Son to me, in order that I might preach him among the Gentiles, I did not confer with flesh and blood, 17 nor did I go up to Jerusalem to those who were apostles before me, but I went away into Arabia; and again I returned to Damascus.

18 Then after three years I went up to Jerusalem to visit Cephas, and remained with him fifteen days. 19 But I saw none of the other apostles except James the Lord's brother. 20 (In what I am writing to you, before God, I do not lie!) 21 Then I went into the regions of Syria and Cili′cia. 22 And I was still not known by sight to the churches of Christ in Judea; 23 they only heard it said, "He who once persecuted us is now preaching the faith he once tried to destroy." 24 And they glorified God because of me.

Eph 3:1-13 (§222)

3 For this reason I, Paul, a prisoner for Christ Jesus on behalf of you Gentiles— 2 assuming that you have heard of the stewardship of God's grace that was given to me for you, 3 how the mystery was made known to me by revelation, as I have written briefly. 4 When you read this you can perceive my insight into the mystery of Christ, 5 which was not made known to the sons of men in other generations as it has now been revealed to his holy apostles and prophets by the Spirit; 6 that is, how the Gentiles are fellow heirs, members of the same body, and partakers of the promise in Christ Jesus through the gospel.

7 Of this gospel I was made a minister

1 Cor 15:1-11 (§131)

15 Now I would remind you, brethren, in what terms I preached to you the gospel, which you received, in which you stand, 2 by which you are saved, if you hold it fast—unless you believed in vain.

3 For I delivered to you as of first im-

▶1:15-24 Acts 9:1-19
But Saul, still breathing threats and murder against the disciples of the Lord, went to the high priest 2 and asked him for letters to the synagogues at Damascus, so that if he found any belonging to the Way, men or women, he might bring them bound to Jerusalem. 3 Now as he journeyed he approached Damascus, and suddenly a light from heaven flashed about him. 4 And he fell to the ground and heard a voice saying to him, "Saul, Saul, why do you persecute me?" 5 And he said, "Who are you, Lord?" And he said, "I am Jesus, whom you are persecuting; 6 but rise and enter the city, and you will be told what you are to do." 7 The men who were traveling with him stood speechless, hearing the voice but seeing no one. 8 Saul arose from the ground; and when his eyes were opened, he could see nothing; so they led him by the hand and brought him into Damascus. 9 And for three days he was without sight, and neither ate nor drank.

10 Now there was a disciple at Damascus named Anani′as. The Lord said to him in a vision, "Anani′as." And he said, "Here I am, Lord." 11 And the Lord said to him, "Rise and go to the street called Straight, and inquire in the house of Judas for a man of Tarsus named Saul; for behold, he is praying, 12 and he has seen a man named Anani′as come in and lay his hands on him so that he might regain his sight." 13 But Anani′as answered, "Lord, I have heard from many about this man, how much evil he has done to thy saints at Jerusalem; 14 and here he has authority from the chief priests to bind all who call upon thy name." 15 But the Lord said to him, "Go, for he is a chosen instrument of mine to carry my name before the Gentiles and kings and the sons of Israel; 16 for I will show him how much he must suffer for the sake of my name." 17 So Anani′as departed and entered the house. And laying his hands on him he said, "Brother Saul, the Lord Jesus who appeared to you on the road by which you came, has sent me that you may regain your sight and be filled with the Holy Spirit." 18 And immediately something like scales fell from his eyes and he regained his sight. Then he rose and was baptized, 19 and took food and was strengthened.

For several days he was with the disciples at Damascus.

26:12-18
12 "Thus I journeyed to Damascus with the authority and commission of the chief priests. 13 At midday, O king, I saw on the way a light from heaven, brighter than the sun, shining round me and those who journeyed with me. 14 And when we had all fallen to the ground, I heard a voice saying to me in the Hebrew language, 'Saul, Saul, why do you persecute me? It hurts you to kick against the goads.' 15 And I said, 'Who are you, Lord?' And the Lord said, 'I am Jesus whom you are persecuting. 16 But rise and stand upon your feet; for I have appeared to you for this purpose, to appoint you to serve and bear witness to the things in which you have seen me and to those in which I will appear to you, 17 delivering you from the people and from the Gentiles—to whom I send you 18 to open their eyes, that they may turn from darkness to light and from the power of Satan to God, that they may receive forgiveness of sins and a place among those who are sanctified by faith in me.'

22:6-11
6 "As I made my journey and drew near to Damascus, about noon a great light from heaven suddenly shone about me. 7 And I fell to the ground and heard a voice saying to me, 'Saul, Saul, why do you persecute me?' 8 And I answered, 'Who are you, Lord?' And he said to me, 'I am Jesus of Nazareth whom you are persecuting.' 9 Now those who were with me saw the light but did not hear the voice of the one who was speaking to me. 10 And I said, 'What shall I do, Lord?' And the Lord said to me, 'Rise, and go into Damascus, and there you will be told all that is appointed for you to do.' 11 And when I could not see because of the brightness of that light, I was led by the hand

195

Phil 3:2-11 (§247)

2 Look out for the dogs, look out for the evil-workers, look out for those who mutilate the flesh. 3 For we are the true circumcision, who worship God in spirit, and glory in Christ Jesus, and put no confidence in the flesh. 4 Though I myself have reason for confidence in the flesh also. If any other man thinks he has reason for confidence in the flesh, I have more: 5 circumcised on the eighth day, of the people of Israel, of the tribe of Benjamin, a Hebrew born of Hebrews; as to the law a Pharisee, 6 as to zeal a persecutor of the church, as to righteousness under the law blameless. 7 But whatever gain I had, I counted as loss for the sake of Christ. 8 Indeed I count everything as loss because of the surpassing worth of knowing Christ

Jesus my Lord. For his sake I have suffered the loss of all things, and count them as refuse, in order that I may gain Christ 9 and be found in him, not having a righteousness of my own, based on law, but that which is through faith in Christ, the righteousness from God that depends on faith; 10 that I may know him and the power of his resurrection, and may share his sufferings, becoming like him in his death, 11 that if possible I may attain the resurrection from the dead.

196. I did not confer with flesh and blood

196

Phil 3:2-11 (§247)

2 Look out for the dogs, look out for the evil-workers, look out for those who mutilate the flesh. 3 For we are the true circumcision, who worship God in spirit, and glory in Christ Jesus, and put no confidence in the flesh. 4 Though I myself have reason for confidence in the flesh also. If any other man thinks he has reason for confidence in the flesh, I have more: 5 circumcised on the

Eph (cont)
according to the gift of God's grace which was given me by the working of his power. 8 To me, though I am the very least of all the saints, this grace was

1 Cor (cont)
portance what I also received, that Christ died for our sins in accordance with the scriptures, 4 that he was buried, that he was raised on the third day in accordance with the scriptures, 5 and that he appeared to Cephas, then to the twelve. 6 Then he appeared to more than five hundred brethren at one time, most of whom are still alive, though some have fallen asleep. 7 Then he appeared to James, then to all the apostles. 8 Last of all, as to one untimely born, he appeared also to me. 9 For I am the

by those who were with me, and came into Damascus.

▶ 1:17-21 *cf Acts 9:19-30

Col 1:24-2:3 (§260)

24 Now I rejoice in my sufferings for your sake, and in my flesh I complete what is lacking in Christ's afflictions for the sake of his body, that is, the church, 25 of which I became a minister according to the divine office which was given to me for you, to make the word of God

eighth day, of the people of Israel, of the tribe of Benjamin, a Hebrew born of Hebrews; as to the law a Pharisee, 6 as to zeal a persecutor of the church, as to righteousness under the law blameless.

given, to preach to the Gentiles the unsearchable riches of Christ, 9 and to make all men see what is the plan of the mystery hidden for ages in God who created all things; 10 that through the church the manifold wisdom of God might now be made known to the principalities and powers in the heavenly places. 11 This was according to the eternal purpose which he has realized in Christ Jesus our Lord, 12 in whom

least of the apostles, unfit to be called an apostle, because I persecuted the church of God. 10 But by the grace of God I am what I am, and his grace toward me was not in vain. On the con-

fully known, 26 the mystery hidden for ages and generations but now made manifest to his saints. 27 To them God chose to make known how great among the Gentiles are the riches of the glory of this mystery, which is Christ in you, the hope of glory. 28 Him we proclaim, warning every man and teaching every

7 But whatever gain I had, I counted as loss for the sake of Christ. 8 Indeed I count everything as loss because of the surpassing worth of knowing Christ Jesus my Lord. For his sake I have suffered the loss of all things, and count them as refuse, in order that I may gain Christ 9 and be found in him, not having a righteousness of my own, based on law, but that which is through faith in Christ, the righteousness from God that

we have boldness and confidence of access through our faith in him. 13 So I ask you not to lose heart over what I am suffering for you, which is your glory.

trary, I worked harder than any of them, though it was not I, but the grace of God which is with me. 11 Whether then it was I or they, so we preach and so you believed.

man in all wisdom, that we may present every man mature in Christ. 29 For this I toil, striving with all the energy which he mightily inspires within me. 2 For I want you to know how greatly I strive for you, and for those at La-odi-ce'a, and for all who have not seen my face, 2 that their hearts may

depends on faith; 10 that I may know him and the power of his resurrection, and may share his sufferings, becoming like him in his death, 11 that if possible I may attain the resurrection from the dead.

Phil 3:12-16 (§248)

12 Not that I have already obtained this or am already perfect; but I press on to make it my own, because Christ Jesus has made me his own. 13 Brethren, I do not consider that I have made it my own; but one thing I do, forgetting what lies behind and straining forward to what lies ahead, 14 I press on toward the goal for the prize of the upward call of God in Christ Jesus. 15 Let those of us who are mature be thus minded; and if in anything you are otherwise minded, God will reveal that also to you. 16 Only let us hold true to what we have attained.

be encouraged as they are knit together in love, to have all the riches of assured understanding and the knowledge of God's mystery, of Christ, 3 in whom are hid all the treasures of wisdom and knowledge.

▶ 1:17 2 Cor 11:5,
5 I think that I am not in the least inferior to these superlative apostles.
12:11
11 I have been a fool! You forced me to it, for I ought to have been commended by you. For I was not at all inferior to these superlative apostles, even though I am nothing.
Gal 2:2,
2 I went up by revelation; and I laid before them (but privately before those who were of repute) the gospel which I preach among the Gentiles, lest somehow I should be running or had run in vain.

6, 6And from those who were reputed to be something (what they were makes no difference to me; God shows no partiality)—those, I say, who were of repute added nothing to me;
9 9 and when they perceived the grace that was given to me, James and Cephas and John, who were reputed to be pillars, gave to me and Barnabas the right hand of fellowship, that we should go to the Gentiles and they to the circumcised;
▶ 1:20 2 Cor 1:23,
23 But I call God to witness against me—it was to spare you that I refrained from coming to Corinth.

11:31 31 The God and Father of the Lord Jesus, he who is blessed for ever, knows that I do not lie.

13:2 2 While they were worshiping the Lord and fasting, the Holy Spirit said, "Set apart for me Barnabas and Saul for the work to which I have called them."

▶ 1:23 Acts 8:3
3 But Saul was ravaging the church, and entering house after house, he dragged off men and women and committed them to prison.

197. We should go to the Gentiles

197

Rom 11:13-16 (§47)

13 Now I am speaking to you Gentiles. Inasmuch then as I am an apostle to the Gentiles, I magnify my ministry 14 in order to make my fellow Jews jealous, and thus save some of them. 15 For if their rejection means the reconciliation of the world, what will their acceptance mean but life from the dead? 16 If the dough offered as first fruits is holy, so is the whole lump; and if the root is holy, so are the branches.

Rom 15:22-29 (§63)

22 This is the reason why I have so often been hindered from coming to you. 23 But now, since I no longer have any room for work in these regions, and since I have longed for many years to come to you, 24 I hope to see you in passing as I go to Spain, and to be sped on my journey there by you, once I have enjoyed your company for a little. 25 At present, however, I am going to Jerusalem with aid for the saints. 26 For Macedo'nia and Acha'ia have been pleased to make some contribution for the poor among the saints at Jerusalem; 27 they were pleased to do it, and indeed they are in debt to them, for if the Gentiles have come to share in their spiritual blessings, they ought also to be of service to them in material blessings. 28 When therefore I have completed this, and have delivered to them what has been raised, I shall go on by way of you to Spain; 29 and I know that when I come to you I shall come in the fulness of the blessing of Christ.

1 Cor 3:10-15 (§80)

10 According to the grace of God given to me, like a skilled master builder I laid a foundation, and another man is building upon it. Let each man take care how he builds upon it. 11 For no other foundation can any one lay than that which is laid, which is Jesus Christ. 12 Now if any one builds on the foundation with gold, silver, precious stones, wood, hay, straw— 13 each man's work will become manifest; for the Day will disclose it, because it will be revealed with fire, and the fire will test what sort of work each one has done. 14 If the work which any man has built on the foundation survives, he will receive a reward. 15 If any man's work is burned up, he will suffer loss, though he himself will be saved, but only as through fire.

1 Cor 9:19-23 (§107)

19 For though I am free from all men, I have made myself a slave to all, that I might win the more. 20 To the Jews I became as a Jew, in order to win Jews; to those under the law I became as one under the law—though not being myself under the law—that I might win those under the law. 21 To those outside the law I became as one outside the law—not being without law toward God but under the law of Christ—that I might win those outside the law. 22 To the weak I became weak, that I might win the weak. I have become all things to all men, that I might by all means save some. 23 I do it all for the sake of the gospel, that I may share in its blessings.

2 Cor 8:1-7 (§171)

8 We want you to know, brethren, about the grace of God which has been shown in the churches of Macedo'nia, 2 for in a severe test of affliction, their abundance of joy and their extreme poverty have overflowed in a wealth of liberality on their part. 3 For they gave according to their means, as I can testify, and beyond their means, of their own free will, 4 begging us earnestly for the favor of taking part in the relief of the saints— 5 and this, not as we expected, but first they gave themselves to the Lord and to us by the will of God. 6 Accordingly we have urged Titus that as he had already made a beginning, he should also complete among you this gracious work. 7 Now as you excel in everything—in faith, in utterance, in knowledge, in all earnestness, and in your love for us—see that you excel in this gracious work also.

1 Cor 15:1-11 (§131)

15 Now I would remind you, brethren, in what terms I preached to you the gospel, which you received, in which you stand, 2 by which you are saved, if you hold it fast—unless you believed in vain.

3 For I delivered to you as of first importance what I also received, that Christ died for our sins in accordance with the scriptures, 4 that he was buried, that he was raised on the third day in accordance with the scriptures, 5 and that he appeared to Cephas, then to the twelve. 6 Then he appeared to more than five hundred brethren at one time, most of whom are still alive, though some have fallen asleep. 7 Then he appeared to James, then to all the apostles. 8 Last of all, as to one untimely born, he appeared also to me. 9 For I am the least of the apostles, unfit to be called an apostle, because I persecuted the church of God. 10 But by the grace of God I am what I am, and his grace toward me was not in vain. On the contrary, I worked harder than any of them, though it was not I, but the grace of God which is with me. 11 Whether then it was I or they, so we preach and so you believed.

Gal 2:1-10

2 Then after fourteen years I went up again to Jerusalem with Barnabas, taking Titus along with me. 2 I went up by revelation; and I laid before them (but privately before those who were of repute) the gospel which I preach among the Gentiles, lest somehow I should be running or had run in vain. 3 But even Titus, who was with me, was not compelled to be circumcised, though he was a Greek. 4 But because of false brethren secretly brought in, who slipped in to spy out our freedom which we have in Christ Jesus, that they might bring us into bondage— 5 to them we did not yield submission even for a moment, that the truth of the gospel might be preserved for you. 6 And from those who were reputed to be something (what they were makes no difference to me; God shows no partiality)—those, I say, who were of repute added nothing to me; 7 but on the contrary, when they saw that I had been entrusted with the gospel to the uncircumcised, just as Peter had been entrusted with the gospel to the circumcised 8 (for he who worked through Peter for the mission to the circumcised worked through me also for the Gentiles), 9 and when they perceived the grace that was given to me, James and Cephas and John, who were reputed to be pillars, gave to me and Barnabas the right hand of fellowship, that we should go to the Gentiles and they to the cir-

2 Cor 9:1-5 (§174)

9 Now it is superfluous for me to write to you about the offering for the saints, 2 for I know your readiness, of which I boast about you to the people of Macedo'nia, saying that Acha'ia has been ready since last year; and your zeal has stirred up most of them. 3 But I am sending the brethren so that our boasting about you may not prove vain in this case, so that you may be ready, as I said you would be; 4 lest if some Macedo'nians come with me and find that you are not ready, we be humiliated—to say nothing of you—for being so confident. 5 So I thought it necessary to urge the brethren to go on to you before me, and arrange in advance for this gift you have promised, so that it may be ready not as an exaction but as a willing gift.

Eph 3:1-13 (§222)

3 For this reason I, Paul, a prisoner for Christ Jesus on behalf of you Gentiles— 2 assuming that you have heard of the stewardship of God's grace that was given to me for you, 3 how the

▶2:1-10 Acts 12:25
25 And Barnabas and Saul returned from Jerusalem when they had fulfilled their mission, bringing with them John whose other name was Mark.
11:27-30
27 Now in these days prophets came down from Jerusalem to Antioch. 28 And one of them named Ag'abus stood up and foretold by the Spirit that there would be a great famine over all the world; and this took place in the days of Claudius. 29 And the disciples determined, every one according to his ability, to send relief to the brethren who lived in Judea; 30 and they did so, sending it to the elders by the hand of Barnabas and Saul.

▶2:2 2 Tim 4:7 7 I have fought the good fight, I have finished the race, I have kept the faith.

▶2:3 Acts 16:3
3 Paul wanted Timothy to accompany him; and he took him and circumcised him because of the Jews that were in those places, for they all knew that his father was a Greek.

▶2:6 Acts 10:34
34 And Peter opened his mouth and said: "Truly I perceive that God shows no partiality,

▶2:7 Acts 9:15, 15 But the Lord said to him, "Go, for he is a chosen instrument of mine to carry my name before the Gentiles and kings and the sons of Israel;

198. I opposed Cephas to his face

198

Rom 2:1-5 (§7)

2 Therefore you have no excuse, O man, whoever you are, when you judge another; for in passing judgment upon him you condemn yourself, because you, the judge, are doing the very same things. 2 We know that the judgment of God rightly falls upon those who do such things. 3 Do you suppose, O man, that when you judge those who do such things and yet do them yourself, you will escape the judgment of God? 4 Or do you presume upon the riches of his kindness and forbearance and patience? Do you not know that God's kindness is meant to lead you to repentance? 5 But by your hard and impenitent heart you are storing up wrath for yourself on the day of wrath when God's righteous judgment will be revealed.

1 Cor 10:23-11:1 (§111)

23 "All things are lawful," but not all things are helpful. "All things are lawful," but not all things build up. 24 Let no one seek his own good, but the good of his neighbor. 25 Eat whatever is sold in the meat market without raising any question on the ground of conscience. 26 For "the earth is the Lord's, and everything in it." 27 If one of the unbelievers invites you to dinner and you are disposed to go, eat whatever is set before you without raising any question on the ground of conscience. 28 (But if some one says to you, "This has been offered in sacrifice," then out of consideration for the man who informed you, and for conscience' sake— 29 I mean his conscience, not yours—do not eat it.) For why should my liberty be determined by another man's scruples? 30 If I partake with thankfulness, why am I denounced because of that for which I give thanks?

31 So, whether you eat or drink, or whatever you do, do all to the glory of God. 32 Give no offense to Jews or to Greeks or to the church of God, 33 just as I try to please all men in everything I do, not seeking my own advantage, but that of many, that they may be saved.

11 1 Be imitators of me, as I am of Christ.

Rom 2:17-24 (§10)

17 But if you call yourself a Jew and rely upon the law and boast of your relation to God 18 and know his will and approve what is excellent, because you are instructed in the law, 19 and if you are sure that you are a guide to the blind, a light to those who are in darkness, 20 a corrector of the foolish, a teacher of children, having in the law the embodiment of knowledge and truth— 21 you then who teach others, will you not teach yourself? While you preach against stealing, do you steal? 22 You who say that one must not commit adultery, do you commit adultery? You who abhor idols, do you rob temples? 23 You who boast in the law, do you dishonor God by breaking the law? 24 For, as it is written, "The name of God is blasphemed among the Gentiles because of you."

Gal 2:11-14

11 But when Cephas came to Antioch I opposed him to his face, because he stood condemned. 12 For before certain men came from James, he ate with the Gentiles; but when they came he drew back and separated himself, fearing the circumcision party. 13 And with him the rest of the Jews acted insincerely, so that even Barnabas was carried away by their insincerity. 14 But when I saw that they were not straightforward about the truth of the gospel, I said to Cephas before them all, "If you, though a Jew, live like a Gentile and not like a Jew, how can you compel the Gentiles to live like Jews?"

Rom 11:13-16 (§47)

13 Now I am speaking to you Gentiles. Inasmuch then as I am an apostle to the Gentiles, I magnify my ministry 14 in order to make my fellow Jews jealous, and thus save some of them. 15 For if their rejection means the

▶2:11-14 Acts 11:27-30
27 Now in these days prophets came down from Jerusalem to Antioch. 28 And one of them named Ag'abus stood up and foretold by the Spirit that there would be a great famine over all the world; and this took place in the days of Claudius. 29 And the disciples determined, every one according to his ability, to send relief to the brethren who lived in Judea; 30 and they did so, sending it to the elders by the hand of Barnabas and Saul.

Acts 12:25
25 And Barnabas and Saul returned from Jerusalem when they had fulfilled their mission, bringing with them John whose other name was Mark.

▶2:12, 14 Acts 10:15,
15 And the voice came to him again a second time, "What God has cleansed, you must not call common."
28
28 and he said to them, "You yourselves know how unlawful it is for a Jew to associate with or to visit any one of another nation; but God has shown me that I should not call any man common or unclean.

▶2:11 Acts 11:19-26
19 Now those who were scattered because of the persecution that arose over Stephen traveled as far as Phoeni'cia and Cyprus and Antioch, speaking the word to none except Jews. 20 But there were some of them, men Cyprus and Cyre'ne, who on coming Antioch spoke to the Greeks' als preaching the Lord Jesus. 21 And t hand of the Lord was with them, and great number that believed turned

Eph (cont)

mystery was made known to me by revelation, as I have written briefly. 4 When you read this you can perceive my insight into the mystery of Christ, 5 which was not made known to the sons of men in other generations as it has now been revealed to his holy apostles and prophets by the Spirit; 6 that is, how the Gentiles are fellow heirs, members of the same body, and partakers of the promise in Christ Jesus through the gospel.

7 Of this gospel I was made a minister according to the gift of God's grace which was given me by the working of his power. 8 To me, though I am the very least of all the saints, this grace was given, to preach to the Gentiles the unsearchable riches of Christ, 9 and to make all men see what is the plan of the mystery hidden for ages in God who created all things; 10 that through the church the manifold wisdom of God

Gal (cont)

cumcised; 10 only they would have us remember the poor, which very thing I was eager to do.

1 Cor (cont)

1 Cor 16:1-4 (§138)

16 Now concerning the contribution for the saints: as I directed the churches of Galatia, so you also are to do. 2 On the first day of every week,

1 Tim 2:7

7 For this I was appointed a preacher and apostle (I am telling the truth, I am not lying), a teacher of the Gentiles in faith and truth.

Col 1:24-2:3 (§260)

24 Now I rejoice in my sufferings for your sake, and in my flesh I complete what is lacking in Christ's afflictions for the sake of his body, that is, the church, 25 of which I became a minister according to the divine office which was given to me for you, to make the word of God fully known, 26 the mystery hidden for ages and generations but now made manifest to his saints. 27 To them God chose to make known how great among the Gentiles are the riches of the glory of this mystery, which is Christ in you, the hope of glory. 28 Him we proclaim,

might now be made known to the principalities and powers in the heavenly places. 11 This was according to the eternal purpose which he has realized in Christ Jesus our Lord, 12 in whom we have boldness and confidence of access through our faith in him. 13 So I ask you not to lose heart over what I am suffering for you, which is your glory.

each of you is to put something aside and store it up, as he may prosper, so that contributions need not be made when I come. 3 And when I arrive, I will send those whom you accredit by letter to carry your gift to Jerusalem. 4 If it seems advisable that I should go also, they will accompany me.

▶ 2:9 Acts 12:17
17 But motioning to them with his hand to be silent, he described to them how the Lord had brought him out of the prison. And he said, "Tell this to James and to the brethren." Then he departed and went to another place.

▶ 2:10 Acts 24:17
17 Now after some years I came to bring to my nation alms and offerings.

▶ 2:2, 6, 9 1:17
17 nor did I go up to Jerusalem to those who were apostles before me, but I went away into Arabia; and again I returned to Damascus.

warning every man and teaching every man in all wisdom, that we may present every man mature in Christ. 29 For this I toil, striving with all the energy which he mightily inspires within me.

2 For I want you to know how greatly I strive for you, and for those at La-odice′a, and for all who have not seen my face, 2 that their hearts may be encouraged as they are knit together in love, to have all the riches of assured understanding and the knowledge of God's mystery, of Christ, 3 in whom are hid all the treasures of wisdom and knowledge.

2 Cor 11:5,
5 I think that I am not in the least inferior to these superlative apostles. 11:23,
23 Are they servants of Christ? I am a better one—I am talking like a madman—with far greater labors, far more imprisonments, with countless beatings, and often near death.
12:11
11 I have been a fool! You forced me to it, for I ought to have been commended by you. For I was not at all inferior to these superlative apostles, even though I am nothing.

▶ 2:2 Phil 2:16
16 holding fast the word of life, so that in the day of Christ I may be proud that I did not run in vain or labor in vain.

1 Cor 15:58
58 Therefore, my beloved brethren, be steadfast, immovable, always abounding in the work of the Lord, knowing that in the Lord your labor is not in vain.

1 Tes 3:5
5 For this reason, when I could bear it no longer, I sent that I might know your faith, for fear that somehow the tempter had tempted you and that our labor would be in vain.

▶ 2:4 1 Cor 9:1-2
Am I not free? Am I not an apostle? Have I not seen Jesus our Lord? Are not you my workmanship in the Lord? 2 If to others I am not an apostle, at least I am to you; for you are the seal of my apostleship in the Lord.

1 Thes 2:13-16
13 And we also thank God constantly for this, that when you received the word of God which you heard from us, you accepted it not as the word of men but as what it really is, the word of God, which is at work in you believers. 14 For you, brethren, became imitators of the churches of God in Christ Jesus which are in Judea; for you suffered the same things from your own countrymen as they did from the Jews, 15 who killed both the Lord Jesus and the prophets, and drove us out, and displease God and oppose all men 16 by hindering us from speaking to the Gentiles that they may be saved—so as always to fill up the measure of their sins. But God's wrath has come upon them at last!

▶ 2:6 Rom 1:5
5 so I am eager to preach the gospel to you also who are in Rome.

▶ 2:7 Rom 2:11
11 For God shows no partiality.

198. I opposed Cephas to his face

198

Rom (cont)

reconciliation of the world, what will their acceptance mean but life from the dead? 16 If the dough offered as first fruits is holy, so is the whole lump; and if the root is holy, so are the branches.

the Lord. 22 News of this came to the ears of the church in Jerusalem, and they sent Barnabas to Antioch. 23 When he came and saw the grace of God, he was glad; and he exhorted them all to remain faithful to the Lord with steadfast purpose; 24 for he was a good man, full of the Holy Spirit and of faith. And a large company was added to the

Lord. 25 So Barnabas went to Tarsus to look for Saul; 26 and when he had found him, he brought him to Antioch. For a whole year they met with the church, and taught a large company of people; and in Antioch the disciples were for the first time called Christians.

1 Tim 5:20
20 As for those who persist in sin, rebuke them in the presence of all, so that the rest may stand in fear.

▶ 2:12 Acts 11:2
2 So when Peter went up to Jerusalem, the circumcision party criticized him, 3 saying, "Why did you go to uncircumcised men and eat with them?"

Acts 15:1
But some men came down from Judea and were teaching the brethren, "Unless you are circumcised according to the custom of Moses, you cannot be saved."

▶ 2:12 Phil 3:2
2 Look out for the dogs, look out for the evil-workers, look out for those who mutilate the flesh.

Gal 6:12-13
12 It is those who want to make a good showing in the flesh that would compel you to be circumcised, and only in order that they may not be persecuted for the cross of Christ. 13 For even those who receive circumcision do not themselves keep the law, but they desire to have you circumcised that they may glory in your flesh.

▶ 2:14 5:11
11 But if I, brethren, still preach circumcision, why am I still persecuted? In that case the stumbling block of the cross has been removed.

199

Rom 3:9-20 (§13)

9 What then? Are we Jews any better off? No, not at all; for I have already charged that all men, both Jews and Greeks, are under the power of sin, 10 as it is written:

"None is righteous, no, not one;
11 no one understands, no one seeks for God.
12 All have turned aside, together they have gone wrong;
no one does good, not even one."
13 "Their throat is an open grave,
they use their tongues to deceive."
"The venom of asps is under their lips."
14 "Their mouth is full of curses and bitterness."
15 "Their feet are swift to shed blood,
16 in their paths are ruin and misery,
17 and the way of peace they do not know."
18 "There is no fear of God before their eyes."

19 Now we know that whatever the law says it speaks to those who are under the law, so that every mouth may be stopped, and the whole world may be held accountable to God. 20 For no human being will be justified in his sight by works of the law, since through the law comes knowledge of sin.

Rom 6:1-14 (§23-24)

6 What shall we say then? Are we to continue in sin that grace may abound? 2 By no means! How can we who died to sin still live in it? 3 Do you not know that all of us who have been baptized into Christ Jesus were baptized into his death? 4 We were buried therefore with him by baptism into death, so that as Christ was raised from the dead by the glory of the Father, we too might walk in newness of life.

5 For if we have been united with him in a death like his, we shall certainly be united with him in a resurrection like his. 6 We know that our old self was crucified with him so that the sinful body might be destroyed, and we might no longer be enslaved to sin. 7 For he who has died is freed from sin. 8 But if we have died with Christ, we believe that we shall also live with him. 9 For we know that Christ being raised from the dead will never die again; death no longer has dominion over him. 10 The death he died he died to sin, once for all, but the life he lives he lives to God. 11 So you also must consider yourselves dead to sin and alive to God in Christ Jesus.

12 Let not sin therefore reign in your mortal bodies, to make you obey their

2 Cor 5:14-21 (§164)

14 For the love of Christ controls us, because we are convinced that one has died for all; therefore all have died. 15 And he died for all, that those who live might live no longer for themselves but for him who for their sake died and was raised.

16 From now on, therefore, we regard no one from a human point of view; even though we once regarded Christ from a human point of view, we regard him thus no longer. 17 Therefore, if any one is in Christ, he is a new creation; the old has passed away, behold, the new has come. 18 All this is from God, who through Christ reconciled us to himself and gave us the ministry of reconciliation; 19 that is, in Christ God was reconciling the world to himself, not counting their trespasses against them, and entrusting to us the message of reconciliation. 20 So we are ambassadors for Christ, God making his appeal through us. We beseech you on behalf of Christ, be reconciled to God. 21 For our sake he made him to be sin who knew no sin, so that in him we might become the righteousness of God.

Gal 2:15-21

15 We ourselves, who are Jews by birth and not Gentile sinners, 16 yet who know that a man is not justified by works of the law but through faith in Jesus Christ, even we have believed in Christ Jesus, in order to be justified by faith in Christ, and not by works of the law, because by works of the law shall no one be justified. 17 But if, in our endeavor to be justified in Christ, we ourselves were found to be sinners, is Christ then an agent of sin? Certainly not! 18 But if I build up again those things which I tore down, then I prove myself a transgressor. 19 For I through the law died to the law, that I might live to God. 20 I have been crucified with Christ; it is no longer I who live, but Christ who lives in me; and the life I now live in the flesh I live by faith in the Son of God, who loved me and gave himself for me. 21 I do not nullify the grace of God; for if justification were through the law, then Christ died to no purpose.

Eph 2:1-10 (§220)

2 And you he made alive, when you were dead through the trespasses and sins 2 in which you once walked, following the course of this world, following the prince of the power of the air, the spirit that is now at work in the sons of disobedience. 3 Among these we all once lived in the passions of our flesh, following the desires of body and mind, and so we were by nature children of wrath, like the rest of mankind. 4 But God, who is rich in mercy, out of the great love with which he loved us,

yield yourselves to God as men who have been brought from death to life, and your members to God as instruments of righteousness. 14 For sin will have no dominion over you, since you are not under law but under grace.

▶2:15 James 2:24
24 You see that a man is justified by works and not by faith alone.

▶2:16 Acts 13:39
39 and by him every one that believes is freed from everything from which you could not be freed by the law of Moses.

15:10-11
10 Now therefore why do you make trial of God by putting a yoke upon the neck of the disciples which neither our fathers nor we have been able to bear? 11 But we believe that we shall be saved through the grace of the Lord Jesus, just as they will."

▶2:15 Rom 9:1-5
I am speaking the truth in Christ, I am not lying; my conscience bears me witness in the Holy Spirit, 2 that I have great sorrow and unceasing anguish in my heart. 3 For I could wish that I myself were accursed and cut off from Christ for the sake of my brethren, my kinsmen by race. 4 They are Israelites, and to them belong the sonship, the glory, the covenants, the giving of the law, the worship, and the promises; 5 to them belong the patriarchs, and of their race, according to the flesh, is the Christ. God who is over all be blessed for ever. Amen.

Eph 4:17-24
17 Now this I affirm and testify in the Lord, that you must no longer live as the Gentiles do, in the futility of their minds; 18 they are darkened in their understanding, alienated from the life of God because of the ignorance that is in them, due to their hardness of heart; 19 they have become callous and have given themselves up to licentiousness, greedy to practice every kind of uncleanness. 20 You did not so learn Christ!—21 assuming that you have heard about him and were taught in him, as the truth is in Jesus. 22 Put off your old nature which belongs to your former manner of life and is corrupt through deceitful lusts, 23 and be renewed in the spirit of your minds, 24 and put on the new nature, created after the likeness of God in true righteousness and holiness.

200

Rom 8:9-17 (§30)

9 But you are not in the flesh, you are in the Spirit, if in fact the Spirit of God dwells in you. Any one who does not have the Spirit of Christ does not belong to him. 10 But if Christ is in you, although your bodies are dead because of sin, your spirits are alive because of righteousness. 11 If the Spirit of him who raised Jesus from the dead dwells in you, he who raised Christ Jesus from the dead will give life to your mortal bodies also through his Spirit which dwells in you.

12 So then, brethren, we are debtors, not to the flesh, to live according to the flesh—13 for if you live according to the flesh you will die, but if by the Spirit you put to death the deeds of the body you will live. 14 For all who are led by the Spirit of God are sons of God. 15 For you did not receive the spirit of slavery to fall back into fear, but you have received the spirit of sonship. When we cry, "Abba! Father!" 16 it is the Spirit himself bearing witness with our spirit that we are children of God, 17 and if children, then heirs, heirs of God and fellow heirs with Christ, provided we suffer with him in order that we may also be glorified with him.

Rom 10:14-17 (§42)

14 But how are men to call upon him in whom they have not believed? And how are they to believe in him of whom they have never heard? And how are they to hear without a preacher? 15 And how can men preach unless they are sent? As it is written, "How beautiful are the feet of those who preach good news!" 16 But they have not all obeyed the gospel; for Isaiah says, "Lord, who has believed what he has heard from us?" 17 So faith comes from what is heard, and what is heard comes by the preaching of Christ.

Rom 16:17-20a (§67)

17 I appeal to you, brethren, to take note of those who create dissensions and difficulties, in opposition to the doctrine which you have been taught; avoid them. 18 For such persons do not serve our Lord Christ, but their own appetites, and by fair and flattering words they deceive the hearts of the simple-minded. 19 For while your obedience is known to all, so that I rejoice over you, I would have you wise as to what is good and guileless as to what is evil; 20 then the God of peace will soon crush Satan under your feet.

200. Works of the law or hearing with faith

Gal 3:1-5

3 O foolish Galatians! Who has bewitched you, before whose eyes Jesus Christ was publicly portrayed as crucified? 2 Let me ask you only this: Did you receive the Spirit by works of the law, or by hearing with faith? 3 Are you so foolish? Having begun with the Spirit, are you now ending with the flesh? 4 Did you experience so many things in vain?—if it really is in vain. 5 Does he who supplies the Spirit to you and works miracles among you do so by works of the law, or by hearing with faith?

▶3:2, 5 Heb 4:2
2 For good news came to us just as to them; but the message which they heard did not benefit them, because it did not meet with faith in the hearers.

▶3:3 Acts 22:17-21
17 "When I had returned to Jerusalem and was praying in the temple, I fell into a trance 18 and saw him saying to me, 'Make haste and get quickly out of Jerusalem, because they will not accept your testimony about me.' 19 And I said, 'Lord, they themselves know that in every synagogue I imprisoned and beat those who believed in thee. 20 And when the blood of Stephen thy witness was shed, I also was standing by and approving, and keeping the garments of those who killed him.' 21 And he said to me, 'Depart; for I will send you far away to the Gentiles.' "

▶3:1 1:6,
6 I am astonished that you are so quickly deserting him who called you in the grace of Christ and turning to a different gospel—

5:12,
12 I wish those who unsettle you would mutilate themselves!

6:7,
7 Do not be deceived; God is not mocked, for whatever a man sows, that he will also reap.

6:17
17 Henceforth let no man trouble me; for I bear on my body the marks of Jesus.

2 Thes 2:11
11 Therefore God sends upon them a strong delusion, to make them believe what is false,

Rom 11:7-10
7 What then? Israel failed to obtain what it sought. The elect obtained it, but the rest were hardened, 8 as it is written,
"God gave them a spirit of stupor, eyes that should not see and ears that should not hear,
down to this very day."

Phil 3:2-11 (§247)

2 Look out for the dogs, look out for the evil-workers, look out for those who mutilate the flesh. 3 For we are the true circumcision, who worship God in spirit, and glory in Christ Jesus, and put no confidence in the flesh. 4 Though I myself have reason for confidence in the flesh also. If any other man thinks he has reason for confidence in the flesh, I have more: 5 circumcised on the eighth day, of the people of Israel, of the tribe of Benjamin, a Hebrew born of Hebrews; as to the law a Pharisee, 6 as to zeal a persecutor of the church, as to righteousness under the law blameless. 7 But whatever gain I had, I counted as loss for the sake of Christ. 8 Indeed I count everything as loss because of the surpassing worth of knowing Christ Jesus my Lord. For his sake I have suffered the loss of all things, and count them as refuse, in order that I may gain Christ 9 and be found in him, not having a righteousness of my own, based on law, but that which is through faith in Christ, the righteousness from God that depends on faith; 10 that I may know him and the power of his resurrection, and may share his sufferings, becoming like him in his death, 11 that if possible I may attain the resurrection from the dead.

Eph (cont)

5 even when we were dead through our trespasses, made us alive together with Christ (by grace you have been saved), 6 and raised us up with him, and made us sit with him in the heavenly places in Christ Jesus, 7 that in the coming ages he might show the immeasurable riches of his grace in kindness toward us in Christ Jesus. 8 For by grace you have been saved through faith; and this is not your own doing, it is the gift of God— 9 not because of works, lest any man should boast. 10 For we are his workmanship, created in Christ Jesus for good works, which God prepared beforehand, that we should walk in them.

Rom (cont)

Rom 8:9-17 (§30)

9 But you are not in the flesh, you are in the Spirit, if in fact the Spirit of God dwells in you. Any one who does not have the Spirit of Christ does not belong to him. 10 But if Christ is in you, although your bodies are dead because of sin, your spirits are alive because of righteousness. 11 If the Spirit of him who raised Jesus from the dead dwells in you, he who raised Christ Jesus from the dead will give life to your mortal bodies also through his Spirit which dwells in you.

12 So then, brethren, we are debtors, not to the flesh, to live according to the flesh—13 for if you live according to the flesh you will die, but if by the Spirit you put to death the deeds of the body you will live. 14 For all who are led by the Spirit of God are sons of God. 15 For you did not receive the spirit of slavery to fall back into fear, but you have received the spirit of sonship. When we cry, "Abba! Father!" 16 it is the Spirit himself bearing witness with our spirit that we are children of God, 17 and if children, then heirs, heirs of God and fellow heirs with Christ, provided we suffer with him in order that we may also be glorified with him.

Rom 9:30-33 (§39)

30 What shall we say, then? That Gentiles who did not pursue righteousness have attained it, that is, righteousness through faith; 31 but that Israel who pursued the righteousness which is based on law did not succeed in fulfilling that law. 32 Why? Because they did not pursue it through faith, but as if it were based on works. They have stumbled over the stumbling stone, 33 as it is written,

"Behold, I am laying in Zion a stone
that will make men stumble,
a rock that will make them fall;
and he who believes in him will not
be put to shame."

Rom 11:1-6 (§44)

11 I ask, then, has God rejected his people? By no means! I myself am an Israelite, a descendant of Abraham, a member of the tribe of Benjamin. 2 God has not rejected his people whom he foreknew. Do you not know what the scripture says of Eli′jah, how he pleads with God against Israel? 3 "Lord, they have killed thy prophets, they have demolished thy altars, and I alone am left, and they seek my life." 4 But what is God's reply to him? "I have kept for myself seven thousand men who have not bowed the knee to Ba′al." 5 So too at the present time there is a remnant, chosen by grace. 6 But if it is by grace, it is no longer on the basis of works; otherwise grace would no longer be grace.

25   25 Husbands, love your wives, as Christ loved the church and gave himself up for her,

*cf Col 2:11-14

1 Cor 1:13   13 Is Christ divided? Was Paul crucified for you? Or were you baptized in the name of Paul?

Gal 5:24,   24And those who belong to Christ Jesus have crucified the flesh with its passions and desires.

6:14   14 But far be it from me to glory except in the cross of our Lord Jesus Christ, by which the world has been crucified to me, and I to the world.

▶2:20 (God) read in God and Christ: p46BD*G it(few) Pelagius

▶2:16 Rom 3:28.   28 For we hold that a man is justified by faith apart from works of law.

4:5   5And to one who does not work but trusts him who justifies the ungodly, his faith is reckoned as righteousness.

▶2:17 Rom 3:3,   3 What if some were unfaithful? Does their faithlessness nullify the faithfulness of God?

7:13   13 Did that which is good, then, bring death to me? By no means! It was sin, working death in me through what is good, in order that sin might be shown to be sin, and through the commandment might become sinful beyond measure.

▶2:18 2 Cor 13:10,   10 I write this while I am away from you, in order that when I come I may not have to be severe in my use of the authority which the Lord has given me for building up and not for tearing down.

10:8   8 For even if I boast a little too much of our authority, which the Lord gave for building you up and not for destroying you, I shall not be put to shame.

▶2:20 Rom 14:8   8 If we live, we live to the Lord, and if we die, we die to the Lord; so then, for us, whether we live or whether we die, we are the Lord's.

Eph 5:2,   2And walk in love, as Christ loved us and gave himself up for us, a fragrant offering and sacrifice to God.

200. Works of the law or hearing with faith

200

Col 2:8-15 (§262)

8 See to it that no one makes a prey of you by philosophy and empty deceit, according to human tradition, according to the elemental spirits of the universe, and not according to Christ. 9 For in him the whole fulness of deity dwells bodily, 10 and you have come to fulness of life in him, who is the head of all rule and authority. 11 In him also you were circumcised with a circumcision made without hands, by putting off the body of flesh in the circumcision of Christ; 12 and you were buried with him in baptism, in which you were also raised with him through faith in the working of God, who raised him from the dead. 13And you, who were dead in trespasses and the uncircumcision of your flesh, God made alive together with him, having forgiven us all our trespasses, 14 having canceled the bond which stood against us with its legal demands; this he set aside, nailing it to the cross. 15 He disarmed the principalities and powers and made a public example of them, triumphing over them in him.

1 Thes 1:2-10 (§276)

2 We give thanks to God always for you all, constantly mentioning you in our prayers, 3 remembering before our God and Father your work of faith and labor of love and steadfastness of hope in our Lord Jesus Christ. 4 For we know, brethren beloved by God, that he has chosen you; 5 for our gospel came to you not only in word, but also in power and in the Holy Spirit and with full conviction. You know what kind of men we proved to be among you for your sake. 6And you became imitators of us and of the Lord, for you received the word in much affliction, with joy inspired by the Holy Spirit; 7 so that you became an example to all the believers in Macedo′nia and in Acha′ia. 8 For not only has the word of the Lord sounded forth from you in Macedo′nia and Acha′ia, but your faith in God has gone forth everywhere, so that we need not say anything. 9 For they themselves report concerning us what a welcome we had among you, and how you turned to God from idols, to serve a living and true God, 10 and to wait for his Son from heaven, whom he raised from the dead, Jesus who delivers us from the wrath to come.

9 And David says,
"Let their table become a snare and a trap,
a pitfall and a retribution for them;
10 let their eyes be darkened so that they cannot see,
and bend their backs for ever."

▶3:5 1 Cor 2:4,   4 and my speech and my message were not in plausible words of wisdom, but in demonstration of the Spirit and of power,

2 Cor 12:12   12 The signs of a true apostle were performed among you in all patience, with signs and wonders and mighty works.

201

Rom 4:1-8 (§16)

4 What then shall we say about Abraham, our forefather according to the flesh? 2 For if Abraham was justified by works, he has something to boast about, but not before God. 3 For what does the scripture say? "Abraham believed God, and it was reckoned to him as righteousness." 4 Now to one who works, his wages are not reckoned as a gift but as his due. 5 And to one who does not work but trusts him who justifies the ungodly, his faith is reckoned as righteousness. 6 So also David pronounces a blessing upon the man to whom God reckons righteousness apart from works:
7 "Blessed are those whose iniquities are forgiven, and whose sins are covered;
8 blessed is the man against whom the Lord will not reckon his sin."

Rom 15:7-13 (§61)

7 Welcome one another, therefore, as Christ has welcomed you, for the glory of God. 8 For I tell you that Christ became a servant to the circum-cised to show God's truthfulness, in order to confirm the promises given to the patriarchs, 9 and in order that the Gentiles might glorify God for his mercy. As it is written,
"Therefore I will praise thee among the Gentiles,
and sing to thy name";
10 and again it is said,
"Rejoice, O Gentiles, with his people";
11 and again,
"Praise the Lord, all Gentiles,
and let all the peoples praise him";
12 and further Isaiah says,
"The root of Jesse shall come,
he who rises to rule the Gentiles;
in him shall the Gentiles hope."
13 May the God of hope fill you with all joy and peace in believing, so that by the power of the Holy Spirit you may abound in hope.

Gal 3:6-9

6 Thus Abraham "believed God, and it was reckoned to him as righteousness." 7 So you see that it is men of faith who are the sons of Abraham. 8 And the scripture, foreseeing that God would justify the Gentiles by faith, preached the gospel beforehand to Abraham, saying, "In you shall all the nations be blessed." 9 So then, those who are men of faith are blessed with Abraham who had faith.

▶3:8 Acts 3:25
25 You are the sons of the prophets and of the covenant which God gave to your fathers, saying to Abraham, 'And in your posterity shall all the families of the earth be blessed.'

▶3:7 3:29,
29 And if you are Christ's, then you are Abraham's offspring, heirs according to promise.

4:7, 7 So through God you are no longer a slave but a son, and if a son then an heir.

4:31 31 So, brethren, we are not children of the slave but of the free woman.

▶3:8 Rom 3:21
21 But now the righteousness of God has been manifested apart from law, although the law and the prophets bear witness to it,

▶3:6 Gen 15:6 6 And
he believed the LORD; and he reckoned it to him as righteousness.

202. Redeemed from curse of the law

202

Rom 2:25-29 (§11)

25 Circumcision indeed is of value if you obey the law; but if you break the law, your circumcision becomes uncircumcision. 26 So, if a man who is uncircumcised keeps the precepts of the law, will not his uncircumcision be regarded as circumcision? 27 Then those who are physically uncircumcised but keep the law will condemn you who have the written code and circumcision but break the law. 28 For he is not a real Jew who is one outwardly, nor is true circumcision something external and physical. 29 He is a Jew who is one inwardly, and real circumcision is a matter of the heart, spiritual and not literal. His praise is not from men but from God.

Rom 3:9-20 (§13)

9 What then? Are we Jews any better off? No, not at all; for I have already charged that all men, both Jews and Greeks, are under the power of sin,
10 as it is written:
"None is righteous, no, not one;
11 no one understands, no one seeks for God.
12 All have turned aside, together they have gone wrong;
no one does good, not even one."
13 "Their throat is an open grave,
they use their tongues to deceive."
"The venom of asps is under their lips."
14 "Their mouth is full of curses and bitterness."
15 "Their feet are swift to shed blood,
16 in their paths are ruin and misery,
17 and the way of peace they do not know."
18 "There is no fear of God before their eyes."
19 Now we know that whatever the law says it speaks to those who are under the law, so that every mouth may be stopped, and the whole world may be held accountable to God. 20 For no human being will be justified in his sight by works of the law, since through the law comes knowledge of sin.

Rom 1:16-17 (§3)

16 For I am not ashamed of the gospel: it is the power of God for salvation to every one who has faith, to the Jew first and also to the Greek. 17 For in it the righteousness of God is revealed through faith for faith; as it is written, "He who through faith is righteous shall live."

Rom 10:5-13 (§41)

5 Moses writes that the man who practices the righteousness which is based on the law shall live by it. 6 But the righteousness based on faith says, Do not say in your heart, "Who will ascend into heaven?" (that is, to bring Christ down) 7 or "Who will descend into the abyss?" (that is, to bring Christ up from the dead). 8 But what does it say? The word is near you, on your lips and in your heart (that is, the word of faith which we preach); 9 because, if you confess with your lips that Jesus is Lord and believe in your heart that God raised him from the dead, you will be saved. 10 For man believes with his heart and so is justified, and he confesses with his lips and so is saved. 11 The scripture says, "No one who believes in him will be put to shame." 12 For there is no distinction between Jew and Greek; the same Lord is Lord of all and bestows his riches upon all who call upon him. 13 For, "every one who calls upon the name of the Lord will be saved."

Gal 3:10-14

10 For all who rely on works of the law are under a curse; for it is written, "Cursed be every one who does not abide by all things written in the book of the law, and do them." 11 Now it is evident that no man is justified before God by the law; for "He who through faith is righteous shall live"; 12 but the law does not rest on faith, for "He who does them shall live by them." 13 Christ redeemed us from the curse of the law, having become a curse for us—for it is written, "Cursed be every one who hangs on a tree"—14 that in Christ Jesus the blessing of Abraham might come upon the Gentiles, that we might receive the promise of the Spirit through faith.

▶ 3:13 Acts 5:30
30 The God of our fathers raised Jesus whom you killed by hanging him on a tree.

▶ 3:14 Acts 2:33
33 Being therefore exalted at the right hand of God, and having received from the Father the promise of the Holy Spirit, he has poured out this which you see and hear.

▶ 3:10-14 Phil 3:2-11
2 Look out for the dogs, look out for the evil-workers, look out for those who mutilate the flesh. 3 For we are the true circumcision, who worship God in spirit, and glory in Christ Jesus, and put no confidence in the flesh. 4 Though I myself have reason for confidence in the flesh also. If any other man thinks he has reason for confidence in the flesh, I have more: 5 circumcised on the eighth day, of the people of Israel, of the tribe of Benjamin, a Hebrew born of Hebrews; as to the law a Pharisee, 6 as to zeal a persecutor of the church, as to righteousness under the law blameless. 7 But whatever gain I had, I counted as loss for the sake of Christ. 8 Indeed I count everything as loss because of the surpassing worth of knowing Christ Jesus my Lord. For his sake I have suffered the loss of all things, and count them as refuse, in order that I may gain Christ 9 and be found in him, not having a righteousness of my own, based on law, but that which is through faith in Christ, the righteousness from God that depends on faith; 10 that I may know him and the power of his resurrection, and may share his sufferings, becoming like him in his death, 11 that if possible I may attain the resurrection from the dead.

▶3:8 Gen 12:3,   ³ I will bless those who bless you, and him who curses you I will curse; and by you all the families of the earth shall bless themselves."

18:18   ¹⁸ seeing that Abraham shall become a great and mighty nation, and all the nations of the earth shall bless themselves by him?

202. Redeemed from curse of the law

Rom 7:7-13
7 What then shall we say? That the law is sin? By no means! Yet, if it had not been for the law, I should not have known sin. I should not have known what it is to covet if the law had not said, "You shall not covet." ⁸ But sin, finding opportunity in the commandment, wrought in me all kinds of covetousness. Apart from the law sin lies dead. ⁹ I was once alive apart from the law, but when the commandment came, sin revived and I died; ¹⁰ the very

commandment which promised life proved to be death to me. ¹¹ For sin, finding opportunity in the commandment, deceived me and by it killed me. ¹² So the law is holy, and the commandment is holy and just and good. 13 Did that which is good, then, bring death to me? By no means! It was sin, working death in me through what is good, in order that sin might be shown to be sin, and through the commandment might become sinful beyond measure.

Rom 10:4   ⁴ For Christ is the end of the law, that every one who has faith may be justified.
▶3:10, 12 5:3   ³ I testify again to every man who receives circumcision that he is bound to keep the whole law.
▶3:13 Rom 8:3   ³ For God has done what the law, weakened by the flesh, could not do: sending his own Son in the likeness of sinful flesh and for sin, he condemned sin in the flesh,

2 Cor 5:21
²¹ For our sake he made him to be sin who knew no sin, so that in him we might become the righteousness of God.
▶ 3:10 Deut 27:26
26 " 'Cursed be he who does not confirm the words of this law by doing them.' And all the people shall say, 'Amen.'
▶3:12 Lev 18:5
⁵ You shall therefore keep my statutes and my ordinances, by doing which a man shall live: I am the LORD.

▶3:11 Hab 2:4 (*cf. Rom 1:17)
⁴ Behold, he whose soul is not upright in him shall fail,
but the righteous shall live by his faith.

▶ 3:13 Deut 21:23
²³ his body shall not remain all night upon the tree, but you shall bury him the same day, for a hanged man is accursed by God; you shall not defile your land which the LORD your God gives you for an inheritance.

▶ 3:14 (promise) read blessing: p⁴⁶D*G it(few)
Marcion

241

203

Rom 4:13-15 (§18)

13 The promise to Abraham and his descendants, that they should inherit the world, did not come through the law but through the righteousness of faith. 14 If it is the adherents of the law who are to be the heirs, faith is null and the promise is void. 15 For the law brings wrath, but where there is no law there is no transgression.

2 Cor 3:4-6 (§155)

4 Such is the confidence that we have through Christ toward God. 5 Not that we are competent of ourselves to claim anything as coming from us; our competence is from God, 6 who has made us competent to be ministers of a new covenant, not in a written code but in the Spirit; for the written code kills, but the Spirit gives life.

Gal 3:15-18

15 To give a human example, brethren: no one annuls even a man's will, or adds to it, once it has been ratified. 16 Now the promises were made to Abraham and to his offspring. It does not say, "And to offsprings," referring to many; but, referring to one, "And to your offspring," which is Christ. 17 This is what I mean: the law, which came four hundred and thirty years afterward, does not annul a covenant previously ratified by God, so as to make the promise void. 18 For if the inheritance is by the law, it is no longer by promise; but God gave it to Abraham by a promise.

▶ 3:17 Acts 7:6
6 And God spoke to this effect, that his posterity would be aliens in a land belonging to others, who would enslave them and ill-treat them four hundred years.

▶ 3:17-18 2 Cor 1:20
20 For all the promises of God find their Yes in him. That is why we utter the Amen through him, to the glory of God.

Rom 15:8-9a 8 For I tell you that Christ became a servant to the circumcised to show God's truthfulness, in order to confirm the promises given to the patriarchs, 9 and in order that the Gentiles might glorify God for his mercy.

▶ 3:16 Gen 12:7 7 Then the Lord appeared to Abram, and said, "To your descendants I will give this land." So he built there an altar to the Lord, who had appeared to him.

204. Why the law?

204

Rom 5:12-21 (§22)

12 Therefore as sin came into the world through one man and death through sin, and so death spread to all men because all men sinned—13 sin indeed was in the world before the law was given, but sin is not counted where there is no law. 14 Yet death reigned from Adam to Moses, even over those whose sins were not like the transgression of Adam, who was a type of the one who was to come.

15 But the free gift is not like the trespass. For if many died through one man's trespass, much more have the grace of God and the free gift in the grace of that one man Jesus Christ abounded for many. 16 And the free gift is not like the effect of that one man's sin. For the judgment following one trespass brought condemnation, but the free gift following many trespasses brings justification. 17 If, because of one man's trespass, death reigned through that one man, much more will those who receive the abundance of grace and the free gift of righteousness reign in life through the one man Jesus Christ. 18 Then as one man's trespass led to

condemnation for all men, so one man's act of righteousness leads to acquittal and life for all men. 19 For as by one man's disobedience many were made sinners, so by one man's obedience many will be made righteous. 20 Law came in, to increase the trespass; but where sin increased, grace abounded all the more, 21 so that, as sin reigned in death, grace also might reign through righteousness to eternal life through Jesus Christ our Lord.

Rom 9:1-5 (§35)

9 I am speaking the truth in Christ, I am not lying; my conscience bears me witness in the Holy Spirit, 2 that I have great sorrow and unceasing anguish in my heart. 3 For I could wish that I myself were accursed and cut off from Christ for the sake of my brethren, my kinsmen by race. 4 They are Israelites, and to them belong the sonship, the glory, the covenants, the giving of the law, the worship, and the promises; 5 to them belong the patriarchs, and, of their race, according to the flesh, is the Christ. God who is over all be blessed for ever. Amen.

Gal 3:19-20

19 Why then the law? It was added because of transgressions, till the offspring should come to whom the promise had been made; and it was ordained by angels through an intermediary. 20 Now an intermediary implies more than one; but God is one.

Rom 10:1-4 (§40)

10 Brethren, my heart's desire and prayer to God for them is that they may be saved. 2 I bear them witness that they have a zeal for God, but it is not enlightened. 3 For, being ignorant of the righteousness that comes from God, and seeking to establish their own, they did not submit to God's righteousness. 4 For Christ is the end of the law, that every one who has faith may be justified.

▶ 3:19 Acts 7:53
53 you who received the law as delivered by angels and did not keep it."

Heb 9:15
15 Therefore he is the mediator of a new covenant, so that those who are called may receive the promised eternal inheritance, since a death has occurred which redeems them from the trangressions under the first covenant.

▶ 3:20 1 Tim 2:5
5 For there is one God, and there is one mediator between God and men, the man Christ Jesus,

▶ 3:19 4:4 4 But when the time had fully come, God sent forth his Son, born of woman, born under the law,

203

204. Why the law?

204

205

Rom 3:9-20 (§13)

9 What then? Are we Jews any better off? No, not at all; for I have already charged that all men, both Jews and Greeks, are under the power of sin, 10 as it is written:

"None is righteous, no, not one;
11 no one understands, no one seeks for God.
12 All have turned aside, together they have gone wrong;
no one does good, not even one."
13 "Their throat is an open grave,
they use their tongues to deceive."
"The venom of asps is under their lips."
14 "Their mouth is full of curses and bitterness."
15 "Their feet are swift to shed blood,
16 in their paths are ruin and misery,
17 and the way of peace they do not know."
18 "There is no fear of God before their eyes."

19 Now we know that whatever the law says it speaks to those who are under the law, so that every mouth may be stopped, and the whole world may be held accountable to God. 20 For no

human being will be justified in his sight by works of the law, since through the law comes knowledge of sin.

Rom 6:11-14 (§24) 11 So you also must consider yourselves dead to sin and alive to God in Christ Jesus.

12 Let not sin therefore reign in your mortal bodies, to make you obey their passions. 13 Do not yield your members to sin as instruments of wickedness, but yield yourselves to God as men who have been brought from death to life, and your members to God as instruments of righteousness. 14 For sin will have no dominion over you, since you are not under law but under grace.

Rom 7:7-13 (§27)

7 What then shall we say? That the law is sin? By no means! Yet, if it had not been for the law, I should not have known sin. I should not have known what it is to covet if the law had not said, "You shall not covet." 8 But sin, finding opportunity in the commandment, wrought in me all kinds of covetousness. Apart from the law sin lies dead. 9 I was once alive apart from the law, but when the commandment

2 Cor 1:15-22 (§149)

15 Because I was sure of this, I wanted to come to you first, so that you might have a double pleasure; 16 I wanted to visit you on my way to Macedo′nia, and to come back to you from Macedo′nia and have you send me on my way to Judea. 17 Was I vacillating when I wanted to do this? Do I make my plans like a worldly man, ready to say Yes and No at once? 18 As surely as God is faithful, our word to you has not been Yes and No. 19 For the Son of God, Jesus Christ, whom we preached among you, Silva′nus and Timothy and I, was not Yes and No; but in him it is always Yes. 20 For all the promises of God find their Yes in him. That is why we utter the Amen through him, to the glory of God. 21 But it is God who establishes us with you in Christ, and has commissioned us; 22 he has put his seal upon us and given us his Spirit in our hearts as a guarantee.

Gal 3:21-25

21 Is the law then against the promises of God? Certainly not; for if a law had been given which could make alive, then righteousness would indeed be by the law. 22 But the scripture consigned all things to sin, that what was promised to faith in Jesus Christ might be given to those who believe.

23 Now before faith came, we were confined under the law, kept under restraint until faith should be revealed. 24 So that the law was our custodian until Christ came, that we might be justified by faith. 25 But now that faith has come, we are no longer under a custodian;

12 So the law is holy, and the commandment is holy and just and good.

13 Did that which is good, then, bring death to me? By no means! It was sin, working death in me through what is good, in order that sin might be shown to be sin, and through the commandment might become sinful beyond measure.

Rom 11:25-32 (§49)

25 Lest you be wise in your own conceits, I want you to understand this mystery, brethren: a hardening has come upon part of Israel, until the full number of the Gentiles come in, 26 and so all Israel will be saved; as it is written,

"The Deliverer will come from Zion,
he will banish ungodliness from Jacob";
27 "and this will be my covenant with them
when I take away their sins."

28 As regards the gospel they are enemies of God, for your sake; but as regards election they are beloved for the sake of their forefathers. 29 For the gifts and the call of God are irrevocable. 30 Just as you were once disobedient to God but now have received mercy because of their disobedience, 31 so they have now been disobedient in order that by the mercy shown to you they also may receive mercy. 32 For God has consigned all men to disobedience, that he may have mercy upon all.

came, sin revived and I died; 10 the very commandment which promised life proved to be death to me. 11 For sin, finding opportunity in the commandment, deceived me and by it killed me.

▶ 3:25 Acts 21:21 21 and they have been told about you that you teach all the Jews who are among the Gentiles to forsake Moses, telling them not to circumcise their children or observe the customs.

▶ 3:21 2:21 21 I do not nullify the grace of God; for if justification were through the law, then Christ died to no purpose.

Rom 8:2 2 For the law of the Spirit of life in Christ Jesus has set me free from the law of sin and death.

▶ 3:22 4:30, 30 But what does the scripture say? "Cast out the slave and her son; for the son of the slave shall not inherit with the son of the free woman."

31 31 So, brethren, we are not children of the slave but of the free woman.

▶ 3:25 Rom 10:4, 4 For Christ is the end of the law, that every one who has faith may be justified.

206. Neither Jew nor Greek

206

Rom 10:5-13 (§41)

5 Moses writes that the man who practices the righteousness which is based on the law shall live by it. 6 But the righteousness based on faith says, Do not say in your heart, "Who will ascend into heaven?" (that is, to bring Christ down) 7 or "Who will descend into the abyss?" (that is, to bring Christ up from the dead). 8 But what does it say? The word is near you, on your lips and in your heart (that is, the word of faith which we preach); 9 because, if you confess with your lips that Jesus is Lord and believe in your heart that God raised him from the dead, you will be saved. 10 For man believes with his heart and so is justified, and he confesses with his lips and so is saved. 11 The scripture says, "No one who believes in him will be put to shame." 12 For there is no distinction between Jew and Greek; the same Lord is Lord of all and bestows his riches upon all who call upon him. 13 For, "every one who calls upon the name of the Lord will be saved."

1 Cor 12:12-13 (§118)

12 For just as the body is one and has many members, and all the members of the body, though many, are one body, so it is with Christ. 13 For by one Spirit we were all baptized into one body—Jews or Greeks, slaves or free—and all were made to drink of one Spirit.

Gal 3:26-29

26 for in Christ Jesus you are all sons of God, through faith. 27 For as many of you as were baptized into Christ have put on Christ. 28 There is neither Jew nor Greek, there is neither slave nor free, there is neither male nor female; for you are all one in Christ Jesus. 29 And if you are Christ's, then you are Abraham's offspring, heirs according to promise.

Eph 2:11-22 (§221)

11 Therefore remember that at one time you Gentiles in the flesh, called the uncircumcision by what is called the circumcision, which is made in the flesh by hands—12 remember that you were at that time separated from Christ, alienated from the commonwealth of Israel, and strangers to the covenants of promise, having no hope and without God in the world. 13 But now in Christ Jesus you who once were far off have been brought near in the blood of Christ. 14 For he is our peace, who has made us both one, and has broken down the dividing wall of hostility, 15 by abolishing in his flesh the law of commandments and ordinances, that he might create in himself one new man in place of the two, so making peace, 16 and might reconcile us both to God in one body through the cross, thereby bringing the hostility to an end. 17 And he came and preached peace to you who were far off and peace to those who were near; 18 for through him we both have access in one Spirit to the Father. 19 So then you are no longer strangers and sojourners, but you are fellow citizens

▶ 3:29 3:7, 7 So you see that it is men of faith who are the sons of Abraham.

4:7, 7 So through God you are no longer a slave but a son, and if a son then an heir.

4:31 31 So, brethren, we are not children of the slave but of the free woman.

3:31 ³¹ Do we then overthrow the law by this faith? By no means! On the contrary, we uphold the law.

▶3:23-25 2 Cor 3:7-11
7 Now if the dispensation of death, carved in letters on stone, came with such splendor that the Israelites could not look at Moses' face because of its brightness, fading as this was, ⁸ will not the dispensation of the Spirit be attended with greater splendor? ⁹ For if there was splendor in the dispensation of condemnation, the dispensation of righteousness must far exceed it in splendor. ¹⁰ Indeed, in this case, what once had splendor has come to have no splendor at all, because of the splendor that surpasses it. ¹¹ For if what faded away came with splendor, what is permanent must have much more splendor..

▶3:21 (God) *omit* of God: p⁴⁶ B it(few) Ambrosiaster

Col 3:5-11 (§226)

5 Put to death therefore what is earthly in you: fornication, impurity, passion, evil desire, and covetousness, which is idolatry. ⁶ On account of these the wrath of God is coming. ⁷ In these you once walked, when you lived in them. ⁸ But now put them all away: anger, wrath, malice, slander, and foul talk from your mouth. ⁹ Do not lie to one another, seeing that you have put off the old nature with its practices ¹⁰ and have put on the new nature, which is being renewed in knowledge after the image of its creator. ¹¹ Here there cannot be Greek and Jew, circumcised and uncircumcised, barbarian, Scyth′ian, slave, free man, but Christ is all, and in all.

206. Neither Jew nor Greek

Eph (cont)
with the saints and members of the household of God, ²⁰ built upon the foundation of the apostles and prophets, Christ Jesus himself being the cornerstone, ²¹ in whom the whole structure is joined together and grows into a holy temple in the Lord; ²² in whom you also are built into it for a dwelling place of God in the Spirit.

207. No longer a slave, but a son

207

Rom 5:1-5 (§20)

5 Therefore, since we are justified by faith, we have peace with God through our Lord Jesus Christ. 2 Through him we have obtained access to this grace in which we stand, and we rejoice in our hope of sharing the glory of God. 3 More than that, we rejoice in our sufferings, knowing that suffering produces endurance, 4 and endurance produces character, and character produces hope, 5 and hope does not disappoint us, because God's love has been poured into our hearts through the Holy Spirit which has been given to us.

Rom 8:9-17 (§30)

9 But you are not in the flesh, you are in the Spirit, if in fact the Spirit of God dwells in you. Any one who does not have the Spirit of Christ does not belong to him. 10 But if Christ is in you, although your bodies are dead because of sin, your spirits are alive because of righteousness. 11 If the Spirit of him who raised Jesus from the dead dwells in you, he who raised Christ Jesus from the dead will give life to your mortal bodies also through his Spirit which dwells in you.

12 So then, brethren, we are debtors, not to the flesh, to live according to the flesh—13 for if you live according to the flesh you will die, but if by the Spirit you put to death the deeds of the body you will live. 14 For all who are led by the Spirit of God are sons of God. 15 For you did not receive the spirit of slavery to fall back into fear, but you have received the spirit of sonship. When we cry, "Abba! Father!" 16 it is the Spirit himself bearing witness with our spirit that we are children of God, 17 and if children, then heirs, heirs of God and fellow heirs with Christ, provided we suffer with him in order that we may also be glorified with him.

Gal 4:1-7

4 I mean that the heir, as long as he is a child, is no better than a slave, though he is the owner of all the estate; 2 but he is under guardians and trustees until the date set by the father. 3 So with us; when we were children, we were slaves to the elemental spirits of the universe. 4 But when the time had fully come, God sent forth his Son, born of woman, born under the law, 5 to redeem those who were under the law, so that we might receive adoption as sons. 6And because you are sons, God has sent the Spirit of his Son into our hearts, crying, "Abba! Father!" 7 So through God you are no longer a slave but a son, and if a son then an heir.

▶ 4:3 Col 2:8,
8 See to it that no one makes a prey of you by philosophy and empty deceit, according to human tradition, according to the elemental spirits of the universe, and not according to Christ.

2:20
20 If with Christ you died to the elemental spirits of the universe, why do you live as if you still belonged to the world? Why do you submit to regulations,

▶ 4:4 3:19
19 Why then the law? It was added because of transgressions, till the offspring should come to whom the promise had been made; and it was ordained by angels through an intermediary.

Eph 1:10,
10 as a plan for the fulness of time, to unite all things in him, things in heaven and things on earth.

Rom 1:3-4 3 the gospel concerning his Son, who was descended from David according to the flesh 4 and designated Son of God in power according to the Spirit of holiness by his resurrection from the dead, Jesus Christ our Lord,

▶ 4:7 3:7,
7 So you see that it is men of faith who are the sons of Abraham.

3:29, 29And if you are Christ's, then you are Abraham's offspring, heirs according to promise.

208. How can you turn back?

208

Rom 14:5-12 (§58)

5 One man esteems one day as better than another, while another man esteems all days alike. Let every one be fully convinced in his own mind. 6 He who observes the day, observes it in honor of the Lord. He also who eats, eats in honor of the Lord, since he gives thanks to God; while he who abstains, abstains in honor of the Lord and gives thanks to God. 7 None of us lives to himself, and none of us dies to himself. 8 If we live, we live to the Lord, and if we die, we die to the Lord; so then, whether we live or whether we die, we are the Lord's. 9 For to this end Christ died and lived again, that he might be Lord both of the dead and of the living. 10 Why do you pass judgment on your brother? Or you, why do you despise your brother? For we shall all stand before the judgment seat of God; 11 for it is written,
"As I live, says the Lord, every knee shall bow to me,
and every tongue shall give praise to God."
12 So each of us shall give account of himself to God.

1 Cor 8:4-6 (§103)

4 Hence, as to the eating of food offered to idols, we know that "an idol has no real existence," and that "there is no God but one." 5 For although there may be so-called gods in heaven or on earth—as indeed there are many "gods" and many "lords"—6 yet for us there is one God, the Father, from whom are all things and for whom we exist, and one Lord, Jesus Christ, through whom are all things and through whom we exist.

1 Cor 12:1-3 (§116)

12 Now concerning spiritual gifts, brethren, I do not want you to be uninformed. 2 You know that when you were heathen, you were led astray to dumb idols, however you may have been moved. 3 Therefore I want you to understand that no one speaking by the Spirit of God ever says "Jesus be cursed!" and no one can say "Jesus is Lord" except by the Holy Spirit.

Gal 4:8-11

8 Formerly, when you did not know God, you were in bondage to beings that by nature are no gods; 9 but now that you have come to know God, or rather to be known by God, how can you turn back again to the weak and beggarly elemental spirits, whose slaves you want to be once more? 10 You observe days, and months, and seasons, and years! 11 I am afraid I have labored over you in vain.

▶ 4:8 1 Thes 4:5
'not in the passion of lust like heathen who do not know God;

▶ 4:9 Col 2:8
8 See to it that no one makes a prey of you by philosophy and empty deceit, according to human tradition, according to the elemental spirits of the universe, and not according to Christ.

4:31   ³¹ So, brethren, we are not children of the slave but of the free woman.

Rom 6:15-23

15 What then? Are we to sin because we are not under law but under grace? By no means! ¹⁶ Do you not know that if you yield yourselves to any one as obedient slaves, you are slaves of the one whom you obey, either of sin, which leads to death, or of obedience, which leads to righteousness? ¹⁷ But thanks be to God, that you who were once slaves of sin have become obedient from the heart to the standard of teaching to which you were committed,

¹⁸ and, having been set free from sin, have become slaves of righteousness. ¹⁹ I am speaking in human terms, because of your natural limitations. For just as you once yielded your members to impurity and to greater and greater iniquity, so now yield your members to righteousness for sanctification. 20 When you were slaves of sin, you were free in regard to righteousness. ²¹ But then what return did you get from the things of which you are now ashamed? The end of those things is death. ²² But now that you have been set free from sin and have become slaves of God, the return you get is sanctifica-

tion and its end, eternal life. ²³ For the wages of sin is death, but the free gift of God is eternal life in Christ Jesus our Lord.

Eph 1:14,   ¹⁴ which is the guarantee of our inheritance until we acquire possession of it, to the praise of his glory.

18   ¹⁸ having the eyes of your hearts enlightened, that you may know what is the hope to which he has called you, what are the riches of his glorious inheritance in the saints,

1 Cor 7:20-24,   ²⁰ Every one should remain in the state in which he was called. ²¹ Were you a slave when called? Never mind. But if you can gain your freedom, avail yourself of the opportunity.ʳ ²² For he who was called in the Lord as a slave is a freedman of the Lord. Likewise he who was free when called is a slave of Christ. ²³ You were bought with a price; do not become slaves of men. ²⁴ So, brethren, in whatever state each was called, there let him remain with God.

6:20   ²⁰ you were bought with a price. So glorify God in your body.

208. How can you turn back?

Col 2:16-23 (§263-264)

16 Therefore let no one pass judgment on you in questions of food and drink or with regard to a festival or a new moon or a sabbath. ¹⁷ These are only a shadow of what is to come; but the substance belongs to Christ. ¹⁸ Let no one disqualify you, insisting on self-abasement and worship of angels, taking his stand on visions, puffed up without reason by his sensuous mind, ¹⁹ and not holding fast to the Head, from whom the whole body, nourished and knit together through its joints and ligaments, grows with a growth that is from God.

20 If with Christ you died to the elemental spirits of the universe, why do you live as if you still belonged to the world? Why do you submit to regulations, ²¹ "Do not handle, Do not taste, Do not touch" ²² (referring to things which all perish as they are used), according to human precepts and doctrines? ²³ These have indeed an appearance of wisdom in promoting rigor of devotion and self-abasement and severity to the body, but they are of no value in checking the indulgence of the flesh.

1 Thes 1:2-10 (§276)

2 We give thanks to God always for you all, constantly mentioning you in our prayers, ³ remembering before our God and Father your work of faith and labor of love and steadfastness of hope in our Lord Jesus Christ. ⁴ For we know, brethren beloved by God, that he has chosen you; ⁵ for our gospel came to you not only in word, but also in power and in the Holy Spirit and with full conviction. You know what kind of men we proved to be among you for your sake. ⁶And you became imitators of us and of the Lord, for you received the word in much affliction, with joy inspired by the Holy Spirit; ⁷ so that you became an example to all the believers in Macedo´nia and in Acha´ia. ⁸ For not only has the word of the Lord sounded forth from you in Macedo´nia and Acha´ia, but your faith in God has gone forth everywhere, so that we need not say anything. ⁹ For they themselves report concerning us what a welcome we had among you, and how you turned to God from idols, to serve a living and true God, ¹⁰ and to wait for his Son

from heaven, whom he raised from the dead, Jesus who delivers us from the wrath to come.

209

1 Cor 2:1-5 (§76)

2 When I came to you, brethren, I did not come proclaiming to you the testimony of God in lofty words or wisdom. ² For I decided to know nothing among you except Jesus Christ and him crucified. ³And I was with .you in weakness and in much fear and trembling; ⁴ and my speech and my message were not in plausible words of wisdom, but in demonstration of the Spirit and of power, ⁵that your faith might not rest in the wisdom of men but in the power of God.

1 Cor 4:14-21 (§86)

14 I do not write this to make you ashamed, but to admonish you as my beloved children. ¹⁵ For though you have countless guides in Christ, you do not have many fathers. For I became your father in Christ Jesus through the gospel. ¹⁶ I urge you, then, be imitators of me. ¹⁷ Therefore I sent to you Timothy, my beloved and faithful child in the Lord, to remind you of my ways in Christ, as I teach them everywhere in every church. ¹⁸ Some are arrogant, as though I were not coming to you. ¹⁹ But I will come to you soon, if the

2 Cor 7:5-13a (§169)

5 For even when we came into Macedo′nia, our bodies had no rest but we were afflicted at every turn—fighting without and fear within. ⁶ But God, who comforts the downcast, comforted us by the coming of Titus, ⁷ and not only by his coming but also by the comfort with which he was comforted in you, as he told us of your longing, your mourning, your zeal for me, so that I rejoiced still more. ⁸ For even if I made you sorry with my letter, I do not regret it (though I did regret it), for I see that that letter grieved you, though only for a while. ⁹As it is, I rejoice, not because you were grieved, but because you were grieved into repenting; for you felt a godly grief, so that you suffered no loss through us. ¹⁰ For godly grief produces a repentance that

Lord wills, and I will find out not the talk of these arrogant people but their power. ²⁰ For the kingdom of God does not consist in talk but in power. ²¹ What do you wish? Shall I come to you with a rod, or with love in a spirit of gentleness?

Gal 4:12-20

12 Brethren, I beseech you, become as I am, for I also have become as you are. You did me no wrong; ¹³ you know it was because of a bodily ailment that I preached the gospel to you at first; ¹⁴ and though my condition was a trial to you, you did not scorn or despise me, but received me as an angel of God, as Christ Jesus. ¹⁵ What has become of the satisfaction you felt? For I bear you witness that, if possible, you would have plucked out your eyes and given them to me. ¹⁶ Have I then become your enemy by telling you the truth?

leads to salvation and brings no regret, but worldly grief produces death. ¹¹ For see what earnestness this godly grief has produced in you, what eagerness to clear yourselves, what indignation, what alarm, what longing, what zeal, what punishment! At every point you have proved yourselves guiltless in the matter. ¹² So although I wrote to you, it was not on account of the one who did the wrong, nor on account of the one who suffered the wrong, but in order that your zeal for us might be revealed

¹⁷ They make much of you, but for no good purpose; they want to shut you out, that you may make much of them. ¹⁸ For a good purpose it is always good to be made much of, and not only when I am present with you. ¹⁹ My little children, with whom I am again in travail until Christ be formed in you! ²⁰ I could wish to be present with you now and to change my tone, for I am perplexed about you.

to you in the sight of God. ¹³ Therefore we are comforted.

2 Cor 12:1-10 (§185)

12 I must boast; there is nothing to be gained by it, but I will go on to visions and revelations of the Lord. ² I know a man in Christ who fourteen years ago was caught up to the third heaven—whether in the body or out of the body I do not know, God knows. ³And I know that this man was caught up into Paradise—whether in the body or out of the body I do not know, God knows—⁴ and he heard things that cannot be told, which man may not utter. ⁵ On behalf of this man I will boast, but on my own behalf I will not boast, ex-

▶ 4:13 Acts 16:6
6 And they went through the region of Phryg′ia and Galatia, having been forbidden by the Holy Spirit to speak the word in Asia.

▶ 4:12 1 Cor 11:1
¹ Be imitators of me, as I am of Christ.

▶ 4:13 2 Cor 10:10   10 For they say, "His letters are weighty and strong, but his bodily presence is weak, and his speech of no account."

▶ 4:14 1:8   8 But even if we, or an angel from heaven, should preach to you a gospel contrary to that which we preached to you, let him be accursed.

▶ 4:17 Phil 2:21   21 They all look after their own interests, not those of Jesus Christ.

Gal 6:12-13   12 It is those who want to make a good showing in the flesh that would compel you to be circumcised, and only in order that they may not be persecuted for the cross of Christ. ¹³ For even those who receive circumcision do not themselves

210. Not children of the slave but of the free woman

210

Rom 9:6-13 (§36)

6 But it is not as though the word of God had failed. For not all who are descended from Israel belong to Israel, ⁷ and not all are children of Abraham because they are his descendants; but "Through Isaac shall your descendants be named." ⁸ This means that it is not the children of the flesh who are the children of God, but the children of the promise are reckoned as descendants. ⁹ For this is what the promise said, "About this time I will return and Sarah shall have a son." ¹⁰And not only so, but also when Rebecca had conceived children by one man, our forefather Isaac, ¹¹ though they were not yet born and had done nothing either good or bad, in order that God's purpose of election might continue, not because of works but because of his call, ¹² she was told, "The elder will serve the younger." ¹³As it is written, "Jacob I loved, but Esau I hated."

2 Cor 3:12-18 (§157)

12 Since we have such a hope, we are very bold, ¹³ not like Moses, who put a veil over his face so that the Israelites might not see the end of the fading splendor. ¹⁴ But their minds were hardened; for to this day, when they read the old covenant, that same veil remains unlifted, because only through Christ is it taken away. ¹⁵ Yes, to this day whenever Moses is read a veil lies over their minds; ¹⁶ but when a man turns to the Lord the veil is removed. ¹⁷ Now the Lord is the Spirit, and where the Spirit of the Lord is, there is freedom. ¹⁸And we all, with unveiled face, beholding the glory of the Lord, are being changed into his likeness from one degree of glory to another; for this comes from the Lord who is the Spirit.

Gal 4:21-31

21 Tell me, you who desire to be under law, do you not hear the law? ²² For it is written that Abraham had two sons, one by a slave and one by a free woman. ²³ But the son of the slave was born according to the flesh, the son of the free woman through promise. ²⁴ Now this is an allegory: these women are two covenants. One is from Mount Sinai, bearing children for slavery; she is Hagar. ²⁵ Now Hagar is Mount Sinai in Arabia;ⁱ she corresponds to the present Jerusalem, for she is in slavery with her children. ²⁶ But the Jerusalem above is free, and she is our mother.
²⁷ For it is written,

"Rejoice, O barren one who does not bear;
break forth and shout, you who are not in travail;
for the children of the desolate one are many more
than the children of her that is married."

²⁸ Now we, brethren, like Isaac, are children of promise. ²⁹ But as at that time he who was born according to the flesh persecuted him who was born ac-

cording to the Spirit, so it is now. ³⁰ But what does the scripture say? "Cast out the slave and her son; for the son of the slave shall not inherit with the son of the free woman." ³¹ So, brethren, we are not children of the slave but of the free woman.

▶ 4:21-31 3:22
²² But the scripture consigned all things to sin, that what was promised to faith in Jesus Christ might be given to those who believe.

Rom 4:13-25

13 The promise to Abraham and his descendants, that they should inherit the world, did not come through the law but through the righteousness of faith. ¹⁴ If it is the adherents of the law who are to be the heirs, faith is null and the promise is void. ¹⁵ For the law brings wrath, but where there is no law there is no transgression. ¹⁶ That is why it depends on faith, in order that the promise may rest on grace and be guaranteed to all his descendants—not only to the adherents of the law but also to those who share the faith of Abraham, for he is the father of us all, ¹⁷ as it is written, "I have made you the father of many nations"—in the presence of the God in whom he believed, who gives life to the dead and calls into existence the things that do not exist. ¹⁸ In hope he believed against hope, that he should become the father of many nations; as he had been told, "So shall your descendants be." ¹⁹ He did not weaken in faith when he considered his own body, which was as good as dead because he was about a hundred years old, or when he considered the barrenness of Sarah's womb. ²⁰ No distrust made him waver concerning the promise of God, but he grew strong in his faith as he gave glory to God, ²¹ fully convinced that God was able to do what he had promised. ²² That is why his faith was "reckoned to him as righteousness." ²³ But the words, "it was reckoned to him," were written not for his sake alone, ²⁴ but for ours also. It will be reckoned to us who believe in him that raised from the dead Jesus our Lord, ²⁵ who was put to death for our trespasses and raised for our justification.

▶ 4:31 3:7,
⁷ So you see that it is men of faith who are the sons of Abraham.

209

2 Cor (cont)

cept of my weaknesses. 6 Though if I wish to boast, I shall not be a fool, for I shall be speaking the truth. But I refrain from it, so that no one may think more of me than he sees in me or hears from me. 7And to keep me from being too elated by the abundance of revelations, a thorn was given me in the flesh, a messenger of Satan, to harass me, to keep me from being too elated. 8 Three times I besought the Lord about this, that it should leave me; 9 but he said to me, "My grace is sufficient for you, for my power is made perfect in weakness." I will all the more gladly boast of my weaknesses, that the power of Christ may rest upon me. 10 For the sake of Christ, then, I am content with weaknesses, insults, hardships, persecutions, and calamities; for when I am weak, then I am strong.

keep the law, but they desire to have you circumcised that they may glory in your flesh.

▶ 4:19 1 Thes 2:7,
7 But we were gentle among you, like a nurse taking care of her children.

1 Thes 1:2-10 (§276)

2 We give thanks to God always for you all, constantly mentioning you in our prayers, 3 remembering before our God and Father your work of faith and labor of love and steadfastness of hope in our Lord Jesus Christ. 4 For we know, brethren beloved by God, that he has chosen you; 5 for our gospel came to you not only in word, but also in power and in the Holy Spirit and with full conviction. You know what kind of men we proved to be among you for your sake. 6And you became imitators of us and of the Lord, for you received the word in much affliction, with joy inspired by the Holy Spirit; 7 so that you became an example to all the believers in Macedo′nia and in Acha′ia. 8 For not only has the word of the Lord sounded forth from you in Macedo′nia and Acha′ia, but your faith in God has gone forth everywhere, so that we need not say anything. 9 For they themselves report concerning us what a welcome we had among you, and how you turned to God from idols, to serve a living and true God, 10 and to wait for his Son from heaven, whom he raised from the

11   11 for you know how, like a father with his children, we exhorted each one of you and encouraged you and charged you

dead, Jesus who delivers us from the wrath to come.

210. Not children of the slave but of the free woman

210

29,
29And if you are Christ's, then you are Abraham's offspring, heirs according to promise.

4:7   7 So through God you are no longer a slave but a son, and if a son then an heir.

▶ 4:22 Gen 16:15,
15 And Hagar bore Abram a son; and Abram called the name of his son, whom Hagar bore, Ish′mael.

21:2,   2And Sarah conceived, and bore Abraham a son in his old age at the time of which God had spoken to him.

9   9 But Sarah saw the son of Hagar the Egyptian, whom she had borne to Abraham, playing with her son Isaac.

▶ 4:27 Is 54:1
"Sing, O barren one, who did not bear;
break forth into singing and cry aloud,
you who have not been in travail!
For the children of the desolate one will be more
than the children of her that is married, says the LORD.

▶4:30 Gen 21:10-12 10 So she said to Abraham, "Cast out this slave woman with her son; for the son of this slave woman shall not be heir with my son Isaac." 11And the thing was very displeasing to Abraham on account of his son. 12 But God said to Abraham, "Be not displeased because of the lad and because of your slave woman; whatever Sarah says to you, do as she tells you, for

through Isaac shall your descendants be named.

▶4:25 (Arabia) read for Sinai is a mountain in Arabia: p46SCG it vg cop(sa) Origen(Latin)

4:28 (we) read you: P46BD*G it(few) syr(pal) cop(sa) Irenaeus

211

Rom 2:6-11 (§8)

6 For he will render to every man according to his works: 7 to those who by patience in well-doing seek for glory and honor and immortality, he will give eternal life; 8 but for those who are factious and do not obey the truth, but obey wickedness, there will be wrath and fury. 9 There will be tribulation and distress for every human being who does evil, the Jew first and also the Greek, 10 but glory and honor and peace for every one who does good, the Jew first and also the Greek. 11 For God shows no partiality.

Rom 2:25-29 (§11)

25 Circumcision indeed is of value if you obey the law; but if you break the law, your circumcision becomes uncircumcision. 26 So, if a man who is uncircumcised keeps the precepts of the law, will not his uncircumcision be regarded as circumcision? 27 Then those who are physically uncircumcised but keep the law will condemn you who have the written code and circumcision but break the law. 28 For he is not a real Jew who is one outwardly, nor is true circumcision something external and

▶ 5:2 Acts 15:1-2
But some men came down from Judea and were teaching the brethren, "Unless you are circumcised according to the custom of Moses, you cannot be saved." 2And when Paul and Barnabas had no small dissension and debate with them, Paul and Barnabas and some of the others were appointed

1 Cor 5:6-8 (§88)

6 Your boasting is not good. Do you not know that a little leaven leavens the whole lump? 7 Cleanse out the old leaven that you may be a new lump, as you really are unleavened. For Christ, our paschal lamb, has been sacrificed. 8 Let us, therefore, celebrate the festival, not with the old leaven, the leaven of malice and evil, but with the unleavened bread of sincerity and truth.

1 Cor 7:17-24 (§97)

17 Only, let every one lead the life which the Lord has assigned to him, and in which God has called him. This is my rule in all the churches. 18 Was any one at the time of his call already circumcised? Let him not seek to remove the marks of circumcision. Was any one at the time of his call uncircumcised? Let him not seek circumcision. 19 For neither circumcision counts for anything nor uncircumcision, but keeping the commandments of God. 20 Every one should remain in the state in which he was called. 21 Were you a slave when called? Never mind. But if you can gain your freedom, avail yourself of the opportunity. 22 For he who was called in the Lord as a slave is a freedman of the Lord. Likewise he who was free when called is a slave of Christ. 23 You were bought with a price; do not become slaves of men. 24 So, brethren, in whatever state each was called, there let him remain with God.

physical. 29 He is a Jew who is one inwardly, and real circumcision is a matter of the heart, spiritual and not literal. His praise is not from men but from God.

Rom 6:15-23 (§25)

15 What then? Are we to sin because we are not under law but under grace? By no means! 16 Do you not know that if you yield yourselves to any one as obedient slaves, you are slaves of the one whom you obey, either of sin, which leads to death, or of obedience, which leads to righteousness? 17 But thanks be to God, that you who were once slaves of sin have become obedient from the heart to the standard of teaching to which you were committed, 18 and, having been set free from sin, have become slaves of righteousness. 19 I am speaking in human terms, because of your natural limitations. For just as you once yielded your members to impurity and to greater and greater iniquity, so now yield your members to righteousness for sanctification.

20 When you were slaves of sin, you were free in regard to righteousness. 21 But then what return did you get from the things of which you are now

Gal 5:1-12

5

For freedom Christ has set us free; stand fast therefore, and do not submit again to a yoke of slavery.

2 Now I, Paul, say to you that if you receive circumcision, Christ will be of no advantage to you. 3 I testify again to every man who receives circumcision that he is bound to keep the whole law. 4 You are severed from Christ, you who would be justified by the law; you have fallen away from grace. 5 For through the Spirit, by faith, we wait for the hope of righteousness. 6 For in Christ Jesus neither circumcision nor uncircumcision is of any avail, but faith working through love. 7 You were running well; who hindered you from obeying the truth? 8 This persuasion is not from him who calls you. 9 A little leaven leavens the whole lump. 10 I have confidence in the Lord that you will take no other view than mine; and he who is troubling you will bear his judgment, whoever he is. 11 But if I, brethren, still preach circumcision, why am I still persecuted? In that case the stumbling block of the cross has been removed. 12 I wish those who unsettle you would mutilate themselves!

ashamed? The end of those things is death. 22 But now that you have been set free from sin and have become slaves of God, the return you get is sanctification and its end, eternal life. 23 For the wages of sin is death, but the free gift of God is eternal life in Christ Jesus our Lord.

Rom 9:30-33 (§39)

30 What shall we say, then? That Gentiles who did not pursue righteousness have attained it, that is, righteousness through faith; 31 but that Israel who pursued the righteousness which is based on law did not succeed in fulfilling that law. 32 Why? Because they did not pursue it through faith, but as if

▶ 5:6 1 Tim 1:5   5 whereas the aim of our charge is love that issues from a pure heart and a good conscience and sincere faith.

▶ 5:2 Gal 6:15
15 For neither circumcision counts for anything, nor uncircumcision, but a new creation.

▶ 5:3 6:13,   13 For even those who receive circumcision do not themselves keep the law, but they desire to have you circumcised that they may glory in your flesh.

3:1 O foolish Galatians! Who has bewitched you, before whose eyes Jesus Christ was publicly portrayed as crucified?

12,   12 but the law does not rest on faith, for "He who does them shall live by them."
5:14
14 For the whole law is fulfilled in one word, "You shall love your neighbor as yourself."

▶ 5:5 Rom 8:22-25, 22 We know that the whole creation has been groaning in travail together until now; 23 and not only the creation, but we ourselves, who have the first fruits of the Spirit, groan inwardly as we wait for adoption as sons, the redemption of our bodies. 24 For in this hope we were saved. Now hope that is seen is not hope. For who hopes for what he sees? 25 But if we hope for what we do not see, we wait for it with patience.

212

Rom 6:15-23 (§25)

15 What then? Are we to sin because we are not under law but under grace? By no means! 16 Do you not know that if you yield yourselves to any one as obedient slaves, you are slaves of the one whom you obey, either of sin, which leads to death, or of obedience, which leads to righteousness? 17 But thanks be to God, that you who were once slaves of sin have become obedient from the heart to the standard of teaching to which you were committed, 18 and, having been set free from sin, have become slaves of righteousness. 19 I am speaking in human terms, because of your natural limitations. For just as you once yielded your members to impurity and to greater and greater iniquity, so now yield your members to righteousness for sanctification.

20 When you were slaves of sin, you were free in regard to righteousness. 21 But then what return did you get from the things of which you are now ashamed? The end of those things is death. 22 But now that you have been set free from sin and have become slaves of God, the return you get is sanctifica-

▶ 5:13 5:1
For freedom Christ has set us free; stand fast therefore, and do not submit again to a yoke of slavery.

1 Cor 9:19-23 (§107)

19 For though I am free from all men, I have made myself a slave to all, that I might win the more. 20 To the Jews I became as a Jew, in order to win Jews; to those under the law I became as one under the law—though not being myself under the law—that I might win those under the law. 21 To those outside the law I became as one outside the law—not being without law toward God but under the law of Christ —that I might win those outside the law. 22 To the weak I became weak, that I might win the weak. I have become all things to all men, that I might by all means save some. 23 I do it all for the sake of the gospel, that I may share in its blessings.

tion and its end, eternal life. 23 For the wages of sin is death, but the free gift of God is eternal life in Christ Jesus our Lord.

Rom 13:8-10 (§55)

8 Owe no one anything, except to love one another; for he who loves his neighbor has fulfilled the law. 9 The commandments, "You shall not com-

▶ 5:14 5:3   3 I testify again to every man who receives circumcision that he is bound to keep the whole law.

mit adultery, You shall not kill, You shall not steal, You shall not covet," and any other commandment, are summed up in this sentence, "You shall love your neighbor as yourself." 10 Love does no wrong to a neighbor; therefore love is the fulfilling of the law.

Rom 3:31
31 Do we then overthrow the law by this faith? By no means! On the contrary, we uphold the law.

212. Called to freedom

Gal 5:13-15

13 For you were called to freedom, brethren; only do not use your freedom as an opportunity for the flesh, but through love be servants of one another. 14 For the whole law is fulfilled in one word, "You shall love your neighbor as yourself." 15 But if you bite and devour one another take heed that you are not consumed by one another.

▶ 5:14 Lev 19:18
18 You shall not take vengeance or bear any grudge against the sons of your own people, but you shall love your neighbor as yourself: I am the LORD.

211

Rom (cont)
it were based on works. They have stumbled over the stumbling stone, [33] as it is written,

"Behold, I am laying in Zion a stone
　　that will make men stumble,
a rock that will make them fall;
and he who believes in him will not
　　be put to shame."

15:13
[13] May the God of hope fill you with all joy and peace in believing, so that by the power of the Holy Spirit you may abound in hope.
▶ 5:6 6:15
[15] For neither circumcision counts for anything, nor uncircumcision, but a new creation.

▶ 5:10 3:1
O foolish Galatians! Who has bewitched you, before whose eyes Jesus Christ was publicly portrayed as crucified?

▶ 5:11 1 Cor 1:22-24
[22] For Jews demand signs and Greeks seek wisdom, [23] but we preach Christ crucified, a stumbling block to Jews and folly to Gentiles, [24] but to those who are called, both Jews and Greeks, Christ the power of God and the wisdom of God.

Gal 6:12　　　　　　[12] It is those who want to make a good showing in the flesh that would compel you to be circumcised, and only in order that they may not be persecuted for the cross of Christ.

▶ 5:12 Phil 3:2　　For we are the true circumcision, who worship God in spirit, and glory in Christ Jesus, and put no confidence in the flesh.

212. Called to freedom

212

213. Walk by the Spirit

213

Rom 1:29-32 (§6)

29 They were filled with all manner of wickedness, evil, covetousness, malice. Full of envy, murder, strife, deceit, malignity, they are gossips, 30 slanderers, haters of God, insolent, haughty, boastful, inventors of evil, disobedient to parents, 31 foolish, faithless, heartless, ruthless. 32 Though they know God's decree that those who do such things deserve to die, they not only do them but approve those who practice them.

Rom 7:14-25 (§28)

14 We know that the law is spiritual; but I am carnal, sold under sin. 15 I do not understand my own actions. For I do not do what I want, but I do the very thing I hate. 16 Now if I do what I do not want, I agree that the law is good. 17 So then it is no longer I that do it, but sin which dwells within me. 18 For I know that nothing good dwells within me, that is, in my flesh. I can will what is right, but I cannot do it. 19 For I do not do the good I want, but the evil I do not want is what I do. 20 Now if I do what I do not want, it is no longer I that do it, but sin which dwells within me.

21 So I find it to be a law that when I want to do right, evil lies close at hand. 22 For I delight in the law of God, in my inmost self, 23 but I see in my members another law at war with the law of my mind and making me captive to the law of sin which dwells in my members. 24 Wretched man that I am! Who will deliver me from this body of death? 25 Thanks be to God through Jesus Christ our Lord! So then, I of myself serve the law of God with my mind, but with my flesh I serve the law of sin.

Rom 8:1-8 (§29)

8 There is therefore now no condemnation for those who are in Christ Jesus. 2 For the law of the Spirit of life in Christ Jesus has set me free from the law of sin and death. 3 For God has done what the law, weakened by the flesh, could not do: sending his own Son in the likeness of sinful flesh and for sin, he condemned sin in the flesh, 4 in order that the just requirement of the law might be fulfilled in us, who walk not according to the flesh but according to the Spirit. 5 For those who live according to the flesh set their minds on the things of the flesh, but those who live according to the Spirit set their minds on the things of the Spirit. 6 To set the mind on the flesh is death, but to set the mind on the Spirit is life and peace. 7 For the mind that is set on the flesh is hostile to God; it does not submit to God's law, indeed it cannot; 8 and those who are in the flesh cannot please God.

1 Cor 6:9-11 (§91)

9 Do you not know that the unrighteous will not inherit the kingdom of God? Do not be deceived; neither the immoral, nor idolaters, nor adulterers, nor sexual perverts, 10 nor thieves, nor the greedy, nor drunkards, nor revilers, nor robbers will inherit the kingdom of God. 11 And such were some of you. But you were washed, you were sanctified, you were justified in the name of the Lord Jesus Christ and in the Spirit of our God.

1 Cor 10:1-13 (§109)

10 I want you to know, brethren, that our fathers were all under the cloud, and all passed through the sea, 2 and all were baptized into Moses in the cloud and in the sea, 3 and all ate the same supernatural food 4 and all drank the same supernatural drink. For they drank from the supernatural Rock which followed them, and the Rock was Christ. 5 Nevertheless with most of them God was not pleased; for they were overthrown in the wilderness.

6 Now these things are warnings for us, not to desire evil as they did. 7 Do not be idolaters as some of them were; as it is written, "The people sat down to eat and drink and rose up to dance." 8 We must not indulge in immorality as some of them did, and twenty-three thousand fell in a single day. 9 We must not put the Lord to the test, as some of them did and were destroyed by serpents; 10 nor grumble, as some of them did and were destroyed by the Destroyer. 11 Now these things happened to them as a warning, but they were written down for our instruction, upon whom the end of the ages has come. 12 Therefore let any one who thinks that he stands take heed lest he fall. 13 No temptation has overtaken you that is not common to man. God is faithful, and he will not let you be tempted beyond your strength, but with the temptation will also provide the way of escape, that you may be able to endure it.

Rom 13:11-14 (§56)

11 Besides this you know what hour it is, how it is full time now for you to wake from sleep. For salvation is nearer to us now than when we first believed; 12 the night is far gone, the day is at hand. Let us then cast off the works of darkness and put on the armor of light; 13 let us conduct ourselves becomingly as in the day, not in reveling and drunkenness, not in debauchery and licentiousness, not in quarreling and jealousy. 14 But put on the Lord Jesus Christ, and make no provision for the flesh, to gratify its desires.

2 Cor 6:1-10 (§165)

6 Working together with him, then, we entreat you not to accept the grace of God in vain. 2 For he says,

"At the acceptable time I have listened to you,
and helped you on the day of salvation."

Behold, now is the acceptable time; behold, now is the day of salvation. 3 We put no obstacle in any one's way, so that no fault may be found with our ministry, 4 but as servants of God we commend ourselves in every way: through great endurance, in afflictions, hardships, calamities, 5 beatings, imprisonments, tumults, labors, watching, hunger; 6 by purity, knowledge, forbearance, kindness, the Holy Spirit, genuine love, 7 truthful speech, and the power of God; with the weapons of righteousness for the right hand and for the left; 8 in honor and dishonor, in ill repute and good repute. We are treated as impostors, and yet are true; 9 as unknown, and yet well known; as dying, and behold we live; as punished, and yet not killed; 10 as sorrowful, yet always rejoicing; as poor, yet making many rich; as having nothing, and yet possessing everything.

2 Cor 8:1-7 (§171)

8 We want you to know, brethren, about the grace of God which has been shown in the churches of Macedonia, 2 for in a severe test of affliction, their abundance of joy and their extreme poverty have overflowed in a wealth of liberality on their part. 3 For they gave according to their means, as I can testify, and beyond their means, of their own free will, 4 begging us earnestly for the favor of taking part in the relief of the saints— 5 and this, not as we expected, but first they gave themselves to the Lord and to us by the will of God. 6 Accordingly we have urged Titus that as he had already made a beginning, he should also complete among you this gracious work. 7 Now as you excel in everything—in faith, in utterance, in knowledge, in all earnestness, and in your love for us—see that you excel in this gracious work also.

1 Cor 5:9-13 (§89)

9 I wrote to you in my letter not to associate with immoral men; 10 not at all meaning the immoral of this world, or the greedy and robbers, or idolaters, since then you would need to go out of the world. 11 But rather I wrote to you not to associate with any one who bears the name of brother if he is guilty of immorality or greed, or is an idolater, reviler, drunkard, or robber—not even to eat with such a one. 12 For what have I to do with judging outsiders? Is it not those inside the church whom you are to judge? 13 God judges those outside. "Drive out the wicked person from among you."

Gal 5:16-26

16 But I say, walk by the Spirit, and do not gratify the desires of the flesh. 17 For the desires of the flesh are against the Spirit, and the desires of the Spirit are against the flesh; for these are opposed to each other, to prevent you from doing what you would. 18 But if you are led by the Spirit you are not under the law. 19 Now the works of the flesh are plain: fornication, impurity, licentiousness, 20 idolatry, sorcery, enmity, strife, jealousy, anger, selfishness, dissension, party spirit, 21 envy, drunkenness, carousing, and the like. I warn you, as I warned you before, that those who do such things shall not inherit the kingdom of God. 22 But the fruit of the Spirit is love, joy, peace, patience, kindness, goodness, faithfulness, 23 gentleness, self-control; against such there is no law. 24 And those who belong to Christ Jesus have crucified the flesh with its passions and desires.

25 If we live by the Spirit, let us also walk by the Spirit. 26 Let us have no self-conceit, no provoking of one another, no envy of one another.

2 Cor 12:19-21 (§188)

19 Have you been thinking all along that we have been defending ourselves before you? It is in the sight of God that we have been speaking in Christ, and all for your upbuilding, beloved. 20 For I fear that perhaps I may come and find you not what I wish, and that you may find me not what you wish; that perhaps there may be quarreling, jealousy, anger, selfishness, slander, gossip, conceit, and disorder. 21 I fear that when I come again my God may humble me before you, and I may have to mourn over many of those who sinned before and have not repented of the impurity, immorality, and licentiousness which they have practiced.

Eph 4:1-10 (§225)

4 I therefore, a prisoner for the Lord, beg you to lead a life worthy of the calling to which you have been called, 2 with all lowliness and meekness, with patience, forbearing one another in love, 3 eager to maintain the unity of the Spirit in the bond of peace. 4 There is one body and one Spirit, just as you were called to the one hope that belongs to your call, 5 one Lord, one faith, one baptism, 6 one God and Father of us all, who is above all and through all and in all. 7 But grace was given to each of us according to the measure of Christ's gift. 8 Therefore it is said,

"When he ascended on high he led a host of captives,
and he gave gifts to men."

9 (In saying, "He ascended," what does it mean but that he had also descended into the lower parts of the earth? 10 He who descended is he who also ascended far above all the heavens, that he might fill all things.)

Eph 4:17-32 (§227)

17 Now this I affirm and testify in the Lord, that you must no longer live as the Gentiles do, in the futility of their minds; 18 they are darkened in their understanding, alienated from the life of God because of the ignorance that is in them, due to their hardness of heart; 19 they have become callous and have given themselves up to licentiousness, greedy to practice every kind of uncleanness. 20 You did not so learn Christ!— 21 assuming that you have heard about him and were taught in him, as the truth is in Jesus. 22 Put off your old nature which belongs to your former manner of life and is corrupt through deceitful lusts, 23 and be renewed in the spirit of your minds, 24 and put on the new nature, created after the likeness of God in true righteousness and holiness.

25 Therefore, putting away falsehood, let every one speak the truth with his neighbor, for we are members one of another. 26 Be angry but do not sin; do not let the sun go down on your anger, 27 and give no opportunity to the devil. 28 Let the thief no longer steal, but rather let him labor, doing honest work with his hands, so that he may be able to give to those in need. 29 Let no evil talk come out of your mouths, but only such as is good for edifying, as fits the occasion, that it may impart grace to those who hear. 30 And do not grieve the Holy Spirit of God, in whom you were sealed for the day of redemption. 31 Let all bitterness and wrath and anger and clamor and slander be put away from you, with all malice, 32 and be kind to

▶ 5:18, 23 1 Tim 1:9 — 9 understanding this, that the law is not laid down for the just but for the lawless and disobedient, for the ungodly and sinners, for the unholy and profane, for murderers of fathers and murderers of mothers, for manslayers,

▶ 5:23 Acts 24:25 — 25 And as he argued about justice and self-control and future judgment, Felix was alarmed and said, "Go away for the present; when I have an opportunity I will summon you."

▶ 5:16-17 3:1-5 — O foolish Galatians! Who has bewitched you, before whose eyes Jesus Christ was publicly portrayed as crucified? 2 Let me ask you only this: Did you receive the Spirit by works of the law, or by hearing with faith? 3 Are you so foolish? Having begun with the Spirit, are you now ending with the flesh? 4 Did you experience so many things in vain?—if it really is in vain. 5 Does he who supplies the Spirit to you and works miracles among you do so by works of the law, or by hearing with faith?

▶ 5:23 1 Cor 7:9 — 9 But if they cannot exercise self-control, they should marry. For it is better to marry than to be aflame with passion.

▶ 5:24 2:20 — 20 I have been crucified with Christ; it is no longer I who live, but Christ who lives in me; and the life I now live in the flesh I live by faith in the Son of God, who loved me and gave himself for me.

213

Phil 4:8-9 (§252)

8 Finally, brethren, whatever is true, whatever is honorable, whatever is just, whatever is pure, whatever is lovely, whatever is gracious, if there is any excellence, if there is anything worthy of praise, think about these things. 9 What you have learned and received and heard and seen in me, do; and the God of peace will be with you.

Eph (cont)

one another, tenderhearted, forgiving one another, as God in Christ forgave you.

Eph 5:3-14 (§230)

3 But fornication and all impurity or covetousness must not even be named among you, as is fitting among saints. 4 Let there be no filthiness, nor silly talk, nor levity, which are not fitting; but instead let there be thanksgiving. 5 Be sure of this, that no fornicator or impure man, or one who is covetous (that is, an idolater), has any inheritance in the kingdom of Christ and of God. 6 Let no one deceive you with empty words, for it is because of these things that the wrath of God comes upon the sons of disobedience. 7 Therefore do not associate with them, 8 for once you were darkness, but now you are light in the Lord; walk as children of light 9 (for the fruit of light is found in all that is good and right and true), 10 and try to learn what is pleasing to the Lord. 11 Take no part in the unfruitful works of darkness, but instead expose them. 12 For it is a shame even to speak of the things that they do in secret; 13 but when anything is exposed by the light it becomes visible, for anything that becomes visible is light. 14 Therefore it is said,

"Awake, O sleeper, and arise from the dead,
and Christ shall give you light."

Col 3:5-17 (§266-267)

5 Put to death therefore what is earthly in you: fornication, impurity, passion, evil desire, and covetousness, which is idolatry. 6 On account of these the wrath of God is coming. 7 In these you once walked, when you lived in them. 8 But now put them all away: anger, wrath, malice, slander, and foul talk from your mouth. 9 Do not lie to one another, seeing that you have put off the old nature with its practices 10 and have put on the new nature, which is being renewed in knowledge after the image of its creator. 11 Here there cannot be Greek and Jew, circumcised and uncircumcised, barbarian, Scyth´ian, slave, free man, but Christ is all, and in all.

12 Put on then, as God's chosen ones, holy and beloved, compassion, kindness, lowliness, meekness, and patience, 13 forbearing one another and, if one has a complaint against another, forgiving each other; as the Lord has forgiven you, so you also must forgive. 14 And above all these put on love, which binds everything together in perfect harmony. 15 And let the peace of Christ rule in your hearts, to which indeed you were called in the one body. And be thankful. 16 Let the word of Christ dwell in you richly, teach and admonish one another in all wisdom, and sing psalms and hymns and spiritual songs with thankfulness in your hearts to God. 17 And whatever you do, in word or deed, do everything in the name of the Lord Jesus, giving thanks to God the Father through him.

▶ 5:21 (envy) *add* murder: A C D G Koine Lect it vg syr cop(bo) Ambrosiaster

Rom 15:1-6 (§60)

15 We who are strong ought to bear with the failings of the weak, and not to please ourselves; 2 let each of us please his neighbor for his good, to edify him. 3 For Christ did not please himself; but, as it is written, "The reproaches of those who reproached thee fell on me." 4 For whatever was written in former days was written for our instruction, that by steadfastness and by the encouragement of the scriptures we might have hope. 5 May the God of steadfastness and encouragement grant you to live in such harmony with one another, in accord with Christ Jesus, 6 that together you may with one voice glorify the God and Father of our Lord Jesus Christ.

1 Cor 2:6-16 (§77)

6 Yet among the mature we do impart wisdom, although it is not a wisdom of this age or of the rulers of this age, who are doomed to pass away. 7 But we impart a secret and hidden wisdom of God, which God decreed before the ages for our glorification. 8 None of the rulers of this age understood this; for if they had, they would not have crucified the Lord of glory. 9 But, as it is written,

"What no eye has seen, nor ear heard,

nor the heart of man conceived,

what God has prepared for those who love him,"

10 God has revealed to us through the Spirit. For the Spirit searches everything, even the depths of God. 11 For what person knows a man's thoughts except the spirit of the man which is in him? So also no one comprehends the thoughts of God except the Spirit of God. 12 Now we have received not the spirit of the world, but the Spirit which is from God, that we might understand the gifts bestowed on us by God. 13And we impart this in words not taught by human wisdom but taught by the Spirit, interpreting spiritual truths to those who possess the Spirit.

14 The unspiritual man does not receive the gifts of the Spirit of God, for they are folly to him, and he is not able to understand them because they are spiritually discerned. 15 The spiritual man judges all things, but is himself to be judged by no one. 16 "For who has known the mind of the Lord so as to instruct him?" But we have the mind of Christ.

1 Cor 9:1-14 (§105)

9 Am I not free? Am I not an apostle? Have I not seen Jesus our Lord? Are not you my workmanship in the Lord? 2 If to others I am not an apostle, at least I am to you; for you are the seal of my apostleship in the Lord.

3 This is my defense to those who would examine me. 4 Do we not have the right to our food and drink? 5 Do we not have the right to be accompanied by a wife, as the other apostles and the brothers of the Lord and Cephas? 6 Or is it only Barnabas and I who have no right to refrain from working for a living? 7 Who serves as a soldier at his own expense? Who plants a vineyard without eating any of its fruit? Who tends a flock without getting some of the milk?

8 Do I say this on human authority? Does not the law say the same? 9 For it is written in the law of Moses, "You shall not muzzle an ox when it is tread-

2 Cor 2:5-11 (§151)

5 But if any one has caused pain, he has caused it not to me, but in some measure—not to put it too severely—to you all. 6 For such a one this punishment by the majority is enough; 7 so you should rather turn to forgive and comfort him, or he may be overwhelmed by excessive sorrow. 8 So I beg you to reaffirm your love for him. 9 For this is why I wrote, that I might test you and know whether you are obedient in everything. 10Any one whom you forgive, I also forgive. What I have forgiven, if I have forgiven anything, has been for your sake in the presence of Christ, 11 to keep Satan from gaining the advantage over us; for we are not ignorant of his designs.

2 Cor 8:8-15 (§172)

8 I say this not as a command, but to prove by the earnestness of others that your love also is genuine. 9 For you know the grace of our Lord Jesus Christ, that though he was rich, yet for your sake he became poor, so that by his poverty you might become rich. 10And in this matter I give my advice: it is best for you now to complete what a year ago you began not only to do but to desire, 11 so that your readiness in desiring it may be matched by your completing it out of what you have. 12 For if the readiness is there, it is acceptable according to what a man has, not according to what he has not. 13 I do not mean that others should be eased and you burdened, 14 but that as a matter of equality your abundance at the present time should supply their want, so that their abundance may supply your want, that there may be equality. 15As it is written, "He who gathered ing out the grain." Is it for oxen that God is concerned? 10 Does he not speak entirely for our sake? It was written for our sake, because the plowman should plow in hope and the thresher thresh in hope of a share in the crop. 11 If we have sown spiritual good among you, is it too much if we reap your material benefits? 12 If others share this rightful claim upon you, do not we still more?

Nevertheless, we have not made use of this right, but we endure anything rather than put an obstacle in the way of the gospel of Christ. 13 Do you not know that those who are employed in the temple service get their food from the temple, and those who serve at the altar share in the sacrificial offerings? 14 In the same way, the Lord commanded that those who proclaim the gospel should get their living by the gospel.

Gal 6:1-6

6 Brethren, if a man is overtaken in any trespass, you who are spiritual should restore him in a spirit of gentleness. Look to yourself, lest you too be tempted. 2 Bear one another's burdens, and so fulfil the law of Christ. 3 For if any one thinks he is something, when he is nothing, he deceives himself. 4 But let each one test his own work, and then his reason to boast will be in himself alone and not in his neighbor. 5 For each man will have to bear his own load.

6 Let him who is taught the word share all good things with him who teaches.

much had nothing over, and he who gathered little had no lack."

2 Cor 13:5-10 (§190)

5 Examine yourselves, to see whether you are holding to your faith. Test yourselves. Do you not realize that Jesus Christ is in you?—unless indeed you fail to meet the test! 6 I hope you will find out that we have not failed. 7 But we pray God that you may not do wrong—not that we may appear to have met the test, but that you may do what is right, though we may seem to have failed. 8 For we cannot do anything against the truth, but only for the truth. 9 For we are glad when we are weak and you are strong. What we pray for is your improvement. 10 I write this while I am away from you, in order that when I come I may not have to be severe in my use of the authority which the Lord has given me for building up and not for tearing down.

▶6:1 1 Thes 2:7

7 But we were gentle among you, like a nurse taking care of her children.

1 Cor 4:21

21 What do you wish? Shall I come to you with a rod, or with love in a spirit of gentleness?

▶6:2 1 Cor 9:21

21 To those outside the law I became as one outside the law—not being without law toward God but under the law of Christ —that I might win those outside the law.

▶6:3 1 Cor 8:2

2 If any one imagines that he knows something, he does not yet know as he ought to know.

▶6:5 Rom 14:12

12 So each of us shall give account of himself to God.

▶6:6 Rom 15:27

27 they were pleased to do it, and indeed they are in debt to them, for if the Gentiles have come to share in their spiritual blessings, they ought also to be of service to them in material blessings.

2 Thes 3:14-15 (§301)

14 If any one refuses to obey what we say in this letter, note that man, and have nothing to do with him, that he may be ashamed. 15 Do not look on him as an enemy, but warn him as a brother.

215

Rom 6:15-23 (§25)

15 What then? Are we to sin because we are not under law but under grace? By no means! 16 Do you not know that if you yield yourselves to any one as obedient slaves, you are slaves of the one whom you obey, either of sin, which leads to death, or of obedience, which leads to righteousness? 17 But thanks be to God, that you who were once slaves of sin have become obedient from the heart to the standard of teaching to which you were committed, 18 and, having been set free from sin, have become slaves of righteousness. 19 I am speaking in human terms, because of your natural limitations. For just as you once yielded your members to impurity and to greater and greater iniquity, so now yield your members to

▶ 6:9 Heb 12:3
3 Consider him who endured from sinners such hostility against himself, so that you may not grow weary or faint-hearted.

1 Cor 15:42-50 (§136)

42 So is it with the resurrection of the dead. What is sown is perishable, what is raised is imperishable. 43 It is sown in dishonor, it is raised in glory. It is sown in weakness, it is raised in power. 44 It is sown a physical body, it is raised

righteousness for sanctification.

20 When you were slaves of sin, you were free in regard to righteousness. 21 But then what return did you get from the things of which you are now ashamed? The end of those things is death. 22 But now that you have been set free from sin and have become slaves of God, the return you get is sanctification and its end, eternal life. 23 For the wages of sin is death, but the free gift of God is eternal life in Christ Jesus our Lord.

▶ 6:7 2 Cor 9:6
6 The point is this: he who sows sparingly will also reap sparingly, and he who sows bountifully will also reap bountifully.

a spiritual body. If there is a physical body, there is also a spiritual body. 45 Thus it is written, "The first man Adam became a living being"; the last Adam became a life-giving spirit. 46 But it is not the spiritual which is first but the physical, and then the spiritual. 47 The first man was from the earth, a man of dust; the second man is from heaven. 48 As was the man of dust, so are those who are of the dust; and as is the man of heaven, so are those who are of heaven. 49 Just as we have borne the image of the man of dust, we shall also bear the image of the man of heaven. 50 I tell you this, brethren: flesh and blood cannot inherit the kingdom of God, nor does the perishable inherit the imperishable.

▶ 6:8 Rom 8:6, 13
6 To set the mind on the flesh is death, but to set the mind on the Spirit is life and peace.

13 for if you live according to the flesh you will die, but if by the Spirit you put to death the deeds of the body you will live.

Gal 6:7-10

7 Do not be deceived; God is not mocked, for whatever a man sows, that he will also reap. 8 For he who sows to his own flesh will from the flesh reap corruption; but he who sows to the Spirit will from the Spirit reap eternal life. 9 And let us not grow weary in well-doing, for in due season we shall reap, if we do not lose heart. 10 So then, as we have opportunity, let us do good to all men, and especially to those who are of the household of faith.

216. A new creation

216

Rom 2:17-24 (§10)

17 But if you call yourself a Jew and rely upon the law and boast of your relation to God 18 and know his will and approve what is excellent, because you are instructed in the law, 19 and if you are sure that you are a guide to the blind, a light to those who are in darkness, 20 a corrector of the foolish, a teacher of children, having in the law the embodiment of knowledge and truth— 21 you then who teach others, will you not teach yourself? While you preach against stealing, do you steal? 22 You who say that one must not commit adultery, do you commit adultery? You who abhor idols, do you rob temples? 23 You who boast in the law, do you dishonor God by breaking the law? 24 For, as it is written, "The name of God is blasphemed among the Gentiles because of you."

Rom 2:25-29 (§11)

25 Circumcision indeed is of value if you obey the law; but if you break the law, your circumcision becomes uncircumcision. 26 So, if a man who is uncircumcised keeps the precepts of the law, will not his uncircumcision be re-

1 Cor 16:21-22 (§144)

21 I, Paul, write this greeting with my own hand. 22 If any one has no love for the Lord, let him be accursed. Our Lord, come!

1 Cor 7:17-24 (§97)

17 Only, let every one lead the life which the Lord has assigned to him, and in which God has called him. This is my rule in all the churches. 18 Was any one at the time of his call already circumcised? Let him not seek to remove the marks of circumcision. Was any one at the time of his call uncircumcised? Let him not seek circumcision. 19 For neither circumcision counts for any-

garded as circumcision? 27 Then those who are physically uncircumcised but keep the law will condemn you who have the written code and circumcision but break the law. 28 For he is not a real Jew who is one outwardly, nor is true circumcision something external and physical. 29 He is a Jew who is one inwardly, and real circumcision is a matter of the heart, spiritual and not literal. His praise is not from men but from God.

thing nor uncircumcision, but keeping the commandments of God. 20 Every one should remain in the state in which he was called. 21 Were you a slave when called? Never mind. But if you can gain your freedom, avail yourself of the opportunity. 22 For he who was called in the Lord as a slave is a freedman of the Lord. Likewise he who was free when called is a slave of Christ. 23 You were bought with a price; do not become slaves of men. 24 So, brethren, in whatever state each was called, there let him remain with God.

Gal 6:11-17

11 See with what large letters I am writing to you with my own hand. 12 It is those who want to make a good showing in the flesh that would compel you to be circumcised, and only in order that they may not be persecuted for the cross of Christ. 13 For even those who receive circumcision do not themselves keep the law, but they desire to have you circumcised that they may glory in your flesh. 14 But far be it from me to glory except in the cross of our Lord Jesus Christ, by which the world has been crucified to me, and I to the world. 15 For neither circumcision counts for anything, nor uncircumcision, but a new creation. 16 Peace and mercy be upon all who walk by this rule, upon the Israel of God.

17 Henceforth let no man trouble me; for I bear on my body the marks of Jesus.

▶ 6:12 Acts 15:1-2
But some men came down from Judea and were teaching the brethren, "Unless you are circumcised according to the custom of Moses, you cannot be saved." 2 And when Paul and Barnabas had no small dissension and debate with them, Paul and Barnabas and some of the others were appointed to go up to Jerusalem to the apostles and the elders about this question.

▶ 6:12-13 4:17
17 They make much of you, but for no good purpose; they want to shut you out, that you may make much of them.

▶ 6:12 5:11
11 But if I, brethren, still preach circumcision, why am I still persecuted? In that case the stumbling block of the cross has been removed.

▶ 6:13 5:3
3 I testify again to every man who receives circumcision that he is bound to keep the whole law.

Phil 3:6
6 as to zeal a persecutor of the church, as to righteousness under the law blameless.

▶ 6:14 2 Cor 10:13-18
13 But we will not boast beyond limit, but will keep to the limits God has apportioned us, to reach even to you. 14 For we are not overextending ourselves, as though we did not reach you; we were the first to come all the way to you with the gospel of Christ. 15 We do not boast beyond limit, in other men's labors; but our hope is that as your faith increases, our field among you may be greatly enlarged, 16 so that we may preach the gospel in lands beyond you, without boasting of work already done in another's field. 17 "Let him who boasts, boast of the Lord." 18 For it is not the man who commends himself that is accepted, but the man whom the Lord commends.

Rom 3:27-31,
27 Then what becomes of our boasting? It is excluded. On what principle? On the principle of works? No, but on the principle of faith. 28 For we hold that a man is justified by faith apart from works of law. 29 Or is God the God of Jews only? Is he not the God of Gentiles also? Yes, of Gentiles also, 30 since God is one; and he will justify the circumcised on the ground of their faith and the uncircumcised through their faith. 31 Do we then overthrow the law by this faith? By no means! On the contrary, we uphold the law.

15:14-21
14 I myself am satisfied about you, my brethren, that you yourselves are full of goodness, filled with all knowledge, and able to instruct one another. 15 But on some points I have written to you very boldly by way of reminder, because of the grace given me by God 16 to be a minister of Christ Jesus to the Gentiles in the priestly service of the gospel of God, so that the offering of the Gentiles may be acceptable, sanctified by the Holy Spirit. 17 In Christ Jesus, then, I have reason to be proud of my work for God. 18 For I will not venture to speak of anything except what Christ has wrought through me to win obedience from the Gentiles, by word and deed, 19 by the power of signs and wonders, by the power of the Holy Spirit, so that from Jerusalem and as far round as Illyricum I have fully preached the gospel of Christ, 20 thus making it my ambition to preach the gospel, not where Christ has already been named, lest I build on another man's foundation, 21 but as it is written,
"They shall see who have never been told of him,
and they shall understand who have never heard of him."

2 Thes 3:6-13 (§300)

215

6 Now we command you, brethren, in the name of our Lord Jesus Christ, that you keep away from any brother who is living in idleness and not in accord with the tradition that you received from us. 7 For you yourselves know how you ought to imitate us; we were not idle when we were with you, 8 we did not eat any one's bread without paying, but with toil and labor we worked night and day, that we might not burden any of you. 9 It was not because we have not that right, but to give you in our conduct an example to imitate. 10 For even when we were with you, we gave you this command: If any one will not work, let him not eat. 11 For we hear that some of you are living in idleness, mere busybodies, not doing any work. 12 Now such persons we command and exhort in the Lord Jesus Christ to do their work in quietness and to earn their own living. 13 Brethren, do not be weary in well-doing.

216. A new creation

216

Col 4:16-18a (§273)

16And when this letter has been read among you, have it read also in the church of the La-odice´ans; and see that you read also the letter from La-odice´a. 17And say to Archip´pus, "See that you fulfil the ministry which you have received in the Lord."

18 I, Paul, write this greeting with my own hand. Remember my fetters.

1 Thes 5:27 (§292)

27 I adjure you by the Lord that this letter be read to all the brethren.

2 Thes 3:17 (§303)

17 I, Paul, write this greeting with my own hand. This is the mark in every letter of mine; it is the way I write.

1 Cor 1:26-31,

26 For consider your call, brethren; not many of you were wise according to worldly standards, not many were powerful, not many were of noble birth; 27 but God chose what is foolish in the world to shame the wise, God chose what is weak in the world to shame the strong, 28 God chose what is low and despised in the world, even things that are not, to bring to nothing things that are, 29 so that no human being might boast in the presence of God. 30 He is the source of your life in Christ Jesus, whom God made our wisdom, our righteousness and sanctification and redemption; 31 therefore, as it is written, "Let him who boasts, boast of the Lord."

▶ 6:15 5:2,

2 Now I, Paul, say to you that if you receive circumcision, Christ will be of no advantage to you.

6
6 For in Christ Jesus neither circumcision nor uncircumcision is of any avail, but faith working through love.

2 Cor 5:17
17 Therefore, if any one is in Christ, he is a new creation; the old has passed away, behold, the new has come.

▶ 6:17 2 Cor 4:10,

10 always carrying in the body the death of Jesus, so that the life of Jesus may also be manifested in our bodies.

Col 1:24
24 Now I rejoice in my sufferings for your sake, and in my flesh I complete what is lacking in Christ's afflictions for the sake of his body, that is, the church,

217

Rom 16:20b (§68)	1 Cor 16:23-24 (§145)	2 Cor 13:14 (§192)	**Gal 6:18**	Eph 6:23-24 (§236)
The grace of our Lord Jesus Christ be with you.	23 The grace of the Lord Jesus be with you. 24 My love be with you all in Christ Jesus. Amen.	14 The grace of the Lord Jesus Christ and the love of God and the fellowship of the Holy Spirit be with you all.	18 The grace of our Lord Jesus Christ be with your spirit, brethren. Amen.	23 Peace be to the brethren, and love with faith, from God the Father and the Lord Jesus Christ. 24 Grace be with all who love our Lord Jesus Christ with love undying.

▶6:18 2 Tim 4:22
22 The Lord be with your spirit. Grace be with you.

*cf 1 Tim 6:21b
*cf Tit 3:15c

Phil 4:23 (§255)	Col 4:18b (§274)	1 Thes 5:28 (§293)	2 Thes 3:18 (§304)	Phm 25 (§311)
23 The grace of the Lord Jesus Christ be with your spirit.	Grace be with you.	28 The grace of our Lord Jesus Christ be with you.	18 The grace of our Lord Jesus Christ be with you all.	25 The grace of the Lord Jesus Christ be with your spirit.

217

218

Rom 1:1-7 (§1)

1 Paul, a servant of Jesus Christ, called to be an apostle, set apart for the gospel of God 2 which he promised beforehand through his prophets in the holy scriptures, 3 the gospel concerning his Son, who was descended from David according to the flesh 4 and designated Son of God in power according to the Spirit of holiness by his resurrection from the dead, Jesus Christ our Lord, 5 through whom we have received grace and apostleship to bring about the obedience of faith for the sake of his name among all the nations, 6 including yourselves who are called to belong to Jesus Christ;
7 To all God's beloved in Rome, who are called to be saints:
Grace to you and peace from God our Father and the Lord Jesus Christ.

1 Cor 1:1-3 (§71)

1 Paul, called by the will of God to be an apostle of Christ Jesus, and our brother Sos′thenes,
2 To the church of God which is at Corinth, to those sanctified in Christ Jesus, called to be saints together with all those who in every place call on the name of our Lord Jesus Christ, both their Lord and ours:
3 Grace to you and peace from God our Father and the Lord Jesus Christ.

2 Cor 1:1-2 (§146)

1 Paul, an apostle of Christ Jesus by the will of God, and Timothy our brother.
To the church of God which is at Corinth, with all the saints who are in the whole of Acha′ia:
2 Grace to you and peace from God our Father and the Lord Jesus Christ.

Gal 1:1-5 (§193)

1 Paul an apostle—not from men nor through man, but through Jesus Christ and God the Father, who raised him from the dead— 2 and all the brethren who are with me,
To the churches of Galatia:
3 Grace to you and peace from God the Father and our Lord Jesus Christ, 4 who gave himself for our sins to deliver us from the present evil age, according to the will of our God and Father; 5 to whom be the glory for ever and ever. Amen.

Eph 1:1-2

1 Paul, an apostle of Christ Jesus by the will of God,
To the saints who are also faithful in Christ Jesus:
2 Grace to you and peace from God our Father and the Lord Jesus Christ.

▶1:1 Acts 18:19
19And they came to Ephesus, and he left them there; but he himself went into the synagogue and argued with the Jews.

*cf Acts 19:1-20:1

Phil 1:1-2 (§237)

1 Paul and Timothy, servants of Christ Jesus,

To all the saints in Christ Jesus who are at Philippi, with the bishops and deacons:

2 Grace to you and peace from God our Father and the Lord Jesus Christ.

Col 1:1-2 (§256)

1 Paul, an apostle of Christ Jesus by the will of God, and Timothy our brother,

2 To the saints and faithful brethren in Christ at Colos'sae:

Grace to you and peace from God our Father.

1 Thes 1:1 (§275)

1 Paul, Silva'nus, and Timothy,
To the church of the Thessalo'-nians in God the Father and the Lord Jesus Christ:

Grace to you and peace.

2 Thes 1:1-2 (§294)

1 Paul, Silva'nus, and Timothy,
To the church of the Thessalo'-nians in God our Father and the Lord Jesus Christ:

2 Grace to you and peace from God the Father and the Lord Jesus Christ.

Phm 1-3 (§305)

1 Paul, a prisoner for Christ Jesus, and Timothy our brother,

To Phile'mon our beloved fellow worker 2 and Ap'phia our sister and Archip'pus our fellow soldier, and the church in your house:

3 Grace to you and peace from God our Father and the Lord Jesus Christ.

▶ 1:1 (are) *add* at Ephesus: S^c AB^{3}DG Koine Lect it vg syr cop Ambrosiaster; *text:* p^{46}S*B* Origen

219

Rom 3:21-26 (§14)

21 But now the righteousness of God has been manifested apart from law, although the law and the prophets bear witness to it, 22 the righteousness of God through faith in Jesus Christ for all who believe. For there is no distinction; 23 since all have sinned and fall short of the glory of God, 24 they are justified by his grace as a gift, through the redemption which is in Christ Jesus, 25 whom God put forward as an expiation by his blood, to be received by faith. This was to show God's righteousness, because in his divine forbearance he had passed over former sins; 26 it was to prove at the present time that he himself is righteous and that he justifies him who has faith in Jesus.

Rom 8:28-30 (§33)

28 We know that in everything God works for good with those who love him, who are called according to his purpose. 29 For those whom he foreknew he also predestined to be conformed to the image of his Son, in order that he might be the first-born among many brethren. 30 And those whom he predestined he also called; and those whom he called he also justified; and those whom he justified he also glorified.

Rom 9:19-29 (§38)

19 You will say to me then, "Why does he still find fault? For who can resist his will?" 20 But who are you, a man, to answer back to God? Will what is molded say to its molder, "Why have you made me thus?" 21 Has the potter no right over the clay, to make out of the same lump one vessel for beauty and another for menial use? 22 What if God, desiring to show his wrath and to make known his power, has endured with much patience the vessels of wrath made for destruction, 23 in order to make known the riches of his glory for the vessels of mercy, which he has prepared beforehand for glory, 24 even us whom he has called, not from the Jews only but also from the Gentiles? 25 As indeed he says in Hose'a,
"Those who were not my people
I will call 'my people,'
and her who was not beloved
I will call 'my beloved.'"

1 Cor 15:20-28 (§133)

20 But in fact Christ has been raised from the dead, the first fruits of those who have fallen asleep. 21 For as by a man came death, by a man has come also the resurrection of the dead. 22 For as in Adam all die, so also in Christ shall all be made alive. 23 But each in his own order: Christ the first fruits, then at his coming those who belong to Christ. 24 Then comes the end, when he delivers the kingdom to God the Father after destroying every rule and every authority and power. 25 For he must reign until he has put all his enemies under his feet. 26 The last enemy to be destroyed is death. 27 "For God has put all things in subjection under his feet." But when it says, "All things are put in subjection under him," it is plain that he is excepted who put all things under him. 28 When all things are subjected to him, then the Son himself will also be subjected to him who put all things under him, that God may be everything to every one.

26 "And in the very place where it was said to them, 'You are not my people,'
they will be called 'sons of the living God.'"
27 And Isaiah cries out concerning Israel: "Though the number of the sons of Israel be as the sand of the sea, only a remnant of them will be saved; 28 for the Lord will execute his sentence upon the earth with rigor and dispatch."
29 And as Isaiah predicted,
"If the Lord of hosts had not left us children,
we would have fared like Sodom and been made like Gomor'rah."

Rom 9:6-13 (§36)

6 But it is not as though the word of God had failed. For not all who are descended from Israel belong to Israel, 7 and not all are children of Abraham because they are his descendants; but "Through Isaac shall your descendants be named." 8 This means that it is not the children of the flesh who are the children of God, but the children of the promise are reckoned as descendants. 9 For this is what the promise said, "About this time I will return and Sarah shall have a son." 10 And not only so, but also when Rebecca had conceived chil-

2 Cor 1:3-11 (§147)

3 Blessed be the God and Father of our Lord Jesus Christ, the Father of mercies and God of all comfort, 4 who comforts us in all our affliction, so that we may be able to comfort those who are in any affliction, with the comfort with which we ourselves are comforted by God. 5 For as we share abundantly in Christ's sufferings, so through Christ we share abundantly in comfort too. 6 If we are afflicted, it is for your comfort and salvation; and if we are comforted, it is for your comfort, which you experience when you patiently endure the same sufferings that we suffer. 7 Our hope for you is unshaken; for we know that as you share in our sufferings, you will also share in our comfort.
8 For we do not want you to be ignorant, brethren, of the affliction we experienced in Asia; for we were so utterly, unbearably crushed that we despaired of life itself. 9 Why, we felt that we had received the sentence of death; but that was to make us rely not on ourselves but on God who raises the dead; 10 he delivered us from so deadly a peril, and he will deliver us; on him we have set our hope that he will deliver us again. 11 You also must help us by prayer, so that many will give thanks on our behalf for the blessing granted us in answer to many prayers.

2 Cor 1:15-22 (§149)

15 Because I was sure of this, I wanted to come to you first, so that you might have a double pleasure; 16 I wanted to visit you on my way to Macedo'nia, and to come back to you from Macedo'nia and have you send me on my way to Judea. 17 Was I vacillating when I wanted to do this? Do I make my plans like a worldly man, ready to say Yes and No at once? 18 As surely as God is faithful, our word to you has not been Yes and No. 19 For the Son of

God, Jesus Christ, whom we preached among you, Silva'nus and Timothy and I, was not Yes and No; but in him it is always Yes. 20 For all the promises of God find their Yes in him. That is why we utter the Amen through him, to the glory of God. 21 But it is God who establishes us with you in Christ, and has commissioned us; 22 he has put his seal upon us and given us his Spirit in our hearts as a guarantee.

Eph 1:3-23

3 Blessed be the God and Father of our Lord Jesus Christ, who has blessed us in Christ with every spiritual blessing in the heavenly places, 4 even as he chose us in him before the foundation of the world, that we should be holy and blameless before him. 5 He destined us in love to be his sons through Jesus Christ, according to the purpose of his will, 6 to the praise of his glorious grace which he freely bestowed on us in the Beloved. 7 In him we have redemption through his blood, the forgiveness of our trespasses, according to the riches of his grace 8 which he lavished upon us. 9 For he has made known to us in all wisdom and insight the mystery of his will, according to his purpose which he set forth in Christ 10 as a plan for the fulness of time, to unite all things in him, things in heaven and things on earth.
11 In him, according to the purpose of him who accomplishes all things according to the counsel of his will, 12 we who first hoped in Christ have been destined and appointed to live for the praise of his glory. 13 In him you also, who have heard the word of truth, the gospel of your salvation, and have believed in him, were sealed with the promised Holy Spirit, 14 which is the guarantee of our inheritance until we acquire possession of it, to the praise of his glory.
15 For this reason, because I have heard of your faith in the Lord Jesus and your love toward all the saints, 16 I do not cease to give thanks for you, remembering you in my prayers, 17 that the God of our Lord Jesus Christ, the Father of glory, may give you a spirit of wisdom and of revelation in the knowledge of him, 18 having the eyes of your hearts enlightened, that you may know what is the hope to which he has called you, what are the riches of his glorious inheritance in the saints, 19 and what is the immeasurable greatness of his power in us who believe, according to the working of his great might 20 which he accomplished in Christ when he raised him from the dead and made him sit at his right hand in the heavenly places, 21 far above all rule and authority and power and dominion, and above every

dren by one man, our forefather Isaac, 11 though they were not yet born and had done nothing either good or bad, in order that God's purpose of election might continue, not because of works but because of his call, 12 she was told, "The elder will serve the younger." 13 As it is written, "Jacob I loved, but Esau I hated."

▶ 1:4 Heb 4:3
3 For we who have believed enter that rest, as he has said,
"As I swore in my wrath,
'They shall never enter my rest,'"
although his works were finished from the foundation of the world.

▶ 1:5 Acts 13:48
48 And when the Gentiles heard this, they were glad and glorified the word of God; and as many as were ordained to eternal life believed.

▶ 1:7 Acts 2:38, 38 And Peter said to them, "Repent, and be baptized every one of you in the name of Jesus Christ for the forgiveness of your sins; and you shall receive the gift of the Holy Spirit.

20:28 28 Take heed to yourselves and to all the flock, in which the Holy Spirit has made you overseers, to care for the church of God which he obtained with the blood of his own Son.
Heb 9:22
22 Indeed, under the law almost everything is purified with blood, and without the shedding of blood there is no forgiveness of sins.

▶ 1:10 Tit 1:3
3 and at the proper time manifested in his word through the preaching with which I have been entrusted by command of God our Savior;

▶ 1:11 Acts 2:23
23 this Jesus, delivered up according to the definite plan and foreknowledge of God, you crucified and killed by the hands of lawless men.

▶ 1:18 Acts 20:32 32 And now I commend you to God and to the word of his grace, which is able to build you up and to give you the inheritance among all those who are sanctified.

▶ 1:20 Acts 2:24 24 But God raised him up, having loosed the pangs of death, because it was not possible for him to be held by it.

▶ 1:7 Col 1:14 14 in whom we have redemption, the forgiveness of sins.

▶ 1:10 Gal 4:4 4 But when the time had fully come, God sent forth his Son, born of woman, born under the law,

▶ 1:13-14 2 Cor 1:22, 22 he has put his seal upon us and given us his Spirit in our hearts as a guarantee.
5:5 5 He who has prepared us for this very thing is God, who has given us the Spirit as a guarantee.
Gal 3:2 2 Let me ask you only this: Did you receive the Spirit by works of the law, or by hearing with faith?

Eph 4:3 3 eager to maintain the unity of the Spirit in the bond of peace.
Rom 4:11 11 He received circumcision as a sign or seal of the righteousness which he had by faith while he was still uncircumcised. The purpose was to make him the father of all who believe without being circumcised and who thus have righteousness reckoned to them

▶ 1:15 Col 1:4 4 because we have heard of your faith in Christ Jesus and of the love which you have for all the saints,

▶ 1:20 Col 3:1-4
If then you have been raised with Christ, seek the things that are above, where Christ is, seated at the right hand of God. 2 Set your minds on things that are above, not on things that are on earth. 3 For you have died, and your life is hid with Christ in God. 4 When Christ who is our life appears, then you also will appear with him in glory.

▶ 1:22-23 4:15,
15 Rather, speaking the truth in love, we are to grow up in every way into him who is the head, into Christ,

Phil 2:1-11 (§242)

2 So if there is any encouragement in Christ, any incentive of love, any participation in the Spirit, any affection and sympathy, [2] complete my joy by being of the same mind, having the same love, being in full accord and of one mind. [3] Do nothing from selfishness or conceit, but in humility count others better than yourselves. [4] Let each of you look not only to his own interests, but also to the interests of others. [5] Have this mind among yourselves, which is yours in Christ Jesus, [6] who, though he was in the form of God, did not count equality with God a thing to be grasped, [7] but emptied himself, taking the form of a servant, being born in the likeness of men. [8] And being found in human form he humbled himself and became obedient unto death, even death on a cross. [9] Therefore God has highly exalted him and bestowed on him the name which is above every name, [10] that at the name of Jesus every knee should bow, in heaven and on earth and under the earth, [11] and every tongue confess that Jesus Christ is Lord, to the glory of God the Father.

Col 1:15-20 (§258)

[15] He is the image of the invisible God, the first-born of all creation; [16] for in him all things were created, in heaven and on earth, visible and invisible, whether thrones or dominions or principalities or authorities—all things were created through him and for him. [17] He is before all things, and in him all things hold together. [18] He is the head of the body, the church; he is the beginning, the first-born from the dead, that in everything he might be pre-eminent. [19] For in him all the fulness of God was pleased to dwell, [20] and through him to reconcile to himself all things, whether on earth or in heaven, making peace by the blood of his cross.

Col 1:24-2:3 (§260)

[24] Now I rejoice in my sufferings for your sake, and in my flesh I complete what is lacking in Christ's afflictions for the sake of his body, that is, the church, [25] of which I became a minister according to the divine office which was given to me for you, to make the word of God fully known, [26] the mystery hidden for ages and generations but now made manifest to his saints. [27] To them God chose to make known how great among the Gentiles are the riches of the glory of this mystery, which is Christ in you, the hope of glory. [28] Him we proclaim, warning every man and teaching every man in all wisdom, that we may present every man mature in Christ. [29] For this I toil, striving with all the energy which he mightily inspires within me.

2 For I want you to know how greatly I strive for you, and for those at La-odice′a, and for all who have not seen my face, [2] that their hearts may be encouraged as they are knit together in love, to have all the riches of assured understanding and the knowledge of God's mystery, of Christ, [3] in whom are hid all the treasures of wisdom and knowledge.

Phm 4-7 (§306)

[4] I thank my God always when I remember you in my prayers, [5] because I hear of your love and of the faith which you have toward the Lord Jesus and all the saints, [6] and I pray that the sharing of your faith may promote the knowledge of all the good that is ours in Christ. [7] For I have derived much joy and comfort from your love, my brother, because the hearts of the saints have been refreshed through you.

219

Eph (cont)

name that is named, not only in this age but also in that which is to come; [22] and he has put all things under his feet and has made him the head over all things for the church, [23] which is his body, the fulness of him who fills all in all.

5:23

[23] For the husband is the head of the wife as Christ is the head of the church, his body, and is himself its Savior.

Col 1:18,

[18] He is the head of the body, the church; he is the beginning, the first-born from the dead, that in everything he might be pre-eminent.

2:19

[19] and not holding fast to the Head, from whom the whole body, nourished and knit together through its joints and ligaments, grows with a growth that is from God.

Rom 12:5

[5] so we, though many, are one body in Christ, and individually members one of another.

1 Cor 12:12,

[12] For just as the body is one and has many members, and all the members of the body, though many, are one body, so it is with Christ.

27

[27] Now you are the body of Christ and individually members of it.

▶ 1:23 4:12,

[12] to equip the saints for the work of ministry, for building up the body of Christ,

5:30

[30] because we are members of his body.

▶ 1:15 (love) *omit* your love: p[46]S*AB cop(bo)

Origen

220

Rom 3:21-26 (§14)

21 But now the righteousness of God has been manifested apart from law, although the law and the prophets bear witness to it, 22 the righteousness of God through faith in Jesus Christ for all who believe. For there is no distinction; 23 since all have sinned and fall short of the glory of God, 24 they are justified by his grace as a gift, through the redemption which is in Christ Jesus, 25 whom God put forward as an expiation by his blood, to be received by faith. This was to show God's righteousness, because in his divine forbearance he had passed over former sins; 26 it was to prove at the present time that he himself is righteous and that he justifies him who has faith in Jesus.

Rom 3:27-31 (§15)

27 Then what becomes of our boasting? It is excluded. On what principle? On the principle of works? No, but on the principle of faith. 28 For we hold that a man is justified by faith apart from works of law. 29 Or is God the God of Jews only? Is he not the God of Gentiles also? Yes, of Gentiles also, 30 since God is one; and he will justify the circumcised on the ground of their faith and the uncircumcised through their faith. 31 Do we then overthrow the law by this faith? By no means! On the contrary, we uphold the law.

Rom 6:1-10 (§23)

6 What shall we say then? Are we to continue in sin that grace may abound? 2 By no means! How can we who died to sin still live in it? 3 Do you not know that all of us who have been baptized into Christ Jesus were baptized into his death? 4 We were buried therefore with him by baptism into death, so that as Christ was raised from the dead by the glory of the Father, we too might walk in newness of life.

5 For if we have been united with him in a death like his, we shall certainly be united with him in a resurrection like his. 6 We know that our old self was crucified with him so that the sinful body might be destroyed, and we might no longer be enslaved to sin. 7 For he who has died is freed from sin. 8 But if we have died with Christ, we believe that we shall also live with him. 9 For we know that Christ being raised from the dead will never die again; death no longer has dominion over him. 10 The death he died he died

1 Cor 3:1-4 (§78)

3 But I, brethren, could not address you as spiritual men, but as men of the flesh, as babes in Christ. 2 I fed you with milk, not solid food; for you were not ready for it; and even yet you are not ready, 3 for you are still of the flesh. For while there is jealousy and strife among you, are you not of the flesh, and behaving like ordinary men? 4 For when one says, "I belong to Paul," and another, "I belong to Apol'los," are you not merely men?

1 Cor 4:6-7 (§84)

6 I have applied all this to myself and Apol'los for your benefit, brethren, that you may learn by us not to go beyond what is written, that none of you may be puffed up in favor of one against another. 7 For who sees anything different in you? What have you that you did not receive? If then you received it, why do you boast as if it were not a gift?

Rom 9:14-18 (§37)

14 What shall we say then? Is there injustice on God's part? By no means! 15 For he says to Moses, "I will have mercy on whom I have mercy, and I will have compassion on whom I have compassion." 16 So it depends not upon man's will or exertion, but upon God's mercy. 17 For the scripture says to Pharaoh, "I have raised you up for the very purpose of showing my power in you, so that my name may be proclaimed in all the earth." 18 So then he has mercy upon whomever he wills, and he hardens the heart of whomever he wills.

Rom 11:1-6 (§44)

11 I ask, then, has God rejected his people? By no means! I myself am an Israelite, a descendant of Abraham, a member of the tribe of Benjamin. 2 God has not rejected his people whom he foreknew. Do you not know what the scripture says of Eli'jah, how he pleads with God against Israel? 3 "Lord, they have killed thy prophets, they have demolished thy altars, and I alone am left, and they seek my life." 4 But what is God's reply to him? "I have kept for myself seven thousand men who have not bowed the knee to Ba'al." 5 So too at the present time there is a remnant, chosen by grace. 6 But if it is by grace, it is no longer on the basis of works; otherwise grace would no longer be grace.

to sin, once for all, but the life he lives he lives to God.

Rom 11:17-24 (§48)

17 But if some of the branches were broken off, and you, a wild olive shoot, were grafted in their place to share the richness of the olive tree, 18 do not boast over the branches. If you do boast, remember it is not you that support the root, but the root that supports you. 19 You will say, "Branches were broken off so that I might be grafted in." 20 That is true. They were broken off because of their unbelief, but you stand fast only through faith. So do not become proud, but stand in awe. 21 For if God did not spare the natural branches, neither will he spare you. 22 Note then the kindness and the severity of God: severity toward those who have fallen, but God's kindness to you, provided you continue in his kindness; otherwise you too will be cut off. 23 And even the others, if they do not persist in their unbelief, will be grafted in, for God has the power to graft them in again. 24 For if you have been cut from what is by nature a wild olive tree, and grafted, contrary to nature, into a cultivated olive tree, how much more will these natural branches be grafted back into their own olive tree.

Rom 12:3-8 (§52)

3 For by the grace given to me I bid every one among you not to think of himself more highly than he ought to think, but to think with sober judgment, each according to the measure of faith which God has assigned him. 4 For as in one body we have many members, and all the members do not have the same function, 5 so we, though many, are one body in Christ, and individually members one of another. 6 Having gifts that differ according to the grace given to us, let us use them: if prophecy, in proportion to our faith; 7 if service, in our serving; he who teaches, in his teaching; 8 he who exhorts, in his exhortation; he who contributes, in liberality; he who gives aid, with zeal; he who does acts of mercy, with cheerfulness.

Gal 2:15-21 (§199)

15 We ourselves, who are Jews by birth and not Gentile sinners, 16 yet who know that a man is not justified by works of the law but through faith in Jesus Christ, even we have believed in Christ Jesus, in order to be justified by faith in Christ, and not by works of the law, because by works of the law shall no one be justified. 17 But if, in our endeavor to be justified in Christ, we ourselves were found to be sinners, is Christ then an agent of sin? Certainly not! 18 But if I build up again those things which I tore down, then I prove myself a transgressor. 19 For I through the law died to the law, that I might live to God. 20 I have been crucified with Christ; it is no longer I who live, but Christ who lives in me; and the life I now live in the flesh I live by faith in the Son of God, who loved me and gave himself for me. 21 I do not nullify the grace of God; for if justification were through the law, then Christ died to no purpose.

Eph 2:1-10

2 And you he made alive, when you were dead through the trespasses and sins 2 in which you once walked, following the course of this world, following the prince of the power of the air, the spirit that is now at work in the sons of disobedience. 3 Among these we all once lived in the passions of our flesh, following the desires of body and mind, and so we were by nature children of wrath, like the rest of mankind. 4 But God, who is rich in mercy, out of the great love with which he loved us, 5 even when we were dead through our trespasses, made us alive together with Christ (by grace you have been saved), 6 and raised us up with him, and made us sit with him in the heavenly places in Christ Jesus, 7 that in the coming ages he might show the immeasurable riches of his grace in kindness toward us in Christ Jesus. 8 For by grace you have been saved through faith; and this is not your own doing, it is the gift of God— 9 not because of works, lest any man should boast. 10 For we are his workmanship, created in Christ Jesus for good works, which God prepared beforehand, that we should walk in them.

▶ 2:2-3 Acts 26:18 18 to open their eyes, that they may turn from darkness to light and from the power of Satan to God, that they may receive forgiveness of sins and a place among those who are sanctified by faith in me.'
▶ 2:3-4 Tit 3:3-7 3 For we ourselves were once foolish, disobedient, led astray, slaves to various passions and pleasures, passing our days in malice and envy, hated by men and hating one another; 4 but when the goodness and loving kindness of God our Savior appeared, 5 he saved us, not because of

deeds done by us in righteousness, but in virtue of his own mercy, by the washing of regeneration and renewal in the Holy Spirit, 6 which he poured out upon us richly through Jesus Christ our Savior, 7 so that we might be justified by his grace and become heirs in hope of eternal life.

▶ 2:7 Tit 3:4 4 but when the goodness and loving kindness of God our Savior appeared,
▶ 2:9 2 Tim 1:9 9 who saved us and called us with a holy calling, not in virtue of our works but in virtue of his own purpose and the grace which he gave us in Christ Jesus ages ago,

Tit 3:5 5 he saved us, not because of deeds done by us in righteousness, but in virtue of his own mercy, by the washing of regeneration and renewal in the Holy Spirit,
▶ 2:10 Tit 2:14 14 who gave himself for us to redeem us from all iniquity and to purify for himself a people of his own who are zealous for good deeds.

▶ 2:3 Rom 1:24-28 24 Therefore God gave them up in the lusts of their hearts to impurity, to the dishonoring of their bodies among themselves, 25 because they exchanged the truth about God for a lie and worshiped and served the creature rather than the Creator, who is blessed for ever! Amen.
26 For this reason God gave them up to dishonorable passions. Their women exchanged natural relations for unnatural, 27 and the men likewise gave up natural relations with women and

were consumed with passion for one another, men committing shameless acts with men and receiving in their own persons the due penalty for their error.
28 And since they did not see fit to acknowledge God, God gave them up to a base mind and to improper conduct.

220

Col 2:8-15 (§262)

8 See to it that no one makes a prey of you by philosophy and empty deceit, according to human tradition, according to the elemental spirits of the universe, and not according to Christ. 9 For in him the whole fulness of deity dwells bodily, 10 and you have come to fulness of life in him, who is the head of all rule and authority. 11 In him also you were circumcised with a circumcision made without hands, by putting off the body of flesh in the circumcision of Christ; 12 and you were buried with him in baptism, in which you were also raised with him through faith in the working of God, who raised him from the dead. 13And you, who were dead in trespasses and the uncircumcision of your flesh, God made alive together with him, having forgiven us all our trespasses, 14 having canceled the bond which stood against us with its legal demands; this he set aside, nailing it to the cross. 15 He disarmed the principalities and powers and made a public example of them, triumphing over them in him.

Col 3:1-11 (§265-266)

3 If then you have been raised with Christ, seek the things that are above, where Christ is, seated at the right hand of God. 2 Set your minds on things that are above, not on things that are on earth. 3 For you have died, and your life is hid with Christ in God. 4 When Christ who is our life appears, then you also will appear with him in glory.

5 Put to death therefore what is earthly in you: fornication, impurity, passion, evil desire, and covetousness, which is idolatry. 6 On account of these the wrath of God is coming. 7 In these you once walked, when you lived in them. 8 But now put them all away: anger, wrath, malice, slander, and foul talk from your mouth. 9 Do not lie to one another, seeing that you have put off the old nature with its practices 10 and have put on the new nature, which is being renewed in knowledge after the image of its creator. 11 Here there cannot be Greek and Jew, circumcised and uncircumcised, barbarian, Scyth′ian, slave, free man, but Christ is all, and in all.

Gal 5:16-17

16 But I say, walk by the Spirit, and do not gratify the desires of the flesh. 17 For the desires of the flesh are against the Spirit, and the desires of the Spirit are against the flesh; for these are opposed to each other, to prevent you from doing what you would.

Rom 8:9-13

9 But you are not in the flesh, you are in the Spirit, if in fact the Spirit of God dwells in you. Any one who does not have the Spirit of Christ does not belong to him. 10 But if Christ is in you, although your bodies are dead because of sin, your spirits are alive because of righteousness. 11 If the Spirit of him who raised Jesus from the dead dwells in you, he who raised Christ Jesus from the dead will give life to your mortal bodies also through his Spirit which dwells in you. 12 So then, brethren, we are debtors, not to the flesh, to live according to the flesh—13 for if you live according to the flesh you will die, but if by the Spirit you put to death the deeds of the body you will live.

▶ 2:4 Rom 2:4

4 Or do you presume upon the riches of his kindness and forbearance and patience? Do you not know that God's kindness is meant to lead you to repentance?

▶ 2:9 1 Cor 1:29,

29 so that no human being might boast in the presence of God. 31 31 therefore, as it is written, "Let him who boasts, boast of the Lord."

2 Cor 10:13-17

13 But we will not boast beyond limit, but will keep to the limits God has apportioned us, to reach even to you. 14 For we are not overextending ourselves, as though we did not reach you; we were the first to come all the way to you with the gospel of Christ. 15 We do not boast beyond limit, in other men's labors; but our hope is that as your faith increases, our field among you may be greatly enlarged, 16 so that we may preach the gospel in lands beyond you, without boasting of work already done in another's field. 17 "Let him who boasts, boast of the Lord."

Rom 5:6-11 (§21)

6 While we were still weak, at the right time Christ died for the ungodly. 7 Why, one will hardly die for a righteous man—though perhaps for a good man one will dare even to die. 8 But God shows his love for us in that while we were yet sinners Christ died for us. 9 Since, therefore, we are now justified by his blood, much more shall we be saved by him from the wrath of God. 10 For if while we were enemies we were reconciled to God by the death of his Son, much more, now that we are reconciled, shall we be saved by his life. 11 Not only so, but we also rejoice in God through our Lord Jesus Christ, through whom we have now received our reconciliation.

Rom 9:1-5 (§35)

9 I am speaking the truth in Christ, I am not lying; my conscience bears me witness in the Holy Spirit, 2 that I have great sorrow and unceasing anguish in my heart. 3 For I could wish that I myself were accursed and cut off from Christ for the sake of my brethren, my kinsmen by race. 4 They are Israelites, and to them belong the sonship, the glory, the covenants, the giving of the law, the worship, and the promises; 5 to them belong the patriarchs, and of their race, according to the flesh, is the Christ. God who is over all be blessed for ever. Amen.

Rom 11:11-12 (§46)

11 So I ask, have they stumbled so as to fall? By no means! But through their trespass salvation has come to the Gentiles, so as to make Israel jealous. 12 Now if their trespass means riches for the world, and if their failure means riches for the Gentiles, how much more will their full inclusion mean!

Rom 11:17-24 (§48)

17 But if some of the branches were broken off, and you, a wild olive shoot, were grafted in their place to share the richness of the olive tree, 18 do not boast over the branches. If you do boast, remember it is not you that support the root, but the root that supports you. 19 You will say, "Branches were broken off so that I might be grafted in." 20 That is true. They were broken off because of their unbelief, but you stand fast only through faith. So do not become proud, but stand in awe. 21 For if God did not spare the natural branches, neither will he spare you. 22 Note then the kindness and the severity of God: severity toward those who have fallen, but God's kindness to you, provided you continue in his kindness; otherwise you too will be cut off. 23 And even the others, if they do not

1 Cor 3:5-9 (§79)

5 What then is Apol′los? What is Paul? Servants through whom you believed, as the Lord assigned to each. 6 I planted, Apol′los watered, but God gave the growth. 7 So neither he who plants nor he who waters is anything, but only God who gives the growth. 8 He who plants and he who waters are equal, and each shall receive his wages according to his labor. 9 For we are God's fellow workers; you are God's field, God's building.

1 Cor 3:16-17 (§81)

16 Do you not know that you are God's temple and that God's Spirit dwells in you? 17 If any one destroys God's temple, God will destroy him. For God's temple is holy, and that temple you are.

1 Cor 6:12-20 (§92)

12 "All things are lawful for me," but not all things are helpful. "All things are lawful for me," but I will not be enslaved by anything. 13 "Food is meant for the stomach and the stomach for food"—and God will destroy both one and the other. The body is not meant for immorality, but for the Lord, and the Lord for the body. 14 And God raised the Lord and will also raise us up by his power. 15 Do you not know that your bodies are members of Christ? Shall I therefore take the members of Christ and make them members of a prostitute? Never! 16 Do you not know that he who joins himself to a prostitute becomes one body with her?

persist in their unbelief, will be grafted in, for God has the power to graft them in again. 24 For if you have been cut from what is by nature a wild olive tree, and grafted, contrary to nature, into a cultivated olive tree, how much more will these natural branches be grafted back into their own olive tree.

Rom 15:7-13 (§61)

7 Welcome one another, therefore, as Christ has welcomed you, for the glory of God. 8 For I tell you that Christ became a servant to the circumcised to show God's truthfulness, in order to confirm the promises given to the patriarchs, 9 and in order that the Gentiles might glorify God for his mercy. As it is written,
"Therefore I will praise thee among the Gentiles,
and sing to thy name";
10 and again it is said,
"Rejoice, O Gentiles, with his people";
11 and again,
"Praise the Lord, all Gentiles,
and let all the peoples praise him";

2 Cor 5:14-21 (§164)

14 For the love of Christ controls us, because we are convinced that one has died for all; therefore all have died. 15 And he died for all, that those who live might live no longer for themselves but for him who for their sake died and was raised.

16 From now on, therefore, we regard no one from a human point of view; even though we once regarded Christ from a human point of view, we regard him thus no longer. 17 Therefore, if any one is in Christ, he is a new creation; the old has passed away, behold, the new has come. 18 All this is from God, who through Christ reconciled us to himself and gave us the ministry of reconciliation; 19 that is, in Christ God was reconciling the world to himself, not counting their trespasses against them, and entrusting to us the message of reconciliation. 20 So we are ambassadors for Christ, God making his appeal through us. We beseech you on behalf of Christ, be reconciled to God. 21 For our sake he made him to be sin who knew no sin, so that in him we might become the righteousness of God.

For, as it is written, "The two shall become one flesh." 17 But he who is united to the Lord becomes one spirit with him. 18 Shun immorality. Every other sin which a man commits is outside the body; but the immoral man sins against his own body. 19 Do you not know that your body is a temple of the Holy Spirit within you, which you have from God? You are not your own; 20 you were bought with a price. So glorify God in your body.

1 Cor 12:1-3 (§116)

12 Now concerning spiritual gifts, brethren, I do not want you to be uninformed. 2 You know that when you were heathen, you were led astray to dumb idols, however you may have been moved. 3 Therefore I want you to understand that no one speaking by the Spirit of God ever says "Jesus be cursed!" and no one can say "Jesus is Lord" except by the Holy Spirit.

12 and further Isaiah says,
"The root of Jesse shall come,
he who rises to rule the Gentiles;
in him shall the Gentiles hope."
13 May the God of hope fill you with all joy and peace in believing, so that by the power of the Holy Spirit you may abound in hope.

1 Cor 12:12-13 (§118)

12 For just as the body is one and has many members, and all the members of the body, though many, are one body, so it is with Christ. 13 For by one Spirit we were all baptized into one body—Jews or Greeks, slaves or free—and all were made to drink of one Spirit.

Eph 2:11-22

11 Therefore remember that at one time you Gentiles in the flesh, called the uncircumcision by what is called the circumcision, which is made in the flesh by hands—12 remember that you were at that time separated from Christ, alienated from the commonwealth of Israel, and strangers to the covenants of promise, having no hope and without God in the world. 13 But now in Christ Jesus you who once were far off have been brought near in the blood of Christ. 14 For he is our peace, who has made us both one, and has broken down the dividing wall of hostility, 15 by abolishing in his flesh the law of commandments and ordinances, that he might create in himself one new man in place of the two, so making peace, 16 and might reconcile us both to God in one body through the cross, thereby bringing the hostility to an end. 17 And he came and preached peace to you who were far off and peace to those who were near; 18 for through him we both have access in one Spirit to the Father. 19 So then you are no longer strangers and sojourners, but you are fellow citizens with the saints and members of the household of God, 20 built upon the foundation of the apostles and prophets, Christ Jesus himself being the cornerstone, 21 in whom the whole structure is joined together and grows into a holy temple in the Lord; 22 in whom you also are built into it for a dwelling place of God in the Spirit.

▶ 2:17 Acts 10:36   36 You know the word which he sent to Israel, preaching good news of peace by Jesus Christ (he is Lord of all)

▶ 2:19 1 Tim 3:15   15 if I am delayed, you may know how one ought to behave in the household of God, which is the church of the living God, the pillar and bulwark of the truth.

▶ 2:11 Rom 2:28-29,   28 For he is not a real Jew who is one outwardly, nor is true circumcision something external and physical. 29 He is a Jew who is one inwardly, and real circumcision is a matter of the heart, spiritual and not literal. His praise is not from men but from God.

4:11-12   11 He received circumcision as a sign or seal of the righteousness which he had by faith while he was still uncircumcised. The purpose was to make him the father of all who believe without being circumcised and who thus have righteousness reckoned to them, 12 and likewise the father of the circumcised who are not merely circumcised but also follow the example of the faith which our father Abraham had before he was circumcised.

Gal 3:15-18

15 To give a human example, brethren: no one annuls even a man's will, or adds to it, once it has been ratified. 16 Now the promises were made to Abraham and to his offspring. It does not say, "And to offsprings," referring to many; but, referring to one, "And to your offspring," which is Christ. 17 This is what I mean: the law, which came four hundred and thirty years afterward, does not annul a covenant previously ratified by God, so as to make the promise void. 18 For if the

Col 1:21-23 (§259)

21 And you, who once were estranged and hostile in mind, doing evil deeds, 22 he has now reconciled in his body of flesh by his death, in order to present you holy and blameless and irreproachable before him, 23 provided that you continue in the faith, stable and steadfast, not shifting from the hope of the gospel which you heard, which has been preached to every creature under heaven, and of which I, Paul, became a minister.

Col 1:15-20 (§258)

15 He is the image of the invisible God, the first-born of all creation; 16 for in him all things were created, in heaven and on earth, visible and invisible, whether thrones or dominions or principalities or authorities—all things were created through him and for him. 17 He is before all things, and in him all things hold together. 18 He is the head of the body, the church; he is the beginning, the first-born from the dead, that in everything he might be pre-eminent. 19 For in him all the fulness of God was pleased to dwell, 20 and through him to reconcile to himself all things, whether on earth or in heaven, making peace by the blood of his cross.

---

inheritance is by the law, it is no longer by promise; but God gave it to Abraham by a promise.

▶ 2:12 1 Thes 4:13
13 But we would not have you ignorant, brethren, concerning those who are asleep, that you may not grieve as others do who have no hope.

▶ 2:15-16 Col 1:20
20 and through him to reconcile to himself all things, whether on earth or in heaven, making peace by the blood of his cross.

Gal 3:28   28 There is neither Jew nor Greek, there is neither slave nor free, there is neither male nor female; for you are all one in Christ Jesus.

Col 3:11   11 Here there cannot be Greek and Jew, circumcised and uncircumcised, barbarian, Scyth'ian, slave, free man, but Christ is all, and in all.

▶2:18 Rom 5:2
2 Through him we have obtained access to this grace in which we stand, and we rejoice in our hope of sharing the glory of God.

222

1 Paul, a servant of Jesus Christ, called to be an apostle, set apart for the gospel of God [2] which he promised beforehand through his prophets in the holy scriptures, [3] the gospel concerning his Son, who was descended from David according to the flesh [4] and designated Son of God in power according to the Spirit of holiness by his resurrection from the dead, Jesus Christ our Lord, [5] through whom we have received grace and apostleship to bring about the obedience of faith for the sake of his name among all the nations, [6] including yourselves who are called to belong to Jesus Christ;

7 To all God's beloved in Rome, who are called to be saints:
Grace to you and peace from God our Father and the Lord Jesus Christ.

13 Now I am speaking to you Gentiles. Inasmuch then as I am an apostle to the Gentiles, I magnify my ministry [14] in order to make my fellow Jews jealous, and thus save some of them. [15] For if their rejection means the reconciliation of the world, what will their acceptance mean but life from the dead? [16] If the dough offered as first fruits is holy, so is the whole lump; and if the root is holy, so are the branches.

33 O the depth of the riches and wisdom and knowledge of God! How unsearchable are his judgments and how inscrutable his ways!
[34] "For who has known the mind of the Lord,
or who has been his counselor?"
[35] "Or who has given a gift to him
that he might be repaid?"
[36] For from him and through him and to him are all things. To him be glory for ever. Amen.

14 I myself am satisfied about you, my brethren, that you yourselves are full of goodness, filled with all knowledge, and able to instruct one another. [15] But on some points I have written to you very boldly by way of reminder, because of the grace given me by God [16] to be a minister of Christ Jesus to the Gentiles in the priestly service of the gospel of God, so that the offering of the Gentiles may be acceptable, sanctified by the Holy Spirit. [17] In Christ Jesus, then, I have reason to be proud of my work for God. [18] For I will not venture to speak of anything except

10 According to the grace of God given to me, like a skilled master builder I laid a foundation, and another man is building upon it. Let each man take care how he builds upon it. [11] For no other foundation can any one lay than that which is laid, which is Jesus Christ. [12] Now if any one builds on the foundation with gold, silver, precious stones, wood, hay, straw— [13] each man's work will become manifest; for the Day will disclose it, because it will be revealed with fire, and the fire will test what sort of work each one has done. [14] If the work which any man has built on the foundation survives, he will receive a reward. [15] If any man's work is burned up, he will suffer loss, though he himself will be saved, but only as through fire.

4 This is how one should regard us, as servants of Christ and stewards of the mysteries of God. [2] Moreover it is required of stewards that they be found trustworthy. [3] But with me it is a very small thing that I should be judged by you or by any human court. I do not even judge myself. [4] I am not aware of anything against myself, but I am not thereby acquitted. It is the Lord who judges me. [5] Therefore do not pronounce judgment before the time, before the Lord comes, who will bring to light the things now hidden in darkness and will disclose the purposes of the heart. Then every man will receive his commendation from God.

15 But I have made no use of any of these rights, nor am I writing this to secure any such provision. For I would rather die than have any one deprive me of my ground for boasting. [16] For if I preach the gospel, that gives me no ground for boasting. For necessity is

far round as Illyr′icum I have fully preached the gospel of Christ, [20] thus making it my ambition to preach the gospel, not where Christ has already been named, lest I build on another man's foundation, [21] but as it is written,
"They shall see who have never been told of him,
and they shall understand who have never heard of him."
what Christ has wrought through me to win obedience from the Gentiles, by word and deed, [19] by the power of signs and wonders, by the power of the Holy Spirit, so that from Jerusalem and as

laid upon me. Woe to me if I do not preach the gospel! [17] For if I do this of my own will, I have a reward; but if not of my own will, I am entrusted with a commission. [18] What then is my reward? Just this: that in my preaching I may make the gospel free of charge, not making full use of my right in the gospel.

15 But when he who had set me apart before I was born, and had called me through his grace, [16] was pleased to reveal his Son to me, in order that I might preach him among the Gentiles, I did not confer with flesh and blood, [17] nor did I go up to Jerusalem to those who were apostles before me, but I went away into Arabia; and again I returned to Damascus.

18 Then after three years I went up to Jerusalem to visit Cephas, and remained with him fifteen days. [19] But I saw none of the other apostles except James the Lord's brother. [20] (In what I am writing to you, before God, I do not lie!) [21] Then I went into the regions of Syria and Cili′cia. [22] And I was still not known by sight to the churches of Christ in Judea; [23] they only heard it said, "He who once persecuted us is now preaching the faith he once tried to destroy." [24] And they glorified God because of me.

2 Then after fourteen years I went up again to Jerusalem with Barnabas, taking Titus along with me. [2] I went up by revelation; and I laid before them (but privately before those who were of repute) the gospel which I preach among the Gentiles, lest somehow I should be running or had run in vain. [3] But even Titus, who was with me, was not compelled to be circumcised, though he was a Greek. [4] But because of false brethren secretly brought in, who slipped in to spy out our freedom which we have in Christ Jesus, that they might bring us into bondage— [5] to them we did not yield submission even for a moment, that the truth of the gospel might be preserved for you. [6] And from those who were reputed to be something (what they were makes no difference to me; God shows no partiality)—those, I say, who were of repute added nothing to me; [7] but on the contrary, when they saw that I had been entrusted with the gospel to the uncircumcised, just as Peter had been entrusted with the gospel to the circumcised [8] (for he who worked through Peter for the mission to the circumcised worked through me also for the Gentiles), [9] and when they perceived the grace that was given to me, James and Cephas and John, who were reputed to be pillars, gave to me and Barnabas the right hand of fellowship, that we should go to the Gentiles and they to the cir-

3 For this reason I, Paul, a prisoner for Christ Jesus on behalf of you Gentiles— [2] assuming that you have heard of the stewardship of God's grace that was given to me for you, [3] how the mystery was made known to me by revelation, as I have written briefly. [4] When you read this you can perceive my insight into the mystery of Christ, [5] which was not made known to the sons of men in other generations as it has now been revealed to his holy apostles and prophets by the Spirit; [6] that is, how the Gentiles are fellow heirs, members of the same body, and partakers of the promise in Christ Jesus through the gospel.

7 Of this gospel I was made a minister according to the gift of God's grace which was given me by the working of his power. [8] To me, though I am the very least of all the saints, this grace was given, to preach to the Gentiles the unsearchable riches of Christ, [9] and to make all men see what is the plan of the mystery hidden for ages in God who created all things; [10] that through the church the manifold wisdom of God might now be made known to the principalities and powers in the heavenly places. [11] This is according to the eternal purpose which he has realized in Christ Jesus our Lord, [12] in whom we have boldness and confidence of access through our faith in him. [13] So I ask you not to lose heart over what I am suffering for you, which is your glory.

cumcised; [10] only they would have us remember the poor, which very thing I was eager to do.

4 I mean that the heir, as long as he is a child, is no better than a slave, though he is the owner of all the estate; [2] but he is under guardians and trustees until the date set by the father. [3] So with us; when we were children, we were slaves to the elemental spirits of the universe. [4] But when the time had fully come, God sent forth his Son, born of woman, born under the law, [5] to redeem those who were under the law, so that we might receive adoption as sons. [6] And because you are sons, God has sent the Spirit of his Son into our hearts, crying, "Abba! Father!" [7] So through God you are no longer a slave but a son, and if a son then an heir.

▶ 3:1 Acts 23:18 — 18 So he took him and brought him to the tribune and said, "Paul the prisoner called me and asked me to bring this young man to you, as he has something to say to you."

2 Tim 1:8,
8 Do not be ashamed then of testifying to our Lord, nor of me his prisoner, but share in suffering for the gospel in the power of God,

12,
I do. But I am not ashamed, for I know whom I have believed, and I am sure that he is able to guard until that Day what has been entrusted to me.

16
16 May the Lord grant mercy to the household of Onesiph′orus, for he often refreshed me; he was not ashamed of my chains,

12 and therefore I suffer as

▶ 3:3 Acts 26:16-18
16 But rise and stand upon your feet; for I have appeared to you for this purpose, to appoint you to serve and bear witness to the things in which you have seen me and to those in which I will appear to you, [17] delivering you from the people and from the Gentiles —to whom I send you [18] to open their eyes, that they may turn from darkness to light and from the power of Satan to God, that they may receive forgiveness of sins and a place among those who are sanctified by faith in me.'

▶ 3:12 Heb 4:16
16 Let us then with confidence draw near to the throne of grace, that we may receive mercy and find grace to help in time of need.

▶ 3:13 2 Tim 2:10
10 Therefore I endure everything for the sake of the elect, that they also may obtain salvation in Christ Jesus with its eternal glory.

▶ 3:1 4:1
I therefore, a prisoner for the Lord, beg you to lead a life worthy of the calling to which you have been called.

Phil 1:12-20
12 I want you to know, brethren, that what has happened to me has really served to advance the gospel, [13] so that it has become known throughout the whole praetorian guard and to all the rest that my imprisonment is for Christ; [14] and most of the brethren have been made confident in the Lord because of my imprisonment, and are much more

bold to speak the word of God without fear.
15 Some indeed preach Christ from envy and rivalry, but others from good will. [16] The latter do it out of love, knowing that I am put here for the defense of the gospel; [17] the former proclaim Christ out of partisanship, not sincerely but thinking to afflict me in my imprisonment. [18] What then? Only that in every way, whether in pretense or in truth, Christ is proclaimed; and in that I rejoice.
19 Yes, and I shall rejoice. For I know that through your prayers and the help of the Spirit of Jesus Christ this

222

Col 1:24-2:3 (§260)

24 Now I rejoice in my sufferings for your sake, and in my flesh I complete what is lacking in Christ's afflictions for the sake of his body, that is, the church, 25 of which I became a minister according to the divine office which was given to me for you, to make the word of God fully known, 26 the mystery hidden for ages and generations but now made manifest to his saints. 27 To them God chose to make known how great among the Gentiles are the riches of the glory of this mystery, which is Christ in you, the hope of glory. 28 Him we proclaim, warning every man and teaching every man in all wisdom, that we may present every man mature in Christ. 29 For this I toil, striving with all the energy which he mightily inspires within me.

2 For I want you to know how greatly I strive for you, and for those at La-odice′a, and for all who have not seen my face, 2 that their hearts may be encouraged as they are knit together in love, to have all the riches of assured understanding and the knowledge of God's mystery, of Christ, 3 in whom are hid all the treasures of wisdom and knowledge.

---

will turn out for my deliverance, 20 as it is my eager expectation and hope that I shall not be at all ashamed, but that with full courage now as always Christ will be honored in my body, whether by life or by death.

Phm 1,

1 Paul, a prisoner for Christ Jesus, and Timothy our brother,
To Phile′mon our beloved fellow worker

---

9   9 yet for love's sake I prefer to appeal to you—I, Paul, an ambassador and now a prisoner also for Christ Jesus—

Col 4:3,

3 and pray for us also, that God may open to us a door for the word, to declare the mystery of Christ, on account of which I am in prison,

18a

18 I, Paul, write this greeting with my own hand. Remember my fetters.

▶ 3:2-3 1 Cor 15:8-10

8 Last of all, as to one untimely born, he appeared also to me. 9 For I am the least of the apostles, unfit to be called an apostle, because I persecuted the church of God. 10 But by the grace of God I am what I am, and his grace toward me was not in vain. On the contrary, I worked harder than any of them, though it was not I, but the grace of God which is with me.

▶ 3:4 2 Cor 11:6

6 Even if I am unskilled in speaking, I am not in knowledge; in every way we have made this plain to you in all things.

1 Cor 13:2

2 And if I have prophetic powers, and understand all mysteries and all knowledge, and if I have all faith, so as to remove mountains, but have not love, I am nothing.

▶ 3:5 Rom 16:25

25 Now to him who is able to strengthen you according to my gospel and the preaching of Jesus Christ, according to the revelation of the mystery which was kept secret for long ages

▶ 3:12 Rom 5:2

2 Through him we have obtained access to this grace in which we stand, and we rejoice in our hope of sharing the glory of God.

▶ 3:13 2 Cor 4:16

16 So we do not lose heart. Though our outer nature is wasting away, our inner nature is being renewed every day.

▶ 3:9 (all men) *omit* all: S*A Origen

223

Rom 8:31-39 (§34)

31 What then shall we say to this? If God is for us, who is against us? 32 He who did not spare his own Son but gave him up for us all, will he not also give us all things with him? 33 Who shall bring any charge against God's elect? It is God who justifies; 34 who is to condemn? Is it Christ Jesus, who died, yes, who was raised from the dead, who is at the right hand of God, who indeed intercedes for us? 35 Who shall separate us from the love of Christ? Shall tribulation, or distress, or persecution, or famine, or nakedness, or peril, or sword? 36 As it is written,

"For thy sake we are being killed all the day long;
we are regarded as sheep to be slaughtered."

37 No, in all these things we are more than conquerors through him who loved us. 38 For I am sure that neither death, nor life, nor angels, nor principalities, nor things present, nor things to come, nor powers, 39 nor height, nor depth, nor anything else in all creation, will be able to separate us from the love of God in Christ Jesus our Lord.

▶3:14-19 Col 1:9-14
9 And so, from the day we heard of it, we have not ceased to pray for you, asking that you may be filled with the knowledge of his will in all spiritual wisdom and understanding, 10 to lead a life worthy of the Lord, fully pleasing to him, bearing fruit in every good work

1 Cor 3:18-23 (§82)

18 Let no one deceive himself. If any one among you thinks that he is wise in this age, let him become a fool that he may become wise. 19 For the wisdom of this world is folly with God. For it is written, "He catches the wise in their craftiness," 20 and again, "The Lord knows that the thoughts of the wise are futile." 21 So let no one boast of men. For all things are yours, 22 whether Paul or Apol′los or Cephas or the world or life or death or the present or the future, all are yours; 23 and you are Christ's; and Christ is God's.

and increasing in the knowledge of God. 11 May you be strengthened with all power, according to his glorious might, for all endurance and patience with joy, 12 giving thanks to the Father, who has qualified us to share in the inheritance of the saints in light. 13 He has delivered us from the dominion of darkness and transferred us to the kingdom of his beloved Son, 14 in whom we have redemption, the forgiveness of sins.

2 Cor 4:16-5:5 (§161)

16 So we do not lose heart. Though our outer nature is wasting away, our inner nature is being renewed every day. 17 For this slight momentary affliction is preparing for us an eternal weight of glory beyond all comparison, 18 because we look not to the things that are seen but to the things that are unseen; for the things that are seen are transient, but the things that are unseen are eternal.

5 For we know that if the earthly tent we live in is destroyed, we have a building from God, a house not made with hands, eternal in the heavens. 2 Here indeed we groan, and long to put on our heavenly dwelling, 3 so that by putting it on we may not be found naked. 4 For while we are still in this tent, we sigh with anxiety; not that we would be unclothed, but that we would be further clothed, so that what is mortal may be swallowed up by life. 5 He who has prepared us for this very thing is God, who has given us the Spirit as a guarantee.

▶3:16 Rom 9:23   23 in order to make known the riches of his glory for the vessels of mercy, which he has prepared beforehand for glory,

▶3:17 Gal 2:20   20 I have been crucified with Christ; it is no longer I who live, but Christ who lives in me; and the life I now live in the flesh I live by faith in the Son of God, who loved me and gave himself for me.

▶3:19 Col 2:9-10   9 For in him the whole fulness of deity dwells bodily, 10 and you have come to fulness of life in him, who is the head of all rule and authority.

Eph 3:14-19

14 For this reason I bow my knees before the Father, 15 from whom every family in heaven and on earth is named, 16 that according to the riches of his glory he may grant you to be strengthened with might through his Spirit in the inner man, 17 and that Christ may dwell in your hearts through faith; that you, being rooted and grounded in love, 18 may have power to comprehend with all the saints what is the breadth and length and height and depth, 19 and to know the love of Christ which surpasses knowledge, that you may be filled with all the fulness of God.

Phil 4:7   7 And the peace of God, which passes all understanding, will keep your hearts and your minds in Christ Jesus.

224. To God be glory

224

Rom 16:25-27 (§70)

25 Now to him who is able to strengthen you according to my gospel and the preaching of Jesus Christ, according to the revelation of the mystery which was kept secret for long ages 26 but is now disclosed and through the prophetic writings is made known to all nations, according to the command of the eternal God, to bring about the obedience of faith—27 to the only wise God be glory for evermore through Jesus Christ! Amen.

2 Cor 9:6-15 (§175)

6 The point is this: he who sows sparingly will also reap sparingly, and he who sows bountifully will also reap bountifully. 7 Each one must do as he has made up his mind, not reluctantly or under compulsion, for God loves a cheerful giver. 8 And God is able to provide you with every blessing in abundance, so that you may always have enough of everything and may provide in abundance for every good work. 9 As it is written,

"He scatters abroad, he gives to the poor;
his righteousness endures for ever."

10 He who supplies seed to the sower and bread for food will supply and multiply your resources and increase the harvest of your righteousness. 11 You will be enriched in every way for great generosity, which through us will produce thanksgiving to God; 12 for the rendering of this service not only supplies the wants of the saints but also overflows in many thanksgivings to God. 13 Under the test of this service, you will glorify God by your obedience in acknowledging the gospel of Christ, and by the generosity of your contribution for them and for all others; 14 while they long for you and pray for you, because of the surpassing grace of God in you. 15 Thanks be to God for his inexpressible gift!

Eph 3:20-21

20 Now to him who by the power at work within us is able to do far more abundantly than all that we ask or think, 21 to him be glory in the church and in Christ Jesus to all generations, for ever and ever. Amen.

Col 2:4-7 (§261)

4 I say this in order that no one may delude you with beguiling speech. 5 For though I am absent in body, yet I am with you in spirit, rejoicing to see your good order and the firmness of your faith in Christ.

6 As therefore you received Christ Jesus the Lord, so live in him, 7 rooted and built up in him and established in the faith, just as you were taught, abounding in thanksgiving.

223

▶3:14 (Father) *add* of our Lord Jesus Christ: ScDG Koine Lect it vg syr(pes har) Origen(Latin)

▶ 3:19 (you) *read* he: p⁴⁶B cop(sa)

224. To God be glory

224

225

Rom 12:1-8 (§51-52)

12 I appeal to you therefore, brethren, by the mercies of God, to present your bodies as a living sacrifice, holy and acceptable to God, which is your spiritual worship. 2 Do not be conformed to this world but be transformed by the renewal of your mind, that you may prove what is the will of God, what is good and acceptable and perfect.

3 For by the grace given to me I bid every one among you not to think of himself more highly than he ought to think, but to think with sober judgment, each according to the measure of faith which God has assigned him. 4 For as in one body we have many members, and all the members do not have the same function, 5 so we, though many, are one body in Christ, and individually members one of another. 6 Having gifts that differ according to the grace given to us, let us use them: if prophecy, in proportion to our faith; 7 if service, in our serving; he who teaches, in his teaching; 8 he who exhorts, in his exhortation; he who contributes, in liberality; he who gives aid, with zeal; he who does acts of mercy, with cheerfulness.

1 Cor 1:10-17 (§73)

10 I appeal to you, brethren, by the name of our Lord Jesus Christ, that all of you agree and that there be no dissensions among you, but that you be united in the same mind and the same judgment. 11 For it has been reported to me by Chloe's people that there is quarreling among you, my brethren. 12 What I mean is that each one of you says, "I belong to Paul," or "I belong to Apollos," or "I belong to Cephas," or "I belong to Christ." 13 Is Christ divided? Was Paul crucified for you? Or were you baptized in the name of Paul? 14 I am thankful that I baptized none of you except Crispus and Gaius; 15 lest any one should say that you were baptized in my name. 16 (I did baptize also the household of Stephanas. Beyond that, I do not know whether I baptized any one else.) 17 For Christ did not send me to baptize but to preach the gospel, and not with eloquent wisdom, lest the cross of Christ be emptied of its power.

1 Cor 8:4-6 (§103)

4 Hence, as to the eating of food offered to idols, we know that "an idol has no real existence," and that "there is no God but one." 5 For although there may be so-called gods in heaven or on earth—as indeed there are many "gods" and many "lords"—6 yet for us there is one God, the Father, from whom are all things and for whom we exist, and one Lord, Jesus Christ, through whom are all things and through whom we exist.

1 Cor 12:4-13 (§117-118)

4 Now there are varieties of gifts, but the same Spirit; 5 and there are varieties of service, but the same Lord; 6 and there are varieties of working, but it is the same God who inspires them all in every one. 7 To each is given the manifestation of the Spirit for the common good. 8 To one is given through the Spirit the utterance of wisdom, and to another the utterance of knowledge according to the same Spirit, 9 to another faith by the same Spirit, to another gifts of healing by the one Spirit, 10 to another the working of miracles, to another prophecy, to another the ability to distinguish between spirits, to another various kinds of tongues, to another the interpretation of tongues. 11 All these are inspired by one and the same Spirit, who apportions to each one individually as he wills.

12 For just as the body is one and has many members, and all the members of the body, though many, are one body, so it is with Christ. 13 For by one Spirit we were all baptized into one body—Jews or Greeks, slaves or free—and all were made to drink of one Spirit.

2 Cor 10:1-6 (§176)

10 I, Paul, myself entreat you, by the meekness and gentleness of Christ—I who am humble when face to face with you, but bold to you when I am away!— 2 I beg of you that when I am present I may not have to show boldness with such confidence as I count on showing against some who suspect us of acting in worldly fashion. 3 For though we live in the world we are not carrying on a worldly war, 4 for the weapons of our warfare are not worldly but have divine power to destroy strongholds. 5 We destroy arguments and every proud obstacle to the knowledge of God, and take every thought captive to obey Christ, 6 being ready to punish every disobedience, when your obedience is complete.

2 Cor 6:1-10 (§165)

6 Working together with him, then, we entreat you not to accept the grace of God in vain. 2 For he says,
"At the acceptable time I have listened to you,
and helped you on the day of salvation."
Behold, now is the acceptable time; behold, now is the day of salvation. 3 We put no obstacle in any one's way, so that no fault may be found with our ministry, 4 but as servants of God we commend ourselves in every way: through great endurance, in afflictions, hardships, calamities, 5 beatings, imprisonments, tumults, labors, watching, hunger; 6 by purity, knowledge, forbearance, kindness, the Holy Spirit, genuine love, 7 truthful speech, and the power of God; with the weapons of righteousness for the right hand and for the left; 8 in honor and dishonor, in ill repute and good repute. We are treated as impostors, and yet are true; 9 as unknown, and yet well known; as dying, and behold we live; as punished, and yet not killed; 10 as sorrowful, yet always rejoicing; as poor, yet making many rich; as having nothing, and yet possessing everything.

Gal 5:16-26 (§213)

16 But I say, walk by the Spirit, and do not gratify the desires of the flesh. 17 For the desires of the flesh are against the Spirit, and the desires of the Spirit are against the flesh; for these are opposed to each other, to prevent you from doing what you would. 18 But if you are led by the Spirit you are not under the law. 19 Now the works of the flesh are plain: fornication, impurity, licentiousness, 20 idolatry, sorcery, enmity, strife, jealousy, anger, selfishness, dissension, party spirit, 21 envy, drunkenness, carousing, and the like. I warn you, as I warned you before, that those who do such things shall not inherit the kingdom of God. 22 But the fruit of the Spirit is love, joy, peace, patience, kindness, goodness, faithfulness, 23 gentleness, self-control; against such there is no law. 24 And those who belong to Christ Jesus have crucified the flesh with its passions and desires.

25 If we live by the Spirit, let us also walk by the Spirit. 26 Let us have no self-conceit, no provoking of one another, no envy of one another.

Gal 3:26-29 (§206)

26 for in Christ Jesus you are all sons of God, through faith. 27 For as many of you as were baptized into Christ have put on Christ. 28 There is neither Jew nor Greek, there is neither slave nor free, there is neither male nor female; for you are all one in Christ Jesus. 29 And if you are Christ's, then you are Abraham's offspring, heirs according to promise.

Eph 4:1-10

4 I therefore, a prisoner for the Lord, beg you to lead a life worthy of the calling to which you have been called, 2 with all lowliness and meekness, with patience, forbearing one another in love, 3 eager to maintain the unity of the Spirit in the bond of peace. 4 There is one body and one Spirit, just as you were called to the one hope that belongs to your call, 5 one Lord, one faith, one baptism, 6 one God and Father of us all, who is above all and through all and in all. 7 But grace was given to each of us according to the measure of Christ's gift. 8 Therefore it is said,
"When he ascended on high he led a host of captives,
and he gave gifts to men."
9 (In saying, "He ascended," what does it mean but that he had also descended into the lower parts of the earth? 10 He who descended is he who also ascended far above all the heavens, that he might fill all things.)

▶4:1 3:1
For this reason I, Paul, a prisoner for Christ Jesus on behalf of you Gentiles—
Phil 1:12
12 I want you to know, brethren, that what has happened to me has really served to advance the gospel,

Phm 1,
1 Paul, a prisoner for Christ Jesus, and Timothy our brother,
To Philemon our beloved fellow worker

Col 4:18a
18 I, Paul, write this greeting with my own hand. Remember my fetters.

Col 1:10 10 to lead a life worthy of the Lord, fully pleasing to him, bearing fruit in every good work and increasing in the knowledge of God.

1 Thes 2:12 12 to lead a life worthy of God, who calls you into his own kingdom and glory.

Phil 1:27 27 Only let your manner of life be worthy of the gospel of Christ, so that whether I come and see you or am absent, I may hear of you that you stand firm in one spirit, with one mind striving side by side for the faith of the gospel,

225

Phil 4:10-20 (§253)

10 I rejoice in the Lord greatly that now at length you have revived your concern for me; you were indeed concerned for me, but you had no opportunity. 11 Not that I complain of want; for I have learned, in whatever state I am, to be content. 12 I know how to be abased, and I know how to abound; in any and all circumstances I have learned the secret of facing plenty and hunger, abundance and want. 13 I can do all things in him who strengthens me.

14 Yet it was kind of you to share my trouble. 15And you Philippians yourselves know that in the beginning of the gospel, when I left Macedo'nia, no church entered into partnership with me in giving and receiving except you only; 16 for even in Thessaloni'ca you sent me help once and again. 17 Not that I seek the gift; but I seek the fruit which increases to your credit. 18 I have received full payment, and more; I am filled, having received from Epaphrodi'-tus the gifts you sent, a fragrant offering, a sacrifice acceptable and pleasing to God. 19And my God will supply every need of yours according to his riches in glory in Christ Jesus. 20 To our God and Father be glory for ever and ever. Amen.

Phil 4:8-9 (§252)

8 Finally, brethren, whatever is true, whatever is honorable, whatever is just, whatever is pure, whatever is lovely, whatever is gracious, if there is any excellence, if there is anything worthy of praise, think about these things. 9 What you have learned and received and heard and seen in me, do; and the God of peace will be with you.

Phil 1:27-30 (§241)

27 Only let your manner of life be worthy of the gospel of Christ, so that whether I come and see you or am absent, I may hear of you that you stand firm in one spirit, with one mind striving side by side for the faith of the gospel, 28 and not frightened in anything by your opponents. This is a clear omen to them of their destruction, but of your salvation, and that from God. 29 For it has been granted to you that for the sake of Christ you should not only believe in him but also suffer for his sake, 30 engaged in the same conflict which you saw and now hear to be mine.

Col 3:12-17 (§267)

12 Put on then, as God's chosen ones, holy and beloved, compassion, kindness, lowliness, meekness, and patience, 13 forbearing one another and, if one has a complaint against another, forgiving each other; as the Lord has forgiven you, so you also must forgive. 14And above all these put on love, which binds everything together in perfect harmony. 15And let the peace of Christ rule in your hearts, to which indeed you were called in the one body. And be thankful. 16 Let the word of Christ dwell in you richly, teach and admonish one another in all wisdom, and sing psalms and hymns and spiritual songs with thankfulness in your hearts to God. 17And whatever you do, in word or deed, do everything in the name of the Lord Jesus, giving thanks to God the Father through him.

Col 1:15-20 (§258)

15 He is the image of the invisible God, the first-born of all creation; 16 for in him all things were created, in heaven and on earth, visible and invisible, whether thrones or dominions or principalities or authorities—all things were created through him and for him. 17 He is before all things, and in him all things hold together. 18 He is the head of the body, the church; he is the beginning, the first-born from the dead, that in everything he might be pre-eminent. 19 For in him all the fulness of God was pleased to dwell, 20 and through him to reconcile to himself all things, whether on earth or in heaven, making peace by the blood of his cross.

1 Thes 4:1-8 (§284)

4 Finally, brethren, we beseech and exhort you in the Lord Jesus, that as you learned from us how you ought to live and to please God, just as you are doing, you do so more and more. 2 For you know what instructions we gave you through the Lord Jesus. 3 For this is the will of God, your sanctification: that you abstain from unchastity; 4 that each one of you know how to take a wife for himself in holiness and honor 5 not in the passion of lust like heathen who do not know God; 6 that no man transgress, and wrong his brother in this matter, because the Lord is an avenger in all these things, as we solemnly forewarned you. 7 For God has not called us for uncleanness, but in holiness. 8 Therefore whoever disregards this, disregards not man but God, who gives his Holy Spirit to you.

2 Thes 2:1-12 (§296)

2 Now concerning the coming of our Lord Jesus Christ and our assembling to meet him, we beg you, brethren, 2 not to be quickly shaken in mind or excited, either by spirit or by word, or by letter purporting to be from us, to the effect that the day of the Lord has come. 3 Let no one deceive you in any way; for that day will not come, unless the rebellion comes first, and the man of lawlessness is revealed, the son of perdition, 4 who opposes and exalts himself against every so-called god or object of worship, so that he takes his seat in the temple of God, proclaiming himself to be God. 5 Do you not remember that when I was still with you I told you this? 6And you know what is restraining him now so that he may be revealed in his time. 7 For the mystery of lawlessness is already at work; only he who now restrains it will do so until he is out of the way. 8And then the lawless one will be revealed, and the Lord Jesus will slay him with the breath of his mouth and destroy him by his appearing and his coming. 9 The coming of the lawless one by the activity of Satan will be with all power and with pretended signs and wonders, 10 and with all wicked deception for those who are to perish, because they refused to love the truth and so be saved. 11 Therefore God sends upon them a strong delusion, to make them believe what is false, 12 so that all may be condemned who did not believe the truth but had pleasure in unrighteousness.

Phm 8-14 (§307)

8 Accordingly, though I am bold enough in Christ to command you to do what is required, 9 yet for love's sake I prefer to appeal to you—I, Paul, an ambassador and now a prisoner also for Christ Jesus—10 I appeal to you for my child, Ones'imus, whose father I have become in my imprisonment. 11 (Formerly he was useless to you, but now he is indeed useful to you and to me.) 12 I am sending him back to you, sending my very heart. 13 I would have been glad to keep him with me, in order that he might serve me on your behalf during my imprisonment for the gospel; 14 but I preferred to do nothing without your consent in order that your goodness might not be by compulsion but of your own free will.

▶4:2 4:32   32 and be kind to one another, tenderhearted, forgiving one another, as God in Christ forgave you.

2 Cor 8:7   7 Now as you excel in everything—in faith, in utterance, in knowledge, in all earnestness, and in your love for us—see that you excel in this gracious work also.

▶4:7 1 Cor 7:7   7 I wish that all were as I myself am. But each has his own special gift from God, one of one kind and one of another.

▶4:8-10 Rom 10:6-8   6 But the righteousness based on faith says, Do not say in your heart, "Who will ascend into heaven?" (that is, to bring Christ down) 7 or "Who will descend into the abyss?" (that is, to bring Christ up from the dead). 8 But what does it say? The word is near you, on your lips and in your heart (that is, the word of faith which we preach);

▶4:8 Ps 68:18   18 Thou didst ascend the high mount, leading captives in thy train, and receiving gifts among men, even among the rebellious, that the Lord God may dwell there.

Rom 12:3-8 (§52)

3 For by the grace given to me I bid every one among you not to think of himself more highly than he ought to think, but to think with sober judgment, each according to the measure of faith which God has assigned him. 4 For as in one body we have many members, and all the members do not have the same function, 5 so we, though many, are one body in Christ, and individually members one of another. 6 Having gifts that differ according to the grace given to us, let us use them: if prophecy, in proportion to our faith; 7 if service, in our serving; he who teaches, in his teaching; 8 he who exhorts, in his exhortation; he who contributes, in liberality; he who gives aid, with zeal; he who does acts of mercy, with cheerfulness.

1 Cor 2:6-16 (§77)

6 Yet among the mature we do impart wisdom, although it is not a wisdom of this age or of the rulers of this age, who are doomed to pass away. 7 But we impart a secret and hidden wisdom of God, which God decreed before the ages for our glorification. 8 None of the rulers of this age understood this; for if they had, they would not have crucified the Lord of glory. 9 But, as it is written,
"What no eye has seen, nor ear heard,
nor the heart of man conceived,
what God has prepared for those who love him,"
10 God has revealed to us through the Spirit. For the Spirit searches everything, even the depths of God. 11 For what person knows a man's thoughts except the spirit of the man which is in him? So also no one comprehends the thoughts of God except the Spirit of God. 12 Now we have received not the spirit of the world, but the Spirit which is from God, that we might understand the gifts bestowed on us by God. 13 And we impart this in words not taught by human wisdom but taught by the Spirit, interpreting spiritual truths to those who possess the Spirit.
14 The unspiritual man does not receive the gifts of the Spirit of God, for they are folly to him, and he is not able to understand them because they are spiritually discerned. 15 The spiritual man judges all things, but is himself to be judged by no one. 16 "For who has known the mind of the Lord so as to instruct him?" But we have the mind of Christ.

1 Cor 3:1-4 (§78)

3 But I, brethren, could not address you as spiritual men, but as men of the flesh, as babes in Christ. 2 I fed you with milk, not solid food; for you were not ready for it; and even yet you are not ready, 3 for you are still of the flesh. For while there is jealousy and strife among you, are you not of the flesh, and behaving like ordinary men? 4 For when one says, "I belong to Paul," and another, "I belong to Apol'los," are you not merely men?

1 Cor 12:4-11 (§117)

4 Now there are varieties of gifts, but the same Spirit; 5 and there are varieties of service, but the same Lord; 6 and there are varieties of working, but it is the same God who inspires them all in every one. 7 To each is given the manifestation of the Spirit for the common good. 8 To one is given through the Spirit the utterance of wisdom, and to another the utterance of knowledge according to the same Spirit, 9 to another faith by the same Spirit, to another gifts of healing by the one Spirit, 10 to another the working of miracles, to another prophecy, to another the ability to distinguish between spirits, to another various kinds of tongues, to another the interpretation of tongues. 11 All these are inspired by one and the same Spirit, who apportions to each one individually as he wills.

1 Cor 12:14-26 (§119)

14 For the body does not consist of one member but of many. 15 If the foot should say, "Because I am not a hand, I do not belong to the body," that would not make it any less a part of the body. 16 And if the ear should say, "Because I am not an eye, I do not belong to the body," that would not make it any less a part of the body. 17 If the whole body were an eye, where would be the hearing? If the whole body were an ear, where would be the sense of smell? 18 But as it is, God arranged the organs in the body, each one of them, as he chose. 19 If all were a single organ, where would the body be? 20 As it is, there are many parts, yet one body. 21 The eye cannot say to the hand, "I have no need of you," nor again the head to the feet, "I have no need of you." 22 On the contrary, the parts of the body which seem to be weaker are indispensable, 23 and those parts of the body which we think less honorable we invest with the greater honor, and our unpresentable parts are treated with greater modesty, 24 which our more presentable parts do not require. But God has so composed the body, giving the greater honor to the inferior part, 25 that there may be no discord in the body, but that the members may have the same care for one another. 26 If one member suffers, all suffer together; if one member is honored, all rejoice together.

1 Cor 12:27-31 (§120)

27 Now you are the body of Christ and individually members of it. 28 And God has appointed in the church first apostles, second prophets, third teachers, then workers of miracles, then healers, helpers, administrators, speakers in various kinds of tongues. 29 Are all apostles? Are all prophets? Are all teachers? Do all work miracles? 30 Do all possess gifts of healing? Do all speak with tongues? Do all interpret? 31 But earnestly desire the higher gifts.
And I will show you a still more excellent way.

Eph 4:11-16

11 And his gifts were that some should be apostles, some prophets, some evangelists, some pastors and teachers, 12 to equip the saints for the work of ministry, for building up the body of Christ, 13 until we all attain to the unity of the faith and of the knowledge of the Son of God, to mature manhood, to the measure of the stature of the fulness of Christ; 14 so that we may no longer be children, tossed to and fro and carried about with every wind of doctrine, by the cunning of men, by their craftiness in deceitful wiles. 15 Rather, speaking the truth in love, we are to grow up in every way into him who is the head, into Christ, 16 from whom the whole body, joined and knit together by every joint with which it is supplied, when each part is working properly, makes bodily growth and upbuilds itself in love.

▶ 4:11 *cf Acts 13:1, 15:32, 35, 1 Tim 5:17

▶ 4:12 *cf 2 Tim 3:16-17

▶ 4:11-16 1 Cor 1:4-5
4 I give thanks to God always for you because of the grace of God which was given you in Christ Jesus, 5 that in every way you were enriched in him with all speech and all knowledge—

▶ 4:12 1:23,
23 For the husband is the head of the wife as Christ is the head of the church, his body, and is himself its Savior.

5:30
30 because we are members of his body.

▶ 4:13-16 1 Cor 13:11,
11 When I was a child, I spoke like a child, I thought like a child, I reasoned like a child; when I became a man, I gave up childish ways.

14:20
20 Brethren, do not be children in your thinking; be babes in evil, but in thinking be mature.

226

Phil 3:12-16 (§248)

12 Not that I have already obtained this or am already perfect; but I press on to make it my own, because Christ Jesus has made me his own. 13 Brethren, I do not consider that I have made it my own; but one thing I do, forgetting what lies behind and straining forward to what lies ahead, 14 I press on toward the goal for the prize of the upward call of God in Christ Jesus. 15 Let those of us who are mature be thus minded; and if in anything you are otherwise minded, God will reveal that also to you. 16 Only let us hold true to what we have attained.

Col 2:16-19 (§263)

16 Therefore let no one pass judgment on you in questions of food and drink or with regard to a festival or a new moon or a sabbath. 17 These are only a shadow of what is to come; but the substance belongs to Christ. 18 Let no one disqualify you, insisting on self-abasement and worship of angels, taking his stand on visions, puffed up without reason by his sensuous mind, 19 and not holding fast to the Head, from whom the whole body, nourished and knit together through its joints and ligaments, grows with a growth that is from God.

Rom 16:19 19 For while your obedience is known to all, so that I rejoice over you, I would have you wise as to what is good and guileless as to what is evil

▶4:15 1 Cor 11:3 3 But I want you to understand that the head of every man is Christ, the head of a woman is her husband, and the head of Christ is God.

Eph 1:22-23, 22 and he has put all things under his feet and has made him the head over all things for the church, 23 which is his body, the fulness of him who fills all in all.

5:23 23 which is his body, the fulness of him who fills all in all.

Col 2:19 19 and not holding fast to the Head, from whom the whole body, nourished and knit together through its joints and ligaments, grows with a growth that is from God.

227

Rom 1:29-32 (§6)

29 They were filled with all manner of wickedness, evil, covetousness, malice. Full of envy, murder, strife, deceit, malignity, they are gossips, 30 slanderers, haters of God, insolent, haughty, boastful, inventors of evil, disobedient to parents, 31 foolish, faithless, heartless, ruthless. 32 Though they know God's decree that those who do such things deserve to die, they not only do them but approve those who practice them.

Rom 13:11-14* (§56)

11 Besides this you know what hour it is, how it is full time now for you to wake from sleep. For salvation is nearer to us now than when we first believed; 12 the night is far gone, the day is at hand. Let us then cast off the works of darkness and put on the armor of light; 13 let us conduct ourselves becomingly as in the day, not in reveling and drunkenness, not in debauchery and licentiousness, not in quarreling and jealousy. 14 But put on the Lord Jesus Christ, and make no provision for the flesh, to gratify its desires.

Rom 1:18-28 (§4-5)

18 For the wrath of God is revealed from heaven against all ungodliness and wickedness of men who by their wickedness suppress the truth. 19 For what can be known about God is plain to them, because God has shown it to them. 20 Ever since the creation of the world his invisible nature, namely, his eternal power and deity, has been clearly perceived in the things that have been made. So they are without excuse; 21 for although they knew God they did not honor him as God or give thanks to him, but they became futile in their thinking and their senseless minds were darkened. 22 Claiming to be wise, they became fools, 23 and exchanged the glory of the immortal God for images resembling mortal man or birds or animals or reptiles.

24 Therefore God gave them up in the lusts of their hearts to impurity, to the dishonoring of their bodies among themselves, 25 because they exchanged the truth about God for a lie and worshiped and served the creature rather than the Creator, who is blessed for ever! Amen.

26 For this reason God gave them up to dishonorable passions. Their women exchanged natural relations for unnatural, 27 and the men likewise gave up natural relations with women and were consumed with passion for one another, men committing shameless acts with men and receiving in their own persons the due penalty for their error.

1 Cor 6:9-11 (§91)

9 Do you not know that the unrighteous will not inherit the kingdom of God? Do not be deceived; neither the immoral, nor idolaters, nor adulterers, nor sexual perverts, 10 nor thieves, nor the greedy, nor drunkards, nor revilers, nor robbers will inherit the kingdom of God. 11 And such were some of you. But you were washed, you were sanctified, you were justified in the name of the Lord Jesus Christ and in the Spirit of our God.

28 And since they did not see fit to acknowledge God, God gave them up to a base mind and to improper conduct.

Rom 11:25-32 (§49)

25 Lest you be wise in your own conceits, I want you to understand this mystery, brethren: a hardening has come upon part of Israel, until the full number of the Gentiles come in, 26 and so all Israel will be saved; as it is written,

"The Deliverer will come from Zion,
   he will banish ungodliness from
      Jacob";
27 "and this will be my covenant with
      them
   when I take away their sins."

28 As regards the gospel they are enemies of God, for your sake; but as regards election they are beloved for the sake of their forefathers. 29 For the gifts and the call of God are irrevocable. 30 Just as you were once disobedient to God but now have received mercy because of their disobedience, 31 so they have now been disobedient in order that by the mercy shown to you they also may receive mercy. 32 For God has consigned all men to disobedience, that he may have mercy upon all.

2 Cor 12:19-21 (§188)

19 Have you been thinking all along that we have been defending ourselves before you? It is in the sight of God that we have been speaking in Christ, and all for your upbuilding, beloved. 20 For I fear that perhaps I may come and find you not what I wish, and that you may find me not what you wish; that perhaps there may be quarreling, jealousy, anger, selfishness, slander, gossip, conceit, and disorder. 21 I fear that when I come again my God may humble me before you, and I may have to mourn over many of those who sinned before and have not repented of the impurity, immorality, and licentiousness which they have practiced.

Gal 5:16-26 (§213)

16 But I say, walk by the Spirit, and do not gratify the desires of the flesh. 17 For the desires of the flesh are against the Spirit, and the desires of the Spirit are against the flesh; for these are opposed to each other, to prevent you from doing what you would. 18 But if you are led by the Spirit you are not under the law. 19 Now the works of the flesh are plain: fornication, impurity, licentiousness, 20 idolatry, sorcery, enmity, strife, jealousy, anger, selfishness, dissension, party spirit, 21 envy, drunkenness, carousing, and the like. I warn you, as I warned you before, that those who do such things shall not inherit the kingdom of God. 22 But the fruit of the Spirit is love, joy, peace, patience, kindness, goodness, faithfulness, 23 gentleness, self-control; against such there is no law. 24 And those who belong to Christ Jesus have crucified the flesh with its passions and desires.

25 If we live by the Spirit, let us also walk by the Spirit. 26 Let us have no self-conceit, no provoking of one another, no envy of one another.

Eph 4:17-24

17 Now this I affirm and testify in the Lord, that you must no longer live as the Gentiles do, in the futility of their minds; 18 they are darkened in their understanding, alienated from the life of God because of the ignorance that is in them, due to their hardness of heart; 19 they have become callous and have given themselves up to licentiousness, greedy to practice every kind of uncleanness. 20 You did not so learn Christ!— 21 assuming that you have heard about him and were taught in him, as the truth is in Jesus. 22 Put off your old nature which belongs to your former manner of life and is corrupt through deceitful lusts, 23 and be renewed in the spirit of your minds, 24 and put on the new nature, created after the likeness of God in true righteousness and holiness.

▶ 4:17-18 Gal 2:15

15 We ourselves, who are Jews by birth and not Gentile sinners,

▶ 4:18 2 Thes 2:11-12

11 Therefore God sends upon them a strong delusion, to make them believe what is false, 12 so that all may be condemned who did not believe the truth but had pleasure in unrighteousness.

Rom 11:7-10

7 What then? Israel failed to obtain what it sought. The elect obtained it, but the rest were hardened, 8 as it is written,
   "God gave them a spirit of stupor,
   eyes that should not see and ears that
      should not hear,
      down to this very day."

9 And David says,
   "Let their table become a snare and a
      trap,
   a pitfall and a retribution for them;
10 let their eyes be darkened so that they
      cannot see,
   and bend their backs for ever."

▶ 4:21 3:2

2 assuming that you have heard of the stewardship of God's grace that was given to me for you,

▶ 4:22 4:25

25 Therefore, putting away falsehood, let every one speak the truth with his neighbor, for we are members one of another.

227

Col 3:5-11　(§266)

5 Put to death therefore what is earthly in you: fornication, impurity, passion, evil desire, and covetousness, which is idolatry. 6 On account of these the wrath of God is coming　7 In these you once walked, when you lived in them. 8 But now put them all away: anger, wrath, malice, slander, and foul talk from your mouth. 9 Do not lie to one another, seeing that you have put off the old nature with its practices 10 and have put on the new nature, which is being renewed in knowledge after the image of its creator. 11 Here there cannot be Greek and Jew, circumcised and uncircumcised, barbarian, Scyth'ian, slave, free man, but Christ is all, and in all.

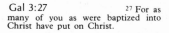

Gal 3:27

27 For as many of you as were baptized into Christ have put on Christ.

Eph 6:11,

11 Put on the whole armor of God, that you may be able to stand against the wiles of the devil.

14

14 Stand therefore, having girded your loins with truth, and having put on the breastplate of righteousness,

1 Thes 5:8

8 But, since we belong to the day, let us be sober, and put on the breastplate of faith and love, and for a helmet the hope of salvation.

228

Rom 1:29-32 (§6)

29 They were filled with all manner of wickedness, evil, covetousness, malice. Full of envy, murder, strife, deceit, malignity, they are gossips, 30 slanderers, haters of God, insolent, haughty, boastful, inventors of evil, disobedient to parents, 31 foolish, faithless, heartless, ruthless. 32 Though they know God's decree that those who do such things deserve to die, they not only do them but approve those who practice them.

Rom 13:11-14 (§56)

11 Besides this you know what hour it is, how it is full time now for you to wake from sleep. For salvation is nearer to us now than when we first believed; 12 the night is far gone, the day is at hand. Let us then cast off the works of darkness and put on the armor of light; 13 let us conduct ourselves becomingly as in the day, not in reveling and drunkenness, not in debauchery and licentiousness, not in quarreling and jealousy. 14 But put on the Lord Jesus Christ, and make no provision for the flesh, to gratify its desires.

Rom 12:9-21 (§53)

9 Let love be genuine; hate what is evil, hold fast to what is good; 10 love one another with brotherly affection; outdo one another in showing honor; 11 Never flag in zeal, be aglow with the Spirit, serve the Lord. 12 Rejoice in your hope, be patient in tribulation, be constant in prayer. 13 Contribute to the needs of the saints, practice hospitality. 14 Bless those who persecute you; bless and do not curse them. 15 Rejoice with those who rejoice, weep with those who weep. 16 Live in harmony with one another; do not be haughty, but associate with the lowly; never be conceited. 17 Repay no one evil for evil, but take thought for what is noble in the sight of all. 18 If possible, so far as it depends upon you, live peaceably with all. 19 Beloved, never avenge yourselves, but leave it to the wrath of God; for it is written, "Vengeance is mine, I will repay, says the Lord." 20 No, "if your enemy is hungry, feed him; if he is thirsty, give him drink; for by so doing you will heap burning coals upon his head." 21 Do not be overcome by evil, but overcome evil with good.

1 Cor 6:9-11 (§91)

9 Do you not know that the unrighteous will not inherit the kingdom of God? Do not be deceived; neither the immoral, nor idolaters, nor adulterers, nor sexual perverts, 10 nor thieves, nor the greedy, nor drunkards, nor revilers, nor robbers will inherit the kingdom of God. 11 And such were some of you. But you were washed, you were sanctified, you were justified in the name of the Lord Jesus Christ and in the Spirit of our God.

1 Cor 5:9-13 (§89)

9 I wrote to you in my letter not to associate with immoral men; 10 not at all meaning the immoral of this world, or the greedy and robbers, or idolaters, since then you would need to go out of the world. 11 But rather I wrote to you not to associate with any one who bears the name of brother if he is guilty of immorality or greed, or is an idolater, reviler, drunkard, or robber—not even to eat with such a one. 12 For what have I to do with judging outsiders? Is it not those inside the church whom you are to judge? 13 God judges those outside. "Drive out the wicked person from among you."

2 Cor 6:1-10 (§165)

6 Working together with him, then, we entreat you not to accept the grace of God in vain. 2 For he says,
"At the acceptable time I have listened to you,
and helped you on the day of salvation."
Behold, now is the acceptable time; behold, now is the day of salvation. 3 We put no obstacle in any one's way, so that no fault may be found with our ministry, 4 but as servants of God we commend ourselves in every way: through great endurance, in afflictions, hardships, calamities, 5 beatings, imprisonments, tumults, labors, watching, hunger; 6 by purity, knowledge, forbearance, kindness, the Holy Spirit, genuine love, 7 truthful speech, and the power of God; with the weapons of righteousness for the right hand and for the left; 8 in honor and dishonor, in ill repute and good repute. We are treated as impostors, and yet are true; 9 as unknown, and yet well known; as dying, and behold we live; as punished, and yet not killed; 10 as sorrowful, yet always rejoicing; as poor, yet making many rich; as having nothing, and yet possessing everything.

2 Cor 12:19-21 (§188)

19 Have you been thinking all along that we have been defending ourselves before you? It is in the sight of God that we have been speaking in Christ, and all for your upbuilding, beloved. 20 For I fear that perhaps I may come and find you not what I wish, and that you may find me not what you wish; that perhaps there may be quarreling, jealousy, anger, selfishness, slander, gossip, conceit, and disorder. 21 I fear that when I come again my God may humble me before you, and I may have to mourn over many of those who sinned before and have not repented of the impurity, immorality, and licentiousness which they have practiced.

Gal 5:16-26 (§213)

16 But I say, walk by the Spirit, and do not gratify the desires of the flesh. 17 For the desires of the flesh are against the Spirit, and the desires of the Spirit are against the flesh; for these are opposed to each other, to prevent you from doing what you would. 18 But if you are led by the Spirit you are not under the law. 19 Now the works of the flesh are plain: fornication, impurity, licentiousness, 20 idolatry, sorcery, enmity, strife, jealousy, anger, selfishness, dissension, party spirit, 21 envy, drunkenness, carousing, and the like. I warn you, as I warned you before, that those who do such things shall not inherit the kingdom of God. 22 But the fruit of the Spirit is love, joy, peace, patience, kindness, goodness, faithfulness, 23 gentleness, self-control; against such there is no law. 24 And those who belong to Christ Jesus have crucified the flesh with its passions and desires.

25 If we live by the Spirit, let us also walk by the Spirit. 26 Let us have no self-conceit, no provoking of one another, no envy of one another.

Eph 4:25-32

25 Therefore, putting away falsehood, let every one speak the truth with his neighbor, for we are members one of another. 26 Be angry but do not sin; do not let the sun go down on your anger, 27 and give no opportunity to the devil. 28 Let the thief no longer steal, but rather let him labor, doing honest work with his hands, so that he may be able to give to those in need. 29 Let no evil talk come out of your mouths, but only such as is good for edifying, as fits the occasion, that it may impart grace to those who hear. 30 And do not grieve the Holy Spirit of God, in whom you were sealed for the day of redemption. 31 Let all bitterness and wrath and anger and clamor and slander be put away from you, with all malice, 32 and be kind to one another, tenderhearted, forgiving one another, as God in Christ forgave you.

▶4:28 Acts 20:35   35 In all things I have shown you that by so toiling one must help the weak, remembering the words of the Lord Jesus, how he said, 'It is more blessed to give than to receive.' "

▶4:25 Rom 12:5   5 so we, though many, are one body in Christ, and individually members one of another.

Eph 5:30   30 because we are members of his body.

1 Cor 12:12,
12 For just as the body is one and has many members, and all the members of the body, though many, are one body, so it is with Christ.

27
27 Now you are the body of Christ and individually members of it.

▶4:28 1 Cor 4:12   12 and we labor, working with our own hands. When reviled, we bless; when persecuted, we endure;

▶4:30 2 Cor 1:22   22 he has put his seal upon us and given us his Spirit in our hearts as a guarantee.

Eph 1:13   13 In him you also, who have heard the word of truth, the gospel of your salvation, and have believed in him, were sealed with the promised Holy Spirit,

Rom 4:11   11 He received circumcision as a sign or seal of the righteousness which he had by faith while he was still uncircumcised. The purpose was to make him the father of all who believe without being circumcised and who thus have righteousness reckoned to them,

▶4:31 5:3-14   3 But fornication and all impurity or covetousness must not even be named among you, as is fitting among saints. 4 Let there be no filthiness, nor silly talk, nor levity, which are not fitting; but instead let there be thanksgiving. 5 Be sure of this, that no fornicator or impure man, or one who is covetous (that is, an idolater), has any inheritance in the kingdom of Christ and of God. 6 Let no one deceive you with empty words, for it is because of these things that the wrath of God comes upon the sons of disobedience. 7 Therefore do not associate with them, 8 for once you were darkness, but now you are light in the Lord; walk as children of light 9 (for the fruit of light is found in all that is good and right and true), 10 and try to learn what is pleasing to the Lord. 11 Take no part in the unfruitful works of darkness, but instead expose them. 12 For it is a shame even to speak of the things that they do in secret; 13 but when anything is exposed by the light it becomes visible, for anything that becomes visible is light. 14 Therefore it is said,

228

Phil 4:8-9 (§252)

8 Finally, brethren, whatever is true, whatever is honorable, whatever is just, whatever is pure, whatever is lovely, whatever is gracious, if there is any excellence, if there is anything worthy of praise, think about these things. 9 What you have learned and received and heard and seen in me, do; and the God of peace will be with you.

Col 3:5-11 (§266)

5 Put to death therefore what is earthly in you: fornication, impurity, passion, evil desire, and covetousness, which is idolatry. 6 On account of these the wrath of God is coming. 7 In these you once walked, when you lived in them. 8 But now put them all away: anger, wrath, malice, slander, and foul talk from your mouth. 9 Do not lie to one another, seeing that you have put off the old nature with its practices 10 and have put on the new nature, which is being renewed in knowledge after the image of its creator. 11 Here there cannot be Greek and Jew, circumcised and uncircumcised, barbarian, Scyth'ian, slave, free man, but Christ is all, and in all.

Col 3:12-17 (§267)

12 Put on then, as God's chosen ones, holy and beloved, compassion, kindness, lowliness, meekness, and patience, 13 forbearing one another and, if one has a complaint against another, forgiving each other; as the Lord has forgiven you, so you also must forgive. 14And above all these put on love, which binds everything together in perfect harmony. 15And let the peace of Christ rule in your hearts, to which indeed you were called in the one body. And be thankful. 16 Let the word of Christ dwell in you richly, teach and admonish one another in all wisdom, and sing psalms and hymns and spiritual songs with thankfulness in your hearts to God. 17And whatever you do, in word or deed, do everything in the name of the Lord Jesus, giving thanks to God the Father through him.

1 Thes 5:12-22 (§288)

12 But we beseech you, brethren, to respect those who labor among you and are over you in the Lord and admonish you, 13 and to esteem them very highly in love because of their work. Be at peace among yourselves. 14And we exhort you, brethren, admonish the idlers, encourage the fainthearted, help the weak, be patient with them all. 15 See that none of you repays evil for evil, but always seek to do good to one another and to all. 16 Rejoice always, 17 pray constantly, 18 give thanks in all circumstances; for this is the will of God in Christ Jesus for you. 19 Do not quench the Spirit, 20 do not despise prophesying, 21 but test everything; hold fast what is good, 22 abstain from every form of evil.

2 Thes 3:6-13 (§300)

6 Now we command you, brethren, in the name of our Lord Jesus Christ, that you keep away from any brother who is living in idleness and not in accord with the tradition that you received from us. 7 For you yourselves know how you ought to imitate us; we were not idle when we were with you, 8 we did not eat any one's bread without paying, but with toil and labor we worked night and day, that we might not burden any of you. 9 It was not because we have not that right, but to give you in our conduct an example to imitate. 10 For even when we were with you, we gave you this command: If any one will not work, let him not eat. 11 For we hear that some of you are living in idleness, mere busybodies, not doing any work. 12 Now such persons we command and exhort in the Lord Jesus Christ to do their work in quietness and to earn their own living. 13 Brethren, do not be weary in well-doing.

"Awake, O sleeper, and arise from the dead,
and Christ shall give you light."
▶4:32 4:2
2 with all lowliness and meekness, with patience, forbearing one another in love,

2 Cor 8:7   7 Now as you excel in everything—in faith, in utterance, in knowledge, in all earnestness, and in your love for us—see that you excel in this gracious work also.

229

1 Cor 5:6-8 (§88)

6 Your boasting is not good. Do you not know that a little leaven leavens the whole lump? 7 Cleanse out the old leaven that you may be a new lump, as you really are unleavened. For Christ, our paschal lamb, has been sacrificed. 8 Let us, therefore, celebrate the festival, not with the old leaven, the leaven of malice and evil, but with the unleavened bread of sincerity and truth.

2 Cor 2:14-17 (§153)

14 But thanks be to God, who in Christ always leads us in triumph, and through us spreads the fragrance of the knowledge of him everywhere. 15 For we are the aroma of Christ to God among those who are being saved and among those who are perishing, 16 to one a fragrance from death to death, to the other a fragrance from life to life. Who is sufficient for these things? 17 For we are not, like so many, peddlers of God's word; but as men of sincerity, as commissioned by God, in the sight of God we speak in Christ.

Eph 5:1-2

5 Therefore be imitators of God, as beloved children. 2And walk in love, as Christ loved us and gave himself up for us, a fragrant offering and sacrifice to God.

▶ 5:1 1 Cor 11:1
1 Be imitators of me, as I am of Christ.

1 Thes 1:6 6And you became imitators of us and of the Lord, for you received the word in much affliction, with joy inspired by the Holy Spirit;

Phil 2:5 5 Have this mind among yourselves, which is yours in Christ Jesus,

▶ 5:2 5:25 25 Husbands, love your wives, as Christ loved the church and gave himself up for her,

Gal 2:20 20 I have been crucified with Christ; it is no longer I who live, but Christ who lives in me;

and the life I now live in the flesh I live by faith in the Son of God, who loved me and gave himself for me.

230. Immorality must not even be named among you

230

Rom 1:29-32 (§6)

29 They were filled with all manner of wickedness, evil, covetousness, malice. Full of envy, murder, strife, deceit, malignity, they are gossips, 30 slanderers, haters of God, insolent, haughty, boastful, inventors of evil, disobedient to parents, 31 foolish, faithless, heartless, ruthless. 32 Though they know God's decree that those who do such things deserve to die, they not only do them but approve those who practice them.

Rom 13:11-14 (§56)

11 Besides this you know what hour it is, how it is full time now for you to wake from sleep. For salvation is nearer to us now than when we first believed; 12 the night is far gone, the day is at hand. Let us then cast off the works of darkness and put on the armor of light; 13 let us conduct ourselves becomingly as in the day, not in reveling and drunkenness, not in debauchery and licentiousness, not in quarreling and jealousy. 14 But put on the Lord Jesus Christ, and make no provision for the flesh, to gratify its desires.

Rom 2:1-5 (§7)

2 Therefore you have no excuse, O man, whoever you are, when you judge another; for in passing judgment upon him you condemn yourself, because you, the judge, are doing the very same things. 2 We know that the judgment of God rightly falls upon those who do such things. 3 Do you suppose, O man, that when you judge those who do such things and yet do them yourself, you will escape the judgment of God? 4 Or do you presume upon the riches of his kindness and forbearance and patience? Do you not know that God's

▶ 5:8 *cf Acts 26:16-18

1Cor 5:9-13 (§89)

9 I wrote to you in my letter not to associate with immoral men; 10 not at all meaning the immoral of this world, or the greedy and robbers, or idolaters, since then you would need to go out of the world. 11 But rather I wrote^i to you not to associate with any one who bears the name of brother if he is guilty of immorality or greed, or is an idolater, reviler, drunkard, or robber—not even to eat with such a one. 12 For what have I to do with judging outsiders? Is it not those inside the church whom you are to judge? 13 God judges those outside. "Drive out the wicked person from among you."

1Cor 6:9-11 (§91)

9 Do you not know that the unrighteous will not inherit the kingdom of God? Do not be deceived; neither the immoral, nor idolaters, nor adulterers, nor sexual perverts, 10nor thieves, nor the greedy, nor drunkards, nor revilers, nor robbers will inherit the kingdom of God. 11And such were some of you. But you were washed, you were sanctified, you were justified in the name of the Lord Jesus Christ and in the Spirit of our God.

1 Cor 7:32-35 (§99)

32 I want you to be free from anxieties. The unmarried man is anxious about the affairs of the Lord, how to please the Lord; 33 but the married man

▶ 5:3, 5 4:17-32

17 Now this I affirm and testify in the Lord, that you must no longer live as the Gentiles do, in the futility of their minds; 18 they are darkened in their understanding, alienated from the life of God because of the ignorance that is in them, due to their hardness of heart; 19 they have become callous and have

2 Cor 12:19-21 (§188)

19 Have you been thinking all along that we have been defending ourselves before you? It is in the sight of God that we have been speaking in Christ, and all for your upbuilding, beloved. 20 For I fear that perhaps I may come and find you not what I wish, and that you may find me not what you wish; that perhaps there may be quarreling, jealousy, anger, selfishness, slander, gossip, conceit, and disorder. 21 I fear that when I come again my God may humble me before you, and I may have to mourn over many of those who sinned before and have not repented of the impurity, immorality, and licentiousness which they have practiced.

2 Cor 6:14-7:1 (§167)

14 Do not be mismated with unbelievers. For what partnership have righteousness and iniquity? Or what fellowship has light with darkness? 15 What accord has Christ with Be'lial?^{i} Or what has a believer in common with an unbeliever? 16 What agreement has the temple of God with idols? For we are the temple of the living God; as God said,
"I will live in them and move among them,
and I will be their God,
and they shall be my people.
17 Therefore come out from them,
and be separate from them, says the Lord,
and touch nothing unclean;
then I will welcome you,
18 and I will be a father to you,
and you shall be my sons and daughters,
says the Lord Almighty."

is anxious about worldly affairs, how to please his wife, 34 and his interests are divided. And the unmarried woman or girl^x is anxious about the affairs of the Lord, how to be holy in body and spirit; but the married woman is anxious about worldly affairs, how to please her husband. 35 I say this for your own benefit, not to lay any restraint upon you, but to promote good order and to secure your undivided devotion to the Lord.

Gal 5:16-26 (§213)

16 But I say, walk by the Spirit, and do not gratify the desires of the flesh. 17 For the desires of the flesh are against the Spirit, and the desires of the Spirit are against the flesh; for these are opposed to each other, to prevent you from doing what you would. 18 But if you are led by the Spirit you are not under the law. 19 Now the works of the flesh are plain: fornication, impurity, licentiousness, 20 idolatry, sorcery, enmity, strife, jealousy, anger, selfishness, dissension, party spirit, 21 envy,^{k} drunkenness, carousing, and the like. I warn you, as I warned you before, that those who do such things shall not inherit the kingdom of God. 22 But the fruit of the Spirit is love, joy, peace, patience, kindness, goodness, faithfulness, 23 gentleness, self-control; against such there is no law. 24And those who belong to Christ Jesus have crucified the flesh with its passions and desires.

25 If we live by the Spirit, let us also walk by the Spirit. 26 Let us have no self-conceit, no provoking of one another, no envy of one another.

Eph 5:3-14

3 But fornication and all impurity or covetousness must not even be named among you, as is fitting among saints. 4 Let there be no filthiness, nor silly talk, nor levity, which are not fitting; but instead let there be thanksgiving. 5 Be sure of this, that no fornicator or impure man, or one who is covetous (that is, an idolater), has any inheritance in the kingdom of Christ and of God. 6 Let no one deceive you with empty words, for it is because of these things that the wrath of God comes upon the sons of disobedience. 7 Therefore do not associate with them, 8 for once you were darkness, but now you are light in the Lord; walk as children of light 9 (for the fruit of light is found in all that is good and right and true), 10 and try to learn what is pleasing to the Lord. 11 Take no part in the unfruitful works of darkness, but instead expose them. 12 For it is a shame even to speak of the things that they do in secret; 13 but when anything is exposed by the light it becomes visible, for anything that becomes visible is light. 14 Therefore it is said,
"Awake, O sleeper, and arise from the dead,
and Christ shall give you light."

7 Since we have these promises, beloved, let us cleanse ourselves from every defilement of body and spirit, and make holiness perfect in the fear of God.

given themselves up to licentiousness, greedy to practice every kind of uncleanness. 20 You did not so learn Christ!— 21 assuming that you have heard about him and were taught in him, as the truth is in Jesus. 22 Put off your old nature which belongs to your former manner of life and is corrupt through deceitful lusts, 23 and be renewed in the spirit of your minds, 24 and put on the new nature, created after the likeness of God in true righteousness and holiness.
25 Therefore, putting away falsehood, let every one speak the truth with his neighbor, for we are members one of another. 26 Be angry but do not sin; do not let the sun go down on your anger, 27 and give no opportunity to the devil.

28 Let the thief no longer steal, but rather let him labor, doing honest work with his hands, so that he may be able to give to those in need. 29 Let no evil talk come out of your mouths, but only such as is good for edifying, as fits the occasion, that it may impart grace to those who hear. 30And do not grieve the Holy Spirit of God, in whom you were sealed for the day of redemption. 31 Let all bitterness and wrath and anger and clamor and slander be put away from you, with all malice, 32 and be kind to one another, tenderhearted, forgiving one another, as God in Christ forgave you.

Rom 8:32

[32] He who did not spare his own Son but gave him up for us all, will he not also give us all things with him?

▶ 5:2 (loved us) *read* loved you: S*AB it(few) cop Clement

(for us) *read* for you: B it(few) cop Origen

230. Immorality must not even be named among you

Col 3:5-11* (§266)

5 Put to death therefore what is earthly in you: fornication, impurity, passion, evil desire, and covetousness, which is idolatry. [6] On account of these the wrath of God is coming. [7] In these you once walked, when you lived in them. [8] But now put them all away: anger, wrath, malice, slander, and foul talk from your mouth. [9] Do not lie to one another, seeing that you have put off the old nature with its practices [10] and have put on the new nature, which is being renewed in knowledge after the image of its creator. [11] Here there cannot be Greek and Jew, circumcised and uncircumcised, barbarian, Scyth'ian, slave, free man, but Christ is all, and in all.

Col 2:4-7 (§261)

[4] I say this in order that no one may delude you with beguiling speech. [5] For though I am absent in body, yet I am with you in spirit, rejoicing to see your good order and the firmness of your faith in Christ.

6 As therefore you received Christ Jesus the Lord, so live in him, [7] rooted and built up in him and established in the faith, just as you were taught, abounding in thanksgiving.

1 Thes 5:1-11 (§287)

5 But as to the times and the seasons, brethren, you have no need to have anything written to you. [2] For you yourselves know well that the day of the Lord will come like a thief in the night. [3] When people say, "There is peace and security," then sudden destruction will come upon them as travail comes upon a woman with child, and there will be no escape. [4] But you are not in darkness, brethren, for that day to surprise you like a thief. [5] For you are all sons of light and sons of the day; we are not of the night or of darkness. [6] So then let us not sleep, as others do, but let us keep awake and be sober. [7] For those who sleep sleep at night, and those who get drunk are drunk at night. [8] But, since we belong to the day, let us be sober, and put on the breastplate of faith and love, and for a helmet the hope of salvation. [9] For God has not destined us for wrath, but to obtain salvation through our Lord Jesus Christ, [10] who died for us so that whether we wake or sleep we might live with him. [11] Therefore encourage one another and build one another up, just as you are doing.

▶ 5:6 Col 2:8

[8] See to it that no one makes a prey of you by philosophy and empty deceit, according to human tradition, according to the elemental spirits of the universe, and not according to Christ.

▶ 5:10 Rom 8:8

[8] and those who are in the flesh cannot please God.

Gal 1:10

10 Am I now seeking the favor of men, or of God? Or am I trying to please men? If I were still pleasing men, I should not be a servant of Christ.

1 Thes 2:4,

[4] but just as we have been approved by God to be entrusted with the gospel, so we speak, not to please men, but to please God who tests our hearts.

4:1

Finally, brethren, we beseech and exhort you in the Lord Jesus, that as you learned from us how you ought to live and to please God, just as you are doing, you do so more and more.

▶ 5:14 Rom 13:11

11 Besides this you know what hour it is, how it is full time now for you to wake from sleep. For salvation is nearer to us now than when we first believed;

▶ 5:9 (light) *read* spirit: p[46] D [c] Koine syr(har) Chrysostom

231

Rom 1:18-23 (§4)

18 For the wrath of God is revealed from heaven against all ungodliness and wickedness of men who by their wickedness suppress the truth. 19 For what can be known about God is plain to them, because God has shown it to them. 20 Ever since the creation of the world his invisible nature, namely, his eternal power and deity, has been clearly perceived in the things that have been made. So they are without excuse; 21 for although they knew God they did not honor him as God or give thanks to him, but they became futile in their thinking and their senseless minds were darkened. 22 Claiming to be wise, they became fools, 23 and exchanged the glory of the immortal God for images resembling mortal man or birds or animals or reptiles.

Rom 14:5-12 (§58)

5 One man esteems one day as better than another, while another man esteems all days alike. Let every one be fully convinced in his own mind. 6 He who observes the day, observes it in

1 Cor 14:26-33a (§128)

26 What then, brethren? When you come together, each one has a hymn, a lesson, a revelation, a tongue, or an interpretation. Let all things be done for edification. 27 If any speak in a tongue, let there be only two or at most three, and each in turn; and let one interpret. 28 But if there is no one to interpret, let each of them keep silence in church and speak to himself and to God. 29 Let two or three prophets speak, and let the others weigh what is

honor of the Lord. He also who eats, eats in honor of the Lord, since he gives thanks to God; while he who abstains, abstains in honor of the Lord and gives thanks to God. 7 None of us lives to himself, and none of us dies to himself. 8 If we live, we live to the Lord, and if we die, we die to the Lord; so then, whether we live or whether we die, we are the Lord's. 9 For to this end Christ died and lived again, that he might be Lord both of the dead and of the living. 10 Why do you pass judgment on your brother? Or you, why do you de-

said. 30 If a revelation is made to another sitting by, let the first be silent. 31 For you can all prophesy one by one, so that all may learn and all be encouraged; 32 and the spirits of prophets are subject to prophets. 33 For God is not a God of confusion but of peace.

1 Cor 10:23-11:1 (§111)

23 "All things are lawful," but not all things are helpful. "All things are lawful," but not all things build up. 24 Let no one seek his own good, but the good of his neighbor. 25 Eat whatever is sold in the meat market without raising any question on the ground of conscience. 26 For "the earth is the Lord's, and everything in it." 27 If one of the unbelievers invites you to dinner and you

spise your brother? For we shall all stand before the judgment seat of God; 11 for it is written,
"As I live, says the Lord, every knee shall bow to me,
and every tongue shall give praise to God."
12 So each of us shall give account of himself to God.

are disposed to go, eat whatever is set before you without raising any question on the ground of conscience. 28 (But if some one says to you, "This has been offered in sacrifice," then out of consideration for the man who informed you, and for conscience' sake— 29 I mean his conscience, not yours—do not eat it.) For why should my liberty be determined by another man's scruples? 30 If I partake with thankfulness, why am I denounced because of that for which I give thanks?

31 So, whether you eat or drink, or whatever you do, do all to the glory of God. 32 Give no offense to Jews or to Greeks or to the church of God, 33 just as I try to please all men in everything I do, not seeking my own advantage, but that of many, that they may be

11

saved. 1 Be imitators of me, as I am of Christ.

1 Cor 14:13-19 (§126)

13 Therefore, he who speaks in a tongue should pray for the power to interpret. 14 For if I pray in a tongue, my spirit prays but my mind is unfruitful. 15 What am I to do? I will pray with the spirit and I will pray with the

Eph 5:15-20

15 Look carefully then how you walk, not as unwise men but as wise, 16 making the most of the time, because the days are evil. 17 Therefore do not be foolish, but understand what the will of the Lord is. 18 And do not get drunk with wine, for that is debauchery; but be filled with the Spirit, 19 addressing one another in psalms and hymns and spiritual songs, singing and making melody to the Lord with all your heart, 20 always and for everything giving thanks in the name of our Lord Jesus Christ to God the Father.

mind also; I will sing with the spirit and I will sing with the mind also. 16 Otherwise, if you bless with the spirit, how can any one in the position of an outsider say the "Amen" to your thanksgiving when he does not know what you are saying? 17 For you may give thanks well enough, but the other man is not edified. 18 I thank God that I speak in tongues more than you all; 19 nevertheless, in church I would rather speak five words with my mind, in order to instruct others, than ten thousand words in a tongue.

▶ 5:19 *cf Acts 16:25

▶ 5:16 1 Cor 7:26   26 I think that in view of the present distress it is well for a person to remain as he is.

▶ 5:20 1 Thes 5:18   18 give thanks in all circumstances; for this is the will of God in Christ Jesus for you.

▶ 5:19 1 Cor 14:40   40 but all things should be done decently and in order.

232. Be subject to one another

232

1 Cor 7:32-35 (§99)

32 I want you to be free from anxieties. The unmarried man is anxious about the affairs of the Lord, how to please the Lord; 33 but the married man is anxious about worldly affairs, how to please his wife, 34 and his interests are divided. And the unmarried woman or girl is anxious about the affairs of the Lord, how to be holy in body and spirit; but the married woman is anxious about worldly affairs, how to please her husband. 35 I say this for your own benefit, not to lay any restraint upon you, but to promote good order and to secure your undivided devotion to the Lord.

1 Cor 11:2-16 (§112)

2 I commend you because you remember me in everything and maintain the traditions even as I have delivered them to you. 3 But I want you to understand that the head of every man is Christ, the head of a woman is her husband, and the head of Christ is God. 4 Any man who prays or prophesies with his head covered dishonors his head, 5 but any woman who prays or prophesies with her head unveiled dishonors

2Cor 11:1-6 (§179)

11

I wish you would bear with me in a little foolishness. Do bear with me! 2 I feel a divine jealousy for you, for I betrothed you to Christ to present you as a pure bride to her one husband. 3 But I am afraid that as the serpent deceived Eve by his cunning, your thoughts will be led astray from a sincere and pure devotion to Christ. 4 For if some one comes and preaches another Jesus than the one we preached, or if you receive a different spirit from the one you received, or if you accept a different gospel from the one you accepted, you submit to it readily enough.

her head—it is the same as if her head were shaven. 6 For if a woman will not veil herself, then she should cut off her hair; but if it is disgraceful for a woman to be shorn or shaven, let her wear a veil. 7 For a man ought not to cover his head, since he is the image and glory of God; but woman is the glory of man. 8 (For man was not made from woman, but woman from man. 9 Neither was man created for woman, but woman for

5 I think that I am not in the least inferior to these superlative apostles. 6 Even if I am unskilled in speaking, I am not in knowledge; in every way we have made this plain to you in all things.

man.) 10 That is why a woman ought to have a veil on her head, because of the angels. 11 (Nevertheless, in the Lord woman is not independent of man nor man of woman; 12 for as woman was made from man, so man is now born of woman. And all things are from God.) 13 Judge for yourselves; is it proper for a woman to pray to God with her head uncovered? 14 Does not nature itself teach you that for a man to wear long hair is degrading to him, 15 but if a woman has long hair, it is her pride? For her hair is given to her for a covering. 16 If any one is disposed to be contentious, we recognize no other practice, nor do the churches of God.

1 Cor 14:33b-36 (§129)

As in all the churches of the saints, 34 the women should keep silence in the churches. For they are not permitted to speak, but should be subordinate, as even the law says. 35 If there is anything

Eph 5:21-6:9

21 Be subject to one another out of reverence for Christ. 22 Wives, be subject to your husbands, as to the Lord. 23 For the husband is the head of the wife as Christ is the head of the church, his body, and is himself its Savior. 24 As the church is subject to Christ, so let wives also be subject in everything to their husbands. 25 Husbands, love your wives, as Christ loved the church and gave himself up for her, 26 that he might sanctify her, having cleansed her by the washing of water with the word, 27 that he might present the church to himself in splendor, without spot or wrinkle or any such thing, that she might be holy and without blemish. 28 Even so husbands should love their wives as their own bodies. He who loves his wife loves himself. 29 For no man ever hates his own flesh, but nourishes

they desire to know, let them ask their husbands at home. For it is shameful for a woman to speak in church. 36 What! Did the word of God originate with you, or are you the only ones it has reached?

▶ 5:22-6:9 *cf 1 Pet 2:13-3:7

*cf Rom 13:1-7

Tit 2:1-10

But as for you, teach what befits sound doctrine. 2 Bid the older men be temperate, serious, sensible, sound in faith, in love, and in steadfastness. 3 Bid the older women likewise to be reverent in behavior, not to be slanderers or slaves to drink; they are to teach what is good, 4 and so train the young women to love their husbands and children, 5 to be sensible, chaste, domestic, kind, and submissive to their husbands, that the word of God may not be discredited. 6 Likewise urge the younger men to control themselves. 7 Show yourself in all respects a model of good deeds, and in your teaching show integrity, gravity, 8 and sound speech that cannot be censured, so that an opponent may be put to shame, having nothing evil to say of us. 9 Bid slaves to be submissive to their masters and to give satisfaction in every respect; they are not to be refractory, 10 nor to pilfer, but to show entire and true fidelity, so that in everything they may adorn the doctrine of God our Savior.

231

Col 3:12-17 (§267)

12 Put on then, as God's chosen ones, holy and beloved, compassion, kindness, lowliness, meekness, and patience, 13 forbearing one another and, if one has a complaint against another, forgiving each other; as the Lord has forgiven you, so you also must forgive. 14 And above all these put on love, which binds everything together in perfect harmony. 15 And let the peace of Christ rule in your hearts, to which indeed you were called in the one body. And be thankful. 16 Let the word of Christ dwell in you richly, teach and admonish one another in all wisdom, and sing psalms and hymns and spiritual songs with thankfulness in your hearts to God. 17 And whatever you do, in word or deed, do everything in the name of the Lord Jesus, giving thanks to God the Father through him.

232. Be subject to one another

232

Eph (cont)

and cherishes it, as Christ does the church, 30 because we are members of his body. 31 "For this reason a man shall leave his father and mother and be joined to his wife, and the two shall become one flesh." 32 This mystery is a profound one, and I am saying that it refers to Christ and the church; 33 however, let each one of you love his wife as himself, and let the wife see that she respects her husband.

6 Children, obey your parents in the Lord, for this is right. 2 "Honor your father and mother" (this is the first commandment with a promise), 3 "that it may be well with you and that you may live long on the earth." 4 Fathers, do not provoke your children to anger, but bring them up in the discipline and instruction of the Lord.

5 Slaves, be obedient to those who are your earthly masters, with fear and trembling, in singleness of heart, as to Christ; 6 not in the way of eyeservice, as men-pleasers, but as servants of Christ, doing the will of God from the heart, 7 rendering service with a good will as to the Lord and not to men, 8 knowing that whatever good any one

Col 3:18-4:1 (§268)

18 Wives, be subject to your husbands, as is fitting in the Lord. 19 Husbands, love your wives, and do not be harsh with them. 20 Children, obey your parents in everything, for this pleases the Lord. 21 Fathers, do not provoke your children, lest they become discouraged. 22 Slaves, obey in everything those who are your earthly masters, not with eyeservice, as men-pleasers, but in singleness of heart, fearing the Lord. 23 Whatever your task, work heartily, as serving the Lord and not men, 24 knowing that from the Lord you will receive the inheritance as your reward; you are serving the Lord Christ. 25 For the wrongdoer will be paid back for the wrong he has done, and there is no partiality.

4 Masters, treat your slaves justly and fairly, knowing that you also have a Master in heaven.

does, he will receive the same again from the Lord, whether he is a slave or free. 9 Masters, do the same to them, and forbear threatening, knowing that he who is both their Master and yours is in heaven, and that there is no partiality with him.

5:26 Acts 22:16
16 And now ny do you wait? Rise and be baptized, d wash away your sins, calling on his me.'

Tit 2:14
14 who gave himself for us to redeem us from all iniquity and to purify for himself a people of his own who are zealous for good deeds.

3:5
5 he saved us, not because of deeds done by us in righteousness, but in virtue of his own mercy, by the washing of regeneration and renewal in the Holy Spirit,

▶ 6:4 2 Tim 3:15
15 and how from childhood you have been acquainted with the sacred writings which are able to instruct you for salvation through faith in Christ Jesus.

▶ 6:5 1 Tim 6:1
Let all who are under the yoke of slavery regard their masters as worthy of all honor, so that the name of God and the teaching may not be defamed.

▶ 6:9 Acts 10:34
34 And Peter opened his mouth and said: "Truly I perceive that God shows no partiality,

▶ 5:23 1:22-23,
22 and he has put all things under his feet and has made him the head over all things for the church, 23 which is his body, the fulness of him who fills all in all.

4:15 15 Rather, speaking the truth in love, we are to grow up in every way into him who is the head, into Christ,

Col 1:18,
18 He is the head of the body, the church; he is the beginning, the first-born from the dead, that in everything he might be pre-eminent.

2:19
19 and not holding fast to the Head, from whom the whole body, nourished and knit together through its joints and ligaments, grows with a growth that is from God.

▶ 5:25 5:2
2 And walk in love, as Christ loved us and gave himself up for us, a fragrant offering and sacrifice to God.

Gal 2:20
20 I have been crucified with Christ; it is no longer I who live, but Christ who lives in me; and the life I now live in the flesh I live by faith in the Son of God, who loved me and gave himself for me.

▶ 5:27 *cf 1:4

▶ 5:30 *cf 1:23, 4:12, 4:25 1 Cor 12:12, 27, Rom 12:4-5

▶ 6:6 *cf Rom 13:1 1 Cor 7:22 1 Thes 2:4 Gal 1:10

▶ 6:8 *cf 2 Cor 11:15b ▶ 6:9 *cf Rom 2:11, 3:22b

▶ 5:31 Gen 2:24
24 Therefore a man leaves his father and his mother and cleaves to his wife, and they become one flesh.

▶ 6:3 Deut 5:16
16 " 'Honor your father and your mother, as the LORD your God commanded you; that your days may be prolonged, and that it may go well with you, in the land which the LORD your God gives you.

*cf 'Rom 8:32

▶ 6:2 Ex 20:12
12 "Honor your father and your mother, that your days may be long in the land which the LORD your God gives you.

▶ 5:22 (subject) omit be subject: p46B Origen

▶ 6:1 (Lord) omit in the Lord: BD*G it(few) Marcion

283

233

Rom 13:11-14 (§56)

11 Besides this you know what hour it is, how it is full time now for you to wake from sleep. For salvation is nearer to us now than when we first believed; 12 the night is far gone, the day is at hand. Let us then cast off the works of darkness and put on the armor of light; 13 let us conduct ourselves becomingly as in the day, not in reveling and drunkenness, not in debauchery and licentiousness, not in quarreling and jealousy. 14 But put on the Lord Jesus Christ, and make no provision for the flesh, to gratify its desires.

1 Cor 16:13-14 (§141)

13 Be watchful, stand firm in your faith, be courageous, be strong. 14 Let all that you do be done in love.

2 Cor 10:1-6 (§176)

10 I, Paul, myself entreat you, by the meekness and gentleness of Christ—I who am humble when face to face with you, but bold to you when I am away!— 2 I beg of you that when I am present I may not have to show boldness with such confidence as I count on showing against some who suspect us of acting in worldly fashion. 3 For though we live in the world we are not carrying on a worldly war, 4 for the weapons of our warfare are not worldly but have divine power to destroy strongholds. 5 We destroy arguments and every proud obstacle to the knowledge of God, and take every thought captive to obey Christ, 6 being ready to punish every disobedience, when your obedience is complete.

Eph 6:10-17

10 Finally, be strong in the Lord and in the strength of his might. 11 Put on the whole armor of God, that you may be able to stand against the wiles of the devil. 12 For we are not contending against flesh and blood, but against the principalities, against the powers, against the world rulers of this present darkness, against the spiritual hosts of wickedness in the heavenly places. 13 Therefore take the whole armor of God, that you may be able to withstand in the evil day, and having done all, to stand. 14 Stand therefore, having girded your loins with truth, and having put on the breastplate of righteousness, 15 and having shod your feet with the equipment of the gospel of peace; 16 besides all these, taking the shield of faith, with which you can quench all the flaming darts of the evil one. 17 And take the helmet of salvation, and the sword of the Spirit, which is the word of God.

▶ 6:10 2 Tim 2:1
You then, my son, be strong in the grace that is in Christ Jesus,

▶ 6:12 Acts 26:16-18
16 But rise and stand upon your feet; for I have appeared to you for this purpose, to appoint you to serve and bear witness to the things in which you have seen me and to those in which I will appear to you, 17 delivering you from the people and from the Gentiles —to whom I send you 18 to open their eyes, that they may turn from darkness to light and from the power of Satan to God, that they may receive forgiveness of sins and a place among those who are sanctified by faith in me.'

▶ 6:15 Acts 10:36   36 You know the word which he sent to Israel, preaching good news of peace by Jesus Christ (he is Lord of all),

▶ 6:11 2 Cor 6:7   7 truthful speech, and the power of God; with the weapons of righteousness for the right hand and for the left;

▶ 6:12 Gal 4:3,   3 So with us; when we were children, we were slaves to the elemental spirits of the universe.

234. Pray at all times in the Spirit

234

Rom 8:26-27 (§32)

26 Likewise the Spirit helps us in our weakness; for we do not know how to pray as we ought, but the Spirit himself intercedes for us with sighs too deep for words. 27 And he who searches the hearts of men knows what is the mind of the Spirit, because the Spirit intercedes for the saints according to the will of God.

Rom 15:30-33 (§64)

30 I appeal to you, brethren, by our Lord Jesus Christ and by the love of the Spirit, to strive together with me in your prayers to God on my behalf, 31 that I may be delivered from the unbelievers in Judea, and that my service for Jerusalem may be acceptable to the saints, 32 so that by God's will I may come to you with joy and be refreshed in your company. 33 The God of peace be with you all. Amen.

Eph 6:18-20

18 Pray at all times in the Spirit, with all prayer and supplication. To that end keep alert with all perseverance, making supplication for all the saints, 19 and also for me, that utterance may be given me in opening my mouth boldly to proclaim the mystery of the gospel, 20 for which I am an ambassador in chains; that I may declare it boldly, as I ought to speak.

▶ 6:18 1 Tim 2:1
First of all, then, I urge that supplications, prayers, intercessions, and thanksgivings be made for all men,

▶ 6:20 Acts 21:33
33 Then the tribune came up and arrested him, and ordered him to be bound with two chains. He inquired who he was and what he had done.

▶ 6:19 3:3,   3 how the mystery was made known to me by revelation, as I have written briefly.

9-10   9 and to make all men see what is the plan of the mystery hidden for ages in God who created all things; 10 that through the church the manifold wisdom of God might now be made known to the principalities and powers in the heavenly places.

▶ 6:20 3:1,
For this reason I, Paul, a prisoner for Christ Jesus on behalf of you Gentiles—
4:1 I therefore, a prisoner for the Lord, beg you to lead a life worthy of the calling to which you have been called,

▶ Phil 1:12-20
12 I want you to know, brethren, that what has happened to me has really served to advance the gospel, 13 so that it has become known throughout the whole praetorian guard and to all the rest that my imprisonment is for Christ; 14 and most of the brethren have been

233

1 Thes 5:1-11 (§287)

5 But as to the times and the seasons, brethren, you have no need to have anything written to you. [2] For you yourselves know well that the day of the Lord will come like a thief in the night. [3] When people say, "There is peace and security," then sudden destruction will come upon them as travail comes upon a woman with child, and there will be no escape. [4] But you are not in darkness, brethren, for that day to surprise you like a thief. [5] For you are all sons of light and sons of the day; we are not of the night or of darkness. [6] So then, let us not sleep, as others do, but let us keep awake and be sober. [7] For those who sleep sleep at night, and those who get drunk are drunk at night. [8] But, since we belong to the day, let us be sober, and put on the breastplate of faith and love, and for a helmet the hope of salvation. [9] For God has not destined us for wrath, but to obtain salvation through our Lord Jesus Christ, [10] who died for us so that whether we wake or sleep we might live with him. [11] Therefore en-

courage one another and build one another up, just as you are doing.

9
that you have come to know God, or rather to be known by God, how can you turn back again to the weak and beggarly elemental spirits, whose slaves you want to be once more? [9] but now

Col 2:8,
8 See to it that no one makes a prey of you by philosophy and empty deceit, according to human tradition, according to the elemental spirits of the universe, and not according to Christ.

20
20 If with Christ you died to the elemental spirits of the universe, why do you live as if you still belonged to the world? Why do you submit to regulations,

▶ 6:12 (we) *read* you: p[46]BD*G it(some) syr(pes pal) Ambrosiaster

---

234. Pray at all times in the Spirit

234

Col 4:2-3 (§269)

2 Continue steadfastly in prayer, being watchful in it with thanksgiving; [3] and pray for us also, that God may open to us a door for the word, to declare the mystery of Christ, on account of which I am in prison,

*cf Col 1:24-2:3(§260)

1 Thes 5:25 (§290)

25 Brethren, pray for us.

2 Thes 3:1-5 (§299)

3 Finally, brethren, pray for us, that the word of the Lord may speed on and triumph, as it did among you, [2] and that we may be delivered from wicked and evil men; for not all have faith. [3] But the Lord is faithful; he will strengthen you and guard you from evil. [4] And we have confidence in the Lord about you, that you are doing and will do the things which we command. [5] May the Lord direct your hearts to the love of God and to the steadfastness of Christ.

---

made confident in the Lord because of my imprisonment, and are much more bold to speak the word of God without fear.
15 Some indeed preach Christ from envy and rivalry, but others from good will. [16] The latter do it out of love, knowing that I am put here for the defense of the gospel; [17] the former pro-

claim Christ out of partisanship, not sincerely but thinking to afflict me in my imprisonment. [18] What then? Only that in every way, whether in pretense or in truth, Christ is proclaimed; and in that I rejoice.
19 Yes, and I shall rejoice. For I know that through your prayers and the help of the Spirit of Jesus Christ this

will turn out for my deliverance, [20] as it is my eager expectation and hope that I shall not be at all ashamed, but that with full courage now as always Christ will be honored in my body, whether by life or by death.

Phm 1,
1 Paul, a prisoner for Christ Jesus, and Timothy our brother,
To Phile'mon our beloved fellow worker

9
[9] yet for love's sake I prefer to appeal to you—I, Paul, an ambassador and now a prisoner also for Christ Jesus—

Col 4:3,
[3] and pray for us also, that God may open to us a door for the word, to declare the mystery of Christ, on account of which I am in prison,
18a
18 I, Paul, write this greeting with my own hand. Remember my fetters.

235

1 Cor 4:14-21 (§86)

14 I do not write this to make you ashamed, but to admonish you as my beloved children. 15 For though you have countless guides in Christ, you do not have many fathers. For I became your father in Christ Jesus through the gospel. 16 I urge you, then, be imitators of me. 17 Therefore I sent to you Timothy, my beloved and faithful child in the Lord, to remind you of my ways in Christ, as I teach them everywhere in every church. 18 Some are arrogant, as though I were not coming to you. 19 But I will come to you soon, if the Lord wills, and I will find out not the talk of these arrogant people but their power. 20 For the kingdom of God does not consist in talk but in power. 21 What do you wish? Shall I come to you with a rod, or with love in a spirit of gentleness?

1 Cor 16:10-12 (§140)

10 When Timothy comes, see that you put him at ease among you, for he is doing the work of the Lord, as I am. 11 So let no one despise him. Speed him on his way in peace, that he may return

to me; for I am expecting him with the brethren.

12 As for our brother Apol′los, I strongly urged him to visit you with the other brethren, but it was not at all his will to come now. He will come when he has opportunity.

Eph 6:21-22

21 Now that you also may know how I am and what I am doing, Tych′icus the beloved brother and faithful minister in the Lord will tell you everything. 22 I have sent him to you for this very purpose, that you may know how we are, and that he may encourage your hearts.

▶6:21 *cf Tit3:12

▶6:22 *cf 1 Cor 16:18, 1 Thes 3:1-5, 2 Cor 7:6-7

236. Peace and grace

236

Rom 16:20b (§68)

The grace of our Lord Jesus Christ be with you.

1 Cor 16:23-24 (§145)

23 The grace of the Lord Jesus be with you. 24 My love be with you all in Christ Jesus. Amen.

2 Cor 13:14 (§192)

14 The grace of the Lord Jesus Christ and the love of God and the fellowship of the Holy Spirit be with you all.

Gal 6:18 (§217)

18 The grace of our Lord Jesus Christ be with your spirit, brethren. Amen.

Eph 6:23-24

23 Peace be to the brethren, and love with faith, from God the Father and the Lord Jesus Christ. 24 Grace be with all who love our Lord Jesus Christ with love undying.

▶6:24 *cf 1 Tim 6:21b, 2 Tim 4:22, Tit 3:15c

235

Phil 2:25-3:1(§246)

25 I have thought it necessary to send to you Epaphrodi′tus my brother and fellow worker and fellow soldier, and your messenger and minister to my need, 26 for he has been longing for you all, and has been distressed because you heard that he was ill. 27 Indeed he was ill, near to death. But God had mercy on him, and not only on him but on me also, lest I should have sorrow upon sorrow. 28 I am the more eager to send him, therefore, that you may rejoice at seeing him again, and that I may be less anxious. 29 So receive him in the Lord with all joy; and honor such men, 30 for he nearly died for the work of Christ, risking his life to complete your service to me.

3 Finally, my brethren, rejoice in the Lord. To write the same things to you is not irksome to me, and is safe for you.

Col 4:7-9 (§271)

7 Tych′icus will tell you all about my affairs; he is a beloved brother and faithful minister and fellow servant in the Lord. 8 I have sent him to you for this very purpose, that you may know how we are and that he may encourage your hearts, 9 and with him Ones′imus, the faithful and beloved brother, who is one of yourselves. They will tell you of everything that has taken place here.

236. Peace and grace

236

Phil 4:23(§255)

23 The grace of the Lord Jesus Christ be with your spirit.

Col 4:18b (§274)

Grace be with you.

1 Thes 5:28 (§293)

28 The grace of our Lord Jesus Christ be with you.

2 Thes 3:18 (§304)

18 The grace of our Lord Jesus Christ be with you all.

Phm 25 (§311)

25 The grace of the Lord Jesus Christ be with your spirit.

237. Paul and Timothy, to the saints at Philippi

237

Rom 1:1-7 (§1)

1 Paul, a servant of Jesus Christ, called to be an apostle, set apart for the gospel of God 2 which he promised beforehand through his prophets in the holy scriptures, 3 the gospel concerning his Son, who was descended from David according to the flesh 4 and designated Son of God in power according to the Spirit of holiness by his resurrection from the dead, Jesus Christ our Lord, 5 through whom we have received grace and apostleship to bring about the obedience of faith for the sake of his name among all the nations, 6 including yourselves who are called to belong to Jesus Christ; 7 To all God's beloved in Rome, who are called to be saints: Grace to you and peace from God our Father and the Lord Jesus Christ.

1 Cor 1:1-3 (§71)

1 Paul, called by the will of God to be an apostle of Christ Jesus, and our brother Sos'thenes, 2 To the church of God which is at Corinth, to those sanctified in Christ Jesus, called to be saints together with all those who in every place call on the name of our Lord Jesus Christ, both their Lord and ours: 3 Grace to you and peace from God our Father and the Lord Jesus Christ.

2 Cor 1:1-2 (§146)

1 Paul, an apostle of Christ Jesus by the will of God, and Timothy our brother. To the church of God which is at Corinth, with all the saints who are in the whole of Acha'ia: 2 Grace to you and peace from God our Father and the Lord Jesus Christ.

Gal 1:1-5 (§193)

1 Paul an apostle—not from men nor through man, but through Jesus Christ and God the Father, who raised him from the dead— 2 and all the brethren who are with me, To the churches of Galatia: 3 Grace to you and peace from God the Father and our Lord Jesus Christ, 4 who gave himself for our sins to deliver us from the present evil age, according to the will of our God and Father; 5 to whom be the glory for ever and ever. Amen.

Eph 1:1-2 (§218)

1 Paul, an apostle of Christ Jesus by the will of God, To the saints who are also faithful in Christ Jesus: 2 Grace to you and peace from God our Father and the Lord Jesus Christ.

▶ 1:1 Acts 16:12-40

12 and from there to Philippi, which is the leading city of the district of Macedo'nia, and a Roman colony. We remained in this city some days; 13 and on the sabbath day we went outside the gate to the riverside, where we supposed there was a place of prayer; and we sat down and spoke to the women who had come together. 14 One who heard us was a woman named Lydia, from the city of Thyati'ra, a seller of purple goods, who was a worshiper of God. The Lord opened her heart to give heed to what was said by Paul. 15 And when she was baptized, with her household, she besought us, saying, "If you have judged me to be faithful to the Lord, come to my house and stay." And she prevailed upon us.

16 As we were going to the place of prayer, we were met by a slave girl who had a spirit of divination and brought her owners much gain by soothsaying. 17 She followed Paul and us, crying, "These men are servants of the Most High God, who proclaim to you the way of salvation." 18 And this she did for many days. But Paul was annoyed, and turned and said to the spirit, "I charge you in the name of Jesus Christ to come out of her." And it came out that very hour.

19 But when her owners saw that their hope of gain was gone, they seized Paul and Silas and dragged them into the market place before the rulers; 20 and when they had brought them to the magistrates they said, "These men are Jews and they are disturbing our city. 21 They advocate customs which it is not lawful for us Romans to accept or practice." 22 The crowd joined in attacking them; and the magistrates tore the garments off them and gave orders to beat them with rods. 23 And when they had inflicted many blows upon them, they threw them into prison, charging the jailer to keep them safely. 24 Having received this charge, he put them into the inner prison and fastened their feet in the stocks.

25 But about midnight Paul and Silas were praying and singing hymns to God, and the prisoners were listening to them, 26 and suddenly there was a great earthquake, so that the foundations of the prison were shaken; and immediately all the doors were opened and every one's fetters were unfastened. 27 When the jailer woke and saw that the prison doors were open, he drew his sword and was about to kill himself, supposing that the prisoners had escaped. 28 But Paul cried with a loud voice, "Do not harm yourself, for we are all here." 29 And he called for lights and rushed in, and trembling with fear he fell down before Paul and Silas, 30 and brought them out and said, "Men, what must I do to be saved?" 31 And they said, "Believe in the Lord Jesus, and you will be saved, you and your household." 32 And they spoke the word of the Lord to him and to all that were in his house. 33 And he took them the same hour of the night, and washed their wounds, and he was baptized at once, with all his family. 34 Then he brought them up into his house, and set food before them; and he rejoiced with all his household that he had believed in God.

35 But when it was day, the magistrates sent the police, saying, "Let those men go." 36 And the jailer reported the words to Paul, saying, "The magistrates have sent to let you go; now therefore come out and go in peace." 37 But Paul said to them, "They have beaten us publicly, uncondemned, men who are Roman citizens, and have thrown us into prison; and do they now cast us out secretly? No! let them come themselves and take us out." 38 The police

238. I thank my God

238

Rom 1:8-15 (§2)

8 First, I thank my God through Jesus Christ for all of you, because your faith is proclaimed in all the world. 9 For God is my witness, whom I serve with my spirit in the gospel of his Son, that without ceasing I mention you always in my prayers, 10 asking that somehow by God's will I may now at last succeed in coming to you. 11 For I long to see you, that I may impart to you some spiritual gift to strengthen you, 12 that is, that we may be mutually encouraged by each other's faith, both yours and mine. 13 I want you to know, brethren, that I have often intended to come to you (but thus far have been prevented), in order that I may reap some harvest among you as well as among the rest of the Gentiles. 14 I am under obligation both to Greeks and to barbarians, both to the wise and to the foolish: 15 so I am eager to preach the gospel to you also who are in Rome.

Rom 15:14-21 (§62)

14 I myself am satisfied about you, my brethren, that you yourselves are full of goodness, filled with all knowledge, and able to instruct one another. 15 But on some points I have written to you very boldly by way of reminder, because of the grace given me by God 16 to be a minister of Christ Jesus to the Gentiles in the priestly service of the gospel of God, so that the offering of the Gentiles may be acceptable, sanctified by the Holy Spirit. 17 In Christ Jesus, then, I have reason to be proud of my work for God. 18 For I will not venture to speak of anything except what Christ has wrought through me to win obedience from the Gentiles, by word and deed, 19 by the power of signs and wonders, by the power of the Holy Spirit, so that from Jerusalem and as far round as Illyr'icum I have fully preached the gospel of Christ, 20 thus making it my ambition to preach the gospel, not where Christ has already been named, lest I build on another man's foundation, 21 but as it is written,

"They shall see who have never been told of him,
and they shall understand who have never heard of him."

1 Cor 1:4-9 (§72)

4 I give thanks to God always for you because of the grace of God which was given you in Christ Jesus, 5 that in every way you were enriched in him with all speech and all knowledge— 6 even as the testimony to Christ was confirmed among you— 7 so that you are not lacking in any spiritual gift, as you wait for the revealing of our Lord Jesus Christ; 8 who will sustain you to the end, guiltless in the day of our Lord Jesus Christ. 9 God is faithful, by whom you were called into the fellowship of his Son, Jesus Christ our Lord.

▶ 1:5 Acts 2:42 **42 And they devoted themselves to the apostles' teaching and fellowship, to the breaking of bread and the prayers.**

16:12-40

12 and from there to Philippi, which is the leading city of the district of Macedo'nia, and a Roman colony. We remained in this city some days; 13 and on the sabbath day we went outside the gate to the riverside, where we supposed there was a place of prayer; and we sat down and spoke to the women who had come together. 14 One who heard us was a woman named Lydia, from the city of Thyati'ra, a seller of purple goods, who was a worshiper of God. The Lord opened her heart to give heed to what was said by Paul. 15 And when she was baptized, with her household, she besought us, saying, "If you have judged me to be faithful to the Lord, come to my house and stay." And she prevailed upon us.

16 As we were going to the place of prayer, we were met by a slave girl who had a spirit of divination and brought her owners much gain by soothsaying. 17 She followed Paul and us, crying, "These men are servants of the Most High God, who proclaim to you the way of salvation." 18 And this she did for many days. But Paul was annoyed, and turned and said to the spirit, "I charge you in the name of Jesus Christ to come out of her." And it came out that very hour.

19 But when her owners saw that their hope of gain was gone, they seized Paul and Silas and dragged them into the market place before the rulers; 20 and when they had brought them to the magistrates they said, "These men are Jews and they are disturbing our city. 21 They advocate customs which it is not lawful for us Romans to accept or practice." 22 The crowd joined in attacking them; and the magistrates tore the garments off them and gave orders to beat them with rods. 23 And when they had inflicted many blows upon them, they threw them into prison, charging the jailer to keep them safely. 24 Having received this charge, he put them into the inner prison and fastened their feet in the stocks.

25 But about midnight Paul and Silas were praying and singing hymns to God, and the prisoners were listening to them, 26 and suddenly there was a great earthquake, so that the foundations of the prison were shaken; and immediately all the doors were opened and every one's fetters were unfastened. 27 When the jailer woke and saw that the prison doors were open, he drew his sword and was about to kill himself, supposing that the prisoners had escaped. 28 But Paul cried with a loud voice, "Do not harm yourself, for we are all here." 29 And he called for lights and rushed in, and trembling with fear he fell down before Paul and Silas, 30 and brought them out and said, "Men, what must I do to be saved?" 31 And they said, "Believe in the Lord Jesus, and you will be saved, you and your household." 32 And they spoke the word of the Lord to him and to all that were in his house. 33 And he took them the same hour of the night, and washed their wounds, and he was baptized at once, with all his family. 34 Then he brought them up into his house, and set food before them; and he rejoiced with all his household that he had believed in God.

35 But when it was day, the magistrates sent the police, saying, "Let those men go." 36 And the jailer reported the words to Paul, saying, "The magistrates have sent to let you go; now therefore come out and go in peace." 37 But Paul said to them, "They have beaten us publicly, uncondemned, men who are Roman citizens, and have thrown us into prison; and do they now cast us out secretly? No! let them come themselves and take us out." 38 The police reported these words to the magistrates, and they were afraid when they heard that they were Roman citizens; 39 so they came and apologized to them. And they took them out and asked them to leave the city. 40 So they went out of the prison, and visited Lydia; and when they had seen the brethren, they exhorted them and departed.

▶ 1:7 Acts 21:33

33 Then the tribune came up and arrested him, and ordered him to be bound with two chains. He inquired who he was and what he had done.

2 Tim 1:8,

8 Do not be ashamed then of testifying to our Lord, nor of me his prisoner, but share in suffering for the gospel in the power of God,

12,

12 and therefore I suffer as I do. But I am not ashamed, for I know whom I have believed, and I am sure that he is able to guard until that Day what has been entrusted to me.

237

Phil 1:1-2

1 Paul and Timothy, servants of Christ Jesus,
To all the saints in Christ Jesus who are at Philippi, with the bishops and deacons:
2 Grace to you and peace from God our Father and the Lord Jesus Christ.

Col 1:1-2 (§256)

1 Paul, an apostle of Christ Jesus by the will of God, and Timothy our brother,
2 To the saints and faithful brethren in Christ at Colos'sae:
Grace to you and peace from God our Father.

1 Thes 1:1 (§275)

1 Paul, Silva'nus, and Timothy,
To the church of the Thessalo'-nians in God the Father and the Lord Jesus Christ:
Grace to you and peace.

2 Thes 1:1-2 (§294)

1 Paul, Silva'nus, and Timothy,
To the church of the Thessalo'-nians in God our Father and the Lord Jesus Christ:
2 Grace to you and peace from God the Father and the Lord Jesus Christ.

Phm 1-3 (§305)

1 Paul, a prisoner for Christ Jesus, and Timothy our brother,
To Phile'mon our beloved fellow worker 2 and Ap'phia our sister and Archip'pus our fellow soldier, and the church in your house:
3 Grace to you and peace from God our Father and the Lord Jesus Christ.

---

reported these words to the magistrates, and they were afraid when they heard that they were Roman citizens; 39 so they came and apologized to them. And they took them out and asked them to leave the city. 40 So they went out of the prison, and visited Lydia; and when they had seen the brethren, they exhorted them and departed.

▶1:1 Acts 16:1
And he came also to Derbe and to Lystra. A disciple was there, named Timothy, the son of a Jewish woman who was a believer; but his father was a Greek.

▶1:1 1 Tim 3:1-2
The saying is sure: If any one aspires to the office of bishop, he desires a noble task. 2 Now a bishop must be above reproach, the husband of one wife, temperate, sensible, dignified, hospitable, an apt teacher,

▶1:1 1 Tim 3:8-10
8 Deacons likewise must be serious, not double-tongued, not addicted to much wine, not greedy for gain; 9 they must hold the mystery of the faith with a clear conscience. 10And let them also be tested first; then if they prove themselves blameless let them serve as deacons.

▶1:1 1 Thes 2:2
2 but though we had already suffered and been shamefully treated at Philippi, as you know, we had courage in our God to declare to you the gospel of God in the face of great opposition.

Tit 1:7
7 For a bishop, as God's steward, must be blameless; he must not be arrogant or quick-tempered or a drunkard or violent or greedy for gain,

238. I thank my God

238

Phil 1:3-11

3 I thank my God in all my remembrance of you, 4 always in every prayer of mine for you all making my prayer with joy, 5 thankful for your partnership in the gospel from the first day until now. 6And I am sure that he who began a good work in you will bring it to completion at the day of Jesus Christ. 7 It is right for me to feel thus about you all, because I hold you in my heart, for you are all partakers with me of grace, both in my imprisonment and in the defense and confirmation of the gospel. 8 For God is my witness, how I yearn for you all with the affection of Christ Jesus. 9And it is my prayer that your love may abound more and more, with knowledge and all discernment, 10 so that you may approve what is excellent, and may be pure and blameless for the day of Christ, 11 filled with the fruits of righteousness which come through Jesus Christ, to the glory and praise of God.

Col 1:3-14 (§257)

3 We always thank God, the Father of our Lord Jesus Christ, when we pray for you, 4 because we have heard of your faith in Christ Jesus and of the love which you have for all the saints, 5 because of the hope laid up for you in heaven. Of this you have heard before in the word of the truth, the gospel 6 which has come to you, as indeed in the whole world it is bearing fruit and growing—so among yourselves, from the day you heard and understood the grace of God in truth, 7 as you learned it from Ep'aphras our beloved fellow servant. He is a faithful minister of Christ on our behalf 8 and has made known to us your love in the Spirit.

9 And so, from the day we heard of it, we have not ceased to pray for you, asking that you may be filled with the knowledge of his will in all spiritual wisdom and understanding, 10 to lead a life worthy of the Lord, fully pleasing to him, bearing fruit in every good work and increasing in the knowledge of God. 11May you be strengthened with all power, according to his glorious might,

1 Thes 1:2-10 (§276)

2 We give thanks to God always for you all, constantly mentioning you in our prayers, 3 remembering before our God and Father your work of faith and labor of love and steadfastness of hope in our Lord Jesus Christ. 4 For we know, brethren beloved by God, that he has chosen you; 5 for our gospel came to you not only in word, but also in power and in the Holy Spirit and with full conviction. You know what kind of men we proved to be among you for your sake. 6And you became imitators of us and of the Lord, for you received the word in much affliction, with joy inspired by the Holy Spirit; 7 so that you became an example to all the believers in Macedo'nia and in Acha'ia. 8 For not only has the word of the Lord sounded forth from you in Macedo'nia and Acha'ia, but your faith in God has

for all endurance and patience with joy, 12 giving thanks to the Father, who has qualified us to share in the inheritance of the saints in light. 13 He has delivered us from the dominion of darkness and transferred us to the kingdom of his beloved Son, 14 in whom we have redemption, the forgiveness of sins.

2 Thes 1:3-12 (§295)

3 We are bound to give thanks to God always for you, brethren, as is fitting, because your faith is growing abundantly, and the love of every one of you for one another is increasing. 4 Therefore we ourselves boast of you in the churches of God for your steadfastness and faith in all your persecutions and in the afflictions which you are enduring.

5 This is evidence of the righteous judgment of God, that you may be made worthy of the kingdom of God, for which you are suffering—6 since indeed God deems it just to repay with affliction those who afflict you, 7 and to grant rest with us to you who are af-

gone forth everywhere, so that we need not say anything. 9 For they themselves report concerning us what a welcome we had among you, and how you turned to God from idols, to serve a living and true God, 10 and to wait for his Son from heaven, whom he raised from the dead, Jesus who delivers us from the wrath to come.

*cf 1 Thes 3:6-13 (§282-283)

Phm 4-7 (§306)

4 I thank my God always when I remember you in my prayers, 5 because I hear of your love and of the faith which you have toward the Lord Jesus and all the saints, 6 and I pray that the sharing of your faith may promote the knowledge of all the good that is ours in Christ. 7 For I have derived much joy and comfort from your love, my brother, because the hearts of the saints have been refreshed through you.

flicted, when the Lord Jesus is revealed from heaven with his mighty angels in flaming fire, 8 inflicting vengeance upon those who do not know God and upon those who do not obey the gospel of our Lord Jesus. 9 They shall suffer the punishment of eternal destruction and exclusion from the presence of the Lord and from the glory of his might, 10 when he comes on that day to be glorified in his saints, and to be marveled at in all who have believed, because our testimony to you was believed. 11 To this end we always pray for you, that our God may make you worthy of his call, and may fulfil every good resolve and work of faith by his power, 12 so that the name of our Lord Jesus may be glorified in you, and you in him, according to the grace of our God and the Lord Jesus Christ.

16
16 May the Lord grant mercy to the household of Onesiph'orus, for he often refreshed me; he was not ashamed of my chains.

▶1:5 4:15-16
15And you Philippians yourselves know that in the beginning of the gospel, when I left Macedo'nia, no church entered into partnership with me in giving and receiving except you only; 16 for even in Thessaloni'ca you sent me help once and again.

1 Cor 9:23
23 I do it all for the sake of the gospel, that I may share in its blessings.

▶1:6, 10 1 Thes 5:2, 2 For yourselves know well that the day of the Lord will come like a thief in the night.

4
4 But you are not in darkness, brethren, for that day to surprise you like a thief.

1 Cor 1:7-8
7 so that you are not lacking in any spiritual gift, as you wait for the revealing of our Lord Jesus Christ; 8 who will sustain you to the end, guiltless in the day of our Lord Jesus Christ.

Phil 2:16
16 holding fast the word of life, so that in the day of Christ I may be proud that I did not run in vain or labor in vain.

2 Thes 2:2-3
2 not to be quickly shaken in mind or excited, either by spirit or by word, or by letter purporting to be from us, to the effect that the day of the Lord has come. 3 Let no one deceive you in any way; for that day will not come, unless the rebellion comes first, and the man of lawlessness is revealed, the son of perdition,

▶1:7 Eph 3:1,
For this reason I, Paul, a prisoner for Christ Jesus on behalf of you Gentiles—

4:1 I therefore, a prisoner for the Lord, beg you to lead a life worthy of the calling to which you have been called.

Phm 1,
1 Paul, a prisoner for Christ Jesus, and Timothy our brother,
To Phile'mon our beloved fellow worker

9
9 yet for love's sake I prefer to appeal to you—I, Paul, an ambassador and now a prisoner also for Christ Jesus—

▶1:8 Gal 1:20
20 (In what I am writing to you, before God, I do not lie!)

Col 4:3,
3 and pray for us also, that God may open to us a door for the word, to declare the mystery of Christ, on account of which I am in prison,

18a
18 I, Paul, write this greeting with my own hand. Remember my fetters.

*cf 2 Cor 1:23, 11:31

▶1:10 *cf 4:8

▶1:11 *cf Rom 6:21-22, Gal 5:22, Rom 7:4-5

239

Rom 1:16-17 (§3)

16 For I am not ashamed of the gospel: it is the power of God for salvation to every one who has faith, to the Jew first and also to the Greek. 17 For in it the righteousness of God is revealed through faith for faith; as it is written, "He who through faith is righteous shall live."

Rom 2:6-11 (§8)

6 For he will render to every man according to his works: 7 to those who by patience in well-doing seek for glory and honor and immortality, he will give eternal life; 8 but for those who are factious and do not obey the truth, but obey wickedness, there will be wrath and fury. 9 There will be tribulation and distress for every human being who does evil, the Jew first and also the Greek, 10 but glory and honor and peace for every one who does good, the Jew first and also the Greek. 11 For God shows no partiality.

1 Cor 15:1-11 (§131)

15 Now I would remind you, brethren, in what terms I preached to you the gospel, which you received, in which you stand, 2 by which you are saved, if you hold it fast —unless you believed in vain.

3 For I delivered to you as of first importance what I also received, that Christ died for our sins in accordance with the scriptures, 4 that he was buried, that he was raised on the third day in accordance with the scriptures, 5 and that he appeared to Cephas, then to the twelve. 6 Then he appeared to more than five hundred brethren at one time, most of whom are still alive, though some have fallen asleep. 7 Then he appeared to James, then to all the apostles. 8 Last of all, as to one untimely born, he appeared also to me. 9 For I am the least of the apostles, unfit to be called an apostle, because I persecuted the church of God. 10 But by the grace of God I am what I am, and his grace toward me was not in vain. On the contrary, I worked harder than any of them, though it was not I, but the grace of God which is with me. 11 Whether then it was I or they, so we preach and so you believed.

▶ 1:12, 13 2 Tim 2:9 9 the gospel for which I am suffering and wearing fetters like a criminal. But the word of God is not fettered.

▶ 1:13 Acts 28:30
30 And he lived there two whole years at his own expense, and welcomed all who came to him,

▶ 1:14 Acts 4:31, 31And when they had prayed, the place in which they were gathered together was shaken; and they were all filled with the Holy Spirit and spoke the word of God with boldness.

28:31
31 preaching the kingdom of God and teaching about the Lord Jesus Christ quite openly and unhindered.

▶ 1:13 Eph 3:1,
For this reason I, Paul, a prisoner for Christ Jesus on behalf of you Gentiles—

4:1 I therefore, a prisoner for the Lord, beg you to lead a life worthy of the calling to which you have been called,

240. Christ will be honored in my body

240

Rom 14:5-12 (§58)

5 One man esteems one day as better than another, while another man esteems all days alike. Let every one be fully convinced in his own mind. 6 He who observes the day, observes it in honor of the Lord. He also who eats, eats in honor of the Lord, since he gives thanks to God; while he who abstains, abstains in honor of the Lord and gives thanks to God. 7 None of us lives to himself, and none of us dies to himself. 8 If we live, we live to the Lord, and if we die, we die to the Lord; so then, whether we live or whether we die, we are the Lord's. 9 For to this end Christ died and lived again, that he might be Lord both of the dead and of the living.

10 Why do you pass judgment on your brother? Or you, why do you despise your brother? For we shall all stand before the judgment seat of God; 11 for it is written,
"As I live, says the Lord, every knee shall bow to me,
and every tongue shall give praise to God."
12 So each of us shall give account of himself to God.

1 Cor 4:14-21 (§86)

14 I do not write this to make you ashamed, but to admonish you as my beloved children. 15 For though you have countless guides in Christ, you do not have many fathers. For I became your father in Christ Jesus through the gospel. 16 I urge you, then, be imitators of me. 17 Therefore I sent to you Timothy, my beloved and faithful child in the Lord, to remind you of my ways in Christ, as I teach them everywhere in every church. 18 Some are arrogant, as though I were not coming to you. 19 But I will come to you soon, if the Lord wills, and I will find out not the talk of these arrogant people but their power. 20 For the kingdom of God does not consist in talk but in power. 21 What do you wish? Shall I come to you with a rod, or with love in a spirit of gentleness?

2 Cor 4:7-12 (§159)

7 But we have this treasure in earthen vessels, to show that the transcendent power belongs to God and not to us. 8 We are afflicted in every way, but not crushed; perplexed, but not driven to despair; 9 persecuted, but not forsaken; struck down, but not destroyed; 10 always carrying in the body the death of Jesus, so that the life of Jesus may also be manifested in our bodies. 11 For while we live we are always being given up to death for Jesus' sake, so that the life of Jesus may be manifested in our mortal flesh. 12 So death is at work in us, but life in you.

2 Cor 5:6-10 (§162)

6 So we are always of good courage; we know that while we are at home in the body we are away from the Lord, 7 for we walk by faith, not by sight. 8 We are of good courage, and we would rather be away from the body and at home with the Lord. 9 So whether we are at home or away, we make it our aim to please him. 10 For we must all appear before the judgment seat of Christ, so that each one may receive good or evil, according to what he has done in the body.

▶ 1:19 Acts 16:7 7And when they had come opposite My'sia, they attempted to go into Bithyn'ia, but the Spirit of Jesus did not allow them;

▶ 1:19 2 Cor 1:11
11 You also must help us by prayer, so that many will give thanks on our behalf for the blessing granted us in answer to many prayers.

▶ 1:20 1 Cor 6:20 20 you were bought with a price. So glorify God in your body.

▶ 1:21 Gal 2:20 20 I have been crucified with Christ; it is no longer I who live, but Christ who lives in me; and the life I now live in the flesh I live by faith in the Son of God, who loved me and gave himself for me.

Rom 8:10
But if Christ is in you, although your bodies are dead because of sin, your spirits are alive because of righteousness.

Col 3:4
4 When Christ who is our life appears, then you also will appear with him in glory.

Phil 1:12-18

239

12 I want you to know, brethren, that what has happened to me has really served to advance the gospel, 13 so that it has become known throughout the whole praetorian guard and to all the rest that my imprisonment is for Christ; 14 and most of the brethren have been made confident in the Lord because of my imprisonment, and are much more bold to speak the word of God without fear.

15 Some indeed preach Christ from envy and rivalry, but others from good will. 16 The latter do it out of love, knowing that I am put here for the defense of the gospel; 17 the former proclaim Christ out of partisanship, not sincerely but thinking to afflict me in my imprisonment. 18 What then? Only that in every way, whether in pretense or in truth, Christ is proclaimed; and in that I rejoice.

Phm 1,

1 Paul, a prisoner for Christ Jesus, and Timothy our brother,
To Philemon our beloved fellow worker

9

9 yet for love's sake I prefer to appeal to you—I, Paul, an ambassador and now a prisoner also for Christ Jesus—

Col 4:3,

3 and pray for us also, that God may open to us a door for the word, to declare the mystery of Christ, on account of which I am in prison,

18a

18 I, Paul, write this greeting with my own hand. Remember my fetters.

Phil 4:22

22 All the saints greet you, especially those of Caesar's household.

▶ 1:14 2 Thes 3:4

4 And we have confidence in the Lord about you, that you are doing and will do the things which we command.

▶ 1:15, 17 Rom 2:8

8 but for those who are factious and do not obey the truth, but obey wickedness, there will be wrath and fury.

240. Christ will be honored in my body

Phil 1:19-26

Phm 21-22 (§309)

240

19 Yes, and I shall rejoice. For I know that through your prayers and the help of the Spirit of Jesus Christ this will turn out for my deliverance, 20 as it is my eager expectation and hope that I shall not be at all ashamed, but that with full courage now as always Christ will be honored in my body, whether by life or by death. 21 For to me to live is Christ, and to die is gain. 22 If it is to be life in the flesh, that means fruitful labor for me. Yet which I shall choose I cannot tell. 23 I am hard pressed between the two. My desire is to depart and be with Christ, for that is far better. 24 But to remain in the flesh is more necessary on your account. 25 Convinced of this, I know that I shall remain and continue with you all, for your progress and joy in the faith, 26 so that in me you may have ample cause to glory in Christ Jesus, because of my coming to you again.

21 Confident of your obedience, I write to you, knowing that you will do even more than I say. 22 At the same time, prepare a guest room for me, for I am hoping through your prayers to be granted to you.

241

2 Cor 1:23-2:4 (§150)

23 But I call God to witness against me—it was to spare you that I refrained from coming to Corinth. 24 Not that we lord it over your faith; we work with you for your joy, for you stand firm in your faith. **2** 1 For I made up my mind not to make you another painful visit. 2 For if I cause you pain, who is there to make me glad but the one whom I have pained? 3And I wrote as I did, so that when I came I might not suffer pain from those who should have made me rejoice, for I felt sure of all of you, that my joy would be the joy of you all. 4 For I wrote you out of much affliction and anguish of heart and with many tears, not to cause you pain but to let you know the abundant love that I have for you.

Eph 4:1-10 (§225)

4 I therefore, a prisoner for the Lord, beg you to lead a life worthy of the calling to which you have been called, 2 with all lowliness and meekness, with patience, forbearing one another in love, 3 eager to maintain the unity of the Spirit in the bond of peace. 4 There is one body and one Spirit, just as you were called to the one hope that belongs to your call, 5 one Lord, one faith, one baptism, 6 one God and Father of us all, who is above all and through all and in all. 7 But grace was given to each of us according to the measure of Christ's gift. 8 Therefore it is said,
"When he ascended on high he led a host of captives,
and he gave gifts to men."

▶ 1:27 Acts 4:32
32 Now the company of those who believed were of one heart and soul, and no one said that any of the things which he possessed was his own, but they had everything in common.

▶ 1:29 Acts 5:41,
41 Then they left the presence of the council, rejoicing that they were counted worthy to suffer dishonor for the name.

14:22   22 strengthening the souls of the disciples, exhorting them to continue in the faith, and saying that through many tribulations we must enter the kingdom of God.

▶ 1:30 Acts 16:22
22 The crowd joined in attacking them; and the magistrates tore the garments off them and gave orders to beat them with rods.

1 Tim 6:12
12 Fight the good fight of the faith; take hold of the eternal life to which you were called when you made the good confession in the presence of many witnesses.

2 Tim 4:7   7 I have fought the good fight, I have finished the race, I have kept the faith.

242. Obedient unto death

242

Rom 2:6-11 (§8)

6 For he will render to every man according to his works: 7 to those who by patience in well-doing seek for glory and honor and immortality, he will give eternal life; 8 but for those who are factious and do not obey the truth, but obey wickedness, there will be wrath and fury. 9 There will be tribulation and distress for every human being who does evil, the Jew first and also the Greek, 10 but glory and honor and peace for every one who does good, the Jew first and also the Greek. 11 For God shows no partiality.

Rom 8:1-8 (§29)

8 There is therefore now no condemnation for those who are in Christ Jesus. 2 For the law of the Spirit of life in Christ Jesus has set me free from the law of sin and death. 3 For God has done what the law, weakened by the flesh, could not do: sending his own Son in the likeness of sinful flesh and for sin, he condemned sin in the flesh, 4 in order that the just requirement of the law might be fulfilled in us, who walk not according to the flesh but according to the Spirit. 5 For those who live according to the flesh set their minds on the things of the flesh, but those who live according to the Spirit set their minds on the things of the Spirit. 6 To set the mind on the flesh is death, but to set the mind on the Spirit is life and peace. 7 For the mind that is set on the flesh is hostile to God; it does

1 Cor 13:4-7 (§122)

4 Love is patient and kind; love is not jealous or boastful; 5 it is not arrogant or rude. Love does not insist on its own way; it is not irritable or resentful; 6 it does not rejoice at wrong, but rejoices in the right. 7 Love bears all things, believes all things, hopes all things, endures all things.

not submit to God's law, indeed it cannot; 8 and those who are in the flesh cannot please God.

Rom 8:9-17 (§30)

9 But you are not in the flesh, you are in the Spirit, if in fact the Spirit of God dwells in you. Any one who does not have the Spirit of Christ does not belong to him. 10 But if Christ is in you, although your bodies are dead because of sin, your spirits are alive because of righteousness. 11 If the Spirit of him who raised Jesus from the dead dwells in you, he who raised Christ Jesus from the dead will give life to your mortal bodies also through his Spirit which dwells in you.
12 So then, brethren, we are debtors, not to the flesh, to live according to the flesh—13 for if you live according to the flesh you will die, but if by the Spirit you put to death the deeds of the body you will live. 14 For all who are led by the Spirit of God are sons of God. 15 For you did not receive the spirit of slavery to fall back into fear, but you have received the spirit of sonship. When we cry, "Abba! Father!" 16 it is

2 Cor 8:8-15 (§172)

8 I say this not as a command, but to prove by the earnestness of others that your love also is genuine. 9 For you know the grace of our Lord Jesus Christ, that though he was rich, yet for your sake he became poor, so that by his poverty you might become rich. 10And in this matter I give my advice: it is best for you now to complete what a year ago you began not only to do but to desire, 11 so that your readiness in desiring it may be matched by your completing it out of what you have. 12 For if the readiness is there, it is acceptable according to what a man has, not according to what he has not. 13 I do not mean that others should be eased and you burdened, 14 but that as a matter of equality your abundance at the present time should supply their want, so that their abundance may supply your want, that there may be equality. 15As it is written, "He who gathered much had nothing over, and he who gathered little had no lack."

Rom 10:5-13 (§41)

5 Moses writes that the man who practices the righteousness which is based on the law shall live by it. 6 But the righteousness based on faith says, Do not say in your heart, "Who will ascend into heaven?" (that is, to bring Christ down) 7 or "Who will descend into the abyss?" (that is, to bring Christ up from the dead). 8 But what does it say? The word is near you, on your lips and in your heart (that is, the word of faith which we preach); 9 because, if you confess with your lips that Jesus is Lord and believe in your heart that God

raised him from the dead, you will be saved. 10 For man believes with his heart and so is justified, and he confesses with his lips and so is saved. 11 The scripture says, "No one who believes in him will be put to shame." 12 For there is no distinction between Jew and Greek; the same Lord is Lord of all and bestows his riches upon all who call upon him. 13 For, "every one who calls upon the name of the Lord will be saved."

Rom 12:9-21 (§53)

9 Let love be genuine; hate what is evil, hold fast to what is good; 10 love one another with brotherly affection; outdo one another in showing honor. 11 Never flag in zeal, be aglow with the Spirit, serve the Lord. 12 Rejoice in your hope, be patient in tribulation, be constant in prayer. 13 Contribute to the needs of the saints, practice hospitality.
14 Bless those who persecute you; bless and do not curse them. 15 Rejoice with those who rejoice, weep with those who weep. 16 Live in harmony with one another; do not be haughty, but asso-

Eph 4:1-10 (§225)

4 I therefore, a prisoner for the Lord, beg you to lead a life worthy of the calling to which you have been called, 2 with all lowliness and meekness, with patience, forbearing one another in love, 3 eager to maintain the unity of the Spirit in the bond of peace. 4 There is one body and one Spirit, just as you were called to the one hope that belongs to your call, 5 one Lord, one faith, one baptism, 6 one God and Father of us all, who is above all and through all and in all. 7 But grace was given to each of us according to the measure of Christ's gift. 8 Therefore it is said,
"When he ascended on high he led a host of captives,
and he gave gifts to men."
9 (In saying, "He ascended," what does

ciate with the lowly; never be conceited. 17 Repay no one evil for evil, but take thought for what is noble in the sight of all. 18 If possible, so far as it depends upon you, live peaceably with all. 19 Beloved, never avenge yourselves, but leave it to the wrath of God; for it is written, "Vengeance is mine, I will repay, says the Lord." 20 No, "if your enemy is hungry, feed him; if he is thirsty, give him drink; for by so doing you will heap burning coals upon his head." 21 Do not be overcome by evil, but overcome evil with good.

cf Rom 15:1-6 (§60)

▶2:7, 9 Heb 2:9   9 But we see Jesus, who for a little while was made lower than the angels, crowned with glory and honor because of the suffering of death, so that by the grace of God he might taste death for every one.

▶2:8 Heb 5:8   8Although he was a Son, he learned obedience through what he suffered;
▶2:9 Acts 2:33
33 Being therefore exalted at the right hand of God, and having received from the Father the promise of the Holy Spirit, he has poured out this which you see and hear.

▶2:9-11 Heb 1:1-4,
In many and various ways God spoke of old to our fathers by the prophets; 2 but in these last days he has spoken to us by a Son, whom he appointed the heir of all things, through whom also he created the world. 3 He reflects the glory of God and bears the very stamp of his nature, upholding the universe by his word of power. When he had made purification for sins, he sat down at the right hand of the Majesty on high, 4 having become as much superior to angels as the name he has obtained is more excellent than theirs.

12:2   2 looking to Jesus the pioneer and perfecter of our faith, who for the joy that was set before him endured the cross, despising the shame, and is seated at the right hand of the throne of God.

▶2:2 4:2
2 I entreat Eu-o′dia and I entreat Syn′tyche to agree in the Lord.
▶2:3 Col 3:12,
12 Put on then, as God's chosen ones, holy and beloved, compassion, kindness, lowliness, meekness, and patience.

Phil 1:27-30

27 Only let your manner of life be worthy of the gospel of Christ, so that whether I come and see you or am absent, I may hear of you that you stand firm in one spirit, with one mind striving side by side for the faith of the gospel, 28 and not frightened in anything by your opponents. This is a clear omen to them of their destruction, but of your salvation, and that from God. 29 For it has been granted to you that for the sake of Christ you should not only believe in him but also suffer for his sake, 30 engaged in the same conflict which you saw and now hear to be mine.

Eph (cont)

9 (In saying, "He ascended," what does it mean but that he had also descended into the lower parts of the earth? 10 He

▶ 1:27 2:24
24 and I trust in the Lord that shortly I myself shall come also.

Col 2:4-7 (§261)

4 I say this in order that no one may delude you with beguiling speech. 5 For though I am absent in body, yet I am with you in spirit, rejoicing to see your good order and the firmness of your faith in Christ. 6 As therefore you received Christ Jesus the Lord, so live in him, 7 rooted and built up in him and established in the faith, just as you were taught, abounding in thanksgiving.

who descended is he who also ascended far above all the heavens, that he might fill all things.)

▶ 1:30 Rom 15:30-32
30 I appeal to you, brethren, by our Lord Jesus Christ and by the love of the Spirit, to strive together with me in your prayers to God on my behalf, 31 that I may be delivered from the unbelievers in Judea, and that my service for Jerusalem may be acceptable to the saints, 32 so that by God's will I may come to you with joy and be refreshed in your company.

1 Thes 3:6-10 (§282)

6 But now that Timothy has come to us from you, and has brought us the good news of your faith and love and reported that you always remember us kindly and long to see us, as we long to see you—7 for this reason, brethren, in all our distress and affliction we have been comforted about you through your faith; 8 for now we live, if you stand fast in the Lord. 9 For what thanksgiving can we render to God for you, for all the joy which we feel for your sake before our God, 10 praying earnestly night and day that we may see you face to face and supply what is lacking in your faith?

2 Thes 1:3-12 (§295)

3 We are bound to give thanks to God always for you, brethren, as is fitting, because your faith is growing abundantly, and the love of every one of you for one another is increasing. 4 Therefore we ourselves boast of you in the churches of God for your steadfastness and faith in all your persecutions and in the afflictions which you are enduring. 5 This is evidence of the righteous judgment of God, that you may be made worthy of the kingdom of God, for which you are suffering—6 since indeed God deems it just to repay with affliction those who afflict you, 7 and to grant rest with us to you who are afflicted, when the Lord Jesus is revealed from heaven with his mighty angels in

Phm 21-22 (§309)

21 Confident of your obedience, I write to you, knowing that you will do even more than I say. 22 At the same time, prepare a guest room for me, for I am hoping through your prayers to be granted to you.

flaming fire, 8 inflicting vengeance upon those who do not know God and upon those who do not obey the gospel of our Lord Jesus. 9 They shall suffer the punishment of eternal destruction and exclusion from the presence of the Lord and from the glory of his might, 10 when he comes on that day to be glorified in his saints, and to be marveled at in all who have believed, because our testimony to you was believed. 11 To this end we always pray for you, that our God may make you worthy of his call, and may fulfil every good resolve and work of faith by his power, 12 so that the name of our Lord Jesus may be glorified in you, and you in him, according to the grace of our God and the Lord Jesus Christ.

242. Obedient unto death

242

Phil 2:1-11

2 So if there is any encouragement in Christ, any incentive of love, any participation in the Spirit, any affection and sympathy, 2 complete my joy by being of the same mind, having the same love, being in full accord and of one mind. 3 Do nothing from selfishness or conceit, but in humility count others better than yourselves. 4 Let each of you look not only to his own interests, but also to the interests of others. 5 Have this mind among yourselves, which is yours in Christ Jesus, 6 who, though he was in the form of God, did not count equality with God a thing to be grasped, 7 but emptied himself, taking the form of a servant, being born in the likeness of men. 8 And being found in human form he humbled himself and became obedient unto death, even death on a cross. 9 Therefore God has highly exalted him and bestowed on him the name which is above every name, 10 that at the name of Jesus every knee should bow, in heaven and on earth and under the earth, 11 and every tongue confess that Jesus Christ is Lord, to the glory of God the Father.

Eph (cont)

it mean but that he had also descended into the lower parts of the earth? 10 He who descended is he who also ascended far above all the heavens, that he might fill all things.)

Eph 1:3-23 (§219)

3 Blessed be the God and Father of our Lord Jesus Christ, who has blessed

Gal 5:25

25 If we live by the Spirit, let us also walk by the Spirit.

▶ 2:4 1 Cor 10:24,
24 Let no one seek his own good, but the good of his neighbor.

us in Christ with every spiritual blessing in the heavenly places, 4 even as he chose us in him before the foundation of the world, that we should be holy and blameless before him. 5 He destined us in love to be his sons through Jesus Christ, according to the purpose of his will, 6 to the praise of his glorious grace which he freely bestowed on us in the Beloved. 7 In him we have redemption through his blood, the forgiveness of our trespasses, according to the riches of his grace 8 which he lavished upon us. 9 For he has made known to us in all wisdom and insight the mystery of his will, according to his purpose which he set forth in Christ 10 as a plan for the fulness of time, to unite all things in him, things in heaven and things on earth.

11 In him, according to the purpose of him who accomplishes all things according to the counsel of his will, 12 we who first hoped in Christ have been destined and appointed to live for the praise of his glory. 13 In him you also, who have heard the word of truth, the gospel of your salvation, and have believed in him, were sealed with the promised Holy Spirit, 14 which is the guarantee of our inheritance until we acquire possession of it, to the praise of his glory.

15 For this reason, because I have heard of your faith in the Lord Jesus and your love toward all the saints, 16 I do not cease to give thanks for you, re-

Gal 6:2, 2 Bear one another's burdens, and so fulfil the law of Christ.

▶ 2:7 Gal 4:4 4 But when the time had fully come, God sent forth his Son, born of woman, born under the law,

membering you in my prayers, 17 that the God of our Lord Jesus Christ, the Father of glory, may give you a spirit of wisdom and of revelation in the knowledge of him, 18 having the eyes of your hearts enlightened, that you may know what is the hope to which he has called you, what are the riches of his glorious inheritance in the saints, 19 and what is the immeasurable greatness of his power in us who believe, according to the working of his great might 20 which he accomplished in Christ when he raised him from the dead and made him sit at his right hand in the heavenly places, 21 far above all rule and authority and power and dominion, and above every name that is named, not only in this age but also in that which is to come; 22 and he has put all things under his feet and has made him the head over all things for the church, 23 which is his body, the fulness of him who fills all in all.

▶ 2:7, 9 2 Cor 13:4
4 For he was crucified in weakness, but lives by the power of God. For we are weak in him, but in dealing with you we shall live with him by the power of God.

▶ 2:9-11 Rom 14:9
9 For to this end Christ died and lived again, that he might be Lord both of the dead and of the living.

*cf 1 Cor 10:33

▶ 2:11 1 Cor 12:3
3 Therefore I want you to understand that no one speaking by the Spirit of God ever says "Jesus be cursed!" and no one can say "Jesus is Lord" except by the Holy Spirit.

243

2 Cor 7:13b-16 (§170)

And besides our own comfort we rejoiced still more at the joy of Titus, because his mind has been set at rest by you all. 14 For if I have expressed to him some pride in you, I was not put to shame; but just as everything we said to you was true, so our boasting before Titus has proved true. 15 And his heart goes out all the more to you, as he remembers the obedience of you all, and the fear and trembling with which you received him. 16 I rejoice, because I have perfect confidence in you.

▶ 2:12 Col 2:5
5 For though I am absent in body, yet I am with you in spirit, rejoicing to see your good order and the firmness of your faith in Christ.

1 Cor 5:3
3 For though absent in body I am present in spirit, and as if present, I have already pronounced judgment

▶ 2:13 1 Thes 2:13
13 And we also thank God constantly for this, that when you received the word of God which you heard from us, you accepted it not as the word of men but as what it really is, the word of God, which is at work in you believers.

244. Do all things without grumbling

244

Rom 12:1-2 (§51)

12 I appeal to you therefore, brethren, by the mercies of God, to present your bodies as a living sacrifice, holy and acceptable to God, which is your spiritual worship. 2 Do not be conformed to this world but be transformed by the renewal of your mind, that you may prove what is the will of God, what is good and acceptable and perfect.

2 Cor 1:12-14 (§148)

12 For our boast is this, the testimony of our conscience that we have behaved in the world, and still more toward you, with holiness and godly sincerity, not by earthly wisdom but by the grace of God. 13 For we write you nothing but what you can read and understand; I hope you will understand fully, 14 as you have understood in part, that you can be proud of us as we can be of you, on the day of the Lord Jesus.

▶ 2:15 Acts 2:40
40 And he testified with many other words and exhorted them, saying, "Save yourselves from this crooked generation."

▶ 2:16 Acts 5:20 20 "Go and stand in the temple and speak to the people all the words of this Life."

▶ 2:15 Eph 1:4, 4 even as he chose us in him before the foundation of the world, that we should be holy and blameless before him.

5:27
27 that he might present the church to himself in splendor, without spot or wrinkle or any such thing, that she might be holy and without blemish.

2 Cor 6:13 13 In return—I speak as to children—widen your hearts also.

Gal 4:19, 19 My little children, with whom I am again in travail until Christ be formed in you!

21-23
21 Tell me, you who desire to be under law, do you not hear the law? 22 For it is written that Abraham had two sons, one by a slave and one by a free woman. 23 But the son of the slave was born according to the flesh, the son of the free woman through promise.

Phm 10 10 I appeal to you for my child, Ones'imus, whose father I have become in my imprisonment.

1 Cor 14:20
20 Brethren, do not be children in your thinking; be babes in evil, but in thinking be mature.

Eph 5:1
Therefore be imitators of God, as beloved children.

▶ 2:16 Gal 2:2 2 I went up by revelation; and I laid before them (but privately before those who were of repute) the gospel which I preach among the Gentiles, lest somehow I should be running or had run in vain.

1 Cor 15:58
58 Therefore, my beloved brethren, be steadfast, immovable, always abounding in the work of the Lord, knowing that in the Lord your labor is not in vain.

1 Thes 3:5 5 For this reason, when I could bear it no longer, I sent that I might know your faith, for fear that somehow the tempter had tempted you and that our labor would be in vain.

1 Cor 1:7-8 7 so that you are not lacking in any spiritual gift, as you wait for the revealing of our Lord Jesus Christ; 8 who will sustain you to the end, guiltless in the day of our Lord Jesus Christ.

Phil 2:12-13

12 Therefore, my beloved, as you have always obeyed, so now, not only as in my presence but much more in my absence, work out your own salvation with fear and trembling; [13] for God is at work in you, both to will and to work for his good pleasure.

Phm 21-22 (§309)

21 Confident of your obedience, I write to you, knowing that you will do even more than I say. [22] At the same time, prepare a guest room for me, for I am hoping through your prayers to be granted to you.

243

244. Do all things without grumbling

244

Phil 2:14-18

14 Do all things without grumbling or questioning, [15] that you may be blameless and innocent, children of God without blemish in the midst of a crooked and perverse generation, among whom you shine as lights in the world, [16] holding fast the word of life, so that in the day of Christ I may be proud that I did not run in vain or labor in vain. [17] Even if I am to be poured as a libation upon the sacrificial offering of your faith, I am glad and rejoice with you all. [18] Likewise you also should be glad and rejoice with me.

1 Thes 5:1-11 (§287)

5 But as to the times and the seasons, brethren, you have no need to have anything written to you. [2] For you yourselves know well that the day of the Lord will come like a thief in the night. [3] When people say, "There is peace and security," then sudden destruction will come upon them as travail comes upon a woman with child, and there will be no escape. [4] But you are not in darkness, brethren, for that day to surprise you like a thief. [5] For you are all sons of light and sons of the day; we are not of the night or of darkness. [6] So then, let us not sleep, as others do, but let us keep awake and be sober. [7] For those who sleep sleep at night, and those who get drunk are drunk at night. [8] But, since we belong to the day, let us be sober, and put on the breastplate of faith and love, and for a helmet the hope of salvation. [9] For God has not destined us for wrath, but to obtain salvation through our Lord Jesus Christ, [10] who died for us so that whether we wake or sleep we might live with him. [11] Therefore encourage one another and build one another up, just as you are doing.

Phil 1:6,

[6] And I am sure that he who began a good work in you will bring it to completion at the day of Jesus Christ.

10

[10] so that you may approve what is excellent, and may be pure and blameless for the day of Christ,

2 Thes 2:2-3

[2] not to be quickly shaken in mind or excited, either by spirit or by word, or by letter purporting to be from us, to the effect that the day of the Lord has come. [3] Let no one deceive you in any way; for that day will not come, unless the rebellion comes first, and the man of lawlessness is revealed, the son of perdition,

2 Cor 1:14

[14] as you have understood in part, that you can be proud of us as we can be of you, on the day of the Lord Jesus.

▶ 2:17-18 Rom 12:15 [15] Rejoice with those who rejoice, weep with those who weep.

▶ 2:17 Phil 4:18 [18] I have received full payment, and more; I am filled, having received from Epaphrodi′-tus the gifts you sent, a fragrant offering, a sacrifice acceptable and pleasing to God.

▶ 2:18 3:1,

Finally, my brethren, rejoice in the Lord. To write the same things to you is not irksome to me, and is safe for you.

4:4,

[4] Rejoice in the Lord always; again I will say, Rejoice.

8

[8] Finally, brethren, whatever is true, whatever is honorable, whatever is just, whatever is pure, whatever is lovely, whatever is gracious, if there is any excellence, if there is anything worthy of praise, think about these things.

245

Rom 16:1-2* (§65)

16 I commend to you our sister Phoebe, a deaconess of the church at Cen'chre-ae, 2 that you may receive her in the Lord as befits the saints, and help her in whatever she may require from you, for she has been a helper of many and of myself as well.

1 Cor 16:10-12* (§140)

10 When Timothy comes, see that you put him at ease among you, for he is doing the work of the Lord, as I am. 11 So let no one despise him. Speed him on his way in peace, that he may return to me; for I am expecting him with the brethren.

12 As for our brother Apol'los, I strongly urged him to visit you with the other brethren, but it was not at all his will to come now. He will come when he has opportunity.

1 Cor 16:15-18* (§142)

15 Now, brethren, you know that the household of Steph'anas were the first converts in Acha'ia, and they have devoted themselves to the service of the saints; 16 I urge you to be subject to such men and to every fellow worker and laborer. 17 I rejoice at the coming of Steph'anas and Fortuna'tus and Acha'icus, because they have made up for your absence; 18 for they refreshed my spirit as well as yours. Give recognition to such men.

1 Cor 4:14-21 (§86)

14 I do not write this to make you ashamed, but to admonish you as my

2 Cor 3:1-3* (§154)

3 Are we beginning to commend ourselves again? Or do we need, as some do, letters of recommendation to you, or from you? 2 You yourselves are our letter of recommendation, written on your[c] hearts, to be known and read by all men; 3 and you show that you are a letter from Christ delivered by us,

beloved children. 15 For though you have countless guides in Christ, you do not have many fathers. For I became your father in Christ Jesus through the gospel. 16 I urge you, then, be imitators of me. 17 Therefore I sent to you Timothy, my beloved and faithful child in the Lord, to remind you of my ways in Christ, as I teach them everywhere in every church. 18 Some are arrogant, as though I were not coming to you. 19 But I will come to you soon, if the Lord wills, and I will find out not the talk of these arrogant people but their power. 20 For the kingdom of God does not consist in talk but in power. 21 What do you wish? Shall I come to you with a rod, or with love in a spirit of gentleness?

written not with ink but with the Spirit of the living God, not on tablets of stone but on tablets of human hearts.

2 Cor 8:16-24* (§173)

16 But thanks be to God who puts the same earnest care for you into the heart of Titus. 17 For he not only accepted our appeal, but being himself very earnest he is going to you of his own accord. 18 With him we are sending the brother who is famous among all the churches for his preaching of the gospel; 19 and not only that, but he has been appointed by the churches to travel with us in this gracious work which we are carrying on, for the glory of the Lord and to show our good will. 20 We intend that no one should blame us about this liberal gift which we are administering, 21 for we aim at what is honorable not only in the Lord's sight but also in the sight of men. 22And with them we are sending our brother whom we have often tested and found earnest in many matters, but who is now more earnest than ever because of his great confidence in you. 23As for Titus, he is my partner and fellow worker in your service; and as for our brethren, they are messengers of the

churches, the glory of Christ. 24 So give proof, before the churches, of your love and of our boasting about you to these men.

▶ 2:19 Acts 16:1
And he came also to Derbe and to Lystra. A disciple was there, named Timothy, the son of a Jewish woman who was a believer; but his father was a Greek.

▶ 2:21 2 Tim 4:10,
10 For Demas, in love with this present world, has deserted me and gone to Thessaloni'ca; Crescens has gone to Galatia, Titus to Dalmatia.

16   16At my first defense no one took my part; all deserted me. May it not be charged against them!

▶ 2:19-24 2:25-30.
25 I have thought it necessary to send to you Epaphrodi'tus my brother and fellow worker and fellow soldier, and your messenger and minister to my need, 26 for he has been longing for you

all, and has been distressed because you heard that he was ill. 27 Indeed he was ill, near to death. But God had mercy on him, and not only on him but on me also, lest I should have sorrow upon sorrow. 28 I am the more eager to send him, therefore, that you may rejoice at

seeing him again, and that I may be less anxious. 29 So receive him in the Lord with all joy; and honor such men, 30 for he nearly died for the work of Christ, risking his life to complete your service to me.

246. Receive Epaphroditus in the Lord

246

Rom 16:1-2 (§65)

16 I commend to you our sister Phoebe, a deaconess of the church at Cen'chre-ae, 2 that you may receive her in the Lord as befits the saints, and help her in whatever she may require from you, for she has been a helper of many and of myself as well.

1 Cor 16:10-12 (§140)

10 When Timothy comes, see that you put him at ease among you, for he is doing the work of the Lord, as I am. 11 So let no one despise him. Speed him on his way in peace, that he may return to me; for I am expecting him with the brethren.

12 As for our brother Apol'los, I strongly urged him to visit you with the other brethren, but it was not at all his will to come now. He will come when he has opportunity.

1 Cor 16:15-18 (§142)

15 Now, brethren, you know that the household of Steph'anas were the first converts in Acha'ia, and they have devoted themselves to the service of the saints; 16 I urge you to be subject to such men and to every fellow worker and laborer. 17 I rejoice at the coming of Steph'anas and Fortuna'tus and Acha'icus, because they have made up for your absence; 18 for they refreshed my spirit as well as yours. Give recognition to such men.

2 Cor 3:1-3 (§154)

3 Are we beginning to commend ourselves again? Or do we need, as some do, letters of recommendation to you, or from you? 2 You yourselves are our letter of recommendation, written on your hearts, to be known and read by all men; 3 and you show that you are a letter from Christ delivered by us, written not with ink but with the Spirit of the living God, not on tablets of stone but on tablets of human hearts.

2 Cor 8:16-24 (§173)

16 But thanks be to God who puts the same earnest care for you into the heart of Titus. 17 For he not only accepted our appeal, but being himself very earnest he is going to you of his own accord. 18 With him we are sending the brother who is famous among all the churches for his preaching of the gospel; 19 and not only that, but he has been appointed by the churches to travel with us in this gracious work which we are carrying on, for the glory of the Lord and to show our good will. 20 We intend that no one should blame us about this liberal gift which we are administering, 21 for we aim at what is honorable not only in the

Lord's sight but also in the sight of men. 22And with them we are sending our brother whom we have often tested and found earnest in many matters, but who is now more earnest than ever because of his great confidence in you. 23As for Titus, he is my partner and fellow worker in your service; and as for our brethren, they are messengers of the churches, the glory of Christ. 24 So give proof, before the churches, of your love and of our boasting about you to these men.

▶ 2:30 4:14-18
14 Yet it was kind of you to share my trouble. 15And you Philippians yourselves know that in the beginning of the gospel, when I left Macedo'nia, no church entered into partnership with me in giving and receiving except you only; 16 for even in Thessaloni'ca you sent me help once and again. 17 Not that I seek the gift; but I seek the fruit which increases to your credit. 18 I have received full payment, and more; I am filled, having received from Epaphrodi'tus the gifts you sent, a fragrant offering, a sacrifice acceptable and pleasing to God.

▶ 3:1 1 Thes 5:16
16 Rejoice always.

Phil 4:1
Therefore, my brethren, whom I love and long for, my joy and crown, stand firm thus in the Lord, my beloved.

Phil 2:19-24

19 I hope in the Lord Jesus to send Timothy to you soon, so that I may be cheered by news of you. 20 I have no one like him, who will be genuinely anxious for your welfare. 21 They all look after their own interests, not those of Jesus Christ. 22 But Timothy's worth you know, how as a son with a father he has served with me in the gospel. 23 I hope therefore to send him just as soon as I see how it will go with me; 24 and I trust in the Lord that shortly I myself shall come also.

Phm 8-14* (§307)

8 Accordingly, though I am bold enough in Christ to command you to do what is required, 9 yet for love's sake I prefer to appeal to you—I, Paul, an ambassador and now a prisoner also for Christ Jesus—10 I appeal to you for my child, Ones′imus, whose father I have become in my imprisonment. 11 (Formerly he was useless to you, but now he is indeed useful to you and to me.) 12 I am sending him back to you, sending my very heart. 13 I would have been glad to keep him with me, in order that he might serve me on your behalf during my imprisonment for the gospel; 14 but I preferred to do nothing without your consent in order that your goodness might not be by compulsion but of your own free will.

245

4:2-3

2 I entreat Eu-o′dia and I entreat Syn′tyche to agree in the Lord. 3And I ask you also, true yokefellow, help these women, for they have labored side by side with me in the gospel together with Clement and the rest of my fellow workers, whose names are in the book of life.

▶ 2:21 Gal 4:17,
17 They make much of you, but for no good purpose; they want to shut you out, that you may make much of them.

6:12-13
is those who want to make a good showing in the flesh that would compel you to be circumcised, and only in order that they may not be persecuted for the cross of Christ. 13 For even those who receive circumcision do not themselves keep the law, but they desire to have you circumcised that they may glory in your flesh.

12 It

▶ 2:24 1:27
27 Only let your manner of life be worthy of the gospel of Christ, so that whether I come and see you or am absent, I may hear of you that you stand firm in one spirit, with one mind striv-

ing side by side for the faith of the gospel,

246. Receive Epaphroditus in the Lord

Phil 2:25-3:1

25 I have thought it necessary to send to you Epaphrodi′tus my brother and fellow worker and fellow soldier, and your messenger and minister to my need, 26 for he has been longing for you all, and has been distressed because you heard that he was ill. 27 Indeed he was ill, near to death. But God had mercy on him, and not only on him but on me also, lest I should have sorrow upon sorrow. 28 I am the more eager to send him, therefore, that you may rejoice at seeing him again, and that I may be less anxious. 29 So receive him in the Lord with all joy; and honor such men, 30 for he nearly died for the work of Christ, risking his life to complete your service to me.

3 Finally, my brethren, rejoice in the Lord. To write the same things to you is not irksome to me, and is safe for you.

Phm 8-14 (§307)

8 Accordingly, though I am bold enough in Christ to command you to do what is required, 9 yet for love's sake I prefer to appeal to you—I, Paul, an ambassador and now a prisoner also for Christ Jesus—10 I appeal to you for my child, Ones′imus, whose father I have become in my imprisonment. 11 (Formerly he was useless to you, but now he is indeed useful to you and to me.) 12 I am sending him back to you, sending my very heart. 13 I would have been glad to keep him with me, in order that he might serve me on your behalf during my imprisonment for the gospel; 14 but I preferred to do nothing without your consent in order that your goodness might not be by compulsion but of your own free will.

246

247

Rom 2:17-24 (§10)

17 But if you call yourself a Jew and rely upon the law and boast of your relation to God 18 and know his will and approve what is excellent, because you are instructed in the law, 19 and if you are sure that you are a guide to the blind, a light to those who are in darkness, 20 a corrector of the foolish, a teacher of children, having in the law the embodiment of knowledge and truth— 21 you then who teach others, will you not teach yourself? While you preach against stealing, do you steal? 22 You who say that one must not commit adultery, do you commit adultery? You who abhor idols, do you rob temples? 23 You who boast in the law, do you dishonor God by breaking the law? 24 For, as it is written, "The name of God is blasphemed among the Gentiles because of you."

Rom 2:25-29 (§11)

25 Circumcision indeed is of value if you obey the law; but if you break the law, your circumcision becomes uncircumcision. 26 So, if a man who is uncircumcised keeps the precepts of the law, will not his uncircumcision be regarded as circumcision? 27 Then those who are physically uncircumcised but keep the law will condemn you who have the written code and circumcision but break the law. 28 For he is not a real Jew who is one outwardly, nor is true circumcision something external and physical. 29 He is a Jew who is one inwardly, and real circumcision is a

▶ 3:4-7 Acts 8:3,
3 But Saul was ravaging the church, and entering house after house, he dragged off men and women and committed them to prison.

*cf 22:3-21,

matter of the heart, spiritual and not literal. His praise is not from men but from God.

Rom 3:21-26 (§14)

21 But now the righteousness of God has been manifested apart from law, although the law and the prophets bear witness to it, 22 the righteousness of God through faith in Jesus Christ for all who believe. For there is no distinction; 23 since all have sinned and fall short of the glory of God, 24 they are justified by his grace as a gift, through the redemption which is in Christ Jesus, 25 whom God put forward as an expiation by his blood, to be received by faith. This was to show God's righteousness, because in his divine forbearance he had passed over former sins; 26 it was to prove at the present time that he himself is righteous and that he justifies him who has faith in Jesus.

Rom 3:27-31 (§15)

27 Then what becomes of our boasting? It is excluded. On what principle? On the principle of works? No, but on the principle of faith. 28 For we hold that a man is justified by faith apart from works of law. 29 Or is God the God of Jews only? Is he not the God of Gentiles also? Yes, of Gentiles also, 30 since God is one; and he will justify the circumcised on the ground of their faith and the uncircumcised through their faith. 31 Do we then overthrow the law by this faith? By no means! On the contrary, we uphold the law.

23:6
6 But when Paul perceived that one part were Sadducees and the other Pharisees, he cried out in the council, "Brethren, I am a Pharisee, a son of Pharisees; with respect to the hope and the resurrection of the dead I am on trial."

*cf Acts 26:4-23

▶ 3:2 Gal 5:11-12
11 But if I, brethren, still preach circumcision, why am I still persecuted? In that case the stumbling block of the cross has been removed. 12 I wish those who unsettle you would mutilate themselves!

2 Cor 3:4-6 (§155)

4 Such is the confidence that we have through Christ toward God. 5 Not that we are competent of ourselves to claim anything as coming from us; our competence is from God, 6 who has made us competent to be ministers of a new covenant, not in a written code but in the Spirit; for the written code kills, but the Spirit gives life.

2 Cor 11:21b-29 (§183)

But whatever any one dares to boast of—I am speaking as a fool—I also dare to boast of that. 22 Are they Hebrews? So am I. Are they Israelites? So am I. Are they descendants of Abraham? So am I. 23 Are they servants of Christ? I am a better one—I am talking like a madman—with far greater labors, far more

Rom 9:30-33 (§39)

30 What shall we say, then? That Gentiles who did not pursue righteousness have attained it, that is, righteousness through faith; 31 but that Israel who pursued the righteousness which is based on law did not succeed in fulfilling that law. 32 Why? Because they did not pursue it through faith, but as if it were based on works. They have stumbled over the stumbling stone, 33 as it is written,

"Behold, I am laying in Zion a stone
   that will make men stumble,
a rock that will make them fall;
and he who believes in him will not
   be put to shame."

▶ 3:10-11 Rom 6:3-5   3 Do you not know that all of us who have been baptized into Christ Jesus were baptized into his death? 4 We were buried therefore with him by baptism into death, so that as Christ was raised

Gal 1:13-14 (§195)   13 For you have heard of my former life in Judaism, how I persecuted the church of God violently and tried to destroy it; 14 and I advanced in Judaism beyond many of my own age among my people, so extremely zealous was I for the traditions of my fathers.

imprisonments, with countless beatings, and often near death. 24 Five times I have received at the hands of the Jews the forty lashes less one. 25 Three times I have been beaten with rods; once I was stoned. Three times I have been shipwrecked; a night and a day I have been adrift at sea; 26 on frequent journeys, in danger from rivers, danger from robbers, danger from my own people, danger from Gentiles, danger in the city, danger in the wilderness, danger at sea, danger from false brethren; 27 in toil and hardship, through many a sleepless night, in hunger and thirst, often without food, in cold and exposure. 28 And, apart from other things, there is the daily pressure upon me of my anxiety for all the churches. 29 Who is weak, and I am not weak? Who is made to fall, and I am not indignant?

Rom 10:1-4 (§40)

10

Brethren, my heart's desire and prayer to God for them is that they may be saved. 2 I bear them witness that they have a zeal for God, but it is not enlightened. 3 For, being igno-

from the dead by the glory of the Father, we too might walk in newness of life.
5 For if we have been united with him in a death like his, we shall certainly be united with him in a resurrection like his.

Gal 2:15-21 (§199) 15 We ourselves, who are Jews by birth and not Gentile sinners, 16 yet who know that a man is not justified by works of the law but through faith in Jesus Christ, even we have believed in Christ Jesus, in order to be justified by faith in Christ, and not by works of the law, because by works of the law shall no one be justified. 17 But if, in our endeavor to be justified in Christ, we ourselves were found to be sinners, is Christ then an agent of sin? Certainly not! 18 But if I build up again those things which I tore down, then I prove myself a transgressor. 19 For I through the law died to the law, that I might live to God. 20 I have been crucified with Christ; it is no longer I who live, but Christ who lives in me; and the life I now live in the flesh I live by faith in the Son of God, who loved me and gave himself for me. 21 I do not nullify the grace of God; for if justification were through the law, then Christ died to no purpose.

rant of the righteousness that comes from God, and seeking to establish their own, they did not submit to God's righteousness. 4 For Christ is the end of the law, that every one who has faith may be justified.

Rom 11:1-6 (§44)

11

I ask, then, has God rejected his people? By no means! I myself am an Israelite, a descendant of Abraham, a member of the tribe of

248

1 Cor 9:24-27 (§108)

24 Do you not know that in a race all the runners compete, but only one receives the prize? So run that you may obtain it. 25 Every athlete exercises self-control in all things. They do it to receive a perishable wreath, but we an imperishable. 26 Well, I do not run aimlessly, I do not box as one beating the air; 27 but I pommel my body and subdue it, lest after preaching to others I myself should be disqualified.

248. Prize of the upward call of God in Christ Jesus

Gal 1:15-24 (§196) 15 But when he who had set me apart before I was born, and had called me through his grace, 16 was pleased to reveal his Son to me, in order that I might preach him among the Gentiles, I did not confer with flesh and blood, 17 nor did I go up to Jerusalem to those who were apostles before me, but I went away into Arabia; and again I returned to Damascus.

18 Then after three years I went up to Jerusalem to visit Cephas, and remained with him fifteen days. 19 But I saw none of the other apostles except James the Lord's brother. 20 (In what I am writing to you, before God, I do not lie!) 21 Then I went into the regions of Syria and Cilicia. 22 And I was still not known by sight to the churches of Christ in Judea; 23 they only heard it

Eph 4:11-16 (§226) 11 And his gifts were that some should be apostles, some prophets, some evangelists, some pastors and teachers, 12 to equip the saints for the work of ministry, for building up the body of Christ, 13 until we all attain to the unity of the faith and of the knowledge of the Son of God, to mature manhood, to the measure of the stature of the fulness of Christ; 14 so that we may no longer be children, tossed to and fro and carried about with every wind of doctrine, by the cunning of men, by their craftiness in deceitful

said, "He who once persecuted us is now preaching the faith he once tried to destroy." 24 And they glorified God because of me.

▶ 3:12, 14 Heb 12:1-2
Therefore, since we are surrounded by so great a cloud of witnesses, let us also lay aside every weight, and sin which clings so closely, and let us run with perseverance the race that is set before us, 2 looking to Jesus the pioneer and perfecter of our faith, who for the joy that was set before

him endured the cross, despising the shame, and is seated at the right hand of the throne of God.

▶ 3:12 Acts 9:5-6   5 And he said, "Who are you, Lord?" And he said, "I am Jesus, whom you are persecuting; 6 but rise and enter the city, and you will be told what you are to do."

1 Tim 6:12,
12 Fight the good fight of the faith; take hold of the eternal life to which you were called when you made the good confession in the presence of many witnesses.

6:19   19 thus laying up for themselves a good foundation for the future, so that they may take hold of the life which is life indeed.

2 Tim 4:8   8 Henceforth there is laid up for me the crown of righteousness, which the Lord, the righteous judge, will award to me on that Day, and not only to me but also to all who have loved his appearing.

▶ 3:14 2 Tim 1:9,   9 who saved us and called us with a holy calling, not in virtue of our works but in virtue of his own purpose and the grace which he gave us in Christ Jesus ages ago,

247

Phil 3:2-11

2 Look out for the dogs, look out for the evil-workers, look out for those who mutilate the flesh. ³ For we are the true circumcision, who worship God in spirit, and glory in Christ Jesus, and put no confidence in the flesh. ⁴ Though I myself have reason for confidence in the flesh also. If any other man thinks he has reason for confidence in the flesh, I have more: ⁵ circumcised on the eighth day, of the people of Israel, of the tribe of Benjamin, a Hebrew born of Hebrews; as to the law a Pharisee, ⁶ as to zeal a persecutor of the church, as to righteousness under the law blameless. ⁷ But whatever gain I had, I counted as loss for the sake of Christ. ⁸ Indeed I count everything as loss because of the surpassing worth of knowing Christ

Jesus my Lord. For his sake I have suffered the loss of all things, and count them as refuse, in order that I may gain Christ ⁹ and be found in him, not having a righteousness of my own, based on law, but that which is through faith in Christ, the righteousness from God that depends on faith; ¹⁰ that I may know him and the power of his resurrection, and may share his sufferings, becoming like him in his death, ¹¹ that if possible I may attain the resurrection from the dead.

Rom (cont)

Benjamin. ² God has not rejected his people whom he foreknew. Do you not know what the scripture says of Elijah, how he pleads with God against Israel? ³ "Lord, they have killed thy prophets, they have demolished thy altars, and I alone am left, and they seek my life." ⁴ But what is God's reply to him? "I have kept for myself seven thousand men who have not bowed the knee to Ba'al." ⁵ So too at the present time there is a remnant, chosen by grace. ⁶ But if it is by grace, it is no longer on the basis of works; otherwise grace would no longer be grace.

▶3:3 (Spirit) *read* worship by the Spirit of God: S*AB CDᶜG Koine Lect cop Origen; *omit* God: p⁴⁶ *text:* SᶜD* it vg syr Origen

248. Prize of the upward call of God in Christ Jesus

248

Phil 3:12-16

12 Not that I have already obtained this or am already perfect; but I press on to make it my own, because Christ Jesus has made me his own. ¹³ Brethren, I do not consider that I have made it my own; but one thing I do, forgetting what lies behind and straining forward to what lies ahead, ¹⁴ I press on toward the goal for the prize of the upward call of God in Christ Jesus. ¹⁵ Let those of us

who are mature be thus minded; and if in anything you are otherwise minded, God will reveal that also to you. ¹⁶ Only let us hold true to what we have attained.

Eph (cont)

wiles. ¹⁵ Rather, speaking the truth in love, we are to grow up in every way into him who is the head, into Christ, ¹⁶ from whom the whole body, joined and knit together by every joint with which it is supplied, when each part is working properly, makes bodily growth and upbuilds itself in love.

4:7
⁷ I have fought the good fight, I have finished the race, I have kept the faith.

▶3:13-14 1 Cor 15:8-11
⁸ Last of all, as to one untimely born, he appeared also to me. ⁹ For I am the least of the apostles, unfit to be called an apostle, because I persecuted the church of God. ¹⁰ But by the grace of God I am what I am, and his grace toward me was not in vain. On the contrary, I worked harder than any of them, though it was not I, but the grace of God which is with me. ¹¹ Whether then it was I or they, so we preach and so you believed.

▶3:15 1 Cor 2:6
6 Yet among the mature we do impart wisdom, although it is not a wisdom of this age or of the rulers of this age, who are doomed to pass away.

Col 4:12
¹² Ep'aphras, who is one of yourselves, a servant of Christ Jesus, greets you, always remembering you earnestly in his prayers, that you may stand mature and fully assured in all the will of God.

1 Cor 14:20
20 Brethren, do not be children in your thinking; be babes in evil, but in thinking be mature.

249

Rom 9:1-5 (§35)

9 I am speaking the truth in Christ, I am not lying; my conscience bears me witness in the Holy Spirit, 2 that I have great sorrow and unceasing anguish in my heart. 3 For I could wish that I myself were accursed and cut off from Christ for the sake of my brethren, my kinsmen by race. 4 They are Israelites, and to them belong the sonship, the glory, the covenants, the giving of the law, the worship, and the promises; 5 to them belong the patriarchs, and of their race, according to the flesh, is the Christ. God who is over all be blessed for ever. Amen.

Rom 11:25-32 (§49)

25 Lest you be wise in your own conceits, I want you to understand this mystery, brethren: a hardening has come upon part of Israel, until the full number of the Gentiles come in, 26 and so all Israel will be saved; as it is written,

"The Deliverer will come from Zion,
   he will banish ungodliness from
   Jacob";

27 "and this will be my covenant with
   them
   when I take away their sins."

28 As regards the gospel they are enemies of God, for your sake; but as regards election they are beloved for the sake of their forefathers. 29 For the gifts and the call of God are irrevocable. 30 Just as you were once disobedient to God but now have received mercy because of their disobedience, 31 so they have now been disobedient in order that by the mercy shown to you they also may receive mercy. 32 For God has consigned all men to disobedience, that he may have mercy upon all.

Rom 16:17-20a (§67)

17 I appeal to you, brethren, to take

1 Cor 10:23-11:1 (§111)

23 "All things are lawful," but not all things are helpful. "All things are lawful," but not all things build up. 24 Let no one seek his own good, but the good of his neighbor. 25 Eat whatever is sold in the meat market without raising any question on the ground of conscience. 26 For "the earth is the Lord's, and everything in it." 27 If one of the unbelievers invites you to dinner and you are disposed to go, eat whatever is set before you without raising any question on the ground of conscience. 28 (But if some one says to you, "This has been offered in sacrifice," then out of consideration for the man who informed you, and for conscience' sake— 29 I mean his conscience, not yours—do not eat it.) For why should my liberty be determined by another man's scruples? 30 If I partake with thankfulness, why am I denounced because of that for which I give thanks?

31 So, whether you eat or drink, or whatever you do, do all to the glory of God. 32 Give no offense to Jews or to Greeks or to the church of God, 33 just as I try to please all men in everything I do, not seeking my own advantage, but that of many, that they may be

note of those who create dissensions and difficulties, in opposition to the doctrine which you have been taught; avoid them. 18 For such persons do not serve our Lord Christ, but their own appetites, and by fair and flattering words they deceive the hearts of the simple-minded. 19 For while your obedience is known to all, so that I rejoice over you, I would have you wise as to what is good and guileless as to what is evil; 20 then the God of peace will soon crush Satan under your feet.

2 Cor 4:13-15 (§160)

13 Since we have the same spirit of faith as he had who wrote, "I believed, and so I spoke," we too believe, and so we speak, 14 knowing that he who raised the Lord Jesus will raise us also with Jesus and bring us with you into his presence. 15 For it is all for your sake, so that as grace extends to more and more people it may increase thanksgiving, to the glory of God.

11 saved. 1 Be imitators of me, as I am of Christ.

1 Cor 15:20-28 (§133)

20 But in fact Christ has been raised from the dead, the first fruits of those who have fallen asleep. 21 For as by a man came death, by a man has come also the resurrection of the dead. 22 For as in Adam all die, so also in Christ shall all be made alive. 23 But each in his own order: Christ the first fruits, then at his coming those who belong to Christ. 24 Then comes the end, when he delivers the kingdom to God the Father after destroying every rule and every authority and power. 25 For he must reign until he has put all his enemies under his feet. 26 The last enemy to be destroyed is death. 27 "For God has put all things in subjection under his feet." But when it says, "All things are put in subjection under him," it is plain that he is excepted who put all things under him. 28 When all things are subjected to him, then the Son himself will also be subjected to him who put all things under him, that God may be everything to every one.

1 Cor 15:42-50 (§136)

42 So is it with the resurrection of the dead. What is sown is perishable, what is raised is imperishable. 43 It is sown in dishonor, it is raised in glory. It is

sown in weakness, it is raised in power. 44 It is sown a physical body, it is raised a spiritual body. If there is a physical body, there is also a spiritual body. 45 Thus it is written, "The first man Adam became a living being"; the last Adam became a life-giving spirit. 46 But it is not the spiritual which is first but the physical, and then the spiritual. 47 The first man was from the earth, a man of dust; the second man is from heaven. 48 As was the man of dust, so are those who are of the dust; and as is the man of heaven, so are those who are of heaven. 49 Just as we have borne the image of the man of dust, we shall also bear the image of the man of heaven. 50 I tell you this, brethren: flesh and blood cannot inherit the kingdom of God, nor does the perishable inherit the imperishable.

▶ 3:19 2 Tim 3:4
4 treacherous, reckless, swollen with conceit, lovers of pleasure rather than lovers of God,

Tit 1:12   12 One of themselves, a prophet of their own, said, "Cretans are always liars, evil beasts, lazy gluttons."

▶ 3:20 Tit 2:13   13 awaiting our blessed hope, the appearing of the glory of our great God and Savior Jesus Christ,

▶ 3:20-21 2 Cor 5:1-5
For we know that if the earthly tent we live in is destroyed, we have a building from God, a house not made with hands, eternal in the heavens. 2 Here indeed we groan, and long to put on our heavenly dwelling, 3 so that by

putting it on we may not be found naked. 4 For while we are still in this tent, we sigh with anxiety; not that we would be unclothed, but that we would be further clothed, so that what is mortal may be swallowed up by life. 5 He who has prepared us for this very

thing is God, who has given us the Spirit as a guarantee.

250. I entreat Euodia and Syntyche

250

▶ 4:3 Rev 3:5,   5 He who conquers shall be clad thus in white garments, and I will not blot his name out of the book of life; I will confess his name before my Father and before his angels.

20:15   15 and if any one's name was not found written in the book of life, he was thrown into the lake of fire.

▶ 4:1 Phil 1:8,   8 For God is my witness, how I yearn for you all with the affection of Christ Jesus.

2:26   26 for he has been longing for you all, and has been distressed because you heard that he was ill.

1 Cor 15:58   58 Therefore, my beloved brethren, be steadfast, immovable, always abounding in the work of the Lord, knowing that in the Lord your labor is not in vain.

Eph 6:13   13 Therefore take the whole armor of God, that you may be able to withstand in the evil day, and having done all, to stand.

Phil 3:17-21

17 Brethren, join in imitating me, and mark those who so live as you have an example in us. 18 For many, of whom I have often told you and now tell you even with tears, live as enemies of the cross of Christ. 19 Their end is destruction, their god is the belly, and they glory in their shame, with minds set on earthly things. 20 But our commonwealth is in heaven, and from it we await a Savior, the Lord Jesus Christ, 21 who will change our lowly body to be like his glorious body, by the power which enables him even to subject all things to himself.

1 Thes 1:2-10 (§276)

2 We give thanks to God always for you all, constantly mentioning you in our prayers, 3 remembering before our God and Father your work of faith and labor of love and steadfastness of hope in our Lord Jesus Christ. 4 For we know, brethren beloved by God, that he has chosen you; 5 for our gospel came to you not only in word, but also in power and in the Holy Spirit and with full conviction. You know what kind of men we proved to be among you for your sake. 6 And you became imitators of us and of the Lord, for you received the word in much affliction, with joy inspired by the Holy Spirit; 7 so that you became an example to all the believers in Macedo'nia and in Acha'ia. 8 For not only has the word of the Lord sounded forth from you in Macedo'nia and Acha'ia, but your faith in God has gone forth everywhere, so that we need not say anything. 9 For they themselves report concerning us what a welcome we had among you, and how you turned to God from idols, to serve a living and true God, 10 and to wait for his Son from heaven, whom he raised from the dead, Jesus who delivers us from the wrath to come.

1 Thes 4:13-18 (§286)

13 But we would not have you ignorant, brethren, concerning those who are asleep, that you may not grieve as others do who have no hope. 14 For since we believe that Jesus died and rose again, even so, through Jesus, God will bring with him those who have fallen asleep. 15 For this we declare to you by the word of the Lord, that we who are alive, who are left until the coming of the Lord, shall not precede those who have fallen asleep. 16 For the Lord himself will descend from heaven with a cry of command, with the archangel's call, and with the sound of the trumpet of God. And the dead in Christ will rise first; 17 then we who are alive, who are left, shall be caught up together with them in the clouds to meet the Lord in the air; and so we shall always be with the Lord. 18 Therefore comfort one another with these words.

2 Thes 3:6-13 (§300)

6 Now we command you, brethren, in the name of our Lord Jesus Christ, that you keep away from any brother who is living in idleness and not in accord with the tradition that you received from us. 7 For you yourselves know how you ought to imitate us; we were not idle when we were with you, 8 we did not eat any one's bread without paying, but with toil and labor we worked night and day, that we might not burden any of you. 9 It was not because we have not that right, but to give you in our conduct an example to imitate. 10 For even when we were with you, we gave you this command: If any one will not work, let him not eat. 11 For we hear that some of you are living in idleness, mere busybodies, not doing any work. 12 Now such persons we command and exhort in the Lord Jesus Christ to do their work in quietness and to earn their own living. 13 Brethren, do not be weary in well-doing.

2 Thes 2:1-12 (§296)

2 Now concerning the coming of our Lord Jesus Christ and our assembling to meet him, we beg you, brethren, 2 not to be quickly shaken in mind or excited, either by spirit or by word, or by letter purporting to be from us, to the effect that the day of the Lord has come. 3 Let no one deceive you in any way; for that day will not come, unless the rebellion comes first, and the man of lawlessness is revealed, the son of perdition, 4 who opposes and exalts himself against every so-called god or object of worship, so that he takes his seat in the temple of God, proclaiming himself to be God. 5 Do you not remember that when I was still with you I told you this? 6 And you know what is restraining him now so that he may be revealed in his time. 7 For the mystery of lawlessness is already at work; only he who now restrains it will do so until he is out of the way. 8 And then the lawless one will be revealed, and the Lord Jesus will slay him with the breath of his mouth and destroy him by his appearing and his coming. 9 The coming of the lawless one by the activity of Satan will be with all power and with pretended signs and wonders, 10 and with all wicked deception for those who are to perish, because they refused to love the truth and so be saved. 11 Therefore God sends upon them a strong delusion, to make them believe what is false, 12 so that all may be condemned who did not believe the truth but had pleasure in unrighteousness.

*cf 2 Thes 1:3-12 (§295)

249

Col 3:1-4,

If then you have been raised with Christ, seek the things that are above, where Christ is, seated at the right hand of God. 2 Set your minds on things that are above, not on things that are on earth. 3 For you have died, and your life is hid with Christ in God.

4 When Christ who is our life appears, then you also will appear with him in glory.

1:5

5 because of the hope laid up for you in heaven. Of this you have heard before in the word of the truth, the gospel

Eph 2:6

6 and raised us up with him, and made us sit with him in the heavenly places in Christ Jesus,

▶ 3:20 Eph 2:12

12 remember that you were at that time separated from Christ, alienated from the commonwealth of Israel, and strangers to the covenants of promise, having no hope and without God in the world.

Phil 4:1-3

4 Therefore, my brethren, whom I love and long for, my joy and crown, stand firm thus in the Lord, my beloved.
2 I entreat Eu-o'dia and I entreat Syn'tyche to agree in the Lord. 3 And I ask you also, true yokefellow, help these women, for they have labored side by side with me in the gospel together with Clement and the rest of my fellow workers, whose names are in the book of life.

Col 4:12

12 Ep'aphras, who is one of yourselves, a servant of Christ Jesus, greets you, always remembering you earnestly in his prayers, that you may stand mature and fully assured in all the will of God.

1 Thes 3:8

8 for now we live, if you stand fast in the Lord.

▶ 4:2 2:2

2 complete my joy by being of the same mind, having the same love, being in full accord and of one mind.

250. I entreat Euodia and Syntyche

1 Thes 2:17-20 (§280)

17 But since we were bereft of you, brethren, for a short time, in person not in heart, we endeavored the more eagerly and with great desire to see you face to face; 18 because we wanted to come to you—I, Paul, again and again—but Satan hindered us. 19 For what is our hope or joy or crown of boasting before our Lord Jesus at his coming? Is it not you? 20 For you are our glory and joy.

250

251

Rom 12:9-21 (§53)

9 Let love be genuine; hate what is evil, hold fast to what is good; 10 love one another with brotherly affection; outdo one another in showing honor. 11 Never flag in zeal, be aglow with the Spirit, serve the Lord. 12 Rejoice in your hope, be patient in tribulation, be constant in prayer. 13 Contribute to the needs of the saints, practice hospitality.

14 Bless those who persecute you; bless and do not curse them. 15 Rejoice with those who rejoice, weep with those who weep. 16 Live in harmony with one another; do not be haughty, but associate with the lowly; never be conceited. 17 Repay no one evil for evil, but take thought for what is noble in the sight of all. 18 If possible, so far as it depends upon you, live peaceably with all. 19 Beloved, never avenge yourselves, but leave it to the wrath of God; for it is written, "Vengeance is mine, I will repay, says the Lord." 20 No, "if your enemy is hungry, feed him; if he is thirsty, give him drink; for by so doing you will heap burning coals upon his head." 21 Do not be overcome by evil, but overcome evil with good.

▶ 4:6 1 Tim 2:1,
First of all, then, I urge that supplications, prayers, intercessions, and thanksgivings be made for all men,

1 Cor 7:32-35 (§99)

32 I want you to be free from anxieties. The unmarried man is anxious about the affairs of the Lord, how to please the Lord; 33 but the married man is anxious about worldly affairs, how to please his wife, 34 and his interests are divided. And the unmarried woman or girl is anxious about the affairs of the Lord, how to be holy in body and spirit; but the married woman is anxious about worldly affairs, how to please her husband. 35 I say this for your own benefit, not to lay any restraint upon you, but to promote good order and to secure your undivided devotion to the Lord.

1 Cor 13:4-7 (§122)

4 Love is patient and kind; love is not jealous or boastful; 5 it is not arrogant or rude. Love does not insist on its own way; it is not irritable or resentful; 6 it does not rejoice at wrong, but rejoices in the right. 7 Love bears all things, believes all things, hopes all things, endures all things.

5:5
5 She who is a real widow, and is left all alone, has set her hope on God and continues in supplications and prayers night and day;

2 Cor 13:11-13 (§191)

11 Finally, brethren, farewell. Mend your ways, heed my appeal, agree with one another, live in peace, and the God of love and peace will be with you. 12 Greet one another with a holy kiss. 13 All the saints greet you.

▶ 4:4-7 2:1-5
So if there is any encouragement in Christ, any incentive of love, any participation in the Spirit, any affection and sympathy, 2 complete my joy by being of the same mind, having the same love, being in full accord and of one mind. 3 Do nothing from selfishness or conceit, but in humility count others better than yourselves. 4 Let each of you look not only to his own interests, but also to the interests of others. 5 Have this mind among yourselves, which is yours in Christ Jesus,

▶ 4:4 2:18,
18 Likewise you also should be glad and rejoice with me.

1 Thes 5:16   16 Rejoice always,

Eph 4:25-32 (§228)

25 Therefore, putting away falsehood, let every one speak the truth with his neighbor, for we are members one of another. 26 Be angry but do not sin; do not let the sun go down on your anger, 27 and give no opportunity to the devil. 28 Let the thief no longer steal, but rather let him labor, doing honest work with his hands, so that he may be able to give to those in need. 29 Let no evil talk come out of your mouths, but only such as is good for edifying, as fits the occasion, that it may impart grace to those who hear. 30 And do not grieve the Holy Spirit of God, in whom you were sealed for the day of redemption. 31 Let all bitterness and wrath and anger and clamor and slander be put away from you, with all malice, 32 and be kind to one another, tenderhearted, forgiving one another, as God in Christ forgave you.

3:1 Finally, my brethren, rejoice in the Lord. To write the same things to you is not irksome to me, and is safe for you.

252. What you have learned and received and seen in me, do

252

Rom 10:14-17 (§42)

14 But how are men to call upon him in whom they have not believed? And how are they to believe in him of whom they have never heard? And how are they to hear without a preacher? 15 And how can men preach unless they are sent? As it is written, "How beautiful are the feet of those who preach good news!" 16 But they have not all obeyed the gospel; for Isaiah says, "Lord, who has believed what he has heard from us?" 17 So faith comes from what is heard, and what is heard comes by the preaching of Christ.

▶ 4:8 1:10,
that you may approve what is excellent, and may be pure and blameless for the day of Christ,

1 Cor 11:2-16 (§112)

2 I commend you because you remember me in everything and maintain the traditions even as I have delivered them to you. 3 But I want you to understand that the head of every man is Christ, the head of a woman is her husband, and the head of Christ is God. 4 Any man who prays or prophesies with his head covered dishonors his head, 5 but any woman who prays or prophesies with her head unveiled dishonors her head—it is the same as if her head were shaven. 6 For if a woman will not veil herself, then she should cut off her hair; but if it is disgraceful for a woman to be shorn or shaven, let her wear a veil. 7 For a man ought not to cover his head, since he is the image and glory of God; but woman is the glory of man. 8 (For man was not made from woman, but woman from man. 9 Neither was man created for woman, but woman for man.) 10 That is why a woman ought to have a veil on her head, because of the angels. 11 (Nevertheless, in the Lord woman is not independent of man nor man of woman; 12 for as woman was made from man, so man is now born of woman. And all things are from God.) 13 Judge for yourselves; is it proper for a woman to pray to God with her head uncovered? 14 Does not nature itself teach you that for a man to wear long hair is degrading to him, 15 but if a

10 so

3:1 Finally, my brethren, rejoice in the Lord. To write the same things to you is not irksome to me, and is safe for you.

2 Cor 6:1-10 (§165)

6 Working together with him, then, we entreat you not to accept the grace of God in vain. 2 For he says,
"At the acceptable time I have listened to you,
and helped you on the day of salvation."
Behold, now is the acceptable time; behold, now is the day of salvation. 3 We put no obstacle in any one's way, so that no fault may be found with our ministry, 4 but as servants of God we commend ourselves in every way: through great endurance, in afflictions, hardships, calamities, 5 beatings, imprisonments, tumults, labors, watching, hunger; 6 by purity, knowledge, forbearance, kindness, the Holy Spirit, genuine love, 7 truthful speech, and the power of God; with the weapons of righteousness for the right hand and for the left; 8 in honor and dishonor, in ill repute and good repute. We are treated as impostors, and yet are true; 9 as unknown, and yet well known; as dying,

woman has long hair, it is her pride? For her hair is given to her for a covering. 16 If any one is disposed to be contentious, we recognize no other practice, nor do the churches of God.

▶ 4:9 1 Cor 4:16,
16 I urge you, then, be imitators of me.

14:33   33 For God is not a God of confusion but of peace.

Gal 5:16-26 (§213)

16 But I say, walk by the Spirit, and do not gratify the desires of the flesh. 17 For the desires of the flesh are against the Spirit, and the desires of the Spirit are against the flesh; for these are opposed to each other, to prevent you from doing what you would. 18 But if you are led by the Spirit you are not under the law. 19 Now the works of the flesh are plain: fornication, impurity, licentiousness, 20 idolatry, sorcery, enmity, strife, jealousy, anger, selfishness, dissension, party spirit, 21 envy, drunkenness, carousing, and the like. I warn you, as I warned you before, that those who do such things shall not inherit the kingdom of God. 22 But the fruit of the Spirit is love, joy, peace, patience, kindness, goodness, faithfulness, 23 gentleness, self-control; against such there is no law. 24 And those who belong to Christ Jesus have crucified the flesh with its passions and desires.

25 If we live by the Spirit, let us also walk by the Spirit. 26 Let us have no self-conceit, no provoking of one another, no envy of one another.

7:15,
15 But if the unbelieving partner desires to separate, let it be so; in such a case the brother or sister is not bound. For God has called us to peace.

Eph 4:1-10 (§225)

4 I therefore, a prisoner for the Lord, beg you to lead a life worthy of the calling to which you have been called, 2 with all lowliness and meekness, with patience, forbearing one another in love, 3 eager to maintain the unity of the Spirit in the bond of peace. 4 There is one body and one Spirit, just

and behold we live; as punished, and yet not killed; 10 as sorrowful, yet always rejoicing; as poor, yet making many rich; as having nothing, and yet possessing everything.

2 Cor 8:1-7 (§171)

8 We want you to know, brethren, about the grace of God which has

11:1   1 Be imitators of me, as I am of Christ.

Phil 4:4-7

4 Rejoice in the Lord always; again I will say, Rejoice. 5 Let all men know your forbearance. The Lord is at hand. 6 Have no anxiety about anything, but in everything by prayer and supplication with thanksgiving let your requests be made known to God. 7 And the peace of God, which passes all understanding, will keep your hearts and your minds in Christ Jesus.

1 Thes 5:12-22 (§288)

12 Put on then, as God's chosen ones, holy and beloved, compassion, kindness, lowliness, meekness, and patience, 13 forbearing one another and, if one has a complaint against another, forgiving each other; as the Lord has forgiven you, so you also must forgive. 14 And above all these put on love, which binds everything together in perfect harmony. 15 And let the peace of Christ rule in your hearts, to which indeed you were called in the one body. And be thankful. 16 Let the word of Christ dwell in you richly, teach and admonish one another in all wisdom, and sing psalms and hymns and spiritual songs with thankfulness in your hearts to God. 17 And whatever you do, in word or deed, do everything in the name of the Lord Jesus, giving thanks to God the Father through him.

4:7 Col 3:15-16

15 And let the peace of Christ rule in your hearts, to which indeed you were called in the one body. And be thankful. 16 Let the word of Christ dwell in you richly, teach and admonish one another in all wisdom, and sing psalms and hymns and spiritual songs with thankfulness in your hearts to God.

252. What you have learned and received and seen in me, do

252

Phil 4:8-9

8 Finally, brethren, whatever is true, whatever is honorable, whatever is just, whatever is pure, whatever is lovely, whatever is gracious, if there is any excellence, if there is anything worthy of praise, think about these things. 9 What you have learned and received and heard and seen in me, do; and the God of peace will be with you.

Col 3:12-17 (§267)

12 But we beseech you, brethren, to respect those who labor among you and are over you in the Lord and admonish you, 13 and to esteem them very highly in love because of their work. Be at peace among yourselves. 14 And we exhort you, brethren, admonish the idlers, encourage the fainthearted, help the weak, be patient with them all. 15 See that none of you repays evil for evil, but always seek to do good to one another and to all. 16 Rejoice always, 17 pray constantly, 18 give thanks in all circumstances; for this is the will of God in Christ Jesus for you. 19 Do not quench the Spirit, 20 do not despise prophesying, 21 but test everything; hold fast what is good, 22 abstain from every form of evil.

Eph (cont)

as you were called to the one hope that belongs to your call, 5 one Lord, one faith, one baptism, 6 one God and Father of us all, who is above all and through all and in all. 7 But grace was given to each of us according to the measure of Christ's gift. 8 Therefore it is said,

"When he ascended on high he led a host of captives, and he gave gifts to men."

9 (In saying, "He ascended," what does it mean but that he had also descended into the lower parts of the earth? 10 He who descended is he who also ascended far above all the heavens, that he might fill all things.)

2 Cor (cont)

been shown in the churches of Macedo'nia, 2 for in a severe test of affliction, their abundance of joy and their extreme poverty have overflowed in a wealth of liberality on their part. 3 For they gave according to their means, as I can testify, and beyond their means, of their own free will, 4 begging us earnestly for the favor of taking part in the relief of the saints— 5 and this, not as we expected, but first they gave themselves to the Lord and to us by the will of God.

6 Accordingly we have urged Titus that as he had already made a beginning, he should also complete among you this gracious work. 7 Now as you excel in everything—in faith, in utterance, in knowledge, in all earnestness, and in your love for us—see that you excel in this gracious work also.

Eph 5:1

Therefore be imitators of God, as beloved children.

2 Thes 3:7,

7 For you yourselves know how you ought to imitate us; we were not idle when we were with you,

9,

9 It was not because we have not that right, but to give you in our conduct an example to imitate.

16

16 Now may the Lord of peace himself give you peace at all times in all ways. The Lord be with you all.

Rom 15:33

33 The God of peace be with you all. Amen.

1 Thes 5:23

23 May the God of peace himself sanctify you wholly; and may your spirit and soul and body be kept sound and blameless at the coming of our Lord Jesus Christ.

2 Cor 13:11

11 Finally, brethren, farewell. Mend your ways, heed my appeal, agree with one another, live in peace, and the God of love and peace will be with you.

253

Rom 12:1-2 (§51)

12 I appeal to you therefore, brethren, by the mercies of God, to present your bodies as a living sacrifice, holy and acceptable to God, which is your spiritual worship. 2 Do not be conformed to this world but be transformed by the renewal of your mind, that you may prove what is the will of God, what is good and acceptable and perfect.

1 Cor 9:1-14 (§105)

9 Am I not free? Am I not an apostle? Have I not seen Jesus our Lord? Are not you my workmanship in the Lord? 2 If to others I am not an apostle, at least I am to you; for you are the seal of my apostleship in the Lord. 3 This is my defense to those who would examine me. 4 Do we not have the right to our food and drink? 5 Do we not have the right to be accompanied by a wife, as the other apostles and the brothers of the Lord and Cephas? 6 Or is it only Barnabas and I who have no right to refrain from working for a living? 7 Who serves as a soldier at his own expense? Who plants a vineyard without eating any of its fruit? Who tends a flock without getting some of the milk? 8 Do I say this on human authority? Does not the law say the same? 9 For it is written in the law of Moses, "You shall not muzzle an ox when it is treading out the grain." Is it for oxen that God is concerned? 10 Does he not speak entirely for our sake? It was written for our sake, because the plowman should plow in hope and the thresher thresh in hope of a share in the crop. 11 If we have sown spiritual good among you, is it too much if we reap your material benefits? 12 If others share this rightful claim upon you, do not we still more? Nevertheless, we have not made use of this right, but we endure anything rather than put an obstacle in the way of

2 Cor 2:14-17 (§153)

14 But thanks be to God, who in Christ always leads us in triumph, and through us spreads the fragrance of the knowledge of him everywhere. 15 For we are the aroma of Christ to God among those who are being saved and among those who are perishing, 16 to one a fragrance from death to death, to the other a fragrance from life to life. Who is sufficient for these things? 17 For we are not, like so many, peddlers of God's word; but as men of sincerity, as commissioned by God, in the sight of God we speak in Christ.

2 Cor 6:1-10 (§165)

6 Working together with him, then, we entreat you not to accept the grace of God in vain. 2 For he says,
"At the acceptable time I have listened to you,
and helped you on the day of salvation."
Behold, now is the acceptable time; behold, now is the day of salvation. 3 We put no obstacle in any one's way, so that no fault may be found with our ministry, 4 but as servants of God we

the gospel of Christ. 13 Do you not know that those who are employed in the temple service get their food from the temple, and those who serve at the altar share in the sacrificial offerings? 14 In the same way, the Lord commanded that those who proclaim the gospel should get their living by the gospel.

commend ourselves in every way: through great endurance, in afflictions, hardships, calamities, 5 beatings, imprisonments, tumults, labors, watching, hunger; 6 by purity, knowledge, forbearance, kindness, the Holy Spirit, genuine love, 7 truthful speech, and the power of God; with the weapons of righteousness for the right hand and for the left; 8 in honor and dishonor, in ill repute and good repute. We are treated as impostors, and yet are true; 9 as unknown, and yet well known; as dying, and behold we live; as punished, and yet not killed; 10 as sorrowful, yet always rejoicing; as poor, yet making many rich; as having nothing, and yet possessing everything.

2 Cor 7:2-4 (§168)

2 Open your hearts to us; we have wronged no one, we have corrupted no one, we have taken advantage of no one. 3 I do not say this to condemn you, for I said before that you are in our hearts, to die together and to live together. 4 I have great confidence in you; I have great pride in you; I am filled with comfort. With all our affliction, I am overjoyed.

2 Cor 11:7-11 (§180)

7 Did I commit a sin in abasing myself so that you might be exalted, because I preached God's gospel without cost to you? 8 I robbed other churches by accepting support from them in order to serve you. 9 And when I was with you and was in want, I did not

Eph 5:1-2 (§229)

5 Therefore be imitators of God, as beloved children. 2 And walk in love, as Christ loved us and gave himself up for us, a fragrant offering and sacrifice to God.

burden any one, for my needs were supplied by the brethren who came from Macedo'nia. So I refrained and will refrain from burdening you in any way. 10 As the truth of Christ is in me, this boast of mine shall not be silenced in the regions of Acha'ia. 11 And why? Because I do not love you? God knows I do!

2 Cor 12:1-10 (§185)

12 I must boast; there is nothing to be gained by it, but I will go on to visions and revelations of the Lord. 2 I know a man in Christ who fourteen years ago was caught up to the third heaven—whether in the body or out of the body I do not know, God knows. 3 And I know that this man was caught up into Paradise—whether in the body or out of the body I do not know, God knows—4 and he heard things that cannot be told, which man may not utter. 5 On behalf of this man I will boast, but on my own behalf I will not boast, except of my weaknesses. 6 Though if I wish to boast, I shall not be a fool, for I shall be speaking the truth. But I refrain from it, so that no one may think more of me than he sees in me or hears from me. 7 And to keep me from being too elated by the abundance of revela-

▶4:10 2 Jn 4,

4 I rejoiced greatly to find some of your children following the truth, just as we have been commanded by the Father.

3 Jn 3

3 For I greatly rejoiced when some of the brethren arrived and testified to the truth of your life, as indeed you do follow the truth.

▶4:11 1 Tim 6:6-8

6 There is great gain in godliness with contentment; 7 for we brought nothing into the world, and we cannot take anything out of the world; 8 but if we have food and clothing, with these we shall be content.

▶4:13 2 Tim 4:17

17 But the Lord stood by me and gave me strength to proclaim the message fully, that all the Gentiles might hear it. So I was rescued from the lion's mouth.

▶4:16 Acts 17:1-9

Now when they had passed through Amphip'olis and Apollo'nia, they came to Thessaloni'ca, where there was a synagogue of the Jews. 2 And Paul went in, as was his

custom, and for three weeks he argued with them from the scriptures, 3 explaining and proving that it was necessary for the Christ to suffer and to rise from the dead, and saying, "This Jesus, whom I proclaim to you, is the Christ." 4 And some of them were persuaded, and

254. Greetings

254

Rom 16:3-16 (§66)

3 Greet Prisca and Aquila, my fellow workers in Christ Jesus, 4 who risked their necks for my life, to whom not only I but also all the churches of the Gentiles give thanks; 5 greet also the church in their house. Greet my beloved Epae'netus, who was the first convert in Asia for Christ. 6 Greet Mary, who has worked hard among you. 7 Greet Androni'cus and Ju'nias, my kinsmen and my fellow prisoners; they are men of note among the apostles, and they were in Christ before me. 8 Greet Amplia'tus, my beloved in the Lord. 9 Greet Urba'nus, our fellow worker in Christ, and my beloved Stachys. 10 Greet Apel'les, who is approved in Christ. Greet those who belong to the family of Aristobu'lus. 11 Greet my

1 Cor 16:19-20 (§143)

19 The churches of Asia send greetings. Aquila and Prisca, together with the church in their house, send you hearty greetings in the Lord. 20 All the brethren send greetings. Greet one another with a holy kiss.

kinsman Hero'dion. Greet those in the Lord who belong to the family of Narcis'sus. 12 Greet those workers in the Lord, Tryphae'na and Trypho'sa. Greet the beloved Persis, who has worked hard in the Lord. 13 Greet Rufus, eminent in the Lord, also his mother and mine. 14 Greet Asyn'critus, Phlegon, Hermes, Pat'robas, Hermas, and the brethren who are with them. 15 Greet Philol'ogus, Julia, Nereus and his sister, and Olym'pas, and all the

2 Cor 13:11-13 (§191)

11 Finally, brethren, farewell. Mend your ways, heed my appeal, agree with one another, live in peace, and the God of love and peace will be with you. 12 Greet one another with a holy kiss. 13 All the saints greet you.

saints who are with them. 16 Greet one another with a holy kiss. All the churches of Christ greet you.

Rom 16:21-23 (§69)

21 Timothy, my fellow worker, greets you; so do Lucius and Jason and Sosip'ater, my kinsmen. 22 I Tertius, the writer of this letter, greet you in the Lord. 23 Ga'ius, who is host to me and to the whole church, greets you. Eras'tus, the city treasurer, and our brother Quartus, greet you.

▶4:22 1:13   13 so that
it has become known throughout the whole praetorian guard and to all the rest that my imprisonment is for Christ;

*cf 2 Tim 4:19-21, Tit 3:15

Phil 4:10-20

10 I rejoice in the Lord greatly that now at length you have revived your concern for me; you were indeed concerned for me, but you had no opportunity. 11 Not that I complain of want; for I have learned, in whatever state I am, to be content. 12 I know how to be abased, and I know how to abound; in any and all circumstances I have learned the secret of facing plenty and hunger, abundance and want. 13 I can do all things in him who strengthens me.

14 Yet it was kind of you to share my trouble. 15And you Philippians yourselves know that in the beginning of the gospel, when I left Macedo′nia, no church entered into partnership with me in giving and receiving except you only; 16 for even in Thessaloni′ca you sent me help once and again. 17 Not that I seek the gift; but I seek the fruit which increases to your credit. 18 I have received full payment, and more; I am filled, having received from Epaphrodi′tus the gifts you sent, a fragrant offering, a sacrifice acceptable and pleasing to God. 19And my God will supply every need of yours according to his riches in glory in Christ Jesus. 20 To our God and Father be glory for ever and ever. Amen.

2 Cor (cont)

tions, a thorn was given me in the flesh, a messenger of Satan, to harass me, to keep me from being too elated. 8 Three times I besought the Lord about this, that it should leave me; 9 but he said to me, "My grace is sufficient for you, for my power is made perfect in weakness." I will all the more gladly boast of my weaknesses, that the power of Christ may rest upon me. 10 For the sake of Christ, then, I am content with weaknesses, insults, hardships, persecutions, and calamities; for when I am weak, then I am strong.

joined Paul and Silas; as did a great many of the devout Greeks and not a few of the leading women. 5 But the Jews were jealous, and taking some wicked fellows of the rabble, they gathered a crowd, set the city in an uproar, and attacked the house of Jason, seeking to bring them out to the people. 6And when they could not find them, they dragged Jason and some of the brethren before the city authorities, crying, "These men who have turned the world upside down have come here also, 7 and Jason has received them; and they are all acting against the decrees of Caesar, saying that there is another king, Jesus." 8And the people and the city authorities were disturbed when they heard this. 9And when they had taken security from Jason and the rest, they let them go.

▶ **4:12 Eph 4:2**
2 with all lowliness and meekness, with patience, forbearing one another in love,

▶ **4:15-16 1:5**
5 thankful for your partnership in the gospel from the first day until now.

▶ **4:19 Col 1:27**   27 To them God chose to make known how great among the Gentiles are the riches of the glory of this mystery, which is Christ in you, the hope of glory.

▶ **4:10 1 Cor 1:12**   12 What I mean is that each one of you says, "I belong to Paul," or "I belong to Apol′los," or "I belong to Cephas," or "I belong to Christ."

▶ **4:14-18 2:30**   30 for he nearly died for the work of Christ, risking his life to complete your service to me.

Rom 9:23   23 in order to make known the riches of his glory for the vessels of mercy, which he has prepared beforehand for glory,

Phm 13   13 I would have been glad to keep him with me, in order that he might serve me on your behalf during my imprisonment for the gospel;

Eph 3:16
16 that according to the riches of his glory he may grant you to be strengthened with might through his Spirit in the inner man,

254. Greetings

Phil 4:21-22

21 Greet every saint in Christ Jesus. The brethren who are with me greet you. 22All the saints greet you, especially those of Caesar's household.

Col 4:10-15 (§272)

10 Aristar′chus my fellow prisoner greets you, and Mark the cousin of Barnabas (concerning whom you have received instructions—if he comes to you, receive him), 11 and Jesus who is called Justus. These are the only men of the circumcision among my fellow workers for the kingdom of God, and they have been a comfort to me. 12 Ep′aphras, who is one of yourselves, a servant of Christ Jesus, greets you, always remembering you earnestly in his prayers, that you may stand mature and fully assured in all the will of God. 13 For I bear him witness that he has worked hard for you and for those in La-odice′a and in Hi-erap′olis. 14 Luke the beloved physician and Demas greet you. 15 Give my greetings to the brethren at La-odice′a, and to Nympha and the church in her house.

1 Thes 5:26 (§291)

26 Greet all the brethren with a holy kiss.

Phm 23-24 (§310)

23 Ep′aphras, my fellow prisoner in Christ Jesus, sends greetings to you, 24 and so do Mark, Aristar′chus, Demas, and Luke, my fellow workers.

255

Rom 16:20b (§68)

The grace of our Lord Jesus Christ be with you.

1 Cor 16:23-24 (§145)

23 The grace of the Lord Jesus be with you. 24 My love be with you all in Christ Jesus. Amen.

2 Cor 13:14 (§192)

14 The grace of the Lord Jesus Christ and the love of God and the fellowship of the Holy Spirit be with you all.

Gal 6:18 (§217)

18 The grace of our Lord Jesus Christ be with your spirit, brethren. Amen.

Eph 6:23-24 (§236)

23 Peace be to the brethren, and love with faith, from God the Father and the Lord Jesus Christ. 24 Grace be with all who love our Lord Jesus Christ with love undying.

▶4:23 2 Tim 4:22

22 The Lord be with your spirit. Grace be with you.

Phil 4:23

23 The grace of the Lord Jesus Christ be with your spirit.

Col 4:18b (§274)

Grace be with you.

1 Thes 5:28 (§293)

28 The grace of our Lord Jesus Christ be with you.

2 Thes 3:18 (§304)

18 The grace of our Lord Jesus Christ be with you all.

Phm 25 (§311)

25 The grace of the Lord Jesus Christ be with your spirit.

255

256

Rom 1:1-7 (§1)

1 Paul, a servant of Jesus Christ, called to be an apostle, set apart for the gospel of God [2] which he promised beforehand through his prophets in the holy scriptures, [3] the gospel concerning his Son, who was descended from David according to the flesh [4] and designated Son of God in power according to the Spirit of holiness by his resurrection from the dead, Jesus Christ our Lord, [5] through whom we have received grace and apostleship to bring about the obedience of faith for the sake of his name among all the nations, [6] including yourselves who are called to belong to Jesus Christ;

[7] To all God's beloved in Rome, who are called to be saints:

Grace to you and peace from God our Father and the Lord Jesus Christ.

1 Cor 1:1-3 (§71)

1 Paul, called by the will of God to be an apostle of Christ Jesus, and our brother Sos'thenes,

[2] To the church of God which is at Corinth, to those sanctified in Christ Jesus, called to be saints together with all those who in every place call on the name of our Lord Jesus Christ, both their Lord and ours:

[3] Grace to you and peace from God our Father and the Lord Jesus Christ.

2 Cor 1:1-2 (§146)

1 Paul, an apostle of Christ Jesus by the will of God, and Timothy our brother.

To the church of God which is at Corinth, with all the saints who are in the whole of Acha'ia:

[2] Grace to you and peace from God our Father and the Lord Jesus Christ.

Gal 1:1-5 (§193)

1 Paul an apostle—not from men nor through man, but through Jesus Christ and God the Father, who raised him from the dead— [2] and all the brethren who are with me,

To the churches of Galatia:

[3] Grace to you and peace from God the Father and our Lord Jesus Christ, [4] who gave himself for our sins to deliver us from the present evil age, according to the will of our God and Father; [5] to whom be the glory for ever and ever. Amen.

Eph 1:1-2 (§218)

1 Paul, an apostle of Christ Jesus by the will of God,

To the saints who are also faithful in Christ Jesus:

[2] Grace to you and peace from God our Father and the Lord Jesus Christ.

▶ 1:1-2 *cf 1 Tim 1:1-2, 2 Tim 1:1-2, Tit 1:1-4, Acts 16:1-5

Phil 1:1-2 (§237)

1 Paul and Timothy, servants of Christ Jesus,

To all the saints in Christ Jesus who are at Philippi, with the bishops and deacons:

2 Grace to you and peace from God our Father and the Lord Jesus Christ.

Col 1:1-2

1 Paul, an apostle of Christ Jesus by the will of God, and Timothy our brother,

2 To the saints and faithful brethren in Christ at Colos'sae:

Grace to you and peace from God our Father.

1 Thes 1:1 (§275)

1 Paul, Silva'nus, and Timothy,

To the church of the Thessalo'nians in God the Father and the Lord Jesus Christ:

Grace to you and peace.

2 Thes 1:1-2 (§294)

1 Paul, Silva'nus, and Timothy,

To the church of the Thessalo'nians in God our Father and the Lord Jesus Christ:

2 Grace to you and peace from God the Father and the Lord Jesus Christ.

Phm 1-3 (§305)

1 Paul, a prisoner for Christ Jesus, and Timothy our brother,

To Phile'mon our beloved fellow worker 2 and Ap'phia our sister and Archip'pus our fellow soldier, and the church in your house:

3 Grace to you and peace from God our Father and the Lord Jesus Christ.

256

Rom 1:8-15 (§2)

8 First, I thank my God through Jesus Christ for all of you, because your faith is proclaimed in all the world. 9 For God is my witness, whom I serve with my spirit in the gospel of his Son, that without ceasing I mention you always in my prayers, 10 asking that somehow by God's will I may now at last succeed in coming to you. 11 For I long to see you, that I may impart to you some spiritual gift to strengthen you, 12 that is, that we may be mutually encouraged by each other's faith, both yours and mine. 13 I want you to know, brethren, that I have often intended to come to you (but thus far have been prevented), in order that I may reap some harvest among you as well as among the rest of the Gentiles. 14 I am under obligation both to Greeks and to barbarians, both to the wise and to the foolish: 15 so I am eager to preach the gospel to you also who are in Rome.

1 Cor 1:4-9 (§72)

4 I give thanks to God always for you because of the grace of God which was given you in Christ Jesus, 5 that in every way you were enriched in him with all speech and all knowledge— 6 even as the testimony to Christ was confirmed among you— 7 so that you are not lacking in any spiritual gift, as you wait for the revealing of our Lord Jesus Christ; 8 who will sustain you to the end, guiltless in the day of our Lord Jesus Christ. 9 God is faithful, by whom you were called into the fellowship of his Son, Jesus Christ our Lord.

▶1:5 Acts 23:6
6 But when Paul perceived that one part were Sad'ducees and the other Pharisees, he cried out in the council, "Brethren, I am a Pharisee, a son of Pharisees; with respect to the hope and the resurrection of the dead I am on trial."

2 Tim 4:8   8 Henceforth there is laid up for me the crown of righteousness, which the Lord, the righteous judge, will award to me on that Day, and not only to me but also to all who have loved his appearing.

Tit 1:2 | 2 in hope of eternal life which God, who never lies, promised ages ago

▶1:10 Acts 17:31
31 because he has fixed a day on which he will judge the world in righteousness by a man whom he has appointed, and of this he has given assurance to all men by raising him from the dead."

▶1:12 Acts 20:32   32And now I commend you to God and to the word of his grace, which is able to build you up and to give you the inheritance among all those who are sanctified.

▶1:4-5 1 Cor 13:13   13 So faith, hope, love abide, these three; but the greatest of these is love.

Eph 1:15-18
15 For this reason, because I have heard of your faith in the Lord Jesus and your love toward all the saints, 16 I do not cease to give thanks for you, remembering you in my prayers, 17 that the God of our Lord Jesus Christ, the Father of glory, may give you a spirit of wisdom and of revelation in the knowledge of him, 18 having the eyes of your hearts enlightened, that you may know what is the hope to which he has called you, what are the riches of his glorious inheritance in the saints,

Gal 5:5-6   5 For through the Spirit, by faith, we wait for the hope of righteousness. 6 For in Christ Jesus neither circumcision nor uncircumcision is of any avail, but faith working through love.

1 Thes 1:3, 3 remembering before our God and Father your work of faith and labor of love and steadfastness of hope in our Lord Jesus Christ.

5:8   8 But, since we belong to the day, let us be sober, and put on the breastplate of faith and love, and for a helmet the hope of salvation.

▶1:5 Eph 1:13   13 In him you also, who have heard the word of truth, the gospel of your salvation, and have believed in him, were sealed with the promised Holy Spirit,

▶1:6 Col 1:23   23 provided that you continue in the faith, stable and steadfast, not shifting from the hope of the gospel which you heard, which has been preached to every creature under heaven, and of which I, Paul, became a minister.

Eph 2:6
6 and raised us up with him, and made us sit with him in the heavenly places in Christ Jesus,

2 Cor 5:1
For we know that if the earthly tent we live in is destroyed, we have a building from God, a house not made with hands, eternal in the heavens.

Col 3:1
If then you have been raised with Christ, seek the things that are above, where Christ is, seated at the right hand of God.

Phil 3:20-21   20 But our commonwealth is in heaven, and from it we await a Savior, the Lord Jesus Christ, 21 who will change our lowly body to be like his glorious body, by the power which enables him even to subject all things to himself.

Rom 10:18
18 But I ask, have they not heard? Indeed they have; for
"Their voice has gone out to all the earth,
and their words to the ends of the world."

▶1:7 Phm 23
23 Ep'aphras, my fellow prisoner in Christ Jesus, sends greetings to you,

Col 4:12-13
12 Ep'aphras, who is one of yourselves, a servant of Christ Jesus, greets you, always remembering you earnestly in his prayers, that you may stand mature and fully assured in all the will of God. 13 For I bear him witness that he has worked hard for you and for those in La-odice'a and in Hi-erap'olis.

▶1:9 Eph 1:15-17
15 For this reason, because I have heard of your faith in the Lord Jesus

Phil 1:3-11 (§238)

3 I thank my God in all my remembrance of you, 4 always in every prayer of mine for you all making my prayer with joy, 5 thankful for your partnership in the gospel from the first day until now. 6 And I am sure that he who began a good work in you will bring it to completion at the day of Jesus Christ. 7 It is right for me to feel thus about you all, because I hold you in my heart, for you are all partakers with me of grace, both in my imprisonment and in the defense and confirmation of the gospel. 8 For God is my witness, how I yearn for you all with the affection of Christ Jesus. 9 And it is my prayer that your love may abound more and more, with knowledge and all discernment, 10 so that you may approve what is excellent, and may be pure and blameless for the day of Christ, 11 filled with the fruits of righteousness which come through Jesus Christ, to the glory and praise of God.

Col 1:3-14

3 We always thank God, the Father of our Lord Jesus Christ, when we pray for you, 4 because we have heard of your faith in Christ Jesus and of the love which you have for all the saints, 5 because of the hope laid up for you in heaven. Of this you have heard before in the word of the truth, the gospel 6 which has come to you, as indeed in the whole world it is bearing fruit and growing—so among yourselves, from the day you heard and understood the grace of God in truth, 7 as you learned it from Ep′aphras our beloved fellow servant. He is a faithful minister of Christ on our behalf 8 and has made known to us your love in the Spirit.

9 And so, from the day we heard of it, we have not ceased to pray for you, asking that you may be filled with the knowledge of his will in all spiritual wisdom and understanding, 10 to lead a life worthy of the Lord, fully pleasing to him, bearing fruit in every good work and increasing in the knowledge of God. 11 May you be strengthened with all power, according to his glorious might, for all endurance and patience with joy, 12 giving thanks to the Father, who has qualified us to share in the inheritance of the saints in light. 13 He has delivered us from the dominion of darkness and transferred us to the kingdom of his beloved Son, 14 in whom we have redemption, the forgiveness of sins.

1 Thes 1:2-10 (§276)

2 We give thanks to God always for you all, constantly mentioning you in our prayers, 3 remembering before our God and Father your work of faith and labor of love and steadfastness of hope in our Lord Jesus Christ. 4 For we know, brethren beloved by God, that he has chosen you; 5 for our gospel came to you not only in word, but also in power and in the Holy Spirit and with full conviction. You know what kind of men we proved to be among you for your sake. 6 And you became imitators of us and of the Lord, for you received the word in much affliction, with joy inspired by the Holy Spirit; 7 so that you became an example to all the believers in Macedo′nia and in Acha′ia. 8 For not only has the word of the Lord sounded forth from you in Macedo′nia and Acha′ia, but your faith in God has gone forth everywhere, so that we need not say anything. 9 For they themselves report concerning us what a welcome we had among you, and how you turned to God from idols, to serve a living and true God, 10 and to wait for his Son from heaven, whom he raised from the dead, Jesus who delivers us from the wrath to come.

2 Thes 1:3-12 (§295)

3 We are bound to give thanks to God always for you, brethren, as is fitting, because your faith is growing abundantly, and the love of every one of you for one another is increasing. 4 Therefore we ourselves boast of you in the churches of God for your steadfastness and faith in all your persecutions and in the afflictions which you are enduring.

5 This is evidence of the righteous judgment of God, that you may be made worthy of the kingdom of God, for which you are suffering—6 since indeed God deems it just to repay with affliction those who afflict you, 7 and to grant rest with us to you who are afflicted, when the Lord Jesus is revealed from heaven with his mighty angels in flaming fire, 8 inflicting vengeance upon those who do not know God and upon those who do not obey the gospel of our Lord Jesus. 9 They shall suffer the punishment of eternal destruction and exclusion from the presence of the Lord and from the glory of his might, 10 when he comes on that day to be glorified in his saints, and to be marveled at in all who have believed, because our testimony to you was believed. 11 To this end we always pray for you, that our God may make you worthy of his call, and may fulfil every good resolve and work of faith by his power, 12 so that the name of our Lord Jesus may be glorified in you, and you in him, according to the grace of our God and the Lord Jesus Christ.

Phm 4-7 (§306)

4 I thank my God always when I remember you in my prayers, 5 because I hear of your love and of the faith which you have toward the Lord Jesus and all the saints, 6 and I pray that the sharing of your faith may promote the knowledge of all the good that is ours in Christ. 7 For I have derived much joy and comfort from your love, my brother, because the hearts of the saints have been refreshed through you.

---

and your love toward all the saints, 16 I do not cease to give thanks for you, remembering you in my prayers, 17 that the God of our Lord Jesus Christ, the Father of glory, may give you a spirit of wisdom and of revelation in the knowledge of him,

Rom 15:14

14 I myself am satisfied about you, my brethren, that you yourselves are full of goodness, filled with all knowledge, and able to instruct one another.

▶ 1:10 Rom 6:21-22

21 But then what return did you get from the things of which you are now ashamed? The end of those things is death. 22 But now that you have been set free from sin and have become slaves of God, the return you get is sanctification and its end, eternal life.

Gal 5:22

22 But the fruit of the Spirit is love, joy, peace, patience, kindness, goodness, faithfulness,

Rom 7:4-5

4 Likewise, my brethren, you have died to the law through the body of Christ, so that you may belong to another, to him who has been raised from the dead in order that we may bear fruit for God. 5 While we were living in the flesh, our sinful passions, aroused by the law, were at work in our members to bear fruit for death.

Phil 1:11

11 filled with the fruits of righteousness which come through Jesus Christ, to the glory and praise of God.

1 Thes 2:12

12 to lead a life worthy of God, who calls you into his own kingdom and glory.

Eph 4:1

1 I therefore, a prisoner for the Lord, beg you to lead a life worthy of the calling to which you have been called.

1 Cor 7:32-35

32 I want you to be free from anxieties. The unmarried man is anxious about the affairs of the Lord, how to please the Lord; 33 but the married man is anxious about worldly affairs, how to please his wife, 34 and his interests are divided. And the unmarried woman or girl is anxious about the affairs of the Lord, how to be holy in body and spirit; but the married woman is anxious about worldly affairs, how to please her husband. 35 I say this for your own benefit, not to lay any restraint upon you, but to promote good order and to secure your undivided devotion to the Lord.

Rom 8:8

8 and those who are in the flesh cannot please God.

Gal 1:10

10 Am I now seeking the favor of men, or of God? Or am I trying to please men? If I were still pleasing men, I should not be a servant of Christ.

1 Thes 2:4

4 but just as we have been approved by God to be entrusted with the gospel, so we speak, not to please men, but to please God who tests our hearts.

▶ 1:12 Eph 1:18

18 having the eyes of your hearts enlightened, that you may know what is the hope to which he has called you, what are the riches of his glorious inheritance in the saints,

Col 3:24

24 knowing that from the Lord you will receive the inheritance as your reward; you are serving the Lord Christ.

▶ 1:13 Eph 2:2

2 in which you once walked, following the course of this world, following the prince of the power of the air, the spirit that is now at work in the sons of disobedience.

▶ 1:14 Eph 1:7

7 In him we have redemption through his blood, the forgiveness of our trespasses, according to the riches of his grace

▶ 1:7 (on our) read your: Sᶜ Dᶜ Koine Lect it(most) vg syr cop Ephraem; text: p⁴⁶S*ABD(Greek) G Ambrosiaster

▶ 1:12 (us) read you: SB cop(sa) Ambrosiaster: text: AC DG Koine Lect it vg cop (bo) Origen(Latin) Ambrosiaster

Rom 5:6-11 (§21)

6 While we were still weak, at the right time Christ died for the ungodly. 7 Why, one will hardly die for a righteous man—though perhaps for a good man one will dare even to die. 8 But God shows his love for us in that while we were yet sinners Christ died for us. 9 Since, therefore, we are now justified by his blood, much more shall we be saved by him from the wrath of God. 10 For if while we were enemies we were reconciled to God by the death of his Son, much more, now that we are reconciled, shall we be saved by his life. 11 Not only so, but we also rejoice in God through our Lord Jesus Christ, through whom we have now received our reconciliation.

Rom 8:28-30 (§33)

28 We know that in everything God works for good with those who love him, who are called according to his purpose. 29 For those whom he foreknew he also predestined to be conformed to the image of his Son, in order that he might be the first-born among many brethren. 30 And those whom he predestined he also called; and those whom he called he also justified; and those whom he justified he also glorified.

Rom 11:13-16 (§47)

13 Now I am speaking to you Gentiles. Inasmuch then as I am an apostle to the Gentiles, I magnify my ministry 14 in order to make my fellow Jews jealous, and thus save some of them. 15 For if their rejection means the reconciliation of the world, what will their acceptance mean but life from the dead? 16 If the dough offered as first fruits is holy, so is the whole lump; and if the root is holy, so are the branches.

Rom 11:33-36 (§50)

33 O the depth of the riches and wisdom and knowledge of God! How unsearchable are his judgments and how inscrutable his ways! 34 "For who has known the mind of the Lord,
or who has been his counselor?"
35 "Or who has given a gift to him
that he might be repaid?"
36 For from him and through him and to him are all things. To him be glory for ever. Amen.

▶ 1:15-16 *cf 1 Tim 1:17

1 Cor 8:4-6 (§103)

4 Hence, as to the eating of food offered to idols, we know that "an idol has no real existence," and that "there is no God but one." 5 For although there may be so-called gods in heaven or on earth—as indeed there are many "gods" and many "lords"—6 yet for us there is one God, the Father, from whom are all things and for whom we exist, and one Lord, Jesus Christ, through whom are all things and through whom we exist.

1 Cor 15:20-28 (§133)

20 But in fact Christ has been raised from the dead, the first fruits of those who have fallen asleep. 21 For as by a man came death, by a man has come also the resurrection of the dead. 22 For as in Adam all die, so also in Christ shall all be made alive. 23 But each in his own order: Christ the first fruits, then at his coming those who belong to Christ. 24 Then comes the end, when he delivers the kingdom to God the Father after destroying every rule and every authority and power. 25 For he must reign until he has put all his enemies under his feet. 26 The last enemy to be destroyed is death. 27 "For God z has put all things in subjection under his feet." But when it says, "All things are put in subjection under him," it is plain that he is excepted who put all things under him. 28 When all things are subjected to him, then the Son himself will also be subjected to him who put all things under him, that God may be everything to every one.

1 Cor 15:42-50 (§136)

42 So is it with the resurrection of the dead. What is sown is perishable, what is raised is imperishable. 43 It is sown in dishonor, it is raised in glory. It is sown in weakness, it is raised in power. 44 It is sown a physical body, it is raised a spiritual body. If there is a physical body, there is also a spiritual body. 45 Thus it is written, "The first man Adam became a living being"; the last Adam became a life-giving spirit. 46 But it is not the spiritual which is first but the physical, and then the spiritual. 47 The first man was from the earth, a man of dust; the second man is from heaven. 48 As was the man of dust, so are those who are of the dust; and as is the

▶ 1:15-16 3:10

10 and have put on the new nature, which is being renewed in knowledge after the image of its creator:

2 Cor 4:4,

4 in their case the god of this world has blinded the minds of the unbelievers, to keep them from seeing the light of the gospel of the glory of Christ, who is the likeness of God.

18

18 because we look not to the things that are seen but to the things that are unseen; for the things that are seen are transient, but the things that are unseen are eternal.

*cf Col 3:10

2 Cor 5:14-21 (§164)

14 For the love of Christ controls us, because we are convinced that one has died for all; therefore all have died. 15 And he died for all, that those who live might live no longer for themselves but for him who for their sake died and was raised.

16 From now on, therefore, we regard no one from a human point of view; even though we once regarded Christ from a human point of view, we regard him thus no longer. 17 Therefore, if any one is in Christ, he is a new creation; the old has passed away, behold, the new has come. 18 All this is from God, who through Christ reconciled us to himself and gave us the ministry of reconciliation; 19 that is, in Christ God was reconciling the world to himself, not counting their trespasses against them, and entrusting to us the message of reconciliation. 20 So we are ambassadors for Christ, God making his appeal through us. We beseech you on behalf of Christ, be reconciled to God. 21 For our sake he made him to be sin who knew no sin, so that in him we might become the righteousness of God.

man of heaven, so are those who are of heaven. 49 Just as we have borne the image of the man of dust, we shall also bear the image of the man of heaven. 50 I tell you this, brethren: flesh and blood cannot inherit the kingdom of God, nor does the perishable inherit the imperishable.

▶ 1:18 1 Cor 12:12,

12 For just as the body is one and has many members, and all the members of the body, though many, are one body, so it is with Christ.

27

27 Now you are the body of Christ and individually members of it.

Eph 4:15,

15 Rather, speaking the truth in love, we are to grow up in every way into him who is the head, into Christ,

5:23

23 For the husband is the head of the wife as Christ is the head of the church, his body, and is himself its Savior.

Col 2:19

19 and not holding fast to the Head, from whom the whole body, nourished and knit together through its joints and ligaments, grows with a growth that is from God.

Rom 12:5

5 so we, though many, are one body in Christ, and individually members one of another.

▶ 1:19 2:9

9 For in him the whole fulness of deity dwells bodily,

Eph 1:3-23 (§219)

3 Blessed be the God and Father of our Lord Jesus Christ, who has blessed us in Christ with every spiritual blessing in the heavenly places, 4 even as he chose us in him before the foundation of the world, that we should be holy and blameless before him. 5 He destined us in love to be his sons through Jesus Christ, according to the purpose of his will, 6 to the praise of his glorious grace which he freely bestowed on us in the Beloved. 7 In him we have redemption through his blood, the forgiveness of our trespasses, according to the riches of his grace 8 which he lavished upon us. 9 For he has made known to us in all wisdom and insight the mystery of his will, according to his purpose which he set forth in Christ 10 as a plan for the fulness of time, to unite all things in him, things in heaven and things on earth.

11 In him, according to the purpose of him who accomplishes all things according to the counsel of his will, 12 we who first hoped in Christ have been destined and appointed to live for the praise of his glory. 13 In him you also, who have heard the word of truth, the gospel of your salvation, and have believed in him, were sealed with the promised Holy Spirit, 14 which is the guarantee of our inheritance until we acquire possession of it, to the praise of his glory.

15 For this reason, because I have heard of your faith in the Lord Jesus and your love toward all the saints, 16 I do not cease to give thanks for you, remembering you in my prayers, 17 that the God of our Lord Jesus Christ, the Father of glory, may give you a spirit of wisdom and of revelation in the knowledge of him, 18 having the eyes of your hearts enlightened, that you may know what is the hope to which he has called you, what are the riches of his glorious inheritance in the saints, 19 and what is the immeasurable greatness of his power in us who believe, according to the working of his great might 20 which he accomplished in Christ when he raised him from the dead and made him sit at his right hand in the heavenly places, 21 far above all rule and authority and power and dominion, and above every

▶ 1:20 Eph 2:13 13 In him you also, who have heard the word of truth, the gospel of your salvation, and have believed in him, were sealed with the promised Holy Spirit,

Eph (cont)

name that is named, not only in this age but also in that which is to come; 22 and he has put all things under his feet and has made him the head over all things for the church, 23 which is his body, the fulness of him who fills all in all.

Eph 4:1-10 (§225)

4 I therefore, a prisoner for the Lord, beg you to lead a life worthy of the calling to which you have been called, 2 with all lowliness and meekness, with patience, forbearing one another in love, 3 eager to maintain the unity of the Spirit in the bond of peace. 4 There is one body and one Spirit, just as you were called to the one hope that belongs to your call, 5 one Lord, one faith, one baptism, 6 one God and Father of us all, who is above all and through all and in all. 7 But grace was given to each of us according to the measure of Christ's gift. 8 Therefore it is said,

"When he ascended on high he led a host of captives,
and he gave gifts to men."

9 (In saying, "He ascended," what does it mean but that he had also descended into the lower parts of the earth? 10 He who descended is he who also ascended far above all the heavens, that he might fill all things.)

Eph 2:11-22 (§221)

11 Therefore remember that at one time you Gentiles in the flesh, called the uncircumcision by what is called the circumcision, which is made in the flesh by hands—12 remember that you were at that time separated from Christ, alienated from the commonwealth of Israel, and strangers to the covenants of promise, having no hope and without God in the world. 13 But now in Christ Jesus you who once were far off have been brought near in the blood of Christ. 14 For he is our peace, who has made us both one, and has broken down the dividing wall of hostility, 15 by abolishing in his flesh the law of commandments and ordinances, that he might create in himself one new man in place of the two, so making peace, 16 and might reconcile us both to God in one body through the cross, thereby bringing the hostility to an end. 17And he

Col 1:15-20

15 He is the image of the invisible God, the first-born of all creation; 16 for in him all things were created, in heaven and on earth, visible and invisible, whether thrones or dominions or principalities or authorities—all things were created through him and for him. 17 He is before all things, and in him all things hold together. 18 He is the head of the body, the church; he is the beginning, the first-born from the dead, that in everything he might be pre-eminent. 19 For in him all the fulness of God was pleased to dwell, 20 and through him to reconcile to himself all things, whether on earth or in heaven, making peace by the blood of his cross.

came and preached peace to you who were far off and peace to those who were near; 18 for through him we both have access in one Spirit to the Father. 19 So then you are no longer strangers and sojourners, but you are fellow citizens with the saints and members of the household of God, 20 built upon the foundation of the apostles and prophets, Christ Jesus himself being the cornerstone, 21 in whom the whole structure is joined together and grows into a holy temple in the Lord; 22 in whom you also are built into it for a dwelling place of God in the Spirit.

▶ 1:20 (cross) *add* through him: p46SACDᶜ Koine(some) Lect syr cop(bo) Chrysostom; *text:* BD*G Koine (some) it vg cop(sa) Origen

259

Rom 11:13-16 (§47)

13 Now I am speaking to you Gentiles. Inasmuch then as I am an apostle to the Gentiles, I magnify my ministry 14 in order to make my fellow Jews jealous, and thus save some of them. 15 For if their rejection means the reconciliation of the world, what will their acceptance mean but life from the dead? 16 If the dough offered as first fruits is holy, so is the whole lump; and if the root is holy, so are the branches.

Rom 12:1-2 (§51)

12 I appeal to you therefore, brethren, by the mercies of God, to present your bodies as a living sacrifice, holy and acceptable to God, which is your spiritual worship. 2 Do not be conformed to this world but be transformed by the renewal of your mind, that you may prove what is the will of God, what is good and acceptable and perfect.

1 Cor 15:51-58 (§137)

51 Lo! I tell you a mystery. We shall not all sleep, but we shall all be changed, 52 in a moment, in the twinkling of an eye, at the last trumpet. For the trumpet will sound, and the dead will be raised imperishable, and we shall be changed. 53 For this perishable nature must put on the imperishable, and this mortal nature must put on immortality. 54 When the perishable puts on the imperishable, and the mortal puts on immortality, then shall come to pass the saying that is written:
"Death is swallowed up in victory."
55 "O death, where is thy victory?
O death, where is thy sting?"
56 The sting of death is sin, and the power of sin is the law. 57 But thanks be to God, who gives us the victory through our Lord Jesus Christ.
58 Therefore, my beloved brethren, be steadfast, immovable, always abounding in the work of the Lord, knowing that in the Lord your labor is not in vain.

2 Cor 4:13-15 (§160)

13 Since we have the same spirit of faith as he had who wrote, "I believed, and so I spoke," we too believe, and so we speak, 14 knowing that he who raised the Lord Jesus will raise us also with Jesus and bring us with you into his presence. 15 For it is all for your sake, so that as grace extends to more and more people it may increase thanksgiving, to the glory of God.

Eph 2:11-22 (§221)

11 Therefore remember that at one time you Gentiles in the flesh, called the uncircumcision by what is called the circumcision, which is made in the flesh by hands—12 remember that you were at that time separated from Christ, alienated from the commonwealth of Israel, and strangers to the covenants of promise, having no hope and without God in the world. 13 But now in Christ Jesus you who once were far off have been brought near in the blood of Christ. 14 For he is our peace, who has made us both one, and has broken down the dividing wall of hostility, 15 by abolishing in his flesh the law of commandments and ordinances, that he might create in himself one new man in place of the two, so making peace, 16 and might reconcile us both to God in one body through the cross, thereby bringing the hostility to an end. 17And he came and preached peace to you who were far off and peace to those who were near; 18 for through him we both have access in one Spirit to the Father. 19 So then you are no longer strangers and sojourners, but you are fellow citizens with the saints and members of the household of God, 20 built upon the foundation of the apostles and prophets, Christ Jesus himself being the cornerstone, 21 in whom the whole structure is joined together and grows into a holy temple in the Lord; 22 in whom you also are built into it for a dwelling place of God in the Spirit.

▶ 1:21 Eph 2:1,
And you he made alive, when you were dead through the trespasses and sins

4:18 18 they are darkened in their understanding, alienated from the life of God because of the ignorance that is in them, due to their hardness of heart;

▶ 1:22 2 Cor 11:2
2 I feel a divine jealousy for you, for I betrothed you to Christ to present you as a pure bride to her one husband.

Eph 5:27
27 that he might present the church to himself in splendor, without spot or wrinkle or any such thing, that she might be holy and without blemish.

Rom 5:10
10 For if while we were enemies we were reconciled to God by the death of his Son, much more, now that we are reconciled, shall we be saved by his life.

2 Cor 5:18 18All this is from God, who through Christ reconciled us to himself and gave us the ministry of reconciliation;

Col 1:21-23

21 And you, who once were estranged and hostile in mind, doing evil deeds, [22] he has now reconciled in his body of flesh by his death, in order to present you holy and blameless and irreproachable before him, [23] provided that you continue in the faith, stable and steadfast, not shifting from the hope of the gospel which you heard, which has been preached to every creature under heaven, and of which I, Paul, became a minister.

Eph 1:3

3 Blessed be the God and Father of our Lord Jesus Christ, who has blessed us in Christ with every spiritual blessing in the heavenly places,

▶ 1:23 2:6-7

6 As therefore you received Christ Jesus the Lord, so live in him, [7] rooted and built up in him and established in the faith, just as you were taught, abounding in thanksgiving.

Eph 3:7

7 Of this gospel I was made a minister according to the gift of God's grace which was given me by the working of his power.

Rom 10:14-17

14 But how are men to call upon him in whom they have not believed? And how are they to believe in him of whom they have never heard? And how are they to hear without a preacher? [15]And how can men preach unless they are sent? As it is written, "How beautiful are the feet of those who preach good news!" [16]But they have not all obeyed the gospel; for Isaiah says, "Lord, who has believed what he has heard from us?" [17] So faith comes from what is heard, and what is heard comes by the preaching of Christ.

*cf Gal 5:1, Phil 4:1, 1 Cor 15:58

Rom 9:19-29 (§38)

19 You will say to me then, "Why does he still find fault? For who can resist his will?" 20 But who are you, a man, to answer back to God? Will what is molded say to its molder, "Why have you made me thus?" 21 Has the potter no right over the clay, to make out of the same lump one vessel for beauty and another for menial use? 22 What if God, desiring to show his wrath and to make known his power, has endured with much patience the vessels of wrath made for destruction, 23 in order to make known the riches of his glory for the vessels of mercy, which he has prepared beforehand for glory, 24 even us whom he has called, not from the Jews only but also from the Gentiles? 25 As indeed he says in Hose´a,

"Those who were not my people
I will call 'my people,'
and her who was not beloved
I will call 'my beloved.' "

26 "And in the very place where it was said to them, 'You are not my people,'
they will be called 'sons of the living God.' "

27 And Isaiah cries out concerning Israel: "Though the number of the sons of Israel be as the sand of the sea, only a remnant of them will be saved; 28 for the Lord will execute his sentence upon the earth with rigor and dispatch." 29 And as Isaiah predicted,

"If the Lord of hosts had not left us children,
we would have fared like Sodom and been made like Gomor´rah."

Rom 16:25-27 (§70)

25 Now to him who is able to strengthen you according to my gospel and the preaching of Jesus Christ, according to the revelation of the mystery which was kept secret for long ages 26 but is now disclosed and through the prophetic writings is made known to all nations, according to the command of the eternal God, to bring about the obedience of faith—27 to the only wise God be glory for evermore through Jesus Christ! Amen.

1 Cor 1:4-9 (§72)

4 I give thanks to God always for you because of the grace of God which was given you in Christ Jesus, 5 that in every way you were enriched in him with all speech and all knowledge—6 even as the testimony to Christ was confirmed among you—7 so that you are not lacking in any spiritual gift, as you wait for´the revealing of our Lord Jesus Christ; 8 who will sustain you to the end, guiltless in the day of our Lord Jesus Christ. 9 God is faithful, by whom you were called into the fellowship of his Son, Jesus Christ our Lord.

1 Cor 2:6-16 (§77)

6 Yet among the mature we do impart wisdom, although it is not a wisdom of this age or of the rulers of this age, who are doomed to pass away. 7 But we impart a secret and hidden wisdom of God, which God decreed before the ages for our glorification. 8 None of the rulers of this age understood this; for if they had, they would not have crucified the Lord of glory. 9 But, as it is written,

"What no eye has seen, nor ear heard,
nor the heart of man conceived,
what God has prepared for those who love him,"

10 God has revealed to us through the Spirit. For the Spirit searches everything, even the depths of God. 11 For what person knows a man's thoughts except the spirit of the man which is in him? So also no one comprehends the thoughts of God except the Spirit of God. 12 Now we have received not the spirit of the world, but the Spirit which is from God, that we might understand the gifts bestowed on us by God. 13 And we impart this in words not taught by human wisdom but taught by the Spirit, interpreting spiritual truths to those who possess the Spirit.

14 The unspiritual man does not receive the gifts of the Spirit of God, for they are folly to him, and he is not able to understand them because they are spiritually discerned. 15 The spiritual man judges all things, but is himself to be judged by no one. 16 "For who has known the mind of the Lord so as to instruct him?" But we have the mind of Christ.

1 Cor 4:1-5 (§83)

4 This is how one should regard us, as servants of Christ and stewards of the mysteries of God. 2 Moreover it is required of stewards that they be found trustworthy. 3 But with me it is a very small thing that I should be judged by you or by any human court. I do not even judge myself. 4 I am not aware of anything against myself, but I am not

2 Cor 11:21b-29 (§183)

But whatever any one dares to boast of—I am speaking as a fool—I also dare to boast of that. 22 Are they Hebrews? So am I. Are they Israelites? So am I. Are they descendants of Abraham? So am I. 23 Are they servants of Christ? I am a better one—I am talking like a madman—with far greater labors, far more imprisonments, with countless beatings, and often near death. 24 Five times I have received at the hands of the Jews the forty lashes less one. 25 Three times I have been beaten with rods; once I was stoned. Three times I have been shipwrecked; a night and a day I have been adrift at sea; 26 on frequent journeys, in danger from rivers, danger from robbers, danger from my own people, danger from Gentiles, danger in the city, danger in the wilderness, danger at sea, danger from false brethren; 27 in toil and hardship, through many a sleepless night, in hunger and thirst, often without food, in cold and exposure. 28 And, apart from other things, there is the daily pressure upon me of my anxiety for all the churches. 29 Who is weak, and I am not weak? Who is made to fall, and I am not indignant?

thereby acquitted. It is the Lord who judges me. 5 Therefore do not pronounce judgment before the time, before the Lord comes, who will bring to light the things now hidden in darkness and will disclose the purposes of the heart. Then every man will receive his commendation from God.

Gal 1:15-24 (§196)

15 But when he who had set me apart before I was born, and had called me through his grace, 16 was pleased to reveal his Son to me, in order that I might preach him among the Gentiles, I did not confer with flesh and blood, 17 nor did I go up to Jerusalem to those who were apostles before me, but I went away into Arabia; and again I returned to Damascus.

18 Then after three years I went up to Jerusalem to visit Cephas, and remained with him fifteen days. 19 But I saw none of the other apostles except James the Lord's brother. 20 (In what I am writing to you, before God, I do not lie!) 21 Then I went into the regions of Syria and Cili´cia. 22 And I was still not known by sight to the churches of Christ in Judea; 23 they only heard it said, "He who once persecuted us is now preaching the faith he once tried to destroy." 24 And they glorified God because of me.

Eph 1:3-23 (§219)

3 Blessed be the God and Father of our Lord Jesus Christ, who has blessed us in Christ with every spiritual blessing in the heavenly places, 4 even as he chose us in him before the foundation of the world, that we should be holy and blameless before him. 5 He destined us in love to be his sons through Jesus Christ, according to the purpose of his will, 6 to the praise of his glorious grace which he freely bestowed on us in the Beloved. 7 In him we have redemption through his blood, the forgiveness of our trespasses, according to the riches of his grace 8 which he lavished upon us. 9 For he has made known to us in all wisdom and insight the mystery of his will, according to his purpose which he set forth in Christ 10 as a plan for the fulness of time, to unite all things in him, things in heaven and things on earth.

11 In him, according to the purpose of him who accomplishes all things according to the counsel of his will, 12 we who first hoped in Christ have been destined and appointed to live for the praise of his glory. 13 In him you also, who have heard the word of truth, the gospel of your salvation, and have believed in him, were sealed with the promised Holy Spirit, 14 which is the guarantee of our inheritance until we acquire possession of it, to the praise of his glory.

15 For this reason, because I have heard of your faith in the Lord Jesus and your love toward all the saints, 16 I do not cease to give thanks for you, remembering you in my prayers, 17 that the God of our Lord Jesus Christ, the Father of glory, may give you a spirit of wisdom and of revelation in the knowledge of him, 18 having the eyes of your hearts enlightened, that you may know what is the hope to which he has called you, what are the riches of his glorious inheritance in the saints, 19 and what is the immeasurable greatness of his power in us who believe, according to the working of his great might 20 which he accomplished in Christ when he raised him from the dead and made him sit at his right hand in the heavenly places, 21 far above all rule and authority and power and dominion, and above every name that is named, not only in this age but also in that which is to come; 22 and he has put all things under his feet and has made him the head over all things for the church, 23 which is his body, the fulness of him who fills all in all.

Eph 3:1-13 (§222)

3 For this reason I, Paul, a prisoner for Christ Jesus on behalf of you

---

▶1:24 2 Tim 1:8,

8 Do not be ashamed then of testifying to our Lord, nor of me his prisoner, but share in suffering for the gospel in the power of God,

12,

12 and therefore I suffer as I do. But I am not ashamed, for I know whom I have believed, and I am sure that he is able to guard until that Day what has been entrusted to me.

16,

16 May the Lord grant mercy to the household of Onesiph´orus, for he often refreshed me; he was not ashamed of my chains,

2:10

10 Therefore I endure everything for the sake of the elect, that they also may obtain salvation in Christ Jesus with its eternal glory.

▶1:27 1 Tim 1:1

Paul, an apostle of Christ Jesus by command of God our Savior and of Christ Jesus our hope,

▶1:28 Acts 20:31

31 Therefore be alert, remembering that for three years I did not cease night or day to admonish every one with tears.

Col 1:24-2:3

24 Now I rejoice in my sufferings for your sake, and in my flesh I complete what is lacking in Christ's afflictions for the sake of his body, that is, the church, 25 of which I became a minister according to the divine office which was given to me for you, to make the word of God fully known, 26 the mystery hidden for ages and generations but now made manifest to his saints. 27 To them God chose to make known how great among the Gentiles are the riches of the glory of this mystery, which is Christ in you, the hope of glory. 28 Him we proclaim warning every man and teaching every man in all wisdom, that we may present every man mature in Christ. 29 For this I toil, striving with all the energy which he mightily inspires within me.

2 For I want you to know how greatly I strive for you, and for those at La-odice'a, and for all who have not seen my face, 2 that their hearts may be encouraged as they are knit together in love, to have all the riches of assured understanding and the knowledge of God's mystery, of Christ, 3 in whom are hid all the treasures of wisdom and knowledge.

Gentiles— 2 assuming that you have heard of the stewardship of God's grace that was given to me for you, 3 how the mystery was made known to me by revelation, as I have written briefly. 4 When you read this you can perceive my insight into the mystery of Christ, 5 which was not made known to the sons of men in other generations as it has now been revealed to his holy apostles and prophets by the Spirit; 6 that is, how the Gentiles are fellow heirs, members of the same body, and partakers of the promise in Christ Jesus through the gospel.

7 Of this gospel I was made a minister according to the gift of God's grace which was given me by the working of his power. 8 To me, though I am the very least of all the saints, this grace was given, to preach to the Gentiles the unsearchable riches of Christ, 9 and to make all men see what is the plan of the mystery hidden for ages in God who created all things; 10 that through the church the manifold wisdom of God might now be made known to the principalities and powers in the heavenly places. 11 This was according to the eternal purpose which he has realized in Christ Jesus our Lord, 12 in whom we have boldness and confidence of access through our faith in him. 13 So I ask you not to lose heart over what I am suffering for you, which is your glory.

▶ 1:24 2 Cor 4:11,
11 For while we live we are always being given up to death for Jesus' sake, so that the life of Jesus may be manifested in our mortal flesh.
6:4 4 but as servants of God we commend ourselves in every way: through great endurance, in afflictions, hardships, calamities,

*cf Phil 1:12-13, 1 Thes 2:2

▶ 2:2 4:12
12 Ep'aphras, who is one of yourselves, a servant of Christ Jesus, greets you, always remembering you earnestly in his prayers, that you may stand mature and fully assured in all the will of God.

▶ 1:26 1 Cor 13:2
2And if I have prophetic powers, and understand all mysteries and all knowledge, and if I have all faith, so as to remove mountains, but have not love, I am nothing.

▶ 2:1 *cf 4:13-17

▶ 1:27 Rom 5:2
2 Through him we have obtained access to this grace in which we stand, and we rejoice in our hope of sharing the glory of God.

Gal 2:20   20 I have been crucified with Christ; it is no longer I who live, but Christ who lives in me; and the life I now live in the flesh I live by faith in the Son of God, who loved me and gave himself for me.

▶ 1:28 Phil 3:15   15 Let those of us who are mature be thus minded; and if in anything you are otherwise minded, God will reveal that also to you.

261

1 Cor 7:32-35 (§99)

32 I want you to be free from anxieties. The unmarried man is anxious about the affairs of the Lord, how to please the Lord; 33 but the married man is anxious about worldly affairs, how to please his wife, 34 and his interests are divided. And the unmarried woman or girl is anxious about the affairs of the Lord, how to be holy in body and spirit; but the married woman is anxious about worldly affairs, how to please her husband. 35 I say this for your own benefit, not to lay any restraint upon you, but to promote good order and to secure your undivided devotion to the Lord.

Eph 5:3-14 (§230)

3 But fornication and all impurity or covetousness must not even be named among you, as is fitting among saints. 4 Let there be no filthiness, nor silly talk, nor levity, which are not fitting; but instead let there be thanksgiving. 5 Be sure of this, that no fornicator or impure man, or one who is covetous (that is, an idolater), has any inheritance in the kingdom of Christ and of God. 6 Let no one deceive you with empty words, for it is because of these things that the wrath of God comes upon the sons of disobedience. 7 Therefore do not associate with them, 8 for once you were darkness, but now you are light in the Lord; walk as children of light 9 (for the fruit of light is found in all that is good and right and true), 10 and try to learn what is pleasing to the Lord. 11 Take no part in the unfruitful works of darkness, but instead expose them. 12 For it is a shame even to speak of the things that they do in secret; 13 but when anything is exposed by the light it becomes visible, for anything that becomes visible is light. 14 Therefore it is said,

▶ 2:5 Acts 16:5 5 So the churches were strengthened in the faith, and they increased in numbers daily.

▶ 2:4 Rom 16:18 18 For such persons do not serve our Lord Christ, but their own appetites, and by fair and flattering words they deceive the hearts of the simple-minded.

▶ 2:5 1 Cor 5:3, 3 For though absent in body I am present in spirit, and as if present, I have already pronounced judgment

14:40 40 but all things should be done decently and in order.

▶ 2:6-7 1:23 23 provided that you continue in the faith, stable and steadfast, not shifting from the hope of the gospel which you heard, which has been preached to every creature under heaven, and of which I, Paul, became a minister.

▶ 2:7 Eph 3:17, 17 and that Christ may dwell in your hearts through faith; that you, being rooted and grounded in love,

262. See that no one makes prey of you

Rom 6:1-10 (§23)

6 What shall we say then? Are we to continue in sin that grace may abound? 2 By no means! How can we who died to sin still live in it? 3 Do you not know that all of us who have been baptized into Christ Jesus were baptized into his death? 4 We were buried therefore with him by baptism into death, so that as Christ was raised from the dead by the glory of the Father, we too might walk in newness of life. 5 For if we have been united with him in a death like his, we shall certainly be united with him in a resurrection like his. 6 We know that our old self was crucified with him so that the sinful body might be destroyed, and we might no longer be enslaved to sin. 7 For he who has died is freed from sin. 8 But if we have died with Christ, we believe that we shall also live with him. 9 For we know that Christ being raised from the dead will never die again; death no longer has dominion over him. 10 The death he died he died to sin, once for all, but the life he lives he lives to God

1 Cor 15:1-11 (§131)

15 Now I would remind you, brethren, in what terms I preached to you the gospel, which you received, in which you stand, 2 by which you are saved, if you hold it fast —unless you believed in vain. 3 For I delivered to you as of first importance what I also received, that Christ died for our sins in accordance with the scriptures, 4 that he was buried, that he was raised on the third day in accordance with the scriptures, 5 and that he appeared to Cephas, then to the twelve. 6 Then he appeared to more than five hundred brethren at one time, most of whom are still alive, though some have fallen asleep. 7 Then he appeared to James, then to all the apostles. 8 Last of all, as to one untimely born, he appeared also to me. 9 For I am the least of the apostles, unfit to be called an apostle, because I persecuted the church of God. 10 But by the grace of God I am what I am, and his grace toward me was not in vain. On the contrary, I worked harder than any of them, though it was not I, but the grace of God which is with me. 11 Whether then it was I or they, so we preach and so you believed.

Gal 3:1-5 (§200)

3 O foolish Galatians! Who has bewitched you, before whose eyes Jesus Christ was publicly portrayed as crucified? 2 Let me ask you only this: Did you receive the Spirit by works of the law, or by hearing with faith? 3 Are you so foolish? Having begun with the Spirit, are you now ending with the flesh? 4 Did you experience so many things in vain?—if it really is in vain. 5 Does he who supplies the Spirit to you and works miracles among you do so by works of the law, or by hearing with faith?

Gal 3:21-29 (§205-206)

21 Is the law then against the promises of God? Certainly not; for if a law had been given which could make alive, then righteousness would indeed be by the law. 22 But the scripture consigned all things to sin, that what was promised to faith in Jesus Christ might be given to those who believe. 23 Now before faith came, we were confined under the law, kept under restraint until faith should be revealed. 24 So that the law was our custodian until Christ came, that we might be justi-

Eph 2:1-10 (§220)

2 And you he made alive, when you were dead through the trespasses and sins 2 in which you once walked, following the course of this world, following the prince of the power of the air, the spirit that is now at work in the sons of disobedience. 3 Among these we all once lived in the passions of our flesh, following the desires of body and mind, and so we were by nature children of wrath, like the rest of mankind. 4 But God, who is rich in mercy, out of the great love with which he loved us, 5 even when we were dead through our trespasses, made us alive together with Christ (by grace you have been saved), fied by faith. 25 But now that faith has come, we are no longer under a custodian; 26 for in Christ Jesus you are all sons of God, through faith. 27 For as many of you as were baptized into Christ have put on Christ. 28 There is neither Jew nor Greek, there is neither slave nor free, there is neither male nor female; for you are all one in Christ Jesus. 29 And if you are Christ's, then you are Abraham's offspring, heirs according to promise.

▶ 2:12 Acts 2:24 24 But God raised him up, having loosed the pangs of death, because it was not possible for him to be held by it.

▶ 2:14 Acts 3:19 19 Repent therefore, and turn again, that your sins may be blotted out, that times of refreshing may come from the presence of the Lord,

▶ 2:8 2:22 22 (referring to things which all perish as they are used), according to human precepts and doctrines?
Eph 5:6 6 Let no one deceive you with empty words, for it is because of these things that the wrath of God comes upon the sons of disobedience.

Gal 1:14 14 and I advanced in Judaism beyond many of my own age among my people, so extremely zealous was I for the traditions of my fathers.

2 Thes 2:15, 15 So then, brethren, stand firm and hold to the traditions which you were taught by us, either by word of mouth or by letter.

3:6 6 Now we command you, brethren, in the name of our Lord Jesus Christ, that you keep away from any brother who is living in idleness and not in accord with the tradition that you received from us.

261

Phil 1:27-30 (§241)

27 Only let your manner of life be worthy of the gospel of Christ, so that whether I come and see you or am absent, I may hear of you that you stand firm in one spirit, with one mind striving side by side for the faith of the gospel, 28 and not frightened in anything by your opponents. This is a clear omen to them of their destruction, but of your salvation, and that from God. 29 For it has been granted to you that for the sake of Christ you should not only believe in him but also suffer for his sake, 30 engaged in the same conflict which you saw and now hear to be mine.

Eph (cont)

"Awake, O sleeper, and arise from the dead,
and Christ shall give you light."

4:21, ²¹ assuming that you have heard about him and were taught in him, as the truth is in Jesus.

Col 2:4-7

⁴ I say this in order that no one may delude you with beguiling speech. ⁵ For though I am absent in body, yet I am with you in spirit, rejoicing to see your good order and the firmness of your faith in Christ.

6 As therefore you received Christ Jesus the Lord, so live in him, ⁷ rooted and built up in him and established in the faith, just as you were taught, abounding in thanksgiving.

2:20, ²⁰ built upon the foundation of the apostles and prophets, Christ Jesus himself being the cornerstone,

22 ²² in whom you also are built into it for a dwelling place of God in the Spirit.

1 Thes 2:1-8 (§277)

2 For you yourselves know, brethren, that our visit to you was not in vain; ² but though we had already suffered and been shamefully treated at Philippi, as you know, we had courage in our God to declare to you the gospel of God in the face of great opposition. ³ For our appeal does not spring from error or uncleanness, nor is it made with guile; ⁴ but just as we have been approved by God to be entrusted with the gospel, so we speak, not to please men, but to please God who tests our hearts. ⁵ For we never used either words of flattery, as you know, or a cloak for greed, as God is witness; ⁶ nor did we seek glory from men, whether from you or from others, though we might have made demands as apostles of Christ. ⁷ But we were gentle among you, like a nurse taking care of her children. ⁸ So, being affectionately desirous of you, we were ready to share with you not only the gospel of God but also our own selves, because you had become very dear to us.

Rom 6:17 ¹⁷ But thanks be to God, that you who were once slaves of sin have become obedient from the heart to the standard of teaching to which you were committed,

2 Thes 2:13-15 (§297)

13 But we are bound to give thanks to God always for you, brethren beloved by the Lord, because God chose you from the beginning to be saved, through sanctification by the Spirit and belief in the truth. ¹⁴ To this he called you through our gospel, so that you may obtain the glory of our Lord Jesus Christ. ¹⁵ So then, brethren, stand firm and hold to the traditions which you were taught by us, either by word of mouth or by letter.

262. See that no one makes prey of you

262

Eph (cont)

⁶ and raised us up with him, and made us sit with him in the heavenly places in Christ Jesus, ⁷ that in the coming ages he might show the immeasurable riches of his grace in kindness toward us in Christ Jesus. ⁸ For by grace you have been saved through faith; and this is not your own doing, it is the gift of God— ⁹ not because of works, lest any man should boast. 10 For we are his workmanship, created in Christ Jesus for good works, which God prepared beforehand, that we should walk in them.

Gal (cont)

Gal 4:8-11 (§208)

8 Formerly, when you did not know God, you were in bondage to beings that by nature are no gods; ⁹ but now that you have come to know God, or rather to be known by God, how can you turn back again to the weak and beggarly elemental spirits, whose slaves you want to be once more? 10 You observe days, and months, and seasons, and years! 11 I am afraid I have labored over you in vain.

▶ 2:9 1:19
¹⁹ For in him all the fulness of God was pleased to dwell,

Col 2:8-15

8 See to it that no one makes a prey of you by philosophy and empty deceit, according to human tradition, according to the elemental spirits of the universe, and not according to Christ. ⁹ For in him the whole fulness of deity dwells bodily, 10 and you have come to fulness of life in him, who is the head of all rule and authority. 11 In him also you were circumcised with a circumcision made without hands, by putting off the body of flesh in the circumcision of Christ; ¹² and you were buried with him in baptism, in which you were also raised with him through faith in the working of God, who raised him from the dead. 13 And you, who were dead in trespasses and the uncircumcision of your flesh, God made alive together with him, having forgiven us all our trespasses, 14 having canceled the bond which stood against us with its legal demands; this he set aside, nailing it to the cross. 15 He disarmed the principalities and powers and made a public example of them, triumphing over them in him.

▶ 2:10 Eph 1:21-23,
²¹ far above all rule and authority and power and dominion, and above every name that is named, not only in this age but also in that which is to come; ²² and he has put all things under his feet and has made him the head over all things for the church, ²³ which is his body, the fulness of him who fills all in all.

4:15, ¹⁵ Rather, speaking the truth in love, we are to grow up in every way into him who is the head, into Christ,

5:23 ²³ For the husband is the head of the wife as Christ is the head of the church, his body, and is himself its Savior.

▶ 2:11 Rom 2:28-29
²⁸ For he is not a real Jew who is one outwardly, nor is true circumcision something external and physical. ²⁹ He is a Jew who is one inwardly, and real circumcision is a matter of the heart, spiritual and not literal. His praise is not from men but from God.

▶ 2:13 Rom 6:11 ¹¹ So you also must consider yourselves dead to sin and alive to God in Christ Jesus.

▶ 2:15 Eph 1:21
²¹ far above all rule and authority and power and dominion, and above every name that is named, not only in this age but also in that which is to come;

2 Cor 2:14
14 But thanks be to God, who in Christ always leads us in triumph, and through us spreads the fragrance of the knowledge of him everywhere.

263

Rom 14:5-12 (§58)

5 One man esteems one day as better than another, while another man esteems all days alike. Let every one be fully convinced in his own mind. 6 He who observes the day, observes it in honor of the Lord. He also who eats, eats in honor of the Lord, since he gives thanks to God; while he who abstains, abstains in honor of the Lord and gives thanks to God. 7 None of us lives to himself, and none of us dies to himself. 8 If we live, we live to the Lord, and if we die, we die to the Lord; so then, whether we live or whether we die, we are the Lord's. 9 For to this end Christ died and lived again, that he might be Lord both of the dead and of the living. 10 Why do you pass judgment on your brother? Or you, why do you despise your brother? For we shall all stand before the judgment seat of God; 11 for it is written,

"As I live, says the Lord, every knee
    shall bow to me,
and every tongue shall give praise to
    God."

12 So each of us shall give account of himself to God.

▶ 2:16 1 Tim 4:1-3
Now the Spirit expressly says that in later times some will depart from the faith by giving heed to deceitful spirits and doctrines of demons, 2 through the pretensions of liars whose consciences are seared, 3 who forbid marriage and enjoin abstinence from foods which God created to be received

1 Cor 4:1-5 (§83)

4 This is how one should regard us, as servants of Christ and stewards of the mysteries of God. 2 Moreover it is required of stewards that they be found trustworthy. 3 But with me it is a very small thing that I should be judged by you or by any human court. I do not even judge myself. 4 I am not aware of anything against myself, but I am not thereby acquitted. It is the Lord who judges me. 5 Therefore do not pronounce judgment before the time, before the Lord comes, who will bring to light the things now hidden in darkness and will disclose the purposes of the heart. Then every man will receive his commendation from God.

with thanksgiving by those who believe and know the truth.
▶ 2:17 Heb 3:5.
5 They serve a copy and shadow of the heavenly sanctuary; for when Moses was about to erect the tent, he was instructed by God, saying, "See that you make everything according to the pattern which was shown you on the mountain."

2 Cor 12:1-10 (§185)

12 I must boast; there is nothing to be gained by it, but I will go on to visions and revelations of the Lord. 2 I know a man in Christ who fourteen years ago was caught up to the third heaven—whether in the body or out of the body I do not know, God knows. 3And I know that this man was caught up into Paradise—whether in the body or out of the body I do not know, God knows—4 and he heard things that cannot be told, which man may not utter. 5 On behalf of this man I will boast, but on my own behalf I will not boast, except of my weaknesses. 6 Though if I wish to boast, I shall not be a fool, for I shall be speaking the truth. But I refrain from it, so that no one may think more of me than he sees in me or hears from me. 7And to keep me from being too elated by the abundance of revelations, a thorn was given me in the flesh, a messenger of Satan, to harass me, to keep me from being too elated. 8 Three times I besought the Lord about this, that it should leave me; 9 but he said to me, "My grace is sufficient for you, for

10:1 For since the law has but a shadow of the good things to come instead of the true form of these realities, it can never, by the same sacrifices which are continually offered year after year, make perfect those who draw near.

▶ 2:18 *cf Heb 12:22-29

Gal 4:8-11 (§208)

8 Formerly, when you did not know God, you were in bondage to beings that by nature are no gods; 9 but now that you have come to know God, or rather to be known by God, how can you turn back again to the weak and beggarly elemental spirits, whose slaves you want to be once more? 10 You observe days, and months, and seasons, and years! 11 I am afraid I have labored over you in vain.

my power is made perfect in weakness." I will all the more gladly boast of my weaknesses, that the power of Christ may rest upon me. 10 For the sake of Christ, then, I am content with weaknesses, insults, hardships, persecutions, and calamities; for when I am weak, then I am strong.

▶ 2:16 Rom 14:17
17 For the kingdom of God is not food and drink but righteousness and peace and joy in the Holy Spirit;

▶ 2:19 Eph 1:22-23,
22 and he has put all things under his feet and has made him the head over all things for the church, 23 which is his body, the fulness of him who fills all in all.

Eph 4:11-16 (§226)

11And his gifts were that some should be apostles, some prophets, some evangelists, some pastors and teachers, 12 to equip the saints for the work of ministry, for building up the body of Christ, 13 until we all attain to the unity of the faith and of the knowledge of the Son of God, to mature manhood, to the measure of the stature of the fulness of Christ; 14 so that we may no longer be children, tossed to and fro and carried about with every wind of doctrine, by the cunning of men, by their craftiness in deceitful wiles. 15 Rather, speaking the truth in love, we are to grow up in every way into him who is the head, into Christ, 16 from whom the whole body, joined and knit together by every joint with which it is supplied, when each part is working properly, makes bodily growth and upbuilds itself in love.

2:21-22,
21 in whom the whole structure is joined together and grows into a holy temple in the Lord; 22 in whom you also are built into it for a dwelling place of God in the Spirit.

264. **If with Christ you died**

264

Rom 6:11-14 (§24)

11 So you also must consider yourselves dead to sin and alive to God in Christ Jesus. 12 Let not sin therefore reign in your mortal bodies, to make you obey their passions. 13 Do not yield your members to sin as instruments of wickedness, but yield yourselves to God as men who have been brought from death to life, and your members to God as instruments of righteousness. 14 For sin will have no dominion over you, since you are not under law but under grace.

▶ 2:22 Tit 1:14
14 instead of giving heed to Jewish myths or to commands of men who reject the truth.

▶ 2:23 1 Tim 4:1-3,
Now the Spirit expressly says that in later times some will depart from the faith by giving heed to deceitful spirits and doctrines of demons, 2 through the pretensions of liars whose consciences are seared, 3 who forbid marriage and enjoin abstinence from foods which God created to be received

with thanksgiving by those who believe and know the truth.
8

*cf 1 Tim 4:8

▶ 2:20 Gal 4:3
3 So with us; when we were children, we were slaves to the elemental spirits of the universe.

▶ 2:22 2:8
8 See to it that no one makes a prey of you by philosophy and empty deceit, according to human tradition, according to the elemental spirits of the universe, and not according to Christ.

▶ 2:23 Rom 13:14
14 But put on the Lord Jesus Christ, and make no provision for the flesh, to gratify its desires.

263

Col 2:16-19

16 Therefore let no one pass judgment on you in questions of food and drink or with regard to a festival or a new moon or a sabbath. 17 These are only a shadow of what is to come; but the substance belongs to Christ. 18 Let no one disqualify you, insisting on self-abasement and worship of angels, taking his stand on visions, puffed up without reason by his sensuous mind, 19 and not holding fast to the Head, from whom the whole body, nourished and knit together through its joints and ligaments, grows with a growth that is from God.

4:15, 15 Rather, speaking the truth in love, we are to grow up in every way into him who is the head, into Christ, **5:23** 23 For the husband is the head of the wife as Christ is the head of the church, his body, and is himself its Savior.

1 Cor 12:12, 12 For just as the body is one and has many members, and all the members of the body, though many, are one body, so it is with Christ.

27 27 Now you are the body of Christ and individually members of it.

Rom 12:5 5 so we, though many, are one body in Christ, and individually members one of another.

▶ 2:18 (visions) *read* what he has not seen: S^{c}CD^{c}G Koine Lect it(most) vg syr Origen: *text:* p^{46} S*ABD* it(few) cop Marcion Origen

264. If with Christ you died

264

Col 2:20-23

20 If with Christ you died to the elemental spirits of the universe, why do you live as if you still belonged to the world? Why do you submit to regulations, 21 "Do not handle, Do not taste, Do not touch" 22 (referring to things which all perish as they are used), according to human precepts and doctrines? 23 These have indeed an appearance of wisdom in promoting rigor of devotion and self-abasement and severity to the body, but they are of no value in checking the indulgence of the flesh.

265

Rom 6:11-14 (§24) [11] So you also must consider yourselves dead to sin and alive to God in Christ Jesus.

[12] Let not sin therefore reign in your mortal bodies, to make you obey their passions. [13] Do not yield your members to sin as instruments of wickedness, but yield yourselves to God as men who have been brought from death to life, and your members to God as instruments of righteousness. [14] For sin will have no dominion over you, since you are not under law but under grace.

Rom 8:1-8 (§29)

8 There is therefore now no condemnation for those who are in Christ Jesus. [2] For the law of the Spirit of life in Christ Jesus has set me free from the law of sin and death. [3] For God has done what the law, weakened by the flesh, could not do: sending his own Son in the likeness of sinful flesh and for sin, he condemned sin in the flesh, [4] in order that the just requirement of the law might be fulfilled in us, who walk not according to the flesh but according to the Spirit. [5] For those who live according to the flesh set their minds on the things of the flesh, but those who live according to the Spirit set their minds on the things of the Spirit. [6] To set the mind on the flesh is death, but to set the mind on the Spirit is life and peace. [7] For the mind that is set on the flesh is hostile to God; it does not submit to God's law, indeed it cannot; [8] and those who are in the flesh cannot please God.

2 Cor 4:13-15 (§160)

[13] Since we have the same spirit of faith as he had who wrote, "I believed, and so I spoke," we too believe, and so we speak, [14] knowing that he who raised the Lord Jesus will raise us also with Jesus and bring us with you into his presence. [15] For it is all for your sake, so that as grace extends to more and more people it may increase thanksgiving, to the glory of God.

Eph 2:1-10 (§220)

2 And you he made alive, when you were dead through the trespasses and sins [2] in which you once walked, following the course of this world, following the prince of the power of the air, the spirit that is now at work in the sons of disobedience. [3] Among these we all once lived in the passions of our flesh, following the desires of body and mind, and so we were by nature children of wrath, like the rest of mankind. [4] But God, who is rich in mercy, out of the great love with which he loved us, [5] even when we were dead through our trespasses, made us alive together with Christ (by grace you have been saved), [6] and raised us up with him, and made us sit with him in the heavenly places in Christ Jesus, [7] that in the coming ages he might show the immeasurable riches of his grace in kindness toward us in Christ Jesus. [8] For by grace you have been saved through faith; and this is not your own doing, it is the gift of God— [9] not because of works, lest any man should boast. [10] For we are his workmanship, created in Christ Jesus for good works, which God prepared beforehand, that we should walk in them.

▶ 3:2-4 Phil 3:20-21

[20] But our commonwealth is in heaven, and from it we await a Savior, the Lord Jesus Christ, [21] who will change our lowly body to be like his glorious body, by the power which enables him even to subject all things to himself.

▶ 3:3-4 Rom 6:4

[4] We were buried therefore with him by baptism into death, so that as Christ was raised from the dead by the glory of the Father, we too might walk in newness of life.

265

Col 3:1-4

3 If then you have been raised with Christ, seek the things that are above, where Christ is, seated at the right hand of God. [2] Set your minds on things that are above, not on things that are on earth. [3] For you have died, and your life is hid with Christ in God. [4] When Christ who is our life appears, then you also will appear with him in glory.

▶ 3:4 (our) *read* your: p[46]SC D*G it vg cop(bo) Origen; *text:* BD[c] Koine Lect syr cop(sa) Origen

266. Put to death what is earthly

266

Rom 1:29-32 (§6)

29 They were filled with all manner of
wickedness, evil, covetousness, malice.
Full of envy, murder, strife, deceit,
malignity, they are gossips, 30 slanderers, haters of God, insolent, haughty,
boastful, inventors of evil, disobedient
to parents, 31 foolish, faithless, heartless,
ruthless. 32 Though they know God's
decree that those who do such things
deserve to die, they not only do them
but approve those who practice them.

Rom 2:1-5 (§7)

2 Therefore you have no excuse, O
man, whoever you are, when you
judge another; for in passing judgment
upon him you condemn yourself, because you, the judge, are doing the very
same things. 2 We know that the judgment of God rightly falls upon those
who do such things. 3 Do you suppose,
O man, that when you judge those who
do such things and yet do them yourself,
you will escape the judgment of God?
4 Or do you presume upon the riches of
his kindness and forbearance and
patience? Do you not know that God's
kindness is meant to lead you to repentance? 5 But by your hard and impenitent heart you are storing up
wrath for yourself on the day of wrath
when God's righteous judgment will be
revealed.

Rom 6:11-14 (§24) 11 So you also must
consider yourselves dead to sin and
alive to God in Christ Jesus.
12 Let not sin therefore reign in your
mortal bodies, to make you obey their
passions. 13 Do not yield your members
to sin as instruments of wickedness, but
yield yourselves to God as men who
have been brought from death to life,
and your members to God as instruments of righteousness. 14 For sin will
have no dominion over you, since you
are not under law but under grace.

Rom 8:9-17 (§30)

9 But you are not in the flesh, you are
in the Spirit, if in fact the Spirit of God
dwells in you. Any one who does not
have the Spirit of Christ does not belong
to him. 10 But if Christ is in you, although your bodies are dead because of
sin, your spirits are alive because of
righteousness. 11 If the Spirit of him
who raised Jesus from the dead dwells
in you, he who raised Christ Jesus from
the dead will give life to your mortal
bodies also through his Spirit which
dwells in you.
12 So then, brethren, we are debtors,
not to the flesh, to live according to the
flesh—13 for if you live according to the
flesh you will die, but if by the Spirit
you put to death the deeds of the body
you will live. 14 For all who are led by
the Spirit of God are sons of God.
15 For you did not receive the spirit of
slavery to fall back into fear, but you
have received the spirit of sonship.
When we cry, "Abba! Father!" 16 it is
the Spirit himself bearing witness with
our spirit that we are children of God,
17 and if children, then heirs, heirs of
God and fellow heirs with Christ, provided we suffer with him in order that
we may also be glorified with him.

1 Cor 5:9-13 (§89)

9 I wrote to you in my letter not to
associate with immoral men; 10 not at all
meaning the immoral of this world, or
the greedy and robbers, or idolaters,
since then you would need to go out of
the world. 11 But rather I wrote to you
not to associate with any one who bears
the name of brother if he is guilty of
immorality or greed, or is an idolater,
reviler, drunkard, or robber—not even
to eat with such a one. 12 For what have
I to do with judging outsiders? Is it not
those inside the church whom you are
to judge? 13 God judges those outside.
"Drive out the wicked person from
among you."

1 Cor 6:9-11 (§91)

9 Do you not know that the unrighteous will not inherit the kingdom
of God? Do not be deceived; neither the
immoral, nor idolaters, nor adulterers,
nor sexual perverts, 10 nor thieves, nor
the greedy, nor drunkards, nor revilers,
nor robbers will inherit the kingdom of
God. 11 And such were some of you. But
you were washed, you were sanctified,
you were justified in the name of the
Lord Jesus Christ and in the Spirit of
our God.

1 Cor 10:1-13 (§109)

10 I want you to know, brethren,
that our fathers were all under the
cloud, and all passed through the sea,
2 and all were baptized into Moses in
the cloud and in the sea, 3 and all ate
the same supernatural food 4 and all
drank the same supernatural drink.
For they drank from the supernatural
Rock which followed them, and the
Rock was Christ. 5 Nevertheless with
most of them God was not pleased; for
they were overthrown in the wilderness.
6 Now these things are warnings for
us, not to desire evil as they did. 7 Do
not be idolaters as some of them were;
as it is written, "The people sat down
to eat and drink and rose up to dance."
8 We must not indulge in immorality as
some of them did, and twenty-three
thousand fell in a single day. 9 We
must not put the Lord to the test, as
some of them did and were destroyed by
serpents; 10 nor grumble, as some of
them did and were destroyed by the
Destroyer. 11 Now these things happened to them as a warning, but they
were written down for our instruction,
upon whom the end of the ages has
come. 12 Therefore let any one who
thinks that he stands take heed lest he
fall. 13 No temptation has overtaken you
that is not common to man. God is
faithful, and he will not let you be
tempted beyond your strength, but with
the temptation will also provide the way
of escape, that you may be able to endure it.

Rom 13:1-14 (§54-56)

13 Let every person be subject to
the governing authorities. For
there is no authority except from God,
and those that exist have been instituted by God. 2 Therefore he who
resists the authorities resists what God
has appointed, and those who resist will
incur judgment. 3 For rulers are not a
terror to good conduct, but to bad.
Would you have no fear of him who is in
authority? Then do what is good, and
you will receive his approval, 4 for he is
God's servant for your good. But if you
do wrong, be afraid, for he does not
bear the sword in vain; he is the servant
of God to execute his wrath on the
wrongdoer. 5 Therefore one must be
subject, not only to avoid God's wrath
but also for the sake of conscience. 6 For
the same reason you also pay taxes, for
the authorities are ministers of God,
attending to this very thing. 7 Pay all of
them their dues, taxes to whom taxes
are due, revenue to whom revenue is
due, respect to whom respect is due,
honor to whom honor is due.
8 Owe no one anything, except to
love one another; for he who loves his
neighbor has fulfilled the law. 9 The
commandments, "You shall not commit adultery, You shall not kill, You
shall not steal, You shall not covet," and
any other commandment, are summed
up in this sentence, "You shall love your
neighbor as yourself." 10 Love does no
wrong to a neighbor; therefore love is
the fulfilling of the law.
11 Besides this you know what hour it
is, how it is full time now for you to
wake from sleep. For salvation is nearer
to us now than when we first believed;
12 the night is far gone, the day is at
hand. Let us then cast off the works of
darkness and put on the armor of light;
13 let us conduct ourselves becomingly
as in the day, not in reveling and
drunkenness, not in debauchery and
licentiousness, not in quarreling and
jealousy. 14 But put on the Lord Jesus
Christ, and make no provision for the
flesh, to gratify its desires.

2 Cor 4:16-5:5 (§161)

16 So we do not lose heart. Though
our outer nature is wasting away, our
inner nature is being renewed every
day. 17 For this slight momentary
affliction is preparing for us an eternal
weight of glory beyond all comparison,
18 because we look not to the things that
are seen but to the things that are unseen; for the things that are seen are
transient, but the things that are unseen
are eternal.
5 For we know that if the earthly
tent we live in is destroyed, we have
a building from God, a house not made
with hands, eternal in the heavens.
2 Here indeed we groan, and long to put
on our heavenly dwelling, 3 so that by
putting it on we may not be found
naked. 4 For while we are still in this
tent, we sigh with anxiety; not that we
would be unclothed, but that we would
be further clothed, so that what is
mortal may be swallowed up by life.
5 He who has prepared us for this very
thing is God, who has given us the
Spirit as a guarantee.

Gal 3:26-29 (§206)

26 for in Christ Jesus you are all
sons of God, through faith. 27 For as
many of you as were baptized into
Christ have put on Christ. 28 There is
neither Jew nor Greek, there is neither
slave nor free, there is neither male nor
female; for you are all one in Christ
Jesus. 29 And if you are Christ's, then
you are Abraham's offspring, heirs according to promise.

Gal 5:16-26 (§213)

16 But I say, walk by the Spirit, and
do not gratify the desires of the flesh.
17 For the desires of the flesh are against
the Spirit, and the desires of the Spirit
are against the flesh; for these are opposed to each other, to prevent you
from doing what you would. 18 But if
you are led by the Spirit you are not
under the law. 19 Now the works of the
flesh are plain: fornication, impurity,
licentiousness, 20 idolatry, sorcery, enmity, strife, jealousy, anger, selfishness,
dissension, party spirit, 21 envy, drunkenness, carousing, and the like. I warn
you, as I warned you before, that those
who do such things shall not inherit the
kingdom of God. 22 But the fruit of the
Spirit is love, joy, peace, patience, kindness, goodness, faithfulness, 23 gentleness, self-control; against such there is
no law. 24 And those who belong to
Christ Jesus have crucified the flesh
with its passions and desires.
25 If we live by the Spirit, let us also
walk by the Spirit. 26 Let us have no
self-conceit, no provoking of one another, no envy of one another.

2 Cor 12:19-21 (§188)

19 Have you been thinking all along
that we have been defending ourselves
before you? It is in the sight of God that
we have been speaking in Christ, and all
for your upbuilding, beloved. 20 For
I fear that perhaps I may come and find
you not what I wish, and that you may
find me not what you wish; that perhaps
there may be quarreling, jealousy, anger, selfishness, slander, gossip, conceit,
and disorder. 21 I fear that when I come
again my God may humble me before
you, and I may have to mourn over
many of those who sinned before and
have not repented of the impurity, immorality, and licentiousness which they
have practiced.

1 Cor 12:12-13 (§118)

12 For just as the body is one and has
many members, and all the members of
the body, though many, are one body,
so it is with Christ. 13 For by one Spirit
we were all baptized into one body—
Jews or Greeks, slaves or free—and all
were made to drink of one Spirit.

Eph 4:17-24 (§227)

17 Now this I affirm and testify in the
Lord, that you must no longer live as
the Gentiles do, in the futility of their
minds; 18 they are darkened in their understanding, alienated from the life of
God because of the ignorance that is in
them, due to their hardness of heart;
19 they have become callous and have
given themselves up to licentiousness,
greedy to practice every kind of uncleanness. 20 You did not so learn
Christ!— 21 assuming that you have
heard about him and were taught in

1 Cor 15:42-50 (§136)

42 So is it with the resurrection of the
dead. What is sown is perishable, what
is raised is imperishable. 43 It is sown in
dishonor, it is raised in glory. It is
sown in weakness, it is raised in power.
44 It is sown a physical body, it is raised
a spiritual body. If there is a physical
body, there is also a spiritual body.
45 Thus it is written, "The first man
Adam became a living being"; the last
Adam became a life-giving spirit. 46 But
it is not the spiritual which is first but
the physical, and then the spiritual.
47 The first man was from the earth, a
man of dust; the second man is from
heaven. 48 As was the man of dust, so are
those who are of the dust; and as is the
man of heaven, so are those who are of
heaven. 49 Just as we have borne the
image of the man of dust, we shall
also bear the image of the man of
heaven. 50 I tell you this, brethren:
flesh and blood cannot inherit the kingdom of God, nor does the perishable
inherit the imperishable.

▶ 3:7 Tit 3:3 3 For we ourselves were once foolish, disobedient, led astray, slaves to various passions and pleasures, passing our days in malice and envy, hated by men and hating one another;

▶ 3:11 Acts 28:2 2 And the natives showed us unusual kindness, for they kindled a fire and welcomed us all, because it had begun to rain and was cold.

▶ 3:7 Eph 2:3, 3 Among these we all once lived in the passions of our flesh, following the desires of body and mind, and so we were by nature children of wrath, like the rest of mankind.

5:6 6 Let no one deceive you with empty words, for it is because of these things that the wrath of God comes upon the sons of disobedience.

▶ 3:8 Eph 4:26, 26 Be angry but do not sin; do not let the sun go down on your anger,

31 31 Let all bitterness and wrath and anger and clamor and slander be put away from you, with all malice,

266

Eph(cont)

him, as the truth is in Jesus. 22 Put off your old nature which belongs to your former manner of life and is corrupt through deceitful lusts, 23 and be renewed in the spirit of your minds, 24 and put on the new nature, created after the likeness of God in true righteousness and holiness.

Eph 5:3-14 (§230)

3 But fornication and all impurity or covetousness must not even be named among you, as is fitting among saints. 4 Let there be no filthiness, nor silly talk, nor levity, which are not fitting; but instead let there be thanksgiving. 5 Be sure of this, that no fornicator or impure man, or one who is covetous (that is, an idolater), has any inheritance in the kingdom of Christ and of God. 6 Let no one deceive you with empty words, for it is because of these things that the wrath of God comes upon the sons of disobedience. 7 Therefore do not associate with them, 8 for once you were darkness, but now you are light in the Lord; walk as children of light 9 (for the fruit of light is found in all that is good and right and true), 10 and try to learn what is pleasing to the Lord. 11 Take no part in the unfruitful works of darkness, but instead expose them. 12 For it is a shame even to speak of the things that they do in secret; 13 but when anything is exposed by the light it becomes visible, for anything that becomes visible is light. 14 Therefore it is said,
"Awake, O sleeper, and arise from the dead,
and Christ shall give you light."

Col 3:5-11

5 Put to death therefore what is earthly in you: fornication, impurity, passion, evil desire, and covetousness, which is idolatry. 6 On account of these the wrath of God is coming. 7 In these you once walked, when you lived in them. 8 But now put them all away: anger, wrath, malice, slander, and foul talk from your mouth. 9 Do not lie to one another, seeing that you have put off the old nature with its practices 10 and have put on the new nature, which is being renewed in knowledge after the image of its creator. 11 Here there cannot be Greek and Jew, circumcised and uncircumcised, barbarian, Scyth'ian, slave, free man, but Christ is all, and in all.

▶ 3:9 Eph 4:25
25 Therefore, putting away falsehood, let every one speak the truth with his neighbor, for we are members one of another.

▶ 3:10 1:15
15 He is the image of the invisible God, the first-born of all creation;

▶ 3:11 Rom 10:12
12 For there is no distinction between Jew and Greek; the same Lord is Lord of all and bestows his riches upon all who call upon him.

▶ 3:6 (coming) *add* upon the sons of disobedience: S ACDG Koine Lect it vg syr cop(bo) Clement; *text:* p46B cop(sa) Clement

267

Rom 12:9-21 (§53)

9 Let love be genuine; hate what is evil, hold fast to what is good; 10 love one another with brotherly affection; outdo one another in showing honor. 11 Never flag in zeal, be aglow with the Spirit, serve the Lord. 12 Rejoice in your hope, be patient in tribulation, be constant in prayer. 13 Contribute to the needs of the saints, practice hospitality.

14 Bless those who persecute you; bless and do not curse them. 15 Rejoice with those who rejoice, weep with those who weep. 16 Live in harmony with one another; do not be haughty, but associate with the lowly; never be conceited. 17 Repay no one evil for evil, but take thought for what is noble in the sight of all. 18 If possible, so far as it depends upon you, live peaceably with all. 19 Beloved, never avenge yourselves, but leave it to the wrath of God; for it is written, "Vengeance is mine, I will repay, says the Lord." 20 No, "if your enemy is hungry, feed him; if he is thirsty, give him drink; for by so doing you will heap burning coals upon his head." 21 Do not be overcome by evil, but overcome evil with good.

Rom 15:1-6 (§60)

15

We who are strong ought to bear with the failings of the weak, and not to please ourselves; 2 let each of us please his neighbor for his good, to edify him. 3 For Christ did not please himself; but, as it is written, "The reproaches of those who reproached thee fell on me." 4 For whatever was written in former days was written for our instruction, that by steadfastness and by the encourage-

▶ 3:16 Acts 16:25
25 But about midnight Paul and Silas were praying and singing hymns to God, and the prisoners were listening to them,

1 Cor 10:23-11:1 (§111)

23 "All things are lawful," but not all things are helpful. "All things are lawful," but not all things build up. 24 Let no one seek his own good, but the good of his neighbor. 25 Eat whatever is sold in the meat market without raising any question on the ground of conscience. 26 For "the earth is the Lord's, and everything in it." 27 If one of the unbelievers invites you to dinner and you are disposed to go, eat whatever is set before you without raising any question on the ground of conscience. 28 (But if some one says to you, "This has been offered in sacrifice," then out of consideration for the man who informed you, and for conscience' sake— 29 I mean his conscience, not yours—do not eat it.) For why should my liberty be determined by another man's scruples? 30 If I partake with thankfulness, why am I denounced because of that for which I give thanks?

31 So, whether you eat or drink, or whatever you do, do all to the glory of God. 32 Give no offense to Jews or to Greeks or to the church of God, 33 just as I try to please all men in everything I do, not seeking my own advantage, but that of many, that they may be saved.

11

1 Be imitators of me, as I am of Christ.

▶ 3:12 2 Cor 8:7
7 Now as you excel in everything—in faith, in utterance, in knowledge, in all earnestness, and in your love for us—see that you excel in this gracious work also.

ment of the scriptures we might have hope. 5 May the God of steadfastness and encouragement grant you to live in such harmony with one another, in accord with Christ Jesus, 6 that together you may with one voice glorify the God and Father of our Lord Jesus Christ.

2 Cor 6:1-10 (§165)

6

Working together with him, then, we entreat you not to accept the grace of God in vain. 2 For he says,
"At the acceptable time I have listened to you,
and helped you on the day of salvation."
Behold, now is the acceptable time; behold, now is the day of salvation. 3 We put no obstacle in any one's way, so that no fault may be found with our ministry, 4 but as servants of God we commend ourselves in every way: through great endurance, in afflictions, hardships, calamities, 5 beatings, imprisonments, tumults, labors, watching, hunger; 6 by purity, knowledge, forbearance, kindness, the Holy Spirit, genuine love, 7 truthful speech, and the power of God; with the weapons of righteousness for the right hand and for the left; 8 in honor and dishonor, in ill repute and good repute. We are treated as impostors, and yet are true; 9 as unknown, and yet well known; as dying, and behold we live; as punished, and yet not killed; 10 as sorrowful, yet always rejoicing; as poor, yet making many rich; as having nothing, and yet possessing everything.

1 Cor 14:26-33a (§128)

26 What then, brethren? When you come together, each one has a hymn, a lesson, a revelation, a tongue, or an interpretation. Let all things be done for edification. 27 If any speak in a tongue, let there be only two or at most three, and each in turn; and let one interpret. 28 But if there is no one to interpret, let each of them keep silence

▶ 3:13 2 Cor 2:7
you should rather turn to forgive and comfort him, or he may be overwhelmed by excessive sorrow.

Gal 5:16-26 (§213)

16 But I say, walk by the Spirit, and do not gratify the desires of the flesh. 17 For the desires of the flesh are against the Spirit, and the desires of the Spirit are against the flesh; for these are opposed to each other, to prevent you from doing what you would. 18 But if you are led by the Spirit you are not under the law. 19 Now the works of the flesh are plain: fornication, impurity, licentiousness, 20 idolatry, sorcery, enmity, strife, jealousy, anger, selfishness, dissension, party spirit, 21 envy, drunkenness, carousing, and the like. I warn you, as I warned you before, that those who do such things shall not inherit the kingdom of God. 22 But the fruit of the Spirit is love, joy, peace, patience, kindness, goodness, faithfulness, 23 gentleness, self-control; against such there is no law. 24 And those who belong to Christ Jesus have crucified the flesh with its passions and desires.

25 If we live by the Spirit, let us also walk by the Spirit. 26 Let us have no self-conceit, no provoking of one another, no envy of one another.

in church and speak to himself and to God. 29 Let two or three prophets speak, and let the others weigh what is said. 30 If a revelation is made to another sitting by, let the first be silent. 31 For you can all prophesy one by one, so that all may learn and all be encouraged; 32 and the spirits of prophets are subject to prophets. 33 For God is not a God of confusion but of peace.

▶ 3:14 1 Cor 13:13 13 So faith, hope, love abide, these three; but the greatest of these is love.

Eph 4:1-10 (§225)

4

I. therefore, a prisoner for the Lord, beg you to lead a life worthy of the calling to which you have been called, 2 with all lowliness and meekness, with patience, forbearing one another in love, 3 eager to maintain the unity of the Spirit in the bond of peace. 4 There is one body and one Spirit, just as you were called to the one hope that belongs to your call, 5 one Lord, one faith, one baptism, 6 one God and Father of us all, who is above all and through all and in all. 7 But grace was given to each of us according to the measure of Christ's gift. 8 Therefore it is said,
"When he ascended on high he led a host of captives,
and he gave gifts to men."
9 (In saying, "He ascended," what does it mean but that he had also descended into the lower parts of the earth? 10 He who descended is he who also ascended far above all the heavens, that he might fill all things.)

Eph 5:15-20 (§231)

15 Look carefully then how you walk, not as unwise men but as wise, 16 making the most of the time, because the days are evil. 17 Therefore do not be foolish, but understand what the will of the Lord is. 18 And do not get drunk with wine, for that is debauchery; but be filled with the Spirit, 19 addressing one another in psalms and hymns and spiritual songs, singing and making melody to the Lord with all your heart, 20 always and for everything giving thanks in the name of our Lord Jesus Christ to God the Father.

▶ 3:15 Phil 4:7 7 And the peace of God, which passes all understanding, will keep your hearts and your minds in Christ Jesus.

Eph 4:32
32 and be kind to one another, tenderhearted, forgiving one another, as God in Christ forgave you.

7 so

268. Subject in the Lord

268

1 Cor 7:32-35 (§99)

32 I want you to be free from anxieties. The unmarried man is anxious about the affairs of the Lord, how to please the Lord; 33 but the married man is anxious about worldly affairs, how to please his wife, 34 and his interests are divided. And the unmarried woman or girl is anxious about the affairs of the Lord, how to be holy in body and spirit; but the married woman is anxious about worldly affairs, how to please her husband. 35 I say this for your own benefit, not to lay any restraint upon you, but to promote good order and to secure your undivided devotion to the Lord.

Eph 5:21-6:9* (§232)

21 Be subject to one another out of reverence for Christ. 22 Wives, be subject to your husbands, as to the Lord. 23 For the husband is the head of the wife as Christ is the head of the church, his body, and is himself its Savior. 24 As the church is subject to Christ, so let wives also be subject in everything to their husbands. 25 Husbands, love your wives, as Christ loved the church and gave himself up for her, 26 that he might sanctify her, having cleansed her by the washing of water with the word, 27 that he might present the church to himself in splendor, without spot or wrinkle or any such thing, that she might be holy and without blemish.

▶ 3:18-4:1 1 Tim 6:1
Let all who are under the yoke of slavery regard their masters as worthy of all honor, so that the name of God and the teaching may not be defamed.

*cf 1 Pet 2:13-3:7

▶ 3:24 Acts 20:32 32 And now I commend you to God and to the word of his grace, which is able to build you up and to give you the inheritance among all those who are sanctified.

▶ 3:25 Acts 10:34
34 And Peter opened his mouth and said: "Truly I perceive that God shows no partiality,

▶ 3:18-4:1 1 Cor 11:3,
3 But I want you to understand that the head of every man is Christ, the head of a woman is her husband, and the head of Christ is God.

14:34
34 the women should keep silence in the churches. For they are not permitted to speak, but should be subordinate, as even the law says.

267

Phil 4:8-9 (§252)

8 Finally, brethren, whatever is true, whatever is honorable, whatever is just, whatever is pure, whatever is lovely, whatever is gracious, if there is any excellence, if there is anything worthy of praise, think about these things. 9 What you have learned and received and heard and seen in me, do; and the God of peace will be with you.

Col 3:12-17

12 Put on then, as God's chosen ones, holy and beloved, compassion, kindness, lowliness, meekness, and patience, 13 forbearing one another and, if one has a complaint against another, forgiving each other; as the Lord has forgiven you, so you also must forgive. 14 And above all these put on love, which binds everything together in perfect harmony. 15 And let the peace of Christ rule in your hearts, to which indeed you were called in the one body. And be thankful. 16 Let the word of Christ dwell in you richly, teach and admonish one another in all wisdom, and sing psalms and hymns and spiritual songs with thankfulness in your hearts to God. 17 And whatever you do, in word or deed, do everything in the name of the Lord Jesus, giving thanks to God the Father through him.

Rom 14:6 6 He who observes the day, observes it in honor of the Lord. He also who eats, eats in honor of the Lord, since he gives thanks to God; while he who abstains, abstains in honor of the Lord and gives thanks to God.

268. Subject in the Lord

268

Eph(cont)

28 Even so husbands should love their wives as their own bodies. He who loves his wife loves himself. 29 For no man ever hates his own flesh, but nourishes and cherishes it, as Christ does the church, 30 because we are members of his body. 31 "For this reason a man shall leave his father and mother and be joined to his wife, and the two shall become one flesh." 32 This mystery is a profound one, and I am saying that it refers to Christ and the church; 33 however, let each one of you love his wife as himself, and let the wife see that she respects her husband.

6 Children, obey your parents in the Lord, for this is right. 2 "Honor

Col 3:18-4:1

18 Wives, be subject to your husbands, as is fitting in the Lord. 19 Husbands, love your wives, and do not be harsh with them. 20 Children, obey your parents in everything, for this pleases the Lord. 21 Fathers, do not provoke your children, lest they become discouraged. 22 Slaves, obey in everything those who are your earthly masters, not with eyeservice, as men-pleasers, but in singleness of heart, fearing the Lord. 23 Whatever your task, work heartily,

your father and mother" (this is the first commandment with a promise), 3 "that it may be well with you and that you may live long on the earth." 4 Fathers, do not provoke your children

as serving the Lord and not men, 24 knowing that from the Lord you will receive the inheritance as your reward; you are serving the Lord Christ. 25 For the wrongdoer will be paid back for the wrong he has done, and there is no partiality.

4 Masters, treat your slaves justly and fairly, knowing that you also have a Master in heaven.

5 Slaves, be obedient to those who are your earthly masters, with fear and trembling, in singleness of heart, as to

to anger, but bring them up in the discipline and instruction of the Lord.

Christ; 6 not in the way of eyeservice, as men-pleasers, but as servants of Christ, doing the will of God from the heart, 7 rendering service with a good will as to the Lord and not to men, 8 knowing that whatever good any one

does, he will receive the same again from the Lord, whether he is a slave or free. 9 Masters, do the same to them, and forbear threatening, knowing that he who is both their Master and yours is in heaven, and that there is no partiality with him.

Rom 13:1 Let every person be subject to the governing authorities. For there is no authority except from God, and those that exist have been instituted by God.

▶ 3:24 1:12 12 giving thanks to the Father, who has qualified us to share in the inheritance of the saints in light.

▶ 3:25 Rom 2:11, 11 For God shows no partiality.

3:22b, For there is no distinction;

13:4 4 for he is God's servant for your good. But if you do wrong, be afraid, for he does not bear the sword in vain; he is the servant of God to execute his wrath on the wrongdoer.

269

Rom 15:30-33 (§64)

30 I appeal to you, brethren, by our Lord Jesus Christ and by the love of the Spirit, to strive together with me in your prayers to God on my behalf, ³¹ that I may be delivered from the unbelievers in Judea, and that my service for Jerusalem may be acceptable to the saints, ³² so that by God's will I may come to you with joy and be refreshed in your company. ³³ The God of peace be with you all. Amen.

1 Cor 16:13-14 (§141)

13 Be watchful, stand firm in your faith, be courageous, be strong. ¹⁴ Let all that you do be done in love.

2 Cor 2:12-13 (§152)

12 When I came to Tro'as to preach the gospel of Christ, a door was opened for me in the Lord; ¹³ but my mind could not rest because I did not find my brother Titus there. So I took leave of them and went on to Macedo'nia.

Eph 6:18-20 (§234)

¹⁸ Pray at all times in the Spirit, with all prayer and supplication. To that end keep alert with all perseverance, making supplication for all the saints, ¹⁹ and also for me, that utterance may be given me in opening my mouth boldly to proclaim the mystery of the gospel, ²⁰ for which I am an ambassador in chains; that I may declare it boldly, as I ought to speak.

▶4:2 Acts 1:14
¹⁴All these with one accord devoted themselves to prayer, together with the women and Mary the mother of Jesus, and with his brothers.

▶4:3 Acts 14:27
²⁷And when they arrived, they gathered the church together and declared all that God had done with them, and how he had opened a door of faith to the Gentiles.

▶4:2 1 Thes 5:6
6 So then, let us not sleep, as others do, but let us keep awake and be sober.

▶4:3 Phm 1,
1 Paul, a prisoner for Christ Jesus, and Timothy our brother,
To Phile'mon our beloved fellow worker

9
⁹ yet for love's sake I prefer to appeal to you—I, Paul, an ambassador and now a prisoner also for Christ Jesus—

Col 4:18a
18 I, Paul, write this greeting with my own hand. Remember my fetters.

270

1 Cor 6:1-8 (§90)

6 When one of you has a grievance against a brother, does he dare go to law before the unrighteous instead of the saints? ² Do you not know that the saints will judge the world? And if the world is to be judged by you, are you incompetent to try trivial cases? ³ Do you not know that we are to judge angels? How much more, matters pertaining to this life! ⁴ If then you have such cases, why do you lay them before those who are least esteemed by the church? ⁵ I say this to your shame. Can it be that there is no man among you wise enough to decide between members of the brotherhood, ⁶ but brother goes to law against brother, and that before unbelievers?

7 To have lawsuits at all with one another is defeat for you. Why not rather suffer wrong? Why not rather be defrauded? ⁸ But you yourselves wrong and defraud, and that even your own brethren.

1 Cor 14:13-19 (§126)

13 Therefore, he who speaks in a tongue should pray for the power to interpret. ¹⁴ For if I pray in a tongue, my spirit prays but my mind is unfruitful. ¹⁵ What am I to do? I will pray with the spirit and I will pray with the mind also; I will sing with the spirit and I will sing with the mind also. ¹⁶ Otherwise, if you bless with the spirit, how can any one in the position of an outsider say the "Amen" to your thanksgiving when he does not know what you are saying? ¹⁷ For you may give thanks well enough, but the other man is not edified. ¹⁸ I thank God that I speak in tongues more than you all; ¹⁹ nevertheless, in church I would rather speak five words with my mind, in order to instruct others, than ten thousand words in a tongue.

▶4:5 Eph 5:15-16
15 Look carefully then how you walk, not as unwise men but as wise, ¹⁶ making the most of the time, because the days are evil.

▶4:6 Eph 4:29
²⁹ Let no evil talk come out of your mouths, but only such as is good for edifying, as fits the occasion, that it may impart grace to those who hear.

269

Col 4:2-4

2 Continue steadfastly in prayer, being watchful in it with thanksgiving; 3 and pray for us also, that God may open to us a door for the word, to declare the mystery of Christ, on account of which I am in prison, 4 that I may make it clear, as I ought to speak.

1 Thes 5:25 (§290)

25 Brethren, pray for us.

2 Thes 3:1-5 (§299)

3 Finally, brethren, pray for us, that the word of the Lord may speed on and triumph, as it did among you, 2 and that we may be delivered from wicked and evil men; for not all have faith. 3 But the Lord is faithful; he will strengthen you and guard you from evil. 4 And we have confidence in the Lord about you, that you are doing and will do the things which we command. 5 May the Lord direct your hearts to the love of God and to the steadfastness of Christ.

Phm 21-22 (§268)

21 Confident of your obedience, I write to you, knowing that you will do even more than I say. 22 At the same time, prepare a guest room for me, for I am hoping through your prayers to be granted to you.

Eph 3:1

For this reason I, Paul, a prisoner for Christ Jesus on behalf of you Gentiles—

*cf. Phil 1:12-20

270. Conduct yourself wisely towards outsiders

270

Col 4:5-6

5 Conduct yourselves wisely toward outsiders, making the most of the time. 6 Let your speech always be gracious, seasoned with salt, so that you may know how you ought to answer every one.

1 Thes 4:9-12 (§285)

9 But concerning love of the brethren you have no need to have any one write to you, for you yourselves have been taught by God to love one another; 10 and indeed you do love all the brethren throughout Macedo′nia. But we exhort you, brethren, to do so more and more, 11 to aspire to live quietly, to mind your own affairs, and to work with your hands, as we charged you; 12 so that you may command the respect of outsiders, and be dependent on nobody.

271

21 Now that you also may know how I am and what I am doing, Tych'icus the beloved brother and faithful minister in the Lord will tell you everything. 22 I have sent him to you for this very purpose, that you may know how we are, and that he may encourage your hearts.

▶ 4:7 Acts 20:4 ⁴ Sop'ater of Beroe'a, the son of Pyrrhus, accompanied him; and of the Thessalo'nians, Aristar'chus and Secun'dus; and Ga'ius of Derbe, and Timothy; and the Asians, Tych'icus and Troph'imus.

▶ 4:8 1 Cor 16:18 ¹⁸ for they refreshed my spirit as well as yours. Give recognition to such men.

*cf Tit 3:12

272. Greetings

272

Rom 16:3-16 (§66)

3 Greet Prisca and Aquila, my fellow workers in Christ Jesus, 4 who risked their necks for my life, to whom not only I but also all the churches of the Gentiles give thanks; 5 greet also the church in their house. Greet my beloved Epae'netus, who was the first convert in Asia for Christ. 6 Greet Mary, who has worked hard among you. 7 Greet Androni'cus and Ju'nias, my kinsmen and my fellow prisoners; they are men of note among the apostles, and they were in Christ before me. 8 Greet Amplia'tus, my beloved in the Lord. 9 Greet Urba'nus, our fellow worker in Christ, and my beloved Stachys. 10 Greet Apel'les, who is approved in Christ. Greet those who belong to the family of Aristobu'lus. 11 Greet my kinsman Hero'dion. Greet those in the Lord who belong to the family of Narcis'sus. 12 Greet those workers in the Lord, Tryphae'na and Trypho'sa. Greet the beloved Persis, who has worked hard in the Lord. 13 Greet Rufus, eminent in the Lord, also his mother and mine. 14 Greet Asyn'critus, Phlegon, Hermes, Pat'robas, Hermas,

1 Cor 16:19-20 (§143)

19 The churches of Asia send greetings. Aquila and Prisca, together with the church in their house, send you hearty greetings in the Lord. ²⁰All the brethren send greetings. Greet one another with a holy kiss.

and the brethren who are with them. ¹⁵ Greet Philol'ogus, Julia, Nereus and his sister, and Olym'pas, and all the saints who are with them. ¹⁶ Greet one another with a holy kiss. All the churches of Christ greet you.

Rom 16:21-23 (§69)

21 Timothy, my fellow worker, greets you; so do Lucius and Jason and Sosip'ater, my kinsmen.
22 I Tertius, the writer of this letter, greet you in the Lord.
23 Ga'ius, who is host to me and to the whole church, greets you. Eras'tus, the city treasurer, and our brother Quartus, greet you.

2 Cor 13:11-13 (§191)

11 Finally, brethren, farewell. Mend your ways, heed my appeal, agree with one another, live in peace, and the God of love and peace will be with you. 12 Greet one another with a holy kiss. ¹³All the saints greet you.

▶ 4:10-12 Acts 19:29 ²⁹ So the city was filled with the confusion; and they rushed together into the theater, dragging with them Ga'ius and Aristar'chus, Macedo'nians who were Paul's companions in travel.

▶ 4:10-11 Acts 27:2 ²And embarking in a ship of Adramyt'tium, which was about to sail to the ports along the coast of Asia, we put to sea, accompanied by Aristar'chus, a Macedo'nian from Thessaloni'ca.

▶ 4:10 Acts 4:36, ³⁶ Thus Joseph who was surnamed by the apostles Barnabas (which means, Son of encouragement), a Levite, a native of Cyprus,

12:12, 12 When he realized this, he went to the house of Mary, the mother of John whose other name was Mark, where many were gathered together and were praying.

15:37, ³⁷And Barnabas wanted to take with them John called Mark.

39 ³⁹And there arose a sharp contention, so that they separated from each other; Barnabas took Mark with him and sailed away to Cyprus,

271

Phil 2:25-3:1 (§246)

25 I have thought it necessary to send to you Epaphrodi′tus my brother and fellow worker and fellow soldier, and your messenger and minister to my need, 26 for he has been longing for you all, and has been distressed because you heard that he was ill. 27 Indeed he was ill, near to death. But God had mercy on him, and not only on him but on me also, lest I should have sorrow upon sorrow. 28 I am the more eager to send him, therefore, that you may rejoice at seeing him again, and that I may be less anxious. 29 So receive him in the Lord with all joy; and honor such men, 30 for he nearly died for the work of Christ, risking his life to complete your service to me.

3 Finally, my brethren, rejoice in the Lord. To write the same things to you is not irksome to me, and is safe for you.

Col 4:7-9

7 Tych′icus will tell you all about my affairs; he is a beloved brother and faithful minister and fellow servant in the Lord. 8 I have sent him to you for this very purpose, that you may know how we are and that he may encourage your hearts, 9 and with him Ones′imus, the faithful and beloved brother, who is one of yourselves. They will tell you of everything that has taken place here.

Phm 8-14 (§307)

8 Accordingly, though I am bold enough in Christ to command you to do what is required, 9 yet for love's sake I prefer to appeal to you—I, Paul, an ambassador and now a prisoner also for Christ Jesus—10 I appeal to you for my child, Ones′imus, whose father I have become in my imprisonment. 11 (Formerly he was useless to you, but now he is indeed useful to you and to me.) 12 I am sending him back to you, sending my very heart. 13 I would have been glad to keep him with me, in order that he might serve me on your behalf during my imprisonment for the gospel; 14 but I preferred to do nothing without your consent in order that your goodness might not be by compulsion but of your own free will.

272. Greetings

272

Phil 4:21-22 (§254)

21 Greet every saint in Christ Jesus. The brethren who are with me greet you. 22 All the saints greet you, especially those of Caesar's household.

Col 4:10-15

10 Aristar′chus my fellow prisoner greets you, and Mark the cousin of Barnabas (concerning whom you have received instructions—if he comes to you, receive him), 11 and Jesus who is called Justus. These are the only men of the circumcision among my fellow workers for the kingdom of God, and they have been a comfort to me. 12 Ep′aphras, who is one of yourselves, a servant of Christ Jesus, greets you, always remembering you earnestly in his prayers, that you may stand mature and fully assured in all the will of God. 13 For I bear him witness that he has worked hard for you and for those in La-odice′a and in Hi-erap′olis. 14 Luke the beloved physician and Demas greet you. 15 Give my greetings to the brethren at La-odice′a, and to Nympha and the church in her house.

1 Thes 5:26 (§291)

26 Greet all the brethren with a holy kiss.

Phm 23-24 (§310)

23 Ep′aphras, my fellow prisoner in Christ Jesus, sends greetings to you, 24 and so do Mark, Aristar′chus, Demas, and Luke, my fellow workers.

---

2 Tim 4:11   11 Luke alone is with me. Get Mark and bring him with you; for he is very useful in serving me.

▶4:14 **2 Tim 4:10**   10 For Demas, in love with this present world, has deserted me and gone to Thessaloni′ca; Crescens has gone to Galatia, Titus to Dalmatia.

▶4:12-13 **1:7**   7 as you learned it from Ep′aphras our beloved fellow servant. He is a faithful minister of Christ on our behalf

▶4:12 **2:2**   2 that their hearts may be encouraged as they are knit together in love, to have all the riches of assured understanding and the knowledge of God's mystery, of Christ,

▶4:13-15 **2:1**   For I want you to know how greatly I strive for you, and for those at La-odice′a, and for all who have not seen my face,

273

1 Cor 16:21-22 (§144)

21 I, Paul, write this greeting with my own hand. 22 If any one has no love for the Lord, let him be accursed. Our Lord, come!

Gal 6:11-17 (§216)

11 See with what large letters I am writing to you with my own hand. 12 It is those who want to make a good showing in the flesh that would compel you to be circumcised, and only in order that they may not be persecuted for the cross of Christ. 13 For even those who receive circumcision do not themselves keep the law, but they desire to have you circumcised that they may glory in your flesh. 14 But far be it from me to glory except in the cross of our Lord Jesus Christ, by which the world has been crucified to me, and I to the world. 15 For neither circumcision counts for anything, nor uncircumcision, but a new creation. 16 Peace and mercy be upon all who walk by this rule, upon the Israel of God.

17 Henceforth let no man trouble me; for I bear on my body the marks of Jesus.

▶ 4:17 2 Tim 4:5
5As for you, always be steady, endure suffering, do the work of an evangelist, fulfil your ministry.

▶ 4:16-17 2:1
For I want you to know how greatly I strive for you, and for those at La-odice′a, and for all who have not seen my face,

▶ 4:17 Phm 2
2 and Ap′phia our sister and Archip′pus our fellow soldier, and the church in your house:

▶ 4:18a 4:3
3 and pray for us also, that God may open to us a door for the word, to declare the mystery of Christ, on account of which I am in prison,

Eph 3:1
For this reason I, Paul, a prisoner for Christ Jesus on behalf of you Gentiles—

*cf Phil 1:12-20

Phm 1,
1 Paul, a prisoner for Christ Jesus, and Timothy our brother,
To Phile′mon our beloved fellow worker

274. Grace

274

Rom 16:20b (§68)
The grace of our Lord Jesus Christ be with you.

1 Cor 16:23-24 (§145)
23 The grace of the Lord Jesus be with you. 24 My love be with you all in Christ Jesus. Amen.

2 Cor 13:14 (§192)
14 The grace of the Lord Jesus Christ and the love of God and the fellowship of the Holy Spirit be with you all.

Gal 6:18 (§217)
18 The grace of our Lord Jesus Christ be with your spirit, brethren. Amen.

Eph 6:23-24 (§236)
23 Peace be to the brethren, and love with faith, from God the Father and the Lord Jesus Christ. 24 Grace be with all who love our Lord Jesus Christ with love undying.

▶ 4:18b 1 Tim 6:21, 21 for by professing it some have missed the mark as regards the faith.
Grace be with you.

2 Tim 4:22
22 The Lord be with your spirit. Grace be with you.

Tit 3:15
15 All who are with me send greetings to you. Greet those who love us in the faith.
Grace be with you all.

Col 4:16-18a

16And when this letter has been read among you, have it read also in the church of the La-odice'ans; and see that you read also the letter from La-odice'a. 17And say to Archip'pus, "See that you fulfil the ministry which you have received in the Lord."

18 I, Paul, write this greeting with my own hand. Remember my fetters.

1 Thes 5:27 (§292)

27 I adjure you by the Lord that this letter be read to all the brethren.

2 Thes 3:17 (§303)

17 I, Paul, write this greeting with my own hand. This is the mark in every letter of mine; it is the way I write.

273

9   9 yet for love's sake
I prefer to appeal to you—I, Paul, an ambassador and now a prisoner also for Christ Jesus—

Col 4:3,

3 and pray for us also, that God may open to us a door for the word, to declare the mystery of Christ, on account of which I am in prison,

274. Grace

Phil 4:23 (§255)

23 The grace of the Lord Jesus Christ be with your spirit.

Col 4:18b

Grace be with you.

1 Thes 5:28 (§293)

28 The grace of our Lord Jesus Christ be with you.

2 Thes 3:18 (§304)

18 The grace of our Lord Jesus Christ be with you all.

Phm 25 (§311)

25 The grace of the Lord Jesus Christ be with your spirit.

274

Rom 1:1-7 (§1)

275

1 Paul, a servant of Jesus Christ, called to be an apostle, set apart for the gospel of God [2] which he promised beforehand through his prophets in the holy scriptures, [3] the gospel concerning his Son, who was descended from David according to the flesh [4] and designated Son of God in power according to the Spirit of holiness by his resurrection from the dead, Jesus Christ our Lord, [5] through whom we have received grace and apostleship to bring about the obedience of faith for the sake of his name among all the nations, [6] including yourselves who are called to belong to Jesus Christ;

[7] To all God's beloved in Rome, who are called to be saints:

Grace to you and peace from God our Father and the Lord Jesus Christ.

1 Cor 1:1-3 (§71)

1 Paul, called by the will of God to be an apostle of Christ Jesus, and our brother Sos'thenes,

2 To the church of God which is at Corinth, to those sanctified in Christ Jesus, called to be saints together with all those who in every place call on the name of our Lord Jesus Christ, both their Lord and ours;

3 Grace to you and peace from God our Father and the Lord Jesus Christ.

2 Cor 1:1-2 (§146)

1 Paul, an apostle of Christ Jesus by the will of God, and Timothy our brother.

To the church of God which is at Corinth, with all the saints who are in the whole of Acha'ia:

2 Grace to you and peace from God our Father and the Lord Jesus Christ.

Gal 1:1-5(§193)

1 Paul an apostle—not from men nor through man, but through Jesus Christ and God the Father, who raised him from the dead— [2] and all the brethren who are with me,

To the churches of Galatia:

3 Grace to you and peace from God the Father and our Lord Jesus Christ, [4] who gave himself for our sins to deliver us from the present evil age, according to the will of our God and Father; [5] to whom be the glory for ever and ever. Amen.

Eph 1:1-2 (§218)

1 Paul, an apostle of Christ Jesus by the will of God,
To the saints who are also faithful[a] in Christ Jesus:

2 Grace to you and peace from God our Father and the Lord Jesus Christ.

▶ 1:1 Acts 16:1.
And he came also to Derbe and to Lystra. A disciple was there, named Timothy, the son of a Jewish woman who was a believer; but his father was a Greek.

17:1-9
Now when they had passed through Amphipolis and Apollonia, they came to Thessaloni'ca, where there was a synagogue of the Jews. [2] And Paul went in, as was his custom, and for three weeks he argued with them from the scriptures, [3] explaining and proving that it was necessary for the Christ to suffer and to rise from the dead, and saying, "This Jesus, whom I proclaim to you, is the Christ." [4] And some of them were persuaded, and joined Paul and Silas; as did a great many of the devout Greeks and not a few of the leading women. [5] But the Jews were jealous, and taking some wicked fellows of the rabble, they gathered a crowd, set the city in an uproar, and attacked the house of Jason, seeking to bring them out to the people. [6] And when they could not find them, they dragged Jason and some of the brethren before the city authorities, crying, "These men who have turned the world upside down have come here also, [7] and Jason has received them; and they are all acting against the decrees of Caesar, saying that there is another king, Jesus." [8] And the people and the city authorities were disturbed when they heard this. [9] And when they had taken security from Jason and the rest, they let them go.

275

Phil 1:1-2 (§237)

1 Paul and Timothy, servants of Christ Jesus,

To all the saints in Christ Jesus who are at Philippi, with the bishops and deacons:

2 Grace to you and peace from God our Father and the Lord Jesus Christ.

Col 1:1-2 (§256)

1 Paul, an apostle of Christ Jesus by the will of God, and Timothy our brother,

2 To the saints and faithful brethren in Christ at Colos′sae:

Grace to you and peace from God our Father.

1 Thes 1:1

1 Paul, Silva′nus, and Timothy,

To the church of the Thessalo′-nians in God the Father and the Lord Jesus Christ:

Grace to you and peace.

2 Thes 1:1-2 (§294)

1 Paul, Silva′nus, and Timothy,

To the church of the Thessalo′-nians in God our Father and the Lord Jesus Christ:

2 Grace to you and peace from God the Father and the Lord Jesus Christ.

Phm 1-3 (§305)

1 Paul, a prisoner for Christ Jesus, and Timothy our brother,

To Phile′mon our beloved fellow worker 2 and Ap′phia our sister and Archip′pus our fellow soldier, and the church in your house:

3 Grace to you and peace from God our Father and the Lord Jesus Christ.

276. We give thanks to God

276

Rom 1:8-15 (§2)

8 First, I thank my God through Jesus Christ for all of you, because your faith is proclaimed in all the world. [9] For God is my witness, whom I serve with my spirit in the gospel of his Son, that without ceasing I mention you always in my prayers, [10] asking that somehow by God's will I may now at last succeed in coming to you. [11] For I long to see you, that I may impart to you some spiritual gift to strengthen you, [12] that is, that we may be mutually encouraged by each other's faith, both yours and mine. [13] I want you to know, brethren, that I have often intended to come to you (but thus far have been prevented), in order that I may reap some harvest among you as well as among the rest of the Gentiles. [14] I am under obligation both to Greeks and to barbarians, both to the wise and to the foolish: [15] so I am eager to preach the gospel to you also who are in Rome.

Rom 10:5-13 (§41)

5 Moses writes that the man who practices the righteousness which is based on the law shall live by it. [6] But the righteousness based on faith says, Do not say in your heart, "Who will ascend into heaven?" (that is, to bring Christ down) [7] or "Who will descend into the abyss?" (that is, to bring Christ up from the dead). [8] But what does it say? The word is near you, on your lips and in your heart (that is, the word of faith which we preach); [9] because, if you confess with your lips that Jesus is Lord and believe in your heart that God raised him from the dead, you will be saved. [10] For man believes with his heart and so is justified, and he confesses with his lips and so is saved. [11] The scripture says, "No one who believes in him will be put to shame." [12] For there is no distinction between Jew and Greek; the same Lord is Lord of all and bestows his riches upon all who call upon him. [13] For, "every one who calls upon the name of the Lord will be saved."

Rom 15:14-21 (§62)

14 I myself am satisfied about you, my brethren, that you yourselves are full of goodness, filled with all knowledge, and able to instruct one another. [15] But on some points I have written to you very boldly by way of reminder, because of the grace given me by God [16] to be a minister of Christ Jesus to the Gentiles in the priestly service of the gospel of God, so that the offering of the Gentiles may be acceptable, sanctified by the Holy Spirit. [17] In Christ Jesus, then, I have reason to be proud of my work for God. [18] For I will not venture to speak of anything except what Christ has wrought through me to win obedience from the Gentiles, by word and deed, [19] by the power of signs and wonders, by the power of the Holy Spirit, so that from Jerusalem and as far round as Illyr'icum I have fully preached the gospel of Christ, [20] thus making it my ambition to preach the gospel, not where Christ has already been named, lest I build on another man's foundation, [21] but as it is written,

"They shall see who have never been
told of him,
and they shall understand who have
never heard of him."

1 Cor 1:4-9 (§72)

4 I give thanks to God always for you because of the grace of God which was given you in Christ Jesus, [5] that in every way you were enriched in him with all speech and all knowledge— [6] even as the testimony to Christ was confirmed among you— [7] so that you are not lacking in any spiritual gift, as you wait for the revealing of our Lord Jesus Christ; [8] who will sustain you to the end, guiltless in the day of our Lord Jesus Christ. [9] God is faithful, by whom you were called into the fellowship of his Son, Jesus Christ our Lord.

1 Cor 2:1-5 (§76)

2 When I came to you, brethren, I did not come proclaiming to you the testimony of God in lofty words or wisdom. [2] For I decided to know nothing among you except Jesus Christ and him crucified. [3] And I was with you in weakness and in much fear and trembling; [4] and my speech and my message were not in plausible words of wisdom, but in demonstration of the Spirit and of power, [5] that your faith might not rest in the wisdom of men but in the power of God.

1 Cor 10:14-22 (§110)

14 Therefore, my beloved, shun the worship of idols. [15] I speak as to sensible men; judge for yourselves what I say. [16] The cup of blessing which we bless, is it not a participation in the blood of Christ? The bread which we break, is it not a participation in the body of Christ? [17] Because there is one bread, we who are many are one body, for we all partake of the one bread. [18] Consider the people of Israel; are not those who eat the sacrifices partners in the altar? [19] What do I imply then? That food offered to idols is anything, or that an idol is anything? [20] No, I imply that what pagans sacrifice they offer to demons and not to God. I do not want you to be partners with demons. [21] You cannot drink the cup of the Lord and the cup of demons. You cannot partake of the table of the Lord and the table of demons. [22] Shall we provoke the Lord to jealousy? Are we stronger than he?

2 Cor 8:1-7 (§171)

8 We want you to know, brethren, about the grace of God which has been shown in the churches of Macedo'nia, [2] for in a severe test of affliction, their abundance of joy and their extreme poverty have overflowed in a wealth of liberality on their part. [3] For they gave according to their means, as I can testify, and beyond their means, of their own free will, [4] begging us earnestly for the favor of taking part in the relief of the saints— [5] and this, not as we expected, but first they gave themselves to the Lord and to us by the will of God. [6] Accordingly we have urged Titus that as he had already made a beginning, he should also complete among you this gracious work. [7] Now as you excel in everything—in faith, in utterance, in knowledge, in all earnestness, and in your love for us—see that you excel in this gracious work also.

2 Cor 9:1-5 (§174)

9 Now it is superfluous for me to write to you about the offering for the saints, [2] for I know your readiness, of which I boast about you to the people of Macedo'nia, saying that Acha'ia has been ready since last year; and your zeal has stirred up most of them. [3] But I am sending the brethren so that our boasting about you may not prove vain in this case, so that you may be ready, as I said you would be; [4] lest if some Macedo'nians come with me and find that you are not ready, we be humiliated—to say nothing of you—for being so confident. [5] So I thought it necessary to urge the brethren to go on to you before me, and arrange in advance for this gift you have promised, so that it may be ready not as an exaction but as a willing gift.

Gal 3:1-5 (§200)

3 O foolish Galatians! Who has bewitched you, before whose eyes Jesus Christ was publicly portrayed as crucified? [2] Let me ask you only this: Did you receive the Spirit by works of the law, or by hearing with faith? [3] Are you so foolish? Having begun with the Spirit, are you now ending with the flesh? [4] Did you experience so many things in vain?—if it really is in vain. [5] Does he who supplies the Spirit to you and works miracles among you do so by works of the law, or by hearing with faith?

Gal 4:12-20 (§209)

12 Brethren, I beseech you, become as I am, for I also have become as you are. You did me no wrong; [13] you know it was because of a bodily ailment that I preached the gospel to you at first; [14] and though my condition was a trial to you, you did not scorn or despise me, but received me as an angel of God, as Christ Jesus. [15] What has become of the satisfaction you felt? For I bear you witness that, if possible, you would have plucked out your eyes and given them to me. [16] Have I then become your enemy by telling you the truth? [17] They make much of you, but for no good purpose; they want to shut you out, that you may make much of them. [18] For a good purpose it is always good to be made much of, and not only when I am present with you. [19] **My little children, with whom I am again in travail until Christ be formed in you!** [20] I could wish to be present with you now and to change my tone, for I am perplexed about you.

Gal 4:8-11 (§208)

8 Formerly, when you did not know God, you were in bondage to beings that by nature are no gods; [9] but now that you have come to know God, or rather to be known by God, how can you turn back again to the weak and beggarly elemental spirits, whose slaves you want to be once more? [10] You observe days, and months, and seasons, and years! [11] I am afraid I have labored over you in vain.

▶1:5 Acts 13:52

[52] And the disciples were filled with joy and with the Holy Spirit.

▶1:6 Acts 17:5-10

[5] But the Jews were jealous, and taking some wicked fellows of the rabble, they gathered a crowd, set the city in an uproar, and attacked the house of Jason, seeking to bring them out to the people. [6] And when they could not find them, they dragged Jason and some of the brethren before the city authorities, crying, "These men who have turned the world upside down have come here also, [7] and Jason has received them; and they are all acting against the decrees of Caesar, saying that there is another king, Jesus." [8] And the people and the city authorities were disturbed when they heard this. [9] And when they had taken security from Jason and the rest, they let them go.

10 The brethren immediately sent Paul and Silas away by night to Beroe'a; and when they arrived they went into the Jewish synagogue.

▶1:7 Acts 18:12

12 But when Gallio was proconsul of Acha'ia, the Jews made a united attack upon Paul and brought him before the tribunal,

▶1:9 Acts 14:15

[15] "Men, why are you doing this? We also are men, of like nature with you, and bring you good news, that you should turn from these vain things to a living God who made the heaven and the earth and the sea and all that is in them.

▶1:10 Acts 2:24,

[24] But God raised him up, having loosed the pangs of death, because it was not possible for him to be held by it.

Tit 2:13

[13] awaiting our blessed hope, the appearing of the glory of our great God and Savior Jesus Christ,

▶1:2 2:13

13 And we also thank God constantly for this, that when you received the word of God which you heard from us, you accepted it not as the word of men but as what it really is, the word of God, which is at work in you believers.

▶1:3 5:8

[8] But, since we belong to the day, let us be sober, and put on the breastplate of faith and love, and for a helmet the hope of salvation.

1Cor 13:13

[13] So faith, hope, love abide, these three; but the greatest of these is love.

Gal 5:5-6

[5] For through the Spirit, by faith, we wait for the hope of righteousness. [6] For in Christ Jesus neither circumcision nor uncircumcision is of any avail, but faith working through love.

Eph 1:15-18

For this reason, because I have heard of your faith in the Lord Jesus and your love toward all the saints, [16] I do not cease to give thanks for you, remembering you in my prayers, [17] that the God of our Lord Jesus Christ, the Father of glory, may give you a spirit of wisdom and of revelation in the knowledge of him, [18] having the eyes of your hearts enlightened, that you may know what is the hope to which he has called you, what are the riches of his glorious inheritance in the saints,

Col 1:4-5

[4] because we have heard of your faith in Christ Jesus and of the love which you have for all the saints, [5] because of the hope laid up for you in heaven. Of this you have heard before in the word of the truth, the gospel

▶1:4 Rom 9:11,

[11] though they were not yet born and had done nothing either good or bad, in order that God's purpose of election might continue, not because of works but because of his call,

11:7

7 What then? Israel failed to obtain what it sought. The elect obtained it, but the rest were hardened,

Eph 1:4

[4] even as he chose us in him before the foundation of the world, that we should be holy and blameless before him.

Col 3:12

12 Put on then, as God's chosen ones, holy and beloved, compassion, kindness, lowliness, meekness, and patience,

▶1:5 2:13

13 And we also thank God constantly for this, that when you received the word of God which you heard from us, you accepted it not as the word of men but as what it really is, the word of God, which is at work in you believers.

276

Phil 1:3-11 (§238)

3 I thank my God in all my remembrance of you, 4 always in every prayer of mine for you all making my prayer with joy, 5 thankful for your partnership in the gospel from the first day until now. 6And I am sure that he who began a good work in you will bring it to completion at the day of Jesus Christ. 7 It is right for me to feel thus about you all, because I hold you in my heart, for you are all partakers with me of grace, both in my imprisonment and in the defense and confirmation of the gospel. 8 For God is my witness, how I yearn for you all with the affection of Christ Jesus. 9And it is my prayer that your love may abound more and more, with knowledge and all discernment, 10 so that you may approve what is excellent, and may be pure and blameless for the day of Christ, 11 filled with the fruits of righteousness which come through Jesus Christ, to the glory and praise of God.

Phil 3:17-21 (§249)

17 Brethren, join in imitating me, and mark those who so live as you have an example in us. 18 For many, of whom I have often told you and now tell you even with tears, live as enemies of the cross of Christ. 19 Their end is destruction, their god is the belly, and they glory in their shame, with minds set on earthly things. 20 But our commonwealth is in heaven, and from it we await a Savior, the Lord Jesus Christ, 21 who will change our lowly body to be like his glorious body, by the power which enables him even to subject all things to himself.

Col 1:3-14 (§257)

3 We always thank God, the Father of our Lord Jesus Christ, when we pray for you, 4 because we have heard of your faith in Christ Jesus and of the love which you have for all the saints, 5 because of the hope laid up for you in heaven. Of this you have heard before in the word of the truth, the gospel 6 which has come to you, as indeed in the whole world it is bearing fruit and growing—so among yourselves, from the day you heard and understood the grace of God in truth, 7 as you learned it from Ep´aphras our beloved fellow servant. He is a faithful minister of Christ on our behalf 8 and has made known to us your love in the Spirit.

9 And so, from the day we heard of it, we have not ceased to pray for you, asking that you may be filled with the knowledge of his will in all spiritual wisdom and understanding, 10 to lead a life worthy of the Lord, fully pleasing to him, bearing fruit in every good work and increasing in the knowledge of God. 11May you be strengthened with all power, according to his glorious might, for all endurance and patience with joy, 12 giving thanks to the Father, who has qualified us to share in the inheritance of the saints in light. 13 He has delivered us from the dominion of darkness and transferred us to the kingdom of his beloved Son, 14 in whom we have redemption, the forgiveness of sins.

1 Thes 1:2-10

2 We give thanks to God always for you all, constantly mentioning you in our prayers, 3 remembering before our God and Father your work of faith and labor of love and steadfastness of hope in our Lord Jesus Christ. 4 For we know, brethren beloved by God, that he has chosen you; 5 for our gospel came to you not only in word, but also in power and in the Holy Spirit and with full conviction. You know what kind of men we proved to be among you for your sake. 6And you became imitators of us and of the Lord, for you received the word in much affliction, with joy inspired by the Holy Spirit; 7 so that you became an example to all the believers in Macedo´nia and in Acha´ia. 8 For not only has the word of the Lord sounded forth from you in Macedo´nia and Acha´ia, but your faith in God has gone forth everywhere, so that we need not say anything. 9 For they themselves report concerning us what a welcome we had among you, and how you turned to God from idols, to serve a living and true God, 10 and to wait for his Son from heaven, whom he raised from the dead, Jesus who delivers us from the wrath to come.

2 Thes 1:3-12 (§295)

3 We are bound to give thanks to God always for you, brethren, as is fitting, because your faith is growing abundantly, and the love of every one of you for one another is increasing. 4 Therefore we ourselves boast of you in the churches of God for your steadfastness and faith in all your persecutions and in the afflictions which you are enduring.

5 This is evidence of the righteous judgment of God, that you may be made worthy of the kingdom of God, for which you are suffering—6 since indeed God deems it just to repay with affliction those who afflict you, 7 and to grant rest with us to you who are afflicted, when the Lord Jesus is revealed from heaven with his mighty angels in flaming fire, 8 inflicting vengeance upon those who do not know God and upon those who do not obey the gospel of our Lord Jesus. 9 They shall suffer the punishment of eternal destruction and exclusion from the presence of the Lord and from the glory of his might, 10 when he comes on that day to be glorified in his saints, and to be marveled at in all who have believed, because our testimony to you was believed. 11 To this end we always pray for you, that our God may make you worthy of his call, and may fulfil every good resolve and work of faith by his power, 12 so that the name of our Lord Jesus may be glorified in you, and you in him, according to the grace of our God and the Lord Jesus Christ.

2 Thes 2:13-15 (§297)

13 But we are bound to give thanks to God always for you, brethren beloved by the Lord, because God chose you from the beginning to be saved, through sanctification by the Spirit and belief in the truth. 14 To this he called you through our gospel, so that you may obtain the glory of our Lord Jesus Christ. 15 So then, brethren, stand firm and hold to the traditions which you were taught by us, either by word of mouth or by letter.

Phm 4-7 (§306)

4 I thank my God always when I remember you in my prayers, 5 because I hear of your love and of the faith which you have toward the Lord Jesus and all the saints, 6 and I pray that the sharing of your faith may promote the knowledge of all the good that is ours in Christ. 7 For I have derived much joy and comfort from your love, my brother, because the hearts of the saints have been refreshed through you.

▶1:6 2:14
14 For you, brethren, became imitators of the churches of God in Christ Jesus which are in Judea; for you suffered the same things from your own countrymen as they did from the Jews,

2 Thes 3:7-9 7 For you yourselves know how you ought to imitate us; we were not idle when we were with you, 8 we did not eat any one's bread without paying, but with toil and labor we worked night and day, that we might not burden any of you. 9 It was not because we have not that right, but to give you in our conduct an example to imitate.

1 Cor 11:1
1 Be imitators of me, as I am of Christ.

▶ 1:7 2:14
14 For you, brethren, became imitators of the churches of God in Christ Jesus which are in Judea; for you suffered the same things from your own countrymen as they did from the Jews,

▶1:8 Rom 10:18
18 But I ask, have they not heard? Indeed they have; for
"Their voice has gone out to all the earth,
and their words to the ends of the world."

▶1:9 1 Cor 12:2
2 You know that when you were heathen, you were led astray to dumb idols, however you may have been moved.

▶ 1:10 4:14
14 For since we believe that Jesus died and rose again, even so, through Jesus, God will bring with him those who have fallen asleep.

Rom 5:9
9 Since, therefore, we are now justified by his blood, much more shall we be saved by him from the wrath of God.

Col 1:5
5 because of the hope laid up for you in heaven. Of this you have heard before in the word of the truth, the gospel

277

Rom 16:17-20a (§67)

17 I appeal to you, brethren, to take note of those who create dissensions and difficulties, in opposition to the doctrine which you have been taught; avoid them. 18 For such persons do not serve our Lord Christ, but their own appetites, and by fair and flattering words they deceive the hearts of the simple-minded. 19 For while your obedience is known to all, so that I rejoice over you, I would have you wise as to what is good and guileless as to what is evil; 20 then the God of peace will soon crush Satan under your feet.

▶ 2:2 Acts 14:5.
5 When an attempt was made by both Gentiles and Jews, with their rulers, to molest them and to stone them,

16:19-24,
19 But when her owners saw that their hope of gain was gone, they seized Paul and Silas and dragged them into the market place before the rulers;

1 Cor 4:14-21 (§86)

14 I do not write this to make you ashamed, but to admonish you as my beloved children. 15 For though you have countless guides in Christ, you do not have many fathers. For I became your father in Christ Jesus through the gospel. 16 I urge you, then, be imitators of me. 17 Therefore I sent to you Timothy, my beloved and faithful child in the Lord, to remind you of my ways in Christ, as I teach them everywhere in every church. 18 Some are arrogant, as though I were not coming to you. 19 But I will come to you soon, if the Lord wills, and I will find out not the talk of these arrogant people but their power. 20 For the kingdom of God does not consist in talk but in power. 21 What do you wish? Shall I come to you with a rod, or with love in a spirit of gentleness?

1 Cor 9:15-18 (§106)

15 But I have made no use of any of these rights, nor am I writing this to secure any such provision. For I would rather die than have any one deprive me of my ground for boasting. 16 For if I preach the gospel, that gives me no

20 and when they had brought them to the magistrates they said, "These men are Jews and they are disturbing our city. 21 They advocate customs which it is not lawful for us Romans to accept or practice." 22 The crowd joined in attacking them; and the magistrates tore the garments off them and gave orders to beat them with rods. 23 And when they had inflicted many blows

2 Cor 4:1-6 (§158)

4 Therefore, having this ministry by the mercy of God, we do not lose heart. 2 We have renounced disgraceful, underhanded ways; we refuse to practice cunning or to tamper with God's word, but by the open statement of the truth we would commend ourselves to every man's conscience in the sight of God. 3 And even if our gospel is veiled, it is veiled only to those who are perishing. 4 In their case the god of this world has blinded the minds of the unbelievers, to keep them from seeing the light of the gospel of the glory of Christ, who is the likeness of God. 5 For what we preach is not ourselves, but Jesus Christ as Lord, with ourselves as your

ground for boasting. For necessity is laid upon me. Woe to me if I do not preach the gospel! 17 For if I do this of my own will, I have a reward; but if not of my own will, I am entrusted with a commission. 18 What then is my reward? Just this: that in my preaching I may make the gospel free of charge, not making full use of my right in the gospel.

upon them, they threw them into prison, charging the jailer to keep them safely. 24 Having received this charge, he put them into the inner prison and fastened their feet in the stocks.

*cf 17:1-9

servants for Jesus' sake. 6 For it is the God who said, "Let light shine out of darkness," who has shone in our hearts to give the light of the knowledge of the glory of God in the face of Christ.

2 Cor 6:1-10 (§165)

6 Working together with him, then, we entreat you not to accept the grace of God in vain. 2 For he says,
"At the acceptable time I have listened to you,
and helped you on the day of salvation."
Behold, now is the acceptable time; behold, now is the day of salvation. 3 We put no obstacle in any one's way, so that no fault may be found with our ministry, 4 but as servants of God we commend ourselves in every way: through great endurance, in afflictions, hardships, calamities, 5 beatings, imprisonments, tumults, labors, watching, hunger; 6 by purity, knowledge, forbearance, kindness, the Holy Spirit, genuine love, 7 truthful speech, and the power of God; with the weapons of righteousness for the right hand and for the left; 8 in honor and dishonor, in ill repute and good repute. We are treated

▶ 2:4 1 Tim 1:11 11 in accordance with the glorious gospel of the blessed God with which I have been entrusted.

▶ 2:5 Acts 20:33 33 I coveted no one's silver or gold or apparel.

as impostors, and yet are true; 9 as unknown, and yet well known; as dying, and behold we live; as punished, and yet not killed; 10 as sorrowful, yet always rejoicing; as poor, yet making many rich; as having nothing, and yet possessing everything.

2 Cor 7:2-4 (§168)

2 Open your hearts to us; we have wronged no one, we have corrupted no one, we have taken advantage of no one. 3 I do not say this to condemn you, for I said before that you are in our hearts, to die together and to live together. 4 I have great confidence in you; I have great pride in you; I am filled with comfort. With all our affliction, I am overjoyed.

2 Cor 10:1-6 (§176)

10 I, Paul, myself entreat you, by the meekness and gentleness of Christ—I who am humble when face to face with you, but bold to you when I am away!— 2 I beg of you that when I am present I may not have to show boldness with such confidence as I count on showing against some who suspect us of acting in worldly fashion.

▶ 2:7 2 Tim 2:24-25 24 And the Lord's servant must not be quarrelsome but kindly to every one, an apt teacher, forbearing, 25 correcting his opponents with gentleness. God may perhaps grant that they will repent and come to know the truth,

278. You remember our labor and toil

278

1 Cor 4:8-13 (§85)

8 Already you are filled! Already you have become rich! Without us you have become kings! And would that you did reign, so that we might share the rule with you! 9 For I think that God has exhibited us apostles as last of all, like men sentenced to death; because we have become a spectacle to the world, to angels and to men. 10 We are fools for Christ's sake, but you are wise in Christ. We are weak, but you are strong. You are held in honor, but we in disrepute. 11 To the present hour we hunger and thirst, we are ill-clad and buffeted and homeless, 12 and we labor, working with our own hands. When reviled, we bless; when persecuted, we endure; 13 when slandered, we try to conciliate; we have become, and are now, as the refuse of the world, the offscouring of all things.

1 Cor 4:14-21 (§86)

14 I do not write this to make you ashamed, but to admonish you as my beloved children. 15 For though you have countless guides in Christ, you do not have many fathers. For I became your father in Christ Jesus through the

▶ 2:11 Acts 20:31, 31 Therefore be alert, remembering that for three years I did not cease night or day to admonish every one with tears.

Heb 5:13-14 13 for every one who lives on milk is unskilled in the word of righteousness, for he is a child. 14 But solid food is for the mature, for those who have their faculties trained by practice to distinguish good from evil.

2 Cor 1:12-14 (§148)

12 For our boast is this, the testimony of our conscience that we have behaved in the world, and still more toward you, with holiness and godly sincerity, not by earthly wisdom but by the grace of God. 13 For we write you nothing but what you can read and understand; I hope you will understand fully, 14 as you have understood in part, that you can be proud of us as we can be of you, on the day of the Lord Jesus.

gospel. 16 I urge you, then, be imitators of me. 17 Therefore I sent to you Timothy, my beloved and faithful child in the Lord, to remind you of my ways in Christ, as I teach them everywhere in every church. 18 Some are arrogant, as though I were not coming to you. 19 But I will come to you soon, if the Lord wills, and I will find out not the talk of these arrogant people but their power. 20 For the kingdom of God does not consist in talk but in power. 21 What do you wish? Shall I come to you with a rod, or with love in a spirit of gentleness?

1 Pet 2:2 2 Like newborn babes, long for the pure spiritual milk, that by it you may grow up to salvation;

1 Cor 9:1-14 (§105)

9 Am I not free? Am I not an apostle? Have I not seen Jesus our Lord? Are not you my workmanship in the Lord? 2 If to others I am not an apostle, at least I am to you; for you are the seal of my apostleship in the Lord.
3 This is my defense to those who would examine me. 4 Do we not have the right to our food and drink? 5 Do we not have the right to be accompanied by a wife, as the other apostles and the brothers of the Lord and Cephas? 6 Or is it only Barnabas and I who have no right to refrain from working for a living? 7 Who serves as a soldier at his own expense? Who plants a vineyard without eating any of its fruit? Who tends a flock without getting some of the milk?
8 Do I say this on human authority? Does not the law say the same? 9 For it is written in the law of Moses, "You shall not muzzle an ox when it is treading out the grain." Is it for oxen that God is concerned? 10 Does he not speak entirely for our sake? It was written for our sake, because the plowman should plow in hope and the thresher thresh in

hope of a share in the crop. 11 If we have sown spiritual good among you, is it too much if we reap your material benefits? 12 If others share this rightful claim upon you, do not we still more?
Nevertheless, we have not made use of this right, but we endure anything rather than put an obstacle in the way of the gospel of Christ. 13 Do you not know that those who are employed in the temple service get their food from the temple, and those who serve at the altar share in the sacrificial offerings? 14 In the same way, the Lord commanded that those who proclaim the gospel should get their living by the gospel.

Phil 1:5 5 thankful for your partnership in the gospel from the first day until now.

▶ 2:10 Eph 1:4, 4 even as he chose us in him before the foundation of the world, that we should be holy and blameless before him.

▶ 2:9 2 Cor 11:8-9 8 I robbed other churches by accepting support from them in order to serve you. 9 And when I was with you and was in want, I did not burden any one, for my needs were supplied by the brethren who came from Macedo'nia. So I refrained and will refrain from burdening you in any way.

12:13-14 13 For in what were you less favored than the rest of the churches, except that I myself did not burden you? Forgive me this wrong!
14 Here for the third time I am ready to come to you. And I will not be a burden, for I seek not what is yours but you; for children ought not to lay up for their parents, but parents for their children.

2 Cor (cont)

3 For though we live in the world we are not carrying on a worldly war, 4 for the weapons of our warfare are not worldly but have divine power to destroy strongholds. 5 We destroy arguments and every proud obstacle to the knowledge of God, and take every thought captive to obey Christ, 6 being ready to punish every disobedience, when your obedience is complete.

2 Cor 12:14-18 (§187)

14 Here for the third time I am ready to come to you. And I will not be a burden, for I seek not what is yours but you; for children ought not to lay up for their parents, but parents for their children. 15 I will most gladly spend and be spent for your souls. If I love you the more, am I to be loved the less? 16 But granting that I myself did not burden you, I was crafty, you say, and got the better of you by guile. 17 Did I take advantage of you through any of those whom I sent to you? 18 I urged Titus to go, and sent the brother with him. Did Titus take advantage of you? Did we not act in the same spirit? Did we not take the same steps?

Heb 5:13-14   13 for every one who lives on milk is unskilled in the word of righteousness, for he is a child. 14 But solid food is for the mature, for those who have their faculties trained by practice to distinguish good from evil.

Col 2:4-7 (§261)

4 I say this in order that no one may delude you with beguiling speech. 5 For though I am absent in body, yet I am with you in spirit, rejoicing to see your good order and the firmness of your faith in Christ.

6 As therefore you received Christ Jesus the Lord, so live in him, 7 rooted and built up in him and established in the faith, just as you were taught, abounding in thanksgiving.

1 Pet 2:2   2 Like newborn babes, long for the pure spiritual milk, that by it you may grow up to salvation;

1 Thes 2:1-8

2 For you yourselves know, brethren, that our visit to you was not in vain; 2 but though we had already suffered and been shamefully treated at Philippi, as you know, we had courage in our God to declare to you the gospel of God in the face of great opposition. 3 For our appeal does not spring from error or uncleanness, nor is it made with guile; 4 but just as we have been approved by God to be entrusted with the gospel, so we speak, not to please men, but to please God who tests our hearts. 5 For we never used either words of flattery, as you know, or a cloak for greed, as God is witness; 6 nor did we seek glory from men, whether from you or from others, though we might have made demands as apostles of Christ. 7 But we were gentle among you, like a nurse taking care of her children. 8 So, being affectionately desirous of you, we were ready to share with you not only the gospel of God but also our own selves, because you had become very dear to us.

▶ 2:8 Acts 20:24   24 But I do not account my life of any value nor as precious to myself, if only I may accomplish my course and the ministry which I received from the Lord Jesus, to testify to the gospel of the grace of God.

▶ 2:2 *cf 2 Cor 11:21b-29

▶ 2:4 *cf Gal 1:10 Eph 3:2 1 Cor 4:5

▶ 2:6 *cf Phm 8

▶ 2:7 *cf 1 Cor 3:2, 4:14, 21, 2 Cor 6:13 Gal 4:19, 21-31 Phil 2:22 1 Cor 14:20 Eph 5:1

▶ 2:8 *cf 3:6 Phil 1:10, 4:1

277

▶ 2:7 (gentle) read babes: p65 SBC*D*G it vg cop(bo) Clement; text: AC2Dc Koine Lect syr cop(sa) Clement

278. You remember our labor and toil

Phil 4:10-20 (§253)

10 I rejoice in the Lord greatly that now at length you have revived your concern for me; you were indeed concerned for me, but you had no opportunity. 11 Not that I complain of want; for I have learned, in whatever state I am, to be content. 12 I know how to be abased, and I know how to abound; in any and all circumstances I have learned the secret of facing plenty and hunger, abundance and want. 13 I can do all things in him who strengthens me.

14 Yet it was kind of you to share my trouble. 15 And you Philippians yourselves know that in the beginning of the gospel, when I left Macedo'nia, no church entered into partnership with me in giving and receiving except you only; 16 for even in Thessaloni'ca you sent me help once and again. 17 Not that I seek the gift; but I seek the fruit which increases your credit. 18 I have received full payment, and more; I am filled, having received from Epaphrodi'tus the gifts you sent, a fragrant offering, a sacrifice acceptable and pleasing to God. 19 And my God will supply

every need of yours according to his riches in glory in Christ Jesus. 20 To our God and Father be glory for ever and ever. Amen.

1 Thes 2:9-12

9 For you remember our labor and toil, brethren; we worked night and day, that we might not burden any of you, while we preached to you the gospel of God. 10 You are witnesses, and God also, how holy and righteous and blameless was our behavior to you believers; 11 for you know how, like a father with his children, we exhorted each one of you and encouraged you and charged you 12 to lead a life worthy of God, who calls you into his own kingdom and glory.

2 Thes 3:6-13 (§300)

6 Now we command you, brethren, in the name of our Lord Jesus Christ, that you keep away from any brother who is living in idleness and not in accord with the tradition that you received from us. 7 For you yourselves know how you ought to imitate us; we were not idle when we were with you, 8 we did not eat any one's bread without paying, but with toil and labor we worked night and day, that we might not burden any of you. 9 It was not because we have not that right, but to give you in our conduct an example to imitate. 10 For even when we were with you, we gave you this command: If any one will not work, let him not eat. 11 For we hear that some of you are living in idleness, mere busybodies, not doing any work. 12 Now such persons we command and exhort in the Lord Jesus Christ to do their work in quietness and to earn their own living. 13 Brethren, do not be weary in well-doing.

278

5:27   27 that he might present the church to himself in splendor, without spot or wrinkle or any such thing, that she might be holy and without blemish.

Col 1:22   22 he has now reconciled in his body of flesh by his death, in order to present you holy and blameless and irreproachable before him.

1 Cor 1:30   30 He is the source of your life in Christ Jesus, whom God made our wisdom, our righteousness and sanctification and redemption;

1 Thes 5:23   23 May the God of peace himself sanctify you wholly; and may your spirit and soul and body be kept sound and blameless at the coming of our Lord Jesus Christ.

▶ 2:11 *cf 2:7 Rom 4:11 1 Cor 3:2, 2 Cor 6:13 Gal 4:19

*cf Phil 2:22 1 Cor 14:20 Eph 5:1 Gal 4:21-31

279

Rom 10:14-17 (§42)

14 But how are men to call upon him in whom they have not believed? And how are they to believe in him of whom they have never heard? And how are they to hear without a preacher? 15And how can men preach unless they are sent? As it is written, "How beautiful are the feet of those who preach good news!" 16 But they have not all obeyed the gospel; for Isaiah says, "Lord, who has believed what he has heard from us?" 17 So faith comes from what is heard, and what is heard comes by the preaching of Christ.

Rom 16:17-20a (§67)

17 I appeal to you, brethren, to take note of those who create dissensions and difficulties, in opposition to the doctrine which you have been taught; avoid them. 18 For such persons do not serve our Lord Christ, but their own appetites, and by fair and flattering words they deceive the hearts of the simple-minded. 19 For while your obedience is known to all, so that I rejoice over you, I would have you wise as to what is good and guileless as to what is evil; 20 then the God of peace will soon crush Satan under your feet.

▶ 2:14, 16 Acts 17:5. 5 But the Jews were jealous, and taking some wicked fellows of the rabble, they gathered a crowd, set the city in an uproar, and attacked the house of Jason, seeking to bring them out to the people.

1 Cor 1:18-25 (§74)

18 For the word of the cross is folly to those who are perishing, but to us who are being saved it is the power of God. 19 For it is written,
"I will destroy the wisdom of the wise,
and the cleverness of the clever I will thwart."
20 Where is the wise man? Where is the scribe? Where is the debater of this age? Has not God made foolish the wisdom of the world? 21 For since, in the wisdom of God, the world did not know God through wisdom, it pleased God through the folly of what we preach to save those who believe. 22 For Jews demand signs and Greeks seek wisdom, 23 but we preach Christ crucified, a stumbling block to Jews and folly to Gentiles, 24 but to those who are called, both Jews and Greeks, Christ the power of God and the wisdom of God. 25 For the foolishness of God is wiser than men, and the weakness of God is stronger than men.

13 13 But when the Jews of Thessaloni'ca learned that the word of God was proclaimed by Paul at Beroe'a also, they came there too, stirring up and inciting the crowds.

Gal 1:6-12 (§194)

6 I am astonished that you are so quickly deserting him who called you in the grace of Christ and turning to a different gospel—7 not that there is another gospel, but there are some who trouble you and want to pervert the gospel of Christ. 8 But even if we, or an angel from heaven, should preach to you a gospel contrary to that which we preached to you, let him be accursed. 9As we have said before, so now I say again, If any one is preaching to you a gospel contrary to that which you received, let him be accursed.

10 Am I now seeking the favor of men, or of God? Or am I trying to please men? If I were still pleasing men, I should not be a servant of Christ.

11 For I would have you know, brethren, that the gospel which was preached by me is not man's gospel. 12 For I did not receive it from man, nor was I taught it, but it came through a revelation of Jesus Christ.

▶ 2:15 Acts 2:23, 23 this Jesus, delivered up according to the definite plan and foreknowledge of God, you crucified and killed by the hands of lawless men.

7:52, 52 Which of the prophets did not your fathers persecute? And they killed those who announced beforehand the coming of the Righteous One, whom you have now betrayed and murdered,

21:13 13 Then Paul answered, "What are you doing, weeping and breaking my heart? For I am ready not only to be imprisoned but even to die at Jerusalem for the name of the Lord Jesus."

280. You are our glory and joy

280

Rom 15:22-29 (§63)

22 This is the reason why I have so often been hindered from coming to you. 23 But now, since I no longer have any room for work in these regions, and since I have longed for many years to come to you, 24 I hope to see you in passing as I go to Spain, and to be sped on my journey there by you, once I have enjoyed your company for a little. 25At present, however, I am going to Jerusalem with aid for the saints. 26 For Macedo'nia and Acha'ia have been pleased to make some contribution for the poor among the saints at Jerusalem; 27 they were pleased to do it, and indeed they are in debt to them, for if the Gentiles have come to share in their spiritual blessings, they ought also to be of service to them in material blessings. 28 When therefore I have completed this, and have delivered to them what has been raised, I shall go on by way of you to Spain; 29 and I know that when I come to you I shall come in the fulness of the blessing of Christ.

▶ 2:17-18 Rom 1:11, 11 For I long to see you, that I may impart to you some spiritual gift to strengthen you,

*cf Phm 22, Col 2:1

1 Cor 4:14-21 (§86)

14 I do not write this to make you ashamed, but to admonish you as my beloved children. 15 For though you have countless guides in Christ, you do not have many fathers. For I became your father in Christ Jesus through the gospel. 16 I urge you, then, be imitators of me. 17 Therefore I sent to you Timothy, my beloved and faithful child in the Lord, to remind you of my ways in Christ, as I teach them everywhere in every church. 18 Some are arrogant, as though I were not coming to you. 19 But I will come to you soon, if the Lord wills, and I will find out not the talk of these arrogant people but their power. 20 For the kingdom of God does not consist in talk but in power. 21 What do you wish? Shall I come to you with a rod, or with love in a spirit of gentleness?

1 Cor 16:5-9 (§139)

5 I will visit you after passing through Macedo'nia, for I intend to pass through Macedo'nia, 6 and perhaps I will stay with you or even spend the winter, so that you may speed me on my journey, wherever I go. 7 For I do not want to see you now just in passing; I hope to spend some time with you, if the Lord permits. 8 But I will stay in Ephesus until Pentecost, 9 for a wide door for effective work has opened to me, and there are many adversaries.

13 13 I want you to know, brethren, that I have often intended to come to you (but thus far have been prevented), in order that I may reap some harvest among you as well as among the rest of the Gentiles.

▶ 2:19 3:13, 13 so that he may establish your hearts unblamable in holiness before our God and Father, at the coming of our Lord Jesus with all his saints.

2 Cor 1:15-22 (§149)

15 Because I was sure of this, I wanted to come to you first, so that you might have a double pleasure; 16 I wanted to visit you on my way to Macedo'nia, and to come back to you from Macedo'nia and have you send me on my way to Judea. 17 Was I vacillating when I wanted to do this? Do I make my plans like a worldly man, ready to say Yes and No at once? 18As surely as God is faithful, our word to you has not been Yes and No. 19 For the Son of God, Jesus Christ, whom we preached among you, Silva'nus and Timothy and I, was not Yes and No; but in him it is always Yes. 20 For all the promises of God find their Yes in him. That is why we utter the Amen through him, to the glory of God. 21 But it is God who establishes us with you in Christ, and has commissioned us; 22 he has put his seal upon us and given us his Spirit in our hearts as a guarantee.

2 Cor 2:12-13 (§152)

12 When I came to Tro'as to preach the gospel of Christ, a door was opened for me in the Lord; 13 but my mind could not rest because I did not find my brother Titus there. So I took leave of them and went on to Macedo'nia.

2 Cor 7:5-13a (§169)

5 For even when we came into Macedo'nia, our bodies had no rest but we were afflicted at every turn—fighting without and fear within. 6 But God, who comforts the downcast, comforted us by the coming of Titus, 7 and not only by his coming but also by the comfort with which he was comforted in you, as he told us of your longing, your mourning, your zeal for me, so that I rejoiced still more. 8 For even if I made you sorry with my letter, I do not regret it (though I did regret it), for I see that that letter grieved you, though only for a while. 9As it is, I rejoice, not because you were grieved, but because you were grieved into repenting; for you felt a godly grief, so that you suffered no loss through us. 10 For godly grief produces a repentance that leads to salvation and brings no regret, but worldly grief produces death. 11 For see what earnestness this godly grief has produced in you, what eagerness to clear yourselves, what indignation, what alarm, what longing, what zeal, what punishment! At every point you have proved yourselves guiltless in the matter. 12 So although I wrote to you, it was not on account of the one who did the wrong, nor on account of the one who suffered the wrong, but in order that your zeal for us might be revealed to you in the sight of God. 13 Therefore we are comforted.

4:15, 15 For this we declare to you by the word of the Lord, that we who are alive, who are left until the coming of the Lord, shall not precede those who have fallen asleep.

5:23 23 May the God of peace himself sanctify you wholly; and may your spirit and soul and body be kept sound and blameless at the coming of our Lord Jesus Christ.

Phil 2:16

16 holding fast the word of life, so that in the day of Christ I may be proud that I did not run in vain or labor in vain.

1 Thes 2:13-16

13 And we also thank God constantly for this, that when you received the word of God which you heard from us, you accepted it not as the word of men but as what it really is, the word of God, which is at work in you believers. 14 For you, brethren, became imitators of the churches of God in Christ Jesus which are in Judea; for you suffered the same things from your own countrymen as they did from the Jews, 15 who killed both the Lord Jesus and the prophets, and drove us out, and displease God and oppose all men 16 by hindering us from speaking to the Gentiles that they may be saved—so as always to fill up the measure of their sins. But God's wrath has come upon them at last!

▶2:16 Acts 9:23,
23 When many days had passed, the Jews plotted to kill him,

13:45, 45 But when the Jews saw the multitudes, they were filled with jealousy, and contradicted what was spoken by Paul, and reviled him.

50, 50 But the Jews incited the devout women of high standing and the leading men of the city, and stirred up persecution against Paul and Barnabas, and drove them out of their district.

14:2, 2 But the unbelieving Jews stirred up the Gentiles and poisoned their minds against the brethren.
5, 5 When an attempt was made by both Gentiles and Jews, with their rulers, to molest them and to stone them,

19 19 But Jews came there from Antioch and Ico nium; and having persuaded the people, they stoned Paul and dragged him out of the city, supposing that he was dead.

*cf 18:12, 21:21, 27, 25:2,7 ▶2:13*cf 1:2, 5, 3:9 1 Cor 11:2

▶ 2:14*cf 1:6 Gal 4:12, 15 1 Thes 1:7 1 Cor 11:1, 4:16 Phil 3:17

▶ 2:16*cf Rom 1:18, 11:25

280. You are our glory and joy

Phil 4:1-3 (§250)

4 Therefore, my brethren, whom I love and long for, my joy and crown, stand firm thus in the Lord, my beloved.
2 I entreat Eu-o'dia and I entreat Syn'tyche to agree in the Lord. 3And I ask you also, true yokefellow, help these women, for they have labored side by side with me in the gospel together with Clement and the rest of my fellow workers, whose names are in the book of life.

1Thes 2:17-20

17 But since we were bereft of you, brethren, for a short time, in person not in heart, we endeavored the more eagerly and with great desire to see you face to face; 18 because we wanted to come to you—I, Paul, again and again—but Satan hindered us. 19 For what is our hope or joy or crown of boasting before our Lord Jesus at his coming? Is it not you? 20 For you are our glory and joy.

2 Thes 1:4
4 Therefore we ourselves boast of you in the churches of God for your steadfastness and faith in all your persecutions and in the afflictions which you are enduring.

281

Rom 8:31-39 (§34)

31 What then shall we say to this? If God is for us, who is against us? 32 He who did not spare his own Son but gave him up for us all, will he not also give us all things with him? 33 Who shall bring any charge against God's elect? It is God who justifies; 34 who is to condemn? Is it Christ Jesus, who died, yes, who was raised from the dead, who is at the right hand of God, who indeed intercedes for us? 35 Who shall separate us from the love of Christ? Shall tribulation, or distress, or persecution, or famine, or nakedness, or peril, or sword? 36As it is written,

"For thy sake we are being killed all the day long;

we are regarded as sheep to be slaughtered."

37 No, in all these things we are more than conquerors through him who loved us. 38 For I am sure that neither death, nor life, nor angels, nor principalities, nor things present, nor things to come, nor powers, 39 nor height, nor depth, nor anything else in all creation, will be able to separate us from the love of God in Christ Jesus our Lord.

▶3:1 Acts 17:15   15 Those who conducted Paul brought him as far as Athens; and receiving a command for Silas and Timothy to come to him as soon as possible, they departed.

1 Cor 4:8-13 (§85)

8 Already you are filled! Already you have become rich! Without us you have become kings! And would that you did reign, so that we might share the rule with you! 9 For I think that God has exhibited us apostles as last of all, like men sentenced to death; because we have become a spectacle to the world, to angels and to men. 10 We are fools for Christ's sake, but you are wise in Christ. We are weak, but you are strong. You are held in honor, but we in disrepute. 11 To the present hour we hunger and thirst, we are ill-clad and buffeted and homeless, 12 and we labor, working with our own hands. When reviled, we bless; when persecuted, we endure; 13 when slandered, we try to conciliate; we have become, and are now, as the refuse of the world, the offscouring of all things.

▶3:3 2 Thes 1:4

4 Therefore we ourselves boast of you in the churches of God for your steadfastness and faith in all your persecutions and in the afflictions which you are enduring.

2 Cor 1:3-11 (§147)

3 Blessed be the God and Father of our Lord Jesus Christ, the Father of mercies and God of all comfort, 4 who comforts us in all our affliction, so that we may be able to comfort those who are in any affliction, with the comfort with which we ourselves are comforted by God. 5 For as we share abundantly in Christ's sufferings, so through Christ we share abundantly in comfort too. 6 If we are afflicted, it is for your comfort and salvation; and if we are comforted, it is for your comfort, which you experience when you patiently endure the same sufferings that we suffer. 7 Our hope for you is unshaken; for we know that as you share in our sufferings, you will also share in our comfort.

8 For we do not want you to be ignorant, brethren, of the affliction we experienced in Asia; for we were so utterly, unbearably crushed that we despaired of life itself. 9 Why, we felt that we had received the sentence of death; but that was to make us rely not on ourselves but on God who raises the dead; 10 he delivered us from so deadly

▶3:2 Acts 16:1   And he came also to Derbe and to Lystra. A disciple was there, named Timothy, the son of a Jewish woman who was a believer; but his father was a Greek.

a peril, and he will deliver us; on him we have set our hope that he will deliver us again. 11 You also must help us by prayer, so that many will give thanks on our behalf for the blessing granted us in answer to many prayers.

2 Cor 7:5-13a (§169)

5 For even when we came into Macedo'nia, our bodies had no rest but we were afflicted at every turn—fighting without and fear within. 6 But God, who comforts the downcast, comforted us by the coming of Titus, 7 and not only by his coming but also by the comfort with which he was comforted in you, as he told us of your longing, your mourning, your zeal for me, so that I rejoiced still more. 8 For even if I made you sorry with my letter, I do not regret it (though I did regret it), for I see that that letter grieved you, though only for a while. 9As it is, I rejoice, not because you were grieved, but because you were grieved into repenting; for you felt a godly grief, so that you suffered no loss through us. 10 For godly grief produces a repentance that leads to salvation and brings no regret, but worldly grief produces death. 11 For

▶3:3 Acts 9:16,   16 for I will show him how much he must suffer for the sake of my name.

14:22   22 strengthening the souls of the disciples, exhorting them to continue in the faith, and saying that through many tribulations we must enter the kingdom of God.

see what earnestness this godly grief has produced in you, what eagerness to clear yourselves, what indignation, what alarm, what longing, what zeal, what punishment! At every point you have proved yourselves guiltless in the matter. 12 So although I wrote to you, it was not on account of the one who did the wrong, nor on account of the one who suffered the wrong, but in order that your zeal for us might be revealed to you in the sight of God. 13 Therefore we are comforted.

2 Cor 11:21b-29 (§183)

But whatever any one dares to boast of—I am speaking as a fool—I also dare to boast of that. 22Are they Hebrews? So am I. Are they Israelites? So am I. Are they descendants of Abraham? So am I. 23Are they servants of Christ? I am a better one—I am talking like a madman—with far greater labors, far more imprisonments, with countless beatings, and often near death. 24 Five times I have received at the hands of the Jews the forty lashes less one. 25 Three times I have been beaten with rods; once I was stoned. Three times I have been shipwrecked; a night and a day I have

▶3:5 Gal 2:2,   2 I went up by revelation; and I laid before them (but privately before those who were of repute) the gospel which I preach among the Gentiles, lest somehow I should be running or had run in vain.

---

282. We live, if you stand fast in the Lord

282

2 Cor 1:3-11 (§147)

3 Blessed be the God and Father of our Lord Jesus Christ, the Father of mercies and God of all comfort, 4 who comforts us in all our affliction, so that we may be able to comfort those who are in any affliction, with the comfort with which we ourselves are comforted by God. 5 For as we share abundantly in Christ's sufferings, so through Christ we share abundantly in comfort too. 6 If we are afflicted, it is for your comfort and salvation; and if we are comforted, it is for your comfort, which you experience when you patiently endure the same sufferings that we suffer. 7 Our hope for you is unshaken; for we know that as you share in our sufferings, you will also share in our comfort.

8 For we do not want you to be ignorant, brethren, of the affliction we experienced in Asia; for we were so utterly, unbearably crushed that we despaired of life itself. 9 Why, we felt that we had received the sentence of death; but that was to make us rely not on ourselves but on God who raises the dead; 10 he delivered us from so deadly

a peril, and he will deliver us; on him we have set our hope that he will deliver us again. 11 You also must help us by prayer, so that many will give thanks on our behalf for the blessing granted us in answer to many prayers.

▶3:6 Acts 18:5   5 When Silas and Timothy arrived from Macedo'nia, Paul was occupied with preaching, testifying to the Jews that the Christ was Jesus.

▶3:6 2:8   8 So, being affectionately desirous of you, we were ready to share with you not only the gospel of God but also our own selves, because you had become very dear to us.

Phil 4:1,   Therefore, my brethren, whom I love and long for, my joy and crown, stand firm thus in the Lord, my beloved.

1:8   8 For God is my witness, how I yearn for you all with the affection of Christ Jesus.

▶3:7-8 Rom 11:20   20 That is true. They were broken off because of their unbelief, but you stand fast only through faith. So do not become proud, but stand in awe.

1 Cor 15:1   Now I would remind you, brethren, in what terms I preached to you the gospel, which you received, in which you stand,

281

Phil 4:10-20 (§253)

10 I rejoice in the Lord greatly that now at length you have revived your concern for me; you were indeed concerned for me, but you had no opportunity. 11 Not that I complain of want; for I have learned, in whatever state I am, to be content. 12 I know how to be abased, and I know how to abound; in any and all circumstances I have learned the secret of facing plenty and hunger, abundance and want. 13 I can

2 Cor (cont)

been adrift at sea; 26 on frequent journeys, in danger from rivers, danger from robbers, danger from my own people, danger from Gentiles, danger in the city, danger in the wilderness, danger at sea, danger from false brethren; 27 in toil and hardship, through many a sleepless night, in hunger and thirst, often without food, in cold and exposure. 28 And, apart from other things, there is the daily pressure upon me of my anxiety for all the churches. 29 Who is weak, and I am not weak? Who is made to fall, and I am not indignant?

6:1 Brethren, if a man is overtaken in any trespass, you who are spiritual should restore him in a spirit of gentleness. Look to yourself, lest you too be tempted.

do all things in him who strengthens me.

14 Yet it was kind of you to share my trouble. 15 And you Philippians yourselves know that in the beginning of the gospel, when I left Macedo′nia, no church entered into partnership with me in giving and receiving except you only; 16 for even in Thessaloni′ca you sent me help once and again. 17 Not that I seek the gift; but I seek the fruit which increases to your credit. 18 I have received full payment, and more; I am filled, having received from Epaphrodi′tus the gifts you sent, a fragrant offering, a sacrifice acceptable and pleasing to God. 19 And my God will supply every need of yours according to his riches in glory in Christ Jesus. 20 To our God and Father be glory for ever and ever. Amen.

1 Cor 15:58

58 Therefore, my beloved brethren, be steadfast, immovable, always abounding in the work of the Lord, knowing that in the Lord your labor is not in vain.

1 Thes 3:1-5

3 Therefore when we could bear it no longer, we were willing to be left behind at Athens alone, 2 and we sent Timothy, our brother and God's servant in the gospel of Christ, to establish you in your faith and to exhort you, 3 that no one be moved by these afflictions. You yourselves know that this is to be our lot. 4 For when we were with you, we told you beforehand that we were to suffer affliction; just as it has come to pass, and as you know. 5 For this reason, when I could bear it no longer, I sent that I might know your faith, for fear that somehow the tempter had tempted you and that our labor would be in vain.

Phil 2:16

16 holding fast the word of life, so that in the day of Christ I may be proud that I did not run in vain or labor in vain.

1 Cor 7:5

5 Do not refuse one another except perhaps by agreement for a season, that you may devote yourselves to prayer; but then come together again, lest Satan tempt you through lack of self-control.

282. We live, if you stand fast in the Lord

282

1 Thes 3:6-10

6 But now that Timothy has come to us from you, and has brought us the good news of your faith and love and reported that you always remember us kindly and long to see us, as we long to see you—7 for this reason, brethren, in all our distress and affliction we have been comforted about you through your faith; 8 for now we live, if you stand fast in the Lord. 9 For what thanksgiving can we render to God for you, for all the joy which we feel for your sake before our God, 10 praying earnestly night and day that we may see you face to face and supply what is lacking in your faith?

▶ **3:7 2 Thes 1:4**

4 Therefore we ourselves boast of you in the churches of God for your steadfastness and faith in all your persecutions and in the afflictions which you are enduring.

3:9 2:13,

13 And we also thank God constantly for this, that when you received the word of God which you heard from us, you accepted it not as the word of men but as what it really is, the word of God, which is at work in you believers.

1:2,

2 We give thanks to God always for you all, constantly mentioning you in our prayers,

5

5 for our gospel came to you not only in word, but also in power and in the Holy Spirit and with full conviction. You know what kind of men we proved to be among you for your sake.

▶ **3:10 Rom 1:11-12**

11 For I long to see you, that I may impart to you some spiritual gift to strengthen you, 12 that is, that we may be mutually encouraged by each other's faith, both yours and mine.

Col 2:1

For I want you to know how greatly I strive for you, and for those at La-odice′a, and for all who have not seen my face,

283

1 Cor 1:4-9 (§72)

4 I give thanks to God always for you because of the grace of God which was given you in Christ Jesus, 5 that in every way you were enriched in him with all speech and all knowledge— 6 even as the testimony to Christ was confirmed among you— 7 so that you are not lacking in any spiritual gift, as you wait for the revealing of our Lord Jesus Christ; 8 who will sustain you to the end, guiltless in the day of our Lord Jesus Christ. 9 God is faithful, by whom you were called into the fellowship of his Son, Jesus Christ our Lord.

▶ 3:11-13 1 Thes 5:23-24

23 May the God of peace himself sanctify you wholly; and may your spirit and soul and body be kept sound and blameless at the coming of our Lord Jesus Christ. 24 He who calls you is faithful, and he will do it.

2 Thes 3:16

16 Now may the Lord of peace himself give you peace at all times in all ways. The Lord be with you all.

▶ 3:12 4:9

9 But concerning love of the brethren you have no need to have any one write to you, for you yourselves have been taught by God to love one another;

2 Thes 1:3

3 We are bound to give thanks to God always for you, brethren, as is fitting, because your faith is growing abundantly, and the love of every one of you for one another is increasing.

▶ 3:13 4:15,

15 For this we declare to you by the word of the Lord, that we who are alive, who are left until the coming of the Lord, shall not precede those who have fallen asleep.

2:19   19 For what is
our hope or joy or crown of boasting before our Lord Jesus at his coming? Is it not you?

2 Thes 1:7, .   7 and to
grant rest with us to you who are afflicted, when the Lord Jesus is revealed from heaven with his mighty angels in flaming fire,

10   10 when
he comes on that day to be glorified in his saints, and to be marveled at in all who have believed, because our testimony to you was believed.

Eph 1:4,   4 even as he
chose us in him before the foundation of the world, that we should be holy and blameless before him.

284. We beseech you in the Lord

284

Rom 12:1-2 (§51)

12 I appeal to you therefore, brethren, by the mercies of God, to present your bodies as a living sacrifice, holy and acceptable to God, which is your spiritual worship. 2 Do not be conformed to this world but be transformed by the renewal of your mind, that you may prove what is the will of God, what is good and acceptable and perfect.

1 Cor 1:10-17 (§73)

10 I appeal to you, brethren, by the name of our Lord Jesus Christ, that all of you agree and that there be no dissensions among you, but that you be united in the same mind and the same judgment. 11 For it has been reported to me by Chloe's people that there is quarreling among you, my brethren. 12 What I mean is that each one of you says, "I belong to Paul," or "I belong to Apollos," or "I belong to Cephas," or "I belong to Christ." 13 Is Christ divided? Was Paul crucified for you? Or were you baptized in the name of Paul? 14 I am thankful that I baptized none of you except Crispus and Gaius; 15 lest any one should say that you were baptized in my name. 16 (I did baptize also the household of Stephanas. Beyond that, I do not know whether I baptized any one else.) 17 For Christ did not send me to baptize but to preach the gospel, and not with eloquent wisdom, lest the cross of Christ be emptied of its power.

1 Cor 7:1-7 (§93)

7 Now concerning the matters about which you wrote. It is well for a man not to touch a woman. 2 But because of the temptation to immorality, each man should have his own wife and each woman her own husband. 3 The husband should give to his wife her conjugal rights, and likewise the wife to her husband. 4 For the wife does not rule over her own body, but the husband does; likewise the husband does not rule

2 Cor 10:1-6 (§176)

10 I, Paul, myself entreat you, by the meekness and gentleness of Christ—I who am humble when face to face with you, but bold to you when I am away!— 2 I beg of you that when I am present I may not have to show boldness with such confidence as I count on showing against some who suspect us of acting in worldly fashion. 3 For though we live in the world we are not carrying on a worldly war, 4 for the

over his own body, but the wife does. 5 Do not refuse one another except perhaps by agreement for a season, that you may devote yourselves to prayer; but then come together again, lest Satan tempt you through lack of self-control. 6 I say this by way of concession, not of command. 7 I wish that all were as I myself am. But each has his own special gift from God, one of one kind and one of another.

1 Cor 7:32-35 (§99)

32 I want you to be free from anxieties. The unmarried man is anxious about the affairs of the Lord, how to please the Lord; 33 but the married man is anxious about worldly affairs, how to please his wife, 34 and his interests are divided. And the unmarried woman or girl is anxious about the affairs of the Lord, how to be holy in body and spirit; but the married woman is anxious about worldly affairs, how to please her husband. 35 I say this for your own benefit,

weapons of our warfare are not worldly but have divine power to destroy strongholds. 5 We destroy arguments and every proud obstacle to the knowledge of God, and take every thought captive to obey Christ, 6 being ready to punish every disobedience, when your obedience is complete.

not to lay any restraint upon you, but to promote good order and to secure your undivided devotion to the Lord.

*cf 1 Cor 5:1-8(§87-88)

1 Cor 7:39-40 (§101)

39 A wife is bound to her husband as long as he lives. If the husband dies, she is free to be married to whom she wishes, only in the Lord. 40 But in my judgment she is happier if she remains as she is. And I think that I have the Spirit of God.

1 Cor 14:37-40 (§130)

37 If any one thinks that he is a prophet, or spiritual, he should acknowledge that what I am writing to you is a command of the Lord. 38 If any one does not recognize this, he is not recognized. 39 So, my brethren, earnestly desire to prophesy, and do not forbid speaking in tongues; 40 but all things should be done decently and in order.

Eph 4:1-10 (§225)

4 I therefore, a prisoner for the Lord, beg you to lead a life worthy of the calling to which you have been called, 2 with all lowliness and meekness, with patience, forbearing one another in love, 3 eager to maintain the unity of the Spirit in the bond of peace. 4 There is one body and one Spirit, just as you were called to the one hope that belongs to your call, 5 one Lord, one faith, one baptism, 6 one God and Father of us all, who is above all and through all and in all. 7 But grace was given to each of us according to the measure of Christ's gift. 8 Therefore it is said,

"When he ascended on high he led a host of captives,
and he gave gifts to men."

9 (In saying, "He ascended," what does it mean but that he had also descended into the lower parts of the earth? 10 He who descended is he who also ascended far above all the heavens, that he might fill all things.)

▶ 4:1 4:10

10 and indeed you do love all the brethren throughout Macedonia. But we exhort you, brethren, to do so more and more,

▶ 4:5 Gal 4:8

8 Formerly, when you did not know God, you were in bondage to beings that by nature are no gods;

1 Cor 15:34

34 Come to your right mind, and sin no more. For some have no knowledge of God. I say this to your shame.

▶ 4:8 2 Thes 3:14

14 If any one refuses to obey what we say in this letter, note that man, and have nothing to do with him, that he may be ashamed.

1 Cor 11:16,

16 If any one is disposed to be contentious, we recognize no other practice, nor do the churches of God.

7:17

17 Only, let every one lead the life which the Lord has assigned to him, and in which God has called him. This is my rule in all the churches.

*cf Phil 4:18

Col 1:21-23(§259)

21 And you, who once were estranged and hostile in mind, doing evil deeds, 22 he has now reconciled in his body of flesh by his death, in order to present you holy and blameless and irreproachable before him, 23 provided that you continue in the faith, stable and steadfast, not shifting from the hope of the gospel which you heard, which has been preached to every creature under heaven, and of which I, Paul, became a minister.

1 Thes 3:11-13

11 Now may our God and Father himself, and our Lord Jesus, direct our way to you; 12 and may the Lord make you increase and abound in love to one another and to all men, as we do to you, 13 so that he may establish your hearts unblamable in holiness before our God and Father, at the coming of our Lord Jesus with all his saints.

2 Thes 2:16-17 (§298)

16 Now may our Lord Jesus Christ himself, and God our Father, who loved us and gave us eternal comfort and good hope through grace, 17 comfort your hearts and establish them in every good work and word.

5:27

27 that he might present the church to himself in splendor, without spot or wrinkle or any such thing, that she might be holy and without blemish.

Phil 1:10

10 so that you may approve what is excellent, and may be pure and blameless for the day of Christ,

284. We beseech you in the Lord

284

1 Thes 4:1-8

4 Finally, brethren, we beseech and exhort you in the Lord Jesus, that as you learned from us how you ought to live and to please God, just as you are doing, you do so more and more. 2 For you know what instructions we gave you through the Lord Jesus. 3 For this is the will of God, your sanctification: that you abstain from unchastity; 4 that each one of you know how to take a wife for himself in holiness and honor 5 not in the passion of lust like heathen who do not know God; 6 that no man transgress, and wrong his brother in this matter, because the Lord is an avenger in all these things, as we solemnly forewarned you. 7 For God has not called us for uncleanness, but in holiness. 8 Therefore whoever disregards this, disregards not man but God, who gives his Holy Spirit to you.

2 Thes 2:1-12 (§296)

2 Now concerning the coming of our Lord Jesus Christ and our assembling to meet him, we beg you, brethren, 2 not to be quickly shaken in mind or excited, either by spirit or by word, or by letter purporting to be from us, to the effect that the day of the Lord has come. 3 Let no one deceive you in any way; for that day will not come, unless the rebellion comes first, and the man of lawlessness is revealed, the son of perdition, 4 who opposes and exalts himself against every so-called god or object of worship, so that he takes his seat in the temple of God, proclaiming himself to be God. 5 Do you not remember that when I was still with you I told you this? 6 And you know what is restraining him now so that he may be revealed in his time. 7 For the mystery of lawlessness is already at work; only he who now restrains it will do so until he is out of the way. 8 And then the lawless one will be revealed, and the Lord Jesus will slay him with the breath of his mouth and destroy him by his appearing and his coming. 9 The coming of the lawless one by the activity of Satan will be with all power and with pretended signs and wonders, 10 and with all wicked deception for those who are to perish, because they refused to love the truth and so be saved. 11 Therefore God sends upon them a strong delusion, to make them believe what is false, 12 so that all may be condemned who did not believe the truth but had pleasure in unrighteousness.

Phm 8-14 (§307)

8 Accordingly, though I am bold enough in Christ to command you to do what is required, 9 yet for love's sake I prefer to appeal to you—I, Paul, an ambassador and now a prisoner also for Christ Jesus—10 I appeal to you for my child, Ones'imus, whose father I have become in my imprisonment. 11 (Formerly he was useless to you, but now he is indeed useful to you and to me.) 12 I am sending him back to you, sending my very heart. 13 I would have been glad to keep him with me, in order that he might serve me on your behalf during my imprisonment for the gospel; 14 but I preferred to do nothing without your consent in order that your goodness might not be by compulsion but of your own free will.

285

Rom 12:9-21 (§53)

9 Let love be genuine; hate what is evil, hold fast to what is good; 10 love one another with brotherly affection; outdo one another in showing honor. 11 Never flag in zeal, be aglow with the Spirit, serve the Lord. 12 Rejoice in your hope, be patient in tribulation, be constant in prayer. 13 Contribute to the needs of the saints, practice hospitality. 14 Bless those who persecute you; bless and do not curse them. 15 Rejoice with those who rejoice, weep with those who weep. 16 Live in harmony with one another; do not be haughty, but associate with the lowly; never be conceited. 17 Repay no one evil for evil, but take thought for what is noble in the sight of all. 18 If possible, so far as it depends upon you, live peaceably with all. 19 Beloved, never avenge yourselves, but leave it to the wrath of God; for it is written, "Vengeance is mine, I will repay, says the Lord." 20 No, "if your enemy is hungry, feed him; if he is thirsty, give him drink; for by so doing you will heap burning coals upon his head." 21 Do not be overcome by evil, but overcome evil with good.

▶ 4:11-12 Acts 20:34-35
34 You yourselves know that these hands ministered to my necessities, and to those who were with me. 35 In all things I have shown you that by so toiling one must help the weak, remembering the words of the Lord Jesus, how he said, 'It is more blessed to give than to receive.' "

1 Cor 13:4-7 (§122)

4 Love is patient and kind; love is not jealous or boastful; 5 it is not arrogant or rude. Love does not insist on its own way; it is not irritable or resentful; 6 it does not rejoice at wrong, but rejoices in the right. 7 Love bears all things, believes all things, hopes all things, endures all things.

Rom 13:8-10 (§55)

8 Owe no one anything, except to love one another; for he who loves his neighbor has fulfilled the law. 9 The commandments, "You shall not commit adultery, You shall not kill, You shall not steal, You shall not covet," and any other commandment, are summed up in this sentence, "You shall love your neighbor as yourself." 10 Love does no wrong to a neighbor; therefore love is the fulfilling of the law.

▶ 4:11 Acts 18:3,
3 and because he was of the same trade he stayed with them, and they worked, for by trade they were tentmakers.

1 Tim 2:2
2 for kings and all who are in high positions, that we may lead a quiet and peaceable life, godly and respectful in every way.

Gal 5:13-15 (§212)

13 For you were called to freedom, brethren; only do not use your freedom as an opportunity for the flesh, but through love be servants of one another. 14 For the whole law is fulfilled in one word, "You shall love your neighbor as yourself." 15 But if you bite and devour one another take heed that you are not consumed by one another.

▶ 4:9 3:12, 12 and may the Lord make you increase and abound in love to one another and to all men, as we do to you,

5:1, But as to the times and the seasons, brethren, you have no need to have anything written to you.

2 Cor 9:1
Now it is superfluous for me to write to you about the offering for the saints,

---

286. Those who have fallen asleep and we who are alive

286

1 Cor 15:12-28 (§132-133)

12 Now if Christ is preached as raised from the dead, how can some of you say that there is no resurrection of the dead? 13 But if there is no resurrection of the dead, then Christ has not been raised; 14 if Christ has not been raised, then our preaching is in vain and your faith is in vain. 15 We are even found to be misrepresenting God, because we testified of God that he raised Christ, whom he did not raise if it is true that the dead are not raised. 16 For if the dead are not raised, then Christ has not been raised. 17 If Christ has not been raised, your faith is futile and you are still in your sins. 18 Then those also who have fallen asleep in Christ have perished. 19 If for this life only we have hoped in Christ, we are of all men most to be pitied.

20 But in fact Christ has been raised from the dead, the first fruits of those who have fallen asleep. 21 For as by a man came death, by a man has come also the resurrection of the dead. 22 For as in Adam all die, so also in Christ shall all be made alive. 23 But each in his own order: Christ the first fruits, then

2 Cor 4:13-15 (§160)

13 Since we have the same spirit of faith as he had who wrote, "I believed, and so I spoke," we too believe, and so we speak, 14 knowing that he who raised the Lord Jesus will raise us also with Jesus and bring us with you into his presence. 15 For it is all for your sake, so that as grace extends to more and more people it may increase thanksgiving, to the glory of God.

at his coming those who belong to Christ. 24 Then comes the end, when he delivers the kingdom to God the Father after destroying every rule and every authority and power. 25 For he must reign until he has put all his enemies under his feet. 26 The last enemy to be destroyed is death. 27 "For God has put all things in subjection under his feet." But when it says, "All things are put in subjection under him," it is plain that he is excepted who put all things under him. 28 When all things are subjected to him, then the Son himself will also be subjected to him who put all things under him, that God may be everything to every one.

2 Cor 4:16-5:5 (§161)

16 So we do not lose heart. Though our outer nature is wasting away, our inner nature is being renewed every day. 17 For this slight momentary affliction is preparing for us an eternal weight of glory beyond all comparison, 18 because we look not to the things that are seen but to the things that are unseen; for the things that are seen are transient, but the things that are unseen are eternal.

1 Cor 15:51-58 (§137)

51 Lo! I tell you a mystery. We shall not all sleep, but we shall all be changed, 52 in a moment, in the twinkling of an eye, at the last trumpet. For the trumpet will sound, and the dead will be raised imperishable, and we shall be changed. 53 For this perishable nature must put on the imperishable, and this mortal nature must put on immortality. 54 When the perishable puts on the imperishable, and the mortal puts on immortality, then shall come to pass the saying that is written:
"Death is swallowed up in victory."
55 "O death, where is thy victory?

5 For we know that if the earthly tent we live in is destroyed, we have a building from God, a house not made with hands, eternal in the heavens. 2 Here indeed we groan, and long to put on our heavenly dwelling, 3 so that by putting it on we may not be found naked. 4 For while we are still in this tent, we sigh with anxiety; not that we would be unclothed, but that we would be further clothed, so that what is mortal may be swallowed up by life. 5 He who has prepared us for this very thing is God, who has given us the Spirit as a guarantee.

O death, where is thy sting?"
56 The sting of death is sin, and the power of sin is the law. 57 But thanks be to God, who gives us the victory through our Lord Jesus Christ.

58 Therefore, my beloved brethren, be steadfast, immovable, always abounding in the work of the Lord, knowing that in the Lord your labor is not in vain.

▶ 4:17 Acts 8:39
39 And when they came up out of the water, the Spirit of the Lord caught up Philip; and the eunuch saw him no more, and went on his way rejoicing.

▶ 4:13 Eph 2:12
12 remember that you were at that time separated from Christ, alienated from the commonwealth of Israel, and strangers to the covenants of promise, having no hope and without God in the world.

▶ 4:14 1:10
10 and to wait for his Son from heaven, whom he raised from the dead, Jesus who delivers us from the wrath to come.

▶ 4:15 2:19,
19 For what is our hope or joy or crown of boasting before our Lord Jesus at his coming? Is it not you?

3:13,
13 so that he may establish your hearts unblamable in holiness before our God and Father, at the coming of our Lord Jesus with all his saints.

5:23
23 May the God of peace himself sanctify you wholly; and may your spirit and soul and body be kept sound and blameless at the coming of our Lord Jesus Christ.

285

Col 4:5-6 (§270)

5 Conduct yourselves wisely toward outsiders, making the most of the time. 6 Let your speech always be gracious, seasoned with salt, so that you may know how you ought to answer every one.

1 Thes 4:9-12

9 But concerning love of the brethren you have no need to have any one write to you, for you yourselves have been taught by God to love one another; 10 and indeed you do love all the brethren throughout Macedo′nia. But we exhort you, brethren, to do so more and more, 11 to aspire to live quietly, to mind your own affairs, and to work with your hands, as we charged you; 12 so that you may command the respect of outsiders, and be dependent on nobody.

2 Thes 3:6-13 (§300)

6 Now we command you, brethren, in the name of our Lord Jesus Christ, that you keep away from any brother who is living in idleness and not in accord with the tradition that you received from us. 7 For you yourselves know how you ought to imitate us; we were not idle when we were with you, 8 we did not eat any one's bread without paying, but with toil and labor we worked night and day, that we might not burden any of you. 9 It was not because we have not that right, but to give you in our conduct an example to imitate. 10 For even when we were with you, we gave you this command: If any one will not work, let him not eat. 11 For we hear that some of you are living in idleness, mere busybodies, not doing any work. 12 Now such persons we command and exhort in the Lord Jesus Christ to do their work in quietness and to earn their own living. 13 Brethren, do not be weary in well-doing.

▶4:10 4:1
Finally, brethren, we beseech and exhort you in the Lord Jesus, that as you learned from us how you ought to live and to please God, just as you are doing, you do so more and more.

▶ 4:11-12 1 Cor 10:31-33
31 So, whether you eat or drink, or whatever you do, do all to the glory of God. 32 Give no offense to Jews or to Greeks or to the church of God, 33 just as I try to please all men in everything I do, not seeking my own advantage, but that of many, that they may be saved.

▶4:11 Eph 4:28
28 Let the thief no longer steal, but rather let him labor, doing honest work with his hands, so that he may be able to give to those in need.

▶ 4:12 1 Cor 14:23
23 If, therefore, the whole church assembles and all speak in tongues, and outsiders or unbelievers enter, will they not say that you are mad?

286. **Those who have fallen asleep and we who are alive**

286

Phil 3:17-21 (§249)

17 Brethren, join in imitating me, and mark those who so live as you have an example in us. 18 For many, of whom I have often told you and now tell you even with tears, live as enemies of the cross of Christ. 19 Their end is destruction, their god is the belly, and they glory in their shame, with minds set on earthly things. 20 But our commonwealth is in heaven, and from it we await a Savior, the Lord Jesus Christ, 21 who will change our lowly body to be like his glorious body, by the power which enables him even to subject all things to himself.

1 Thes 4:13-18

13 But we would not have you ignorant, brethren, concerning those who are asleep, that you may not grieve as others do who have no hope. 14 For since we believe that Jesus died and rose again, even so, through Jesus, God will bring with him those who have fallen asleep. 15 For this we declare to you by the word of the Lord, that we who are alive, who are left until the coming of the Lord, shall not precede those who have fallen asleep. 16 For the Lord himself will descend from heaven with a cry of command, with the archangel's call, and with the sound of the trumpet of God. And the dead in Christ will rise first; 17 then we who are alive, who are left, shall be caught up together with them in the clouds to meet the Lord in the air; and so we shall always be with the Lord. 18 Therefore comfort one another with these words.

2 Thes 2:1-12 (§296)

2 Now concerning the coming of our Lord Jesus Christ and our assembling to meet him, we beg you, brethren, 2 not to be quickly shaken in mind or excited, either by spirit or by word, or by letter purporting to be from us, to the effect that the day of the Lord has come. 3 Let no one deceive you in any way; for that day will not come, unless the rebellion comes first, and the man of lawlessness is revealed, the son of perdition, 4 who opposes and exalts himself against every so-called god or object of worship, so that he takes his seat in the temple of God, proclaiming himself to be God. 5 Do you not remember that when I was still with you I told you this? 6 And you know what is restraining him now so that he may be revealed in his time. 7 For the mystery of lawlessness is already at work; only he who now restrains it will do so until he is out of the way. 8 And then the lawless one will be revealed, and the Lord Jesus will slay him with the breath of his mouth and destroy him by his appearing and his coming. 9 The coming of the lawless one by the activity of Satan will be with all power and with pretended signs and wonders, 10 and with all wicked deception for those who are to perish, because they refused to love the truth and so be saved. 11 Therefore God sends upon them a strong delusion, to make them believe what is false, 12 so that all may be condemned who did not believe the truth but had pleasure in unrighteousness.

Phil 1:21-26 21 For to me to live is Christ, and to die is gain. 22 If it is to be life in the flesh, that means fruitful labor for me. Yet which I shall choose I cannot tell. 23 I am hard pressed between the two. My desire is to depart and be with Christ, for that is far better. 24 But to remain in the flesh is more necessary on your account. 25 Convinced of this, I know that I shall remain and continue with you all, for your progress and joy in the faith, 26 so that in me you may have ample cause to glory in Christ Jesus, because of my coming to you again.

▶ 4:16 2 Thes 1:7, 7 and to grant rest with us to you who are afflicted, when the Lord Jesus is revealed from heaven with his mighty angels in flaming fire,

10 10 when he comes on that day to be glorified in his saints, and to be marveled at in all who have believed, because our testimony to you was believed.

▶ 4:18 5:11 11 Therefore encourage one another and build one another up, just as you are doing.

287

Rom 8:28-30 (§33)

28 We know that in everything God works for good with those who love him, who are called according to his purpose. 29 For those whom he foreknew he also predestined to be conformed to the image of his Son, in order that he might be the first-born among many brethren. 30And those whom he predestined he also called; and those whom he called he also justified; and those whom he justified he also glorified.

Rom 9:19-29 (§38)

19 You will say to me then, "Why does he still find fault? For who can resist his will?" 20 But who are you, a man, to answer back to God? Will what is molded say to its molder, "Why have you made me thus?" 21 Has the potter no right over the clay, to make out of the same lump one vessel for beauty and another for menial use? 22 What if God, desiring to show his wrath and to make known his power, has endured with much patience the vessels of wrath made for destruction, 23 in order to make known the riches of his glory for the vessels of mercy, which he has prepared beforehand for glory, 24 even us whom he has called, not from the Jews only but also from the Gentiles? 25As indeed he says in Hose´a,

"Those who were not my people
I will call 'my people,'
and her who was not beloved
I will call 'my beloved.' "

26 "And in the very place where it was said to them, 'You are not my people,'
they will be called 'sons of the living God.' "

27 And Isaiah cries out concerning Israel: "Though the number of the sons of Israel be as the sand of the sea, only a remnant of them will be saved; 28 for the Lord will execute his sentence upon the earth with rigor and dispatch." 29And as Isaiah predicted,

"If the Lord of hosts had not left us children,
we would have fared like Sodom and been made like Gomor´rah."

Rom 13:11-14 (§56)

11 Besides this you know what hour it is, how it is full time now for you to wake from sleep. For salvation is nearer

1 Cor 7:25-31 (§98)

25 Now concerning the unmarried, I have no command of the Lord, but I give my opinion as one who by the Lord's mercy is trustworthy. 26 I think that in view of the present distress it is well for a person to remain as he is. 27Are you bound to a wife? Do not seek to be free. Are you free from a wife? Do not seek marriage. 28 But if you marry, you do not sin, and if a girl marries she does not sin. Yet those who marry will have worldly troubles, and I would spare you that. 29 I mean, brethren, the appointed time has grown very short; from now on, let those who have wives live as though they had none, 30 and those who mourn as though they were not mourning, and those who rejoice as though they were not rejoicing, and those who buy as though they had no goods, 31 and those who deal with the world as though they had no dealings with it. For the form of this world is passing away.

1 Cor 16:13-14 (§141)

13 Be watchful, stand firm in your faith, be courageous, be strong. 14 Let all that you do be done in love.

to us now than when we first believed; 12 the night is far gone, the day is at hand. Let us then cast off the works of darkness and put on the armor of light; 13 let us conduct ourselves becomingly as in the day, not in reveling and drunkenness, not in debauchery and licentiousness, not in quarreling and jealousy. 14 But put on the Lord Jesus Christ, and make no provision for the flesh, to gratify its desires.

Rom 14:5-12 (§58)

5 One man esteems one day as better than another, while another man esteems all days alike. Let every one be fully convinced in his own mind. 6 He who observes the day, observes it in honor of the Lord. He also who eats, eats in honor of the Lord, since he gives thanks to God; while he who abstains, abstains in honor of the Lord and gives thanks to God. 7 None of us lives to himself, and none of us dies to himself. 8 If we live, we live to the Lord, and if we die, we die to the Lord; so then, whether we live or whether we die, we are the Lord's. 9 For to this end Christ died and lived again, that he might be

2 Cor 10:1-6 (§176)

10 I, Paul, myself entreat you, by the meekness and gentleness of Christ—I who am humble when face to face with you, but bold to you when I am away!— 2 I beg of you that when I am present I may not have to show boldness with such confidence as I count on showing against some who suspect us of acting in worldly fashion. 3 For though we live in the world we are not carrying on a worldly war, 4 for the weapons of our warfare are not worldly but have divine power to destroy strongholds. 5 We destroy arguments and every proud obstacle to the knowledge of God, and take every thought captive to obey Christ, 6 being ready to punish every disobedience, when your obedience is complete.

Lord both of the dead and of the living. 10 Why do you pass judgment on your brother? Or you, why do you despise your brother? For we shall all stand before the judgment seat of God; 11 for it is written,

"As I live, says the Lord, every knee shall bow to me,
and every tongue shall give praise to God."

12 So each of us shall give account of himself to God.

Eph 6:10-17 (§233)

10 Finally, be strong in the Lord and in the strength of his might. 11 Put on the whole armor of God, that you may be able to stand against the wiles of the devil. 12 For we are not contending against flesh and blood, but against the principalities, against the powers, against the world rulers of this present darkness, against the spiritual hosts of wickedness in the heavenly places. 13 Therefore take the whole armor of God, that you may be able to withstand in the evil day, and having done all, to stand. 14 Stand therefore, having girded your loins with truth, and having put on the breastplate of righteousness, 15 and having shod your feet with the equipment of the gospel of peace; 16 besides all these, taking the shield of faith, with which you can quench all the flaming darts of the evil one. 17And take the helmet of salvation, and the sword of the Spirit, which is the word of God.

Eph 5:3-14 (§230)

3 But fornication and all impurity or covetousness must not even be named among you, as is fitting among saints. 4 Let there be no filthiness, nor silly talk, nor levity, which are not fitting; but instead let there be thanksgiving. 5 Be sure of this, that no fornicator or impure man, or one who is covetous (that is, an idolater), has any inheritance in the kingdom of Christ and of God. 6 Let no one deceive you with empty words, for it is because of these things that the wrath of God comes upon the sons of disobedience. 7 Therefore do not associate with them, 8 for once you were darkness, but now you are light in the Lord; walk as children of light 9 (for the fruit of light is found in all that is good and right and true), 10 and try to learn what is pleasing to the Lord. 11 Take no part in the unfruitful works of darkness, but instead expose them. 12 For it is a shame even to speak of the things that they do in secret; 13 but when anything is exposed by the light it becomes visible, for anything that becomes visible is light. 14 Therefore it is said,

"Awake, O sleeper, and arise from the dead,
and Christ shall give you light."

▶ 5:1 Acts 1:7
7 He said to them, "It is not for you to know times or seasons which the Father has fixed by his own authority.

▶ 5:7 Acts 2:15
15 For these men are not drunk, as you suppose, since it is only the third hour of the day;

▶ 5:4 Acts 26:18
18 to open their eyes, that they may turn from darkness to light and from the power of Satan to God, that they may receive forgiveness of sins and a place among those who are sanctified by faith in me.'

▶ 5:1 4:9
9 But concerning love of the brethren you have no need to have any one write to you, for you yourselves have been taught by God to love one another;

2 Cor 9:1
Now it is superfluous for me to write to you about the offering for the saints,

▶ 5:2 1 Cor 1:8,
8 who will sustain you to the end, guiltless in the day of our Lord Jesus Christ.

5:5 5 you are to deliver this man to Satan for the destruction of the flesh, that his spirit may be saved in the day of the Lord Jesus.

2 Cor 1:14
14 as you have understood in part, that you can be proud of us as we can be of you, on the day of the Lord Jesus.

Phil 1:6,
6And I am sure that he who began a good work in you will bring it to completion at the day of Jesus Christ.

10, 10 so that you may approve what is excellent, and may be pure and blameless for the day of Christ,

1 Cor 13:13 13 So faith, hope, love abide, these three; but the greatest of these is love.

2:16
16 holding fast the word of life, so that in the day of Christ I may be proud that I did not run in vain or labor in vain.

▶ 5:8 1:3 3 remembering before our God and Father your work of faith and labor of love and steadfastness of hope in our Lord Jesus Christ.

Gal 5:5-6 5 For through the Spirit, by faith, we wait for the hope of righteousness. 6 For in Christ Jesus neither circumcision nor uncircumcision is of any avail, but faith working through love.

Eph 1:15-18
15 For this reason, because I have heard of your faith in the Lord Jesus and your love toward all the saints, 16 I do not cease to give thanks for you, remembering you in my prayers, 17 that the God of our Lord Jesus Christ, the Father of glory, may give you a spirit of wisdom and of revelation in the knowledge of him, 18 having the eyes of your hearts enlightened, that you may know what is the hope to which he has called you, what are the riches of his glorious inheritance in the saints,

Col 1:4-5
4 because we have heard of your faith in Christ Jesus and of the love which you have for all the saints, 5 because of the hope laid up for you in

heaven. Of this you have heard before in the word of the truth, the gospel

2 Cor 6:7 7 truthful speech, and the power of God; with the weapons of righteousness for the right hand and for the left;

▶ 5:11 4:18
18 Therefore comfort one another with these words.

Phil 2:14-18 (§244)

14 Do all things without grumbling or questioning, 15 that you may be blameless and innocent, children of God without blemish in the midst of a crooked and perverse generation, among whom you shine as lights in the world, 16 holding fast the word of life, so that in the day of Christ I may be proud that I did not run in vain or labor in vain. 17 Even if I am to be poured as a libation upon the sacrificial offering of your faith, I am glad and rejoice with you all. 18 Likewise you also should be glad and rejoice with me.

1 Thes 5:1-11

5 But as to the times and the seasons, brethren, you have no need to have anything written to you. 2 For you yourselves know well that the day of the Lord will come like a thief in the night. 3 When people say, "There is peace and security," then sudden destruction will come upon them as travail comes upon a woman with child, and there will be no escape. 4 But you are not in darkness, brethren, for that day to surprise you like a thief. 5 For you are all sons of light and sons of the day; we are not of the night or of darkness. 6 So then, let us not sleep, as others do, but let us keep awake and be sober. 7 For those who sleep sleep at night, and those who get drunk are drunk at night. 8 But, since we belong to the day, let us be sober, and put on the breastplate of faith and love, and for a helmet the hope of salvation. 9 For God has not destined us for wrath, but to obtain salvation through our Lord Jesus Christ, 10 who died for us so that whether we wake or sleep we might live with him. 11 Therefore encourage one another and build one another up, just as you are doing.

2 Thes 2:1-12 (§296)

2 Now concerning the coming of our Lord Jesus Christ and our assembling to meet him, we beg you, brethren, 2 not to be quickly shaken in mind or excited, either by spirit or by word, or by letter purporting to be from us, to the effect that the day of the Lord has come. 3 Let no one deceive you in any way; for that day will not come, unless the rebellion comes first, and the man of lawlessness is revealed, the son of perdition, 4 who opposes and exalts himself against every so-called god or object of worship, so that he takes his seat in the temple of God, proclaiming himself to be God. 5 Do you not remember that when I was still with you I told you this? 6 And you know what is restraining him now so that he may be revealed in his time. 7 For the mystery of lawlessness is already at work; only he who now restrains it will do so until he is out of the way. 8 And then the lawless one will be revealed, and the Lord Jesus will slay him with the breath of his mouth and destroy him by his appearing and his coming. 9 The coming of the lawless one by the activity of Satan will be with all power and with pretended signs and wonders, 10 and with all wicked deception for those who are to perish, because they refused to love the truth and so be saved. 11 Therefore God sends upon them a strong delusion, to make them believe what is false, 12 so that all may be condemned who did not believe the truth but had pleasure in unrighteousness.

288

Rom 12:9-21 (§53)

9 Let love be genuine; hate what is evil, hold fast to what is good; 10 love one another with brotherly affection; outdo one another in showing honor. 11 Never flag in zeal, be aglow with the Spirit, serve the Lord. 12 Rejoice in your hope, be patient in tribulation, be constant in prayer. 13 Contribute to the needs of the saints, practice hospitality.

14 Bless those who persecute you; bless and do not curse them. 15 Rejoice with those who rejoice, weep with those who weep. 16 Live in harmony with one another; do not be haughty, but associate with the lowly; never be conceited. 17 Repay no one evil for evil, but take thought for what is noble in the sight of all. 18 If possible, so far as it depends upon you, live peaceably with all. 19 Beloved, never avenge yourselves, but leave it to the wrath of God; for it is written, "Vengeance is mine, I will repay, says the Lord." 20 No, "if your enemy is hungry, feed him; if he is thirsty, give him drink; for by so doing you will heap burning coals upon his head." 21 Do not be overcome by evil, but overcome evil with good.

1 Cor 16:15-18 (§142)

15 Now, brethren, you know that the household of Steph′anas were the first converts in Acha′ia, and they have devoted themselves to the service of the saints; 16 I urge you to be subject to such men and to every fellow worker and laborer. 17 I rejoice at the coming of Steph′anas and Fortuna′tus and Acha′icus, because they have made up for your absence; 18 for they refreshed my spirit as well as yours. Give recognition to such men.

Eph 4:25-32 (§228)

25 Therefore, putting away falsehood, let every one speak the truth with his neighbor, for we are members one of another. 26 Be angry but do not sin; do not let the sun go down on your anger, 27 and give no opportunity to the devil. 28 Let the thief no longer steal, but rather let him labor, doing honest work with his hands, so that he may be able to give to those in need. 29 Let no evil talk come out of your mouths, but only such as is good for edifying, as fits the occasion, that it may impart grace to those who hear. 30 And do not grieve the Holy Spirit of God, in whom you were sealed for the day of redemption. 31 Let all bitterness and wrath and anger and clamor and slander be put away from you, with all malice, 32 and be kind to one another, tenderhearted, forgiving one another, as God in Christ forgave you.

*cf Eph 5:15-20

▶ 5:12-13 Heb 13:7-17

7 Remember your leaders, those who spoke to you the word of God; consider the outcome of their life, and imitate their faith. 8 Jesus Christ is the same yesterday and today and for ever. 9 Do not be led away by diverse and strange teachings; for it is well that the heart be strengthened by grace, not by foods, which have not benefited their adherents. 10 We have an altar from which those who serve the tent have no right to eat. 11 For the bodies of those animals whose blood is brought into the sanctuary by the high priest as a sacrifice for sin are burned outside the camp. 12 So Jesus also suffered outside the gate in order to sanctify the people through his own blood. 13 Therefore let us go forth to him outside the camp, and bear the abuse he endured. 14 For here we have no lasting city, but we seek the city which is to come. 15 Through him then let us continually offer up a sacrifice of praise to God, that is, the fruit of lips that acknowledge his name. 16 Do not neglect to do good and to share what you have, for such sacrifices are pleasing to God.

17 Obey your leaders and submit to them; for they are keeping watch over your souls, as men who will have to give account. Let them do this joyfully, and not sadly, for that would be of no advantage to you.

▶ 5:12 1 Tim 5:17

17 Let the elders who rule well be considered worthy of double honor, especially those who labor in preaching and teaching;

▶ 5:16-18 Col 3:16-17

16 Let the word of Christ dwell in you richly, teach and admonish one another in all wisdom, and sing psalms and hymns and spiritual songs with thankfulness in your hearts to God. 17 And whatever you do, in word or deed, do everything in the name of the Lord Jesus, giving thanks to God the Father through him.

1 Thes 5:12-22

12 But we beseech you, brethren, to respect those who labor among you and are over you in the Lord and admonish you, 13 and to esteem them very highly in love because of their work. Be at peace among yourselves. 14And we exhort you, brethren, admonish the idlers, encourage the fainthearted, help the weak, be patient with them all. 15 See that none of you repays evil for evil, but always seek to do good to one another and to all. 16 Rejoice always, 17 pray constantly, 18 give thanks in all circumstances; for this is the will of God in Christ Jesus for you. 19 Do not quench the Spirit, 20 do not despise prophesying, 21 but test everything; hold fast what is good, 22 abstain from every form of evil.

2 Thes 3:6-13 (§300)

6 Now we command you, brethren, in the name of our Lord Jesus Christ, that you keep away from any brother who is living in idleness and not in accord with the tradition that you received from us. 7 For you yourselves know how you ought to imitate us; we were not idle when we were with you, 8 we did not eat any one's bread without paying, but with toil and labor we worked night and day, that we might not burden any of you. 9 It was not because we have not that right, but to give you in our conduct an example to imitate. 10 For even when we were with you, we gave you this command: If any one will not work, let him not eat. 11 For we hear that some of you are living in idleness, mere busybodies, not doing any work. 12 Now such persons we command and exhort in the Lord Jesus Christ to do their work in quietness and to earn their own living. 13 Brethren, do not be weary in well-doing.

289

1 Cor 1:4-9 (§72)

4 I give thanks to God always for you because of the grace of God which was given you in Christ Jesus, 5 that in every way you were enriched in him with all speech and all knowledge— 6 even as the testimony to Christ was confirmed among you—7 so that you are not lacking in any spiritual gift, as you wait for the revealing of our Lord Jesus Christ; 8 who will sustain you to the end, guiltless in the day of our Lord Jesus Christ. 9 God is faithful, by whom you were called into the fellowship of his Son, Jesus Christ our Lord.

▶ 5:23-23 3:11-13
11 Now may our God and Father himself, and our Lord Jesus, direct our way to you; 12 and may the Lord make you increase and abound in love to one another and to all men, as we do to you, 13 so that he may establish your hearts unblamable in holiness before our God

and Father, at the coming of our Lord Jesus with all his saints.
2 Thes 2:16-17
16 Now may our Lord Jesus Christ himself, and God our Father, who loved us and gave us eternal comfort and good hope through grace, 17 comfort your hearts and establish them in every good work and word.

Rom 15:13
13 May the God of hope fill you with all joy and peace in believing, so that by the power of the Holy Spirit you may abound in hope.

▶ 5:23 2:19, 19 For what is our hope or joy or crown of boasting before our Lord Jesus at his coming? Is it not you?

4:15, 15 For this we declare to you by the word of the Lord, that we who are alive, who are left until the coming of the Lord, shall not precede those who have fallen asleep.

*cf Rom 15:33

*cf 1 Cor 7:15, 14:33

290. Pray for us

290

Rom 15:30-33 (§64)

30 I appeal to you, brethren, by our Lord Jesus Christ and by the love of the Spirit, to strive together with me in your prayers to God on my behalf, 31 that I may be delivered from the unbelievers in Judea, and that my service for Jerusalem may be acceptable to the saints, 32 so that by God's will I may come to you with joy and be refreshed in your company. 33 The God of peace be with you all. Amen.

Eph 6:18-20 (§234)
18 Pray at all times in the Spirit, with all prayer and supplication. To that end keep alert with all perseverance, making supplication for all the saints, 19 and also for me, that utterance may be given me in opening my mouth boldly to proclaim the mystery of the gospel, 20 for which I am an ambassador in chains; that I may declare it boldly, as I ought to speak.

▶5:25 1 Jn 5:13-15
13 I write this to you who believe in the name of the Son of God, that you may know that you have eternal life. 14And this is the confidence which we have in him, that if we ask anything according to his will he hears us. 15And if we know that he hears us in whatever we ask, we know that we have obtained the requests made of him.

James 5:13
13 Is any one among you suffering? Let him pray. Is any cheerful? Let him sing praise.

Heb 13:18-19
18 Pray for us, for we are sure that we have a clear conscience, desiring to act honorably in all things. 19 I urge you the more earnestly to do this in order that I may be restored to you the sooner.

▶5:25 2 Cor 1:11
11 You also must help us by prayer, so that many will give thanks on our behalf for the blessing granted us in answer to many prayers.

1 Thes 5:23-24

23 May the God of peace himself sanctify you wholly; and may your spirit and soul and body be kept sound and blameless at the coming of our Lord Jesus Christ. 24 He who calls you is faithful, and he will do it.

2 Thes 3:16 (§302)

16 Now may the Lord of peace himself give you peace at all times in all ways. The Lord be with you all.

289

2:10 10 You are witnesses, and God also, how holy and righteous and blameless was our behavior to you believers;

Col 1:22 22 he has now reconciled in his body of flesh by his death, in order to present you holy and blameless and irreproachable before him.

▶ 5:24 1 Cor 10:13 13 No temptation has overtaken you that is not common to man. God is faithful, and he will not let you be tempted beyond your strength, but with the temptation will also provide the way of escape, that you may be able to endure it.

2 Cor 1:18 18As surely as God is faithful, our word to you has not been Yes and No.

290. Pray for us

Col 4:2-4 (§269)

2 Continue steadfastly in prayer, being watchful in it with thanksgiving; 3 and pray for us also, that God may open to us a door for the word, to declare the mystery of Christ, on account of which I am in prison, 4 that I may make it clear, as I ought to speak.

1 Thes 5:25

25 Brethren, pray for us.

2 Thes 3:1-5 (§299)

3 Finally, brethren, pray for us, that the word of the Lord may speed on and triumph, as it did among you, 2 and that we may be delivered from wicked and evil men; for not all have faith. 3 But the Lord is faithful; he will strengthen you and guard you from evil. 4And we have confidence in the Lord about you, that you are doing and will do the things which we command. 5 May the Lord direct your hearts to the love of God and to the steadfastness of Christ.

Phm 21-22 (§309)

21 Confident of your obedience, I write to you, knowing that you will do even more than I say. 22At the same time, prepare a guest room for me, for I am hoping through your prayers to be granted to you.

290

291

Rom 16:3-16 (§66)

3 Greet Prisca and Aquila, my fellow workers in Christ Jesus, 4 who risked their necks for my life, to whom not only I but also all the churches of the Gentiles give thanks; 5 greet also the church in their house. Greet my beloved Epae′netus, who was the first convert in Asia for Christ. 6 Greet Mary, who has worked hard among you. 7 Greet Androni′cus and Ju′nias, my kinsmen and my fellow prisoners; they are men of note among the apostles, and they were in Christ before me. 8 Greet Amplia′tus, my beloved in the Lord. 9 Greet Urba′nus, our fellow worker in Christ, and my beloved Stachys. 10 Greet Apel′les, who is approved in Christ. Greet those who belong to the family of Aristobu′lus. 11 Greet my kinsman Hero′dion. Greet those in the Lord who belong to the family of Narcis′sus. 12 Greet those workers in the Lord, Tryphae′na and Trypho′sa. Greet the beloved Persis, who has worked hard in the Lord. 13 Greet Rufus, eminent in the Lord, also his mother and mine. 14 Greet Asyn′critus, Phlegon, Hermes, Pat′robas, Hermas,

▶ 5:26 *cf 2 Tim 4:19-21, Tit 3:15

1 Cor 16:19-20 (§143)

19 The churches of Asia send greetings. Aquila and Prisca, together with the church in their house, send you hearty greetings in the Lord. 20 All the brethren send greetings. Greet one another with a holy kiss.

and the brethren who are with them. 15 Greet Philol′ogus, Julia, Nereus and his sister, and Olym′pas, and all the saints who are with them. 16 Greet one another with a holy kiss. All the churches of Christ greet you.

Rom 16:21-23 (§69)

21 Timothy, my fellow worker, greets you; so do Lucius and Jason and Sosip′ater, my kinsmen.
22 I Tertius, the writer of this letter, greet you in the Lord.
23 Ga′ius, who is host to me and to the whole church, greets you. Eras′tus, the city treasurer, and our brother Quartus, greet you.

2 Cor 13:11-13 (§191)

11 Finally, brethren, farewell. Mend your ways, heed my appeal, agree with one another, live in peace, and the God of love and peace will be with you. 12 Greet one another with a holy kiss. 13 All the saints greet you.

292

1 Cor 16:21-22 (§144)

21 I, Paul, write this greeting with my own hand. 22 If any one has no love for the Lord, let him be accursed. Our Lord, come!

292. Read this letter to the brethren

Gal 6:11-17 (§216)

11 See with what large letters I am writing to you with my own hand. 12 It is those who want to make a good showing in the flesh that would compel you to be circumcised, and only in order that they may not be persecuted for the cross of Christ. 13 For even those who receive circumcision do not themselves keep the law, but they desire to have you circumcised that they may glory in your flesh. 14 But far be it from me to glory except in the cross of our Lord Jesus Christ, by which the world has been crucified to me, and I to the world. 15 For neither circumcision counts for anything, nor uncircumcision, but a new creation. 16 Peace and mercy be upon all who walk by this rule, upon the Israel of God.

17 Henceforth let no man trouble me; for I bear on my body the marks of Jesus.

Phil 4:21-22 (§254)

21 Greet every saint in Christ Jesus. The brethren who are with me greet you. 22All the saints greet you, especially those of Caesar's household.

Col 4:10-15 (§272)

10 Aristar'chus my fellow prisoner greets you, and Mark the cousin of Barnabas (concerning whom you have received instructions—if he comes to you, receive him), 11 and Jesus who is called Justus. These are the only men of the circumcision among my fellow workers for the kingdom of God, and they have been a comfort to me. 12 Ep'aphras, who is one of yourselves, a servant of Christ Jesus, greets you, always remembering you earnestly in his prayers, that you may stand mature and fully assured in all the will of God. 13 For I bear him witness that he has worked hard for you and for those in La-odice'a and in Hi-erap'olis. 14 Luke the beloved physician and Demas greet you. 15 Give my greetings to the brethren at La-odice'a, and to Nympha and the church in her house.

1 Thes 5:26

26 Greet all the brethren with a holy kiss.

Phm 23-24 (§310)

23 Ep'aphras, my fellow prisoner in Christ Jesus, sends greetings to you, 24 and so do Mark, Aristar'chus, Demas, and Luke, my fellow workers.

291

292. Read this letter to the brethren

292

Col 4:16-18a (§273)

16And when this letter has been read among you, have it read also in the church of the La-odice'ans; and see that you read also the letter from La-odice'a. 17And say to Archip'pus, "See that you fulfil the ministry which you have received in the Lord."

18 I, Paul, write this greeting with my own hand. Remember my fetters.

1 Thes 5:27

27 I adjure you by the Lord that this letter be read to all the brethren

2 Thes 3:17 (§303)

17 I, Paul, write this greeting with my own hand. This is the mark in every letter of mine; it is the way I write.

293. Grace

293

Rom 16:20b (§68)

The grace of our Lord Jesus Christ be with you.

1 Cor 16:23-24 (§145)

23 The grace of the Lord Jesus be with you. 24 My love be with you all in Christ Jesus. Amen.

2 Cor 13:14 (§192)

14 The grace of the Lord Jesus Christ and the love of God and the fellowship of the Holy Spirit be with you all.

Gal 6:18 (§217)

18 The grace of our Lord Jesus Christ be with your spirit, brethren. Amen.

Eph 6:23-24 (§236)

23 Peace be to the brethren, and love with faith, from God the Father and the Lord Jesus Christ. 24 Grace be with all who love our Lord Jesus Christ with love undying.

*cf 1 Tim 6:21b, 2 Tim 4:22, Tit 3:15c

Phil 4:23 (§255)	Col 4:18b (§274)	1 Thes 5:28	2 Thes 3:18 (§304)	Phm 25 (§311)
23 The grace of the Lord Jesus Christ be with your spirit.	Grace be with you.	28 The grace of our Lord Jesus Christ be with you.	18 The grace of our Lord Jesus Christ be with you all.	25 The grace of the Lord Jesus Christ be with your spirit.

293

294

Rom 1:1-7 (§1)

1 Paul, a servant of Jesus Christ, called to be an apostle, set apart for the gospel of God 2 which he promised beforehand through his prophets in the holy scriptures, 3 the gospel concerning his Son, who was descended from David according to the flesh 4 and designated Son of God in power according to the Spirit of holiness by his resurrection from the dead, Jesus Christ our Lord, 5 through whom we have received grace and apostleship to bring about the obedience of faith for the sake of his name among all the nations, 6 including yourselves who are called to belong to Jesus Christ;

7 To all God's beloved in Rome, who are called to be saints:

Grace to you and peace from God our Father and the Lord Jesus Christ.

1 Cor 1:1-3 (§71)

1 Paul, called by the will of God to be an apostle of Christ Jesus, and our brother Sos'thenes,

2 To the church of God which is at Corinth, to those sanctified in Christ Jesus, called to be saints together with all those who in every place call on the name of our Lord Jesus Christ, both their Lord and ours:

3 Grace to you and peace from God our Father and the Lord Jesus Christ.

2 Cor 1:1-2 (§146)

1 Paul, an apostle of Christ Jesus by the will of God, and Timothy our brother.

To the church of God which is at Corinth, with all the saints who are in the whole of Acha'ia:

2 Grace to you and peace from God our Father and the Lord Jesus Christ.

Gal 1:1-5 (§193)

1 Paul an apostle—not from men nor through man, but through Jesus Christ and God the Father, who raised him from the dead— 2 and all the brethren who are with me,

To the churches of Galatia:

3 Grace to you and peace from God the Father and our Lord Jesus Christ, 4 who gave himself for our sins to deliver us from the present evil age, according to the will of our God and Father; 5 to whom be the glory for ever and ever. Amen.

Eph 1:1-2 (§218)

1 Paul, an apostle of Christ Jesus by the will of God,

To the saints who are also faithful in Christ Jesus:

2 Grace to you and peace from God our Father and the Lord Jesus Christ.

▶ 1:1 Acts 16:1.

And he came also to Derbe and to Lystra. A disciple was there, named Timothy, the son of a Jewish woman who was a believer; but his father was a Greek.

17:1-9

Now when they had passed through Amphip'olis and Apollo'nia, they came to Thessaloni'ca, where there was a synagogue of the Jews. 2And Paul went in, as was his custom, and for three weeks he argued with them from the scriptures, 3 explaining and proving that it was necessary for the Christ to suffer and to rise from the dead, and saying, "This Jesus, whom I proclaim to you, is the Christ." 4And some of them were persuaded, and joined Paul and Silas; as did a great many of the devout Greeks and not a few of the leading women. 5 But the Jews were jealous, and taking some wicked fellows of the rabble, they gathered a crowd, set the city in an uproar, and attacked the house of Jason, seeking to bring them out to the people. 6And when they could not find them, they dragged Jason and some of the brethren before the city authorities, crying, "These men who have turned the world upside down have come here also, 7 and Jason has received them; and they are all acting against the decrees of Caesar, saying that there is another king, Jesus." 8And the people and the city authorities were disturbed when they heard this. 9And when they had taken security from Jason and the rest, they let them go.

Phil 1:1-2 (§237)

1 Paul and Timothy, servants of Christ Jesus,
To all the saints in Christ Jesus who are at Philippi, with the bishops and deacons:
2 Grace to you and peace from God our Father and the Lord Jesus Christ.

Col 1:1-2 (§256)

1 Paul, an apostle of Christ Jesus by the will of God, and Timothy our brother,
2 To the saints and faithful brethren in Christ at Colos´sae:
Grace to you and peace from God our Father.

1 Thes 1:1 (§275)

1 Paul, Silva´nus, and Timothy,
To the church of the Thessalo´nians in God the Father and the Lord Jesus Christ:
Grace to you and peace.

2 Thes 1:1-2

1 Paul, Silva´nus, and Timothy,
To the church of the Thessalo´nians in God our Father and the Lord Jesus Christ:
2 Grace to you and peace from God the Father and the Lord Jesus Christ.

Phm 1-3 (§305)

1 Paul, a prisoner for Christ Jesus, and Timothy our brother,
To Phile´mon our beloved fellow worker 2 and Ap´phia our sister and Archip´pus our fellow soldier, and the church in your house:
3 Grace to you and peace from God our Father and the Lord Jesus Christ.

294

295

Rom 1:8-15 (§2)

8 First, I thank my God through Jesus Christ for all of you, because your faith is proclaimed in all the world. 9 For God is my witness, whom I serve with my spirit in the gospel of his Son, that without ceasing I mention you always in my prayers, 10 asking that somehow by God's will I may now at last succeed in coming to you. 11 For I long to see you, that I may impart to you some spiritual gift to strengthen you, 12 that is, that we may be mutually encouraged by each other's faith, both yours and mine. 13 I want you to know, brethren, that I have often intended to come to you (but thus far have been prevented), in order that I may reap some harvest among you as well as among the rest of the Gentiles. 14 I am under obligation both to Greeks and to barbarians, both to the wise and to the foolish: 15 so I am eager to preach the gospel to you also who are in Rome.

1 Cor 1:4-9 (§72)

4 I give thanks to God always for you because of the grace of God which was given you in Christ Jesus, 5 that in every way you were enriched in him with all speech and all knowledge— 6 even as the testimony to Christ was confirmed among you—7 so that you are not lacking in any spiritual gift, as you wait for the revealing of our Lord Jesus Christ; 8 who will sustain you to the end, guiltless in the day of our Lord Jesus Christ. 9 God is faithful, by whom you were called into the fellowship of his Son, Jesus Christ our Lord.

1 Cor 3:10-15 (§80)

10 According to the grace of God given to me, like a skilled master builder I laid a foundation, and another man is building upon it. Let each man take care how he builds upon it. 11 For no other foundation can any one lay than that which is laid, which is Jesus Christ. 12 Now if any one builds on the foundation with gold, silver, precious stones, wood, hay, straw—13 each man's work will become manifest; for the Day will disclose it, because it will be revealed with fire, and the fire will test what sort of work each one has done. 14 If the work which any man has built on the foundation survives, he will receive a reward. 15 If any man's work is burned up, he will suffer loss, though he himself will be saved, but only as through fire.

2 Cor 1:3-11 (§147)

3 Blessed be the God and Father of our Lord Jesus Christ, the Father of mercies and God of all comfort, 4 who comforts us in all our affliction, so that we may be able to comfort those who are in any affliction, with the comfort with which we ourselves are comforted by God. 5 For as we share abundantly in Christ's sufferings, so through Christ we share abundantly in comfort too. 6 If we are afflicted, it is for your comfort and salvation; and if we are comforted, it is for your comfort, which you experience when you patiently endure the same sufferings that we suffer. 7 Our hope for you is unshaken; for we know that as you share in our sufferings, you will also share in our comfort.

8 For we do not want you to be ignorant, brethren, of the affliction we experienced in Asia; for we were so utterly, unbearably crushed that we despaired of life itself. 9 Why, we felt that we had received the sentence of death; but that was to make us rely not on ourselves but on God who raises the dead; 10 he delivered us from so deadly a peril, and he will deliver us; on him we have set our hope that he will deliver us again. 11 You also must help us by prayer, so that many will give thanks on our behalf for the blessing granted us in answer to many prayers.

2 Cor 7:2-4 (§168)

2 Open your hearts to us; we have wronged no one, we have corrupted no one, we have taken advantage of no one. 3 I do not say this to condemn you, for I said before that you are in our hearts, to die together and to live together. 4 I have great confidence in you; I have great pride in you; I am filled with comfort. With all our affliction, I am overjoyed.

▶ 1:5 Acts 14:22   22 strengthening the souls of the disciples, exhorting them to continue in the faith, and saying that through many tribulations we must enter the kingdom of God.

▶ 1:3 1 Thes 4:9,

9 But concerning love of the brethren you have no need to have any one write to you, for you yourselves have been taught by God to love one another;

3:12   12 and may the Lord make you increase and abound in love to one another and to all men, as we do to you,

2 Thes 2:13

13 But we are bound to give thanks to God always for you, brethren beloved by the Lord, because God chose you from the beginning to be saved, through sanctification by the Spirit and belief in the truth

▶ 1:4 2 Cor 9:1-3

Now it is superfluous for me to write to you about the offering for the saints, 2 for I know your readiness, of which I boast about you to the people of Macedo'nia, saying that Acha'ia has been ready since last year; and your zeal has stirred up most of them. 3 But I am sending the brethren so that our boasting about you may not prove vain in this case, so that you may be ready, as I said you would be;

▶ 1:5-10 Rom 12:14-21

14 Bless those who persecute you; bless and do not curse them. 15 Rejoice with those who rejoice, weep with those who weep. 16 Live in harmony with one another; do not be haughty, but associate with the lowly; never be conceited. 17 Repay no one evil for evil, but take thought for what is noble in the sight of all. 18 If possible, so far as it depends upon you, live peaceably with all. 19 Beloved, never avenge yourselves, but leave it to the wrath of God; for it is written, "Vengeance is mine, I will repay, says the Lord." 20 No, "if your enemy is hungry, feed him; if he is thirsty, give him drink; for by so doing you will heap burning coals upon his head." 21 Do not be overcome by evil, but overcome evil with good.

▶ 1:5 1 Thes 2:12

12 to lead a life worthy of God, who calls you into his own kingdom and glory.

▶ 1:6 Rom 12:19

19 Beloved, never avenge yourselves, but leave it to the wrath of God; for it is written, "Vengeance is mine, I will repay, says the Lord."

2 Cor 7:5

5. For even when we came into Macedo'nia, our bodies had no rest but we were afflicted at every turn—fighting without and fear within.

▶ 1:7 1 Thes 3:13,

13 so that he may establish your hearts unblamable in holiness before our God and Father, at the coming of our Lord Jesus with all his saints.

4:16   16 For the Lord himself will descend from heaven with a cry of command, with the archangel's call, and with the sound of the trumpet of God. And the dead in Christ will rise first;

2 Thes 2:8   8 And then the lawless one will be revealed, and the Lord Jesus will slay him with the breath of his mouth and destroy him by his appearing and his coming.

▶ 1:8 Rom 2:8   8 but for those who are factious and do not obey the truth, but obey wickedness, there will be wrath and fury.

▶ 1:9 Col 1:11

11 May you be strengthened with all power, according to his glorious might, for all endurance and patience with joy,

▶ 1:10 2:1,

Now concerning the coming of our Lord Jesus Christ and our assembling to meet him, we beg you, brethren,

Phil 1:3-11 (§238)

3 I thank my God in all my remembrance of you, 4 always in every prayer of mine for you all making my prayer with joy, 5 thankful for your partnership in the gospel from the first day until now. 6 And I am sure that he who began a good work in you will bring it to completion at the day of Jesus Christ. 7 It is right for me to feel thus about you all, because I hold you in my heart, for you are all partakers with me of grace, both in my imprisonment and in the defense and confirmation of the gospel. 8 For God is my witness, how I yearn for you all with the affection of Christ Jesus. 9 And it is my prayer that your love may abound more and more, with knowledge and all discernment, 10 so that you may approve what is excellent, and may be pure and blameless for the day of Christ, 11 filled with the fruits of righteousness which come through Jesus Christ, to the glory and praise of God.

Phil 1:27-30 (§241)

27 Only let your manner of life be worthy of the gospel of Christ, so that whether I come and see you or am absent, I may hear of you that you stand firm in one spirit, with one mind striving side by side for the faith of the gospel, 28 and not frightened in anything by your opponents. This is a clear omen to them of their destruction, but of your salvation, and that from God. 29 For it has been granted to you that for the sake of Christ you should not only believe in him but also suffer for his sake, 30 engaged in the same conflict which you saw and now hear to be mine.

Phil 3:17-21 (§249)

17 Brethren, join in imitating me, and mark those who so live as you have an example in us. 18 For many, of whom I have often told you and now tell you even with tears, live as enemies of the cross of Christ. 19 Their end is destruction, their god is the belly, and they glory in their shame, with minds set on earthly things. 20 But our commonwealth is in heaven, and from it we await a Savior, the Lord Jesus Christ, 21 who will change our lowly body to be like his glorious body, by the power which enables him even to subject all things to himself.

Col 1:3-14 (§257)

3 We always thank God, the Father of our Lord Jesus Christ, when we pray for you, 4 because we have heard of your faith in Christ Jesus and of the love which you have for all the saints, 5 because of the hope laid up for you in heaven. Of this you have heard before in the word of the truth, the gospel 6 which has come to you, as indeed in the whole world it is bearing fruit and growing—so among yourselves, from the day you heard and understood the grace of God in truth, 7 as you learned it from Ep′aphras our beloved fellow servant. He is a faithful minister of Christ on our behalf 8 and has made known to us your love in the Spirit.

9 And so, from the day we heard of it, we have not ceased to pray for you, asking that you may be filled with the knowledge of his will in all spiritual wisdom and understanding, 10 to lead a life worthy of the Lord, fully pleasing to him, bearing fruit in every good work and increasing in the knowledge of God. 11 May you be strengthened with all power, according to his glorious might, for all endurance and patience with joy, 12 giving thanks to the Father, who has qualified us to share in the inheritance of the saints in light. 13 He has delivered us from the dominion of darkness and transferred us to the kingdom of his beloved Son, 14 in whom we have redemption, the forgiveness of sins.

1 Thes 2-10 (§276)

2 We give thanks to God always for you all, constantly mentioning you in our prayers, 3 remembering before our God and Father your work of faith and labor of love and steadfastness of hope in our Lord Jesus Christ. 4 For we know, brethren beloved by God, that he has chosen you; 5 for our gospel came to you not only in word, but also in power and in the Holy Spirit and with full conviction. You know what kind of men we proved to be among you for your sake. 6 And you became imitators of us and of the Lord, for you received the word in much affliction, with joy inspired by the Holy Spirit; 7 so that you became an example to all the believers in Macedo′nia and in Acha′ia. 8 For not only has the word of the Lord sounded forth from you in Macedo′nia and Acha′ia, but your faith in God has gone forth everywhere, so that we need not say anything. 9 For they themselves report concerning us what a welcome we had among you, and how you turned to God from idols, to serve a living and true God, 10 and to wait for his Son from heaven, whom he raised from the dead, Jesus who delivers us from the wrath to come.

2 Thes 1:3-12

3 We are bound to give thanks to God always for you, brethren, as is fitting, because your faith is growing abundantly, and the love of every one of you for one another is increasing. 4 Therefore we ourselves boast of you in the churches of God for your steadfastness and faith in all your persecutions and in the afflictions which you are enduring.

5 This is evidence of the righteous judgment of God, that you may be made worthy of the kingdom of God, for which you are suffering—6 since indeed God deems it just to repay with affliction those who afflict you, 7 and to grant rest with us to you who are afflicted, when the Lord Jesus is revealed from heaven with his mighty angels in flaming fire, 8 inflicting vengeance upon those who do not know God and upon those who do not obey the gospel of our Lord Jesus. 9 They shall suffer the punishment of eternal destruction and exclusion from the presence of the Lord and from the glory of his might, 10 when he comes on that day to be glorified in his saints, and to be marveled at in all who have believed, because our testimony to you was believed. 11 To this end we always pray for you, that our God may make you worthy of his call, and may fulfil every good resolve and work of faith by his power, 12 so that the name of our Lord Jesus may be glorified in you, and you in him, according to the grace of our God and the Lord Jesus Christ.

Phm 4-7 (§306)

4 I thank my God always when I remember you in my prayers, 5 because I hear of your love and of the faith which you have toward the Lord Jesus and all the saints, 6 and I pray that the sharing of your faith may promote the knowledge of all the good that is ours in Christ. 7 For I have derived much joy and comfort from your love, my brother, because the hearts of the saints have been refreshed through you.

---

8   8 And then the lawless one will be revealed, and the Lord Jesus will slay him with the breath of his mouth and destroy him by his appearing and his coming.

1 Thes 2:19,   19 For what is our hope or joy or crown of boasting before our Lord Jesus at his coming? Is it not you?

5:23   23 May the God of peace himself sanctify you wholly; and may your spirit and soul and body be kept sound and blameless at the coming of our Lord Jesus Christ.

1 Cor 15:23   23 But each in his own order: Christ the first fruits, then at his coming those who belong to Christ.

1:11 Gal 5:6 6 For in Christ Jesus neither circumcision nor uncircumcision is of any avail, but faith working through love.

Rom 1:18-23 (§4)

18 For the wrath of God is revealed from heaven against all ungodliness and wickedness of men who by their wickedness suppress the truth. 19 For what can be known about God is plain to them, because God has shown it to them. 20 Ever since the creation of the world his invisible nature, namely, his eternal power and deity, has been clearly perceived in the things that have been made. So they are without excuse; 21 for although they knew God they did not honor him as God or give thanks to him, but they became futile in their thinking and their senseless minds were darkened. 22 Claiming to be wise, they became fools, 23 and exchanged the glory of the immortal God for images resembling mortal man or birds or animals or reptiles.

Rom 1:24-28 (§5)

24 Therefore God gave them up in the lusts of their hearts to impurity, to the dishonoring of their bodies among themselves, 25 because they exchanged the truth about God for a lie and worshiped and served the creature rather than the Creator, who is blessed for ever! Amen.

26 For this reason God gave them up to dishonorable passions. Their women exchanged natural relations for unnatural, 27 and the men likewise gave up natural relations with women and were consumed with passion for one another, men committing shameless acts with men and receiving in their own persons the due penalty for their error.

Rom 2:6-11 (§8)

6 For he will render to every man according to his works: 7 to those who by patience in well-doing seek for glory and honor and immortality, he will give eternal life; 8 but for those who are factious and do not obey the truth, but obey wickedness, there will be wrath and fury. 9 There will be tribulation and distress for every human being who does evil, the Jew first and also the Greek, 10 but glory and honor and peace for every one who does good, the Jew first and also the Greek. 11 For God shows no partiality.

Rom 11:7-10 (§45)

7 What then? Israel failed to obtain what it sought. The elect obtained it, but the rest were hardened, 8 as it is

1 Cor 7:25-31 (§98)

25 Now concerning the unmarried, I have no command of the Lord, but I give my opinion as one who by the Lord's mercy is trustworthy. 26 I think that in view of the present distress it is well for a person to remain as he is. 27 Are you bound to a wife? Do not seek to be free. Are you free from a wife? Do not seek marriage. 28 But if you marry, you do not sin, and if a girl marries she does not sin. Yet those who marry will have worldly troubles, and I would spare you that. 29 I mean, brethren, the appointed time has grown very short; from now on, let those who have wives live as though they had none, 30 and those who mourn as though they were not mourning, and those who rejoice as though they were not rejoicing, and those who buy as though they had no goods, 31 and those who deal with the world as though they had no dealings with it. For the form of this world is passing away.

1 Cor 10:1-13 (§109)

10 I want you to know, brethren, that our fathers were all under the cloud, and all passed through the sea, 2 and all were baptized into Moses in the cloud and in the sea, 3 and all ate the same supernatural food 4 and all drank the same supernatural drink. For they drank from the supernatural Rock which followed them, and the Rock was Christ. 5 Nevertheless with most of them God was not pleased; for they were overthrown in the wilderness.

6 Now these things are warnings for us, not to desire evil as they did. 7 Do not be idolaters as some of them were; as it is written, "The people sat down to eat and drink and rose up to dance." 8 We must not indulge in immorality as some of them did, and twenty-three thousand fell in a single day. 9 We

written,
"God gave them a spirit of stupor,
eyes that should not see and ears that
should not hear,
down to this very day."
9 And David says,
"Let their table become a snare and a
trap,
a pitfall and a retribution for them;
10 let their eyes be darkened so that they
cannot see,
and bend their backs for ever."

2 Cor 12:11-13 (§186)

11 I have been a fool! You forced me to it, for I ought to have been commended by you. For I was not at all inferior to these superlative apostles, even though I am nothing. 12 The signs of a true apostle were performed among you in all patience, with signs and wonders and mighty works. 13 For in what were you less favored than the rest of the churches, except that I myself did not burden you? Forgive me this wrong!

2 Cor 11:12-15 (§181)

12 And what I do I will continue to do, in order to undermine the claim of those who would like to claim that in their boasted mission they work on the same terms as we do. 13 For such men are false apostles, deceitful workmen, disguising themselves as apostles of Christ. 14 And no wonder, for even Satan disguises himself as an angel of light. 15 So it is not strange if his servants also disguise themselves as servants of righteousness. Their end will correspond to their deeds.

1 Cor 15:20-28 (§133)

20 But in fact Christ has been raised from the dead, the first fruits of those who have fallen asleep. 21 For as by a man came death, by a man has come also the resurrection of the dead. 22 For as in Adam all die, so also in Christ shall all be made alive. 23 But each in his own order: Christ the first fruits, then at his coming those who belong to Christ. 24 Then comes the end, when he delivers the kingdom to God the Father after destroying every rule and every authority and power. 25 For he must reign until he has put all his enemies

must not put the Lord to the test, as some of them did and were destroyed by serpents; 10 nor grumble, as some of them did and were destroyed by the Destroyer. 11 Now these things happened to them as a warning, but they were written down for our instruction, upon whom the end of the ages has come. 12 Therefore let any one who thinks that he stands take heed lest he fall. 13 No temptation has overtaken you that is not common to man. God is faithful, and he will not let you be tempted beyond your strength, but with the temptation will also provide the way of escape, that you may be able to endure it.

under his feet. 26 The last enemy to be destroyed is death. 27 "For God has put all things in subjection under his feet." But when it says, "All things are put in subjection under him," it is plain that he is excepted who put all things under him. 28 When all things are subjected to him, then the Son himself will also be subjected to him who put all things under him, that God may be everything to every one.

▶ 2:1 Heb 10:25
25 not neglecting to meet together, as is the habit of some, but encouraging one another, and all the more as you see the Day drawing near.

▶ 2:3 1 Tim 4:1,
Now the Spirit expressly says that in later times some will depart from the faith by giving heed to deceitful spirits and doctrines of demons,

Heb 3:12
12 Take care, brethren, lest there be in any of you an evil, unbelieving heart, leading you to fall away from the living God.

▶ 2:5 Acts 20:29-30
29 I know that after my departure fierce wolves will come in among you, not sparing the flock; 30 and from among your own selves will arise men speaking perverse things, to draw away the disciples after them.

▶ 2:8 1 Tim 6:14,
14 I charge you to keep the commandment unstained and free from reproach until the appearing of our Lord Jesus Christ;

2 Tim 1:10,
10 and now has manifested through the appearing of our Savior Christ Jesus, who abolished death and brought life and immortality to light through the gospel.

2 Tim 4:1,
I charge you in the presence of God and of Christ Jesus who is to judge the living and the dead, and by his appearing and his kingdom:

8
8 Henceforth there is laid up for me the crown of righteousness, which the Lord, the righteous judge, will award to me on that Day, and not only to me but also to all who have loved his appearing.

Tit 2:13
13 awaiting our blessed hope, the appearing of the glory of our great God and Savior Jesus Christ,

▶ 2:10 1 Tim 2:4
4 who desires all men to be saved and to come to the knowledge of the truth.

▶ 2:11 2 Tim 4:4
4 and will turn away from listening to the truth and wander into myths.

▶ 2:1, 8 1:10
10 when he comes on that day to be glorified in his saints, and to be marveled at in all who have believed, because our testimony to you was believed.

1 Thes 2:19,
19 For what is our hope or joy or crown of boasting before our Lord Jesus at his coming? Is it not you?

3:13,
13 so that he may establish your hearts unblamable in holiness before our God and Father, at the coming of our Lord Jesus with all his saints.

5:23,
23 May the God of peace himself sanctify you wholly; and may your spirit and soul and body be kept sound and blameless at the coming of our Lord Jesus Christ.

4:15
15 For this we declare to you by the word of the Lord, that we who are alive, who are left until the coming of the Lord, shall not precede those who have fallen asleep.

1 Cor 15:23
23 But each in his own order: Christ the first fruits, then at his coming those who belong to Christ.

▶ 2:2 1 Cor 1:8,
8 who will sustain you to the end, guiltless in the day of our Lord Jesus Christ.

Phil 3:17-21 (§249)

17 Brethren, join in imitating me, and mark those who so live as you have an example in us. 18 For many, of whom I have often told you and now tell you even with tears, live as enemies of the cross of Christ. 19 Their end is destruction, their god is the belly, and they glory in their shame, with minds set on earthly things. 20 But our commonwealth is in heaven, and from it we await a Savior, the Lord Jesus Christ, 21 who will change our lowly body to be like his glorious body, by the power which enables him even to subject all things to himself.

1 Thes 4:13-18 (§286)

13 But we would not have you ignorant, brethren, concerning those who are asleep, that you may not grieve as others do who have no hope. 14 For since we believe that Jesus died and rose again, even so, through Jesus, God will bring with him those who have fallen asleep. 15 For this we declare to you by the word of the Lord, that we who are alive, who are left until the coming of the Lord, shall not precede those who have fallen asleep. 16 For the Lord himself will descend from heaven with a cry of command, with the archangel's call, and with the sound of the trumpet of God. And the dead in Christ will rise first; 17 then we who are alive, who are left, shall be caught up together with them in the clouds to meet the Lord in the air; and so we shall always be with the Lord. 18 Therefore comfort one another with these words.

1 Thes 5:1-11 (§287)

5 But as to the times and the seasons, brethren, you have no need to have anything written to you. 2 For you yourselves know well that the day of the Lord will come like a thief in the night. 3 When people say, "There is peace and security," then sudden destruction will come upon them as travail comes upon a woman with child, and there will be no escape. 4 But you are not in darkness, brethren, for that day to surprise you like a thief. 5 For you are all sons of light and sons of the day; we are not of the night or of darkness. 6 So then, let us not sleep, as others do, but let us keep awake and be sober. 7 For those who sleep sleep at night, and those who get drunk are drunk at night. 8 But, since we belong to the day, let us be sober, and put on the breastplate of faith and love, and for a helmet the hope of salvation. 9 For God has not destined us for wrath, but to obtain salvation through our Lord Jesus Christ, 10 who died for us so that whether we wake or sleep we might live with him. 11 Therefore encourage one another and build one another up, just as you are doing.

2 Thes 2:1-12

2 Now concerning the coming of our Lord Jesus Christ and our assembling to meet him, we beg you, brethren, 2 not to be quickly shaken in mind or excited, either by spirit or by word, or by letter purporting to be from us, to the effect that the day of the Lord has come. 3 Let no one deceive you in any way; for that day will not come, unless the rebellion comes first, and the man of lawlessness is revealed, the son of perdition, 4 who opposes and exalts himself against every so-called god or object of worship, so that he takes his seat in the temple of God, proclaiming himself to be God. 5 Do you not remember that when I was still with you I told you this? 6 And you know what is restraining him now so that he may be revealed in his time. 7 For the mystery of lawlessness is already at work; only he who now restrains it will do so until he is out of the way. 8 And then the lawless one will be revealed, and the Lord Jesus will slay him with the breath of his mouth and destroy him by his appearing and his coming. 9 The coming of the lawless one by the activity of Satan will be with all power and with pretended signs and wonders, 10 and with all wicked deception for those who are to perish, because they refused to love the truth and so be saved. 11 Therefore God sends upon them a strong delusion, to make them believe what is false, 12 so that all may be condemned who did not believe the truth but had pleasure in unrighteousness.

5:5 5 you are to deliver this man to Satan for the destruction of the flesh, that his spirit may be saved in the day of the Lord Jesus.

2 Cor 1:14

14 as you have understood in part, that you can be proud of us as we can be of you, on the day of the Lord Jesus.

Phil 1:6,

6 And I am sure that he who began a good work in you will bring it to completion at the day of Jesus Christ.

10, 10 so that you may approve what is excellent, and may be pure and blameless for the day of Christ,

2:16

16 holding fast the word of life, so that in the day of Christ I may be proud that I did not run in vain or labor in vain.

1 Thes 5:2 2 For you yourselves know well that the day of the Lord will come like a thief in the night.

▶ 2:3 Col 2:4

4 I say this in order that no one may delude you with beguiling speech.

▶ 2:4 1 Cor 8:5-6

5 For although there may be so-called gods in heaven or on earth—as indeed there are many "gods" and many "lords"—6 yet for us there is one God, the Father, from whom are all things and for whom we exist, and one Lord, Jesus Christ, through whom are all things and through whom we exist.

▶ 2:5 1 Thes 3:4

4 For when we were with you, we told you beforehand that we were to suffer affliction; just as it has come to pass, and as you know.

▶ 2:6 Rom 8:18-23

18 I consider that the sufferings of this present time are not worth comparing with the glory that is to be revealed to us. 19 For the creation waits with eager longing for the revealing of the sons of God; 20 for the creation was subjected to futility, not of its own will but by the will of him who subjected it in hope; 21 because the creation itself will be set free from its bondage to decay and obtain the glorious liberty of the children of God. 22 We know that the whole creation has been groaning in travail together until now; 23 and not only the creation, but we ourselves, who have the first fruits of the Spirit, groan inwardly as we wait for adoption as sons, the redemption of our bodies.

▶ 2:8 1:7 7 and to grant rest with us to you who are afflicted, when the Lord Jesus is revealed from heaven with his mighty angels in flaming fire,

1 Thes 4:6 6 that no man transgress, and wrong his brother in this matter, because the Lord is an avenger in all these things, as we solemnly forewarned you.

▶ 2:9 *cf 2 Cor 4:4

▶ 2:10 *cf 1 Cor 1:18

▶ 2:3 (lawlessness) read sin: ADG Koine Lect it vg syr Irenaeus(Latin); text: SB cop Marcion

297

Rom 2:6-11 (§8)

6 For he will render to every man according to his works: 7 to those who by patience in well-doing seek for glory and honor and immortality, he will give eternal life; 8 but for those who are factious and do not obey the truth, but obey wickedness, there will be wrath and fury. 9 There will be tribulation and distress for every human being who does evil, the Jew first and also the Greek, 10 but glory and honor and peace for every one who does good, the Jew first and also the Greek. 11 For God shows no partiality.

Rom 8:28-30 (§33)

28 We know that in everything God works for good with those who love him, who are called according to his purpose. 29 For those whom he foreknew he also predestined to be conformed to the image of his Son, in order that he might be the first-born among many brethren. 30And those whom he predestined he also called; and those whom he called he also justified; and those whom he justified he also glorified.

1 Cor 16:13-14 (§141)

13 Be watchful, stand firm in your faith, be courageous, be strong. 14 Let all that you do be done in love.

▶ **2:13 1:3**
3 We are bound to give thanks to God always for you, brethren, as is fitting, because your faith is growing abundantly, and the love of every one of you for one another is increasing.

Eph 1:4
4 even as he chose us in him before the foundation of the world, that we should be holy and blameless before him.

▶ **2:14 Phil 3:21**
21 who will change our lowly body to be like his glorious body, by the power which enables him even to subject all things to himself.

▶ **2:15 Gal 5:1**
For freedom Christ has set us free; stand fast therefore, and do not submit again to a yoke of slavery.

1 Cor 11:2
2 I commend you because you remember me in everything and maintain the traditions even as I have delivered them to you.

Rom 6:17
17 But thanks be to God, that you who were once slaves of sin have become obedient from the heart to the standard of teaching to which you were committed,

298

298. May our Lord comfort your hearts

2 Cor 1:3-11 (§147)

3 Blessed be the God and Father of our Lord Jesus Christ, the Father of mercies and God of all comfort, 4 who comforts us in all our affliction, so that we may be able to comfort those who are in any affliction, with the comfort with which we ourselves are comforted by God. 5 For as we share abundantly in Christ's sufferings, so through Christ we share abundantly in comfort too. 6 If we are afflicted, it is for your comfort and salvation; and if we are comforted, it is for your comfort, which you experience when you patiently endure the same sufferings that we suffer. 7 Our hope for you is unshaken; for we know that as you share in our sufferings, you will also share in our comfort.

8 For we do not want you to be ignorant, brethren, of the affliction we experienced in Asia; for we were so utterly, unbearably crushed that we despaired of life itself. 9 Why, we felt that we had received the sentence of death; but that was to make us rely not on ourselves but on God who raises the dead; 10 he delivered us from so deadly a peril, and he will deliver us; on him we have set our hope that he will deliver us again. 11 You also must help us by prayer, so that many will give thanks on our behalf for the blessing granted us in answer to many prayers.

▶ **2:16 Tit 3:7**
7 so that we might be justified by his grace and become heirs in hope of eternal life.

▶ **2:16-17 1 Thes 5:23-24**
23 May the God of peace himself sanctify you wholly; and may your spirit and soul and body be kept sound and blameless at the coming of our Lord Jesus Christ. 24 He who calls you is faithful, and he will do it.

2 Thes 3:16
16 Now may the Lord of peace himself give you peace at all times in all ways. The Lord be with you all.

▶ **2:17 1 Thes 4:18,**
18 Therefore comfort one another with these words.

5:11,
11 Therefore encourage one another and build one another up, just as you are doing.

Eph 2:10
10 For we are his workmanship, created in Christ Jesus for good works, which God prepared beforehand, that we should walk in them.

297

Phil 4:8-9 (§252)

8 Finally, brethren, whatever is true, whatever is honorable, whatever is just, whatever is pure, whatever is lovely, whatever is gracious, if there is any excellence, if there is anything worthy of praise, think about these things. 9 What you have learned and received and heard and seen in me, do; and the God of peace will be with you.

Col 2:4-7 (§261)

4 I say this in order that no one may delude you with beguiling speech. 5 For though I am absent in body, yet I am with you in spirit, rejoicing to see your good order and the firmness of your faith in Christ.

6 As therefore you received Christ Jesus the Lord, so live in him, 7 rooted and built up in him and established in the faith, just as you were taught, abounding in thanksgiving.

2 Thes 2:13-15

13 But we are bound to give thanks to God always for you, brethren beloved by the Lord, because God chose you from the beginning to be saved, through sanctification by the Spirit and belief in the truth. 14 To this he called you through our gospel, so that you may obtain the glory of our Lord Jesus Christ. 15 So then, brethren, stand firm and hold to the traditions which you were taught by us, either by word of mouth or by letter.

2 Thes 3:6

6 Now we command you, brethren, in the name of our Lord Jesus Christ, that you keep away from any brother who is living in idleness and not in accord with the tradition that you received from us.

298. May our Lord comfort your hearts

298

1 Thes 3:11-13 (§283)

11 Now may our God and Father himself, and our Lord Jesus, direct our way to you; 12 and may the Lord make you increase and abound in love to one another and to all men, as we do to you, 13 so that he may establish your hearts unblamable in holiness before our God and Father, at the coming of our Lord Jesus with all his saints.

2 Thes 2:16-17

16 Now may our Lord Jesus Christ himself, and God our Father, who loved us and gave us eternal comfort and good hope through grace, 17 comfort your hearts and establish them in every good work and word.

299

Rom 15:30-33 (§64)

30 I appeal to you, brethren, by our Lord Jesus Christ and by the love of the Spirit, to strive together with me in your prayers to God on my behalf, 31 that I may be delivered from the unbelievers in Judea, and that my service for Jerusalem may be acceptable to the saints, 32 so that by God's will I may come to you with joy and be refreshed in your company. 33 The God of peace be with you all. Amen.

2 Cor 7:13b-16 (§170)

And besides our own comfort we rejoiced still more at the joy of Titus, because his mind has been set at rest by you all. 14 For if I have expressed to him some pride in you, I was not put to shame; but just as everything we said to you was true, so our boasting before Titus has proved true. 15 And his heart goes out all the more to you, as he remembers the obedience of you all, and the fear and trembling with which you received him. 16 I rejoice, because I have perfect confidence in you.

Eph 6:18-20 (§234)

18 Pray at all times in the Spirit, with all prayer and supplication. To that end keep alert with all perseverance, making supplication for all the saints, 19 and also for me, that utterance may be given me in opening my mouth boldly to proclaim the mystery of the gospel, 20 for which I am an ambassador in chains; that I may declare it boldly, as I ought to speak.

▶ 3:2 *cf Acts 17:5-10

▶ 3:1 2 Cor 1:11　11 You also must help us by prayer, so that many will give thanks on our behalf for the blessing granted us in answer to many prayers.

▶ 3:3 2 Cor 1:18　18 As surely as God is faithful, our word to you has not been Yes and No.

1 Cor 1:9,　9 God is faithful, by whom you were called into the fellowship of his Son, Jesus Christ our Lord.

10:13　13 No temptation has overtaken you that is not common to man. God is faithful, and he will not let you be tempted beyond your strength, but with the temptation will also provide the way of escape, that you may be able to endure it.

1 Thes 5:24　24 He who calls you is faithful, and he will do it.

300. If any one will not work

300

1 Cor 9:1-14 (§105)

9 Am I not free? Am I not an apostle? Have I not seen Jesus our Lord? Are not you my workmanship in the Lord? 2 If to others I am not an apostle, at least I am to you; for you are the seal of my apostleship in the Lord.

3 This is my defense to those who would examine me. 4 Do we not have the right to our food and drink? 5 Do we not have the right to be accompanied by a wife, as the other apostles and the brothers of the Lord and Cephas? 6 Or is it only Barnabas and I who have no right to refrain from working for a living? 7 Who serves as a soldier at his own expense? Who plants a vineyard without eating any of its fruit? Who tends a flock without getting some of the milk?

8 Do I say this on human authority? Does not the law say the same? 9 For it is written in the law of Moses, "You shall not muzzle an ox when it is treading out the grain." Is it for oxen that God is concerned? 10 Does he not speak entirely for our sake? It was written for our sake, because the plowman should plow in hope and the thresher thresh in hope of a share in the crop. 11 If we have sown spiritual good among you, is it too much if we reap your material benefits? 12 If others share this rightful claim upon you, do not we still more?

Nevertheless, we have not made use of this right, but we endure anything rather than put an obstacle in the way of the gospel of Christ. 13 Do you not know that those who are employed in the temple service get their food from the temple, and those who serve at the altar share in the sacrificial offerings? 14 In the same way, the Lord commanded that those who proclaim the gospel should get their living by the gospel.

Eph 4:25-32 (§228)

25 Therefore, putting away falsehood, let every one speak the truth with his neighbor, for we are members one of another. 26 Be angry but do not sin; do not let the sun go down on your anger, 27 and give no opportunity to the devil. 28 Let the thief no longer steal, but rather let him labor, doing honest work with his hands, so that he may be able to give to those in need. 29 Let no evil talk come out of your mouths, but only such as is good for edifying, as fits the occasion, that it may impart grace to those who hear. 30 And do not grieve the Holy Spirit of God, in whom you were sealed for the day of redemption. 31 Let all bitterness and wrath and anger and clamor and slander be put away from you, with all malice, 32 and be kind to one another, tenderhearted, forgiving one another, as God in Christ forgave you.

▶ 3:8 Acts 18:3　3 and because he was of the same trade he stayed with them, and they worked, for by trade they were tentmakers.

▶ 3:11 1 Tim 5:13　13 Besides that, they learn to be idlers, gadding about from house to house, and not only idlers but gossips and busybodies, saying what they should not.

▶ 3:6 2:15,　15 So then, brethren, stand firm and hold to the traditions which you were taught by us, either by word of mouth or by letter.

1 Cor 7:6,　6 I say this by way of concession, not of command.

299

Col 4:2-4 (§269)

2 Continue steadfastly in prayer, being watchful in it with thanksgiving; 3 and pray for us also, that God may open to us a door for the word, to declare the mystery of Christ, on account of which I am in prison, 4 that I may make it clear, as I ought to speak.

1 Thes 5:25 (§290)

25 Brethren, pray for us.

2 Thes 3:1-5

3 Finally, brethren, pray for us, that the word of the Lord may speed on and triumph, as it did among you, 2 and that we may be delivered from wicked and evil men; for not all have faith. 3 But the Lord is faithful; he will strengthen you and guard you from evil. 4 And we have confidence in the Lord about you, that you are doing and will do the things which we command. 5 May the Lord direct your hearts to the love of God and to the steadfastness of Christ.

Phm 21-22(§309)

21 Confident of your obedience, I write to you, knowing that you will do even more than I say. 22 At the same time, prepare a guest room for me, for I am hoping through your prayers to be granted to you.

Eph 6:10-11,

10 Finally, be strong in the Lord and in the strength of his might. 11 Put on the whole armor of God, that you may be able to stand against the wiles of the devil.

13

13 Therefore take the whole armor of God, that you may be able to withstand in the evil day, and having done all, to stand.

Col 1:11

11 May you be strengthened with all power, according to his glorious might, for all endurance and patience with joy,

▶ 3:4 1 Thes 4:10

10 and indeed you do love all the brethren throughout Macedo'nia. But we exhort you, brethren, to do so more and more,

2 Cor 2:3

3 And I wrote as I did, so that when I came I might not suffer pain from those who should have made me rejoice, for I felt sure of all of you. that my joy would be the joy of you all.

▶ 3:5 Rom 15:5

5 May the God of steadfastness and encouragement grant you to live in such harmony with one another, in accord with Christ Jesus,

300. If any one will not work

300

Phil 3:17-21 (§249)

17 Brethren, join in imitating me, and mark those who so live as you have an example in us. 18 For many, of whom I have often told you and now tell you even with tears, live as enemies of the cross of Christ. 19 Their end is destruction, their god is the belly, and they glory in their shame, with minds set on earthly things. 20 But our commonwealth is in heaven, and from it we await a Savior, the Lord Jesus Christ, 21 who will change our lowly body to be like his glorious body, by the power which enables him even to subject all things to himself.

1 Thes 2:9-12 (§278)

9 For you remember our labor and toil, brethren; we worked night and day, that we might not burden any of you, while we preached to you the gospel of God. 10 You are witnesses, and God also, how holy and righteous and blameless was our behavior to you believers; 11 for you know how, like a father with his children, we exhorted each one of you and encouraged you and charged you 12 to lead a life worthy of God, who calls you into his own kingdom and glory.

1 Thes 4:9-12 (§285)

9 But concerning love of the brethren you have no need to have any one write to you, for you yourselves have been taught by God to love one another; 10 and indeed you do love all the brethren throughout Macedo'nia. But we exhort you, brethren, to do so more and more, 11 to aspire to live quietly, to mind your own affairs, and to work with your hands, as we charged you; 12 so that you may command the respect of outsiders, and be dependent on nobody.

2 Thes 3:6-13

6 Now we command you, brethren, in the name of our Lord Jesus Christ, that you keep away from any brother who is living in idleness and not in accord with the tradition that you received from us. 7 For you yourselves know how you ought to imitate us; we were not idle when we were with you, 8 we did not eat any one's bread without paying, but with toil and labor we worked night and day, that we might not burden any of you. 9 It was not because we have not that right, but to give you in our conduct an example to imitate. 10 For even when we were with you, we gave you this command: If any one will not work, let him not eat. 11 For we hear that some of you are living in idleness, mere busybodies, not doing any work. 12 Now such persons we command and exhort in the Lord Jesus Christ to do their work in quietness and to earn their own living. 13 Brethren, do not be weary in well-doing.

1 Thes 5:12-22 (§288)

12 But we beseech you, brethren, to respect those who labor among you and

are over you in the Lord and admonish you, 13 and to esteem them very highly in love because of their work. Be at peace among yourselves. 14 And we exhort you, brethren, admonish the idlers, encourage the fainthearted, help the weak, be patient with them all. 15 See that none of you repays evil for evil, but always seek to do good to one another and to all. 16 Rejoice always, 17 pray constantly, 18 give thanks in all circumstances; for this is the will of God in Christ Jesus for you. 19 Do not quench the Spirit, 20 do not despise prophesying, 21 but test everything; hold fast what is good, 22 abstain from every form of evil.

10,

10 To the married I give charge, not I but the Lord, that the wife should not separate from her husband

12,

12 To the rest I say, not the Lord, that if any brother has a wife who is an unbeliever, and she consents to live with him, he should not divorce her.

11:23,

23 For I received from the Lord what I also delivered to you, that the Lord Jesus on the night when he was betrayed took bread,

15:3

3 For I delivered to you as of first importance what I also received, that Christ died for our sins in accordance with the scriptures,

Gal 6: 5

5 For each man will have to bear his own load.

*cf 1 Cor 11:2 Rom 6:17 Col 2:6-7

▶ 3:7, 9 *cf 1 Thes 2:13-16, 1:2-10 Gal 4:12 1 Cor 11:1, 4:16 Phil 3:17

▶ 3:8 *cf 2 Cor 11:9, 12:13-16 1 Cor 4:12

▶ 3:10 *cf 1 Thes 3:4 ▶ 3:12 *cf Phm 8-9 ▶ 3:13 *cf Gal 6:9

301

1 Cor 5:9-13 (§89)

9 I wrote to you in my letter not to associate with immoral men; 10 not at all meaning the immoral of this world, or the greedy and robbers, or idolaters, since then you would need to go out of the world. 11 But rather I wrote to you not to associate with any one who bears the name of brother if he is guilty of immorality or greed, or is an idolater, reviler, drunkard, or robber—not even to eat with such a one. 12 For what have I to do with judging outsiders? Is it not those inside the church whom you are to judge? 13 God judges those outside. "Drive out the wicked person from among you."

1 Cor 14:37-40 (§130)

37 If any one thinks that he is a prophet, or spiritual, he should acknowledge that what I am writing to you is a command of the Lord. 38 If any one does not recognize this, he is not recognized. 39 So, my brethren, earnestly desire to prophesy, and do not forbid speaking in tongues; 40 but all things should be done decently and in order.

1 Cor 16:21-22 (§144)

21 I, Paul, write this greeting with my own hand. 22 If any one has no love for the Lord, let him be accursed. Our Lord, come!

▶ 3:14-15 1 Cor 11:2,

2 I commend you because you remember me in everything and maintain the traditions even as I have delivered them to you.

16,

16 If any one is disposed to be contentious, we recognize no other practice, nor do the churches of God.

7:17

17 Only, let every one lead the life which the Lord has assigned to him, and in which God has called him. This is my rule in all the churches.

302. May the Lord give you peace

302

Rom 15:30-33 (§64)

30 I appeal to you, brethren, by our Lord Jesus Christ and by the love of the Spirit, to strive together with me in your prayers to God on my behalf, 31 that I may be delivered from the unbelievers in Judea, and that my service for Jerusalem may be acceptable to the saints, 32 so that by God's will I may come to you with joy and be refreshed in your company. 33 The God of peace be with you all. Amen.

▶ 3:16 2:16-17

16 Now may our Lord Jesus Christ himself, and God our Father, who loved us and gave us eternal comfort and good hope through grace, 17 comfort your hearts and establish them in every good work and word.

1 Thes 3:11-13

11 Now may our God and Father himself, and our Lord Jesus, direct our way to you; 12 and may the Lord make you increase and abound in love to one another and to all men, as we do to you, 13 so that he may establish your hearts unblamable in holiness before our God and Father, at the coming of our Lord Jesus with all his saints.

*cf Rom 15:13, 1 Cor 7:15, 14:33

301. If anyone refuses to obey what we say.

2 Thes 3:14-15

14 If any one refuses to obey what we say in this letter, note that man, and have nothing to do with him, that he may be ashamed. 15 Do not look on him as an enemy, but warn him as a brother.

301

302. May the Lord give you peace

1 Thes 5:23-24 (§289)

23 May the God of peace himself sanctify you wholly; and may your spirit and soul and body be kept sound and blameless at the coming of our Lord Jesus Christ. 24 He who calls you is faithful, and he will do it.

2 Thes 3:16

16 Now may the Lord of peace himself give you peace at all times in all ways. The Lord be with you all.

302

303

1 Cor 16:21-22 (§144)

21 I, Paul, write this greeting with my own hand. 22 If any one has no love for the Lord, let him be accursed. Our Lord, come!

Gal 6:11-17 (§216)

11 See with what large letters I am writing to you with my own hand. 12 It is those who want to make a good showing in the flesh that would compel you to be circumcised, and only in order that they may not be persecuted for the cross of Christ. 13 For even those who receive circumcision do not themselves keep the law, but they desire to have you circumcised that they may glory in your flesh. 14 But far be it from me to glory except in the cross of our Lord Jesus Christ, by which the world has been crucified to me, and I to the world. 15 For neither circumcision counts for anything, nor uncircumcision, but a new creation. 16 Peace and mercy be upon all who walk by this rule, upon the Israel of God.

17 Henceforth let no man trouble me; for I bear on my body the marks of Jesus.

304. Grace

304

Rom 16:20b (§68)

The grace of our Lord Jesus Christ be with you.

1 Cor 16:23-24 (§145)

23 The grace of the Lord Jesus be with you. 24 My love be with you all in Christ Jesus. Amen.

2 Cor 13:14 (§192)

14 The grace of the Lord Jesus Christ and the love of God and the fellowship of the Holy Spirit be with you all.

Gal 6:18 (§217)

18 The grace of our Lord Jesus Christ be with your spirit, brethren. Amen.

Eph 6:23-24 (§236)

23 Peace be to the brethren, and love with faith, from God the Father and the Lord Jesus Christ. 24 Grace be with all who love our Lord Jesus Christ with love undying.

▶ 3:18 *cf 1 Tim 6:21b, 2 Tim 4:22, Tit 3:15c

Col 4:16-18a (§273)

¹⁶And when this letter has been read among you, have it read also in the church of the La-odice′ans; and see that you read also the letter from La-odice′a. ¹⁷And say to Archip′pus, "See that you fulfil the ministry which you have received in the Lord."

18 I, Paul, write this greeting with my own hand. Remember my fetters.

1 Thes 5:27(§292)

27 I adjure you by the Lord that this letter be read to all the brethren.

2 Thes 3:17

17 I, Paul, write this greeting with my own hand. This is the mark in every letter of mine; it is the way I write.

303

304. Grace

Phil 4:23 (§255)

23 The grace of the Lord Jesus Christ be with your spirit.

Col 4:18b (§274)

Grace be with you.

1 Thes 5:28 (§293)

28 The grace of our Lord Jesus Christ be with you.

2 Thes 3:18

¹⁸ The grace of our Lord Jesus Christ be with you all.

Phm 25 (§311)

25 The grace of the Lord Jesus Christ be with your spirit.

304

305

Rom 1:1-7 (§1)

1 Paul, a servant of Jesus Christ, called to be an apostle, set apart for the gospel of God [2] which he promised beforehand through his prophets in the holy scriptures, [3] the gospel concerning his Son, who was descended from David according to the flesh [4] and designated Son of God in power according to the Spirit of holiness by his resurrection from the dead, Jesus Christ our Lord, [5] through whom we have received grace and apostleship to bring about the obedience of faith for the sake of his name among all the nations, [6] including yourselves who are called to belong to Jesus Christ;

7 To all God's beloved in Rome, who are called to be saints:

Grace to you and peace from God our Father and the Lord Jesus Christ.

▶ 2 2 Tim 2:3
[3] Share in suffering as a good soldier of Christ Jesus.

1 Cor 1:1-3 (§71)

1 Paul, called by the will of God to be an apostle of Christ Jesus, and our brother Sos'thenes,

2 To the church of God which is at Corinth, to those sanctified in Christ Jesus, called to be saints together with all those who in every place call on the name of our Lord Jesus Christ, both their Lord and ours:

3 Grace to you and peace from God our Father and the Lord Jesus Christ.

▶ 1-3 *cf 1 Tim 1:1-2, 2 Tim 1:1-2, Tit1:1-4

2 Cor 1:1-2 (§146)

1 Paul, an apostle of Christ Jesus by the will of God, and Timothy our brother.

To the church of God which is at Corinth, with all the saints who are in the whole of Acha'ia:

2 Grace to you and peace from God our Father and the Lord Jesus Christ.

Gal 1:1-5 (§193)

1 Paul an apostle—not from men nor through man, but through Jesus Christ and God the Father, who raised him from the dead— [2] and all the brethren who are with me,

To the churches of Galatia:

3 Grace to you and peace from God the Father and our Lord Jesus Christ, [4] who gave himself for our sins to deliver us from the present evil age, according to the will of our God and Father; [5] to whom be the glory for ever and ever. Amen.

Eph 1:1-2 (§218)

1 Paul, an apostle of Christ Jesus by the will of God,

To the saints who are also faithful in Christ Jesus:

2 Grace to you and peace from God our Father and the Lord Jesus Christ.

306. I thank my God

306

Rom 1:8-15 (§2)

8 First, I thank my God through Jesus Christ for all of you, because your faith is proclaimed in all the world. [9] For God is my witness, whom I serve with my spirit in the gospel of his Son, that without ceasing I mention you always in my prayers, [10] asking that somehow by God's will I may now at last succeed in coming to you. [11] For I long to see you, that I may impart to you some spiritual gift to strengthen you, [12] that is, that we may be mutually encouraged by each other's faith, both yours and mine. [13] I want you to know, brethren, that I have often intended to come to you (but thus far have been prevented), in order that I may reap some harvest among you as well as among the rest of the Gentiles. [14] I am under obligation both to Greeks and to barbarians, both to the wise and to the foolish: [15] so I am eager to preach the gospel to you also who are in Rome.

▶ 6 Phil 1:9
[9] And it is my prayer that your love may abound more and more, with knowledge and all discernment,

1 Cor 1:4-9 (§72)

4 I give thanks to God always for you because of the grace of God which was given you in Christ Jesus, [5] that in every way you were enriched in him with all speech and all knowledge— [6] even as the testimony to Christ was confirmed among you— [7] so that you are not lacking in any spiritual gift, as you wait for the revealing of our Lord Jesus Christ; [8] who will sustain you to the end, guiltless in the day of our Lord Jesus Christ. [9] God is faithful, by whom you were called into the fellowship of his Son, Jesus Christ our Lord.

▶ 6-7 1 Thes 3:7
[7] for this reason, brethren, in all our distress and affliction we have been comforted about you through your faith;

2 Cor 7:2-4 (§168)

2 Open your hearts to us; we have wronged no one, we have corrupted no one, we have taken advantage of no one. [3] I do not say this to condemn you, for I said before that you are in our hearts, to die together and to live together. [4] I have great confidence in you; I have great pride in you; I am filled with comfort. With all our affliction, I am overjoyed.

▶ 7 2 Cor 1:3-7,
3 Blessed be the God and Father of our Lord Jesus Christ, the Father of mercies and God of all comfort, [4] who comforts us in all our affliction, so that we may be able to comfort those who are in any affliction, with the comfort with which we ourselves are comforted by God. [5] For as we share abundantly in Christ's sufferings, so through Christ we share abundantly in comfort too. [6] If we are afflicted, it is for your comfort and salvation; and if we are comforted, it is for your comfort, which you experience when you patiently endure the same sufferings that we suffer. [7] Our hope for you is unshaken; for we know that as you share in our sufferings, you will also share in our comfort.

7:13   [13] Therefore we are comforted.
And besides our own comfort we rejoiced still more at the joy of Titus, because his mind has been set at rest by you all.

1 Cor 16:18 [18] for they refreshed my spirit as well as yours. Give recognition to such men.

305. Paul and Timothy to Philemon

Phil 1:1-2 (§237)

1 Paul and Timothy, servants of Christ Jesus,
To all the saints in Christ Jesus who are at Philippi, with the bishops and deacons:
2 Grace to you and peace from God our Father and the Lord Jesus Christ.

Col 1:1-2 (§256)

1 Paul, an apostle of Christ Jesus by the will of God, and Timothy our brother,
2 To the saints and faithful brethren in Christ at Colos′sae:
Grace to you and peace from God our Father.

1 Thes 1:1 (§275)

1 Paul, Silva′nus, and Timothy,
To the church of the Thessalo′nians in God the Father and the Lord Jesus Christ:
Grace to you and peace.

2 Thes 1:1-2 (§294)

1 Paul, Silva′nus, and Timothy,
To the church of the Thessalo′nians in God our Father and the Lord Jesus Christ:
2 Grace to you and peace from God the Father and the Lord Jesus Christ.

Phm 1-3

1 Paul, a prisoner for Christ Jesus, and Timothy our brother,
To Phile′mon our beloved fellow worker 2 and Ap′phia our sister and Archip′pus our fellow soldier, and the church in your house:
3 Grace to you and peace from God our Father and the Lord Jesus Christ.

305

306. I thank my God

Phil 1:3-11 (§238)

3 I thank my God in all my remembrance of you, 4 always in every prayer of mine for you all making my prayer with joy, 5 thankful for your partnership in the gospel from the first day until now. 6 And I am sure that he who began a good work in you will bring it to completion at the day of Jesus Christ. 7 It is right for me to feel thus about you all, because I hold you in my heart, for you are all partakers with me of grace, both in my imprisonment and in the defense and confirmation of the gospel. 8 For God is my witness, how I yearn for you all with the affection of Christ Jesus. 9 And it is my prayer that your love may abound more and more, with knowledge and all discernment, 10 so that you may approve what is excellent, and may be pure and blameless for the day of Christ, 11 filled with the fruits of righteousness which come through Jesus Christ, to the glory and praise of God.

Col 1:3-14 (§257)

3 We always thank God, the Father of our Lord Jesus Christ, when we pray for you, 4 because we have heard of your faith in Christ Jesus and of the love which you have for all the saints, 5 because of the hope laid up for you in heaven. Of this you have heard before in the word of the truth, the gospel 6 which has come to you, as indeed in the whole world it is bearing fruit and growing—so among yourselves, from the day you heard and understood the grace of God in truth, 7 as you learned it from Ep′aphras our beloved fellow servant. He is a faithful minister of Christ on our behalf 8 and has made known to us your love in the Spirit.
9 And so, from the day we heard of it, we have not ceased to pray for you, asking that you may be filled with the knowledge of his will in all spiritual wisdom and understanding, 10 to lead a life worthy of the Lord, fully pleasing to him, bearing fruit in every good work and increasing in the knowledge of God. 11 May you be strengthened with all

1 Thes 1:2-10 (§276)

2 We give thanks to God always for you all, constantly mentioning you in our prayers, 3 remembering before our God and Father your work of faith and labor of love and steadfastness of hope in our Lord Jesus Christ. 4 For we know, brethren beloved by God, that he has chosen you; 5 for our gospel came to you not only in word, but also in power and in the Holy Spirit and with full conviction. You know what kind of men we proved to be among you for your sake. 6 And you became imitators of us and of the Lord, for you received the word in much affliction, with joy inspired by the Holy Spirit; 7 so that you became an example to all the believers in Macedo′nia and in Acha′ia. 8 For not only has the word of the Lord sounded forth from you in Macedo′nia power, according to his glorious might, for all endurance and patience with joy, 12 giving thanks to the Father, who has qualified us to share in the inheritance of the saints in light. 13 He has delivered us from the dominion of darkness and transferred us to the kingdom of his beloved Son, 14 in whom we have redemption, the forgiveness of sins.

2 Thes 1:3-12 (§295)

3 We are bound to give thanks to God always for you, brethren, as is fitting, because your faith is growing abundantly, and the love of every one of you for one another is increasing. 4 Therefore we ourselves boast of you in the churches of God for your steadfastness and faith in all your persecutions and in the afflictions which you are enduring.
5 This is evidence of the righteous judgment of God, that you may be made worthy of the kingdom of God, for which you are suffering—6 since indeed God deems it just to repay with affliction those who afflict you, 7 and to grant rest with us to you who are afflicted, when the Lord Jesus is revealed from heaven with his mighty angels in and Acha′ia, but your faith in God has gone forth everywhere, so that we need not say anything. 9 For they themselves report concerning us what a welcome we had among you, and how you turned to God from idols, to serve a living and true God, 10 and to wait for his Son from heaven, whom he raised from the dead, Jesus who delivers us from the wrath to come.

Phm 4-7

4 I thank my God always when I remember you in my prayers, 5 because I hear of your love and of the faith which you have toward the Lord Jesus and all the saints, 6 and I pray that the sharing of your faith may promote the knowledge of all the good that is ours in Christ. 7 For I have derived much joy and comfort from your love, my brother, because the hearts of the saints have been refreshed through you.

flaming fire, 8 inflicting vengeance upon those who do not know God and upon those who do not obey the gospel of our Lord Jesus. 9 They shall suffer the punishment of eternal destruction and exclusion from the presence of the Lord and from the glory of his might, 10 when he comes on that day to be glorified in his saints, and to be marveled at in all who have believed, because our testimony to you was believed. 11 To this end we always pray for you, that our God may make you worthy of his call, and may fulfil every good resolve and work of faith by his power, 12 so that the name of our Lord Jesus may be glorified in you, and you in him, according to the grace of our God and the Lord Jesus Christ.

306

2 Cor 7:4
4 I have great confidence in you; I have great pride in you; I am filled with comfort. With all our affliction, I am overjoyed.

Phm 20 20 Yes, brother, I want some benefit from you in the Lord. Refresh my heart in Christ.

▶ 6 (ours *read* yours: p⁶¹SG Koine it(some) vg syr cop Chrysostom; *text*: ACD Lect (some) it(few) Ambrosiaster

307

Rom 12:1-2 (§51)

12 I appeal to you therefore, brethren, by the mercies of God, to present your bodies as a living sacrifice, holy and acceptable to God, which is your spiritual worship. 2 Do not be conformed to this world but be transformed by the renewal of your mind, that you may prove what is the will of God, what is good and acceptable and perfect.

Rom 16:1-2 (§65)

16 I commend to you our sister Phoebe, a deaconess of the church at Cen′chre-ae, 2 that you may receive her in the Lord as befits the saints, and help her in whatever she may require from you, for she has been a helper of many and of myself as well.

▶ 11 2 Tim 4:11
11 Luke alone is with me. Get Mark and bring him with you; for he is very useful in serving me.

1 Cor 1:10-17 (§73)

10 I appeal to you, brethren, by the name of our Lord Jesus Christ, that all of you agree and that there be no dissensions among you, but that you be united in the same mind and the same judgment. 11 For it has been reported to me by Chlo′e's people that there is quarreling among you, my brethren. 12 What I mean is that each one of you says, "I belong to Paul," or "I belong to Apol′los," or "I belong to Cephas," or "I belong to Christ." 13 Is Christ divided? Was Paul crucified for you? Or were you baptized in the name of Paul? 14 I am thankful that I baptized none of you except Crispus and Ga′ius; 15 lest any one should say that you were baptized in my name. 16 (I did baptize also the household of Steph′anas. Beyond that, I do not know whether I baptized any one else.) 17 For Christ did not send me to baptize but to preach the gospel, and not with eloquent wisdom, lest the cross of Christ be emptied of its power.

*cf 1 Cor 7:17-24 (§97)
*cf 1 Cor 16:10-12 (§140)
*cf 1 Cor 16:15-18 (§142)

▶ 14 1 Tim 6:2
2 Those who have believing masters must not be disrespectful on the ground that they are brethren; rather they must serve all the better since those who benefit by their service are believers and beloved. Teach and urge these duties.

2 Cor 3:1-3 (§154)

3 Are we beginning to commend ourselves again? Or do we need, as some do, letters of recommendation to you, or from you? 2 You yourselves are our letter of recommendation, written on your hearts, to be known and read by all men; 3 and you show that you are a letter from Christ delivered by us, written not with ink but with the Spirit of the living God, not on tablets of stone but on tablets of human hearts.

2 Cor 8:16-24 (§173)

16 But thanks be to God who puts the same earnest care for you into the heart of Titus. 17 For he not only accepted our appeal, but being himself very earnest he is going to you of his own accord. 18 With him we are sending the brother who is famous among all the churches for his preaching of the gospel; 19 and not only that, but he has been appointed by the churches to travel with us in this gracious work which we are carrying on, for the glory of the Lord and to show our good will. 20 We intend that no one should blame us about this liberal gift which we are administering, 21 for we aim at what is honorable not only in the

▶ 8-9 2 Thes 3:6,
6 Now we command you, brethren, in the name of our Lord Jesus Christ, that you keep away from any brother who is living in idleness and not in accord with the tradition that you received from us.

10,
10 For even when we were with you, we gave you this command: If any one will not work, let him not eat.

Lord's sight but also in the sight of men. 22 And with them we are sending our brother whom we have often tested and found earnest in many matters, but who is now more earnest than ever because of his great confidence in you. 23 As for Titus, he is my partner and fellow worker in your service; and as for our brethren, they are messengers of the churches, the glory of Christ. 24 So give proof, before the churches, of your love and of our boasting about you to these men.

*cf 2 Cor 10:1-6 (§176)

12
12 Now such persons we command and exhort in the Lord Jesus Christ to do their work in quietness and to earn their own living.

Eph 4:1-10 (§225)

4 I therefore, a prisoner for the Lord, beg you to lead a life worthy of the calling to which you have been called, 2 with all lowliness and meekness, with patience, forbearing one another in love, 3 eager to maintain the unity of the Spirit in the bond of peace. 4 There is one body and one Spirit, just as you were called to the one hope that belongs to your call, 5 one Lord, one faith, one baptism, 6 one God and Father of us all, who is above all and through all and in all. 7 But grace was given to each of us according to the measure of Christ's gift. 8 Therefore it is said,

"When he ascended on high he led a
host of captives,
and he gave gifts to men."

9 (In saying, "He ascended," what does it mean but that he had also descended into the lower parts of the earth? 10 He who descended is he who also ascended far above all the heavens, that he might fill all things.)

2 Cor 8:8
8 I say this not as a command, but to prove by the earnestness of others that your love also is genuine.

308. Receive him as you would receive me

308

Rom 13:8-10 (§55)

8 Owe no one anything, except to love one another; for he who loves his neighbor has fulfilled the law. 9 The commandments, "You shall not commit adultery, You shall not kill, You shall not steal, You shall not covet," and any other commandment, are summed up in this sentence, "You shall love your neighbor as yourself." 10 Love does no wrong to a neighbor; therefore love is the fulfilling of the law.

Rom 16:1-2 (§65)

16 I commend to you our sister Phoebe, a deaconess of the church at Cen′chre-ae, 2 that you may receive her in the Lord as befits the saints, and help her in whatever she may require from you, for she has been a helper of many and of myself as well.

Rom 15:7-13 (§61)

7 Welcome one another, therefore, as Christ has welcomed you, for the glory of God. 8 For I tell you that Christ became a servant to the circumcised to show God's truthfulness, in order to confirm the promises given to the patriarchs, 9 and in order that the Gentiles might glorify God for his

▶ 17 Phil 1:5,
5 thankful for your partnership in the gospel from the first day until now.

1 Cor 7:17-24 (§97)

17 Only, let every one lead the life which the Lord has assigned to him, and in which God has called him. This is my rule in all the churches. 18 Was any one at the time of his call already circumcised? Let him not seek to remove the marks of circumcision. Was any one at the time of his call uncircumcised? Let him not seek circumcision. 19 For neither circumcision counts for anything nor uncircumcision, but keeping the commandments of God. 20 Every one should remain in the state in which he was called. 21 Were you a slave when called? Never mind. But if you can gain your freedom, avail yourself of the opportunity. 22 For he who was called in the Lord as a slave is a freedman of the Lord. Likewise he who was free when called is a slave of Christ. 23 You were bought with a price; do not become slaves of men. 24 So, brethren, in whatever state each was called, there let him remain with God.

mercy. As it is written,
"Therefore I will praise thee among
the Gentiles,
and sing to thy name";

4:15
15 And you Philippians yourselves know that in the beginning of the gospel, when I left Macedo′nia, no church entered into partnership with me in giving and receiving except you only;

2 Cor 3:1-3 (§154)

3 Are we beginning to commend ourselves again? Or do we need, as some do, letters of recommendation to you, or from you? 2 You yourselves are our letter of recommendation, written on your hearts, to be known and read by all men; 3 and you show that you are a letter from Christ delivered by us, written not with ink but with the Spirit of the living God, not on tablets of stone but on tablets of human hearts.

2 Cor 8:16-24 (§173)

16 But thanks be to God who puts the same earnest care for you into the heart of Titus. 17 For he not only accepted our appeal, but being himself very earnest

1 Cor 16:10-12 (§140)

10 When Timothy comes, see that you put him at ease among you, for he is doing the work of the Lord, as I am. 11 So let no one despise him. Speed him on his way in peace, that he may return to me; for I am expecting him with the

10 and again it is said,
"Rejoice, O Gentiles, with his
people";

11 and again,

Rom 14:1
As for the man who is weak in faith, welcome him, but not for disputes over opinions.

▶ 19 1 Cor 16:21
21 I, Paul, write this greeting with my own hand.

he is going to you of his own accord. 18 With him we are sending the brother who is famous among all the churches for his preaching of the gospel; 19 and not only that, but he has been appointed by the churches to travel with us in this gracious work which we are carrying on, for the glory of the Lord and to show our good will. 20 We intend that no one should blame us about this liberal gift which we are administering, 21 for we aim at what is honorable not only in the Lord's sight but also in the sight of men. 22 And with them we are sending our brother whom we have often tested and found earnest in many matters, but who is now more earnest than ever because

brethren.

12 As for our brother Apol′los, I strongly urged him to visit you with the other brethren, but it was not at all his will to come now. He will come

"Praise the Lord, all Gentiles,
and let all the peoples praise him";
12 and further Isaiah says,
"The root of Jesse shall come,
he who rises to rule the Gentiles;
in him shall the Gentiles hope."

2 Thes 3:17
17 I, Paul, write this greeting with my own hand. This is the mark in every letter of mine; it is the way I write.

of his great confidence in you. 23 As for Titus, he is my partner and fellow worker in your service; and as for our brethren, they are messengers of the churches, the glory of Christ. 24 So give proof, before the churches, of your love and of our boasting about you to these men.

when he has opportunity.

13 May the God of hope fill you with all joy and peace in believing, so that by the power of the Holy Spirit you may abound in hope.

Gal 6:11
11 See with what large letters I am writing to you with my own hand.

▶ 20 7 7 For I have derived much joy and comfort from your love, my brother, because the hearts of the saints have been refreshed through you.

307. I appeal to you for Onesimus

Phil 2:19-24 (§245)

19 I hope in the Lord Jesus to send Timothy to you soon, so that I may be cheered by news of you. 20 I have no one like him, who will be genuinely anxious for your welfare. 21 They all look after their own interests, not those of Jesus Christ. 22 But Timothy's worth you know, how as a son with a father he has served with me in the gospel. 23 I hope therefore to send him just as soon as I see how it will go with me; 24 and I trust in the Lord that shortly I myself shall come also.

Phil 2:25-3:1 (§246)

25 I have thought it necessary to send to you Epaphrodi′tus my brother and fellow worker and fellow soldier, and your messenger and minister to my need, 26 for he has been longing for you all, and has been distressed because you heard that he was ill. 27 Indeed he was ill, near to death. But God had mercy on him, and not only on him but on me also, lest I should have sorrow upon sorrow. 28 I am the more eager to send him, therefore, that you may rejoice at seeing him again, and that I may be less anxious. 29 So receive him in the Lord

Col 4:7-9 (§271)

7 Tych′icus will tell you all about my affairs; he is a beloved brother and faithful minister and fellow servant in the Lord. 8 I have sent him to you for this very purpose, that you may know how we are and that he may encourage your hearts, 9 and with him Ones′imus, the faithful and beloved brother, who is one of yourselves. They will tell you of everything that has taken place here.

with all joy; and honor such men, 30 for he nearly died for the work of Christ, risking his life to complete your service to me.

3 Finally, my brethren, rejoice in the Lord. To write the same things to you is not irksome to me, and is safe for you.

1 Thes 4:1-8 (§284)

4 Finally, brethren, we beseech and exhort you in the Lord Jesus, that as you learned from us how you ought to live and to please God, just as you are doing, you do so more and more. 2 For you know what instructions we gave you through the Lord Jesus. 3 For this is the will of God, your sanctification: that you abstain from unchastity; 4 that each one of you know how to take a wife for himself in holiness and honor 5 not in the passion of lust like heathen who do not know God; 6 that no man transgress, and wrong his brother in this matter, because the Lord is an avenger in all these things, as we solemnly forewarned you. 7 For God has not called us for uncleanness, but in holiness. 8 Therefore whoever disregards this, disregards not man but God, who gives his Holy Spirit to you.

Phm 8-14

8 Accordingly, though I am bold enough in Christ to command you to do what is required, 9 yet for love's sake I prefer to appeal to you—I, Paul, an ambassador and now a prisoner also for Christ Jesus—10 I appeal to you for my child, Ones′imus, whose father I have become in my imprisonment. 11 (Formerly he was useless to you, but now he is indeed useful to you and to me.) 12 I am sending him back to you, sending my very heart. 13 I would have been glad to keep him with me, in order that he might serve me on your behalf during my imprisonment for the gospel; 14 but I preferred to do nothing without your consent in order that your goodness might not be by compulsion but of your own free will.

307

1 Cor 7:6,
6 I say this by way of concession, not of command.

10,
10 To the married I give charge, not I but the Lord, that the wife should not separate from her husband

12
12 To the rest I say, not the Lord, that if any brother has a wife who is an unbeliever, and she consents to live with him, he should not divorce her.

Phm 14
14 but I preferred to do nothing without your consent in order that your goodness might not be by compulsion but of your own free will.

▶9 **Eph 3:1**
For this reason I, Paul, a prisoner for Christ Jesus on behalf of you Gentiles—

*cf 4:1 Phm 1, 10, 13 Col 4:3, 18a Phil 1:12-20
▶10 *cf 2 Cor 6:13 Phil 2:22 1 Cor 4:14-15, 14:20 Gal 4:19, 4:21-31 Eph 5:1
▶13 *cf Phil 2:30   ▶14 *cf 1 Cor 7:6, 35 2 Cor 9:7

308. Receive him as you would receive me

Phm 15-20

15 Perhaps this is why he was parted from you for a while, that you might have him back for ever, 16 no longer as a slave but more than a slave, as a beloved brother, especially to me but how much more to you, both in the flesh and in the Lord. 17 So if you consider me your partner, receive him as you would receive me. 18 If he has wronged you at all, or owes you anything, charge that to my account. 19 I, Paul, write this with my own hand, I will repay it—to say nothing of your owing me even your own self. 20 Yes, brother, I want some benefit from you in the Lord. Refresh my heart in Christ.

308

309

1 Cor 4:14-21 (§86)

14 I do not write this to make you ashamed, but to admonish you as my beloved children. 15 For though you have countless guides in Christ, you do not have many fathers. For I became your father in Christ Jesus through the gospel. 16 I urge you, then, be imitators of me. 17 Therefore I sent to you Timothy, my beloved and faithful child in the Lord, to remind you of my ways in Christ, as I teach them everywhere in every church. 18 Some are arrogant, as though I were not coming to you. 19 But I will come to you soon, if the Lord wills, and I will find out not the talk of these arrogant people but their power. 20 For the kingdom of God does not consist in talk but in power. 21 What do you wish? Shall I come to you with a rod, or with love in a spirit of gentleness?

1 Cor 16:5-9 (§139)

5 I will visit you after passing through Macedo'nia, for I intend to pass through Macedo'nia, 6 and perhaps I will stay with you or even spend the winter, so that you may speed me on my journey, wherever I go. 7 For I do not want to see

2 Cor 1:15-22 (§149)

15 Because I was sure of this, I wanted to come to you first, so that you might have a double pleasure; 16 I wanted to visit you on my way to Macedo'nia, and to come back to you from Macedo'nia and have you send me on my way to Judea. 17 Was I vacillating when I wanted to do this? Do I make my plans like a worldly man, ready to say Yes and No at once? 18 As surely as God is faithful, our word to you has not been Yes and No. 19 For the Son of God, Jesus Christ, whom we preached among you, Silva'nus and Timothy and I, was not Yes and No; but in him it is always Yes. 20 For all the promises of God find their Yes in him. That is why we utter the Amen through him, to the glory of God. 21 But it is God who establishes us with you in Christ, and

has commissioned us; 22 he has put his seal upon us and given us his Spirit in our hearts as a guarantee.

you now just in passing; I hope to spend some time with you, if the Lord permits. 8 But I will stay in Ephesus until Pentecost, 9 for a wide door for effective work has opened to me, and there are many adversaries.

▶ 21 2 Cor 2:3 ³And I wrote as I did, so that when I came I might not suffer pain from those who should have made me rejoice, for I felt sure of all of you, that my joy would be the joy of you all.

Rom 1:5 ⁵ through whom we have received grace and apostleship to bring about the obedience of faith for the sake of his name among all the nations,

2 Thes 3:4 ⁴And we have confidence in the Lord about you, that you are doing and will do the things which we command.

▶ 22 Rom 1:11, ¹¹ For I long to see you, that I may impart to you some spiritual gift to strengthen you,

15:23 ²³ But now, since I no longer have any room for work in these regions, and since I have longed for many years to come to you,

310. Greetings

310

Rom 16:3-16 (§66)

3 Greet Prisca and Aquila, my fellow workers in Christ Jesus, 4 who risked their necks for my life, to whom not only I but also all the churches of the Gentiles give thanks; 5 greet also the church in their house. Greet my beloved Epae'netus, who was the first convert in Asia for Christ. 6 Greet Mary, who has worked hard among you. 7 Greet Androni'cus and Ju'nias, my kinsmen and my fellow prisoners; they are men of note among the apostles, and they were in Christ before me. 8 Greet Amplia'tus, my beloved in the Lord. 9 Greet Urba'nus, our fellow worker in Christ, and my beloved Stachys. 10 Greet Apel'les, who is approved in Christ. Greet those who belong to the family of Aristobu'lus. 11 Greet my kinsman Hero'dion. Greet those in the Lord who belong to the family of Narcis'sus. 12 Greet those workers in the Lord, Tryphae'na and Trypho'sa. Greet the beloved Persis, who has worked hard in the Lord. 13 Greet Rufus, eminent in the Lord, also his mother and mine. 14 Greet Asyn'critus, Phlegon, Hermes, Pat'robas, Hermas,

1 Cor 16:19-20 (§143)

19 The churches of Asia send greetings. Aquila and Prisca, together with the church in their house, send you hearty greetings in the Lord. 20 All the brethren send greetings. Greet one another with a holy kiss.

and the brethren who are with them. 15 Greet Philol'ogus, Julia, Nereus and his sister, and Olym'pas, and all the saints who are with them. 16 Greet one another with a holy kiss. All the churches of Christ greet you.

Rom 16:21-23 (§69)

21 Timothy, my fellow worker, greets you; so do Lucius and Jason and Sosip'ater, my kinsmen. 22 I Tertius, the writer of this letter, greet you in the Lord. 23 Ga'ius, who is host to me and to the whole church, greets you. Eras'tus, the city treasurer, and our brother Quartus, greet you.

2 Cor 13:11-13 (§191)

11 Finally, brethren, farewell. Mend your ways, heed my appeal, agree with one another, live in peace, and the God of love and peace will be with you. 12 Greet one another with a holy kiss. 13 All the saints greet you.

▶ 24 Acts 12:12, 12 When he realized this, he went to the house of Mary, the mother of John whose other name was Mark, where many were gathered together and were praying.

19:29, ²⁹ So the city was filled with the confusion; and they rushed together into the theater, dragging with them Ga'ius and Aristar'chus, Macedo'nians who were Paul's companions in travel.

27:2 ²And embarking in a ship of Adramyt'tium, which was about to sail to the ports along the coast of Asia, we put to sea, accompanied by Aristar'chus, a Macedo'nian from Thessalo-ni'ca.

2 Tim 4:10 ¹⁰ For Demas, in love with this present world, has deserted me and gone to Thessaloni'ca; Crescens has gone to Galatia, Titus to Dalmatia.

Phil 1:19-26 (§240)

19 Yes, and I shall rejoice. For I know that through your prayers and the help of the Spirit of Jesus Christ this will turn out for my deliverance, 20 as it is my eager expectation and hope that I shall not be at all ashamed, but that with full courage now as always Christ will be honored in my body, whether by life or by death. 21 For to me to live is Christ, and to die is gain. 22 If it is to be life in the flesh, that means fruitful labor for me. Yet which I shall choose I cannot tell. 23 I am hard pressed between the two. My desire is to depart and be with Christ, for that is far better. 24 But to remain in the flesh is more necessary on your account. 25 Convinced of this, I know that I shall remain and continue with you all, for your progress and joy in the faith, 26 so that in me you may have ample cause to glory in Christ Jesus, because of my coming to you again.

Phil 1:27-30 (§241)

27 Only let your manner of life be worthy of the gospel of Christ, so that whether I come and see you or am absent, I may hear of you that you stand firm in one spirit, with one mind striving side by side for the faith of the gospel, 28 and not frightened in anything by your opponents. This is a clear omen to them of their destruction, but of your salvation, and that from God. 29 For it has been granted to you that for the sake of Christ you should not only believe in him but also suffer for his sake, 30 engaged in the same conflict which you saw and now hear to be mine.

Phil 2:19-24 (§245)

19 I hope in the Lord Jesus to send Timothy to you soon, so that I may be cheered by news of you. 20 I have no one like him, who will be genuinely anxious for your welfare. 21 They all look after their own interests, not those of Jesus Christ. 22 But Timothy's worth you know, how as a son with a father he has served with me in the gospel. 23 I hope therefore to send him just as soon as I see how it will go with me; 24 and I trust in the Lord that shortly I myself shall come also.

Phil 2:12-13 (§243)

12 Therefore, my beloved, as you have always obeyed, so now, not only as in my presence but much more in my absence, work out your own salvation with fear and trembling; 13 for God is at work in you, both to will and to work for his good pleasure.

1 Thes 5:25 (§290)

25 Brethren, pray for us.

Phm 21-22

21 Confident of your obedience, I write to you, knowing that you will do even more than I say. 22 At the same time, prepare a guest room for me, for I am hoping through your prayers to be granted to you.

309

310. Greetings

Phil 4:21-22 (§254)

21 Greet every saint in Christ Jesus. The brethren who are with me greet you. 22 All the saints greet you, especially those of Caesar's household.

Col 4:10-15 (§272)

10 Aristar'chus my fellow prisoner greets you, and Mark the cousin of Barnabas (concerning whom you have received instructions—if he comes to you, receive him), 11 and Jesus who is called Justus. These are the only men of the circumcision among my fellow workers for the kingdom of God, and they have been a comfort to me. 12 Ep'aphras, who is one of yourselves, a servant of Christ Jesus, greets you, always remembering you earnestly in his prayers, that you may stand mature and fully assured in all the will of God. 13 For I bear him witness that he has worked hard for you and for those in La-odice'a and in Hi-erap'olis. 14 Luke the beloved physician and Demas greet you. 15 Give my greetings to the brethren at La-odice'a, and to Nympha and the church in her house.

1 Thes 5:26 (§291)

26 Greet all the brethren with a holy kiss.

Phm 23-24

23 Ep'aphras, my fellow prisoner in Christ Jesus, sends greetings to you, 24 and so do Mark, Aristar'chus, Demas, and Luke, my fellow workers.

310

311

Rom 16:20b (§68)

The grace of our Lord Jesus Christ be with you.

▶ 25 2 Tim 4:22
22 The Lord be with your spirit. Grace be with you.

1 Cor 16:23-24 (§145)

23 The grace of the Lord Jesus be with you. 24 My love be with you all in Christ Jesus. Amen.

2 Cor 13:14 (§192)

14 The grace of the Lord Jesus Christ and the love of God and the fellowship of the Holy Spirit be with you all.

Gal 6:18 (§217)

18 The grace of our Lord Jesus Christ be with your spirit, brethren. Amen.

Eph 6:23-24 (§236)

23 Peace be to the brethren, and love with faith, from God the Father and the Lord Jesus Christ. 24 Grace be with all who love our Lord Jesus Christ with love undying.

Phil 4:23 (§255)	Col 4:18b (§274)	1 Thes 5:28 (§293)	2 Thes 3:18 (§304)	Phm 25
23 The grace of the Lord Jesus Christ be with your spirit.	Grace be with you.	28 The grace of our Lord Jesus Christ be with you.	[18] The grace of our Lord Jesus Christ be with you all.	25 The grace of the Lord Jesus Christ be with your spirit.

311

Index of Primary Paragraphs

3:12-16/§248 §108, 155, 196, 226
3:17-21/§249 §35, 49, 67, 131, 132, 133, 135, 136, 160, 276, 286, 295, 296
4:1-3/§250 §73, 280
4:4-7/§251 §53, 99
4:8-9/§252 §42, 112, 165, 171, 213, 225, 228, 267
4:10-20/§253 §51, 73, 105, 153, 165, 168, 180, 185, 186, 225, 278, 281
4:21-22/§254 §66, 69, 143, 191, 272, 291, 310
4:23/§255 §68, 145, 192, 217, 236, 274, 293, 304, 311

Colossians

1:1-2/§256 §1, 71, 146, 193, 218, 237, 275, 294, 305
1:3-14/§257 §2, 43, 62, 72, 238, 276, 295, 306
1:15-20/§258 §21, 33, 50, 103, 133, 136, 164, 219, 221, 225
1:21-23/§259 §21, 42, 47, 221
1:24-2:3/§260 §38, 47, 49, 70, 77, 83, 121, 134, 158, 183, 196, 197, 219, 222
2:4-7/§261 §99, 223, 230, 241, 277, 297
2:8-15/§262 §23, 131, 132, 200, 220
2:16-19/§263 §58, 83, 185, 208, 226
2:20-23/§264 §24, 208
3:1-4/§265 §24, 29, 160, 220
3:5-11/§266 §6, 24, 30, 41, 56, 89, 91, 109, 118, 136, 137, 161, 188, 206, 213, 220, 227, 228, 230
3:12-17/§267 §53, 58, 60, 111, 126, 128, 165, 171, 213, 225, 228, 231, 252
3:18-4:1/§268 §99, 232
4:2-4/§269 §64, 141, 152, 234, 290, 299
4:5-6/§270 §90, 127, 285
4:7-9/§271 §235, 307
4:10-15/§272 §66, 69, 143, 191, 254, 291, 310
4:16-18a/§273 §144, 216, 292, 303
4:18b/§274 §68, 145, 192, 217, 236, 255, 293, 304, 311

1 Thessalonians

1:1/§275 §1, 71, 146, 193, 218, 237, 256, 294, 305
1:2-10/§276 §2, 41, 43, 62, 72, 76, 116, 171, 174, 186, 200, 208, 209, 238, 249, 257, 295, 306
2:1-8–§277 §67, 86, 106, 153, 158, 165, 167, 168, 176, 183, 187, 194, 261
2:9-12/§278 §85, 86, 105, 148, 180, *186*, 300
2:13-16/§279 §42, 74, 111, 194
2:17-20/§280 §63, 86, 139, 149, 152, 169, 250
3:1-5/§281 §34, 86, 134, 147, 152, 169, 183
3:6-10/§282 §147, 150, *238*, 241
3:11-13/§283 §72, *238*, 298
4:1-8/§284 §5, 51, 73, 93, 99, 225, 307

4:9-12/§285 §53, 55, 122, 270, 300
4:13-18/§286 §132, 133, 137, 160, 249, 296
5:1-11/§287 §33, 38, 56, 58, 98, 141, 176, 230, 233, 244, 296
5:12-22/§288 §53, 128, 142, 228, 251, 300
5:23-24/§289 §191, 302
5:25/§290 §64, 234, 269, 299, 309
5:26/§291 §66, 69, 143, 191, 254, 272, 310
5:27/§292 §144, 216, 273, 303
5:28/§293 §68, 145, 192, 217, 236, 255, 274, 304, 311

2 Thessalonians

1:1-2/§294 §1, 71, 146, 193, 218, 237, 256, 275, 305
1:3-12/§295 §2, 72, 80, 147, 168, 238, 241, 249, 257, 276, 306
2:1-12/§296 §4, 5, 8, 45, 51, 73, 98, 109, 133, 181, 186, 225, 249, 284, 286, 287
2:13-15/§297 §8, 33, 91, 141, 261, 276
2:16-17/§298 §147, 169, 283
3:1-5/§299 §64, 170, 234, 269, 290
3:6-13/§300 §85, 86, 105, 111, 215, 228, 249, 278, 285, 288
3:14-15/§301 §87, 89, 112, 130, 214
3:16/§302 §64, 128, 191, 289
3:17/§303 §144, 216, 273, 292
3:18/§304 §68, 145, 192, 217, 236, 255, 274, 293, 311

Philemon

1-3/§305 §1, 71, 146, 193, 218, 237, 256, 275, 294
4-7/§306 §2, 72, 123, 168, 219, 238, 257, 276, 295
8-14/§307 §51, 65, 73, 97, 122, 130, 140, 142, 154, 173, 225, 245, 246, 271, 284
15-20/§308 §55, 61, 65, 90, 97, 122, 140, 142, 154, 173
21-22/§309 §63, 86, 139, 149, 240, 241, 243, 269, 290
23-24/§310 §66, 69, 143, 191, 254, 272, 291
25/§311 §68, 145, 192, 217, 236, 255, 274, 293, 304

Index of Acts and Pastoral Epistles in Notes

Acts

1:3-4	§131
1:7	§287
1:14	§25, 53, 269
1:24	§32
2:4-8	*§124*
2:13	§127
2:15	§287
2:17	*§124*
2:21	§41, 71
2:23	§219, 279
2:24	§19, 23, 34, 41, 92, 131, 132, 133, 160, 193, 219, 262, 276
2:31	§131
2:33	§20, 202, 242
2:38	§23, 73, 219
2:39	§35
2:40	§193, 244
2:42	§110, 238
3:6	§165
3:14	§164
3:19	§262
3:21	§31
3:25	§35, 201
3:26	§4, 61
4:2	§132
4:13	§157
4:29	§157
4:31	§239
4:32	§241
4:34	§172
4:36	*§272*
5:12	§186
5:20	§244
5:30	§202
5:32	§30
5:40	*§85*
5:41	§241
6:3-4	*§120*
7:2	§77
7:6	§203
7:48	§161
7:51	§11
7:52	§279
7:53	§204

8:3	§131, 195, 196, 247
8:16	§23
8:31	§42
8:39	§185, 286
9:1-19	§196
9:3	§105, 131
9:5-6	§248
9:13	§64
9:14	§71
9:15	§1, 47, 62, 193, 196, 197
9:16	§165, 183, 281
9:17	§105
9:19-22	§196
9:21	§71, 195
9:22-23	§196
9:23	§183, 279
9:24-25	§184
9:26-30	§196
10:15, 28	§59, 198
10:34	§8, 15, 197, 232, 268
10:35	§11, 15
10:36	§41, 221, 233
10:42	§9, 162
10:45	§20
11:2-3	§198
11:18	§169
11:19-26	§198
11:27-30	§197, 198
11:29	§138, 171, 197
11:30	§196
12:12	§272, 310
12:17	§197
12:25	§197, 198
13:1	§69, *120*, 226
13:2	§196
13:15	§52
13:27	§77
13:32	§35
13:39	§13, 15, 29, 199
13:45, 50	§183, 279
13:46	§46
13:48	§219
13:52	§276

Passages listed in italics are not quoted in the notes.